A Treasury of Russian Literature

A Treasury of

Russian Literature

BEING A COMPREHENSIVE SELECTION OF MANY OF
THE BEST THINGS BY NUMEROUS AUTHORS IN
PRACTICALLY EVERY FIELD OF THE RICH
LITERATURE OF RUSSIA FROM ITS BEGINNINGS TO
THE PRESENT, WITH MUCH MATERIAL NOW FIRST
MADE AVAILABLE IN ENGLISH, AND ALL OF THE
ACCEPTED FAVORITES NEWLY TRANSLATED OR
THEIR CURRENT TRANSLATIONS
THOROUGHLY REVISED. SELECTED AND EDITED,
WITH A FOREWORD AND BIOGRAPHICAL AND
CRITICAL NOTES, BY

Bernard Guilbert Guerney

NEW YORK · THE VANGUARD PRESS

*The pleasant labors involved
in this work are dedicated to
FRANCES WINWAR
as a mark of the Editor's long
friendship and earnest esteem*

THE RUSSIAN TONGUE

*In the days of doubts, in the days of op-
pressive reflections concerning the destinies
of my native land, thou alone art my
stay and my staff, O great, mighty,
true, and free Russian tongue! Wert
thou not, how could one do aught
but fall into despair at the
sight of all that is taking
place at home? But it is
past all belief that such
a tongue is given to
any but a great
* people! **
TURGENEV'S
Senilia

*

Là, sotto i giorni rubelosi e brevi . . .
Nasce una gente a ciu'l morir non dole
PETRARCH

There, where the days are clouded o'er and short,
A people is a-borning that does not grieve in dying

Introduction

Sixty centuries of civilization have produced three literatures which are acknowledged as supremely great: Greek, English, and Russian. It would be supererogatory if not presumptuous to try to determine here which of these three is the superlative one. There need be but little hesitancy, however, in saying that Russian literature is as vast and overwhelming as the land that produced it, and that the men who produced that literature were as valiant and courageous as the heroic warriors who have, for more than two years now, been breasting back, with their sole might, the greatest part of the hordes of a troglodytal enemy, and who at the present writing seem likely to wrest the victory from him.

It is a literature worthy of a great land and a great people, and the present work is a modest tribute to both.

A great Russian writer's tribute to his land and language is given in an epigraph; the opinion of most non-Russians on the literature of Russia may perhaps be best given here in the words of an able British critic, who claims that "its chief gift to mankind is an expression made with a naturalness and sincerity that are matchless, and a love of reality which is unique—for all Russian literature, whether in prose or verse, is rooted in reality," and who speaks of its "great heart; a heart that is large enough to embrace the world and to drown all the sorrows therein with the immensity of its sympathy, its fraternity, its pity, its charity, and its love."

It may also be safely said that no other literature offers so many striking and curious aspects as the Russian. It goes back to the tenth century for its beginnings as a formal literature, yet the term Russian Literature is practically synonymous with Modern Russian Literature— and, as such, it is still not two centuries old. Yet, though the youngest of literatures, it conveys the greatest impression of maturity. The book from the Russian publication of which it dates as a modern literature was first published neither in Russian nor in Russia, but in French and in England.[1] The language of this young literature was first used as a literary instrument only ninety years before the publication of the *Satires;*[2] its very alphabet came into being only during the reign of Peter the Great.[3] The first collection of Russian folk poems was made not by a Russian but by an Englishman.[4] One of its most interesting (and voluminous) practitioners was strong on wit and verve but weak on Russian orthography, and has a definite place in French literature as well.[5]

The accepted founder of this modern literature, who is also the founder of Russian modern culture and science, was a self-taught peasant.[6] And so recent is this literature that one man was able to achieve several "firsts" therein.[7] Russia's literary equivalent of the Age of Queen Anne preceded her Elizabethan Age. The Golden Age of its poetry is supposed to have lasted exactly eleven years, of its novel for less than forty years.[8] Russia had no printed novels before 1750, and no printed books before 1564. It was only about 1825 that rumors of this literature began to reach Europe; it did not become generally

[1] The *Satires* of Prince Antioch Cantemir (1708-44); first published in the author's own land and language in 1762, twelve years after its publication in a French version in London and eighteen years after his death.

[2] The *Life* (written by himself in 1672-73) of Arch-presbyter Avvacum (Habakkuk), who spent nine years in Siberia, fourteen in an earth-work prison in Northeast Russia, and was burned at the stake in 1681. His book is racy, vigorous, and delightfully humorous, and is to this day a model of apt, forceful, concise Russian.

[3] Born 1672, ascended throne, 1682, died, 1725. Peter himself was a born writer; many of his written dicta have become folk sayings. And Wilhelm Mons, his Empress' lover, wrote authentic Russian love poems—in German characters.

[4] Richard James, 1619.

[5] Catherine the Great (born 1729, ascended throne, 1762, died, 1796). Scholarly historian, fairy-tale writer, epistolographer, satirist, humorist, and, above all, dramatist —wrote tragedies, comedies, historical plays, comic operas, and humble adaptations, honestly acknowledged, from Shakespeare. Freer from suspicion of ghostly collaborators than any other Royal Author.

[6] Michailo Lomonossov (born between 1708-15; died, 1765), the Russian Johnson *cum* Franklin. Fixed standards for the language, introduced a new prosody, and as didactic poet is equalled in grandeur only by Derzhavin.

[7] Alexander Petrovich Sumarocov (1717-77); Russia's first professional man of letters, first modern dramatist, first to steal *Hamlet,* first director of the first theater in Petersburg (founded 1756), first fabulist, journalist, critic, and, while not first as poet, decidedly an inventive and melodious one.

[8] Poetry: From publication of Pushkin's *Russlan and Liudmilla* in 1820 to 1831, when Pushkin turned to prose. Novel: from publication of *Dead Souls* in 1842 to Dostoievski's death in 1881. Such metallic tags do not ring true, for a number of good reasons, but the reader is entitled to know them.

known until 1875, and to this day vast tracts of it are still unexplored by non-Russian readers.

No other literature calls forth so many superlatives. No other has shown so much excellence in so short a time in so many fields of writing (except the essay); in poetry, in drama, in the short story, and, above all, the novel. No other has been so misunderstood (with the best intentions in the world), so misinterpreted, and (at least in English) so mistranslated. It is richer in picaresques than even the Spanish; no other is richer in fable, satire, sheer humor—and no other has so undeserved a reputation for gloom and morbidity. No other has so consistently and puissantly been used as a mighty and sanctified weapon for justice and right; no other will assay comparatively so little dross; [9] no other (save the Greek) comes so near to De Quincey's concept of a literature of power and the function thereof.

At the same time, no other country shows so curious a strain of self-depreciation in its critics. Briefly, the attitude is that because Scandinavia had its sagas, Iceland its eddas, and Germany its Nibelungenlied, Russia cannot call her *bylini* her own. Yet it is definitely known that German tradition and Norse saga borrowed Russia's Ilya of Murom. It is also this Derivative School which accepts the apparent poverty of early Russian literature as a mysterious visitation of God. The answer to the first claim is: Purveyors are we all, and that the Russians have stolen as the bees steal and not as the ants. The world's nearest (and only) approach to an indigenous and homogeneous literature is the Greek. What happened to Russian literature in the seventeenth and eighteenth centuries is merely what happened to the English in the thirteenth and fourteenth. The espaliers may have been imported, but no other literature is so deeply, so firmly rooted in its native soil. It is for that very reason that Russian Emigré Literature can hardly be said to have flourished.

The answer to the apparent poverty of early Russian literature lies as much in sober history as in Divine influence. History says, coldly, that Russia's abandonment of paganism served to isolate her rather than to broaden her horizons. In Russia the persecution of all secular folk art, especially anything written, was particularly virulent and persistent. Geographically and politically, Russia was likewise isolated. When England began to traffic with Russia, King Sigismund of Poland

---

[9] A very sketchy survey of English criticism reveals no fewer than fourteen Russian novels, each one of them the "greatest in the world"; one list, of the world's six greatest books, gives two novels of Tolstoi's and one of Dostoievski's.

pleaded hard with Queen Elizabeth not to send British craftsmen to Russia, lest the young Ilya of Murom awaken in his might.

Russian literature is so amazing that it may be likened only to its own Ilya Murometz. Yet still more amazing is the fact that Russia produced any literature at all. Prison and literature seem to have been inseparable in old Russia. One of her earliest writers has no other name than Daniel of the Oubliette. And Necrassov, in the nineteenth century, draws the lot of the honest Russian writer in a quatrain: "Fate was preparing for him a glorious path and the resounding name of an intercessor for the people—and consumption, and Siberia." Prison— and censorship. Political censorship, theatrical censorship, moral censorship, spiritual censorship. Chapbook, broadside, or Tolstoi—everything had to run the gantlet.

Yet, while life was hard for the people, whether muzhiks or writers, the Russians should not be thought of as moody mystics. "Is there any place where no enjoyments are to be found?" writes Gogol. "They exist even in Petersburg, despite its austere, morose appearance. A cruel frost of thirty degrees may crackle through its streets; that child of the North, the snowstorm witch, squeals and whines as she sweeps snowdrifts over the sidewalks, blinding the eyes, powdering the coat collars of fur, and mustaches, and the muzzles of shaggy animals; yet invitingly, even through the crisscross flurry of the snowflakes, a small window sends its light from somewhere above, even from a fourth floor—there, in a cozy little room, by the light of unassuming stearine candles, to the hum of a samovar, a conversation that warms the heart and the soul is being carried on, a radiant page of some inspired Russian poet, one of those whom God has bestowed in reward upon His Russia, is being read aloud, and the young heart of some youth beats with such exalted ardor as is not to be found even under a sky warmed by a meridian sun."

Naturally, it is not meant to imply that there is no such thing as a most fascinating and exceedingly rich *informal* Russian literature from very early times—folk poetry, folk tales, folk legends, folklore. But, for obvious reasons of space, the call of the folklorelei must be resisted, just as one has to forego the very interesting Ukrainian literature or the very many literatures written in non-Russian languages and yet considered part of Soviet literature. We are here concerned with the formal literature of Great Russia, and folklore is included only where it has been transmuted into literary forms.

And there is, definitely, an Old Russian Literature and a Middle one. If the reader were hovering over the vast domain of Russian letters in some Wellsian time-and-space machine, he would see first a dreary tundra covered with such Church-Slavonic moss as chronicles, legal codes, peace treaties; morasses of liturgies, swangs of "theological eloquence," the sloughs of hagiographies—in short, the Dismal Swamp of Theology. This lasts until almost the end of the twelfth century, when amid the quaggy, level plain we come upon *Igor,* a monolith as lofty as a tor and as mysterious (if we refuse to accept an historical explanation for it) as Stonehenge or the monstrous figures on Easter Island.

And, although there is a further stretch of fens and bogs—more church calendars, genealogies, annals, more hagiologies—the ground does become tussocky; folk literature takes on written forms; there is a Slavic equivalent of *Faustus;* there is the first picaresque; there are chapbooks and woodcut broadsides, so popular that specimens have survived all the zeal of all the censorships.

Old Russia is coming to an end. It is the end of the seventeenth century; Ilya is stirring as the Westernizing sandaled pilgrims come to him. The ground becomes firmer; tussocks are replaced by hills; in the eighteenth century there are mountains; in the nineteenth we reach the Alps and the Himalayas.

In the second decade of this our century there is a terrific upheaval; here we have the beginnings of a Russian Emigré Literature (which must always remain little more than a footnote); in the third decade Russian Literature takes on the name of Soviet Literature. And in the present decade all the world is in flames and bathed in blood as it battles a monstrous aberration. To all intents and purposes (and rightly so) the war communiqués are the most absorbing literature of today.

Yet, with all due diffidence, a prophecy may be ventured on. Russia has never been conquered, nor has her indomitable spirit ever been crushed. Even during the siege of Leningrad she has brought forth Shostakovich's Seventh Symphony; her poets still produce poems which sweep over Russia from the battle lines to the Urals. On the whole, however, literature functions slowly. Russia's prominent writers are now covering (and dying on) her war fronts. But just as the Battle of the River of Sorrow produced *Igor;* as the Napoleonic Invasion produced *War and Peace,* the Crimean Campaign, *Sebastopol,* the Russo-Turkish War, *Four Days,* and the Russo-Japanese, *Tsushima,* so will Russia transmute its present titanic struggle into future masterpieces.

This anthology may be called a Grand Tour of Russian Literature—both in prose and verse: the first attempt of the sort in forty years. It is representative and comprehensive without pretending to be exhaustive or formalistic. No matter how widely read the reader may be, it is hoped that he will find herein some pieces unfamiliar to him; even the old favorites have been given new settings in English which are believed to be somewhat nearer to the spirit and truth of the originals. Most anthologies from the Russian are usually labeled *The Best Russian This* and *The Greatest Russian That*. The plain truth is that any book of this sort, if it is honestly carried through, will consist of the best and greatest; this book merely tries to live up to its unassuming title of Treasury. Many of the anthologies currently appearing in a praise-worthy effort to satisfy the present interest in Russia claim, laudably enough, to give an understanding of Russian life, or of Russian history, or of Russian literary biography. While the present work is neither grimly pointed in one inexorable direction, nor claims to be a shot-gun prescription, it really is a double-barreled affair. Since the selections were made with a certain amount of firsthand knowledge of the Russian language and literature, the reader cannot but get a fair idea of the life of Russia as portrayed and interpreted by her literary masters; if he cares to read the unpretentious sketches preceding the selections, he will find that collectively they constitute not only an informal history of Russian literature, but also contain a not inconsiderate amount of literary biography and give a certain historical background. And, while a bibliography was not feasible, an attempt was made to indicate, wherever possible, certain preferences in the matter of translations—a not unimportant point in reading any literature not in its own language.

Comparatively large as this Treasury is, it yet contains, naturally, a mere handful of treasures. Nevertheless there is some catholicity and considerable variety. It is not a *Beauties of Russian Literature*—hence there has been an avoidance of snippets and extracts; practically all the selections are complete, and abridgement was but little resorted to.

Above all, the selectivity was guided by a certain belief that great things need not necessarily be soporific, that best (or even good) writing need not be over-solemn, and that boredom is not quite synonymous with appreciation. In brief, if this book can contribute to the reader's enjoyment, and incidentally add to his knowledge (and possibly appreciation) of Russia, its modest aims will have been fulfilled.

New York, 1943   BERNARD GUILBERT GUERNEY.

Acknowledgments – and a Request

The Editor's warmest thanks are hereby extended to: David Orans and Mrs. Louis Orans, as Trustees, for granting the Editor access to the library of the late Louis Orans—a collection exceptionally complete in texts of the Russian classics; to Morris Orans for the full use of his highly specialized reference library, with invaluable material on all aspects of Russia; and to Irina Aleksander for numerous points of information which could not be derived from books but only from a residence in Russia more recent than the Editor's. As for those who have offered valuable suggestions and assisted in the more humdrum tasks connected with the physical preparation of this book, the Editor's thanks are offered to them also, even though they have preferred to remain anonymous.

As in the past, any comments, criticisms, or suggestions will be appreciated.

B. G. G.

Contents

PAGE

A Treasury of Russian Literature

Friar Nestor

1 0 5 6 – C. 1 1 1 4

NESTOR ENTERED the Monastery of the Grottoes in Kiev at the age of seventeen. The Chronicle (titled in one of the fourteenth-century manuscripts as *Relations of Times Gone By; How the Land of Russia Began, Who First Reigned at Kiev, and How the Land of Russia Was Formed*) is traditionally ascribed to him, but it has been rather well established that only a small part thereof is his, and that it was Abbot Sylvester who edited the whole and continued it into the twelfth century. Nor is his title as Russia's First Chronicler undisputed. Like most chronicles, Nestor's is a quaint melange, not without charm in its naïveté, of folk tales, legends, superstitions, professional piety, and small grains of history as authentic as any other. But, covering as it does the period from 862 to 1110 A. D., its value as a chief source for the early history of Russia cannot be exaggerated.

The subjoined may be considered as not uninteresting in showing the transition of Russia from worship of the highly poetic Slavic pantheon to monotheism. Vladimir, son of Svyatoslav (also known as St. Vladimir), was Grand Prince of Kiev from 980 to his death in 1015. He was baptized "in the year 6496," or 988 A. D., upon his marriage to Princess Anna of Greece.

How Vladimir of Kiev and All Russia Were Baptized

IT SO FELL OUT, by the will of God, that Vladimir was ailing with his eyes, and his vision failed him, and he was greatly troubled thereat. The Empress counseled him: If thou wouldst be free of thy affliction, accept baptism without delay. If not, thou wilt not be rid thereof.

Thereupon Vladimir said: If it be truly thus, then is your Christian God great indeed. And he issued orders for his baptism. The Bishop of Corsun, together with the other priests of the Empress, received Vladimir as a catechumen and did baptize him, and at the moment of the laying on of hands the Prince recovered his vision and saw. When Vladimir perceived this sudden healing, he rendered praises to God, saying: Now have I first found the true God.

When his court witnessed this, many likewise accepted baptism. The Prince was baptized in the Church of St. Basil, which is at Corsun, in the market place thereof. . . . Those who have not the right knowledge say he was baptized in Kiev; others, again, tell it otherwise.

Thereafter Vladimir took with him the Empress . . . and the priests of Corsun, together with the holy relics of Clement and of his disciple Phœbus, and sundry church utensils and holy icons, for his own use. . . . The captured city of Corsun he gave back to the Greeks as a marriage offering, for the sake of the Empress, and wended back to Kiev.

Upon his return he commanded the idols to be cast down, and certain ones to be hacked into splinters, and others still to be consigned to the flames; but as for Perun [the Slavic Zeus], him he ordered to be tied to the tail of a horse and dragged down the Borichev slope to a stream, and set a dozen men to beating him with rods, not as if the wood itself had any feelings, but to put to scorn the demon that had

Translated by Bernard Guilbert Guerney. Copyright, 1943, by the Vanguard Press, Inc.

by means of the idol so greatly seduced the people, and so that he might receive his meed of chastisement at the hands of mortals. As the idol was being dragged along the stream toward the Dnieper, those who were still pagans (inasmuch as they were still unbaptized) did lament him greatly, and he was cast into the Dnieper. Vladimir, standing by, saith: Should the waters carry him to any place on the banks, thrust him off, until he be past the rapids, when ye may abandon him.

These orders they obeyed. When the idol had floated beyond the rapids and was set loose, the wind bore it onto a sandbank, which, because of this, bears the name of Perun's Bank and is so known to this very day.

Thereafter Vladimir caused to be proclaimed throughout the city: Whosoever fails to appear at the river tomorrow, be he rich or poor, or a beggar, or a craftsman, the same shall find himself in my disfavor.

Hearing this, the people came with gladness and rejoicing, saying: Were this not a good thing, the Prince and his nobles would not have accepted it.

Next morning Vladimir set forth with the priests of the Empress and those of Corsun to the Dnieper, whither the people had flocked in countless multitudes. They went into the water, some standing therein breast-high, some up to their necks, while those who were younger kept close to the bank, holding those who were youngest of all, the while their elders waded deeper into the river. And the priests on the bank offered up their prayers, and there was much rejoicing in heaven and on earth at the sight of so many people saved. But the Devil groaned, saying: Woe is me! I am being driven forth from here. Here I had meant to have my safe dwelling place, for the teachings of the Apostles were not preached here, and they knew not God, and I rejoiced in the worship they offered up to me. But now I am overcome, not by Apostles or holy martyrs, but by common, ignorant folk. No longer shall I hold sway in these lands.

Vladimir was happy in that he and his people had found God and, casting up his eyes to heaven, he spake: God, it is Thou Who hast created heaven and earth! Guard these, Thy new people, and allow them, O Lord, to discover the true God, such as the Christians know. Strengthen the true and steadfast faith within them and help me, O Lord, against mine enemy, so that, in reliance upon Thee and Thy power, I may escape any ambush he may set for me!

The people, having received baptism, all wended their way home, and Vladimir commanded churches to be built, and that they be builded where the idols had thereto stood. He built the Church of St. Basil on the hill where the great idol Perun had once stood, as well as the idols of the other gods to whom the Prince and his people had once offered sacrifices. And he began building churches and placing priests therein throughout the towns, and to lead the people to baptism in all the towns and hamlets. He dispatched men to take the sons of noblemen and to put them to book learning. But the mothers of these children wept for them, for they were not yet strong in their faith, and they wept for them as for the dead.[1]

[1] As Russian mothers were to weep for their children when Peter the Great also took their sons away to "put them to book learning."—*Translator.*

Poet Unknown

FL. 1185

The Lay of the Host of Igor, already mentioned in the Introduction, is a magnificent monument not only of Russian but world poetry. It is not only higher in poetic content but infinitely more readable than the *Nibelungenlied* and the *Chanson de Roland*. Its nearest approach is the *Kalevala*. As poet, its author is ranked as not inferior to Pushkin.

The poem is in all probability an eyewitness account of the rash campaign of Igor, Prince of Novgorod, against the paynim Polovtsi, or Cumanians, and was written, according to some scholars, very shortly after Igor's defeat at the River Kayala in 1185; according to others, no later than 1188. As to the author, we have only the internal evidence of the poem to go by. He seems in many ways to have been a Slavic parallel of Lord Bacon: Courtier; scholar (versed in Homer, almost certainly) ; perhaps a minstrel, probably a warrior; decidedly—with his realization of the need of unity—a statesman; an ardent patriot, and apparently more pagan than churchly.

The discovery of the work and its subsequent destinies are as fascinating as anything else about the *Lay*. That prince of Russian bibliophiles and archæologues, Count Alexei Ivanovich Musin-Pushkin, who had unearthed and publicized many all-important early written memorials of Russia (such as the first Russian legal code, Nestor's *Chronicle*, and so on), bought, in 1795, a lot of eight pieces from a monk. The *Lay*, in a sixteenth-century manuscript, was the fifth item. A transcript was made for Catherine the Great, and the poem was published, together with a translation into modern Russian, in 1800. Then, reversing the legend of the Phoenix, the manuscript, together with much of the *editio princeps*, many other precious rarities, and the Musin-Pushkin mansion housing them, perished in the great Moscow Fire during the Napoleonic invasion of 1812. Thus, unless another miracle reveals another manuscript (or other manuscripts), the *Lay* will remain the palæographer's nightmare—and the exegete's dream.

Quite naturally, the publication of the poem raised a scholarly tempest, similar to the controversy over Ossian. Pushkin took to the cathedra at the University of Moscow to defend its authenticity, incidentally throwing several hitherto undisputed Russian literary geniuses to the lions. That authenticity has by now been proven—among other things, by a quotation from the poem in a manuscript dated 1307, and by a very palpable imitation of the *Lay* in a poem (late fourteenth or early fifteenth century) dealing with the Battle of Kulicovo (1380).

To list the translators of the *Lay* into modern Russian would be to call a roll of many of Russia's great poets. Pushkin's last creative work consists of notes on, and studies of, the poem; he meant to translate it, but evinced a strange diffidence about his powers to do justice to the earlier poet. A manuscript translation found among his papers was erroneously publicized as his, but proved to be Zhucovski's, with marginalia by Pushkin. In 1902 there were, according to Leo Wiener, thirty-five translations into modern Russian, numerous translations into Little Russian, Polish, Bohemian, Serbian, Bulgarian, German and French—six in the last language alone. The Russian translations are far more numerous by now, and partial translations are almost innumerable. But in English, oddly enough, the work had to wait over a hundred years for its first complete translation: in Professor Wiener's prose.

The following translation can, therefore, lay claim to but one small distinction at present: it is the first attempt to English a Russian classic in a form that the translator (together with others) feels to be an approach to the intent of the poem. It has been translated into modern Russian in practically every manner conceivable, from literal to patterned prose, from the most formal schemes of meter and rhyme to *vers libre*.

For the "original" text a modern recension of the Catherine II transcript and two very modern redactions of the *editio princeps* have been followed; fourteen translations into modern Russian (two of them literal) have been consulted, ranging from Zhucovski's to that of Ivan Novicov, one of the latest and apparently the most successful as well as scholarly to date, since he has followed the methods of translation suggested by Pushkin.

Since the present abridged version is intended primarily for supposititious enjoyment, the translator has tried to make the reader's path as easy as possible through the obscure and corrupt passages; while, to avoid notes, which could easily run to a hundred pages and more, the historical, the mythological, geographical and genealogical details were made as self-explanatory as possible.

The Lay of the Host of Igor, Son of Svyatoslav, Grandson of Oleg

I

WOULD IT seemly be, my brethren all,
To begin in the ancient strain,
In most ancient words,
This song about warlike deeds,
About the Host of Igor,
Igor, son of Svyatoslav?

Nay, that song should begin as befits
A tale of our own time,
And not with the subtle art
Of Boyan the Bard.

For whenever Boyan, that most wondrous bard,
Would a song create to some hero's glory,
His thoughts soared away
Like a flying squirrel
Over a tree's bark—
Like a tawny wolf
Over brown turf—
Like an eagle gray
Under the very clouds.
He sang, he recalled
The internecine wars
That began with time itself.

Translated by Bernard Guilbert Guerney. Copyright, 1943, by the Vanguard Press, Inc.

He would loosen then
Falcons half a score
'Gainst a flock of swans:
As each falcon-hero swooped
Down upon a swan,
That hero's song would be sung:
Boyan sang thereon
To Yaroslav of old;
To Mstislav the Brave
Who with his own hands slew
The giant Rededya,
Before the very eyes of all the Kasog horde;
To Roman the Fair, son of Svyatoslav.

But this Boyan, my brethren all,
Did not truly loose
Falcons half a score
On a flock of swans:
But his fingers ten, that such wonders wrought,
On the living strings would place;
And those strings themselves
Would pour forth their songs
To the glory of
The brave, doughty knights.

II

Let us then begin, brethren mine,
This our song, our lay,
With Vladimir of the times of old,
And come down to Igor of this our own day,
Who his mind did gird with all fortitude,
And his heart within him whet
With all manliness,
And, with war fervor filled,
Did his brave troops lead
Against the Polovtsi,

And against their land,
That beyond the land
Of fair Russia lies.

And 'twas then Igor
Eyed the radiant sun—
And thereafter saw
That sun darkness spread
Over all his troops.

Thereupon Igor
To his nobles spake:

"Oh, my brethren all,
And my comrades brave!
Better slain to be
Than be taken slave.
Let us, brethren mine,
Mount our wind-swift steeds;
Let us feast our eyes
On blue-watered Don!"

And a longing seized
On the Prince's mind,
And the omen dread
Fled his yearning great
To behold and brave
The broad mighty Don.

Thereupon he spake:
"I would fain break lance
On the gory field 'gainst the Polovtsi;
Fain would I with ye,
Mighty Russian men,
Either lay my head
Down in eternal sleep,
Or from helmet deep
The Don's water quaff."

And Vsevolod, the Fierce Wild Ox,
Unto Igor spake:
"My only brother, thou, thou only one,
Thou most radiant Igor!
Yet both of us foster-sons of radiant Svyatoslav!
Saddle, then, brother mine,
Thy wind-swift steeds,
For mine are already fully trained,
For mine already are saddled at Kursk!
As for my Kurians, they are tried in war:
Swaddled to the blowing of war-horns,
Cradled within helmets,
Suckled upon the sharp tips of spears.
All the paths to them are familiar,
All the wellsprings in the ravines to them are known.
Their bows are drawn taut,
Their quivers gape ready,
Their swords are whetted;
They skim over the plains
Like tawny wolves,
Seeking, for their Prince,
                    Glory,
And, for themselves,
                    Honor."

And Igor the Prince
Set his foot in his stirrup of gold
And rode off over
The vast open plain.

The eclipsed sun
On his path darkness spread;
The sudden night,
Moaning over the nearing storm,
Awakened every fowl;
Every tiny beast
Whimpered.

Deev, the bird-demon of darkness,
Fluttered on a tree and cawed

From its very top,
Bidding each outland take heed:

    Volga,
    And the Sea's Marge,
    And Posulia,
    And Surozh,
    And Corsun,
    And thine,
    Great Idol of Tmutarakan!

And the Polovtsi
Heeded the evil Deev;
Over ways untrod
They have raced unto
The broad mighty Don;
Their carts, in the dead of night,
Send forth an unearthly screech,
For all the world like
A frightened flock
Of bewildered swans!

Igor his host Don-ward leads.

And now birds in thick oak groves
Misfortunes forebode for him;
The wolves in deep ravines
Howl down evil on his head;
The eagles hawk forth a throaty call
For all wild beasts upon bones to feast;
The vixen loudly yelps
At his scarlet shield.

O my land,
My land of Russia,
Thou art left behind now,
Beyond the great Grave Mound art thou!

Long is the murk of night.
The dawn has held back its light.
The mists have veiled the plains.

The trilling of nightingales
>Has become stilled.
The cawing talk of jackdaws
>Has awakened.

Russia's mighty men
Have thrown a weir
Of scarlet shields
Across the great plain:
Seeking, for their Prince,
>>Glory,
And, for themselves,
>>Honor.

III

Early Friday morn
They crushed underfoot
The Pagan troops
Of the Polovtsi;
And, scattering like arrows
Over the field,
They drove before them
The fair Polovets maids;
They bore off with these
>Gold,
>And gossamers,
>And precious samites.

With horsecloths,
And with purple palls,
And other fine weaves
So cunningly wrought by the Polovtsi,
They builded a way,
They carpeted a path,
Over swamps, over quagmires,
For the brave son

Of Svyatoslav!
>   Scarlet his banner,
>   White his oriflamme;
>   Scarlet his pennon,
>   Silver its staff.

The brave Severski eyrie,
Seed of Oleg, Oleg son of Svyatoslav,
Slumbers on the plain:
Far have they winged their way!
Never had they submitted to wrong:
Nor to falcon, nor to gerfalcon,
Nor to thee, thou black raven,
Thou Polovchanin, foul and vile!

The Khan Ghza by now runs
Like a tawny wolf;
The Khan Konchak
Shows him the way
To the mighty Don.

And next day, at morn,
At the morn's earliest hour,
A glow red as blood
Heralds the dawn;
And black clouds
Move up from the sea,
And would fain veil over
The four sons—
The four doughty Chiefs.

And within those black clouds
Blue lightnings quiver.

A great storm is brewing;
The rain will come slanting
Like arrows
From the mighty Don;
Many a spear

Is fated to be broken here;
Many a saber
To be blunted here
Against the helmets,
Against the helmets of the Polovtsi,
Here, on the River Kayala,
The River of Sorrow,
Nigh the mighty Don!

O my land,
My land of Russia,
Thou art left behind now,
Beyond the great Grave Mound art thou!

And the winds,
Grandsons of Stribog, the god of all winds,
Dart in from the sea like arrows
Against the brave troops of Igor.
The earth rumbles,
The rivers flow turbidly,
Dust hovers over the plains and veils them,
The banners flutter in the wind:
'Tis the Polovtsi
Streaming from the Don,
Streaming from the sea;
And they the Russian troops
Encircle.

And the plains are barred:
The Seed of the Fiend barred them
With their rallying battle cry,
But the brave men of Russia
Barred them
With their scarlet shields.

Thou, Vsevolod, thou Fierce Wild Ox!
Thou standest thy ground,
Beating off the foe;
Thou wingest arrows against the warriors,

Thou thunderest against their helmets
With swords of chilled steel.
Wheresoever thou boundest, Wild Ox,
With the gold of thy helmet flashing,
There the pagans lay down
Their Polovetz heads. . . .
With thy tempered sword
Their Avar-forged helmets are cleft,
Cleft by thee, Wild Ox Vsevolod!

For why should he think of wounds,
Brethren mine,
Who has rank forgot,
And his life forgot,
And his Chernigov town,
And his sire's gold throne,
And the days and ways
Of his own loved wife—
The most beauteous one,
Daughter of the great Glyeb clan!

IV

Troy on a time knew wars.
The troublous years of Yaroslav are long since over.
Oleg, son of Svyatoslav, waged campaigns in his day also.
This Oleg
Wielded his sword as a hammer sedition to forge;
With his arrows he sowed the earth.

Thus in those olden times,
The times of Oleg the Woe-Bringing One,
Dissension was sown, e'en as grain,
And, e'en as grain, dissensions were garnered,
And therein was wasted the substance of the Russian,
That grandson of Dazhbog, the god of all fruitfulness:
Amid the dissensions of princes

The days of mankind
Were shortened.

And throughout the Russian land then
Rarely did the plowmen
Hail one another
Across the fields:
But, to make up for that,
How oft the corbies
Cawed,
The corpses among them sharing;
And the jackdaws also,
In their own tongue were choosing:
"Whither shall we fly now
To hold a fine feast?"
  Thus was it in those frays,
  And in those campaigns;
  But such a carnage as this
  Had never yet been heard of.

From early morn till even,
And from even to daybreak,
Fly arrows with barbs of chilled steel,
Swords thunder against helmets,
Spears of tempered steel crack
On an unfamiliar battlefield,
In the Polovetz land.

And the black ground
Under the horses' hooves
Was sown with bones
And watered with blood:
  And they came up
  As a crop of sorrow
  Throughout the Russian land.

  What is that din I hear,
  What rings in my ear—
  There, far away,
Early, before the break of day?

'Tis Igor, facing his troops about:
He feels for his brother,
For Vsevolod.

Thus they fought for a day;
They fought for another day;
But toward noon of the third day
The banners of Igor
Fell.

And it was then and there
That the brothers parted,
Near the swift-flowing Kayala,
On the bank of that River of Sorrow.

And the wine of blood
Thereupon ran short;
It was there the brave Russian men
Brought their feast to an end.
They gave their hosts their fill of drink,
But they themselves laid down their lives
For the Russian land.

The grasses wilt
From pity,
And each tree bends down to the earth
In sorrow.

Thus did it befall,
O brethren mine,
That a year of sadness came;
Thus the desert dust hid
The mighty war force.

Obida, Maid of Wrong,
Stirred mightily the Russian folk,
The grandsons of Dazhbog;
She plashed her wings,
Her swan-wings,
In the blue sea
Near the Don;

And, as she plashed thus,
She yearning aroused
For the weal that had been.

Among the princes there is
Dissension—
But for us common folk the pagans are
Sheer ruination!
For noble brother began contending against brother:
    "This is mine!
      And that also is mine!"
And of that which is small
The princes began saying:
    "It is great!"
And they began to forge
Discord for their own selves,
The while vile pagans
Descended upon the Russian land,
Coming from every quarter,
Reaping victories!

Oh, far, far has the falcon strayed;
    Slaying, driving the foul birds
      To the sea!
But Igor's mighty host
Will never rise to life again!

V

Throughout the Russian land
Voplenitza, the Keener, bewailed
His defeat,
And Zhalnitza, the Sorrowing,
Writhed in agony,
The burning grief within her
Like ever-replenished labdanum
Within a funereal torch
Fashioned from a horn.

The women of Russia shed bitter tears:
Lamenting, keening:
"No more are our dear ones,
Our beloved ones,
To be thought of in our thoughts,
To be minded in our minds,
To be eyed by our eyes;
And as for gold and silver—
Embroider not a stitch in either
Upon our raiment black!"

But the princes for themselves
Still discord forged;
While the pagans, for their part,
Ranging in victory
Over the Russian land,
Demanded tribute: from each household
The silver value of a squirrel skin.

Thus had the two,
Igor and Vsevolod,
Brave sons of Svyatoslav,
Through their own willfulness
Awakened an old evil anew;
And yet that evil had been subdued
By their own foster sire, Svyatoslav,
The awesome, the great
Kiev Prince.

Like a thunderstorm he
The pagans had overwhelmed,
With his mighty hosts,
With his chilled-steel swords;
He had trodden down
The land of the Polovtsi;
He had trampled down its knolls
Level with its ravines;
He had stirred up the beds
Of its rivers and lakes;

He had drained dry
Its torrents and its swamps. . . .

As for Kobyak, their pagan lord,
Him, near the Crescent-Shored Sea,
He had snatched, like a whirlwind,
From the very midst of his Polovets hordes,
Mighty, ironclad.
And Kobyak fell dead
In Kiev,
In the great Council Hall
Of Svyatoslav.
Now did the Tongue-tied Ones [Germans],
And the Venetians,
Now did the Moravians also,
And the Greeks,
Sing the glory of Svyatoslav,
Yet condemn and pity
His princely son Igor,
For that he had thrown his substance overboard,
For that he had poured Russian gold
To the bottom of that Polovets river,
The River Kayala.

For Igor
Had changed his golden saddle
        Of a prince
For the wooden saddle
        Of a slave.

VI

And walls of towns
Grew desolate.
And merriment died out
Within the towns.

On that third day,
The day of defeat,
There was utter darkness:
Two suns had dimmed,
Both pillars of scarlet fire were extinguished,
And with them two young kinsmen—moons,
That had followed the suns in war,
Dimmed and set within the sea;
While Oleg, their grandsire,
And Svyatoslav their foster sire,
Were enshrouded in gloom.

Thus on the river, the River Kayala,
Gloom overcast light;
And over all the land of Russia
The outlanders scattered and roamed,
Like a pack of hunting leopards;
And they inundated it like to a tidal wave;
And the violence of those paynims
Still more unbridled grew.

By now disgrace glory did replace,
By now thralldom had already mounted freedom,
By now Deev, Spirit of Evil,
Had come down upon the land,
While the fair maids of the Goths,
Chinking ill-got Russian gold,
Have raised their voices in song
By the shore of the blue sea;
Their song is of hoary times:
They celebrate the old revenge
Of Sharu-Khan
Against Oleg.

But as for us, now,
My fighting comrades all:
We have grown weary, longing
After our old mirth.

VII

Svyatoslav the Great thereon
Uttered golden speech,
Not unmixed with tears;
Thuswise did he speak:

"Oh, my foster sons, most dear—
Igor and Vsevolod!
Too soon did ye begin
With your swords to taunt
The land of the Polovtsi,
And for yourselves glory seek.
But your encounter was inglorious,
And ingloriously did ye spill
Their vile pagan blood.

Let your hearts so brave
Be girt with hardened steel,
And tempered with courage true.
But what was it ye wrought
For my time-silvered head?

For ye said:
"We are men by our own selves!
Whatever glory the future hold
We shall grasp for ourselves;
As for the glory that is past,
We twain shall share it between us also!"

Well, now,
Brethren mine—
Is a miracle to take place?
Is an old man to turn into a youth?
Yet when a falcon molts
He beats off other birds
Till they fly high above him:
He will let none harm his nest!

But herein lies the ill:
The other princes are no help to me. . . .

The years have turned a dour face upon us:
At Rimov now
The people groan loud
Under the swords of the Polovtsi,
And Vladimir, brother to Vsevolod's wife,
Groans from his wounds.
Sorrow and woe are the lot
Of this princely son of Glyeb!

Oh, thou Grand Prince of Suzdal,
Vsevolod,
Whom men call the Great Nest!
Art thou not thinking
Of winging here from afar,
The golden throne of thy father
To safeguard?
For thou couldst all Volga
Scatter in drops with thy oars—
Couldst drain the Don dry
With thy helmets!

Wert thou here
The Polovtsi would fetch, as slaves,
A *nogata* of fifty coppers
                    For a female,
And a *rezana* of twenty coppers
                    For a male.

And even on dry land
Thou couldst send forth
Living crossbows—
The doughty sons
Of Glyeb!

Set your feet, then, ye princes,
In your stirrups of gold:

To avenge the wrong done in our time—
To avenge the land of Russia,
To avenge the wounds upon Igor,
The brave son of Svyatoslav!

Thou Yaroslav,
Called Brains-for-Eight-Men,
Thou Prince of Galicia!
Loftily thou sittest
On thy throne of beaten gold;
The Carpathian Mountains
Thou hast propped up
With thy ironclad troops,
After barring a king's path,
After locking the gates of the Danube,
After shifting armies in huge masses
Over cloud-capped heights,
After fitting out vessels
To sail the Danube.

Thy thunderous threats
Flow through many lands;
Thou openest the gates for Kiev;
Thou bringest down with arrows
From thy sire's throne
Soldans many lands away.

Send an arrow, then,
O Sovereign One,
At Konchak, the vile caitiff.
To avenge the land of Russia—
To avenge the wounds upon Igor,
The brave son of Svyatoslav!

For by now
The light of the day has dimmed
For Igor;
And the trees of the forest
Have shed all their leaves—
But not of their own will;

Along the Rossa River,
Along the Sula River,
The towns have been apportioned
Among the invaders.

But Igor's mighty host
Will never rise to life again!

The Don is calling unto you, great Prince,
And it summons all the princes—
Yet it was but the brave princes
Of the seed of Oleg
That were the first to reach the brunt of the fray. . . .

Bar the gates of the steppes, then,
With your keen-barbed arrows—
    To avenge the land of Russia,
    To avenge the wounds upon Igor,
    The brave son of Svyatoslav!

VIII

By now the Sula River
No longer flows in a silver stream
To the town of Pereyaslavl;
And the Dvina flows through a swamp
Toward the camps of the ferocious invaders,
With the battle cry of the paynim echoing over it!

Oh, Yaroslav, Prince of Chernigov!
And all ye grandsons of Vseslav,
Who was son of Bryachislav—
Lower ye your banners all;
Your blunted swords into the ground thrust,
For ye have by now fallen away
From the glory of your grandsire;
For through your dissensions

Ye were the first to bring on the onslaught of
the paynim
Upon the land of Russia,
Upon the goodly domain of Vseslav;
'Tis because of your very feuds
That the oppression has come
From the land of the Polovtsi!

Oh, how can Russia but moan,
Recalling the years of its beginnings,
And its first princes!

I X

'Tis not spears
Humming through the air over the Danube;
'Tis the voice of Yaroslavna,
Igor's wife, I hear;
Like a linnet unseen, at early morn
She sends forth her call:

"I shall fly like the linnet,"
She utters,
"Over the Danube,
That I knew as a maid;
I shall dip my sleeve,
Trimmed with beaver pelt,
In the Kayala;
I shall cleanse the wounds and blood
On the stiffened body
Of my prince. . . ."

Early in the day
On the city wall
Of Putivl
Yaroslavna laments:

"O thou wind, thou mighty wind!
Wherefore, Lord of Air,
Dost thou blow oppression
Upon our fair land?
On thy peaceful wings
Thou dost the pagans' arrows steer
'Gainst the fighting hosts
Of my beloved ones—
Wherefore?
Would it not content thee
To blow high under a cloud,
Or upon the blue sea
The great ships to rock?
Wherefore, Lord of Air,
Have you strewn over the feather grass
My joy?"

      Early in the day
      On the city wall
      Of Putivl
      Yaroslavna laments:

"O Dnieper, thou Son of Flowing Glory!
Thou hast pierced stony mountains
Throughout the land of the Polovtsi;
And upon thy bosom thou hast rocked
The galleys of Svyatoslav
To the very camp of Khan Kobyak;
Bring to me my weal,
O Sovereign One,
That I may cherish him,
That I may not have to send after him,
Tears out to sea,
In the early dawn."

      Early in the day
      On the city wall
      Of Putivl
      Yaroslavna laments:

"O thou radiant,
Thou thrice-radiant
Sun!
Thou art warm and joyous toward all!
Wherefore, then, Sovereign One,
Against the fighting host
Of my beloved one
Dost thou send
Thy burning ray?
On the waterless plain
Through thirst thou hast made
Their bows to shrink,
Through misery thou hast made
Their quivers to warp."

X

The sea has reared up at midnight;
The waterspouts advance amid murk:
To Igor the Prince
God showeth the way
Out of the land
Of the Polovtsi,
To the land of Russia—
To his foster sire's
Throne of gold.

The evening glow
Has died out;
Igor hovers
Between sleep and waking:
Igor, in his mind
Scans the plains
From the great Don
To the Lesser Donets.

Ovlur the Polovets
(A Russian on his mother's side)
Whistled for a steed
At midnight, beyond the river.
That whistle is likewise meant
As signal to the Prince.
But the Prince comes not!
Ovlur softly called:
The earth quaked,
The grass swished,
The tents of the Polovtsi
Swayed.

    And Igor the Prince
Bounded to the river-reeds
Like an ermine;
Cast himself in the water
Like a white wild duck;
He leapt upon, sped away
On a wind-swift steed;
He sprang off the steed
And like a tawny wolf
Loped away to the meadows
Of the Donets;
He soared
Like a falcon
That hunts under the fog-banks
Wild geese, wild swans
    To break its fast
    And for noontide fare
    And for evening feast.

And even as Igor like a falcon
Flies,
So Ovlur even as a wolf
Runs;
    Their bodies scatter
    The ice-chill dew:
They had foundered
Their wind-swift steeds!

And the Donets spake:
"Igor, thou Prince!
There will be no dearth
Of praise for thee,
And of sore vexation
For Konchak,
And of rejoicing
For the land of Russia!"

And Igor spake:
"O thou, Donets!
For thee, also,
There is no dearth of praise:
For thee, who gently bore
The Prince on thy waves;
Who spread for him a carpet
Of green grass
On thy silvery banks;
Who clothed him
In thy warm mists,
Who shaded him
Under thy green trees,
Who guarded him
Like a wild duck on thy waters,
Like a gull on thy currents,
Like a black duck on thy winds.

"How different," saith the Prince,
"The Stugna River was!
Riotous were its currents
After its gluttonous swallowing-up
Of other streams,
And it shattered boats to splinters
Against the bushes on its banks!
Thus, for that youthful Prince,
Rostislav,
Did it bar the way,
Did it shut off the Dnieper;
And on the Stugna's dark bank
The mother of Rostislav

The young Prince bewailed,
And through pity for him
The flowers drooped,
And through sorrow for him
The trees hung their heads
Down to the ground."

'Tis not the magpies
Setting up their chattering:
'Tis the Khans Ghza and Konchak
Riding on Igor's trail.

And the ravens then kept from cawing,
And the jackdaws kept still,
And the crows kept from chattering.
And other birds crept along silently;
The woodpeckers alone
Kept crawling
With a slow crawl over tree bark,
Pecking away with their beaks,
Warning Igor
Of the river ahead.

The nightingales, with lissome songs,
Proclaimed the dawn.

And Khan Ghza spake to Khan Konchak:
"Since the falcon is flying to his nest,
Let us kill his young falcon
With our arrows of gold!"

And Khan Konchak said unto Khan Ghza:
"Nay, since the falcon is flying to his nest,
Then we shall fetter his new-fledged falcon
With the fetters of a fair maid."

And Khan Ghza said unto Khan Konchak:
"Yet if we should fetter him
With the fetters of a fair maid,
We shall lose both the new-fledged falcon

And our fair maid,
And, in all likelihood,
All the falcons shall swoop down,
Upon the plains of our own land
Our own fowl
Slaying."

XI

The sun sheds its light
In the sky—
Igor the Prince sheds his
On the land of Russia!

How the fair maids sing
Along the Danube—
And how their voices blend,
Floating across the sea to Kiev!

Over the steep Borichev slope,
Into the heart of Kiev,
Rides Igor,
Toward the Many-Towered Church,
The Church of the Mother of God.

All the lands rejoice!
All the towns make merry!

Having sung a song
To the old princes,
Let us sing a song
To the young ones also:

"Glory
To Igor, son of Svyatoslav—
To the Fierce Wild Ox, Vsevolod—
To Vladimir, son of Igor!

All hail
To the princes and their knightly band,
Who fought on the battlefield
Against the troops of the infidels
For all Christian men!

To the princes—
        Glory!
And to their knightly band—
Ay, verily—
        Glory!"

Apocrypha

THE APOCRYPHAL LITERATURE in Russia is a vast one and for the most part fascinating. Its Oriental sources and its transmission through pilgrims, traders, travelers, are equally obvious. While many of the stories are biblical Apocrypha (of both Testaments), the reader should not imagine them as paralleling the tidy and comparatively short Apocrypha he or she is familiar with in English; a much nearer and truer analogy is that of the *Gesta Romanorum* and the bestiaries, lapidaries, and so forth, of the Middle Ages. Of the two-score groupings (or thereabouts), the largest is that of stories dealing with King Solomon, from which the following selection has been taken; it has been traced to the Talmud. The Kitovras occurs in Russian literature of the fourteenth century, but the story itself is from a manuscript of the fifteenth; the monster is most probably our old friend the centaur, but theses have been written to claim him for the unicorn family, and even to link him with Leviathan, all of which, of course, need not spoil the reader's enjoyment.

The rendering is, by choice, a rather free one.

Of the Kitovras

AND NEXT SOLOMON, in his wisdom, would learn of the Kitovras. He had learned that this monster dwelt in a far-off wilderness. And Solomon knew other things also; he therefore ordered a rope to be

Translated by Bernard Guilbert Guerney. Copyright, 1943, by the Vanguard Press, Inc.

woven of metal strands, and a hoop of chilled metal to be forged, and upon the latter he had engraved an incantation, invoking the name of God. And he sent forth the chiefest man at his court, and huntsmen with him, and he bade them take along many skins of wine and many skins of mead, and the fleece of many sheep. And those he sent arrived at the place designated, and, lo, there were three wells there, even as Solomon had told them, but the Kitovras was not there.

Following the instructions given them by the Wise King, they drained the three wells and closed the inlets thereof with the fleece; two of the wells they filled with wine, and the third with mead, and thereafter concealed themselves in ambush, for they had been told that the monster came to those wells to drink.

And he came in due time, and lay him down to drink, but, beholding the wine, he said: None gains wisdom from drinking wine.

But since his thirst was exceedingly great, he said shortly: Yet art thou the wine that makes the heart of man rejoice.

And thereupon he drank dry the two wells of wine, and the third of mead. Now the wine had coursed through his blood and made him drowsy, and he lay him down, and his sleep was a deep one. Thereupon the chiefest man at Solomon's court drew near him with his men, and he placed the hoop about the monster's neck, and his men bound him with the rope woven of metal strands. And in due time the Kitovras awoke and would have rent his fetters, but the chiefest man at Solomon's court spake to him: The name of the Lord is upon thee and forbids thee.

And the monster, beholding the name of the Lord upon the hoop about his neck, submitted and went peacefully whither he was led.

Now a Kitovras will never follow a path that winds or is crooked, but ever a straight one; such is his habit. And when he arrived at Jerusalem, they had to level the road for him, and even palaces had to be razed, for he would not go if the road was not straight as an arrow.

They came to a widow's house; she was lamenting, and she begged him for alms, saying: I am a widow, and poor. And he hid behind a house, and brake two of his ribs, and they went on.

As he was led through the market place he heard a man chaffering at a cobbler's stall: Hast thou not sandals that will last for seven years?

And the Kitovras laughed mightily.

And he saw another man, a teller of fortunes, and again the Kitovras laughed.

And he saw a marriage being performed as they passed a house, and he wept. . . .

Then, when they came to the palace, Solomon questioned the Kitovras, for all these things had been reported to him.

And Solomon asked: Wherefore didst thou break two of thy ribs when the poor widow begged alms of thee?

And the Kitovras answered: A soft word can break bones, but a hard one stirreth up wrath.

And Solomon asked: Wherefore didst thou laugh so loud at the man who wanted sandals that would last seven years?

And the Kitovras answered: I did but look at him, and I saw that he would not last even seven days.

And Solomon asked: Wherefore didst thou laugh at the man telling fortunes?

And the Kitovras answered: He was telling men and women of that which is hidden, yet he himself knew not that a hoard of gold lay buried under where he stood.

Thereupon the Wise King bade men go and dig and ascertain. They went, and when they came back they brought back the pot of gold they had dug up.

And Solomon asked: And wherefore didst thou weep at the sight of the wedding ceremony?

And the Kitovras answered: I wept out of pity for the groom, for I knew he would not live out the month.

And the Wise King once more sent forth men, and they came back and told him: The bridegroom had dropped dead as he was leading the bride over the threshold of his house. . . .

Folk Epos

FOLK BALLADRY is just as thriving an institution in Russia, even at this day, as it is in the more remote regions of our own Appalachians; the modern Russian *skiziteli*, or reciters, deal, however, with somewhat different subjects (battles, great events, popular heroes) than the crimes, feuds, and train wrecks so dear to the hillbilly balladeer. But, along with the topical Russian ballads, the ancient *byliny* (tales of things that have been) or *stariny* as they are also called (tales of the times of old) retain their popularity to this day, being told or chanted around the bunkhouse fire by the lumberjacks in the North of Russia and in the forecastles of fishing boats on the Lake of Onezh, the White Sea, and even the Arctic Ocean. These older *byliny* with their accompanying chants are transmitted from father to son, the inherent charm surviving despite all the variations, incongruities, and anachronisms due to such a mode of transmission, and certain families are famous as reciters.

With that diffidence peculiar to Russians in matters literary, Russian critics have attempted to prove that the *bylina* is of non-Slavic origin and that it is not even actual folk poetry but the work of minstrels, thus having come down from the court to the common folk. There are a great many of these critics, and the theories are as many as the critics; to date, however, all of the former remain conjectural and very, very far from conclusive.

The most popular *byliny*, dealing with the fabulous lives and exploits of *bogatyri*, the Men of Might or folk heroes, belong to the Kiev and Novgorod Cycles; very, very roughly, and in a very, very Scythian way, these *bogatyri* may be said to correspond to the goodly knights of King Arthur or the paladins of Charlemagne. And by all odds the greatest of all the doughty men surrounding Prince Vladimir, enthroned on a throne of gold in the hill-builded city of Kiev, was Ilya of Murom (although he never did reach the innermost circle), two episodes of whose Gargantuan life are given below, and who has offered inspiration to many poets, painters, and composers of Russia. (Glière has written a symphony about him which is played occasionally by the leading American symphony orchestras.)

Needless to say, this folk epos has offered a field which has been lovingly explored and cultivated by the ethnologists and folklorists (the first collection was published in 1804, based upon transcriptions made by Kirsha Danilov, a Siberian Cossack). Thus there are several possible interpretations of Ilya. There is passable evidence that he was an historical character (*c.* 1188); certain Russians call themselves Ilya's Peasants even now, and certain woodsmen in the practically virgin forests of Murom are noted for their exceptional stature, build, and strength. Other scholars classify him as a Russian saint, or even as the Prophet

Elijah. He may even be regarded as one of the Thunder-gods, of the company of Jove, Thor, Indra, and the Slavic Perun. Or you may choose the generally accepted theory (to which the present writer inclines), which does not necessarily deny his historicity: that Ilya of Murom is a personification of the Russian peasantry, just as the Monstrous Idol is a personification of the barbaric Southern hordes that invaded Russia.

The Oliver Twistian reader is referred to the prose versions of these *byliny* in Isabel F. Hapgood's *The Epic Songs of Russia* (preferably the 1916 edition) or, better still, to the decidedly more scholarly and interesting treatment, with some approach to rhythm, of N. Kershaw Chadwick, in *Russian Heroic Poetry* (Cambridge University Press, 1932).

Ilya of Murom and the Sandaled Pilgrims

WHO IS THERE who would tell us of the things of old,
Of the things of old, of the things that have been,
Of that Ilya, of Ilya of Murom,
Of Ilya Murometz, the son of Ivanov?
He sat, never stirring for three-and-thirty years;
They of the begging brotherhood came unto him,
Jesus the Christ himself, and His Apostles two.
"Go thou, Ilya, and fetch us somewhat to drink!"
"Begging brethren, I can stir neither hand nor foot!"
"Get thee up, Ilya—do not us deceive!"
Ilya heaved and rose, all unkempt and dazed;
He brought back a bowl bigger than a pail—

Translated by Bernard Guilbert Guerney. Copyright, 1943, by the Vanguard Press, Inc.

To the begging brethren he did offer it;
But the begging men made him drink himself,
And when he had drunk they did question him:
"Dost thou feel, Ilya, much of strength in thee?"
"If there were a pillar reared to the very sky,
If a ring of gold were to that pillar fixed—
I would seize that ring, all Holy Russia heave!"
"Go you now, Ilya, another bowlful fetch!"
Ilya offered them a second bowl with water filled,
But the pilgrims made him drink thereof himself.
Ilya drained it off without drawing breath—
A big bowlful, bigger than a pail.
They thereon began for to question him:
"Dost thou feel, Ilya, much of strength in thee?"
"Of my strength, I vow, I have but half now."
So the sandaled pilgrims unto Ilya spake:
"Thou, Ilya, shalt be a great man of might,
In a fray to face death is not thy fate's scroll:
Thou mayst fight, mayst smite, any man of might,
And with any pagan horde mayst battle do;
But never offer fight to one Sviatogor—
'Tis all earth itself can do to bear his full weight;
Go not forth to fight 'gainst Samson, that man of might—
He hath upon his head seven hairs by angels blest.
Contend not against the line of the Mikulovs—
Our dank mother-earth hath great love for him;
Likewise, wage no fight against V'Oleg, Seslav's own son;
If he cannot lay thee low through main strength
He will bring thee down by his wit and craft.
Get thee, Ilya, a steed worthy of a man of might,
Fare thee forth into the open field, wide as any sea,
Buy thee there a first-foaled colt,
Put him in a stall for all of three months;
For three nights let that colt in an orchard loose,
And let that colt roll in three morning dews.
Lead him then to a high spiked fence:
When the colt takes to leaping over that spiked fence,
To that side of it, and then back again,
Thou mayst ride him then, wheresoe'er thou wilt—
He will bear thee well."

And with that the pilgrims vanished in thin air.
Ilya went to his begetter, to his own sire,
Where he was tending to his husbandry;
There was a burned patch to be cleared of charred oak-stumps.
Ilya cleared away all the oak-tree stumps,
In a river deep he cast every one,
And, his task all done, wended his way home.

B. G. G.

Ilya of Murom and the Most Monstrous Idol

The monstrous pagan Idol came to the throne city of Kiev,
Breathing threats, striving to inspire great fear—
It came to that mighty Prince, to Vladimir,
And took a stand in the Prince's courtyard,
And sent an envoy to the Prince, to Vladimir,
Asking that Prince Vladimir, of the throne of Kiev,
Might send a champion against him,
A foeman worthy of the Idol's strength.
And the envoy came before Vladimir,
And the envoy spake to him these words:
"Thou Vladimir, Prince of the throne of Kiev!
Send thou forth a champion into the open field,
A champion and a foeman great of strength,
So that he may stand up against the Monstrous Idol."
Thereupon Vladimir the Prince he became afeard,
Most dreadfully afeard, and woebegone besides.
Thereupon Ilya spake to him these words:
"Be thou not woebegone, Vladimir, be not thou grieved:
In battle to fall is not written in my fate's scroll;
I will ride forth into the open field, the sea-wide field,
And that Monstrous Idol of the pagans slay."
Ilya shod himself in slippers fashioned of soft silk,
Over his shoulder he slung a wallet of velvet black,
On his comely head he put a cap from the land of Greece,

Translated by Bernard Guilbert Guerney. Copyright, 1943, by the Vanguard Press, Inc.

And fared forth to meet the Monstrous Idol of the infidel.
But it was no small oversight he had been guilty of:
He had not taken along his war-club of chilled steel,
And he had not taken with him his razor-keen sword.
He walked along a path, and fell into deep thought:
"There, I am setting forth against the monstrous heathen Idol,
Yet what if I come upon him in an ill hour, at the wrong time,
Whatever will I have to overcome the Monstrous Idol with?"
At that very hour, at that very time,
Ivan the Great, in pilgrim dress, came toward him;
In his hand he bore a staff weighing three hundred pounds or more.
Ilya to him spake these words:
"Ho, there, Ivan, thou hulk, thou pilgrim man,
Let me have thy staff for but a little while—
I have to go to the Monstrous Idol of the heathen men."
But Ivan the Great, the mighty pilgrim man,
Would not yield to him his staff, fit for a hero's hand.
Ilya then spake to him these words:
"Ho, there, Ivan, thou hulk, thou pilgrim man!
Let thee and me fight man to man—
For a death in fight is not writ on my fate's scroll;
I shall kill thee and thy staff will be mine."
Thereon Great Ivan, mighty pilgrim man, was most sorely wroth;
He raised that staff high above his head
And plunged it deep into the dank earth.
Then went off the mighty pilgrim man, sobbing like a babe.
It was all Ilya of Murom could do
That staff to loosen from out the dank earth.
And he came to the palace of white stones built,
Where this Monstrous Idol of the pagans dwelt,
He came to the Idol and he greeted him.
The Monstrous Idol spake unto Ilya:
"Ho, there, wanderer, thou pilgrim man!
How big is your man of might, Ilya of Murom?"
Unto him Ilya in these words did speak:
"Ilya is in size just the way I be."
Then to him the monstrous pagan Idol said:
"Does this Ilya of yours eat a lot of bread?
Does this Ilya of yours drink a lot of ale?"
Then to him Ilya spoke in these words:

"Ilya eats as much as I myself eat,
Ilya drinks as much as I myself drink."
The monstrous heathen Idol then said unto him:
"What a mighty man your Ilya must be!
Take me, now; I drink seventy quarts of ale and more at a meal,
I eat two hundred and fifty pounds of bread and more at a meal."
Ilya unto him then in these words spake:
"Our Ilya of Murom was sired by a farming man,
And his father had a cow that ate its fool head off;
It drank a lot and it ate a lot—but it up and burst."
The Monstrous Idol, he liked that speech none too much;
He snatched out his dagger great, of cold-tempered steel,
And threw it at the wandering pilgrim man
With all of his strength, his mighty strength.
And Ilya of Murom, he just ducked a mite, off to one side,
And that knife of cold-tempered steel near his ear whizzed by
To the opposite wall, between windows two.
The mighty heart of Ilya of Murom was inflamed thereat,
He snatched off his comely head the cap from the land of Greece,
And threw it in the face of the monstrous heathen Idol;
And then he clove the Monstrous Idol in twain,
And thereon they chanted dirges for the Monstrous Idol.

B. G. G.

Athanassii Nikitin

FIFTEENTH CENTURY

~

ATHANASSII NIKITIN set forth, in or about 1468, for India, on a commercial venture, and did not return until 1474. While he was apparently as adventurous as Marco Polo, he does not seem to have fared as well as a trader. His account, couched in a most sober style even when he tells the most fantastic details, is unique in Russian literature as an early travel narrative. The selection is taken from *India in the Fifteenth Century,* a publication of the Hakluyt Society (London, 1857); the translation of Count Wielhorski has been revised.

Traveler's Tales

ALL THE HINDUS walk on foot; they are fast walkers. They are all naked and barefooted, and carry a shield in one hand and a sword in the other. Some of the serving men go armed with long bows; the arrows likewise are long.

Elephants are much used in battle. Men on foot are sent ahead, the Khorassanians being mounted; both men and horses are in full armor. Large scythe blades are attached to the trunks and tusks of the elephants, and the animals are covered by plates of steel, with cunningly wrought designs thereon. Each elephant carries a citadel upon its back,

Translated by Bernard Guilbert Guerney. Copyright, 1943, by the Vanguard Press, Inc.

and each citadel holds a dozen men in armor, with guns and barbs for weapons. . . .

In Aland [Aladinand?] there is a bird called the *gukkuk,* that flies at night, and calls out *gukkuk!*—and if it lights on the roof of any house a man will die therein; and if any man attempts to kill it, fire will be seen issuing from its beak.

Huge wildcats prowl about of nights and catch fowls. As for the apes, they live in the thick woods and have a Prince of their own, who is attended by a host of armed followers. When any ape is caught, a complaint reaches the Prince and an army is sent forth to recapture the missing. And when they come to a town they pull down the houses and beat the people. And their armies, so it is said, are vast in numbers. They speak their own tongue and bring forth many young, and when the offspring looks neither like its father nor its mother, it is thrown out on a highroad. Thus they are often caught by the Hindus, who teach them every sort of handicraft or sell them at night (so that they may not find their way home), or teach them to dance. . . .

Gabriel Romanovich
Derzhavin
1 7 4 3 – 1 8 1 6

AMONG THE bizarre lives of poets anywhere, Derzhavin's is not the least bizarre. He was of Tatar blood; he received most of his education from a country deacon, a bell ringer, and, later, from a German convict; the best years of his life were spent in the barracks; yet from rake, tosspot, rowdy, cardsharp, and perpetrator of a series of acts all within the compass of the hangman's tarry noose he became brilliant soldier, Governor, Secretary to Catherine the Great, Senator, Treasurer, Minister (of all things!) of Justice, and— Russia's greatest poet of the eighteenth century. And all this in a series of rises and falls, falls and rises. He played a leading part in suppressing the Pugachev uprising—and, for his pains, came within an ace of being hanged at the same time that Pugachev himself was quartered. Catherine complained that he was not "merely rude" during his reports "but actually cursed." Paul I disgraced him for a "sassy" answer;

Alexander I for an "unseemly" one. "I am hot-tempered," Derzhavin himself wrote, "and the very Devil for telling the truth!"

He laid the foundation of his fortunes with, and became Catherine's "own author" through, his *Ode to Felicia;* time and again he repaired those fortunes with those odes of his. Yet they are at their best and sincerest only while he is away from court. There they assume satiric under- and over-tones. One of the greatest, *To Potentates and Judges,* which had taken years in the writing, was banned by the censors; Catherine herself suppressed the entire first printing of the *Ode on the Taking of Warsaw.*

Together with Lomonossov, Derzhavin remains the founder of Russian poetics, master of Russian didacticism (even though here his supremacy is challenged again by the same Lomonossov) and, above all, what Gogol called him: Singer of Grandeur.

God *

I AM the link of all the worlds in being,
I am of nature the uttermost degree,
I am the center of all things that are living,
The first stroke e'er drawn by the Divinity.
My body molders into a dust corrupt—
My mind bids lightning the heavens to disrupt;
King, slave, worm, god—all these I am!
Yet though so wondrous every way,
Whence have I come? No one can say:
Yet from myself I could not stem.
    Thy own creation I, Creator,
Of Thy great Wisdom I a thing—
Life Source, of good Disseminator,
Soul of my soul and its true King!
So that Thy own Truth its laws might keep,
My deathless life thou mad'st to overleap
Death's abyss of finality;
So that my spirit mortality attain
And that through death I might regain,
Father, Thy immortality!
1784

                          B. G. G.

Plaint

THEY caught a sweet-voiced bird,
And tightly clutch the wildwood thing;
Instead of song but squeaks are heard—
But they keep at it: "Sing, bird, sing!"

* From *God, An Ode.*

Ivan Ivanovich
Dmitriev
1 7 6 0 – 1 8 3 7

THIS FABULIST and sentimental lyricist was, among other things, the great encourager of Krylov. It was Dmitriev's truly remarkable parody-satire, *In Foreign Accents,* which dealt what amounted to a fatal blow to Russian pseudoclassicism and fulsome ode writing.

Epigram

"I HAVE been robbed! The thieves have ruined me!"
  "I sympathize, I share your grief."
"They stole a batch of my own poetry—"
  "I sympathize—with the poor thief."

B. G. G.

Poets

THE ancients aimed at stars; our aims quite lower are;
The ancients struck the lyre—we strum on a guitar.
The ancients strove for fame; to them love was a god:
We are content with coppers or with a lordling's nod.

Ivan Andreievich
Krylov

1 7 6 8 OR 6 9 – 1 8 4 4

IVAN ANDREIEVICH KRYLOV, the foremost fabulist in a country rich in fabulists, was the son of a poor army officer. He came to Petersburg in 1782, soon entered literary and theatrical circles, and began his career as a writer of comedies and tragedies. In 1789 he commenced publication of a satirical periodical, *The Ghostly Post Office,* and in 1791 organized, with others, a printing plant, where he published his *Spectator,* to which he contributed some of his best satires.

Krylov opposed, with spirit and wit, serfdom, bureaucracy, the reactionary nobility and the stagnating bourgeoisie, and was against the sentimental, the conservative, and the false in literature. The persecutions which Catherine the Great (who had founded the first satirical periodical in Russia and was a satirist of note, if not of things too near home) had begun against radical literature, and

which led to the arrest and banishment of many of the best writers and spirits of the time, affected Krylov as well; in 1792 his plant was raided and he was placed under surveillance. Leaving Petersburg, he passed over a decade in the provinces in extreme hardship, reduced, like Gogol after him, to the lowliest task of the Russian intellectual—tutoring the impossible hobbledehoys of the rich.

He did not return to Petersburg until 1806, when, through the good offices of Olenin, grandee and Mæcenas, he obtained a sinecure in the Public Library and a pension.

He played the violin, had the utmost contempt for dress, an utter disregard of his surroundings, more than a streak of Oblomovism (he read utter trash lying on a divan at the library, merely to kill time), and believed in digging his grave with his teeth.

He published the first of his immortal fables in 1806, under the encouragement of another fabulist, the poet Dmitriev. The first few show the influence of classicism; the vast majority represent the very pinnacle of Krylov's creativeness and are written with wit, clarity, and an observation drawn from a vast fund of worldly wisdom.

With that same curious self-depreciation of their own literature (alluded to elsewhere in this book) so peculiar to the Slavs, Russian critics have pointed out Krylov's indebtedness to La Fontaine (as if La Fontaine himself had not borrowed freely from Aesop and Bidpai) and others. As a matter of cold, scholarly analysis, of the more than two hundred fables of Krylov only thirty-eight are borrowed. Krylov gave the fable new content. That his fables are just as applicable today as when they first appeared can be easily seen from the selections here given.

There are any number of these fables in English, in literal prose and in verse; the best of the latter the Editor has been able to find is that of I. Henry Harrison (*Kriloff's Original Fables,* London, 1883), from which the selections have been made.

The Cat and the Cook

A COOK whose learning passed for great,
　His kitchen left one evening late,
Intent (he was a man of goodly life)
On pothouse ale in memory of his wife,
　Who died that day a year before;
And, as he had of eatables a store,
　To keep them safe from mouse or rat
　He placed on guard a favorite Cat.
What's this he sees on his return? The floor
All strewn with piecrust, Tommy on the stretch
Behind a cask, a chicken in his jaws,
And purring softly, at a bone he gnaws.
"Ah, glutton! Ah, thou nasty wretch!"
The Cook's tongue for abuse was much respected:

The translations of these three fables by Krylov are by Henry I. Harrison, from *Kriloff's Original Fables,* London, 1883.

"Is't not a shame in thee to desecrate these walls?
[Tom the while a nice tidbit inspected.]
What, thou, that everyone a fine Cat called,
A model for all mildness past belief—
O thou—fie, blush for thy disgrace!
The neighbors all shall cry out to thy face:
'Tomcat's a rogue! Tomcat's a thief!'
Nor yard nor kitchen now shall Tommy see;
From hungry wolves the sheepfold should be free;
The scandal he, the pest, the eyesore of our streets!"
(Tom listens, yes; but still—he eats!)
Our orator, once set on morals preaching,
Could find no end unto his flow of teaching.
What then? While he his own words followed,
Tommy the last piece of the roast had swallowed.

And I would teach our Cook, the dunce,
By letters on the wall carved big:
To waste no time in talking like a prig,
But force employ at once.

1812

The Swan, the Pike, and the Crab

WHEN partners with each other don't agree,
Each project must a failure be,
And out of it no profit come, but sheer vexation.

A Swan, a Pike, and Crab once took their station
In harness, and would drag a loaded cart;
But when the moment came for them to start,
They sweat, they strain, and yet the cart stands still; what's lacking?
The load must, as it seemed, have been but light;
The Swan, though, to the clouds takes flight,
The Pike into the water pulls, the Crab keeps backing.

Now which of them was right, which wrong, concerns us not:
The cart is still upon the selfsame spot.

1814

The Ape and the Spectacles

AN APE in old age suffered much from blindness,
But, being told, through human kindness,
That such a weakness need not long endure,
A pair of spectacles the cure,
He went at once and bought a dozen pair.

The Ape the spectacles turns o'er and o'er,
His forehead's hot with them, his tail quite sore;
He smells at them, and licks them round with care;
And still the spectacles are useless quite.
"Confound them," quoth the Ape, "and every fool
That listens to the lies of human spite;
I'm cheated like a boy at school,
For spectacles set no eyes right."
Thus saying, on the nearest stone he dashes them,
And into sparkling splinters smashes them.

The same thing happens not to apes alone:
Where they should profit by the thing they own,
The ignorant to loss will always turn it;
And worse with fools who for their rank are known,
They will not only spoil a thing, but spurn it.

1815

Vassílii Andreievich
Zhucovski
1 7 8 3 – 1 8 5 2

THE FIRST POET whom the Russians took to their hearts as a poet for himself alone, and not as a representative of some school or literary mode, was the illegitimate son of a landowner by the name of Bunin (there is a connection here with Ivan Bunin) and a captive Turkish woman, and took his name from an impoverished hanger-on of the Bunins. In 1797 the poet entered the University of Moscow; here, for the next five years, in the family of I. P. Turgenev, Director of the University, he first found himself in the right milieu.

He began as a translator from the German, but first attracted attention in 1802 with his translation of Gray's *Elegy*. He took part in the bloody Battle of Borodino (September 7, 1812); in 1815 he became a member of the famous Arzamas circle, which was unrelentingly even if jocosely carrying on a struggle against the conservatism of classical poetry; and in 1817 was appointed Reader at Court and tutor to the Czarevich who was later to become Alexander II. His life at court for a quarter of a century inevitably transformed him, as somebody has aptly put it, into an "Ossian in a powdered wig."

His craftsmanship is superb; not one of the poets before Pushkin (who considered Zhucovski his master), with the exception of Batiushcov, perhaps, can compare with him in the music of language. His role as a representative of the so-called sentimental style was a tremendous one.

Zhucovski presents a peculiar problem in representation. Three-quarters of his output are translations, which played an enormous part in the history of Russian literature. Translations helped to form Zhucovski's own style, which in its turn influenced the development of Russian poetry greatly. Also, the peculiar Russians consider what they describe as *artistic translation* on a par with so-called *original* or *creative* work. Pushkin, himself a master translator, called Zhucovski the Genius of Translation. In other words, if Virgil and Chaucer are *original* authors, why not consider Zhucovski an original? Just because he was honest about acknowledging his debts instead of stealing outright?

Hence a single exception has been made in his case, and Mr. Spiegel has acquitted himself well in the peculiar and ticklish task of translating a translation; *The Midnight Muster at Waterloo,* the reader is assured, is much better in Zhucovski's Russian and Mr. Spiegel's English than is the original in the rather stolid German of Seidlitz.

Song

WHEN I was loved, in raptures and in bliss lost,
Like an ensorceled dream the whole of my life ran;
But you forgot me—where is happiness' ghost?
Ah, but your love my happiness was then!

When I was loved, I sang, by you inspired;
My soul to live upon your praise was fain:
But you forgot me—my moment's gift expired;
Ah, but your love my genius was then!

When I was loved, gifts of sweet charity
My hand how often bore to poverty's poor den!
But you forgot—heart's pity is a rarity;
Ah, but your love my kindliness was then!

B. G. G.

The Midnight Muster at Waterloo

AT MIDNIGHT, the ghostliest hour,
The drummer from his coffin rises
And, pacing his beat to and fro,
An alert on his drum loudly sounds.
And within dark graves his loud drum
The infantry mighty awakens;
The stalwart young Chasseurs spring up,
Spring up, too, the Grenadier graybeards—
From under bleak Russia's deep snows,
From Italy's green, fertile valleys,
From Africa's sun-parchèd wastes,
And Palestine's sands deep and burning.

At midnight, the ghostliest hour,
The bugler from his grave emerges
And, riding his steed to and fro,
On his trumpet a loud alert sounds.
And his trumpet within dark graves
The cavalry mighty awakens:
The silver-haired Hussars spring up,
And Cuirassiers, fierce and mustachioed;
And flying from North and from South,
From East and from West come forth rushing
On steeds light and swift as the wind
The squadrons in endless succession.

At midnight, the ghostliest hour,
From his sepulcher comes the Commander;
His uniform hid by his surtout,
He wears a cocked hat and a saber,
And, his old charger bestriding,
He rides, his Grand Army saluting.

His Marshals behind him ride slowly,
Behind him his aides, too, are riding,
While his soldiers return his greeting.
Then his steed before them he reins,
To ghostly but martial strains
His troops, as they march by, reviewing.
Next all of his Generals he
In a close knot about him gathers,
And in the ear of the nearest
He whispers his password and slogan.
The Generals then to the men
That password impart and that slogan:
And *France!* is the password they hear,
While the slogan is *Saint Helena!*

And thus for his soldiers of old,
His army's grand muster reviewing,
At midnight, the ghostliest hour,
From his death has their Emperor risen.

MORRIS SPIEGEL

Remembrance

OF THOSE loved way-companions who made dear
With their companionship our world of strife and stir,
 Say not with sadness: *They are no longer here!*
 But say with gratitude: *They were.*

B. G. G.

Alexander Sergheievich
Pushkin
1 7 9 9 – 1 8 3 7

"THERE IS no extremity to which this unhappy young man may not go," read the letter handed to Pushkin by the Ministry of Foreign Affairs, after his first exile, for transmission to his new superior, "but neither is there any perfection which he could not attain through the sublimity of his gifts. . . ."

Alexander Sergheievich Pushkin was born in Moscow, June 6 (May 26, Old Style), 1799. His maternal great-grandfather was Ibrahim Hannibal, supposedly an Abyssinian petty prince, whom the poet proudly immortalized in *The Negro of Peter the Great*. The poet's lackadaisical father came from one of the oldest families of *boyars* or nobles, whose names run like a rogue's yarn through the bizarre tapestry of Russian history. Four Pushkins signed the document choosing the Romanovs for ascension to the Russian throne; another Pushkin was made a head shorter by Peter the Great; Ibrahim Hannibal himself had a taste of Siberia. Hardly a staid clan, the Pushkins.

The poet's early education was of a most preposterous nature, in a fantastically chaotic circus of a household, under a succession of shiftless tutors—for the most part Frenchmen spewed forth by the Revolution. One instance of the weird nature of his early education will suffice: a German was appointed to teach the future supreme lord of the Russian language precisely that subject. One saving influence was his old nurse, Arina Rodionovna, a marvelous storyteller, who has been called the intermediary between the poet and the Russian folk; his love for her was lifelong, and she is immortalized in his verse. Another was the vast library—French, of course. Pushkin's love of the book began when he was about eight; he spent whole nights reading, and even at eleven his knowledge of French literature was astonishing. His precociousness was not confined to reading; he started writing at nine (in French), and his first poem appeared in print in 1814. He entered the newly founded aristocratic Lyceum in 1811, and was graduated in 1817.

1817 to 1820 were spent in Petersburg, in the Ministry of Foreign Affairs, and in living the life of the dandy. Yet it was during this period that one of his greatest and longest folk poems was written; its publication in 1820 marked a real departure from Classicism and placed Pushkin in the front ranks as a writer. In the same year he first ran afoul of the powers, through his *Ode to Liberty* and other political poems which were circulated in manuscript, and, after narrowly escaping Siberia, he was exiled to Ekaterinoslav and Kishenev, at that time hellholes in the South of Russia. 1820 also marked his first trip, for health, to the Caucasus, and his introduction to the poetry of Byron. In Kishenev he met many of the future Decembrists (participants of the unsuccessful uprising of December 14 [26, New Style], 1825). In 1823 he was transferred to Odessa, in Russia proper. But here, too, a letter of his, atheistic in tenor, was intercepted; he was dismissed from service and ordered to live at Mihailovskoe, a family estate in Pskov, under the surveillance, among others, of policemen, priests, and even of his father. During this exile ("Books! For God's sake, send me books!") he imbibed folklore from Arina Rodionovna, worked on *Oneghin*, wrote *Boris Godunov.*

The abortive uprising of December 1825, accompanying the accession of Nicholas I to the throne, involved Pushkin. He was pardoned by the Emperor, who offered his protection, appointed himself Pushkin's censor (which did not prevent even the imperially approved writings from being subsequently banned by the regular censorship), and placed the poet under the unrelenting surveillance of the infamous Section III, a secret police within the secret police. Twice was Pushkin in serious danger again: over *André Chénier* and the *Gabrieliad:* the poet had to deny the authorship of the latter to escape exile.

1829 was marked by another trip to the Caucasus. And another repeated attempt to go abroad was frustrated. In 1830 he wrote the *Tales of Belkin.* In 1831 he married N. N. Goncharova, almost half as young as himself, whose great beauty was hardly matched by her brains. In 1834 the Emperor appointed Pushkin to a post which necessitated his constant attendance at court; the poet was unable to refuse.

A court intrigue, which resulted in an anonymous letter calling Pushkin a cuckold, led to a duel with a fop, one George Heckeren, Baron d'Anthès, brother-in-law to his wife. On February 8 (New Style), 1837, the poet ("Pushkin fights a duel a day," one of his fair friends had once written of him jocosely) received a serious pistol wound from which he died two days later.

Czarism and Philistinism had scored again.

It is insulting to call Pushkin the Russian Byron—just as it would be honoring Byron too greatly to call him the British Pushkin. Byron's "influence" on Pushkin has been vastly exaggerated. Pushkin's greatest mentor was Zhucovski. The author of *Russlan and Ludmilla* was "influenced" by Voltaire, the Koran, Arina Rodionovna, Shakespeare; the germ of *The Golden Cockerel* was derived from our own Washington Irving.

As for Pushkin's influence—that is too vast a subject even to touch upon here. That influence extends down to the present-day Zoshchenko. If, Dostoievski claimed, all contemporary Russian prose writers of significance had emerged from under Gogol's *Overcoat,* his own *Crime and Punishment* had been fostered under the mantle of *The Queen of Spades.* Pushkin is a true original. He is a master poet—it is unfortunate that his true genius is not always apparent in translations—storyteller, historian, critic; he fashioned the inherent strength, grace, delicacy, vigor, savor, color and music of the Russian language into a superb literary instrument second (by a narrow margin) only to the supreme one—English. The greatest lyricist and romanticist of Russia was also its greatest realist; if Gogol had not written *The In-spector General* as a play, Pushkin would have done it as a short story.

He gave to Russian literature both form and new content, showed the way to a true representation of national life, and drew the strength and beauty of his creations from the soul and the actuality of the people. His genius brought back from the fabulous land of Lukomorie, the Land of the Crescent-Shaped Sea Marge, that spirit of Russia of which he sang.

After all, Pushkin was killed at the height of his powers. The papers found after his death indicate some of the vast projects he had in mind. Who can now tell to what still greater heights he might have risen, what supreme figures in world literature he may have surpassed?

No; it is more just to accept the other, equally familiar tag for Pushkin: the Shakespeare of Russia.

An anthology can represent only a few facets of Pushkin. He is here represented as lyricist, short story writer, and a teller of fairy tales—the particular fairy tale here included may also be considered a political satire.

The most complete representation in English of Pushkin's poetry and prose is Avrahm Yarmolinsky's volume, with an able biographical sketch, *The Works of Alexander Pushkin* (Random House, N. Y.). His *Gabrieliad* has also been Englished—after a fashion.

The Queen of Spades

The Queen of Spades denotes secret ill-will.
From the latest Fortune-Teller

I

And in cold, nasty weather
They would all get together,
Frequently.
They played for big stakes
(Lord forgive their mistakes!)
Ardently.
And they played more and more,
And chalked up the score,
Big and plain.
Thus, in cold, nasty weather
They spent time together
Not in vain.

K. TH. RYLEIEV *and* A. A. BESTUZHEV

THEY WERE PLAYING CARDS at the home of Narumov, of the Horse Guards. The long winter night went by without their perceiving it; it was going on five in the morning when they sat down to supper. Those who had come out ahead of the game ate with great appetite; the others sat in abstraction before their empty plates. But when champagne appeared, the conversation grew more lively, and everyone took part in it.

"How did you come out, Surin?" asked the host.

"I lost, as usual. I must confess I'm unlucky; I systematically refrain from raising my stakes, I never get excited, nothing can make me lose my head—and yet I keep on losing all the time!"

"And you've never been tempted? Never gambled on a flush? I marvel at your firmness."

"But what do you think of Hermann!" remarked one of the guests, indicating a young officer in the uniform of the Engineers. "Never in

Translated especially for this work by Ethel O. Bronstein. Copyright, 1943, by the Vanguard Press, Inc.

his life has he picked up a card; never in his life has he doubled a stake; yet he sits with us until five in the morning and watches us play!"

"I find cards most entertaining," said Hermann, "but I am in no position to sacrifice the essential in the hope of acquiring the superfluous."

"Hermann's a German; he's calculating, that's all!" remarked Tomski. "But if there's anybody whom I can't understand it's my grandmother, Countess Anna Fedotovna."

"How? What's that?" clamored the guests.

"I can't conceive," Tomski continued, "why in the world my grandmother doesn't go in for banker or stuss."

"Why," Narumov queried, "what's so remarkable about an old lady of eighty refraining from punting?"

"Then you know nothing about her, I take it?"

"Not a thing, really!"

"Oh? Listen to this, then: you must know that, some sixty years ago, my grandmother went to Paris and became all the rage there. People would run after her just to catch a glimpse of *la Vénus moscovite;* Armand, Duc de Richelieu—grandnephew of the Cardinal, if you'll remember—dangled after her, and grandmother maintains that he all but shot himself because of her hardheartedness. Ladies used to play faro in those days. On one occasion, at Court, she lost—much too much!—to the Duc d'Orléans, on her word. On getting home, as she was peeling the beauty-patches off her face and getting out of her hoop-skirts, she informed my grandfather of her gaming loss and ordered him to pay it. My late grandfather, as far as I remember, was regarded by my grandmother as a sort of major-domo. He dreaded her like fire; just the same, when he heard how staggering the loss was, he lost his temper entirely, fetched his accounts, pointed out to her that in half a year they had run through half a million, that their estates were near Moscow and in Saratov, both of which were nowhere near Paris, and flatly refused to pay this gambling debt. Grandmother slapped his face for him and went to bed alone, as a sign of her disfavor.

"The next day she summoned her husband, hoping that the domestic discipline had had its effect on him, but found that he was not to be moved. For the first time in her life she was reduced to giving him reasons and explanations; she thought she would shame him, condescendingly pointing out that there were debts *and* debts, and that, after all, there was a difference between a prince and a coachmaker.

But it was no go! Grandfather was up in arms. No—and that was that! Grandmother didn't know what to do.

"A very remarkable man happened to be one of her closest friends. You've heard of Count St. Germain, of whom so many marvelous things are told. You know that he palmed himself off as the Wandering Jew, as the inventor of the Elixir of Life and the Philosopher's Stone, and so forth. He was ridiculed as a charlatan, while Casanova states, in his *Memoirs,* that he was a spy; be that as it may, St. Germain, despite all the mystery surrounding him, had a most respectable appearance and was a most amiable man in society. Grandmother still loves him madly and becomes angry if anyone speaks of him with disrespect. Grandmother knew that St. Germain had considerable sums of money at his disposal. She decided to have recourse to him and wrote him a note requesting him to come to her without any delay. The queer old stick came at once and found her dreadfully woebegone. She described to him her husband's barbarous behavior, painting it in the blackest hues, and concluded by saying that she placed all her hope in his friendship and amiability. St. Germain grew thoughtful.

" 'I could oblige you with such a sum,' said he, 'but I know you wouldn't rest easy till you had repaid me, and I don't want to lead you into fresh difficulties. There's another way: you can win back what you owe.'

" 'But, my dear Count,' my grandmother answered, 'I tell you we have no money whatsoever.'

" 'There's no money required in this case,' St. Germain countered. 'Please deign to hear me out.'

"Thereupon he revealed to her a secret for which everyone of us would be willing to pay dearly—"

The young gamblers redoubled their attention. Tomski lit his pipe, took a deep draw on it, and went on:

"That same evening my grandmother was in attendance at Versailles, *au jeu de la Reine*—at the Queen's game. The Duc d'Orléans kept the bank, grandmother apologized lightly for not having brought the money to pay her debt, making up some innocent little story to excuse this oversight, and began to punt against him. She picked three cards and played them one after the other: each of the three broke the bank, and grandmother recouped completely everything she had lost."

"Mere chance!" said one of the guests.

"A fairy tale!" remarked Hermann.

"Trick cards, perhaps?" a third chimed in. "An extra spot or so applied in a special light powder—a flick of the finger and it's gone—"

"I don't think so," Tomski replied impressively.

"What!" Narumov cried out. "You have a grandmother who can hit upon three lucky cards in a row, and you haven't yet gotten the cabalistics of it out of her?"

"Hell, no!" answered Tomski. "She had four sons, my father being one of them; all four are desperate gamblers; yet she never revealed her secret to a single one of them, even though it wouldn't have been a bad thing for them, or, for that matter, for me. But here's what my uncle, Count Ivan Ilyich, used to tell me, assuring me on his honor it's all true. The late Chaplitski, the same who died in beggary after squandering millions, once lost something like three hundred thousand when he was a young man—if I remember right it was to Zorich, one of the favorites of Catherine the Great. Chaplitski was desperate. Grandmother, who always looked upon the follies of youth with a stern eye, nevertheless took pity on him. She told him what three cards to pick, stipulating that he play them one after the other, and exacted his word of honor that he would never gamble thereafter. Chaplitski went back to the man who had beaten him; they sat down to play. Chaplitski staked fifty thousand on the first card, and broke the bank; he doubled his stake, and won, then quadrupled the stake and won for the third time, not only recouping his losses but coming out ahead of the game. . . .

"However, it's time to go to bed—it's a quarter to six already."

True enough, dawn was breaking by now; the young men drained their glasses and dispersed.

II

"Il paraît que monsieur est
décidément pour les suivantes."
"Que voulez-vous, madame?
Elles sont plus fraîches." [1]
SOCIETY SMALL TALK

The old Countess was sitting before the mirror in her boudoir. Three maids hovered around her. One held a rouge pot; another, a box of

---

[1] "It appears that Monsieur shows a decided preference for serving-wenches." "What would you, Madame? They're so much fresher."

hairpins; the third, a towering mobcap with flame-colored ribbons. The Countess had not the slightest claim to a beauty long since faded, but she still maintained all the habits of her youth, adhered strictly to the fashions of the seventies, and expended just as much time and care over her dressing as she used to do all of sixty years ago. A young lady, her protégée, was sitting by a window, bent over an embroidery-frame.

"Greetings, *Grand'maman,*" said a young officer entering the room. "*Bon jour,* Mademoiselle Lise. *Grand'maman,* I've a favor to ask of you."

"What is it, Paul?"

"Allow me to present one of my friends to you and to bring him to the ball on Friday."

"Bring him along to the ball and you can present him then and there. Were you at ——'s yesterday?"

"Of course! It was a very gay affair; we danced until five. How pretty Yeletskaya looked!"

"Come, dear man! What's so pretty about her? Could she hold up a candle to her grandmother, the Grand Duchess Darya Petrovna? By the way, the Grand Duchess Darya Petrovna must have grown very old, I guess?"

"Grown very old? Why, what do you mean?" Tomski answered without stopping to think. "It's all of seven years by now that she's been dead."

The girl raised her head and made a sign to the young man. He remembered that the death of any of her contemporaries was being kept from the old Countess, and bit his lip. But the Countess heard this news, which was really news to her, with considerable indifference.

"She died!" she said. "Why, I didn't even know that! We were appointed Ladies-in-Waiting together, and as we were being presented, Her Majesty—"

And the Countess, for the hundredth time, told this anecdote to her grandson.

"Well, Paul," she said when she had finished, "you may help me get up now. Lizanka, where's my snuffbox?"

And the Countess, accompanied by her maids, went behind a screen to finish her toilette. Tomski remained with the young lady.

"Who is the gentleman you want to present?" Lizaveta Ivanovna asked quietly.

"Narumov. Do you know him?"

"No. Is he a military man or a civilian?"

"He's a military man."

"In the Engineers?"

"No! In the Cavalry. And what made you think he was in the Engineers?"

The girl burst out laughing—but did not answer a word.

"Paul!" the Countess called out from behind the screen. "Send me some new novel or other, but *please* not a modern one."

"What do you mean, *Grand'maman?*"

"I mean a novel in which the hero doesn't strangle either his father or his mother, and in which there aren't any drowned corpses. I'm horribly afraid of people who drown!"

"There are no novels free from that nowadays. Unless you would like me to send you some Russian ones?"

"Why, *are* there any Russian novels? Send them along, dear man— send them along, please!"

"Excuse me, *Grand'maman*—I must hurry. Excuse me, Lizaveta Ivanovna! Whatever made you think Narumov was in the Engineers?"

And Tomski went out of the boudoir.

Lizaveta Ivanovna was left alone; she dropped her work and began to look out of the window. Presently, on the other side of the street, from behind the house on the corner, a young officer appeared. Her cheeks became mantled with color, she went back to her work, and bent her head so low that it almost touched the embroidery. Just then the Countess came in, fully dressed.

"Order the carriage, Lizanka," she said, "and let's go for a drive."

Lizanka got up from the embroidery-frame and began putting her work away.

"What are you about, my girl? Are you deaf, or what?" the Countess began to shout. "Order them to get the carriage ready as soon as possible."

"Right away!" the young lady answered softly, and ran out into the anteroom.

A manservant entered and handed the Countess some books sent by the Grand Duke Paul Alexandrovich.

"Good! Thank him," said the Countess. "Lizanka, Lizanka! Why, where are you running to?"

"To get dressed."

"You'll have time, my dear girl. Sit here. Open the first volume; read it aloud."

The girl took the book and read several lines.

"Louder!" said the Countess. "What's the matter with you, my girl? Have you lost your voice, or what? Wait a bit; move that footstool closer to me; no, nearer! Well?"

Lizaveta Ivanovna read two pages more. The Countess yawned.

"Drop that book," she said. "What rubbish! Send it back to the Grand Duke Paul, and tell them to thank him. . . . Now, where's that carriage?"

"The carriage is ready," said Lizaveta Ivanovna after a glance into the street.

"But how is it you're not dressed?" asked the Countess. "I always have to wait for you! This is intolerable, my girl!"

Liza ran to her room. No more than two minutes had elapsed when the Countess began to ring with all her might. Three maids ran in through one door and a valet through another.

"Why can't I get you to answer?" the Countess demanded of them. "Tell Lizaveta Ivanovna I'm waiting for her."

Lizaveta Ivanovna entered, in manteau and bonnet.

"At last, my girl!" said the Countess. "What finery! What's it for? To captivate whom? What's the weather like? It seems windy."

"Not at all, Your Ladyship, Ma'am! It's very calm indeed, Ma'am!" the valet informed her.

"You always say the first thing that pops into your head! Open the ventilator. Just as I thought: it's windy! And a very cold wind, at that! Send the carriage back! We're not going, Lizanka; you needn't have dressed yourself up like that."

"And that's my life!" Lizaveta Ivanovna reflected.

Lizaveta Ivanovna was, indeed, a most unfortunate being. "What bitter fare," says Dante, "is others' bread; how hard the path to go upward and downward by another's stair." And who should know the bitterness of dependence if not the poor protégée of an old lady of quality? Countess —— was, to be sure, not cruel at heart, but she was self-willed, as a woman pampered by society would be, miserly, and immersed in chill egotism, as are all old people who have had their fill of love in their day and are out of touch with the present. She took part in all the vanities of high society; dragged herself to balls, where she would sit in the corner, bedizened in old-fashioned finery and berouged, like a hideous yet indispensable ornament of the ball-room; the guests as they arrive would walk up to her with low bows, as if in accordance with an established rite, and after that not a soul paid any attention to her. At home, she received the whole town, observing the strictest etiquette, but without recognizing a single face. Her numerous house serfs, grown fat and gray in her anteroom and maids' quarters, did as they pleased, vying with one another in robbing the moribund old woman.

Lizaveta Ivanovna was the martyr of the household. She poured the tea—and received reprimands for the excessive consumption of sugar; she read novels aloud—and was held accountable for all the faults of each author; she accompanied the Countess on her outings—and had to answer for the weather and the state of the cobbled roadway. She was assigned a salary which was never paid her in full, yet at the same time it was demanded of her that she dress like everyone else—that is, that she dress like the very few. Out in society she played the most pathetic of roles. Everybody knew her and nobody noticed her; at balls she danced only when there was a partner short in the quadrille, and the ladies would take her by the arm whenever they had to go to the powder-room to put something to rights about their attire. She had self-esteem, felt her position keenly, and looked about her in impatient expectancy of a deliverer; but the young men, calculating even in their fickle vanity, would not deign to notice her, even though Lizaveta Ivanovna was a hundred times more charming than the barefaced and coldhearted prospective brides on whom they danced attendance. How many times, quietly leaving the boring, sumptuous drawing room, would she go off to cry in her miserable room, which contained a screen covered with wallpaper, a bureau, a small mirror, and a painted bedstead, and where a tallow candle burned in a brass candlestick!

One day—this happened two days after the evening of cards described at the beginning of this tale, and a week previous to the scene we have just left—one day Lizaveta Ivanovna, as she sat at the window over her embroidery-frame, chanced to look out into the street—and saw a young officer in the uniform of the Engineers standing there motionless and with his eyes directed toward her window. She lowered her head and resumed her work; five minutes later she looked again: the young officer was still standing on the same spot. Since she was not in the habit of flirting with passing officers, she stopped looking into the street and went on with her embroidery for nearly two hours, without once raising her head. Dinner was served. She got up, began putting away her embroidery-frame and, chancing to look out into the street once more, again caught sight of the officer. This struck her as rather odd. After dinner she went up to the window with a somewhat uneasy feeling, but the officer was no longer there—and she did not give him any further thought.

Two days later, as she was going out to the carriage with the Countess, she caught sight of him again. He was standing by the very entrance, his face masked by his beaver collar; his black eyes glittered from under his hat. Lizaveta Ivanovna grew frightened without herself knowing why, and entered the carriage in inexplicable agitation.

On her return home she ran over to the window: the officer was standing in his former place, his eyes fixed upon her. She left the window, tortured by curiosity and troubled by a feeling completely new to her.

From that time forth not a day passed without the young man's putting in an appearance at a certain hour under the windows of the house. Without any prearrangement, certain relations were established between them. As she sat at her work in her place, she could sense his approach; lifting her head, she would watch him longer and longer each day. The young man, it seemed, felt grateful to her for this: she perceived, with the keen vision of youth, how quickly a flush mantled his pale cheeks each time their glances met. A week more, and she gave him a smile. . . .

When Tomski had asked the Countess for permission to present his friend, the poor girl's heart had begun to beat fast. But when she learned that Narumov was not in the Engineers but the Horse Guards, she regretted having betrayed her secret to the frivolous Tomski by her indiscreet question.

Hermann was the son of a Russianized German who had left him a very small patrimony. Firmly convinced of the necessity for making his independence secure, Hermann refrained from touching even his interest and lived entirely on his salary, without permitting himself the slightest indulgence. However, he was secretive and ambitious, and his associates rarely had an opportunity to laugh at his excessive thrift. He had strong passions and an ardent imagination, but his firmness of character saved him from the usual vagaries of youth. Thus, for instance, although a gambler at heart, he never touched cards, for he had coldly calculated that his circumstances did not permit him (as he put it) *to sacrifice the essential in the hope of acquiring the superfluous*—yet for all that, he would pass night after night sitting at card tables, and follow, with a feverish agitation, the various turns of the game.

The anecdote of the three cards affected his imagination deeply and would not leave his mind all night long.

"What would happen," he kept thinking all evening on the following day, as he wandered about Petersburg, "what would happen if the old Countess were to reveal her secret to me? If she were to designate those three unfailing cards to me! Why shouldn't I try my luck? I ought to get an introduction to her, worm my way into her good graces —become her lover, perhaps; but all that demands time, whereas she's all of eighty-seven; she can die in a week—in a couple of days! And then there's the story itself—can anyone believe it? No: Calculation, Moderation, and Industry: there are my three unfailing cards; there's what will increase my fortune threefold and even sevenfold, and bring me security and independence!"

Meditating in this fashion, he found himself on one of the principal streets of Petersburg, before a house of old-fashioned architecture. The street was blocked with vehicles, as carriage after carriage rolled up to the brightly lit entrance. At every minute the carriage doors opened, and the shapely foot of some belle would emerge, or a high boot with jingling spur, or the clocked stocking and patent-leather pump of a diplomat. Capes and fur coats flitted past the majestic doorman. Hermann stopped.

"Whose house is that?" he asked the policeman in a striped sentry-box at the corner.

"Countess ——'s," answered the policeman.

Hermann felt his pulse quicken. The amazing anecdote came to his imagination again. He began pacing to and fro near the house, thinking of its mistress and her wonderful faculty. It was late when he came back to his own modest quarters; it was long before he could fall asleep; and when sleep did overcome him, he dreamt of cards, of the gaming table covered with green baize, of heaped-up bank notes and mounds of gold pieces. He played card after card, placed his stakes without the least hesitation, and won with never a break, raking in the gold and stuffing the notes in his pockets.

When he awoke, quite late, he sighed at the loss of his imaginary wealth, went out to roam about the city again, and again found himself before the house of Countess ——. An unknown force, it seemed, was drawing him to it. He stopped, and fixed his eyes upon its windows. In one of them he caught sight of a little dark head apparently bent

over a book or some work. The pretty head lifted. Hermann glimpsed
a rosy little face and a pair of dark eyes.

That moment decided his fate.

III

*Vous m'écrivez, mon ange,
des lettres de quatre pages
plus vite que je ne puis les
lire.*[1]
FROM A CORRESPONDENCE

No sooner had Lizaveta Ivanovna taken off her manteau and bonnet
than the Countess sent for her again and ordered the carriage once
more. They went down to it. Just as two footmen had lifted the old
woman and thrust her in through the carriage door, Lizaveta Ivanovna
saw her young Engineer standing by the very wheel. He seized her
hand. She was beside herself with fright; the young man vanished—
and she found a letter in her hand. She hid it inside her glove and
throughout the entire drive neither heard nor saw anything. The
Countess was in the habit of asking questions every minute while they
were in the carriage: Who was that they had met?—What was the
name of that bridge?—What did that sign say? On this occasion Lizaveta Ivanovna answered at random and so very wide of the mark that
she provoked the Countess.

"What's come over you, my girl? Are you in a daze, or what? Either
you aren't listening to me, or you don't understand me! Thank heaven,
I don't lisp, and I'm not so old that I haven't my wits about me!"

Lizaveta Ivanovna was not listening to her. When they returned
home, she ran to her room and took the letter (it was not sealed) out
of her glove. She read it. The letter contained a declaration of love:
it was tender, deferential—and taken word for word out of a sentimental German novel. But Lizaveta Ivanovna knew no German and
was very pleased with the epistle.

Nevertheless, the letter she had accepted troubled her exceedingly.
It was the first time she had ever entered into secret, close relations with
a young man. His presumption horrified her. She reproached herself
with imprudent behavior and did not know what to do: should she

---

[1] My angel, you write me four-page letters more quickly than I am able to read them.

stop sitting at the window and, by her indifference, cool the young officer's inclination to pursue her further? Should she send the letter back to him? Should she answer him coldly and in positive terms? She had no one with whom to take counsel; she had no friend or preceptress. At last Lizaveta Ivanovna decided to answer the letter.

She sat down at her small desk, got out quill and paper, and sank into thought. She began her letter several times—and tore it up each time: her expressions seemed to her either too condescending or too severe. Finally, she succeeded in writing a few lines with which she remained satisfied.

"I am sure," she wrote, "that your intentions are honorable and that you would not wish to offend me by an unconsidered action, but our acquaintance must not begin in such fashion. I am returning your letter to you, and I hope that, hereafter, I shall have no reason to complain of a lack of respect which I do not merit."

The next day, seeing Hermann approaching, Lizaveta Ivanovna rose from her embroidery-frame, went out into the drawing room, opened the ventilator, and tossed the letter out into the street, trusting to the young officer's adroitness. Hermann darted forward, picked up the letter, and stepped into a confectioner's shop. On breaking the seal, he found his own letter and Lizaveta Ivanovna's answer. He had expected as much, and returned home very much fascinated by his intrigue.

Three days later a young, bright-eyed miss brought Lizaveta Ivanovna a note from a fashionable shop. Lizaveta Ivanovna opened it with misgivings, anticipating a dun, but suddenly recognized Hermann's handwriting.

"My dear, you've made a mistake," she said. "This note isn't for me."

"Oh, but it is for you, sure enough!" answered the pert girl without concealing a sly smile. "Be kind enough to read it."

Lizaveta Ivanovna ran her eyes over the note. Hermann requested a meeting.

"Impossible!" said Lizaveta Ivanovna, frightened both at the urgency of his request and the means he had taken for its delivery. "This is certainly not for me!" And she tore the letter into tiny pieces.

"If the letter isn't for you, then why did you tear it up?" asked the shopgirl. "I'd have taken it back to the party who sent it."

"Please, my dear," said Lizaveta Ivanovna, flaring up at her remark, "from now on don't bring me any notes! And as for the one who sent you, tell him he ought to be ashamed of himself!"

But Hermann would not desist. She received a letter from him every day, transmitted in one way or another. No longer were these letters translations from the German. Hermann wrote them inspired by passion, and spoke in his own language: both the inflexibility of his desires and the disordered state of an unbridled imagination were expressed in them. Lizaveta Ivanovna no longer thought of sending them back; she drank them in; she began to answer them—and her notes were becoming longer and more tender from hour to hour. At last she threw the following letter to him from the window:

"There's a ball tonight at the A——an Ambassador's. The Countess is going. We shall be there until about two. This is your opportunity to see me alone. As soon as the Countess has left, her servants will probably disperse. The doorman will be left in the vestibule, but he usually goes off to his own cubbyhole. Come at half-past eleven. Go right up the steps. If you should find anyone in the hall, just ask whether the Countess is home. They will tell you she isn't, and there won't be much left for you to do but to come back and try again. But probably you won't meet anyone. The maids will be sitting in their own room. From the vestibule turn left and go straight to the Countess's bedroom. There, behind a screen, you will see two small doors: the one at the right leads to the study, which the Countess never enters; the one at the left into a corridor, and there you will find a narrow winding stairway: it leads to my room."

Hermann quivered like a tiger as he waited for the appointed time. At ten that evening he was already standing outside the Countess's house. The weather was frightful; the wind howled, the snow fell in large wet flakes; the lanterns burned dimly; the streets were deserted. Occasionally a jehu would amble by with his gaunt nag, on the lookout for a belated fare. Hermann stood there, in his light tunic, feeling neither the wind nor the snow. At last the Countess's carriage drew up. Hermann saw how the bent old woman, wrapped in a sable cloak, was practically carried out under the arms by flunkies, and how, in a wrap that did not give much warmth, with fresh flowers adorning her head, her protégée flitted behind the Countess. The doors of the carriage slammed; it lumbered off over the powdery snow. The doorman closed the doors. The windows grew dark. Hermann began to walk up and down beside the house that now seemed deserted; he walked up to a street lamp and looked at his watch: it was twenty minutes past eleven. He remained under the street lamp, his eyes fixed on the hands of his watch as he waited for the remaining minutes to pass.

At exactly half-past eleven Hermann went up the steps of the Countess's mansion and entered the brightly lit vestibule. The door-man was not around. Hermann ran up the stairs, opened the door into an anteroom, and saw a servant asleep under the lamp, seated in an ancient, soiled armchair. With a light firm step Hermann walked past him. The drawing room and the parlor were dark, the lamp from the anteroom lighting them but feebly.

Hermann entered the bedroom. Before an ark filled with ancient images a golden lampad glowed warmly. Armchairs and sofas, most of their gilt worn off, upholstered in faded silk, their cushions stuffed with down, were ranged in depressing symmetry against walls covered with Chinese wallpaper. Two portraits painted in Paris by Mme. Lebrun hung on a wall. One depicted a man about forty, ruddy and stout, in a light green uniform with a star of some order; the other, a young aquiline-nosed beauty with a rose in her powdered hair, done into ringlets at the temples. Every nook and corner was cluttered with porcelain shepherds and shepherdesses, clocks made by the celebrated Leroy, little boxes, diavolos, fans and all sorts of feminine knickknacks, invented at the end of the eighteenth century together with Mont-golfier's balloon and Mesmer's magnetism.

Hermann went behind the screen. There stood a small iron cot; at the right was a door leading into the study; at the left another, lead-ing into a corridor. Hermann opened it; he saw a narrow winding stair-way which led to the room of the poor protégée. . . . But he turned back and entered the dark study.

Time dragged by. All was still. Twelve o'clock struck in the parlor; one after another, the clocks in all the rooms struck midnight—and everything grew still again. Hermann stood leaning against the cold tile stove. He was calm; his heart beat evenly, like that of a man who has decided on a course of action that is hazardous but inevitable. The clocks struck the first, then the second hour of the morning—and he heard the distant rattle of a carriage. He was overcome by an excite-ment beyond his control. The carriage drove up and stopped. He heard the clatter of the carriage-step being let down. Commotion sprang up throughout the house. People started running about, voices were heard, and the house was lighted up. Three elderly chambermaids ran into the bedroom, and the Countess, more dead than alive, came in and sank into a deep, high-backed leather wing-chair. Hermann peeked through the keyhole: Livazeta Ivanovna went past him. He heard her hurried steps on the treads of her stairs. Something resembling the gnawing of conscience stirred in his heart, but was stilled again. He was petrified.

The Countess began to undress before her mirror. Her maids unpinned her mobcap trimmed with roses; they took the powdered wig off her gray, closely-cropped head. Hairpins rained about her. The yellow dress, embroidered with silver, fell down about her swollen feet. Hermann was witness to the revolting mysteries of her toilette. Finally, the Countess remained in her nightgown and nightcap; in that costume, more suitable to her old age, she seemed less horrible and outrageous.

Like old people in general, the Countess suffered from insomnia. After undressing she sat down by the window in the wing chair and dismissed the chambermaids. The candles were carried out and the room was again lit only by the solitary icon-lamp. The Countess sat there, all yellow, moving her pendulous lips, her body rocking from side to side. Her turbid eyes expressed nothing but complete absence of thought; looking at her, one might have thought that the rocking of the frightful old woman proceeded not from her will but from the action of secret galvanism.

Suddenly that dead face altered indescribably. Her lips ceased moving, her eyes became animated: a strange man was standing before the Countess.

"Don't be frightened; for God's sake don't be frightened!" he said in a clear and quiet voice. "I have no intention of harming you; I have come to implore a certain favor of you."

The old woman was looking at him in silence and, it seemed, without hearing him. Hermann surmised that she was deaf and, bending to her very ear, he repeated what he had just said. The old woman remained as silent as before.

"You have it in your power," Hermann went on, "to bring about my life's happiness, and it would entail no cost to you: I know that you can guess three winning cards in a row—"

Hermann paused. The Countess, apparently, had grasped what was being demanded of her; she seemed to be groping for words with which to answer.

"It was a jest," she said at last. "I swear to you it was a jest!"

"This is not a matter to jest about," Hermann retorted angrily. "Remember Chaplitski, whom you helped to win back his losses."

The Countess became visibly embarrassed. Her features betrayed a powerful agitation of the soul, but she soon sank back into her former insensibility.

"Can you," Hermann persisted, "designate to me those three infallible cards?"

The Countess remained silent; Hermann resumed:

"For whom should you guard your secret? For your grandchildren? They're rich even without that; why, they're actually unaware of the value of money. Your three cards would be of no avail to a profligate. He who cannot guard his patrimony will die a beggar in the end, even if all the demons exerted themselves in his behalf. I am no profligate; I know the value of money. Your three cards will not be wasted on me. Well? . . ."

He stopped and awaited her answer with trepidation. The Countess maintained her silence; Hermann got down on his knees.

"If ever," he said, "your heart has known the feeling of love, if you remember its raptures, if you even once smiled at the cry of a new-born son, if anything human ever throbbed in your breast, then I implore you, by the feelings of a wife, a mistress, a mother—by all that is held holy in life—do not deny my plea! Reveal your secret to me! Of what good is it to you? Perhaps it is bound up with some horrible sin, with the loss of eternal bliss, with some diabolical compact. . . . Reflect: you are old, you have not long to live—I am ready to take your sin upon my soul. Do but reveal your secret to me. Consider that a man's happiness lies in your hands; that not only I but my children, my grandchildren and great-grandchildren will bless your memory and hold it sacred. . . ."

The old woman did not answer a word.

Hermann got up from his knees.

"You old witch!" said he, clenching his teeth. "In that case I'll make you answer—"

With these words he drew a pistol out of his pocket.

At sight of the pistol the Countess evinced strong emotion for the second time. She began to nod her head and raised an arm, as if to shield herself from the shot. . . . Then she rolled backward—and remained motionless.

"Stop acting childishly," said Hermann, taking her hand. "I am asking you for the last time: do you want to designate your three cards to me? Yes or no?"

The Countess made no answer. Hermann perceived that she had died.

I V

7 *Mai* 18—
Homme sans moeurs et sans religion.[1]
FROM A CORRESPONDENCE

Lizaveta Ivanovna, still in her ballroom finery, was sitting in her room, plunged in thought. On arriving home she had hastened to dismiss the sleepy wench who had grudgingly offered her services, telling her that she would undress herself, and had entered her room in trepidation, hoping to find Hermann there—and wishing she might not find him. At first glance she was convinced of his absence and thanked fate for whatever obstacle had hindered their meeting. Without undressing, she sat down and fell to recalling all the circumstances which, in so short a time, had seduced her to such lengths. Not even three weeks had passed since the first time she had noticed the young man from her window—and here she was already carrying on a correspondence with him, and he had already succeeded in inducing her to grant him a tryst at night! She knew his name only because some of his letters had been signed; she had never spoken with him, had never heard his voice, had never even heard of him until that very evening. A strange thing! That very evening at the ball Tomski, angry with the young Duchess Pauline—because she, contrary to her custom, flirted not with him but someone else—had wanted to pay her back by a show of indifference: he had sought out Lizaveta Ivanovna and danced an endless mazurka with her. During all that time he twitted her about her partiality for officers in the Engineers, assuring her that he knew much more than she could suppose, and some of his jokes were so close to the mark that several times Lizaveta Ivanovna thought her secret was known to him.

"From whom did you find out all this?" she asked, laughing.

"From a friend of the person you know," answered Tomski. "From a very remarkable man!"

"And who may this remarkable man be?"

"His name is Hermann."

Lizaveta Ivanovna said nothing in reply, but her hands and feet turned to ice.

"This Hermann," Tomski went on, "is truly a character out of a

[1] A man without morals or religion.

romantic novel; he has the profile of Napoleon—and the soul of Mephistopheles. I think this man must have at least three malefactions on his soul. . . . How pale you've become!"

"I've a headache. But what was it this Hermann—or whatever his name is—told you?"

"Hermann is very much displeased with his friend: he says that, in his place, he would have acted altogether differently. I even surmise that Hermann himself has designs upon you; at any rate, he listens to the infatuated exclamations of his friend with anything but indifference."

"But where did he see me?"

"At church, or perhaps when you were out on a drive! God alone knows what Hermann is up to! Perhaps in your room, while you were asleep; he is capable of it—"

Three ladies, coming up to Tomski and offering him his choice of a partner under the mask-words of *"Oubli ou regret?"* [1] interrupted the conversation, which was becoming excruciatingly tantalizing for Lizaveta Ivanovna. The lady chosen by Tomski was none other than the Duchess Pauline. She contrived to clear things up with him, after having made an extra turn around the room and still another near her chair. Tomski on coming back to his own place gave no further thought either to Hermann or Lizaveta Ivanovna. She felt it imperative to renew the interrupted conversation, but the mazurka ended, and shortly after the old Countess made her departure.

Tomski's words were nothing more than the badinage appropriate to a mazurka, but they sank deeply into the soul of the young dreamer. The portrait sketched by Tomski bore a resemblance to the picture she herself had formed, and such a character, by now vulgarized through the latest novels, both frightened and captivated her imagination. She sat, with her bared arms crossed, her head, still bedecked with flowers, sunk forward on her décolletée bosom. . . . Suddenly the door opened and Hermann entered. She began to tremble.

"Where have you been?" she asked in a frightened whisper.

"In the bedroom of the old Countess," Hermann replied. "I've just come away from her. The Countess is dead."

"My God! What are you saying?"

"And it seems," Hermann continued, "I am the cause of her death."

Lizaveta Ivanovna glanced at him, and Tomski's words resounded in her heart: *This man must have at least three malefactions on his soul!*

[1] "Oblivion or regret?"

Hermann sat down on the window sill near her and told her everything that had happened.

Lizaveta Ivanovna heard him out with horror. And so those passionate letters, those flaming demands, this audacious, determined pursuit—all this had not been love! Money—that was what his soul had hungered after! It was not she who could allay his desires and make him happy! The poor protégée had been nothing but the blind accomplice of the brigand, the murderer of her aged benefactress! . . . She burst into bitter tears in her belated, agonizing repentance.

Hermann watched her in silence; his heart, too, was in torture, but neither the poor girl's tears nor her striking loveliness in her grief troubled his obdurate soul. He felt no remorse at the thought of the dead old woman. Only one thing horrified him: the irretrievable loss of the secret which he had expected to enrich him.

"You're a monster!" Lizaveta Ivanovna uttered at last.

"I did not desire her death," Hermann retorted. "My pistol is unloaded."

They fell silent.

Morning was at hand. Lizaveta Ivanovna extinguished the dying candle; a wan light was diffused through her room. She dried her tear-stained eyes and raised them to look at Hermann: he sat on the window sill, his hands folded and his brows knit in a sinister frown. In this attitude there was something about him amazingly reminiscent of portraits of Napoleon. This resemblance overwhelmed even Lizaveta Ivanovna.

"How will you get out of the house?" she asked at last. "I was thinking of taking you down the secret staircase, but it would be necessary to go past the bedroom, and I'm afraid."

"Tell me how to find this secret staircase; I'll find my way out."

Lizaveta Ivanovna rose, took a key out of the bureau, put it into Hermann's hand, and gave him detailed directions. Hermann pressed her cold, unresponsive hand, kissed her bowed head, and went out.

He descended the winding stairway and once more entered the Countess' bedroom. The dead old woman sat there, rigid as stone: her face wore an expression of profound calm. Hermann stopped in front of her; he gazed at her a long time, as if wishing to assure himself of the horrible truth. Finally he went into the study, groped for and found the door concealed by wallpaper, and began to descend the dark staircase, agitated by strange sensations. Up this same stairway, he mused, perhaps all of sixty years ago, into that same bedroom, at just such an hour, his hair dressed *à l'oiseau royal*,[1] pressing his three-cornered hat to a heart beating fast under an embroidered long coat, some fortunate youth, now long turned to dust in his grave, had been making his stealthy way—and this night the heart of his most ancient mistress had ceased to beat. . . .

Hermann found the door at the foot of the staircase, which he opened with the same key, and found himself in an open passageway which let him out into the street.

V

"That night the deceased Baroness von W—— appeared to me. She was all in white, and said to me: 'Greetings, Sir Councilor!'"

SWEDENBORG

At nine in the morning, three days after the fatal night, Hermann went to the celebrated monastery of V——, where a requiem mass was to be sung over the remains of the departed Countess. Though he felt no repentance, he nevertheless could not completely still the voice of conscience that kept repeating to him: "You are the murderer of the old woman!" Having but little real faith, he was hagridden by a host of superstitions. He believed that the dead Countess could exercise a baneful influence on his life—and decided to attend her funeral in order to beg for and obtain her forgiveness.

The church was full. Hermann could barely force his way through the throng. The coffin rested on a sumptuous catafalque under a baldachin of velvet. The woman now gone to her long rest lay with her hands crossed on her breast, in lace cap and gown of white satin. Round about stood the members of her household: the servants in black caftans, with armorial ribbons over their shoulders and candles in their hands; her relatives—her children, grandchildren, and great-grandchildren—all in deep mourning. Nobody wept; tears would have been *une affectation*. The Countess was so old that her death could not stun anyone, and her relatives had long regarded her as one who had lived beyond her time. A youthful prelate delivered the funeral oration. In

[1] After the style of the royal bird—that is, the heron.

simple and moving terms he described the peaceful passing away of this righteous woman, whose long years had been a quiet, touching preparation for an end befitting a Christian.

"The Angel of Death came upon her," said the orator, "as she was keeping vigil amid pious meditations and awaiting the Bridegroom that cometh at midnight."

The service concluded with sad decorum. The relatives were the first to come forward to bid the body farewell. Then followed the multitudinous guests, who had come to pay their last homage to one who had ever so many years ago been a participant in their frivolous diversions. And after them came all the domestics. The last to approach was the ancient "lady's lady" or housekeeper, a serf-woman of the same age as the deceased. Two young girls supported her under the arms as they led her along. It was beyond her strength to bow down to the ground—yet she was the only one to shed a few tears as she kissed the cold hand of her mistress.

After she had turned away, Hermann summoned up the resolution to approach the casket. He prostrated himself, and lay without moving for several minutes on the cold floor strewn with fir needles. Finally he rose, pale as the dead woman herself, went up the steps of the catafalque, and bent over the casket. . . . At that moment it appeared to him that the dead woman gave him a mocking glance, puckering up one eye. Hastily drawing back, Hermann missed a step and crashed to the ground, falling flat on his back. They picked him up. At the very same time, Lizaveta Ivanovna was carried out in a faint to the church porch. This incident disturbed for several minutes the solemn pomp of the somber ceremonial. A subdued murmur arose among the onlookers, and a gaunt Court Chamberlain, a near relative of the deceased, whispered into the ear of an Englishman standing next to him that the young officer was her son on the wrong side of the blanket, to which the Englishman replied with a chill "Oh?"

Hermann was extremely upset all that day. Dining in an obscure tavern, he drank a great deal, contrary to his custom, in the hope of silencing his inner disquietude. But the wine merely enfevered his imagination still more. When he returned home he threw himself on his bed without undressing and fell fast asleep.

When he awoke it was already night. His room was flooded with moonlight. He glanced at his watch; it was a quarter to three. Sleep had left him; he sat down on the bed and meditated on the funeral of the old Countess.

At that moment someone peered in from the street through the window—and immediately stepped back. Hermann paid not the least attention to this occurrence. A minute later he heard someone opening the door in the entry. Hermann thought it was his orderly, drunk as usual, returning from a nocturnal prowl. But the step he heard was an unfamiliar one: someone was softly shuffling along in slippers. The door opened; a white-garbed woman entered. Hermann took her for his old wet-nurse, and wondered what could have brought her at such an hour. But the woman in white, gliding along, suddenly confronted him—and Hermann recognized the Countess.

"I have come to you against my will," she said in a firm voice, "but I am under a command to fulfill your request. The trey, the seven, and the ace will win for you in that order—but only under these conditions: that you stake on only one card in twenty-four hours, and never play again in your life thereafter. As for my death, I forgive you—provided you marry my protégée, Lizaveta Ivanovna."

With the last word she turned quietly, went to the door, and disappeared, her slippers shuffling. Hermann heard the outer door slam in the entry and saw someone again peer in at his window.

It was a long time before Hermann could come back to himself. He went out into the other room. His orderly was sleeping on the floor; it was all Hermann could do to rouse him. As usual, the orderly was drunk; there was no getting anything sensible out of him. The door into the entry was locked. Hermann went back to his room, lit the candle, and wrote down an account of his apparition.

VI

"Attendez!" [1]
"How dared you say *Attendez!* to me?"
"Your Excellency, I said: '*Attendez*—Sir!'"

Two fixed ideas can no more co-exist in the nature of morality than two bodies can occupy one and the same space in the physical world. *Trey, seven, ace*—these soon obscured the image of the dead old woman in Hermann's imagination. *Trey, seven, ace*—they never left his mind

[1] "Hold on!"—as a gambling term it is a suggestion to hedge on a bet, or to refrain entirely from betting.—*Translator.*

and were perpetually on his lips. If he laid eyes on a young woman, he would say: "How shapely she is! . . . Nothing short of a trey of hearts!" If he was asked: "What time is it?" he would answer: "Five minutes to a seven of—" Every paunchy man called up an ace in his mind. *Trey, seven, ace* haunted him in his sleep, taking on every guise possible. The trey bloomed before him in the shape of a magnificent, luxuriant flower; the seven presented itself as a Gothic portal; the ace, as an enormous spider. All his thoughts coalesced into one: to avail himself of the secret which had cost him so dear. He began thinking of resigning and traveling. He wanted to wrest a treasure-trove from the bewitched goddess Fortune in the open gambling hells of Paris. But chance relieved him of going to any trouble.

A syndicate of wealthy gamblers was organized in Moscow under the chairmanship of the celebrated Chekalinski, who had spent all his life at cards, and who had at one time amassed millions by accepting IOU's when he won and by paying in cold cash when he lost. His experience of many years had earned for him the confidence of his associates, while the open house he kept, his famous chef, and his own geniality and affability had gained him the respect of the public. He came to Petersburg. The young people flocked to him, neglecting dances for cards and preferring the temptations of faro to the fascinations of gallantry. Narumov took Hermann with him to Chekalinski's.

They passed through a succession of magnificent rooms, with obsequious flunkies at every step. Several generals and privy councilors were playing whist; young men were lounging and sprawling on the divans upholstered in brocaded silks, eating ice cream or smoking pipes. In the main room, at a long table with a score or so of gamblers crowded around it, sat the host, keeping the bank. He was a man of about sixty, of the most respectable appearance: his head was silvery gray; his full, rosy face wore an expression of geniality; his eyes twinkled, animated by a never-failing smile. Narumov presented Hermann to him. Chekalinski shook hands with him cordially, begged him to make himself at home, and went on dealing.

The game lasted a long time. There were more than thirty cards on the table. Chekalinski stopped after every deal to give the players time to arrange their hands, tallied the losses, listened attentively to the players' demands, and even more attentively straightened out the extra corner turned down by the hand of some gambler too absent-minded to put up the additional stake signified thereby. But at last the game came to an end. Chekalinski shuffled the cards and prepared to deal again.

"Let me stake on a card," said Hermann, stretching out his hand from behind a stout man who was also about to punt. Chekalinski smiled and bowed in silence in token of courteous acquiescence. Narumov laughingly congratulated Hermann on breaking his long abstention at last, and wished him beginner's luck.

"Here goes!" said Hermann, writing his stake in chalk above his card.

"How much, Sir?" asked the banker, screwing up his eyes. "I can't quite make it out, Sir."

"Forty-seven thousand," answered Hermann.

At these words every head in the room turned instantaneously, and all eyes were directed at him.

"He's gone out of his mind!" thought Narumov.

"Allow me to point out to you," Chekalinski said with his unfailing smile, "that you're playing a very high game—nobody here has ever yet staked more than two hundred and seventy-five on a single card."

"Well, what is it to be?" retorted Hermann. "Are you covering my card or not?"

Chekalinski bowed with the same air of submissive acquiescence.

"I merely wanted to inform you that, since I am honored by the confidence of my associates, I cannot play except for spot cash. For my own part, of course, I'm convinced that your word is enough, but, for the sake of keeping the game and tallies straight, I must ask you to put up money on your card."

The young Engineer took a bank note out of his pocket and handed it to Chekalinski, who, after a cursory glance at it, placed it on Hermann's card. Chekalinski began to deal for stuss. A nine lay to the right of Hermann's card and, to its left, a trey.

"My card won!" said Hermann, showing his card.

A murmur arose among the players. Chekalinski frowned, but the smile immediately came back to his face.

"Would you care to have your winnings now?"

"If you will be so good."

Chekalinski took several bank notes out of his pocket and settled on the spot. Hermann took his money and left the table. Narumov was in a daze. Hermann drank a glass of lemonade and went home.

On the evening of the following day he again appeared at Chekalinski's. The host was dealing. Hermann walked up to the table; the players immediately made room for him. Chekalinski bowed to him affably.

Hermann waited for a new game, picked his card, and staked thereon his own forty-seven thousand and his winnings of the evening before. Chekalinski began to deal. A jack turned up to the right of Hermann's card, a seven to its left.

Hermann showed his seven.

The cry of astonishment was general. Chekalinski was obviously disconcerted. He counted out ninety-four thousand and passed the sum over to Hermann. The latter accepted it with *sang-froid* and instantly withdrew.

On the following evening Hermann appeared at the gaming-table again. Everyone had been expecting him. The Generals and Privy Councilors dropped their whist in order to watch such extraordinary play. The young officers jumped up from their divans; all the flunkies gathered in the main salon. Everybody surrounded Hermann. The other players did not pick any cards, impatiently waiting to see how he would wind up. Hermann stood by the table, preparing to play alone against the pale yet still smiling Chekalinski. Each broke the seal on a fresh deck of cards. Chekalinski shuffled his deck. Hermann picked a card from his and placed his stake, snowing under the card with a heap of bank notes. The situation resembled a duel. A profound silence reigned throughout the room.

Chekalinski began to deal; his hands were shaking. A queen came up to the right, an ace to the left.

"The ace has won!" said Hermann, and turned up his card.

"Your queen is done for," said Chekalinski amiably.

Hermann shuddered: true enough, instead of an ace he held the queen of spades. He could not believe his own eyes, unable to understand how he could have missed.

At that moment it seemed to him that the queen of spades puckered up her eye and smiled mockingly. The extraordinary resemblance stunned him.

"The old woman!" he screamed in horror.

Chekalinski drew the forfeited bank notes toward him. Hermann was still standing motionless. When he at last left the table, noisy discussion sprang up throughout the room.

"He played splendidly!" the players commented.

Chekalinski shuffled the cards anew; the game resumed its ordinary course.

CONCLUSION

Hermann went out of his mind. He is now confined in the Obuhov Hospital, in cell No. 17; he never responds to any questions, but mutters with remarkable rapidity: "Trey, seven, ace! Trey, seven, queen! . . ."

Lizaveta Ivanovna married a very agreeable young man; he has some sort of post and is possessed of considerable means—he is the son of a former steward to the old Countess. She is bringing up a girl, a poor relation of hers.

Tomski has been promoted to a captaincy, and is engaged to be married to the Duchess Pauline.

The Tale of the Golden Cockerel [1]

IN A realm that shall be nameless,
In a country bright and blameless,
Lived the mighty Czar Dadon,
Second in renown to none.
Fierce and bold, he would belabor
Without scruple every neighbor.
But he fancied, as he aged,
That enough wars had been waged—
Having earned a rest, he took it.
But his neighbors would not brook it,
And they harassed the old Czar,
And they ruthlessly attacked him,
And they harried and they hacked him.
Therefore, lest his realm be lost,
He maintained a mighty host.

Translated by Babette Deutsch. From *The Works of Alexander Pushkin,* selected and edited by Avrahm Yarmolinsky. Reprinted by permission of Random House, Inc.

[1] The germ of this poem remained a puzzle until 1933, when Anna Ahmatova pointed out its source in Washington Irving's *Alhambra,* a French translation of which (published in 1832, also the year of its publication in the original) is known to have been in Pushkin's library. The reader will be richly repaid by rereading, after this poem, Irving's chapters, "The House of the Weathercock" and "Legend of the Arabian Astrologer."
                                                                                    G.

Though his captains were not napping,
They not seldom took a rapping:
In the South they're fortified—
From the East their foemen ride;
Mend the breach, as is commanded—
On the shore an army's landed
That has come from oversea.
Czar Dadon, so vexed was he,
Was upon the point of weeping,
Didn't find it easy sleeping.
Never was life bitterer!
So to the astrologer,
To the wise old eunuch, pleading
For his help, an envoy's speeding.
To the eunuch he bows low,
And the mage consents to go
At Dadon's behest, appearing
At the court: a sign most cheering.
In his bag, as it befell,
He'd a golden cockerel.
"Set this bird," the mage directed,
"On a pole that's soon erected;
And my golden cockerel
Will protect thee very well.
When there is no sign of riot,
He will sit serene and quiet,
But if ever there should be
Threat of a calamity,
Should there come from any quarter
Raiders ripe for loot and slaughter,
Then my golden cockerel
Will arouse: his comb will swell,
He will crow, and up and doing,
Turn to where the danger's brewing."
In return the mage is told
He shall have a heap of gold,
And good Czar Dadon instanter
Promises the kind enchanter:
"Once thy wish to me is known,
'Twill be granted as my own."

On his perch, by the Czar's orders,
Sits the cock and guards the borders—
And when danger starts to peep
He arises, as from sleep,
Crows, and ruffles up his feathers,
Turns to where the trouble gathers,
Sounds his warning clear and true,
Crying: "Cock-a-doodle-doo!
Slug-a-bed, lie still and slumber,
Reign with never care or cumber!"
And the neighbors dared not seek
Any quarrel, but grew meek:
Czar Dadon there was no trapping,
For they could not catch him napping.

Peacefully two years go by,
And the cock sits quietly.
But one day, by noises shaken,
Czar Dadon is forced to waken.
Cries a captain: "Czar and Sire,
Rise, thy children's need is dire!
Trouble comes, thy realm to shatter."
"Gentlemen, what is the matter?"
Yawns Dadon. "What do you say?
Who is there? What trouble, pray?"
Says the captain: "Fear is growing,
For the cockerel is crowing:
The whole city's terrified."
The Czar looked out and spied
The gold cockerel a-working—
Toward the East he kept on jerking.
"Quickly now! Make no delay!
Take to horse, men, and away!"
Toward the East the army's speeding
That the Czar's first-born is leading.
Now the cockerel is still,
And the Czar may sleep his fill.

Eight full days go by like magic,
But no news comes, glad or tragic:

Did they fight or did they not?
Not a word Dadon has got.
Hark! Again the cock is crowing—
A new army must be going
Forth to battle; Czar Dadon
This time sends his younger son
To the rescue of his brother.
And this time, just as the other,
The young cock grows still, content.
But again no news is sent.
And again eight days go flitting,
And in fear the folk are sitting;
And once more the cockerel crows,
And a third host eastward goes.
Czar Dadon himself is leading,
Not quite certain of succeeding.

They march on, by day, by night,
And they soon are weary, quite.
Czar Dadon, in some vexation,
Vainly seeks an indication
Of a fight; a battleground,
Or a camp, or funeral-mound.
Strange! But as the eighth day's ending,
We find Czar Dadon ascending
Hilly pathways, with his men—
What does his gaze light on then?
'Twixt two mountain-peaks commanding
Lo! a silken tent is standing.
Wondrous silence rules the scene,
And behold, in a ravine
Lies the slaughtered army! Chastened
By the sight, the old Czar hastened
To the tent. . . . Alas, Dadon!
Younger son and elder son
Lie unhelmed, and either brother
Has his sword stuck in the other.
In the field, alackaday,
Masterless, their coursers stray,

On the trampled grass and muddy,
On the silken grass now bloody. . . .
Czar Dadon howled fearfully:
"Children, children! Woe is me!
Both our falcons have been taken
In the nets! I am forsaken!"
All his army howled and moaned
Till the very valleys groaned—
From the shaken mountains darted
Echoes. Then the tent flaps parted. . . .
Suddenly upon the scene
Stood the young Shamakhan queen!
Bright as dawn, with gentle greeting
She acknowledged this first meeting
With the Czar, and old Dadon,
Like a night-bird in the sun,
Stood stock-still and kept on blinking
At the maid, no longer thinking
Of his sons, the dead and gone.
And she smiled at Czar Dadon—
Bowing, took his hand and led him
Straight into her tent, and fed him
Royally, and then her guest
Tenderly she laid to rest
On a couch with gold brocaded,
By her silken curtains shaded.
Seven days and seven nights
Czar Dadon knew these delights,
And, of every scruple ridden,
Did, bewitched, what he was bidden.

Long enough he had delayed—
To his army, to the maid,
Czar Dadon was now declaring
That they must be homeward faring.
Faster than Dadon there flies
Rumor, spreading truth and lies.
And the populace have straightway
Come to meet them at the gateway.

Now behind the coach they run,
Hail the queen and hail Dadon,
And most affable they find him. . . .
Lo! there in the crowd behind him
Who should follow Czar Dadon,
Hair and beard white as a swan,
And a Moorish hat to top.him,
But the mage? There's none to stop him;
Up he comes: "My greetings, Sire."
Says the Czar: "What's thy desire?
Pray, come closer. What's thy mission?"
"Czar," responded the magician,
"We have our accounts to square;
Thou hast sworn, thou art aware,
For the help that I accorded,
Anything thy realm afforded
Thou wouldst grant me: my desire,
As thy own, fulfilling, Sire.
'Tis this maiden I am craving:
The Shamakhan queen." "Thou'rt raving!"
Shrieked Dadon forthwith, amazed,
While his eyes with anger blazed.
"Gracious! Hast thou lost thy senses?
Who'd have dreamed such consequences
From the words that once I said!"
Cried the Czar. "What's in thy head?
Yes, I promised, but what of it?
There are limits, and I'll prove it.
What is any maid to thee?
How dare thou thus speak to me?
Other favors I am able
To bestow: take from my stable
My best horse, or, better far,
Henceforth rank as a boyar;
Gold I'll give thee willingly—
Half my czardom is for thee."
"Nought is offered worth desiring,"
Said the mage. "I am requiring
But one gift of thee. I mean,
Namely, the Shamakhan queen."

Then the Czar, with anger spitting,
Cried: "The devil! 'Tis not fitting
That I listen to such stuff.
Thou'lt have nothing. That's enough!
To thy cost thou hast been sinning—
Reckoned wrong from the beginning.
Now be off while thou'rt yet whole!
Take him out, God bless my soul!"
The enchanter, ere they caught him,
Would have argued, but bethought him
That with certain mighty folk
Quarreling is not a joke,
And there was no word in answer
From the white-haired necromancer.
With his scepter the Czar straight
Rapped the eunuch on his pate;
He fell forward: life departed.
Forthwith the whole city started
Quaking—but the maiden, ah!
Hee-hee-hee! and Ha-ha-ha!
Feared no sin and was not queasy.
Czar Dadon, though quite uneasy,
Gave the queen a tender smile
And rode forward in fine style.
Suddenly there is a tinkling
Little noise, and in a twinkling,
While all stood and stared anew,
From his perch the cockerel flew
To the royal coach, and lighted
On the pate of the affrighted
Czar Dadon, and there, elate,
Flapped his wings, and pecked the pate,
And soared off . . . and as it flitted,
Czar Dadon his carriage quitted:
Down he fell, and groaned at most
Once, and then gave up the ghost.
And the queen no more was seen there:
'Twas as though she'd never been there—
Fairy tales, though far from true,
Teach good lads a thing or two.

As Leaden as the Aftermath of Wine *

AS LEADEN as the aftermath of wine
Is the dead mirth of my delirious days; .
And as wine waxes strong with age, so weighs
More heavily the past on my decline.
My path is dim. The future's troubled sea
Foretokens only toil and grief to me.
But oh! my friends, I do not ask to die!
I crave more life, more dreams, more agony!
Midmost the care, the panic, the distress,
I know that I shall taste of happiness.
Once more I shall be drunk on strains divine,
Be moved to tears by musings that are mine;
And haply when the last sad hour draws nigh,
Love with a farewell smile may gild the sky.

MAURICE BARING

Remembrance *

WHEN the loud day for men who sow and reap
    Grows still, and on the silence of the town
The unsubstantial veils of night and sleep,
    The need of the day's labor, settle down,
Then for me in the stillness of the night
    The wasting, watchful hours drag on their course,
And in the idle darkness comes the bite
    Of all the burning serpents of remorse;

* Reprinted from *Lost Lectures* by Maurice Baring, by permission and special arrangement with Alfred A. Knopf, Inc. Copyright, 1932, by Alfred A. Knopf, Inc.

Dreams seethe; and fretful infelicities
    Are swarming in my overburdened soul,
And Memory before my wakeful eyes
    With noiseless hand unwinds her lengthy scroll.
Then, as with loathing I peruse the years,
    I tremble, and I curse my natal day,
Wail bitterly, and bitterly shed tears,
    But cannot wash the woeful script away.

MAURICE BARING

I Loved You Once

I LOVED YOU once; that love perchance may yet
Like hidden embers in my soul remain;
But let that not dismay you, and forget:
I would not want to bring you the least pain.

I loved in silence, loved you hopelessly,
Now with a timid, now a jealous, mind;
I loved so deeply, loved so tenderly—
God grant such love you in some other find!

B. G. G.

Life's Stage Coach

ALTHOUGH at times 'tis overfilled,
The coach rolls light, its horses fleet;
Hoar Father Time, a coachman skilled,
Drives it, and never leaves his seat.

When in the morn we take our places,
Slow comfort scorning, on we dash,
And urge Time on (our blood, too, races),
And shout: "Give all your team the lash!"

But noontide finds our spirits cool,
We now can feel each jar and jolt;
We fear ravines, the downhill pull,
And shout: "Drive easier, you dolt!"

Relentless still the coach wheels spin;
By evening we the jolts endure,
And, dozing, roll on to the Inn,
While Time still holds the reins secure.

B. G. G.

The Lay of Oleg the Wise

WISE OLEG to the war now fares forth again,
    The Hazars have awaked his ire;
For rapine and raid Hazar hamlet and plain
    Is subjected to falchion and fire.
In mail of Byzance the great prince takes the lead
Of his companions brave, on his faithful steed.

From the darksome fir forest, to meet that array,
    Forth paces a gray-haired magician:
To none but Perun did that sorcerer pray,
    Fulfilling a prophet's dread mission;
His life he has spent all in penance and pain—
And beside that enchanter Oleg drew rein.

From T. B. Shaw's *Pushkin the Russian Poet*, Blackwood's, London, 1845.

"Now rede me, enchanter, beloved of Perun,
 The good and the ill fate before me:
Will my neighboring foes be rejoicing right soon
 As the earth of the grave is piled o'er me?
Reveal all the truth, fear me not, and for meed,
Choose among them—and take thou the best battle steed."

"True enchanters care never for prince or for peer,
 And gifts are but needlessly given;
The wise tongue ne'er stumbleth for falsehood or fear—
 'Tis the friend of the councils of Heaven!
The years of the future are clouded and dark,
Yet on thy fair forehead thy fate I can mark:

"Remember now firmly the words of my tongue;
 For the warrior finds rapture in glory:
On the gates of Byzantium thy buckler is hung,
 Thy name shall be deathless in story;
Wild waves and broad kingdoms are subject to thee,
The foe, in amaze, envies thy destiny.

"And not the blue sea with its treacherous wave,
 Tempestuous in ominous power,
Nor arrow, nor sling, nor assassin's glaive
 Shall shorten thy years by an hour:
Within thy strong armor no wound shalt thy know—
A guardian unseen shall ward off every blow.

"Thy steed fears not hardship, nor danger, nor pain;
 His lord's lightest accent he heareth:
Now stands still though arrows fall round him like rain,
 Now o'er the red plain he careereth.
He fears not the winter, he fears not to bleed—
Yet thy death thou shalt meet through thy good battle-steed!"

Oleg smiled a moment, but then his fair brow
 And his gaze somber grew in a frown;
In silence he leaned in his saddle, and slow
 The Prince from his courser came down;
And as though from a friend he were parting with pain,
He stroked his broad neck and his dark flowing mane.

"Farewell, my companion, leal servant and bold!
  We must part—such is destiny's power:
Rest thee now; I swear, in thy stirrup of gold
  No foot shall be set from this hour.
Farewell—yet recall him you bore in the fray—
My squires, now I pray ye, lead my steed away!

"The softest of carpets his horsecloths shall be,
  Now lead him away to the meadow;
On the choicest of corn he shall feed daintily,
  He shall drink of the well in the shadow."
Then straightway departed the squires with the steed,
And to valiant Oleg a new courser they lead.

Oleg and his comrades are feasting, I trow;
  Their mead-cups are merrily clashing;
Their locks are as white as the dawn-lighted snow
  On the ridge of a grave-mound flashing:
They talk of old times, of the days of their pride,
And the frays where together they struck side by side.

"But where," quoth Oleg, "is my good battle horse?
  My mettlesome charger—how fares he?
Is he playful as ever, as fleet in the course—
  His age and his freedom how bears he?"
They answer and say: On the hill by the stream
He has long slept the slumber that knows not a dream.

Oleg bowed his head, and thought clouded his brow:
  "How can mortals the future divine?
A mad, lying dotard, Enchanter, art thou!
  Had I spurned that prediction of thine,
My steed to this day would have ridden with me!"
Then the bones of his charger Oleg wished to see.

Oleg rides forth with Igor at his side,
  His old friends behind him are streaming;
And they see on a knoll by Dnieper's swift tide
  Where the steed's noble bones lie gleaming:
They are washed by the rains, dust over them blows,
And waving above them the feather-grass grows.

Then the Prince set his foot on the courser's white skull,
   Saying: "Sleep, my old friend, in thy glory!
Thy lord hath outlived thee, his days are nigh full:
   At his funeral feast, red and gory,
'Tis not thou 'neath the ax that shall redden the sod,
That my dust may be pleasured to quaff thy brave blood.

"And am I to find my destruction in this?
   My death in a skeleton seeking?"
From the skull of the courser a snake, with a hiss,
   Crept forth as the hero was speaking:
Round his legs, like a ribbon, it twined its black ring,
And the Prince shrieked aloud as he felt the keen sting.

The mead-cups are foaming, they circle around—
   At Oleg's great death-feast they are ringing;
Prince Igor and Olga they sit on the mound,
   The warriors the death-chant are singing.
And they talk of old times, of the days of their pride,
And the frays where together they struck side by side.

                       T. B. SHAW

Michael Urievich
Lermontov

1814 – 1841

IN THE GALAXY of those poets "whom God has bestowed in reward on His Russia," as Gogol puts it, Lermontov ranks as a star second in magnitude only to the greatest, Pushkin. In fact, some critics maintain that in expressiveness, mellifluousness, and power Lermontov has no peer. Many parallels could be drawn between the two poets as champions of freedom, as victims of an inimical social order, and even in the manner of their untimely deaths. But while Pushkin was killed at the height of his powers, leaving much mature work, Lermontov was killed on the threshold of full development, and his work, amazing as it is, must be considered to a large extent juvenilia. Yet that juvenilia indicates that he may well have gone on to equal if not surpass Pushkin. And while Pushkin has, since 1937, become a little more than a name in English, Lermontov, in English, is still hardly even a name.

Like Pushkin's, Lermontov's ancestry is not without fantastic elements. He was descended from the George Learmont who came to Russia in the seventeenth century, who claimed descent from the Learmont who fought with Malcolm against Macbeth, which Learmont claimed his descent from the legendary Thomas the Rhymer of the eleventh century, who claimed his descent from none other than Ler, the Caledonian god of the sea.

Lermontov's aristocratic mother had, against her family's wishes, married a genteel but poor retired army captain; on her death in 1817 the father had to surrender his three-year-old son to the latter's maternal grandmother. Pushkin's grandmother had been one of his saving influences; Lermontov's, rich and domineering, spoiled him on her country estate. He went to an aristocratic boarding school in 1828, going from there to the University of Moscow in 1830 and leaving it, after a dispute with one of the professors, in 1832. He then entered a military school, from which, in 1834, he was graduated, with the rank of Cornet, into the Hussars. The feud between Moscow and Petersburg was an old one; Lermontov, a Muscovite, was considered not quite top-notch by Petersburg society, but make his way in it he did. "Mocking, caustic, adroit," a poetess recalled him, "at the same time with a full and brilliant mind, rich, independent, he became the soul of a society of young people, the first in its conversations, its pleasures, its sprees."

He had begun writing at thirteen; between 1828 and 1832 he had written fifteen narrative poems, three dramas, over three hundred lyrics. (A considerable amount of his work has been lost; a little was rescued in retranslations from the German.) He first appeared in print in 1835, when *Hajji Abrek,* a poem, was published without his knowledge. But it was not until 1837 that he made an enormous impression with his poem on the death of Pushkin—circulated in manuscript copies, of course. One of these reached Nicholas I, with an anonymous inscription: *A Call to Revolution.* Lermontov was arrested and through imperial orders exiled, transferred to a regiment of dragoons in the Caucasus, with orders to leave in forty-eight hours. But through his grandmother's exertions he was back in Petersburg fourteen months later. (Throughout his military career he was generally in hot water, and as much in the guardhouse as out of it.)

1840 was marked by the appearance, in book form, of his novel *A Hero of Our Times* (a work which has had the very curious compliment paid to it of being the basis for a British forgery-hoax), and the publication of a volume of his poetry; Belinski hailed the appearance of a "new brilliant luminary, a star of the first magnitude." But in the spring of the same year Lermontov fought a duel with the son of the French Envoy, which brought new repressions upon the poet. He was arrested and incarcerated. Belinski visited him in the guardhouse. This was not the first meeting, but it was the first time the great critic and spiritual leader saw the young poet without the latter's mask of a fop. "The first time I saw this man as a real man," Belinski wrote. "A profound and a mighty spirit.. . . Oh, this will be a Russian poet as lofty as the Great Ivan tower.! A wonderful nature." Belinski was gladdened by Lermontov's "cerebrally chill and mordant view of life and man . . . which yet evinces the seeds of a faith in the worth both of the one and the other."

As an upshot of the duel, Lermontov was again banished to the Caucasus, this time to a regiment of infantry. (As a royal author Nicholas I shared with Catherine the Great only a majestic disregard of orthography; the misspelling of the Russian equivalent for "This very day!" penned by his own hand on the order of expulsion is enough to make any Russian schoolboy—no relation to Macaulay's—wince.)

For a series of daring actions under

fire Lermontov was cited for a decoration; the Emperor not merely rejected the citation but ordered
Lermontov removed as head of a
Cossack command. On leave in
Petersburg in 1841 the poet applied
for retirement, since he wanted to
devote himself entirely to literature;
the request was denied, and he was
ordered to return to his regiment. On
the way back he stopped over at
Pyatigorsk. At this spa his sneers at
Martynov, an old acquaintance, a
fopling and a minor-league Lothario, brought about a quarrel,
duly fanned by the usual coterie of
snobs and aristocratic cuckolds. One
of the fantastic conditions (Lermontov's) of the ensuing duel was that
it be fought on the edge of a precipice—and it was Lermontov who,
wounded, fell over that edge. "A

dog's death," said Petersburg aristocracy on learning of the intransi-
gent's passing, "befits a dog."

Of the shorter lyrics here given,
The Angel and *Lonely and Far a
White Sail Soars* were written at
seventeen; the longer poem' about
Ivan the Terrible and the bold trader
Kalashnicov (first published in
1838) is one of the best and most
loved things in Russian, and ought
to be of interest to students of
fistiana, if no one else; the Turkish
fairy tale is a much more interesting
representation of Lermontov's prose
than the extracts from his novel
usually given. In addition to his great
talent as a poet, Lermontov was an
excellent draftsman; unfortunately,
pictorial representation does not
come within the province of this
work.

Ashik-Kerib

A TURKISH FAIRY TALE

A LONG TIME AGO, in the town of Tiflis, there lived a certain rich Turk.
Much gold had Allah bestowed upon him, yet dearer than all gold to
him was his own daughter, Maghul-Megheri. Fair are the stars in
heaven; but there are angels dwelling behind the stars, and the angels
are still fairer; even thus was Maghul-Megheri fairer than all the maids
in Tiflis.

There was also in the town of Tiflis a poor lad by the name of Ashik-
Kerib. The Prophet had bestowed nought upon him save an exalted
heart and the gift of making songs; playing his *saaz,* his dulcimer, and
singing the glory of the ancient knights of Turkestan, he attended wed-

Translated by Bernard Guilbert Guerney. Copyright, 1943, by the Vanguard Press,
Inc.

dings to entertain the rich folk at their rejoicing. And it was at one of these weddings that he first beheld Maghul-Megheri, and they came to love each other. There was but little hope, however, of Ashik-Kerib's gaining her hand, and he became as dismal as the sky in winter.

And so one day he happened to be lying on the grass in a garden, underneath a grapevine, where he finally fell asleep. At that very time Maghul-Megheri chanced to pass by with her companions, and one of them, chancing to see the sleeping *ashik,* or dulcimer-player, fell behind and approached him.

"Why art thou sleeping under the grapevine?" she chanted. "Arise, thou madman, for thy gazelle is passing by."

He awakened; the girl flitted off like a tiny bird. Maghul-Megheri had heard her song and fell to chiding her.

"If thou didst but know to whom I sang that song," the other answered, "thou wouldst thank me: 'twas none other than thy Ashik-Kerib."

"Bring me to him," said Maghul-Megheri, and they went off. Beholding his sad countenance, Maghul-Megheri fell to questioning and consoling him.

"What else should I do save grieve?" Ashik-Kerib told her. "I love thee, yet never wilt thou be mine."

"Ask my father for my hand," she said. "And my father will give the wedding at his own expense and will give me enough for us both to live on."

" 'Tis well," he answered. "Mayhap Ayak-Agha will not begrudge anything for the happiness of his daughter, yet who knows whether thou mayst not reproach me in the future because I had nothing of my own, and because I owe everything to thee? Nay, dear Maghul-Megheri, I have taken a task upon my soul: I vow to travel through the world for seven years and either amass wealth for myself or perish in the far-off deserts; if thou consent to this, then at the expiration of the time thou wilt be mine."

Consent she did, but added that if he failed to return on the day agreed upon she would become the wife of Kurdush-Bey, who had long been courting her.

Ashik-Kerib went to his mother, received her blessing, kissed his little sister, slung a pouch over his shoulder, took up a calender's staff, and went forth from the town of Tiflis.

And lo, a horseman overtook him. Ashik-Kerib looked, and saw it was Kurdush-Bey.

"May thy travels be pleasant!" the Bey shouted to him. "Whichever thy way may lie, pilgrim, I'll keep thee company!"

The *ashik* was none too happy to have such a companion, yet there was nought he could do in the matter. For a long time they went along together, until at last they beheld a river ahead of them. There was no bridge across it, nor was there any ford.

"Swim thou across it first," said Kurdush-Bey, "and I'll follow thee."

Ashik-Kerib cast off his outer garments and swam off. Having gotten across the river, he looked back—and cried: "Woe! O Allah Akbar!" He saw that Kurdush-Bey, having taken his garments, had started back for Tiflis; all one could see was the dust trailing after him, even as a serpent trails over a level field.

Having galloped back to Tiflis, the Bey took Ashik-Kerib's garments to the latter's aged mother.

"Thy son is drowned in a deep river," he told her. "Here be his garments."

In a grief beyond all words the mother threw herself upon the garments of her son and shed scalding tears thereon; thereafter she took them and bore them to her future daughter-in-law, Maghul-Megheri.

"My son is drowned," she imparted to her. "It was Kurdush-Bey that brought back his garments; now art thou free."

Maghul-Megheri smiled.

"Believe it not," she answered her. "These be but the inventions of Kurdush-Bey. No man will I have to husband before the seven years are up."

And, taking her lute down from the wall, she softly began to chant a favorite song of Ashik-Kerib's.

In the meanwhile our pilgrim came, barefooted and naked, to a certain village. The good people clothed and fed him; thereupon, to repay their kindness, he sang them some wonderful songs. And thus did he go from village to village, from town to town, and his fame spread far and wide.

And at last he came to the city of Khalaf. As was his wont, he entered a coffeehouse, asked for a *saaz,* and struck up a song.

It so happened that a certain Pasha who was very fond of minstrels was living at the time in Khalaf. Many had been brought before him, but not one had proven to his liking. His servants were worn out with running all over town, seeking new minstrels for him. Suddenly, as they passed by one of the coffeehouses, they heard an amazing voice and hurried within.

"Come with us to the Pasha," they cried, "or thou wilt pay for thy refusal with thy head!"

"I am a free man, a pilgrim from the city of Tiflis," Ashik-Kerib told them. "If I want to, I go; if I do not want to, I go not. I sing when I feel like it, and your Pasha is no chief over me."

However, despite this, they seized him and brought him before the Pasha.

"Sing!" demanded the Pasha, and Ashik-Kerib began to sing. And in his song he sang the praises of his Maghul-Megheri, and this song was so much to the proud Pasha's liking that he let Ashik-Kerib stay at his court. Silver and gold rained down upon him; he went about in rich, sleek garments. A happy life and a gay one did Ashik-Kerib lead, and he waxed very rich. Whether he forgot his Maghul-Megheri or no, this slave knows not; but in any event, the time of waiting decided upon was running out. The last year of the seven was about to come to an end soon, yet he was not making the least preparation for departure.

At this time a certain merchant was about to set out from the city of Tiflis with a caravan of forty camels and eighty slaves. So Maghul-Megheri summoned him to her and gave him a salver of gold.

"Take thou this salver," she told him, "and whatever town thou mayst come to, display it prominently on thy counter, and make it known everywhere that whosoever will acknowledge the ownership of this salver, and proves his claim thereto, will receive the same, and its weight in gold to boot."

The merchant set out; at every halting place did he carry out the commission he had been entrusted with by Maghul-Megheri, but none would admit himself the owner of the golden salver. He had already sold almost all his wares and had come to the city of Khalaf with whatever he had left. He made known everywhere the instructions he had received from Maghul-Megheri. Hearing thereof, Ashik-Kerib came running to the caravan-serai of the merchant from Tiflis, and beheld the golden salver on the stall of the merchant.

" 'Tis mine!" he said, and laid his hands thereon.

"Of a verity 'tis thine," said the merchant. "For I have recognized thee, Ashik-Kerib. Betake thee, then, with all speed to Tiflis; thy Maghul-Megheri bade me tell thee that the time agreed upon is running out and if thou art not present there at the appointed day she will marry another."

Ashik-Kerib clutched his head in despair; but three days remained to the fateful hour. However, he mounted a steed, took with him a bag of gold coins, and galloped off, without sparing his mount. Finally his racer foundered, falling down bereft of all breath upon Mount Arzinghan, which is between Arzinian and Arzeroum. What was he to do? From Arzinian to Tiflis is a two months' ride, yet all that remained to him was but two days.

"Almighty Allah!" he cried out. "If Thou dost not help me now, then there is nothing on earth I can do." And he was about to throw himself off a precipice. But suddenly he saw a man on a white steed below him, and he heard a loud voice:

"What art thou about to do, O *oghlan* [youth]?"

"I would die," answered the *ashik*.

"Come down here, in that case, and I will slay thee."

Ashik-Kerib scrambled down the precipice, somehow.

"Follow me," said the horseman awesomely.

"But how am I to follow thee?" asked the *ashik*. "Thy steed flies along like the wind, whereas I am burdened down with my bag."

"True enough; hang thy bag on my saddle and follow me."

But Ashik-Kerib fell behind, no matter how hard he tried to run.

"Come, why art thou lagging behind?" asked the horseman.

"But how am I not to follow thee? Thy steed is fleeter than thought, whereas I am exhausted."

"True enough; mount behind me on my steed and tell me the whole truth: whither dost thou have to go?"

"Oh, would I might but get even to Arzeroum now!" answered Ashik-Kerib.

"Close thy eyes, then." Ashik-Kerib closed his eyes. "Now open them," said the horseman. The *ashik* opened his eyes and looked: before him the walls of Arzeroum showed whitely and its minarets gleamed.

"I am at fault, Agha," said the *ashik*. "I erred; I meant to say that I had to go to Kars."

"There, now," answered the horseman. "I warned thee to tell me the very truth. So be it; close thy eyes again. . . . Now open them."

Ashik-Kerib could not believe his own senses and that he was now beholding Kars. He fell on his knees and spake:

"Guilty, Agha, thrice guilty is thy slave Ashik-Kerib; but thou knowest thyself that if a man resolve to lie in the morning he is bound to lie to the very evening; 'tis Tiflis I really have to reach."

"What an untruthful fellow thou art!" said the horseman angrily.

"Well, there's no help for it; I forgive thee. Close thy eyes. . . . Now open them," he added after the lapse of a minute. The *ashik* cried out for joy: they were at the gates of Tiflis.

Having rendered his sincere thanks, and as he was taking his bag off the saddle, Ashik-Kerib spake to the horseman:

"Great is thy good deed, Agha; yet do thou a greater for me. If I tell anyone that I covered the way from Arzinian to Tiflis in one day's span, none will believe me; let me have something wherewith to prove that claim."

"Bend down," said the horseman with a smile, "and take a clod of earth from under the hoof of my steed, and put that clod within the bosom of thy cloak; and then, should any take to disbelieving the truth of thy words, bid them bring to thee some blind woman who has been sightless for seven years, anoint her eyes with that clod—and she will see."

Ashik-Kerib took the clod from under the hoof of the white steed, but no sooner had he raised his head than the steed and rider vanished. Thereupon he was convinced in his soul that his protector had been none other than Haderiliaz, or St. George, as the *giaours* call him.

Only late at evening did Ashik-Kerib find his house. He knocked on the door with a trembling hand, calling on his *ana*, his mother: "Ana, Ana, open the door to me! I am a guest sent by God, and chilled and hungry; I beg thee, for the sake of thy wandering son, to let me in."

"For the shelter of wayfarers there are the houses of the rich and powerful," the feeble voice of the old woman answered him. "There are weddings being held throughout the city—go thou there; there thou canst pass the night in pleasure."

"Ana," he answered, "there is none I know here and therefore I repeat my plea: for the sake of thy wandering son, let me in!"

Thereupon his sister spake to the mother:

"I will get up, Mother, and open the door for him."

"Thou worthless one!" said the mother. "Glad art thou to receive young people and to regale them, for it is seven years now that I have lost my sight because of the tears I have shed."

But the daughter, without heeding her reproaches, got up and let in Ashik-Kerib. After uttering the usual salutation, he sat down and with secret emotion began looking about him. And he saw that his sweet-sounding *saaz* was hanging on the wall in a dusty cover, and he fell to questioning his mother:

"What hast thou hanging there on the wall?"

"What an inquisitive guest thou art!" she answered him. "Let it suffice thee that thou wilt be given a piece of bread and on the morrow sent on thy way with God's blessing."

"I have already told thee," he retorted, "that thou art my own mother, and that this is my sister, and therefore I ask thee to explain to me what thou hast hanging on the wall."

"It's a *saaz*, a *saaz*!" the old woman answered angrily, refusing to believe him.

"And what do you mean by a *saaz*?"

"I mean it is something to play on and sing songs to."

And thereupon Ashik-Kerib begged her to permit his sister to take down the *saaz* and show it to him.

"It cannot be," answered the old woman. "That *saaz* belongs to my unfortunate son; for seven long years has it been hanging on the wall, and the hand of no man living has touched it."

But his sister arose, took the *saaz* down off the wall, and handed it to him. Thereupon he lifted up his eyes to heaven and rendered up a prayer as follows: "O Almighty Allah! If I am fated to attain my desired goal, then my seven-stringed *saaz* will be just as attuned as on the day when I played it last!" And he struck the copper strings, and the strings answered in harmony, and he began to sing: "I am but a poor *kerib*, a wanderer, and poor are my words; yet did the great Haderiliaz help me to get down the steep precipice. Even though I be poor and poor are my words, recognize me, my mother, recognize thy own wanderer."

Whereupon his mother burst into tears and asked him:

"What name do they call thee?"

"Raschid [Simple-Hearted One]," answered he.

"Thou hast spoken; now hearken, Raschid," said she. "With thy words thou hast cut my heart into small pieces. This night I saw in a dream—for 'tis but in my dreams I can see—that my hair had turned all white. 'Tis seven years now that I have become blind because of my tears; tell me, thou who hast his voice—when will my son come?"

And twice, with tears, did she repeat her plea. In vain did he call himself her son—she would not believe. And, after the lapse of a few minutes, he begged her:

"Give me thy leave, O my mother, to take the *saaz* and to venture forth; there is a wedding being held near by, I have heard; my sister will guide me thither; I shall play and sing, and everything that I may obtain thereby I shall bring back here and share with the two of you."

"I will not allow it," answered the old woman. "Ever since my son has been away his *saaz* has not been out of the house."

But he began to vow that he would not harm a single string. "If even one string snap," Ashik-Kerib persisted, "then I will hold myself responsible with all my worldly goods."

So the old woman ran her fingers over his wallet and, learning that it was filled with coin, allowed him to go. Having guided him to the wealthy house where the wedding feast was in noisy progress, the sister remained at the door, to watch what would befall.

It was Maghul-Megheri who dwelt in this house, and it was on this night that she was to become the wife of Kurdush-Bey. Kurdush-Bey was feasting with his kinsmen and friends, while Maghul-Megheri sat behind a richly wrought *chatra,* or drapery, with her female companions, holding in one hand a chalice with poison and in the other a keen dagger: she had taken a vow to die before she would lay her head down on the couch of Kurdush-Bey.

And she heard behind her *chatra* that a stranger had arrived, who had said: *"Salaam aleikoum!* Peace be unto you! Ye are making merry here and feasting; allow me, then, a poor pilgrim, to sit down with you, and I shall sing you a song in requital."

"Why not!" said Kurdush-Bey. "The singers of songs and the dancers ought to be permitted in here, inasmuch as there is a wedding going on. Sing something, then, *ashik,* and I will send thee away with a handful of gold." And thereafter Kurdush-Bey asked Ashik-Kerib: "What do they call thee, pilgrim!"

"Shindi-gherursez."

"What a name!" the other cried out with laughter. "It's the first time I hear its like."

"When my mother was lying in labor over me, many of the neighbors came to her door to ask whether God hath sent her a son or a daughter, and it was the same answer they all got: *shindi gherursez* [you will soon find out]."

After which he picked up his *saaz* and began to sing:

"In the town of Khalaf I drank Missirian wine, but God gave me wings and I flew hither in three days."

Kurdush-Bey's brother was a man of but little sense; he snatched out his dagger and cried:

"Thou liest! How can anyone get here from Khalaf in three days?"

"But wherefore wouldst thou slay me?" countered the *ashik*. "It is usual for singers from all the four ends of the world to gather in the same spot; nor am I taking anything from you for my song; you may believe me or not, just as you wish."

"Let him go on," said the bridegroom, and Ashik-Kerib began his song anew:

"The morning prayer I said in the vale of Arzinian; the noontime prayer in the city of Arzeroum; the prayer before sunset in the city of Kars, and the evening prayer in Tiflis. Allah gave me wings, and I have flown hither; may God grant that I fall victim to the white steed if I lie; he leapt swiftly, like a dancer on the tightrope, from mountain to ravine, from ravine to mountain; Mevlian, our Lord, gave wings to Ashik, and he flew to the wedding of Maghul-Megheri."

Thereupon Maghul-Megheri, recognizing his voice, tossed the poison to one side and the dagger to the other.

"So that is how thou keepest thy vow?" said one of her companions. "Thou wilt, then, be the wife of Kurdush-Bey this night?"

"Thou hast not recognized it, but I have recognized the voice so dear to me," answered Maghul-Megheri and, picking up a pair of shears, she cut an opening in the *chatra*. And when she had looked and recognized of a certainty the face of Ashik-Kerib, she cried out and rushed to him and put her arms about his neck, and both of them fell down unconscious. Kurdush-Bey's brother threw himself at them with a dagger, intending to stab both of them to death, but Kurdush-Bey stopped him, uttering:

"Calm thyself, and know: Whatever is written upon a man's forehead at birth he is not fated to forego."

Regaining consciousness, Maghul-Megheri turned red for shame, hid her face with her hand, and disappeared behind the *chatra*.

"Now, of a truth, one can see thou art Ashik-Kerib," said the bridegroom. "But inform us how thou couldst in so short a time traverse so great a distance?"

"In proof of the truth," answered Ashik-Kerib, "my sword will cleave a stone; but if I lie, may my neck be thinner than a hair. But, best of all, bring to me a blind woman who hath not for seven years beheld God's daylight, and I shall restore her sight."

Ashik-Kerib's sister, who had been standing close to the door in the entry, no sooner heard this than she ran to her mother.

"Mother!" she cried out. "He is of a surety my brother and of a surety thy son, Ashik-Kerib," and, taking the old woman by the hand, she brought her to the feast. Thereupon Ashik-Kerib took the clod of earth from out his bosom, dissolved it in water, and anointed his mother's eyes therewith, saying as he did so:

"Know all ye men how mighty and great is Haderiliaz," and his mother opened her eyes and saw. After that none durst doubt the verity of his words, and Kurdush-Bey relinquished to him the unutterably beautiful Maghul-Megheri.

Whereupon, in his joy, Ashik-Kerib said unto him:

"Hearken, Kurdush-Bey, I will console thee: my sister is in no way inferior to the bride that was to be thine; I am rich, she will have no less silver and gold than Maghul-Megheri; therefore, do thou take her unto thyself—and may both of you be as happy as I am with my dear, beloved Maghul-Megheri."

The Chalice of Life

OUR AVID LIPS to life's cup cling
(Though our eyes close in dread),
Its golden brim first moistening
With tears our own eyes shed.

But when ere death the veil shall fall—
The veil that bound our eyes—
And all that had bewitched us—all
Falls with the veil and dies,

Then, then will empty seem
The golden cup of hours:
The draught it held was but a dream—
Not e'en the cup was ours!

B. G. G.

Lonely and Far a White Sail Soars

LONELY and far a white sail soars
Amid the ocean's bluish spray. . . .
What does it seek on distant shores?
What has it left in its own bay?
The wind howls, and the mast bends, creaking
In protest to the rising seas. . . .
Alas, the sail no joy is seeking,
And it is not from joy it flees.
Beneath, the azure current churns,
Above, the aureate sunlight glows;
Yet for a storm the sail still yearns—
As though in storms one found repose!

　　　　　　　　　　　　　B. G. G.

The Angel

AT MIDNIGHT an angel was soaring on high,
And his chant seemed to rival the hush of the sky.
The stars and the moon and the clouds in a throng
Listened enrapt to the heavenly song.

He sang of the souls that are stainless and white,
Who in gardens of Paradise dream in delight;
His music rose high like a jubilant flame,
A luminous hymn to the Holiest Name.

He carried a soul to the portals of birth,
Down to the vales of the grief-harrowed earth;
But the sound of his chant the new soul had caught,
And forever retained its wondrous, great Thought.

And long that soul languished amid earthly woe,
Yet yearned for the song it had heard long ago,
And no weary earth-song could for it blight
The long-cherished chant of the angel in flight.

MORRIS SPIEGEL

Testament *

I WANT TO be alone with you,
A moment quite alone.
The minutes left to me are few,
They say I'll soon be gone.
And you are going home on leave,
Then say . . . but why? I do believe
There's not a soul who'll greatly care
To hear about me over there.

And yet if someone questions you,
Whoever it may be—
Tell them a bullet hit me through
The chest—and did for me.
And say I died, and for the Czar,
And say what fools the doctors are:
And that I shook you by the hand,
And spoke about my native land.

* Reprinted from *Have You Anything to Declare?* by Maurice Baring, by permission of and special arrangement with Alfred A. Knopf, Inc. Copyright, 1937, by Alfred A. Knopf, Inc.

My father and my mother, both,
   By now are surely dead—
To tell the truth, I would be loath
   To send them tears to shed.
If one of them is living, say
I'm bad at writing home, and they
Have told the regiment to pack—
And that I shan't be coming back.

We had a neighbor, as you know,
   And you remember I
And she—How very long ago
   It is we said good-by!
She won't ask after me, nor care,
But tell her ev'rything, don't spare
Her empty heart; and let her cry;
To her it doesn't signify.

                MAURICE BARING

A SONG OF

Czar Ivan Vassilievich the Terrible

OF HIS YOUNG BODYGUARD, AND OF

Kalashnicov,

THE BOLD TRADING MAN

Oh, all hail to thee, thou Czar Ivan Vassilievich!
'Tis of thee that our song we made,
And thy favorite, the young bodyguard,
And of that trader bold, of Kalashnicov;
We have made that song in the style of old,
We sang it to the twang of a psaltery,
And we chanted it, and recited it.
All the Christian folk solace found therein,
While that noble great, Matvei Romadanovski,
Handed us a bowl of spiced foaming mead;

While his lady-wife, lily-white of face,
Brought to us, on a silver tray,
A fine napkin worked with designs in silk.
For three days, three nights did they us regale,
And to our song harked, nor could hear enough.

I

'TIS NOT the fair sun, shining in the sky,
Nor are those cloudlets blue that admire him:
'Tis the Awesome Czar, Ivan Vassilievich,
Sitting at his board, in his crown of gold,
While behind him stand all his dapifers,
And across from him sit his earls and knights,
And on each hand stand his brave bodyguards;
To God's glory the Czar quaffs and feasts,
And his own soul's mirth, and to pleasure him.
With a smile the Czar bade his gold bowl filled
With a wine most sweet, brought from overseas,
And to offer it to his bodyguards.
And thereof all drank, and the Czar's praise sang.
Only one of them, but one bodyguard,
A most lusty wight, bold in love and fight,
In that golden bowl did not wet his lips;
His dark eyes looked down on the oaken floor,
His fair head sank down on his mighty breast,
For within that breast dwelt a carking thought.
Thereupon the Czar knit his eyebrows black,
And he fixed the lad with his piercing eyes,
Even as a hawk from the heavens' height
Eyes a pigeon young with its light gray wings—
Yet the warrior youth never raised his eyes.
Thereupon the Czar struck his weighty staff
Hard upon the floor—and its heavy tip
Deep within the boards of hewn oak sank;
Yet not even this made the brave lad start.
Thereupon the Czar spake an awesome word,
And the goodly youth came awake at last.

"Ho, there, son of Kiribei, our servant true and leal—
Hast thou disloyal thoughts in thy bosom hid?
Or dost envy feel for our glory great?
Or hast weary grown of thy honored task?
When the moon doth rise, all the stars rejoice,
For they have more light for their skyey jaunts;
But if any star in a small cloud hide,
It will earthward fall in a headlong flight. . . .
It but ill befits thee, then, son of Kiribei,
When the Czar rejoices his joy to disdain,
For by birth thou art a Scuratov true,
And thou fostered wert by the Malutin clan!"
　　The son of Kiribei thereon spake, and said,
With obeisance low, to the Awesome Czar:
　　"Our Sovereign Lord, Ivan Vassilievich!
Do not thou upraid thy unworthy slave;
There is never wine the heart's flames can quench,
There is never viand that black thought can sate!
But if thy wrath I roused, wreak thy royal will:
Order them to slay me, to lop off my head,
For it heavy lies on my shoulders broad,
Of itself it droops to dank mother earth."
　　Unto him then spake Czar Vassilievich:
"Why, what grief can crush a stout lad like thee?
Has the cloth of gold of thy robe rubbed thin?
Has thy sable cap far too long been worn?
Has thy purse grown lean, of its gold all shorn?
Or hast nicked the edge of thy chilled-steel sword?
Or hast lamed thy steed, through some blacksmith's fault?
Or hast been knocked down by some trader's son,
In a bare-fist fight on Moscow River held?"
　　The son of Kiribei then this answer made:
"Such a bewitched fist has not yet been born,
Nor in noble line nor in trading clan;
Gaily runs my steed from Cabardinian steppes;
Like a mirror gleams my sword, its edge razor-keen;
And on gala days, through thy royal largess,
No worse than the next I myself array.
　　When I mount and ride my mettlesome steed,
To pace him and race him beyond Moscow River,

My broad sash of silk about me I tighten,
On the side of my head I perch my cap,
'Tis of velvet made, with darkest sable trimmed;
Nigh gates of hewn timbers all the fair maids stand,
And the young wives, for to eye and sigh, and to smile at me.
Only one eyes not, only one sighs not
But with striped headdress her fair face doth hide.
    In all Holy Russia, our own Motherland,
You may seek and never find a beauty so great:
Statelily she walks, like to a young swan;
Sweetly her eyes gaze, like a young dove's;
If she utter a word, nightingales sing;
Her rose cheeks blush with a living flame,
Like the glow at morn in God's own sky;
Her braids ruddy are, with the sheen of gold,
With bright ribbands are they interlaced,
On her shoulders they glide as though they had life,
Her white bosom sweet they caress and kiss.
In a trading clan was she born and bred,
Alena Dmitrevna is the name she bears.
    When my eyes behold her I am not my own self:
My strong arms fall listless by my side,
My quick-darting eyes darken and grow dim;
Weary, dreary then do I feel, Great Czar,
Grieving on this earth by my lone self.
I no solace find in steeds swift as wind,
My robes of cloth of gold no solace for me hold,
And no need have I of a gold-stuffed purse. . . ."
    And Ivan Vassilievich spake thereon, and laughed:
"Well, my servant leal! In thy sorry plight,
In thy woe so great, I shall try to help.
Here, take thou my gem-studded ring,
Take thou, too, strings of orient pearls.
Some matchmaker seek, a crone wise and shrewd,
And send her thou then with the precious gifts
To thy love, to Alena Dmitrevna;
If she love thee well, hold thy wedding feast.
If she love thee not, be not wroth with me."
    Oh, all hail to thee, Czar Ivan Vassilievich!

But thou hast been gulled by thy crafty slave,
He hath not told thee all the truth, forsooth,
Hath to thee ne'er told that the lady fair
In the Church of God had been truly wed,
Had been truly wed to a trader young,
As our law demands, our own Christian law.

Ho there, lads, sing—but let your psaltery ring!
Ho there, lads, drink—but let not your wits sink!
Pleasure ye the heart of the goodly knight,
And his lady-wife, lily-white of face!

II

At the counter of his shop the young trader sits,
A well-built brave lad, Stepan, son of Paramon,
And his last name is Kalashnicov.
His bolts of silk on the counter he spreads,
With beguiling speech tries buyers to lure,
His gold and silver he counts and recounts.
But this day has not been a good day for him:
The rich gentlefolk have been going right by,
Going right by, but none stepped within.

The vespers have been rung and sung in every church,
The evening glow is murky beyond Kremlin's walls,
Small clouds gather in the sky;
They are driven by a gathering, chanting storm;
The broad market place is deserted now.
Stepan, son of Paramon, locks the oak shop door
With a spring lock wrought in the Tongue-Tied Land,
A huge surly hound outside he chains,
And sunk in deep thought for his home he starts,
Across Moscow River, where his young wife waits.

But when he comes at last to his well-built house,
Stepan, son of Paramon, doth wonder much:
His young wife greets him not when he opes the door,

No white cloth is spread on the oaken board,
While the light but barely glows where the icons hang.
And he calls to him his old household drudge:
"Tell me, now, Eremeievna, tell me everything:
Where has she gone to, where does she keep herself
At so late an hour, my Alena Dmitrevna?
And my children dear—what about them?
I guess they ran and played till they tired out,
And were early tucked in their little beds?"

   "Oh, my master dear, Stepan Paramonovich!
'Tis a wonder wondrous that I have to tell:
For Alena Dmitrevna had to vespers gone—
But the priest just passed with his fair young wife,
They have lit their lights and sat down to sup,
Yet from the parish church thy wife has not come back.
And thy little ones neither sleep nor play—
They cry grievously; there's no hushing them."

   In distressing thought did Kalashincov
At the window stand, looking at the street,
And that street was dark with the darkest night;
The white snow fell, spreading far and wide,
The white snow swirled, hiding every track.
Then within the entry he heard the door slam,
And thereafter steps, hasty, faltering;
He spun round and saw—Christ's power be with us!—
Standing before him his own wedded wife.
Pale she was, all pale, and her head was bare;
Her thick russet braids all unbraided were,
Sprinkled o'er with snow and with rime bedewed;
Her beclouded eyes with a crazed look stared,
Her lips whispered words none could understand.

   "Where, my wife, my wife, hast thou roaming been?
In what courtyard, now, or upon what square,
That thy hair is all in disorder now,
That thy raiment is torn all to shreds?
Thou hast lusted with, thou hast feasted with
All the nobles' sons, that I will be bound!
Not for that we wed 'fore the holy icons,
Not for that, my wife, we gold rings exchanged. . . .

With an iron lock will I lock thee up
Behind oaken doors, all with iron trimmed,
So that God's own light thou'lt no more behold,
That my honest name thou'll no more besmirch. . . ."
When she heard such words poor Alena Dmitrevna
Trembled grievously, like a frightened dove,
Quivered ceaselessly, like an aspen leaf,
Weeping brokenly with bitter, bitter tears,
And sank down on her knees at her husband's feet:
"Oh, my own true lord, dear to me as the sun,
Either slay me now or else hear me out!
The things thou sayest are as a pointed blade—
Because of them my poor heart is rent;
I am not afeard of any cruel death,
Nor am I afeard of what other folks may say,
But I am afeard that I may lose thy love.
When the vespers ended I did homeward turn,
Walking down the street, going all alone;
Then methought I heard snow crunching not far behind:
I looked back and saw, running fleet as wind,
A man after me. My knees all but failed,
Yet my silken scarf quickly my face veiled.
And he my hands seized in a vise-like grip,
And thus spake to me in a whisper soft:
'What doth thee affright, my beauty beautiful?
For no thief am I, slaying passers-by—
'Tis the Czar I serve, the Most Awesome Czar,
And all men call me the son of Kiribei,
And the foster child of the Malutins proud. . . .'
I was frightened then more than e'er before;
In my poor head all was in a dizzy whirl.
And he fell to kissing, to caressing me,
And whilst kissing me he spoke without cease:
'Do but tell me what thy heart longeth for,
My beloved one, my most precious one!
Is it gold thou wishest, or is it orient pearls?
Dost wish for bright gems or patterned cloth of gold?
Like a very queen I shall thee array,
All the women will envy thy display—
Only save thou me from a self-willed death;

If thou wouldst but love, wouldst but clasp me close—
If for but one time, if but in farewell!'
And he me caressed, and he did me kiss;
And each kiss accursed, like a living flame,
Still my face is searing, still on my cheeks burns!
And the neighbor women through their gates peered out,
Laughing, and their fingers pointed at us twain. . . .
Then from out his hands I broke loose at last,
And started off for home in a headlong flight,
But that villain's hands clutched my broidered shawl
That thou gavest me, and my Bokhara scarf.
He had me disgraced, hath put me to shame,
I that honest was, and without a stain—
And the vixen neighbors, what won't they say the now?
And how could I now ever people face?
Do not thou let me, thy own wedded wife,
Be the mock of vile and affronting men!
Whom have I but thee to seek protection from?
To whom could I now turn, from whom could I ask aid?
In all the wide, wide world I but an orphan am;
My own father under the cold sod lies,
And my mother lies by my father's side,
While my elder brother, as thyself thou knowest,
In a foreign land hath vanished without trace,
While my younger brother still is but a child—
Still is but a child, with a child's mind. . . ."
  Thus to him did speak Alena Dmitrevna,
Weeping all the while, weeping scalding tears.

  Stepan, son of Paramon, thereon sent a man
For to bring to him his younger brethren two.
And his brethren came to him, and to him bowed low,
And thereafter unto him spake they in these words:
  "Our eldest brother, do unto us impart
What to thee hath happed, what to thee befell,
That made thee send for us in the dark of night,
In the dark of night, in the frosty night?"
  "I will tell ye now, dearest brethren mine,
What a sore misfortune hath befallen me:
Our clan, so long in honor held, has been disgraced, to shame put,

By the Czar's evil bodyguard, the son of Kiribei;
And the wrong is such as no soul can bear,
And no stout heart can e'er put up with it.
So, tomorrow, when the fights are held
On the Moscow River, before the very Czar,
I, too, will fight hard 'gainst the Czar's own bodyguard,
I will fight to my dying breath, to very death;
But if he beat me—step ye forth and fight
For Holy Mother Truth, for what is the right.
Be not faint of heart, dearest brethren mine!
Younger you than I, fresher your strength is,
Ye have gathered less sins on your soul than I—
Mayhap the Lord to you may more gracious be!"
   And his brethren then thus did answer him:
"Whither the wind blows in the firmament,
Thither, too, the small clouds in obedience rush;
When the eagle, gray-winged, with a loud cry calls,
To a blood-drenched vale where a battle raged,
Calls for a feast through the night as a ghastly last rite,
To him flock the eaglets from near and afar.
Our eldest brother thou, our second sire,
Do as thou deemest best, as thou knowest best;
And be sure, our own, we will thee ne'er fail."

   Ho there, lads, sing—but let your psaltery ring!
   Ho there, lads, drink—but let not your wits sink!
   Pleasure ye the heart of the goodly knight,
   And his lady-wife, lily-white of face!

III

Over Moscow great, with its golden domes,
Over Kremlin's wall, all of white stones built,
From beyond far woods, from beyond blue hills,
On the snug roofs of hewn timber shedding light,
The gray cloudlets scattering in disordered flight,
The dawn's scarlet glow rises in the sky;

It has tossed wide its lovelocks of gold,
It has laved itself in the drifts of powdery snow;
As a most fair maid looks in her mirror small,
It looks into the clear sky, smilingly.

Wherefore, scarlet dawn-glow, has thou waked this day?
Wherefore art thou so sprightly, wherefore dost thou play?

How Moscow's fighting men, stout of heart, came, flocked
To the fisticuffs on Moscow River's ice,
For a holiday spree, for to amuse themselves!
And the Czar drove up, with his knightly band,
And his nobles all, and his bodyguards,
And he ordered to be staked out a silver chain,
With the links thereof soldered with virgin gold.
With that chain they squared a ring of an hundred feet,
Of an hundred feet and five and seventy more,
For them that would fight, fight it out man to man.
And thereupon the Czar, Ivan Vassilievich, bade
That a call be called in a ringing voice:
"Oh, where are ye all, ye stouthearted men?
Pleasure ye the Czar, our own Father dear,
Step ye forth the now into the great ring;
To him that wins a bout the Czar a gift will give,
But him that defeat will receive, the Lord will forgive!"
And the mettlesome son of Kiribei stepped forth,
Bowed from the waist in silence before the Czar,
From off his mighty shoulders his velvet cloak he cast,
Propped his good right hand on his oak-stump hip,
With the other fixed his scarlet cap,
And awaited what good foe might against him come.
Thrice the loud call they did loudly call—
Not a fighting man would as much as budge,
They do but stand there and each other nudge.
The young bodyguard struts freely like a fighting cock,
The chickenhearted fighters he doth jeer and mock:
"Ye have grown so meek; ye think twice, I guess!
So be it, then; since 'tis a holiday, I vow
I'll let my foe off alive, if he do repent,
I shall but pleasure the Czar, our own Sire."

But the throng sudden parts to either side—
And through it comes Stepan, son of Paramon,
The young trading man, the bold fighting man,
Who bears the name of Kalashnicov.
First of all he bowed low before the Awesome Czar,
Then to the Kremlin white, and the churches holy,
And only then to all the Russian folk there.
Blazing are his eyes that are a falcon's eyes;
On the young bodyguard fixes he his gaze.
Facing him, a firm stance he takes,
On his hands he draws the hard fighting gloves snug,
His mighty shoulders he flexes with a shrug,
And at his curly beard he doth most gently tug.

And to him then spake the son of Kiribei:
"Do but tell me now, thou stouthearted lad,
From what line, what clan, thou art by birth,
And what name it is that men call thee by?
So that we may know at thy funeral mass,
And likewise that I know whom to boast about."

To him Stepan, son of Paramon, answer made:
"Why, the name they call me by is Stepan Kalashnicov,
And I was born the son of an honest man,
And I have lived according to the Lord's own law,
Nor ever disgraced another man's wife,
Nor ever moon's man been in the lonely night,
Nor e'er myself hid from the heavens' light. . . .
And 'twas nought but truth thou didst say but now:
For one of us will a funeral mass be sung,
And that no later than on the morrow, at the hour of noon;
And but one of us will all the boasting do,
As he revels and feasts with his goodly friends;
But 'twas not to chaff, not to make folks laugh
I against thee come, thou vile paynim's son—
I come to fight to my dying breath, to the very death!"

But when he heard that, the son of Kiribei
Turned all white of face, like the autumn snow;
Over his bold eyes spread a veil of mist,
And a chill ran down 'twixt his shoulders broad,
He could say no word, for on his open lips it froze. . . .

And thereafter in silence the two drew apart;
The two men of might their great fight did start.

The son of Kiribei swung his arm wide then,
Landing the first blow on Kalashnicov, the trading man,
And that blow he landed right square on his breast;
Every rib shook in that stalwart chest,
On his heels rocked Stepan, son of Paramon;
On his breast a copper crucifix hung,
With holy relics therein from Kiev town—
And that cross was bent, and sank in the flesh:
Trickling like dew from under it came drops of blood—
And thereon thought Stepan, son of Paramon:
"Whatsoever is bound to be, that will be fulfilled;
I'll stand up for what's right to the very last!"
So he deftly turned, firmly braced himself,
Gathered into him every ounce of strength,
And at his hated foe struck, driving true and straight,
At his left temple, with all his shoulder's weight.
And the young bodyguard let out but one low moan,
Swayed a little, and keeled over dead;
He crashed down on the cold, cold snow,
On the cold, cold snow, like a young pine tree,
Like a young pine tree, in the thick pine woods,
Cut at resinous roots by the woodsman's ax.
And on seeing that, the Czar, Czar Ivan Vassilievich,
With great wrath was wroth, and on the ground he stamped,
And a thundercloud gathered on his brows;
He bade his men the bold trading man seize,
And then to his awesome presence to be brought.
    And thus unto him spake the Orthodox Czar:
"Answer me in all truth, in all conscience,
Was't through thy own will or unwillingly
Thou didst do to death my servant leal and true,
My best fighting man, son of Kiribei?"
    "I will tell thee true, thou Orthodox Czar:
I did him to death of my own free will,
But wherefore and why I shall not tell thee,
I will tell that only to the Lord God Himself.

Bid me my guilty head on the headsman's block place,
But withhold not from my children small,
Withhold thou not from my widow young,
And from my brethren two, thy mercy and thy grace."
   "A good thing for thee, thou goodly lad,
Thou bold fighting man, and thou trader's son,
That thou answer made as thy conscience bade.
To thy widow young and thy orphans poor
I shall grant a sum from my treasury;
Thy brethren shall I bid from this very day,
Freely to trade, without taxes or stay,
Throughout the far-flung Russian domain;
But as for thee, my goodly lad, do betake thee now
To the towering black Execution Dock,
And there lay down thy head, thy so restless head.
I will bid them hone-whet an ax of the finest steel,
Bid the hangman don-put on new garb from head to heel,
Order the Great Bell to ring, to peal,
So as all the good folk in Moscow may know
My grace I withheld not from thee also."

See how the folk gather on the Red Square;
The Great Bell tolls, clangs so dolefully,
Spreading far and wide the evil news.
Over the high scaffold on Execution Dock,
In a blood-red shirt with buttons bright,
Swinging a great ax whetted razor-keen,
Rubbing his hands the hangman gaily struts,
Biding there for the bold fighting man to come;
But the bold fighting man, the great trading man,
To his brethren twain is saying farewell:
   "There, my brethren two, friends of my own blood,
Let us kiss, embrace, since for the last time we part.
Say farewell for me to Alena Dmitrevna,
Bid her not to grieve for me overmuch;
To my little ones tell no word of me;
Say farewell for me to my parents' house;
Say farewell for me to all my bosom friends,
And pray ye yourselves in the Church of God,
For my soul—my soul, full of mortal sin!"

And they put to death Stepan Kalashnicov,
With a cruel death, and an ignominious;
And his hapless head rolled in blood on the scaffold boards.

Beyond Moscow River did they bury him,
In an open field, where three highways meet—
The Tula Road, the Ryazan, and the Vladimir.
And a hillock of sods they raised over it,
And a cross of maple wood they put over it.
And the riotous winds wander freely and howl
Over his small grave, lonely and without name,
And the good folk go by that lonely grave:
>When an old man goes by, he crosses himself;
>When a fine lad goes by, he preens himself;
>When a young maid goes by, she weeps to herself.
But when they that sing to the psaltery go by, they strike up a song!

>*Ho there, lads brave and strong!*
>*And ye psaltery players young,*
>*Whose voices ring in song.*
>*Fitly your song began—bring it to a fit end:*
>*To all men due deserts and honor extend!*
>*To the openhanded knight—glory!*
>*And to his beauteous lady-wife—glory!*
>*And to all the Christian folk—glory!*

Alexei Vassilievich
Koltsov

1 8 0 8 - 1 8 4 2

KOLTSOV is the Russian approximation of Burns.

From the beginning of the nineteenth century the cultured, upper-class poets had been seeking to engraft Russian poetry with the artless forms of the folk song and to express therein the forthright emotion, the outlook of the people. But what was really needed was a poet of genius, sprung from the people itself. Koltsov was that poet—Russia's first genuine folk poet.

This burgher of Voronezh, who acted as a sort of commission merchant for the peasants, who had only a year and a half of the most elementary schooling, acquiring an education from whatever books came his way, became a protégé of Belinski's and was the first to reveal the wealth of poetry hidden deep in the soul of the peasant—who at that time was no more than a chattel slave.

Koltsov died of tuberculosis at the age of thirty-four.

I Will Saddle a Steed

I WILL saddle a steed,
A steed fleet as wind;
I will soar, will fly
Light as any hawk,

Over leas, over seas
To a far-off land.
I will overtake,
Will bring back my youth!
Will array myself
As the youth I was,
And once more the eyes
Of fair maidens please!
But—no paths e'er lead
To things past recall;
Never will the sun
In the West arise!

FRANCES WINWAR

Nicholas Vassilievich
Gogol

1 8 0 9 – 1 8 5 2

ARISTOPHANES, Cervantes, Dickens, Erasmus, Gogol, Heine, Lucian, Martial, Molière, Rabelais, Swift, Voltaire. . . . The list is deliberately alphabetical. There are so many analogies and contrasts! Both Gogol and Molière were good actors and better playwrights (if we may mention a third actor-playwright, from the reports that have come down to us we can concede that Gogol was a better actor than Shakespeare); Gogol, however, never became a professional actor; also, despite the magnificent stageful of characters to the credit of each master of comedy and satire, it would be as loose to style Molière a Gallic Gogol as it would be to style Gogol a Slavic Molière. The satyricon of Gogol is full-bodied, red, and rich; the satyricon of Molière is fine, glaucous, and dry. A comparison of Harpagon and Pliushkin will instantly occur to the reader. Harpagon is great, indisputably, yet leaning toward mummy; Pliushkin is living skin-bones-and-phlegm. As for poor Scrooge, he is paler than Marley's ghost by comparison with the latter. (Gogol, incidentally, translated and adapted, despite his dislike of French, Molière's *Sganarelle.*)

Rabelais? You can easily note Gogol's love of the infinitesimal detail, of cataloguing, of the gusty, lusty word, of an exuberant vocabulary, of robustness, of exaggeration (where he is akin to the great American humorists). He is of kin, too, to Thomas Wolfe. Notice, merely, how both Wolfe and Gogol delight in the color, smell, taste, richness and copiousness of earthy man's poetry—good food. And both the Russian and the American shake hands on this, across the centuries, with that Frenchman, Rabelais-Alcofribas.

Swift? There are two supreme examples of death-grin sardonicism in world satire. One, if you will recall, is Swift's *Modest Proposal, etc.* The reader of *Dead Souls* will have no difficulty in recalling the second: the scene where Chichicov, the zombie dealer, is haggling over dead souls with Korobochca, the immortal widow woman.

A comparison with Dickens is inevitable. (Both Gogol and Dickens were admittedly talented, if not professional, character actors, and superb as readers.) In character drawing the English master is just about Gogol's only peer. But Gogol can be savage on occasion; is never sugar-waterily sentimental; decidedly (despite his conjectured virginity) better at creating feminine characters; and not only was not a reformer but resented even the tag of liberal that some critics bestowed on him. If *Dead Souls* is an indictment of serfdom, it is so without the author's awareness. *Dead Souls* is by no means the Russian *Uncle Tom's Cabin.* That honor goes to Turgenev's *Hunting Sketches,* published in 1852, the year of Gogol's death and of the publication of the second part of *Dead Souls.* In *The Inspector General* ("It'll be funnier than the devil!" he wrote to Pushkin, who gave him the theme for the play, just as he had done for *Dead Souls.*) Gogol's admitted aim was to "dump in a single heap all that is vile in Russia," yet serfdom is not in that heap at all. This inability to perceive the root of all Russia's evil forms the paradox of Gogol, Russia's first Naturalist, Russia's greatest satirist. (In a literature that is, oddly, richer in the picaresque than even the Span-ish, Gogol has created not one but two superb petty knaves: Chichicov and Hlestacov.)

Gogol-Yanovski (later he dropped the Yanovski; *gogol* is a species of wild duck) was born in a family of petty squires in the Ukraine—Russia's mother lode of great humorists and the more cheerful poets. His Micawberish father was passionately fond of theatricals; he directed, he acted, he even wrote two comedies in Ukrainian which are assigned a high place in the literature of that language. He it was who coached Nicholas in theater and developed his power of improvisation. His mother may, to some extent, be considered his collaborator; she supplied him, by request, with the details of Ukrainian folkways, which Gogol so fully and superbly utilized in his unbelievably fine and original stories of Little Russia. He may have studied law, but apparently never even attempted to practice it. He quit civil service, unable to stomach the bureaucratic milieu.

He had very hard sledding in Petersburg; like Krylov, he was reduced to tutoring the scions of the wealthy. For that matter, his first two books (poetry, under pseudonyms) were as ghastly failures as the first ventures of Poe. His reading, during his one and only tryout for the professional stage, had been "expressive, masterly, and absolutely natural," but since it was utterly devoid of the artificiality and affectation then in vogue, it did not make a favorable impression on the "theatrical aristarchs." He did not even bother returning for the verdict on his audition. Similarly, while no Beau Brummell, he was neither deformed nor repulsive, nor was he an unmitigated failure at teaching, which he tried only after attaining success, and acquiring the genuine friendship of Zhucovski, Pushkin, and others; these friendships he won through his *Evenings on a Farm near Dikanka, Published by Rood Panko, the Beekeeper*—a fresh, fantastic book, and of an unprecedented genre. As a matter of fact, he held two teaching positions. His first two or three lectures as a professor of history were unbelievably brilliant displays of fireworks and showmanship; thereafter, owing to lack of time for preparation, the pyrotechnics petered out. (Turgenev, then unknown, was one of those who attended these lectures.)

He was afflicted with Cossack wanderlust, and at one time actually started out for America with the intention of settling there. Incidentally, he was passionately fond of drawing and, while no Du Maurier, is as good a draftsman as Thackeray, at least. The final burning of the second, and probably the outline of the third, part of *Dead Souls* (he had burned previous drafts once or twice before) is one of the most harrowing calamities of literature, and as poignant an incident as the suicide of Chatterton.

We are indebted for this loss to the influence of Gogol's evil demon, an ignorant Orthodox priest who finally turned Gogol's latent mysticism into the downright religious mania that ruined him as a creative artist. And even his deathbed call for a ladder, for long considered delirious gibberish, was only an echoing of a Russian saint's similar call; it need not necessarily be regarded as raving, unless quoting Jeremiah be regarded as delirium.

Gogol was, throughout his life, harassed by censorship. He had, grovelingly, to distort the *Captain Kopeikin* story so that *Dead Souls* might see the light; every effort was made to suppress *The Inspector General,* and the censors would have succeeded had it not been for the hearty laughter and applause of Nicholas I at the first performance—May 1 (New Style), 1836, at the Alexandrovski Theater in Petersburg. The play's reception, needless to say, was a stormy one; but the Czar is supposed to have said, with just the right touch of chuckling demagogic bravado: "Everybody got his—but I most of all!"

The Overcoat is a *must* in any Russian anthology, in view of Dostoievski's *mot* (see commentary preceding the Pushkin selections).

A great deal of Gogol is available in English. However, the main trouble with almost all the English translations is not that they are Victorian, but that they were not good even when the great Queen was alive.

It is with intense satisfaction, therefore, after having been able to retranslate *Dead Souls,* that the Editor is now able to give two more masterpieces of Gogol's in much-needed new versions.

The Overcoat

IN the Bureau of . . . but it might be better not to mention the Bureau by its precise name. There is nothing more touchy than all these Bureaus, Regiments, Chancelleries of every sort, and, in a word, every sort of person belonging to the administrative classes. Nowadays every civilian, even, considers all of society insulted in his own person. Quite recently, so they say, a petition came through from a certain Captain of Rural Police in some town or other (I can't recall its name), in which he explained clearly that the whole social structure was headed for ruin and that his sacred name was actually being taken entirely in vain, and, in proof, he documented his petition with the enormous tome of some romantic work or other wherein, every ten pages or so, a Captain of Rural Police appeared—in some passages even in an out-and-out drunken state. And so, to avoid any and all unpleasantnesses, we'd better call the Bureau in question *a certain Bureau.* And so, in *a certain Bureau* there served a *certain clerk*—a clerk whom one could hardly style very remarkable: quite low of stature, somewhat pockmarked, somewhat rusty-hued of hair, even somewhat purblind, at first glance; rather bald at the temples, with wrinkles along both cheeks, and his face of that complexion which is usually called hemorrhoidal. Well, what would you? It's the Petersburg climate that's to blame. As far as his rank is concerned (for among us the rank must be made known first of all), why, he was what they call a Perpetual Titular Councilor— a rank which, as everybody knows, various writers who have a praiseworthy wont of throwing their weight about among those who are in no position to hit back, have twitted and exercised their keen wits against often and long. This clerk's family name was Bashmachkin. It's quite evident, by the very name, that it sprang from *bashmak* or shoe, but at what time, just when and how it sprang from a shoe— of that nothing is known. For not only this clerk's father but his grandfather and even his brother-in-law, and absolutely all the Bashmachkins, walked about in boots, merely resoling them three times a year.

Translated by Bernard Guilbert Guerney. Copyright, 1943, by the Vanguard Press, Inc.

His name and patronymic were Akakii Akakiievich. It may, perhaps, strike the reader as somewhat odd and out of the way, but the reader may rest assured that the author has not gone out of his way at all to find it, but that certain circumstances had come about of themselves in such fashion that there was absolutely no way of giving him any other name. And the precise way this came about was as follows. Akakii Akakiievich was born—unless my memory plays me false—on the night of the twenty-third of March. His late mother, a government clerk's wife, and a very good woman, was all set to christen her child, all fit and proper. She was still lying in bed, facing the door, while on her right stood the godfather, a most excellent man by the name of Ivan Ivanovich Eroshkin, who had charge of some Department or other in a certain Administrative Office, and the godmother, the wife of the precinct police officer, a woman of rare virtues, by the name of Arina Semenovna Byelobrushkina. The mother was offered the choice of any one of three names: Mokii, Sossii—or the child could even be given the name of that great martyr, Hozdavat. "No," the late lamented had reflected, "what sort of names are these?" In order to please her they opened the calendar at another place—and the result was again three names: Triphilii, Dula, and Varahasii. "What a visitation!" said the elderly woman. "What names all these be! To tell you the truth, I've never even heard the likes of them. If it were at least Baradat or Baruch, but why do Triphilii and Varahasii have to turn up?" They turned over another page—and came up with Pavsikahii and Vahtissii. "Well, I can see now," said the mother, "that such is evidently his fate. In that case it would be better if he were called after his father. His father was an Akakii—let the son be an Akakii also." And that's how Akakii Akakiievich came to be Akakii Akakiievich.

The child was baptized, during which rite he began to bawl and made terrible faces as if anticipating that it would be his lot to become a Perpetual Titular Councilor. And so that's the way it had all come about. We have brought the matter up so that the reader might see for himself that all this had come about through sheer inevitability and it had been utterly impossible to bestow any other name upon Akakii Akakiievich.

When, at precisely what time, he entered the Bureau, and who gave him the berth, were things which no one could recall. No matter how many Directors and his superiors of one sort or another came and went, he was always to be seen in the one and the same spot, in the same posture, in the very same post, always the same Clerk of Correspondence, so that subsequently people became convinced that he evidently had come into the world just the way he was, all done and set, in a uniform frock and bald at the temples. No respect whatsoever was shown him in the Bureau. The porters not only didn't jump up from their places whenever he happened to pass by, but didn't even as much as glance at him, as if nothing more than a common housefly had passed through the reception hall. His superiors treated him with a certain chill despotism. Some assistant or other of some Head of a Department would simply shove papers under his nose, without as much as saying "Transcribe these," or "Here's a rather pretty, interesting little case," or any of those small pleasantries that are current in well-conducted administrative institutions. And he would take the work, merely glancing at the paper, without looking up to see who had put it down before him and whether that person had the right to do so; he took it and right then and there went to work on it. The young clerks made fun of him and sharpened their wits at his expense, to whatever extent their quill-driving wittiness sufficed, retailing in his very presence the various stories made up about him; they said of his landlady, a crone of seventy, that she beat him, and asked him when their wedding would take place; they scattered torn paper over his head, maintaining it was snow.

But not a word did Akakii Akakiievich say in answer to all this, as if there were actually nobody before him. It did not even affect his work: in the midst of all these annoyances he did not make a single clerical error. Only when the jest was past all bearing, when they jostled his arm, hindering him from doing his work, would he say: "Leave me alone! Why do you pick on me?" And there was something odd about his words and in the voice with which he uttered them. In that voice could be heard something that moved one to pity—so much so that one young man, a recent entrant, who, following the example of the others, had permitted himself to make fun of Akakii Akakiievich, stopped suddenly, as if pierced to the quick, and from that time on everything seemed to change in his eyes and appeared in a different light. Some sort of preternatural force seemed to repel him from the companions he had made, having taken them for decent, sociable people. And for a long time afterward, in the very midst of his most cheerful moments, the little squat clerk would appear before him, with the small bald patches on each side of his forehead, and he would hear his heart-piercing words "Leave me alone! Why do you pick on me?" And in these heart-piercing words he caught the ringing sound of others: "I am your brother." And the poor young man would cover his eyes with his hand, and many a time in his life thereafter did he shudder, seeing how much inhumanity there is in man, how much hidden ferocious coarseness lurks in refined, cultured worldliness and, O God! even in that very man whom the world holds to be noble and honorable. . . .

It is doubtful if you could find anywhere a man whose life lay so much in his work. It would hardly do to say that he worked with zeal; no, it was a labor of love. Thus, in this transcription of his, he visioned some sort of diversified and pleasant world all its own. His face expressed delight; certain letters were favorites of his and, whenever he came across them he would be beside himself with rapture: he'd chuckle, and wink, and help things along by working his lips, so that it seemed as if one could read on his face every letter his quill was outlining. If rewards had been meted out to him commensurately with his zeal, he might have, to his astonishment, actually found himself among the State Councilors; but, as none other than those wits, his own co-workers, expressed it, all he'd worked himself up to was a button in a buttonhole too wide, and piles in his backside.

However, it would not be quite correct to say that absolutely no attention was paid him. One Director, being a kindly man and wishing to reward him for his long service, gave orders that some work of a more important nature than the usual transcription be assigned to him; to be precise, he was told to make a certain referral to another Administrative Department out of a docket already prepared; the matter consisted, all in all, of changing the main title as well as some pronouns here and there from the first person singular to the third person singular. This made so much work for him that he was all of a sweat, kept mopping his forehead, and finally said: "No, better let me transcribe something." Thenceforth they left him to his transcription for all time. Outside of this transcription, it seemed, nothing existed for him.

He gave no thought whatsoever to his dress; the uniform frock coat on him wasn't the prescribed green at all, but rather of some rusty-flour hue. His collar was very tight and very low, so that his neck, even though it wasn't a long one, seemed extraordinarily long emerging therefrom, like those gypsum kittens with nodding heads which certain outlanders balance by the dozen atop their heads and peddle throughout Russia. And, always, something was bound to stick to his coat: a wisp of hay or some bit of thread; in addition to that, he had a peculiar knack whenever he walked through the streets of getting under some window at the precise moment when garbage of every sort was being thrown out of it, and for that reason always bore off on his hat watermelon and cantaloupe rinds and other such trifles. Not once in all his life had he ever turned his attention to the everyday things and doings out in the street—something, as everybody knows, that is always watched with eager interest by Akakii Akakiievich's confrère, the young government clerk, the penetration of whose lively gaze is so extensive that he will even take in somebody on the opposite sidewalk who has ripped loose his trouser strap—a thing that never fails to evoke a sly smile on the young clerk's face. But even if Akakii Akakiievich did look at anything, he saw thereon nothing but his own neatly, evenly penned lines of script, and only when some horse's nose, bobbing up from no one knew where, would be placed on his shoulder and let a whole gust of wind in his face through its nostrils, would he notice that he was not in the middle of a line of script but, rather, in the middle of the roadway.

On coming home he would immediately sit down at the table, gulp down his cabbage soup and bolt a piece of veal with onions, without noticing in the least the taste of either, eating everything together with the flies and whatever else God may have sent at that particular time of the year. On perceiving that his belly was beginning to swell out, he'd get up from the table, take out a small bottle of ink, and transcribe the papers he had brought home. If there were no homework, he would deliberately, for his own edification, make a copy of some paper for himself, especially if the document were remarkable not for its beauty of style but merely addressed to some new or important person.

Even at those hours when the gray sky of Petersburg becomes entirely extinguished and all the pettifogging tribe has eaten its fill and finished dinner, each as best he could, in accordance with the salary he receives and his own bent, when everybody has already rested up after the scraping of quills in various departments, the running around, the unavoidable cares about their own affairs and the affairs of others, and all that which restless man sets himself as a task voluntarily and to an even greater extent than necessary—at a time when the petty bureaucrats hasten to devote whatever time remained to enjoyment: he who is of the more lively sort hastening to the theater; another for a saunter through the streets, devoting the time to an inspection of certain pretty little hats; still another to some evening party, to spend that time in paying compliments to some comely young lady, the star of a small bureaucratic circle; a fourth (and this happened most frequently of all) would simply go for a call on a confrère in a flat up three or four flights of stairs, consisting of two small rooms with an entry and a kitchen and one or two attempts at the latest improvements—a kerosene lamp instead of candles, or some other elegant little thing that had cost many sacrifices, such as going without dinners or good times—in short, even at the time when all the petty bureaucrats scatter through the small apartments of their friends for a session of dummy whist, sipping tea out of tumblers and nibbling at cheap zwieback, drawing deep at their pipes, the stems thereof as long as walking sticks, retailing, during the shuffling and dealing, some bit of gossip or other from high society that had reached them at long last (something which no Russian, under any circumstances, and of whatever estate he be, can ever deny himself), or even, when there was nothing whatsoever to talk about, retelling the eternal chestnut of the commandant to whom people came to say that the tail of the horse on the Falconetti monument had been docked —in short, even at the time when every soul yearns to be diverted, Akakii Akakiievich did not give himself up to any diversion. No man could claim having ever seen him at any evening gathering. Having had his sweet fill of quill-driving, he would lie down to sleep, smiling at the thought of the next day: just what would God send him on the morrow?

Such was the peaceful course of life of a man who, with a yearly salary of four hundred, knew how to be content with his lot, and that course might even have continued to a ripe old age had it not been for sundry calamities, such as are strewn along the path of life, not only of Titular, but even Privy, Actual, Court, and all others sorts of Councilors, even those who never give any counsel to anybody nor ever accept any counsel from others for themselves.

There is, in Petersburg, a formidable foe of all those whose salary runs to four hundred a year or thereabouts. This foe is none other than our Northern frost—even though, by the bye, they do say that it's the most healthful thing for you. At nine in the morning, precisely at that hour when the streets are thronged with those on their way to sundry bureaus, it begins dealing out such powerful and penetrating fillips to all noses, without any discrimination, that the poor bureaucrats absolutely do not know how to hide them. At this time, when even those who fill the higher posts feel their foreheads aching because of the frost and the tears come to their eyes, the poor Titular Councilors are sometimes utterly defenseless. The sole salvation, if one's overcoat is of the thinnest, lies in dashing, as quickly as possible, through five or six blocks and then stamping one's feet plenty in the porter's room, until the faculties and gifts for administrative duties, which have been frozen on the way, are thus thawed out at last.

For some time Akakii Akakiievich had begun to notice that the cold was somehow penetrating his back and shoulders with especial ferocity, despite the fact that he tried to run the required distance as quickly as possible. It occurred to him, at last, that there might be some defects about this overcoat. After looking it over rather thoroughly at home he discovered that in two or three places—in the back and at the shoulders, to be exact—it had become no better than the coarsest of sacking; the cloth was rubbed to such an extent that one could see through it, and the lining had crept apart. The reader must be informed that Akakii Akakiievich's overcoat, too, was a butt for the jokes of the petty bureaucrats; it had been deprived of the honorable name of an overcoat, even, and dubbed a *negligée*. And, really, it was of a rather queer cut; its collar grew smaller with every year, inasmuch as it was utilized to supplement the other parts of the garment. This supplementing was not at all a compliment to the skill of the tailor, and the effect really was baggy and unsightly.

Perceiving what the matter was, Akakii Akakiievich decided that the overcoat would have to go to Petrovich the tailor, who lived somewhere up four flights of backstairs and who, despite a squint-eye and pockmarks all over his face, did quite well at repairing bureaucratic as well as all other trousers and coats—of course, be it understood, when he was in a sober state and not hatching some nonsartorial scheme in his head. One shouldn't, really, mention this tailor at great length, but since there is already a precedent for each character in a tale being clearly defined, there's no help for it, and so let's trot out Petrovich as well. In the beginning he had been called simply Gregory and had been the serf of some squire or other; he had begun calling himself Petrovich only after obtaining his freedom papers and taking to drinking rather hard on any and every holiday—at first on the red-letter ones and then, without any discrimination, on all those designated by the church: wherever there was a little cross marking the day on the calendar. In this respect he was loyal to the customs of our grandsires, and, when bickering with his wife, would call her a worldly woman and a German frau. And, since we've already been inadvertent enough to mention his wife, it will be necessary to say a word or two about her as well; but, regrettably, little was known about her—unless, perhaps, the fact that Petrovich had a wife, or that she even wore a house-cap and not a kerchief; but as for beauty, it appears that she could hardly boast of any; at least the soldiers in the Guards were the only ones with hardihood enough to bend down for a peep under her cap, twitching their mustache as they did so and emitting a certain peculiar sound.

As he clambered up the staircase that led to Petrovich—the staircase, to render it its just due, was dripping all over from water and slops and thoroughly permeated with that alcoholic odor which makes the eyes smart and is, as everybody knows, unfailingly present on all the backstairs of all the houses in Petersburg—as he clambered up this staircase Akakii Akakiievich was already conjecturing how stiff Petrovich's asking-price would be and mentally determined not to give him more than two rubles. The door was open, because the mistress of the place, being busy preparing some fish, had filled the kitchen with so much smoke that one actually couldn't see the very cockroaches for it. Akakii Akakiievich made his way through the kitchen, unperceived even by the mistress herself, and at last entered the room wherein he beheld Petrovich, sitting on a wide table of unpainted deal with his feet tucked in under him like a Turkish Pasha. His feet, as is the wont of tailors seated at their work, were bare, and the first thing that struck one's eyes was the big toe of one, very familiar to Akakii Akakiievich, with some sort of deformed nail, as thick and strong as a turtle's shell. About Petrovich's neck were loops of silk and cotton thread, while some sort of ragged garment was lying on his knees. For the last three minutes he had been trying to put a thread through the eye of a needle, couldn't hit the mark, and because of that was very wroth against the darkness of the room and even the thread itself, grumbling under his breath: "She won't go through, the heathen! You've spoiled my heart's blood, you damned good-for-nothing!"

Akakii Akakiievich felt upset because he had come at just the moment when Petrovich was very angry; he liked to give in his work when the latter was already under the influence or, as his wife put it, "He's already full of rot-gut, the one-eyed devil!" In such a state Petrovich usually gave in willingly and agreed to everything; he even bowed and was grateful every time. Afterward, true enough, his wife would come around and complain weepily that, now, her husband had been drunk and for that reason had taken on the work too cheaply; but all you had to do was to tack on another ten kopecks—and the thing was in the bag. But now, it seemed, Petrovich was in a sober state, and for that reason on his high horse, hard to win over, and bent on boosting his prices to the devil knows what heights. Akakii Akakiievich surmised this and, as the saying goes, was all set to make back tracks, but the deal had already been started. Petrovich puckered up his one good eye against him very fixedly and Akakii Akakiievich involuntarily said, "Greetings, Petrovich!" "Greetings to you, Sir," said Petrovich and looked askance at Akakiievich's hands, wishing to see what sort of booty the other bore.

"Well, now, I've come to see you, now, Petrovich!"

Akakii Akakiievich, the reader must be informed, explained himself for the most part in prepositions, adverbs, and such verbal oddments as have absolutely no significance. But if the matter was exceedingly difficult, he actually had a way of not finishing his phrase at all, so that, quite frequently, beginning his speech with such words as "This, really, is perfectly, you know—" —he would have nothing at all to follow up with, and he himself would be likely to forget the matter, thinking that he had already said everything in full.

"Well, just what is it?" asked Petrovich, and at the same time, with his one good eye, surveyed the entire garment, beginning with the collar and going on to the sleeves, the back, the coat-skirts, and the buttonholes, for it was all very familiar to him, inasmuch as it was all his own handiwork. That's a way all tailors have; it's the first thing a tailor will do on meeting you.

"Why, what I'm after, now, Petrovich . . . the overcoat, now, the cloth . . . there, you see, in all the other places it's strong as can be . . . it's gotten a trifle dusty and only seems to be old, but it's really new, there's only one spot . . . a little sort of . . . in the back . . . and also one shoulder, a trifle rubbed through—and this shoulder, too, a trifle—do you see? Not a lot of work, really—"

Petrovich took up the *negligée,* spread it out over the table as a preliminary, examined it for a long time, shook his head, and then groped with his hand on the window sill for a round snuffbox with the portrait of some general or other on its lid—just which one nobody could tell, inasmuch as the place occupied by the face had been holed through with a finger and then pasted over with a small square of paper. After duly taking tobacco, Petrovich held the *negligée* taut in his hands and scrutinized it against the light, and again shook his head; after this he turned it with the lining up and again shook his head, again took off the lid with the general's face pasted over with paper and, having fully loaded both nostrils with snuff, covered the snuffbox, put it away, and, at long last, gave his verdict:

"No, there's no fixin' this thing: your wardrobe's in a bad way!"

Akakii Akakiievich's heart skipped a beat at these words.

"But why not, Petrovich?" he asked, almost in the imploring voice of a child. "All that ails it, now . . . it's rubbed through at the shoulders. Surely you must have some small scraps of cloth or other—"

"Why, yes, one could find the scraps—the scraps will turn up," said Petrovich. "Only there's no sewing them on: the whole thing's all rotten: touch a needle to it—and it just crawls apart on you."

"Well, let it crawl—and you just slap a patch right on to it."

"Yes, but there's nothing to slap them little patches on to; there ain't nothing for the patch to take hold on—there's been far too much wear. It's cloth in name only, but if a gust of wind was to blow on it it would scatter."

"Well, now, you just fix it up. That, really, now . . . how can it be?"

"No," said Petrovich decisively, "there ain't a thing to be done. The whole thing's in a bad way. You'd better, when the cold winter spell comes, make footcloths out of it, because stockings ain't so warm. It's them Germans that invented them stockings, so's to rake in more money for themselves. [Petrovich loved to needle the Germans whenever the chance turned up.] But as for that there overcoat, it looks like you'll have to make yourself a new one."

At the word *new* a mist swam before Akakii Akakiievich's eyes and everything in the room became a hotchpotch. All he could see clearly was the general on the lid of Petrovich's snuffbox, his face pasted over with a piece of paper.

"A new one? But how?" he asked, still as if he were in a dream. "Why, I have no money for that."

"Yes, a new one," said Petrovich with a heathenish imperturbability.

"Well, if there's no getting out of it, how much, now—"

"You mean, how much it would cost?"

"Yes."

"Why, you'd have to cough up three fifties and a bit over," pronounced Petrovich and significantly pursed up his lips at this. He was very fond of strong effects, was fond of somehow nonplusing somebody, utterly and suddenly, and then eyeing his victim sidelong, to see what sort of wry face the nonplusee would pull after his words.

"A hundred and fifty for an overcoat!" poor Akakii Akakiievich cried out—cried out perhaps for the first time since he was born, for he was always distinguished for his low voice.

"Yes, Sir!" said Petrovich. "And what an overcoat, at that! If you put a marten collar on it and add a silk-lined hood it might stand you even two hundred."

"Petrovich, please!" Akakii Akakiievich was saying in an imploring voice, without grasping and without even trying to grasp the words uttered by Petrovich and all his effects. "Fix it somehow or other, now, so's it may do a little longer, at least—"

"Why, no, that'll be only having the work go to waste and spending your money for nothing," said Petrovich, and after these words Akakii Akakiievich walked out annihilated. But Petrovich, after his departure, remained as he was for a long time, with meaningfully pursed lips and without resuming his work, satisfied with neither having lowered himself nor having betrayed the sartorial art.

Out in the street, Akakii Akakiievich walked along like a somnambulist. "What a business, now, what a business," he kept saying to himself. "Really, I never even thought that it, now . . . would turn out like that. . . ." And then, after a pause, added: "So that's it! That's how it's turned out after all! Really, now, I couldn't even suppose that it . . . like that, now—" This was followed by another long pause, after which he uttered aloud: "So that's how it is! This, really, now, is something that's beyond all, now, expectation . . . well, I never! What a fix, now!"

Having said this, instead of heading for home, he started off in an entirely different direction without himself suspecting it. On the way a chimney sweep caught him square with his whole sooty side and covered his whole shoulder with soot; enough quicklime to cover his whole hat tumbled down on him from the top of a building under construction. He noticed nothing of all this and only later, when he ran up against a policeman near his sentry box (who, having placed his halberd near him, was shaking some tobacco out of a paper cornucopia on to his calloused palm), did Akakii Akakiievich come a little to himself, and that only because the policeman said: "What's the idea of shoving your face right into mine? Ain't the sidewalk big enough for you?" This made him look about him and turn homeward.

Only here did he begin to pull his wits together; he perceived his situation in its clear and real light; he started talking to himself no longer in snatches but reasoningly and frankly, as with a judicious friend with whom one might discuss a matter most heartfelt and intimate. "Well, no," said Akakii Akakiievich, "there's no use reasoning with Petrovich now; he's, now, that way. . . . His wife had a chance to give him a drubbing, it looks like. No, it'll be better if I come to him on a Sunday morning; after Saturday night's good time he'll be squinting his eye and very sleepy, so he'll have to have a hair of the dog that bit him, but his wife won't give him any money, now, and just then I'll up with ten kopecks or so and into his hand with it—so he'll be more reasonable to talk with, like, and the overcoat will then be sort of. . . ."

That was the way Akakii Akakiievich reasoned things out to himself, bolstering up his spirits. And, having bided his time till the next Sunday and spied from afar that Petrovich's wife was going off somewhere out of the house, he went straight up to him. Petrovich, sure enough, was squinting his eye hard after the Saturday night before, kept his head bowed down to the floor, and was no end sleepy; but, for all that, as soon as he learned what was up, it was as though the Devil himself nudged him.

"Can't be done," said he. "You'll have to order a new overcoat."

Akakii Akakiievich thrust a ten-kopeck coin on him right then and there.

"I'm grateful to you, Sir; I'll have a little something to get me strength back and will drink to your health," said Petrovich, "but as for your overcoat, please don't fret about it; it's of no earthly use any more. As for a new overcoat, I'll tailor a glorious one for you; I'll see to that."

Just the same, Akakii Akakiievich started babbling again about fixing the old one, but Petrovich simply would not listen to him and said: "Yes, I'll tailor a new one for you without fail; you may rely on that, I'll try my very best. We might even do it the way it's all the fashion now—the collar will button with silver catches under appliqué."

It was then that Akakii Akakiievich perceived that there was no doing without a new overcoat, and his spirits sank utterly. Really, now, with what means, with what money would he make this overcoat? Of course he could rely, in part, on the coming holiday bonus, but this money had been apportioned and budgeted ahead long ago. There was an imperative need of outfitting himself with new trousers, paying the shoemaker an old debt for a new pair of vamps to an old pair of boot-legs, and he had to order from a sempstress three shirts and two pair of those nethergarments which it is impolite to mention in print; in short, all the money was bound to be expended entirely, and even if the Director were so gracious as to decide on giving him five and forty, or even fifty rubles as a bonus, instead of forty, why, even then only the veriest trifle would be left over, which, in the capital sum required for the overcoat, would be as a drop in a bucket. Even though Akakii Akakiievich was, of course, aware of Petrovich's maggot of popping out with the devil knows how inordinate an asking price, so that even his wife herself could not restrain herself on occasion from crying out: "What, are you going out of your mind, fool that you are! There's times when he won't take on work for anything, but the Foul One has egged him on to ask a bigger price than all of him is worth"—even though he knew, of course, that Petrovich would probably undertake the work for eighty rubles, nevertheless and notwithstanding where was he to get those eighty rubles? Half of that sum might, perhaps, be found; half of it could have been found, maybe even a little more—but where was he going to get the other half?

But first the reader must be informed where the first half was to come from. Akakii Akakiievich had a custom of putting away a copper or so from every ruble he expended, into a little box under lock and key, with a small opening cut through the lid for dropping money therein. At the expiration of every half-year he made an accounting of the entire sum accumulated in coppers and changed it into small silver. He had kept this up a long time, and in this manner, during the course of several years, the accumulated sum turned out to be more than forty rubles. And so he had half the sum for the overcoat on hand; but where was he to get the other half? Where was he to get the other forty rubles? Akakii Akakiievich mulled the matter over and over and decided that it would be necessary to curtail his ordinary expenses, for the duration of a year at the very least; banish the indulgence in tea of evenings; also, of evenings, to do without lighting candles, but, if there should be need of doing something, to go to his landlady's room and work by her candle; when walking along the streets he would set his foot as lightly and carefully as possible on the cobbles and flagstones, walking almost on tiptoes, and thus avoid wearing out his soles prematurely; his linen would have to be given as infrequently as possible to the laundress and, in order that it might not become too soiled, every time he came home all of it must be taken off, the wearer having to remain only in his jean bathrobe, a most ancient garment and spared even by time itself.

It was, the truth must be told, most difficult for him in the beginning to get habituated to such limitations, but later it did turn into a matter of habit, somehow, and everything went well; he even became perfectly trained to going hungry of evenings; on the other hand, however, he had spiritual sustenance, always carrying about in his thoughts the eternal idea of the new overcoat. From this time forth it seemed as if his very existence had become somehow fuller, as though he had taken unto himself a wife, as though another person was always present with him, as though he were not alone but as if an amiable feminine helpmate had consented to traverse the path of life side by side with him—and this feminine helpmate was none other than this very same overcoat, with a thick quilting of cotton wool, with a strong lining that would never wear out.

He became more animated, somehow, even firmer of character, like a man who has already defined and set a goal for himself. Doubt, indecision—in a word, all vacillating and indeterminate traits—vanished of themselves from his face and actions. At times a sparkle appeared in his eyes; the boldest and most daring of thoughts actually flashed through his head: Shouldn't he, after all, put marten on the collar? Meditations on this subject almost caused him to make absent-minded blunders. And on one occasion, as he was transcribing a paper, he all but made an error, so that he emitted an almost audible "Ugh," and made the sign of the cross.

During the course of each month he would make at least one call on Petrovich, to discuss the overcoat: Where would it be best to buy the cloth, and of what color, and at what price—and even though somewhat preoccupied he always came home satisfied, thinking that the time would come, at last, when all the necessary things would be bought and the overcoat made.

The matter went even more quickly than he had expected. Contrary to all his anticipations, the Director designated a bonus not of forty or forty-five rubles for Akakii Akakiievich, but all of sixty. Whether he had a premonition that Akakii Akakiievich needed a new overcoat, or whether this had come about of its own self, the fact nevertheless remained: Akakii Akakiievich thus found himself the possessor of an extra twenty rubles. This circumstance hastened the course of things. Some two or three months more of slight starvation—and lo! Akakii Akakiievich had accumulated around eighty rubles. His heart, in general quite calm, began to palpitate. On the very first day possible he set out with Petrovich to the shops. The cloth they bought was very good, and no great wonder, since they had been thinking over its purchase as much as half a year before and hardly a month had gone by without their making a round of the shops to compare prices; but then, Petrovich himself said that there couldn't be better cloth than that. For lining they chose calico, but of such good quality and so closely woven that, to quote Petrovich's words, it was still better than silk and, to look at, even more showy and glossy. Marten they did not buy, for, to be sure, it was expensive, but instead they picked out the best catskin the shop boasted—catskin that could, at a great enough distance, be taken for marten.

Petrovich spent only a fortnight in fussing about with the making of the overcoat, for there was a great deal of stitching to it, and if it hadn't been for that it would have been ready considerably earlier. For his work Petrovich took twelve rubles—he couldn't have taken any less; everything was positively sewn with silk thread, with a small double stitch, and after the stitching Petrovich went over every seam with his own teeth, pressing out various figures with them.

It was on . . . it would be hard to say on precisely what day, but it was, most probably, the most triumphant day in Akakii Akakiievich's life when Petrovich, at last, brought the overcoat. He brought it in the morning, just before Akakii Akakiievich had to set out for his Bureau. Never, at any other time, would the overcoat have come in so handy, because rather hard frosts were already setting in and, apparently, were threatening to become still more severe. Petrovich's entrance with the overcoat was one befitting a good tailor. Such a portentous expression appeared on his face as Akakii Akakiievich had never yet beheld. Petrovich felt to the fullest, it seemed, that he had performed no petty labor and that he had suddenly evinced in himself that abyss which lies between those tailors who merely put in linings and alter and fix garments and those who create new ones.

He extracted the overcoat from the bandanna in which he had brought it. (The bandanna was fresh from the laundress; it was only later on that he thrust it in his pocket for practical use.) Having drawn out the overcoat, he looked at it quite proudly and, holding it in both hands, threw it deftly over the shoulders of Akakii Akakiievich, pulled it and smoothed it down the back with his hand, then draped it on Akakii Akakiievich somewhat loosely. Akakiievich, as a man along in his years, wanted to try it on with his arms through the sleeves. Petrovich helped him on with it: it turned out to be fine, even with his arms through the sleeves. In a word, the overcoat proved to be perfect and had come in the very nick of time. Petrovich did not let slip the opportunity of saying that he had done the work so cheaply only because he lived in a place without a sign, on a side street, and, besides, had known Akakii Akakiievich for a long time; *but* on the Nevski Prospect they would have taken seventy-five rubles from him for the labor alone. Akakii Akakiievich did not feel like arguing the matter with Petrovich and, besides, he had a dread of all the fancy sums with which Petrovich liked to throw dust in people's eyes. He paid the tailor off, thanked him, and walked right out in the new overcoat on his way to the Bureau. Petrovich walked out at his heels and, staying behind on the street, for a long while kept looking after the overcoat from afar, and then deliberately went out of his way so that, after cutting across a crooked lane, he might run out again into the street and have another glance at his overcoat from a different angle—that is, full front.

In the meantime Akakii Akakiievich walked along feeling in the most festive of moods. He was conscious every second of every minute that he had a new overcoat on his shoulders, and several times even smiled slightly because of his inward pleasure. In reality he was a gainer on two points: for one, the overcoat was warm, for the other, it was a fine thing. He did not notice the walk at all and suddenly found himself at the Bureau; in the porter's room he took off his overcoat, looked it all over, and entrusted it to the particular care of the doorman. None knows in what manner everybody in the Bureau suddenly learned that Akakii Akakiievich had a new overcoat, and that the *negligée* was no longer in existence. They all immediately ran out into the vestibule to inspect Akakii Akakiievich's new overcoat. They fell to congratulating him, to saying agreeable things to him, so that at first he could merely smile, and in a short time became actually embarrassed. And when all of them, having besieged him, began telling him that the new overcoat ought to be baptized and that he ought, at the least, to get up an evening party for them, Akakii Akakiievich was utterly at a loss, not knowing what to do with himself, what answers to make, nor how to get out of inviting them. It was only a few minutes later that he began assuring them, quite simple-heartedly, that it wasn't a new overcoat at all, that it was just an ordinary overcoat, that in fact it was an old overcoat. Finally one of the bureaucrats—some sort of an Assistant to a Head of a Department, actually—probably in order to show that he was not at all a proud stick and willing to mingle even with those beneath him, said: "So be it, then; I'm giving a party this evening and ask all of you to have tea with me; today, appropriately enough, happens to be my birthday."

The clerks, naturally, at once thanked the Assistant to a Head of a Department and accepted the invitation with enthusiasm. Akakii Akakiievich attempted to excuse himself at first, but all began saying that it would show disrespect to decline, that it would be simply a shame and a disgrace, and after that there was absolutely no way for him to back out. However, when it was all over, he felt a pleasant glow as he reminded himself that this would give him a chance to take a walk in his new overcoat even in the evening. This whole day was for Akakii Akakiievich something in the nature of the greatest and most triumphant of holidays.

Akakii Akakiievich returned home in the happiest mood, took off the overcoat, and hung it carefully on the wall, once more getting his fill of admiring the cloth and the lining, and then purposely dragged out, for comparison, his former *negligée,* which by now had practically disintegrated. He glanced at it and he himself had to laugh, so great was the difference! And for a long while thereafter, as he ate dinner, he kept on smiling slightly whenever the present state of the *negligée* came to his mind. He dined gayly, and after dinner did not write a single stroke; there were no papers of any kind, for that matter; he just simply played the sybarite a little, lounging on his bed, until it became dark. Then, without putting matters off any longer, he dressed, threw the overcoat over his shoulders, and walked out into the street.

We are, to our regret, unable to say just where the official who had extended the invitation lived; our memory is beginning to play us false—very much so—and everything in Petersburg, no matter what, including all its streets and houses, has become so muddled in our mind that it's quite hard to get anything out therefrom in any sort of decent shape. But wherever it may have been, at least this much is certain: that official lived in the best part of town; consequently a very long way from Akakii Akakiievich's quarters. First of all Akakii Akakiievich had to traverse certain deserted streets with but scant illumination; however, in keeping with his progress toward the official's domicile, the streets became more animated; the pedestrians flitted by more and more often; he began meeting even ladies, handsomely dressed; the men he came upon had beaver collars on their overcoats; more and more rarely did he encounter jehus with latticed wooden sleighs, studded over with gilt nails—on the contrary, he kept coming across first-class drivers in caps of raspberry-hued velvet, their sleighs lacquered and with bearskin robes, while the carriages had decorated seats for the drivers and raced down the roadway, their wheels screeching over the snow.

Akakii Akakiievich eyed all this as a novelty—it was several years by now since he had set foot out of his house in the evening. He stopped with curiosity before the illuminated window of a shop to look at a picture, depicting some handsome woman or other, who was taking off her shoe, thus revealing her whole leg (very far from ill-formed), while behind her back some gentleman or other, sporting side whiskers and a handsome goatee, was poking his head out of the door of an adjoining room. Akakii Akakiievich shook his head and smiled, after which he went on his way. Why had he smiled? Was it because he had encountered something utterly unfamiliar, yet about which, nevertheless, everyone preserves a certain instinct? Or did he think, like so many other petty clerks, "My, the French they are a funny race! No use talking! If there's anything they get a notion of, then, sure enough, there it is!" And yet, perhaps, he did not think even that; after all, there's no way of insinuating one's self into a man's soul, of finding out all that he might be thinking about.

At last he reached the house in which the Assistant to a Head of a Department lived. The Assistant to a Head of a Department lived on a grand footing; there was a lantern on the staircase; his apartment was only one flight up. On entering the foyer of the apartment Akakii Akakiievich beheld row after row of galoshes. In their midst, in the center of the room, stood a samovar, noisy and emitting clouds of steam. The walls were covered with hanging overcoats and capes, among which were even such as had beaver collars or lapels of velvet. On the other side of the wall he could hear much noise and talk, which suddenly became distinct and resounding when the door opened and a flunky came out with a tray full of empty tumblers, a cream pitcher, and a basket of biscuits. It was evident that the bureaucrats had gathered long since and had already had their first glasses of tea.

Akakii Akakiievich, hanging up his overcoat himself, entered the room and simultaneously all the candles, bureaucrats, tobacco-pipes and card tables flickered before him, and the continuous conversation and the scraping of moving chairs, coming from all sides, struck dully on his ears. He halted quite awkwardly in the center of the room, at a loss and trying to think what he ought to do. But he had already been noticed, was received with much shouting, and everyone immediately went to the foyer and again inspected his overcoat. Akakii Akakiievich, even though he was somewhat embarrassed, still could not but rejoice on seeing them all bestow such praises on his overcoat, since he was a man with an honest heart. Then, of course, they all dropped him and his overcoat and, as is usual, directed their attention to the whist tables.

All this—the din, the talk, and the throng of people—all this was somehow a matter of wonder to Akakii Akakiievich. He simply did not know what to do, how to dispose of his hands, his feet, and his whole body; finally he sat down near the cardplayers, watched their cards, looked now at the face of this man, now of that, and after some time began to feel bored, to yawn—all the more so since his usual bedtime had long since passed. He wanted to say good-by to his host but they wouldn't let him, saying that they absolutely must toast his new acquisition in a goblet of champagne. An hour later supper was served, consisting of mixed salad, cold veal, meat pie, patties from a pastry cook's, and champagne. They forced Akakii Akakiievich to empty two goblets, after which he felt that the room had become ever so much more cheerful. However, he absolutely could not forget that it was already twelve o'clock and that it was long since time for him to go home. So that his host might not somehow get the idea of detaining him, he crept out of the room, managed to find his overcoat—which, not without regret, he saw lying on the floor; then, shaking the overcoat and taking every bit of fluff off it, he threw it over his shoulders and made his way down the stairs and out of the house.

It was still dusk out in the street. Here and there small general stores, those round-the-clock clubs for domestics and all other servants, were still open; other shops, which were closed, nevertheless showed, by a long streak of light along the crack either at the outer edge or the bottom, that they were not yet without social life and that, probably, the serving wenches and lads were still winding up their discussions and conversations, thus throwing their masters into utter bewilderment as to their whereabouts. Akakii Akakiievich walked along in gay spirits; he even actually made a sudden dash, for some unknown reason, after some lady or other, who had passed by him like a flash of lightning, and every part of whose body was filled with buoyancy. However, he stopped right then and there and resumed his former exceedingly gentle pace, actually wondering himself at the sprightliness that had come upon him from none knows where.

Soon he again was passing stretch after stretch of those desolate streets which are never too gay even in the daytime, but are even less so in the evening. Now they had become still more deserted and lonely; he came upon glimmering street lamps more and more infrequently— the allotment of oil was now evidently decreasing; there was a succession of wooden houses and fences, with never another soul about; the snow alone glittered on the street, and the squat hovels, with their shutters closed in sleep, showed like depressing dark blotches. He approached a spot where the street was cut in two by an unending square, with the houses on the other side of it barely visible—a square that loomed ahead like an awesome desert.

Far in the distance, God knows where, a little light flickered in a policeman's sentry box that seemed to stand at the end of the world. Akakii Akakiievich's gay mood somehow diminished considerably at this point. He set foot in the square, not without a premonition of something evil. He looked back and on each side of him—it was as though he were in the midst of a sea. "No, it's better even not to look," he reflected and went on with his eyes shut. And when he did open them to see if the end of the square were near, he suddenly saw standing before him, almost at his very nose, two strangers with mustaches— just what sort of men they were was something he couldn't even make out. A mist arose before his eyes and his heart began to pound.

"Why, that there overcoat is mine!" said one of the men in a thunderous voice, grabbing him by the collar. Akakii Akakiievich was just about to yell "Police!" when the other put a fist right up to his mouth, a fist as big as any government clerk's head, adding: "There, you just let one peep out of you!"

All that Akakii Akakiievich felt was that they had taken the overcoat off him, given him a kick in the back with the knee, and that he had fallen flat on his back in the snow, after which he felt nothing more. In a few minutes he came to and got up on his feet, but there was no longer anybody around. He felt that it was cold out in that open space and that he no longer had the overcoat, and began to yell; but his voice, it seemed, had no intention whatsoever of reaching the other end of the square. Desperate, without ceasing to yell, he started off at a run across the square directly toward the sentry box near which the policeman was standing and, leaning on his halberd, was watching the running man, apparently with curiosity, as if he wished to know why the devil anybody should be running toward him from afar and yelling. Akakii Akakiievich, having run up to him, began to shout in a stifling voice that he, the policeman, had been asleep, that he was not watching and couldn't see that a man was being robbed. The policeman answered that he hadn't seen anything, that he had seen two men of some sort stop him in the middle of the square, but he had thought they were friends of Akakii Akakiievich's, and that instead of cursing him out for nothing he'd better go on the morrow to the Inspector, and the Inspector would find out who had taken his overcoat.

Akakii Akakiievich ran home in utter disorder; whatever little hair still lingered on his temples and the nape of his neck was all disheveled; his side and his breast and his trousers were all wet with snow. The old woman, his landlady, hearing the dreadful racket at the door, hurriedly jumped out of bed and, with a shoe on only one foot, ran down to open the door, modestly holding the shift at her breast with one hand; but, on opening the door and seeing Akakii Akakiievich in such a state, she staggered back. When he had told her what the matter was, however, she wrung her hands and said that he ought to go directly to the Justice of the Peace; the District Officer of Police would take him in, would make promises to him and then lead him about by the nose; yes, it would be best of all to go straight to the Justice. Why, she was even acquainted with him, seeing as how Anna, the Finnish woman who had formerly been her cook, had now gotten a place as a nurse at the Justice's; that she, the landlady herself, sees the Justice often when he drives past her house, and also that he went to church every Sunday, praying, yet at the same time looking so cheerfully at all the folks, and that consequently, as one could see by all the signs, he was a kindhearted man. Having heard this solution of his troubles through to the end, the saddened Akakii Akakiievich shuffled off to his room, and how he passed the night there may be left to the discernment of him who can in any degree imagine the situation of another.

Early in the morning he set out for the Justice's, but was told there that he was sleeping; he came at ten o'clock, and was told again, "He's sleeping." He came at eleven; they told him, "Why, His Honor's not at home." He tried at lunchtime, but the clerks in the reception room would not let him through to the presence under any circumstances and absolutely had to know what business he had come on and what had occurred, so that, at last, Akakii Akakiievich for once in his life wanted to evince firmness of character and said sharply and categorically that he had to see the Justice personally, that they dared not keep him out, that he had come from his own Bureau on a Government matter, and that now, when he'd lodge a complaint against them, why, they would see, then. The clerks dared not say anything in answer to this and one of them went to call out the Justice of the Peace.

The Justice's reaction to Akakii Akakiievich's story of how he had been robbed of his overcoat was somehow exceedingly odd. Instead of turning his attention to the main point of the matter, he began interrogating Akakii Akakiievich: Just why had he been coming home at so late an hour? Had he, perhaps, looked in at, or hadn't he actually visited, some disorderly house? Akakii Akakiievich became utterly confused and walked out of the office without himself knowing whether the investigation about the overcoat would be instituted or not.

This whole day he stayed away from his Bureau (the only time in

his life he had done so). On the following day he put in an appearance,
all pale and in his old *negligée,* which had become more woebegone
than ever. The recital of the robbery of the overcoat, despite the fact
that there proved to be certain ones among his co-workers who did not
let pass even this opportunity to make fun of Akakii Akakiievich,
nevertheless touched many. They decided on the spot to make up a
collection for him, but they collected the utmost trifle, inasmuch as
the petty officials had spent a lot even without this, having subscribed
for a portrait of the Director and for some book or other, at the
invitation of the Chief of the Department, who was a friend of the
writer's; and so the sum proved to be most trifling. One of them, moved
by compassion, decided, at the least, to aid Akakii Akakiievich with
good advice telling him that he oughtn't to go to the precinct officer
of the police, because, even though it might come about that the precinct
officer, wishing to merit the approval of his superiors, might locate the
overcoat in some way, the overcoat would in the end remain with the
police, if Akakii Akakiievich could not present legal proofs that it
belonged to him; but that the best thing of all would be to turn to a
certain important person; that this important person, after conferring
and corresponding with the proper people in the proper quarters, could
speed things up.

There was no help for it; Akakii Akakiievich summoned up his
courage to go to the important person. Precisely what the important
person's post was and what the work of that post consisted of, has
remained unknown up to now. It is necessary to know that the certain
important person had only recently become an Important Person, but,
up to then, had been an unimportant person. However, his post was
not considered an important one even now in comparison with more
important ones. But there will always be found a circle of people who
perceive the importance of that which is unimportant in the eyes of
others. However, he tried to augment his importance by many other
means, to wit: he inaugurated the custom of having the subordinate
clerks meet him while he was still on the staircase when he arrived at
his office; another, of no one coming directly into his presence, but
having everything follow the most rigorous precedence: a Collegiate
Registrar was to report to the Provincial Secretary, the Provincial Secretary to a Titular one, or whomever else it was necessary to report to,
and only thus was any matter to come to him. For it is thus in our
Holy Russia that everything is infected with imitativeness; everyone
apes his superior and postures like him. They even say that a certain

Titular Councilor, when they put him at the helm of some small individual chancellery, immediately had a separate room for himself partitioned off, dubbing it the Reception Center, and had placed at the door some doormen or other with red collars and gold braid, who turned the doorknob and opened the door for every visitor, even though there was hardly room in the Reception Center to hold even an ordinary desk.

The manners and ways of the important person were imposing and majestic, but not at all complex. The chief basis of his system was strictness. "Strictness, strictness, and—strictness," he was wont to say, and when uttering the last word he usually looked very significantly into the face of the person to whom he was speaking, even though, by the way, there was no reason for all this, inasmuch as the half-score of clerks constituting the whole administrative mechanism of his chancellery was under the proper state of fear and trembling even as it was: catching sight of him from afar the staff would at once drop whatever it was doing and wait, at attention, until the Chief had passed through the room. His ordinary speech with his subordinates reeked of strictness and consisted almost entirely of three phrases: "How dare you? Do you know whom you're talking to? Do you realize in whose presence you are?" However, at soul he was a kindly man, treated his friends well, and was obliging; but the rank of General had knocked him completely off his base. Having received a General's rank he had somehow become muddled, had lost his sense of direction, and did not know how to act. If he happened to be with his equals he was still as human as need be, a most decent man, in many respects—even a man not at all foolish; but whenever he happened to be in a group where there were people even one rank below him, why, there was no holding him; he was taciturn, and his situation aroused pity, all the more since he himself felt that he could have passed the time infinitely more pleasantly. In his eyes one could at times see a strong desire to join in some circle and its interesting conversation, but he was stopped by the thought: Wouldn't this be too much unbending on his part, wouldn't it be a familiar action, and wouldn't he lower his importance thereby? And as a consequence of such considerations he remained forever aloof in that invariably taciturn state, only uttering some monosyllabic sounds at rare intervals, and had thus acquired the reputation of a most boring individual.

It was before such an *important person* that our Akakii Akakiievich appeared, and he appeared at a most inauspicious moment, quite inopportune for himself—although, by the bye, most opportune for the important person. The important person was seated in his private office and had gotten into very, very jolly talk with a certain recently arrived old friend and childhood companion whom he had not seen for several years. It was at this point that they announced to the important person that some Bashmachkin or other had come to see him. He asked abruptly, "Who is he?" and was told, "Some petty clerk or other." "Ah. He can wait; this isn't the right time for him to come," said the important man.

At this point it must be said that the important man had fibbed a little: he had the time; he and his old friend had long since talked over everything and had been long eking out their conversation with protracted silences, merely patting each other lightly on the thigh from time to time and adding, "That's how it is, Ivan Abramovich!" and "That's just how it is, Stepan Varlaamovich!" But for all that he gave orders for the petty clerk to wait a while just the same, in order to show his friend, a man who had been long out of the Civil Service and rusticating in his village, how long petty clerks had to cool their heels in his anteroom.

Finally, having had his fill of talk, yet having had a still greater fill of silences, and after each had smoked a cigar to the end in a quite restful armchair with an adjustable back, he at last appeared to recall the matter and said to his secretary, who had halted in the doorway with some papers for a report, "Why, I think there's a clerk waiting out there. Tell him he may come in."

On beholding the meek appearance of Akakii Akakiievich and his rather old, skimpy frock coat, he suddenly turned to him and asked, "What is it you wish?"—in a voice abrupt and firm, which he had purposely rehearsed beforehand in his room at home in solitude and before a mirror, actually a week before he had received his present post and his rank of General.

Akakii Akakiievich already had plenty of time to experience the requisite awe, was somewhat abashed, and, as best he could, in so far as his poor freedom of tongue would allow him, explained, adding even more *now's* than he would have at another time, that his overcoat had been perfectly new, and that, now, he had been robbed of it in a perfectly inhuman fashion, and that he was turning to him, now, so that he might interest himself through his . . . now . . . might correspond with the Head of Police or somebody else, and find his overcoat, now.

. . . Such conduct, for some unknown reason, appeared familiar to the General.

"What are you up to, my dear Sir?" he resumed abruptly. "Don't you know the proper procedure? Where have you come to? Don't you know how matters ought to be conducted? As far as this is concerned, you should have first of all submitted a petition to the Chancellery; it would have gone from there to the head of the proper Division, then would have been transferred to the Secretary, and the Secretary would in due time have brought it to my attention—"

"But, Your Excellency," said Akakii Akakiievich, trying to collect whatever little pinch of presence of mind he had, yet feeling at the same time that he was in a dreadful sweat, "I ventured to trouble you, Your Excellency, because secretaries, now . . . aren't any too much to be relied upon—"

"What? What? What?" said the important person. "Where did you get such a tone from? Where did you get such notions? What sort of rebellious feeling has spread among the young people against the administrators and their superiors?" The important person had, it seems, failed to notice that Akakii Akakiievich would never see fifty again, consequently, even if he could have been called a young man it could be applied only relatively, that is, to someone who was already seventy. "Do you know whom you're saying this to? Do you realize in whose presence you are? Do you realize? Do you realize, I'm asking you!" Here he stamped his foot, bringing his voice to such an overwhelming note that even another than an Akakii Akakiievich would have been frightened. Akakii Akakiievich was simply bereft of his senses, swayed, shook all over, and simply could not stand on his feet. If a couple of doormen had not run up right then and there to support him he would have slumped to the floor; they carried him out in a practically cataleptic state. But the important person, satisfied because the effect had surpassed even anything he had expected, and inebriated by the idea that a word from him could actually deprive a man of his senses, looked out of the corner of his eye to learn how his friend was taking this and noticed, not without satisfaction, that his friend was in a most indeterminate state and was even beginning to experience fear on his own account.

How he went down the stairs, how he came out into the street— that was something Akakii Akakiievich was no longer conscious of. He felt neither his hands nor his feet; never in all his life had he been dragged over such hot coals by a General—and a General outside his bureau, at that! With his mouth gaping, stumbling off the sidewalk, he breasted the blizzard that was whistling and howling through the streets; the wind, as is its wont in Petersburg, blew upon him from all the four quarters, from every cross lane. In a second it had blown a quinsy down his throat, and he crawled home without the strength to utter a word; he became all swollen and took to his bed. That's how effective a proper hauling over the coals can be at times!

On the next day he was running a high fever. Thanks to the magnanimous all-round help of the Petersburg climate, the disease progressed more rapidly than could have been expected, and when the doctor appeared he, after having felt the patient's pulse, could not strike on anything to do save prescribing hot compresses, and that solely so that the sick man might not be left without the beneficial help of medicine; but, on the whole, he announced on the spot that in another day and a half it would be curtains for Akakii Akakiievich, after which he turned to the landlady and said, "As for you, Mother, don't you be losing any time for nothing; order a pine coffin for him right now, because a coffin of oak will be beyond his means."

Whether Akakii Akakiievich heard the doctor utter these words, so fateful for him, and, even if he did hear them, whether they had a staggering effect on him, whether he felt regrets over his life of hard sledding—about that nothing is known, inasmuch as he was all the time running a temperature and was in delirium. Visions, each one stranger than the one before, appeared before him ceaselessly: now he saw Petrovich and was ordering him to make an overcoat with some sort of traps to catch thieves, whom he ceaselessly imagined to be under his bed, at every minute calling his landlady to pull out from under his blanket one of them who had actually crawled under there; then he would ask why his old *negligée* was hanging in front of him, for he had a new overcoat; then once more he had a hallucination that he was standing before the General, getting a proper raking over the coals, and saying, "Forgive me, Your Excellency!"; then, finally, he actually took to swearing foully, uttering such dreadful words that his old landlady could do nothing but cross herself, having never in her life heard anything of the sort from him, all the more so since these words followed immediately after "Your Excellency!"

After that he spoke utter nonsense, so that there was no understanding anything; all one could perceive was that his incoherent words and thoughts all revolved about that overcoat and nothing else.

Finally poor Akakii Akakiievich gave up the ghost. Neither his room nor his things were put under seal; in the first place because he had no heirs, and in the second because there was very little left for anybody to inherit, to wit: a bundle of goose quills, a quire of white governmental paper, three pairs of socks, two or three buttons that had come off his trousers, and the *negligée* which the reader is already familiar with. Who fell heir to all this treasure-trove, God knows; I confess that even the narrator of this tale was not much interested in the matter. They bore Akakii Akakiievich off and buried him. And Petersburg was left without Akakii Akakiievich, as if he had never been therein. There vanished and disappeared a being protected by none, endeared to no one, of no interest to anyone, a being that actually had failed to attract to itself the attention of even a naturalist who wouldn't let a chance slip of sticking an ordinary housefly on a pin and of examining it through a microscope; a being that had submissively endured the jests of the whole chancellery and that had gone to its grave without any extraordinary fuss, but before which, nevertheless, even before the very end of its life, there had flitted a radiant guest in the guise of an overcoat, which had animated for an instant a poor life, and upon which being calamity had come crashing down just as unbearably as it comes crashing down upon the heads of the mighty ones of this earth!

A few days after his death a doorman was sent to his house from the Bureau with an injunction for Akakii Akakiievich to appear immediately; the Chief, now, was asking for him; but the doorman had to return empty-handed, reporting back that "he weren't able to come no more," and, to the question, "Why not?" expressed himself in the words, "Why, just so; he up and died; they buried him four days back." Thus did they learn at the Bureau about the death of Akakii Akakiievich, and the very next day a new pettifogger, considerably taller than Akakii Akakiievich, was already sitting in his place and putting down the letters no longer in such a straight hand, but considerably more on the slant and downhill.

But whoever could imagine that this wouldn't be all about Akakii Akakiievich, that he was fated to live for several noisy days after his death, as though in reward for a life that had gone by utterly unnoticed? Yet that is how things fell out, and our poor history is taking on a fantastic ending.

Rumors suddenly spread through Petersburg that near the Kalinkin Bridge, and much farther out still, a dead man had started haunting of nights, in the guise of a petty government clerk, seeking for some overcoat or other that had been purloined from him and, because of that stolen overcoat, snatching from all and sundry shoulders, without differentiating among the various ranks and titles, all sorts of overcoats: whether they had collars of catskin or beaver, whether they were quilted with cotton wool, whether they were lined with raccoon, with fox, with bear—in a word, every sort of fur and skin that man has ever thought of for covering his own hide. One of the clerks in the Bureau had seen the dead man with his own eyes and had immediately recognized in him Akakii Akakiievich. This had inspired him with such horror, however, that he started running for all his legs were worth and for that reason could not make him out very well but had merely seen the other shake his finger at him from afar. From all sides came an uninterrupted flow of complaints that backs and shoulders—it wouldn't matter so much if they were merely those of Titular Councilors, but even those of Privy Councilors were affected—were exposed to the danger of catching thorough colds, because of this oft-repeated snatching-off of overcoats.

An order was put through to the police to capture the dead man, at any cost, dead or alive, and to punish him in the severest manner as an example to others—and they all but succeeded in this. To be precise, a policeman at a sentry box on a certain block of the Kirushkin Lane had already gotten a perfect grip on the dead man by his coat collar, at the very scene of his malefaction, while attempting to snatch off the frieze overcoat of some retired musician, who in his time had tootled a flute. Seizing the dead man by the collar, the policeman had summoned two of his colleagues by shouting and had entrusted the ghost to them to hold him, the while he himself took just a moment to reach down in his bootleg for his snuffbox, to relieve temporarily a nose that had been frostbitten six times in his life; but the snuff, probably, was of such a nature as even a dead man could not stand. Hardly had the policeman, after stopping his right nostril with a finger, succeeded in drawing half a handful of rapee up his left, than the dead man sneezed so heartily that he completely bespattered the eyes of all the three myrmidons. While they were bringing their fists up to rub their eyes, the dead man vanished without leaving as much as a trace, so that they actually did not know whether he had really been in their hands or not.

From then on the policemen developed such a phobia of dead men that they were afraid to lay hands even on living ones and merely shouted from a distance, "Hey, there, get going!" and the dead government clerk began to do his haunting even beyond the Kalinkin Bridge, inspiring not a little fear in all timid folk.

However, we have dropped entirely a certain *important person,* who, in reality, had been all but the cause of the fantastic trend taken by what is, by the bye, a perfectly true story. First of all, a sense of justice compels us to say that the *certain important person,* soon after the departure of poor Akakii Akakiievich, done to a turn in the raking over the hot coals, had felt something in the nature of compunction. He was no stranger to compassion; many kind impulses found access to his heart, despite the fact that his rank often stood in the way of their revealing themselves. As soon as the visiting friend had left his private office, he actually fell into a brown study over Akakii Akakiievich. And from that time on, almost every day, there appeared before him the pale Akakii Akakiievich, who had not been able to stand up under an administrative hauling over the coals. The thought concerning him disquieted the certain important person to such a degree that, a week later, he even decided to send a clerk to him to find out what the man had wanted, and how he was, and whether it were really possible to help him in some way. And when he was informed that Akakii Akakiievich had died suddenly in a fever he was left actually stunned, hearkening to the reproaches of conscience, and was out of sorts the whole day.

Wishing to distract himself to some extent and to forget the unpleasant impression this news had made upon him, he set out for an evening party to one of his friends, where he found a suitable social gathering, and, what was best of all, all the men there were of almost the same rank, so that he absolutely could not feel constrained in any way. This had an astonishing effect on the state of his spirits. He relaxed, became amiable and pleasant to converse with—in a word, he passed the time very agreeably. At supper he drank off a goblet or two of champagne—a remedy which, as everybody knows, has not at all an ill effect upon one's gaiety. The champagne predisposed him to certain extracurricular considerations; to be precise, he decided not to go home yet but to drop in on a certain lady of his acquaintance, a Caroline Ivanovna —a lady of German extraction, apparently, toward whom his feelings and relations were friendly. It must be pointed out the important person was no longer a young man, that he was a good spouse, a respected *paterfamilias.* He had two sons, one of whom was already serving in a chancellery, and a pretty daughter of sixteen, with a somewhat humped yet very charming little nose, who came to kiss his hand every day, adding, *"Bonjour,* papa," as she did so. His wife, a woman who still had not lost her freshness and was not even in the least hard to look at, would allow him to kiss her hand first, then, turning her own over, kissed the hand that was holding hers.

Yet the important person, who, by the bye, was perfectly contented with domestic tendernesses, found it respectable to have a lady friend in another part of the city. This lady friend was not in the least fresher or younger than his wife, but such are the enigmas that exist in this world, and to sit in judgment upon them is none of our affair. And so the important person came down the steps, climbed into his sleigh, and told his driver, "To Carolina Ivanovna's!"—while he himself, after muffling up rather luxuriously in his warm overcoat, remained in that pleasant state than which no better could even be thought of for a Russian—that is, when one isn't even thinking of his own volition, but the thoughts in the meanwhile troop into one's head by themselves, each more pleasant than the other, without giving one even the trouble of pursuing them and seeking them. Filled with agreeable feelings, he lightly recalled all the gay episodes of the evening he had spent, all his *mots* that had made the select circle go off into peals of laughter; many of them he even repeated in a low voice and found that they were still just as amusing as before, and for that reason it is not to be wondered at that even he chuckled at them heartily.

Occasionally, however, he became annoyed with the gusty wind which, suddenly escaping from God knows where and no one knows for what reason, simply cut the face, tossing tatters of snow thereat, making the collar of his overcoat belly out like a sail, or suddenly, with unnatural force, throwing it over his head and in this manner giving him ceaseless trouble in extricating himself from it.

Suddenly the important person felt that someone had seized him rather hard by his collar. Turning around, he noticed a man of no great height, in an old, much worn frock coat, and, not without horror, recognized in him Akakii Akakiievich. The petty clerk's face was wan as snow and looked utterly like the face of a dead man. But the horror of the important person passed all bounds when he saw that the mouth of the man became twisted and, horribly wafting upon him the odor of the grave, uttered the following speech: "Ah, so there you are, now, at last! At last I have collared you, now! Your overcoat is just the one I need! You didn't put yourself out any about mine, and on top of that hauled me over the coals—so now let me have yours!"

The poor important person almost passed away. No matter how firm of character he was in his chancellery and before his inferiors in general, and although after but one look merely at his manly appearance and his figure everyone said, "My, what character he has!"—in this instance, nevertheless, like quite a number of men who have the appearance of doughty knights, he experienced such terror that, not without reason, he even began to fear an attack of some physical disorder. He even hastened to throw his overcoat off his shoulders himself and cried out to the driver in a voice that was not his own, "Go home—fast as you can!"

The driver, on hearing the voice that the important person used only at critical moments and which he often accompanied by something of a far more physical nature, drew his head in between his shoulders just to be on the safe side, swung his whip, and flew off like an arrow. In just a little over six minutes the important person was already at the entrance to his own house. Pale, frightened out of his wits, and minus his overcoat, he had come home instead of to Caroline Ivanovna's, somehow made his way stumblingly to his room, and spent the night in quite considerable distress, so that the next day, during the morning tea, his daughter told him outright, "You're all pale today, papa." But papa kept silent and said not a word to anybody of what had befallen him, and where he had been, and where he had intended to go.

This adventure made a strong impression on him. He even badgered his subordinates at rarer intervals with his, "How dare you? Do you realize in whose presence you are?"—and even if he did utter these phrases he did not do so before he had first heard through to the end just what was what. But still more remarkable is the fact that from that time forth the apparition of the dead clerk ceased its visitations utterly; evidently the General's overcoat fitted him to a *t*; at least, no cases of overcoats being snatched off anybody were heard of any more, anywhere. However, many energetic and solicitous people simply would not calm down and kept on saying from time to time that the dead government clerk was still haunting the remoter parts of the city.

And, sure enough, one policeman at a sentry box in Colomna had with his own eyes seen the apparition coming out of a house; but, being by nature somewhat puny, so that on one occasion an ordinary well-grown shoat, darting out of a private yard, had knocked him off his feet, to the profound amusement of the cab drivers who were standing around, from whom he had exacted a copper each for humiliating him so greatly, to buy snuff with—well, being puny, he had not dared to halt him but simply followed him in the dark until such time as the apparition suddenly looked over its shoulder and, halting, asked him, "What are you after?" and shook a fist at him whose like for size was not to be found among the living. The policeman said, "Nothing," and at once turned back. The apparition, however, was considerably taller by now and was sporting a pair of enormous mustachios; setting its steps apparently in the direction of the Obuhov Bridge, it disappeared utterly in the darkness of night.

1839-1842.

The Inspector General

CHARACTERS

ANTON ANTONOVICH SKVOZNIK-DMUHANOVSKI, *The Mayor*

He has already grown gray in serving the public and, in his own way, is very, very far from being a foolish man. Even though he is a taker of bribes, he nevertheless carries himself with very great dignity; he is rather serious— even a moralist, to some extent; he speaks neither too loudly nor too softly, neither too much nor too little. His every word is fraught with significance. His features are coarse and harsh, like those of every man who has started in an exacting service at the bottom of the ladder. His transitions from fear to joy, from abasement to arrogance, are quite rapid—those of a man with but roughly developed spiritual tendencies. He is generally togged out in his uniform frock coat, the buttons and buttonholes being prominent features, and in jackboots, highly polished and spurred. His hair is grizzled and closely cropped.

LUKA LUKICH HLOPOV, *Superintendent of Schools*

AMOS FEDOROVICH LYAPKIN-TYAPKIN, *The Judge*

A man who has read five or six books and is hence somewhat inclined to freethinking. A great hand for making conjectures, and for that reason lends profundity to his every word. The actor portraying him must always preserve a significant mien. He speaks in a bass, with a rather excessive drawl, hoarsely and strangled, like one of those grandfather clocks that go through a great deal of hissing as a preliminary to striking.

ARTEMII PHILIPOVICH ZEMLYANIKA, *Director of Charities*

A very stout, unwieldy, and clumsy man but, for all that, as foxy as they come and a knave. No end obliging and as active as can be.

IVAN KUZMICH SHPEKIN, *The Postmaster*

So simplehearted that he is naïve.

PETER IVANOVICH BOBCHINSKI
and
PETER IVANOVICH DOBCHINSKI

Both landowners—but of those who prefer to live in town instead of on their estates. Both are rather squat, rather short, both inquisitive and extraordinarily like each other. Both have neat little bay-windows. Both speak in a patter, helping that patter along with gestures and their hands—excessively so. DOBCHINSKI is a trifle taller and more serious than BOBCHINSKI, but BOBCHINSKI is more free-and-easy and lively than DOBCHINSKI.

IVAN ALEXANDROVICH HLESTACOV, *a government clerk from the capital*

A young man (twenty-three), very slender, very thin—somewhat on the silly side and, as the saying goes, there's nobody home. One of those fellows who, in the Civil Service, are called the lamest of lame-brains. He speaks and acts without any consideration of anything. He is utterly incapable of giving undivided attention to any one idea. His speech is jerky, and his words pop out in an utterly unexpected way. The more ingenuousness and simplicity the actor evinces in this role the more successful he will be. HLESTACOV's dress is the last word in style.

OSSIP, *Hlestacov's Servant*

Like all servants who are getting on in years. He is serious of speech; his eyes are somewhat cast down; he is a moralist and fond of sermonizing to himself moral lectures intended for his master. His voice is almost always even; when he speaks with his master it takes on a stern, abrupt, and even a somewhat rude tone. He is far more intelligent than his master and therefore catches on to things more quickly, but he doesn't like to talk too much and, as a knave, prefers to keep his mouth shut. He is dressed in a long jacket, either gray or blue, and much worn.

CHRISTIAN IVANOVICH HÜBNER, *District Doctor*

FEDOR ANDREIEVICH LULUCOV
IVAN LAZAREVICH RASTACOVSKI
STEPAN IVANOVICH KOROBKIN
Retired Officials

Prominent citizens in the town.

STEPAN ILYICH UHOVERTOV, *Inspector of Police*

SVISTUNOV
PUGOVITZIN *Policemen*
DERZHIMORDA

Typical bullies—while Derzhimorda is the prototype of all uniformed, small-town bullies.

ABDULIN, *A Shopkeeper*

MISHKA, *The Mayor's Servant*

WAITER *at the inn*

A GENDARME

ANNA ANDREIEVNA, *The Mayor's Wife*

A provincial coquette, not entirely elderly yet, her education about evenly divided between romantic novels and album verse, and cares about the pantry and the maid-servants. Very inquisitive, and evinces vanity and conceit whenever there is a chance. Occasionally gets the upper hand of her husband, merely because he cannot find a ready answer. But this dominance is utilized only for trifles and consists of lectures and sneers. She has four complete changes of costume during the play.

MARIA ANTONOVNA, *The Mayor's*
Daughter

WIFE OF THE SUPERINTENDENT
OF SCHOOLS

KOROBKIN'S WIFE

THEVRONIA PETROVNA POSHLEP-
KINA, *The Locksmith's Wife*

CORPORAL'S WIDOW

———

GUESTS (both sexes); *Shopkeepers;*
Townspeople; Petitioners.

The parts not commented upon above do not require any special explanations.
Their originals are almost always before our eyes.

The cast should pay particular attention to the last tableau. The concluding
speech (the GENDARME'S) *must stun everybody, suddenly and simultaneously,*
like an electric shock. The entire group must shift its poses in an instant. The
exclamation of astonishment must escape all the feminine characters simulta-
neously, as if from but a single pair of lungs. Failure to carry out this business
exactly may ruin the whole effect.

No use blaming the mirror if it's your own mug that's crooked.

FOLK SAYING

ACT I, Scene 1

A room in the MAYOR'S *house. Early morning.*
At rise: MISHKA *is dusting hurriedly; straightens out chairs and table,*
looks over room, exits.
ANNA *enters, casts housewifely look over room, unnecessarily shifts*
a vase and adjusts a curtain, and, after another look, exits.
MARIA *runs on girlishly, looks around her, peeps through windows, and,*
hearing someone approaching, scampers off in girlish fright.
The MAYOR *stomps on; looks over the room absent-mindedly; he*
seems worried and takes a few steps through the room.
Enter two POLICEMEN; *they flank the door. They are followed by:*
The DIRECTOR OF CHARITIES, *The* SUPERINTENDENT OF SCHOOLS, *The*
JUDGE, *and The* DISTRICT DOCTOR.
They gather around the table amid a general atmosphere of expectancy.

MAYOR: I've called you together, gentlemen, to let you in on a most
unpleasant bit of news. There's an Inspector General on his way here.
And not only that, but he has secret instructions, too.
DIRECTOR OF CHARITIES: What! An Inspector General?

JUDGE: An Inspector General?

MAYOR: An Inspector General, straight from the capital, and traveling incognito.

JUDGE: There's a fix for you.

DIRECTOR OF CHARITIES: Well, there hasn't been much trouble lately, so now we'll have plenty and to spare.

SUPERINTENDENT OF SCHOOLS: Good Lord! And with secret instructions, mind you!

MAYOR: It's just as though I felt this coming. I kept dreaming all last night of a couple of rats—and most unusual they were, somehow. Really, I'd never seen anything like them—all black, and of a most unnatural size! They came, sniffed around, and then ran off. Here, I'll read you a letter I've just received from Chmihov (*turning to* DIRECTOR OF CHARITIES)—you know him. Here's what he writes: "Dear friend and benefactor"—(*mumbles in a low voice to himself, his eyes running quickly through the letter*)—"to inform you . . ." Ah, here it is: "hasten to inform you, among other things, of the arrival of a government official with instructions to inspect the whole province and particularly (*raises his right index finger with great significance*)—our district. I have learned this from most reliable sources, even though he pretends to be a private individual. Since I know that you are no more innocent of certain little transgressions than other people, inasmuch as you are a clever fellow and dislike to let slip anything that may come to hand." (*Pause.*) Oh, well, we're all friends here! (*Resumes reading.*) "I advise you to take certain precautions, for he may arrive at any moment—if he has not arrived already and is not stopping somewhere incognito. Yesterday I—" Well, from there on he deals with family matters: "Sister Anne has come to visit us with her husband; her brother has grown very fat but still plays the fiddle"—and so on. There, that's the situation!

JUDGE: Yes, the situation is an extraordinary one—simply extraordinary! There's something back of all this.

SUPERINTENDENT OF SCHOOLS (*to* MAYOR): But what's all this for? What brought this on? Why should the Inspector General be coming here?

MAYOR: Why, indeed! It must be fate, evidently! (*Sighs.*) Up to now, glory be, they were getting after the other towns; now they've caught up with us.

JUDGE (*to* MAYOR): I think there's a deeper motive here, and one

of a political nature, rather. This visit means that this country is . . . yes
. . . this country is about to declare war and the Department of State,
now—you see?—has sent an official to find out if there is any disloyalty
anywhere.

MAYOR: You sure have taken in a lot of territory! And yet you're
supposed to be intelligent! Disloyalty—in a county seat! Where do you
think our town is, on a foreign border? Why, if you were to gallop at
top speed for three years in any direction you wouldn't come to any
other country!

JUDGE: No, I must tell you you haven't grasped . . . you don't . . .
the Government . . . the Government has some thoroughly considered
ends in view; it doesn't matter that we're so far in the sticks—the
Government still has something in the back of its mind—

MAYOR: Whether it has or not, at least I've warned you, gentlemen.
Look sharp; I've taken certain steps as far as those things under my
jurisdiction are concerned; I advise you to do likewise in your departments. (*Turning to* DIRECTOR OF CHARITIES.) You especially! Beyond
a doubt the official, as he is passing through, will want to see before anything else the charitable institutions under your supervision—therefore, do everything possible to make things look decent; you might put
clean gowns on the patients in the hospital—and the patients themselves ought not to look as if they'd just been through a blacksmith's
shop—the way they usually do when no visitors are expected.

DIRECTOR OF CHARITIES: Oh, well, that's a small matter. The clean
gowns can be managed, if you like.

MAYOR: Right! Also, the patient's case-history ought to be written
out on a card at the head of the bed, in Latin—or even in Greek.
(*Turning to* DISTRICT DOCTOR.) That's your department, since you're
the District Doctor. Write down who the patient is, what day and month
—and year—the patient was admitted. It's a pity your patients smoke
such strong tobacco that you sneeze your head off the minute you set
foot in the hospital. Also, it mightn't be a bad idea if there weren't so
many of them—their number will immediately be put down to poor
management or the inefficiency of the Doctor.

DIRECTOR OF CHARITIES: Oh, as far as treatment goes, we (*patting*
DISTRICT DOCTOR'S *arm*) don't go in for any fancy medicines—the
more chances you give nature the better. Our patients are all simple folk:
if any one of 'em is going to pop off, pop off he will anyway; and if he's
going to get well, he'll get well just so. And besides, it would be rather
difficult for our friend here (*patting* DISTRICT DOCTOR'S *back*) to make

himself understood—he doesn't know a damned word in our language.

DISTRICT DOCTOR (*mouths out something that sounds like a cross between*): *Ja* and *Oui*.

MAYOR (*to* JUDGE): And I'd advise you also to turn your attention to our administrative buildings. Take your anteroom, now, where the litigants usually come—your court attendants have gotten into keeping their geese there, together with the goslings, and they're forever getting underfoot. It's a praiseworthy thing, of course, for any man to go in for poultry-raising and things like that, and really, why shouldn't a man go in for raising poultry, even if he is a court-attendant? Only, don't you know, it sort of doesn't look right to do so in such a place. I meant to remark on this to you even before, but somehow it kept slipping my mind all the time.

JUDGE: Why, I'll issue immediate orders to have every fowl removed to my kitchen this very day. You might drop in for dinner, if you like.

MAYOR: Besides that, it really looks bad to have all sorts of ragged wash hanging out to dry in the courtroom itself. And right over the closet where you keep all the papers you've got your hunting crop hung up. I know you're fond of hunting, but just the same, for the time being, it might be better to remove it and then, when the Inspector General will have gone on his way, you can hang it up again, if you like. Then there's your clerk. (*Sighs.*) Of course, he's a walking, or rather staggering, encyclopedia of the law, but he always smells as if he had just crawled out of a distillery—and that's not so good, either. I meant to tell you about this, too, ages ago, but my mind was taken off by something—I can't recall just what. There are certain palliatives if, as he claims, that is his natural odor; you might suggest that he go in for garlic, or scallions, or some similar vegetable diet. The District Doctor might help out in this case with some preparation.

DISTRICT DOCTOR (*mouths out same cross between*): *Ja* and *Oui*.

JUDGE: No, this is something beyond all help by now. He claims his nurse injured him when he was a child and that he's been giving off a slight reek of whiskey ever since.

MAYOR: Well, I merely remarked on it. As for internal arrangements and what the letter calls "slight transgressions," there's really nothing much I can say. Why, it's an odd thing even to talk about. There isn't a man living that hasn't some . . . irregularities on his conscience. Surely, all that must have been so arranged by the Lord God Himself, and it's all in vain that the freethinkers talk against it.

JUDGE: Well, what do you consider transgressions? There are transgressions—and transgressions. I tell the whole world I take bribes—but what do those bribes consist of? Why, greyhound pups! That's an entirely different matter!

MAYOR: Well, whether you take them in the form of pups or of something else, they're all bribes.

JUDGE: Oh, never! On the other hand, if somebody gets a fur-lined coat worth half a thousand, and his wife gets a shawl—

MAYOR: Well, suppose you do take your bribes in greyhound pups—what of it? But to make up for that you don't believe in God, you never set foot in a church, whereas I, at least, am firm in my faith and go to church every Sunday. But you—oh, I'm on to you! If you just start talking about the creation of the world it's enough to make one's hair stand on end.

JUDGE: Why, I arrived at all that by my own self—through my own intelligence.

MAYOR: All I have to say is that there are some cases where too much intelligence is worse than none at all. However, I merely mentioned the county courthouse in passing, whereas, if the truth were told, hardly anyone will ever look in there. It's such an enviable spot—the Lord God Himself watches over it. On the other hand, you (*turning to the* SUPERINTENDENT OF SCHOOLS), as the Superintendent of Schools, ought to be particularly careful as far as the teachers are concerned. They are, of course, men of learning and received their education in different colleges, and so on, but just the same they have some mighty queer ways about them—things that go hand in hand with their learned calling, naturally. One of them—the fellow with the fat face, for instance, I can't recall his name—well, he simply can't get along without making a face every time he gets up on the platform. Like this (*mugging*). And then he starts in fiddling with his necktie and ironing out his beard. Of course, if he pulls a face like that at a pupil it isn't so bad; perhaps that's even just as it should be—I'm no judge of that. But you just judge for yourself: if he should ever pull anything like that on a visitor, things might go very badly. The Inspector General, or somebody else, might consider that the face was meant for his benefit. And the devil alone knows what the upshot might be.

SUPERINTENDENT OF SCHOOLS: But really, what am I to do with him? I've spoken to him several times already. Why, just the other day, when one of our foremost citizens happened to drop in on his class, this teacher pulled a face that was a masterpiece even for him. His heart was in the right place when he did it, but just the same it meant a bawling-out for me: Why were radical ideas being implanted in the minds of our young people, and so on.

MAYOR: I am compelled to make a similar remark to you about the professor of history. He has a slue of learning in that head of his—anybody can see that; and he has accumulated no end of information—only why does he have to explain things with such earnestness that he forgets himself? I happened to hear one of his lectures; well, while he was speaking about the Assyrians and the Babylonians things weren't so very bad; but when he came to Alexander of Macedonia—well, I simply couldn't begin telling you what came over him! I thought there was a fire, by God! He dashes off the platform and, with all his might and main, smashes a chair against the floor! Well, now, Alexander the Great is a hero and all that—but why smash chairs? The public funds are bound to suffer thereby—

SUPERINTENDENT: Yes, he's a hotheaded fellow! I've already reprimanded him several times for this trait of his. "Well," he says, "do whatever you like, but I'm willing to lay down my life for scholarship!"

MAYOR: Yes. Such, evidently, is the inexplicable decree of the fates: the man of learning is bound to be either a drunkard or to pull faces that are enough to curdle milk.

SUPERINTENDENT: May God save me from ever having to teach! You're afraid of everything then; everyone interferes, everyone wants to show that he, too, has scholarship.

MAYOR: Things wouldn't be so bad if it weren't for that damned incognito! Suppose he were to drop in? "Ah, so you're all here, my dear Sirs? And who," he'll say, "who is the Judge?"—"Lyapkin-Tyapkin."—"Well, fetch this Lyapkin-Tyapkin here! And who is the Director of Charities?"—"Zemlyanika."—"Well, fetch this Zemlyanika here!"—There, that's what's bad!

POSTMASTER (*entering*): Will you please explain to me, gentlemen, just what's what? Who's the official on his way here?

MAYOR: Why, haven't you heard?

POSTMASTER: I did hear something from Bobchinski. He dropped in to see me at the Post Office.

MAYOR: Well, what do you think of all this?

POSTMASTER: What do I think? Why, I think it means we're going to be at war with the Turks.

JUDGE: Just what I said! I was thinking the very same thing.

MAYOR: Both of you are shooting at the moon!

POSTMASTER: No, really—we're going to have a war with the Turks. It's those damned Frenchmen, always messing things up.

MAYOR: What's all this talk of a war with the Turks? It's all very simple; it'll be us that will catch it and not the Turks. That's something we already know—I have a letter.

POSTMASTER: Ah, in that case the war with the Turks is all off.

MAYOR (*to* POSTMASTER): Well, now, where do you stand?

POSTMASTER: Well, what about me? Where do *you* stand?

MAYOR: Where do I stand, now? It isn't that I'm afraid, exactly, but still, to a very slight extent . . . I'm uneasy about the businessmen and the gentry. They're saying that they're fed up with me; but, by God, even if I did accept a little something from this one or that one, it really was without any prejudice. I'm even wondering (*taking the* POST-MASTER *by the arm and leading him off to one side*)—I'm even wondering if there weren't some complaints against me. For really, now, why should an Inspector General be heading this way? I say, couldn't you—for all our sakes—take every letter that goes through the Post Office—both the incoming and the outgoing, and sort of . . . unseal each one a little, don't you know, and kind of glance it through, to see if it doesn't contain some complaint or other, or simply an exchange of information? If it doesn't, it can be sealed up again—or it may be delivered just as it is, "opened by mistake," don't you know—

POSTMASTER: Oh, I know, I know. You don't have to teach me. I do it not so much out of precaution but more out of curiosity; I'm no end fond of finding out if there's anything new going on in the world. And it's mighty interesting reading, let me tell you. Now and then there's a letter that's simply delightful to read—what vivid descriptions, what tender passages! And what lofty morality—better than in any metropolitan daily!

MAYOR: Well, now, tell me—haven't you read anything about a certain official coming from the capital?

POSTMASTER: No, there wasn't a word about any official from the capital—but there's a great deal about two other officials from two other cities. What a pity it is, though, that you don't get to look over the mail; there are some dandy items. One, for instance, where a certain Lieutenant describes a ball to a friend of his, in a most playful mood. Very, very good. He described that ball with great feeling—very great feeling. I've purposely kept that letter by me. Would you like to have me read it to you?

MAYOR: Well, this is hardly the time for it. So do me that favor—

if you should come across a complaint, or someone informing, just hold the letter back, without the least hesitation.

POSTMASTER: With the greatest of pleasure.

JUDGE: Watch out; you'll get into trouble some day over that.

POSTMASTER: Oh, Lord!

MAYOR (*glaring at the* JUDGE): It's nothing, it's nothing! It would be another matter if you were to use such letters publicly—but this is all in the family.

JUDGE: Yes, this is beginning to look like a grand mess! I must own up I was coming to you (*turning to* MAYOR) to present you with a fine pup. Own sister to the hound, you know. You must have heard about the lawsuit that two of our landowners have started recently—and now I'm in the seventh heaven: I hunt rabbits with dogs on both their lands.

MAYOR: My dear fellow, I have no heart now for your rabbits; I've got that damned incognito stuck in my head. I expect the door to fly open any minute—and bingo!

BOBCHINSKI (*piling in with* DOBCHINSKI; *both are out of breath*): Something extraordinary has happened!

DOBCHINSKI: The news is so utterly unexpected!

ALL: What is it? What is it?

DOBCHINSKI: Whoever would have thought it? We come to the hotel—

BOBCHINSKI (*breaking in on him*): Peter Ivanovich here and I come to the hotel—

DOBCHINSKI (*breaking in in his turn*): Oh, now, Peter Ivanovich, if you'll only let me I'll tell everything—

BOBCHINSKI: Oh, no, if you'll only let me, now! Let me, do! You'd hardly be able to tell it, if it comes to that—

DOBCHINSKI: And you'll get all muddled up and won't remember everything.

BOBCHINSKI: Yes, I'll remember—I will, so help me! Don't interrupt, now—let me tell the story. Don't interrupt! Do me a favor, gentlemen—tell Peter Ivanovich not to interrupt—

MAYOR: Come, speak, for the love of God! What's up? My heart is down in my boots. Sit down, gentlemen! Help yourselves to chairs. Here's one for you, Bobchinski, and one for you, Dobchinski. (*All seat themselves around the two* PETER IVANOVICHES.) Well, now, out with it!

BOBCHINSKI: Allow me, allow me—I'll tell everything in order. No sooner did I leave you, after you received the letter that confused you

so much, than I immediately dropped in on—now please don't interrupt, Peter Dobchinski! I already know everything—*everything*—
EVERYTHING! Well, then, if you please, I dropped in on Korobkin.
But, not finding this Korobkin at home, I turned in at Rastacovski's, and
not finding Rastacovski in either, I dropped in on Shpekin, the Postmaster, you see, so's to tell him of the news you received, and as I was
coming from there, I met Peter Dobchinski—

DOBCHINSKI: Near that place where they sell hot cakes—

BOBCHINSKI: Right—near the place where they sell hot cakes. Very
well. Having met Dobchinski, I said to him: "Have you heard the news
our Mayor has received by mail, from a most reliable source?" But he'd
already heard this (*turning to* MAYOR) from your housekeeper, whom
you had sent to Pochechuev's house to fetch something—I don't know
just what it was—

DOBCHINSKI: A small brandy keg—

BOBCHINSKI (*pushing* DOBCHINSKI's *hands away*): A small brandy
keg. And so Dobchinski and I started off for Pochechuev's house—
come, Dobchinski, don't you interrupt me now! Please don't interrupt!
So we started off for Pochechuev's house, but on the way Dobchinski
says to me, he says: "You've no idea what a rumpus my stomach is raising! I haven't eaten a thing since morning, and my stomach is simply
crying for food"—that's Dobchinski's stomach, mind you. "And,"
he says, "they've just delivered some fresh salmon at the hotel, so we
might just as well have a bite." No sooner had we stepped into the hotel
than a young man—

DOBCHINSKI: Not at all of a bad appearance, in civilian clothes—

BOBCHINSKI: Yes, yes—not at all of a bad appearance, and in civilian
clothes. Well, he strolls through the room, don't you know, with such
a thoughtful expression—such a serious face. And the way he carried
himself! And (*fluttering his fingers near his forehead*) he seems to
have a lot up here—oh, a lot! It was just as though I had a hunch, and
I said to Dobchinski here, I said: "There's more here than meets the
eye! Yes, sir! By that time Dobchinski had already made a sign to the
owner—you know him: his name is Vlass; his wife was confined three
weeks ago—a boy, it was, and what a lively one, to be sure—he's going to run a hotel, just like his daddy. So, having called this Vlass over,
Dobchinski here ups and asks him, on the quiet: "Who," he asks, "may
that young man be?" To which Vlass answers: "This young man," he
says—I wish you wouldn't interrupt now, Dobchinski; please don't
interrupt! You could never tell the story, so help me—never. You

lithp! you have but one tooth in your head, I know, and that one whistles. "This young man," Vlass says, "is a government official"—that's just what he said! "He's come from the capital now, and his name," Vlass says, "is Hlestacov, and he's on his way north, and," he says, "he's behaving mighty queer; he's staying here for the second week now, hardly ever sets foot outside the place, calls for everything on credit, and won't lay out as much as a copper in cash." The minute he said that to me, it was just as though a light broke in on me from up above. "Ah!" I says to Dobchinski—

DOBCHINSKI: No, Bobchinski, it was me that said "Ah!"

BOBCHINSKI: All right, you said "Ah!" first, and then I said "Ah!" too. "Ah!" said Dobchinski and I. "And what reason would he have for staying here if his way lies north?" Yes, Sir! Well, now, he and none other is that very official—

MAYOR: What official?

BOBCHINSKI: The official you were notified about, if you please—the Inspector General.

MAYOR (*thoroughly frightened*): Whatever are you saying—the Lord be with you! It can't be he!

DOBCHINSKI: It is he! He'll neither pay nor go away. Even his transportation pass specifies that he's traveling north.

BOBCHINSKI: It is he, it is he—honest to God it is he! What an observant fellow—he took in everything. He noticed that Dobchinski and I were eating salmon—the main reason we had chosen salmon was on account of Dobchinski's stomach—well, he looked right into our plates, too. Why, I was simply scared stiff!

MAYOR: Lord have mercy on us sinners! What room has he got at the hotel?

DOBCHINSKI: Number Five—under a flight of stairs.

BOBCHINSKI: The same room where those army officers had a fight last year, the day they arrived.

MAYOR: And has he been here long?

DOBCHINSKI: Why, it must be two weeks by now.

MAYOR: Two weeks! (*Aside.*) May the Lord and all His saints deliver us! The Corporal's widow was flogged within these two weeks! No provisions were issued to the convicts! The people are carrying on in the streets—and the streets themselves are downright filthy! It's a disgrace and a shame! (*Clutches his head.*)

DIRECTOR OF CHARITIES (*to* MAYOR): Well, what do you say? Shall we start for the hotel and pay him a formal call?

JUDGE: No, no! Let the clergy and the businessmen of the town call on him first. Even according to procedure—

MAYOR: No, no! Let me attend to everything in my own way. Life has had its difficult moments before this—but they passed, and there were even times when I was thanked. Who knows, perhaps God will deliver us this time as well. (*To* BOBCHINSKI.) He's a young man, you say?

BOBCHINSKI: Yes, a young man; twenty-three, or a little over twenty-four.

MAYOR: So much the better; you can get things out of a youngster much quicker. It's hell when you come up against an old devil, but with a young fellow everything is right on the surface. You get everything set in your own bailiwicks, gentlemen, while I'll go by myself—or even with Dobchinski here, if you like—privately, sort of strolling by, don't you know, and just dropping in to find out if our transient visitors are having any unpleasant experiences in our town. Hey, there, Svistunov!

SVISTUNOV (*rushing forward from his post near the door*): What do you wish, Sir?

MAYOR: Go this minute and fetch the Inspector of Police—or no, I'll need you. Tell somebody else to go and bring the Inspector of Police to me here, as soon as possible, and then you come back here. (SVISTUNOV *bustles out, almost at a run.*)

DIRECTOR OF CHARITIES (*to* JUDGE): Come, come! There really may be some trouble.

JUDGE: Why, what have you to be afraid of? All you have to do is slap clean gowns on your patients and you've covered up everything.

DIRECTOR OF CHARITIES: Gowns my eye! The patients are supposed to be on a strict diet, but there's such a reek of cabbage in all the corridors that you have to hold your nose.

JUDGE: As for me, I feel quite calm. Really, now, who'd ever think of dropping in at a county courthouse? And if anyone should ever get it into his head to look over any of the papers, he'd curse the day he was ever born. It's fifteen years now that I've been on the bench, yet if I ever as much as glance at a report I just sigh and give it up as a bad job. Solomon himself wouldn't be able to decide what's true in it and what isn't. (*Exeunt* JUDGE, DIRECTOR OF CHARITIES, SUPERINTENDENT OF SCHOOLS, *and* POSTMASTER; *in the doorway they collide with the returning* SVISTUNOV.)

MAYOR: Well, is the carriage ready?

SVISTUNOV: Right at the door.

MAYOR: Go outside and—or, no, hold on! Go and fetch me . . . why, where are all the other police? Didn't I give orders for Prohorov to be here, too? Where is he?

SVISTUNOV: He's at the station house; the only thing is he's out of the running.

MAYOR: What do you mean by that?

SVISTUNOV: Why, just this—he was brought in this morning dead drunk. We've thrown two buckets of water over him so far, but he hasn't come to yet.

MAYOR (*clutching his hair*): Oh, my God, my God! Go on out, fast as you can—or wait; run up to my room first—do you hear—and bring me my sword and my new hat. (*To* DOBCHINSKI.) Well, let's go.

BOBCHINSKI: Me too, me too! Let me go along too!

MAYOR: No, no, Bobchinski—you can't, you can't! It'd be awkward, and, besides, there'd be no room for you in the carriage.

BOBCHINSKI: That's nothing, that's nothing, I'll manage somehow; I could even trot behind your carriage, if you'll let me hold on. All I want is just one tiny peep through the crack of the door, don't you know, to see how the young man acts—

MAYOR (*to* SVISTUNOV, *as he takes sword from him*): Run right away, take some of the police, and let each one of them take . . . Just see how nicked and banged up that sword is! That damned little shop-keeper Abdulin sees right well that the boss of the town has an old sword but never thinks of sending him a new one! Oh, what a wise crowd! As it is, I'm thinking they're already drawing up complaints on the sly. (*Turning to* SVISTUNOV *again*.) Let each one of your men take a street in hand—what in hell am I saying? Not a street but a broom—let each man take a broom in hand and sweep the whole street that leads to the hotel, and sweep it clean—the street, I mean—do you hear me? And you watch out—you, you, I mean! I'm on to you; you pretend to be friendly but steal silver spoons and shove them in your bootleg. Watch out! I've got my ear to the ground. What did you pull on that shopkeeper Chernayev—eh? He gave you two yards of broadcloth for a uniform —so what did you do but swipe the whole bolt? Watch out! You're taking bribes 'way above what your rank entitles you to!—On your way now! (*Exit* SVISTUNOV; *enter* INSPECTOR OF POLICE, *whom the* MAYOR *addresses*.) Ah, there you are! Tell me, for God's sake—did you get lost in the shuffle? What does it look like for the Inspector of Police to be away at such a time?

INSPECTOR OF POLICE: I was here all the time—right at your gate.

MAYOR: Very well, listen: The official from the capital has arrived. What steps have you taken?

INSPECTOR OF POLICE: Why, I've followed your instructions exactly. I sent Pugovitzin and a few policemen under him to clean up the sidewalks.

MAYOR: And where's Derzhimorda?

INSPECTOR OF POLICE: Derzhimorda has gone off with the fire engine.

MAYOR: And Prohorov is drunk?

INSPECTOR OF POLICE: Drunk as a lord.

MAYOR: How did you ever allow such a thing to happen?

INSPECTOR OF POLICE: Why, the Lord only knows how it all came about. There was a brawl just outside the town yesterday; Prohorov went out there to preserve law and order, but was shipped back fried, somehow.

MAYOR: Tell you what you do: Pugovitzin, now, is a pretty tall fellow, even for a cop; so, for the looks of things, you station him at the bridge. And then break up the old fence around where the shoemaker lives, as fast as you can, and make it look as if we were planning to build something there. The more demolition there's going on, the greater the inference that the head of the town is active. Oh, my God— why, I forgot that there are about forty cartloads of all sorts of garbage dumped behind that fence. What an atrocious town this is! No sooner is a monument put up on any spot—or even a fence, for that matter— than they'll pile up all sorts of rubbish there! The devil alone knows where it all comes from! (*Sighs.*) And another thing: should this newly arrived official get to asking anybody working for the city if they're satisfied, let 'em say: "Yes, Your Honor"—but if any one of 'em should turn out to be dissatisfied—well, I'll really give him something to be dissatisfied about later on. Ah, me, but I have sinned; I have sinned much! (*Picks up cardboard hatbox instead of his hat.*) May God grant that all this blow over as soon as possible, and after that I'll put up such a candle as no one has ever yet put up; I'll make each son of a bitch of a shopkeeper in this town come across with a hundred pounds of wax for that candle. Oh, my God, my God! Come, let's go, Dobchinski! (*Puts on hatbox instead of hat.*)

INSPECTOR OF POLICE: Sir, that's a hatbox and not a hat.

MAYOR (*hurling hatbox to one side*): So it is, so it is—and to hell with it! Yes, and if he should ask why the chapel for the hospital hasn't been built yet—for which a certain sum was appropriated five years ago—don't forget to say that construction was begun on it but that it burned down. I even submitted a report to that effect. Otherwise, like as not, somebody may get absent-minded and blab his fool head off and say that it was never as much as started. And you might tell Derzhimorda not to be so free with his fists; that fellow gives shiners to everybody, just on general principles—both to the just and the unjust. Let's go, let's go, Dobchinski! (*Goes out but immediately returns.*) Yes, and don't let the soldiers out into the street without their full equipment; they're such a crummy lot they'll put their uniforms on, true enough—but there won't be a thing underneath. (*Exeunt all.* ANNA, *wife of the* MAYOR, *and* MARIA, *his daughter, dash on.*)

ANNA: Where are they now? Where are they? Oh, Lord! (*Opening door.*) Where's my husband? Anton! Tony! (*Speaks fast.*) And it's all your fault! It's all on account of you! You had to start fussing around. "Just this pin! Just this collar!" (*Runs up to window, leans out, and calls.*) Tony, where are you going? Where? What? Did he come? You mean it's the Inspector General? Has he a mustache? What kind of a mustache?

MAYOR (*off*): Later on, later on, my love!

ANNA: Later on? What an idea—he'll tell me later! I won't have it later! Just one word is all I want—what is he, a Colonel? Eh? (*Contemptuously, withdrawing from window.*) He went off. Oh, I'll make him pay for this! And it's all this girl's fault: "Mamma dear, mamma dear, wait, I'll just pin up my collar! I'll be ready right away!" There, that's what you get for your "Right away"! And we didn't get to find out anything. And it's all her confounded coquetry: she heard that the Postmaster was here and right off started primping before the mirror —now from this side, now from the other. She imagines he's after her! In reality he only makes a face at you the minute your back is turned.

MARIA: Well, Mother dear, what can we do about it now? We'll find out everything in a couple of hours anyway.

ANNA: In a couple of hours? Thanks, no end! I'm ever so much obliged to you for that answer! How is it you never thought of saying that in a month we can find out still better? (*Leans out of window.*) Avdotya! Eh? Well, Avdotya, have you heard somebody has just come to town? You haven't? How stupid you are! He shoos you away? Let him! You just go ahead and get it out of him! You couldn't? That's the trouble with you—all you have on your mind is men and all that sort of nonsense. Eh? They went off too fast? Why, you should have run after the carriage. Go on, go on with you—this very minute! Do you hear me?

Run and find out where they went. And be sure to find out everything, to the last detail. Find out who the stranger is and what he looks like— you hear me? Look through the keyhole and find out everything—and also what color his eyes are, whether they're dark or not, and come back in a minute or so—do you hear? Hurry, hurry, hurry, hurry! (*She keeps shouting until the curtain comes down upon her and* MARIA, *both of them standing at the window.*)

Curtain

ACT I, Scene 2

An attic room at the hotel—little more than a cubbyhole. A bed, a table, and a chair comprise practically all the furnishings.
A valise, an empty bottle, boots, a clothes brush, and other such articles are strewn about the room.

OSSIP (*discovered lounging on his master's bed with his boots on*): Oh, hell, but I want to eat! My stomach is raising as much of a racket as a whole regimental band! There, we'll never manage to reach home—and that's that. Well, what can you do about it? It's going on two months now that the great man left the capital. He squandered all his money on the way, the little darling; now he's stuck here with his tail betwixt his legs and is lying low. Why, there was plenty—plenty and to spare—for traveling expenses; but no, he has to show off in every town we come to, you see. (*Mimics* HLESTACOV.) "I say, Ossip, go and look at the rooms, and pick out the best; and you might order the very best they have for dinner—I can't dine poorly, I must dine well." It wouldn't matter so much if he really amounted to something— but then he's nothing but a common pen-pusher, at the very bottom of the Civil Service! He'll scrape up an acquaintance with every passing stranger and then sit down to cards with him—and now just see what his cards have brought him to! Eh, I'm fed up with such a life! On the level, it's much better in the country; there may not be so much going on but, on the other hand, there's less to worry you: you get yourself a wench, and loll in bed all day and eat dumplings. Of course, if the truth were told, there's no disputing that life in the capital is best of all. You must have money, naturally, but living there is grand and refined—theayters, and trained dogs dancing for your amusement, and everything else your heart may desire. And then there's house-maids and such, flirting with you now and then—what girls! (*Smirks and shakes his head.*) Hell, everybody treats you fine; you never hear an impolite word. If you get tired of walking, you just jump in a cab and sit there like a lord—and if you don't feel like paying the driver you don't have to, really—there's hardly a house that hasn't got an exit on some other street; all you've got to do is to give him the slip, quick, and then the devil himself won't ever find you. There's one bad thing, though: one day you eat swell but the next you all but pass away from hunger—like now, f'r instance. And it's him that's to blame for every-thing. What can one do with a fellow like that? His old man sends him money for living expenses—and that's all he needs: he's off on a spree the minute he gets it. He won't go a step on foot; not a day passes but he sends me out to get theayter tickets for him; but inside of a week, the first thing you know he's sending me out to sell a brand-new suit as a cast off. Sometimes he'll let everything go, down to his last shirt, until he's got nothing left but his worn-out uniform. Honest to God! The finest cloth, mind you; he'll spend as much as a hundred and fifty for the coat alone—and then sell it for twenty; as for the pants, there's no need even mentioning them—they're practically given away. And what's the reason for all this? It's all because he won't get down to business; instead of going to his office he traipses around or plays cards. Oh, if your old man was ever to find out! He wouldn't give a damn that you're working for the Government but just let your pants down and let you have it so hot you'd be eating your meals off a mantel for a week. If you've got a job, attend to it. Why, just now the pro-prietor said he wouldn't send up any more meals till you've settled for what you've had up to now; well, and what'll happen if we don't? (*Sighs.*) Oh, Lord, what wouldn't I do for a bowl of soup! I feel I could eat up the whole world now. I think there's somebody coming; it must be he, for sure. (*Hastily gets off the bed.*)

HLESTACOV (*entering*): Here, take these. (*Hands cap and cane to* OSSIP.) Ah, loafing on my bed again?

OSSIP: What would I want to be loafing on your bed for? Do you think I never saw a bed before, or what?

HLESTACOV: You're lying; you were so loafing on it—see how you mussed it all up.

OSSIP: Why, what would I be wanting with it? Do you think I don't know what a bed is? I have me own legs and I can stand—what do I need your bed for?

HLESTACOV (*pacing the room*): Take a look—maybe there's a pinch of tobacco left in the wrapper.

OSSIP: Well, now, how should there be any left there? You smoked the last shred four days ago.

HLESTACOV (*still pacing the room, twists his mouth in all sorts of ways, then in a loud and assured voice*): Listen, Ossip! I say, now—

OSSIP: What do you want?

HLESTACOV (*in a voice just as loud but no longer as assured*): You go there—

OSSIP: Where?

HLESTACOV (*in a voice not at all assured nor loud—in fact very near begging*): Why, go down to the dining room . . . tell them . . . to send up something for my dinner—

OSSIP: Well, no, I don't feel like going there at all.

HLESTACOV: How dare you, you idiot!

OSSIP: Why, just so; it won't make no difference even if I was to go—nothing will come of it. The proprietor said not to serve you no more dinners.

HLESTACOV: How dare you refuse? What sort of nonsense is this?

OSSIP: And that's not all, neither, "I," he says, "will even go to the Mayor; it's the third week now that I haven't seen the color of your master's money. Why, you and your master," he says, "are both dead beats, and your master is up to all sorts of tricks. We, now," he says, "have seen plenty of such con-men and scoundrels."

HLESTACOV: Well, I can see you're only too happy to be telling me all this, you brute.

OSSIP: "If things go on like this," he says, "every man jack will be coming to this place, make himself to home, run up a bill, and in the end you won't be able to kick him out, even. I got no intentions of fooling around," he says, "I'm going straight off to lodge a complaint, so's to get him out of here—and into jail."

HLESTACOV: There, there, you fool, that'll do! Go on, go on— tell him what I said. What a coarse brute!

OSSIP: Why, I'd better call the proprietor himself to come up to you.

HLESTACOV: Who wants the proprietor, now? You go and tell him yourself.

OSSIP: Oh, now, really—

HLESTACOV: Go ahead, then, and the devil take you! Go on—call the proprietor! (*Exit* OSSIP.) Oh, but I'm famished! Dreadfully famished. I took a little walk, just so, thinking maybe my hunger would pass—but no, it won't, the devil take it! Well, if I hadn't gone off on a bat on the way here, there would have been money enough to take me home. That damned Infantry Captain all but knocked the props from under me—he can deal the most amazing hands to himself at stuss! He sat in at the game for no more than a quarter of an hour or so—and did he trim me! But completely. And yet, for all that, how I'd have liked to have another go at him! Only circumstances were against it. Circumstances are everything. What a vile hick town this is! They won't give you a thing on credit at the food stores. Why, that's downright mean. (*Whistles: at first an aria from* Robert le Diable, *then the* Red Sarafan, *and finally trails off into something that's neither here nor there.*) Well, I guess nobody wants to come up.

WAITER (*entering*) : The proprietor told me to ask what you wanted.

HLESTACOV: Ah, there, my good fellow! And how are you?

WAITER: Well enough, glory be.

HLESTACOV: And how's everything around the place? Everything going nicely, eh?

WAITER: Yes, glory be—quite nicely.

HLESTACOV: Place all filled up?

WAITER: Oh, yes, quite—glory be.

HLESTACOV: I say, my good man, my lunch hasn't been sent up yet; so won't you hurry things up a bit, please; you see, I've something to attend to right after lunch.

WAITER: Well, now, the proprietor said he weren't going to send up nothing more on the cuff. Why, he was all set to go and lodge a complaint with the Mayor today.

HLESTACOV: Why, what's the idea of complaining? Judge for yourself, my dear fellow—what's to be done, now? Why, I *must* eat. If things go on like this I'm liable to waste away to nothing. I'm as hungry as hungry can be—and that's no joke, either.

WAITER: Right, Sir. But the boss said: "I ain't giving him no more dinners till he's paid for those he's already et." Them's his very words.

HLESTACOV: Come, now, reason with him—persuade him.

WAITER: Why, what kind of arguments could I give him?

HLESTACOV: You just explain to him, in all seriousness, that I must eat. Money isn't everything! He thinks just because it may do no harm for a coarse lout like himself to go hungry for a day, others can go hungry as well. Who ever heard of such a thing!

WAITER: I'll talk with him, if you like. (*Exit.*)

HLESTACOV: (*solo*): It'll be rotten if he refuses outright to give me anything to eat. Never have I wanted to eat so much as now. Should I put some of my clothes in circulation, perhaps? Sell my trousers, maybe? No; it's better to starve but come home with the latest outfit from the capital. What a pity that I couldn't get a carriage on credit from some first-class livery stable, for it would have been a fine thing, deuce take it, to arrive in the old home town in a fine carriage, to drive up at a devilish speed to the grand entrance of some neighboring squire, with all the carriage lanterns lit and Ossip perched behind, tagged out as a flunky. I can just imagine what a stir that would create! "Who's that? What's up?" And just then a footman enters (*Drawing himself up and impersonating a footman.*) "Ivan Alexandrovich Hlestacov, from Petersburg; are you at home?" Why, the yokels don't even know what "at home" means! If some country bumpkin of a squire does come to see them, he barges right into the drawing room, bear that he is. A fellow can walk up to one of the neighbor's pretty little daughters: "How delighted I am, Madam——" (*Rubs his hands, bowing and scraping.*) Ugh! (*Makes a wry face.*) I'm actually nauseated, that's how badly I want to eat. (*Enter* OSSIP.) Well, how did you make out?

OSSIP: They're bringing up lunch.

HLESTACOV (*clapping his hands and bouncing on a chair*): Goody, goody, goody!

WAITER (*entering with a loaded tray*): This is the last time, now, that the boss is giving you anything.

HLESTACOV: Oh, your boss! I don't give a whoop for your boss! What have you there?

WAITER: Soup and a roast.

HLESTACOV: What, only two courses?

WAITER: That's all, Sir.

HLESTACOV: How preposterous! I refuse to accept that! You just tell your boss this will never do! What does he think he's doing? This isn't enough——

WAITER: No, the boss says even this is much too much.

HLESTACOV: And why is there no gravy?

WAITER: There just isn't any.

HLESTACOV: And why isn't there? I saw with my own eyes as I was passing through the kitchen that there were a great many things being prepared. And in the dining room this morning I saw two chubby little men putting away salmon and lots of other things.

WAITER: Well, there is gravy—and at the same time there ain't.

HLESTACOV: What do you mean by that?

WAITER: Why, there just ain't.

HLESTACOV: But what about the salmon, and the steaks, and the chops?

WAITER: That's for them as are the real thing—

HLESTACOV: Oh, you fool!

WAITER: Yes, Sir.

HLESTACOV: You're something of a swine. How is it they eat those things and I don't? Why can't I have the same, the devil take it? Aren't they just guests, the same as I am?

WAITER: Why, everybody knows they ain't in the same class.

HLESTACOV: What class are they in then?

WAITER: They're real guests. Everybody knows they pay hard cash.

HLESTACOV: I don't want to argue with you, you fool. (*Ladles out some soup and eats.*) You call this soup? You must have put plain dishwater into the tureen; it hasn't the least taste—but plenty of smell! I don't want this soup—bring me a different kind!

WAITER: I'll take it away then. The boss said if you didn't like it, it was all right with him.

HLESTACOV (*protecting the food with his arms*): There, there, there! Leave it alone, you fool. You must have gotten used to treating others like that—I'm different, fellow! You can't do this to me—and I advise you not to try. (*Eats.*) Oh, Lord, what soup! (*But he continues to eat.*) I don't think anybody in all this world has ever yet tasted a soup like that; there are some feathers floating around in it instead of good, honest fat. (*Fishes out a bit of chicken and cuts it up.*) Oh, oh, oh—what chicken! Let me have the roast. There's a little soup left over it—you may have it, Ossip. (*Tackling the roast.*) What kind of roast is this? This is no roast.

WAITER: Well, what would you call it?

HLESTACOV: The devil alone knows what it is, only it's not a roast. It's just a boot sole, well done. (*Eating.*) What cheats, what scoundrels! Look at the food they give you! One mouthful is enough to make your jaw ache for a week. (*Picking his teeth with his fingers.*) What low-down creatures! Just like splinters—can't pull them out, even, no matter how you try; stuff like that will ruin your teeth. What cheats! (*Wipes mouth with napkin.*) Anything else?

WAITER: No.

HLESTACOV: Scoundrels! Cheats! Why, if there were only a little gravy, at least, or a bit of pastry—the good-for-nothings! All they know is to take the stranger in. (WAITER *and* OSSIP *clear off the dishes and carry them out.*) Honestly, it's just as if I hadn't eaten at all; I've simply whetted my appetite. If I had any change at all I'd send out for a loaf.

OSSIP (*entering*): The Mayor has just arrived for some reason, and is making inquiries about you.

HLESTACOV (*frightened*): There it is! What a damned beast that proprietor is—he's already managed to start proceedings! What if he should really lug me off to jail? Well, what of it? As long as I'm treated as a gentleman I may as well go. . . . No, no, I don't want to go! The town is chock-full of officers and natives promenading around—and, as if for spite, I've been putting on airs and winking at a certain merchant's daughter. She winked right back at me, if it comes to that. No, I don't want to go. Why, who does the proprietor think he is? When you come to think of it, how dare he do such a thing? Really, what does he take me for, now? A plain businessman or a manual laborer? (*Screwing up courage and drawing himself up.*) I'll walk right up to him and tell him right to his face: "How dare you! How—" (*A knock on the door, doorknob turns*—HLESTACOV *turns pale and shrinks into himself.* MAYOR *enters, followed by* DOBCHINSKI, *and stops.* HLESTACOV *and the* MAYOR, *both equally frightened, stare at each other for a few moments, their eyes popping.*)

MAYOR (*recovering a little and standing at attention*): Hope you are well, Sir!

HLESTACOV (*bowing*): My respects, Sir!

MAYOR: Pardon my intrusion—

HLESTACOV: Not at all.

MAYOR: It is my duty, as Chief Magistrate of this town, to see that no advantage is taken of transients and people of standing—

HLESTACOV (*stammering a little at first but, toward the end of the speech, quite loudly*): Well, what can one do. . . . It's hardly my fault. . . . I really intend to pay—I expect money from home— (BOBCHINSKI *peers in at the door.*) He is far more at fault than I am; he serves me beef as tough as shoe leather; as for his soups, the devil knows what he puts in 'em; I just had to throw some out of the window. He starves me for days at a time. And his tea is most peculiar; you could never tell it's tea by its smell—it stinks of fish. Why should I, then . . . I never heard of such a thing!

MAYOR (*taken aback*): Do forgive me—I'm not to blame, really. The beef I inspect at the markets is always good. It's brought in by reliable dealers, sober and well-behaved people. I really don't know where he gets his. But if anything isn't just so, why, then. . . . May I suggest that you come with me to other quarters—

HLESTACOV: No, I don't want to. I know just what you mean by other quarters—the jail. Why, what right have you got to say that to me? How dare you? Why, I'll . . . I work for the Government at the capital! (*Putting on a bold front.*) Why, I—I—I—

MAYOR (*aside*): Oh, good Lord, how angry he is! He has found out everything—those damned shopkeepers have spilled everything.

HLESTACOV (*blustering*): Why, if you were to come down with all your men I wouldn't go! I'll take the matter directly to the Prime Minister! (*Thumping the table.*) Who do you think you are, you . . . you—

MAYOR (*drawing himself up at attention, with his whole body trembling*): Have pity on me—don't ruin me! I have a wife and little ones . . . You don't have to ruin a man!

HLESTACOV: I simply won't have it! What's all that got to do with me? Just because you have a wife and little ones I have to sit in prison? That's just dandy! (BOBCHINSKI *peeks in through door and, thoroughly frightened, hides himself.*) No, thanks ever so much, but I won't have it!

MAYOR (*trembling*): It's all due to my inexperience—by God, it's all my inexperience. And shortage of funds. . . . You may judge for yourself: my official salary wouldn't keep me in tea and what goes with it. And if there have been any bribes, why, they were the merest trifles— something for the table, or enough cloth for a suit. As for that Corporal's widow who runs a shop, and whom I'm supposed to have flogged —why, that's just slander, by God! It was invented by those who would wrong me; they're the sort who are ready to attempt my life—

HLESTACOV: Well, what of it? I have nothing to do with them. (*Thoughtfully.*) However, I don't know why you talk of those who would wrong you and of some Corporal's widow or other. A Corporal's wife is something else entirely; but as for me, you dare not flog me— you've a long way to go before you can do that. What else? Look whom we have here! I'll pay—I'll pay my hotel bill, but I haven't anything just now. That's precisely why I'm stuck here—because I haven't got a copper on me.

MAYOR (*aside*): Oh, what a fox! Just see what he's aiming at! What a smoke screen he puts up! Let anybody that wants to try to make him out. A fellow doesn't know what side to tackle him from. Oh, well, come what may, let's have a try at him! Can't lose much by making a blind stab. (*Aloud.*) If you are really short of cash, or anything else, why I'm at your service, at a moment's notice. It's my duty to help out transients.

HLESTACOV: Yes, yes, lend me some money. I'll pay off the proprietor. All I'd like to have is a couple of hundred—or even less.

MAYOR (*offering him a sheaf of bank notes*): Exactly two hundred; you don't even have to bother counting them.

HLESTACOV (*accepting the money*): Thanks ever so much. I'll send this back to you the minute I get to my country estate. I don't put off things like that. You're a noble fellow, I can see that. Things are entirely different now.

MAYOR (*aside*): Well, glory be to God, he took the money. Looks as if things will go smoothly from here on. Just the same, I shoved four hundred on him instead of two.

HLESTACOV: Hey there, Ossip! (*Enter* OSSIP.) Call that waiter in here! (*Exit* OSSIP. HLESTACOV *turns to the* MAYOR *and* DOBCHINSKI.) But why are you standing? Be good enough to sit down. (*Urging the reluctant* DOBCHINSKI.) Do sit down, I beg of you!

MAYOR: It doesn't matter; we'll just stand.

HLESTACOV: Be good enough to sit down. I can now see perfectly the goodness of your natures and your hospitality; for I must confess that I was already thinking that you had come to— (*To* DOBCHINSKI.) Do sit down! (MAYOR *and* DOBCHINSKI *take seats.* BOBCHINSKI *peeks in at the door and listens.*)

MAYOR (*aside*): I should have acted more boldly. He wants to be considered incognito. Very well; we, too, will put up a bluff; we'll act as if we weren't at all aware just who and what he is. (*Aloud.*) As we—Peter Ivanovich Dobchinski here—he's a landowner hereabouts —and I—as we were walking by in the line of duty, we purposely dropped in here, to find out whether the guests were being treated right, because I'm not like some other mayors, who'll have nothing to do with anything; but, outside of any call of duty, out of Christian regard for my fellow men, I want a good reception to be extended to every mortal, and in this instance, as if in reward, chance has afforded me such a pleasant acquaintance!

HLESTACOV: Same here—I'm very happy also. Had it not been for you, I confess I'd have been stuck here for a long time; I had no earthly idea how I was to square the bill.

MAYOR (*aside*): Tell us another! He didn't know how he was to pay the bill! (*Aloud.*) May I make so bold as to ask you—where, and to what places, you wish to travel?

HLESTACOV: I'm on my way to the Saratov province—to my own country estate.

MAYOR (*aside, his face assuming an ironic expression*): To the Saratov province, indeed! Why, he doesn't even blush! Oh, you've got to be up on your toes with this fellow! (*Aloud.*) That's a very good idea, traveling. As for reaching there, they're saying that on the one hand there's a lot of bother in getting horses but, on the other hand, there's nothing like a trip for diverting the mind. For I guess it's mostly for your own pleasure that you're going there?

HLESTACOV: No, my father demands that I come; the old gentleman is angry because up to now I haven't worked myself up to anything worth while at the capital. He's under the impression that the minute you get there they start out handing decorations to you. Yes, I'd like to send him there and see how much headway he'd make in some department.

MAYOR (*aside*): Just listen, if you please, to the line he hands out— he even dragged in his old man! (*Aloud.*) And are you planning to stay there long?

HLESTACOV: Really, I don't know. For my father is a stubborn old pepper pot and as stupid as a log. I'll let him have it straight from the shoulder: "Do as you like," I'll tell him, "but I can't live out of the capital. For after all, for what earthly reason should I ruin my life among a lot of hayseeds? The demands of the present day aren't what they used to be; my soul longs for civilized ways."

MAYOR (*aside*): What a masterly liar! He lies and he lies, but there's never a loose end to give him away. And yet he isn't much to look at, and a kind of short little fellow—looks as if you could squash him on your thumbnail. But you just wait—I'll catch you slipping up yet. I'll sure make you tell us more! (*Aloud.*) That was a very just remark you were pleased to make. What can one accomplish out in the sticks? Why, take this very town; you don't sleep of nights, trying to do your best for your country, without sparing anything, but as for any reward, nobody knows when it'll come. (*Looks over the room.*) This room seems sort of damp, doesn't it?

HLESTACOV: It's a rat hole, and I've never seen the like of the bedbugs here—they bite like dogs.

MAYOR: Well, now! Such a distinguished guest—and he has to suffer! And from whom, mind you? From worthless bedbugs, who should never have come into this world! Like as not, this room is dark as well?

HLESTACOV: Oh, yes, pitch-dark. The proprietor has gotten into the habit of not giving me any candles. At times one feels like doing something, or reading; you may get a notion of writing something, but you can't; it's dark in here—so dark!

MAYOR: Dare I request that you. . . . But no, I'm not worthy of it—

HLESTACOV: Why, what is it?

MAYOR: No, no! I'm not worthy of it—I'm not worthy of it!

HLESTACOV: Come, what's it all about?

MAYOR: If I may make so bold—I've a fine room for you in my house, light, and so comfortable. . . . But no; I myself feel that it would be too great an honor. . . . Don't be angry at me! Really, by God, I suggested it to you out of sheer simpleheartedness—

HLESTACOV: On the contrary, I'll accept with pleasure, if you like. It would be far more pleasant for me in a private home than in this pothouse.

MAYOR: Oh, that would make me ever so happy! And it'll make my wife ever so happy, too! For that's just my nature: I've been taught to practice hospitality ever since my childhood—especially if the guest is a civilized person. Don't get the idea that I'm saying this just out of flattery. No, that's one vice I'm free from; I say this with all my soul.

HLESTACOV: Thank you ever so much. I'm the same way myself: I've no great love for two-faced people. I find your frankness and cordiality very much to my liking, and I'll confess I never ask for anything more than loyalty and respect—and respect and loyalty. (*Enter* WAITER *and* OSSIP. BOBCHINSKI *peeks in at door.*)

WAITER: Did you call, Sir?

HLESTACOV: Yes, let's have the bill.

WAITER: I already handed you a second bill just a while back.

HLESTACOV: I no longer remember what your silly bills were. Come, now, what did they amount to?

WAITER: You ordered a full dinner the first day, while on the second you had just a snack of smoked salmon, and after that you began putting everything on the cuff—

HLESTACOV: You fool—are you going to start itemizing everything? How much do I owe altogether?

MAYOR (*to* HLESTACOV): Don't upset yourself—he can wait. (*To* WAITER.) Go on, git! The money will be sent you.

HLESTACOV: An excellent idea, that! (*Puts away his money. Exit* WAITER. BOBCHINSKI *peeks in through door.*)

MAYOR: Would you care to inspect some of the institutions in the town, such as the Department of Public Charities, and so on?

HLESTACOV: Why, what would I find there?

MAYOR: Oh, look them over just so; you'll see how the administration carries on . . . the general system . . . it might be of interest to a visitor—

HLESTACOV: With the greatest of pleasure; I'm at your service.

(BOBCHINSKI *puts his head in through door.*)

MAYOR: Also, you may wish, later on, to go from there to the District School, to see our method of teaching the various subjects.

HLESTACOV: By all means, by all means.

MAYOR: After that, if you like, you can visit the prison and the town hoosegows—I mean jails—to see how we treat our prisoners.

HLESTACOV: But why pick on jails? It would be better if we inspected just the charitable institutions.

MAYOR: Whatever you wish. Do you intend to go in your carriage, or will you share my buggy with me?

HLESTACOV: Why, I'd better go with you in your buggy.

MAYOR (*to* DOBCHINSKI): Well, there won't be any room for you now.

DOBCHINSKI: It doesn't matter; I'll manage.

MAYOR (*to* DOBCHINSKI, *in a low voice*): Listen, you run along— but, what I mean, run as fast as your legs will carry you—and deliver two notes for me; one to Zemlyanika, at the Department of Public Charities, and the other to my wife. (*To* HLESTACOV.) I'll make so bold as to ask your permission to dash off just a line to my wife in your presence, so that she may prepare herself to receive our distinguished guest—

HLESTACOV: Oh, but whatever for? However, here's the ink; the only thing is, I don't know about paper . . . unless you use this bill—

MAYOR: It won't take me but a minute. (*Writes, at the same time talking to himself.*) There, we'll see how things will go after a good lunch and a nice, potbellied bottle. Yes, we have a provincial Madeira— not much to look at, but it's strong enough to knock an elephant off its feet. If only I could find out just who he is and to what extent I must be on my guard against him! (*Having finished, the* MAYOR *hands the notes to* DOBCHINSKI, *who approaches the door, but at that moment it flies open and* BOBCHINSKI, *who had been eavesdropping on the other side, tumbles in. General exclamations.* BOBCHINSKI *picks himself up.*)

HLESTACOV: I say, you haven't hurt yourself by any chance?

BOBCHINSKI: Not at all, not at all—nothing out of the way—just a bump on the bridge of my nose. I'll run over to the Doctor's; he's got a certain kind of plaster, and the bump will go away in no time. (*Exit* DOBCHINSKI, *clucking.*)

MAYOR (*makes a gesture of disapproval to* BOBCHINSKI, *then turns to* HLESTACOV): It's really nothing. This way, please, I beg you! And I'll tell your man to bring your things over. (*To* OSSIP.) You bring everything over to my place—the Mayor's, now; anybody will show you the way. (*To* HLESTACOV.) Right this way! (*Lets* HLESTACOV *precede him, but, before following him, manages to turn around and say reproachfully to* BOBCHINSKI.) What a man you are! You couldn't find any other place to flop! And you had to stretch out at full length— it looked like hell! (*Exits, followed by* BOBCHINSKI.)

Curtain

ACT II

Setting same as ACT I, Scene 1. At rise: ANNA *and* MARIA *are standing near the window, in the same poses as at Curtain of ACT I, Scene 1.*

ANNA: There, we've been waiting a whole hour, and it's all your fault, with your stupid primping. You were all dressed, but, no, you had to fuss around. I shouldn't have listened to the girl at all! How provoking! Not a soul in sight; you might think it was on purpose. You'd think the whole town died out.

MARIA: But really, Mamma dear, we'll find out everything in just a minute or two. Why, Avdotya is bound to be back soon. (*Looks attentively through window and emits a little scream.*) Ah, Mamma dear, Mamma dear, somebody's coming! There, at the end of the street!

ANNA: Where do you see anybody coming? You're forever imagining one thing or another. Well, yes, there is somebody coming. But just who can it be? Rather short . . . in a frock coat . . . whoever could it be? Eh? I must say it's provoking! Who in the world could it be?

MARIA: It's Dobchinski, Mamma dear.

ANNA: How could it be Dobchinski? You're always making things up out of thin air. It's not Dobchinski at all. (*Waves her handkerchief.*) I say, walk a little faster! A little faster!

MARIA: Really, Mamma dear, it is Dobchinski.

ANNA: There you go—just to be arguing! I'm telling you it isn't Dobchinski.

MARIA: Well, now? Well, now, Mamma dear? You can see for yourself it's Dobchinski.

ANNA: Well, yes, it's Dobchinski. I can see that now—so what are you arguing about? (*Shouting through window.*) Walk faster! Faster! You walk so slowly! Well, now, where are they? Eh? Oh, you can tell me from there—it doesn't matter. What? Is he very stern? Eh? And what about my husband? My husband, I said! (*Stepping away from window a little, with vexation.*) What a stupid creature—he won't tell me a thing until he's inside! (*Enter* DOBCHINSKI, *all out of breath.*) There, now, tell me please—doesn't your conscience bother you? I depended upon you as the only decent man, but everybody dashed out and you had to go right after them! And up to this minute I can't get a sensible word out of anybody. Aren't you ashamed of yourself? Why, I was godmother to your little boy and girl, and that's how you acted toward me!

DOBCHINSKI: As God is my witness, dear lady, I ran so hard to pay my respects to you that I can't catch my breath. Greetings, Maria Antonovna.

MARIA: How d'you do?

ANNA: Well, what's what? Come, tell me all about it.

DOBCHINSKI: Your husband sent you this little note—

ANNA (*taking note*): Well, who is he? A General?

DOBCHINSKI: No, he isn't, but he's every bit as good as any General. So well educated, and his every action is so impressive.

ANNA: Ah, then it must be the very same man they wrote my husband about.

DOBCHINSKI: He's the real thing. I was the first one to find this out—together with Bobchinski.

ANNA: Do tell me everything at last! What happened, and how did it happen?

DOBCHINSKI: Well, glory be to God, everything went off auspiciously. At first he received your husband a trifle sternly, true enough; he was huffy and said that nothing about the hotel suited him, for one thing, but he wouldn't come here either, and that he didn't feel like sitting in jail for his sake; but later on, when he found out how innocent your husband was and when he had talked a little more intimately with him, he at once changed his ideas, and, glory be, everything went well. They've gone off now to inspect the charitable institutions. But I really must tell you that your husband was thinking whether a secret complaint hadn't been lodged against him; I myself had a bit of a scare, too.

ANNA: Why, what have you to be afraid of? You aren't in any government service.

DOBCHINSKI: Oh, just on general principles. You know how it is— when a high dignitary speaks you naturally feel scared.

ANNA: Oh, well! However, all this is nonsense—tell me what he looks like? Is he old or young, now?

DOBCHINSKI: He's young—a young man of twenty-three or close to it, yet he talks just as if he were an old man. "I'll come to your house," he says, "if you like," and (*gesturing vaguely*) this and that—it was all done so grandly. "I," he says, "am fond both of reading and writing; but I find it's a nuisance because this room is a trifle dark."

ANNA: But what's he like, you provoking man—dark-haired or light?

DOBCHINSKI: No, he's more on the auburn side, and his eyes dart here and there ever so quickly, like little animals of some sort—it actually makes you feel uneasy.

ANNA: Let's see what Tony writes me. (*Reads.*) "I write you in haste, dearest, to inform you that my situation was a most lamentable one; but, placing my trust in the mercy of God, for two pickles, extra, and a half-portion of caviar, one-twenty-five—" (*Stops reading.*) I can't understand a thing: what have pickles and caviar to do with all this?

DOBCHINSKI: Why, your husband wrote on scrap paper, he was in such a hurry; there must have been some bill written on it.

ANNA: Ah, yes—that's it. (*Resumes reading.*) ". . . but, placing my trust in the mercy of God . . . it seems as if everything will come out right. Get a room ready as quickly as you can for a distinguished guest—the one with the yellow wallpaper; as for dinner, don't bother preparing anything extra, because we are going to have a bite at the Department of Public Charities, with its Director. But as for wines, order as much as possible; tell that shopkeeper Abdulin to send his best, for otherwise I will turn his whole wine cellar upside down myself. Kissing your hand, my dearest, I remain yours, Anton Skvoznik-Dmuhanovski—" Oh, my God, this must surely be attended to as soon as possible. Hey, who's there? Mishka!

DOBCHINSKI (*making a dash for the door and shouting*) : Mishka! Mishka! Mishka! (*Enter* MISHKA.)

ANNA: Look here: Dash over to Abdulin's shop . . . hold on, I'll give you a note. (*Sitting down at a desk and speaking as she writes.*) You give this note to Sidor, the coachman; let him run over to Abdulin's shop and bring the wine back from there. And you yourself get that room (*pointing*) ready for the guest—and do it right! Put a bed in there, and a washbasin, and everything else. (*Exit* MISHKA.)

DOBCHINSKI: Well, I'll run along now to see how they're doing with their inspection—

ANNA: Go ahead, go ahead—I'm not detaining you. (*Exit* DOBCHIN-SKI.) Well, daughter, we'll have to get busy dressing. He's from the capital; God forbid he should make fun of us over something or other. Your blue dress with the little pleats would be the most becoming—

MARIA (*with disgust*) : No, Mamma dear; I don't like that blue dress at all. Not only does Lyapkin-Tyapkin's wife dress in blue, but so does Zemlyanika's daughter, too. No, I'd better put on something bright.

ANNA: Something bright, indeed! Really, you're saying that only to be contrary. The blue will look ever so much better on you, because I want to wear straw-yellow. I'm very fond of straw-yellow.

MARIA: Ah, Mamma dear, straw-yellow is so unbecoming to you!

ANNA: Straw-yellow is unbecoming to me?

MARIA: Yes. I'll stake anything you like it won't become you. One must have absolutely dark eyes to wear straw-yellow.

ANNA: That's just dandy! And aren't my eyes dark? As dark as dark can be! What nonsense the girl spouts! How can they be anything but dark when I always take the queen of clubs for myself whenever I tell fortunes by cards?

MARIA: Ah, Mamma dear, you're more like the queen of hearts!

ANNA: Bosh—absolute bosh! I never was a queen of hearts. (*Exit hurriedly with* MARIA, *but is still heard, off.*) What things pop into your head! Queen of hearts, indeed! God knows what nonsense you talk! (*As they exit, the door of the room* ANNA *had indicated opens and* MISHKA *sweeps out rubbish.* OSSIP *comes in through main door, lugging a valise on his head.*)

OSSIP: Where do I put this?

MISHKA: This way, Uncle—right this way.

OSSIP: Hold on; give us a chance to rest. What a dog's life! Every load seems heavy on an empty belly.

MISHKA: Tell me, Uncle—will the General be here soon?

OSSIP: What general?

MISHKA: Why, your master.

OSSIP: My master? But what sort of a general is he?

MISHKA: Why, ain't he a general?

OSSIP (*hedging*): He is—only the other way around.

MISHKA: Well, is he more important than a real general or less?

OSSIP: More!

MISHKA: So that's it! No wonder they're raising such a fuss in our house!

OSSIP: Look here, young fellow—I can see you're a bright lad; suppose you fix up a bite of something for me.

MISHKA: Why, Uncle, there's nothing ready yet that would be to your liking. You wouldn't want to eat anything plain; but when your master sits down at table you'll get some of the same food.

OSSIP: Well, now, what have you got in the way of plain fare?

MISHKA: Cabbage soup, buckwheat groats, and meat pies.

OSSIP: Bring on your soup, your groats and meat pies! It don't matter —we'll eat anything. Come on, let's lug this in. Is there another way out from there?

MISHKA: There is. (*Exit both, carrying the large suitcase into the adjoining room. Both halves of main door are flung open by two* POLICEMEN, *who flank the entrance. Enter* HLESTACOV, *followed by* MAYOR, *then the* DIRECTOR OF CHARITIES, *the* SUPERINTENDENT OF SCHOOLS, *and* DOBCHINSKI *and* BOBCHINSKI, *the latter with a plaster on the bridge of his nose.* MAYOR *makes a Jovelike gesture at a scrap of paper on the floor; the* POLICEMEN *rush helter-skelter to pick it up, colliding with each other.*)

HLESTACOV: Fine institutions you've got here. What I like is that you let your visitors see everything; in other towns they wouldn't show me a thing.

MAYOR: In other towns, if I may make so bold as to inform you, the town administrators and officials are more concerned with their own welfare, as it were; but here, if one may say so, we have no other thought save to earn the recognition of our superiors by good order and vigilance.

HLESTACOV: That was a very fine lunch; I ate entirely too much. Why, do you have lunches like that every day?

MAYOR: It was especially arranged for so pleasant a guest.

HLESTACOV: I love a good meal. For that's what one lives for—to pluck the blossoms of pleasure. What do they call that fish we had?

DIRECTOR OF CHARITIES (*trotting up to* HLESTACOV): Salted scrod, Sir.

HLESTACOV: Very tasty. Where was it we lunched? At the hospital, wasn't it?

DIRECTOR: Right, Sir! Just one of our eleemosynary institutions.

HLESTACOV: I remember, I remember. There were a lot of cots standing empty there. And have all the patients recovered? There didn't seem to be many of them around.

DIRECTOR: There's half a score or so of them left; all the others have recovered. That's the way it goes—it's the way things are arranged. Ever since I've assumed the post—perhaps this may seem actually incredible to you—all the patients recover like . . . like flies. No sooner does a patient set foot in the infirmary than he gets well—and not so much through the aid of any medicines as through sheer honesty and efficient organization.

MAYOR: And, if I may make so bold as to inform you, the responsibility of being Mayor is ever so harrowing! There are so many problems —take sanitation alone, and repairs, and rectifications. . . . In short, the most intelligent of men might find himself in difficulties; yet, God be thanked, everything runs smoothly. Another Mayor, of course, might strive for his own benefit; but, believe me, that even when one lies down to sleep one keeps thinking—Lord God, how can I arrange things so that my superiors may perceive my zeal? I ask for nothing more. Whether they reward me or not, at least I shan't be perturbed at heart. When good order is maintained throughout the town, when all the streets are swept, the prisoners well kept, and there are only a few drunkards—what more could I desire? I swear I want no honors. Of course, that sort of thing is enticing, but before virtue all else is but dross and vanity.

DIRECTOR (*aside*): Listen to that scalawag laying it on! It's a gift from Heaven!

HLESTACOV: Very, very true. I confess I myself am occasionally fond of intellectual pursuits—at times in prose, and at others tossing off some slight verse.

BOBCHINSKI (*to* DOBCHINSKI): Quite right, Peter Ivanovich, quite right! His remarks are so . . . so . . . you know! One can see that he has studied the humanities.

HLESTACOV: Tell me, please, don't you go in for diversions of any sort? Haven't you gatherings where one may, for instance, indulge in a little game of cards?

MAYOR (*aside*): Oho, brother, I know what you're driving at! (*Aloud.*) God save us from anything of the sort! There isn't even a hint at such gatherings here. I never as much as held a card in my hands; I couldn't play cards if my life actually depended on it. I never could bear to look at them with indifference; why, if I should but happen somehow to catch sight of a king of diamonds, let's say, I'm overcome with such disgust that I simply have to spit. One time it so happened that I built a house of cards, just to amuse the children, don't you know—and all that night the accursed things kept plaguing me in my dreams. God be with them that play—how can anyone kill precious time over cards?

SUPERINTENDENT OF SCHOOLS (*aside*): And yet that scoundrel took me over for a hundred on points, only three days ago!

MAYOR: I'd rather utilize the time for the good of the State.

HLESTACOV: Oh, really now, you're making a fuss over nothing at all. It all depends on how you look at a thing. If, for instance, you were to start hedging when you've lost three quarters of your stakes, then, naturally. . . . No, it's no use talking, it's intriguing to play a game of cards now and then. (*Enter* ANNA *and* MARIA.)

MAYOR: May I make so bold as to present my family: my wife and my daughter.

HLESTACOV (*bowing and scraping*): Delighted, Madam, in having the pleasure, as it were, of meeting you—

ANNA: It's still a greater pleasure for us to meet such a personage.

HLESTACOV (*posturing*): Pardon me, but mine is so much greater!

ANNA: How can that be! You're pleased to say so only for the sake of a compliment. Be seated, I beg of you.

HLESTACOV: Merely to stand near you constitutes happiness; however, since you absolutely insist, I'll sit down. How happy I am to be sitting near you at last!

ANNA: Pardon me, but I dare not accept the compliment as being really intended for me . . . . I think you must have found traveling very unpleasant after life in the capital?

HLESTACOV: Extremely unpleasant. Having become used to living in society, *comprenez vous,* and then to find yourself suddenly on the road—the filthy inns, the surrounding gloom of boorishness. I must confess, if it weren't for such good fortune which (*glancing at* ANNA *and showing off before her*) has rewarded me for everything. . . .

ANNA: Really, it must be so unpleasant for you!

HLESTACOV: However, Madam, at this moment I am in a most pleasant mood!

ANNA: But that's out of the question—you do me too much honor. I do not merit it.

HLESTACOV: But why in the world not? You do merit it!

ANNA: I live in the backwoods—

HLESTACOV: Yes, but the backwoods, by the bye, also has its points—knolls, brooks, and rills. Well, naturally, no one would compare it with the capital. Ah, the capital! What life, really! You may think, perhaps, that I'm merely a pen-pusher; but no, the Head of the Department is on a friendly footing with me. He'll slap me on the back, like this: "Come and have dinner with me, dear fellow!" I drop in at the office for only a couple of minutes a day, merely to tell 'em to do this thing that way and that thing this way. And immediately a special clerk—and what an old rat he is!—starts scraping away with his pen. (*Imitates a scratchy pen.*) They even wanted to give me a much higher rank, but, I thought to myself, what's the use? And the doorman runs after me with a brush: "Permit me, Sir—I want to shine your shoes!" (*To* MAYOR.) But why are you standing? Please do sit down, gentlemen!

MAYOR		Your rank is such that we can well keep on standing—
DIRECTOR	(*simultaneously*):	We'll stand—
SUPERINTENDENT		Please don't mind us—

HLESTACOV: Never mind ranks—I'm asking you to sit down. (MAYOR *and the others sit down.*) I'm not fond of ceremonies; on the contrary, I actually try to slip by without attracting attention—so I do. But you simply can't hide yourself—you can't, you can't! All I have to do is to go out somewheres, and they all start saying at once: "There," they say, "goes Hlestacov!" And on one occasion they actually took me for a Commander-in-Chief. The soldiers rushed right out of the guard-room and presented arms. It was only later on that an officer, whom I know very well, explained to me: "Why, brother, we actually took you for the Commander-in-Chief!"

ANNA: Do tell!

HLESTACOV: I know ever so many pretty little actresses. For, after all, I've written all sorts of amusing little pieces for the stage. I mingle with all the writers. Pushkin and I are like that. (*Puts middle finger over index finger.*) Many's the time I've said to him: "Well, how are things going, Pushkin, old thing?"—and he'd come right back at me with, "Why, old thing, things are just so-so, somehow!" Most original fellow!

ANNA: So you write, too? It must be so pleasant to feel oneself a writer. You probably publish in the magazines as well?

HLESTACOV: Oh, yes—in the magazines as well. However, I've done ever so many things: *The Marriage of Figaro, Robert Le Diable, Norma.* . . . By now I don't remember even the titles. And it all came about by sheer chance; I didn't want to write, but the theatrical managers kept pestering me, "Please, dear fellow, write something for us!" So I thought to myself: "All right, dear fellows, so I will—just to get rid of you!" And right then and there—I don't think it took me more than a single evening, I dashed off everything—and did I astonish all of them! (*Slight pause.*) I have an exceptional facility of imagination. I am really the backbone of the *Morning Telegraph;* my sea novel, *The Frigate Hope,* is still a best-seller, and everything that came out under the name of Baron Brambeus—

ANNA (*breaking in on him*): Do tell! So you were that famous colyumist?

HLESTACOV: Why, of course. Why, there isn't a poet whose poems I don't doctor. The biggest publisher in the country pays me a retainer of forty thousand a year for that alone.

ANNA: Then *Uri Miloslavski* must also be your work—

HLESTACOV: Yes, it is.

ANNA: There, I guessed it right off!

MARIA: Ah, Mamma dear, it says right on the title page it was written by some Zagoskin.

ANNA: There you go! I simply knew you'd start an argument even over that—

HLESTACOV (*hardly batting an eye*): Oh, yes, that's right; that's really by Zagoskin; but there's another novel by the same name—well, that one is mine.

ANNA: Well, it surely must be yours I read. How well written it is!

HLESTACOV: To confess the truth, I live by my pen. My house is the best in the whole capital. Everybody knows it! They call it Hlestacov House—just like that. (*Addressing everybody.*) If you're ever in the capital, gentlemen, do me a favor and drop in on me; I urge you, most heartily. And then, I also give grand affairs.

ANNA: I can imagine how tasteful and magnificent they must be.

HLESTACOV: Well, really, they're past all description. In the center of the table is a watermelon—and that watermelon costs a mere seven hundred. Soup in special cans, just arrived by steamer direct from Paris —open a can, and the steam is like—like nothing on earth. Not a day passes without my having to attend dances. There, in the capital, we have formed our own circle for whist. The Minister of Foreign Affairs, the French Ambassador, and the British, and the German, and me. And you get so fagged out playing it's really a shame. When you run up to the fourth floor all you have strength to say to the cook is, "Here, old girl, take my coat"—hold on, though: why, I'm mixing everything up; I've actually forgotten I live on the first floor. My staircase alone is— well, simply priceless! And it's ever so curious to peep in at my reception hall, at an hour when I haven't even opened my eyes. The counts and dukes are milling about and buzz like so many bumblebees; all you can hear is their *bzz, bzz, bzz!* Occasionally you'll find the Premier there— just hanging around. . . . (*The* MAYOR *and the others are so awed that they rise from their chairs.*) Even my letters are addressed "Your Excellency." Once I had charge of a whole Department, actually. Most odd, that was. The Director had gone off—but where to nobody seemed to know. Well, naturally, all sorts of discussions sprang up: How was his place to be filled, who was going to fill it, what was to be done. Many of the generals were willing enough and tackled the job, but, when they got right down to it—we-e-ell, no, the matter was entirely too complicated. It was easy enough, at first glance, but when you got a closer look at it, it turned out to be the devil and all. Later on they see that there's no help for it—so they turn to me. And that very moment all the streets are simply swarming with dashing messengers, and messengers, and more messengers—no end of messengers, and all of 'em dashing about like mad. You can just imagine, there were thirty-five thousand messengers alone! Wasn't that some situation, I ask you? "Ivan Alexandrovich, come and take charge of that Department!" I was somewhat taken aback, I confess; I had come out in my dressing gown and was just about to turn 'em down, but then I thought to myself: Suppose word of my refusal reaches the Emperor? And then there's my service record to be considered, too . . . "Very well, gentlemen," I said, "if you like I'll accept the post; I accept it," I tell 'em: "The only thing is, watch out! I won't stand for any guff from anybody. You've got to be up on your toes when you work for me. You know me!" And really, whenever I used to pass through the Department it was simply like an earthquake; there wasn't a soul there that didn't quake and quiver like an aspen leaf. (*The* MAYOR *and the others quake in apprehension;* HLESTAKOV *works himself up to a real fever pitch.*) Oh, I don't like to fool around! I hauled all of them over the coals. (*Pause.*) Why, even the Imperial Council is afraid of me. And really, why not? That's the sort of man I am! I don't let anybody stand in my way. I always tell everybody "I, I myself know my own self." I'm all over—all over! I drop in at the Palace every day. They'd make me Field Marshal on the morrow—at a moment's notice from me—(*Slips, and all but flops on the floor, but is deferentially caught and supported by the* OFFICIALS.)

MAYOR (*approaching him and trying to speak, his whole body quaking*): B-b-ut. . . . Yo . . . yo . . . yo. . . .

HLESTACOV (*sharply*): What is it?

MAYOR: B-b-ut. . . . Yo . . . yo . . . yo. . . .

HLESTACOV (*as before*): I can't make out a word. It doesn't make sense.

MAYOR: Yo . . . yo. . . . Your Lexecency—Your Excellency may wish to rest. Here's your room, and everything you need—

HLESTACOV: Rest? Nonsense! However, if you like, I'm ready to take a rest. Your lunch was eckshellent, gemmen! I'm gratified—I'm gratified. (*Declaiming.*) Scrod, *scrod,* SCROD! (*Exit, solicitously followed by the* MAYOR, *into the side room.*)

BOBCHINSKI (*to* DOBCHINSKI): There's a man for you, Peter Ivanovich. There's a man that's a man! Never in my life have I been in the presence of so important a personage—I all but passed out, I was that scared. What do you think, Peter Ivanovich: who is he? What's his rank, I mean?

DOBCHINSKI: I think he's nothing short of a general, Peter Ivanovich.

BOBCHINSKI: Well, in my opinion no general is fit to lace the shoes of this fellow! But if he is a general, then he must be a generalissimo at the very least. You heard him: he's got the whole Imperial Council backed up against the wall. Let's go and tell everything to the judge and to Korobkin. Good-by, Anna Andreievna!

DOBCHINSKI: Good-by, dearest lady! (*Exeunt* DOBCHINSKI *and* BOBCHINSKI.)

DIRECTOR OF CHARITIES (*to* SUPERINTENDENT OF SCHOOLS): It's simply frightening! But just why, a body can't tell. Why, we aren't even wearing our uniforms! Well, now, suppose he gets up after a good night's sleep and then dashes off a confidential report to the capital? (*Walks thoughtfully to door with* SUPERINTENDENT OF SCHOOLS, *then turns to* ANNA.) Good-by, Ma'am!

SUPERINTENDENT OF SCHOOLS: Good-by! (*Exeunt both.*)

ANNA: Ah, what an agreeable fellow!

MARIA: Ah! The darling!

ANNA: But mind you, what fine deportment! One can perceive a man from the capital right off. His ways, and all that sort of thing. . . . Ah, but that's fine! I'm awfully fond of young men like that. I've simply lost my head over him. However, I proved very much to his liking; I noticed he was eying me all the time—

MARIA: Ah, Mamma dear—it was me he was looking at!

ANNA: Oh, get away from me with your impertinence! That remark is entirely out of place in this instance.

MARIA: No, Mamma dear, he really was.

ANNA: There you go! God forbid that you should ever keep from arguing! It just couldn't be, and that's that. When did he look at you? And what reason did he have to look at you?

MARIA: Really, Mamma dear, he kept looking at me all the time. Why, he glanced at me the moment he began talking about literature, and when he was telling us about how he played whist with the ambassadors he looked at me also.

ANNA: Well, maybe he did, one little time, and even then he did it just so, just to be nice. "Eh," he must have said to himself, "let's take a look at her—might as well."

MAYOR (*tiptoeing in from* HLESTACOV'S *room*): Shhhh—sh!

ANNA. What is it?

MAYOR: Really, I'm none too happy now I got him drunk. Well, now, supposing even half of what he said is true? (*Falls into thought.*) But still, how could it be anything but the truth? Once you've got plenty of drink under your belt you come right out with everything. Whatever you've got in your heart is right at the tip of your tongue. Of course, he did touch things up a bit. But then, nobody ever says anything without some added touches. He plays whist with prime ministers and is a regular visitor at Court. So really, now, the more I think of it—the devil knows what's going on in my head, for I'm sure I don't know; it's just as if I were standing up on some belfry, or as if they were about to hang me.

ANNA: But me, now—I wasn't in the least put out; I simply saw him as a well-brought-up man of the world, a man of the highest quality, but as for his rank and position, why, I simply don't take them into consideration, even.

MAYOR: Oh, you women! That one word is enough to settle all argument. All you think of is fuss and feathers. And you'll always pop up with some silly thing or other. You will get off with nothing but a flogging—but your husband's goose will be gone and done for. You, my darling, treated him just as familiarly as if he were some Dobchinski or other.

ANNA: That's something I'd advise you not to worry your head about. There's a little something we know about him. (*Looks at her daughter.*)

MAYOR. (*solo*): Oh, what's the use of talking with you! What a thing to happen, really! I still can't get over my fright. (*Opening door and calling.*) Mishka, call Svistunov and Derzhimorda; their beat is just a little beyond the gates. (*Short pause after closing door.*) Odd how mixed up everything has become in the world; if only people would be impressive to look at, but no, every man is puny and small and as thin as a match—how can a body tell who he is? You take a military man, now —at least his uniform tells you what he is; but even he, when he puts on civilian dress, will look like a fly with its wings snipped off. However, he sure did hold back at that hotel. He sprang such allegories and equivocations on me that it looked as if I'd never get anything sensible out of him. But there, he did give in in the end. And he actually let spill more than he should have. You can see right off he's still a youngster. (*Enter* OSSIP, *polishing a boot. All make a dash for him, beckoning with their fingers.*)

ANNA: Come here, old fellow!

MAYOR: Shhh! Well? Is he sleeping?

OSSIP: No, not yet; he's still stretching himself every once in a while.

ANNA: Look here . . . what's your name?

OSSIP: Ossip, Ma'am.

MAYOR (*to his wife and daughter*): There, that'll do you, that'll do you! (*To* OSSIP.) Now, then, my friend, have they fed you well?

OSSIP: They did that, thanking you most humbly—they fed me right well.

ANNA: Well, now, tell me: there must be ever so many counts and dukes calling on your master?

OSSIP (*aside*): What's the use of saying anything! If they fed me well now, it means they're going to feed me still better later on. (*Aloud.*) Yes, there's counts calling on him, amongst others.

MARIA: Ossip, darling, your master is such a good-looking little fellow!

ANNA: But tell me please, Ossip—is your master—

MAYOR: Now stop that, please! You merely hinder me with such idle talk. Come, what can you tell me, friend?

ANNA: And what might your master's rank be?

OSSIP: His rank? Why, the usual thing—

MAYOR: Oh, my God, how you keep on with your silly pumping! You won't give me a chance to ask anything that matters. (*To* OSSIP.) Well, my friend, what sort of man is your master? Strict? Is he fond of bawling people out, or isn't he? Eh?

OSSIP: Yes, he's fond of having everything in order. What he's after is having everything regular-like.

MAYOR: Why, I like your face, so I do! You must be a kindhearted fellow, friend. Well, now—

ANNA: See here, how does your master look in his uniform?

MAYOR: Come, that'll do you two chatterboxes. This is a most urgent matter. It concerns life and death! (*To* OSSIP.) As I was saying, I do like you, ever so much. When you're traveling it can't do the least harm to have an extra glass of tea or something; it's cold now. So here's a couple of cart wheels for tea.

OSSIP (*accepting the coins*): Thank you, ever so humbly. May God grant you all good health for helping a poor man.

MAYOR: Fine, fine; that makes me happy, too. Well, now, friend—

ANNA: I say, Ossip, what sort of eyes does your master prefer, now?

MARIA: Ossip, darling! What a 'cute little nose your master has!

MAYOR: Hold on, now, give me a chance! (*To* OSSIP.) And now, friend—to what things does your master pay the most attention? What appeals to him most when he's traveling, that is?

OSSIP: It all depends on whatever turns up. He likes best of all to be well received—he likes good entertainment.

MAYOR: Good entertainment?

OSSIP: Yes, good entertainment. There, now, I may be nothing but a serf, yet even so he looks out that I'm treated right, too. By God, whenever we used to stop anywhere, he'd always ask me, "Well, Ossip, were you treated right?"—"Not so well, Your Excellency," I might tell him. "Eh," he'd say, "our host has a mean nature, Ossip. You remind me," he'd say, "when we get back to the capital." But I'd think to myself: "Eh, (*makes a resigned gesture*) God be with that fellow; I'm a simple man."

MAYOR: Fine, fine, and what you're saying is good common sense. I gave you something for tea just now—so here's something else for cookies to go with it.

OSSIP: Why are you so good to me, Your Honor? (*Pocketing the coin.*) In that case I'll drink to Your Honor's health.

ANNA: You come to me, Ossip; you'll get something additional.

MARIA: Ossip, darling, kiss your master for me! (HLESTACOV *is heard coughing slightly in the adjoining room.*)

MAYOR: Shhh! (*Gets up on tiptoes; rest of scene in* sotto voce.) God save you from making a noise! That'll do you two; go to your rooms.

ANNA: Come along, Maria! I'll tell you exactly what I noticed about our guest; it's something I can tell you only when we're alone. (*Exeunt* ANNA *and* MARIA.)

MAYOR: Oh, they'll have plenty to talk about! I think if you were to listen you'd have to stick your fingers in your ears. (*Turning to* OSSIP.) Well, friend—(DERZHIMORDA *and* SVISTUNOV *clump in.*) Shhh! What clumsy bears, clumping with their boots! Barging in with as much noise as if somebody was dumping a load off a cart! Where in the hell were you?

DERZHIMORDA: I wuz carryin' out orders—

MAYOR: Shhhh! (*Clapping hand over* DERZHIMORDA'S *mouth.*) Listen to him cawing like a crow! (*Mimicking.*) "I wuz carryin' out orders!" Sounds like a foghorn. (*To* OSSIP.) Well, friend, you run along and get whatever your master needs. You can call for anything and everything in the house. (*Exit* OSSIP.) As for you two, you stand on the front steps and don't stir from the spot! And don't let a single stranger into the house—especially the storekeepers! If you'll let even one of 'em in, I'll skin you alive. The minute you see anyone at all coming with a complaint—or even without a complaint, but maybe the fellow looks like the kind of a fellow that would want to lodge a complaint against me—you just let him have it right in the neck! Like this! Let him have it good and hot! (*Kicks, to demonstrate.*) You hear me? Shh! Shhhhhhh! (*Tiptoes out, after* DERZHIMORDA *and* SVISTUNOV.)

Curtain

ACT III, Scene 1

Scene same. Next morning. Enter, cautiously and almost on tiptoes, JUDGE, DIRECTOR OF CHARITIES, POSTMASTER, SUPERINTENDENT OF SCHOOLS, *and* DOBCHINSKI *and* BOBCHINSKI. *All act as if on dress parade, and the officials are in their uniforms. The whole scene, until* HLESTACOV'S *entrance, is in* sotto voce.

JUDGE (*arranging everybody in a semicircle*): For God's sake, gentlemen, get in a circle without wasting time, and try to be as orderly as possible! God be with him—he not only attends at Court but also bawls out the Imperial Council! Straighten up! A soldierlike bearing, gentlemen—you mustn't fall down on that soldierlike bearing! You, Peter Ivanovich—trot over to this side; and you, Peter Ivanovich, stand right here. (DOBCHINSKI *and* BOBCHINSKI *trot over to the places indicated.*)

DIRECTOR OF CHARITIES: Have it your way, Judge, but we really ought to take some . . . action.

JUDGE: And what, precisely?

DIRECTOR OF CHARITIES: Well, you know what.

JUDGE: Palm oil?

DIRECTOR OF CHARITIES: Well, yes—why not palm oil—

JUDGE: A dangerous thing, devil take it; he may raise a hullabaloo, working for the State as he does. Unless, perhaps, we were to do it in the guise of a contribution from the gentry, for some sort of a monument?

POSTMASTER: Or else: "Here, now, some money has come through the mails—and no one knows to whom it belongs!"

DIRECTOR OF CHARITIES: Watch out he doesn't post you somewhere to hell and back again. Look here, that's not the way things are done in a well-regulated State. Why is there a whole squadron of us here? We ought to present ourselves one by one and, when each is eye to eye with him, then . . . do whatever has to be done, and there are no ears to overhear. That's how things are done in a well-regulated social order. There, now, Judge—you'll be the first to start the ball rolling.

JUDGE: Why, it would be better if you did; it was in your Department that our important visitor broke bread.

DIRECTOR OF CHARITIES: Well, it might be better, after all, if the Superintendent of Schools took the initiative—as one who enlightens the youth and all that.

SUPERINTENDENT OF SCHOOLS: I can't, gentlemen, I simply can't. To tell you the truth, my upbringing has been such that if anyone, even one step above me in rank, starts talking to me my heart simply sinks into my boots and it's as if the cat has stolen my tongue. No, gentlemen, you must excuse me—you really must.

DIRECTOR OF CHARITIES: Well, Judge, it looks like there's nobody to do it outside of yourself. You never utter a word but it sounds as if Cicero himself were speaking with your tongue.

JUDGE: Come, now! Come, now—Cicero indeed! What will you

think of next? Just because once in a while one becomes deeply interested in discussing a pack of house-dogs or a racing bloodhound—

ALL (*badgering him*): No, dogs aren't all you can talk about—you
could have straightened out the trouble at the building of the Tower of
Babel! No, Judge, don't leave us in a lurch! Be like a father to us! Really,
Judge—

JUDGE: Do let me alone, gentlemen! (*At this moment* HLESTACOV
*is heard clearing his throat and walking about in his room—All try to
head off one another in a panic rush to the door—which, naturally,
leads to certain casualties. But, for all that, the protests are also in* sotto
voce.)

BOBCHINSKI'S VOICE: Ouch! Dobchinski, Dobchinski, you're standing on my foot!

VOICE OF DIRECTOR OF CHARITIES: Gentlemen, let me out of here
before I pass away! You've crushed me completely—(*A few more
"Ouch!"'s; finally all push through, leaving stage empty for a few
seconds.*)

HLESTACOV (*solo, entering with sleep-laden eyes*): I must have had
some snooze, it looks like. Wherever do they get such soft mattresses
and feather beds? I was actually roasting. It looks as if they'd given me
something stronger than water; my head is still throbbing. A man can
pass his time most pleasantly here, I can see that. I love open-handed
hospitality and it pleases me all the more, I must admit, when I'm being
entertained from the bottom of the heart and not out of any selfish interest. Then, too, the Mayor's daughter isn't at all hard to look at, and
her mother, for that matter, is an old fiddle on which one could still
play a tune. . . . Yes, I don't know why, but really this sort of life
is to my liking.

JUDGE (*entering and stopping, in an aside*): Lord God, see me
through this safely! My knees are simply caving in. (*Aloud, straightening up and clutching the sword at his side.*) I have the honor of presenting myself: Lyapkin-Tyapkin, Collegiate Assessor and Judge of the
District Court in this town!

HLESTACOV: Be seated, please. So you're the Judge here?

JUDGE: I was chosen for a three-year term by the gentry, ever so long
ago, and I've continued on the bench right up to now.

HLESTACOV: I say, though, is there much in being a judge?

JUDGE: During my three-year terms I was proposed for the Order of
St. Vladimir, Fourth Class, with the commendation of my superiors.

(*Aside.*) I've got the money right in my fist—and my fist feels as if it were on fire.

HLESTACOV: Why, I like the Order of St. Vladimir. The Order of St. Anna, Third Class, isn't so much by comparison.

JUDGE (*aside, thrusting out his fist little by little*): Lord God, I don't know what I'm sitting on. Just as though I were on pins and needles.

HLESTACOV: What's that you've got in your hand?

JUDGE (*losing his head and dropping the bank notes on the floor*): Not a thing, Sir—

HLESTACOV: What do you mean, not a thing? Isn't that money I see on the floor?

JUDGE (*shivering from head to foot*): By no means, Sir. (*Aside.*) Oh, God, I'm as good as up on charges right now! I can hear the Black Maria rattling up to fetch me away.

HLESTACOV (*picking up the bank notes*): Yes, it's money, sure enough.

JUDGE (*aside*): Well, it's all over; I'm lost—lost!

HLESTACOV: Tell you what: suppose you let me have this as a loan—

JUDGE (*hastily*): Of course, Sir, of course—with the greatest of pleasure! (*Aside.*) A little more boldly, now! Get me out of this, Most Holy Mother of God!

HLESTACOV: I've sort of run low on funds on my travels, don't you know, what with one thing and another. However, I'll send this right back to you from my country estate—

JUDGE: Good gracious, don't give it a thought! Why, this is such an honor. . . . Of course, with all my feeble powers . . . my striving and zeal for my superiors . . . I shall try to merit—(*Gets up from chair and stands at attention, his hands at his sides.*) I dare not impose my presence on you any further. Have you any instructions for me perhaps?

HLESTACOV: What instructions?

JUDGE: I mean, aren't you issuing any instructions for the District Court here?

HLESTACOV: Whatever for? For I have absolutely no concern with it at present; no, there are no instructions. Thanks, ever so much.

JUDGE (*aside, bowing and scraping as he makes his getaway*): Well, the town is all ours now!

HLESTACOV: Fine fellow, the Judge.

POSTMASTER (*drawing himself up as he enters and clutching the sword at his side*) : I have the honor of presenting myself: Court Councilor Shpekin, the Postmaster.

HLESTACOV: Ah, do come in. I'm very fond of pleasant company. Sit down! You've always lived in this town—isn't that right?

POSTMASTER: Just so, Sir.

HLESTACOV: Why, I like this little town. Of course, it hasn't got so much of a population—well, what of that? After all, it isn't a capital. Isn't that so—it isn't a capital, after all?

POSTMASTER: Absolutely so, Sir.

HLESTACOV: For it's only at the capital that you'll find the *bon ton*— and no provincial geese. What's your opinion—isn't that so?

POSTMASTER: Just so, Sir. (*Aside.*) I must say, though, that he isn't at all uppity; he asks about everything.

HLESTACOV: But just the same, you must admit that even in a small town it's possible to live one's life happily.

POSTMASTER: Just so, Sir.

HLESTACOV: What, to my way of thinking, does a man need? All one needs is to be respected, to be loved sincerely—isn't that so?

POSTMASTER: That is absolutely correct.

HLESTACOV: To tell you the truth, I'm glad you are of the same opinion as myself. Of course, they'll call me an odd stick, but then that's the sort of nature I have. (*Soliloquizes, even while he is looking right into the* POSTMASTER'S *eyes.*) Guess I might as well make a touch from this Postmaster! (*Aloud.*) What an odd thing to happen to me; I ran absolutely short of funds during my travels. Could you possibly let me have three hundred as a loan?

POSTMASTER: Why not? I would deem it the greatest happiness. There you are, Sir. At your service, with all my heart.

HLESTACOV: Very grateful to you. For, I must confess, I have a mortal dislike of denying myself anything while I'm traveling—and, besides, why in the world should I? Isn't that so?

POSTMASTER: Just so, Sir. (*Stands up, draws himself erect, and holds on to his sword.*) I dare not impose my presence on you any longer . . . Perhaps you have some criticism as to the management of the Post Office, Sir?

HLESTACOV: No, not at all. (*Exit* POSTMASTER, *bowing and scraping.*) Postmaster, it seems to me that you, too, are a very fine fellow. At least you're obliging; I like people like that.

VOICE (*off, quite audibly*) : What are you so scared about?

SUPERINTENDENT OF SCHOOLS (*he doesn't exactly enter, but is practically shoved through the door, right after the above speech; draws himself up, not without trembling, and clutches the sword at his side)*: I have the honor of presenting myself: Titular Councilor Hlopov, Superintendent of Schools—

HLESTACOV: Ah, do come in! Sit down, sit down! Care for a cigar? (*Offering cigar.*)

SUPERINTENDENT OF SCHOOLS (*soliloquizing as he hesitates*): There's a comeuppance! That's something I'd never foreseen. To take or not to take?

HLESTACOV: Take it, take it! It's a rather decent smoke. Of course not the same thing as at the capital. There, my friend, I'm used to corona-corona-coronas, at twenty-five the hundred; you simply have to blow a kiss after smoking one. Here's a light—get it going. (*Offers light.* SUPERINTENDENT OF SCHOOLS *tries to light cigar, at the same time trembling all over.*) You're lighting it from the wrong end.

SUPERINTENDENT OF SCHOOLS (*soliloquizing, as he drops the cigar from sheer fright and gives up, with a hopeless gesture*): The devil take it all! My damned timidity has been the ruin of me!

HLESTACOV: You, I can see, are no great lover of cigars. Yet I confess they're a weakness of mine. And also as far as the feminine sex is concerned—I simply can't remain indifferent. What about you? Which do you prefer—blondes or brunettes? (*The* SUPERINTENDENT OF SCHOOLS *is at a total loss as to what to say.*) Now, do be frank with me —is it blondes or brunettes?

SUPERINTENDENT OF SCHOOLS: I dare not venture on an opinion.

HLESTACOV: No, no—don't try to wriggle out of it. I want to find out your taste, without fail.

SUPERINTENDENT OF SCHOOLS: I make so bold as to report. . . . (*Aside.*) Why, I myself don't know what I'm saying!

HLESTACOV: Ah, ah! So you won't tell me. Probably some little brunette has already smitten your heart. Confess—hasn't she? (*The* SUPERINTENDENT OF SCHOOLS *can't utter a word.*) Ah, ah! You've turned red—you see, you see! But why don't you say something?

SUPERINTENDENT OF SCHOOLS: I'm overcome with timidity, Your Hon . . . Excell . . . High. . . . (*Aside.*) My confounded tongue has sold me out! It has sold me out!

HLESTACOV: Overcome by timidity, are you? Well, there really is something about my eyes that inspires timidity. At least I know that there isn't a woman living who can resist them—isn't that so?

SUPERINTENDENT OF SCHOOLS: Just so, Sir.

HLESTACOV: However, a deucedly odd thing has happened to me: I've run entirely out of funds on the road. Could you possibly let me have a loan of three hundred?

SUPERINTENDENT OF SCHOOLS (*soliloquizing as he gropes in his pocket*): What a fix I'll be in if I haven't the money on me! I have it, I have it! (*Takes out bank notes and offers them with fear and trembling.*)

HLESTACOV: Thanks, ever so much.

SUPERINTENDENT OF SCHOOLS (*drawing himself up and clutching his sword*): I dare not impose my presence on you any longer—

HLESTACOV: Good-by!

SUPERINTENDENT OF SCHOOLS (*aside, as he scuttles out, practically at a run*): There, glory be to God! Chances are he won't as much as look in at my classes.

DIRECTOR OF CHARITIES (*drawing himself up as he enters and clutching his sword*): I have the honor of presenting myself: Court Councilor Zemlyanika, Director of Charities!

HLESTACOV: How d'you do; I beg you to be seated.

DIRECTOR OF CHARITIES: I had the honor of accompanying you on your tour of inspection and of receiving you personally in the eleemosynary institutions entrusted to my care.

HLESTACOV: Ah, yes, I remember. You tendered me a most excellent luncheon.

DIRECTOR OF CHARITIES: Only too happy to exert myself in the service of our native land!

HLESTACOV: It's a weakness of mine, I confess, but I do love good food. Tell me, please—it seems to me that you were somewhat shorter yesterday—isn't that so?

DIRECTOR OF CHARITIES: That's very possible. (*After a brief silence.*) I may say that I spare no effort and fulfill my duties zealously. (*Inching forward together with his chair and speaking in a low voice.*) It's the Postmaster here who does absolutely nothing; all his affairs are much neglected; the outgoing mail is always held up . . . you can find out the specific details yourself, if you wish. The Judge, too—he's the one who was here a little while before me—all he knows is to go riding after rabbits; he keeps dogs in the courthouse, and his whole conduct— if I may be frank with you—of course it's for the good of the State that I must do this, even though he's related to me and is a friend of mine—his conduct is most prejudicial. There's a certain landowner hereabouts; they call him Dobchinski—you've seen him around, I dare say. Well, no sooner does this Dobchinski step out of his house than the Judge is already there, sitting with Dobchinski's wife. I'm ready to take my oath on that. And make a point of looking the little Dobchinskis over; there isn't a one that looks like Dobchinski, but every one of them, even the little girl, is the spit and image of the Judge—

HLESTACOV: You don't say! Why, I'd never even think that.

DIRECTOR OF CHARITIES: And then there's the Superintendent of the Schools here. I don't know how the Administration could ever entrust him with such a post. He's worse than any Red, and he instills the youth with such pernicious doctrines as it would be difficult even to describe. If you care to give me instructions to that effect, I could report on all this ever so much better in black and white—

HLESTACOV: Very well—let it be done in black and white. It'll please me very much. I'm sort of fond, don't you know, of reading something amusing whenever I'm bored. What's your name? I keep forgetting it.

DIRECTOR OF CHARITIES: Zemlyanika.

HLESTACOV: Ah, yes—Zemlyanika. Well, now, tell me, please: have you any little ones?

DIRECTOR OF CHARITIES: Why, naturally, Sir: five—two of them are grown up by now.

HLESTACOV: You don't say! Already grown up? And what do you . . . how are they—

DIRECTOR OF CHARITIES: You are pleased to ask, I take it, what they are called?

HLESTACOV: That's it; how are they called?

DIRECTOR OF CHARITIES: Nicolai, Ivan, Elizaveta, Maria, and Perepetuya.

HLESTACOV: Fine, fine!

DIRECTOR OF CHARITIES: I dare not impose my presence upon you any further . . . to infringe upon the time dedicated to your consecrated duties—(*Bowing and scraping as a preliminary to leaving.*)

HLESTACOV (*seeing him to the door*): No, not at all. All that you've told me is most amusing. Please pay me another call sometime. I love that sort of-thing, very much. (DIRECTOR OF CHARITIES *steps through door;* HLESTACOV *closes it but immediately goes back and, opening it, calls after him.*) Hey, there! What do they call you? I keep forgetting your full name.

DIRECTOR OF CHARITIES (*in doorway*): Artemii Philipovich Zemlyanika.

HLESTACOV: If you'll be so kind, Artemii Philipovich: I'm in an odd fix—I've run all out of funds during my travels. Have you four hundred on you by any chance that you could lend me—

DIRECTOR OF CHARITIES (*proffering bank notes*): I have.

HLESTACOV: It comes in quite handy, I must say. Thanks, ever so much. (*Exit* DIRECTOR OF CHARITIES. *Enter* BOBCHINSKI *and* DOBCHINSKI.)

BOBCHINSKI: I have the honor of presenting myself: Peter Ivanovich Bobchinski. I'm a landowner, living in this town.

DOBCHINSKI: Peter Ivanovich Dobchinski, a landowner.

HLESTACOV: Ah, I've already seen you around. (*To* BOBCHINSKI.) I believe you fell that time—and how is your nose now?

BOBCHINSKI: Glory be—Please don't worry on that score; there's a scab on it now—a perfect scab.

HLESTACOV: A fortunate thing, that scab. Happy to hear about it. (*With unexpected abruptness.*) Got any money on you?

BOBCHINSKI: Money? What money?

HLESTACOV: A thousand—to lend me.

BOBCHINSKI: I swear to God I have no such sum on me. But perhaps you have, Peter Ivanovich?

DOBCHINSKI: Not on me, I haven't. All my funds, I must inform you, are placed with the Board of Guardians.

HLESTACOV: Well, if you haven't all of a thousand, have you a hundred or so, perhaps?

BOBCHINSKI (*rummaging through his pockets*): Have you a hundred on you, Peter Ivanovich? All I have is forty, in bank notes.

DOBCHINSKI (*looking in his wallet*): All I have is twenty-five.

BOBCHINSKI: Oh, look a little better, Peter Ivanovich! I know you have a hole in your right-hand pocket—surely something must have slipped down the lining of the coat.

DOBCHINSKI: No, really, there's nothing even in the lining.

HLESTACOV: Well, it doesn't really matter. I thought I'd ask. Very well—sixty-five will do. It doesn't matter. (*Accepts money.*)

DOBCHINSKI: I make so bold as to make a request of you, concerning a certain very delicate matter.

HLESTACOV: Just what is it?

DOBCHINSKI: It's of a very delicate nature; my eldest son, may it please you, was born to me before my marriage.

HLESTACOV: Really?

DOBCHINSKI: In a manner of speaking, that is; but he was born to me just as if in wedlock, and I consummated everything properly afterward, through the legal bonds of matrimony, Sir. So, may it please you, I would like him to be an entirely legitimate son of mine, as it were, Sir, and to have him bear the same name as myself: Dobchinski, Sir.

HLESTACOV: Very well, let him be called thus! It can be done.

DOBCHINSKI: I wouldn't trouble you, but I feel sorry for him, on account of his capabilities. He's a lad of great promise; he can recite all sorts of verse and, if a jackknife is handy, he can whittle out a tiny carriage right on the spot, as deftly as any sleight-of-hand artist. There, Peter Ivanovich knows that, too.

BOBCHINSKI: Yes, he's quite a capable lad.

HLESTACOV: Fine, fine—I'll exert myself in this matter; I'll put in a word or two. All this will be managed—I hope. Yes, yes! (*To* BOB-CHINSKI.) Perhaps there's something you wish to say to me?

BOBCHINSKI: Of course—I have a most important request—

HLESTACOV: Well, what is it? What about?

BOBCHINSKI: I beg of you most humbly, when you go to the capital tell all those different high dignitaries, all those senators and admirals, now—tell them that, now, "Your Serenity—or Your Excellency— there's a Peter Ivanovich Bobchinski living in such-and-such a town." Tell 'em just that: "There's a Peter Ivanovich Bobchinski living in such-and-such a town."

HLESTACOV: Very good.

BOBCHINSKI: And should you have occasion to speak to the Sovereign, then tell it to the Sovereign as well; that, now, "Your Imperial Majesty, there's a Peter Ivanovich Bobchinski living in such-and-such a town—"

HLESTACOV: Very good!

DOBCHINSKI: Excuse us for having put you out so with our presence.

BOBCHINSKI: Excuse us for having put you out so with our presence.

HLESTACOV: Not at all, not at all. It has been a great pleasure for me. (*Gets rid of them. Solo.*) There's certainly a slue of officials here. It seems to me, however, that they must take me for a State dignitary. I must have thrown plenty of dust in their eyes yesterday. What a pack of fools! I guess I'll write about all this to the capital, to Tryapichkin. He dashes off articles and things now and then; let him give them a thorough going-over. Hey, there, Ossip! (OSSIP *pops his head through doorway.*) Fetch me paper and ink.

OSSIP: Right away! (*Disappears.*)

HLESTACOV: And as for Tryapichkin, really, if he ever sinks his teeth into anybody, he's a caution! He wouldn't spare his own father to put a joke over. And he's fond of the coin, too. However, these officials are a kindly lot; that's a good trait of theirs, making me all those loans. Let's see, now, how much money I have exactly. There's three hundred —that's from the Judge. There's another three hundred—that's from the Postmaster. Six hundred, seven hundred, eight hundred—what a filthy bill! Eight hundred, nine hundred . . . Oho, it's over a thousand! Well, now, my Captain of Infantry! Well, you just cross my path now! We'll see who will trim whom at stuss! (*Enter* OSSIP, *with paper and ink.*) Well, you fool, you see how they receive and entertain me? (*Begins writing.*)

OSSIP: Yes, glory be to God! The only thing is . . . You know what?

HLESTACOV: Well, what is it?

OSSIP: Make your getaway. Honest to God, it's time.

HLESTACOV (*writing*): What bosh! Why should I?

OSSIP: Oh, just so. God be with all of them! You've had a fine time here for a couple of days; well, let that do you. What's the use of getting tangled up with them for long? Give 'em up! Cut it too fine—and somebody else will come along. By God, that's so, Ivan Alexandrovich! And you can hire such dandy horses here—how they'd dash off with you!

HLESTACOV (*writing*): No. I want to stay on here for a while. We'll go tomorrow, perhaps.

OSSIP: Don't talk of tomorrow! Really, Ivan Alexandrovich, let's get away from here. It's sure a great honor for you, but just the same, you know, it would be better to make tracks as quickly as we can. They must have taken you for somebody else, sure enough—and your father will be ever so angry at you for delaying so long. So really, we ought to dash away in a blaze of glory! And they'd give us fine horses here—

HLESTACOV (*writing*): Very well, then. Only first of all send off this letter, and you might as well get an order for the post horses at the same time. But watch out that you get good horses. Tell the drivers that I'll give a cart wheel to each one of 'em—so's they'll dash along as if I were an Imperial Courier! And so's they'll sing their songs for me! (*Continuing to write.*) I can just imagine it: Tryapichkin will die laughing—

OSSIP: I'll send it off with one of the men here, Sir, whilst I'd better be packing, so's not to waste time.

HLESTACOV (*writing*): Good idea. But bring me a candle.

OSSIP (*going out and speaking off*): Hey there, brother! You'll bring a letter over to the post office, and tell the Postmaster to frank it, and tell 'em to bring up their best troika for my master—a courier's troika—and they'd best be quick about it; as for the mileage, tell 'em my master rides free; tell 'em the mileage is at government expense. And snap it up, all around, for otherwise, now, my master will be angry. Hold on, the letter isn't ready yet.

HLESTACOV (*still writing*): I'm curious—where's he living now? On Post Office Street or Gorohovaya? For he, too, likes to change his rooms often—it's cheaper than paying rent. I'll take a chance and address this to Post Office Street. (*Folds letter, forming it into an envelope, and addresses it.* OSSIP *brings in candle.* HLESTACOV *seals letter.*)

DERZHIMORDA'S VOICE (*off*): Hey there, you with the beard! The orders is not to let nobody in, I'm telling you!

HLESTACOV (*handing letter to* OSSIP): There, get that off.

SHOPKEEPERS (*off*): Let us through, like a good man! You can't keep us out! We're here on business—

DERZHIMORDA'S VOICE: Move on, move on, now! Break it up! He ain't seeing nobody; he's sleeping now. (*Hubbub increases.*)

HLESTACOV: What's going on there, Ossip? See what that noise is.

OSSIP (*looking through window*): Some shopkeepers or other; they want to come in but the policeman won't let them through. They're waving papers—probably want to see you.

HLESTACOV (*walking up to window*): Well, what is it you wish, my dear friends?

SHOPKEEPERS (*off*): We appeal to Your Worship! Sir, order them to accept our petition!

HLESTACOV: Let 'em in—let 'em in! Let 'em come in. Ossip, tell 'em they can come in (*Exit* OSSIP. HLESTACOV *receives the petitions through the window, unrolls one of them and reads it aloud.*) "To His Nobly Born Serenity, Master of Finance, from Abdulin the Merchant—" what the devil is all this; there isn't any such rank or title, as a matter of fact! (*The* SHOPKEEPERS *troop in.*) Well, what is it you wish, my dear friends?

SHOPKEEPERS (*bowing very low*): We prostrate ourselves before Your Worship!—We appeal to your mercy!

HLESTACOV: But just what is it you want?

SHOPKEEPERS: Save us from ruin, Sir!—We suffer grievous and most unjust oppression!

HLESTACOV: From whom?

ABDULIN: Why, it's all because of the Mayor of this here town. Sir, there has never been such another Mayor as this one. He puts such wrongs upon us as are past all describing. He's been the death of us, entirely, what with his billeting and all—we might as well put our heads in the noose. He don't act rightly, he don't. He grabs you by the beard and calls you a furriner and a vagabond. Honest to God! If it were a matter of our not having paid him proper respects, now, in anything; but no, we always does the right thing; we never kick about comin' across with whatever's owin' to him, cloth for his wife's dresses, say, or his daughter's. But no; all that is too little for him, you see. So help us God—so help us! He'll barge into the store and take whatever comes to his hand; if he lays his eyes on a bolt of cloth, he'll say: "Eh, my dear fellow, that's a fine piece of cloth—bring it over to my house!" Well, naturally, you bring it over—and yet there may be all of fifty yards in that bolt.

HLESTACOV: Really, now? Ah, what a swindler he is!

ABDULIN: Honest to God, there's nobody can recall such another Mayor! You simply gotta hide everything in the shop as soon as you catch sight of him—

ANOTHER SHOPKEEPER: We're not saying anything, even, about delicacies of any sort—but he'll grab at all sorts of trash: prunes that may have been mouldering in a barrel for seven years, that no clerk of mine would touch, even—but no, he'll sink his whole paw in that there barrel—

THIRD SHOPKEEPER: When his birthday rolls around, on St. Anthony's day, it sure don't look like we'd overlooked him in any way; there's nary a thing lacking. But no, you gotta to come across with more offerings later—he's got a birthday for every Saint on the calendar! So what can a body do? You give him birthday presents on all the other days as well.

HLESTACOV: Why, he's no better than a highwayman!

ABDULIN: Aye, aye, by God! But you just dare to let a peep out of you, and he'll march a whole regiment up to your house and billet them on you. And, if there's the least objections, he gives orders to put a lock on the shop-door. "I," he says, "ain't goin' to subject you to no corporal punishment, nor to put you to no torture. Them things," he says, "is forbidden by law, but, my dear friend, I'll have you livin' off of herring—and that without a drop of water!"

HLESTACOV: Oh, what a swindler! Why, he ought to be sent straight to Siberia for that!

ABDULIN: Why, it don't really matter where Your Worship may pack him off to—so long, that is, as he's as far from us as possible. Don't disdain our marks of hospitality, our Father. We offer you these here heads of sugar, and this hamper of wine.

HLESTACOV: No, you really must not think that of me; I never take any bribes whatsoever. On the other hand, if you were to suggest lending me three hundred, for example, it might be an entirely different matter; a loan is something I can accept.

SHOPKEEPERS: If you will favor us, our Father!—(*Dig up bills and coins.*) Better take five hundred, only help us out!

HLESTACOV: I won't have a word to say against a loan. If you like, I'll accept it.

ABDULIN (*offering* HLESTACOV *the money on a silver platter*): There, if it please you—take the silver platter at the same time.

HLESTACOV: Very well; I can take the little silver platter as well.

SHOPKEEPERS (*bowing*): Do take the sugar, too, at the same time.

HLESTACOV: Oh, no; I never take any bribes of any sort—

OSSIP: Why don't you take them things, Your Honor? Take 'em! They'll come in handy on the road. Let's have them sugar loaves here, and that hamper! Let's have everything. It'll all come in useful. What you got there—a bit of rope? Let's have that bit of rope too! Even a bit of rope can come in handy; if a cart breaks down, or something like that, it can be spliced together.

ABDULIN: So do us that favor, Your Serenity. For if you don't help us out with our petition, now, then we really don't know what's to become of us; we might as well put our heads in a noose.

HLESTACOV: Absolutely, absolutely! I'll do my best. (*Exit* SHOPKEEPERS.)

WOMAN'S VOICE (*off*): No, you dassen't keep me out! I'll complain against you to the great man himself! Don't you push me so hard—it hurts!

HLESTACOV: Who's that? (*Walks up to window.*) And what's the matter with you, mother?

VOICES OF TWO WOMEN: I ask for your mercy, Father! Master, order them to let us in—hear us out!

HLESTACOV (*through window*): Let 'em come in.

KEYSMITH'S WIFE (*bowing very low before* HLESTACOV *as she rushes on*): I ask your mercy!

CORPORAL'S WIDOW (*same business*): I ask your mercy!

HLESTACOV: Why, who might you women be?

CORPORAL'S WIDOW: I'm the widow of Ivanov—a corporal, he was.

KEYSMITH'S WIFE: I'm a keysmith's wife, living in this town—Thebronia Petrova Poshlepkina; my father was—

HLESTACOV: Hold on; speak one at a time. (*To* KEYSMITH'S WIFE.) What is it you want?

KEYSMITH'S WIFE: I crave your mercy! I am complaining against the Mayor! May God send him every sort of evil, so that neither his children, nor he himself, swindler that he is, nor his uncles, nor his aunts, may have good or gain in anything!

HLESTACOV: Come, what is it?

KEYSMITH'S WIFE: Why, he ordered my husband to be clipped short for a soldier, and yet it weren't our turn yet, swindler that he is! And besides, it's agin the law: my husband's a married man.

HLESTACOV: How could he ever do such a thing?

KEYSMITH'S WIFE: He done it! The swindler, he done it! May God strike him down in this world and the next! And if he's got an aunt, may every nasty thing befall her, and if his father be living, may he croak, the dog, or choke forever and ever, swindler that he is. It was the tailor's son that should have been took, and he's a miserable little drunkard to boot, only his parents come across wth an expensive present, so the Mayor he went after the son of Panteleievna, the merchant's wife; well, Panteleievna in her turn sent the Mayor's wife three bolts of linen; so then he tackles me: "What do you want with a husband?" he says. "He's of no use to you any more." But I'm the one that knows whether he's of any use or not; that's my affair, you scalawag, you. "He's a thief," he says, "he mayn't have stolen nothing yet, but that don't make no difference," he says, "he's goin' to steal; and even without that he'll be took for a recruit next year." Why, what will it be like for me without a husband, you scalawag, you? I'm a weak human critter, you low-down thief, you! May all your kin and kindred never see God's own daylight, and if you've got a mother-in-law, may even your mother-in-law—

HLESTACOV (*getting the old woman out of the room*): Very good, very good! (*Turning to the* CORPORAL'S WIDOW.) Well, and what about you?

KEYSMITH'S WIFE (*leaving*): So don't forget, our Father! Be merciful to us! (*Exit.*)

CORPORAL'S WIDOW: I've come to complain against the Mayor, Father—

HLESTACOV: Yes, but what is it? For what reason? Tell me in a few words.

CORPORAL'S WIDOW: He flogged me, Father.

HLESTACOV: How did that happen?

CORPORAL'S WIDOW: Through a mistake, my Father. Us women folk, now, got in a free-for-all on the market place, but the police didn't get there in time and they caught me instead. And they let me have it so good and hot that I couldn't sit down for two days.

HLESTACOV: But what can one do about it now?

CORPORAL'S WIDOW: Well, naturally, there's nothing to be done now. But you might order him to pay a fine for that there mistake. There ain't no use of me turning down any bit of good luck, and the money would come in right handy now.

HLESTACOV: Very good, very good. Run along, run along. I'll look into it. (*Shoos her out. Hands, waving petitions, are thrust in through window.*) Who else is out there? (*Walks up to window.*) I don't want 'em, I don't want 'em! Don't need 'em, don't need 'em! (*Leaving window.*) I'm fed up with 'em, the devil take it! Don't let anybody in, Ossip!

OSSIP (*shouting out of the window*): Get going! Get going! Come around tomorrow. (*Door is pushed open and some sort of woebegone figure in a shoddy overcoat emerges—unshaven, with a swollen lip and his cheek tied up. Several others appear behind him.*) Get out, get out! What's the idea of barging in here? (*Shoves against intruder's belly and squeezes through door together with him, at the same time slamming door to.*)

MARIA (*entering girlishly*): Ah!

HLESTACOV: What has frightened you so, Ma'am?

MARIA: No, I wasn't frightened—

HLESTACOV (*posturing*): I must say, Ma'am, I'm very much pleased at being taken for the sort of man who. . . . Where did you intend to go, if I may ask?

MARIA: Really, I wasn't going anywhere in particular.

HLESTACOV: But just why weren't you going anywhere in particular?

MARIA: I thought perhaps Mamma dear was here—

HLESTACOV: No, I'd really like to know why you weren't going anywhere in particular—

MARIA: I've intruded on you. You must have been engaged in important matters.

HLESTACOV (*posturing more than ever*): Why, what are important matters compared with your eyes? . . . You couldn't possibly intrude on me; on the contrary, your presence is such a pleasure!

MARIA: You talk just the way they do in the capital—

HLESTACOV: Only to such a bewitching person as yourself. May I offer you a chair—it would make me so happy. But no, you ought to have a throne and not a mere chair—

MARIA: Really, I don't know. . . . I really did have to go. (*Sits down.*)

HLESTACOV: What a beautiful kerchief!

MARIA: Oh, now you're making fun of me! Anything to have a laugh at us provincials!

HLESTACOV: Oh, how I wish I were your kerchief, that I might clasp your little lily-white neck!

MARIA: I absolutely can't understand what you're admiring so; it's just an ordinary kerchief. . . . What queer weather we're having today—

HLESTACOV: But what does any weather matter, Ma'am, compared with your lips?

MARIA: You persist in saying such odd things. . . . I'd like to ask you to write some sort of a little poem for my album instead. You probably know a lot of poems.

HLESTACOV: For you, Ma'am—anything you desire. Merely demand whatever sort of poem you wish.

MARIA: Something sort of. . . . Something good—new.

HLESTACOV: Oh, what do poems matter! I know no end of them.

MARIA: Yes, but tell me—just what will you write?

HLESTACOV: Oh, what's the use of repeating the lines—I can write them down without that!

MARIA: I'm ever so fond of poems—

HLESTACOV: Yes, I've a great stock of them, of all sorts. Well, if you like, I'll give you this one of mine: "All the world's a stage, and all the men and women merely players." Well, now, I've written others, too. Can't remember 'em all now; however, it doesn't really matter. Instead of that I'd rather symbolize my love which, because of your glance—(*Edges his chair nearer.*)

MARIA: Love! I don't understand love. I've never even known what love is—(*Moves her chair away.*)

HLESTACOV: But why do you move your chair away? It'll be better if we sit closer to each other.

MARIA (*moving her chair away*): But why closer? It's just as well if there's some distance between us.

HLESTACOV (*edging his chair nearer*): But why the distance—it's just as well if we're closer.

MARIA (*moving away*): But what's all this for?

HLESTACOV (*edging nearer*): Why, it merely seems to you that the chairs are close together, but what you ought to do is imagine that they're at a distance from each other. How happy it would make me, Ma'am, if I could clasp you in my embraces—

MARIA (*glancing out of the window*): What was that? Something seems to have flown past. Is it a magpie? Or some other bird?

HLESTACOV (*kissing her shoulder and glancing through window*): That's a magpie.

MARIA (*getting up indignantly*): No, this is too much! What impudence!

HLESTACOV (*detaining her*): Forgive me, Ma'am! I did it out of love, purely out of love.

MARIA: You must consider me some sort of a country girl—(*Makes an effort to leave.*)

HLESTACOV (*still detaining her*): Yes, out of love,—really, it was out of love. Don't be angry at me, Maria Antonovna—I was only joking! I'm ready to get down on my knees to beg your forgiveness. (*Falls on his knees.*) Forgive me—do forgive me! There, you see, I'm on my knees before you!

ANNA (*entering and catching sight of* HLESTACOV *kneeling*): Ah, what a situation!

HLESTACOV (*scrambling to his feet*): Eh, the devil take it!

ANNA (*turning on her daughter*): What is the meaning of this, Miss? What sort of behavior is this?

MARIA: Why, Mamma dear, I—

ANNA: Get out of here! Do you hear me—out, out, and don't dare show me your face again! (*Exit* MARIA, *in girlish tears.* ANNA *turns to* HLESTACOV.) Excuse me, please, but I must confess I am so astonished—

HLESTACOV (*aside*): She, too, is most appealing—very far from bad. (*Throws himself on his knees before* ANNA.) Madam, you can see that I am consumed by love!

ANNA: What, you're on your knees? Ah, get up, get up; the floor is so dusty here!

HLESTACOV: I must learn on my knees—absolutely on my knees!—what my fate is to be: life or death!

ANNA: Really, you must excuse me, but I still can't grasp fully the significance of your words. If I'm not mistaken you're making a request for my daughter's hand—

HLESTACOV: No, it's you I'm in love with! My life hangs on a thread. If you do not crown my undying love, then I am unworthy of earthly existence. With my heart being consumed by flames I supplicate your hand—

ANNA: But, if you will permit me to remark, I am, in a sort of a way . . . married!

HLESTACOV: Oh, that! Love knows no such distinctions, and one of our greatest poets has said: " 'Tis but the laws that condemn." We shall withdraw to some shady stream. Your hand—I crave your hand!

MARIA (*dashing in unexpectedly*): Mamma dear, Papa dear said for you to—(*Cries out as she sees* HLESTACOV *kneeling.*) Ah, what a situation!

ANNA: Well, what's got into you? You run in all of a sudden like a cat with conniption fits. There, what do you find so astonishing? What ideas have you gotten into your head? Really, you're like some three-year-old child. It doesn't look in the least as if the girl were eighteen—it doesn't, it doesn't at all! I don't know when you'll become more prudent, when you're going to conduct yourself like a decently brought up young lady, when you will know what the proprieties are, or what decorous demeanor is.

MARIA (*through her tears*): Really, Mamma dear, I had no idea—

ANNA: There's a draft or something blowing through your head all the time; you are taking Judge Lyapkin-Tyapkin's daughters as your example. Why should you look at them? You shouldn't look at them. You have other examples before you; you have your own mother before your own eyes. There, that's the sort of example you ought to follow.

HLESTACOV (*seizing* MARIA'S *hand but addressing the mother*): Do not oppose our well-being—bless a constant love!

ANNA (*in astonishment*): So it's she whom you—

HLESTACOV: Decide: is it life or death?

ANNA (*to* MARIA): There, you see, you fool? There, you see, it's because of you, because of such an insignificant little baggage, that our guest was pleased to get down on his knees. But no, you have to burst in all of a sudden like a madwoman. There, really, it would serve you right if I were deliberately to refuse him; you aren't worthy of such good fortune. (HLESTACOV *gets up, brushes his knees.*)

MARIA: I won't act like that in the future, Mamma dear; I won't, honest!

MAYOR (*dashing in, much upset, to* HLESTACOV): Your Excellency! Do not ruin me! Do not ruin me!

HLESTACOV: What is the matter with you?

MAYOR: Those shopkeepers were complaining to Your Excellency. I assure you on my honor that not even half of what they're saying is true. They themselves deceive the public and give false weights and measures. The Corporal's widow told you a pack of lies if she claimed I flogged her. She lies! I swear to God she lies. She flogged her own self.

HLESTACOV: The Corporal's widow be damned. I have other things on my mind.

MAYOR: Don't you believe her—don't you believe her! They're all such liars—not even a child that high would believe them. Why, the whole town knows them for liars by now. And as for swindling, I make so bold as to inform you that they're swindlers whose like the world hasn't yet produced.

ANNA: Do you know what honor Ivan Alexandrovich is bestowing upon us? He is asking for the hand of our daughter.

MAYOR: What? What? You're out of your head, Mother! Please restrain your wrath, Your Excellency! She's a little touched—and her mother was the same way.

HLESTACOV: Yes, I really am asking for your daughter's hand. I am in love with her.

MAYOR: I find it impossible to believe, Your Excellency.

ANNA: Not even when you're told so?

HLESTACOV: I'm telling you this in all seriousness. I may go out of my head because of love!

. MAYOR: I dare not believe; I am unworthy of such an honor.

HLESTACOV: Yes. If you won't consent to give me Maria Antonovna's hand, I'm ready to do the devil knows what.

MAYOR: I cannot believe it; you are pleased to jest, Your Excellency.

ANNA: Ah, what a blockhead you really are! When he's trying to get the idea into your head!

MAYOR: I cannot believe it.

HLESTACOV: Give her to me—give her to me! I am a desperate man;

I am ready for anything; if I shoot myself you'll be hauled up for trial before the court.

MAYOR: Ah, my God! I'm innocent, body and soul—I swear it, I swear it. Please don't be angry! I'll do whatever your mercy may command me to do! To tell you the truth, my head right now is. . . . I don't rightly know myself what's going on in there. I've become such an utter fool now as never before—

ANNA: Well, give them your blessing! (HLESTACOV *approaches the* MAYOR, *leading* MARIA *by the hand.*)

MAYOR: Ay, may God bless you both—but I'm innocent, I tell you! (HLESTACOV *kisses* MARIA, *while the* MAYOR *stares at them.*) What the devil! It's really true! (*Rubs his eyes.*) They're kissing. Ah, my sainted aunt, they're kissing! He's her bridegroom, sure enough! (*Shouts and hops about in joy.*) Ah, Tony! Ah, Tony! Ah, you Mayor! So that's the way things are going now!

OSSIP (*entering*): The horses are waiting.

HLESTACOV: Ah . . . very well. I'll be ready right away.

MAYOR: What? Are you leaving us?

HLESTACOV: Yes, I'm leaving.

MAYOR: But just when, may I ask? You yourself were pleased to hint, it seems, at a wedding.

HLESTACOV: Why, it'll be for just a minute, so to say. For a single day, to see an uncle of mine—a rich old codger—and I'll start back no later than tomorrow.

MAYOR: I dare not detain you in any way and hope for your propitious return.

HLESTACOV: Of course, of course, I'll be back in a wink. Good-by, my love . . . no, I simply can't express all I feel. Good-by, dearest! (*Kisses* MARIA'S *hand.*)

MAYOR: Isn't there anything you need for your trip, perhaps? You were pleased to say, I think, that you were short of cash.

HLESTACOV: Oh, no, no need of that at all. (*After a moment's reflection.*) On the other hand, why not, if you feel so inclined—

MAYOR: How much would you like?

HLESTACOV: Well, you gave me two hundred that time—that is, not two hundred but four—I wouldn't want to take advantage of your error; so, if you like, give me the same amount now, so's to make it an even eight hundred.

MAYOR: In a moment! (*Takes bills out of his wallet.*) And, as if on purpose, it's all in crisp, new bills.

HLESTACOV: Ah, yes, just so. (*Takes bills and examines them.*) A very good thing, that. For they do say it brings new luck to be given new bills.

MAYOR: Precisely, Sir.

HLESTACOV: Good-by, Anton Antonovich! I'm very much indebted to you for your hospitality. I confess with all my heart that I've never been so well received anywhere. Good-by, Anna Andreievna! Good-by, Maria Antonovna, my love! (*Exit, followed by* OSSIP *and all the others.*)

(*Off*):

HLESTACOV'S VOICE: Good-by, Maria Antonovna, my soul's angel!

MAYOR'S VOICE: But how can you ride in that wretched post carriage?

HLESTACOV'S VOICE: Why, I've gotten used to that. Springs make my head ache.

DRIVER'S VOICE: Whoa, there!

MAYOR'S VOICE: Cover the seat with something, at least—even a mat. Would you care to? I'll order a mat to be brought.

HLESTACOV: No, what in the world for? It's a trifling matter. On the other hand—yes, let 'em bring a mat, if you like.

MAYOR'S VOICE: Hey, there, Avdotya! Go to the storeroom and take out a rug. The best one, the Persian one with the blue background! And be quick about it.

DRIVER'S VOICE: Whoa, there!

MAYOR'S VOICE: When may we expect you, then?

HLESTACOV'S VOICE: Tomorrow, or the day after.

OSSIP'S VOICE: Is that the rug? Let's have it here. Put it down—that's it! Now let's have some hay on this side.

DRIVER'S VOICE: Whoa, there!

OSSIP'S VOICE: Here, put some hay on this side. Right here! Some more! That's fine. Now it'll be grand! (*Slaps rug.*) Now you can take your seat, Your Honor!

HLESTACOV'S VOICE: Good-by, Anton Antonovich!

MAYOR'S VOICE: Good-by, Your Excellency!

FEMININE VOICES: Good-by, Ivan Alexandrovich!

HLESTACOV'S VOICE: Good-by, Mamma dear! (*Sound of a short kiss. Pause. Sound of a prolonged kiss.*)

DRIVER'S VOICE: Giddap, me darlin'! (*Sound of jingle bells, receding.*)

Curtain
(*Slow, coming down completely only as the
last sound of the jingle bells dies away*)

ACT III, Scene 2

Scene: Same evening. At Rise: MAYOR, ANNA, *and* MARIA.

MAYOR: Well, now, Anna Andreievna? Eh? Did you ever think of such a thing as this? What a rich prize, devil take it! There, own up—you never even dreamt of it. From an ordinary Mayor's lady and then—holy hell—to become related to such a devil of a fellow!

ANNA: Not at all. I knew it all along. It's such a rarity for you because you're so common; you've never met any decent people.

MAYOR: Mother, I myself am a decent person. But really, now, when one stops to think of it, Anna Andreievna—what fine-feathered birds you and I have now become! Eh, Anna Andreievna? We can fly high now, the devil take it! You just wait—now's the time when I'll make it hot for all those who were so ready to lodge complaints and denunciations against me! (*Opening door a trifle.*) Hey, who's there? (*Enter* PUGOVITZIN.) Ah, it's you, Pugovitzin! Brother, you just summon all the shopkeepers here. I'll fix those dogs! So they're going to complain against me, are they? Why, the damned pack of Judases! You just wait, my darlings! Up to now I've been just going easy with you; you'll find out what real hell is now! Make a list of every man jack who as much as came here to complain against me. And, above all, make a note of all those writing fellows—all those writing gents, now, who made up the petitions for the others. And proclaim it to everybody, so that all men may know: that, now, just look at what an honor God has bestowed upon your Mayor; he's going to marry his daughter off not to just any old commoner, but to such a grand man as the world has never yet seen, and who can do everything—everything, everything, everything! Proclaim it to everybody, so that all men may know. Cry it out to all the people; ring all the bells till they crack, the devil take it! If there's going to be a celebration, let it be an all-out one! (PUGOVITZIN *withdraws.*) So that's the way things are going, eh, Anna Andreievna? Well, what are our plans now—where are we going to live? Here or at the capital?

ANNA: At the capital, naturally. How could we ever stay on here?

MAYOR: Well, if it's the capital, the capital it is! But it would be well to stay on right here. Well, now, I guess we'll send mayoring to the devil, eh, Anna Andreievna?

ANNA: Naturally! The idea of being a mere Mayor now!

MAYOR: Sure; we can go after a big position in society now. Don't you think, Anna Andreievna? For he's like that (*crosses index and middle fingers of right hand*)—with all the prime ministers and calls at Court; with a pull like that one can work things so's to get in right among the generals. What do you think, Anna Andreievna, can I get in among all those generals, or can't I?

ANNA: I should say so! Of course you can!

MAYOR: Ah, the devil take it, it's swell to be a general! They'll sling a pretty ribbon over my shoulder—and which do you think is better, Anna Andreievna: the red, for the Order of St. Anna, or the blue, for the White Eagle?

ANNA: The blue, of course.

MAYOR: See what the woman has set her heart on! Even a red ribbon would be good enough. Do you know why one wants to be a general? Because, if you have occasion to travel anywhere, you have aides and state couriers galloping ahead of you everywhere you go, demanding horses! And when you get to a post station there won't be anybody getting any horses; every living soul has to bide its turn. All those titled persons, and captains and mayors. But you don't give a good damn, even. You're dining at some governor's—and you simply snub a mayor if you see one standing around! (*Sniggers; sends out peal after peal of laughter; his laughter is simply killing him.*) There, damn it, that's what's so attractive!

ANNA: Anything that is coarse always appeals to you. You must remember that we'll have to change our course of life entirely, that our friends will no longer consist of a hound-loving Judge with whom you go chasing rabbits, or a charity-monger like Zemlyanika; on the contrary, your friends will be of the most ree-fined deportment: counts, and all sorts of society people. The only thing is, I'm really worried about you. At times you'll come out with some such phrase as is never heard in good society.

MAYOR: Damn it, what of it? Words will never hurt you.

ANNA: That sort of thing was well enough when you were Mayor. But life in the capital is altogether different.

MAYOR: Why, they say you can get two particular kinds of fish there so tasty they make your mouth water at the first bite—sea-eels and smelts—

ANNA: All he thinks of is seafood! I absolutely will have things my way. Our house must be the first one at the capital, and my boudoir must be so exquisitely lighted and so scented with ambergris that nobody will be able to set foot in it without puckering up the eyes—like this! (*Blinks her eyes and sniffs daintily.*) Ah, how splendid all this is! (*Enter* SHOPKEEPERS, *sheepishly.*)

MAYOR: Ah, greetings to you, my fine-feathered friends!

SHOPKEEPERS (*bowing deeply*): Greetings to you, Father!

MAYOR: Well, my darlings, how are you getting along? How are your goods moving? So, you tea-swilling, yardstick-swinging swine got a notion of complaining against me, did you? You archknaves, you super-swindlers, you master-cheats and sea-monsters! You're going to complain, eh? Well? Did it get you much? Thought they'd just grab me and clap me into jail! Do you know, may seven devils and a witch take you, that—

ANNA: Ah, my God, what language you're using!

MAYOR (*ruffled*): Eh, I have more than language to think of right now! (*Goes back to badgering the* SHOPKEEPERS.) Do you know that the very same official to whom you were complaining is now going to marry my daughter? What? Eh? What have you got to say now? Now I'll show you! Ooo-oo-oo-oooh! (*Singles out* ABDULIN.) You cheat the public. You'll get a contract from the Treasury, swindle it to the tune of a hundred thousand by supplying rotten cloth, and then sacrifice twenty yards to me—and you expect a medal for it? Why, if they were to know that, they'd take you and. . . . Look at the way he shoves his belly out! He's a businessman; you dassen't touch him; "We won't take no back seat even for no gentry!" Why, a gentleman—damn your ugly-looking puss—a gentleman goes in for learning; even though they may beat him at school it's for a good purpose, so's he'll know whatever is useful. But what about you? You begin with knavish tricks; your boss beats you if you aren't skilled at cheating. While you're still a brat and don't know your paternoster yet, you're already giving short measure, and, soon as your belly fills out and you've got your pockets stuffed, you start in putting on airs! My, my, what a rare fellow! Just because you can drink seventeen samovars dry in a day you think it entitles you to put on airs? Why, I spit in your face, you and your airs!

ABDULIN (*leading the chorus of deeply bowing* SHOPKEEPERS): We're at fault, Anton Antonovich!

MAYOR: Complain, will you? (*Again singling out* ABDULIN.) But who was it helped you to put over that crooked deal when you were building the bridge, and who entered twenty thousand for lumber when there wasn't even a hundred's worth? It was me that helped you, you goat-beard! That's something you forgot. If I'd told on you it would have been my turn to pack you off to Siberia. What have you to say to that? Eh?

ABDULIN: We're at fault before God, Anton Antonovich. The sly Evil One tripped us up. And we'll take our oaths not to complain from now on. We'll make it up to you in any way you like, only don't be angry!

MAYOR: Don't be angry, eh? There, you're groveling at my feet now. Why? Because I've got the upper hand. But if things were going ever so little your way, wny, you dog, you'd grind me into the very mud— and sink me in with a piledriver, on top of everything!

SHOPKEEPERS (*bowing to the* MAYOR'S *very feet*): Don't ruin us, Anton Antonovich!

MAYOR: "Don't ruin us!" Now it's "Don't ruin us!" But what were you saying before? (*Ferociously menacing.*) Why, I ought to take you and—(*With an "I-give-you-up!" gesture.*) Well, let God forgive you! Enough! I'm not the sort to bear a grudge. Only, mind you, walk the chalk line from now on! I'm not marrying my daughter off to just any ordinary squire. So let your congratulations be in keeping—d'you understand? Don't think you can get away with some measly side of salted sturgeon or a head of sugar! There, go, and God go with ye!

(SHOPKEEPERS *crawl out. Enter* JUDGE *and* DIRECTOR OF CHARITIES.)

JUDGE (*in the very doorway*): Am I to believe the rumors, Anton Antonovich? Fortune̦has been very good to you!

DIRECTOR OF CHARITIES: I have the honor of congratulating you on your exceptional good fortune! I was sincerely glad when I heard of it! (*Approaches* ANNA *and kisses her hand.*) Anna Andreievna! (*Repeats business with* MARIA.) Maria Antonovna!

RASTACOVSKI (*entering*): I congratulate Anton Antonovich! May God prolong the lives of yourself and the young couple and give you a numerous posterity—grandchildren and great-grandchildren! Anna Andreievna! (*Approaches* ANNA *and kisses her hand.*) Maria Antonovna! (*Repeats business. Enter* KOROBKIN *and his* WIFE, *and* LULUCOV.)

KOROBKIN: I have the honor of congratulating Anton Antonovich! (*Approaching* ANNA *and kissing her hand.*) Anna Andreievna! (*Repeating business with* MARIA.) Maria Antonovna!

KOROBKIN'S WIFE: I congratulate you with all my heart on your new good fortune, Anna Andreievna!

LULUCOV: I have the honor of congratulating you, Anna Andreievna!

(*Kisses her hand; then, turning to spectators, clicks his tongue with a devil-of-a-fellow air.*) Maria Antonovna, I have the honor of congratulating you! (*Kisses her hand and repeats rest of business. Numerous* GUESTS, *of both sexes, in informal dress, who had been drifting in steadily, crowd around, the men first kissing* ANNA'S *hand, then* MARIA'S, *with exclamations of* "Anna Andreievna!" *and* "Maria Antonovna!" *and the women gushing and kissing* ANNA *and* MARIA. BOBCHINSKI *and* DOBCHINSKI *bustle in, making their way through the thronging guests.*)

BOBCHINSKI: I have the honor of congratulating you, Anton Antonovich!

DOBCHINSKI: Anton Antonovich, I have the honor of congratulating you!

BOBCHINSKI: Congratulations on your good fortune!

DOBCHINSKI: Anna Andreievna!

BOBCHINSKI: Anna Andreievna! (*Both approach at the same time for the hand-kissing ritual and bump their foreheads together.*)

DOBCHINSKI (*kissing* MARIA'S *hand*): Maria Antonovna, I have the honor of congratulating you! You'll be ever so happy; you'll wear a dress of gold and eat all sorts of exquisite soups; you'll have a most amusing time—

BOBCHINSKI (*breaking in*): Maria Antonovna! (*Kissing her hand.*) I have the honor of congratulating you! May God grant you all wealth, lots of gold pieces, and a little rascal of a son, so-o big—(*spreading his arms*)—so that you may dandle him on the palm of your hand—yes, Ma'am! And the little one will keep on bawling all the time—(*Imitates a baby crying. A few more guests go through kissing business with* ANNA *and* MARIA.)

SUPERINTENDENT OF SCHOOLS (*entering with his* WIFE): I have the honor—

HIS WIFE (*running ahead of him*): I congratulate you, Anna Andreievna! (*She and* ANNA *kiss each other.*) Really, now, I was overjoyed. "Anna Andreievna is marrying off her daughter," they tell me. "Ah, my God!" I think to myself, and I was that overjoyed I say to my husband: "Listen, Luka dear—what good luck has come to Anna Andreievna! There," I think to myself, "glory be to God!" And I say to him, I say: "I'm so delighted I'm simply burning up with impatience to let Anna Andreievna know. . . . Ah, my God," I think to myself, "Anna Andreievna was just waiting for a good match for her daughter, and now fate has been so good to her, things fell out just the way she wanted them," and really, I was so overjoyed that I couldn't utter a word. I cry and cry—there, I simply sobbed. So then Luka Lukich he says to me: "What are you sobbing about, Nastenka?"—"Luka, dear," I say to him, "I don't rightly know myself why"—and my tears keep flowing like a river—

MAYOR: I beg you to be seated, ladies and gentlemen. (*Through door.*) Hey, Mishka! Fetch a lot of chairs in here! (GUESTS *seat themselves.* MISHKA *brings in more chairs. Enter* INSPECTOR OF POLICE *and three* POLICEMEN.)

INSPECTOR OF POLICE: I have the honor of congratulating you, Your Honor, and of wishing you a long and prosperous life.

MAYOR: Thank you, thank you. Please be seated, ladies and gentlemen. (*More* GUESTS *seat themselves.*)

JUDGE: Now tell us please, Anton Antonovich, just how all this began—the gradual progress of this matter.

MAYOR: The progress was extraordinary: he was pleased to make a personal proposal—

ANNA (*taking the ball away from him*): Most respectfully, and in the most refined manner. Everything was extraordinarily well put. "I, Anna Andreievna," he says, "am doing this solely out of respect for your personal qualities." And such a splendid, cultured person, of the noblest principles. "Anna Andreievna," he says, "would you believe it, I don't value my life at a bent pin; I am doing this only because I respect your rare qualities."

MARIA: Ah, Mamma dear, it was to me he said that!

ANNA: Stop that; you don't know anything, and don't mix into what is none of your affair! "Anna Andreievna," he said, "I am astonished. . . ." He was profuse with such flattering things. . . . And when I wanted to tell him that we simply dared not hope for such an honor, he suddenly fell down on his knees, and that in the most genteel manner: "Anna Andreievna! Don't make me the most miserable of men! Consent to respond to my feelings, otherwise I'll put a violent end to my life!"

MARIA: Really, Mamma dear, he was saying that concerning me.

ANNA: Why, of course. It concerned you also; I don't deny that in the least.

MAYOR: And he even scared us no end, actually—said he would shoot himself. "I'll shoot myself, so I will!" he says.

CHORUS OF GUESTS: You don't say!

JUDGE: What an odd thing to happen!

SUPERINTENDENT OF SCHOOLS: Ay, verily, Fate must have guided things so.

DIRECTOR OF CHARITIES: No, not Fate, my Father. Fate is a tough old turkey; it's Anton Antonovich's meritorious services that have brought him this. (*Aside.*) Luck will always pop into the snout of a swine like that.

JUDGE: I'd just as lief sell you that young hound we were dickering about, Anton Antonovich.

MAYOR: No, I've bigger fish to fry now than that hound pup.

JUDGE: Well, if you don't want it, we'll come to terms on some other dog.

KOROBKIN'S WIFE: Ah, Anna Andreievna, how glad I am over your good luck! You simply can't imagine!

KOROBKIN: And where, if I may ask, is your distinguished guest at present? I heard that he has left for some reason.

MAYOR: Yes, he has gone away for a day on a very important matter—

ANNA: To see an uncle of his, and ask his blessing—

MAYOR: And ask his blessing; but no later than tomorrow. (*Sneezes. The "God bless you's!" blend and swell into a mighty chorus.*) Thank you all! But no later than on the morrow he's coming back. (*Sneezes. Again a swelling chorus of "God bless you's!" Certain voices are heard above the others.*)

POLICE INSPECTOR'S: I wish you health, Your Honor!

BOBCHINSKI'S: A hundred years and a sackful of gold pieces!

DOBCHINSKI'S: May God prolong your life to forty times forty years!

DIRECTOR OF CHARITIES : Drop dead, you skunk!

KOROBKIN'S WIFE'S: May the devil take you!

MAYOR: I humbly thank you. And I wish you the same.

ANNA: We intend to live in the capital now. For here, I confess, the atmosphere is so . . . far too countryfied! Most uncongenial, I confess. And my husband, now—he'll get a general's rank there.

MAYOR: Yes, ladies and gentlemen, I confess I very much want to be a general, the devil take it!

SUPERINTENDENT OF SCHOOLS: And may God grant that you get to be one!

RASTACOVSKI: What's impossible through human means is possible through the Divine.

JUDGE: A great ship needs deep waters.

DIRECTOR OF CHARITIES: All honor to them that have earned honor.

JUDGE (*aside*) : There, he'll show 'em a thing or two if he ever gets to be a general! There's somebody whom a general's rank fits the way a saddle fits a cow! No, brother, you haven't gotten there yet, not by a long shot. There are folks in this town far better than you, and they aren't generals to this day.

DIRECTOR OF CHARITIES (*aside*): Look at what's actually trying to worm himself in among the generals, devil take it! For all you know, he may really get to be one. For there are enough high airs about him—may the cunning Evil One take him. (*Turning to* MAYOR.) When the time comes, Anton Antonovich, don't forget all about us.

JUDGE: And if anything should turn up—some opportunity in administrative matters—don't leave us without your favor.

KOROBKIN: Next year I'm bringing my youngster to the capital, so that he may serve the government; so do me a favor, extend your patronage to him, take the place of a father to the poor lonely lad.

MAYOR: I'm quite ready; for my part, I'm quite ready to exert myself.

ANNA: Tony, dear, you're always ready with your promises. In the first place, you won't have time to think of such things. And how can you, and for what reason should you, burden yourself with promises?

MAYOR: But why not, dearest? One can do so, now and then.

ANNA: Of course one can, but then there's no use extending patronage to all the small fry.

KOROBKIN'S WIFE (sotto voce, *to another* LADY GUEST): Did you hear how she rates us?

LADY GUEST: Why, she was always like that; I know her—you give her an inch and she'll take a yard—

POSTMASTER (*rushing in, all out of breath and waving an open letter*): An amazing thing, ladies and gentlemen! The official whom we took for the Inspector General wasn't the Inspector General—

ALL: What? He wasn't the Inspector General?

POSTMASTER: Not the Inspector General at all; I found this out through a letter—

MAYOR: What are you saying? What are you saying? From what letter?

POSTMASTER: Why, from a letter which he himself wrote. A letter was brought to me at the Post Office. I look at the address, and I see that it's directed to Post Office Street. I was simply stunned. "Well," I thinks to myself, "he must have come across irregularities in my department and is informing the Administration." So I went and unsealed it.

MAYOR: But how could you ever do it?

POSTMASTER: I don't rightly know myself. Some unnatural force must have impelled me. I had already summoned a special courier in order to send it off posthaste—but such curiosity as I had never before experienced overcame me. I couldn't, I couldn't do it—I felt that I simply couldn't, yet at the same time it was drawing me, simply drawing me to open it. In one ear I hear nothing but: "Hey, there, don't break that seal; your goose is cooked if you do!"—but in the other ear there seems to be some demon sitting: "Break the seal! Break the seal! Break the seal!" And no sooner had I pressed down on the wax than fire seemed to shoot right through my veins, and when I had actually unsealed the letter, by God, I was frozen stiff; my hands were trembling and everything turned black before my eyes.

MAYOR: But how dared you unseal the letter of such an influential personage?

POSTMASTER: Why, that's just where the trick comes in: he's not influential and he's no personage!

MAYOR: What is he then, according to you?

POSTMASTER: Nor fish nor flesh nor good red herring; the devil knows what he is.

MAYOR (*flaring up*): What do you mean by that? How dare you call him nor fish nor flesh nor good red herring—and the devil knows what, on top of that? I'll place you under arrest—

POSTMASTER: Who? You?

MAYOR: Yes, me!

POSTMASTER: You're not big enough.

MAYOR: Are you aware that he is marrying my daughter, that I myself am going to be a high dignitary—that I'll bottle you up in Siberia, no less?

POSTMASTER: Eh, Anton Antonovich! Why talk of Siberia—Siberia's a long way off. I'd better read the letter to you. Ladies and gentlemen! May I have your permission?

ALL: Read it! Read it!

POSTMASTER (*reading letter*): "I hasten to inform you, my dearest friend Tryapichkin, of what wonders have befallen me. On my travels I was cleaned out—but thoroughly!—by a certain Captain of Infantry, so that mine host of the local hostelry was all set to put me in the cooler, when out of a clear sky, owing to my physiognomy and dress being those of a citizen of the capital, the whole town took me for a governor-general, or something. And now I am living at the home of the Mayor, having the time of my life, and running after the Mayor's wife and daughter for all I am worth. The only thing is, I haven't made up my mind which one to start up with; I think I'll tackle the mother first, because it looks as if she were ready to grant one any favors right off the bat.—Do you remember what tough times you and I used to have, trying to get our meals without paying for them, and how once, in a pastry shop, the proprietor grabbed me by the collar because I had eaten some tarts and wanted to charge them to the account of His Britannic Majesty? Things are altogether different now. They all lend me money, as much as I wish. And they're all frightfully quaint here. You'd die laughing. I know you write short things of all sorts; find a place for them in your work. First of all, there's the Mayor; he's as stupid as a gray gelding—"

MAYOR: Impossible! There's nothing of the sort in the letter—

POSTMASTER (*showing* MAYOR *the letter*): Read it yourself!

MAYOR: "—as stupid as a gray gelding—" Impossible! You wrote that yourself.

POSTMASTER: How could I possibly sit down to write a letter like that?

DIRECTOR OF CHARITIES: Read on!

POSTMASTER (*resumes reading*): "—there's the Mayor; he's as stupid as a gray gelding—"

MAYOR: Oh, to hell with all that! Must you keep on repeating it—just as though it weren't there without all that repetition!

POSTMASTER (*resumes reading*): Hmm . . . hmm . . . hmm . . . hmm! "—as a gray gelding. The Postmaster, too, is a good-hearted fellow—" (*Cuts short his reading.*) Well, at this point he expresses himself disrespectfully about me as well—

MAYOR: No, you read it!

POSTMASTER: But what for?

MAYOR: No, devil take it, if you're going to read, then read—read everything!

DIRECTOR OF CHARITIES: Allow me, I'll read it. (*Takes letter, puts on spectacles, and reads aloud.*) "The Postmaster is, down to the least detail, just like Mihei, the watchman in our Department; and, just like Mihei, he must be fond of gin-and-bitters, the scoundrel—"

POSTMASTER (*to spectators*): Well, he's just an atrocious brat who ought to be whipped—that's all!

DIRECTOR OF CHARITIES (*going on with his reading*): "The Director of Chari . . . i . . . i—" (*Begins stammering.*)

KOROBKIN: Well, what are you stopping for?

DIRECTOR OF CHARITIES: Why, his handwriting is rather hard to make out. However, one can see he's a good-for-nothing!

KOROBKIN: Let me have it. There, I think my eyes are better than yours! (*Tries to take letter.*)

DIRECTOR OF CHARITIES (*holding on to letter*): No, this place can be skipped—and it's much easier to read further on—

KOROBKIN: Do permit me—I know all about it.

DIRECTOR OF CHARITIES: Well, as for reading it, I'll read it myself—really, it's all easy to read further on.

POSTMASTER: No, you read everything! After all, everything up to now was read out loud.

ALL: Give it up! Give up that letter! (*To* KOROBKIN.) You read it!

DIRECTOR: Just a minute! (*Surrenders letter to* KOROBKIN.) Here, permit me—(*covers part of letter with forefinger*)—read from here on. (*All surround him.*)

POSTMASTER: Read on, read on! Stuff and nonsense! Read the whole thing!

KOROBKIN (*reading*): "The Director of Charities, Zemlyanika, is a perfect swine—in a skullcap—"

DIRECTOR OF CHARITIES (*to the spectators*): That's supposed to be witty. A swine—in a skullcap. Why, whoever saw a swine in a skullcap?

KOROBKIN (*going on with his reading*): "The Superintendent of Schools is saturated—but saturated!—with the fragrance of onions—"

SUPERINTENDENT OF SCHOOLS (*to spectators*): So help me, I've never so much as tasted onions!

JUDGE (*aside*): Glory be, at least there isn't anything there about me!

KOROBKIN: "The Judge—"

JUDGE (*aside*): There it is! (*Aloud.*) Ladies and gentlemen, I think the letter is much too long, and besides, what the devil is there to it—what's the use of reading such rubbish?

SUPERINTENDENT OF SCHOOLS: Don't stop!

POSTMASTER: Don't stop! Keep on reading!

DIRECTOR OF CHARITIES: Yes, you'd better keep on with the reading.

KOROBKIN (*resumes*): "The Judge, Lyapkin-Tyapkin, is *mauvais ton* to the *n*th degree—" (*Pauses.*) That must be French.

JUDGE: Why, the devil knows what it means! Good thing if it means only "swindler"—but maybe it's even worse than that.

KOROBKIN: "But on the whole they're a hospitable and kindhearted lot. Good-by, my dear friend Tryapichkin. I want to go into literature myself, following your example. It's a bore, brother, to lead the life I do; after all, one wants some spiritual food; I perceive that one must really occupy himself with something or other of a lofty nature. Write to me in the Saratov Province—the Village of Podkatilovka." (*Turns letter over and reads address.*) "To the Right Honorable Ivan Vassilievich Tryapichkin, Saint Petersburg, Post Office Street, House Number Ninety-Seven, within the Courtyard, Third Floor, Turn Right."

LADY GUEST: What an unexpected reprimand!

MAYOR: There! When he set out to slit my throat he slit it from ear to ear! I'm killed, killed, killed entirely! I can't see a thing! All I can see before me are some swinish snouts instead of faces, and not another thing! Bring him back—bring him back! (*Waves his arm.*)

POSTMASTER: How can you bring him back? As if on purpose, I ordered the station-master to give him the very best team of three horses, and on top of that the devil himself must have egged me on to give him an order for all the relays of horses ahead.

KOROBKIN'S WIFE: Well, this is an unparalleled mess, sure enough!

JUDGE: But, devil take it, gentlemen! He took three hundred from me as a loan.

DIRECTOR OF CHARITIES: And three hundred from me, too.

POSTMASTER (*with a sigh*): Oh, and three hundred from me as well.

BOBCHINSKI: He took sixty-five from Peter Ivanovich and me—in bills, Sir. Yes, Sir!

JUDGE (*spreading his hands in bewilderment*): But how can this be, gentlemen? Really, now, how was it he took us in like that?

MAYOR (*striking his forehead*): But what about me? But what about me, now, old fool that I am? I've lost my wits through age, like an old ram! Thirty years of my life have I spent in serving the public; never a businessman, never a contractor could take me in; I hornswoggled swindlers who could show tricks to other swindlers; such cheats and knaves as were wise enough to cheat the whole world did I rope in; three governors have I hoodwinked! But what do governors amount to! (*Deprecating gesture.*) As if governors were even in the running—

ANNA: But this can't be, Tony darling; he's engaged to our Maria—

MAYOR (*really stirred up*): "Engaged!" He's engaged in a pig's eye! Don't go shoving that engagement at me! (*In a frenzy.*) There, look—let all the world, let all of Christianity look—look, all of you, how the Mayor has been made a fool of! Call him a fool, call him a fool, the old, low-down villain! (*Shakes his fist in his own face.*) Hey, there, you with the thick nose! You took a squirt, a rag like that for a person of importance! There, he's eating up the road now, rolling along to the tinkling of his jingle bells! He'll spread this story through the whole world, nor will it be enough that you'll be a general laughing stock. . . . Some scribbler, some waster of good white paper will turn up, and he'll plunk you into a comedy—that's what hurts! He won't spare your rank, your title, and all the people will bare their teeth, grinning and clapping their hands. (*Turning on the spectators.*) What are you laughing at? You're laughing at your own selves! (*With a "What's-the-use!" gesture.*) Eh, you! . . . (*Stamps his feet in frenzied malice.*) I'd take all these wasters of good white paper and—(*roars*) oo-oo-oooooh! You scribblers, you damned liberals! Seed of the devil! I'd tie all of you in a knot, I'd grind you all into powder and shove you in the devil's hip pocket! And in his hat as well! (*Shakes his fist and grinds his boot-heel into the floor. After a brief silence.*) I can't come to myself to this very minute. There, verily: Him whom God would chastise He first deprives of reason. Well, now, what was there about this snot-nose that looked like an Inspector General? Nary a thing! There, not even that much. (*Measures off the very tip of his little finger.*) And suddenly they all set up a chorus: "The Inspector General! The Inspector General!" There, now, who was the first to come out with the rumor that he was the Inspector General? Answer me!

DIRECTOR OF CHARITIES (*spreading his hands*): If you were to kill me I couldn't explain how all this came about; I'm dazed and in a fog, it seems; the devil must have led me astray—

JUDGE: Why, who do you think was the first to come out with that rumor? They're the ones! (*Pointing to* DOBCHINSKI *and* BOBCHINSKI.) Those two fine fellows!

BOBCHINSKI: So help me, so help me, it wasn't me; I never even thought any such thing—

DOBCHINSKI: I didn't do a thing—not a single thing—

DIRECTOR OF CHARITIES: Of course it was the two of you!

SUPERINTENDENT OF SCHOOLS: Of course. They came running from the hotel as if they were mad: "He's arrived, he's arrived, and he won't lay out any money. . . ." You sure found a fine bird that time.

MAYOR: Naturally, it had to be you two! You town gossips, you damned liars!

JUDGE: May the devil take both of you with your Inspector General and your stories!

MAYOR: All you do is snoop through the town and mix everybody up, you damned chatterboxes; you breed gossip, you bobtailed magpies, you!

JUDGE: You confounded bunglers!

SUPERINTENDENT OF SCHOOLS: Dunce caps!

DIRECTOR OF CHARITIES: You potbellied toadstools! (*All surround* BOBCHINSKI *and* DOBCHINSKI.)

BOBCHINSKI: Honest to God, it wasn't me—it was Peter Ivanovich—

DOBCHINSKI: Oh, no, Peter Ivanovich, for you were the first to—

BOBCHINSKI: Oh, no—so there! You were the first—

GENDARME (*entering*): The official sent here in the Emperor's name from Petersburg demands your immediate presence. He is stopping at the hotel. (*All are thunderstruck by his words. An outcry of astonishment escapes all the ladies simultaneously; all the characters, suddenly shifting their positions, become petrified.*)

~ ~ TABLEAU ~ ~

The MAYOR *stands in the center, looking like a post, with outspread arms and head thrown back. To his right are his* WIFE *and* DAUGHTER, *each straining toward him with all her body. Behind them is the* POSTMASTER, *who has turned into a living question mark addressed to the spectators. Behind him is the* SUPERINTENDENT OF SCHOOLS, *most guilelessly nonplused. Behind him, near the very side of the proscenium, are three* LADY GUESTS, *leaning together with the most sarcastic expressions on their faces, meant for the* MAYOR *and still more for his* WIFE *and* DAUGHTER. *To the left of the* MAYOR *is the* DIRECTOR OF CHARITIES, *with his head somewhat cocked, as though he were hearkening to something. Behind him is the* JUDGE, *with his arms spread wide, squatting almost to the ground, and with his lips puckered as if to whistle, or to say, "Oh, my sainted aunt! This is it, sure enough!" Behind him is* KOROBKIN, *turning to the spectators with one eye narrowed and putting over a caustic insinuation concerning the* MAYOR. *Behind him, at the very side of the proscenium, are* DOBCHINSKI *and* BOBCHINSKI, *the arrested motion of their hands directed at each other, their mouths gaping and their eyes goggling at each other. The other* GUESTS *remain where they are, like so many pillars of salt. All the characters, thus petrified, retain their positions for almost a minute and a half.*

Slow Curtain

Vissarion Gregorievich
Belinski
1811 – 1848

"Too bad this Belinski is dead. For we'd have made him rot in prison!"

*From the Frenzied Opinions, during a Political Raid, of the
Redoubtable General Dubbelt, Chief of Gendarmerie, Master
Catchpole of Section III, and Leading Censor.*

"Belinski and his *Letter* are my whole religion."

TURGENEV

IN THE BEGINNING of 1847 Gogol issued his *Choice Passages from Correspondence with Friends*, a book which survives merely as a curiosity, as one of those aberrations from which not even the greatest writers· seem immune. Its chief importance lies in its manifestation of the tabific effect of the Church (or Religion, if you prefer) on the Arts. Somewhat milder but equally unmistakable instances of that effect upon mere talent can be clearly seen even in present-day instances; *Choice Passages,* etc., shows the gorge-raising effect on genius.

Belinski reviewed the book in *The Contemporary,* a review which, despite all the censored deletions, was excoriating and devastating. Gogol, misinterpreting Belinski's wrath as being directed at him and not his book, wrote in protest to the critic. Upon receiving Gogol's letter in the small German town of Salzbrunn, Belinski sat down to his famous answer, in which he uncorked all the vials of his righteous wrath. That answer is an unparalleled indictment and exposé of all the abominations of Nicholas I's Russia. (According to the Editor-Translator's best information at present, the *Letter* is given here for the first time in English.)

It attained enormous circulation in endlessly transcribed copies. Ivan Aksacov (son of the great writer) wrote, even though he had no great love for the critic, "The name of Belinski is known to every youth who is at all given to thinking, to everyone longing for a breath of fresh air amid the stinking quagmire of provincial life. There is not a single high-school teacher in the provincial capitals who does not know Belinski's *Letter to Gogol* by heart. . . . We are indebted to Belinski for our salvation, the honest youngsters tell me everywhere in the provinces." And elsewhere he writes, "If you need an honest man who can commiserate with the ills and misfortunes of the oppressed, an honest doctor, an honest examining judge eager to take part in the good fight —seek for such men in the provinces, among the followers of Belinski."

Belinski devoted three mornings to the writing of this letter. He was "silent and absorbed all the time . . . and strangely agitated," P. Annencov, an eyewitness, tells us. When Herzen heard the letter read, he whispered in Annencov's ear, "It is a work of genius—and, apparently, his testament as well." It was.

Not the least irritating thing to the contemporaries of Russia's greatest critic (born in Finland) was his hardly aristocratic origin. He was the son of a poor navy doctor; his childhood in a miserable Russian provincial town was a wretched one. In 1829 he entered the University of Moscow. His first work, a narrative drama, is significant only as an ardent protest against serfdom, but it was considered "immoral" (a word covering even more sins than charity), and led to threats of exile to Siberia and deprivation of all rights, and in 1832 to exclusion from the University. The next two years were marked by extreme poverty. In 1834 his epochal *Literary Reveries* appeared in *Common Talk,* inaugurating real literary criticism in Russia and making Belinski the arbiter of Russian literature until his death and an influential force for a considerable time thereafter. In 1836 *The Telescope,* with which Belinski was connected, was suppressed and he lost his position. Like Krylov and Gogol he was forced to tutor for coppers and sank to what is a lower form of literary endeavor than even translation: he wrote a Russian grammar. He settled in Petersburg in 1839, where he was overworked and underpaid on *The Notes of the Fatherland.*

Belinski has been called everything, from Raging Vissarion to the Father of the Russian Intelligentsia. He was decidedly the father of genuine criticism in Russia, and the foremost of the westernizers (antiisolationists, in the current phrase, who believed in progress along European lines, but more anticlerical and liberalistic). He had the chief three invaluable prerequisites of the authentic critic: intuition, enthusiasm and pugnacity. Sensitive and prophetic, he had championed modern literature as against the classical and romantic, and saw a realistic literature born in 1846-47. His enthusiasm was the first to hail and encourage Lermontov, Gogol, Koltsov, Dostoievski, among many others. He was the leader of the young, the bogy of the conservative, and a literary revolutionary to the last. His part in the development of Russian literature was great; his services to that literature, which he loved passionately and poignantly, were enormous.

1848 was the year of the Great Petrashevski Cabal, which has been incontrovertibly shown to consist of nothing more than literary evenings devoted to Saint-Simon and Fourier. The *Letter to Gogol* had created a staggering impression on Belinski's contemporaries and had thrown the guardians of the Great Throne into fright and terror. Belinski was under the unrelenting surveillance of the notorious Section III, that noble flower of Nicholas I's ineffable regime. The great critic, haunted by privations throughout life, escaped imprisonment and perpetual hard labor in Siberia by dying of tuberculosis caused by those privations, in May of that great year.

Letter to Gogol

YOU ARE only partly right in having perceived in my article an *angered* man: that epithet is too feeble and gentle to express the state into which the reading of your book brought me. But you are altogether wrong in ascribing that state to your opinions—which are, truly, not altogether flattering—concerning those who honor your talent. No, there was a more important reason in my case. An outraged sense of self-esteem can be borne, after all, and I would have had sense enough to let the subject pass in silence if the whole matter consisted only thereof, but one cannot bear an outraged sense of truth, of human dignity—one cannot keep silent when, under the cover of religion and the protection of the knout, falsehood and immorality are preached as truth and virtue.

Yes, I loved you with all the passion with which a man who has blood ties with his land can love its hope, honor, glory—one of its great leaders on the path of consciousness, development, progress.

Translated by Bernard Guilbert Guerney. Copyright, 1943, by the Vanguard Press, Inc.

And you had a fundamental reason to be disturbed, if for but a moment, in your calm spiritual state, upon losing the right to such a love. I am not saying this because I consider my love as a reward for great talent, but because, in this respect, I represent not one person but a multitude of persons, the greater number of whom neither you nor I have seen, and who in their turn have also never seen us. I am in no position to give you the least conception of that indignation which your book aroused in all noble hearts, nor of those screams of savage joy which were set up on its appearance by all your enemies, both the nonliterary (the *Chichicovs,* the *Nozdrevs,* the *Mayors*) [1] and the literary, whose names are well known to you. You yourself perceive that even people who obviously are of the same spirit as the spirit of your book have backed away from it. Even if it had been written as a result of a profound, sincere conviction— even then it would have been bound to create the same impression upon the public. And if it has been received by everybody (with the exception of a few people whom one must see and know in order not to be overjoyed by their approval) as a crafty but far too unceremonious trick of attaining through a celestial means a purely earthly goal, you alone are at fault. And this is not in the least astonishing—the astonishing thing is, however, that you should find it astonishing. I think this is due to the fact that your profound knowledge of Russia is only that of an artist and not of a man of profound thought, the rôle which you so unsuccessfully took upon yourself in this fantastic book of yours. And that, not because you are not a thinking man, but because for so many years you have become accustomed to looking upon Russia from your *beautiful, far-off place*; [2] and yet it is well known that there is nothing easier than to see objects from afar the way we want to see them, inasmuch as in this *beautiful, far-off place* you live an utter stranger to it, within yourself, deep within you, or in the monotony of a circle that is attuned even as you are and impotent to resist your influence upon it. For that reason you have not observed that Russia sees its salvation not in mysticism, not in asceticism, not in pietism, but in the successes of civilization, of enlightenment, of humanity. It is not preachments that Russia needs (she has heard them aplenty!), nor prayers (she has said them over and over aplenty!), but an awakening among her common folk of a sense of human dignity (for so many ages lost amid the mire and manure) and rights and laws, conforming not with the teaching of the Church but with common sense and justice, and as strict fulfillment of them as is possible. But instead of that Russia presents the horrible spectacle of a land where men traffic in men, not having therefor even that justification which the American plantation owners craftily avail themselves of, affirming that a Negro is not a man; the spectacle of a land where people do not call themselves by names but by sobriquets: Vankas, Vasskas, Steshkas, Palashkas; the spectacle of a country, finally, where there are not only no guarantees whatsoever for one's individuality, honor, property, but where there is even no order maintained by police, instead of which there are only enormous corporations of various administrative thieves and robbers! The livest contemporary national problems in Russia now are: the abolition of the right to own serfs, the abrogation of corporal punishment, the introduction, as far as possible, of a strict fulfillment of at least those laws which already exist. This is felt even by the government itself (which is well aware of what the landowners do with their peasants and how many throats of the former are cut every year by the latter), which is proved by its timid and fruitless half-measures for the benefit of our white Negroes and the comic substitution of a cat-o'-three tails for a knout with but a single lash.

These are the problems with which all Russia is uneasily taken up in her apathetic slumber! And at this very point a great writer, who with his wondrously artistic, profoundly true creations had so mightily assisted in Russia's realization of herself, affording it an opportunity to look at her very self as in a mirror—this writer appears with a book wherein, in the name of Christ and Church, he instructs the landowning barbarian to extract more money out of his peons, instructs him to curse them more. And *that* was not supposed to make me indignant? . . . Why, if you were exposed in an attempt at assassinating me, even then I would not be aroused to as great a hatred of you as over these ignominious lines of yours. . . . And after that you would have people believe in the sincerity of your book's intent! No. If you had been actually filled to overflowing with the truth of Christ and not with the teaching of the Devil, you would have written something altogether different in your new book. You would have told the landowner that, since his peons are his brethren in Christ, and since a brother cannot be slave to his brother, the landowner is consequently bound either to give the peons their freedom or, at the very least, to utilize their labors as much for their benefit as possible, realizing himself, in the very depths of his conscience, in a false position toward them.

And what about your expression *"Oh, you unwashed snout!"* Why, on what Nozdrev, on what Sobakevich did you eavesdrop to get it, to transmit it to the world as a great discovery for the benefit and edification of the muzhiks who, even without that, do not wash themselves because, believing their masters, they themselves do not consider themselves as human beings? And what about your conception of a national Russian system of trial and punishment, the ideal of which you found in the words of a stupid country wife in one of Pushkin's stories [3] and according to the reasoning of which country wife both the innocent and the guilty ought to be flogged alike?

Why, this is often done among us even as it is, although for the most part it is only the innocent one who is flogged among us, if he has nothing to ransom himself with, in which case another proverb applies: He's at fault without any fault! And is it such a book that could have been the result of an arduous inward process, of a high spiritual enlightenment? It cannot be! Either you are ill and ought to be under treatment, or—I dare not finish my thought! . . . Proponent of the knout, apostle of ignorance, champion of obscurantism and Cimmerian darkness, panegyrist of Tatar morals—what are you about? Look under your feet—why, you are standing on the brink of an abyss!

Can it be possible that you, the author of the *Inspector General* and *Dead Souls*—can it be possible that you sincerely, from your very soul, have sung a hymn to the abominable Russian clergy, placing it immeasurably above Catholic clergy? Let us suppose that you do not know that the latter at one time amounted to something, while the former has never been anything save the servant and slave of secular power; yet is it really possible that you are unaware that our clergy is now held in universal contempt by Russian society and the Russian people? About whom is it the Russian folk tell a filthy story? About the priest, the priest's wife, the priest's daughter, and the priest's hired hand. Whom do the Russian folk call a breed of crazy fools? The priests. Isn't the priest in Russia the representative to all Russians of gluttony, miserliness, servility, shamelessness? And apparently you don't know all this? Strange! According to you the Russian folk is the most religious in the world—which is a lie! The basis of religiousness is piety, reverence, fear of God. But the Russian utters the name of God even as he scratches himself. . . . He says of a holy image: If it works, pray before it; if it don't work, use it for a pot cover.

Look a little more intently and you will see that this is a profoundly atheistic folk. There is still a great deal of superstition in it, but there isn't even a trace of religiousness. Superstition passes with the advances of civilization, but religiousness often contrives to live side by side with those advances, a living example of this being France, where even now there are many sincere Catholics among enlightened and cultured people, and where many who have put aside Christianity still stand up stubbornly for some god or other. The Russian folk isn't like that: mystic exaltation is not in its nature; it has too much common sense for that, and clarity and positiveness of mind, and therein, it may be, lies the enormous scope of its historic destinies in the future. Religiousness did not take even among its clergy, for a few isolated, exceptional individuals distinguished for such a chill ascetic consciousness do not prove a thing. But the majority of our clergy has always been distinguished solely for potbellies, scholastic pedantry, and savage ignorance. It is a sin to accuse the Russian folk of religious intolerance and fanaticism; it is rather to be praised for its exemplary indifference to this faith business. Religiousness has manifested itself among us only among the Schismatic sects, so opposed in their spirit to the mass of the people and so insignificant in numbers by comparison with it.[4]

I am not going to dilate on your dithyramb about the love-ties of the Russian folk with its potentates. I will come right out with it: this dithyramb did not meet with sympathy from anyone and has lowered you in the eyes of people who approach you in their general tendency. As far as I personally am concerned, I leave it to your conscience to drink in the contemplation of the divine beauty of autocracy (it's ever so restful, and profitable besides); only continue to contemplate it prudently from your *beautiful, far-off place*; near at hand it isn't so beautiful and not so safe. I will make only one remark: when the religious spirit takes possession of some European, especially a Catholic, he becomes an accuser of unrighteous power, like unto the Hebrew prophets, who denounced the lawless actions of the powerful ones of this earth. But with us, on the contrary, when a man (even a decent one) is overcome by that disorder which is known among the psychiatrists by the name of *religiosa mania,* he will at once proceed to burn more incense to the earthly god than the heavenly, and will also slop over the edges so that even if the thurified one wanted to reward him for his slavish zeal, he yet sees that he would thereby compromise himself in the eyes of society—he is a low-down beast, is our brother, the Russian!

I have also recalled that you affirm in your book as a great and incontrovertible truth that, apparently, literacy is not only of no benefit to the common folk but downright harmful. What can one tell you in answer to that? Yea, may your Byzantine God forgive you for this Byzantine idea—provided that, when you put it down on paper, you were not aware of what you were saying. But you may say, perhaps: "Let us suppose that I had erred, and that all my ideas are false, yet why is my right to err being taken away from me, and why won't people believe in the sincerity of my errors?" Because, I answer you, such a tendency has been no novelty in Russia for a long time. Even quite recently it was exhaustively exploited by Burachok [5] and his fraternity. Of course, there is a great deal more intellect and even talent in your book than in their works (although the book does not exactly abound in either); but, nevertheless, they developed the doctrine they held in common with you with greater energy and greater consistency, boldly reached its ultimate results, rendered full meed to the Byzantine God, leaving nothing over for Satan; whereas you, desiring to put up a taper both to the one and the other, fell into contradiction—defending, for example, Pushkin, literature, and the theater, all of which, from your point of view (if you only had the conscientiousness of consistency), cannot contribute in the least to the salvation of the soul, but can contribute a great deal to its perdition. . . . Whose head, then, could digest the thought of the identity of Gogol and Burachok? You have placed yourself too high in the regard of the Russian people to have it believe the sincerity of such convictions in you. That which seems natural in foolish men cannot seem so in a man of genius. Some people arrived at the notion that your book is the fruit of a mental derangement, close to downright madness. But they soon rejected such a conclusion; it is clear that the book was not written in a day, nor a week, nor a month, but probably in a year, or two, or three; there is a coherence about it; through a careless exposition one can see cogitation, while the hymn to the powers-that-be neatly feathers the nest of the pious author here on earth. That is why they have spread the rumor through Petersburg that you apparently wrote the book to get a berth as a tutor to the son of the Heir Apparent. Even before this there was common knowledge in Petersburg of your letter to Uvarov,[6] wherein you say with mortification that your works about Russia are given a perverted interpretation, and further on reveal dissatisfaction with your former productions and declare that you will rest content with your works only when the Czar will be content with them. Judge for yourself, then: is it to be wondered at that this book of yours has lowered you in the eyes of the public, both as a writer and, what is more, as a man?

You, as far as I can see, do not understand the Russian public very well. Its character is determined by the condition of Russian society, in which fresh forces are seething and straining to burst forth but, crushed by severe oppression, finding no escape, induce only despondence, ennui, apathy. Only in literature alone, despite the Tatar censorship, is there still life and a forward movement. That is why the title of writer is held in such esteem among us, that is why literary success is so easy among us, even for a writer of but small talent. The title of poet, the calling of a litterateur, have long since dimmed among us the tinsel of epaulets and many-hued uniforms. And that is why among us any so-called liberal tendency is especially rewarded by universal attention, even if a talent seem poor, and that is why the popularity of great talents who give themselves up sincerely or insincerely to the service of Orthodoxy, autocracy, and nationalism declines so quickly. Pushkin is a striking example: he had to write but two or three Your-loyal-subject poems and put on the livery of a Chamberlain in order to be deprived suddenly of his people's love! [7] And you err greatly if you are seriously thinking that your book failed, not because of its evil tendency, but because of the trenchancy of the truths which you claim to express to all and sundry. Let us say that you might be able to think this of the writing brethren, but how could the public ever fall into that category? Can it be that in *The Inspector General* and *Dead Souls* you told it less bitter truths, less trenchantly, with lesser verity and talent? For the Old Guard, true enough, raged against you to the verge of frenzy, yet *The Inspector General* and *Dead Souls* did not fail because of that, whereas your latest book has been the most dismal of failures. And herein the public is right: it sees in its writers its only leaders, its paladins against, and saviors from, autocracy, Orthodoxy, and nationalism, and for that reason, always ready to forgive a writer a poor book, it will never forgive him a pernicious one. This demonstrates how much fresh, healthy instinct (even though in embryo) there lies in our society, and it demonstrates that that society has a future. If you love Russia, rejoice together with me at the failure of your book! . . . I will say to you, not without a certain feeling of self-satisfaction, that it seems to me I know the Russian public a little. Your book frightened me with the possibility of a bad influence on the government, on the censorship, but never on the public. When the rumor spread through Petersburg that the government wanted to print your book in an edition of many thousand copies and sell them at the very lowest price, my friends were despondent; but I immediately told them that, despite everything, the book would not meet with success and would be soon forgotten. And, actually, it is now memorable more because of all the articles about it than for itself. Yes, the instinct for truth lies deep within the Russian, even though that instinct is not developed as yet.

Your attitude may even, perhaps, have been sincere, but the idea of bringing it to the attention of the public was most unfortunate. The times of naïve piety have long since gone by, even in our society. It already understands that it makes no difference where a man does his praying, that Christ is sought in Jerusalem only by people who have never borne Him within their breasts, or by those who have lost Him. He who is capable of suffering at the sight of another's suffering, he who finds painful the spectacle of others being oppressed—that man bears Christ in his bosom, and that man has no need of making a pilgrimage on foot to Jerusalem. The resignation preached by you is, in the first place, nothing new and, in the second, smacks on the one hand of fearful pride and, on the other, of the most disgraceful debasement of one's human dignity. The idea of becoming some sort of abstract paragon, of rising superior to all men through resignation, can only be the fruit either of pride or of feeblemindedness, and in both instances inevitably leads to hypocrisy, sanctimoniousness, Celestial quietism. And in addition to that, in your book you allow yourself to express, with cynical nastiness, not only your opinions concerning others (which would have been merely impolite), but even concerning your own self —which is downright vile, for if a man who slaps the cheeks of a fellow-man arouses indignation, then a man who slaps his own arouses nothing but contempt. No, you are merely groping in the dark and are not at all enlightened; you have grasped neither the form nor the spirit of the Christianity of our time. It is not the truth of Christianity's teaching which is wafted from your book, but a sickly fear of death, of the Devil and Hell.

And what sort of language, what sort of phrases do you use? Can it be that you think the use of apocopate elisions means expressing oneself in Biblical language? What a great truth it is that, when a man gives himself up wholly to falsehood, intellect and talent desert him! If your name were not displayed on your book, who would ever think that this pompous and slovenly crazy quilt of words and phrases is the creation of the author of *The Inspector General* and *Dead Souls?*

But, as far as I am concerned, I repeat to you: you were mistaken in thinking my review an expression of vexation at your comment on me as one of your critics. If that had been the only thing that had angered me, it would have been the only thing on which I would have commented with vexation, but should have expressed myself about all the rest calmly, without prejudice. . . . It was your book that lay before me and not your intentions; I read it and reread it a hundred times, and still did not find in it anything except what is in it, and that which is in it stirred me deeply and affronted my soul.

If I gave free rein to my feelings, this letter would shortly turn into a thick notebook. I never thought of writing to you on this subject, even though my desire to do so was excruciating, and though you had given, in print, permission to all and sundry to write to you without any ceremony, solely with the truth in view. Living in Russia I would never have been able to do this, inasmuch as the Shpekins [8] at the Customs unseal the letters of utter strangers not merely for their own pleasure but in the line of duty, to lodge secret information. This summer incipient tuberculosis has driven me abroad, and Necrassov has forwarded your letter to me at Salzbrunn, which I am leaving this very day for Paris with Annencov, through Frankfort-on-the-Main. The unexpected receipt of your letter gave me the opportunity of having my say about everything that was lying on my soul against you on account of your book. I can't say things by halves. I can't be crafty—it isn't in my nature. Let you, or time itself, prove that I erred in my conclusions concerning you. I will be the first to rejoice thereat, but will not repent of what I have told you. Here the matter has to do neither with my personality nor yours, but with a subject not only far higher than myself but even yourself. Here the matter has to do with truth, with Russian society, with Russia.

And here is my last, concluding word: if you have had the misfortune to repudiate with proud resignation your truly great works, you ought now, with sincere resignation, repudiate your last book and to expiate the heavy sin of having brought it into the light of day through bringing forth new creations, which would be reminiscent of your former ones.

Salzbrunn, 15th of *July,* 1847.

---

[1] *Chichicov* is the swindler-hero of *Dead Souls; Nozdrev* is a blusterer and braggart in the same novel; the *Mayor* is the tyrant and boss of a provincial town in *The Inspector General.*

[2] *Dead Souls,* Book One, Chapter 12.

[3] The Commandant's wife, in *The Captain's Daughter.*

[4] In the overlong chronicle of human idiocy, a history of the Russian Old-Faith Schismatics (the Raskolniki or Dissenters, Old Believers, Splitters, Heretics, and Sectarians) would make not the least fascinating and weird section in the chapter headed "Religion." The Great Cleavage began about the middle of the XVIIth century over (of all things!) a matter of translation: the Patriarch Nikon, among other Church reforms, insisted on a revision of the sacred writings; the adherents of the good old religion, Russian style, preferred to cling to the old versions, with all the old errors due to translators, scribes, and copyists. After the split with the Greek Catholic (or Orthodox) Church, the Dissenters proceeded to split into the Priestly Sect and the Nonpriestly Sect. The Priestly Sect split into the Accepters of Austrian Priests and the Nonaccepters of Austrian Priests. The Accepters split into Circuiteers and Anticircuiteers. To go back: of the Nonaccepters the White Priest Sect is the most prominent, accepting only priests who come over from the Orthodox Church. To go back still further: the Nonpriestly Sect fell into almost innumerable sects, taking their names from their founders (Vikulovshchians, Aristovshchians, Ryabinovshchians, etc., etc.); from the region of origin (the Vetcovskoe Accord, the Pomorskoe Accord, etc.); or from some particular tenet: Wanderers or Runners, Medal-Bearers, Nonpayers, Judaizers, Spirit-Wrestlers, Molokani (Puritans), and such really charming sects as Flagellants and Castrators.

Inhuman persecutions made them fly to the most distant regions, thus helping to settle vast but wild Russia; they were dispersed even as far as China and Canada. Unbelievable persecution bred unbelievable fanaticism; to escape their inquisitors the Raskolniki resorted, gloryingly, to self-holocausts, self-noyades, burials alive, the hunger-death, and the Beautiful (or Red) Death: strangulation-by-request. By the beginning of this century the number of these Sectarians (the designation now generally accepted) was estimated at ten million. To get a vivid picture of the early persecutions of these Sectarians, reread Merezhcovski's *Peter and Alexis* (especially Book 10: *The Red Death*); for equally vivid pictures of Russian mysticism under the last Czar, read Bunin's *Aglaia, I Say Nothing* and *The Sacrifice,* in his volume of short stories, *The Gentleman from San Francisco.*

The world certainly does advance. After all, we haven't lynched, mobbed, and imprisoned so very many Jehovah's Witnesses. The crucifying Penitentes of our Southwest and the ophiolators down in Ol' Kaintuck seem to be tolerated, phallic idolatry right on the Merrick Highway arouses no comment, and arborolatry is quite *comme il faut* in the very heart of Harlem—among the whites even more so than the Negroes.

[5] S. A. Burachok (1800-1878), writer; editor of *The Beacon,* a reactionary journal which preached complete stagnation of social life.

[6] S. S. Uvarov (1786-1855) maintained, while Minister of Popular Education, a policy of bringing up the youth in a spirit of "autocracy, Orthodoxy, and nationalism."

[7] This idea of the great critic is profoundly erroneous. At the time of writing he was not in a position to know all the circumstances of the last years of Pushkin's life. The bestowal of a post as Chamberlain was due solely to the desire of Nicholas I to humiliate the poet and to deprive him of any opportunity to leave the Court. Pushkin accepted this favor with sharp indignation but was unable to express it openly.

[8] The letter-opening Postmaster in *The Inspector General.*

Jvan Sergheievich
Turgenev
1 8 1 8 - 1 8 8 3

Turgenev was eminent as a writer, but he was, at the same time, grand
as a man. . . . His conscience was the conscience of a people.

ERNEST RENAN

Even his contempt is not a cold contempt. There is always a soul in his
voice.

GEORG BRANDES

Great fellows the Russians for the telling of a story; the best storytellers
are the Russians, and the best amongst them was Turgenev.

GEORGE MOORE

THE TURGENEVS rank with the
Pushkins and the Tolstois as of the
warp and woof of Russia's history.
And Spasskoe-Lutovinovo, the family estate of the Turgenevs (more
specifically the estate of the great
writer's mother), while it did not become a world shrine like the Tolstois'
Yasnaya Polyana, was more fantastic
than even the Pushkins' Michaelov-
skoe. There were five thousand serfs;
the house serfs alone numbered more
than twoscore—some of them assigned solely to feeding pigeons.
The three-story house was enormous:
it had an orchestra of serf musicians,
a choir of serf singers, a theater of
serf actors, a special police force of
serfs, and a family doctor who had
studied medicine in Germany but
was nevertheless a serf and no whit
better treated than any other. The
writer's grandmother had clubbed
a serf to death with her own hands

for having been too slow in fetching some trifle, and his mother thought nothing of personally knouting a serf or exiling him to a remote village and separating him from his wife and children, and never accorded any serf the dignity of his real Christian name, always tagging on the canine ending of *ka*. Turgenev's mother (see *First Love* for her portrait, as painted by the son himself) seems to have been more than a match for Saltycov's in cruelty and tyranny and Necrassov's father in bestial savagery, even when her dependents were not serfs: her treatment of a young protégée paralleled that of the old Countess' treatment of Lise in the *Queen of Spades*; Ivan was her favorite son—and was beaten the most, "almost daily," according to his own words. As in the cases of Saltycov and Necrassov, the daily scenes of uncurbed seigniorial despotism left a lifelong mark on the soul of the future writer and were the cause of his hatred for and revulsion against serfdom. "In my eyes the foe had a definite image, had a known name," he wrote later. "This foe was serfdom. Under that name I gathered and concentrated all that I had decided to contend against to the bitter end, with which I resolved never to make peace. This was my Hannibal's oath—and I was not the only one who took it then." [1]

As at the Pushkins' Michaelov-

skoe, there was a great library—and the books were also mostly French. French and German were spoken for the most part—Russian was good enough only for the serfs. And just as Pushkin had in his wonderful old nurse his intermediary with the Russian folk, Turgenev, the future great master of Russian prose, first learned the Russian language and its literature from a serf, an old man who used to read to the "young massa" in secret. It was also from serf Nimrods that he acquired his lifelong passion for hunting.

Turgenev entered the University of Moscow at fifteen, a year later changing to the University of Petersburg, where he formed his first literary acquaintances. In 1833 he went to Berlin to round out his studies and there made further literary contacts. It was under the impact of his life abroad that he became an ardent Westernizer, for which he was subjected to attacks by the Slavophiles (professional one-hundred-per-cent Russians). In 1840, after a brief stay in Russia and a journey to Italy, he came back to Berlin, where he shared quarters with M. A. Bakunin, later on to become famous as an anarchist. Next year Turgenev returned to Russia, and in 1842 entered the chancellery of the Minister of the Interior. His reaction to civil service seems to have been similar to that of Gogol

---

[1] Another Turgenev, Nicolai Ivanovich (1789-1871), was also a powerful antagonist of serfdom and was sentenced to death, *in absentia*, for his part in the unfortunately unsuccessful uprising of December 14, 1825. It is to the eternal credit of England that she refused to yield to Nicholas I's demand for his extradition.
—*Editor.*

(even though he worked under V. I. Dahl, the great lexicographer and proverbiologist, also well known as a writer under the pen name of Cossack Luganski), and he resigned in 1843. In the same year he took his first serious literary step with the publication of *Parasha*—without, however, putting his name thereto—and made the acquaintance of Belinski, who had reacted very favorably to the poem. But by 1846 he realized that poetry was not his forte and was contemplating abandoning literature entirely. But his great talent as a prose writer was revealed by a short sketch, *Hor and Kalinich,* published by Necrassov in 1847 and followed by a whole series of similar pieces. These were collected and published as the *Hunting Sketches* (1852) and played an enormous and fruitful role in the emancipation of the serfs. At any rate, the publication of this book and, in the same year, of an essay on the death of Gogol was enough to win him the usual recognition which the government extended to practically all Russians of talent or genius. In Turgenev's case it took the form of a month in the "precinct jail" and two years of forced residence at his country estate. The last half of the fifties and the beginning of the sixties saw the publication of *Rudin* (1856), *A Nest of Gentlefolk* (1858), *On the Eve* (1860) and, most important of all, *Fathers and Sons* (1862), which created an unprecedented furore.

Dickens, the superb master of character, seemed unable to create heroines with anything but sugar-water in their veins. Turgenev, whose heroines are superb creations, seemed unable to fashion his heroes out of anything but the best grade of cardboard. When he needed a strong hero for *On the Eve,* it was pointed out that he had made Insarov, that hero, not a Russian but a Bulgarian. Was the master incapable of producing a real hero who would also be a Russian?

Turgenev, who prided himself on keeping his finger on the pulse of the public, on his sensitivity to the trends of the times, brought forth *Fathers and Sons.* Bazarov was something new in the way of heroes—with a vengeance—and Russian became enriched with the new words *nihilist* and *nihilism.* Words change their meaning with time; it must be pointed out that Bazarov was not a terrorist but a crass materialist, realist, iconoclast, atheist.

Turgenev had created Bazarov *con amore* and with admiration. But the reception accorded this new hero was more than what his creator had bargained for. Every author expects bouquets and brickbats; what hurts is to have the bouquets come from your lifelong foes and the brickbats from those you had considered your friends. And that was exactly what happened to Turgenev. "What a true picture of our impossible youth!" all the reactionaries praised his creation. "This boor and bore Bazarov is nothing but a gross caricature of idealistic Young Russia!" said the revolutionary youth he loved so well. True enough, somewhat later the brilliant and radical young critic Pisarev came nearer the mark and proudly accepted Bazarov as a true type of the realistic young Russian, and, life once more apparently imitating art, the very youngest radicals made Bazarov their ideal and nihilism their religion.

Whatever the stature of *Fathers and Sons* as literature and whatever its historical significance may be, its greatest importance lies in its effect upon the life of its author. He had sensed the trend of the younger generation all too keenly and paid the penalty of the prophet. The hurt inflicted upon him never healed: sixteen years after the publication of *Fathers and Sons,* and only five years before his death, he voiced his feelings in his poem in prose, *Thou Shalt Hear the Judgment of the Fool*—a title taken from Pushkin. Being of less tough fiber than Lescov, who had also had his misunderstandings with the hair-triggered radicals, Turgenev went abroad (where his reputation was by now secure) and did not return to Russia again except for infrequent and short visits. And as if to bear out the claim of the critics that he had written himself out, he produced practically nothing until

1867, when his *Smoke* appeared. His last novel, *Virgin Soil,* was published ten years later.

His last years were spent in agonizing ill health. He died in Bougival (on the Seine, near Paris) ; autopsy revealed cancer of the spine, which had destroyed three vertebrae.

The reader who does not know Russian, French, or German has but Hobson's choice between the translations of Turgenev's "complete" works by Garnett and Hapgood. He will do much better to haunt the stalls of the second-hand booksellers for the many early translations of the individual works done into English not from the original but from French or German versions. In the case of Turgenev this advice is sound, rather than absurd, since he himself had kept an eye on the French versions, at least. He did not deem it unworthy of him to translate Flaubert's *Herodias* into Russian. But, curiously enough, one of his last works was written in French and translated into Russian by someone else, though under his guidance; another he dictated, on what was to be his deathbed, in French, German, and Italian.

Fathers and Sons

Dedicated to the memory of
Vissarion Gregorievich Belinski

I

"WELL, Peter? Anything in sight yet?" was the question asked on May 20, 1859, by a gentleman of a little over forty, in dusty coat and checked trousers, as he came out without his hat on to the low steps of the posting station at S——. He was addressing his servant, an apple-cheeked young fellow, with whitish down on his chin and with tiny, lackluster eyes.

The servant, in whom everything—the turquoise ring in his ear, the streaky hair plastered with grease, and the civility of his movements—indicated a man of the new, perfected generation, glanced with an air of indulgence along the road and made answer:

"No, Sir; nothing in sight yet."

"Nothing in sight?" repeated his master.

"No, Sir, nothing in sight," reiterated the man.

His master sighed, and sat down on a small bench. We will introduce him to the reader while he sits, his feet tucked under, pensively looking about him.

His name is Nicolai Petrovich Kirsanov. He has, twelve miles from the posting station, a fine property of two hundred serfs, or, as he expresses it (since having arranged the division of his land with the peasants and started a "farm"), of nearly five thousand acres. His father, a general in the army, who had fought in 1812 during the Napoleonic invasion, a coarse, half-educated, but not an ill-natured man, and a typical Russian, had been in harness all his life, first in command of a brigade and then of a division, and had lived constantly in the provinces, where, by virtue of his rank, he played a fairly important part. Nicolai Petrovich was born in the South of Russia like his elder brother, Paul, of whom more hereafter. He had been educated at home till he was fourteen, surrounded by cheap tutors, his father's free-

New translation. Copyright, 1943, by the Vanguard Press, Inc.

and-easy but toadying adjutants, and all the usual regimental and staff set. His mother, one of the Kolyazin family, as a girl called Agathe, but as a general's wife Agathocleia Kuzminishna Kirsanova, was one of those matriarchal officer's ladies who take their full share of the duties and dignities of office. She flaunted gorgeous caps and swishing silk dresses; in church she was the first to advance to the cross; she talked a great deal in a loud voice, let her children kiss her hand in the morning, and gave them her blessing at night—in fact, she got everything out of life she could. Nicolai Petrovich, as a general's son— though so far from being distinguished by courage that he even deserved to be called something of a coward—had been intended, like his brother Paul, for the army; but he broke his leg on the very day when the news of his commission came, and, after spending two months in bed, retained a slight limp throughout his life. His father gave him up as a bad job and let him go into the Civil Service. He took his son to Petersburg as soon as he reached eighteen, and placed him in the University. His brother Paul happened about the same time to be made an officer in the Guards. The young men started living together in one set of rooms, under the remote supervision of a cousin on their mother's side, Ilya Kolyazin, an official of high rank. Their father returned to his division and his wife and merely sent his sons at infrequent intervals large sheets of gray paper, scrawled over in a bold clerkly hand. The bottom of these sheets was graced by a signature surrounded by sundry flourishes and curlicues: Petrus Kirsanov, Major General.

In 1835 Nicolai Petrovich left the University, a graduate, and in the same year General Kirsanov was put on the retired list after an unsuccessful review and came to Petersburg with his wife and settled there. He was about to take a house in the Tavricheski Gardens, and had joined the English club, but he died suddenly of an apoplectic fit. Agathocleia Kuzminishna soon followed him; she could not accustom herself to a dull life in the capital; she was consumed by the ennui of existence away from the regiment.

Meanwhile Nicolai Petrovich had already, in his parents' lifetime and to their no slight chagrin, managed to fall in love with the daughter of his landlord, a petty official by the name of Prepolovenski. She was pretty and what was called an "advanced" girl; she used to read the serious articles in the Science columns of the magazines. He married her as soon as his period of mourning was over and, leaving the Civil Service in which his father's influence had procured him a post, was perfectly blissful with his Mary, first in a country villa near the Forestry Institute, afterward in town in a pretty little flat with a spick-and-span staircase and a rather cold drawing room, and then in the country, where he settled finally and where in a short time a son, Arcadii, was born to him. The young couple lived very happily and peacefully; they were scarcely ever apart; they read together, sang and played duets together on the piano; she tended her flowers and looked after the poultry yard; he sometimes went hunting, and busied himself with the estate, while Arcadii grew and grew in the same happy and peaceful way.

Ten years passed like a dream. In 1847 Kirsanov's wife died. He almost succumbed to this blow; in a few weeks his hair turned gray; he was getting ready to go abroad, thinking to find some distraction, at least. But then came the fateful year 1848. He returned unwillingly to the country and, after a rather prolonged period of inactivity, began to take an interest in improvements in the management of his land. In 1855 he brought his son to the University; he spent three winters with him in Petersburg, hardly going out anywhere and trying to make the acquaintance of Arcadii's young companions. The last winter he had not been able to go, and here we see him in the May of 1859, already quite gray, stoutish, and rather bent, waiting for his son, who had just taken his degree, as once he had taken one himself.

The servant, from a feeling of propriety, and also, perhaps, because he was not anxious to remain under the master's eye, had gone to the gate and was smoking a pipe. Nicolai Petrovich bent his head and began staring at the timeworn steps; a big mottled chick was walking sedately over them, treading firmly with its large yellow feet; a muddy cat gave him an unfriendly look, twisting herself coyly around the railing. The sun was scorching; from the half-dark passage of the posting station came an odor of rye bread fresh out of the oven.

Nicolai Petrovich fell to dreaming. "My son—a graduate . . . Arcadii—" were the ideas that kept mulling in his head; he tried to think of something else, and again the same thoughts returned. He remembered his dead wife. "She did not live to see it!" he murmured sadly.

A plump, bluish-gray pigeon flew into the road and hurriedly went to drink in a puddle near the well. Nicolai Petrovich began looking at it, but his ear had already caught the sound of approaching wheels.

"It sounds as if they're coming, Sir," announced the servant, popping in from the gateway.

The father jumped up and fixed his eyes on the road. A carriage appeared with three posting horses harnessed abreast; in the carriage he caught a glimpse of the blue band of a student's cap, the familiar outline of a dear face.

"Arcasha! Arcasha!" cried Kirsanov, and he started to run, waving his arms. A few instants later his lips were pressed to the beardless, dusty, sunburnt cheek of the youthful graduate.

I I

"Let me get some of the dust off first, Dad," said Arcadii in a voice tired from traveling, but boyish and clear as a bell, as he gaily responded to his father's caresses. "I'm making you all dusty."

"Never mind, never mind," the father kept repeating, smiling tenderly, and he brushed the collar of his son's cloak and his own overcoat with his hand. "Let's have a look at you, let's have a look at you!" he added, moving back from him, but immediately he went with hurried steps toward the yard of the station, calling: "This way, this way! And let's get horses at once!"

The father seemed far more excited than his son; he seemed a little confused, a little timid. Arcadii stopped him.

"Dad," he said, "let me introduce you to my great friend, Bazarov, about whom I've so often written to you. He's been so good as to promise to stay with us."

Nicolai Petrovich went back quickly and, going up to a tall man in a long, loose, rough coat with tassels, who had only just got out of the carriage, he warmly pressed the ungloved rough hand, which the latter did not at once hold out to him.

"I am heartily glad," he began, "and very grateful for your kind intention of visiting us. May I ask your name, and your father's?"

"Eugene Vassiliev," answered Bazarov in a lazy but manly voice; and as he turned back the collar of his rough coat Nicolai Petrovich could see his whole face. Long and lean, with a broad forehead, a nose flat at the bridge but pointed at the tip, large greenish eyes, and sandy drooping side whiskers, it was lighted by a tranquil smile and showed self-confidence and intelligence.

"I hope, dear Eugene Vassilyich, you won't be bored at our place," continued Nicolai Petrovich.

Bazarov's thin lips moved just perceptibly, though he made no reply, merely taking off his cap. His long, thick hair did not hide the prominent bumps on his head.

"Well, Arcadii," Nicolai Petrovich began again, turning to his son, "should fresh horses be harnessed at once, or would you prefer to rest here?"

"We'll rest at home, Dad; tell them to harness the horses."

"Right away, right away," the father assented. "Hey, Peter, do you hear? Get things ready, brother; look sharp."

Peter, who as a modernized servant had not approached to kiss the young master's hand, but merely bowed to him from a distance, again vanished through the gateway.

"I came here with the carriage, but there are three horses for your coach, too," said the father fussily, while the son drank some water from a metal dipper brought him by the woman in charge of the station and Bazarov lit a pipe and went up to the driver, who was unharnessing the horses. "There are only two seats in the carriage, and I don't know how your friend will manage—"

"He'll go in the coach," interposed Arcadii in an undertone. "You mustn't stand on ceremony with him, please. He's a fine fellow, so simple—you'll see."

The elder Kirsanov's coachman brought out the horses.

"Come, get a move on, bushy beard!" said Bazarov, addressing the driver of the hired horses.

"Did you hear, Mityuha," put in another driver, standing by with his hands thrust behind him into the opening of his sheepskin coat, "what the gentleman called you? And you are a bushy beard at that."

Mityuha tossed his head so that his hat slipped and pulled the reins off the heated shaft horse.

"Look sharp, look sharp, lads, lend a hand," cried Nicolai Petrovich; "there'll be something to drink our health with!"

In a few minutes the horses were harnessed; the father and son were installed in the carriage; Peter clambered up on the box; Bazarov jumped into the coach and nestled his head down into the leather cushion, and both the vehicles rolled away.

III

"So here you are, a graduate at last, and come home again," said Nicolai Petrovich, patting Arcadii now on the shoulder, now on the knee. "At last!"

"And how is Uncle? Quite well?" asked Arcadii, who, in spite of the genuine, almost childish delight filling his heart, wanted as soon as possible to turn the conversation from the emotional into a commonplace channel.

"Quite well. He was thinking of coming with me to meet you, but for some reason or other he gave up the idea."

"And have you been waiting for me long?" inquired Arcadii.

"Oh, about five hours."

"Dear old Dad!"

Arcadii turned round quickly to his father and kissed his cheek resoundingly. The father laughed softly.

"What a fine horse I have for you!" he began. "You'll see. And your room has been freshly papered."

"And is there a room for Bazarov?"

"We'll find one for him, too."

"Please, Dad, be good to him. I can't tell you how highly I value his friendship."

"Have you made friends with him lately?"

"Yes, quite lately."

"Ah, that's why I didn't see him last winter. What is he taking up?"

"His chief subject is natural science. But he knows everything. Next year he wants to take his doctor's degree."

"Ah! he's studying medicine," observed Nicolai Petrovich, and he was silent for a little. "Peter," he went on, pointing, "aren't those our peasants driving along?"

Peter looked where his master was pointing. Some carts harnessed with unbridled horses were moving rapidly along a narrow side road. In each cart there were one or two peasants in unbuttoned sheepskin coats.

"Yes, Sir," replied Peter.

"Where are they going—to town?"

"To town, I suppose. To the pothouse," he added contemptuously, turning slightly toward the coachman, as though he would appeal to him. But the latter did not budge; he was a man of the old stamp and did not share the modern views of the younger generation.

"I'm having a lot of bother with the peasants this year," Nicolai Petrovich went on, turning to his son. "They won't pay their rent. What's to be done?"

"But do you like your hired hands?"

"Yes," Nicolai Petrovich said through his teeth. "The trouble is they're being set against me and they aren't doing their best yet. They spoil harness. They haven't tilled the land badly, though. But everything will come out right in the end. Why, are you interested in farming now?"

"You've no shade—that's your main trouble," remarked Arcadii, without answering the last question.

"I've had a great awning put up on the north side over the balcony," observed Nicolai Petrovich; "now we can even dine in the open air."

"It'll be too much like a summer villa. However, that's all nonsense. But what fine air here! How delicious it smells! Really, it seems to me you won't find such fragrance anywhere in the world as in the meadows here! And this sky, too—"

Arcadii broke off abruptly, cast a stealthy look behind him, and said no more.

"Of course," observed the father, "you were born here, and so everything is bound to strike you as something extraordinary—"

"Come, Dad, it makes no difference where a man is born."

"Still—"

"No; it makes absolutely no difference."

Nicolai Petrovich gave a sidelong glance at his son, and the carriage went on half a mile farther before the conversation was renewed between them.

"I don't remember whether I wrote you," the father began, "but your old nurse, Yegorovna, is dead."

"Really? Poor old thing! But Procophich is still living?"

"Yes, and not a bit changed. Grumbles as much as ever. In fact, you won't find many changes in Maryino."

"Have you still the same manager?"

"Well, to be sure, I've made a change there. I decided not to keep about me any freed house serfs or at least not to entrust them with duties of any responsibility." (Arcadii glanced toward Peter.) *"Il est libre, en effet,"* [1] observed Nicolai Petrovich in an undertone, "and,

[1] "He is practically free."

besides, he's only a valet. Now I have a townsman as a manager; he seems a practical fellow. I pay him two hundred and fifty rubles a year. But," he added, rubbing his forehead and eyebrows, which was always an indication with him of inward embarrassment, "I told you just now that you wouldn't find changes at Maryino. That's not quite correct. I think it my duty to prepare you, although—"

He hesitated for an instant and then went on in French.

"An austere moralist would regard my frankness as uncalled for; but, in the first place, the matter can't be concealed and secondly, you're aware that I have always had peculiar ideas as regards the relation of father and son. Though, of course, you'd be right in blaming me. At my age . . . In short, this—this girl, about whom you've probably heard already—"

"Phenichka?" Arcadii asked without any embarrassment.

Nicolai Petrovich turned red. "Don't mention her name aloud, please. Well, yes—she's living with me. I have installed her in the house—there were two little rooms there. However, all that can be changed."

"Heavens, Dad, what for?"

"Your friend is going to stay with us . . . it's awkward—"

"Please, don't be uneasy on Bazarov's account. He's above all that."

"Well, after all, you have to be considered," Nicolai Petrovich added. "That small wing of the house is so horrid—that's the worst of it."

"Heavens, Dad," interposed Arcadii, "you seem to be apologizing; how is it you're not ashamed?"

"Of course, I ought to be ashamed," answered the father, turning redder and redder.

"Nonsense, Dad, nonsense; please don't!" Arcadii smiled affectionately. "What a thing to apologize for!" he thought to himself, and his heart was filled with a feeling of condescending tenderness for his kind, softhearted father, mixed with a sense of secret superiority. "Please don't," he repeated once more, instinctively reveling in a consciousness of his own advanced and emancipated condition.

Nicolai Petrovich glanced at him through the fingers of the hand with which he was still rubbing his forehead, and something like a pang went through his heart. But he at once accused himself.

"Here's where our fields start," he said, after a long silence.

"And that's our forest ahead, I think?" asked Arcadii.

"Yes. Only I have sold the timber. They'll be cutting it down this year."

"Why did you sell it?"

"I needed money; besides, that land is to go to the peasants."

"Who don't pay you their rent?"

"That's their affair; however, they'll pay it some day."

"I'm sorry about the forest," observed Arcadii, and he began to look about him.

The country through which they were driving could hardly be called picturesque. Field after field stretched away to the very horizon, fields now sloping gently upward, now dropping down; here and there one could see small woods and winding ravines with low, scanty brushwood—recalling vividly those so very quaintly represented on the old-fashioned maps of the times of Catherine the Great. They also came across small rivers with hollowed-out banks, and tiny ponds with wretched dams, and hamlets with small, squat hovels under dark roofs, their thatching often half gone, and small barns all askew, with walls woven of brushwood and gaping doorways beside neglected threshing floors, and churches, some brick-built, with stucco peeling off here and there, others of wood, with leaning crosses and utterly neglected graveyards.

Arcadii's heart was sinking little by little. As if by arrangement, the peasants they met were all tattered and torn and on the sorriest little nags; the willows, with their trunks stripped of bark and their branches broken, stood like ragged beggars along the roadside; gaunt and shaggy cows that looked as if they had been gnawn were greedily nibbling the grass along the ditches. They looked as though they had just struggled free from the death-dealing claws of some sinister being, and, evoked by the piteous appearance of the weakened, starved beasts, there arose in the midst of the lovely spring day the white phantom of joyless, endless winter with its blizzards and frosts and snows.

"No," Arcadii reflected, "this is no rich region; it scarcely impresses one either with plenty or industry. It can't, it can't go on like this, reforms are absolutely necessary. But how is one to carry them out, how begin?"

Thus did Arcadii ponder. But even as he pondered, the spring was coming into its own. All around him was golden green, everything—trees, bushes, grass—gave off a sheen and undulated sweepingly and gently under the soft breath of a warm breeze; everywhere the larks trilled in endless rivulets of song; the lapwings were enigmatically calling as they hovered over the low-lying meadows or ran noiselessly over the tussocks of grass; the rooks strutted among the half-grown short spring grain, standing out picturesquely black against its tender green; they disappeared in the already whitening rye, their heads alone peeping out at rare intervals amid its misty waves. Arcadii gazed and gazed, and little by little his reflections grew fainter and vanished. He flung off his overcoat and turned to his father, with a face so bright, so very boyish, that the latter gave him another hug.

"We haven't far to go now," remarked Nicolai Petrovich. "All we have to do is top that little hill and we'll be in sight of home. We'll live splendidly, Arcadii; you'll help me in farming the estate, if it isn't a bore to you. We must draw close to each other now and learn to know each other thoroughly, mustn't we?"

"Of course," said Arcadii. "But what a marvelous day this is!"

"To welcome you, my soul. Yes, it's spring in its full glory. However, I agree with Pushkin—do you remember in *Eugene Oneghin*—

> " 'How sad to me thy coming is,
> Spring, spring, the time of love?' "

"Arcadii!" Bazarov's voice called from the coach, "send me a match; I've nothing to light my pipe with."

Nicolai Petrovich stopped, while Arcadii, who had begun listening to him with some surprise, though also not without sympathy, made haste to pull a silver matchbox out of his pocket and sent it to Bazarov by Peter.

"Will you have a cheroot?" shouted Bazarov again.

"Thanks," answered Arcadii.

Peter came back to the carriage and, as he returned the matchbox, also handed Arcadii a thick black cheroot which the latter promptly lit, diffusing about him such a strong and pungent odor of fermented tobacco that Nicolai Petrovich, who had never smoked in his life, willy-nilly had to turn his nose, although he tried to do it as imperceptibly as he could, so as not to hurt his son's feelings.

A quarter of an hour later the two carriages drew up before the steps of a new wooden house, painted gray, with a red iron roof. This was Maryino, also known as New Borough, or, as the peasants had dubbed it, Lackland Croft.

IV

No throng of house serfs ran out on to the steps to meet the masters; the only one to appear was a little girl of twelve, shortly followed by a young lad, very like Peter, dressed in a gray livery jacket with white armorial buttons, the servant of Paul Petrovich Kirsanov. Without speaking, he opened the door of the carriage and then unbuttoned the apron of the coach. Nicolai Petrovich with his son and Bazarov walked through a dark and almost empty hall, from behind the door of which they caught a glimpse of a young woman's face, into a drawing room furnished in the latest taste.

"Home at last," said Nicolai Petrovich, taking off his cap and shaking back his hair. "The most important thing now is to have supper and then rest."

"A meal would not come amiss, certainly," observed Bazarov, stretching himself, and he sank on to a sofa.

"Yes, yes, let's have supper—supper right away." Nicolai Petrovich, for no apparent reason, stamped his feet. "And there's Procophich, just in time."

A man about sixty entered, white-haired, thin, and swarthy, in a brown coat with brass buttons and a pink neckerchief. He smirked, went up to kiss Arcadii's hand, and, after a bow to the guest, retreated to the door and put his hands behind him.

"There he is, Procophich," Nicolai Petrovich began. "He's come back to us at last. Well, how does he look to you?"

"As well as could be," said the old man, and smirked again, but immediately thereafter knit his bushy brows. "Do you wish supper to be served?" he asked impressively.

"Yes, yes, please. But wouldn't you like to go to your room first, Eugene Vassilyich?"

"No, thanks; it is not necessary. Just tell them to bring up my terrible suitcase—and this garment, too," he added, taking off his loose overcoat.

"Certainly. Procophich, take the gentleman's coat." (Procophich, with an air of perplexity, picked up Bazarov's "garment" in both hands and, holding it high above his head, tiptoed out.) "And you, Arcadii, are you going up to your room for a minute?"

"Yes, I must wash," answered Arcadii, and was just starting for the door, but at that instant a man of medium height, dressed in a dark English suit, a fashionable low cravat, and kid shoes, entered the drawing room. This was Paul Petrovich Kirsanov. He looked about forty-five: his close-cropped gray hair shone with a dark luster, like new silver; his face, yellow but free from wrinkles, was exceptionally regular and pure in line, as though carved by a light and delicate chisel, and showed traces of remarkable good looks; especially fine were his clear, black, almond-shaped eyes. The whole mien of Arcadii's uncle, exquisite and thoroughbred, had preserved the gracefulness of youth and that air of striving upward, of spurning the earth, which for the most part is lost after the twenties are past.

Paul Petrovich took out of his trouser pocket his exquisite hand with its long tapering pink nails, a hand which seemed still more beautiful because of the snowy whiteness of the cuff, buttoned with a single big opal, and gave it to his nephew. After a preliminary handshake in the European style, he kissed him thrice after the Russian fashion, that is to say, he touched his cheek three times with his fragrant mustache, and said, "Welcome."

Nicolai Petrovich presented him to Bazarov; Paul Petrovich greeted him with a slight inclination of his supple figure and a slight smile, but he did not offer him his hand, and even put it back in his pocket.

"I'd begun to think you weren't coming today," he began in a musical voice, swaying genially and with a shrug of the shoulders, as he showed his splendid white teeth. "Anything happen on the road by any chance?"

"Nothing happened," answered Arcadii. "We were just delayed a little. But we're as hungry as wolves now. Hurry up Procophich, Dad, and I'll be back right away."

"Wait, I'm coming with you," Bazarov called out, suddenly rising from the sofa. Both young men went out.

"Who is he?" asked Paul Petrovich.

"A friend of Arcadii's. A very clever fellow, according to him."

"Is he going to stay with us?"

"Yes."

"That unkempt creature?"

"Why, yes."

Paul Petrovich drummed with his finger tips on the table.

"I think Arcadii *s'est dégourdi*," [1] he remarked. "I'm glad he has come back."

At supper there was little conversation. Bazarov in particular said practically nothing, but he ate a great deal. Nicolai Petrovich related

---

[1] Is more at his ease.

various incidents in what he called his career as a farmer, talked about the impending government measures, about committees, deputations, the necessity of introducing machinery, and so on. Paul Petrovich paced slowly up and down the dining room (he never ate supper), sipping a glass of red wine at infrequent intervals and more often uttering some remark or rather exclamation, in the nature of "Ah! Aha! Hm!" Arcadii told some news from Petersburg, but he was conscious of a little awkwardness, that awkwardness which usually overtakes a youth when he has just ceased to be a child and has come back to a place where the people are accustomed to regard him as a child and to treat him as such. He made his sentences quite unnecessarily long, avoided the word "dad," and once even replaced it by the word "father," mumbled, it is true, between his teeth; with an exaggerated carelessness he poured into his glass far more wine than he really wanted and drank it all off. Procophich did not take his eyes off him, and merely kept chewing his lips. They all separated as soon as supper was over.

"You've got a rather queer uncle," Bazarov said to Arcadii as he sat in his dressing gown by his bedside, drawing hard at a short pipe. "Just imagine such style in the country! His nails, his nails—you ought to send them to an exhibition!"

"But you don't know," replied Arcadii. "He was a lion in his day. I'll tell you his story some day. For he was a dandy; used to turn all the women's heads."

"Oh, so that's it? So he keeps it up in the memory of the past. It's a pity there's no one here for him to fascinate, though. I kept staring at his amazing collar. Like marble, and his chin's shaved ever so close. Come, Arcadii Nikolaich, isn't that ridiculous?"

"Perhaps; but he's a fine man, really."

"An antique! But your father is a good fellow. He's wasting his time reading poetry, and he hardly knows much about farming, but he's a kindhearted fellow."

"My father is one man in a thousand."

"Did you notice how shy he is?"

Arcadii shook his head as though he himself were not shy.

"An astonishing thing," Bazarov went on, "these little old romantics, they develop their nervous systems till they break down—naturally all balance is upset. However, good night. There's an English washstand in my room, but you can't lock the door. Still, English washstands ought to be encouraged—an English washstand stands for progress!"

Bazarov went away, and a sense of great joyousness came over Arcadii. It is sweet to fall asleep in one's own home, in the familiar bed, under a quilt worked by loving hands, perhaps the hands of his dear nurse, those kind, tender, untiring hands. Arcadii recalled Yegorovna and with a sigh wished her the kingdom of heaven. For himself he made no prayer.

Both he and Bazarov were soon asleep, but others in the house were awake long after. His son's return had excited Nicolai Petrovich. He lay down in bed, but did not put out the candles, and, with head propped on his hand, he thought long thoughts. His brother sat in his study until long past midnight, in a beautifully made, roomy armchair before the fireplace, on which the coals were smoldering into faintly glowing embers. Paul Petrovich had not undressed, save that red Chinese heelless slippers had replaced the kid half boots. He held in his hand the last number of *Galignani's Messenger,* but he was not reading; he gazed fixedly into the grate, where a bluish flame flickered, dying down, then flaring up again. God knows where his thoughts were wandering, but they were not wandering in the past alone; his expression was concentrated and grim, which is not the case when a man is absorbed solely in recollections. And in a small back room, a young woman in a blue, warm, sleeveless jacket, with a white kerchief thrown over her dark hair, was sitting on a large trunk. This was Phenichka. She was now listening, now dozing, now glancing at the open door through which one could see a child's crib and hear the regular breathing of a sleeping baby.

V

The next morning Bazarov woke up before anyone else and went out of the house. "So!" he thought, looking about him. "This hamlet isn't much to look at!"

When Nicolai Petrovich had divided the land with his peasants, he had had to build his new manor house on eleven acres of perfectly flat and barren land. He had contrived a house, outbuildings and a farm, laid out a garden, dug a pond and sunk two wells; but the young trees grew but poorly, very little water had collected in the pond, and that in the wells turned out to be brackish. Only one arbor of lilac bushes and acacia had grown decently; here they occasionally had tea or dinner. It took Bazarov only a few minutes to cover all the little garden paths, to drop in at the cattle yard and stable, and to come upon a couple of little boys, with whom he made friends at once and took along with him to a small swamp about a mile from the house to hunt for frogs.

"What do you want frogs for, Master?" one of the boys asked him.

"Why, I'll tell you," answered Bazarov, who possessed a peculiar knack of inspiring confidence in people of a lower class, though he never tried to win them and behaved casually with them. "I'll cut the frog open and see what's going on in its insides, and, since you and I are the same as frogs, except that we walk on our hind legs, I'll know what's going on in our insides, too."

"And what do you want to know that for?"

"So's not to make a mistake, if you get sick and I have to cure you."

"Are you a doctor, then?"

"Yes."

"Vasska, do you hear, the gentleman says you and I are the same as frogs. Sounds queer!"

"I'm scairt of frogs," observed Vasska, a boy of seven, with head as white as flax, and his feet bare, dressed in a gray cossackeen with a stand-up collar.

"What's there to be scairt of? They don't bite, do they?"

."There, into the water with you, my philosophers," said Bazarov.

Meanwhile Nicolai Petrovich had awakened in his turn, and went in to see Arcadii, whom he found already dressed. Father and son went out on the terrace under the shelter of the awning; near the balustrade, on the table, among great bunches of lilac, the samovar was already boiling. A little girl came up, the same who had been the first to meet them at the steps on their arrival the evening before.

"Theodosia Nicolaevna isn't feeling quite well," she said in a shrill voice. "She can't come. She told me to ask you, do you want to pour out the tea yourself, or should she send Dunyasha?"

"I'll pour it myself—myself," Nicolai Petrovich quickly cut her short. "How do you like your tea, Arcadii—with cream or lemon?"

"With cream," answered Arcadii, and, after a brief silence, called him questioningly: "Dad?"

Nicolai Petrovich looked at his son in embarrassment.

"What is it?" he asked.

Arcadii dropped his eyes.

"Forgive me, Dad, if my question seems out of place," he began, "but you yourself, by your frankness yesterday, encourage me to be frank in my turn—you won't be angry?"

"Go on."

"You embolden me to ask you. . . . Isn't the reason Phen . . . isn't my presence the reason she won't come here to pour the tea?"

Nicolai Petrovich turned his head away a little.

"Perhaps," he said at last. "She supposes that . . . she feels ashamed."

Arcadii looked up at his father quickly.

"She really shouldn't. In the first place, you are aware of my way of thinking." (Arcadii found it very agreeable to be saying all this.) "And, in the second place, could I be willing to hamper your life, your habits, even in the very least? Also, I'm sure you couldn't make a bad choice; if you've allowed her to live under the same roof with you she must be worthy of it. In any event, a son can't act as his father's judge—I least of all, and, least of all, such a father as yourself, who has never hampered my liberty in any way."

Arcadii's voice had been shaky at first, he felt himself magnanimous, yet at the same time he realized he was delivering something in the nature of a lecture to his father; but the sound of one's own discourses has a powerful effect on man, and Arcadii brought out his last words firmly, even effectively.

"Thanks, Arcadii," said Nicolai Petrovich in a muffled voice, and his fingers again strayed over his eyebrows and forehead. "Your suppositions are quite right. Of course, if this girl really were not worthy . . . this is not a frivolous infatuation. It's awkward for me to talk to you about this, but you understand that it's hard for her to come here, in your presence, especially the first day of your return."

"In that case I will go to her!" Arcadii cried out with a fresh access of magnanimous emotions, and he jumped up from his seat. "I'll explain to her that she has no reason to be ashamed before me."

Nicolai Petrovich got up in his turn.

"Arcadii," he began, "as a favor to me—really, how can you! You'll find there—I haven't told you that—"

But Arcadii was no longer listening to him, and ran off the terrace. Nicolai Petrovich looked after him and sank into his chair in confusion. His heart began to palpitate. Did he at that moment realize the inevitable strangeness of the future relations between him and his son? Was he conscious that Arcadii would perhaps have shown him more respect if he had never touched on this subject at all? Did he reproach himself for weakness? It is hard to say. All these emotions were present

within him, but merely as sensations—and even then vague. And the
flush would not leave his face, and his heart palpitated.

He heard hurrying footsteps, and Arcadii came up on the terrace.
"We've made friends, Dad!" he cried with an expression of a certain
tender and kindly triumph. "Theodosia Nicolaevna is really not quite
well today and she'll come a little later. But why didn't you tell me
I had a brother? I'd have kissed him last night, just as I kissed him
now."

Nicolai Petrovich tried to utter something, tried to get up and open
his arms. Arcadii flung himself on his neck.

"What's this? Hugging again?" they heard the voice of Paul Petrovich behind them.

Father and son were equally glad at his appearance at that moment.
There are situations which are touching enough, yet from which one
nevertheless wishes to escape as speedily as possible.

"Why should you be surprised at that?" said Nicolai Petrovich gaily.
"Think of the ages I've been waiting for Arcadii. I haven't had time
to get a good look at him since yesterday."

"I'm not at all surprised," observed Paul Petrovich; "I wouldn't
mind hugging him myself."

Arcadii went up to his uncle, and again felt the touch of his perfumed mustache on his cheeks. Paul Petrovich sat down to the table. He
wore an exquisite morning suit of English cut, and a small fez adorned
his head. This fez and the negligently tied small cravat hinted at the
ease of country life, but the stiff collar of his shirt—not white, it is
true, with a colored design, as called for in morning wear—propped
up his well-shaved chin with the same inexorability as ever.

"Where's your new friend?" he asked Arcadii.

"He's not in the house; he usually gets up early and goes off somewhere. The main thing is not to pay any attention to him; he doesn't
like ceremony."

"Yes, one can see that." Paul Petrovich began leisurely spreading
butter on his bread. "Is he going to stay with us long?"

"It all depends. He's stopping over on the way to his father's."

"And where does his father live?"

"In our own province, over sixty miles from here. He has a small
estate there. He used to be an army doctor."

"Tut, tut, tut! To be sure, I kept asking myself, 'Where have I heard
that name of Bazarov?' Nicolai, if I remember right, wasn't there a
pillroller by the name of Bazarov in our father's division?"

"I believe there was."

"Right, right! So that pillroller was his father. Hm!" Paul Petrovich's mustache twitched. "Well, and what precisely is M'sieu' Bazarov himself?" he asked drawlingly.

"What is Bazarov?" Arcadii smiled. "Would you like me, Uncle, to tell you precisely what he is?"

"If you will be so obliging, Nephew."

"He's a nihilist."

"What!" escaped from Nicolai Petrovich, while Paul Petrovich lifted a knife in the air with a dab of butter on its tip, and froze in surprise.

"He's a nihilist," repeated Arcadii.

"A nihilist," Nicolai Petrovich managed to say. "That's from the Latin, *nihil, nothing,* as far as I can judge; the word must mean a man who—who recognizes nothing?"

"Say 'who respects nothing,' " put in his brother, and he set to work on the butter again.

"Who regards everything from the critical point of view," observed Arcadii.

"Isn't that the very same thing?" inquired the uncle.

"No, it isn't. A nihilist is a man who does not bow down before any authority, who does not accept any principle on faith no matter what an aura of reverence may surround that principle."

"Well, and is that good?" Paul Petrovich broke in on him.

"It all depends, Uncle. It's good for some, but to others it may be poison."

"So that's it. Well, I see it's not in our line. We old-fashioned folk— we imagine that without principles [he pronounced the word softly, after the French, whereas his nephew, on the contrary, made it harsh, even to accenting the first syllable], principles taken on faith, as you put it, there's no use taking a step, nor drawing a breath. *Vous avez changé tout cela.*[1] God give you good health and the rank of a general, while we'll be content to look on and admire, Messieurs les— what do you call them?"

"Nihilists," Arcadii said, speaking very distinctly.

"Yes. There used to be Hegelists, but now you have nihilists. We shall see how you will exist in a void, in a vacuum. And now please ring, brother Nicolai Petrovich—it's time I had my cocoa."

His brother rang the bell and called "Dunyasha!" But instead of

[1] You've changed all that.

Dunyasha, it was Phenichka herself who came out on the terrace. She was a young woman of about three-and-twenty, all dainty white-ness and softness, with dark hair and eyes, red, childishly plump small lips, and delicate little hands. She wore a neat print dress; a new blue kerchief lay lightly on her soft shoulders. She was carrying a large cup of cocoa and, having set it down before Paul Petrovich, she was over-whelmed with confusion; the hot blood rushed in a wave of crimson over the delicate skin of her endearing face. She dropped her eyes and stood at the table, leaning a little on the very tips of her fingers. Appar-ently ashamed of having come in, she at the same time felt she had a right to come.

Paul Petrovich knit his brows sternly while Nicolai Petrovich looked embarrassed.

"Good morning, Phenichka," he got out through his teeth.

"Good morning, Sir," she replied in a voice not loud but resonant, and with a sidelong glance at Arcadii, who gave her a friendly smile, she quietly withdrew. She walked with a slightly rolling gait, but even this was becoming to her.

For some seconds silence reigned on the terrace. Paul Petrovich sipped his cocoa; then suddenly he raised his head.

"Here is M'sieu' Nihilist coming to visit us," he said in an under-tone.

Bazarov was in fact coming through the garden, striding over the flower beds. His linen duster and trousers were covered with mire; a clinging marsh weed was twined round the crown of his battered round hat; in his right hand he held a small sack with something alive stirring therein. He quickly drew near the terrace and let drop with a nod: "Good morning, gentlemen; sorry I'm late for tea: I'll be back right away—I must find a place for my fair captives."

"What have you there—leeches?" asked Paul Petrovich.

"No, frogs."

"Do you eat them—or breed them?"

"I need them for experiments," Bazarov explained indifferently, and went into the house.

"He's going to cut them up then," observed Paul Petrovich. "He has no faith in principles but he has in frogs."

Arcadii looked regretfully at his uncle, and Nicolai Petrovich shrugged his shoulders stealthily. Paul Petrovich himself felt that his witticism had fallen flat, and began to talk about husbandry and the new manager, who had come to him the evening before to complain that a hired hand by the name of Thoma, "was deboshed" and quite unmanageable. "He's such an Æsop," he said among other things; "he's gotten himself a bad name all over; he'll stay here a while and then walk off in a huff like a fool."

VI

Bazarov came back, sat down to the table, and began drinking his tea hurriedly. The two brothers looked at him in silence, while Arcadii stealthily watched his father and his uncle by turn.

"Did you go far from here?" Nicolai Petrovich asked Bazarov at last.

"You've a small swamp here, close to the aspen grove. I started five snipe or so; you might pothunt them, Arcadii."

"You aren't a hunter, then?"

"No."

"You're studying physics, properly speaking?" Paul Petrovich asked in his turn.

"Physics, yes; and natural sciences in general."

"They say the Germans have of late made great strides in those subjects."

"Yes; we can take the Nemtzi as our masters in that," Bazarov answered negligently.

The word *German* instead of the ordinary *Nemtzi* (Tongue-tied Men) Paul Petrovich had used for the sake of irony, which, however, had gone utterly unnoticed.

"Have you such a high opinion of the Nemtzi, then," Paul Petrovich asked with exaggerated courtesy. He was beginning to feel a secret irritation. His aristocratic nature was revolted by Bazarov's absolute nonchalance. This pillroller's son was not only not abashed—he actually gave abrupt and unwilling answers, and there was something churlish, almost insolent, in the tone of his voice.

"The scientific men there are a practical lot."

"So, so. But you probably have no such flattering notion of the Russian men of science?"

"Yes, if you like."

"That's very praiseworthy self-abnegation," Paul Petrovich declared, drawing himself up and throwing his head back. "But how is

this? Arcadii Nicolaich was telling us just now that you do not acknowledge any authorities whatsoever—that you do not believe in them?"

"But why should I acknowledge them? And what should I believe in?
When anyone talks sense, I agree, and that's all."

"And all the Germans talk sense?" asked Paul Petrovich, and his
face assumed an expression as impassive, as remote, as if he had with-
drawn to some empyrean height.

"Not all," replied Bazarov with a short yawn. He obviously did not
care to continue the debate.

Paul Petrovich glanced at Arcadii, as though he would say to him:
"Your friend is most polite, I must say." "For my own part," he began
again, not without some effort, "I am so unregenerate as not to like
Germans. Russian Germans I am not speaking of now; we all know
what sort of creatures they are. But even German Germans aren't anything I can easily stomach. In former days there may have been some
halfway decent ones; they had—well, Schiller, to be sure, Goethe.
My brother, for instance, is very favorably inclined toward them. . . .
But now they've all turned chemists and materialists—"

"A chemist who knows his business is twenty times as useful as any
poet," broke in Bazarov.

"Oh, indeed," commented Paul Petrovich, and, as though falling
asleep, he faintly raised his eyebrows. "You don't recognize art, then,
I take it?"

"The Art of Making Money, or No More Piles!" cried Bazarov with
a contemptuous laugh.

"Yes, Sir, yes, Sir! You will have your joke, I see. So you reject all,
then? Very well. That means you believe in science alone?"

"I have already explained to you that I don't believe in anything.
And what is science—science in general? There are sciences, as there
are trades and callings; but science in general doesn't exist at all."

"Very good, Sir. Well, and in regard to the other conventions accepted in human conduct, do you maintain the same negative attitude?"

"What is this, a grilling?" asked Bazarov.

Paul Petrovich paled a little. . . . Nicolai Petrovich thought it his
duty to interpose in the conversation.

"We'll converse on this subject with you more in detail some day,
my dear Eugene Vassilyich; we'll learn your views and express our own.
For my part, I'm very glad you're studying the natural sciences. I've
heard that Liebig has made some wonderful discoveries in the fertiliza-

tion of soils. You can be of assistance to me in my agricultural work; you may be able to give me some useful advice."

"I'm at your service, Nicolai Petrovich, but where do we compare with Liebig? One has to learn the *a b c* first before beginning to read, and we haven't set eyes on the alphabet yet."

"Well, you certainly are a nihilist, I can see that," thought Nicolai Petrovich. "Just the same, allow me to apply to you on occasion," he added aloud. "And now, brother, I think it's time for us to be going for a talk with the manager."

Paul Petrovich got up from his seat.

"Yes," he said without looking at anyone, "it's a misfortune to live five years in the country like this, far removed from any mighty intellects! First thing you know, you're a fool among fools. You may try not to forget what you've been taught, but *bang* it turns out to be all rubbish, and you're told that sensible men don't waste their time on such trifles and that, if you please, you're plain old hat. What's to be done? Evidently young people are really more intelligent than we are."

Paul Petrovich turned slowly on his heels and slowly went out; his brother followed him.

"What, is he always like that?" Bazarov coolly inquired of Arcadii, as soon as the door had closed behind the two brothers.

"Look, Eugene, you were much too harsh with him," remarked Arcadii. "You have insulted him."

"Come, am I going to pamper them, these small-town aristocrats? For it's all vanity, dandified habits, foppery. He should have continued his career in Petersburg, if that's his bent. However, God be with him! I've found a rather rare specimen of water beetle, *Dytiscus marginatus*. Do you know it? I'll show it to you."

"I promised to tell you the story——" Arcadii began.

"The story of the beetle?"

"Come, that'll do, Eugene. The story of my uncle. You'll see he's not at all the sort of man you imagine him. He deserves sympathy rather than jeers."

"I don't dispute it, but why are you so concerned over him?"

"One must to be just, Eugene."

"How does that follow?"

"No, listen——"

And Arcadii told him his uncle's story.

VII

Paul Petrovich Kirsanov had at first been educated at home, like his younger brother, and afterward in the Corps of Pages. From childhood he was distinguished by remarkable beauty; moreover, he was self-confident, somewhat mocking, and had a somewhat jaundiced humor—he could not fail to please. He began to be seen everywhere as soon as he had received his commission as an officer. He was made much of and he indulged every whim, even making a fool of himself and posing, but even this was becoming in him. Women lost their heads over him; men called him a coxcomb, and in their hearts envied him. He lived, as has been related already, in the same apartments as his brother, whom he loved sincerely, though he was not at all like him. Nicolai Petrovich limped a little, had delicate, pleasing but somewhat melancholy features, small dark eyes, and thin soft hair; he liked to loaf, but at the same time was fond of reading, and was timid in society. Paul Petrovich never spent an evening at home, prided himself on his daring and agility (it was he who had made a fad of athletics among the beaux), and his entire reading consisted of five or six French books. By twenty-eight he was already a captain; a brilliant career lay ahead of him. Suddenly everything changed.

At that time there was seen in Petersburg society, at rare intervals, a woman who has even yet not been forgotten, a Princess R——. She had a well-educated, well-bred, but rather stupid husband, and no children. She had a way of going abroad suddenly, and of returning just as suddenly to Russia, and, in general, led an eccentric life. She had the reputation of being a frivolous coquette, abandoned herself eagerly to every sort of pleasure, danced to exhaustion, laughed and joked with young men, whom she received in the dim light of her drawing room before dinner, while at night she wept and prayed, unable to find peace in anything, and often paced her room till morning, wringing her hands in anguish, or sat, pale and chill, over the Psalms. Day would come, and she was transformed again into a grand lady; she went out anew, laughed, chattered, and simply flung herself headlong into anything which could afford her the least distraction. She was marvelously well proportioned, her braided hair, the hue of gold and as heavy, came down below her knees, but no one would have called her a beauty; the only good point in her whole face was her eyes, and not even the eyes themselves—they were gray, and not large—

but rather their look, which was swift and deep, insouciant to the point of audacity, and pensive to the point of despondence. An enigmatic glance. There was a light of something extraordinary in them, even while her tongue was babbling the most frivolous inanities. She dressed with elaborate care.

Paul Petrovich met her at a ball, danced a mazurka with her, in the course of which she did not utter a single sensible word, and fell passionately in love with her. Being accustomed to making conquests, he soon attained his object in this instance as well, but his easy success did not dampen his ardor. On the contrary, he became still more excruciatingly, still more closely, attached to this woman, in whom, even at the very moment when she yielded herself irretrievably, there still seemed to remain something hallowed and inaccessible, to which none could penetrate. What was hidden in that soul, God alone knows! It seemed as though she were in the power of some mysterious forces, incomprehensible even to herself; they played with her at will, her intellect was not powerful enough to master their caprices. Her whole conduct presented a series of incongruities; the only letters which could have aroused her husband's just suspicions she wrote to a man who was almost a stranger to her, whilst her love had always an element of melancholy; she would no longer laugh and jest with the one she chose as a lover, and listened to him and gazed at him with a look of bewilderment. Sometimes, for the most part suddenly, this bewilderment would pass into chill horror; her face took on a wild, deathlike expression; she locked herself up in her bedroom, and her maid, putting an ear to the keyhole, could hear her smothered sobs. More than once, as he went home after an assignation, Kirsanov felt within him that heart-rending, bitter vexation which follows a total failure.

"What more do I want?" he would ask himself, while his heart ached dully.

He once gave her a ring with a sphinx engraved on the stone.

"What's that?" she asked. "A sphinx?"

"Yes," he answered, "and that sphinx is you."

"I?" she queried, and slowly raising her eyes fixed her enigmatical gaze upon him. "Do you know that's very flattering?" she added with a meaningless smile, yet her eyes still kept the same strange look.

Paul Petrovich suffered even while Princess R—— loved him; but when she grew cold to him (and this happened rather soon), he almost went out of his mind. He was on the rack, and he was jealous; he gave her no peace, trailing her everywhere; she became fed up with his unremitting pursuit and she went abroad. He resigned his commission in spite of the entreaties of his friends, the exhortations of his superiors, and set out after the princess. He spent four years in foreign countries, now pursuing her, now intentionally losing sight of her. He was ashamed of himself, he was disgusted with his own pusillanimity—but nothing availed. Her image, that incomprehensible, almost meaningless but bewitching image, was deeply rooted in his soul.

At Baden he once more regained his old footing with her; it seemed as though she had never loved him so passionately. But in a month it was all at an end: the flame had flickered up for the last time and had gone out forever. He had a premonition of the inevitable parting but he wanted at least to remain her friend, as though friendship with such a woman were possible. She secretly left Baden and thenceforth steadily avoided Kirsanov. He returned to Russia and tried to resume his former life, but he could not get back into the old groove. He wandered from place to place like a victim of slow poisoning; he still went into society, he still retained the habits of a man of the world, he could have boasted of two or three new conquests; but he no longer expected anything much of himself or of others, and he embarked on nothing new. He grew old and gray; to spend his evenings sitting at the club, jaundiced and bored, and arguing with his fellow bachelors, became a necessity for him—a bad symptom, as everybody knows.

Marriage, of course, was something that did not even occur to him. Ten years passed in this way; they passed by colorlessly, fruitlessly, and quickly—frightfully quickly. Nowhere does time fly the way it does in Russia; in prison, they say, it flies even faster. One day, at dinner at the club, Paul Petrovich heard of the death of the Princess R——. She had died at Paris in a state bordering on insanity. He got up from the table, and for a long time he paced about the rooms of the club, stopping now and then near the cardplayers and standing stock-still, but he did not go home before his usual time. Some time later he received a packet addressed to him; in it was the ring he had given the Princess. She had drawn a cruciform line over the sphinx and sent him word that the solution of her enigma lay in the cross.

This happened at the beginning of the year 1848, at the very time when Nicolai Petrovich had come to Petersburg after the loss of his wife. Paul Petrovich had scarcely seen his brother since the latter had settled in the country; the marriage of Nicolai Petrovich had coincided with the very first days of Paul Petrovich's acquaintance with the princess. When he came back from abroad he had gone to his brother with the intention of staying a couple of months with him, in sympathetic enjoyment of his happiness, but he had been able to stand only a week of it. The difference in the positions of the two brothers was too great. In 1848 this difference had grown less; Nicolai Petrovich had lost his wife, Paul Petrovich had lost his memories; after the death of the Princess he tried not to think of her. But to Nicolai there remained the sense of a well-spent life, his son was growing up under his eyes; Paul, on the contrary, a solitary bachelor, was entering upon that indefinite twilight period of regrets that are akin to hopes and hopes that are akin to regrets, when youth is over, while old age has not yet come.

The time was harder for Paul Kirsanov than for any other man; having lost his past, he had lost everything.

"I will not invite you to Maryino now," Nicolai Petrovich said to him one day (he had called his property by that name in honor of his wife); "you were bored there in my dear wife's time, and I think you'd be bored to death now."

"I was stupid and fidgety then," answered Paul. "Since then I have grown quieter, if not wiser. Now, on the contrary, if you'll let me, I'm ready to settle with you for good."

All the answer Nicolai Petrovich made was to embrace him; but a year and a half passed after this conversation before Paul made up his mind to carry out his intention. When he was once settled in the country, however, he did not leave it, even during the three winters which Nicolai spent in Petersburg with his son. He began to read, chiefly English; he arranged his whole life, roughly speaking, in the English style, rarely saw his neighbors, and only went out to the election of the leader of the local nobility, where he was generally taciturn, only occasionally annoying and alarming landowners of the old school by his liberal sallies, yet keeping away from the representatives of the younger generation. Both groups considered him too proud, but both respected him for his fine aristocratic manners, for the stories of his amatory conquests, for the exquisite way he dressed and his custom of staying in the best room in the best hotel, for the fact that he generally dined well, and had once even dined with Wellington at Louis Philippe's table; because he always took with him everywhere a real silver dressing-case and a portable bath; because he was always fragrant with some perfume strikingly in "good form"; because he played whist in masterly fashion, yet always lost; and lastly, they respected him for his irreproachable-honesty as well. Ladies considered him an enchanting melancholic, but he did not cultivate the acquaintance of ladies.

"So you see, Eugene," observed Arcadii, as he finished his story, "how unjustly you judge my uncle! To say nothing of his having more than once helped my father out of difficulties, given him all his money—perhaps you don't know that the property isn't divided. However, he's glad to help anyone; among other things, he always speaks up for the peasants. Although, true enough, when he talks to them he puckers up his face and sniffs eau de cologne."

"His nerves, no doubt," put in Bazarov.

"Perhaps; but his heart is decidedly in the right place. And he's far from being stupid. What useful advice he has given me, especially—especially in regard to relations with women."

"Aha! He's scalded himself on milk, so he warns others even about cold water. We know all about that!"

"In short," continued Arcadii, "he's profoundly unhappy, believe me; it's a sin to despise him."

"Why, who's despising him?" retorted Bazarov. "Just the same, I tell you that a fellow who stakes his whole life on the card of women's love and who, when that card is beaten, turns sour and lets himself go till he's fit for nothing—such a fellow is neither a man, nor even a male. You say he's unhappy, and you ought to know best; but he's not rid of his folly yet. I'm convinced that he in all seriousness imagines himself a sensible person because he reads that wretched *Galignani* and every month or so saves a peasant from a flogging."

"But remember his education, the age in which he grew up," observed Arcadii.

"Education?" broke in Bazarov. "Every man must educate himself, just as I've done, for instance. And as for the age, why should I rely on it? Let it rather rely on me. No, brother, that's going all to pieces, living in a void! And what's all this about mysterious relations between man and woman? We physiologists know what those relations are. You make a thorough study of the anatomy of the eye: where does that enigmatical glance you talk about come in there? That's all romanticism, nonsense, rot, aestheticism. We'd much better go and take a look at the beetle."

And the two friends went off to Bazarov's room, which was already pervaded by a sort of medicosurgical odor, mingled with the smell of cheap tobacco.

VIII

Paul Kirsanov did not long remain present at his brother's interview with his estate manager, a tall, thin man with a sweet consumptive voice and knavish eyes, who to all of Nicolai Petrovich's remarks answered: "Certainly, Sir, you know how it is, Sir," and tried to make the peasants appear thieves and drunkards. The estate, only recently shifted to a new system, creaked like an ungreased wheel, coming apart like homemade furniture of unseasoned wood. Nicolai Petrovich did not lose heart, but quite often he sighed and was gloomy; he felt that the thing could not go on without money, and his money was almost all spent. Arcadii had spoken the truth: Paul had more than once helped his brother; more than once, seeing him struggling and racking his brains, at a loss which way to turn, Paul would slowly walk up to the window, with his hands deep in his pockets, and mutter through his teeth: *"Mais je puis vous donner de l'argent,"* [1] and would give him money; but today he had none himself, and he preferred to go away. The petty cares of agricultural management worried him; besides, it constantly struck him that Nicolai, for all his zeal and industry, did not go about things in the right way, though he himself would not have been able to point out precisely wherein Nicolai's mistake lay. "My brother's not practical enough," he reasoned to himself; "they take advantage of him."

Nicolai, on the other hand, had the highest opinion of Paul's practical ability and always asked his advice. "I'm a soft, weak fellow, I've passed all my life in the backwoods," he used to say, "while you haven't seen so much of people for nothing, you know them well—you have an eagle eye." In answer to which Paul Petrovich merely turned away, but did not try to change his brother's opinion.

Leaving Nicolai Petrovich in his study, he walked along the corridor which separated the front part of the house from the back and, on coming to a low door, he stopped in thought, tugged at his mustache, and knocked.

"Who's there? Come in!" sounded Phenichka's voice.

"It's I," said Paul Petrovich, and opened the door.

Phenichka jumped up from the chair on which she was sitting with her baby and, transferring him to the arms of a girl, who at once carried him out of the room, she hastily put straight her kerchief.

---

[1] "Why, I can give you money."

"Pardon me if I disturb you," Paul began, without looking at her; "I only wanted to ask you—they're sending somebody to town today, I think—to order some green tea for me."

"Certainly, Sir," answered Phenichka, "how much do you wish to buy?"

"Oh, half a pound will be enough, I suppose. You've made a change here, I see," he added with a rapid glance around him, which glided over her face as well. "Those curtains there," he explained, seeing she did not understand him.

"Oh, yes, the curtains. Nicolai Petrovich was so good as to make me a present of them, but they've been up a long while now."

"Yes, and it's a long while since I've been to see you. You've a very pretty place here now."

"Thanks to Nicolai Petrovich's kindness," murmured Phenichka.

"Are you more comfortable here than in that small wing you used to have?" inquired Paul Petrovich urbanely, but without the slightest smile.

"Certainly, it's more comfortable, Sir."

"Who's been put in your place there?"

"The laundrymaids are there now."

"Ah!"

Paul Petrovich fell silent. "He'll be going now," thought Phenichka; but he did not go, and she stood before him as if she were rooted to the spot, her fingers feebly fidgeting.

"Why did you send your little one away?" Paul Petrovich began at last. "I love children; let me see him."

Phenichka blushed all over from confusion and delight. She was afraid of Paul Petrovich; he had hardly ever spoken to her.

"Dunyasha," she called, "will you bring Mitya, please." (Phenichka did not treat anyone in the house familiarly.) "But wait a minute—he ought to have something on." She started for the door.

"That doesn't matter," remarked Paul Petrovich.

"I'll be back directly," she answered, and went out quickly.

Paul Petrovich was left alone, and this time he looked around him with special attention. The small low-ceiled room in which he found himself was very clean and cozy. It smelt of the freshly painted floor, of camomile and melissa. Along the walls were ranged chairs with lyre-shaped backs, bought by the late general as far back as the campaign of 1812; in one corner was a high, small bedstead under a muslin canopy, near an ironbound chest with a rounded lid. In the opposite corner a little image-lamp was burning before a big dark icon of St. Nicolai the Wonder-Worker; a tiny porcelain egg hung by a red ribbon from the protruding gold halo down to the saint's breast; on the window sills stood greenish glass jars of last year's jam, carefully tied and with the light showing green through them; on their paper tops Phenichka herself had written in big letters *Gooseberry*—Nicolai Petrovich was particularly fond of this jam. Near the ceiling, on a long cord, hung a cage with a bobtailed siskin; it was constantly chirping and hopping about, and the cage was constantly shaking and swinging, while hempseeds fell with a light tap onto the floor. On the wall, just above a small chest of drawers, hung some rather poor photographs of Nicolai Petrovich in various poses, taken by some itinerant photographer; there, too, hung a photograph of Phenichka herself, which was an absolute failure: an eyeless face wearing a forced smile, in a dingy frame—one could make out nothing more. And above Phenichka, General Yermolov, in a Circassian felt cloak, scowled menacingly upon the Caucasian mountains in the distance, from beneath a little pincushion in the form of a shoe, which came down right over his eyebrows.

Five minutes passed; one could hear fussing and whispering in the next room. Paul Petrovich picked up from the chest of drawers a much-soiled book, an odd volume of Massalski's *The Czar's Archers,* and turned a few pages. The door opened, and Phenichka came in with Mitya in her arms. She had put on him a little red smock with embroidery on the collar, had combed his hair and washed his face; he was breathing hard, his whole body working and his little hands waving in the air, the way all healthy babies do, but his smart smock obviously impressed him, and an air of delight was reflected in every part of his chubby little person. Phenichka had put her own hair in order also and had arranged her kerchief better, but she might well have remained as she was. And really, is there anything in the world more captivating than a good-looking young mother with a healthy baby in her arms?

"What a husky fellow!" Paul Petrovich remarked graciously and tickled Mitya's little double chin with the tapering nail of his index finger. The baby fixed his eyes on the siskin and chuckled.

"That's Uncle," said Phenichka, bending her face down to the boy and bouncing him, while Dunyasha quietly set on the window sill a smoldering incense cone, putting a copper coin under it.

"How many months is he now?" asked Paul Petrovich.

"Six months; it will soon be seven, on the eleventh."

"Isn't it eight, Theodosia Nicolaevna?" put in Dunyasha, not without timidity.

"No, seven; what an idea!" The baby chuckled again, fixed his eyes
on the chest, and suddenly caught hold of his mother's nose and mouth
with all his five little fingers. "You spoiled darling," said Phenichka,
without drawing her face away.

"He looks like my brother," observed Paul Petrovich.

"Who else should he look like?" thought Phenichka.

"Yes," Paul Petrovich went on, as though speaking to himself;
"there's an indubitable likeness." He looked attentively, almost sadly,
at Phenichka.

"That's Uncle," she repeated, but in a whisper by now.

"Ah, Paul! So that's where you are!" they suddenly heard the voice
of Nicolai Petrovich.

Paul quickly turned around and frowned, but his brother was looking at him with such delight, such gratitude, that he could not help
responding with a smile.

"You've a splendid little urchin," he said, and looked at his watch.
"I just dropped in about ordering some tea."

And, assuming an expression of indifference, he went out of the
room.

"Did he come of himself?" Nicolai Petrovich asked Phenichka.

"Yes, Sir; he knocked and came in."

"Well, and has Arcadii been in to see you again?"

"No. Hadn't I better move back into the wing, Nicolai Petrovich?"

"What for?"

"I wonder whether it mightn't be best at first."

"N—no," Nicolai Petrovich brought out hesitatingly, rubbing his
forehead. "We ought to have done it before. How are you, chubby?"
he said, suddenly brightening, and going up to the baby kissed him
on the cheek; then he bent a little and pressed his lips to Phenichka's
hand, which lay white as milk upon Mitya's little red smock.

"Nicolai Petrovich! What are you doing?" she whispered, dropping
her eyes, then slowly raised them. Very charming was the expression
of her eyes when she peeped, as it were, from under her lids, and smiled
tenderly and a little foolishly.

Nicolai Petrovich had made Phenichka's acquaintance three years
before when he had happened to stay overnight at an inn in a remote
district town. He was agreeably struck by the cleanness of the room

assigned to him, by the freshness of the bed linen. Was the woman of the house by any chance a German? it occurred to him; but she proved to be a Russian, a woman of about fifty, neatly dressed, with a comely, clever face and discreet of speech. He entered into conversation with her at tea; he liked her very much. Nicolai Kirsanov had at that time just moved into his new home and, not wishing to keep serfs in the house, was on the lookout for hired servants; the landlady for her part complained of the small number of transients in the town, and the hard times; he proposed to her to come into his house in the capacity of housekeeper; she consented. Her husband had long been dead, leaving her an only daughter—Phenichka. Within a fortnight Arina Savishna (that was the new housekeeper's name) arrived with her daughter at Maryino and settled in a small wing. Nicolai Kirsanov's choice proved a successful one. Arina brought order into the household. As for Phenichka, who was at that time seventeen, no one spoke of her, and scarcely anyone ever saw her; she lived ever so quietly, ever so unassumingly, and only on Sundays did Nicolai Petrovich notice in the parish church, somewhere off on the side, the delicate profile of her small white face. More than a year passed thus.

One morning Arina came into his study and, bowing low as usual, she asked him if he could do anything for her daughter, who had got a spark from the stove in her eye. Nicolai Kirsanov, like all stay-at-homes, dabbled in doctoring, and had even bought a homeopathic medicine cabinet by mail. He at once told Arina to bring the patient to him. Phenichka was much frightened when she heard the master had sent for her; however, she followed her mother. Nicolai Petrovich led her to the window and took her head in both hands. After thoroughly examining her reddened and swollen eye, he prescribed a fomentation, which he made up himself at once, and, tearing his handkerchief in pieces, he showed her how it ought to be applied. Phenichka listened to him attentively and, when he had done, turned to go. "Kiss the master's hand, you silly little thing," said Arina. Nicolai Petrovich did not hold out his hand for her to kiss, and in confusion himself kissed her bent head on the parting.

Phenichka's eye was soon well again, but the impression she had made on Nicolai did not pass away so soon. He was forever haunted by that pure, delicate, timorously lifted face; he felt on his palms that soft hair, and saw those innocent, slightly parted lips, through which pearly teeth gleamed moistly in the sun. He began to watch her with great attention in church, he tried to get into conversation with her. At first she was shy of him, and one day encountering him toward evening in a narrow footpath beaten through a rye field, she ducked into the tall thick rye, overgrown with cornflowers and wormwood, so as not to meet him face to face. He caught sight of her little head through an aureate network of grain ears, through which she was peeping out like a small wild creature, and called out affectionately to her:

"Good evening, Phenichka! I won't bite you!"

"Good evening," she whispered, not coming out of her ambuscade.

By degrees she began to get used to him, but was still shy in his presence, when suddenly Arina, her mother, died of cholera. Which way was Phenichka to turn? She inherited from her mother a love for order, common sense, and sedateness; but she was so young, so lonely. Nicolai Petrovich was himself so good and modest. . . . There is no need to relate the rest.

"So my brother came in to see you just so?" Nicolai Petrovich questioned her. "He knocked and came in?"

"Yes, Sir."

"Well, that's a good thing. Let me swing Mitya a little."

And he began tossing the baby almost up to the ceiling, to his huge delight, and to the considerable uneasiness of the mother, who every time he flew up stretched her arms up toward his bare little legs.

As for Paul, he went back to his artistic study, handsomely papered in a neutral gray tint, with weapons hanging up against a variegated Persian rug; with walnut furniture upholstered in dark green velveteen, with a renaissance bookcase of old black oak, with bronze statuettes on the magnificent writing table, with an open fireplace. He threw himself on the sofa, clasped his hands behind his head, and remained without moving, staring almost in despair at the ceiling. Then, whether he wanted to hide from the very walls that which was reflected in his face, or for some other reason, he got up, drew the heavy window curtains, and again threw himself on the sofa.

IX

On the same day Bazarov, too, made the acquaintance of Phenichka. He was walking with Arcadii in the garden and explaining to him why some of the young trees, especially the oaks, had not done well.

"You ought to have planted silver poplars here for the most part, and spruce firs, and perhaps limes, giving them some black loam. The arbor there has done well," he added, "because acacias and lilac bushes are accommodating good fellows and don't demand much care. Why, there's someone in here!"

The arbor was occupied by Phenichka, with Dunyasha and Mitya. Bazarov stopped, while Arcadii nodded to Phenichka like an old friend.

"Who's that?" Bazarov asked him directly they had passed by. "What a pretty little thing!"

"Whom are you talking about?"

"That's not hard to tell; only one of them was really pretty."

Arcadii, not without embarrassment, explained to him in a few words who Phenichka was.

"Aha!" commented Bazarov. "It's easy to see your father has good taste. I like your father, I swear! He's a grand fellow. However, we ought to become acquainted," he added, and turned back toward the arbor.

"Eugene!" Arcadii called after him apprehensively. "Mind what you're about, for God's sake."

"Don't get upset," Bazarov said reassuringly. "Us city slickers know how to behave."

He took off his cap as he approached Phenichka.

"Allow me to introduce myself," he began with a polite bow. "I'm a harmless person, and a friend of Arcadii Nicolaevich's."

Phenichka got up from the bench and looked at him without speaking.

"What a wonderful baby!" Bazarov went on. "Don't be uneasy, I've never yet put the evil eye on anybody. Why are his cheeks so red? Is he cutting his teeth?"

"Yes, Sir," Phenichka managed to say; "he's cut four teeth already, and now the gums are swollen again."

"Let me see—come, and don't be afraid, I'm a doctor."

Bazarov took the baby up in his arms, and to the great astonishment both of Phenichka and Dunyasha the child made no resistance at all and was not frightened.

"I see, I see. It's nothing, everything's in order. He'll have a good set of teeth. If anything goes wrong, tell me. And are you quite well yourself?"

"I am, thank God."

"Thank God, indeed—that's the great thing. And you?" he added, turning to Dunyasha.

Dunyasha, a girl very prim in the master's chambers but a great giggler outside the gates, merely guffawed in answer.

"Well, that's just fine. Here's your giant."

Phenichka received the baby in her arms.

"How well he behaved with you!" she commented in an undertone.

"Children always behave well for me," answered Bazarov. "I have a way with them."

"Children sense those who love them," Dunyasha remarked.

"Yes, that's true," Phenichka confirmed. "Why, Mitya won't go to some people for anything."

"Would he come to me, now?" asked Arcadii, who, after standing at a distance for some time, had come up to the arbor.

He tried to entice Mitya to come to him, but Mitya threw his head back and wailed, to Phenichka's great embarrassment.

"I'll have better luck next time, when he's had time to get used to me," said Arcadii indulgently, and the two friends walked off.

"What's her name?" asked Bazarov.

"Phenichka—Theodosia," answered Arcadii.

"And her patronymic? One must know that, too."

"Nicolaevna."

"*Bene*. What I like about her is that she's not embarrassed too much. Somebody else, I suppose, would condemn her for that very thing. What nonsense! Why be embarrassed? She's a mother—and that justifies everything."

"She's justified," observed Arcadii, "but my father, now—"

"He's justified, too," Bazarov cut him short.

"Well, no, I don't think so."

"You can't stomach an extra little heir, I suppose."

"I wonder you're not ashamed to attribute such ideas to me!" Arcadii retorted hotly. "I don't consider my father wrong from that point of view. I think he ought to marry her."

"Oho-ho!" Bazarov retorted tranquilly. "What magnanimous fellows we are, to be sure! You still attach significance to marriage—I didn't expect that from you."

The friends walked a few paces in silence.

"I've looked over your father's whole establishment," Bazarov began again. "The livestock is poor, the horses are broken down, he didn't do so well with the buildings, either, and the hands look like confirmed loafers, while the superintendent is either a fool or a knave—I haven't quite found out which yet."

"You're rather hard on everything today, Eugene Vassilyich."

"And the darling little peasants will hornswoggle your father sure as fate. You know the saying: 'The peasant can gobble up the good Lord God Himself.'"

"I'm beginning to agree with my uncle," remarked Arcadii. "You have a downright poor opinion of Russians."

"As though that mattered! The only good point about a Russian is his most abominable opinion of himself. What does matter is that two times two makes four and the rest is all fiddle-faddle."

"And is nature fiddle-faddle?" Arcadii let drop, looking pensively at the bright-colored fields in the distance, beautiful and soft in the light of the sun, already low.

"Nature, too, is fiddle-faddle in your conception of it. Nature is not a temple but a workshop, and man's the workman in it."

At that moment the long-drawn notes of a violoncello floated out to them from the house. Some one was playing Schubert's *Expectation* with much feeling, though with an untrained hand, and the sweet melody spread far and wide.

"What's that?" Bazarov asked in amazement.

"It's my father."

"Your father plays the violoncello?"

"Yes."

"Why, how old is your father?"

"Forty-four."

Bazarov suddenly went off into peals of laughter.

"What are you laughing at?"

"Have a heart! A man of forty-four, a *paterfamilias* and out in these wilds playing on the violoncello!"

Bazarov went on laughing. But Arcadii, much as he revered his preceptor, this time did not even smile.

X

About two weeks passed by. Life at Maryino flowed on in its accustomed course. Arcadii played the sybarite, and Bazarov worked. Everyone in the house had grown used to him, to his careless manners and his mono-syllabic and abrupt speech. Phenichka in particular had become so used to him that one night she sent to wake him up. Mitya had had con-vulsions. And Bazarov had come and, half joking, half yawning after his wont, had stayed two hours with her and relieved the child. On the other hand Paul Kirsanov had grown to detest Bazarov with all the strength of his soul; he regarded him as proud, impudent, cynical, and plebeian. He suspected that Bazarov had no respect for him, that he all but had contempt for him—him, Paul Kirsanov! Nicolai Petrovich was rather afraid of the young "nihilist," and entertained doubts whether his influence over Arcadii was for the good, but he willingly listened to him and was willingly present at his scientific and chemical experiments. Bazarov had brought his microscope with him and busied himself with it for hours on end. The servants, too, took to him, though he poked fun at them; they felt that, after all, he was one with them under the skin, that he was not a master. Dunyasha was always ready to giggle with him and used to cast significant and stealthy glances at him whenever she minced past him like a hen partridge; Peter, a man vain and stupid in the extreme, his forehead forever furrowed with care, a man whose whole merit consisted in his look of civility, the ability to read by syllables, and diligence in brushing his little coat with a little clothesbrush—well, even he smirked and brightened up as soon as Bazarov paid him any attention; the boys on the farm simply ran after the "doctor" like puppies. The old man Procophich was the only one who did not like him; he handed him the dishes at table with a surly face, called him a "horse knacker" and a "fly-by-night," and declared that with his side-whiskers he looked like a pig in a bush. Procophich in his own way was quite as much of an aristocrat as Paul Kirsanov.

The best days of the year had come—the first days of June. The weather kept splendidly fine; in the background there was the recurrent threat of cholera, but the inhabitants of that province had had time to get used to its visitations. Bazarov used to get up very early and go out for two or three miles, not for a walk (he couldn't abide aimless strolls), but to collect specimens of herbs and insects. Occasionally he took Arcadii with him. On the way home an argument would usually spring up between them, and Arcadii usually lost it, even though he spoke more than his companion.

One day they had lingered rather late before starting out; Nicolai Petrovich went to meet them in the garden, and as he reached the arbor he suddenly heard the quick steps and the voices of the two young men. They were walking on the other side of the arbor and could not see him.

"You don't know my father well enough," Arcadii was saying.

"Your father's a good fellow," Bazarov pronounced, "but he's a back number; his act is finished."

Nicolai Petrovich strained his ears. Arcadii made no answer.

The "back number" remained standing motionless for a couple of minutes and then slowly shuffled off home.

"The day before yesterday I saw him reading Pushkin," Bazarov went on in the meantime. "Explain to him, please, that it's of no earthly use. For he isn't a little boy, after all; it's time to drop all such rubbish. The very idea of being a romantic at this time of day! Give him something useful to read."

"Such as what?" asked Arcadii.

"Oh, I think Büchner's *Stoff und Kraft* [1] for a start."

"That's what I think," Arcadii observed approvingly, *"Stoff und Kraft* is written in popular language."

"So that's the fix you and I find ourselves in," Nicolai Petrovich said the same day after dinner to his brother, as he sat in the latter's study. "You and I have become back numbers; our act is finished. Well, what of it? Perhaps Bazarov is actually right; but one thing does pain me, I confess: I had hoped, precisely now, to get on close, intimate terms with Arcadii, but it turns out I've been left behind while he has forged ahead, and we can't understand each other."

"Come, just how has he forged ahead? And in what way is he so very much apart from us, after all?" Paul exclaimed impatiently. "It's that signor, that nihilist, who's knocked all that stuff into his head. I detest that miserable little pillroller; in my opinion, he's simply a quack; I'm convinced, for all his frogs, that he hasn't gone very far even in physics."

"No, brother, you mustn't say that; Bazarov is clever and has genuine knowledge."

"And his conceit's something revolting," Paul broke in again.

"Yes," observed Nicolai, "he is conceited. But evidently there's no getting along without that. There's only one thing I can't get into my head. It would seem I'm doing everything to keep up with the times; I've provided for the peasants, I've started a model farm, so that I'm even called a Red Radical throughout the province; I read, I study,

[1] Matter and Force.

I try in every way to keep abreast of the demands of the day—but they say my act is finished. Why, Brother, I myself am beginning to think that it is."

"Why so?"

"I'll tell you why. This morning I was sitting reading Pushkin. I remember I had happened to turn to *The Gypsies.* All of a sudden Arcadii came up to me and, without speaking, with such a kindly compassion on his face, took the book away from me as gently as if I were a baby and laid another before me—a German book. Then he smiled and went away, carrying Pushkin off with him."

"You don't say! Just what book did he give you?"

"This one."

And Nicolai Petrovich pulled Büchner's famous brochure ("Now in its Ninth Edition") out of his coattail pocket.

Paul turned it in his hands. "Hm!" he lowed. "Arcadii Nicolaich is taking your education in hand. Well, now, did you try to read it?"

"Yes, I did."

"And what happened?"

"Either I'm stupid, or else it's all bosh. Probably I must be stupid."

"Perhaps you've forgotten your German?" Paul queried.

"Oh, I understand German."

Paul Petrovich again turned the book over in his hands, and glanced from under his brows at his brother. Both were silent for a while.

"Oh, by the way," Nicolai began, obviously wishing to change the subject, "I got a letter from Kolyazin."

"Matthew Ilyich?"

"The same. He has come to inspect the province. He's quite a big shot now and writes to me that as a relative he'd like to see us again, and invites you and me and Arcadii to call on him in the town."

"Are you going?" asked Paul.

"No; and you?"

"No, I won't go either. No use in dragging oneself over forty miles for a spoonful of cranberry sauce. *Mathieu* wants to show off before us in all his glory. To the devil with him! It'll be enough if the whole province will burn incense to him—he'll get along without ours. What a great dignitary, to be sure—a Privy Councilor! If I'd kept on in the service, if I'd kept on dragging the stupid official load, I'd have been an adjutant general by now. Besides, you and I are back numbers, you know."

"Yes, Brother; it's time, evidently, to order a coffin and cross one's arms on one's breast," Arcadii's father remarked with a sigh.

"Well, I'm not going to give in quite so soon," his brother muttered. "I have a premonition that pillroller and I will come to grips yet."

They came to grips that very day at evening tea. Paul Petrovich came into the drawing room all ready for the fray, irritable and determined. He was only waiting for a pretext to fall upon the enemy, but for a long while that pretext did not present itself. As a rule, Bazarov said little in the presence of "those little Kirsanov ancients," as he spoke of the brothers, and that evening he felt out of sorts and drank off cup after cup of tea without a word. Paul Petrovich was all ablaze with impatience; his wishes were fulfilled at last.

The conversation turned to one of the neighboring landowners. "Trash; just a miserable little aristocrat," indifferently remarked Bazarov, who had met the fellow in Petersburg.

"Allow me to ask you," began Paul Petrovich, and his lips began to tremble, "according to your conceptions the words 'trash' and 'aristocrat' signify one and the same thing?"

"I said 'just a miserable little aristocrat,'" replied Bazarov, lazily swallowing a sip of tea.

"Precisely so; but I imagine you have the same opinion of aristocrats as of miserable little aristocrats. I think it my duty to inform you that I do not share that opinion. I venture to assert that everyone knows me for a man of liberal ideas and devoted to progress; but for that very reason I respect aristocrats—real aristocrats. Kindly remember, Sir"—at these words Bazarov lifted his eyes and looked at the speaker—"kindly remember, Sir," he repeated, with acrimony, "the English aristocrats. They do not abate one iota of their rights, and for that reason they respect the rights of others; they demand the performance of what is due to them, and for that reason they perform their own duties. The aristocracy has given freedom to England and maintains it there."

"We've heard that song a good many times," retorted Bazarov. "But what are you trying to prove by that?"

"I'm trying to prove by that there, Sir"—(when Paul Petrovich was angry he deliberately indulged in such locutions, though, of course, he knew very well that they were not grammatically permissible. This quirk betrayed a vestige of the traditions of Alexander I's time. The exquisites of that day, on the rare occasions when they spoke their own language, made use of such slipshod forms; as much as to say, "We, of course, are born Russians, at the same time we are great grandees, who are at liberty to disdain the rules of scholars.")—"I'm trying to prove by that there, Sir, that without the sense of personal dignity, without self-respect—and these two sentiments are well developed in the aristocrat—there is no secure foundation for the social . . . *bien public* . . . the social structure. Personal character, Sir—that is the chief thing; a man's personal character must be firm as a rock, inasmuch as everything is built thereon. I am very well aware, for instance, that you're pleased to consider my habits, my dress, my personal neatness, in fact, as ridiculous. But all that proceeds from a sense of self-respect, from a sense of duty—yes, Sir, of duty. I live in the country, in the backwoods, but I will not lower myself. I respect the dignity of man in myself."

"Let me ask you, Paul Petrovich," Bazarov put in, "you respect yourself, and sit twiddling your thumbs—of just what benefit is that to the *bien public*? You'd still be doing the same, even if you didn't respect yourself."

Paul Petrovich turned white.

"That's an entirely different matter. I'm under no compulsion whatever to explain to you now why I sit twiddling my thumbs, as you are pleased to put it. I wish to tell you merely that aristocracy is a principle, and in our time none but immoral or frivolous people can live without principles. I said that to Arcadii the day after he came home and I now repeat it to you. Am I right in my recollection, Nicolai?"

Nicolai nodded his head.

"Aristocracy, liberalism, progress, principles," Bazarov was saying meanwhile. "Come to think of it, what a lot of foreign—and useless—words! A Russian has no need of them, even as a gift."

"What does he need then, according to you? If we listen to you, we find that we're outside humanity, outside its laws. Come, the logic of history demands—"

"But what's the good of that logic to us? We get along without it quite well."

"How do you mean?"

"Why, just this. You don't need logic, I hope, to put a bit of bread in your mouth when you're hungry. What have we to do with these abstractions?"

Paul Petrovich raised his hands in horror.

"I don't understand you, after that. You insult the Russian people. I don't understand how it's possible not to acknowledge principles, rules! By virtue of what do you act then?"

"I've already told you, Uncle, that we don't recognize any authorities," Arcadii interposed.

"We act by virtue of what we recognize as beneficial," observed Bazarov. "At the present time, repudiation is the most beneficial of all —and as we repudiate—"

"Everything?"

"Everything."

"What, not only art and poetry but even . . . it is horrible to say—"

"Everything," repeated Bazarov with indescribable imperturbability.

Paul Petrovich stared at him. He had not expected this; Arcadii fairly glowed with delight.

"Allow me to say something, though," Nicolai Petrovich began. "You repudiate everything, or, speaking more precisely, you destroy everything. But one must be constructive, too, you know."

"That's not our business now. The ground must be cleared first."

"The present state of the people demands it," Arcadii added with an important air. "We are bound to carry out these demands; we have no right to yield to the satisfaction of our personal egoism."

This last phrase apparently was not to Bazarov's liking. There was an odor of philosophy about it, that is to say, of romanticism, for Bazarov called philosophy also romanticism; however, he did not consider it necessary to contravene his young disciple.

"No, no!" Paul Kirsanov cried out with sudden energy. "I'm not willing to believe that you gentlemen really know the Russian people, that you are the representatives of its demands, its aspirations! No; the Russian people is not what you imagine it. It holds its traditions sacred; it is a patriarchal people; it cannot live without faith—"

"I'm not going to dispute that," Bazarov interrupted. "I'm even ready to agree that in *that* you're right."

"But if I'm right—"

"And still it doesn't prove a thing."

"Precisely—it doesn't prove a thing," Arcadii repeated with the confidence of a practiced chess player who has foreseen an apparently dangerous move on the part of his adversary and so is not in the least taken aback by it.

"How does it prove nothing?" muttered Paul Kirsanov, astounded. "You must be going against your own people then?"

"And what if we are?" exclaimed Bazarov. "The people imagine that when it thunders the prophet Ilya's riding across the sky in his chariot. What then? Am I to agree with them? Besides, the people are Russian—but am I not Russian, too?"

"No, you're no Russian after all you've just been saying! I can't acknowledge you as Russian."

"My grandfather plowed the land," answered Bazarov with actual hauteur. "Ask any one of your peasants which of us—you or me—he'd more readily acknowledge as a fellow countryman. You don't even know how to talk to him."

"But you talk to him and hold him in contempt at the same time."

"Well, why not, if he deserves contempt? You condemn my attitude, but who told you that I came by it by chance, that it wasn't brought forth by that very national spirit, in the name of which you are so zealously contending?"

"Come, now! As if nihilists were of much use!"

"Whether they're of use or not is not for us to decide. Why, even you suppose you're not a useless person."

"Gentlemen, gentlemen, no personalities, please!" Nicolai Petrovich cried out and rose from his chair.

Paul Kirsanov smiled and, placing his hand on his brother's shoulder, made him resume his seat.

"Don't be uneasy," he said; "I won't forget myself, precisely because of that sense of dignity which our friend—our friend, the doctor—pokes fun at so cruelly. Let me ask," he resumed, turning again to Bazarov, "do you suppose, by any chance, that your doctrine is a novelty? You imagine so in vain. The materialism you preach has already been in vogue more than once, and has always proved bankrupt."

"Another foreign word!" Bazarov broke in. He was beginning to feel vicious, and his face had taken on a certain coarse and coppery hue. "In the first place, we don't preach a thing; that's not our way."

"What do you do then?"

"I'll tell you what we do. Not so very long ago we used to say that our officials took bribes, that we had no roads, no commerce, no real justice—"

"Oh, I see, you are denunciators—that's what they're called, I believe. I, too, agree with many of your denunciations, but—"

"Then we surmised that talk, perpetual talk and nothing but talk, about our sores was not worth the effort, that it all led to nothing but vulgarity and doctrinarianism; we saw that our clever fellows, the so-called leading men and denunciators, weren't worth a hoot in hell; that we were fussing around with nonsense, talking rubbish about art, about unconscious creativeness, about parliamentarism, trial by jury, and the devil knows what not, when it was really a question of getting our daily bread, when we were stifling under the grossest superstition, when all our stock companies were blowing up, simply because there is a shortage of honest men, when the very emancipation our government's so busy with will hardly do us any good, because our peasant is willing to rob even himself as long as he can get enough ratgut in some ginmill."

"Yes," interposed Paul Petrovich—"yes; you were convinced of all this and decided not to undertake anything seriously yourselves."

"We decided not to undertake anything," Bazarov repeated glumly. He suddenly felt vexed with himself for having been so expansive before this seigneur.

"But to confine yourselves to abuse?"

"To confine ourselves to abuse."

"And that is called nihilism?"

"And that's called nihilism," Bazarov repeated again, this time with peculiar rudeness.

Paul Petrovich puckered up his eyes a little. "So that's it!" he observed in a strangely composed voice. "Nihilism is to cure all our woes, and you, you are our heroes and saviors. So. But why do you berate others—even those same denunciators, say? Don't you do as much chattering as all the others?"

"Whatever faults we have, of that sin we are innocent," Bazarov muttered.

"Well, then? Do you act, or what? Are you preparing for action?"

Bazarov made no answer. Something like a shudder ran through Paul Petrovich, but he at once regained control of himself.

"Hm! . . . Action, demolition . . ." he went on. "But how can one demolish without even knowing why?"

"We demolish because we are a force," observed Arcadii.

Paul Petrovich glanced at his nephew and smiled slightly.

"Yes, a force is not to be called to account," said Arcadii and drew himself up.

"Unhappy boy!" wailed Paul Petrovich; he was absolutely incapable of controlling himself any longer. "If only you, at least, would stop to think *what* you're lending your support to in Russia by your vulgar sententiousness. No; it's enough to make an angel lose his patience. Force! There's force in the savage Kalmuck, in the Mongolian; but of what use is it to us? It is civilization that is precious to us; yes,

yes, my dear Sir, its fruits are precious to us. And don't tell me those fruits are insignificant; the veriest dauber, *un barbouilleur*, the professor who gets a small silver coin for thumping the piano all evening, is—well, even they are more useful than you, because they are the representatives of civilization, and not of brute Mongolian force! You fancy yourselves in the vanguard, but all you're fit for is to squat in a Kalmuck's tent! Force! And recall, at last, you forcible gentlemen, that there are only four men and a half of you in all, whereas there are millions of the others who won't let you trample down their most sacred traditions, who will crush you underfoot!"

"If we're crushed, well and good," observed Bazarov. "Only that's easier said than done. We aren't so few as you suppose."

"What? You seriously suppose you can manage—that you can manage to overcome a whole people?"

"All Moscow was burnt down, you know, by a candle that cost but a copper," answered Bazarov.

"Yes, yes. First a pride almost Satanic, then scoffing. There, that's what youth is infatuated with, that's what schoolboys submit to! Here's one of them sitting beside you, he's almost ready to worship you. Admire your handiwork. [Arcadii turned away and frowned.] And this infection already has spread far. I've been told that in Rome our artists never set foot in the Vatican. Raphael they regard as well-nigh a ninny because, if you please, he has the halo of authority; while they themselves are disgustingly impotent and sterile, and their imagination cannot go beyond *Girl at a Fountain,* even if you were to slay them! And even the girl is drawn most execrably. Fine fellows according to you, are they not?"

"According to me," retorted Bazarov, "Raphael's not worth a belch in a gale of wind, and they're no better than he."

"Bravo! bravo! Listen, Arcadii—that's how young men of today ought to express themselves! And if you come to think of it, how can they help but follow you? Formerly young men had to study; they didn't want to be known as ignoramuses, so they had to work hard whether they liked it or not. But now, all they have to do is say: 'Everything in the world is humbug!' and the trick's done. The young men are delighted. And, really, they were simply dunderheads before, and now they have suddenly blossomed into nihilists."

"There you are—your praiseworthy sense of personal dignity failed to sustain you," Bazarov remarked phlegmatically, while Arcadii was hot all over, and his eyes were flashing. "Our argument has gone too far; it's better to cut it short, I think. But I'll be quite ready to agree with you," he added, getting up, "when you bring forward a single institution in our present mode of life, either domestic or social, which does not call forth complete and merciless repudiation."

"I'll bring forward millions of such institutions," Paul Kirsanov cried out, "millions! Why, take communal land, for instance."

A cold smile curved Bazarov's lips. "Well, when it comes to communal land," he commented, "you'd better talk to your brother. By now he has seen at first hand, I believe, what sort of thing communal land is, and mutual responsibility, and temperance, and other such knick-knacks."

"The family, then, the family as it exists among our peasants!" Paul Kirsanov began to shout.

"And that subject, too, I imagine, it would be better for you yourself not to take up in detail. Ever hear of the patriarchs who try out their daughters-in-law? Take my advice, Paul Petrovich, give yourself a couple of days to think about it; you're not likely to find anything right off. Go through all our classes and think rather carefully over each one, and in the meantime Arcadii and I will—"

"Go on scoffing over everything," Kirsanov broke in.

"No, we will go on dissecting frogs. Come, Arcadii. Good-by for the present, gentlemen!"

The two friends walked out. The brothers were left alone, and at first they merely exchanged glances.

"There," began Paul, "there you have the youth of today! There they are—our successors!"

"Our successors!" Nicolai echoed him with a despondent sigh. He had been sitting on pins and needles all through the discussion and had done nothing but glance stealthily, with a sore heart, at Arcadii. "Do you know what I was reminded of, Brother? I once had a quarrel with our poor mother; she shouted and wouldn't listen to me. At last I said to her, 'Of course, you can't understand me; we belong,' I said, 'to two different generations.' She was dreadfully offended, while I thought, 'There's no help for it. It's a bitter pill, but she'll have to swallow it.' Well, now our turn has come, and our successors can say to us, 'You are not of our generation; swallow your pill.' "

"You're far too magnanimous and modest," Paul Petrovich retorted. "I'm convinced, on the contrary, that you and I are far more in the right than these young gentlemen, though we do perhaps express ourselves in a somewhat old-fashioned language, *vieilli,* and haven't the same inso-

lent self-reliance. . . . And how puffed up the young men are nowadays! You ask one: 'Do you take red wine or white?'—'It is my custom
to prefer red!' he answers in a deep bass, with a face as solemn as if all
creation were looking at him at that instant. . . ."

"Do you care for any more tea?" asked Phenichka, putting her head
in at the door; she had not dared to come into the drawing room while
there was the sound of voices in dispute there.

"No, you can tell them to take the samovar away," answered Nicolai
Petrovich, and he got up to meet her. Paul said *"Bon soir"* to his brother
abruptly and went off to his study.

XI

Half an hour later Nicolai Petrovich went into the garden, to his
favorite arbor. He was overcome by melancholy thoughts. For the first
time he had come to realize clearly the distance between him and his
son; he foresaw that every day it would grow greater and greater. In
vain, then, had he spent whole days sometimes in the winter at Petersburg over the newest books; in vain had he listened to the talk of the
young men; in vain had he rejoiced when he succeeded in putting in
his word, too, in their heated discussions. "My brother says we're right,"
he thought, "and apart from all vanity, I do think myself that they are
farther from the truth than we are, though at the same time I feel there
is something behind them we haven't got, some point of superiority
over us. . . . Is it youth? No; it isn't only youth. Doesn't their superiority consist in there being fewer traces of the slaveowner in them
than in us?"

Nicolai Petrovich's head sank despondently, and he passed his hand
over his face.

"But to renounce poetry?" he thought again. "To have no feeling
for art, for nature . . ."

And he looked around, as though trying to understand how it was
possible to have no feeling for nature. It was already evening; the sun
had hidden behind a small grove of aspens which lay a quarter of a mile
from the garden; its shadow stretched indefinitely across the still fields.
A peasant on a white nag went trotting along the dark, narrow path
very close to the copse; his whole figure was clearly visible, even to the
patch on his shoulder, in spite of his being in the shade; it was pleasant

to see the clean flash of the horse's legs. The sun's rays from the farther side fell full on the copse and, piercing through its thickets, poured such a warm light on the aspen trunks that they looked like pines, and their leafage was almost a dark blue, while above them rose a pale-blue sky, faintly tinged by the glow of sunset. The swallows flew high; the wind had died away; belated bees hummed lazily and drowsily among the lilac blossoms; midges swarmed in a pillar over a solitary branch which stood far out against the sky.

"How beautiful, my God!" thought Nicolai Petrovich, and his favorite verses were almost on his lips; but he remembered Arcadii's *Stoff und Kraft*—and was silent; but still he sat there, still he gave himself up to the sorrowful and solacing consolation of solitary thought. He was fond of occasional reveries; life in the country had developed this tendency in him. Was it so long ago that he had been dreaming the same dreams, waiting for his son at the posting station? Yet since then a change had already taken place; their relations, which were then as yet undefined, had now become defined—and how defined! Again his late wife came back to his imagination, but not as he had known her for many years, not as the good home-loving housewife but as a young girl with a slim figure, innocently searching eyes, and tightly braided hair over her childlike neck. He remembered how he had seen her for the first time. He was still a student then. He had met her on the staircase of his lodging and, jostling her by accident, turned around wishing to apologize and could only mutter, *"Pardon, monsieur,"* while she bowed her head, smiled, and suddenly seemed frightened and ran away, though at the turn of the staircase she glanced at him quickly, assumed a serious air, and blushed. Afterward, the first timid visits, the half-words, the half-smiles, and embarrassment; and melancholy, and yearnings, and at last that gasping rapture. . . . Where had it all fled? She had become his wife, he had been happy as few on earth are happy. . . . "But," he mused, "those delectable first moments, why could they not live an eternal, an undying life?"

He did not try to make his thought clear to himself; but he felt that he longed to retain that beatific time by something stronger than memory; he longed to feel the nearness of his Mary, again to have the sense of her warmth and breathing, and already he was imagining that over him—

"Nicolai Petrovich," Phenichka's voice sounded near him, "where are you?"

He started. He felt no pain, no remorse. He never even admitted the possibility of comparison between his wife and Phenichka, but he was sorry she had thought of coming to look for him. Her voice had brought back to him at once his gray hairs, his age, his reality.

The enchanted world into which he had just set foot, which had just been rising out of the dim waves of the past, had stirred—and vanished.

"Here I am," he answered; "I'll come later, run along." "There they are, the traces of the slaveowner," flashed through his mind. Phenichka peeped into the arbor at him without speaking, and disappeared, while he noticed with astonishment that the night had come on while he had been dreaming. Everything around him had grown dark and hushed. And Phenichka's face had glided by before him ever so pale and slight. He got up and was about to return home; but his heart would not calm down, and he began slowly pacing around the garden, sometimes thoughtfully looking at the ground at his feet, or raising his eyes toward the sky where swarms of stars were twinkling. He walked a great deal, till he was almost tired out, but the uneasiness within him, a kind of yearning, vague, melancholy uneasiness, still would not abate. Oh, how Bazarov would have laughed at him if he had known what was passing within him then! Arcadii himself would have condemned him. He, a man of forty-four, an agriculturist and a landowner, was shedding tears, causeless tears; this was a hundred times worse than the violoncello.

He continued walking and could not summon the resolution to go into the house, into the peaceful and snug nest which looked out at him so hospitably from all its lighted windows; he had not the force to tear himself away from the darkness, the garden, the feel of the fresh air in his face, this pensiveness, this uneasiness.

At a turn in the path he came upon his brother. "What's the matter with you?" Paul asked Nicolai. "You're as white as a ghost; you're not well—why don't you lie down?"

Nicolai in a few words explained his physical mood and withdrew. Paul reached the end of the garden and he, too, grew thoughtful, and he, too, raised his eyes toward the heavens. But in his beautiful dark eyes nothing was reflected but the light of the stars. He was not a born romantic, and his fastidiously dry and sensuous soul, misanthropical after the French manner, was not capable of dreaming.

"You know what?" Bazarov was saying to Arcadii the same night. "A splendid idea has popped into my head. Your father was saying today that he'd had an invitation from that illustrious relative of yours.

Your father's not going, so let you and I dash over to the town, for the great gentleman included you, too, in the invitation. Just see how fine the weather is; we'll have a jaunt and look the town over. We'll have an outing for five or six days and then call it quits."

"And you'll come back here again?"

"No; I must go to my father's. You know, he lives about twenty-five miles from the town we're going to. I haven't seen him for a long while, and my mother, too; I must cheer the old people up. They've been good to me, especially my father. He's as amusing as can be. After all, I'm their only child."

"And will you stay with them long?"

"I don't think so. It'll be boring, most likely."

"And you'll come to us on your way back?"

"I don't know. I'll see. Well, what do you say? Shall we go?"

"If you like," Arcadii agreed languidly.

In his heart he was highly delighted with his friend's proposal, but he deemed himself duty-bound to conceal his feeling. He wasn't a nihilist for nothing!

The next day he set off with Bazarov. The younger part of the household at Maryino was sorry at their going; Dunyasha even had a cry. But the old folks breathed more easily.

XII

The town to which our friends set off was in the jurisdiction of a Governor who was of the youngish sort, a progressive and at the same time a despot, a very frequent phenomenon in Russia. Before the end of the first year of his rule he had contrived to quarrel not only with the local Leader of Nobility, a retired officer of the guards, who kept open house and a stud farm, but even with his own subordinates. The feuds arising from this cause finally assumed such proportions that the ministry in Petersburg had found it necessary to send down a trusted personage with a commission to investigate everything on the spot. The choice of the authorities fell upon Matthew Ilyich Kolyazin, the son of the Kolyazin under whose protection the brothers Kirsanov had once been. He, too, was a "young" man, that is to say, he had only recently passed forty, but he was already aiming at becoming a statesman, and already sported a star on either breast—one, to be sure, a foreign star, by no means of the first magnitude. Like the Governor whom he had come down to pass judgment upon, he was considered a progressive; and though he was already a big shot, he was dissimilar from the majority of big shots. He had the highest opinion of himself; his ambition knew no bounds, but he behaved simply, looked affably, listened condescendingly, and laughed so good-naturedly that on a first acquaintance he might even be taken for "an excellent fellow." On important occasions, however, he knew, as the saying is, how to throw dust in people's eyes. "Energy is essential," he used to say then, *"l'énergie est la première qualité d'un homme d'état;"* [1] but for all that he was usually left holding the bag, and any moderately experienced official could saddle and ride him. Matthew Kolyazin spoke with great respect of Guizot and tried to impress everyone with the idea that he himself did not belong to the class of *routiniers* and reactionary bureaucrats, that not a single phenomenon of social life passed unnoticed by him. All such phrases came very pat to him. He even followed (with dignified indifference, it is true) the development of contemporary literature—just as a grown-up man who meets a procession of small boys in the street may occasionally join it. In reality Kolyazin had not progressed much beyond those professional patriots of Alexander I's time who, in preparation for an evening party at Madame Svyechina's Petersburg salon,[2] would read a page of Condillac in the morning, save that his methods were different, more in keeping with the times. He was an adroit courtier, a great schemer, and nothing more. He had no special aptitude for administrative affairs, no intellect, but he knew how to manage his own affairs—no one could saddle and ride him there; and after all, that's the principal thing.

Kolyazin received Arcadii with the good nature characteristic of the enlightened dignitary—nay, even more, with playfulness. He was astonished, however, when he learned that the cousins he had invited had remained at home in the country. "Your father always was a queer stick," he remarked, toying with the tassels of his magnificent velvet lounging robe, and, suddenly turning to a young official in a discreetly buttoned-up uniform, he exclaimed with a preoccupied air: "What is it?" The young man, whose lips had become glued together from prolonged silence, got up and looked in perplexity at his chief. But having nonplused his subordinate, Kolyazin paid him no further attention. Our

[1] "Energy is the paramount requirement in a statesman."
[2] Sveychina, Sophia (1782-1859), a high-society authoress of mystical tendencies.

dignitaries as a rule are fond of nonplusing their subordinates; the methods to which they have recourse to attain that end are rather multiform. The following device, among others, is in great use, *is quite a favorite,* as the English put it: a dignitary will suddenly cease to understand the simplest words, will assume total deafness. He will ask, for instance, "What day is this?"

"Today is Friday, Your Exce-ce-ce-ce-ce-l-lency," he will be respectfully and stammeringly informed.

"Eh? What? What's that? What's that you say?" the great man repeats in absorption.

"Today is Friday, Your Ex-ce-ce-cellency."

"Eh? What? What's Friday? What Friday are you talking about?"

"Friday, Your Ex-ce-cecece-cecece-ce-cellency—you know, a day of the week."

"So-o-o, you presume to teach me, do you?"

And Kolyazin was a dignitary, after all, though he was reckoned a liberal.

"I advise you, my friend, to go and call on the Governor," he said to Arcadii. "You understand, I'm not advising you to do so because I adhere to old-fashioned ideas about the necessity of paying respect to authorities, but simply because the Governor's a very decent fellow; besides, you probably want to become acquainted with the society hereabout. For you're not a bear, I hope? And he's giving a great ball the day after tomorrow."

"Will you be at this ball?" inquired Arcadii.

"He's giving it in my honor," answered Kolyazin, almost with regret. "Do you dance?"

"Yes, I dance, but rather poorly."

"That's a pity! There are pretty little things here, and besides it's a shame for a young man not to dance. Again, I don't say that because of any old-fashioned notions; I don't in the least think that a man's wit lies in his feet, but Byronism is ridiculous, *il a fait son temps.*" [1]

"But, Uncle, it's not Byronism at all—"

"I'll introduce you to the young ladies here; I'm taking you under my wing," interrupted Kolyazin, and he laughed complacently. "You'll find it warm there, eh?"

A servant entered and announced the arrival of the Director of the Administrative Chamber, a mawkish-eyed old man with wrinkled lips, who was excessively fond of nature, especially on a summer day, when,

[1] "His day is over."

in his words, "every little busy bee takes a little bribe from every little flower."

Arcadii withdrew.

He found Bazarov at the tavern where they were staying and was a long while persuading him to go with him to the Governor's. "Well, there's no help for it," said Bazarov at last. "When you start something you've got to go through with it. We came to look the gentry over—so let's look 'em over!"

The Governor received the young men affably, but he did not ask them to sit down and did not sit down himself. He was in an everlasting bustle and hurry; in the morning he harnessed himself in a tight uniform and an exceedingly stiff cravat; he never ate properly or had enough sleep—always the busy administrator. He bore throughout the province the nickname of Bourdaloue—not after the famous Jesuit preacher, however, but hinting at *bourda*, or overfermented small beer. He invited Kirsanov and Bazarov to his ball, and two minutes later invited them a second time, by now regarding them as brothers and calling them Keisarov.

They were on their way home from the Governor's, when suddenly a short man, in a coat of a cut much affected by professional one-hundred-per-cent Russians, but really a garment of Hungarian origin, leaped out of a vehicle that was passing them, and with a shout of "Eugene Vassilyich!" rushed at Bazarov.

"Ah! It's you, Herr Sitnicov," observed Bazarov, still stepping along the sidewalk. "What fates bring you here?"

"Just imagine, I am here by pure chance," he replied, and turning around to the carriage he waved his hand at least five times and shouted: "Follow us, follow us now!" "My father had business here," he went on, skipping across the gutter, "and so he asked me to attend to it. I heard today of your arrival, and have already been to see you." (The friends did, in fact, on returning to their room, find a card there, with the corners turned down, bearing the name of Sitnicov on one side in French on the other in Slavonic script.) "I hope you're not coming from the Governor's?"

"Your hope is in vain; we're coming straight from him."

"Ah! In that case I'll call on him, too. Eugene Vassilyich, introduce me to your—to the—"

"Sitnicov, Kirsanov," Bazarov muttered without stopping.

"I'm greatly flattered," began Sitnicov, edging along, smirking, and hurriedly pulling off his gloves, which really were far too elegant. "I've heard so much—I'm an old acquaintance of Eugene Vassilyich and, I may say, his disciple. I am indebted to him for my regeneration—"

Arcadii looked at this disciple of Bazarov's. The small but on the whole pleasant features of his well-scrubbed face betrayed an uneasy and stolid tenseness; his small, apparently astonished eyes had a fixed and restless look, and his laugh, too, was restless—some sort of choppy, xylophonic laugh.

"Would you believe it," he went right on, "when Eugene Vassilyich for the first time said before me that it was not right to recognize any authorities, I felt such rapture, just as though my eyes had been opened! Here, I thought, I have at last found a man! By the way, Eugene Vassilyich, you absolutely must drop in on a certain lady here, who is utterly capable of understanding you, and for whom your visit would be a real gala occasion; you've heard of her, I suppose?"

"Who is she?" Bazarov brought out unwillingly.

"Kukshina, *Eudoxie*—Eudoxia Kukshina. She's a remarkable being, *émancipée* in the true sense of the word, an advanced woman. Do you know what? We'll all go together to see her now. She lives only a couple of steps from here. We'll have lunch there. I suppose you haven't lunched yet?"

"Not yet."

"Well, that's fine. She has separated from her husband, you understand—isn't dependent on anyone."

"Is she pretty?" Bazarov broke in.

"N—no, you couldn't call her that."

"Then what the devil are you asking us to see her for?"

"Oh, you are droll, really! She'll give us a bottle of champagne."

"You don't say. One can see a practical man right off. By the way, your father is still in liquor-tax farming?"

"Yes, he is," said Sitnicov hurriedly, and gave a shrill spasmodic laugh. "Well, now? Are we going?"

"I don't know, really."

"You wanted to see people—go' ahead," Arcadii remarked in an undertone.

"And what about you, M'sieu' Kirsanov?" Sitnicov put in. "You must come, too, please; we can't go without you."

"But how can all of us barge in on her like that?"

"That's no matter. Kukshina's a swell person!"

"There will be a bottle of champagne?" asked Bazarov.

"Three!" cried Sitnicov. "That I guarantee."

"What with?"

"My own head."

"Your father's purse would be better. However, let's go."

XIII

The small genteel house in the Moscow style, in which Avdotya Nikitishna (otherwise Eudoxia) Kukshina lived, was in one of the recently burned-down streets of the town; as everybody knows, our provincial towns burn down every five years or so. Near the door, above a visiting card crookedly nailed on, there was a bellpull, and in the hall the visitors were met by someone, not exactly a servant, nor exactly a companion, in a cap—patent tokens of the progressive tendencies of the lady of the house. Sitnicov inquired whether Avdotya Nikitishna was at home.

"Is that you, *Victor?*" a shrill voice sounded from an adjoining room. "Come in."

The woman in the cap immediately vanished.

"I'm not alone," observed Sitnicov, with a sharp look at Arcadii and Bazarov as he deftly shed his Russo-Hungarian overcoat, from beneath which emerged something of the nature of a coachman's baggy velvet jacket.

"It doesn't matter," answered the voice. *"Entrez."*

The young men went in. The room in which they found themselves was more like a study than a drawing room. Papers, letters, thick Russian periodicals, for the most part uncut, were scattered on dusty tables; stray cigarette ends showed whitely all over the place. A lady, still young, was reclining on a leather-covered divan. Her fair hair was rather disheveled; she wore a silk gown, not quite tidy, heavy bracelets on her stubby arms, and a diagonally folded lace fascinator on her head. She got up from the divan and, carelessly drawing a velvet cape trimmed with yellowed ermine over her shoulders, said languidly, "Good morning, *Victor,*" and pressed Sitnicov's hand.

"Bazarov, Kirsanov," he announced abruptly in imitation of Bazarov.

"Delighted," answered Kukshina, and fixed on Bazarov a pair of round eyes, between which a tiny turned-up nose showed forlornly red.

"I know you," she added, and pressed his hand, just as she had Arcadii's.

Bazarov scowled. There was nothing hideous about the small and plain figure of the emancipated woman, but the expression of her face produced a disagreeable effect on the beholder. One involuntarily wanted to ask her, "What's the matter, are you hungry? Or bored? Or shy? What are you fidgeting about?" Both she and Sitnicov were eternally sad at heart. She spoke and moved about with the utmost unconstraint, yet at the same time awkwardly; she obviously regarded herself as a good-natured and simple being, and yet, no matter what she did, it always struck one that that was precisely what she had not wanted to do; everything with her seemed, as children say, done on purpose, that is to say, not simply, not naturally.

"Yes, yes, I know you, Bazarov," she repeated. (She had the habit —peculiar to many provincial and Moscow ladies—of calling men by their surnames from the first day's acquaintance.) "Care for a cigar?"

"A cigar is all right in its way," quickly put in Sitnicov, who by now had sprawled out in an armchair and had his legs up in the air, "but suppose you give us some lunch? We're awfully hungry; and tell them to bring us up a little bottle of champagne."

"Sybarite," commented Eudoxia, and she laughed. (When she laughed the gum above her upper teeth became bared.) "He is a sybarite, isn't he, Bazarov?"

"I like the comforts of life," Sitnicov pronounced with an important air. "Which does not prevent my being a Liberal."

"No, it does prevent it, it does!" Eudoxia shrilled, but just the same she ordered her maid to attend to the lunch as well as the champagne.

"What do you think about it?" she added, turning to Bazarov. "I'm persuaded you share my opinion."

"Well, no," retorted Bazarov. "A piece of meat is better than a piece of bread even from the chemical point of view."

"Why, are you studying chemistry? That is my passion. I've even invented a new sort of plastic myself."

"A plastic? You?"

"Yes, I. And do you know for what purpose? To make unbreakable dolls' heads. I, too, am practical. But all that isn't ready yet. I still have to read Liebig. By the way, have you read Kislyacov's article on Female Labor in the *Moscow Gazette*? Do read it, please. You're interested in feminism, I suppose? And in the schools, too? What does your friend do? What's his name?"

Madame Kukshina let her questions drop one after another with refined negligence without waiting for an answer; spoiled children talk so to their nurses.

"My name is Arcadii Nicolaich Kirsanov," said Arcadii, "and I don't do anything."

Eudoxia went off into peals of laughter. "How charming! What, you don't smoke? Victor, do you know, I'm angry with you."

"What for?"

"They tell me you've begun singing the praises of George Sand again. A retrogressive woman, and that's all there is to it! How can anyone possibly compare her with Emerson? She has no ideas whatsoever on education, or physiology, or anything. I'm certain she hasn't even heard of embryology, yet how could you possibly get along without such knowledge nowadays?" (Here Eudoxia actually threw up her hands.) "Ah, what a wonderful article Elisyevich has written on that subject! He's a gentleman of genius." (Eudoxia's use of "gentleman" for "man" was a consistent one.) "Bazarov, sit by me on the divan. You don't know it, but I'm awfully afraid of you."

"Why so, if I may ask?"

"You're a dangerous gentleman; you're so very critical. Ah, my God! Really, I could laugh—here I am, talking like some landed proprietress out on the steppes. However, I really am a landed proprietress. I manage my property myself; and just imagine, my manager Erophey is a wonderful type, quite like Cooper's Pathfinder—there's something so primitive about him! I've definitely settled here—an unbearable town, isn't it? But what can one do?"

"This town is like every town," Bazarov remarked placidly.

"All its interests are so petty, that's the horrible part! I used to spend my winters in Moscow—but now my lawful spouse, M'sieu' Kukshin, resides there. And besides, Moscow nowadays—really, I don't know—it's no longer the same. I'm thinking of going abroad; last year I was all ready to go."

"To Paris, naturally?" queried Bazarov.

"To Paris *and* Heidelberg."

"Why Heidelberg?"

"Oh, now! Why, Bunsen's there!"

To this Bazarov could find no reply.

"*Pierre* Sapozhnicov—do you know him?"

"No, I don't."

"Oh, now! *Pierre* Sapozhnicov—why, he's *always* at Lidia Hesta-tova's."

"Don't know her either."

"Well, it was he undertook to be my cicerone. Thank God, I'm inde-pendent; I've no children. . . . What was that I said: *thank God* actually! However, it doesn't really matter."

Eudoxia rolled a cigarette with fingers stained a dark brown by nico-tine, licked the edge with her tongue, sucked at the cigarette to see if it drew, and lit up. The maid came in with a tray.

"Well, here's lunch! Will you have an appetizer first? Victor, open the bottle—that's in your department."

"So it is, so it is," mumbled Sitnicov, and again gave vent to his squealing laugh.

"Are there any pretty women here?" inquired Bazarov, as he drank off a third glass.

"Yes, there are," answered Eudoxia, "but then they're all such empty-headed creatures. *Mon amie* Odintsova, for instance, isn't at all bad-looking. It's a pity that her reputation is sort of . . . That wouldn't matter so much, though, but she has no independence in her views, no breadth, nothing of all that. Our whole system of educa-tion ought to be changed. I've already given the matter some thought— our women are very badly educated."

"You can't do a thing with them," put in Sitnicov. "They deserve contempt—and contempt, utter and complete, is all I feel for them!" (The possibility of feeling and expressing contempt was the most agreeable of sensations to Sitnicov; he was particularly severe in his strictures on women, never suspecting that a few months later he was fated to grovel before his wife merely because she was a Princess Durdo-leosova by birth.) "Not a single one of them would be capable of understanding our conversation; not a single one merits being discussed by serious men like us!"

"But there's no need whatsoever for them to understand our con-versation," Bazarov observed.

"Whom do you mean?" Eudoxia put in.

"Pretty women."

"What? Do you share Proudhon's opinion, then?"

Bazarov drew himself up haughtily.

"I don't share anyone's opinions; I have my own."

"Down with all authorities!" shouted Sitnicov, delighted at an opportunity of expressing himself boldly before the man he slavishly admired.

"But even Macaulay—" Kukshina was about to say something.

"Down with Macaulay!" thundered Sitnicov. "Are you going to stick up for these silly women?"

"For silly women, no, but for the rights of women, which I have sworn to defend to the last drop of my blood."

"Down with—" but here Sitnicov brought himself up short. "Why, I'm not denying them," he said.

"No, I see you're a Slavophile."

"No, I'm not a Slavophile—although, of course—"

"No, no, no! You *are* a Slavophile. You're an advocate of patriarchal despotism. All you need is a cat-o'-nine-tails in your hands!"

"A cat-o'-nine-tails is an excellent thing," remarked Bazarov; "but we've got to the last drop."

"Of what?" interrupted Eudoxia.

"Of champagne, most estimable Avdotya Nikitishna, of champagne —not of your blood."

"I can never listen calmly when women are assailed," Eudoxia went on. "It's horrible, horrible! Instead of assailing them, you'd do better to read Michelet's book, *De l'amour*. That's exquisite! Gentlemen, let's talk of love," added Eudoxia, letting her arm fall languidly on a rumpled divan cushion.

A sudden silence ensued. "No, why should we talk of love?" said Bazarov. "But you mentioned an Odintsova just now. That's what you called her, I think? Who is this lady?"

"She's charming, charming!" Sitnicov piped up. "I'll introduce you. Clever girl, rich, a widow. It's a pity she's not yet advanced enough; she ought to become better acquainted with our Eudoxia. I drink to your health, *Eudoxie*! Let's clink glasses! *Et toc, et toc, et tin-tin-tin! Et toc, et toc, et tin-tin-tin!*"

"Victor, you're a scalawag."

The lunch lasted a long while. The first bottle of champagne was followed by another, a third, and even a fourth. Eudoxia chattered without stopping for breath; Sitnicov chimed in with her. They discussed whether marriage was a prejudice or a crime, and whether men were born equal or not. And just what, precisely, does individuality consist of. Things at last reached a point where Eudoxia, flushed from the wine she had drunk, and thumping with flat-nailed fingers the keys of a grand piano all out of tune, took to singing in a hoarse voice—first gypsy songs and then Seymour-Schiff's song, "Drowsy Granada Slumbers," while Sitnicov tied a scarf around his head and represented a swooning lover. At the words:

> "Let thy lips and mine, beloved,
> Blend within a kiss of fire—"

Arcadii's patience came to an end. "Gentlemen, this has begun to look like Bedlam," he remarked aloud.

Bazarov, who had only at rare intervals put it an ironical word in the conversation—he devoted himself to the champagne for the most part—gave a loud yawn, got up, and, without taking leave of their hostess, walked out with Arcadii. Sitnicov jumped up and followed them.

"Well, what do you think of her?" he inquired, skipping obsequiously now to the right, now to the left of them. "Just as I told you, a remarkable personality! If only we had more women like that! She is, in her own way, an expression of the highest morality."

"And is that establishment of your old man's likewise an expression of the highest morality?" observed Bazarov, pointing to a ginmill which they were passing at that instant.

Sitnicov again went off into his squealing laugh. He was very much ashamed of his origin and did not know whether to feel himself flattered or offended at Bazarov's unexpected familiarity.

XIV

A few days later the ball at the Governor's took place. Kolyazin was the real "hero of the occasion." The Leader of Nobility made it known to all and sundry that he had come, properly speaking, out of respect for him; while the Governor, even at the ball, even while he was not bustling about, went right on being the ever-busy administrator. The affability of Kolyazin's demeanor could be equaled only by his stateliness. He was gracious to all, to some with a shade of squeamishness, to others with a shade of respect; he played his rôle *"en vrai chevalier français"* up to the hilt before the ladies, and was continually giving vent to a hearty, sonorous, unshared laugh, such as befits a dignitary. He slapped Arcadii on the back and loudly "dear nephew"-ed him; vouchsafed Bazarov—who was attired in a rather old evening coat—a sidelong glance in passing—absent but condescending—and an indistinct but affable grunt, in which nothing could be distinguished except "I . . ." and "very much"; gave Sitnicov a finger and a smile, though with his head already averted; even to Kukshina, who made her appearance at the ball with dirty gloves and no crinoline, but with a bird of paradise in her hair, he said *"enchantée."* There were scads of people, and no lack of male dancing partners; the civilians were wallflowers for the most part, but the military men danced assiduously, especially one who had spent six weeks in Paris, where he had mastered various daring expletives in the nature of *"zut!" "Ah, fichtrr-zze!" "pst, pst, mon bibi!"* and the like. He pronounced them to perfection with genuine Parisian *chic,* yet at the same time he confused his tenses, used *absolument* in the sense of *certainly*—in short, he expressed himself in that pidgin Great Russo-French which Frenchmen ridicule so when they do not have to assure our sort that we speak French like angels— *"comme des anges."*

Arcadii, as we already know, danced badly, while Bazarov did not dance at all; they both found a nook for themselves, where they were joined by Sitnicov. Assuming a scornful smile and giving vent to venomous comments, he kept looking insolently about him, and was apparently really enjoying himself. Suddenly his face changed and, turning to Arcadii, he said, with some show of embarrassment, "Odintsova is here!"

Arcadii turned and saw a tall woman in a black dress standing at the door of the room. He was struck by the dignity of her carriage. Her bare arms lay gracefully along her slender waist; gracefully some light sprays of fuchsia drooped from her gleaming hair on to her sloping shoulders; her clear eyes looked out from under a somewhat overhanging white brow, with a tranquil and intelligent expression—tranquil, precisely, and not pensive—and a scarcely perceptible smile hovered on her lips. Her face radiated a gracious and gentle force.

"Do you know her?" Arcadii asked Sitnicov.

"Intimately. Would you like me to introduce you?"

"Please—after this quadrille."

Bazarov's attention, too, was directed to Odintsova.

"Who in the world is she?" he remarked. "She's different from the rest of the females here."

After waiting till the end of the quadrille, Sitnicov led Arcadii up to Odintsova, but it hardly seemed as if he were intimately acquainted with her; he himself was embarrassed when he spoke, while she for her part looked at him in some surprise. However, her face assumed a cordial expression when she heard Arcadii's surname. She asked him whether he was not the son of Nicolai Petrovich.

"Yes."

"I've seen your father twice and have heard a great deal about him," she went on. "I am very glad to make your acquaintance."

At that instant some adjutant flew up to her and begged for a quadrille. She consented.

"So you dance?" Arcadii asked respectfully.

"Yes, I dance. Why do you think I don't? Or do I seem too old to you?"

"Really, now, how could I possibly? But since you do dance, permit me to ask you for a mazurka."

Odintsova smiled condescendingly.

"If you wish," she said and looked at Arcadii, not exactly with an air of superiority, but as married sisters look at very young brothers. Odintsova was not much older than Arcadii—she was twenty-nine— but in her presence he felt himself a schoolboy, an adolescent, as though the difference in their ages were far greater. Kolyazin approached her with a majestic air and ingratiating speeches. Arcadii moved away but kept watching her; he could not take his eyes off her even during the quadrille. She talked with equal ease to her partner and to the grand dignitary; she gently turned her head and eyes and twice laughed gently. Her nose—like almost all Russian noses—was a little thick; and her complexion was not perfectly clear; Arcadii made up his mind, for all that, that he had never before met such an attractive woman. He could not get the sound of her voice out of his ears; the very folds of her dress seemed to hang upon her differently from all other women—more gracefully and amply—and her movements were peculiarly smooth and natural.

Arcadii felt some timidity at heart when at the first sounds of the mazurka he began to sit it out beside his partner; he was about to enter into a conversation with her, but merely kept running his hand through his hair and could not find a single word to say. But his timidity and agitation did not last long; Odintsova's tranquillity was imparted to him as well. Before a quarter of an hour had passed he was telling her freely about his father, his uncle, his life in Petersburg and in the country. Odintsova listened to him with courteous sympathy, slightly opening and closing her fan; his talk was broken off when partners came for her; Sitnicov, among others, asked her twice. She would come back, sit down again, take up her fan, and her bosom did not even rise more rapidly while Arcadii again fell to chattering, permeated by the happiness of being near her, talking to her, looking at her eyes, her lovely brow, all her endearing, dignified, clever face. She said little, for her part, but her words evinced a knowledge of life; from some of her observations Arcadii concluded that this young woman had already contrived to feel and think a great many things.

"Who was that you were standing with," she asked him, "when M'sieu' Sitnicov brought you to me?"

"Oh, so you noticed him?" Arcadii asked in his turn. "He has a splendid face, hasn't he? He's a certain Bazarov, a friend of mine."

Arcadii fell to talking about this "friend" of his. He spoke of him in such detail, and with such enthusiasm, that Odintsova turned toward him and gave him an attentive look. Meanwhile the mazurka was drawing to a close. Arcadii felt sorry about having to leave his partner; he had spent nearly an hour so pleasantly with her! He had, it is true, during the whole time continually felt as though she were condescending to him, as though he ought to be grateful to her—but young hearts are not weighed down by that feeling.

The music stopped. *"Merci,"* said Odintsova, getting up. "You promised to come and see me; do bring your friend with you. I'll be very curious to see the man who has the courage not to believe in anything."

The Governor came up to Odintsova, announced that supper was ready, and, with a careworn face, offered her his arm. As she went away, she turned to give a last smile and nod to Arcadii. He bowed low, followed her with his eyes (how graceful her waist seemed to him, the grayish luster of black silk apparently poured over it!), and as he thought, "She has already forgotten my existence this very instant," he was conscious of a certain exquisite humility in his soul.

"Well?" Bazarov questioned him as soon as Arcadii had rejoined him in the corner. "Have a good time? A gentleman has been telling me just now that this lady is—my, my, my! But then the gentleman himself strikes me as very much of a fool. Well, now, according to you, is she really?—my, my, my!"

"I don't quite understand that definition," answered Arcadii.

"Oh, now! What innocence!"

"In that case, I don't understand the gentleman you quote. Odintsova is indisputably most endearing, but she behaves so coldly and austerely, that—"

"Still waters—you know!" Bazarov put in quickly. "She's cold, you say. That's just where the taste comes in. For you like ice cream, don't you?"

"Perhaps," Arcadii muttered. "I can't judge about that. She wishes to make your acquaintance and asked me to bring you to see her."

"I can imagine how you've painted me! However, you did the right thing. Take me along. Whatever she may be—whether she's simply a provincial lioness, or an 'emancipated woman,' à la Kukshina, the fact remains that she's got a pair of shoulders whose like I've not set eyes on for a long while."

Arcadii felt a twinge at Bazarov's cynicism, but—as often happens—he reproached his friend for something else than the precise thing he disliked about him.

"Why are you unwilling to allow freedom of thought in women?" he asked in a low voice.

"Because, brother, as far as my observations go, among women it is only the freaks who go in for freedom of thought."

At this point the conversation came to an end. Both young men left immediately after supper. They were followed by a nervously malicious yet somewhat hesitating laugh from Kukshina, whose vanity had been deeply wounded by neither one nor the other having paid her any attention. She stayed later than anyone at the ball, and at four o'clock in the morning she danced a polka-mazurka through with Sitnicov, in the Parisian style. This edifying spectacle was the final event of the Governor's gala.

X V

"Let's see what species of mammalia this specimen belongs to," Bazarov was saying to Arcadii the following day, as they mounted the staircase of the hotel at which Odintsova was stopping. "I scent something out of the way here."

"I'm surprised at you!" exclaimed Arcadii. "What? You—you, Bazarov!—clinging to that narrow morality which—"

"What a funny fellow you are!" Bazarov cut him short carelessly. "Don't you know that in our dialect and for the likes of us 'something out of the way' means 'everything is hunky-dory'? There's good hunting here, see? Didn't you tell me yourself today that she had made a strange marriage—although, to my way of thinking, marrying a rich old man is by no means a strange business, but, on the contrary, a prudent one. I don't believe the gossip of the town, but I like to think, as our cultivated Governor says, that it's well grounded."

Arcadii made no answer and knocked on the door of the room. A young flunky in livery conducted the two friends into a large room, badly furnished, like all rooms in Russian hotels, but with flowers all over it. Soon Odintsova herself appeared in a simple morning dress. She seemed still younger by the light of the spring sunshine. Arcadii presented Bazarov, and noticed with secret wonder that he seemed embarrassed, while Odintsova remained perfectly tranquil, as she had been the night before. Bazarov himself was conscious of his embarrassment and was irritated by it. "Of all things! Frightened of a petticoat!" he thought, and, sprawled out in an armchair just like Sitnicov, began talking with an exaggerated unrestraint, while Odintsova kept her clear eyes fixed on him.

Anna Sergheievna Odintsova was the daughter of Serghei Nicolaevich Loktev, notorious as an Adonis, an adventurer, and a gambler, who, after cutting a figure and making a splash for fifteen years in Petersburg and Moscow, wound up by losing his shirt, and was forced to retire to the country, where, however, he died shortly, leaving a very small property to his two daughters—Anna, a girl of twenty, and Katya, a child of twelve. Their mother, who came of an impoverished line of princes, the H——s, had died at Petersburg when her husband was in his heyday. Anna's position after her father's death was very difficult. The brilliant education she had received in Petersburg had not fitted her for enduring the cares of domestic life and estate management, or an obscure existence in the country. She knew absolutely no one in the whole neighborhood, and there was no one she could consult. Her father had tried to avoid all contact with the neighbors; he despised them in his way and they despised him in theirs. She did not lose her head, however, and promptly sent for a sister of her mother's, Princess Avdotya Stepanovna H——, a malicious and arrogant old lady, who, on installing herself in her niece's house, appropriated all the best rooms for her own use, scolded and groused from morning till night, and would not go even for a walk in the garden unattended by her one serf, a surly flunky in a threadbare pea-green livery with light blue trimming and a three-cornered hat. Anna put up patiently with all her aunt's quirks, gradually set to work on her sister's education, and, it seemed, had already become reconciled to the idea of withering away in the wilderness.

But destiny had decreed another fate for her. She chanced to be seen by a certain Odintsov, a very wealthy man of forty-six, an eccentric and a hypochondriac, bloated, heavy, and sour; but not stupid and not ill-natured; he fell in love with her and offered her his hand. She consented to become his wife, and he lived six years with her, and on his death settled all his property upon her. Anna Sergheievna remained in the country for nearly a year after his death; then she went abroad with her sister, but visited only Germany; she tired of it and came back to live at her beloved Nikolskoe, which was nearly thirty miles from the town of X——. There she had a magnificent, splendidly furnished house and a beautiful garden, with conservatories; the late Odintsov had never begrudged himself anything. Anna Sergheievna came to the town very rarely, for the most part only on business, and even then she did not stay long. She was not liked in the province; there had been a fearful outcry at her marriage with Odintsov, all sorts of fantastic tales were told about her; it was asserted that she had helped her father in his cardsharping tricks, and even that she had gone abroad out of necessity to conceal certain lamentable consequences. "You understand of what," the indignant gossips would wind up. "She's been through fire and water," they said of her; to which a noted provincial wit usually added the rest of the tag, "And brazen furnaces." All these slanders reached her, but she turned a deaf ear to them; there was much independence and a good deal of determination in her character.

Odintsova sat leaning back in her armchair and listened with folded hands to Bazarov. He, contrary to his wont, was talking a good deal and obviously trying to entertain her—another surprise for Arcadii. He could not decide whether Bazarov was attaining his object. It was difficult to surmise from Anna Sergheievna's face what impression was being made on her; it retained the same expression, affable and refined; her beautiful eyes were lighted up by attention, but an untroubled attention. Bazarov's posturing had affected her unpleasantly for the first few minutes of his visit like a bad odor or a jarring sound; but she saw at once that he was nervous, and found this even flattering. Vulgarity alone repelled her, and no one could have accused Bazarov of vulgarity.

Arcadii was fated to be incessantly surprised that day. He had expected that Bazarov would talk to a clever woman like Odintsova about his convictions and views, while she herself had expressed a desire to listen to the man "who has the courage not to believe in anything." But instead of that Bazarov discoursed on medicine, on homeopathy, and on botany. It turned out that Odintsova had not wasted her time in solitude; she had read a number of good books, and spoke excellent Russian. She led the conversation around to music; but noticing that Bazarov did not appreciate art, she quietly brought it back to botany, even though Arcadii was just launching into a discourse upon the significance of folk melodies. Odintsova continued to treat him as though he were a younger brother; apparently she appreciated the goodness and simpleheartedness of youth in him—and that was all. For over three hours did the conversation last, leisurely, varied, and animated.

The friends at last got up and began to take their leave. Anna Serghievna looked cordially at them, held out her beautiful white hand to both, and, after a moment's thought, said with a hesitating but delightful smile:

"If you aren't afraid of being bored, gentlemen, come to see me at Nikolskoe."

"Oh, Anna Serghievna!" Arcadii exclaimed, "I'd consider it the greatest happiness—"

"And you, M'sieu' Bazarov?"

Bazarov only bowed, and Arcadii had his last surprise: he noticed that his friend was blushing.

"Well," he asked him out in the street, "are you still of the same opinion, that she's—all my, my, my?"

"Who can tell anything about her? Just see how she froze all up!" retorted Bazarov, and after a brief pause added, "She's a perfect grand duchess, a regal personage. She only needs a long train to her dress and a crown on her head."

"Our grand duchesses don't talk such excellent Russian," remarked Arcadii.

"She's been through the mill, brother; she knows what hard-earned bread tastes like!"

"Anyway, she's charming as can be," observed Arcadii.

"What a magnificent body," Bazarov went on. "What a subject for the dissecting table!"

"Stop it, for God's sake, Eugene! You're really going too far."

"Well, don't get angry, you softy. I told you she's first-rate. We must go for a stay with her."

"When?"

"Well, why not the day after tomorrow? What are we going to do here? Drink champagne with Kukshina? Listen to your relative, the Liberal dignitary? Let's dash off the day after tomorrow, then. By the way—my father's patch of ground isn't far from there. This Nikolskoe's on the S—— road, isn't it?"

"Yes."

"*Optime*.[1] Why shilly-shally? It's only fools that do—and those who are too clever. A magnificent body, I'm telling you!"

Three days later the two friends were rolling along the road to Nikolskoe. The day was bright and not too hot, and the well-fed posting horses trotted along in unison, switching their tied and plaited tails. Arcadii looked at the road and, without knowing why, was smiling.

"Congratulate me!" exclaimed Bazarov suddenly. "Today's the twenty-second of June, my birthday. Let's see how well my guardian angel will keep an eye on me. Today they're expecting me home," he added, lowering his voice. "Well, they can go on expecting me. It isn't so important."

XVI

The country house in which Anna Sergheievna lived stood on a sloping exposed hill at no great distance from a yellow stone church with a green roof, white columns, and a fresco over the main portal representing the Resurrection of Christ in the "Italian" style. Sprawling in the foreground of the picture was a swarthy warrior in a helmet, specially conspicuous for his rotund contours. Behind the church a long village stretched in two rows, with chimneys peeping out here and there above the thatched roofs. The manor house was built in the same style as the church, the style known among us as Alexandrine; this house, too, was painted yellow and had a green roof and white columns, and a pediment with an escutcheon on it. The provincial architect had put up both buildings with the approval of the deceased Odintsov, who could not endure—as he expressed it—any idle and arbitrary innovations whatsoever. The house was flanked by the dark trees of an old garden; an avenue of clipped pines led up to the entrance.

Our friends were met in the hall by two well-grown footmen in

[1] "Splendid!"

livery; one of them at once ran for the steward. The steward, a stout man in a black dress coat, promptly appeared and led the visitors by a staircase covered with rugs to a special room, in which two bedsteads were already prepared for them with all necessaries for dressing. It was clear that order reigned supreme in the house; everything was clean, everything was redolent of some decorous fragrance, just the same as in ministerial reception rooms.

"Anna Sergheievna asks you to please come down to her in half an hour," the steward announced. "Are there any orders you would care to give meanwhile?"

"No orders, my dear fellow," answered Bazarov. "Unless you'll be so good as to trouble yourself to bring me a glass of vodka."

"Yes, Sir," said the steward, not without some perplexity, and he withdrew, his boots creaking.

"What *grand genre!*" remarked Bazarov. "That's what they call it in your set, isn't it? She's a grand duchess, and that's all there's to it."

"A fine grand duchess," retorted Arcadii, "to invite two such high and mighty aristocrats as you and me for a stay at the very first meeting."

"Especially me, a future pillroller, and the son of a pillroller, and a village sexton's grandson. . . . You know, I suppose, I'm the grandson of a sexton? Like Speranski," [1] Bazarov added after a brief silence, and his lips curved.

"And she is so self-indulgent—oh, but she is self-indulgent, is this grand lady! Should we put on full dress by any chance?"

Arcadii merely shrugged his shoulders—but he, too, felt a little abashed.

Half an hour later Bazarov and Arcadii went down together into the drawing room. It was a spacious, high-ceilinged room, furnished rather luxuriously but without any particular taste. Heavy, expensive furniture was ranged in the usual stiff order along walls covered with cinnamon-colored paper with gold arabesques; Odintsov had ordered the furniture from Moscow through a friend and agent of his, a wine dealer. Over a divan in the center of one wall hung a portrait of a flabby, fair-haired man—and the portrait seemed to be eying the visitors unfriendlily.

"Must be the late lamented himself," Bazarov whispered to Arcadii and, wrinkling up his nose, he added: "Maybe we'd better clear out quickly."

But at that instant their hostess herself walked in. She had on a light

[1] Count M. M. Speranski (1772-1839), famous statesman.

barège dress; her hair, smoothly combed back behind her ears, gave a girlish expression to her pure and fresh face.

"Thank you for keeping your word," she began. "You must stay a while with me; really, it's not bad here. I'll introduce you to my sister; she plays the piano well. That doesn't mean much to you, M'sieu' Bazarov; but you, I think, M'sieu' Kirsanov, are fond of music. Besides my sister I have an old aunt living with me, and one of our neighbors drops in sometimes to play cards; that makes up our whole circle. And now let's sit down."

Odintsova delivered this whole little speech with peculiar precision, as though she had learned it by heart; then she turned to Arcadii. It turned out that her mother had known Arcadii's mother, and had even been her confidante in her love for Arcadii's father. Arcadii began talking with great warmth of his dead mother; while Bazarov took to looking through albums in the meantime. "What a tame little fellow I'm getting to be," he was thinking to himself.

A beautiful greyhound bitch with a blue collar on ran into the drawing room, tapping on the floor with her nails, immediately followed by a girl of eighteen, black-haired and swarthy, with a somewhat round but pleasing face and small dark eyes. She was carrying a basket filled with flowers.

"And here's my Katya," said Odintsova, indicating her with a motion of her head. Katya made a slight curtsy, settled down beside her sister, and began sorting the flowers. The greyhound, whose name was Fifi, went up, wagging her tail, to each of the visitors in turn, and thrust her cold nose into the hands of each.

"Did you pick all that yourself?" asked Odintsova.

"By myself," answered Katya.

"Is auntie coming to tea?"

"Yes."

When Katya spoke, she had a very endearing smile, timid and candid, and looked up from under her eyebrows with a sort of humorous severity. Everything about her still had the greenness of youth: her voice, and the bloom on her whole face, and her rosy hands with the whitish circles on the palms, and her shoulders just the least bit narrow. . . . She was constantly blushing and breathing rapidly.

Odintsova turned to Bazarov: "You're looking at the photographs only from politeness, Eugene Vassilyich," she began. "That doesn't interest you. You'd better come closer to us, and let's have a discussion about something or other."

Bazarov drew nearer.

"What's your pleasure?" he asked.

"Whatever subject you like. I warn you I'm a dreadfully argumentative person."

"You?"

"Yes. That seems to surprise you. Why?"

"Because, as far as I can judge, you have a calm, cool character, whereas one must be impulsive to be argumentative."

"How can you have had time to understand me so soon? In the first place I am impatient and insistent—ask Katya; and in the second place I am very easily carried away."

Bazarov looked at Anna Sergheievna.

"Perhaps; you ought to know best. And so you are inclined for a discussion. By all means. I was looking through the views of the Saxon mountains in your album, and you remarked that that couldn't interest me. You said so because you suppose me to have no feeling for art, and as a fact I haven't any; but these views might be interesting to me from a geological viewpoint, from the viewpoint of the formation of the mountains, for instance."

"Excuse me; as a geologist you'd rather have recourse to a book, to a special work on the subject, and not a drawing."

"The drawing shows me at a glance what would be spread over ten pages in a book."

Anna Sergheievna was silent for a little while.

"And so you haven't a jot of artistic feeling?" she observed, putting her elbows on the table, and by that very action bringing her face nearer to Bazarov. "However can you get along without it?"

"Why, what does one need it for, may I ask?"

"Well, if only to enable one to recognize and study people."

Bazarov smiled slightly.

"In the first place, that's what experience in life is for; and in the second, I assure you, studying separate individualities isn't worth the bother. All people are like one another, in soul as in body; each of us has a brain, spleen, a heart, and lungs made and arranged alike; and the so-called moral qualities are the very same in all; the slight variations don't mean a thing. A single human specimen is sufficient to judge all the others by. People are like trees in a forest: no arborist is going to bother studying each individual birch."

Katya, who was leisurely matching the flowers, lifted her eyes to Bazarov with a puzzled look and, encountering his rapid and careless glance, crimsoned up to her ears. Anna Sergheievna shook her head.

"Trees in a forest," she repeated his words. "According to you, then, there is no difference between the stupid man and the intelligent one, between the good and the evil?"

"No, there is a difference, just as between a sick man and a healthy one. The lungs of a pulmonary consumptive are not at all in the same condition as yours and mine, though they are made on the same plan. We know approximately what bodily diseases come from; while moral disorders come from bad education, from all the bosh people's heads are stuffed with from their earliest years—from the hideous state of society, in short. Reform society, and there will be no diseases."

Bazarov said all this with such an air as if he were at the same time thinking to himself: "You can believe me or not—it's all one to me!" He was slowly passing his long fingers over his side whiskers, while his eyes strayed over the corners of the room.

"And you suppose," observed Anna Sergheievna, "that when society will have become reformed there will be no stupid and wicked people?"

"At least, in a proper organization of society it will be absolutely one whether a man is stupid or clever, wicked or good."

"Yes, I understand; they will all have one and the same sort of spleen."

"Precisely so, Madam."

Odintsova turned to Arcadii.

"And what's your opinion, Arcadii Nicolaevich?"

"I agree with Eugene," he answered.

Katya looked up at him from under her brows.

"You amaze me, gentlemen," commented Odintsova, "but we'll discuss things further. Now, however, I hear my aunt coming in to tea; we must spare her ears."

Anna Sergheievna's aunt, Princess H——, a wizened little woman with a pinched-up face that looked like a small clenched fist, and staring malicious eyes under a gray scratch wig, came in, and, scarcely bowing to the guests, she sank into a roomy velvet-covered armchair upon which none but she had the right to sit. Katya put a footstool under her feet; the old woman did not thank her, did not even glance at her, her hands merely stirred under the yellow shawl, which practically covered her whole wizened body. The Princess was fond of yellow; her cap, too, had bright yellow ribbons.

"How have you slept, Aunt?" inquired Odintsova, raising her voice.

"That dog is in here again," the old lady growled in reply and, having noticed that Fifi had taken two hesitating steps in her direction, she cried: "Get out! Get out!"

Katya called Fifi and opened the door for her.

Fifi dashed out delighted, in the expectation of being taken for a walk, but, left alone outside the door, she began scratching and whining. The Princess scowled. Katya was about to go out. . . .

"I expect tea is ready," said Odintsova. "Come, gentlemen; Aunt, please come in to tea."

The Princess got up from her armchair without a word and was the first out of the drawing room. They all followed her into the dining room. A little page in livery drew back from the table, with much scraping, another tabooed armchair covered with cushions, into which the Princess sank. She was the first to whom Katya, in pouring out the tea, handed a cup emblazoned with a heraldic crest. The crone put some honey in her cup (she considered it both sinful and extravagant to drink tea with sugar in it, though she never spent a copper herself on anything), and suddenly asked in a hoarse voice, "And what does Prince Ivan write?"—she pronounced it "Preence."

No one made her any reply. Bazarov and Arcadii soon guessed that no attention was paid to her, although she was treated respectfully.

"They keep her here to make themselves important," thought Bazarov. "Princely spawn, you see."

After tea Anna Sergheievna suggested a stroll, but it began to drizzle, and the whole party, with the exception of the Princess, returned to the drawing room. The neighbor, who was a devotee of cards, arrived; his name was Porphyrii Platonich, a stoutish, grayish man with shortish legs that seemed carved; he was most polite and amusing. Anna Sergheievna, who was still talking for the most part with Bazarov, asked him whether he wouldn't like to try his hand against them in old-fashioned preference? Bazarov assented, saying that he ought to prepare himself beforehand for the duties awaiting him as a country medico.

"Watch out for yourself," Anna Sergheievna warned him. "Porphyrii Platonich and I will overwhelm you. And you, Katya," she added, "play something for Arcadii Nicolaevich; he's fond of music, and it'll give us a chance to listen, too."

Katya went unwillingly to the piano; and Arcadii, though he certainly was fond of music, unwillingly followed her; it seemed to him that Odintsova was shunting him off—although like every young man of his age he already felt a certain vague and oppressive emotion surging up in his heart, something like a premonition of love. Katya raised the top of the grand piano and without looking at Arcadii she asked in a low voice:

"What should I play for you?"

"Whatever you like," Arcadii answered indifferently.

"What sort of music do you like best?" Katya asked again, without moving.

"Classical," Arcadii answered in the same tone of voice.

"Do you like Mozart?"

"Yes, I like Mozart."

Katya pulled out Mozart's Sonata-Fantasia in C minor. She played very well, although rather overprecisely and dryly. Without taking her eyes off the notes, she sat upright and stiffly; and only toward the end of the sonata did her face take on a bright glow, and a tiny lock of her loosened hair straggled down over her dark eyebrow.

Arcadii was particularly struck by the last part of the sonata, that part wherein, in the midst of the captivating gaiety of the insouciant air, there suddenly arise pangs of such mournful, almost tragic, sorrowing. But the ideas stirred in him by Mozart's music had nothing to do with Katya. Looking at her, he simply thought: "Well, this young lady doesn't play so badly, and she's not so bad-looking herself."

When she had finished the sonata, Katya, without taking her hands off the keys, asked: "Enough?"

Arcadii declared that he dared not trouble her again, and began talking to her about Mozart, and asked her whether she had chosen that sonata herself or if someone had recommended it to her. But Katya answered him monosyllabically; she went back into her shell, withdrew into herself. Whenever this happened with her, she did not come out again soon; her very face assumed an obstinate, almost stolid, expression at such times. She was not exactly shy but rather diffident and quite overawed by her sister, who had educated her and who naturally had no suspicion of the fact. Arcadii wound up with having to call Fifi to him and patting her on the head with a benevolent smile, in order to save face.

Katya again busied herself with her flowers.

Bazarov meanwhile was losing and losing. Anna Sergheievna played cards in masterly fashion; Porphyrii Platonich, too, could hold his own in the game. Bazarov lost a sum which, though trifling in itself, still was not altogether a pleasant thing. At supper Anna Sergheievna again turned the conversation on botany.

"We'll go for a walk tomorrow morning," she said to Bazarov. "I want you to teach me ,the Latin names of the wild flowers and their peculiarities."

"Of what use would the Latin names be to you?" asked Bazarov.

"Order is needed in everything," she answered.

"What an exquisite woman Anna Sergheievna is!" Arcadii exclaimed when he was alone with his friend in the room assigned to them.

"Yes," answered Bazarov, "a female with brains. And she's seen life, too."

"In what sense do you mean that, Eugene Vassilyich?"

"In a good sense, a good sense, my dear friend, Arcadii Nicolaich! I'm convinced she also manages her estate excellently. However, it isn't she who is the supreme miracle, but her sister."

"What? That dark little thing?"

"Yes, that dark little thing. She's the one who's fresh and untouched and shy and silent, and anything you like. There's someone worth taking in hand. You could fashion her into whatever you desire; but the other's shopworn."

Arcadii made no reply to Bazarov, and each of them got into bed with rather singular thoughts of his own in his head.

Anna Sergheievna, too, thought of her guests that evening. Bazarov had proven to her liking because of the absence of gallantry in him and the very brusquerie of his views. She saw in him something new which she had not chanced to meet before—and she was curious by nature.

Anna Sergheievna was quite a strange creature. Having no prejudices of any kind, having even no strong beliefs, she never retreated before anything and was not going in any particular direction. She saw many things clearly, she was interested in many things, but nothing satisfied her completely, and, besides, she hardly desired complete satisfaction. Her intellect was at the same time inquiring and indifferent; her doubts never quieted down to forgetfulness and never grew strong enough to disturb her. Had she not been rich and independent she would perhaps have thrown herself into the fray, have come to know passion. But life was easy for her, even though she was bored now and then, and she continued to pass day after day with deliberation and with only rare perturbations. Rainbow hues would occasionally burst into glow even before her eyes, but she breathed more freely when they died out and did not regret them. Her imagination may even have been borne away beyond the limits of what is considered permissible by the laws of conventional morality; but even then the blood coursed as quietly as ever through her fascinatingly graceful and tranquil body. Sometimes, stepping out of her scented bath all warm and enervated, she would fall into reveries about the nothingness of life, its misery, toil, labor, and evil. Her soul would be filled with sudden daring, would seethe with noble ardor, but a slight draft would blow from a half-closed window—and there would Anna Sergheievna be, all shrunk into herself and plaintive and almost complaining, and there was only one thing she felt a need of at that instant —not to have that nasty draft blowing on her.

Like all women who have not succeeded in knowing love, she desired something, without herself knowing what. Strictly speaking, she did not desire anything, but it seemed to her that she desired everything. She had hardly been able to endure the late Odintsov (she had married him out of calculation, although probably she would not have consented to become his wife if she had not considered him a kind-hearted man), and had acquired a secret repugnance of all men, whom she could not imagine to herself other than slovenly, heavy, sluggish, and impotently importunate creatures. Once, somewhere abroad, she had met a young handsome Swede, with a chivalrous expression, with honest blue eyes under an open brow; he had made a strong impression on her, but this had not kept her from returning to Russia.

"A strange man, this doctor!" she thought as she lay in her luxurious bed on lace pillows under a light silk coverlet. Anna Sergheievna had inherited from her father a little of his inclination for luxury. She had loved her sinful but good-natured father very much, and he had idolized her, joking with her in a friendly way as though she were an equal, confiding in her fully and asking her advice. Her mother she scarcely remembered.

"This doctor is a strange man!" she repeated to herself. She stretched, smiled, clasped her hands behind her head, then ran her eyes over a couple of pages of a silly French novel, let the book drop—and fell asleep, all pure and cool in her snowy and fragrant linen.

The following morning Anna Sergheievna went off botanizing with Bazarov right after breakfast and returned just before lunch. Arcadii did not go off anywhere and spent about an hour with Katya. He was not bored with her; she herself volunteered to play again the sonata of the day before; but when Odintsova came back at last, when he caught sight of her, his heart momentarily contracted. She came through the garden with a rather tired step; her cheeks were glowing and her eyes shining more brightly than usual under her round straw hat. She was twirling in her fingers the thin stalk of some field flower, her light mantle had slipped down to her elbows, and the wide gray ribbons of her hat clung to her bosom. Bazarov was walking behind her, self-confident and careless as usual, but the expression of his face, even though cheerful and kindly, was not to Arcadii's liking. Muttering "Good morning!" Bazarov went to his room, while Odintsova shook Arcadii's hand absent-mindedly and also went past him.

"Good morning!" Arcadii reflected. "Why, haven't we seen each other already today?"

XVII

Time (a well-known fact) sometimes flies on the wings of a bird, sometimes crawls like a worm; but man is wont to be particularly happy when he does not even notice whether it passes quickly or slowly. It was precisely thus that Arcadii and Bazarov spent fifteen days at Odintsova's. The orderliness she had set up in her house and in her life partly contributed to this result. She adhered strictly to this orderliness herself, and forced others to submit thereto. Everything throughout the day was done at a set time. In the morning, precisely at eight, all assembled for tea; from morning tea till lunch time everyone did as he or she pleased, the hostess herself was occupied with her manager (the estate was on the rent system), her steward, and her head housekeeper. Before dinner all met again for conversation or reading; the evening was devoted to strolling, cards, music; at half-past ten Anna Sergheievna retired to her own room, gave her orders for the following day, and went to bed. Bazarov did not like this measured, somewhat ostentatious regularity in daily life. "It's like moving along rails," he maintained; the liveried flunkies, the decorous stewards, offended his democratic sentiments. He declared that one might as well go the whole hog and dine as the British do, in full dress and white ties. He once spoke plainly upon the subject to Anna Sergheievna. Her attitude was such that no one hesitated to speak his mind freely before her. She heard him out and then replied: "From your point of view you're right—and perhaps in that instance I am being the grand lady; but you can't live in the country without orderliness—you'd be overcome by ennui," and she continued to go on in her own way.

Bazarov grumbled, but the very reason life was so easy for him and Arcadii at Odintsova's was because everything in her house "moved on rails." For all that, a change had taken place in both the young men from the very first days of their stay at Nikolskoe. Bazarov, toward whom Anna Serghejevna was obviously favorably inclined although she seldom agreed with him, began to evince an uneasiness unprecedented in him: he became easily irritable, spoke unwillingly, had an angry look, and could not sit still in one place, just as though something were egging him on. As for Arcadii, who had made up his mind conclusively that he was in love with Odintsova, he had begun to yield to a gentle despondency. However, this despondency did not interfere with his drawing closer to Katya; it even helped him to get on affectionate, friendly terms with her. *"She* does not appreciate me! So be it! But here is a gentle being who does not reject me," he thought, and his heart again knew the sweetness of magnanimous emotions. Katya vaguely realized that he was seeking some sort of consolation in her company and did not deny him or herself the innocent pleasure of a half-shy, half-trusting friendship. They did not talk to each other in Anna Serghejevna's presence: Katya always shrank into herself under the keen eye of her sister, while Arcadii, as befits a man in love, could no longer pay attention to anything else when near the object of his passion. But he felt at his ease only with Katya. He was conscious that it was beyond his power to interest Odintsova; he was shy and at a loss whenever he was left alone with her, and she likewise did not know what to say to him—he was too young for her. With Katya, on the other hand, Arcadii felt at home; he treated her condescendingly, did not discourage her from expressing the impressions aroused in her by music, the reading of novels, verse, and other such trifles, without noticing or realizing that these *trifles* interested him as well. Katya, for her part, did not hinder him from indulging in melancholy. Arcadii was at his ease with Katya, Odintsova was at her ease with Bazarov, and thus it usually came to pass that the two couples, after being a little while together, would go off on their separate ways, especially during the walks. Katya adored nature, and Arcadii loved it, though he dared not confess this; Odintsova was rather indifferent to it, just as Bazarov was. The almost continual separation of the two friends was not without its consequences; the relations between them began to change. Bazarov gave up discussing Odintsova with Arcadii, gave up even abusing her "aristocratic ways"; Katya, it is true, he praised as before, and only advised Arcadii to restrain her sentimental tendencies, but his praises were hurried, his advice dry, and in general he talked to him less than before. He seemed to be avoiding him, seemed to be ashamed of him.

Arcadii noticed all this but kept his observations to himself.

The real cause of all this "newness" was the feeling inspired in Bazarov by Odintsova, a feeling which tortured and maddened him, and which he would at once have denied with scornful laughter and cynical abuse if anyone had even remotely hinted at the possibility of what was taking place in him. Bazarov had a great love for women and for feminine beauty; but love in the ideal or, as he expressed it, romantic sense, he called tommyrot, unforgivable imbecility; he regarded chivalrous sentiments as something in the nature of deformity or disease and had more than once expressed his wonder that Schiller's Toggenburg and all the minnesingers and troubadours had not been clapped into a lunatic asylum.

"If a woman strikes your fancy," he used to say, "try and get somewhere; but if you can't—well, turn your back on her—there are lots of good fish in the sea."

Odintsova had taken his fancy; the widespread rumors about her, the freedom and independence of her ideas, her unmistakable predisposition for him—everything, it seemed, was in his favor, but he soon perceived that he would not "get somewhere" with her and, as for turning his back on her, he found it, to his bewilderment, beyond his power. His blood was on fire directly if he merely thought of her; he could easily have mastered his blood, but something else had gotten into him, something he had never admitted, at which he had always jeered, at which all his pride revolted. In his conversations with Anna Sergheievna he expressed more strongly than ever his indifferent contempt for everything romantic, but when he was alone he recognized with indignation the romantic sentimentalist in himself. Whereupon he would set off to the forest and walk through it with long strides, smashing the branches that came in his way and cursing under his breath both her and himself; or he would get into the hayloft in the barn and, obstinately closing his eyes, try to force himself to sleep, in which, of course, he did not always succeed. Suddenly he would imagine that those chaste hands would one day twine about his neck, that those proud lips would respond to his kisses, those clever eyes would dwell with tenderness—yes, with tenderness—on his, and his head would start spinning, and for an instant he would forget himself, until indignation flared up in him again. He caught himself in all sorts of "shameful" thoughts, as though some fiend were mocking him. Sometimes it seemed to him that a change was taking place in Odintsova as well; that a certain something was emerging in the expression of her face; that perhaps— But at that very point he would stamp his foot or gnash his teeth and shake his fist in his own face.

And yet Bazarov was not altogether mistaken. He had struck Odintsova's imagination; he interested her; she thought a great deal about him. In his absence she was not bored, she was not impatient for his coming, but his appearance immediately enlivened her; she liked to be left alone with him, and liked to talk with him even when he angered her or offended her taste, her refined habits. She was, as it were, eager to test him and at the same time to probe herself.

One day, walking in the garden with her, he suddenly announced in a surly voice that he intended going to his father's place very soon. She paled, as though some pang had gone through her heart, and such a pang that she wondered and mused long after upon its meaning. Bazarov had spoken of his departure with no idea of putting her to the test, of seeing what would come of it; he never "made things up." On the morning of that day he had seen Timotheich, his father's manager, who had taken care of him when he was a child. This Timotheich, a little ancient of much experience and astuteness, with faded yellow hair, a weatherbeaten red face, and tiny tear drops in his narrowed eyes, had unexpectedly appeared before Bazarov, in his short peasant coat of stout grayish-blue cloth, belted with a torn strap, and in tarred boots.

"Ah, old-timer; how are you?" Bazarov had cried out.

"How do you do, friend Eugene Vassilyich?" began the little ancient, and he smiled with delight so that his whole face was suddenly covered with wrinkles.

"What have you come for? They've sent you for me, eh?"

"Heavens, Sir, how could that be?" mumbled Timotheich. (He recalled the strict injunctions he had received from his master on starting.) "We were going to the town on master's business, and we got word of Your Honor, and so here we turned off on our way—to have a look at Your Honor, that is—as if we could even think of troubling you!"

"Come, don't be lying!" Bazarov cut him short. "Would this be your road to the town, now?" Timotheich shifted from foot to foot and made no answer. "Is my father well?"

"Thank God, Sir."

"And my mother?

"And Arina Vlassievna, too, glory be to God."

"They're expecting me, never fear?"

The little ancient held his tiny head to one side.

"Ah, Eugene Vassilyich, how else? As you believe in God, it fair breaks one's heart to look at your parents, so it does."

"There, that'll do, that'll do! Don't lay it on too thick. Tell them I'll be there soon."

"I hear you, Sir," answered Timotheich with a sigh.

As he went out of the house, he pulled his cap down on his head with both hands, clambered into a wretched-looking racing sulky, and went off at a trot, but not in the direction of the town.

On the evening of the same day Odintsova was sitting in her own room with Bazarov while Arcadii walked up and down the drawing room listening to Katya's playing. The Princess had gone upstairs to her own room; she could not bear guests as a rule, and especially these "new crackpates," as she called them. In the main rooms she merely sulked; but then in her own room, before her maid, she made up for it by exploding into such cursing that the cap danced on her head together with the scratch wig. Odintsova was well aware of this.

"How is it you are proposing to leave us?" she began. "And what about your promise?"

Bazarov started.

"What promise, Madam?"

"Have you forgotten? You wanted to give me a few lessons in chemistry."

"It can't be helped, Madam! My father expects me; I can't loiter any longer. However, you can read Pelouse et Frémy, *Notions générales de Chimie*; it's a good book and clearly written. You'll find everything you need in it."

"But do you remember—you assured me a book can't take the place of—I've forgotten how you put it, but you know what I want to say. Do you remember?"

"It can't be helped, Madam!" Bazarov repeated.

"Why leave?" asked Odintsova, dropping her voice.

He glanced at her. She had thrown her head on the back of her easy chair, and had crossed her arms, bare to the elbows, on her breast. She seemed paler in the light of the single lamp covered with a perforated paper shade. An ample white gown hid her completely in its soft folds; the tips of her feet, also crossed, were hardly visible.

"And why stay?" Bazarov countered.

Odintsova turned her head slightly.

"You ask why? Haven't you enjoyed yourself here? Or do you think you won't be missed?"

"I'm sure of it."

Odintsova was silent a while. "You're wrong in thinking so. However, I don't believe you. You couldn't have said that seriously." Bazarov still sat immovable. "Eugene Vassilyich, why don't you say something?"

"Why, what am I to say to you? It isn't worth while missing people, as a general thing—and surely not me."

"Why so?"

"I'm a practical, uninteresting person. I don't know how to converse."

"You're begging for compliments, Eugene Vassilyich."

"That's not a habit of mine. Don't you know yourself that I've nothing in common with the refined aspect of life, that aspect which you prize so much?"

Odintsova bit the corner of her handkerchief.

"You may think what you like, but I'll be bored when you go away."

"Arcadii will stay on," remarked Bazarov.

Odintsova shrugged her shoulders slightly.

"I'll be bored," she repeated.

"Really? At any rate, you won't feel bored long."

"What makes you suppose that?"

"Because you told me yourself that you're bored only when your regular routine is broken. You've ordered your life with such unimpeachable regularity that there can be no place in it for tedium or yearning—for any depressing emotions whatsoever."

"And you find that I am so unimpeachable—that is to say, that I've ordered my life with such regularity?"

"I should say so! Here's an example: in a few minutes it'll strike ten and I know beforehand that you will drive me away."

"No, I won't drive you away, Eugene Vassilyich. You may remain. Open that window—I feel half stifled somehow."

Bazarov got up and gave the window a push. It flew open noisily and suddenly. He had not expected it to open so easily; besides, his hands were shaking. The dark soft night peered into the room with its almost black sky, its faintly rustling trees, and the fresh fragrance of the pure open air.

"Draw the blind and sit down," said Odintsova. "I want to have a talk with you before you go away. Tell me something about yourself— that is something you never talk about."

"I try to talk to you upon improving subjects, Anna Sergheievna."

"You're very modest. But I'd like to know something about you, about your family, about your father, whom you are forsaking us for."

"Why is she saying such things?" Bazarov wondered.

"All that is not in the least entertaining," he uttered aloud. "Especially for you; we are an obscure lot."

"And, according to you, I am an aristocrat?"

Bazarov lifted his eyes to Odintsova.

"Yes," he said with exaggerated brusquerie.

She smiled slightly.

"I see you know me but little, even though you do maintain that all people resemble one another and that it's not worth bothering to study them. I'll tell you my life some day—but you tell me yours first."

"I know you but little," repeated Bazarov. "Perhaps you're right; perhaps every being really is an enigma. Why, take you, for example; you keep aloof from society, you are oppressed by it, and you have invited two students to stay with you. Why do you, with your intellect, with your beauty, live in the country?"

"What? What was it you said?" Odintsova interposed eagerly. "With my—beauty?"

Bazarov scowled.

"Never mind that," he muttered. "I meant to say that I don't understand very well why you have settled in the country."

"You don't understand that. However, you explain it to yourself in some way?"

"Yes. I assume that you remain continually in the same place because you have overpampered yourself, because you're very fond of comfort, of ease, and most indifferent to everything else."

Odintsova again smiled slightly. "You absolutely refuse to believe that I'm capable of being carried away by anything?"

Bazarov glanced at her from under his brows.

"By curiosity, if you like, but not otherwise."

"Really? Well, now I understand why we've become such friends; you're the very same sort of person as myself, you see."

"We've become such friends—" Bazarov uttered in a stifled voice. "Yes! For I'd forgotten that you wish to leave."

Bazarov got up. The lamp burnt dimly in the middle of the dark, fragrant, isolated room; from time to time the blind shook, and the insidious freshness of the night flowed in; one could hear the mysterious whisperings of that night. Odintsova did not stir a single limb; a secret emotion was overcoming her little by little. It was communicated to Bazarov. He suddenly became aware that he was alone with a young and lovely woman.

"Where are you going?" she said slowly.

He made no answer and sank into a chair.

"And so you consider me a placid, pampered, spoiled creature," she went on in the same voice, never taking her eyes off the window. "Whereas I know so much about myself that I am very unhappy."

"You unhappy? What from? It can't be possible you attach the least importance to abominable gossip?"

Odintsova frowned. It annoyed her that he had interpreted her words in such a way.

"Such tittle-tattle does not even amuse me, Eugene Vassilyich, and I am too proud to allow it to disturb me. I am unhappy because—I have no desires, no will to live. You look at me incredulously; you think it's a 'she-aristocrat' who's saying this, all in lace and sitting in a velvet easy chair. Nor am I hiding the fact: I love what you call comfort, but at the same time I have little desire to live. Reconcile that contradiction as best you can. However, that's all romanticism in your eyes."

Bazarov shook his head.

"You're in good health, independent, rich; what more would you have? What do you want?"

"What do I want?" echoed Odintsova, and she sighed. "I'm very weary, I am old. It seems to me I've been living a very long time. Yes, I am old," she added, ever so gently drawing the ends of her mantilla over her bare arms. Her eyes met Bazarov's and she blushed faintly. "I already have so many recollections behind me: my life in Petersburg, wealth, then poverty, then my father's death, my marriage, then the inevitable trip abroad. So many recollections yet there's nothing to recall, and ahead of me—ahead of me lies a long, long road, but there is no goal. I even have no wish to go on."

"You are so disillusioned?" asked Bazarov.

"No, but I am dissatisfied," Odintsova replied, dwelling on each syllable. "I think if I could become strongly attached to something—"

"You want to fall in love," Bazarov interrupted her, "yet love you cannot; therein lies your unhappiness."

Odintsova began to examine the sleeves of her mantilla.

"Am I really incapable of love?" she asked.

"Hardly. Only I was wrong in calling that unhappiness. On the contrary, it is rather the one to whom such a mischance befalls who deserves commiseration."

"When what mischance befalls him?"

"Falling in love."

"And how do you know that?"

"By hearsay," Bazarov answered in irritation.

"You're flirting," he thought; "you're bored and are teasing me for want of something to do, while I—" His heart really seemed to be straining to escape from his breast.

"Besides, you are perhaps too exacting," he said, bending his whole frame forward and playing with the fringe on his armchair.

"Perhaps. My idea is everything or nothing. A life for a life. If you've taken mine, give up thine, and that without regret and without turning back. Otherwise better not begin."

"Well, why not?" observed Bazarov. "Those terms are fair and I'm surprised that so far you—haven't found what you wanted."

"And do you think it would be easy to give oneself up wholly to anything whatsoever?"

"Not easy if you begin reflecting and waiting and keep adding value to yourself—prizing yourself, I mean. But to give yourself up without reflection is very easy."

"How can one help prizing oneself? If I am of no value, whoever would need my devotion?"

"That's really not up to oneself; it's somebody else's business to appraise one's value. The chief thing is to be able to surrender oneself."

Odintsova bent forward from the back of her chair.

"You speak," she began, "as though you've gone through all that."

"It happened to be *à propos,* Anna Sergheievna; all that sort of thing, as you know, isn't in my line."

"But you would be able to surrender?"

"I don't know. I shouldn't like to boast."

Odintsova said nothing, and Bazarov fell silent. The sounds of the piano floated up to them from the drawing room.

"How is it Katya is playing so late?" Odintsova remarked.

Bazarov got up.

"Yes, it really is late now; it's time for you to retire."

"Wait a little; why are you in a hurry? I want to say something to you."

"What is it?"

"Wait a little," whispered Odintsova. Her eyes rested on Bazarov; it seemed as though she were examining him intently.

He strode across the room, then suddenly went up to her, hurriedly said "Good-by!", squeezed her hand so that she almost cried out, and left the room. She raised her crushed fingers to her lips, breathed on them, and suddenly, impulsively getting up from her low chair, she went with rapid steps toward the door, as though she wished to bring Bazarov back.

A maid came into the room with a decanter on a silver tray. Odintsova stopped, told her she could go, and sat down again, and again sank into thought. Her braid came loose and like a dark snake slithered down on her shoulder. The lamp burned long in Anna Sergheievna's room, and for long did she sit without moving, only running her hands from time to time over her arms, nipped at by the chill of night.

Bazarov went back to his bedroom two hours later, his boots wet with dew; he was all ruffled and glum. He found Arcadii at the desk with a book in his hands, and with his coat all buttoned.

"What, not in bed yet?" he asked, apparently in annoyance.

"You've been sitting a long while with Anna Sergheievna this evening," Arcadii remarked without answering his question.

"Yes, I sat with her all the while you and Katerina Sergheievna were playing the piano."

"I was not playing—" Arcadii began—and stopped. He felt the tears were welling up in his eyes, and he did not want to start crying before his sarcastic friend.

XVIII

The following morning when Odintsova came down to morning tea, Bazarov sat a long while bowed over his cup—and then suddenly glanced up at her. She turned around to him as though he had nudged her, and it seemed to him that her face had become a little pale during the night. She soon withdrew to her own room and reappeared only at lunch. The weather was rainy from early morning; there was no possibility of going for a walk. They all assembled in the drawing room. Arcadii took the latest issue of some periodical and began reading it aloud. The Princess, as was her wont, at first assumed an expression of amazement, as though he were doing something improper, then glared at him malevolently, but he paid no attention to her.

"Eugene Vassilyich," said Odintsova, "let's go up to my room. . . . There's something I want to ask you. You mentioned a certain textbook yesterday—"

She got up and went to the door. The Princess looked about her with such an expression as if she would say: "Look, look—see how shocked I am!" and then returned to glaring at Arcadii, but the latter raised his voice and, exchanging glances with Katya, near whom he was sitting, went on reading.

Odintsova went with rapid steps to her study. Bazarov followed her quickly, without raising his eyes, and only his ears caught the delicate swish and rustle of her silk gown gliding before him. Odintsova sank into the same easy chair in which she had sat the previous evening, and Bazarov took up the same position as before.

"Well, what was the name of that book?" she began after a brief silence.

"Pelouse et Frémy, *Notions générales*," Bazarov answered. "However, I might also recommend Ganot, *Traité élémentaire de physique expérimentale* for you. In this book the illustrations are clearer and, in general, this textbook—" Odintsova held out her hand:

"You must forgive me, Eugene Vassilyich, but I didn't invite you here to discuss textbooks. I wanted to renew our conversation of last night. You went away so suddenly—you won't be bored?"

"I'm at your service, Anna Sergheievna. But what was it, now, we were talking about last night?"

Odintsova threw a sidelong glance at Bazarov.

"We were talking of happiness, I believe. I told you about myself. By the way, I mentioned the word 'happiness.' Tell me why it is that even when we are enjoying music, for instance, or a fine evening, or a conversation with sympathetic people—why does it all seem rather an intimation of some boundless happiness existing somewhere than actual happiness—that is, such happiness as we ourselves possess? Why is it? Or perhaps you feel nothing of the sort?"

"You know the saying, 'Happiness is where we are not,' " Bazarov retorted. "Besides, you told me yesterday you are discontented. Whereas I certainly never have such ideas coming into my head."

"Perhaps they seem ridiculous to you?"

"No; but they don't come into my head."

"Really? Do you know, I'd very much like to know what you think about?"

"What? I don't understand you."

"Look, I've long wanted to have a frank talk with you. There's no need to tell you—you know it yourself—that you're out of the ordinary run; you're still young—all life is before you. What are you preparing yourself for? What future awaits you? I mean to say—what goal do you want to attain? What are you going forward to? What is in your soul? In short, who are you, what are you?"

"You surprise me, Anna Sergheievna. You know that I'm studying natural sciences; as for who I am—"

"Yes, who are you?"

"I've already informed you that I'm going to be a general practitioner."

Anna Sergheievna made a movement of impatience.

"Why do you say that? You don't believe it yourself. Arcadii might answer me in that way, but not you."

"Why, what is the matter with Arcadii—"

"Stop! Is it possible you would be content with such a humble career, and aren't you yourself always maintaining that medicine doesn't exist for you? You—with your ambition—a provincial doctor! You answer me like that to put me off, because you have no confidence in me whatsoever. But do you know, Eugene Vassilyich, that I could understand you—I myself have been poor and ambitious like you; I myself may have been through the same trials as you."

"That's all very well, Anna Sergheievna, but you must excuse me. I'm not used to talking freely about myself as a general thing, and there's such a distance between us—"

"What distance? You want to tell me again that I'm an aristocrat? No more of that, Eugene Vassilyich; I think I have proved to you—"

"And even apart from that," broke in Bazarov, "what's the use of talking and thinking about the future, which for the most part does not depend on us? If a chance turns up of doing something—well and good; and if it doesn't turn up—one can at least find satisfaction in not having blabbed too much beforehand."

"You call a friendly conversation blabbing? Or perhaps you consider me, since I am a woman, unworthy of your confidence? For you
despise us all!"

"I don't despise you, Anna Sergheievna, and you know it."

"No, I don't know anything. But let us suppose that I understand
your disinclination to talk of your future career. However, that which
is taking place within you now—"

"That which is taking place!" Bazarov repeated. "As though I were
some sort of realm or society! In any case, all this isn't at all interesting;
and besides, can a man always come right out with everything that is
taking place in him?"

"Why, I don't see why one can't speak freely of everything one has
at heart."

"Can you?" asked Bazarov.

"I can," Odintsova answered after a brief hesitation.

Bazarov bowed his head.

"You are more fortunate than I."

She looked at him questioningly. "Just as you like," she went on,
"but still something tells me that we have not come together for nothing, that we'll be great friends. I'm convinced this—how should I say
it?—intenseness, restraint of yours will vanish at last."

"So you have noticed restraint in me—what else was it you said—
intenseness?"

"Yes."

Bazarov got up and went to the window.

"And you would like to know the reason of this restraint? You would
like to know what is taking place within me?"

"Yes," Odintsova repeated, with a certain dread she as yet did not
understand.

"And you won't become angry?"

"No."

"No?" Bazarov was standing with his back to her. "Let me tell you
then that I love you like a fool, like a madman. . . . There, you've
forced it out of me."

Odintsova held both her hands out before her, but Bazarov was
leaning with his forehead pressed against the window pane. He was
gasping; his whole body was visibly trembling. But it was not the tremor
of youthful timidity, it was not the delectable dread of a first declaration
of love that possessed him; it was passion struggling in him, strong

and painful—passion not unlike rancor, and perhaps akin to it. Odint-sova became both afraid of him and sorry for him.

"Eugene Vassilyich!" she said, and involuntarily there was the ring of tenderness in her voice.

He turned quickly, devoured her with his eyes, and, snatching both her hands, he drew her suddenly to his breast.

She did not free herself from his embrace at once, but within an instant she was standing in a distant corner and watching Bazarov from there. He rushed toward her.

"You have misunderstood me," she whispered hurriedly, in alarm. It seemed that were he to make another step she would scream. Bazarov bit his lips and left the room.

Half an hour later a maid brought Anna Sergheievna a note from Bazarov. It consisted of but one line: "Am I to go today, or may I stay till tomorrow?"

"Why should you go? I did not understand you—you did not understand me," Odintsova answered him, but to herself she thought: "I did not understand myself either."

She did not show herself till dinnertime, and kept pacing her room to and fro, with her hands behind her, stopping infrequently, now at the window, now at the looking glass, and slowly rubbing her handker-chief over her neck, on which she still seemed to feel a burning spot. She asked herself what had induced her to "force," in Bazarov's words, his confidence, and whether she had suspected nothing. "I am to blame," she decided aloud, "but I could not have foreseen this." She fell to musing, and blushed crimson, remembering Bazarov's almost animal face when he had darted toward her.

"But is that really true?" she suddenly uttered, and she stopped short and shook back her curls. She caught sight of herself in the glass; her head thrown back, with a mysterious smile on the half-closed, half-open eyes and lips, seemed to be telling her at that instant something at which she herself became confused.

"No," she decided at last. "God knows what this might lead to; this is no jesting matter; tranquillity is after all the best thing in the world."

Her tranquillity was not shaken; but she felt gloomy and even shed a few tears, without herself knowing why—only it was not from the insult inflicted upon her. She did not feel herself insulted; she was more inclined to feel herself at fault. Under the influence of various vague emotions, the realization of life slipping away, the desire for something new, she had made herself reach a certain point, made herself look beyond it, and had seen behind it not even an abyss, but a void—or hideousness.

XIX

Great as was Odintsova's self-possession, and superior as she was to all prejudice, she none the less felt awkward when she appeared in the dining room for dinner. The meal went off fairly well, however. Porphyrii Platonich arrived and told all sorts of anecdotes; he had just come back from town. Among other things, he informed them that the Governor had ordered his officials on special commissions to wear spurs, since he might send them somewhere on horseback for the sake of greater speed. Arcadii talked in an undertone to Katya, and diplomatically attended to the Princess's wants. Bazarov maintained an obstinate and grim silence. Odintsova looked at him twice—not stealthily but straight in his face, which was stern and jaundiced, with downcast eyes, and contemptuous determination stamped on every feature—and she thought: "No—no—no."

After dinner she went into the garden with all the others, and perceiving that Bazarov wanted to speak to her, she took a few steps to one side and stopped. He went up to her, but even then did not raise his eyes, and said in a stifled voice:

"I have to apologize to you, Anna Sergheievna. It is impossible that you should not be wroth with me."

"No, I'm not angry at you, Eugene Vassilyich," answered Odintsova. "But I am hurt."

"So much the worse. At any rate, I have been punished enough. My position, you will most probably agree, is as foolish as can be. You wrote me, 'Why should you go?' Yet stay I cannot, and do not wish to. Tomorrow I shall no longer be here."

"Eugene Vassilyich, why are you—"

"Why am I going away?"

"No, that isn't what I wanted to say."

"There's no bringing back the past, Anna Sergheievna—and this was bound to come about sooner or later. Consequently I must go. I can only conceive of one condition upon which I could remain, but that condition can never be. For—excuse my impertinence—you don't love me, and will never come to love me."

Bazarov's eyes flashed for an instant under their dark brows.

Anna Sergheievna did not answer him.

"I'm afraid of this man," the thought flashed through her mind.

"Good-by, then," said Bazarov, as though he had surmised her thought, and he turned back to the house.

Anna Sergheievna started after him in a very subdued mood and, calling Katya to her, took her arm. She did not leave her side until the very evening. She did not play cards, and was constantly laughing, which was not at all in keeping with her pale and perplexed face. Arcadii was puzzled and observed her after the manner of all young people—that is, he was constantly questioning himself: "What may the meaning of this be, now?" Bazarov shut himself up in his room; he came back to tea, however. Anna Sergheievna longed to say some kindly word to him but she did not know how to break the ice.

An unexpected incident delivered her from her embarrassing situation: the head butler announced the arrival of Sitnicov.

It is difficult to convey in words what a quail-hen figure the young progressive cut as he fluttered into the room. Though with the toadyism peculiar to him he had decided to go into the country to visit a woman with whom he was scarcely acquainted, who had never invited him, but with whom, according to information he had gathered, such talented and intimate friends of his were staying, he was nevertheless scared to the marrow of his bones; and instead of bringing out the apologies and greetings he had learned by heart beforehand, he muttered some rubbish or other about Eudoxia Kukshina, now, having sent him to inquire after the health of Anna Sergheievna, and that Arcadii Nicolaich, too, had always spoken to him in the highest terms. . . . At this point he faltered and lost his presence of mind to such an extent that he sat down on his own hat. However, since no one showed him the door, and Anna Sergheievna actually presented him to her aunt and her sister, he soon recovered himself and began chattering in all his glory. The introduction of vulgarity is often an advantage in life; it relieves overtautened strings and sobers too self-confident or self-sacrificing emotions by recalling its close kinship to them. With Sitnicov's appearance everything became somehow duller, emptier—and simpler; they all even ate more substantially at supper, and retired to bed half an hour earlier than usual.

"I might now repeat to you," said Arcadii, as he lay in bed, to Bazarov, who was also undressed by now, "what you said to me once: 'Why are you so melancholy? Probably you have fulfilled some sacred duty.' "

For some time past a sort of pretense of free-and-easy banter had sprung up between the two young men, which is always a sign of secret resentment or unvoiced suspicions.

"I'm going to my old man's tomorrow," said Bazarov.

Arcadii raised himself and leaned on his elbow. He felt both surprised and, for some reason or other, pleased.

"Ah!" he said. "And is that why you're sad?"

Bazarov yawned.

"You'll get old before your time if you know too much."

"And Anna Sergheievna?" Arcadii persisted.

"What about Anna Sergheievna?"

"I mean to say, will she let you go?"

"I didn't hire myself out to her."

Arcadii grew thoughtful, while Bazarov lay down and turned his face to the wall.

Some minutes went by in silence.

"Eugene!" Arcadii called out suddenly.

"Well?"

"I'll go along with you tomorrow."

Bazarov made no answer.

"Only I'll go home," Arcadii went on. "We'll go together as far as the Hohlovski settlements, and there you can get horses at Phedot's. I'd be delighted to make the acquaintance of your people, but I'm afraid of being both in their way and yours. You're coming to us again later, of course?"

"I've left all my things with you," Bazarov pointed out, without turning around.

"Why doesn't he ask me why I'm going? And just as suddenly as he?" thought Arcadii. "Really, now, why *am* I going, and why is he?" he continued his reflections. He could find no satisfactory answer to his own questions, while his heart was becoming filled with some corrosive feeling. He felt it would be hard to part from this life to which he had become so accustomed, but for him to stay on alone would be odd, somehow. "Something has happened between them," he reasoned to himself. "Why, then, should I remain as an eyesore after he leaves? She's definitely fed up with me, and I'll lose whatever little regard remains." He began to imagine Anna Sergheievna to himself, then other features little by little came out from behind the lovely image of the young widow.

"I feel sorry about Katya, too!" Arcadii whispered into his pillow, on which a tear had already fallen. Suddenly he tossed back his hair and said loudly:

"What the devil made that dunderhead Sitnicov honor us with a visit?"

Bazarov at first stirred a little in his bed, and only then made his rejoinder:

"Brother, you're still at the foolish stage, I see. The Sitnicovs of this world are indispensable to us. I—do get this through your head—I have need of such blessed idiots. It's not for the gods to bake bricks, after all!"

"Oho!" Arcadii thought to himself, and it was only then that all the bottomless pit of the Bazarovian self-conceit was revealed to him in a flash. "So you and I are gods, are we? That is, you're a god—but am I a blessed idiot, then?"

"Yes," Bazarov repeated glumly, "you're still at the foolish stage."

Odintsova evinced no particular surprise when Arcadii told her the next day that he was leaving with Bazarov; she seemed absent-minded and tired. Katya gave him a serious look, without saying anything, while the Princess actually crossed herself under her shawl so that he couldn't help noticing it.

Sitnicov, on the other hand, was thoroughly flabbergasted. He had just come down to lunch in a new and dandified getup, this time not at all of a Slavophile cut—the evening before he had astonished the valet assigned to him by the wealth of linen he had brought with him, and now all of a sudden his comrades were deserting him! He took a few mincing steps, darted about a little like a harried hare at the edge of a forest, and abruptly, almost in dismay, almost with a wail, announced that he intended to leave. Odintsova made no attempt to detain him.

"I have a most comfortable carriage," added the unhappy young man, turning to Arcadii; "I can give you a lift, while Eugene Vassilyich can take your coach—it'll actually be more convenient that way."

"But, really, it's entirely out of your way and it's quite a long distance to my place."

"That's nothing—nothing at all; I've plenty of time; besides that, I have business in that direction."

"In connection with liquor taxes?" asked Arcadii, showing far too much contempt by now.

But Sitnicov found himself in such desperate straits that he did not even emit his usual laugh.

"I assure you my carriage is exceedingly comfortable," he mumbled, "and there'll be room for all."

"Don't disappoint M'sieu' Sitnicov by a refusal," Anna Sergheievna let drop.

Arcadii glanced at her and inclined his head gravely.

The visitors left after lunch. As she said good-by to Bazarov, Odintsova held out her hand to him and said:

"We'll see each other again, shan't we?"

"As you command," Bazarov answered.

"In that case—we shall."

Arcadii was the first to come out on the front steps; he clambered into Sitnicov's carriage. A steward helped him up respectfully, but Arcadii could have beaten him with pleasure, or have burst into tears. Bazarov took his seat in the coach. When they reached the Hohlovski settlements, Arcadii waited till Phedot, the keeper of the posting station, had harnessed the horses and then, walking up to the coach, he said to Bazarov with his old smile:

"Eugene, take me with you. I want to visit your place."

"Get in," Bazarov said through his teeth.

Sitnicov, who had been leisurely walking around his carriage, whistling briskly, simply let his jaw drop when he heard these words, while Arcadii coolly dragged his luggage out of the carriage, took his seat beside Bazarov, and, after a polite bow to his former fellow traveler, called out: "Let 'er ride!"

The coach rolled away and was soon out of sight. Sitnicov, utterly confused, looked at his coachman, but the latter was merely flicking his short whip over the tail of the off horse. Thereupon Sitnicov jumped into the carriage and, after thundering at two passing peasants, "Put on your hats, you fools!" started off on the wearing drive to town, where he arrived very late, and where, the following day, at Kukshina's, he laced it into the two "disgusting stuck-up sticks and ignoramuses."

As he was getting into Bazarov's coach Arcadii had squeezed his hand hard, and for a long while did not say anything. Apparently Bazarov had understood and appreciated both the handshake and the silence. He had not slept all through the previous night, and had not smoked, and had eaten scarcely anything for several days. His profile, already thinner, stood out glumly and sharply under his cap, which was pulled far down.

"Well, brother," he said at last, "let's have a cheroot. And look—I guess my tongue is yellow."

"It is," Arcadii assured him.

"To be sure—that's why the cheroot is flat. The machine's wobbly."

"You certainly have changed lately," Arcadii observed.

"It's nothing! We'll soon be better. Only it's a bore—my mother's so tenderhearted; if you don't grow a round belly and unless you eat ten times a day, she's simply heartbroken. My father's all right, though; he's gone through everything and known all sorts of ups and downs himself. No, I can't smoke," he added, and he flung the cheroot into the dust of the road.

"It's twenty miles to your place, isn't it?" asked Arcadii.

"Yes. But better ask this sage." He indicated the muzhik sitting on the box, one of Phedot's hired hands.

But the sage only answered, "Who knows—nobody measures the miles hereabouts," and he went on cursing out under his breath the shaft horse for "kicking with her headpiece," that is, jerking her head.

"Yea, verily," Bazarov began, "it's a lesson to you, my youthful friend, a sort of instructive example. What bosh! Every man hangs on a thread, the abyss may yawn under his feet any moment, and yet he must go and think up all sorts of unpleasantnesses for himself and spoil his life."

"What are you hinting at?" asked Arcadii.

"I'm not hinting at anything; I'm coming right out with it: we've both made fools of ourselves. What's the use of talking about it? Still, I've noticed in hospital practice, the man who's furious at his illness is bound to get the upper hand over it."

"I don't quite understand you," observed Arcadii. "It doesn't seem as if you had anything to complain about."

"Well, since you don't quite understand me, I'll tell you this much —to my mind, you're better off making little ones out of big ones in a road chain gang than letting a woman get a firm grip on even a finger." Bazarov had all but come out with his favorite word "romanticism," but checked himself and said, "bosh." "You won't believe me now, but I'm telling you; you and I got into feminine society and we found it pleasant enough; but to leave such society is as good as dousing yourself with cold water on a hot day. A man has no time for such trifles; a man must be untamed, says an excellent Spanish proverb. Take you," he added, turning to the muzhik up on the box, "you look like a clever fellow—have you a wife?"

The peasant turned his flat, purblind face upon both friends:

"A wife? Yes, I have a wife. How else?"

"Do you beat her?"

"My wife? There's all sorts of things happen. She don't get beat without a reason!"

"That's excellent. Well, and does she beat you?"

The peasant began tugging hard at the reins.

"What a thing to say, Sir. You don't think of anything but joking." He was obviously offended.

"You hear, Arcadii Nicolaich? Whereas you and I have gotten a beating—that's what comes of being educated people."

Arcadii gave a forced laugh, while Bazarov turned away and did not open his mouth again throughout the rest of the journey.

The twenty miles seemed all of forty to Arcadii. But at last the small hamlet where Bazarov's parents lived appeared on the slope of a knoll. Alongside of it, in a copse of young birches, could be seen a small house with a thatched roof, yet with a squirish look about it. Two peasants stood with their hats on at the first hut, cursing each other.

"You're a great sow," said one, "worse'n than a little suckling pig."

"And your wife's a witch," retorted the other.

"From the unconstraint of their behavior," Bazarov remarked to Arcadii, "and the playfulness of their turns of speech, you can guess that my father's muzhiks aren't too much oppressed. Why, there he is himself coming out on the steps of his dwelling. That means he must have heard the horses' bells. It's he, it's he—I recognize his figure. Oho-ho! How gray he's grown, though, poor fellow!"

XX

Bazarov leaned out of the coach, while Arcadii craned his head over his companion's shoulder and caught sight on the steps of the little manor house of a tall, gaunt man with rumpled hair and a thin aquiline nose; his old military coat was unbuttoned. He was standing, his legs wide apart, smoking a long pipe, and his eyes were puckered up from the sun.

The horses stopped.

"So you've favored us at last," said Bazarov's father, still going on smoking, though his student-pipe was fairly dancing up and down in his fingers. "Come, get out, get out; let me kiss you."

He put his arms around his son.

"Gene, Gene," they heard a woman's trembling voice. The door was flung open, and a roly-poly, short little old woman in a white cap and a short striped jacket appeared on the threshold. She "oh'd," swayed, and would certainly have fallen if Bazarov had not held her up. Her plump little hands were instantly twined round his neck, her head was pressed to his breast, and there was a complete hush. The only sound to be heard was her broken sobs.

Old Bazarov was breathing hard and narrowing his eyes more than ever.

"There, that's enough, that's enough, Arina! That'll do," he said, exchanging a glance with Arcadii, who had remained motionless near the coach, while the muzhik on the box even turned his head away. "That's not at all necessary! Please—that'll do."

"Ah, Vassilii Ivanovich," faltered the little old woman, "for what ages I haven't seen my dear one, my darling Gene," and, without unclasping her hands, she drew her wrinkled face, all wet with tears, creased and overcome with emotion, a little away from Bazarov and gazed at him with eyes that were somehow blissful and mirth-provoking, and again held him close.

"Well, yes, of course, all this is in the nature of things," commented Vassilii Ivanovich, "but still it would be better if we went inside. Eugene has brought a guest with him. You must excuse it," he added, turning to Arcadii, and scraped his foot a little. "You understand, it's a woman's weakness; a mother's heart, you know—"

His own lips, as well as his eyebrows, were twitching, and his chin quivered. Still, he was obviously trying to control himself and appear almost unmoved.

"Let's go in, Mother, really," said Bazarov, and he led the old woman, all overcome, into the house. Having seated her in an easy chair, he once more hurriedly embraced his father and presented Arcadii to him.

"Glad to make your acquaintance, upon my soul," said Vassilii Ivanovich, "but you mustn't be too exacting; everything here in my house is done in a plain way, on a military footing. Arina Vlassievna, calm yourself, as a favor to me. What's all this weakness? Our guest will have a poor opinion of you."

"My dear sir," said the little old lady through her tears, "I haven't the honor of knowing your name and your father's—"

"Arcadii Nicolaich," Vassilii Ivanovich prompted her in a low voice.

"Excuse a silly old woman like me." The old woman blew her nose and, bending her head to the right and to the left, carefully wiped each eye in turn. "You must excuse me. You see, I thought I should die, that I'd never live to see my da-a-arling."

"Well, here we've lived to see him, Madam," Vassilii Ivanovich put in quickly. "Taniushka," he turned to a barefooted little girl of thirteen in a bright red calico dress who was timidly peeping in at the door, "bring your mistress a glass of water—on a tray, do you hear? And you, gentlemen," he added with a certain old-fashioned playfulness, "let me ask you to step into the study of a retired veteran."

"Let me take you around once more, little Gene," moaned Arina Vlassievna. Bazarov bent down to her. "Why, what a handsome fellow you've become!"

"Well, I don't know about his being handsome," remarked the father, "but as a man, he is what they call *ommfé*.[1] And now I hope, Arina Vlassievna, that, having satisfied your maternal heart, you'll see to satisfying the appetites of our dear guests, because, as you're aware, even nightingales can't be fed on fairy tales."

The little old lady got up from her armchair.

"Vassilii Ivanovich, the table shall be laid this minute. I'll run to the kitchen myself and order the samovar to be brought in; everything shall be ready—everything. Why, I haven't seen him, not given him food or drink these three years—do you think it was easy for me?"

"There, mind, good mother, see to it; don't put us to shame. And you, gentlemen, I beg of you to follow me. And here's Timotheich come to pay his respects to you, Eugene. He, too, I guess, is delighted, the old dog. Eh? Aren't you delighted, you old dog? Be so good as to follow me."

And old Bazarov bustled ahead, scraping and flapping with his slippers trodden down at the heel.

All his little house consisted of six tiny rooms. One of them—the one to which he brought our friends—was called the study. A thick-legged desk, cluttered over with papers black with an accumulation of ancient dust, as though they had been smoked, occupied all the space between the two windows; on the walls were hung Turkish firearms,

[1] *Homme fait*—an impressive man. (A possible origin of the Hollywoodism *oomph*.) —*Editor.*

quirts, a saber, two maps, some sort of anatomical charts, a portrait of Hufeland,[1] a monogram woven in hair in a black frame, and a diploma under glass. A leather divan, worn into hollows and torn here and there, was placed between two enormous closets of Carelian birch; books, small boxes, stuffed birds, jars, and phials were crowded in disorder on the shelves; in one corner stood a broken-down galvanic battery.

"I warned you, my honored guest," Vassilii Ivanovich began, "that we live here as if we were bivouacking, so to say—"

"There, that'll do. What are you apologizing for?" Bazarov interrupted. "Kirsanov knows very well we're no Crœsuses, and that you don't live in a palace. Where are we going to put him, that's the question?"

"Of course, Eugene, of course; I have an excellent room in the wing; he'll be very comfortable there."

"So you've built on a wing, have you?"

"Naturally, Sir; where the bathhouse is, Sir," Timotheich put in his oar.

"That is, next to the bathhouse," Vassilii Ivanovich hastened to add. "It's already summertime . . . I'll run over there right now and see to everything—and you, Timotheich, might bring in their things in the meantime. As for you, Eugene, I'll of course place my study at your disposal. *Suum cuique.*" [2]

"There you have him! A most amusing old codger, and the kindliest soul," Bazarov remarked as soon as his father had left the room. "Just as odd as yours, only in another way. He does chatter too much."

"And your mother seems a splendid woman," Arcadii remarked.

"Yes, there's nothing sly about her. You'll see what a dinner she'll set out for us."

"They didn't expect you today, father of mine; they haven't put in any beef," observed Timotheich, who had just dragged in Bazarov's box.

"We'll manage even without beef. You can't hang a man for being poor. Poverty, so they say, is no disgrace."

"How many serfs does your father own?" Arcadii asked suddenly.

"The estate's not his but mother's; there are fifteen souls, if I remember right."

"Twenty-two in all," Timotheich supplemented with an air of displeasure.

---

[1] Hufeland, Christoph Wilhelm (1762-1836); German physician.—*Editor.*

[2] To every one his own.

The flapping of slippers was heard, and old Bazarov reappeared.

"Your room will be ready for your reception in a few minutes," he cried triumphantly. "Arcadii . . . Nicolaich? I think that is the form you prefer? And here is your attendant," he added, indicating a short-cropped boy who had come in with him, in a blue full-skirted coat out at the elbows and in boots obviously not his own. "They call him Phedka. I must repeat once more, even though my son forbids me to say such things, you mustn't be too exacting. However, the lad knows how to fill a pipe for you. You smoke, of course?"

"For the most part, I smoke cigars," Arcadii informed him.

"And you show excellent judgment. I myself give the preference to cigars, but in our isolated regions it is exceedingly difficult to obtain them."

"There, that's enough of eating humble pie," Bazarov again cut him short. "You'd do much better to sit right here on the divan and let me have a look at you."

Vassilii Ivanovich laughed and sat down. He was very like his son in face, save that his forehead was lower and narrower, and his mouth a little wider, and he was forever fidgeting, shrugging up his shoulder as though his coat cut him under the armpits, blinking, clearing his throat, and gesticulating with his fingers, whereas his son was distinguished by a kind of nonchalant immobility.

"Humble pie!" Vassilii Ivanovich repeated. "You mustn't think, Eugene, that I want to arouse our guest's pity, so to say—'There, now, see what backwoods we are living in!' On the contrary, I'm of the opinion that for a thinking man there is no such thing as backwoods. At least, I try as far as possible not to become a mossy fossil, as they say, not to fall behind the times."

He drew out of his pocket a fresh handkerchief of yellow foulard which he had had time to snatch up on his way to Arcadii's room and, flourishing it in the air now and then, he went on: "I'm not now alluding to the fact that, for example, at the cost of sacrifices not inconsiderable for me, I have put my peasants on the rent system and given up my land to them on half shares in the crops. I regarded that as my duty; prudence itself dictates such a procedure, though other proprietors do not even think of it. I am alluding to the sciences, to culture."

"Yes; I see you have here *The Friend of Good Health* of four years ago," Bazarov put in.

"An old comrade sends it to me out of friendship," Vassilii Ivanovich made haste to answer. "But we have, for instance, some idea even of phrenology," he added, addressing himself, however, principally to Arcadii and pointing to the top of a closet on which stood a small plaster head divided into numbered squares. "We're not unacquainted, either, with Schenlein or Rademacher."

"Why, do people still believe in Rademacher in this province?" asked Bazarov.

The old man had a coughing spell. "In this province. . . . Of course, gentlemen, you know best; how could we catch up with you? You're here to take our places. Even in my day a certain Humoralist by the name of Hoffmann, and a certain Brown with his Vitalism, seemed very ridiculous to us, and yet they had made a great stir at one time. Some newcomer has taken the place of Rademacher among you; you bow down before him, but in another twenty years you'll be laughing even at him."

"For your consolation I'll tell you," observed Bazarov, "that nowadays we laugh at medicine altogether and don't bow down before anyone."

"How can that be? Why, you're going to be a doctor, aren't you?"

"Yes, but the one fact doesn't interfere with the other."

Old Bazarov poked his middle finger into his pipe, where a little smoldering ash still remained. "Well, perhaps, perhaps—I'm not going to argue the point. After all, who am I? A retired army doctor, *volla-too;* [1] now fate has made me take to farming. I served in your grandfather's brigade," he again turned to Arcadii. "Yes, Sir, yes, Sir, I've seen many a sight in my time. And into what kinds of society haven't I been thrown, whom haven't I come in contact with! I, I myself, whom you see before you now, felt the pulse of Prince Wittgenstein and of Zhucovski! As for those who were in the Southern Army, in the Fourteenth Regiment, you understand—" here Vassilii Ivanovich pursed up his lips significantly—"I knew every single one of 'em. Well, naturally, I kept myself to myself—physician, stick to your lancet, and that's that! But your grandfather was a most honorable man, a real soldier."

"Confess, now, he was quite a blockhead," Bazarov remarked lazily.

"Ah, Eugene, how can you say such things! Do consider! Of course, General Kirsanov was not one of the most—"

"Oh, drop him," Bazarov broke in. "I felt great as I was driving along here on seeing your birch grove; it has shot up fine."

Vassilii Ivanovich became animated.

---

[1] *Voilà tout*—that is all.

"Why, you ought to have a look at what a little garden I've got now! I planted every little tree myself. I've fruit, and raspberries, and all kinds of medicinal herbs. However clever you young gentlemen may be, old man Paracelsus uttered the holy truth: *in herbis, verbis et lapidibus.*[1] I've retired from practice, of course, as you know, but two or three times a week I have to go back to my old trade. They come for advice—and I can't very well drive them away. Sometimes the poor have to turn to me for help. As a matter of fact, there are no doctors here at all. There's a certain neighbor here; he's a retired major, but just imagine, he doctors people, too. I asked whether he had ever studied medicine. 'No, he never studied,' they told me, 'he does it more out of philanthropy.' . . . Ha! Ha! out of philanthropy! Eh? Rich, isn't it? Ha! Ha! Ha! Ha!"

"Phedka, fill me a pipe!" Bazarov said sternly.

"Then there was another doctor hereabouts, who had come to visit a patient," old Bazarov persisted in a kind of desperation, "but the patient had already gone *ad patres*. The servant wouldn't give the doctor a chance to say anything. 'You're no longer needed,' he told him. The doctor hadn't expected this; he became confused and asked: 'Well, now, did your master hiccup before his death?' 'He did that, Sir.' 'And did he hiccup a great deal?' 'Yes, a great deal!' 'Ah, well, that's good,' and off he set back home. Ha! Ha! Ha!"

The old man was alone in his laughter. Arcadii forced a smile; Bazarov simply stretched. The conversation went on in this way for about an hour; Arcadii had time to go to his room, which turned out to be the anteroom attached to the bathhouse, but was very snug and clean. At last Taniushka came in and announced that dinner was ready.

Vassilii Ivanovich was the first to get up. "Come, gentlemen! You must be magnanimous and pardon me if I've bored you. I daresay my good wife will entertain you more than I."

The dinner, although gotten together in haste, turned out to be very good, even abundant; only the wine was not quite up to the mark; an almost black sherry, bought by Timotheich in the town from a dealer he knew, it had a faint coppery or resinous bouquet—it was hard to tell which; the flies, too, were a great nuisance. On ordinary days a serf boy used to keep driving them away with a large green branch, but on this occasion old Bazarov had banished him through fear of criticism by the younger generation. The mother had had time to dress up; she had

[1] "Through herbs, words and minerals."

put on a high cap with silk ribbons and a blue flowered shawl. She had another crying spell as soon as she caught sight of her little Gene, but this time her husband had no need to admonish her—she made haste to wipe away her tears herself, for fear of their spotting her shawl.

The young men were the only ones who ate; the master and mistress of the house had dined long before. Phedka waited at table, obviously encumbered by having boots on, something he was not used to; he was assisted by a woman of a masculine cast of face and only one eye, by the name of Anphissushka, who performed the duties of housekeeper, poultry-woman, and laundress. Vassilii Ivanovich paced up and down the room throughout the dinner, and with a perfectly happy and even beatific air talked about the serious anxiety he felt at Napoleon's policy, and the intricacy of the Italian question. Arina Vlassievna took little notice of Arcadii, nor was she very solicitous about his appetite; with her round face, to which the puffy cherry-colored lips and the little moles on her cheeks and over the eyebrows gave a very simple, good-natured expression, propped up by her little closed fist, she did not take her eyes off her son, and kept constantly sighing; she was dying to know for how long he had come, but was afraid to ask him.

"Well, now, suppose he says it's only for two days?" she thought, and her heart would die away.

After the roast Vassilii Ivanovich disappeared for an instant and returned with an opened half bottle of champagne.

"Here," he cried, "though we do live in the backwoods, we have something to make merry with on festive occasions!"

He poured out three goblets and a small wineglass, proposed the health of "our inestimable guests," and tossed off his glass in one breath, in military fashion, and made his wife drink her wineglass to the last drop.

When the time came for preserves, Arcadii, who could not abide anything sweet, thought it his duty, nevertheless, to taste four different kinds which had been freshly made, all the more so since Bazarov flatly refused them and immediately lit a cheroot. Then tea came on the scene with cream, butter, and sweet pretzels, after which old Bazarov took them all into the garden to admire the beauty of the evening.

As they passed a garden seat he whispered to Arcadii:

"This is the spot where I love to meditate, as I watch the setting of the sun; it suits a recluse like me. And there, a little farther off, I have planted some of the trees beloved of Horace."

"What trees?" asked Bazarov, overhearing.

"Why—acacias."

Bazarov began to yawn.

"I imagine it's time our travelers were in the arms of Morpheus," observed Vassilii Ivanovich.

"That is, it's time to sleep," Bazarov seconded him. "That's a thoroughly sound notion. It's time, certainly."

As he said good night to his mother, he kissed her on the forehead, while she embraced him, and stealthily behind his back she gave him her blessing by making the sign of the cross three times. Vassilii Ivanovich conducted Arcadii to his room and wished him "as refreshing repose as I, too, enjoyed at your happy age." And Arcadii actually did sleep excellently in his bathhouse anteroom; there was a smell of mint in it, and two crickets behind the stove vied with each other in their soporific chirping.

Vassilii Ivanovich went from Arcadii's room to the study and, perching on the divan at his son's feet, he was looking forward to having a chat with him; but Bazarov at once sent him away, saying he was sleepy. But he did not fall asleep till morning. With wide-open eyes he stared vindictively into the darkness. The memories of childhood had no power over him, and, besides, he had not yet had time to get rid of his recent bitter impressions.

Arina Vlassievna first prayed to her heart's content, then had a long, long conversation with Anphissushka, who stood stock-still before her mistress and, fixing her solitary eye upon her, communicated in a mysterious whisper all her observations and conjectures in regard to Eugene Vassilyich. The old mother's head was all in a whirl from happiness and wine and tobacco smoke: her husband tried to talk to her, but soon gave it up as a bad job.

Arina Vlassievna was a genuine Russian daughter of the petty nobility of former days; she ought to have lived two centuries before, in the times of old Moscow. She was very devout and emotional; she believed in all sorts of omens, fortune-telling, spells, and dreams; she believed in holy innocents, hobgoblins, wood-demons, in unlucky encounters, in the evil eye, in popular remedies, in salt specially prepared on Holy Thursday, and that the end of the world was at hand; she believed that if on Easter Sunday the lights did not go out at all-night mass there would be a good crop of buckwheat, and that a mushroom ceases to grow after the eye of man beholds it; she believed that the

Devil favored places where there is water, and that every Jew has a small blood-stained patch on his breast; she was afraid of mice, adders, frogs, sparrows, leeches, thunder, cold water, draughts, horses, goats, red-haired people, and black cats, and she considered crickets and dogs as unclean beasts; she never ate veal, or doves, or crayfish, or cheese, or asparagus, or artichokes, or hares, or watermelons—because a cut watermelon suggested the head of John the Baptist; as for oysters, she could not speak of them without a shudder; she was fond of eating well—and fasted rigidly; she slept ten hours out of the twenty-four—and never went to bed at all if Vassilii Ivanovich got a headache; she had never read a single book—except that masterpiece of French sentimentalism, *Alexis, or the Cottage in the Forest*; she wrote one letter in a year, or two at the most, but knew what was what in housewifery, drying fruits and vegetables and making jam, though she never touched a thing with her own hands, and was generally disinclined to budge.

She was very kindhearted, and in her way not at all stupid. She knew that the world consists of masters, whose duty it is to give orders, and common people, whose duty it is to serve them—and therefore she felt no repugnance at servility and prostrations to the ground; but she treated those in subjection to her kindly and gently, never let a single beggar go away empty-handed, and never spoke ill of any one, even though she was occasionally fond of gossip. In her youth she had been very pretty, had played the clavichord, and spoken a little French; but in the course of many years' wanderings with her husband, whom she had married against her will, she had grown stout, and forgotten both music and French.

Her son she loved and feared unutterably; she had given up the management of the property to Vassilii Ivanovich—and no longer took any interest in anything concerning business; she'd "Oh!", flutter her handkerchief, and raise her eyebrows higher and higher in fright as soon as her old husband began to discuss the impending government reforms and his own plans. She was given to hypochondria, and was forever expecting some great misfortune, and would break into tears the moment she recalled anything sad.

Such women are growing scarcer and scarcer nowadays. God knows whether we ought to rejoice at that fact!

XXI

On getting up, Arcadii opened the window—and the first thing that met his view was Vassilii Ivanovich. In a Bokhara dressing gown girt round the waist with a pocket handkerchief the old man was industriously digging in his garden. He perceived his young guest and, leaning on his spade, called out:

"The best of health to you! How have you slept?"

"Splendidly," Arcadii assured him.

"Well, here am I, as you see me, like some Cincinnatus, marking out a bed for late turnips. The time has come now—and glory be to God for it!—when everyone ought to gain his sustenance with his own hands; it's useless to rely on others; one must toil oneself. And it turns out that Jean Jacques Rousseau is right. Half an hour ago, my dear Sir, you might have seen me in a totally different situation. One peasant woman was complaining of looseness—that's how they put it, but in our language it's dysentery—and I—how can I express it best? I poured opium into her, and for another I extracted a tooth. I proposed etherization to her—only she wouldn't consent. All that I do *gratis en amateur*. However, it's no novelty to me, for I'm a plebeian, *homo novus*—I don't spring from any ancient line, like my spouse. But perhaps you'd like to come here into the shade, to breathe the morning freshness a little before tea?"

Arcadii went out to him.

"Welcome once again," said old Bazarov, raising his hand in a military salute to the greasy skullcap covering his head. "You, I know, are accustomed to luxury, to pleasures, but even the great ones of this world do not disdain to spend a brief space under a cottage roof."

"Good heavens," protested Arcadii, "as though I were one of the great ones of this world! Nor am I accustomed to luxury."

"Pardon me, pardon me," Vassilii Ivanovich rejoined with an amiable simper. "Though I'm laid away on the shelf now, I've knocked about the world, too—I can tell a bird by its flight. I'm something of a psychologist, too, in my own way, and a physiognomist. If I hadn't been endowed with this gift—for I'll venture to call it such—I'd have come to grief long ago; a little man like me would have been rubbed out of existence. I tell you, without flattery, I'm sincerely delighted at the friendship I observe between you and my son. I've just seen him;

according to his wont—as you're probably aware—he got up very early and went for a ramble about the neighborhood. Permit me to inquire— have you known my son long?"

"Since last winter."

"Indeed. And permit me to question you further—but hadn't we better sit down? Permit me, as a father, to ask without reserve: What's your opinion of my Eugene?"

"Your son is one of the most remarkable men I've ever met," Arcadii answered with enthusiasm.

The father's eyes suddenly grew round, and his cheeks were suffused with a faint flush. The spade fell out of his hand.

"And so you suppose—" he began—

"I'm convinced," Arcadii put in, "that your son has a great future before him; that he will do honor to your name. I became convinced of that from our very first meeting."

"How—how did that come about?" the father barely managed to say. His broad lips were spread in a triumphant smile, which would not leave them.

"You would like to know how we met?"

"Yes—and in general—"

Arcadii began his story and spoke of Bazarov with still greater warmth, still greater enthusiasm than he had done on the evening when he had danced a mazurka with Odintsova.

Vassilii Ivanovich listened and listened, blinked, rolled his handkerchief up into a wad in both his hands, coughed, rumpled up his hair, and at last could stand it no longer. He bent down to Arcadii and kissed him on his shoulder.

"You've made me perfectly happy," he said, never ceasing to smile. "I must tell you that I—idolize my son. My old wife I won't speak of —we all know what mothers are!—but I dare not show my feelings before him because he doesn't like it. He is averse to every kind of demonstration of feeling; many people even condemn him for such firmness of character and see it as a mark of pride or lack of feeling, but men like him ought not to be measured by the common yardstick— isn't that so? Take but one instance: another fellow in his place would have been a constant drag on his parents; but he, would you believe it, has never from the day he was born taken a copper more than he could help—and that's God's own truth!"

"He's a disinterested, honest man," Arcadii observed.

"Precisely; he's a disinterested man. And I don't merely idolize him, Arcadii Nicolaich, I'm proud of him, and my sole ambition is to have the following lines appear in his biography some day: 'Son of an ordinary army doctor, who, however, was capable of early divining his greatness, and who spared nothing for his education—' " Here the old man's voice broke.

Arcadii pressed his hand hard.

"What do you think," Vassilii Ivanovich asked after a certain silence, "will it be in the field of medicine that he'll attain the celebrity you predict for him?"

"Of course not in medicine, though even in that department he'll be one of the foremost scientists."

"In what then, Arcadii Nicolaich?"

"That would be hard to say now, but he'll be famous."

"He'll be famous!" repeated the old man, and he sank into a reverie.

"Arina Vlassievna sent me to call you in to tea," announced Anphissushka, going by with an immense platter of ripe raspberries.

Vassilii Ivanovich awoke from his trance.

"And will there be cooled cream for the raspberries?"

"There will be, Sir."

"Cold now, mind! Don't stand on ceremony, Arcadii Nicolaich; take more. But how is it Eugene isn't coming?"

"I'm here," they heard Bazarov's voice coming from Arcadii's room.

Vassilii Ivanovich turned around quickly. "Aha! you wanted to pay a visit to your friend, but you were too late, *amice,* and we've already had a long conversation. Now we must go in to tea, Mother summons us. By the way, I want to have a little talk with you."

"What about?"

"There's a peasant here; he's suffering from icterus—"

"You mean jaundice?"

"Yes, a chronic and very obdurate case of icterus. I have prescribed him horse-knop and St.-John's-wort, made him eat carrots and given him soda—but all those are merely palliative measures; we want some more drastic treatment. Even though you laugh at medicine, I feel certain you can give me worth-while advice. But we'll talk of that later. And now let's go in to tea."

Vassilii Ivanovich jumped up briskly from the garden seat and began humming from *Robert le Diable:*

> "One law, one law, one law we shall establish—
> To live for joy, for joy, for joy, for joy!"

"What remarkable vitality!" Bazarov commented, leaving the window.

It was midday. The sun was burning behind its thin veil of unbroken whitish clouds. Everything was hushed; the roosters alone were calling challengingly to one another in the village, producing in everyone who heard them a strange sense of drowsiness and tedium; and somewhere, high up among the treetops, a young sparrow-hawk was incessantly, plaintively cheeping. Arcadii and Bazarov were lying in the shade of a small haystack, having put under them a couple of armfuls of dryly rustling but still green and fragrant grass.

"That aspen," began Bazarov, "reminds me of my childhood; it grows at the edge of a pit where a brick barn had once stood, and in those days I believed firmly that that pit and the aspen possessed a peculiar talismanic power. I was never bored near them. I didn't understand then that I wasn't bored because I was a child. Well, now I'm grown up, the talisman doesn't work."

"How long did you live here altogether?" asked Arcadii.

"Two years on end; then we came from time to time. We led a roving life, traipsing from town to town for the most part."

"And has this house been standing long?"

"Yes. My grandfather himself built it—my mother's father."

"What sort of a man was your grandfather?"

"The devil knows. Some Second Major or other. Served with Suvorov and was always telling stories about the crossing of the Alps. Probably lying."

"No wonder you have a portrait of Suvorov hanging in your drawing room. For my part, I love such little houses as yours; they're so old-fashioned and warm, and there's always a special sort of aroma about them."

"An aroma of icon lamp oil and hart's-clover," Bazarov remarked, yawning. "And what a world of flies in these darling little houses! Ugh!"

"Tell me," Arcadii began after a brief pause, "were you tyrannized as a child?"

"You can see what my parents are like. They aren't the strict kind."

"Do you love them, Eugene?"

"I do, Arcadii!"

"They love you so much!"

Bazarov was silent for a while.

"Do you know what I'm thinking about?" he brought out at last, clasping his hands behind his head.

"No. What is it?"

"I'm thinking life on this earth is a fine thing for my parents! My father at sixty is fussing around, talking about 'palliative' measures, doctoring people, playing the magnanimous master with the peasants—having a spiritual spree, in short. And my mother's happy, too; her day's so chock-full of all sorts of occupations, and oh's and ah's, that she has no time even to stop and think, whereas I—"

"Whereas you—"

"Whereas I'm thinking: Here I am, lying under a haystack. The tiny space I occupy is so infinitesimally small in comparison with the rest of space, in which I am not, and which has nothing to do with me; and the period of time which I may contrive to live through is so insignificant before the face of that eternity in which I never was and never shall be. And in this atom, this mathematical point, the blood is circulating, the brain is working, and this atom is likewise yearning for something. What hideous incongruity! What trifles!"

"Allow me to point out to you that what you're saying applies to all men in general—"

"You're right," Bazarov cut in. "I was going to say that they, for instance—my parents, that is—are busy and don't trouble themselves about their own insignificance; it doesn't stink in their nostrils. Whereas I—I feel nothing but ennui and malice."

"Malice? But why malice?"

"Why? How can you ask why? Why, have you forgotten?"

"I remember everything, but still I don't admit that you have any right to feel malice. You're unlucky, I agree, but still—"

"Eh! Why, Arcadii Nicolaich, I can see you have the same attitude toward love that all the ultra-modern young men have: Here, chick, chick, chick!—but the second the chick comes near you take to your heels with all the strength God gave you. But enough of that. It's actually disgraceful to cry over spilt milk." He turned over on his side. "Oho! there goes a fine, upstanding ant, dragging along a half-dead fly. Drag her along, brother, drag her along! Don't pay any attention to her resistance; take advantage of your right as an animal not to recognize the sentiment of compassion—make the most of it—not like our conscientious self-destructive brotherhood!"

"You should be the last to say that, Eugene! When did you destroy yourself?"

Bazarov raised his head.

"That's the only thing I pride myself on. I haven't destroyed myself, therefore even a creature in skirts won't destroy me. Amen! Finis! You won't hear another word from me about it."

Both the friends lay for some time in silence.

"Yes," Bazarov began again, "man's a strange creature. When one looks from the side, sort of, and from a distance at the smothered life our 'fathers' lead here, what could be better, apparently? Eat, drink, and know you're acting in the most regular, most sensible manner. But, no, ennui will overcome you. One wants to fuss around with people—to abuse them, even, yet still fuss around with them."

"One ought to order one's life so that every moment in it should be of significance," Arcadii uttered reflectively.

"That goes without saying! The significant is sweet, even though it may be false; but one can become reconciled even with the insignificant. But when it comes to petty cares—petty cares are the devil and all!"

"Petty cares don't exist for a man so long as he refuses to recognize them."

"H'm! What you've just said is a commonplace in reverse."

"What? What do you mean by that term?"

"Why, just this: to say, for instance, that education is beneficial is a commonplace; but to say that education is harmful, that's a commonplace in reverse. It's more dandified, apparently, but in reality it's one and the same."

"But where's the truth, now—on which side?"

"Where? I'll answer you like an echo: 'Where?' "

"You're in a melancholy mood today, Eugene."

"Really? The sun must have steamed me up, probably, and besides, one shouldn't eat so many raspberries."

"In that case it mightn't be a bad thing to take a nap," Arcadii observed.

"You're right; only don't look at me—every man's face is stupid when he's asleep."

"But isn't it all the same to you what people think of you?"

"I don't know what to tell you. A real man oughtn't to care; a real man is one whom it's no use thinking about, but whom one must either obey or hate."

"It's a strange thing! I don't hate anybody," Arcadii said after a brief reflection.

"But there are ever so many I hate. You are a softhearted, wishy-washy fellow—where do you come in to hate anybody! You're timid; you have but little self-reliance—"

"And you have?" Arcadii interrupted him. "You have a high opinion of yourself?"

Bazarov was silent for a while.

"When I meet a man who won't back water before me," he said, dwelling on every syllable, "then I'll change my opinion of myself. To hate—that is the thing! Here's an example. You said today as we passed our manager Philip's hut—it's the one that's so fine and clean—well, you said Russia would attain perfection when the last and least peasant had a dwelling just like that, and every one of us must help toward that end. But I felt such a hatred for this last and least peasant, this Philip or Sidor, for whom I'm supposed to strain every nerve and sinew and who won't give me even a *thank you*. And, besides, what would I do with his *thank you*? Well, let's say he does live in a white hut while I'm pushing up the daisies? So what comes next?"

"That'll do, Eugene. To hear you talk today one would be driven willy-nilly to agreeing with those who reproach us with lacking principles."

"You talk like your uncle. There are no such things as principles in general—you still haven't tumbled to that!—but there are sensations. Everything depends on them."

"How so?"

"Why, just so. Take me, for instance—I adhere to a negative attitude, by virtue of my sensation. I find it pleasant to deny; that's the way my brain's made, and that's that! Why do I like chemistry? Why do you like apples? Also by virtue of our sensations. It's all one whole. Deeper than that men will never penetrate. Not everyone will tell you that, and I won't tell you that another time, either."

"Well, now, is honesty a sensation also?"

"I should say so!"

"Eugene—" Arcadii began in a lugubrious voice—

"Eh? What? That's not to your taste?" Bazarov cut him short. "No, brother. If you've decided to mow down everything, don't spare your own legs. However, we've philosophized enough. 'Nature wafts a slumbrous silence,' said Pushkin."

"He never said anything of the sort," Arcadii retorted.

"Well, if he didn't, as a poet he might—and should have said it. By the way, he must have been a military man."

"Pushkin never was a military man!"

"Come, now, on every page of his he has: 'To arms! to arms! for Russia's honor!' "

"What sort of things are you making up! Why, it's downright calumny."

"Calumny? My, my! What a word you've found to frighten me with! Whatever calumny you bring up against a man, he really merits something twenty times worse."

"We'd better go to sleep!" said Arcadii in vexation.

"With the greatest of pleasure," Bazarov replied.

But neither of them slept. Some almost inimical feeling was overcoming the hearts of both. Five minutes later they opened their eyes and glanced at each other in silence.

"Look," Arcadii said suddenly, "a dry maple leaf has come off and is falling to the earth; its fluttering is exactly like the flight of a butterfly. Isn't it strange? That which is dead and most sad resembles the gayest and liveliest."

"Oh, my friend, Arcadii Nicolaich!" cried Bazarov, "I beg but one thing of you—don't wax grandiloquent."

"I talk as best I can. And, finally, this is despotism. An idea came into my head; why shouldn't I utter it?"

"Right, but why shouldn't I utter mine? I think that grandiloquence is downright indecent."

"What's decent then? To bicker?"

"Eh, eh! Why, I see that you really intend to follow in your uncle's footsteps. How that idiot would rejoice if he were to hear you!"

"What did you call Paul Petrovich?"

"I called him by his proper name—an idiot."

"Why, this is unbearable!" Arcadii cried out.

"Aha! Family pride spoke up in you," Bazarov uttered calmly. "It persists most stubbornly in people, I've noticed. A man's ready to abjure everything and break with every prejudice, but to admit that his brother, for instance, who steals handkerchiefs, is a thief—that's more than he can bear. And really, now: *my* brother—mine!—and he shouldn't be a genius? How can that be?"

"It was a simple feeling of justice spoke in me and not at all a feeling of family pride," retorted Arcadii, flaring up. "But since that's a feeling you don't understand, since you haven't that *sensation,* why, you're in no position to judge it."

"In other words, Arcadii Kirsanov is too exalted for my comprehension. I bend my knee and say no more."

"Please, that'll do, Eugene; we'll really wind up quarreling."

"Ah, Arcadii! Do oblige me—let's have a good quarrel for once in earnest—till we're laid out cold, till we exterminate each other."

"But then we may end up by—"

"By fighting?" Bazarov caught him up. "Well, why not? Here, on the hay, in such idyllic surroundings, far from the world and gaze of men, it wouldn't matter. But you'd be no match for me. I'd grab you by the throat right off—"

Bazarov spread out his long and rough fingers. Arcadii turned round and got set, as though in jest, to resist. But his friend's face struck him as so ominous—there was such grimly earnest menace in the smile that distorted his lips and in his smoldering eyes, that Arcadii felt an instinctive timorousness.

"Ah! so that's where you've gone to!" the voice of Vassilii Ivanovich sounded at that instant, and the old army doctor appeared before the young men clad in a homemade linen jacket, and with a straw hat, also homemade. "I've been looking and looking for you. Well, you've picked out an excellent place and are exceedingly well employed. Lying on the *earth,* gazing up to *heaven.* Do you know, there's some sort of special significance in that."

"I never gaze up to heaven except when I want to sneeze," growled Bazarov and, turning to Arcadii, he added in an undertone, "pity he interrupted us."

"There, that'll do," Arcadii whispered, and squeezed his friend's hand on the sly. "But no friendship whatsoever can long endure such shocks."

"I look at you, my youthful friends," old Bazarov was saying in the meantime, shaking his head and leaning his folded arms on a rather cunningly twisted stick of his own carving, with a Turk's figure by way of a knob—"I look at you and cannot refrain from admiration. How much strength there is in you, how much youth in its very flowering, how many abilities, talents! Simply Castor and Pollux!"

"So that's what you're up to—shooting off mythology!" Bazarov remarked. "One can see right off you were a mighty Latinist in your day! Why, I seem to remember you gained a silver medal for Latin prose—eh?"

"The Dioscuri, the Dioscuri!" repeated Vassilii Ivanovich.

"However, that'll do, Father; don't get sentimental."

"Once in a blue moon it's surely permissible," murmured the old man. "However I've sought you out, gentlemen, not to pay you compliments; but, in the first place, to inform you that we'll be dining soon, and secondly, I wanted to prepare you, Eugene. You're a sensible man, you know the world, and you know what women are, and consequently you'll be tolerant. Your mother wished to have a Te Deum sung on the occasion of your arrival. You mustn't imagine that I'm inviting you to attend this thanksgiving—it's over by now; but Father Alexis—"

"That hedge-priest?"

"Well, yes, the priest. He's—he's going to dine with us. I didn't anticipate this, and even advised against it—but somehow it just happened. He misunderstood me. Well, so Arina Vlassievna. . . . Anyway, he's a very worthy and reasonable man—"

"He won't eat up my portion at dinner, I suppose?" asked Bazarov.

Vassilii Ivanovich laughed.

"Goodness, how you talk!"

"Well, I don't ask for anything more. I'm ready to sit down at table with any man."

Vassilii Ivanovich set his hat straight.

"I was certain before I spoke," he said, "that you were above any kind of prejudices. Here am I, an old man going on sixty-two, yet I have none." Vassilii Ivanovich dared not confess that he himself had desired the thanksgiving service. His piety was no lesser than his wife's. "And Father Alexis very much wanted to make your acquaintance. You'll like him, see if you don't. He's not averse to a small game of cards, and—but that's just among ourselves—he even smokes a pipe."

"Well, why not? We'll have a round of humbug whist after dinner, and I'll trim him."

"He! He! He! We'll see! It may work the other way."

"Why? Will you go back to your old tricks?" Bazarov asked with a peculiar emphasis.

The father's bronzed cheeks turned an uneasy red.

"Aren't you ashamed, Eugene? What's over is gone and done with. Well, yes, I'm ready to acknowledge before this gentleman I had that passion in my youth, true enough, but I've paid for it—plenty, too! How hot it is, though! Allow me to sit down with you. I won't be in your way, I hope?"

"Not in the least," Arcadii assured him.

Vassilii Ivanovich, grunting, lowered himself into the hay.

"Your present couch reminds me, my dear Sirs," he began, "of my military bivouacking life, the bandaging points, somewhere like this under a haystack—and even for that we glorified God." He sighed. "I've gone through many, many experiences in my span. For one, if you'll allow me, I might tell you a curious episode of the black plague in Bessarabia."

"For which you got the Vladimir cross?" Bazarov put in. "We know, we know. . . . By the way, why aren't you wearing it?"

"Why, I told you that I have no prejudices," muttered the father (he had only the evening before ordered the small bit of red ribbon to be ripped off his coat), and he proceeded to relate the episode of the plague. "Why, he's fallen asleep," he suddenly whispered to Arcadii, indicating Bazarov and winking good-naturedly. "Eugene! Get up!" he went on aloud. "Let's go in to dinner."

Father Alexis, a handsome and stout man with thick, carefully combed hair, with an embroidered belt around his cassock of lilac silk, appeared to be a person of much adroitness and resourcefulness. He made haste to be the first to offer his hand to Arcadii and Bazarov, as though understanding beforehand that they did not stand in need of his blessing, and he behaved himself in general without constraint. He neither lost face himself nor trod on anybody else's toes; he laughed, *à propos,* at hog-Latin and stood up for his bishop; drank two small glasses of wine but refused a third; accepted a cigar from Arcadii but did not smoke it, saying he would take it home with him.

The only thing not quite agreeable about him was a way he had of constantly raising his hand, slowly and carefully, to catch the flies on his face, sometimes squashing them in the process. He sat down at the green baize table, evincing but a modicum of pleasure, and wound up by taking Bazarov over for two rubles and a half in paper money— they had not the least idea in Arina Vlassievna's house how to reckon in silver coin.

The mother was sitting, as before, near her son (she did not play cards), her cheek, as before, was propped up by her little fist, and she got up only to order some new dainty to be served. She was afraid to caress Bazarov, and he, for his part, gave her no encouragement, did not invite her caresses. Besides, the father had advised her not to "bother" their son too much. "Young people aren't overfond of that sort of thing," he had told her over and over. It's needless to say what the dinner was like that day; Timotheich had *in propria persona* galloped off at early dawn for special beef from Circassia; the manager had gone off in another direction for eel-pouts, gremilles, and crawfish; the countrywives had gotten forty-two coppers for the mushrooms alone. But the mother's eyes, bent undeviatingly on Bazarov, expressed not only devotion and tenderness; one could see sorrow in them also, mingled with curiosity and awe—could see in them a certain resigned reproach.

Bazarov, however, had other things on his mind besides analyzing what his mother's eyes might be expressing; he seldom turned to her, and then only with the briefest of questions. Once he asked her to shake his hand "for luck"; she gently laid her soft little hand on his rough and broad palm.

"Well?" she asked, after waiting a little. "Has it helped you any?"

"Things are going worse than ever," he answered with a careless, mocking smile.

"He plays far too recklessly," pronounced Father Alexis, as if with regret, and he stroked his handsome beard.

"Napoleon's rule, good Father, Napoleon's rule," Vassilii Ivanovich chimed in, and led with an ace.

"It brought him to St. Helena, though," observed Father Alexis, and trumped his ace.

"Wouldn't you like some currant tea, little Gene?" inquired Arina Vlassievna.

Bazarov merely shrugged his shoulders.

"No!" he said to Arcadii the next day, "I'm leaving here tomorrow. I'm bored; I want to work, but you can't work here. I'll go to your village again; besides, I've left all my apparatus there. In your house a fellow can at least shut himself up. While here my father keeps repeating to me: 'My study is at your disposal—nobody'll interfere with you,' and at the same time he himself won't go a step from me. And I'm ashamed somehow to shut myself up from him. Then there's my mother, too. I hear her sighing on the other side of the wall, but if you step out to see her, you can't find a thing to say to her."

"She'll be very much grieved," observed Arcadii, "and so will he."

"I'll come back to them again."

"When?"

"Why, when I start out for Petersburg."

"I feel especially sorry for your mother."

"How come? Has she gotten around you with berries, or what?"

Arcadii let his eyes drop.

"You don't know your mother, Eugene. She's not only a very good woman, she's very clever, really. This morning she talked to me for half an hour, and so sensibly, interestingly."

"I suppose she was expatiating upon me all the while?"

"We didn't talk about you alone."

"Perhaps; you can see better from the sidelines. If a woman can keep up a half hour's conversation, it's always a good sign. But I'm going just the same."

"It won't be very easy for you to break the news to them."

"No, it won't be easy. The devil egged me on to tease my father today—he had ordered one of his tenant serfs to be flogged the other day, and quite right, too—yes, yes, you needn't look at me in such horror—he did quite right, because this fellow is an awful thief and drunkard; only my father had no idea that I, as they say, had become cognizant of the facts. He was very much embarrassed, and now I'll have to upset him more than ever. Never mind! He'll get over it!"

Bazarov had said "Never mind!"—but the whole day passed before he could summon the resolution to inform his father of his intentions. At last, when he was saying good night to him in the study, he let drop with an assumed yawn:

"Yes—I almost forgot to tell you. Send to Phedot's for our horses tomorrow."

Vassilii Ivanovich was dumfounded.

"Why, is M'sieu' Kirsanov leaving us?"

"Yes; and I'm going with him."

The father positively reeled.

"You're going?"

"Yes. I must. Make the arrangements about the horses, please."

"Very well," faltered the old man. "I'll send to Phedot's. Very well. Only—only—what's this all about?"

"I must go to his place for a short time. I'll come back here again later."

"Ah! For a short time—very well." He took out his handkerchief and, blowing his nose, drooped almost to the ground. "Well, what's the use? Everything will be attended to. I'd thought you'd stay with us —a little longer. Three days—after three years it's—it's rather too little; rather too little, Eugene!"

"But, I'm telling you, I'm coming back soon. It's unavoidable."

"Unavoidable—well! Duty before everything. So you want the

horses sent for. Very well. Of course, Arina and I did not anticipate this. Why, she has just begged some flowers from a neighbor—she meant to decorate the room for you." (Vassilii Ivanovich did not even mention that every morning, as soon as dawn broke, standing with only slippers on his bare feet, he held counsel with Timotheich and, peeling off with trembling fingers one tattered ruble note after another, entrusted him with various purchases, with particular emphasis on good things to eat and red wine, which latter, as far as he could observe, the young men liked extremely.) "Freedom is the great thing; that's my rule. One mustn't interfere with people—one mustn't—"

He suddenly ceased and made for the door.

"We'll see each other again soon, Father, really."

But Vassilii Ivanovich, without turning round, merely made a hopeless gesture and was gone. When he got back to his bedroom he found his wife in bed, and began to say his prayers in a whisper, so as not to awaken her. She awoke, however.

"Is that you, Vassilii Ivanovich?" she asked.

"Yes, Mother."

"Have you come from Gene? Do you know, I'm afraid he doesn't sleep so comfortably on that divan. I told Anphissushka to give him your traveling mattress and new pillows; I'd have given him our featherbed, but I seem to remember he doesn't like too soft a bed—"

"Never mind, Mother; don't worry yourself. He's all right. Lord, have mercy on us sinners," he went on with his prayer in a low voice. He felt sorry for his old wife; he did not want to worry her by telling her before morning what a sorrow there was in store for her.

Bazarov and Arcadii went off the next day. From early morning all was dejection in the house; the crockery kept falling out of Anphissushka's hands; even Phedka was all in a daze, and wound up by taking off his boots. Vassilii Ivanovich was bustling about more than ever; he was obviously putting up a brave front, talked loudly, and walked noisily, but his face looked haggard, and his eyes were continually avoiding his son. Arina Vlassievna was crying quietly; she would have lost her head entirely and been unable to control herself at all if her husband had not spent two whole hours early in the morning exhorting her. When Bazarov, after repeated promises to come back certainly not later than in a month's time, tore himself at last from the embraces detaining him and took his seat in the coach; when the horses had started, and the horse-bells began jingling, and the wheels turning, and there was no longer any use in following them with your eyes, and the dust had settled, and Timotheich, all bent and tottering as he walked, had crept back to his cubbyhole; when the little old couple were left alone in their little house, which also seemed to have suddenly shrunk into itself and grown decrepit, Vassilii Ivanovich, after a few more moments of bravely waving his handkerchief on the steps, sank into a chair and let his head drop on to his breast.

"He's forsaken us, he's forsaken us!" he babbled. "He's forsaken us; he became bored here. I'm all alone now, all alone, like this!" And each time he said this he thrust out his hand, with the index finger sticking up. Whereupon Arina Vlassievna drew near him and, putting her gray head close to his gray head, said:

"There's no help for it, Vassya! A son is a slice off the loaf. He's like the falcon—he felt like it, and he winged back to the nest; he felt like it, and he winged away. But you and I are like bumps on a hollow tree, sitting side by side and never budging. Only I shall remain the same to you forever, even as you to me."

Vassilii Ivanovich took his hands away from his face and embraced his wife, his friend, his mate, harder than he had ever clasped her even in youth: she had consoled him in his grief.

XXII

In silence, only rarely exchanging a few insignificant words, our friends reached Phedot's. Bazarov was not altogether satisfied with himself. Arcadii was not satisfied with him, either. In addition, Bazarov was experiencing that causeless melancholy which is known only to very young people. The driver changed the horses and, getting up on to the box, inquired whether he should turn to the right or to the left.

Arcadii was startled. The road to the right led to the town and from there home; the road to the left led to Odintsova's place.

He glanced at Bazarov.

"To the left, Eugene?" he asked.

Bazarov turned away.

"What folly is this?" he muttered.

"I know it's folly," Arcadii answered. "But what harm can it do? Is it the first time we've committed follies?"

Bazarov pulled his cap down over his forehead.

"Do as you think best," he said at last.

"Turn to the left!" Arcadii shouted.

The coach rolled off in the direction of Nikolskoe. But having resolved on the *folly,* the friends were even more stubbornly silent than before and seemed positively sullen.

Directly the major-domo met them on the steps of Odintsova's house, the friends could surmise that they had acted injudiciously in yielding to their suddenly conceived whim. They were evidently not expected. They sat rather a long while in the drawing room, with rather foolish faces. At last Odintsova came in to them. She greeted them with her usual amiability, but was surprised at their speedy return; and, as far as one could judge from the deliberateness of her gestures and words, she was none too overjoyed by it. They made haste to announce that they had only dropped in on their way, and would have to go on to the town within four hours. She confined herself to a slight exclamation, begged Arcadii to remember her to his father, and sent for her aunt. The Princess appeared as if she had just been sleeping, which gave her wrinkled old face an even more ill-natured expression. Katya was not feeling well; she did not leave her room. Arcadii suddenly realized that he had wished to see Katya at least as much as Anna Sergheievna herself.

The four hours went by in insignificant discussion of one thing and another; Anna Sergheievna both listened and spoke without a smile. It was only at the very parting that her former friendliness seemed to stir within her soul.

"I have a fit of hypochondria just now," she said, "but you must pay no attention to that and come again—I say this to both of you— some time later."

Both Bazarov and Arcadii responded with a silent bow, took their seats in their carriage, and without stopping again anywhere went straight home to Maryino, where they arrived safely on the evening of the following day. During the whole way neither one nor the other mentioned even the name of Odintsova. Bazarov, in particular, hardly opened his mouth and kept staring off to one side, away from the road, with a kind of exasperated intensity.

At Maryino everyone was exceedingly delighted to see them. The prolonged silence of his son had begun to make Nicolai Petrovich uneasy; he uttered a cry of joy and bounced on the divan, dangling his legs, when Phenichka ran into his room with sparkling eyes and announced the arrival of the "young masters"; even Paul Petrovich himself felt a certain pleasant excitement and smiled condescendingly as he shook hands with the returned wanderers.

There was much talk and many questions. It was Arcadii who spoke for the most part, especially at supper, which was prolonged long after midnight. Nicolai Petrovich ordered up some bottles of porter which had only just been brought from Moscow and became so festive himself that his cheeks became the color of raspberries, and he kept laughing all the time with a half-childish, half-nervous laughter. Even the servants were infected by the general animation. Dunyasha dashed back and forth like one possessed and was continually slamming doors; while Peter was still trying, at three o'clock in the morning, to play the *Cossack Waltz* on his guitar. The strings gave forth a plaintive and pleasant sound in the still air, but with the exception of a small opening flourish, nothing came of the cultured valet's efforts; nature had denied him musical ability just as she had denied him every other.

But meanwhile things were not going overharmoniously at Maryino, and poor Nicolai Petrovich was having a bad time of it. Difficulties on the farm sprang up every day—cheerless, senseless difficulties. The trouble with the hired hands had become unbearable. Some were asking either to be paid off or to have their wages increased, while others made off with the wages they had received in advance; the horses fell sick; harness was used up as though it were on fire; the work was carelessly done; a threshing machine that had been ordered from Moscow turned out to be useless because of its great weight; another, a winnowing machine, was ruined the first time it was used; half the cattle sheds burned down because an old blind housemaid had, in windy weather, gone with a burning brand to fumigate her cow. True, the old woman maintained that the whole mischief had come about because the master had gotten the notion of introducing new-fangled cheeses and milk products. The overseer had suddenly turned lazy and had even begun to grow fat, as every Russian does when he finds a soft thing. Whenever he caught sight of Nicolai Petrovich in the distance, he would fling a stick at a suckling pig passing by or threaten some half-naked urchin, to show his zeal, but for the most part he just slept.

The peasants who had been put on the rent system did not bring their money at the time due and stole the timber; almost every night the watchmen caught the peasants' horses in the meadows of the "farm," and at times forcibly took them away. Nicolai Petrovich attempted to fix a money fine for damages, but the matter usually ended with the horses, after they had been kept a day or two on the master's fodder, being returned to their owners. To top it all off, the peasants began quarreling among themselves: brothers asked for a division of property, their wives could not get on together in the same house; all of a sudden the fight would boil up, and all, as though at a given signal, would get up on their hind legs, all would at once come running to the countinghouse steps, barging in on the master, often with battered faces and in a drunken state, and demand justice and judgment. Hubbub, screaming, sniveling, feminine squeals would arise, alternating with masculine cursing. One had to examine the contending parties, and shout oneself hoarse, knowing beforehand that it was impossible to arrive at a just decision anyway. There weren't enough hands for the harvest; a neighboring small landowner, with a most decent countenance, contracted to supply him with reapers for a commission of two rubles an acre and had cheated him in the most conscienceless manner; his own peasant women demanded unheard-of sums, and the grain in the meanwhile was going to waste; here they had failed to get on with the mowing, and there the Council of Guardians was threatening and demanding prompt and full payment of interest due on the mortgage.

"I'm at the end of my rope!" Nicolai Petrovich cried more than once in despair. "I can't fight them myself, and as for calling in the police captain, my principles won't allow it, yet you can't do a thing with them without the fear of punishment!"

"*Du calme, du calme,*" Paul Petrovich would remark upon this, but even he hummed to himself, frowned, and tugged at his mustache.

Bazarov kept aloof from these squabbles, and, besides, as a guest, it was not for him to meddle in other people's business. The day after his arrival at Maryino he set to work on his frogs, his infusoria, his chemical compounds, and was forever fussing with them. Arcadii, on the contrary, deemed it his duty, if not to help his father, at least to make a show of being ready to help him. He would patiently hear his father out, and once offered him some advice, not with any idea of its being followed but to show his interest. Running an estate did not arouse any aversion in him; he used even to dream with pleasure of work on the land, but at this time his brain was swarming with other ideas.

Arcadii, to his own astonishment, was thinking incessantly of Nikolskoe. Formerly he would merely have shrugged his shoulders if anyone had told him that he could ever become bored under the same roof with Bazarov—and that roof his father's! Yet he actually was bored and longed to get away. He got the idea of hiking until he was tired, but even that did not help. In conversation with his father one day he found out that the latter had in his possession a number of letters, rather interesting, written by Odintsova's mother to his wife, and he gave his father no rest till he got hold of the letters, for which Nicolai Petrovich had to rummage through twenty drawers and trunks. Having gained possession of these half-crumbling papers, Arcadii seemed to calm down, just as though he had beheld before him a goal toward which he ought now to go.

" 'I say this to both of you,' " he was constantly whispering. She herself had added that! "I'll go, I'll go, devil take it all!" But he would recall the last visit, the cold reception, and his former embarrassment —and timidity would get the better of him.

The "may be" of youth, the secret desire to try one's luck, to prove one's worth by oneself, without the protection of anyone whatever, gained the day at last. Before ten days had passed after his return to Maryino, on the pretext of studying the working of Sunday schools, he was galloping off to town again, and from there to Nikolskoe. Urging the driver on without cease, he flew along like a young officer riding to battle; and he felt both frightened and lighthearted, and was breathless with impatience.

"The main thing is not to think," he kept repeating to himself.

The driver he had happened to get was a lad of spirit; he halted before every tavern, saying, "What about a drop of something?" or "Shouldn't I have a drop, now?"—but then, having had his drop, he did not spare his horses.

And at last the high roof of the familiar house came in sight.

"What am I doing?" flashed through Arcadii's head. "Well, there's no turning back now!"

The three horses dashed along as one; the driver whooped and whistled, urging them on. And now the bridge was rumbling under the hoofs and wheels, now the avenue of clipped pines had come nearer. There was a glimpse of a woman's pink dress amid the dark verdure, a young face peeped out from under the light fringe of a parasol.

He recognized Katya, and she recognized him. Arcadii told the driver to rein in the galloping horses, leaped out of the carriage, and went up to her.

"It's you!" she said, gradually flushing all over. "Let us go to my sister, she's here in the garden; she'll be delighted to see you."

Katya led Arcadii off into the garden. His meeting with her had struck him as a particularly happy omen; he was as glad to see her as if she were of his own kindred. Everything had come about so splendidly; no major-domo, no formal announcement. At a turn in the path he caught sight of Anna Sergheievna. She was standing with her back to him. Hearing footsteps, she slowly turned around.

Arcadii would have become abashed again, but the first words she uttered reassured him at once. "Greetings, runaway!" she said in her even, kindly voice, and went to meet him, smiling and puckering her eyes from the sun and wind. "Where did you find him, Katya?"

"I have brought you something, Anna Sergheievna," he began, "which you certainly don't expect—"

"You have brought yourself; that's best of all."

XXIII

Having seen Arcadii off with mocking regret, and given him to understand that he was not in the least deceived as to the real object of his journey, Bazarov isolated himself completely; he was overtaken by a fever for work. He no longer disputed with Paul Petrovich, all the more so since the latter assumed too aristocratic an air in his presence and expressed his opinions more in sounds than in words. Only on one occasion did Paul Petrovich embark on a controversy with the *nihilist* over a question in vogue at the time concerning the rights of the nobles of the Baltic province; but he himself suddenly stopped, remarking with chill politeness: "However, we are unable to comprehend each other; I, at least, have not the honor of comprehending you."

"Of course not," Bazarov exclaimed. "Man is capable of comprehending anything—how the ether vibrates, and what's going on upon the sun—but when it comes to how another man can blow his nose in a different manner from the way one blows one's own—that is something he's incapable of comprehending."

"What, is that supposed to be a witticism?" Paul Petrovich let drop inquiringly, and he drew off to one side.

However, he occasionally requested permission to be present at Bazarov's experiments, and once even drew his perfumed face, washed with the very best preparation, near the microscope to observe how a transparent infusorium swallowed a green mote of dust, and with great alacrity masticated it by means of some sort of exceedingly minute cogs in its gullet. Nicolai Petrovich visited Bazarov far more frequently than his brother; he could have come every day, "to study," as he expressed it, if his cares on the farm were not distracting him. He did not embarrass the young scientist; he would take a seat somewhere in a corner of the room and look on attentively, at rare intervals permitting himself a discreet question. During dinner- and supper-time he would try to turn the conversation to physics, geology, or chemistry, since all other topics, even agriculture, to say nothing of politics, might lead, if not to collisions, at least to mutual unpleasantness.

He surmised that his brother's hatred of Bazarov had not diminished in the least. One unimportant incident, among many others, confirmed his surmises. Cholera had begun to make its appearance here and there in the vicinity, and had even "carried off" two persons from Maryino itself. In the night Paul Petrovich happened to have a rather severe attack. He went through torments until the morning, but did not have recourse to Bazarov's skill. And on seeing him the following day, in reply to Bazarov's question why he had not sent for him, Paul Petrovich answered, still quite pale but scrupulously groomed and shaven, "Why, I seem to recollect you said yourself you didn't believe in medicine."

Thus the days went by. Bazarov worked away stubbornly and grimly. And meanwhile there was in Nicolai Petrovich's house one being to whom, if he did not exactly open his heart, he at least was glad to talk. That being was Phenichka.

He encountered her for the most part early in the morning, in the garden or the yard; he did not drop in at her room, and she had only once come to his door to ask him whether she ought to let Mitya have his bath or not. She not merely confided in him, she not merely was not afraid of him—she was actually freer and more at her ease with him than with Nicolai Petrovich himself. It is hard to say how this had come about; perhaps it was because she unconsciously felt the absence in Bazarov of all gentility, of all that superiority which both attracts and awes. In her eyes he was both excellent as a doctor and simple as a man. She attended to her baby without constraint in his presence; and once when her head suddenly began to go round and ache, she accepted a spoonful of medicine from his hand. Before Nicolai Petrovich she kept aloof, as it were, from Bazarov; she did so, not out of hypocrisy, but from a certain sense of propriety. Of Paul Petrovich she was more afraid than ever; for some time he had begun to keep an eye on her and would suddenly bob up, as though he had sprung up out of the ground behind her back, in *his suit,* with his immovable vigilant face, and his hands in his pockets.

"It just sends a chill right through you," Phenichka complained to Dunyasha, and the latter would sigh in response and think of another "heartless" man. Bazarov, without himself suspecting it, had become the *cruel tyrant* of her heart.

Phenichka liked Bazarov, but she, too, was to his liking. Even his face would change when he talked to her; it took on a serene, almost kindly expression, and to his wonted nonchalance was added a certain jocose attentiveness. Phenichka was becoming prettier with every day. There is an epoch in the life of young women when they suddenly begin to bloom and become full-blown like summer roses; such an epoch had come to Phenichka. Everything furthered it, even the July sultriness then prevailing. Dressed in a light white dress, she seemed herself lighter and whiter; she was not tanned by the sun, but the heat, from which she could not shield herself, spread a slight flush over her cheeks and ears and, infusing a soft indolence into her entire body, was reflected in a dreamy languor in her pretty eyes. She was almost unable to work; her hands were forever falling into her lap. She scarcely walked at all and was constantly "oh"-ing and complaining with an amusing helplessness.

"You should go oftener for a dip," Nicolai Petrovich told her. He had made a large bathhouse, covered over with canvas, in one of his ponds which had not yet quite dried up.

"Oh, Nicolai Petrovich! You can die before you get to the pond, and you can die on your way back. For there's no shade in the garden at all."

"That's true enough about there being no shade," Nicolai Petrovich would answer, rubbing his forehead.

Once, at seven o'clock in the morning, Bazarov, returning from a walk, came upon Phenichka in the lilac arbor, which was long past flowering but was still thick and green. She was sitting on the garden seat and had, as usual, thrown a white kerchief over her head; near her lay a whole heap of red and white roses still wet with dew. He said good morning to her.

"Ah! Eugene Vassilyich!" she said, and lifted the edge of her kerchief a little to look at him, in doing which her arm was bared to the elbow.

"What are you doing here?" said Bazarov, sitting down beside her. "Are you making a bouquet?"

"Yes, for the table at lunch. Nicolai Petrovich likes it."

"But it's a long while yet to lunch. What a heap of flowers!"

"I picked them now, for it's going to be hot, and you won't be able to go out. It's all you can do to breathe now. I feel quite weak from this heat. I'm really afraid I may get sick."

"What a notion! Let me feel your pulse." Bazarov took her hand, felt for the evenly beating pulse, but did not even begin to count its throbs. "You'll live to be a hundred," he said dropping, her hand.

"Ah, God forbid!" she cried.

"Why? Don't you want a long life?"

"Yes, but a hundred years! We had a grandmother of eighty-five years—and what a martyr she was! Black and deaf and bent and coughing all the time; nothing but a burden to herself. What sort of life is that!"

"So it's better to be young?"

"Well, how else?"

"But just how is it better? Tell me!"

"How can you ask how? Why, here I am now, still young, I can do everything—come and go, and fetch and carry, and I don't have to ask anyone to do anything. What could be better?"

"But to me it's all the same whether I'm young or old."

"How can you say—it's all the same? What you say is impossible."

"Well, judge for yourself, Theodosia Nicolaievna—what good is my youth to me? I live alone, a poor lonely bachelor—"

"That's all up to you."

"That's just it—it isn't up to me! If only someone would take pity on me."

Phenichka gave Bazarov a sidelong look but did not say anything. "What's that book you have there?" she asked a little later.

"That? That's a learned book, very hard."

"But you're still studying? And don't you ever get bored with it? You know everything as it is, I guess."

"It doesn't look that way. You try to read a little of it now."

"But I won't understand anything of it. Is it Russian?" asked Phenichka, taking the heavily bound book in both hands. "What a thick book!"

"Yes, it's Russian."

"I won't understand anything anyway."

"Well, I'm not after your understanding it. I wanted to look at you while you're reading it. When you read, the tip of your little nose moves ever so charmingly."

Phenichka, who had set to work to spell out in a low voice the article on "Creosote" she had come across, laughed and abandoned the book. It slipped from the seat to the ground.

"I like it when you laugh, too," Bazarov said.

"Oh, now!"

"I like it when you talk. It's just like a little brook murmuring."

Phenichka turned her head away.

"How you talk!" she said, running her fingers over the flowers. "And why should you listen to me? You've conversed with such clever ladies."

"Ah, Theodosia Nicolaievna! Believe me, all the clever ladies in the world aren't worth the dimple on your little elbow."

"Why, what you won't think of!" murmured Phenichka, and put her hands under her.

Bazarov picked up the book from the ground.

"That's a medical book; why do you throw it down?"

"A medical book?" Phenichka repeated, and she turned to him. "But do you know what? Ever since you gave me those drops—do you remember?—Mitya sleeps so well! I really can't think how to thank you; you're so kind, really."

"Well, doctors really ought to be paid," Bazarov observed with a smile. "Doctors, as you yourself know, are grasping people."

Phenichka raised her eyes, which seemed still darker from the whitish reflection cast on the upper part of her face, and looked at Bazarov. She did not know whether he was joking or not.

"If you like, we'll be delighted. . . . I'll have to ask Nicolai Petrovich—"

"Why, do you think I want money?" Bazarov broke in. "No, it isn't money I want from you."

"What then?" asked Phenichka.

"What?" repeated Bazarov. "Guess!"

"I'm not so good at guessing."

"Then I'll tell you; I want—one of those roses."

Phenichka broke into laughter again and even clapped her hands, so amusing did Bazarov's request seem to her. She laughed, and at the same time felt flattered. Bazarov was looking at her intently.

"By all means, by all means," she said at last and, bending down to the seat, began picking over the roses. "Which will you have—a red or a white?"

"Red—and not too large."

She straightened up again.

"Here you are," she said, but instantly drew back her outstretched hand and, biting her lips, looked toward the entrance of the arbor, then listened.

"What is it?" asked Bazarov. "Nicolai Petrovich?"

"No . . . he's gone to the fields . . . besides, I'm not afraid of him. But Paul Petrovich. . . . I imagined—"

"What?"

"I imagined he was walking around here. No—there's nobody there. Take it." She gave Bazarov the rose.

"On what grounds are you afraid of him?"

"He always scares me. It isn't that he says anything, but he looks at a body so strangely. And I know you don't like him, either. You remember, you used to argue with him all the time. I don't really know what your argument is about, but I can see you twist him this way and that way."

Phenichka showed with her hands how, in her opinion, Bazarov twisted Paul Petrovich.

Bazarov smiled.

"But what if he were getting the upper hand of me," he asked. "Would you stand up for me?"

"Where do I come to be standing up for you? But, no, no one can get the better of you."

"Do you think so? But I know a hand which could knock me down with one little finger if it liked."

"Whose hand is it?"

"Why, don't you know, really? Sniff the rose you gave me—how gloriously fragrant it is."

Phenichka stretched her little neck forward and put her face close to the flower. The kerchief rolled down from her head on to her shoulders; a soft mass of dark, shining, slightly ruffled hair became visible.

"Wait, I want to sniff it with you," said Bazarov. He bent down and kissed her hard on her parted lips.

She was startled and thrust him back with both her hands on his breast, but her thrust was weak, and he was able to renew and prolong his kiss.

There was a dry cough behind the lilac bushes. Phenichka instantaneously moved away to the other end of the seat. Paul Petrovich appeared, made a slight bow, and having dropped with a sort of malicious despond "You here?", he withdrew. Phenichka at once gathered up all the roses and went out of the arbor.

"That was wrong of you, Eugene Vassilyich," she whispered as she went. There was a note of unfeigned reproach in her whisper.

Bazarov remembered another recent scene, and he felt both shame and contemptuous annoyance. But he immediately tossed back his head, ironically congratulated himself "on his formal induction into the ranks of the Lotharios," and went off to his own room.

As for Paul Petrovich, he left the garden and, pacing slowly, made his way to the forest. He stayed there rather a long while, and when he returned to lunch, Nicolai Petrovich inquired solicitously whether he were quite well—so dark had his face become.

"You know that I sometimes suffer from jaundice," Paul Petrovich answered him calmly.

XXIV

Two hours later he was knocking at Bazarov's door.

"I must apologize for interrupting you in your scientific pursuits," he began, seating himself on a chair near the window and leaning with both hands on a beautiful cane with an ivory knob (he usually walked without a stick), "but I am constrained to ask you to spare me five minutes of your time—no more."

"My time is entirely at your disposal," replied Bazarov, something flitting over his face as soon as Paul Kirsanov had crossed the threshold.

"Five minutes will suffice for me. I've come to put a single question to you."

"A question? What about?"

"I'll tell you if you'll be kind enough to hear me out. At the beginning of your stay in my brother's house, before I had yet renounced the pleasure of conversing with you, I had occasion to hear your opinions on many subjects; but as far as my memory serves, neither between us, nor in my presence, was the subject of single combats, of dueling in general, ever broached. Will you allow me to hear what your opinion on that subject is?"

Bazarov, who had risen to meet Paul Petrovich, perched on the edge of the table and folded his arms.

"My opinion is," he said, "that from a theoretical point of view dueling is an absurdity, but from a practical point of view—it's quite a different matter."

"That is, you wish to say, if I have understood you right, that no matter what your theoretical views on dueling are, you would not, in practice, allow yourself to be insulted without demanding satisfaction?"

"You have guessed my meaning fully."

"Very good, Sir. I am very pleased to hear you say so. Your words extricate me from a state of incertitude."

"Of indecision, you mean to say."

"That is all the same, Sir; I express myself so that you might understand me. I—am not as learned as a seminary rat. Your words save me from a certain deplorable necessity. I have decided to fight you."

Bazarov's eyes were goggling. "With me?"

"You—without fail."

"But what for, pray?"

"I could explain the reason to you," Paul Petrovich began, "but I prefer to pass it over in silence. As far as my taste goes, you are one too many here; I cannot endure you; I despise you; and if that is not enough for you—"

His eyes began flashing. . . . Bazarov's flared up as well.

"Very good, Sir," he assented. "No need of further explanations. You've a whim to try your chivalrous spirit upon me. I might refuse you this pleasure, but let come what may!"

"I am sensible of my obligation to you," replied Paul Kirsanov. "And I can now hope that you will accept my challenge without compelling me to resort to violent measures."

"That is, speaking without any allegories, to that stick?" Bazarov remarked coolly. "That's perfectly correct. It's not at all necessary for you to insult me. And, besides, it might not be altogether without danger. You can remain a gentleman. I accept your challenge, also like a gentleman."

"That is excellent," observed Kirsanov, and placed his cane in the corner. "We will say a few words about the conditions of our duel right away, but first I would like to know whether you consider it necessary to resort to the formality of a trifling quarrel, which might serve as a pretext for my challenge?"

"No; it's best without formalities."

"I think so myself. I presume it is also out of place to go deeply into the real grounds of our difference. We cannot endure each other. What more is necessary?"

"What more indeed?" Bazarov repeated ironically.

"As regards the conditions of the duel itself, seeing that we shall have no seconds—for where are we to get them—"

"Precisely—where are we to get them?"

"—therefore I have the honor to lay the following proposition before you: The combat to take place early tomorrow, at six, let us say, beyond the grove, with pistols, at ten paces—"

"Ten paces? That's right; we do hate each other that far away."

"We might make it eight," remarked Paul Petrovich.

"We might—why not?"

"Two shots; and, to provide against any contingencies, let each one of us put a note in his pocket, in which he accuses himself of his own end."

"Now, that's something I don't entirely approve of," observed Bazarov. "There's something of the French novel about it—doesn't look very plausible somehow."

"Perhaps. You will agree, however, that it would be unpleasant to incur a suspicion of murder?"

"I concur. But there is a means of avoiding that grievous accusation. We shall have no seconds, but we can have a witness."

"And who, precisely, allow me to inquire?"

"Why, Peter."

"What Peter?"

"Your brother's valet. He's a man who stands on the peak of contemporary culture and he will perform his rôle with all the *comme il faut* necessary in such cases."

"I think you are joking, my dear Sir."

"Not at all. After due consideration of my suggestion you will be convinced that it's full of common sense and simplicity. Murder will out, but I'll undertake to prepare Peter in a fitting manner and bring him to the field of honor."

"You persist in jesting," said Kirsanov, getting up from his chair. "But after the courteous readiness you have evinced, I have no right to feel aggrieved at you. And so everything is arranged. By the way, you have no pistols?"

"How should I have pistols, Paul Petrovich? I'm not a professional soldier."

"In that case, I offer you mine. You may rest assured that it's five years now since I used them."

"That's a very consoling piece of news."

Kirsanov took up his cane.

"And now, my dear Sir, it only remains for me to thank you and to leave you to your pursuits. I have the honor to take leave of you."

"Till we have the pleasure of meeting again, my dear Sir," said Bazarov, conducting his visitor to the door.

Kirsanov went out, while Bazarov remained standing a minute before the door and suddenly exclaimed, "What the devil! How fine, and how foolish! What a comedy we put on! The way trained dogs dance on their hind legs. But to decline was out of the question; why, I do believe he'd have struck me, and then—" Bazarov paled at the very thought; all his pride simply reared up. "Then I would have had to strangle him like a kitten."

He went back to his microscope, but his heart was beating, and the composure necessary for taking observations had vanished. "He had seen us today," he thought, "but would he really come to his brother's defense like that? And besides, what's so serious about a kiss? There must be something else to it. Bah! Is he in love with her himself by any chance? Of course he is; it's as clear as day. What a pickle, when you think of it! Things are bad!" he decided at last. "Things are bad, no matter how you look at them. In the first place you'll have to offer your forehead as a target, and in any case, to go away; and there's Arcadii—and that blessed little ladybug, Nicolai Petrovich. Things are bad—bad!"

The day passed somehow peculiarly quietly and listlessly. It was just as though there were no Phenichka; she sat in her little room like a baby mouse in its hole. Nicolai Petrovich had a careworn look. He had been informed that rust had begun to appear on his wheat, on which he had placed his particular hopes. Paul Petrovich crushed everyone, with his icy courtesy—even Procophich. Bazarov had begun a letter to his father, but tore it up and threw it under the table.

"If I die," he thought, "they will find it out; but I won't die. No, I shall knock about in this world a good while yet."

He gave Peter orders to come to him on important business the next morning as soon as it was light. Peter got an idea that he wanted to take him to Petersburg with him. Bazarov went to bed late and all night long was harassed by disordered dreams. Odintsova kept hovering before him—she was at the same time his mother; a small cat with black whiskers was following her, and this small cat was Phenichka; while Paul Kirsanov appeared to him as a great forest which he would have to fight despite everything.

Peter aroused him at four o'clock; Bazarov dressed at once and went out with him.

It was a glorious fresh morning; tiny flecked clouds hovered fleecily against the bleakly clear azure; the dew lay scattered in tiny drops on the leaves and grass and like silver on the spiders' webs; the damp, glistening earth seemed still to preserve rosy traces of the dawn; from all the sky the songs of the larks were showering down. Bazarov reached the grove, sat down in the shade at its edge, and only then disclosed to Peter the nature of the service he expected of him. The refined valet became scared to death; but Bazarov calmed him by the assurance that he would have nothing else to do but stand at a distance and look on, and that he would not incur any sort of responsibility. "Yet at the same time," he added, "just think what an important part will be yours!"

Peter threw up his hands, looked down, and leaned against a birch, his face all green.

The road from Maryino skirted the copse; a light dust lay on it, still unstirred by wheel or foot since the previous day. Bazarov was involuntarily glancing along this road, plucking and nibbling blades of grass, and kept repeating to himself, "What foolishness!" The chill of the early morning made him shiver once or twice. Peter gave him a dejected look, but Bazarov merely smiled; he was in no poltroonish mood.

The stamping of horses' hoofs was heard along the road. A muzhik came into sight from behind the trees. He was driving two hobbled horses before him, and as he passed Bazarov he looked at him somehow strangely, without doffing his hat, which evidently upset Peter as an unlucky omen.

"There, that fellow also got up early," thought Bazarov; "but at least he's doing something useful; but what about us?"

"Looks like he were comin', Sir," Peter whispered suddenly.

Bazarov raised his head and beheld Paul Kirsanov. Dressed in a light checked jacket and snow-white trousers, he was walking rapidly along the road; under his arm he carried a case wrapped up in green cloth.

"I beg your pardon; I believe I've kept you waiting," he observed, bowing first to Bazarov, then to Peter, whom he treated respectfully at that instant, as representing something in the nature of a second. "I was unwilling to wake my man."

"It doesn't matter, Sir," answered Bazarov. "We've only just gotten here ourselves."

"Ah! So much the better!" Kirsanov looked about him. "There's no one in sight; no one will hinder us. May we proceed?"

"Let's."

"You do not, I presume, demand any fresh explanations?"

"I do not."

"Would you care to load?" inquired Paul Petrovich, taking the pistols out of their case.

"No; you load, and I'll pace off the distance. I have long legs," Bazarov added with a smile. "One, two, three—"

"Eugene Vassilyich," Peter babbled with difficulty (he was shaking as though he were in an ague fit), "do as you wish; I'm going to move off."

"Four, five—move off, brother, move off; you may get behind a tree even and stop up your ears, only don't shut your eyes; and if either one of us falls, run and pick him up. Six, seven, eight." Bazarov halted. "Will that do?" he asked, turning to Kirsanov; "Or shall I add on two paces?"

"Just as you wish," the other replied, ramming down the second bullet.

"Well, let's throw in two paces more." Bazarov drew a line on the ground with the toe of his boot. "There's the barrier, then. And by the way, how many paces may each of us go from the barrier? That, too, is an important question. There was no discussion of that point yesterday."

"Ten, I imagine," replied Kirsanov, handing Bazarov both pistols. "Will you be so good as to choose?"

"I will be so good. But, Paul Petrovich, will you agree that our combat is unusual to the point of absurdity? Only look at the countenance of our second."

"You are disposed to laugh at everything," answered Kirsanov. "I do not deny the oddity of our duel, but I deem it my duty to warn you that I intend to fight in earnest. *A bon entendeur, salut!*" [1]

---

[1] "Let him who will, heed!"

"Oh! I don't doubt that we've decided to exterminate each other; but why not laugh, too, and unite *utile dulci*? [1] So, you talk to me in French, and I'll talk to you in Latin."

"I am going to fight in earnest," repeated Kirsanov, and he walked off to his place. Bazarov, for his part, counted off ten paces from the barrier and halted.

"Are you ready?" asked Kirsanov.

"Perfectly."

"We can approach one another then."

Bazarov started forward ever so slowly, and Kirsanov, his left hand thrust in his pocket, gradually raising the muzzle of his pistol, advanced against him.

"He's aiming straight at my nose," thought Bazarov, "and how carefully he narrows his eye, the bandit! It's not a pleasant sensation, though. Guess I'll look at his watch chain."

Something whizzed sharply past Bazarov's very ear, and at the same instant a shot rang out. "I heard it, so nothing happened," he had time to think in a flash. He took one more step and, without taking aim, pressed the trigger.

Kirsanov gave a slight start and clutched at his thigh. A thin stream of blood began to trickle down his white trousers.

Bazarov flung aside his pistol and approached his antagonist. "Are you wounded?" he asked.

"You had the right to call me up to the barrier," said Paul Petrovich, "but this wound is a trifle. According to our agreement, each of us has the right to one more shot."

"Really, you'll excuse me, but that will wait till another time," answered Bazarov, and he put his arm around Kirsanov, who was beginning to turn pale. "Now I'm no longer a duelist but a doctor, and I must examine your wound before anything else. Peter, come here! Peter! Where have you hidden yourself?"

"That's all nonsense—I don't need anyone's aid," Kirsanov declared jerkily, "and—we must—again—" He tried to pull at his mustache, but his hand failed him, his eyes rolled up, and he lost consciousness.

"That's something new! Falling in a faint! Whatever made him do it?" Bazarov exclaimed involuntarily as he lowered Kirsanov on the grass. "Let's have a look at what's wrong." He took out a handkerchief, wiped away the blood, and felt around the wound. "The bone's not touched," he muttered; "the bullet went through at no great depth;

[1] "The useful with the pleasant."

only one muscle, *vastus externus,* was grazed. He'll be doing a jig in three weeks! But that fainting spell! Oh, but these nervous people get me down! What a thin hide, I must say!"

"Is he kilt, Sir?" the quavering voice of Peter asked behind Bazarov's back, sounding more like rustling leaves than a human voice.

Bazarov looked around. "Go fetch some water as quick as you can, brother. Don't worry, he'll outlive both of us yet."

But the perfect servant apparently did not understand his words and did not stir from the spot. Kirsanov slowly opened his eyes.

"He's dying," Peter whispered, and he began crossing himself.

"You're right—what an imbecilic physiognomy," remarked the wounded gentleman with a forced smile.

"Well, go for the water, you devil!" Bazarov shouted.

"It's not necessary. It was just a momentary *vertigo.* Help me to sit up—there, that's it. All I need is something to bind up this scratch and I can reach home on foot, or else you can send a droshky for me. The duel, if you are willing, won't be renewed. You have behaved nobly— today, today, you will note."

"No use raking up the past," rejoined Bazarov. "And as for the future, it's not worth while racking one's head about that, either, for I intend clearing out without any delay. Let me bind up your leg now; your wound's not dangerous, but it's always best to stop the bleeding. But first I must bring this mortal back to his senses."

Bazarov shook Peter by the collar and sent him for a droshky.

"Watch out, don't frighten my brother," Paul Petrovich said to him. "Don't even think of telling him."

Peter flew off, and while he was hurrying for a droshky, the two antagonists sat on the ground and said nothing. Kirsanov tried not to look at Bazarov; he did not want to be reconciled to him in any case; he felt ashamed of his own arrogance, of his failure; he felt ashamed of the whole mess he had stirred up, even though he felt that it could not have ended in a more favorable manner. "At any rate, he won't be hanging around here," he consoled himself, "and that's something to be thankful for." The silence was prolonged, a silence depressing and awkward. Both of them were in no pleasant mood. Each realized that the other understood him. Such a realization is pleasant to friends but always quite unpleasant to those who are not friends, especially when it is impossible either to explain things or to separate.

"Haven't I bound up your leg too tight?" Bazarov asked at last.

"No, not at all; it's fine," answered Kirsanov; and after a brief pause he added: "There's no deceiving my brother; we shall have to tell him we had a blowup over politics."

"Very good," Bazarov assented. "You can say I was berating all Anglomaniacs."

"That will do splendidly. What do you suppose that man is thinking of us now?" Kirsanov went on, indicating the same peasant who had driven the hobbled horses past Bazarov a few minutes before the duel, and who now, coming back along the road, deferentially inclined his head and doffed his hat at the sight of the "gentlefolk."

"Who in the world can tell?" answered Bazarov. "Most probably he's thinking of nothing at all. The Russian peasant is that mysterious stranger about whom Mrs. Radcliffe spoke so much at one time. Who's to understand him! Even he doesn't understand himself!"

"Ah! So that's your idea," Kirsanov began, and suddenly he exclaimed, "Look what your fool Peter has done! Why, it's my brother himself galloping this way!"

Bazarov turned round and saw the pale face of Nicolai Petrovich, who was sitting in the droshky. He jumped out of it before it had stopped and rushed up to his brother.

"What does this mean?" he asked in an agitated voice. "Eugene Vassilyich, what's all this, if you please?"

"Nothing at all," answered Paul, "they have alarmed you for nothing. M'sieu' Bazarov and I had a slight argument, and I've had to pay for it a little."

"But how did it all come about, for God's sake?"

"How am I to explain it to you? M'sieu' Bazarov spoke disrespectfully of Sir Robert Peel. I must hasten to add that I am the only person to blame in all this, while M'sieu' Bazarov conducted himself most worthily. It was I who challenged him."

"But, good heavens, you're bleeding!"

"Well, did you suppose I had water in my veins? But this bloodletting is downright beneficial. Isn't that so, Doctor? Help me to get into the droshky and don't give yourself up to melancholy. I'll be quite well tomorrow. That's it; fine. Drive on, coachman."

Nicolai Petrovich started walking after the droshky; Bazarov tried to remain where he was.

"I must ask you to look after my brother," Nicolai Petrovich said to him, "till we bring another doctor from the town."

Bazarov inclined his head in silence.

An hour later Paul Kirsanov was lying in bed with a skillfully bandaged leg. The whole house was thrown into turmoil; Phenichka had a fainting spell, Nicolai Petrovich kept stealthily wringing his hands, while Kirsanov laughed and joked, especially with Bazarov; he had put on a fine cambric shirt, a dandified morning jacket, and a fez, would not allow the blinds to be lowered, and complained amusingly about the necessity of refraining from food.

Toward night, however, he became feverish; his head began to ache. The doctor arrived from the town. (Nicolai Petrovich would not listen to his brother, and indeed Bazarov himself did not wish him to; he sat the whole day in his room, looking jaundiced and surly, and only paid the briefest of visits to the invalid. Twice he happened to encounter Phenichka, but she leapt away from him with horror.) The new doctor advised cooling drinks; on the whole, however, he confirmed Bazarov's assurances that there was no danger to be foreseen. Nicolai Petrovich told him his brother had wounded himself by accident, to which the doctor's response was, "Hm!" But, having twenty-five silver rubles slipped into his hand on the spot, he observed: "You don't say so! It's a thing that often happens, to be sure."

No one in the house went to bed or undressed. Nicolai Petrovich kept tiptoeing into his brother's room and tiptoeing out again; the latter dozed off, then moaned a little, told him in French, *"Couchez-vous,"* and asked for drink. Once Nicolai Petrovich made Phenichka bring Kirsanov a glass of lemonade; Paul gave her an intent look and drank off the glass to the last drop. Toward morning his fever had increased a little; there was slight delirium. At first Kirsanov uttered incoherent words; then suddenly he opened his eyes and, seeing his brother near his bed bending anxiously over him, he said: "Don't you think, Nicolai, that Phenichka has something in common with Nellie?"

"What Nellie, dear Paul?"

"How can you ask? Princess R———. Especially about the upper part of the face. *C'est de la même famille."*[1]

Nicolai Petrovich made no answer, but inwardly he marveled at the tenacity of old passions in man. "It has come to the surface at a moment like this," he reflected.

"Ah, how I love that magnificent being!" moaned Paul Petrovich, despondently clasping his hands behind his head. "I won't stand for any insolent fellow daring to touch . . ." he was babbling a few minutes later.

---

[1] "There's a family likeness."

Nicolai Petrovich merely sighed; he did not even suspect to whom these words referred.

Bazarov presented himself before him at eight o'clock the next day. He had already had time to pack, and to set free all his frogs, insects, and birds.

"You have come to say good-by to me?" said Nicolai Petrovich, getting up to meet him.

"Exactly, Sir."

"I understand you and approve of you fully. My poor brother, of course, is to blame; that's just why he has been punished. He himself told me that he made it impossible for you to act otherwise. I believe that you could not avoid this duel, which—which to a certain extent is explained by the almost constant antagonism of your respective views." (Nicolai Petrovich was confusing his words.) "My brother is a man of the old school, hot-tempered and obstinate. Thank God that it has ended as it has. I have taken all the necessary measures to avoid publicity."

"I'm leaving you my address, in case there's any trouble," Bazarov remarked casually.

"I hope there won't be any, Eugene Vassilyich. . . . I'm very sorry your stay in my house should have such a—such an end. It is all the more distressing to me since Arcadii—"

"I'll probably be seeing him," interrupted Bazarov, in whom explanations and protestations of every sort always aroused a feeling of impatience. "In case I don't, I beg of you to give him my regards, and accept this expression of my regret."

"And I in my turn beg—" answered Nicolai Petrovich, but Bazarov did not wait for the end of the sentence and went out.

Learning that Bazarov was about to depart, Paul Petrovich expressed a desire to see him, and shook his hand. But even here Bazarov remained as cold as ice; he realized that Kirsanov wanted to indulge in magnanimity. He did not have a chance to say good-by to Phenichka; he only exchanged glances with her at the window. Her face struck him as sad. "She'll come to grief, likely as not!" he said to himself. "Oh, well, she'll pull through somehow!" Peter, however, was so overcome that he wept on his shoulder, till Bazarov chilled him with the question: "What have you got—the waterworks?" As for Dunyasha, she was obliged to run off into the grove to hide her emotion.

The culprit who had brought on all this woe got into a light cart, lit a cigar, and when at the third mile, at a turn in the road, the Kirsanov estate with its new house unrolled in a long line, he merely spat and muttering: "The damned squireens!", wrapped himself closer in his overcoat.

It was not long before Paul Kirsanov improved, but he had to keep to his bed for about a week. He bore his captivity, as he called it, rather patiently, but he was far too fussy over his dressing and had everything deodorized with eau de cologne. Nicolai Petrovich read periodicals to him; Phenichka waited on him as before, bringing him bouillon, lemonade, soft-boiled eggs, tea; but a secret horror overcame her every time she entered his room. Paul Petrovich's unexpected action had thoroughly frightened everyone in the house, but her most of all. Procophich alone was not abashed; he discoursed upon how gentlemen used to fight in his day, "but only real noble gentlemen amongst theirselves, but as for any fly-by-night like them there, they'd order 'em whipped in the stable for their impudence." Phenichka's conscience practically did not reproach her, but the thought of the real cause of the quarrel did torture her at times, and besides, Paul Petrovich, too, looked at her so strangely—so that even when her back was turned she felt his eyes upon her. She grew thinner from constant inner perturbation and, as it generally happens, became still more charming.

One day—the incident took place in the morning—Paul Petrovich was feeling better and moved from his bed to the divan, while Nicolai Petrovich, having inquired about his brother's health, went off to the threshing floor. Phenichka brought in a cup of tea and, setting it down on a little table, was about to withdraw. Paul detained her.

"Where are you going in such a hurry, Theodosia Nicolaievna?" he began. "Why, are you busy?"

"No, Sir. . . . Yes, Sir. . . . I have to pour out the morning tea."

"Dunyasha will attend to that without you; sit a little while with a poor sick man. Incidentally, I must have a little talk with you."

Phenichka perched on the edge of an armchair, without a word.

"Listen," said Paul Petrovich, and tugged at his mustache; "I've long been wanting to ask you—you seem to be afraid of me?"

"I, Sir?"

"Yes, you. You never look at me, as though your conscience were not clear."

Phenichka turned red, but she looked at him. He seemed strange to her, somehow, and her heart began to palpitate softly.

"For your conscience is clear, isn't it?" he asked her.

"Why shouldn't it be?" she whispered.

"Goodness knows why! However, whom can you have wronged? Me? That is improbable. Any other people in the house here? That, too, is something unlikely to happen. Unless it's my brother perchance? But then you love him, don't you?"

"I do."

"With all your soul, with all your heart?"

"I love Nicolai Petrovich with all my heart."

"Honestly? Look at me, Phenichka." (It was the first time he had called her that.) "You know, it's a great sin to lie!"

"I'm not lying, Paul Petrovich. Were I to stop loving Nicolai Petrovich, why, I wouldn't want to go on living."

"And you wouldn't give him up for anyone else?"

"Why, for whom could I give him up?"

"For whom indeed! Why, even for that gentleman who has just gone away."

Phenichka got up.

"My Lord God, what are you torturing me for, Paul Petrovich? What have I done to you? How can anyone say such things?"

"Phenichka," Kirsanov uttered in a sorrowful voice, "why, I saw—"

"What did you see, Sir?"

"Why, there—in the arbor."

Phenichka crimsoned to her hair and ears.

"But how was I to blame for that?" she got out with an effort.

Kirsanov raised himself up.

"You were not to blame? No? Not in the least?"

"I love Nicolai Petrovich alone in all the world, and will love him forever!" Phenichka uttered with sudden force, while her throat seemed fairly throbbing with sobs. "As for what you saw, why, even on the Day of Judgment I'll say I'm not to blame and never was, and it'd be better if I were to die right now, if I'm to be suspected of such a thing against my benefactor, Nicolai Petrovich."

But here her voice failed her, and at the same time she felt that Kirsanov had seized and pressed her hand. She looked at him and was simply petrified. He had turned even paler than before; his eyes were shining, and, what was most astonishing of all, a heavy solitary tear was rolling down his cheek.

"Phenichka!" he said in a strange whisper. "Love him—love my brother! Don't play him false for anyone in the world; don't listen to anyone's speeches! Think, what can be more horrible than to love and not be loved! Never forsake my poor Nicolai!"

Phenichka's eyes dried and her terror passed—so great was her astonishment. But what were her feelings when Paul Petrovich—Paul Petrovich himself—put her hand to his lips and simply clung to it, without kissing it and only heaving convulsive sighs from time to time.

"Good Lord!" she thought. "Is he having a fit by any chance?"

But at that instant all his perished life was quivering within him.

The staircase started creaking under rapid footsteps. He thrust her from him and let his head drop back on the pillow. The door opened, and Nicolai Petrovich appeared, cheerful, fresh, and ruddy. Mitya, as fresh and ruddy as his father, in nothing but his little shirt, was bouncing on his chest, catching the big buttons of his father's rough country overcoat with his little bare toes.

Phenichka simply flung herself upon him and, clasping him and her son together in her arms, dropped her head on Nicolai Petrovich's shoulder. He was surprised. Phenichka, the shy and modest Phenichka, had never given him a caress in the presence of a third person.

"What's the matter with you?" he asked and, glancing at his brother, handed Mitya over to her. "You don't feel worse?" he inquired, going up to Paul Petrovich.

The latter buried his face in a cambric handkerchief.

"No—not at all. On the contrary, I'm considerably better."

"You really shouldn't have been so hasty about shifting to the divan. Where are you going?" he added, turning around to Phenichka; but she had already shut the door behind her. "I was bringing in my young hero to show you; he's been pining for his uncle. Why did she carry him off? What's wrong with you, though? Has anything passed between you, or what?"

"Brother!" Paul said solemnly.

Nicolai Petrovich was startled. He had an uncanny feeling, without himself understanding why.

"Brother," Paul repeated, "give me your word you will fulfill one request of mine."

"What request? Tell me."

"It is most important; the whole happiness of your life, in my opinion, depends on it. I've been giving a great deal of thought all this time to what I want to tell you now. Brother, fulfill your obligation, the obligation of an honest and noble-hearted man; put an end to the scandal and the bad example you are setting—you, the best of men!"

"What are you trying to say, Paul?"

"Marry Phenichka. She loves you; she is the mother of your son."

Nicolai Petrovich took a step back and wrung his hands. "Is it you who say that, Paul? You, whom I've always considered the most implacable opponent of such marriages! You say that! But don't you know that it was solely out of respect for you I haven't fulfilled what you've so justly called my duty?"

"You were wrong to respect me in that instance," Paul responded, with a weary smile. "I'm beginning to think Bazarov was right in accusing me of aristocratism. No, dear brother, it's time we stopped posturing and thinking about the world; we're already old folks and resigned; it's high time we laid aside vanity of all kinds. Let us, just as you say, start fulfilling our obligations; and see, we'll obtain happiness in the bargain."

Nicolai rushed to embrace his brother.

"You have opened my eyes completely!" he cried. "Not for nothing have I always declared you the kindest-hearted and wisest fellow in the world, and now I see you are just as reasonable as you are magnanimous."

"Easy, easy," Paul interrupted him. "Don't hurt the leg of your reasonable brother, who at close upon fifty has been fighting a duel like an ensign. And so, this matter is decided: Phenichka will be my—*belle soeur.*"

"My dearest Paul! But what will Arcadii say?"

"Arcadii? He'll exult, naturally! Marriage is against his principles, but then his sentiment of equality will be gratified. And, really, how can one have castes *au dix-neuvième siècle?*"

"Ah, Paul, Paul! Let me kiss you once more! Don't be afraid, I'll be careful."

The brothers embraced.

"What do you think, shouldn't you inform her of your intention right now?" asked Paul.

"Why rush things?" Nicolai objected. "Has there already been any conversation about this between you?"

"A conversation—between us? *Quelle idée!*"

"Well, that's fine. First of all, you must get well, and meanwhile the thing won't run away. We must think it over rather well, and take everything into consideration—"

"But you've decided, haven't you?"

"Of course I've decided, and I thank you with all my soul. I'll leave you now; you must rest—any excitement is bad for you. But we'll talk about it again. Sleep well, my soul, and God grant you health!"

"What is he thanking me like that for?" thought Paul when he was left alone. "As though it didn't depend on him! I'll go away as soon as he's married, somewhere a long way off—to Dresden or Florence—and will live there till I peg out."

Paul moistened his forehead with eau de cologne and closed his eyes. Lit up by the bright light of day, his beautiful emaciated head lay on the white pillow like the head of a dead man.

And indeed he was a dead man.

XXV

At Nikolskoe, Katya and Arcadii were sitting in the garden on a turf seat in the shade of a tall ash tree; Fifi had placed herself on the ground near them, giving her slender body that graceful curve which is known among hunters as "the hare lie." Both Arcadii and Katya were silent; he was holding a half-open book in his hands, while she was picking out of a basket the few crumbs of white bread left in it, and tossing them to a small family of sparrows, who with the poltroonish impudence peculiar to them were hopping and chirruping at her very feet. A faint breeze stirring in the leaves of the ash kept pale-gold flecks of light wavering to and fro over the shady path and over Fifi's tawny back; an even shade fell upon Arcadii and Katya, save that now and then a vivid streak would flare up on her hair. Both were silent, but the very way in which they were silent, in which they were sitting together, was expressive of a trustful *rapprochement*; each of them seemed to be not even thinking of his companion, yet secretly rejoicing at the other's proximity. Their faces, too, had changed since we saw them last; Arcadii seemed calmer, Katya more animated, more spirited.

"Don't you find," Arcadii began, indicating the ash tree, "that the *yassen* is very aptly named? No other tree lets the air through so easily and radiantly (*yassno*)."

Katya raised her eyes and said "Yes," while Arcadii thought, "There's one who doesn't reproach me for expressing myself *grandiloquently*."

"I have no love for Heine," said Katya, indicating with her eyes the book Arcadii was holding, "either when he laughs or when he weeps; I like him when he's pensive and melancholy."

"But I like him when he laughs," Arcadii remarked.

"That's due to old traces of the satirical tendencies still in you."

"Old traces!" thought Arcadii. "If Bazarov were to hear that!"

"Wait a little; we'll make you over."

"Who will? You?"

"Who? My sister; Porphyrii Platonich, our neighbor whom you no longer quarrel with; Auntie, whom you escorted to church the day before yesterday."

"I couldn't very well have refused! And as for Anna Sergheievna, she herself, if you remember, agreed with Eugene in a great many things."

"My sister was under his influence then, just as you were."

"As I was! Why, do you notice that I've already freed myself of his influence?"

Katya let this pass in silence.

"I know," Arcadii went on, "that you never liked him."

"I can form no opinion about him."

"Do you know, Katerina Sergheievna, every time I hear that answer I disbelieve it! There isn't a man whom every one of us could not form an opinion about! That's simply a way of getting out of it."

"Well, I'll say, then, that I don't—exactly dislike him, but I feel that he's alien to me, and that at the same time I am alien to him. And you, too, are alien to him."

"Why do you say that?"

"How shall I put it to you? . . . He's feral, while you and I are tame."

"And I, too, am tame?"

Katya nodded.

Arcadii scratched behind his ear.

"Look, Katerina Sergheievna, that really hurts one's feelings."

"Why, would you wish to be feral?"

"Not feral, no; but strong, energetic."

"That's not something one can just wish. Your friend, now, doesn't even wish for it, yet it's in him."

"Hm! So you suppose he had a great influence on Anna Sergheievna?"

"Yes. But no one can keep the upper hand of her for long," Katya added in a low voice.

"What makes you think that?"

"She's very proud—no, that isn't what I wanted to say. She values her independence very much."

"But who doesn't?" asked Arcadii, and the thought flashed through his mind: "What good is it?"—"What good is it?" flashed through Katya's mind as well. When young people are often together on friendly terms, they are forever coming upon the very same ideas.

Arcadii smiled and, moving a little closer to Katya, he said in a whisper:

"Confess, you're a little afraid of her."

"Of whom?"

"Her," Arcadii repeated significantly.

"And how about you?" Katya asked in her turn.

"I am, too—notice that I said: 'I am, *too*.'"

Katya shook her finger at him.

"I wonder at that," she began. "My sister has never felt so well disposed to you as just now; far more so than on your first visit."

"Really, now!"

"Why, haven't you noticed it? Doesn't that make you glad?"

Arcadii grew thoughtful.

"How could I have earned Anna Sergheievna's good will? Was it possibly through bringing her your mother's letters?"

"Through that, too, and there are other reasons, which I shan't tell you."

"Why not?"

"I shan't tell you."

"Oh! I know—you're very obstinate."

"Yes, I am."

"And observant."

Katya gave him a sidelong look.

"Perhaps that angers you? What are you thinking of?"

"I am thinking how you have come to be so observant—something you really are. You are so shy, so mistrustful; you keep away from everybody—"

"I've lived a great deal by myself; willy-nilly one becomes reflective. But then, do I really keep away from everybody?"

Arcadii flung a grateful glance at Katya.

"That's all very well," he went on, "but people in your position—I mean in your circumstances—don't often possess that gift. Truth has just as hard a time reaching them as it has in reaching kings."

"But I'm not rich."

Arcadii was taken aback and did not understand her at once. "Why, to be sure, the property's all her sister's!" it suddenly occurred to him; he found the thought not unpleasant.

"How well you put that!" he commented.

"What are you referring to?"

"You put it well, simply, without being ashamed and without posing. By the way, I imagine there must always be something peculiar, a kind of vanity of its own, in the feeling of anyone who knows and says he or she is poor."

"I've never experienced anything of that sort, through the kindness of my sister. I mentioned my position only because it happened to come up."

"Just so; but confess that you, too, have a share of that vanity I spoke of just now."

"For instance?"

"For instance, you—forgive my question—you wouldn't marry a rich man, would you?"

"If I loved him very much. No, I think even then I wouldn't marry him."

"There! You see!" Arcadii exclaimed, and after a short wait he added: "And why wouldn't you marry him?"

"Because even folk songs tell us all about unequal matches."

"You want to dominate, perhaps, or—"

"Oh, no! Why should I? On the contrary, I'm ready to submit, if it weren't that inequality is hard to bear. But as for respecting one's self and submitting, that I can understand; that's happiness. But a subordinate existence—no, there's enough of that as it is."

"There's enough of that as it is," Arcadii echoed her. "Yes, yes," he went on, "It's not for nothing that you and Anna Sergheievna are of the same blood; you're just as independent as she is; but you're more secretive. You, I'm certain, would never be the first to give expression to your feeling, however strong and holy it might be—"

"Why, how else should it be?" asked Katya.

"You're equally clever; you've just as much character as she, if not more—"

"Don't compare me with my sister, please," Katya hastily interrupted him. "That's too much to my disadvantage. You seem to forget my sister's a beauty and a clever girl, and—you of all people, Arcadii

Nicolaich, ought not to say such things, and with such a straight face, too."

"What do you mean by 'you of all people'—and what makes you conclude I'm joking?"

"Of course you are."

"You think so? But what if I'm convinced of what I say? What if I find that I actually haven't put the matter strongly enough?"

"I don't understand you."

"Really? Well, now I see—I certainly overestimated your power of observation."

"How?"

Arcadii made no answer and turned away, while Katya found a few more crumbs in the basket and began throwing them to the sparrows, but she swung her arm too vigorously and they flew away, without stopping to peck at them.

"Katerina Sergheievna!" Arcadii began suddenly. "It probably won't matter to you, but I want you to know that I would not exchange you, not only for your sister, but for anyone in the world."

He got up and went quickly away, as though he were frightened at the words that had escaped his tongue.

As for Katya, she let her hands drop together with the basket onto her lap and, with head bent to one side, for a long while followed Arcadii with her eyes. Gradually a crimson flush came faintly out upon her cheeks; her lips did not smile, however, and her dark eyes had a look of perplexity and some other, as yet nameless, feeling.

"Are you alone?" she heard the voice of Anna Sergheievna near her. "I thought you came into the garden with Arcadii."

Katya slowly raised her eyes to her sister (exquisitely, even elaborately dressed, she was standing in the path and tickling Fifi's ears with the tip of her open parasol), and slowly replied:

"Yes, I'm alone."

"So I see," the other answered with a smile. "I suppose he's gone to his room?"

"Yes."

"Were you reading together?"

"Yes."

Anna Sergheievna took Katya by the chin and lifted her face up.

"You haven't been quarreling, I hope?"

"No," said Katya, and she quietly put her sister's hand aside.

"How solemnly you answer! I thought I'd find him here and suggest his coming for a walk with me. That's what he himself is always asking me. They've brought you some shoes from the town; go and try them on—I noticed only yesterday your old ones are quite worn out. In general, you don't pay enough attention to such things, and yet you have such charming little feet! Your hands are pretty, too—the only thing is they're large, so you must make your feet effective. However, you're no coquette."

Anna Sergheievna went on along the path with a light rustle of her beautiful gown; Katya got up from the seat and, taking Heine with her, also went—but not to try on shoes.

"Charming little feet!" she thought as she slowly and lightly mounted the stone steps of the terrace, which were burning with the heat of the sun; "charming little feet, you say. Well, he'll be lying at them!"

But she immediately felt ashamed and ran swiftly upstairs.

Arcadii had gone along the corridor to his room; a butler overtook him and announced that Bazarov was waiting for him in his room.

"Eugene!" Arcadii murmured, almost with dismay. "Has he been here long?"

"He's arrived this minute, Sir, and gave orders not to announce him to Anna Sergheievna, but to show him straight up to you."

"Can any misfortune have happened at home?" thought Arcadii, and, running hurriedly up the stairs, hastened to open the door. The sight of Bazarov at once reassured him, though a more experienced eye might probably have discerned signs of inward agitation in the shrunken figure of the unexpected visitor, though it was as energetic as ever. With a dusty overcoat over his shoulders and cap on his head, he was sitting on the window sill; he did not get up even when Arcadii flung himself with noisy exclamations on his neck.

"This is a surprise! What luck brings you here?" Arcadii kept repeating, bustling about the room like one who both imagines himself and wishes to show himself delighted. "For everything's all right at home—everybody well, eh?"

"Everything's all right, but not everybody is well," said Bazarov. "However, you might stop chattering and instead send for some bread cider for me, then sit down and listen to what I'll tell you in a few but, I hope, pretty vigorous phrases."

Arcadii quieted down, and Bazarov told him about his duel with Paul. Arcadii was very much surprised and even saddened, but did not consider it necessary to show this—he merely asked whether his uncle's wound was really not dangerous, and on receiving the reply that it was most interesting, but not from a medical point of view, he gave a forced smile, yet at heart he felt both uneasy and somehow ashamed. Bazarov seemed to understand him.

"Yes, brother," he let drop, "you see what comes of living with feudal personages. You turn into a feudal personage yourself and find yourself taking part in knightly jousts. And so, my dear Sir, I set off for my paternal nest," Bazarov wound up, "and I've turned in here on the way—to tell you all this, I would say, except that I consider a useless lie a piece of foolishness. No, I turned in here—the devil only knows why. You see, it's a good thing sometimes for a man to take himself by his forelock and pull himself up, like a radish out of its bed; that's just what I did the other day. But I had a hankering for one more look at what I had parted with, at the bed where I was planted."

"I hope those words don't refer to me," Arcadii responded with some emotion. "I hope you're not thinking of parting with me?"

Bazarov turned an intent, almost piercing gaze upon him.

"Would that really grieve you so much? It strikes me *you* have already parted with me. You're such a fresh and spruce little fellow. Probably your affair with Anna Serghieievna is getting on swimmingly."

"What affair of mine with Anna Serghieievna?"

"Why, isn't it on her account you came here from town, my innocent fledgling? By the way, how are those Sunday schools getting on? Or aren't you in love with her? Or have you already reached the stage of playing the modest hero?"

"Eugene, you know I've always been frank with you; I can assure you—I swear it most solemnly before you—you're mistaken."

"Hm! That's a new word," Bazarov remarked in an undertone. "But there's no need for you to get all worked up, for after all it's a matter of absolute indifference to me. A romantic would have said: 'I feel that we are coming to a parting of our ways,' but I simply say that we're fed up with each other."

"Eugene—"

"My dear soul, that's really no misfortune; one gets fed up with much more than that in this world! And now I suppose we'd better say good-by, hadn't we? Ever since I've been here I've felt ever so abominably, as though I'd been steadily reading Gogol's letters to the good lady of the Governor of Kaluga. By the way, I didn't tell them to unharness the horses."

"Good heavens, but this is impossible!"

"But why?"

"I'm not saying anything about myself; but that would be discourteous to the last degree to Anna Sergheievna, who will inevitably wish to see you."

"Oh, you're mistaken there."

"On the contrary, I am certain I'm right," Arcadii retorted. "And what's the use of your pretending? If it comes to that, haven't you come here on her account yourself?"

"That may be true enough, but you're mistaken just the same."

But Arcadii was right. Anna Sergheievna wished to see Bazarov and sent an invitation to him by a butler. Bazarov changed his clothes before going to her: it turned out that he had packed his new suit so as to be able to get at it easily.

Odintsova received him not in the room where he had so unexpectedly declared his love to her, but in the drawing room. She held her finger tips out to him amiably, but her face betrayed an involuntary tenseness.

"Anna Sergheievna," Bazarov hastened to say, "first of all I must reassure you. Before you is a poor mortal who has long since come to his senses, and hopes that others have forgotten his follies as well. I'm going away for a long spell; and even though you'll agree I'm not at all a gentle creature, it would still be far from cheerful for me to carry away with me the thought that you recall me with aversion."

Anna Sergheievna gave a deep sigh like one who has just clambered up on a high mountain, and her face became animated by a smile. She held out her hand a second time to Bazarov and responded to his pressure.

"Let bygones be bygones," she said. "All the more so since, speaking from my conscience, I, too, had transgressed at that time, if not through coquetry, then something else. In a word, let's be the same friends we were. It was all a dream, wasn't it? And who ever remembers dreams?"

"Who remembers them? And, besides, love—why it's really just an assumed feeling."

"Really? I'm most delighted to hear that."

Thus spoke Anna Sergheievna, and thus did Bazarov speak; they both thought they were telling the truth. Was the truth, the whole truth, to be found in their words? They themselves did not know this, and naturally the author knows least of all. But they struck up a conversation which intimated that they had believed each other perfectly.

Anna Sergheievna asked Bazarov, casually, what he had been doing at the Kirsanovs'. He was on the verge of telling her about his duel with Arcadii's uncle, but he checked himself with the thought that she might think he was trying to make himself interesting, and answered that he had been at work all the time.

"As for me," said Anna Sergheievna, "I had an attack of hypochondria at first, God knows why; I was even getting ready to go abroad—imagine! Then it passed off, your friend Arcadii Nicolaich arrived, and I again got back into my rut, into my real role."

"What role is that, may I ask?"

"The role of aunt, preceptress, mother—call it what you will. By the way, do you know that hitherto I had not thoroughly understood your close friendship with Arcadii Nicolaich; I considered him rather insignificant. But now I've come to know him better and have become convinced that he's clever. And above all he's young, young! Not like you and I, Eugene Vassilyich."

"Is he still as timorous in your presence?" asked Bazarov.

"Why, was he—" Anna Sergheievna began, and after a little thought added: "He has become more trustful now; he talks to me. He used to avoid me before. However, I didn't seek his society either. He and Katya are great friends."

Bazarov felt irritated. "It's impossible for a woman not to be crafty!" he reflected.

"You say he used to avoid you," he said with a chill smile. "But it is probably no secret to you that he was in love with you?"

"What! He, too?" escaped from Anna Sergheievna.

"He, too," repeated Bazarov with a submissive bow. "Is it possible you didn't know it and that I've told you something new?"

She dropped her eyes.

"You are mistaken, Eugene Vassilyich."

"I don't think so. But perhaps I shouldn't have mentioned it."— "And in the future don't you be crafty with me!" he added to himself.

"Why not mention it? But I think that here, too, you are attaching too much significance to a passing impression. I'm beginning to suspect you're inclined to exaggeration."

"Let's not talk about it, Anna Sergheievna."

"But why not?" she retorted, yet she herself led the conversation into another channel. She was still ill at ease with Bazarov, even though she had told him and had assured herself that everything had been forgotten. Exchanging the simplest phrases with him, even while jesting with him, she felt a faint spasm of fear. Thus people on a steamer at sea talk and laugh carelessly, for all the world as if they were on dry land; but let the least stoppage occur, let the least sign of anything unusual appear, and immediately there will emerge on every face an expression of peculiar alarm, evidencing a constant consciousness of constant danger.

Her conversation with Bazarov did not last long. She began falling into thoughtfulness, answering absent-mindedly, and suggested at last that they go into the reception room, where they found the Princess and Katya.

"But where is Arcadii Nicolaich?" asked the hostess, and on hearing that he had not shown himself for more than an hour she sent for him. It took some time to find him: he had made his way into the very thickest part of the garden and, with his chin propped on his clasped hands, was sitting plunged in meditations. They were deep and serious, these meditations, but not mournful. He knew Anna Serghejevna was sitting alone with Bazarov, and he felt no jealousy, as he had once felt; on the contrary, his face was softly glowing; he seemed to be at once wondering at something, and rejoicing and coming to some resolve.

XXVI

The late Odintsov had not been fond of innovations, but he had tolerated "a certain play of ennobled taste," and had in consequence erected in his garden, between the hothouse and the pond, a structure after the fashion of a Greek portico—of Russian brick. Along the blind wall at the back of this portico or gallery were placed six niches for statues, which Odintsov had intended to order from abroad. These statues were to represent Solitude, Silence, Meditation, Melancholy, Pudicity, and Sensibility. One of them, the goddess of Silence, with her finger on her lips, had been brought and put in place, but that very same day some urchins on the place had knocked off her nose, and although a plasterer in the neighborhood undertook to put a new nose on her "twice as good as she had before," Odintsov ordered her to be removed, and the goddess found herself in a corner of the threshing barn, where she had stood for many a long year, arousing superstitious terror in the village women. The front part of the temple had long been overgrown with thick shrubbery; only the capitals of the columns could be seen above the dense greenery. In the portico itself it was cool even at midday. Anna Sergheievna disliked visiting this place ever since she had seen an adder there; but Katya often came and sat on the wide stone seat built in under one of the niches. Here in the midst of the shade and coolness she used to read, work, or give herself up to that sensation of perfect peace probably familiar to everyone, the charm of which consists in the conscious, mute watchfulness of the vast wave of life that rolls ceaselessly both around us and within us.

The day after Bazarov's arrival Katya was sitting on this favorite seat of hers. Arcadii was once more sitting by her side. He had beseeched her to come with him to the "portico."

There was still about an hour left before lunch; the dewy morning was already being replaced by a sultry day. Arcadii's face retained the expression of the preceding day; Katya had a preoccupied air. Her sister had, right after their morning tea, called her into her study and, after some preliminary caresses, which always frightened Katya a little, she had advised her to be more guarded in her behavior with Arcadii, and especially to avoid solitary talks with him, supposedly already noticed by her aunt and the whole household. Besides that, even the evening before, Anna Sergheievna had been out of sorts, while Katya herself had felt ill at ease, as though she were conscious of being at fault in some way. As she yielded to Arcadii's entreaty, she said to herself that this would be the last time.

"Katerina Sergheievna," he began with a certain free-and-easy manner begotten of bashfulness, "ever since I've had the happiness of living in the same house with you, I have discussed a great many things with you, and yet there is a certain . . . question . . . of the utmost importance to me which I haven't yet touched upon. You remarked yesterday that I have been made over here," he went on, at once catching and avoiding the questioning gaze Katya had fixed upon him. "I have certainly changed in many ways, and you know that better than anyone else—you to whom I really owe this change."

"I? To me?" said Katya.

"I am not now the conceited boy I was when I came here," Arcadii went on. "I'm not past twenty-three for nothing; as before, I want to be useful, I want to dedicate all my powers to the truth; but I no longer seek my ideals where I sought them before; they present themselves to me—considerably closer. Up to now I had not understood myself; I set myself tasks which were beyond my powers. My eyes have been opened recently, thanks to a certain emotion. . . . I'm expressing myself not quite clearly, but I hope you will understand me."

Katya made no answer but she ceased to gaze at Arcadii.

"I suppose," he began again, by now in a more agitated voice, while above his head a chaffinch sang its song unheedingly among the leaves of the birch—"I suppose it's the duty of every honorable man to be utterly frank with those—with those who—in short, with those who are near to him, and so I—I intend—"

But here Arcadii's eloquence failed him; he forgot what he wanted to say, spoke haltingly, and was forced to fall silent for a brief while. Katya still did not raise her eyes. Apparently she did not understand what he was leading up to with all this, yet at the same time was waiting for something.

"I foresee I shall surprise you," Arcadii began, pulling himself together again with an effort, "especially since this feeling relates in a way—in a way, notice—to you. You reproached me yesterday, if I remember correctly, with a want of seriousness," Arcadii went on, with the air of a man who has got into a bog, feels that he is sinking further and further in at every step, and yet hurries onward in the hope of crossing it as soon as possible. "That reproach is often directed at—falls upon young men even when they cease to deserve it; and if I had more self-confidence—" ("Come, help me, do help me!" Arcadii was thinking in desperation, but, as before, Katya did not turn her head.) "If I could hope—"

"If I could but feel sure of what you say!" the clear voice of Anna Sergheievna broke in on them at that instant.

Arcadii immediately fell silent, while Katya turned pale. A small path ran past the very bushes that screened the portico. Anna Sergheievna was walking along it, accompanied by Bazarov. Katya and Arcadii could not see them but they heard every word, the rustle of their clothes, their very breathing. They took a few steps and, as though on purpose, stopped just in front of the portico.

"You see," Anna Sergheievna continued, "you and I have made a mistake; we're both past our first youth—especially I; we have seen life, we are tired; we're both—why be falsely modest?—clever; at first we aroused each other's interest, our curiosity was stirred, but then—"

"But then I became flat," Bazarov put in.

"You know that that was not the cause of our misunderstanding. But be that as it may, we had no need of each other, that's the main thing; there was too much—how should I put it?—similarity in us. We did not realize this immediately. On the other hand, Arcadii—"

"Have you any use for him?" asked Bazarov.

"Come, now, Eugene Vassilyich. You tell me he is not indifferent to me, and it always seemed to me that he liked me. I know that I'm old enough to be his aunt, but I don't wish to conceal from you that I've come to think more often of him. There's a certain charm about such youthful, fresh emotion—"

"The word *fascination* is more apt in such cases," Bazarov interrupted; one could hear seething spleen in his stifled yet calm voice. "Arcadii was somehow secretive with me yesterday, and spoke neither of you nor of your sister, which is a grave symptom."

"He's just like a brother to Katya," she commented, "and I like that about him, though perhaps I shouldn't have allowed such intimacy between them."

"Is that the—sister in you speaking?" Bazarov brought out drawlingly.

"Of course! But why are we standing? Let's walk on. What a strange talk we are having, aren't we? And could I even have anticipated that I would be talking to you like this? You know that I'm afraid of you— yet at the same time I trust you, because in reality you are very kind."

"In the first place, I'm not at all kind; and in the second, I've lost all significance for you, and so you tell me I am kind. Which is like placing a wreath of flowers on the head of a dead man."

"Eugene Vassilyich, we have no power over—" she began; but a gust of wind swooped down, set the leaves rustling, and bore her words away.

"Of course, you are free—" Bazarov declared a little later. Nothing more could be distinguished; their steps retreated; everything was stilled.

Arcadii turned to Katya. She was sitting in the same position, save that she had bowed her head still lower.

"Katerina Sergheievna," said he in a quivering voice and clasping his hands, "I love you forever and irrevocably, and I love no one but you. I wanted to tell you this, to find out your opinion of me and to ask for your hand, since I am both not rich and feel ready for any sacrifice. You do not answer me? You do not believe me? Do you think I speak frivolously? Recall these last days, then! Can it be that you haven't long since become convinced that all else—do understand me!—that all else has long since vanished without a trace? Look at me, say but one word to me! I love—I love you—believe me!"

She looked at him with a clear and grave gaze and after long thought, with the faintest smile, she replied:

"Yes."

He leapt up from the seat.

"Yes! You said *yes,* Katerina Sergheievna! What does that word mean? Only, that I love you, that you believe me—or—or—I dare not finish—"

"Yes," repeated Katya, and this time he understood her. He snatched her large beautiful hands and, breathless with rapture, pressed them to his heart. He could scarcely stand on his feet and merely kept repeating: "Katya, Katya—" while she began weeping in a guileless way, smiling gently at her own tears. He who has never seen such tears in the eyes of a beloved being has never experienced to what an extent, all faint with gratitude and shame, a man may be happy on earth.

The next day, early in the morning, Anna Sergheievna sent to summon Bazarov to her study and, with a forced laugh, handed him a folded sheet of notepaper. It was a letter from Arcadii; in it he asked for her sister's hand.

Bazarov quickly scanned the letter and made an effort to control himself, so as not to betray the feeling of malevolent joy which instantaneously flared up in his breast.

"So that's how it is," he commented. "And yet, I believe, you were supposing only yesterday that he loved Katerina Sergheievna with a brother's love. Well, what do you intend doing now?"

"What would you advise me?" asked Anna Sergheievna, still laughing.

"Why, I suppose," Bazarov answered, also with a laugh, although he was not at all in a gay mood and had no more inclination to laugh than she had—"I suppose you ought to give the young people your blessing. It's a good match in all respects; Kirsanov's position is passable, he's the only son, and his father's a good-natured fellow, he won't want to thwart him."

Odintsova walked through the room. Her face alternately flushed and paled.

"You think so?" she asked. "Well, I can see no obstacles. I'm glad for Katya's sake—and for Arcadii Nicolaich's. Of course, I'll wait for his father's answer. I'll send him in person to him. But it turns out I was right yesterday when I told you we're both old people already. How was it I didn't see anything? That's what amazes me!"

She again broke into laughter and immediately turned her head away.

"The younger generation of today has become very cunning," remarked Bazarov, and laughed in his turn. "Good-by," he began again after a short silence. "I hope you will bring the matter to the most satisfactory conclusion; as for me, I'll rejoice from a distance."

Odintsova quickly turned to him.

"Why, are you going away? Why shouldn't you stay *now*? Do stay. It's exciting to talk with you—as though one were walking along the edge of a precipice. At first one feels timid, but then one gets courage from somewhere. Do stay."

"Thanks for the suggestion, Anna Sergheievna, and for your flattering opinion of my conversational talents. But I find I've been moving in a sphere which is not my own too long as it is. Flying fishes can stay up in the air for a certain length of time, but they must plunge back into the water soon; allow me, too, to dive back into my own element."

Odintsova looked at Bazarov. His pale face was twitching with a bitter smile.

"This was the man who loved me!" she thought—and she felt pity for him and held out her hand to him with sympathy.

But he, too, understood her.

"No!" he said, taking a step back. "I'm a poor man, but I've never accepted alms so far. Good-by, Madam, and may all be well with you."

"I am convinced we're not seeing each other for the last time," Anna Sergheievna declared with an involuntary gesture.

"Anything can happen in this world!" answered Bazarov, bowed, and walked out.

"So you've gotten a notion of building a nest for yourself?" he was saying the same day to Arcadii, squatting on the floor and packing his suitcase. "Well, why not—it's a good thing. Only you really shouldn't have been so sly about it. I expected something from you in altogether another quarter. Or perhaps you were bowled over yourself?"

"Yes, I certainly didn't expect this when I parted from you," answered Arcadii. "But why are you being sly, telling me yourself, 'It's a good thing,' as though I didn't know your opinion of marriage?"

"Eh, my dear friend!" said Bazarov. "How you talk! You see what I'm doing: there turned out to be an empty space in the suitcase and so I'm filling it up with hay. That's how it is with the suitcase of our life: it doesn't matter what we stuff it with, as long as there is no void. Don't be offended, please; you probably remember the opinion I've always had of Katerina Sergheievna. Many a young lady's called clever simply because she can sigh cleverly; but yours can hold her own and, indeed, she'll hold it so well that she'll have you under her thumb as well—to be sure, though, that's quite as it should be." He slammed the lid to, and got up from the floor. "And now I say again, in farewell— for it's no use deceiving ourselves—we're parting for good, and you feel that yourself—you've acted sensibly; you're not made for our sour, rough, lonely life. There's no daring, no malice in you, but there is a youthful valor, a youthful cockiness, and that's no good in our business. Your sort, you gentry, can never get beyond refined submission or re- fined indignation, and that's just piffle. You won't fight, for instance, and yet you imagine yourselves brave lads—whereas we're aching to fight. Oh, well! Our dust would make your eyes smart, our mud would bemire you, and, besides, you're not grown up enough for us, you can't help admiring yourself, you find it pleasant to upbraid yourself; but we're bored with that—let's have men of another sort! We've got to smash others! You're a fine fellow; but you're a namby-pamby liberal squire's son, after all—*ay volla-too,* as my parent is fond of saying."

"You are parting from me forever, Eugene," Arcadii responded sadly, "and have you nothing else to say to me?"

Bazarov scratched the nape of his neck.

"I have, Arcadii—I do have something else to say to you, but I'm not going to say it, because that's romanticism—which means getting all sirupy. But you just get married as fast as you can, and build yourself a nest, and turn out as many children as you can. They'll be clever, if only because they'll be born at the right time, which is something you and I failed to do. Aha, I see the horses are ready. Time to go! I've said good-by to everyone already. Well, now, should we embrace, perhaps?"

Arcadii flung himself on the neck of his former preceptor and friend, and his tears fairly spurted.

"That's what it means to be young!" Bazarov commented calmly. "But I rely upon Katerina Sergheievna. You'll see how quickly she'll console you!"

"Good-by, brother!" he said to Arcadii, having already clambered into a light cart and, pointing to a pair of jackdaws sitting side by side on the stable roof, he added: "That's meant for you! Consider and reflect!"

"What's all that for?" asked Arcadii.

"What? Are you so weak in natural history, or have you forgotten that the jackdaw is a most respectable domestic bird? That's an example to you! Good-by, Signor!"

The cart began to rattle and rolled away.

Bazarov had spoken the truth. Talking that evening with Katya, Arcadii completely forgot about his preceptor. He was already beginning to submit to her, and Katya sensed this, and was not at all astonished. He was to set off the next day for Maryino, to see his father. Anna Sergheievna did not want to intrude upon the young people, and only out of propriety would not leave them by themselves for too long a time. She magnanimously kept the Princess out of their way; the latter had been reduced to a state of tearful frenzy by the news of the proposed marriage. At first Anna Sergheievna had feared that the sight of their happiness might prove rather trying to herself, but it turned out quite the contrary; this sight not only was not trying to her—it interested her, it even touched her in the end. She felt both gladdened and saddened by this. "It's evident Bazarov was right," she thought: "Curiosity, solely curiosity, and love of ease, and egoism—"

"Children," she said aloud, "what do you say, is love a purely assumed feeling?"

But neither Katya nor Arcadii even understood her. They fought shy of her; the conversation they had involuntarily overheard haunted their minds. But Anna Sergheievna soon set them at rest, nor was this difficult for her—she had set herself at rest.

XXVII

The old Bazarov couple was all the more overjoyed by their son's sudden arrival, since it was quite unexpected. Arina Vlassievna became so flustered, and kept running all through the house so much, that Vassilii Ivanovich compared her to a "hen partridge"; the short tail of her abbreviated jacket did in fact give her something of a birdlike appearance. He himself merely lowed and bit hard on the amber mouthpiece of the pipe on one side of his mouth or, clutching his neck with his fingers, would twist his head as though he were trying whether it were properly screwed on and, suddenly opening his wide mouth, go off into paroxysms of utterly silent laughter.

"I've come to you for all of six weeks, old-timer," Bazarov told him. "I want to work, so don't you hinder me, please."

"You'll forget what my physiognomy looks like, that's how little I'll hinder you!" Vassilii Ivanovich answered him.

He kept his promise. After installing his son as before in his study, he all but hid himself away from him, and kept his wife from all superfluous demonstrations of tenderness.

"You and I, mother, pestered our dear Eugene a trifle on his first visit; we must act a little wiser this time."

Arina Vlassievna agreed with her husband but came out but little ahead of the game, since she saw her son only at meals and was now absolutely afraid to address him.

"Gene, dear," she would say sometimes—but before he had time to look around, she was already nervously fingering the tassels of her reticule and faltering: "Never mind, never mind, I was only—" and afterward she would betake herself to Vassilii Ivanovich and, propping up her cheek, would tell him: "If I could only find out, darling, which Eugene would like for dinner today—cabbage or beet soup?" —"But why didn't you ask him yourself?"—"Why, I'd be pestering him!"

However, Bazarov of his own accord soon ceased shutting himself up; the fever of work shortly forsook him, and was replaced by dreary ennui and a dull unrest. A strange fatigue could be noted in all his movements; even his walk, firm and impetuously bold, became changed. He gave up his solitary walks and began to seek society; he drank tea in the drawing room, strolled about the truck garden with his father, and smoked with him, "keeping mum"; once he even inquired about Father Alexis.

Vassilii Ivanovich at first rejoiced at this change but his joy did not last long. "Gene's breaking my heart," he complained in secret to his wife. "It's not that he's discontented or angry—that wouldn't matter so much; he's aggrieved, he's sorrowing—that's what's terrible. He's always silent. If he'd only scold us! He's losing weight, the color of his face is so bad."

"Lord, Lord!" whispered the little crone. "I'd like to put a blessed amulet around his neck, but of course he won't allow it."

Vassilii Ivanovich several times attempted in the most circumspect manner to question Bazarov about his work, about his health, about Arcadii. But Bazarov's replies were reluctant and casual; and, once noticing that his father was trying gradually to lead up to something in his conversation, he said to him crossly: "Why do you always seem to be tiptoeing around me? That way's worse than the old one."— "There, there, I didn't mean anything!" poor Vassilii Ivanovich answered hastily.

Just as fruitless did his political hints remain. He hoped to awaken his son's sympathy one day by broaching a conversation about the imminent emancipation of the serfs, about progress; but his son merely remarked apathetically: "Yesterday I was passing by a fence, and I heard the peasant boys around here bawling a cheap sentimental street ballad instead of some grand old song. That's progress for you."

Sometimes Bazarov went into the village and in his usual bantering tone entered into conversation with some muzhik: "Come," he would say to him, "expound your views on life to me, brother; for they say all the strength and future of Russia lies in your hands, that you'll start a new epoch in history—you'll give us an authentic language as well as our laws."

The peasant either did not answer at all or would utter such gems as: "Why, we can, lief as not . . . because, so to signify . . . up to whatever limit is set up for us—"

"You just explain to me what your *mir* is," Bazarov interrupted. "And is it the very same *mir*[1] that is said to rest on three fishes?"

"It's the earth, father of mine, that rests on three fishes," the peasant would explain to him soothingly, in a patriarchally good-natured singsong. "But over against our *mir*, now, as everybody knows, there's the masters' will, since you are our fathers. And the stricter the masters' rule, the more the peasant loves it."

After having heard out such a speech one day, Bazarov shrugged his shoulders disdainfully and turned away, while the muzhik ambled onward on his own affairs.

"What was he talking about?" inquired another peasant, middle-aged and of glum appearance, who had been following the other's conversation with Bazarov from a distance, standing on the threshold of his hut. "About arrears, or what?"

"It weren't about no arrears, brother o' mine," answered the first peasant, and by now there wasn't even a trace of patriarchal singsong in his voice; on the contrary, there was a certain scornful gruffness to be heard in it. "He was just battin' away about something or other;

[1] Bazarov is punning execrably on two of several meanings of the word: *Communal Council* and *Universe.—Editor.*

wanted to gab a little. You know how it is yourself; he's a gentleman —so how can he understand anything?"

"How could he?" answered the other muzhik, and, tossing back their hats and pushing down their belts, they proceeded to discuss their affairs and needs.

Alas! Bazarov, shrugging his shoulders disdainfully, Bazarov, who knew how to talk to muzhiks (as he had boasted in a dispute with Paul Kirsanov)—this self-assured Bazarov did not even suspect that in their eyes he was after all only something in the nature of a jack-pudding.

However, he found an occupation for himself at last. One day Vassilii Ivanovich was bandaging a muzhik's wounded leg in his presence, but the old man's hands were trembling and he could not manage the bandages; his son helped him, and from then on began to participate in his practice, though at the same time he never ceased ridiculing both the remedies he himself advised and his father, who immediately availed himself of them. But Bazarov's jeers did not in the least upset Vassilii Ivanovich; they were even a solace to him. Holding his greasy dressing gown across his stomach with two fingers and puffing away at his pipe, he used to listen with enjoyment to his son, and the more malice there was in the latter's outbursts, the more good-naturedly did the happy father laugh, showing every last one of his black teeth. He even used to repeat these outbursts, which were at times flat or pointless, and would, for instance, for several days in a row reiterate without rhyme or reason: "It's no great shakes!"— simply because his son, on learning that he attended matins, had used that expression.

"Glory be to God! He's gotten over his hypochondria!" he whispered to his wife. "What a tongue-lashing he gave me today—it was simply wonderful!"

Moreover, the idea of having such an assistant threw him into raptures; it filled him with pride. "Yes, yes," he would say to some countrywife in a man's thick overcoat and a headdress with points like horns, as he handed her a vial of Goulard's solution or a box of white ointment, "you ought to be thanking God every minute, my good woman, because my son is staying with me; you'll now be treated by the most scientific, most modern methods. Do you understand that? You take even Napoleon, the Emperor of the French— well, even he hasn't a better doctor than that." But the countrywife, who had come to complain that her "innards feel all-overish" (the exact meaning of which words she was not able, however, herself to explain), merely kept bowing low and reaching into her bosom, where she had four eggs tied up in the corner of a towel, by way of a fee.

Bazarov once even pulled out a tooth for a passing dry-goods peddler, and though this tooth was merely an average specimen, Vassilii Ivanovich preserved it as a curiosity and, as he exhibited it to Father Alexis, kept ceaselessly repeating: "Just look at those roots! What strength Eugene has! The peddler simply rose up in the air. If it had been an oak, I think he'd have rooted it up just the same!"

"Most promising!" Father Alexis would comment at last, at a loss as to what answer to make, and how to get rid of the ecstatic old man.

One day a muzhik from a neighboring village brought his brother, ill with typhus, to Vassilii Ivanovich. Lying face down on a truss of straw, the poor fellow was dying; his body was covered with dark splotches; he had long since lost consciousness. Vassilii Ivanovich voiced his regret that no one had thought of turning to medical aid sooner and pronounced the case hopeless. And, in fact, the peasant did not get his brother home alive; he died in the cart.

Three days later Bazarov came into his father's room and asked him if he had any lunar caustic.

"Yes; what do you want it for?"

"I need it—to cauterize a cut."

"For whom?"

"For myself."

"What—yourself? How is that? What sort of a cut? Where is it?"

"Right here, on my finger. I went to the village today—you know, where they brought that peasant with typhus from. They were about to perform an autopsy on him for some reason or other, and I've had no practice on that sort for a long while."

"Well?"

"Well, so I asked the district doctor to let me do it; and so I cut myself."

Vassilii Ivanovich suddenly turned all white and, without uttering a word, rushed to his study, from which he returned at once carrying a bit of lunar caustic. Bazarov was about to take it and leave.

"For dear God's sake," said the father, "let me do this myself."

Bazarov smiled.

"What a devoted practitioner!"

"Don't laugh, please. Let me see your finger. The cut isn't so great. Doesn't that hurt?"

"Press harder; don't be afraid."

Vassilii Ivanovich stopped.

"What do you think, Eugene—wouldn't it be better to cauterize it with a hot iron?"

"That should have been done sooner; but now, if you get down to brass tacks, even the lunar caustic is useless. If I've been infected, it's too late now."

"What—too late—" Vassilii Ivanovich could scarcely articulate the words.

"Of course! It's more than four hours ago."

Vassilii Ivanovich cauterized the cut a little more.

"Why, didn't the district doctor have any lunar caustic?"

"No."

"My God, how is it possible? A doctor—and he hasn't got such an indispensable thing as that!"

"You ought to have a look at his lancets," Bazarov observed, and walked out.

Until late that evening, and all the following day, the father grasped at every possible excuse to drop in at his son's room; and though he not only kept from referring to the cut but even tried to talk about the most irrelevant subjects, he nevertheless looked so persistently into his eyes, and watched him in such trepidation, that Bazarov lost patience and threatened to go away. Vassilii Ivanovich gave him his word to stop worrying, all the more so since Arina Vlassievna (from whom, naturally, he had kept all this secret) was beginning to pester him as to why he did not sleep, and what had come over him. For two whole days he held himself in, though he did not at all like the look of his son, whom he kept watching stealthily. But on the third day, at dinner, he could bear it no longer. Bazarov sat with downcast looks, and would not touch a single dish.

"Why don't you eat, Eugene?" he inquired, putting on a most carefree expression. "The food, I think, is very tastily cooked."

"I don't want to eat, and so I don't eat."

"Have you no appetite? And what about your head?" he added in a timid voice. "Does it ache?"

"It does. And why shouldn't it?"

The mother straightened up and cocked her ears.

"Don't be angry, please, Eugene," Vassilii Ivanovich went on, "but won't you let me feel your pulse?"

Bazarov got up.

"I can tell you without feeling my pulse that I'm running a high temperature."

"And have you had chills?"

"Yes, I've had chills, too. I'll go and lie down, and you can send me some lime-flower tea. I must have caught a cold, probably."

"No wonder I heard you coughing last night," observed Arina Vlassievna.

"I've caught a cold," Bazarov repeated, and withdrew

Arina Vlassievna busied herself about the preparation of the lime-flower tea, while Vassilii Ivanovich went into the next room and clutched his hair in silent despair.

Bazarov did not get up again that day, and passed the whole night in heavy, half-oblivious dozing. At one o'clock in the morning, opening his eyes with an effort, he saw by the light of the image-lamp his father's pale face bending over him, and told him to go away; the latter submitted but immediately tiptoed back and, half-hidden by a closet door, gazed at his son without taking his eyes off him. Arina Vlassievna did not go to bed either, and leaving the study door open the tiniest crack kept constantly coming up to it to listen "how Gene was breathing," and to have a look at Vassilii Ivanovich. She could see nothing but his motionless bent back, but even that afforded her a certain relief.

In the morning Bazarov attempted to get up; his head became dizzy, he had a nasal hemorrhage, and lay down again. Vassilii Ivanovich tended him in silence; Arina Vlassievna came into his room and asked him how he was feeling. He answered "Better," and turned to the wall. The father waved his wife away with both hands; she bit her lips so as not to cry, and went out.

Everything in the house suddenly seemed to darken; all faces became long-drawn; there was a strange hush; a loud-throated rooster was carried away from the yard to the village, unable to comprehend why he should be treated so. Bazarov continued to lie still, with his face turned to the wall. Old Bazarov tried to put various questions to him, but they fatigued Bazarov, and the father sat motionless in his arm-chair, merely cracking his finger joints at rare intervals.

He would go out for a few moments into the garden, stand there like a graven image, as though overwhelmed with unutterable bewilderment (the expression of bewilderment never left his face throughout), and then come back to his son anew, trying to avoid his wife's questions. She caught him by the arm at last, and convulsively, almost menacingly, asked: "What's wrong with him?" Thereupon he came to himself and forced himself to smile to her in reply; but to his own horror, instead of a smile, he found himself taken somehow by a fit of laughter.

He had sent for a doctor at daybreak. He thought it necessary to warn his son of this, for fear he might be angered, somehow.

Bazarov suddenly turned over on the divan, looked dully at his father, and asked for drink.

Vassilii Ivanovich gave him some water and availed himself of the chance to feel his forehead. It was simply on fire.

"Old-timer," Bazarov began, in a hoarse, slow voice, "my goose is cooked; I've caught the infection, and in a few days you'll be burying me."

Vassilii Ivanovich swayed as though someone had knocked his legs from under him.

"Eugene!" he faltered. "What are you saying? God be with you! You've caught a cold—"

"Come, now," Bazarov interrupted him slowly. "A doctor can't be allowed to talk like that. There's every symptom of infection; you know that yourself."

"Where are the symptoms of—infection, Eugene? Good Heavens!"

"And what do you call this?" asked Bazarov and, pulling up his shirt sleeve, he showed his father the ominous red splotches coming out on his arm.

Vassilii Ivanovich shuddered and turned chill with terror.

"Supposing," he said at last, "even supposing—even if there's something like—infection—"

"Pyemia," his son prompted him.

"Well, yes—something in the nature of epidemic—"

"Pyemia," Bazarov repeated sternly and distinctly. "Or have you forgotten your notebooks?"

"Well, yes, yes, have it your way. But just the same we'll cure you!"

"Cure me, fiddlesticks. But that's not the point. I didn't expect I'd die so soon; it's a most unpleasant incident, to tell you the truth. You and mother ought to make the most of your strong religious belief;

here's your chance to put it to the test." He drank a little more water. "But I want to ask you about one thing—while my head is still under my control. Tomorrow or the day after, you know, my brain will hand in its resignation. Even now I'm not quite certain whether I'm expressing myself clearly. While I've been lying here, it seemed to me there were red dogs running around me, while you were making them point at me, as if I were a woodcock. Just as if I were drunk. Do you understand me all right?"

"I assure you, Eugene, you are talking perfectly correctly."

"So much the better. You told me you'd sent for a doctor. You did that to comfort yourself—comfort me, too; send a messenger—"

"To Arcadii Nicolaich?" the old man said eagerly.

"Who's Arcadii Nicolaich?" said Bazarov, as though trying to recall. "Ah, yes! That fledgling! No, let him be; he's among the jackdaws now. Don't be surprised; that's not delirium yet. No, you send a messenger to Odintsova, Anna Sergheievna; she's a landowner around here. You know about her?" Vassilii Ivanovich nodded. "Eugene Bazarov, now, sends his greetings, and sends word he's dying. Will you do that?"

"Yes, I will. But is it a possible thing for you to die, Eugene? Judge for yourself! Where would justice be after that?"

"That's something I know nothing about; you just send that messenger now."

"I'll send him this minute and I'll write a note myself."

"No, what for? Say I send greetings; nothing more is necessary. And now I'll go back to my dogs. A strange thing! I want to fix my thoughts on death and nothing comes of it. All I see is some sort of a blotch—and nothing more."

He turned painfully to the wall again, while his father went out of the study and, having somehow managed to reach his wife's bedroom, simply slumped on his knees before the holy images.

"Pray, Arina, pray!" he moaned. "Our son is dying."

The doctor, the same district doctor who had had no lunar caustic, arrived and, after examining the patient, advised them to maintain a watchful course, and at the same time said a few words about the possibility of recovery.

"Have you ever had occasion to see people in my state *not* set off for the Elysian fields?" asked Bazarov and, suddenly snatching the leg of a heavy table that stood near his divan, he shook it and moved it from its place. "The strength, now, the strength is still there," he uttered, "and yet I must die! The old man at least has had time to be weaned from life, but I. . . . Yes, go and try to renounce death. Death renounces you, and that's that! Who's that crying there?" he added a little later. "Mother? Poor thing! Whom will she feed now with her amazing beet soup? And you, Vassilii Ivanovich, are also turning on the waterworks, it seems? Why, if Christianity doesn't help, be a philosopher, a Stoic, or something. Why, didn't you boast you were a philosopher?"

"A fine philosopher I am!" wailed Vassilii Ivanovich, while the tears fairly pattered down his cheeks.

Bazarov grew worse with every hour; the progress of the disease was rapid, which is usually the case in surgical infections. He still had not lost consciousness, and understood what was said to him; he was still struggling.

"I don't want to rave," he muttered, clenching his fists; "what non-sense all this is!" And immediately he would say: "Come, take ten from eight, what remains?"

His father wandered about like one demented, proposing now one remedy, now another, and was forever covering up his son's feet. "Try a cold pack . . . an emetic . . . mustard plasters on the stom-ach . . . bleed him," he kept saying with an effort. The doctor, whom he had entreated to remain, "yes'd" him, drenched the patient with lemonade, while for himself he requested now a pipe, now "something fortifying and warming"—that is, vodka. Arina Vlassievna sat on a footstool near the door and left only from time to time to pray. A few days before, a looking glass had slipped out of her hands and shattered, and this was something she had always considered an omen of evil; even Anphissushka could say nothing to comfort her. Timotheich had gone off to Odintsova's.

Bazarov passed a bad night. He was in the agonies of high fever. Toward morning he felt a little easier. He asked Arina Vlassievna to comb his hair, kissed her hand, and swallowed two gulps or so of tea. Vassilii Ivanovich revived a little.

"Glory be to God!" he kept repeating. "The crisis has come—the crisis is gone!"

"There, think of it!" commented Bazarov. "See what a word means! He's found it; he said 'crisis,' and is comforted. It's an amazing thing how man believes in words. If he's told he's a fool, for instance, and even if he's not beaten he'll feel blue; call him a clever fellow and he'll be delighted even if you go off without paying him."

This little speech of Bazarov's, recalling his old "outbursts," moved Vassilii Ivanovich greatly.

"Bravo! Excellently put—excellently!" he cried, pretending to clap his hands.

Bazarov smiled sadly.

"What's your opinion, then?" he asked. "Is the crisis gone, or has it come?"

"You're better—that's what I see, that's what makes me rejoice," answered Vassilii Ivanovich.

"Well, that's fine; rejoicings never come amiss. And about her— do you remember? Did you send a messenger?"

"I did that—how else!"

The change for the better did not last long. The disease renewed its onslaughts.

Vassilii Ivanovich was sitting by Bazarov. Some particular anguish seemed to be tormenting the old man. He was on the point of speaking several times—and could not.

"Eugene!" he brought out at last. "My son, my dear one, my beloved son!"

This unusual appeal produced an effect on Bazarov. He turned his head a little and, obviously trying to struggle free from under the load of oblivion weighing upon him, he asked:

"What is it, my father?"

"Eugene," Vassilii Ivanovich went on, and he fell on his knees before Bazarov, though the latter did not open his eyes and could not see him. "Eugene, you're better now; please God, you'll get well, but make use of this time, comfort your mother and me, perform the duty of a Christian! For me to say this to you is awful; but still more awful—for it's forever, Eugene—just think what this means—"

The old man's voice broke, and something strange crept over his son's face, even though he continued to lie with closed eyes.

"I won't refuse, if that can be any comfort to you," he brought out at last. "But it seems to me there's no need for haste. You say yourself I am better."

"You are better, Eugene, you are; but who knows, it's all in God's hands, but having done your duty—"

428]   A TREASURY OF *Russian Literature*

"No, I'll wait," Bazarov cut him short. "I agree with you that the crisis has come. But if we're mistaken—well! For they give the sacrament even to men who're unconscious."

"Eugene, I implore you—"

"I'll wait. And now I want to go to sleep. Don't disturb me."

And he laid his head back on the pillow.

The old man rose from his knees, sat down in the armchair, and, clutching his chin, began biting his fingers.

The sound of a light carriage on springs, that sound which is so particularly noticeable in the wilds of the country, suddenly struck upon his hearing. Nearer and nearer rolled the light wheels; now even the snorting of the horses could be heard. Vassilii Ivanovich jumped up and ran to the little window. A carriage with seats for two, with four horses harnessed abreast, was driving into the court-yard of his little house. Without stopping to consider what this might mean, under the impulse of some senseless joy, he ran out on the front steps. A groom in livery was opening the carriage doors; a lady in a black veil and a black mantle was getting out of it.

"I am Odintsova," she said. "Is Eugene Vassilyich still alive? You are his father? I have brought a doctor with me."

"My benefactress!" Vassilii Ivanovich cried out, and snatching her hand he convulsively pressed it to his lips, while the doctor brought by Anna Sergheievna, a manikin in spectacles, with a German physiognomy, clambered leisurely out of the carriage. "He's still living, my Eugene is still living, and now he'll be saved! Wife! Wife! An angel from heaven has come to us—"

"Good Lord! What does this mean?" babbled the crone, running out of the drawing room, and, unable to grasp anything, she fell right in the entry at the feet of Anna Sergheievna and began kissing her garments like a mad woman.

"What are you doing! What are you doing!" protested Anna Sergheievna, but Arina Vlassievna did not heed her, while Vassilii Ivanovich could only repeat: "An Angel! An Angel!"

"Wo ist der Kranke? Where is it the patient is at?" said the doctor at last, not without some indignation.

Vassilii Ivanovich came to himself.

"Right this way, right this way—please follow me, *werthester Herr Kollege,*" [1] he added, recalling whatever he remembered of German.

---

[1] "My most worthy colleague."

"Ah!" articulated the German with a sour grin.

Vassilii Ivanovich led him into the study.

"The doctor from Anna Sergheievna Odintsova," he said, bending down to his son's very ear, "and she herself is here."

Bazarov suddenly opened his eyes.

"What did you say?"

"I say that Anna Sergheievna Odintsova is here and has brought this medical gentleman to you."

Bazarov let his eyes rove about him. "She's here. . . . I want to see her."

"You shall see her, Eugene; but first we must have a little talk with the doctor. I'll tell him the whole history of your illness, since Sidor Sidorich [this was the name of the district doctor] has gone, and we'll have a little consultation."

Bazarov glanced at the German.

"Well, talk away quickly, only not in Latin; you see, I know the meaning of *jam moritur*." [1]

"Der Herr scheint des Deutschen mächtig zu sein?" [2] began the newly-arrived foster child of Aesculapius, turning to Vassilii Ivanovich.

"Ich . . . habe [3]—Let's better drop German," said the old man.

"Ah, ah! Shoost so! Shoost as you blease—"

And the consultation began.

Half an hour later Anna Sergheievna, conducted by Vassilii Ivanovich, came into the study. The doctor had had time to whisper to her that there was no use in even thinking of the patient's recovery.

She looked at Bazarov—and halted in the doorway, so greatly was she struck by the inflamed and at the same time deathly face, with its turbid eyes fastened upon her. She felt simply frightened, with a sort of cold and agonizing fright; the thought that she would not have felt like that if she had really loved him flashed instantaneously through her head.

"Thanks," he began with an effort. "I did not expect this. It's a good deed. There, we have seen each other again, just as you promised."

"Anna Sergheievna has been so kind—" Vassilii Ivanovich began.

"Father, leave us alone. Anna Sergheievna, you will allow it? It would seem that now—"

[1] "Already dying."

[2] "Sir, I believe you have a knowledge of German?"

[3] "I . . . have."

With a motion of his head he indicated his prostrate body, shorn of all its strength.

Vassilii Ivanovich went out.

"Well, thanks," Bazarov repeated. "This is a regal action. They say that monarchs visit the dying, too."

"Eugene Vassilyich, I hope—"

"Eh, Anna Sergheievna, let's speak the truth. It's all over with me. I'm caught under the wheel. And now it turns out it was useless to think of the future. Death is an old trick, yet it strikes everyone as something new. So far I have no craven fear of it—and later on a coma will come, and—" he whistled and made a feeble nugatory gesture. "Well, what am I to say to you? That I loved you? There was no sense in that even before, and less than ever now. Love is a form, and my own form is already decomposing. I'd do better to say how fine you are! Even now you're standing there, so beautiful—"

Anna Sergheievna gave an involuntary shudder.

"Never mind, don't be upset. Sit over there. Don't come close to me—after all, my illness is contagious."

Anna Sergheievna swiftly crossed the room and sat down in the armchair near the divan on which Bazarov was lying.

"Magnanimous one!" he whispered. "Oh, how near and how young and fresh and pure . . . in this loathsome room! . . . Well, goodby! Live long, that's the best thing of all, and make the most of it while there is time. Just see, what a hideous spectacle: a worm half crushed, but writhing still. And yet I, too, thought: I'd accomplish so many things, I wouldn't die, not me! If there were any problem—well, I was a giant! And now all the problem the giant has is how to die decently, although that makes no difference to anyone either. Never mind; I'm not going to wag my tail."

Bazarov fell silent, and began groping with his hand for the glass. Anna Sergheievna gave him the drink without taking off her glove, and holding her breath apprehensively.

"You will forget me," he began again. "The dead man is no companion for the living. My father will tell you, see, now, what a man Russia is losing. That's nonsense, but don't disillusion an old man. What does it matter what toy will comfort a child—you know. And be kind to mother. People like them aren't to be found in your great world if you were to look for them by daylight with a candle. Russia needs me. No, evidently, she doesn't. And, besides, who is needed? The shoemaker's needed, the tailor's needed, the butcher—sells meat—the butcher—wait a little, I'm getting mixed up. There's a forest here—"

Bazarov put his hand to his brow.

Anna Sergheievna bent down to him.

"Eugene Vassilyich, I'm here—" .

He at once took his hand away and raised himself.

"Good-by," he said with sudden force, and his eyes gleamed with a last gleam. "Good-by. Listen—you know I didn't kiss you that time. Breathe on the dying lamp and let it go out—"

Anna Sergheievna put her lips to his forehead.

"Enough!" he murmured, and dropped back on the pillow. "Now . . . darkness—"

Anna Sergheievna went softly out.

"Well?" Vassilii Ivanovich asked her in a whisper.

"He has fallen asleep," she answered, barely audibly.

Bazarov was not fated to awaken. Toward evening he sank into complete unconsciousness, and the following day he died. Father Alexis performed the last religious rites over him. When they anointed him with the last unction, when the holy oil touched his breast, one eye opened, and it seemed as though at the sight of the priest in his vestments, of the smoking censer, of the tapers before the icon, something like a shudder of horror passed over the death-stricken face.

And when finally he had breathed his last, and a universal lamentation arose throughout the house, Vassilii Ivanovich was seized by a sudden frenzy.

"I said I would rebel," he screamed hoarsely, with his face flaming and distorted, shaking his fist in the air, as though threatening someone, "and I will rebel, I will rebel!"

But Arina Vlassievna, all in tears, hung upon his neck, and both prostrated themselves together.

"Side by side," Anphissushka related afterward in the servants' quarters, "they let their poor heads droop, like lambs at noonday—"

But the sultriness of noonday passes, and evening comes, and night, and then follows the return to the calm refuge, where sleep is sweet for the tortured and the weary.

XXVIII

Six months had passed by. White winter had come with the cruel still-ness of unclouded frosts, with packed, crunching snow, rosy rime on the trees, pale emerald sky, caps of smoke above the chimneys, clouds of steam rushing out of doors opened for an instant, with fresh faces that look stung by the cold, and the hurrying trot of chilled horses.

A January day was drawing to its close; the cold of evening was more keen than ever in the still air, and a blood-red sunset was rapidly dying down. Lights were being lit in the windows of the house at Maryino; Procophich in a black frock coat and white gloves was, with a special solemnity, laying the table for seven. A week before in the small parish church two weddings had taken place quietly and almost without witnesses—those of Arcadii and Katya, and Nicolai Petrovich and Phenichka; and on this day Nicolai Petrovich was giving a farewell dinner for his brother, who was going away to Moscow on business. Anna Sergheievna had also gone there immediately after the wedding, having made very handsome presents to the bridal couples.

Precisely at three o'clock they all gathered around the table. Mitya was placed there too; he had already acquired a nurse in a cap of glazed brocade. Paul Petrovich had the place of honor between Katya and Phenichka; the husbands took their places beside their wives. Our friends had changed of late; they all seemed to have grown better-looking and more mature. Paul Petrovich alone was thinner, which, however, added even more elegance and a still greater air of the grand seigneur to his expressive features. And Phenichka, too, had become a different woman. In a new silk gown, with a wide velvet ornament on her hair, with a thin gold chain around her neck, she sat with deco-rous immobility, respectful toward herself and everything surrounding her, and smiled as though she would say, "I beg your pardon; I'm not to blame." And not she alone—all the others smiled, and also seemed apologetic; they were all a little awkward, a little sorry, and in reality very pleased. They all helped one another with amusing considerate-ness, as though they had all agreed to play out some sort of artless comedy. Katya was the most composed of all; she looked trustingly about her, and one could notice that Nicolai Petrovich was already dotingly fond of her. At the end of dinner he got up and, glass in hand, turned to Paul.

"You are leaving us—you are leaving us, dear brother," he began, "of course not for long, but still I cannot help expressing what I—what we—how much I—how much we—there, that's just the trouble: that I don't know how to make speeches! Arcadii, you make the speech."

"No, Dad, I'm not prepared."

"As though I were so well prepared! Well, Brother, I'll simply say, let me embrace you, wish you all good luck, and come back to us as quick as you can!"

Paul exchanged kisses with everyone, not excluding Mitya, of course; when it came to Phenichka, he also kissed her hand, which she had not yet learned to offer properly, and, drinking off the glass which had been filled again, he pronounced with a deep sigh: "May you be happy, my friends! *Farewell!*" This English flourish passed unnoticed; but just the same they were all moved.

"To the memory of Bazarov," Katya whispered in her husband's ear, as she clinked glasses with him. Arcadii pressed her hand warmly in response, but he did not venture to propose this toast aloud.

This is the end, it would seem? But perhaps some reader would care to know what each of the characters we have introduced is doing in the present, the actual present. We are ready to satisfy him.

Anna Sergheievna has recently married, not of love but out of conviction, one of the future leaders of Russia, a very intelligent man, a lawyer, possessed of strong practical sense, firm will, and remarkable eloquence—still young, good-natured, and cold as ice. They live in great harmony together, and will live perhaps to attain complete happiness—perhaps love. The Princess K—— died, forgotten on the very day of her death. The Kirsanovs, father and son, live at Maryino; their fortunes are on the mend. Arcadii has become zealous in the management of the estate, and the "farm" is now yielding a rather good revenue.

Nicolai Petrovich has been made one of the mediators appointed to carry out the emancipation reforms, and works with all his might and main; he is forever traveling all over the district; delivers long speeches (he maintains the opinion that the lowly muzhiks ought to be "instructed"—that is, reduced to exhaustion by the constant repetition of the same words); and yet, to tell the truth, he does not satisfy fully either the cultured gentry, who talk with heat or melancholy of the *emancipation* (giving the word a French twist by speaking the second syllable through the nose), or to the uncultured gentry, who unceremoniously curse "the damned *'mancipation."* He is too softhearted for both camps.

Katerina Sergheievna has a son, little Nicolai, while Mitya runs about ever so livelily and talks beautifully; Phenichka, now generally dignified as Theodosia Nicolaievna, adores no one so much (next to her husband and son) as her daughter-in-law, and when the latter sits down at the piano, she would not mind spending the whole day at her side.

Incidentally, we might mention Peter. He has become utterly petrified with stupidity and pompousness and has evolved a very high-class accent; however, he, too, is married, and received a respectable dowry with his bride, the daughter of a truck-gardener in town, who had turned down two excellent suitors only because they had no watches, whereas Peter had not only a watch but a pair of patent-leather half boots.

In Dresden, on the Brühl Terrace, between two and four o'clock— the most fashionable time for walking—you may meet a man about fifty, by now altogether gray, and apparently afflicted with gout, but still handsome, exquisitely dressed, and with that special stamp which is gained only by moving a long time in the higher strata of society. That is Paul Petrovich. From Moscow he had gone abroad for the sake of his health, and has settled down in Dresden, where he associates for the most part with Englishmen and Russian visitors. With the Englishmen he behaves simply, almost modestly, but with dignity; they find him a trifle boring but respect him for being, as they put it, *a perfect gentleman.* With Russians he is more free and easy, gives vent to his spleen, and pokes fun at himself and them, but in his case all this is very charming, nonchalant, and proper. He adheres to Slavophile views; this, as everybody knows, is regarded as *très distingué* in the highest society. He reads nothing Russian, but you will find on his desk a silver ashtray in the shape of a muzhik's plaited bast sandal. He is much run after by our tourists. Matthew Ilyich Kolyazin, happening to be among the political outs temporarily, paid him a majestic visit on his way to take the waters in Bohemia. As for the natives (with whom, however, he is but little seen), they all but worship him. No one can obtain a ticket for the court chapel, for the theater, and so on, as quickly and readily as *der Herr Baron von Kirsanoff.* He still does good, as far as it lies within his power; he still is making a modest noise in the world—it is not for nothing that he was once a lion; but life is a burden to him—a heavier burden than he suspects himself. One need but glance at him in the Russian church, when, leaning against the wall, off to one side, he sinks into thought and remains long without stirring, bitterly compressing his lips, then comes to with a start and begins, almost imperceptibly, making the sign of the cross over himself.

Kukshina, too, found herself abroad. She is in Heidelberg at present, and it is no longer natural science she is studying but architecture, in which, according to her, she has discovered new laws. She is still hail-fellow-well-met with students, especially with the young Russians studying physics and chemistry, with whom Heidelberg is crowded, and who, astounding the naïve German professors at first by their sober views of things, later on astound the same professors no less by their utter apathy and absolute laziness.

With two or three just such young chemists, who don't know oxygen from nitrogen, but are filled with skepticism and self-respect, Sitnicov is knocking about Petersburg, also getting ready to be great, and, according to his own assertions, is carrying on Bazarov's "work." There's talk of someone having given him a beating recently, but Sitnicov made sure to pay his assailant out: in an obscure little article, published in an obscure little journal, he has hinted that the man who had beat him was a coward. He calls this irony. His father bullies him as before, while his wife regards him as a harmless little fool— and a litterateur.

There is a small village graveyard in one of the remote nooks of Russia. Like almost all our graveyards, it presents a woebegone appearance; the ditches surrounding it have long been overgrown; the weather-beaten wooden crosses lean over and rot under their once painted gable-boards; the stone slabs are all displaced, as though someone were pushing them up from below; two or three small trees with tattered leaves give a scanty shade; the sheep browse among the graves, and there's none to say them nay. But among these graves there is one untouched by man, untrampled by beast; the birds alone perch thereon and sing at dawn. An iron railing runs around it; two young firs are there, one planted at each end.

Eugene Bazarov is buried in this grave. Often, from the little village not far off, an old couple, decrepit by now, comes to visit it—man and wife. Supporting each other, they move to it with heavy steps; they come close to the railing and get down on their knees. And long and bitterly do they weep, and long and intently do they gaze at the mute stone, under which their son is lying; they exchange some brief phrase, brush the dust from the stone, and set straight a branch on one of the firs, and then pray again, and they cannot forsake this place, where they seem to feel nearer to their son, to their memories of him.

Can it be that their prayers, their tears are fruitless? Can it be that love, holy devoted love, is not omnipotent? Oh, nay! However passionate, sinning, and riotous the heart hidden in the tomb, the flowers growing thereon gaze serenely at us with their innocent eyes; they tell us not of eternal peace alone, of that great peace of "indifferent" nature; they tell us, too, of eternal reconciliation and of life without end.

Theodore Michaelovich
Dostoievski
1 8 2 1 – 1 8 8 1

~

His books resemble Greek tragedies by the magnitude of the spiritual adventures they set forth; they are unlike Greek tragedies in the Christian charity and the faith and hope which goes out of them; they inspire the reader with courage, never with despair, although Dostoievski, face to face with the last extremities of evil, never seeks to hide it or to shun it, but merely to search for the soul of goodness in it. He did not search in vain.

MAURICE BARING

From all that Dostoievski has created, however great in scope, it is evident that it is nothing compared with what he could have created under different social conditions.

MEREZHCOVSKI

Most certainly he wrote only one-tenth of the stories which for years he had planned. . . . The subjects which he had not had time to write were without number.

STRAHOV

THE READER can best grasp the truth of the last two statements (which are in no way derogatory of Dostoievski's actual unbelievable achievements) by grasping two stark, monstrous facts: that all of his masterpieces came literally within a few seconds of never being written, and that the commutation of his death sentence to nine years of forced labor and military servitude, together with the imprisonment before his sentence, shortened his creative life by one third—and that, probably the best third.

Attempts have been made to prove that the Great Plebeian was of gentle blood. Factually, Dostoievski's father, a doctor attached to a public hospital, came of a long line of priests; Theodore grew up in a puritan household that was always haunted by the fear of poverty. From 1835 to 1837 he attended a good private school in Moscow (his native city); from 1837 to 1843 he studied in the School for Military Engineers and, upon graduation, secured a post in the Engineering Department.

Even during his harrowing life as a poverty-stricken student he had dreamed of fame and security; to seek these he resigned his post after a year and tried many things, which proved so many soap bubbles. But literature did smile on him. D. V. Grigorovich, then beginning his own career as a writer, brought Dostoievski's *Poor Folk* to Necrassov, who in his turn showed it to Belinski with the enthusiastic claim that a new Gogol had arisen; the cautious Belinski countered with the opinion that new Gogols grew as thick as mushrooms in the poet-publisher's imagination, but was equally delighted on reading the manuscript and, on its publication in 1846, hailed it as the most outstanding production of the day. Its author became a literary lion, but the salons made him feel like a plebeian jackdaw in peacock feathers (Turgenev was merely one of those who twitted

and ridiculed him), and he broke abruptly with society. This break was the precursor of a far more serious one: just as Necrassov had broken off with "noblemen's poetry," Dostoievski became the promulgator of "the word of the burgher" as against the prose of the noblemen; whole sections of his plebeian novels (a label he proudly accepted) are actually parodies of the "landowning style."

It is very difficult to pick out the worst among Czarism's unbroken chain of crimes against Russian genius, but the case of Dostoievski is by all means the most appalling. There is no case ghastlier, more criminal or more Caliban-like anywhere, at any time.

The Petrashevtsi (or followers of Petrashevski) used to meet in their leader's quarters to discuss Utopian Socialism and read the works of such horrendous fire-brands as Saint-Simon, Fourier, and Owen—with, of course, the usual *agent provocateur* in their guileless midst. After a year's surveillance, on April 23, 1849, thirty-three members of the circle were arrested. Dostoievski, one of the number, was confined in the notorious oubliette of SS. Peter and Paul for eight months. He was found guilty not only of complicity in conducting a private press but of "having circulated a letter [to Gogol] of one Belinski, a journalist, filled with scurrilous expressions against the Orthodox Church and the Supreme Power [here the Czar, and not the Deity is meant]." He was, with twenty others, condemned to be shot.

On December 22, 1849, as Dostoievski stood in a white shroud on the scaffold, and within a few seconds (thirty, as estimated by himself) of the handkerchief being dropped as a signal to the firing squad, the condemned men were reprieved through the "great mercy" of His Imperial Majesty, Nicholas I. One of the men was taken off the scaffold insane. In Dostoievski's case the sentence was commuted to banishment to Siberia, for four years at hard labor and five of military servitude in the ranks (he had been graduated as a Second Lieutenant). He did not return to Petersburg until 1860, and then only after incredible trouble. However, just as the Bastille found its ardent and sentimental defenders in the France of a few years ago, this case of one of the world's greatest writers having the best ten of the thirty productive years of his life turned into a living death finds, to this very day, its jesuitical defenders among certain ex-Russians. This whole business of the execution "tragicomedy," we are chucklingly told, was really nothing but a hearty hoax, a mere good-natured prank. To which one can only juxtapose Dostoievski's own description of the reprieve: "A monstrous and uncalled-for defamation," and his feeling about the commutation: ". . . a time of living burial. I was put in a coffin. The torture was inexpressible and incessant." Siberia intensified his incipient epilepsy to the point where the attacks were recurrent "every few days." And yet, in a book brought out as recently as 1934 and

of all places, in New York, we find the following airy dismissal of the inhuman crime: "Dostoievsky's incarceration was a most paradoxical affair which should be looked upon as a classic in the voluminous history of police blunders both within and without Russia." (Notice the "incarceration.")

Dostoievski came back to Petersburg and renewed his struggle against poverty. In 1861 he started publication of his own periodical, *Time,* which became a success, and in which he published his *House of the Dead* and *The Humiliated and Injured,* rewinning his place in the front ranks as a writer. 1862-3 are marked by his affair with Apollinaria Suslova (see Pauline, in *The Gambler,* for a study of an "infernal woman") and his first trip abroad.

1863 began auspiciously enough, but in May of that year came a catastrophe that terminated in disaster for the author's fortunes and nullified years of his superhuman struggles against adversity: the government, failing to perceive that a certain article was really on all fours with its abysmal reaction, shut down his magazine. Only after ten months of painful and countless negotiations was Dostoievski able to resume publication. Under the new name of *The Epoch* the magazine failed; Dostoievski became involved financially (his debts ran to between ten and eleven thousand dollars, a considerable sum at that time).

1865 was the very nadir of his fortunes. His wife, his child, his brother Michael (a minor yet sincere writer), and his friend Grigoriev died; he was in unbelievable poverty, and to escape debtors' prison was forced to flee abroad. But literature was still his way out. He wrote what many (including the Editor) believe to be his supreme novel, *Crime and Punishment,* and with the proceeds was able to return and stave off his creditors. In 1867 he married again and went abroad for four years. This was a far from happy phase. A disorderly, nomadic life, nostalgia, chronic poverty, unbelievably shameful exploitation, amounting to literary peonage, all took their toll; even his exceptional productivity (*The Idiot, The Eternal Husband, The Fiends* were written during these years) failed to improve his circumstances.

Unbearably wearied, Dostoievski jumped from the frying pan of his chaotic life abroad into the fire of a creditors' siege at home. But now he returned to Petersburg a world-famous author. In 1873 he became the exceedingly well-paid editor of *The Citizen,* a weekly. His popularity was so great that periodicals of the most diverse political trends solicited his participation. In 1874 *Notes of the Fatherland* had to pay double rates to publish *The Adolescent*—a far cry from eight years before, when the over-shrewd Stellovski had acquired not only the copyright to all of Dostoievski's published work but the yet unwritten *Gambler* for the preposterous sum of fifteen hundred dollars.

As a publisher of his own works Dostoievski fared infinitely better than Scott or Mark Twain. Thus the serial publication of *A Writer's Diary* (begun in 1876) was enormously popular and very profitable. Toward the end of the '70's his material conditions had improved vastly, and he was indisputably first among Russian authors. He was becoming something in the nature of prophet, apostle, preceptor of life. In 1880, with the publication, in part, of *The Brothers Karamazov* (a novel he was never to finish), and with his speech on Pushkin (delivered at the unveiling of a monument to the poet) his fame reached its very peak. That speech was his swan song. He had been living on his nerves (literally) for years; he died January 26th of the next year from pulmonary emphysema. The mourners at Necrassov's funeral had been innumerable; those at Dostoievski's have been estimated at forty thousand.

Dostoievski's spiritual and creative life is a series of paradoxes. He is a revolutionary who wanted to be a reactionary and a reactionary who wanted to be a revolutionary. Siberia seems to have had the same curious effect on him that religion had on Gogol. Dostoievski came back to preach the morality of the Divine Spark, the Christian morality-of-the-slave, the mystic balderdash that Orthodoxy was right because it was Slavic. His hopeless struggles in the nets of social conditions prompted his reactionary manifestations and made the clerical-landowning camp hail him as their own pet writer. But his talented and sharp protest places him outside and above the real reactionaries of his time. The speech on Pushkin is enough to prove this. There was within him a conflict between a bitter enmity against the existing social order, as well as against democracy and socialism on one hand and, on the other, his search after individual truth, his love for the humiliated and injured. He was never, as an apologist for Czarist Russia describes him, "a true adept of the Slavic philosophy with its firmly imbedded faith in the socionomic and super-class character of the Russian Czar's power"; he remains what Belinski has called him, "the poet whose Muse loves the people who live in garret and cellar."

Some of the other aspects of the Cruel Genius must, of sheer necessity, be merely mentioned here: his sombre, tragic tone and his sentimentalism; the sadist-masochist complexity of his heroes; his "grotesque naturalism." One can only indulge in phrases concerning the coiled-spring kinetics of his style, his unique mastery of the intuitive psychological (or psychopathological) scalpel. To speak of his enormous influence (even greater outside Russia than within) would be to risk banality: one drop of the true Dostoievski, diluted homeopathically through a dozen novels, has sufficed to make a Wasserman. Here it must suffice to say that the social underground determined the creative thematics of the Genius of the Underground. Dostoievski, who (like Johnson) considered himself a mere literary hack, has, in Merezhcovski's phrase, nevertheless "shown by his life that a man of letters may be as heroic as any warrior, martyr, or lawgiver of the past."

Dostoievski, in his own words, began a lawsuit against the literature of his day. And he himself was the last word in that indictment of the decay of Russian society which led to the sentence and execution of 1917.

Notes from Underground is the quintessence of Dostoievski. Had he written nothing else it would stamp him as a great and original writer who, as explorer and dissector of the soul's most minute nerves and fibers, not merely preceded but out-Freuded Freud. It is the heart and core of Dostoievski—as none other than that Dostoievskian character Nietzsche has pointed out.

Most of Dostoievski's works are available in English, but the translations, with no exceptions known to the Editor, are the weakest of travesties on the elemental force of the original. The reader is therefore most earnestly urged to read him, if at all possible, in any other language in preference to English.

The translation which had of necessity to be used here has been thoroughly revised.

Notes from Underground [1]

A NOVEL

Part I—Underground

I

I AM a sick man. I am a spiteful man. I am an unattractive man. I believe my liver is diseased. However, I know nothing at all about my disease and do not know for certain what ails me. I don't consult a doctor for it, and never have, though I have a respect for medicine and doctors. Besides, I am extremely superstitious, sufficiently so to respect medicine, at any rate (I am well-educated enough not to be superstitious, even though I am). No, I refuse to consult a doctor out of spite. That is something you probably will not understand. Well, I do. Of course, I can't explain whom precisely I am mortifying in this case by my spite: I am perfectly well aware that I cannot "get even" with the doctors by not consulting them; I know better than anyone that by all this I am only injuring myself and no one else. But still, if I don't consult a doctor it is out of spite. My liver is bad, well—let it get worse!

I have been going on like that for a long time—twenty years. Now I am forty. I used to be in the government service, but am no longer. I was a spiteful official. I was rude and took pleasure in being so. I did not take bribes, you see, so I was bound to find a recompense in that, at least. (A poor jest, but I will not cross it out. I wrote it thinking

Translated by Constance Garnett. Thoroughly revised.

[1] The author of the diary and the diary itself are, of course, imaginary. Nevertheless it is clear that such persons as the writer of these notes not only may, but positively must, exist in our society, when we consider the circumstances in the midst of which our society is formed. I have tried to expose to the view of the public, more distinctly than is commonly done, one of the characters of the recent past. He is one of the representatives of a generation still living. In this fragment, entitled *Underground,* this person introduces himself and his views and, as it were, tries to explain the causes owing to which he has made his appearance and was bound to make his appearance in our midst. In the second fragment there are added the actual notes of this person concerning certain events in his life.—*Author's Note.*

it would sound very witty; but now that I have perceived myself that I was merely trying to show off in a despicable way, I will purposely refrain from crossing it out!)

When petitioners would come to my desk for information, I would grind my teeth at them and feel intense enjoyment whenever I succeeded in making anybody unhappy. I almost always did succeed. For the most part they were all timid people—of course, since they were petitioners. But of the uppity ones there was one officer in particular I could not endure. He simply would not be humble, and kept clanking his sword in a disgusting way. I carried on a feud with him for eighteen months over that sword. At last I got the better of him. He left off clanking it. That happened in my youth, though.

But do you know, gentlemen, what was the chief point about my spite? Why, the whole point, the real sting of it lay in the fact that continually, even in the moment of the acutest spleen, I was inwardly conscious with shame that I was not only not a spiteful man but not even an embittered one, that I was simply scaring sparrows at random and amusing myself by it. I might foam at the mouth, but bring me a doll to play with, give me a cup of tea with sugar in it, and I could be appeased. I might even be genuinely touched, though probably I should grind my teeth at myself afterward and lie awake at night from shame for months after. That was my way.

I was lying when I said just now that I was a spiteful official. I was lying from spite. I was simply amusing myself with the petitioners and with the officer, and in reality I never could become spiteful. I was conscious every moment in myself of many, very many elements absolutely opposite to that. I felt them positively swarming in me, these opposed elements. I knew that they had been swarming in me all my life and craving some outlet from me, but let them out I would not. I would not let them, I purposely would not let them come out. They tormented me till I was ashamed; they drove me to convulsions and at last sickened me—how they sickened me! Now, aren't you imagining, gentlemen, that I am expressing remorse over something, that I am asking your forgiveness for something? I am sure you are. However, I assure you I don't care about that.

It was not only that I could not become spiteful; I did not know how to become anything: either spiteful or kind, either a rascal or an honest man, either a hero or an insect. Now I am living out my life in my corner, taunting myself with the spiteful and useless consolation that an intelligent man cannot seriously become anything and it is only the fool who becomes something. Yes, a man in the nineteenth century must and morally ought to be pre-eminently a characterless creature; a man of character, an active man is pre-eminently a limited creature. That is my conviction of forty years. I am forty years old now, and you know forty years is a whole lifetime; you know it is extreme old age. To live longer than forty years is bad manners, it's vulgar, immoral. Who lives beyond forty? Answer that, sincerely and honestly. I will tell you who: fools and good-for-nothings. I tell all old men that to their faces, all these venerable old men, all these silver-haired and reverend ancients! I tell the whole world that to its face! I have a right to say so, for I'll go on living to sixty myself. To seventy! To eighty! Hold on, let me catch my breath.

No doubt, gentlemen, you imagine that I wish to amuse you. You are mistaken in that, too. I am by no means such a mirthful person as you imagine, or may imagine; however, irritated by all this babble (and I feel that you are irritated), you think fit to ask me who am I; my answer is, I am a Collegiate Assessor. I went into Civil Service so as to have something to eat (that and nothing else), and when last year a distant relation left me six thousand rubles in his will I immediately retired from the Service and settled down in my hole. I used to live in this hole before, but now I have settled down in it. My room is a wretched, horrid one on the outskirts of the town. My servant is an old countrywoman, ill-natured from stupidity, and, moreover, there is always a nasty smell about her. I am told that the Petersburg climate is bad for me, and that with my small means it is very expensive to live there. I know all that better than all these sage and experienced counselors and preceptors. But I am remaining in Petersburg; I am not going away from Petersburg! I am not going away because—eh, it absolutely doesn't matter whether I am going away or not going away.

But what can a decent man speak of with most pleasure?

Answer: Of himself.

Well, then, I will talk about myself.

II

And now, gentlemen, whether you care to hear it or not, I want to tell you why I could not become even an insect. I tell you solemnly that I have tried to become an insect, many's the time. But I was not equal even to that. I swear, gentlemen, that to be too conscious is an illness—a real out-and-out illness. For man's everyday needs it would have been quite enough to have the ordinary human consciousness, that is, half or a quarter of the amount which falls to the lot of a cultivated man of our unhappy nineteenth century, especially one who has the fatal ill-luck to inhabit Petersburg, the most theoretical and intentional town on the whole terrestrial globe. (There are intentional and unintentional towns.) It would have been quite enough, for instance, to have the consciousness by which all so-called straightforward persons and men of action live. I'll bet you think I am writing all this from affectation, to be witty at the expense of men of action; and what is more, that from ill-bred affectation I am clanking a sword, like my officer. But, gentlemen, whoever can pride himself on his diseases and even swagger over them?

Although, after all, everyone does do just that; people do pride themselves on their diseases, and I, perhaps, more than anyone else. We will not dispute it; my contention was absurd. And yet I am firmly persuaded that a great deal of consciousness—every sort of consciousness, in fact—is a disease. I stick to that. But let's leave that, too, for a minute. Tell me this: why does it happen that at the very—yes, at the *very*—moments when I am most capable of feeling every refinement of all that is *good and beautiful* (as they used to say at one time), I would, as though on purpose, happen not only to feel but to do such ugly things that—well, in short, such actions as perhaps all men commit, but which, as though purposely, came at the very time when I was most conscious that they ought not to be committed. The more conscious I was of goodness and of all that was *good and beautiful,* the more deeply I sank into my mire and the more ready I was to sink in it altogether. But the chief point was that all this was not accidental in me, as it were, but apparently had to be so. It was as though it were my most normal condition, and not in the least disease or depravity, so that at last all desire in me to struggle against this depravity passed. It ended by my almost (perhaps actually) believing that this was perhaps my normal condition.

But at first, in the beginning, what agonies I endured in that struggle! I did not believe it was the same with other people, and all my life I hid this fact about myself as a secret. I was ashamed (even now, perhaps, I am ashamed); I got to the point of feeling a sort of secret, abnormal, despicable enjoyment in returning home to my hole on some disgustingly inclement Petersburg night, acutely conscious that

that day I had committed a loathsome action again, that what was done could never be undone, and secretly, inwardly gnawing, gnawing at myself for it, rending and consuming myself till at last the bitterness turned into a sort of shameful accursed sweetness, and at last into positive real enjoyment! Yes, into enjoyment—into enjoyment! I insist upon that. I have spoken of this because I keep wanting to know for a fact whether other people feel such enjoyment? I will explain: the enjoyment was just from the too intense consciousness of one's own degradation; it was from feeling that you had reached the last barrier, that it was horrible, but that it could not be otherwise; that there was no escape for you; that you never could become a different man; that even if time and faith were still left you to change into something different you would most likely not wish to change; or if you did wish to, even then you would do nothing, because perhaps in reality there was nothing for you to change into.

And the worst of it, and the root of it all, was that it was all in accord with the normal fundamental laws of overacute consciousness, and with the inertia that was the direct result of those laws, and that consequently one was not only unable to change but could do absolutely nothing. Thus it would follow, as the result of acute consciousness, that one is not to blame in being a scoundrel; as though that were any consolation to the scoundrel once he has come to realize that he actually is a scoundrel. But enough! Eh, I've talked a lot of nonsense, yet what have I explained? How is such enjoyment to be explained? Yet explain it I will. I will get to the bottom of it! That is why I have taken up my pen. . . .

I, for instance, have a great deal of *amour propre*. I am as suspicious and prone to take offense as a hunchback or a dwarf. But, upon my word, I sometimes have had moments when, if I had happened to be slapped in the face, I should, perhaps, have been positively glad of it. I say, in earnest, that I should probably have been able to discover even in that a peculiar sort of enjoyment—the enjoyment, of course, of despair; but in despair there are the most intense enjoyments, especially when one is very acutely conscious of the hopelessness of one's position. And when one is slapped in the face—why, then the consciousness of being rubbed into a pulp would positively overwhelm one. The worst of it is, look at it which way you will, it still turns out that I was always most to blame in everything. And what is most humiliating of all, to blame for no fault of my own but, so to say, through the laws of nature. In the first place, I was to blame because I am cleverer than any of the people surrounding me. (I have always considered myself cleverer than any of the people surrounding me, and sometimes, would you believe it, have been positively ashamed of it. At any rate, I have all my life, as it were, turned my eyes away and never could look people straight in the face.) I was to blame, finally, because even if I had had magnanimity, I should only have had more suffering from the sense of its uselessness. I should certainly have never been able to do anything because of being magnanimous—either to forgive (for my assailant would perhaps have slapped me from the laws of nature, and one cannot forgive the laws of nature) or to forget (for even if the slap were owing to the laws of nature, it is insulting all the same). Finally, even if I had wanted to be anything but magnanimous, had desired on the contrary to avenge myself on my assailant, I could not have avenged myself on anyone for anything, because I should certainly never have made up my mind to do anything, even if I had been able to. Why shouldn't I have made up my mind? I want to say a few words about that in particular.

III

With people who know how to avenge themselves and to stand up for themselves in general, how is it done? Why, when they are possessed, let us suppose, by the feeling of revenge, then for the time being there is nothing else but that feeling left in their whole being. Such a gentleman simply dashes straight for his object like an infuriated bull with its horns down, and nothing but a wall will stop him. (By the way: facing the wall, such gentlemen—that is, the *straightforward* persons and men of action—are genuinely nonplused. For them a wall is not an evasion, as for us who think and consequently do nothing; it is not an excuse for turning aside, an excuse which we always are very glad of, though we scarcely believe in it ourselves, as a rule. No, they are nonplused in all sincerity. The wall has for them something tranquilizing, morally soothing, final—perhaps even something mysterious—but of this wall more later.)

Well, such a straightforward person I regard as the real normal man, as his tender Mother Nature wished to see him when she graciously brought him into being on the earth. I envy such a man till I am green in the face. He is stupid. I am not disputing that, but perhaps, for all we know, the normal man should be stupid. Perhaps it's all very beautiful, in fact. And I am the more persuaded of that suspicion, if one can call it so, by the fact that if you take, for instance, the antithesis of the normal man, that is, the man of acute consciousness, who has come, of course, not out of the lap of nature but out of a retort (this is almost mysticism, gentlemen, but I suspect that this, too, is so), this retort-made man is sometimes so nonplused in the presence of his antithesis that with all his exaggerated consciousness he genuinely thinks of himself as a mouse and not a man. It may be an acutely conscious mouse, yet it is a mouse, while the other is a man, and, therefore, *et cetera, et cetera.* And the worst of it is, he himself, his very own self, looks on himself as a mouse; no one asks him to do so; and that is an important point. Now let us look at this mouse in action. Let us suppose, for instance, that it feels insulted, too (and it almost always does feel insulted), and wants to revenge itself likewise. There may even be a greater accumulation of spite in it than in *l'homme de la nature et de la vérité.* The base and nasty desire to vent that spite on its assailant rankles perhaps even more nastily in it than in *l'homme de la nature et de la vérité.* For through his innate stupidity the latter looks upon his revenge as justice, pure and simple; while in consequence of its acute consciousness the mouse does not believe in the justice of it.

To come at last to the deed itself, to the very act of revenge. Apart from the one fundamental nastiness the luckless mouse succeeds in creating around it, so many other nastinesses in the form of doubts and questions add to the one question so many unsettled questions that there inevitably works up around it a sort of fatal ferment, a stinking mess, made up of its doubts, emotions, and of the contempt spat upon it by the *straightforward* men of action who stand solemnly about it as judges and arbitrators, laughing at it till their healthy sides ache. Of course, the only thing left for it is to dismiss all that with a wave of its paw and, with a smile of assumed contempt in which it does not even itself believe, creep ignominiously into its mousehole. There in its nasty, stinking, underground home our insulted, crushed and ridiculed mouse promptly becomes absorbed in cold, malignant, and, above all, everlasting spite. For forty years together it will remember its injury down to the smallest, most ignominious details, and every time will add, of itself, details still more ignominious, spitefully teasing and tormenting itself with its own imagination. It will itself be ashamed of its imaginings, but yet it will recall everything, it will go over and over every detail, it will invent unheard-of things against itself, pretending that those things might happen, and will forgive nothing. Perhaps it will take to avenging itself, too, but piecemeal, as it were, in trivial ways, from behind the stove, incognito, without believing either in its own right to vengeance or in the success of its revenge, knowing that from all its efforts at revenge it will suffer a hundred times more than he on whom it revenges itself, while the victim, I daresay, will not even know a thing about it. On its deathbed the mouse will recall everything all over again, with interest compounded through all the years, and—

But it is just in that cold, abominable half-despair, half-belief, in that conscious burying of oneself alive for grief in the underworld for forty years, in that acutely recognized and yet partly doubtful hopelessness of one's position, in that hell of unsatisfied, introverted desires, in that fever of oscillations, of resolutions determined for ever and repented of again a minute later—that the savor of that strange enjoyment of which I have spoken lies. It is so subtle, so difficult of analysis, that persons who are a little limited, or even simply persons of strong nerves, will not understand a single atom of it. "Possibly," you will add on your own account with a grin, "people who have never received a slap in the face will not understand it either," and in that way you will politely hint to me that I, too, perhaps, have had the experience of a slap in the face in my life, and therefore speak as one who knows. I'll bet that's what you're thinking. But set your minds at rest, gentlemen, I have not received a slap in the face, though it is absolutely a matter of indifference to me what you may think about it. Possibly I even regret, myself, that I have given so few slaps in the face during my life. But enough—not another word on that subject of such extreme interest to you.

I will continue calmly concerning persons with strong nerves who do not understand a certain refinement of enjoyment. Though in certain circumstances these gentlemen bellow their loudest like bulls, though this, let us suppose, does them the greatest credit, yet, as I have said already, confronted with the impossible they subside at once. The impossible means the stone wall! What stone wall? Why, of course, the laws of nature, the deductions of natural science, mathematics. As soon as they prove to you, for instance, that you are descended from a monkey; there's no use scowling, accept it for a fact. When they prove to you that in reality one drop of your own suet must be dearer to you than a hundred thousand of your fellow creatures, and that this conclusion is the final solution of all the so-called virtues and duties and all such prejudices and fancies, why, you just have to accept it; there's no help for it, for two times two is a law of mathematics. Just try refuting it!

"Upon my word," they will shout at you, "it is no use protesting: it's a case of two times two making four! Nature does not ask your permission, she has nothing to do with your wishes, and whether you like her laws or dislike them, you're bound to accept her as she is, and consequently all her conclusions. A wall, you see, is a wall—" and so on and so on.

Merciful Heavens! But what do I care for the laws of nature and arithmetic, when, for some reason, I dislike those laws and the fact that two times two makes four? Of course I can't break through the wall by battering my head against it if I really haven't the strength to knock it down, but I'm not going to be reconciled to it simply because it is a stone wall and I haven't the strength.

As though such a stone wall really were a consolation and really did contain some word of conciliation, simply because it is as true as that two times two makes four. Oh, absurdity of absurdities! How much better it is to understand all, to recognize all—all the impossibilities and the stone wall; not to be reconciled to one of those impossibilities and stone walls if it disgusts you to be reconciled to it; by the way of the most inevitable, logical combinations to reach the most revolting conclusions on the everlasting theme: that you yourself are somehow to blame even for the stone wall, though again it is as clear as day you are not to blame in the least, and therefore grinding your teeth in silent impotence to sink into luxurious inertia, brooding on the fact that there's no one for you even to feel vindictive against, that you have not, and perhaps never will have, an object for your spite, that it is a sleight of hand, a bit of jugglery, a cardsharper's trick, that it is simply a mess, no knowing what and no knowing who. But in spite of all these uncertainties and juggleries, there is still an ache in you, and the more you do not know, the worse the ache.

IV

"Ha, ha, ha! You'll be finding enjoyment in toothache next," you cry with a laugh.

"Well? There is enjoyment even in toothache," I answer. I had a toothache for a whole month and I know there is. In that case, of course, people aren't silently spiteful but moan; the moans, however, are not candid but malevolent. And it is in their malevolence that the whole point lies. The enjoyment of the sufferer finds expression in those moans; if he did not feel enjoyment in them he would not moan. It is a good example, gentlemen, and I will develop it. Those moans express in the first place all the aimlessness of your pain, which is so humiliating to your consciousness; the whole legal system of nature on which you spit disdainfully, of course, but from which you suffer all the same while nature doesn't. They express the consciousness that you have no enemy to punish, but that you do have pain; the consciousness that in spite of all possible autosuggestionists you are in complete slavery to your teeth; that if someone wishes it, your teeth will leave off aching, and if he does not, they will go on aching another three months; and that, finally, if you are still contumacious and still protest, all that is left you for your own gratification is to beat yourself, or beat your wall with your fists as hard as you can—that, and absolutely nothing more. Well, these mortal insults, these jeers on the part of someone unknown, end at last in an enjoyment which sometimes reaches the highest degree of voluptuousness.

I ask you, gentlemen, listen sometimes to the moans of an educated man of the nineteenth century suffering from toothache on the second or third day of the attack, when he is beginning to moan not as he moaned on the first day—that is, not simply because he has toothache, not just as any coarse peasant, but as a man affected by progress and European civilization, a man who is "divorced from the soil and the national elements," as they express it nowadays. His moans become nasty, disgustingly malevolent, and go on for whole days and nights. And of course he himself knows that he isn't doing himself the least good with his moans; he knows better than anyone that he is only lacerating and harassing himself and others for nothing; he knows that even the audience before whom he is making his efforts, and his whole family, listen to him with loathing, without the least belief in him, and inwardly understand that he might moan differently, more simply, without trills and grace notes, and that he is only amusing himself like that from ill-humor, from malevolency. Well, it is in all these recognitions and disgraces that the voluptuous pleasure lies. As though he would say: "I am worrying you, I am lacerating your hearts, I am keeping everyone in the house awake. Well, stay awake; then you, too, will feel every moment that I have toothache. I am not a hero to you now, as I tried to seem before, but simply a nasty person, an impostor. Well, so be it, then! I am very glad that you see through me. It is nasty for you to hear my despicable moans; well, let it be nasty; there, I'll let you have a nastier quaver in just a moment!" You do not understand even now, gentlemen? No, it seems our development and our consciousness must go further to understand all the intricacies of this pleasure. You laugh? Delighted! My jests, gentlemen, are of course in bad taste, abrupt, involved, lacking in self-confidence. But of course that is because I do not respect myself. Can a man of perception respect himself at all?

V

Come, can a man who attempts to find enjoyment in the very feeling of his own degradation possibly have a spark of respect for himself? I am not saying this now from any mawkish kind of remorse. And, indeed, I could never endure saying: "Forgive me, Papa, I won't do it again"—not because I am incapable of saying that; on the contrary, perhaps just because I have been too capable of it, and how, at that! As though on purpose, I used to get into trouble in cases when I was not to blame in any way. That was the nastiest part of it. At the same time I was genuinely touched and penitent; I used to shed tears and, of course, deceived myself, though I was not acting in the least and there was a sick feeling in my heart at the time. For that, one could not blame even the laws of nature, though the laws of nature have continually all my life offended me more than anything else. It is loathsome to remember it all, but it was loathsome even then. Of course, a minute or so later I would realize wrathfully that it was all a lie, a revolting lie, a stilted lie—I mean all this penitence, this emotion, these vows of reform. You will ask why I upset myself with such antics: the answer is because it was very dull to sit with one's hands folded, and so I began cutting capers. That's it, really. Observe yourselves more carefully, gentlemen, then you will understand that it's so. I invented adventures for myself and made up a life, so as at least to live in some way. How many times it has happened to me— well, for instance, to take offense simply on purpose, for nothing; and you know yourself, of course, that you're offended at nothing, that you're putting on an act, and yet you bring yourself at last to the point of being really offended. All my life have I had an impulse to play such pranks, so that in the end I could not control that impulse in myself.

Another time—twice, in fact—I tried hard to fall in love. I suffered, too, gentlemen, I assure you. In the depth of my heart there was no faith in my suffering, only a faint stir of mockery, yet suffer I did, and that in the real, orthodox way; I was jealous, beside myself—and it was all from ennui, gentlemen, all from ennui; inertia overcame me. You know the direct, legitimate fruit of consciousness is inertia, that is, conscious sitting-with-your-hands-folded. I have referred to this already. I repeat, I repeat with emphasis: all *straightforward* persons and men of action are active just because they are stupid and limited. How explain that? I will tell you: in consequence of their limitation they take immediate and secondary causes for primary ones, and in that way persuade themselves more quickly and easily than other people that they have found an infallible basis for their activity, and their minds are at ease and that, you know, is the chief thing. To begin to act, you know, you must first have your mind completely at ease and no trace of doubt left in it. Why, how am I, for example, to set my mind at rest? Where are the primary causes on which I am to build? Where are my bases? Where am I to get them from? I exercise myself in reflection, and consequently with me every primary cause at once draws after itself another still more primary, and so on to infinity. That is just the essence of every sort of consciousness and reflection. It must be a case of the laws of nature again. What is the result of it in the end? Why, the same unvarying one.

Remember I spoke just now of vengeance. (I am sure you did not take it in.) I said that a man avenges himself because he sees justice in it. Therefore he has found a primary cause—that is, justice. And so he is at rest all around, and consequently he carries out his revenge calmly and successfully, being persuaded that he is doing a just and honest thing. But I see no justice in it, I find no sort of virtue in it, either, and consequently if I attempt to avenge myself, it is only out of spite. Spite, of course, might overcome everything, all my doubts, and so might serve quite successfully in place of a primary cause, precisely because it is not a cause. But what is to be done if I have not even spite (I began with that just now, you know)? In consequence again of those accursed laws of consciousness, anger in me is subject to chemical disintegration. You look into it, the object flies off into air, your reasons evaporate, the criminal is not to be found, the wrong becomes not a wrong but a phantom, something like the toothache, for which no one is to blame, and consequently there is only the same outlet left again—that is, to pound the wall as hard as you can. So you give it up with a wave of the hand because you have not found a fundamental cause. And you try letting yourself be carried away by your feelings, blindly, without reflection, without a primary cause, repelling consciousness at least for a time; you hate or love, just so as not to sit with your hands folded. The day after tomorrow, at the latest, you will begin despising yourself for having knowingly deceived yourself. Result: a soap bubble and inertia. Oh, gentlemen, do you know, perhaps I consider myself an intelligent man only because all my life I have been able neither to begin nor to finish anything. Granted I am a babbler, a harmless, vexatious babbler, like all of us. But what is to be done if the direct and sole vocation of every intelligent man is babbling —that is, the intentional pouring of water through a sieve?

VI

Oh, if I had done nothing simply from laziness! Heavens, how I should have respected myself then! I should have respected myself because I should at least have been capable of being lazy; there would at least have been one positive quality, as it were, in me, in which I could have believed myself. Question: What is he? Answer: A sluggard. How very pleasant it would have been to hear that of oneself! It would mean that I was positively defined, it would mean that there was something to say about me. "Sluggard"—why, it is a calling and vocation, it is a career. Do not jest—it is so. I should then be a member of the best club, by right, and should find my occupation in continually respecting myself. I knew a gentleman who prided himself all his life on being a connoisseur of Lafitte. He considered this as his positive virtue and never doubted himself. He died not simply with a tranquil but with a triumphant conscience, and he was quite right, too. Then I should have chosen a career for myself, I should have been a sluggard and a glutton, not a simple one, but, for instance, one with sympathies for everything good and beautiful. How do you like that? I have long had visions of it. That *good and beautiful* weighs heavily on my mind at forty. But that is at forty; then—oh, then it would have been different! I should have found for myself a form of activity in keeping with it—to be precise, drinking to the health of everything *good and beautiful*. I should have snatched at every opportunity to drop a tear into my glass and then to drain it to all that is *good and beautiful*. I should then have turned everything into the good and the beautiful; in the nastiest, unquestionable trash, I should have sought out the *good and the beautiful*. I should have exuded tears as a wet sponge exudes water. An artist, for instance, paints a picture worthy of Goya. At once I drink to the health of the artist who painted the picture worthy of Goya, because I love all that is *good and beautiful*. An author has written *As You Like It*: at once I drink to the health of *As You Like It* because I love all that is *good and beautiful*.

I should claim respect for doing so. I should persecute anyone who would not show me respect. I should live at ease, I should die with dignity; why, it's charming, utterly charming! And what a good round belly I'd grow, what a triple chin I'd fit myself out with, what a ruby nose I'd color for myself, so that everyone would say, looking at me: "Here is an asset! Here is something real and solid!"

And, say what you like, it is very agreeable to hear such remarks about oneself in this negative age.

VII

But these are all golden dreams. Oh, tell me, who was it first announced, who was it first proclaimed, that man only does nasty things because he does not know his own interests; and that if he were enlightened, if his eyes were opened to his real normal interests, man would at once cease to do nasty things, would at once become good and noble because, being enlightened and understanding his real advantage, he would see his own advantage in the good and nothing else, and we all know that not one man can, consciously, act against his own interests, consequently, so to say, through necessity, he would begin doing good? Oh, the babe! Oh, the pure, innocent child! Why, in the first place, when in all these thousands of years has there been a time when man has acted only from his own interest? What is to be done with the millions of facts that bear witness that men, *consciously*, that is, fully understanding their real interests, have left them in the background and have rushed headlong on another path, to meet peril and danger, compelled to this course by nobody and by nothing, but, as it were, simply disliking the beaten track, and have obstinately, willfully, beaten another difficult, absurd path, seeking it almost in the darkness? So, I suppose, this obstinacy and perversity were pleasanter to them than any advantage. Advantage! What is advantage? And will you take it upon yourself to define with perfect accuracy of what the advantage of man consists? And what if it so happens that a man's advantage, *sometimes,* not only may, but even must, consist in his desiring in certain cases what is harmful to himself and not advantageous? And if so, if there can be such a case, the whole principle falls into dust. What do you think—are there such cases? You laugh; laugh away, gentlemen, but only answer me: have man's advantages been reckoned up with perfect certainty? Are there not some which not only have not been included but cannot possibly be included under any classification?

You see, you gentlemen have, to the best of my knowledge, taken your whole register of human advantages from the averages of statistical figures and politico-economical formulas. Your advantages are prosperity, wealth, freedom, peace—and so on, and so on. So that the man who should, for instance, go openly and knowingly in opposition to all that list would, to your thinking, and indeed mine, too, of course, be an obscurantist or an absolute madman: wouldn't he? But, you know, this is what is surprising: why does it so happen that all these statisticians, sages and lovers of humanity, when they reckon up human advantages, invariably leave out one? They don't even take it into their reckoning in the form in which it should be taken, yet the whole reckoning depends upon that. It would be no great matter, they would simply have to take it, this advantage, and add it to the list. But the trouble is that this strange advantage does not fall under any classification and is out of place in any list. I have a friend, for instance— Eh, gentleman, but of course he is your friend, too; and indeed there is no one—no one!—to whom he is not a friend! When he prepares for any undertaking this gentleman immediately explains to you, elegantly and clearly, exactly how he must act in accordance with the laws of reason and truth. What is more, he will talk to you with animation and passion of the true normal interests of man; with irony he will upbraid the shortsighted fools who do not understand their own interests, nor the true significance of virtue; and, within a quarter of an hour, without any sudden outside provocation, but simply through something inside him which is stronger than all his interests, he will go off on quite a different tack—that is, act in direct opposition to what he has just been saying about himself, in opposition to the laws of reason, in opposition to his own advantage, in fact, in opposition to everything. I warn you that my friend is a compound personality, and therefore it is difficult to blame him as an individual.

The fact is, gentlemen, there apparently must really exist something that is dearer to almost every man than his greatest advantages, or (not to be illogical) there is a most advantageous advantage (the very one omitted, of which we spoke just now) which is more important and more advantageous than all other advantages, for the sake of which a man if necessary is ready to act in opposition to all laws; that is, in opposition to reason, honor, peace, prosperity—in fact, in opposition to all those excellent and useful things if only he can attain that fundamental, most advantageous advantage which is dearer to him than all.

"Yes, but it's an advantage all the same," you will retort. But excuse me, I'll make the point clear, and it isn't a case of playing upon words, either. What matters is that this advantage is remarkable from the very fact that it breaks down all our classifications and continually shatters every system constructed by lovers of mankind for the benefit of mankind. In fact, it upsets everything. But before mentioning this advantage to you, I want to compromise myself personally, and therefore I boldly declare that all these fine systems—all these theories for explaining to mankind its real normal interests, so that inevitably striving to pursue these interests men may at once become good and noble—are, in my opinion, so far, mere logical exercises! Yes, logical exercises. Why, to maintain this theory of the regeneration of mankind by means of the pursuit of its own advantage is to my mind almost the same thing as—as to affirm, for instance, following Buckle, that through civilization mankind becomes softer, and consequently less bloodthirsty and less fitted for warfare. Logically it does seem to follow from his arguments. But man has such a predilection for systems and abstract deductions that he is ready to distort the truth intentionally, he is ready to deny the evidence of his senses only to justify his logic.

I take this example because it is the most glaring instance of it. Only look about you: blood is being spilt in streams, and in the merriest way, as though it were champagne. Take the whole of the nineteenth century in which Buckle lived. Take Napoleon—the Great, and also the present one. Take North America—the eternal Union. Take the farce of Schleswig-Holstein. And what is it that civilization softens in us? The only gain of civilization for mankind is the greater capacity for variety of sensations—and absolutely nothing more. And through the development of this many-sidedness man may come to finding enjoyment in bloodshed. In fact, this has already happened to him. Have you noticed that it is the most civilized gentlemen who have been the subtlest slaughterers, to whom the Attilas and Stenka Razins [1] could not hold a candle? And if they are not so conspicuous as the Attilas and Stenka Razins, it is simply because they are so often met with, are so ordinary and have become so familiar to us. In any case, civilization has made mankind, if not more bloodthirsty, at least more vilely, more loathsomely bloodthirsty.

In the old days man saw justice in bloodshed, and with his conscience at peace exterminated people as he saw fit. Now we do think bloodshed abominable and yet we engage in this abomination, and with more energy than ever. Which is worse? Decide that for yourselves. They say that Cleopatra (excuse an instance from Roman history) was fond of sticking gold pins into her slave-girls' breasts and derived gratification from their screams and writhings. You will say that that was in the comparatively barbarous times; that these are barbarous times, too, because also, comparatively speaking, pins are stuck in even now; that though man has now learned to see more clearly than in barbarous ages, he is still far from having learned to act as reason and science would dictate. But yet you are fully convinced that he will be sure to learn when he gets rid of certain old bad habits, and when common sense and science have completely re-educated human nature and turned it in a normal direction. You are confident that then man will cease from *intentional* error and, so to say, will be compelled not to want to set his will against his normal interests. That is not all; then, you say, science itself will teach man (though to my mind it's a superfluous luxury) that he never has really had any caprice or will of his own, and that he himself is something in the nature of a piano-key or the stop of an organ, and that there are, besides, things called the laws of nature; so that everything he does is not done by his willing it, but is done by itself, by the laws of nature. Consequently we have only to discover these laws of nature, and man will no longer have to answer for his actions and life will become exceedingly easy for him. All

---

[1] Stepan (Stenka) Razin was the leader of a peasant-Cossack rebellion, the objectives of which were the abolition of serfdom and landlordism and the establishment of a Cossack republic. The uprising was marked by mass executions of landlords and officials; Razin's execution was followed by bloody repressions. Stenka Razin has become the Russian counterpart of Robin Hood.—*Editor.*

human actions will then, of course, be tabulated according to these laws, mathematically, like tables of logarithms up to 108,000, and entered in an index; or, better still, there would be published certain edifying works in the nature of encyclopedic lexicons, in which everything will be so clearly calculated and explained that there will be no more incidents or adventures in the world.

Then—it is you who are saying all this—new economic relations will be established, all ready-made and worked out with mathematical exactitude, so that every possible question will vanish in the twinkling of an eye, simply because every possible answer to it will be provided. Then will the Palace of Crystal be built. Then . . . in fact, those will be halcyon days. Of course, there is no guaranteeing (this is my comment) that it will not be, for instance, frightfully dull then (for what will one have to do when everything will be calculated and tabulated?), but on the other hand everything will be extraordinarily rational. Of course boredom may lead you to anything. It is boredom that sets one to sticking golden pins into people, but all that would not matter. What is bad (this is my comment again) is that, I dare say, people will be thankful for the gold pins then. Man is stupid, you know, phenomenally stupid; or rather he is not at all stupid, but he is so ungrateful that you could not find his like in all creation.

I, for instance, would not be in the least surprised if all of a sudden, *à propos* of nothing, in the midst of general prosperity, a gentleman with an ignoble, or rather with a reactionary and ironical, countenance were to arise and, putting his arms akimbo, say to us all: "I say, gentlemen, hadn't we better kick over the whole show and scatter rationalism to the winds, simply to send these logarithms to the devil, and to enable us to live once more at our own sweet foolish will?"

That, again, would not matter; but what is annoying is that he would be sure to find followers—such is the nature of man. And all that for the most foolish reason, which, one would think, was hardly worth mentioning: that is, that man everywhere and at all times, whoever he may be, has preferred to act as he chose and not in the least as his reason and advantage dictated. And one may choose what is contrary to one's own interests, and sometimes one *positively ought* (that is my idea). One's own free, unfettered choice, one's own caprice, however wild it may be, one's own fancy worked up at times to frenzy—is that very *most advantageous advantage* which we have overlooked, which comes under no classification and against which all systems and theories are continually being shattered to atoms. And how do these wiseacres know that man wants a normal, a virtuous choice? What has made them conceive that man must want a rationally advantageous choice? What man wants is simply *independent* choice, whatever that independence may cost and wherever it may lead. And a choice, of course, whose nature only the devil knows.

VIII

"Ha! ha! ha! But you know there is no such thing as choice in reality, say what you like," you will interpose with a chuckle. "Science has succeeded in so far analyzing man that we know already that choice and what is called freedom of will is nothing else than—"

Hold on, gentlemen, I meant to begin with that myself. I confess I was rather frightened. I was just going to say that the devil only knows what choice depends on, and that perhaps that was a very good thing, but I remembered the teachings of science—and pulled myself up short. And here you have begun upon it. Indeed, if a formula for all our desires and caprices is really discovered some day—that is, an explanation of what they depend upon, by which laws they arise, how they develop, what they are aiming at in this case and that, and so on, that is, a real mathematical formula—then, most likely, man will at once cease to feel desire; indeed, he will be certain to cease feeling desire. For who would want to choose by rule? Besides, he will at once be transformed from a human being into an organ-stop or something of the sort; for what is a man without desires, without free will and without choice, if not a stop in an organ? What do you think? Let us reckon the chances—can such a thing happen or not?

"H'm!" you decide. "Our choice is usually mistaken from a false view of our advantage. We sometimes choose absolute nonsense because in our foolishness we see in that nonsense the easiest means for attaining a supposed advantage. But when all that is explained and worked out on paper (which is perfectly possible, for it is contemptible and senseless to suppose that some laws of nature man will never understand), then certainly so-called desires will no longer exist. For if a desire should come into conflict with reason we shall then reason and not desire, because it will be impossible, retaining our reason, to be *senseless* in our desires, and in that way knowingly act against reason and desire to injure ourselves. And as all choice and reasoning can be really calculated—because there will some day be discovered the laws of our so-called free will—so, joking apart, there may one day be something like a table constructed of them, so that we really shall choose in accordance with it. If, for instance, some day they calculate and prove to me that I thumbed my nose at someone because I could not help thumbing my nose at him and that I had to do it in that particular way, what *freedom* is left me, especially if I am a learned man and have taken my degree somewhere? Then I should be able to calculate my whole life for thirty years beforehand. In short, if this could be arranged there would be nothing left for us to do; anyway, that would have to be our understanding. And, in fact, we ought unwearyingly to repeat to ourselves that at such and such a time and in such and such circumstances nature does not ask our leave; that we have got to take her as she is and not fashion her to suit our fancy, and if we really aspire to formulas and tables of rules, and—well, even to the chemical retort—there's no help for it, we must accept the retort, too, or else it will be accepted without our consent."

Yes, but here I come to a stop! Gentlemen, you must excuse me for being overphilosophical; it's the result of forty years underground! Allow me to indulge my fancy. You see, gentlemen, reason is an excellent thing, there's no disputing that, but reason is nothing but reason and satisfies only the rational side of man's nature, while will is a manifestation of the whole life, that is, of the whole human life including reason and all the impulses. And although our life, in this manifestation of it, is often worthless, yet it is life and not simply extracting square roots. Here I, for instance, quite naturally want to live, in order to satisfy all my capacities for life, and not simply my capacity for reasoning, that is, not simply one-twentieth of my capacity for life. What does reason know? Reason only knows what it has succeeded in learning (some things, perhaps, it will never learn; this is a poor comfort, but why not say so frankly?), and human nature acts as a whole, with everything that is in it, consciously or unconsciously, and, even if it goes wrong, it still lives on. I suspect, gentlemen, that you're looking at me with compassion; you tell me again that an enlightened and developed man, such, in short, as the future man will be, cannot consciously desire anything disadvantageous to himself, that this can be proved mathematically. I thoroughly agree it can—by mathematicians. But I repeat for the hundredth time, there is one case, one only, when man may consciously, purposely, desire what is injurious to himself, what is stupid, very stupid—simply in order to have the right to desire for himself even what is very stupid and not to be bound by an obligation to desire only what is sensible.

Of course, this very stupid thing, this caprice of ours, may be in reality, gentlemen, more advantageous for us than anything else on earth, especially in certain cases. And in particular it may be more advantageous than any advantage even when it does us obvious harm and contradicts the soundest conclusions of our reason concerning our advantage—for it preserves for us, at any rate, what is most precious and most important—that is, our personality, our individuality. Some, you see, maintain that this really is the most precious thing for mankind; choice, of course, if it chooses, can be in agreement with reason; and especially if the choice be not abused but kept within bounds. It is profitable and sometimes even praiseworthy. But very often, and even most often, choice is utterly and stubbornly opposed to reason . . . and . . . and . . . do you know that that, too, is profitable, sometimes even praiseworthy?

Gentlemen, let us suppose that man is not stupid. (Indeed, one cannot refuse to suppose that, if only from the one consideration, that, if man is stupid, then who is wise?) But if he is not stupid, he is monstrously ungrateful! Phenomenally ungrateful. In fact, I believe that the best definition of man is the ungrateful biped. But that is not all, that is not his worst defect; his worst defect is his perpetual moral obliquity, perpetual—from the days of the Flood to the Schleswig-Holstein period. Moral obliquity and consequently lack of good sense; for it has long been accepted that lack of good sense is due to no other cause than moral obliquity. Put it to the test and cast your eyes upon the history of mankind. What will you see? Is it a grand spectacle? Grand, if you like. Take the Colossus of Rhodes, for instance, that's worth something. With good reason Mr. Anaevski testifies of it that some say that it is the work of man's hands, while others maintain that it has been created by nature herself. Is history motley with many colors? Maybe it is, at that: if you take the dress uniforms, military and civilian, of all peoples in all ages—that alone is worth something, and if you take the undress uniforms you'll never get to the end of the thing; no historian would be equal to the job. Is it monotonous? Maybe it's monotonous, too: it's all fighting and fighting; they are fighting now, they fought first and they fought last—you will admit that it's almost too monotonous.

In short, one may say anything about the history of the world— anything that might enter the most disordered imagination. The only thing you can't say is that it's rational. The very word sticks in your throat. And, indeed, this is the odd thing that is continually happening: there are continually turning up in life moral and rational persons, sages and lovers of humanity, who make it their object to live all their lives as morally and rationally as possible, to be, so to speak, a light to their neighbors simply in order to show them that it is possible to live morally and rationally in this world. And yet we all know that those very people sooner or later have been false to themselves, playing some queer trick, often a most unseemly one. Now I ask you: what can be expected of man since he is a being endowed with such strange qualities? Shower upon him every earthly blessing, drown him in a sea of happiness, so that nothing but bubbles of bliss can be seen on the surface; give him economic prosperity, such that he should have nothing else to do but sleep, live on cakes and ale and busy himself wth the continuation of his species, and even then out of sheer ingratitude, sheer spite, man would play you some nasty trick. He would even risk his cakes and ale and would deliberately desire the most fatal rubbish, the most uneconomical absurdity, simply to introduce into all this positive good sense his fatal fantastic element. It is just his fantastic dreams, his vulgar folly, that he will desire to retain, simply in order to prove to himself—as though that were so necessary—that men still are men and not the keys of a piano, which the laws of nature threaten to control so completely that soon one will not be able to desire anything but by the calendar. And that is not all: even if man really were nothing but a piano-key, even if this were proved to him by natural science and mathematics, even then he would not become reasonable, but would purposely do something perverse out of simple ingratitude, simply to gain his point. And if he does not find means he will contrive destruction and chaos, will contrive sufferings of all sorts, only to gain his point! He will launch a curse upon the world, and as only man can curse (it is his privilege, the primary distinction between him and other animals), maybe by his curse alone he will attain his object—that is, convince himself that he is a man and not a piano-key! If you say that all this, too, can be calculated and tabulated —chaos and darkness and curses, so that the mere possibility of calculating it all beforehand would stop it all, and reason would reassert itself—then man would purposely go mad in order to be rid of reason and gain his point! I believe in it, I answer for it, for the whole work of man really seems to consist in nothing but proving to himself every minute that he is a man and not a piano-key! It may be at the cost of his skin, it may be by cannibalism! And this being so, can one help being tempted to rejoice that it has not yet come off, and that desire still depends on something we don't know?

You will scream at me (that is, if you condescend to do so) that no one is touching my free will, that all they are concerned with is that my will should of itself, of its own free will, coincide with my own normal interests, with the laws of nature and arithmetic.

Good Heavens, gentlemen, what sort of free will is left when we come to tabulation and arithmetic, when it will all be a case of two times two making four? Two times two makes four without my will. As if free will meant that!

IX

Gentlemen, I am joking, and I know myself that my jokes are not brilliant, but you know one can't take everything as a joke. I am, perhaps, jesting against the grain. Gentlemen, I am tormented by questions; answer them for me. You, for instance, want to cure men of their old habits and reform their will in accordance with science and good sense. But how do you know, not only that it is possible, but also that it is *desirable,* to reform man in that way? And what leads you to the conclusion that man's inclinations *need* reforming? In short, how do you know that such a reformation will be a benefit to man? And to go to the root of the matter—why are you so positively convinced that not to act against his real normal interests as guaranteed by the conclusions of reason and arithmetic is certainly always advantageous for man, and must always be a law for mankind? So far, you know, this is only your supposition. It may be the law of logic, but not the law of humanity. You think, gentlemen, perhaps that I am mad? Allow me to defend myself. I agree that man is pre-eminently a creative animal, predestined to strive consciously for an object and to engage in engineering—that is, incessantly and eternally to make new roads, *wherever they may lead.* But the reason why he wants sometimes to go off at a tangent may be precisely because he is *predestined* to make the road, and perhaps, too, that however stupid the straightforward practical man may be, the thought sometimes will occur to him that the road almost always does lead *somewhere,* and that the destination it leads to is less important than the process of making it, and that the chief thing is to save the well-conducted child from despising engineering, and so giving way to fatal idleness, which, as we all know, is the mother of all the vices.

Man likes to make roads and to create, that's a fact beyond dispute. But why has he such a passionate love for destruction and chaos also? Tell me that! But on that point I want to say a couple of words myself. May it not be that he loves chaos and destruction (there can be no disputing that he does sometimes love them) because he is instinctively afraid of attaining his object and completing the edifice he is constructing? Who knows, perhaps he only loves that edifice from a distance, and is by no means in love with it at close quarters; perhaps he only loves building it and does not want to live in it, but will leave it, when completed, for the use of *les animaux domestiques*—such as the ants, the sheep, and so on. Now the ants have quite a different taste. They have a marvelous edifice of that pattern which endures forever— the ant heap.

With the ant heap the respectable race of ants began and with the ant heap it will probably end, which does the greatest credit to the perseverance and good sense of ants. But man is a frivolous and ludicrous creature, and perhaps, like a chess player, loves the process of the game, not the end of it. And who knows (there is no saying this with certainty), perhaps the only goal on earth to which mankind is striving lies in this incessant process of attaining (in other words, in life itself), and not in the thing to be attained, which must always be expressed as a formula, as positive as that two times two makes four, and such positiveness is not life, gentlemen, but is the beginning of death. Anyway, man has always been afraid of this mathematical certainty, and I am afraid of it now. Granted man does nothing but seek that mathematical certainty, he traverses oceans, he sacrifices his life in the quest; but I assure you, he dreads to succeed, really to find it. He feels that when he has found it there will be nothing for him to look for. When workmen have finished their work they do at least receive their pay, they go to the tavern, then they are taken to the police station—and there is occupation for a week. But where can man go? Anyway, one can observe a certain awkwardness about him when he has attained such objects. He loves the process of attaining, but does not quite like to have attained, and that, of course, is very absurd. In fact, man is a comical creature; there seems to be a kind of jest in it all. But yet mathematical certainty is, after all, something insufferable. Two times two making four seems to me simply a piece of insolence.

Two times two making four is a pert coxcomb who stands with arms akimbo barring your path and spitting. I admit that two times two making four is an excellent thing, but if we are to give everything its due, two times two making five is sometimes a very charming thing, too.

And why are you so firmly, so triumphantly convinced that only the normal and the positive—in other words, only what is conducive to welfare—is for the advantage of man? Is not reason in error as regards advantage? Does not man, perhaps, love something besides well-being? Perhaps he is just as fond of suffering? Perhaps suffering is just as great a benefit to him as well-being? Man is sometimes extraordinarily, passionately in love with suffering, and that's a fact. There is no need to appeal to universal history to prove that; only ask yourself, if you are a man and have lived at all. As far as my personal opinion is concerned, to care only for well-being seems to me positively ill-bred. Whether it's good or bad, it is sometimes very pleasant, too, to smash things. I hold no brief for suffering nor for well-being either. I am standing for . . . my caprice, and for its being guaranteed to me when necessary. Suffering would be out of place in musical comedies, for instance; I know that. In the Palace of Crystal it is unthinkable; suffering means doubt, negation, and what would be the good of a *palace of crystal* if there could be any doubt about it? And yet I think man will never renounce real suffering, that is, destruction and chaos. Why, suffering is the sole origin of consciousness. Though I did lay it down at the beginning that consciousness is the greatest misfortune for man, yet I know man prizes it and would not give it up for any satisfaction. Consciousness, for instance, is infinitely superior to two times two making four. Once you have mathematical certainty there is nothing left to do or to understand. There will be nothing left but to bottle up your five senses and plunge into contemplation. While if you stick to consciousness, even though the same result is attained, you can at least flog yourself at times, and that will, at any rate, liven you up. Reactionary as it is, corporal punishment is better than nothing.

X

You believe in a *palace of crystal* that can never be destroyed—a palace at which one will not be able to put out one's tongue or thumb one's nose on the sly. And perhaps that is just why I am afraid of this edifice, that it is of crystal, and can never be destroyed, and that one can't put one's tongue out at it even on the sly.

You see, if it were not a palace, but a henhouse, I might creep into it to avoid getting wet, and yet I would not call the henhouse a palace out of gratitude to it for keeping me dry. You laugh and say that in such circumstances a henhouse is as good as a mansion. Yes, I answer, if one had to live simply to keep out of the rain.

But what is to be done if I have taken it into my head that that is not the only object in life, and that if one must live one had better live in a mansion? That is my choice, my desire. You will only eradicate it when you have changed my preference. Well, do change it, allure me with something else, give me another ideal. But meanwhile I will not take a henhouse for a mansion. The *palace of crystal* may be an idle dream, it may be that it is inconsistent with the laws of nature and that I have invented it only through my own stupidity, through the old-fashioned irrational habits of my generation. But what does it matter to me that it is inconsistent? That makes no difference, since it exists in my desires, or rather exists as long as my desires exist. Perhaps you are laughing again? Laugh away; I will put up with any mockery rather than pretend that I am sated when I am hungry. I know, anyway, that I will not be put off with a compromise, with a recurring zero, simply because it is consistent with the laws of nature and actually exists. I will not accept as the crown of my desires a block of slum tenements on a lease of a thousand years, and perhaps with a signboard of a dentist hanging out. Destroy my desires, eradicate my ideals, show me something better, and I will follow you. You will say, perhaps, that it is not worth your trouble; but in that case I can give you the same answer. We are discussing things seriously; but if you won't deign to give me your attention, I'll drop your acquaintance. I can retreat into my underground hole.

But while I am alive and have desires I would rather my hand were withered off than bring one brick to such a building! Don't remind me that I have just rejected the *palace of crystal* for the sole reason that one cannot put out one's tongue at it. I did not say that because I am so fond of putting my tongue out. Perhaps the thing I resented was that of all your edifices there has not been one at which one could not put out one's tongue. On the contrary, I would let my tongue be cut off out of gratitude if things could be so arranged that I should lose all desire to put it out. It's not my fault that things cannot be so arranged, and that one must be satisfied with model flats. Then why am I made with such desires? Can I have been constructed simply in order to come to the conclusion that all my construction is a cheat? Can this be my whole purpose? I do not believe it.

But do you know what? I'm convinced that we underground folk ought to be kept in check. Though we may sit forty years underground without speaking, when we do come out into the light of day and break out we talk and talk *and* talk. . . .

XI

The long and the short of it is, gentlemen, that it's better to do nothing! Better conscious inertia! And so hurrah for the underground! Though I have said that I envy the normal man to the last drop of my bile, yet I should not care to be in his place such as he is now (though I shall not cease envying him). No, no; anyway, the underground life is more advantageous. There, at any rate, one can. . . . Oh, but even now I'm lying! I'm lying because I know myself that it is not the underground that is better, but something different, quite different, for which I am thirsting, but which I cannot find. Damn the underground!

I will tell you another thing that would be better, and that is, if I myself believed in anything of what I have just written. I swear to you, gentlemen, there is not one thing, not one word of what I have written that I really believe. That is, I believe it, perhaps, but at the same time I feel and suspect that I am lying like a politician.

"Then why have you written all this?" you will say to me.

"I ought to put you underground for forty years without anything to do and then come to you in your cellar, to find out what stage you have reached! How can a man be left with nothing to do for forty years?"

"Isn't that shameful, isn't that humiliating?" you will say, perhaps, wagging your heads contemptuously. "You thirst for life and try to settle the problems of life by a logical tangle. And how persistent, how insolent are your sallies, and at the same time what a fright you are in! You spout nonsense and are pleased with it; you say impudent things and are in continual alarm and apologizing for them. You declare that you are afraid of nothing and at the same time try to ingratiate yourself in our good opinion. You declare that you are gnashing your teeth and at the same time you try to be witty so as to amuse us. You know that your witticisms are not witty, but you are evidently well satisfied with their literary value. You may, perhaps, have really suffered, but you have no respect for your own suffering. You may have sincerity, but you have no modesty; out of the pettiest vanity you expose your sincerity to publicity and ignominy. You doubtless mean to say something but hide your last word through fear, because you haven't the resolution to utter it and have only a cowardly impudence. You boast of consciousness, but you are not sure of your ground, for though your mind works, yet your heart is darkened and corrupt, and you cannot have a full, genuine consciousness without a pure heart. And how intrusive you are, how you insist and grimace! Lies, lies, lies!"

Of course I have myself made up all the things you say. That, too, is of the underground. I have been for forty years listening to you through a crack under the floor. I have invented them myself, there was nothing else I could invent. It is no wonder that I have learned it all by heart and it has taken a literary form.

But can you really be so credulous as to think that I will print all this and give it to you to read, too? And another problem: Why do I call you "gentlemen," why do I address you as though you really were my readers? Such confessions as I intend to make are never printed nor given to other people to read. Anyway, I am not strong-minded enough for that, and I don't see why I should be. But, you see, a fancy has struck me and I want to realize it at all costs. Let me explain.

Every man has reminiscences which he would not tell to everyone, but only to his friends. He has other matters in his mind which he would not reveal even to his friends, but only to himself, and that in secret. But there are other things which a man is afraid to tell even to himself, and every decent man has a number of such things stored away in his mind. The more decent he is, the greater the number of such things in his mind. Anyway, I have only lately determined to remember some of my early adventures. Till now I have always avoided them, even with a certain uneasiness. Now, when I am not only recalling them, but have actually decided to write an account of them, I want to try the experiment whether one can, even with oneself, be perfectly open and not take fright at the whole truth. I will observe, in parenthesis, that Heine says that a true autobiography is almost an impossibility, and that man is bound to lie about himself. He considers that Rousseau certainly told lies about himself in his *Confessions,* and even intentionally lied, out of vanity. I am convinced that Heine is right;

I quite understand how sometimes one may, out of sheer vanity, attribute regular crimes to oneself, and indeed I can very well conceive that kind of vanity. But Heine judged of people who made their confessions to the public. I write only for myself, and I wish to declare once and for all that if I write as though I were addressing readers, that is simply because it is easier for me to write in that form. It is a form, an empty form—I'll never have readers. I have made this plain already.

I don't wish to be hampered by any restrictions in the compilation of my notes. I shall not attempt any system or method. I will jot things down as I remember them.

But here, perhaps, someone will catch at the word and ask me: "If you really don't reckon on readers, why do you make such compacts with yourself—and on paper, too—as that you won't attempt any system or method, that you'll jot things down as you remember them, and so on, and so on? Why the explanations? Why the apologies?"

"There, now!" I answer.

There is a whole psychology in all this, though. Perhaps it is simply that I am a coward. And perhaps that I purposely imagine an audience before me in order that I may be more dignified while I write. There are perhaps thousands of reasons. Again, what precisely is my object in writing? If it is not for the benefit of the public why should I not simply recall these incidents in my own mind without putting them on paper?

Quite so; but yet it is more imposing on paper. There's something more impressive about it; I'll be better able to criticize myself and improve my style. Besides, I may obtain actual relief from writing. Today, for instance, I'm particularly oppressed by one memory of a distant past. It came back vividly to my mind a few days ago, and has remained haunting me like an annoying tune that one cannot get rid of. And yet get rid of it I must, somehow. I have hundreds of such reminiscences; but at times some one of them stands out from a hundred others and oppresses me. For some reason I believe that if I wrote it down I'd get rid of it. Why not try?

Besides, I'm bored, and I never have anything to do. Writing will be a sort of work. They say work makes man kindhearted and honest. Well, here is a chance for me, anyway.

Snow is falling today, yellow and dingy. It fell yesterday, too, as well as a few days ago. I fancy it is the wet snow that has reminded me of that incident which I cannot shake off now. And so let it be a story *à propos* of the falling snow.

Part II—A propos of the Wet Snow

From out dark error's subjugation
My words of passionate exhortation
  Had wrenched thy fainting spirit free;
And writhing prone in thine affliction
Thou didst recall with malediction
  The vice that had encompassed thee:
And then, thy slumbering conscience fretting
  From recollection's torturing flame,
Thou didst reveal the hideous setting
  Of thy life's current ere I came;
And suddenly I saw thee sicken,
  And weeping, hide thine anguished face,
Revolted, maddened, horror-stricken,
  At memories of foul disgrace.

NECRASSOV
(*Translated by
Juliet Soskice*)

I

AT that time I was only twenty-four. My life was even then gloomy, ill-regulated, and as solitary as that of a savage. I made friends with no one and positively avoided speech, burying myself more and more in my hole. At work in the office I never looked at anyone, and I was perfectly well aware that my companions looked upon me not only as a queer fellow, but even—I always fancied this—with a sort of loathing. I sometimes wondered why it was that nobody else fancied that he was looked upon with aversion. One of the clerks had a most repulsive, pock-marked face, which looked positively villainous. I believe I should not have dared to look at anyone with such an unsightly countenance. Another had such a very dirty old uniform that there was an unpleasant odor in his proximity. Yet neither of these gentlemen showed in any way the slightest self-consciousness, either about his clothes or his countenance or his character. Neither of them ever imagined that he was looked at with disgust; if they had imagined it they would not have minded—so long as their superiors did not look at them in that way.

It is clear to me now that, owing to my unbounded vanity and to the high standard I set for myself, I often looked at myself with furious discontent, which verged on loathing, and so I inwardly attributed the same feeling to everyone. I hated my face, for instance: I thought it disgusting, and even suspected that there was something base in my expression, and so every day when I turned up at the office I tried to behave as independently as possible and to assume a lofty expression, so that I might not be suspected of being abject. "My face may be ugly," I thought, "but let it be lofty, expressive, and, above all, *extremely* intelligent." But I was positively and painfully certain that it was impossible for my countenance ever to express those qualities. And what was worst of all, I thought it actually stupid-looking, and I would have been quite satisfied if I could have looked intelligent. In fact, I would even have put up with looking base if, at the same time, my face could have been thought strikingly intelligent.

Of course, I hated my fellow clerks one and all, and I despised them all, yet at the same time I was, as it were, afraid of them. In fact, it happened at times that I thought more highly of them than of myself. It somehow happened quite suddenly that I alternated between despising them and thinking them superior to myself. A cultivated and decent man cannot be vain without setting a fearfully high standard for himself, and without despising and almost hating himself at certain moments. But whether I despised them or thought them superior, I dropped my eyes almost every time I met anyone. I even made experiments whether I could face so-and-so's looking at me, and I was always the first to drop my eyes. This worried me to distraction. I had a sickly dread, too, of being ridiculous, and so had a slavish passion for the conventional in everything external. I loved to fall into the common rut and had a wholehearted terror of any kind of eccentricity in myself. But how could I live up to it? I was morbidly sensitive, as a man of our age should be. They were all stupid and as like one another as so many sheep. Perhaps I was the only one in the office who fancied that I was a coward and a slave, and I fancied it just because I was more highly developed. But it was not only that I fancied it, it really was so. I *was* a coward and a slave. I say this without the slightest embarrassment. Every decent man of our age must be a coward and a slave. That is his normal condition. Of that I am firmly convinced. He is made and constructed to that very end. And not only at the present time, owing to certain casual circumstances, but always, at all times, a decent man is bound to be a coward and a slave. It is the law of nature for all decent people all over the earth. If any one of them happens to be valiant about something, he need not be comforted nor carried away by that; he would show the white feather just the same before something else. That's how it invariably and inevitably ends. Only donkeys and mules are valiant, and then only till they are up against the wall. It's not worth while to pay attention to them, for they really don't count.

Another circumstance, too, worried me in those days: that there was no one like me and that I was not like anyone else. "I am unique, but they are like all," I thought—and pondered.

From which it's evident that I was still a youngster.

Sometimes the very opposite would happen. It was loathsome sometimes to go to the office; things reached such a point that I often came home ill. But all at once, *à propos* of nothing, there would come a phase of skepticism and indifference (everything happened in phases to me), and I myself would laugh at my intolerance and fastidiousness, I would reproach myself with being *romantic*. At one time I was unwilling to speak to anyone, while at other times I would not merely talk with people but go to the extent of contemplating friendship with them. All my fastidiousness would suddenly, without rhyme or reason, vanish. Who knows, perhaps I never had really had it, and it had simply been affected and gotten out of books. I haven't decided that question even up to now. Once I actually made friends with them, visited their homes, played cards, drank vodka, talked of promotions. But here let me make a digression.

We Russians, speaking generally, have never had those foolish transcendental *romantics* (German, and still more French) on whom nothing produces any effect; if there were an earthquake, if all France perished at the barricades, the French *romantics* would still be the same, they would not even have the decency to affect a change, but would still go on singing their transcendental songs to the hour of their death, because they are fools. We, in Russia, have no fools; that's something everybody knows well. That's what distinguishes our land from others. Consequently these transcendental natures are not found amongst us in their pure form. The idea that they are so found is due to our *realistic* journalists and critics of the day, always on the lookout for Kostanzhoglos[1] and Uncle Peter Ivanichs[2] and foolishly accepting them as our ideal; they have slandered our *romantics,* taking them for the same transcendental sort as in Germany or France. On the contrary,

---

[1] Kostanzhoglos is an impossibly perfect personification of all the ant-and-bee virtues, in *Dead Souls* (Book Two).—*Editor.*

[2] A character in Goncharov's *A Common Story.* The Editor is obliged for this datum to Marc Slonim and Irina Aleksander.

the characteristics of our *romantics* are absolutely and directly opposed to the transcendental European type, and no European standard can be applied to them. (Allow me to make use of this word *romantic*—an old-fashioned and much-respected word which has done good service and is familiar to all.) The characteristics of our *romantic* are to understand everything, *to see everything and to see it often incomparably more clearly than our most realistic minds see it;* to refuse to accept anyone or anything, but at the same time not to despise anything; to give way, to yield, from policy; never to lose sight of a useful practical object (such as rent-free quarters at the government expense, pensions, decorations), to keep an eye on that object through all the enthusiasms and volumes of lyrical poems, and at the same time to preserve *the good and the beautiful* inviolate within them to the hour of their death, and to preserve themselves also, incidentally, like some precious jewel wrapped in cotton wool, if only for the benefit of *the good and the beautiful.* Our *romantic* is a man of great breadth and the greatest rogue of all our rogues, I assure you. I can assure you of that from experience, indeed. Of course, that is, if he is intelligent. But what am I saying? The *romantic* is always intelligent, and I only meant to observe that although we have had foolish romantics they don't count, and they were foolish only because in the flower of their youth they degenerated into Germans and, to preserve their precious jewel more comfortably, settled somewhere out there—by preference in Weimar or the Black Forest.

I, for instance, genuinely despised my official work and did not openly abuse it simply because I was in it myself and got a salary out of it. Anyway, take note, I did not openly abuse it. Our *romantic* would rather go out of his mind—a thing, however, which very rarely happens—than take to open abuse, unless he had some other career in view; and he is never kicked out. At most, they would take him to the lunatic asylum as "the King of Spain" if he should go very mad. But it is only the slim, fair-haired lads who go out of their minds in Russia. Innumerable *romantics* attain later in life to considerable rank in the Service. Their many-sidedness is remarkable! And what a faculty they have for the most contradictory sensations! I was comforted by this thought even in those days, and I am of the same opinion now. That is why there are so many *broad natures* among us who never lose their ideal even in the depths of degradation; and though they never stir a finger for their ideal, though they are arrant thieves and knaves, yet they tearfully cherish their first ideal and are extraordinarily honest at heart. Yes, it is only among us that the most incorrigible rogue can be absolutely and loftily honest at heart without in the least ceasing to be a rogue. I repeat, our *romantics,* frequently, become such accomplished rascals (I use the term *rascals* affectionately), suddenly display such a sense of reality and practical knowledge, that their bewildered superiors and the public generally can only ejaculate in amazement.

Their many-sidedness is really amazing, and goodness knows what it may develop into later on, and what the future has in store for us. It is not a poor material! I do not say this from any foolish or boastful patriotism. But I feel sure that you are again imagining that I am joking. Or perhaps it's just the contrary, and you are convinced that I really think so. Anyway, gentlemen, I shall welcome both views as an honor and a special favor. And do forgive my digression.

I did not, of course, maintain friendly relations with my comrades and soon was at loggerheads with them, and in my youth and inexperience I even gave up bowing to them, as though I had cut off all relations. That, however, only happened to me once. As a rule, I was always alone.

In the first place I spent most of my time at home, reading. I tried to stifle all that was continually seething within me by means of external impressions. And the only external means I had was reading. Reading, of course, was a great help—stirring me, giving me pleasure and pain. Yet at times it bored me fearfully. One longed for movement in spite of everything, and I plunged all at once into dark, underground, loathsome vice of the pettiest kind. My wretched passions were acute, smarting, from my continual, sickly irritability. I had hysterical impulses, accompanied by tears and convulsions. I had no resource except reading—that is, there was nothing in my surroundings which I could respect and which attracted me. I was overwhelmed with depression, too; I had an hysterical craving for incongruity and for contrast, and so I took to vice. I have not said all this to justify myself. . . . But, no—I'm lying. I did want to justify myself. I made that little observation for my own benefit, gentlemen. I don't want to lie. I vowed to myself I wouldn't.

And so, furtively, timidly, in solitude, at night, I indulged in filthy vice, with a feeling of shame which never deserted me, even at the most loathsome moments, and which at such moments nearly made me curse. Already even then I had my underground world in my soul. I was fearfully afraid of being seen, of being met, of being recognized. I visited various obscure haunts.

One night as I was passing a tavern I saw through a lighted window some gentlemen fighting with billiard cues, and saw one of them thrown out of a window. At other times I should have felt very much disgusted, but I was in such a mood at the time that I actually envied the gentleman thrown out of a window—and I envied him so much that I even went into the tavern and into the billiard room. "Perhaps," I thought, "I'll have a fight, too, and they'll throw me out of a window."

I wasn't drunk—but what is one to do? Depression will drive a man to such a pitch of hysteria! But nothing happened. It seemed that I was not even up to being thrown out of a window, and I went away without having had my fight.

An officer put me in my place from the first moment.

I was standing by the billiard table and in my ignorance blocking up the way, and he wanted to pass; he took me by the shoulders and without a word—without a warning or explanation—thrust me from where I was standing to another spot and passed by as though he had not noticed me. I could have forgiven blows, but I could not forgive his having thrust me aside without noticing me.

The devil knows what I would have given for a real, regular quarrel —a more decent, a more *literary* one, so to speak. I had been treated like a fly. This officer was over six feet, while I was a spindly little fellow. But the quarrel was in my hands. I had only to protest and I certainly would have been thrown out of a window. But I changed my mind and preferred to beat a resentful retreat.

From the tavern I went straight home, confused and troubled, and the next night I went out again with the same lewd intentions, still more furtively, abjectly and miserably than before, as it were, with tears in my eyes—but still I did go out again. Don't imagine, though, it was cowardice which made me slink away from the officer: I never have been a coward at heart, though I have always been a coward in action. Don't be in a hurry to laugh—I assure you I can explain it all.

Oh, if only that officer had been one of the sort who would consent to fight a duel! But no, he was one of those gentlemen (alas, long extinct!) who preferred fighting with cues or, like Gogol's Lieutenant Pirogov, appealing to the police. They did not fight duels and would have thought a duel with a civilian like me an utterly unseemly procedure in any case—and they looked upon the duel altogether as something impossible, something freethinking and French. But they were quite ready to bully, especially when they were over six feet.

I did not slink away through cowardice, but through an unbounded vanity. I was afraid not of his six-foot height, nor of getting a sound thrashing and being thrown out of a window; I should have had physical courage enough, I assure you; but I hadn't the moral courage. What I was afraid of was that everyone present, from the insolent marker down to the lowest little stinking, pimply clerk in a greasy collar, would jeer at me and fail to understand when I began to protest and to address them in literary language. For of the point of honor—not of honor, but of the point of honor (*point d'honneur*)—one cannot speak among us except in literary language. You can't allude to the *point of honor* in ordinary language. I was fully convinced (the sense of reality, in spite of all my romanticism!) that they would all simply split their sides with laughter, and that the officer would not simply beat me (that is, without insulting me), but would certainly give me his knee in the back, kick me round the billiard table, and only then, perhaps, have pity and drop me out of a window.

Of course, for me this trivial incident could not end in that. I often met that officer afterward in the street and noticed him very carefully. I'm not quite sure whether he recognized me; I imagine not. I judge from certain signs. But I—I stared at him with spite and hatred, and so it went on—for several years! My resentment grew even deeper with the years. At first I began making stealthy inquiries about this officer. It was difficult for me to do so, for I knew no one. But one day I heard someone shout his last name in the street as I was following him at a distance, as though I were tied to him—and so I learned his last name. Another time I followed him to his flat, and for a small silver coin learned from the janitor where he lived, on which floor, whether he lived alone or with others, and so on—in fact, everything one could learn from a janitor. One morning, though I had never tried my hand with the pen, it suddenly occurred to me to write a satire on this officer in the form of a novel which would unmask his villainy. I wrote the novel with relish. I did unmask his villainy, I even exaggerated it; at first I so altered his last name that it could easily be recognized, but on second thoughts I changed it and sent the story to *Notes of the Fatherland*. But at that time such attacks were not the fashion and my story was not printed. Which was a great vexation to me.

Sometimes I was positively choked with resentment. At last I determined to challenge my enemy to a duel. I composed a splendid, charming letter to him, imploring him to apologize to me and hinting rather plainly at a duel in case of refusal. The letter was so composed that if the officer had had the least understanding of the good and the beautiful he would certainly have flung himself on my neck and have offered me his friendship. And how fine that would have been! How we should have got on together! "He could have shielded me with his higher rank, while I could have improved his mind with my culture, and, well . . . my ideas; and all sorts of things might have happened." Just imagine, this was two years after his insult to me, and my challenge would have been a ridiculous anachronism, in spite of all the ingenuity of my letter in disguising and explaining away the anachronism. But, thank God (to this day I thank the Almighty with tears in my eyes), I did not send the letter to him. Cold shivers run down my back when I think of what might have happened if I had sent it.

And all at once I revenged myself in the simplest way, by a stroke of genius! A brilliant thought suddenly dawned upon me. Sometimes on holidays I used to stroll along the sunny side of the Nevski Prospect about four o'clock in the afternoon. Though it was hardly a stroll so much as a series of innumerable miseries, humiliations and resentments; but no doubt that was just what I wanted. I used to squirm along in a most unseemly fashion, like an eel, continually moving aside to make way for generals, for officers of the guards and hussars, or for ladies. At such moments there used to be a convulsive twinge at my heart, and I used to feel hot all down my back at the mere thought of the wretchedness of my attire, of the wretchedness and abjectness of my little scurrying figure. This was a regular martyrdom; a continual, intolerable humiliation at the thought, which passed into an incessant and direct sensation, that I was a mere fly in the eyes of all this world, a nasty, disgusting fly—more intelligent, more highly developed, more refined in feeling than any of them, of course—but a fly that was continually making way for everyone, insulted and injured by everyone. Why I inflicted this torture upon myself, why I went to the Nevski Prospect, I don't know. I felt simply drawn there at every possible opportunity.

Already then I began to experience a rush of the enjoyment of which I spoke in the first chapter. After my affair with the officer I felt even more drawn there than before: it was on the Nevski Prospect that I met him most frequently; there I could admire him. He, too, went there chiefly on holidays. He, too, turned out of his path for generals and persons of high rank, and he, too, squirmed in and out among them like an eel; but people like me, or even those better dressed, yet like me, he simply walked over; he made straight for them as though there was nothing but empty space before him, and never, under any circumstances, turned aside. I gloated over my resentment, watching him and

—always made way for him resentfully. It exasperated me that even in the street I could not be on an even footing with him.

"Why must you invariably be the first to move aside?" I kept asking myself in hysterical rage, waking up sometimes at three o'clock in the morning. "Why you and not he? There's no regulation about it; there's no written law. Let there be equality about making way, as there usually is when refined people meet: he moves halfway and you move halfway; you pass with mutual respect."

But that never happened, and I always moved aside, while he didn't as much as notice my making way for him. And lo and behold, a bright idea dawned upon me! "What," I thought, "if I meet him and don't move to one side? What if I don't move aside on purpose, even if I bump against him? How would that do?" This audacious idea took such a hold on me that it gave me no peace. I was dreaming of it continually, horribly, and I purposely went more frequently to the Nevski Prospect in order to picture more vividly how I should do it when I did do it. I was delighted. This intention seemed to me more and more practical and feasible.

"Of course I won't really jostle him," I thought, already more good-natured in my joy. "I simply won't turn aside, will run up against him, not very violently, but merely shouldering him—just as much as decency permits. I'll jostle against him just as much as he jostles against me." At last I made up my mind completely. But my preparations took a great deal of time. To begin with, when I carried out my plan I'd have to look rather more decent, and so I had to think of my getup. "In case of emergency, if, for instance, there were any sort of public scandal (and the public there is of the most *recherché*: the Countess walks there; Prince D——walks there; all the literary world is there), I must be well dressed; that inspires respect and of itself puts us on an equal footing in the eyes of society."

With this object I asked for some of my salary in advance and bought at Churkin's a pair of black gloves and a decent hat. Black gloves seemed to me both more dignified and *bon ton* than the lemon-colored ones which I had contemplated at first. "The color is too gaudy; it looks as though one were trying to be conspicuous," and I did not take the lemon-colored ones. I had got ready long beforehand a good shirt, with white bone studs; my overcoat was the only thing that held me back. The coat in itself was a very good one, it kept me warm; but it was quilted and it had a raccoon collar, which was the height of vulgarity. I had to change the collar at any sacrifice, and get one of beaver, like an officer's. For this purpose I began visiting the Drapers' Row and after several attempts I decided upon some cheap German beaver. Though German beaver soon grows stagey and looks wretched, yet at first it looks exceedingly well, and I only needed it for one occasion. I asked the price; even so, it was too expensive. After thinking it over thoroughly I decided to sell my raccoon collar; the rest of the sum (a considerable one for me) I decided to borrow from Anton Antonich Syetochkin, my immediate superior, an unassuming person, though grave and judicious. He never lent money to anyone, but I had, on entering the service, been specially recommended to him by an important personage who had got me my job. I was horribly worried. To borrow from Anton Antonich seemed to me monstrous and shameful. I did not sleep for two or three nights. Indeed, I did not sleep well at that time, I was in a fever; I had a vague sinking at my heart or else a sudden throbbing, throbbing, throbbing! Anton Antonich was surprised at first, then he frowned, then he reflected, and after all lent me the money, receiving from me a written authorization to take from my salary a fortnight later the sum that he had lent me.

In this way everything was at last ready. The handsome beaver replaced the mean-looking raccoon, and I began by degrees to get ready for action. It would never have done to act offhand, at random; the plan had to be carried out skillfully, by degrees. But I must confess that after many efforts I began to despair: we simply could not run into each other. I made every preparation, I was quite determined—it seemed as though we should run into one another directly—and before I knew what I was doing I had stepped aside for him again and he had passed without noticing me. I even prayed as I approached him that God would grant me determination. One time I had made up my mind thoroughly, but it ended in my stumbling and falling at his feet because at the very last instant when I was only six inches from him my courage failed me. He very calmly stepped over me, while I flew to one side like a ball. That night I was ill again, feverish and delirious.

And suddenly it ended most happily. The night before I had made up my mind not to carry out my fatal plan and to abandon it all, and with that object I went to the Nevski Prospect for the last time, just to see how I would abandon it all. Suddenly, three paces from my enemy, I unexpectedly made up my mind—I closed my eyes, and we ran full tilt, shoulder to shoulder, against one another! I did not budge an inch and passed him on a perfectly equal footing! He did not even look round and pretended not to notice it; but he was only pretending,

I am convinced of that. I am convinced of that to this day! Of course, I got the worst of it—he was stronger, but that was not the point. The point was that I had attained my object; I had kept up my dignity, I had not yielded a step and had put myself publicly on an equal social footing with him. I returned home feeling that I was fully avenged for everything. I was delighted. I was triumphant and sang Italian arias. Of course, I will not describe to you what happened to me three days later; if you have read my first chapter you can guess that for yourself. The officer was afterwards transferred; I have not seen him now for fourteen years. What is the dear fellow doing now? Whom is he trampling now?

II

But the period of my dissipation would end, and I always felt very sick afterward. It was followed by remorse—I tried to drive it away: I felt too sick. By degrees, however, I grew used to that, too. I grew used to everything, or rather I voluntarily resigned myself to enduring it. But I had a means of escape that reconciled everything—that was to find refuge in *the good and the beautiful*—in dreams, of course. I was a terrible dreamer, I would dream for three months on end, tucked away in my corner, and you may believe me that at those moments I had no resemblance to the gentleman who, in his chickenhearted perturbation, had put a collar of German beaver on his overcoat. I suddenly became a hero. I would not have admitted my six-foot lieutenant even if he had called on me. I could not even picture him before me then. What were my dreams and how could I satisfy myself with them? It is hard to say now, but at the time I was satisfied with them. Though, indeed, even now, I am to some extent satisfied with them.

Dreams were particularly sweet and vivid after a spell of dissipation; they came with remorse and with tears, with curses and transports. There were moments of such positive intoxication, of such happiness, that there was not the faintest trace of irony within me, on my honor. I had faith, hope, love. I believed blindly at such times that by some miracle, by some external circumstance, all this would suddenly open out, expand; that suddenly a vista of suitable activity—beneficent, good, and, above all, *ready-made* (what sort of activity I had no idea, but the great thing was that it should be all ready for me)—would rise up before me—and I should come out into the light of day, well-nigh riding a white horse and crowned with laurel. Anything but the foremost place I could not conceive for myself, and for that very reason, in reality, I quite contentedly occupied the lowest. Either to be a hero or to grovel in the mud—there was nothing between. That was my ruin, for when I was in the mud I comforted myself with the thought that at other times I was a hero, and the hero was a cloak for the mud: for an ordinary man it was shameful to defile himself, but a hero was too lofty to be utterly defiled, and so he might defile himself. It is worth noting that these attacks of *the good and the beautiful* visited me even during the period of dissipation and just at the times when I was touching bottom. They came in separate spurts, as though reminding me of themselves, but did not banish the dissipation by their appearance. On the contrary, they seemed to add a zest to it by contrast, and were only sufficiently present to serve as an appetizing sauce. That sauce was made up of contradictions and sufferings, of agonizing inward analysis, and all these pangs and pinpricks gave a certain piquancy, even a significance, to my dissipation—in fact, completely answered the purpose of an appetizing sauce. There was a certain depth of meaning in it. And I could hardly have resigned myself to the simple, vulgar, direct debauchery of a clerk and have endured all the filthiness of it. What could have allured me about it then and have drawn me at night into the street? No, I had a lofty way of getting out of it all.

And what loving-kindness, O Lord, what loving-kindness I felt at times in those dreams of mine, in those flights into *the good and the beautiful*. Though it was fantastic love, though it was never applied to anything human in reality, yet there was so much of this love that one did not feel afterward even the impulse to apply it in reality—that would have been superfluous. Everything, however, passed satisfactorily by a lazy and fascinating transition into the sphere of art, that is, into the beautiful forms of life, lying ready, largely stolen from the poets and novelists and adapted to all sorts of needs and uses. I, for instance, was triumphant over everyone; everyone, of course, was in dust and ashes, and was forced spontaneously to recognize my superiority, and I forgave them all. I was a poet and a grand gentleman; I fell in love; I came in for countless millions and immediately devoted them to humanity, and at the same time I confessed before all the people my shameful deeds, which, of course, were not merely shameful but had in them much that was *good and beautiful,* something in the style of Manfred. Everyone would kiss me and weep (what idiots they would be if they didn't), while I'd go barefoot and hungry preaching new ideas and fighting a victorious Austerlitz against the obscurantists. Then the band would play a march, an amnesty would be declared, the Pope would agree to retire from Rome to Brazil; then there would be a ball for the whole of Italy at the Villa Borghese on the shores of the Lake of Como (the Lake of Como being for that purpose transferred to the neighborhood of Rome); then would come a scene in the bushes, and so on, and so on—as though you didn't know all about it!

You will say that it is vulgar and contemptible to drag all this out before everybody after all the tears and transports which I have myself confessed. But why is it contemptible? Can you imagine that I am ashamed of it all, and that it was stupider than anything in your life, gentlemen? And I can assure you that some of these fancies were by no means badly composed. It did not all happen on the shores of Lake Como. And yet you are right—it really is vulgar and contemptible. And most contemptible of all is the fact that I am now attempting to justify myself to you. And even more contemptible than that is my making this remark now. But that's enough, or there will be no end to it: each step will be more contemptible than the last. . . .

I could never stand more than three months of dreaming at a time without feeling an irresistible desire to plunge into society. To plunge into society meant to visit my superior at the office, Anton Antonich Syetochkin. He was the only permanent acquaintance I ever had in my life, and I wonder at the fact myself now. But I only went to see him when that phase came over me and when my dreams had reached such a point of bliss that it became essential at once to embrace my fellows and all mankind; and for that purpose I needed, at least, one human being, actually existing. I had to call on Anton Antonich, however, on Tuesday—his at-home day, so I always had to time my passionate desire to embrace humanity so that it might fall on a Tuesday.

This Anton Antonich lived on the fourth floor in a house in Five Corners, in four low-pitched rooms, each smaller than the next, of a particularly frugal and sere appearance. He had two daughters, and the daughters had an aunt, who used to pour out the tea. Of the daughters one was thirteen and the other fourteen; they both had snub noses, and I was awfully shy in their presence because they were always whispering and giggling together. The master of the house usually sat in his study on a leather couch in front of the table with some gray-headed gentleman, usually a colleague from our office or some other department. I never saw more than two or three visitors there, always the same. They talked about the excise duties, about matters in the Senate, about salaries, about promotions, about His Excellency, and the best means of pleasing him, and so on. I had the patience to sit like a fool beside these people for four hours at a stretch, listening to them without knowing what to say to them or venturing to say a word. I became stupefied, several times I felt myself perspiring, I was overcome by a sort of paralysis; but this was pleasant and good for me. On returning home I deferred for a time my desire to embrace all mankind.

I had, however, one other acquaintance of a sort, Simonov, who was an old schoolfellow. In fact, I had a number of schoolfellows in Petersburg, but I did not associate with them and had even given up nodding to them in the street. I believe I had asked to be transferred into the department I was in simply to avoid their company and to cut off all connection with my hateful childhood. Curses on that school and all those terrible years of penal servitude! In short, I parted from my schoolfellows as soon as I got out into the world. There were two or three left to whom I did nod in the street. One of them was Simonov, who had been in no way distinguished at school, and was of a quiet and equable disposition; but I discovered in him a certain independence of character and even honesty. I don't even suppose that he was particularly stupid. I had at one time spent some rather soulful moments with him, but these had not lasted long and had somehow been suddenly clouded over. He was evidently uncomfortable at these recollections and was, I imagine, always afraid that I might take up the same tone again. I suspected that he had an aversion for me, but still I went on going to see him, not being quite certain of it.

And so on one occasion, unable to endure my solitude and knowing that since it was Thursday Anton Antonich's door would be closed, I thought of Simonov. Climbing up to his fourth-floor flat, I was thinking that the man disliked me and that it was a mistake to go and see him. But as it always happened that such reflections impelled me, as though purposely, to put myself into a false position, I went in. It was almost a year since I had last seen Simonov.

III

I found two of my old schoolfellows with him. They seemed to be discussing an important matter. All of them took scarcely any notice of my entrance, which was strange, for I had not met them for years.

Evidently they looked upon me as something on the level of a common housefly. I had not been treated like that even at school, though they had all hated me. I knew, of course, that they must despise me now for my lack of success in the Service, and for my having let myself sink so low, going about badly dressed, and so on—which seemed to them a sign of my incapacity and insignificance. But I had not expected such contempt. Simonov was positively surprised at my turning up. Even in the old days he had always seemed surprised at my coming. All this disconcerted me. I sat down, feeling rather miserable, and began listening to what they were saying.

They were engaged in warm and earnest conversation about a farewell dinner which they wanted to arrange for the next day to a comrade of theirs called Zvercov, an officer in the army, who was going away to a distant province. This Zvercov, too, had been at school all the time I was there. I had begun to hate him, particularly in the upper grades. In the lower grades he had simply been a pretty, playful boy whom everybody liked. I had hated him, however, even in the lower grades, just because he was a pretty and playful boy. He was always poor at his lessons and got worse and worse as he went on; however, he left with a good certificate, since he had influential people interested in him. During his last year at school he came in for an estate of two hundred serfs, and as almost all of us were poor he took to swaggering among us. He was vulgar in the extreme, but at the same time he was a good-natured fellow, even in his swaggering. In spite of superficial, fantastic and sham notions of honor and dignity, all but very few of us positively groveled before Zvercov, and the more he swaggered the more they groveled. And it was not from any interested motive that they groveled, but simply because he had been favored by the gifts of nature. Moreover, it was, as it were, an accepted idea among us that Zvercov was a specialist in tact and the social graces. This last fact particularly infuriated me. I hated the abrupt self-confident tone of his voice, his admiration of his own witticisms, which were often frightfully stupid, though he was bold in his language; I hated his handsome but stupid face (for which I would, however, have gladly exchanged my intelligent one), and the free-and-easy military manners in fashion in the forties.

I hated the way in which he used to talk of his future conquests of women (he did not venture to begin his attacks upon women until he had the epaulettes of an officer, and was looking forward to them with impatience), and boasted of the duels he would constantly be fighting. I remember how I, invariably so taciturn, suddenly fastened upon

Zvercov, when one day while talking at a leisure moment with his schoolfellows of his future relations with the fair sex, and growing as sportive as a puppy in the sun, he all at once declared that he would not leave a single village girl on his estate unnoticed, that that was his *droit de seigneur,* and that if the peasants dared to protest he would have them all flogged and double the tax on them, the bearded rascals. Our servile rabble applauded, but I attacked him, not from compassion for the girls and their fathers, but simply because they were applauding such an insect. I got the better of him on that occasion, but though Zvercov was stupid he was also lively and impudent, and so laughed it off, and in such a way that my victory was not really complete: the laugh was on his side. He got the better of me on several occasions afterward, but without malice, jestingly, casually. I remained angrily and contemptuously silent and would not answer him.

When we left school he made advances to me; I did not rebuff them, for I was flattered, but we soon parted, and quite naturally. Afterward I heard of his barrack-room success as a lieutenant, and of the fast life he was leading. Then there came other rumors—of his successes in the Service. By then he had taken to cutting me in the street, and I suspected that he was afraid of compromising himself by greeting a personage as insignificant as myself. I saw him once at a theater, in the third tier of boxes. By then he was wearing shoulder straps. He was twisting and turning, ingratiating himself with the daughters of an ancient general. In three years he had become considerably shopworn, though he was still rather handsome and adroit. One could see that by the time he was thirty he would be corpulent.

So it was to this Zvercov that my schoolfellows were going to give a dinner on his departure. They had kept up with him for those three years, though privately they did not consider themselves on an equal footing with him, I am convinced of that.

Of Simonov's two visitors, one was Ferfichkin, a Russianized German —a little fellow with the face of a monkey, a blockhead who was always deriding everyone, a very bitter enemy of mine from our days in the lower grades—a vulgar, impudent, swaggering fellow, who affected a most sensitive feeling of personal honor, though, of course, he was a wretched little coward at heart. He was one of those worshipers of Zvercov who made up to the latter from interested motives, and often borrowed money from him. Simonov's other visitor, Trudolyubov, was a person in no way remarkable—a tall young fellow, in the army, with a cold face, fairly honest, though he worshiped success of every sort, and was capable only of thinking about promotion. He was some sort of distant relation of Zvercov's, and this, foolish as it seems, gave him a certain importance among us. He always thought me of no consequence whatever; his behavior to me, though not quite courteous, was tolerable.

"Well, with seven rubles each," said Trudolyubov, "which is twenty-one rubles for the three of us, we ought to be able to get a good dinner. Zvercov, of course, won't pay."

"Of course not, since we're inviting him," Simonov decided.

"Can you imagine," Ferfichkin interrupted hotly and conceitedly, like some insolent flunky boasting of his master's, the general's, decorations, "can you imagine that Zvercov will let us pay alone? He'll accept from delicacy, but he'll order half a dozen bottles of champagne."

"Do we want half a dozen for the four of us?" observed Trudolyubov, taking notice only of the half dozen.

"It's settled then—the three of us, with Zvercov for the fourth, twenty-one rubles, at the Hôtel de Paris, at five o'clock tomorrow," Simonov, who had been asked to make the arrangements, concluded finally.

"How do you figure twenty-one rubles?" I asked in some agitation, with a show of being offended. "If you count me it won't be twenty-one but twenty-eight rubles."

It seemed to me that to invite myself so suddenly and unexpectedly would be positively graceful, and that they would all be conquered at once and would look upon me with respect.

"Do you want to join, too?" Simonov observed, with no appearance of pleasure, seeming to avoid looking at me. He knew me through and through.

It infuriated me that he knew me so thoroughly.

"Why not? I'm an old schoolfellow of his, too, I believe, and I must own I feel hurt at your having left me out," I said, boiling over again.

"And where were we to find you?" Ferfichkin put in rudely.

"You never were on good terms with Zvercov," Trudolyubov added, frowning.

But I had already grabbed at the idea and would not give it up.

"It seems to me that no one has a right to form an opinion upon that," I retorted in a shaky voice, as though something tremendous had happened. "Perhaps that is just my reason for wishing it now, that I have not always been on good terms with him."

"Oh, there's no making you out—with all these refinements," Trudolyubov jeered.

"We'll put your name down," Simonov decided, addressing me. "Tomorrow at five o'clock, at the Hôtel de Paris."

"What about the money?" Ferfichkin began in an undertone, indicating me to Simonov, but he broke off, for even Simonov was embarrassed.

"That will do," said Trudolyubov, getting up. "If he wants to come so much, let him."

"But it's a private affair, among friends," Ferfichkin said crossly as he, too, picked up his hat. "It's not an official gathering."

They went away. Ferfichkin did not greet me in any way as he went out, Trudolyubov barely nodded. Simonov, with whom I was left tête-à-tête, was in a state of vexation and perplexity, and looked at me queerly. He did not sit down nor did he ask me to.

"H'm . . . yes . . . tomorrow, then. Will you pay your share now? I'm merely asking to make sure," he muttered in embarrassment.

I flushed crimson, and as I did so I remembered that I had owed Simonov fifteen rubles for ages—which I had, indeed, never forgotten, though I had not paid it.

"You will understand, Simonov, that I could have no idea of this when I came here. I'm very much embarrassed that I have forgotten—"

"All right, all right, that doesn't matter. You can pay tomorrow after the dinner. I simply wanted to know. Please don't—"

He broke off and began pacing the room, still more vexed. As he walked he began to stamp with his heels.

"Am I keeping you?" I asked after two minutes of silence.

"Oh!" he said, starting, "for—to be truthful—yes. I have to go and see someone—not far from here," he added in an apologetic voice, somewhat abashed.

"My goodness, why didn't you say so?" I cried, seizing my cap, with an astonishingly free-and-easy air, which was the last thing I should have expected of myself.

"It's close by—not two steps away," Simonov repeated, accompanying me to the front door with a fussy air which did not suit him at all. "So five o'clock, punctually, tomorrow," he called down the stairs after me. He was very glad to get rid of me. I was furious.

"What possessed me—what possessed me to force myself upon them?" I wondered, grinding my teeth as I strode along the street, "for a scoundrel, a swine like that Zvercov! Of course, I'd better not go;

of course, I must just snap my fingers at them. I'm not bound in any way. I'll send Simonov a note by tomorrow's mail—"

But what made me furious was that I knew for certain that I should go, that I should make a point of going; and the more tactless, the more unseemly my going would be, the more certainly I would go.

And there was a positive obstacle to my going: I had no money. All I had was nine rubles. I had to give seven of that to my servant, Apollon, for his monthly wages. That was all I paid him—he had to keep himself.

Not to pay him was impossible, considering his character. But I will talk about that fellow, about that plague of mine, another time.

However, I knew I would go and wouldn't pay him his wages.

That night I had the most hideous dreams. No wonder; all the evening I had been oppressed by memories of my miserable days at school, and I couldn't shake them off. I had been sent to the school by distant relations, upon whom I was dependent and of whom I have heard nothing since; they had sent me there a forlorn, silent boy, already crushed by their reproaches, already troubled by doubt, and looking with savage distrust at everyone. My schoolfellows met me with spiteful and merciless gibes because I was unlike any of them. But I could not endure their taunts; I could not give in to them with the ignoble readiness with which they gave in to one another. I hated them from the first, and shut myself away from everyone in timid, wounded, and disproportionate pride. Their coarseness revolted me. They laughed cynically at my face, at my clumsy figure; and yet what stupid faces they had themselves! In our school the boys' faces seemed in a special way to degenerate and grow stupider. How many fine-looking boys came to us! In a few years they became repulsive. Even at sixteen I wondered at them morosely; even then I was struck by the pettiness of their thoughts, the stupidity of their pursuits, their games, their conversations. They had no understanding of things that were so essential, they took no interest in matters that were so striking, so impressive, that I could not help considering them inferior to myself.

It was not wounded vanity that drove me to this, and for God's sake do not thrust upon me your hackneyed remarks, repeated *ad nauseam,* that "I was only a dreamer," while they even then had an understanding of life. They understood nothing, they had no idea of real life, and I swear that that was what made me most indignant about them. On the contrary, the most obvious, striking reality they accepted with fantastic stupidity and even at that time were accustomed to respect success. Everything that was just, but oppressed and looked down upon, they laughed at heartlessly and shamefully. They took rank for intelligence; even at sixteen they were already talking about a snug berth. Of course, a great deal of it was due to their stupidity, to the bad examples with which they had always been surrounded in their childhood and boyhood. They were monstrously depraved. Of course, a great deal of that, too, was superficial and an assumption of cynicism; of course, there were glimpses of youth and freshness even in their depravity; but even that freshness was not attractive, and showed itself in a certain rakishness.

I hated them horribly, though perhaps I was worse than any of them. They repaid me in the same way, and did not conceal their aversion for me. But by then I did not desire their affection: on the contrary, I continually longed for their humiliation. To escape from their derision I purposely began to make all the progress I could with my studies and forced my way to the very top. This impressed them. Moreover, they all began by degrees to grasp that I had already read books none of them could read, and understood things (not forming part of our school curriculum) of which they had not even heard. They took a savage and sarcastic view of it, but were morally impressed, especially as the teachers began to notice me on those grounds. The mockery ceased, but the hostility remained, and cold and strained relations became permanent between us. In the end I could not put up with it; with years a craving for society, for friends, developed in me. I attempted to get on friendly terms with some of my schoolfellows, but somehow or other my intimacy with them was always strained and soon ended of itself.

Once, indeed, I did have a friend. But I was already a tyrant at heart; I wanted to exercise unbounded sway over him; I tried to instill in him a contempt for his surroundings; I required of him a disdainful and complete break with those surroundings. I frightened him with my passionate affection; I reduced him to tears, to hysterics. He was a simple and devoted soul; but when he devoted himself to me entirely I began to hate him immediately and repulsed him—as though all I needed him for was to win a victory over him, to subjugate him and nothing else. But I could not subjugate all of them; my friend was not at all like them either, he was, in fact, a rare exception. The first thing I did on leaving school was to give up the special job for which I had been destined, so as to break all ties, to curse my past and shake its dust from off my feet. And goodness knows why, after all that, I should go trudging off to Simonov's!

Early next morning I roused myself and jumped out of bed with excitement, as though it were all about to happen at once. But I believed that some radical change in my life was coming, and would come inevitably on that day. Owing to its rarity, perhaps, any external event, however trivial, always made me feel as though some radical change in my life were at hand. I went to the office, however, as usual, but sneaked away home two hours earlier to get ready. The great thing, I thought, was not to be the first to arrive, or they would think me over-joyed at coming. But there were thousands of such great points to consider, and they all agitated and overwhelmed me. I polished my boots a second time with my own hands; nothing in the world would have induced Apollon to clean them twice a day, as he considered that it was more than his duties required of him. I stole the brushes to clean them from the passage, being careful he should not detect it, for fear of his contempt. Then I minutely examined my clothes and thought that everything looked old, worn, and threadbare. I had let myself get too slovenly. My uniform, perhaps, was tidy, but I could hardly go out to dinner in it. The worst of it was that there was a big yellow stain on the knees of my trousers. I had a foreboding that that stain would deprive me of nine-tenths of my personal dignity. I knew, too, that it was very bad to think so. "But this is no time for thinking: now I am in for the real thing," I thought, and my heart sank.

I knew, too, perfectly well even then, that I was monstrously ex-aggerating the facts. But how could I help it? I could not control myself and was already shaking with fever. With despair I pictured to myself how coldly and disdainfully that scoundrel Zvercov would meet me; with what dull-witted, invincible contempt that blockhead Trudolyubov would look at me; with what impudent rudeness that insect Ferfichkin would snigger at me in order to curry favor with Zvercov; how completely Simonov would take it all in, and how he would despise me for the abjectness of my vanity and lack of spirit—and worst of all, how paltry, *unliterary*, commonplace it would all be. Of course, the best thing would be not to go at all. But that was most impossible of all: if I feel impelled to do anything, I seem to be pitchforked into it. I should have jeered at myself ever afterward: "So you fell down, you fell down, you fell down when it came to the *real thing*!" On the contrary, I passionately longed to show all that "rabble" that I was by no means such a spiritless creature as I seemed to myself.

What is more, even in the acutest paroxysm of this cowardly fever, I dreamed of getting the upper hand, of dominating them, carrying them away, making them like me—if only for my "elevation of thought and unmistakable wit." They would abandon Zvercov, he would sit to one side, silent and ashamed, while I would crush him. Then, perhaps, we'd be reconciled and drink to our everlasting friendship; but what was most bitter and most humiliating for me was that I knew even then, knew fully and for certain that I really needed nothing of all this, that I did not really want to crush, to subdue, to attract them, and that I didn't really care a straw for the result, even if I did achieve it. Oh, how I prayed for the day to pass quickly! In unutterable anguish I went to the window, opened the ventilator, and looked out into the troubled darkness of the thickly falling wet snow.

At last my wretched little clock hissed out five. I seized my hat and, trying not to look at Apollon, who had been all day expecting his month's wages, but in his foolishness was unwilling to be the first to speak about it, I slipped out between him and the door and, jumping into a high-class sleigh on which I spent my last half ruble, I drove up in grand style to the Hôtel de Paris.

IV

I had been certain the day before that I should be the first to arrive. But it was not a question of being the first to arrive. Not only were they not there, but I had difficulty in finding our room. The table had not been laid even. What did it mean? After a good many questions I elicited from the waiters that the dinner had been ordered not for five but for six o'clock. This was confirmed at the bar as well. I felt really ashamed to go on questioning them. It was only twenty-five minutes past five. If they had changed the dinner hour they ought at least to have let me know—that's what the mail is for—and not put me in an absurd position in my own eyes and . . . and even before the waiters. I sat down; the servant began laying the table; I felt even more humiliated when he was present. Toward six o'clock they brought in candles, though there were lamps burning in the room. It had not occurred to the waiter, however, to bring them in at once when I arrived. In the next room two gloomy, angry-looking persons were eating their dinners in silence at two different tables. There was a great deal of noise, even shouting, in a room further away; one could hear the laughter of a crowd of people and nasty little shrieks in French: there were ladies at the dinner. It was sickening, in fact. I rarely passed more unpleasant moments, so much so that when they did arrive all together punctually at six I was overjoyed to see them, as though they were my deliverers, and even forgot that I really ought to show resentment.

Zvercov walked in at the head of them; evidently he was the leading spirit. He and all of them were laughing; but, seeing me, Zvercov drew himself up a little and walked up to me deliberately with a slight, rather jaunty bend from the waist. He shook hands with me in a friendly, but not overfriendly, fashion, with a sort of circumspect courtesy like that of a general, as though in giving me his hand he were warding off something. I had imagined, on the contrary, that on coming in he would at once break into his habitual thin, shrill laugh and fall to making his insipid jokes and witticisms. I had been preparing for them ever since the previous day, but I had not expected such conde-scension, such high-official courtesy. So, then, he felt himself ineffably superior to me in every respect! If he only meant to insult me by that high-official tone it would not matter, I thought—I could pay him back for it one way or another. But what if, in reality, without the least desire to be offensive, that muttonhead had a notion in earnest that he was superior to me and could only look at me in a patronizing way? The very supposition made me gasp.

"I was surprised to hear of your desire to join us," he began, lisping and drawling, which was something new. "You and I seem to have seen nothing of each other. You fight shy of us. You shouldn't. We're not such dreadful people as you think. Well, anyway, I am glad to renew our acquaintance."

And he turned carelessly to put down his hat on the window.

"Have you been waiting long?" Trudolyubov inquired.

"I arrived at five o'clock as you told me yesterday," I answered loudly, with an irritability that threatened an explosion.

"Didn't you let him know that we had changed the hour?" said Trudolyubov to Simonov.

"No, I didn't. I forgot," the latter replied, with no sign of regret, and, without even apologizing to me, he went off to order the hors d'oeuvres.

"So you've been here a whole hour? Oh, you poor fellow!" Zvercov cried out ironically, for to his notion this was bound to be extremely funny. That rascal Ferfichkin chimed in with his nasty little snigger, like a puppy yapping. My position struck him, too, as exquisitely ludicrous and embarrassing.

. "It isn't funny at all!" I cried to Ferfichkin, more and more irritated. "It wasn't my fault, but that of others. They neglected to let me know. It was . . . it was . . . it was simply absurd!"

"It's not only absurd, but something else as well," muttered Trudolyubov, naïvely taking my part. "You're too mild about it. It was simply rudeness—unintentional, of course. And how could Simonov— h'm!"

"If a trick like that had been played on me," observed Ferfichkin, "I'd—"

"But you should have ordered something for yourself," Zvercov interrupted, "or simply asked for dinner without waiting for us."

"You'll admit that I might have done that without your permission," I rapped out. "If I waited, it was because—"

"Let us sit down, gentlemen," called out Simonov, coming in. "Everything is ready; I can answer for the champagne; it is capitally iced. You see, I didn't know your address; where was I to look for you?" He suddenly turned to me, but again he seemed to avoid looking at me. Evidently he had something against me. It must have been what had happened yesterday.

All sat down; I did the same. It was a round table. Trudolyubov was on my left, Simonov on my right. Zvercov was sitting opposite, Ferfichkin next to him, between him and Trudolyubov.

"Tell me, are you . . . in a government office?" Zvercov went on being attentive to me. Seeing that I was embarrassed, he seriously thought that he ought to be friendly to me, and, so to speak, cheer me up.

"Does he want me to throw a bottle at his head?" I thought, in a rage. In my novel surroundings I was unnaturally ready to be irritated.

"In the N—— office," I answered jerkily, with my eyes on my plate.

"And ha-ave you a goo-ood berth? I say, what ma-a-de you leave your original job?"

"What ma-a-de me was that I wanted to leave my original job," I drawled more than he, hardly able to control myself. Ferfichkin went off into a guffaw. Simonov looked at me sarcastically. Trudolyubov left off eating and began looking at me with curiosity.

Zvercov winced, but he tried not to notice anything.

"And the remuneration?"

"What remuneration?"

"I mean, your sa-a-lary?"

"Why are you cross-examining me?" However, I told him at once what my salary was. I turned horribly red.

"It's not very handsome," Zvercov observed majestically.

"Yes, you can't afford to dine at cafés on that," Ferfichkin added insolently.

"To my thinking it's very poor," Trudolyubov observed gravely.

"And how thin you have grown! How you have changed!" added Zvercov, with a shade of venom in his voice, scanning me and my attire with a sort of insolent compassion.

"Oh, spare his blushes," cried Ferfichkin, sniggering.

"My dear Sir, allow me to tell you I am not blushing," I broke out at last: "Do you hear? I am dining here, at this café, at my own expense, not at other people's—note that, Mr. Ferfichkin."

"Wha-at? Isn't everyone here dining at his own expense? You seem to be—" Ferfichkin turned on me, becoming as red as a lobster and looking me in the face with fury.

"We won't go into tha-at," I mimicked in answer, feeling I had gone too far. "And I imagine it would be better to talk of something more intelligent."

"You intend to show off your intelligence, I suppose?"

"Don't upset yourself; that would be quite out of place here."

"Why are you jabbering away like that, my good Sir, eh? Have you gone out of your wits in your office?"

"Enough, gentlemen, enough!" Zvercov cried authoritatively.

"How stupid all this is!" muttered Simonov.

"It really is stupid. We've met here, a party of friends, for a farewell dinner to a comrade, and you carry on a fight," said Trudolyubov, rudely addressing himself to me alone. "You invited yourself to join us, so don't disturb the general harmony."

"Enough, enough!" cried Zvercov. "Quit it, gentlemen, it's out of place. Better let me tell you how I nearly got married the day before yesterday—"

And then followed a burlesque narrative of how this gentleman had almost been married two days before. There was not a word about the marriage, however, but the story was adorned with generals, colonels, and gentlemen-in-waiting, while Zvercov almost took the lead among them. It was greeted with approving laughter; Ferfichkin positively squealed.

No one paid any attention to me, and I sat crushed and humiliated.

"Good Heavens, these are not the people for me!" I thought. "And what a fool I have made of myself before them! I let Ferfichkin go too far, though. The brutes imagine they are doing me an honor in letting me sit down with them. They don't understand that it's an honor to them and not to me! I've grown thinner! My clothes! Oh, damn my trousers! Zvercov noticed the yellow stain on the knee as soon as he came in. But what's the use! I must get up at once, this very minute, take my hat and simply go without a word—with contempt! And tomorrow I can send a challenge. The scoundrels! As though I cared about the seven rubles. They may think. . . . Damn it! I don't care about the seven rubles. I'll go this minute!"

Of course I remained. I drank sherry and Lafitte by the glassful in my discomfiture. Being unaccustomed to it, I was quickly affected. My annoyance increased as the wine went to my head. I longed, all of a sudden, to insult them all in a most flagrant manner and then go away. To seize the moment and show what I could do, so that they would say: "He's clever, though he's absurd," and . . . and . . . in fact, damn them all!

I scanned them all insolently with my drowsy eyes. But they seemed to have forgotten me altogether. They were noisy, vociferous, cheerful. Zvercov was talking all the time. I began listening. Zvercov was talking of some exuberant lady whom he had at last led on to declaring her love (of course he was lying like a trooper), and how he had been helped in this affair by an intimate friend of his, a Prince Nicky, an officer in the hussars, who had three thousand serfs.

"And yet this Nicky, who has three thousand serfs, hasn't put in an appearance here tonight to see you off," I cut in suddenly.

For a minute everyone was silent. "You are drunk already." Trudolyubov deigned to notice me at last, glancing contemptuously in my direction. Zvercov, without a word, examined me as though I were an insect. I dropped my eyes. Simonov made haste to fill up the goblets with champagne.

Trudolyubov raised his goblet, as did everyone else but me.

"Your health and good luck on the journey!" he cried to Zvercov. "To old times, to our future, hurrah!"

They all tossed off their goblets and crowded around Zvercov to kiss him. I didn't stir; my full goblet stood untouched before me.

"Why, aren't you going to drink the toast?" roared Trudolyubov, losing patience and turning menacingly to me.

"I want to make a speech separately, on my own account—and then I'll drink to it, Mr. Trudolyubov."

"Spiteful brute!" muttered Simonov.

I drew myself up in my chair and feverishly seized my goblet, prepared for something extraordinary, though I did not know myself precisely what I was going to say.

"*Silence!*" cried Ferfichkin. "Now for a display of wit!"

Zvercov waited very gravely, knowing what was coming.

"Lieutenant Zvercov, Sir," I began, "let me tell you that I hate phrases, phrasemongers, and men who wear corsets—that's the first point, and there's a second one to follow it."

There was a general stir.

"The second point is: I hate loose talk and loose talkers. Especially loose talkers! The third point: I love justice, truth, and honesty." I went on almost mechanically, for I was beginning to shiver with horror myself and had no idea how I had come to be talking like this. "I love thought, Monsieur Zvercov; I love true comradeship, on an equal footing and not—h'm! I love—but, however, why not? I'll drink your health, too, Monsieur Zvercov. Seduce the Circassian girls, shoot the enemies of the fatherland, and—and—here's to your health, Monsieur Zvercov!"

Zvercov got up from his seat, bowed to me, and said:

"I'm very much obliged to you." He was frightfully offended and had turned pale.

"Damn the fellow!" roared Trudolyubov, bringing his fist down on the table.

"Well, he ought to get a punch in the nose for that," squealed Ferfichkin.

"We ought to turn him out," muttered Simonov.

"Not a word, gentlemen, not a move!" cried Zvercov gravely, checking the general indignation. "I thank you all, but I am able to show him myself how much value I attach to his words."

"Mr. Ferfichkin, you will give me satisfaction tomorrow for your words just now!" I said aloud, turning with dignity to Ferfichkin.

"A duel, you mean? Certainly," he answered. But probably I was so ridiculous as I challenged him, and it was so out of keeping with my appearance, that everyone, including Ferfichkin, was prostrate with laughter.

"Yes, let him alone, of course! He's quite drunk," Trudolyubov said with disgust.

"I'll never forgive myself for letting him join us," Simonov muttered again.

"Now is the time to throw a bottle at their heads," I thought to myself. I picked up the bottle—and filled my glass.

"No, I'd better sit on to the end," I went on thinking; "you would be pleased, my friends, if I went away. Nothing will induce me to go. I'll go on sitting here and drinking to the end, on purpose, just to show that I don't think you of the slightest consequence. I'll go on sitting and drinking, because this is a tavern and I paid my entrance money. I'll sit here and drink, for I look upon you as so many pawns, so many inanimate pawns. I'll sit here and drink—and sing if I want to. Yes, sing, for I have the right to—to sing. H'm!"

But I did not sing. I simply tried not to look at any of them. I assumed various attitudes, ever so unconcerned, and waited with impatience for them to speak *first*. But alas, they did not address me! And oh, how I wished at that moment to be reconciled to them! It struck eight, and nine, at last. They moved from the table to the sofa. Zvercov stretched himself on a lounge and put one foot on a round table. Wine was brought there. He did, as a fact, order three bottles on his own account. I, of course, was not invited to join them. They all sat round him on the sofa. They listened to him, almost with reverence. It was evident that they were fond of him.

"What for? What for?" I wondered. From time to time they were moved to drunken enthusiasm and kissed one another. They talked of the Caucasus, of the nature of true passion, of snug berths in the Service, of the income of an hussar called Podharzhevski, whom none of them knew personally, and rejoiced at the hugeness of it, at the extraordinary grace and beauty of a Princess D——, whom none of them had ever seen; then it came to Shakespeare's being immortal.

I smiled contemptuously and walked up and down the other side of the room, opposite the sofa, from the table to the stove and back again. I tried my very utmost to show them that I could do without them, and yet I purposely made a noise with my shoes, thumping my heels. But it was all in vain. They paid no attention. I had the patience to walk up and down in front of them from eight o'clock till eleven, in the same place, from the table to the stove and back again. "I walk up and down to please myself, and no one can prevent me." The waiter who came into the room stopped, from time to time, to look at me. I was somewhat giddy from turning round so often; at moments it seemed to me that I was in delirium. During those three hours I was three times soaked with sweat and dry again.

At times, with an intense, acute pang, I was stabbed to the heart by the thought that ten years, twenty years, forty years would pass, and that even in forty years I would remember with loathing and humiliation those filthiest, most ludicrous, and most awful moments of my life. No one could have gone out of his way to degrade himself more shamelessly, and I fully realized it fully, and yet I went on pacing up and down from the table to the stove. "Oh, if you only knew what thoughts and feelings I am capable of, how cultured I am!" I thought at moments, mentally addressing the sofa on which my enemies were sitting. But my enemies behaved as though I were not in the room. Once—only once—they turned toward me, just when Zvercov was talking about Shakespeare, and I suddenly gave a contemptuous laugh. I laughed in such an affected and disgusting way that they all at once broke off their conversation and silently and gravely for two minutes watched me walking up and down from the table to the stove, *taking no notice of them*. But nothing came of it: they said nothing, and two minutes later they ceased to notice me again. It struck eleven.

"Friends," cried Zvercov, getting up from the sofa, "let us all go *there* now!"

"Of course, of course," the others assented. I turned sharply to Zvercov. I was so harassed, so exhausted, that I would have cut my throat to put an end to it. I was in a fever; my hair, soaked with perspiration, stuck to my forehead and temples.

"Zvercov, I beg your pardon," I said abruptly and resolutely. "Ferfichkin, yours, too, and everyone's, everyone's: I have insulted you all!"

"Aha! A duel is not in your line, old man," Ferfichkin got out venomously through clenched teeth.

It sent a sharp pang to my heart.

"No, it's not the duel I'm afraid of, Ferfichkin! I'm ready to fight you tomorrow, after we're reconciled. I insist upon it, in fact, and you cannot refuse. I want to show you that I am not afraid of a duel. You'll fire first and I'll fire into the air."

"He's comforting himself," said Simonov.

"He's simply raving," said Trudolyubov.

"Look, let us pass. Why are you barring our way? What do you want?" Zvercov answered disdainfully.

They were all flushed; their eyes were bright; they had been drinking heavily.

"I ask for your friendship, Zvercov; I insulted you, but—"

"Insulted? *You* insulted *me?* Understand, Sir, that you never, under any circumstances, could possibly insult *me.*"

"And that's enough for you. Out of the way!" concluded Trudolyubov.

"Olympia is mine, friends, that's agreed!" cried Zvercov.

"We won't dispute your right, we won't dispute your right," the others answered, laughing.

I stood there as though they had spat upon me. The party went noisily out of the room. Trudolyubov struck up some stupid song. Simonov remained behind for a moment to tip the waiters. I suddenly went up to him.

"Simonov, give me six rubles!" I said with desperate resolution.

He looked at me in extreme amazement, with vacant eyes. He, too, was drunk.

"You don't mean you're coming with us?"

"Yes."

"I've no money," he snapped out, and with a scornful laugh he went toward the door.

I clutched at his overcoat. It was a nightmare.

"Simonov, I saw you had money. Why do you refuse me? Am I a scoundrel? Beware of refusing me: if you knew, if you but knew why I'm asking! My whole future, my whole plans depend upon it!"

Simonov pulled out the money and almost flung it at me.

"Take it, if you have no sense of shame!" he uttered pitilessly, and ran to overtake the others.

I was left alone for a moment. Disorder, the remains of dinner, a broken wineglass on the floor, spilt wine, cigarette ends, fumes of drink and delirium in my brain, an agonizing misery in my heart and finally the waiter, who had seen and heard all and was looking inquisitively into my face.

"I'm going there!" I cried. "Either they'll all go down on their knees to beg for my friendship or I'll give Zvercov a slap in the face!"

V

"So this is it, this is it at last—contact with real life," I muttered as I ran headlong down the stairs. "This is very different from the

Pope's leaving Rome and going to Brazil, very different from the ball on Lake Como!"

"You're a scoundrel," a thought flashed through my mind, "if you laugh at this now."

"No matter!" I cried, answering myself. "Now everything is lost!"

There was no trace to be seen of them, but that made no difference— I knew where they had gone.

At the steps stood a solitary nighthawk of a sleigh driver in a rough peasant coat, powdered over with the still-falling snow, wet and seemingly warm. It felt hot and steamy. The little shaggy piebald horse was also covered with snow and wheezing—I remember that very well. I made a rush for the ramshackle sleigh, but as soon as I raised my foot to get into it, the recollection of how Simonov had just given me six rubles seemed to double me up and I tumbled into the sledge like a sack.

"No, I must do a great deal to make up for all this!" I cried. "But I will make up for it or perish on the spot this very night. Get going!" I told the driver.

We set off. My head was all in a whirl.

"They won't go down on their knees to beg for my friendship. That's a mirage, a cheap mirage, revolting, romantic, and fantastical— that's another ball on Lake Como. And so I'm bound to slap Zvercov's face! It's my duty to. And so it's settled; I'm rushing to give him a slap in the face. Hurry up!"

The driver tugged at the reins.

"Soon as I go in I'll let him have it. Should I say a few words by way of preface before giving him a slap in the face? No. I'll simply go in and let him have it. They will all be sitting in the drawing room, and he with Olympia on the sofa. That damned Olympia! She laughed at my looks on one occasion and turned me down. I'll pull Olympia's hair, pull Zvercov's ears! No, better one ear, and drag him by it round the room. Maybe they'll all begin beating me and will kick me out. That's most likely, indeed. No matter! Anyway, I'll first slap him; the initiative will be mine; and by the laws of honor that's everything: he'll be branded and unable to wipe off the slap by any blows, by nothing short of a duel. He'll be forced to fight. And let them beat me now. Let them, the ungrateful wretches! Trudolyubov will beat me hardest, he's so strong; Ferfichkin will be sure to edge in and tug at my hair. But no matter, no matter! That's what I'm going for. The blockheads will be forced at last to see the tragedy of it all! When they drag me to the door I'll call out to them that in reality they're not worth my little finger. Hurry, driver, hurry!" I cried. He started and flicked his whip, so savagely had I shouted.

"We'll fight at daybreak, that's settled. I've done with my job. Ferfichkin made fun of it just now. But where can I get pistols? Nonsense! I'll get my salary in advance and buy them. And powder and bullets? That's the second's business. And how can it all be done by daybreak? And where am I to get a second? I have no friends. Nonsense!" I cried, working myself up more and more. "It's of no consequence! The first person I meet in the street is bound to be my second, just as he would be bound to pull a drowning man out of water. The most peculiar things may happen. Even if I were to ask the director himself to be my second tomorrow, he'd be bound to consent, if only from a feeling of chivalry, and to keep the secret! Anton Antonich—"

The fact is that at that very minute the disgusting absurdity of my plan and the other side of the question was clearer and more vivid to my imagination than it could be to anyone else on earth. But—

"Hurry, driver! Hurry, you! Hurry!"

"Yes, Sir!" said the son of toil, and grunted.

Cold shivers suddenly ran down my back. Wouldn't it be better to . . . go straight home? My God, my God! Why did I invite myself to this dinner yesterday? But no, it's impossible. And my pacing up and down for three hours from the table to the stove? No, they, *they* and no one else must pay for that promenade of mine! They must wipe out that dishonor! Drive on!

And what if they give me into custody? They won't dare! They'll be afraid of the scandal. And what if Zvercov is so contemptuous that he refuses to fight a duel? He's sure to; but in that case I'll show them! I'll turn up at the posting station when he is setting off tomorrow, I'll catch him by the leg, I'll pull off his coat when he gets into the carriage. I'll sink my teeth into his hand, I'll bite him. "See what lengths you can drive a desperate man to!" He may hit me on the head and they may belabor me from behind. I'll shout to the assembled multitude: "Look at this puppy who's driving off to captivate the Circassian girls after letting me spit in his face!"

Of course, after that everything will be over! The office will have vanished off the face of the earth. I shall be arrested, I shall be tried, I shall be dismissed from the Service, thrown in prison, sent to Siberia. Never mind! In fifteen years when they let me out of prison I'll trudge off to him, a beggar, in rags. I shall find him in some provincial town.

He'll be married and happy. He'll have a grown-up daughter. . . . I'll say to him: "Look, monster, at my hollow cheeks and my rags! I've lost everything—my career, my happiness, art, science, *the woman I loved,* and all through you. Here are pistols. I have come to discharge my pistol in the air and—and—I forgive you. Then I'll fire into the air and he'll hear nothing more of me. . . ."

I was actually on the point of tears, though I knew perfectly well at that moment that all this was out of Pushkin's *Sylvio* and Lermontov's *Masquerade.* And all at once I felt horribly ashamed, so ashamed that I stopped the horse, got out of the sleigh, and stood still in the snow in the middle of the street. The driver gazed at me with a gasping wonder.

What was I to do? I could not go on there—it was evidently stupid, and I could not leave things as they were, because that would seem as though . . . Heavens, how could I leave things just so? And after such insults! "No!" I cried, throwing myself into the sleigh again. "It is ordained! It is fate! Drive on, drive on!"

And in my impatience I hit the back of the driver's neck.

"What are you up to? What are you hitting me for?" the peasant shouted, but he whipped up his nag so that it began kicking.

The snow was falling in big wet flakes; I opened my coat in spite of that. I forgot everything else, for I had finally decided on slapping Zvercov's face, and felt with horror that the thing was going to happen *now, at once,* and that *no force could stop it.* The deserted street lamps gleamed sullenly in the snowy darkness like torches at a funeral. The snow drifted under my greatcoat, under my coat, under my cravat, and melted there. I did not wrap myself up—all was lost, anyway.

At last we arrived. I jumped out, almost unconscious, ran up the steps, and began knocking and kicking at the door. I felt fearfully weak, particularly in my legs and knees. The door was opened quickly as though they knew I was coming. As a fact, Simonov had warned them that perhaps another gentleman would arrive, and this was a place in which one had to give notice and to observe certain precautions. It was one of those *millinery emporia* which the police had closed down some time ago. By day it really was a shop; but at night, if one had an introduction, one might visit it for other purposes.

I walked rapidly through the dark shop into the familiar drawing room, where there was only one candle burning, and stood still in amazement: there was no one there. "Where are they?" I asked somebody. But by now, of course, they had separated. Before me was standing a person with a stupid smile, the *madam* herself, who had seen me before. A minute later a door opened and another person came in.

Taking no notice of anything, I strode about the room and, I believe, I talked to myself. I felt as though I had been saved from death and was conscious of this, joyfully, all over: I should have given that slap, I should certainly, certainly have given it! But now they were not here and . . . everything had vanished and changed! I looked around. I could not realize my condition yet. I looked mechanically at the girl who had come in, and had a glimpse of a fresh, young, rather pale face, with straight, dark eyebrows, and with grave, as it were wondering, eyes that attracted me at once; I should have hated her if she had been smiling. I began looking at her more intently and with something like an effort. I had not fully collected my thoughts. There was something simple and good-natured in her face, yet somehow strangely grave. I am sure that this stood in her way here, and no one of those fools had noticed her. She could not, however, have been called a beauty, though she was tall, strong-looking, and well built. She was very simply dressed. Something loathsome stirred within me. I went straight up to her.

I chanced to look into the glass. My harassed face struck me as revolting in the extreme, pale, wrought-up, abject, with disheveled hair. "No matter, I'm glad of it," I thought: "I'm glad I'll seem repulsive to her; I like that."

VI

Somewhere behind a screen a clock began wheezing, as though oppressed by something, as though someone were strangling it. After an unnaturally prolonged wheezing there followed a shrill, nasty, and, as it were, unexpectedly rapid, chime—as though someone were suddenly leaping forward. It struck two. I woke up, though I hadn't really been asleep but lying half conscious.

It was almost completely dark in the narrow, cramped, low-ceiled room, cumbered up with an enormous wardrobe and piles of cardboard boxes and all sorts of frippery and litter. The candle end that had been burning on the table was going out and gave a faint flicker from time to time. In a few minutes there would be complete darkness.

I was not long in coming to myself; everything came back to my mind at once, without an effort, as though it had been in ambush to pounce out on me again. And, indeed, even while I was unconscious a point seemed continually to remain in my memory unforgotten, and round it my dreams moved drearily. But, strange to say, everything that had happened to me in that day seemed to me now, on waking, to be in the far, faraway past, as though I had long, long since lived all that down.

My head was full of fumes. Something seemed to be hovering over me, rousing me, exciting me, and making me restless. Misery and spite seemed surging up in me again and seeking an outlet. Suddenly I saw beside me two wide-open eyes scrutinizing me curiously and persistently. The look in those eyes was coldly detached, sullen, utterly remote, as it were; it weighed upon me.

A grim idea came into my brain and passed all over my body, as a horrible sensation, such as one feels when one goes into a damp and moldy cellar. There was something unnatural in those two eyes, beginning to look at me only now. I recalled, too, that during those two hours I had not said a single word to this creature, and had, in fact, considered it utterly superfluous; in fact, the silence had for some reason gratified me. Now I suddenly realized vividly the hideous idea— revolting as a spider—of vice, which, without love, grossly and shamelessly begins with that in which true love finds its consummation. For a long time we gazed at each other like that, but she did not drop her eyes before mine and her expression did not change, so that at last I felt uncomfortable.

"What is your name?" I asked abruptly, to put an end to it.

"Liza," she answered almost in a whisper, but somehow far from graciously, and she turned her eyes away.

I was silent.

"What weather! The snow is disgusting!" I said, almost to myself, putting my arm under my head despondently and gazing at the ceiling.

She made no answer. This was horrible.

"Have you always lived in Petersburg?" I asked a minute later, almost angrily, turning my head slightly toward her.

"No."

"Where do you come from?"

"From Riga," she answered reluctantly.

"Are you a German?"

"No, Russian."

"Have you been here long?"

"Where?"

"In this house?"

"A fortnight."

She spoke more and more jerkily. The candle went out; I could no longer distinguish her face.

"Have you a father and mother?"

"Yes . . . no. Yes, I have."

"Where are they?"

"There—in Riga."

"Who are they?"

"Oh, nobody in particular."

"Nobody? Why, what do they do?"

"They're tradespeople."

"Have you always lived with them?"

"Yes."

"How old are you?"

"Twenty."

"Why did you leave them?"

"Oh, for no special reason."

That answer meant "Let me alone; I feel sick, sad."

We were silent.

God knows why I did not go away. I felt myself more and more sick and dreary. The images of the previous day began of themselves, apart from my will, flitting through my memory in confusion. I suddenly recalled something I had seen that morning when, full of anxious thoughts, I was hurrying to the office.

"I saw them carrying a coffin out yesterday and they nearly dropped it," I suddenly said aloud, not that I desired to open the conversation, but by accident, as it were.

"A coffin?"

"Yes, in the Hay Market; they were bringing it up out of a cellar."

"From a cellar?"

"Not from a cellar, but from a basement. Oh, you know—from somewhere underground—from a sporting house. It was all so filthy there. Eggshells, rubbish, stink. It was loathsome."

Silence.

"A nasty day to be buried," I began, simply to avoid being silent.

"Nasty—in what way?"

"The snow, the wet." (I yawned.)

"It makes no difference," she said suddenly, after a brief silence.

"No, it's horrid." (I yawned again.) "The gravediggers must have sworn at getting wet from the snow. And there must have been water in the grave."

"Why should there be water in the grave?" she asked with a sort of curiosity, but speaking even more harshly and abruptly than before. I suddenly began to feel provoked.

"Why, there must have been water at the bottom a foot deep. You can't dig a dry grave in Volkovo Cemetery."

"Why?"

"Why? Because the place is quaggy. It's a regular marsh. So they bury them in water. I've seen it myself—many times."

(I had never seen it once; as a matter of fact, I'd never been in Volkovo and had only heard stories of it.)

"Do you mean to say, you don't mind how you die?"

"But why should I die?" she answered, as though defending herself.

"Why, some day you'll die, and you'll die just the same as that dead woman. She was a—girl—like you. She died of consumption."

"A tart would have died in a hospital . . ." (She knows all about it already: she said *tart,* not *girl.*)

"She was in debt to her madam," I retorted, more and more provoked by the discussion; "and went on earning money for her up to the end, though she had consumption. The sleigh drivers standing about were talking about her to some soldiers and telling them so. No doubt they knew her. They were laughing. They were going to meet in a pothouse to drink to her memory."

A great deal of this was my own invention. Silence followed, profound silence. She did not stir.

"And is it better to die in a hospital?"

"Isn't it just the same? Besides, why should I die?" she added irritably.

"If not now, a little later."

"Why a little later?"

"Why, indeed? Now you're young, not bad-looking, fresh, you fetch a high price. But after another year of this life you'll be very different— you'll pop off."

"In a year?"

"Anyway, in a year you'll be worth less," I continued maliciously. "You'll go from here to something lower, to some other house; a year later—to a third, lower and lower, and in seven years you will come to a basement around the Hay Market. That is, if you're lucky. But it would be much worse if you got some disease, tuberculosis, say. All you have to do is catch a chill or something. It's not easy to get over an illness in your way of life. If you catch anything you may not get rid of it. And so you'll die."

"Oh, well, then I'll die," she answered quite vindictively, and she made a quick movement.

"Still, one feels sorry."

"Sorry for whom? Or what?"

"Sorry for life."

Silence.

"Were you ever engaged? Eh?"

"What's it to you?"

"Oh, I'm not cross-examining you. It's nothing to me. Why are you so cross? Of course you may have had your own troubles. What's it to me? It's simply that I felt sorry."

"Sorry for whom?"

"Sorry for you."

"No need," she whispered hardly audibly, and again made a faint movement.

That incensed me at once. What! I was so gentle with her, but she—

"Why, do you think that you're on the right path?"

"I don't think anything."

"That's just what's wrong. You don't think. Come to your senses while there's still time. There still *is* time. You are still young, not bad-looking; you might love, be married, be happy—"

"Not all married women are happy," she snapped in the rude, abrupt tone she had used at first.

"Not all, of course, but anyway it's much better than the life here. Infinitely better. Besides, with love one can live even without happiness. Even in sorrow life is sweet; life is sweet however one lives. But here— what is there except . . . filth? Phew!"

I turned away with disgust; I was no longer reasoning coldly. I myself began to feel what I was saying and warmed to the subject. I was already longing to expound the cherished ideas I had brooded over in my cubbyhole. Something suddenly flared up in me. An object had appeared before me.

"Never mind my being here, I'm no example for you. I am, perhaps, worse than you are. I was drunk when I came here, though," I nevertheless hastened to say in self-defense. "Besides, a man is no example for a woman. It's a different thing. I may degrade and defile myself, but I'm not anybody's slave. I come and go, and that's the end of it.

I shake it off and I'm a different man. But you are a slave from the start. Yes, a slave! You give up everything, your whole freedom. If you want to break your chains afterward, you won't be able to: you'll get more and more tangled. It's an accursed bondage. I know it. I won't speak of anything else, maybe you won't understand, but tell me: no doubt you're in debt to your madam? There, you see," I added, though she made no answer, but only listened in silence, entirely absorbed, "that's bondage for you! You'll never buy your freedom. They'll see to that. It's like selling your soul to the Devil. And besides, perhaps I, too, am just as unlucky—how do you know—and wallow in the mud on purpose, out of misery? You know, men take to drink from grief; well, maybe I'm here from grief. Come, tell me, what is there good here? Here you and I . . . came together . . . just now and didn't say a single word to each other all the time, and it was only afterward you began staring at me like a wild creature, and I at you. Is that love? Is that how one human being should meet another? It's hideous, that's what it is!"

"Yes!" she assented sharply and quickly.

I was positively astounded by the promptitude of this "Yes." So the same thought may have been straying through her mind when she was staring at me just before. So she, too, was capable of certain thoughts? "Damn it all, this was interesting, this was a point of likeness!" I thought, almost rubbing my hands. And indeed it's easy to turn a young soul like that!

It was the exercise of my power that attracted me most.

She turned her head nearer to me, and it seemed to me in the darkness that she propped herself on her arm. Perhaps she was scrutinizing me. How I regretted that I could not see her eyes. I heard her deep breathing.

"Why have you come here?" I asked her, with a note of authority already in my voice.

"Oh, I don't know."

"But how fine it would be to be living in your father's house! It's warm, and no one bothers you; you have a home of your own."

"But what if it's worse than this?"

"I must take the right tone," flashed through my mind. "I may not get far with sentimentality." But it was only a momentary thought. I swear she really did interest me. Besides, I was exhausted and moody. And cunning so easily goes hand-in-hand with feeling.

"Who denies it!" I hastened to answer. "Anything may happen. I am convinced that someone has wronged you, and that you are more sinned against than sinning. Of course, I know nothing of your story, but it's not likely a girl like you has come here of her own inclination. . . ."

"A girl like me?" she whispered, hardly audibly; but I heard it.

Damn it all, I was flattering her. That was horrid. But perhaps it was a good thing. . . . She was silent.

"Look, Liza, I'll tell you about myself. If I had had a home from childhood, I shouldn't be what I am now. I often think that. However bad it may be at home, anyway they are your father and mother, and not enemies, strangers. Once a year, at least, they'll show their love of you. Anyhow, you know you are at home. I grew up without a home, and perhaps that's why I've turned so—unfeeling."

I waited again. "Perhaps she doesn't understand," I thought, "and, indeed, it's absurd, this moralizing."

"If I were a father and had a daughter, I believe I'd really love my daughter more than my sons," I began indirectly, as though talking of something else, to distract her attention. I must confess I blushed.

"Why so?" she asked.

Ah! so she was listening!

"I don't know, Liza. I knew a father who was a stern, austere man, but used to go down on his knees to his daughter, used to kiss her hands, her feet, he couldn't make enough of her, really. When she danced at parties he used to stand for five hours at a stretch, gazing at her. He was mad over her: I understand that! She'd fall asleep tired at night, and he'd wake to kiss her in her sleep and make the sign of the cross over her. He would go about in a dirty old coat, he was stingy to everyone else, but would spend his last penny for her, giving her expensive presents, and it was his greatest delight when she was pleased with what he gave her. Fathers always love their daughters more than the mothers do. Some girls live happily at home! And I believe I'd never let my daughters marry."

"What next?" she asked with a faint smile.

"I'd be jealous, I really should. To think that she should kiss anyone else! That she should love a stranger more than her father! It's painful to imagine it. Of course, that's all nonsense; of course, every father would be reasonable at last. But I believe before I should let her marry I'd worry myself to death; I'd find fault with all her suitors. But I'd end by letting her marry whomever she herself loved. The one whom the daughter loves always seems the worst to the father, you know. That's always so. So many family troubles come from that."

"Some are glad to sell their daughters rather than to marry them off honorably."

Ah, so that was it!

"Such a thing, Liza, happens in those accursed families in which there is neither love nor God," I retorted warmly, "and where there is no love, there is no sense either. There are such families, it's true, but I am not speaking of them. You must have seen wickedness in your own family, if you talk like that. Truly, you must have been unlucky. H'm! That sort of thing mostly comes about through poverty."

"And is it any better with the gentry? Even among the poor, honest people live happily."

"H'm . . . yes. Perhaps. Another thing, Liza, man is fond of reckoning up his troubles, but does not count his joys. If he counted them up as he ought, he'd see that every lot has enough happiness provided for it. And what if all goes well with the family, if the blessing of God is upon it, if the husband is a good one, loves you, cherishes you, never leaves you! There's happiness in such a family! Even sometimes there is happiness in the midst of sorrow; and indeed sorrow is everywhere. If you marry *you will find out for yourself*. But think of the first years of married life with one you love: what happiness, what happiness there sometimes is in it! And indeed it's the usual thing. In those early days even quarrels with one's husband end happily. Some women get up quarrels with their husbands just because they love them. Indeed, I knew a woman like that: she seemed to say that because she loved him she'd torment him and make him feel it. You know that you may torment a man on purpose through love. Women are particularly given to that, thinking to themselves 'I will love him so, I will make so much of him afterward, that it's no sin to torment him a little now.' And all in the house rejoice at the sight of you, and you are happy and gay and peaceful and honored. Then there are some women who are jealous. I knew one such woman; she couldn't restrain herself, but would jump up at night and run off on the sly to find out where he was, if he went off anywhere, whether he was with some other woman. That's a pity. And the woman knows herself it's wrong, and her heart fails her and she suffers, but she loves—it's all through love. And how sweet it is to make up after quarrels, to own herself in the wrong or to forgive him! And they are both suddenly so happy—as though they had met anew, been married over again, as though their love had begun afresh. And no one, no one should know what passes between husband and wife if they love one another. And whatever quarrels there may be between them, they ought not to call in even their own mothers to judge between them and tell tales of one another. They are their own judges. Love is a holy mystery and ought to be hidden from all other eyes, whatever happens. That makes it holier and better. They respect one another more, and much is built on respect. And if once there has been love, if they have been married for love, why should love pass away? Surely one can keep it! It is rare that one can't keep it. And if the husband is kind and straightforward, why should not love last? The first phase of married love will pass, it's true, but then there will come a love that is better still. Then there will be the union of souls, they will have everything in common, there'll be no secrets between them. And once they have children, the most difficult times will seem to them happy, so long as there is love and courage. Even toil will be a joy; you may deny yourself bread for your children and even that will be a joy. They'll love you for it afterward, so you are putting something away for your future. As the children grow up you feel that you're an example, a support for them; that even after you die, your children will always keep your thoughts and feelings, because they have received them from you; they will take on your semblance and likeness. So you see this is a great duty. How can it fail to draw the father and mother nearer? People say it's a trial to have children. Who says that? It is heavenly happiness! Are you fond of little children, Liza? I'm awfully fond of them. You know—a little rosy baby boy at your bosom, and what husband's heart isn't touched, seeing his wife nursing his child! A plump little rosy baby, sprawling and snuggling, chubby little hands and feet, clean tiny little nails, so tiny that it makes one laugh to look at them; eyes that look as if they understand everything. And while it sucks it clutches at your bosom with its little hand and plays. When its father comes up, the child tears itself away from the bosom, flings itself back, looks at its father, laughs, as though it were fearfully funny, and falls to sucking again. Or it will bite its mother's breast when its little teeth are coming, while it looks sideways at her, with its little eyes as though to say, 'Look, I'm biting!' Isn't it happiness when the three are together, husband, wife, and child? One can forgive a great deal for the sake of such moments. Yes, Liza, one must first learn to live oneself before one blames others!"

"It's by pictures, pictures like that one must get at you," I thought to myself, though I did speak with real feeling, and all at once I flushed crimson. "What if she were suddenly to burst out laughing, what should I do then?" That idea drove me to fury. Toward the end of my speech

I really was excited, and now my vanity was somehow wounded. The silence continued. I almost nudged her.

"Why are you—" she began and stopped. But I understood: there was a quiver of something different in her voice, not abrupt, harsh, and unyielding as before, but something soft and shamefaced, so shamefaced that I suddenly felt ashamed and guilty.

"What?" I asked with tender curiosity.

"Why, you—"

"What?"

"Why, you—talk like a book, somehow," she said, and again there was a note of irony in her voice.

That remark sent a pang through my heart. It wasn't what I had been expecting.

I did not understand that she was hiding her feelings under irony, that this is usually the last refuge of modest and chaste-souled people when the privacy of their soul is coarsely and unfeelingly invaded, and that their pride makes them refuse to surrender till the last moment and shrink from giving expression to their feelings before you. I ought to have guessed the truth from the timidity with which she had repeatedly approached her sarcasm, only bringing herself to utter it at last with an effort. But I did not guess, and an evil feeling took possession of me.

"Wait a bit!" I thought.

VII

"Oh, hush, Liza! How can you talk about talking like a book, when it makes even me, an outsider, feel sick? Though I don't look at it as an outsider, for, indeed, it touches me to the heart. Is it possible—is it possible that you do not feel sick at being here yourself? Evidently habit does wonders! God knows what habit can do with anyone. Can you seriously think that you'll never grow old, that you'll never lose your looks, and that they'll keep you here for ever and ever? I say nothing of the loathsomeness of the life here. Though let me tell you this about it—about your present life, I mean; here though you are young now, attractive, nice, with soul and feeling, yet you know as soon as I came to myself just now I felt at once sick at being here with you! One can only come here when one is drunk. But if you were anywhere else, living as good people live, I would perhaps be more than attracted by you, fall in love with you, be glad of a look from you, let alone a word; I'd hang about your door, go down on my knees to you, look upon you as my betrothed and think it an honor. I would not dare to have an impure thought about you. But here, you see, I know that I have only to whistle and you have to come with me whether you like it or not. I don't consult your wishes, but you mine. The lowest laborer hires himself as a work-man but he doesn't make a slave of himself altogether; besides, he knows that he will be free again presently. But when are you free? Only think what you're giving up here! What are you enslaving? Your soul, together with your body; you're selling your soul, which you have no right to dispose of! You give your love to be outraged by every drunk-ard! Love! But that's everything, you know, it's a priceless diamond, it's a maiden's treasure; love—why, a man would be ready to give his soul, to face death to gain that love. But how much is your love worth now? You are sold, all of you, body and soul, and there's no need to strive for love when one can have everything without love. And you know there's no greater insult to a girl than that, do you understand? To be sure, I've heard that they comfort you poor fools, they let you have lovers of your own here. But you know that's simply a farce, that's simply a sham, it's just mockery, and you're taken in by it! Why, do you suppose he really loves you, that lover of yours? I don't believe it. How can he love you when he knows you may be called away from him any minute? He would be a low fellow if he did! Will he have a grain of respect for you? What have you in common with him? He laughs at you and robs you—that's all his love amounts to! You are lucky if he doesn't beat you. Very likely he does beat you, too. Ask him, if you have got one, whether he'll marry you. He'll laugh in your face, if he doesn't spit in it or give you a blow—though maybe he isn't worth a damn himself. And for what have you ruined your life, if you come to think of it? For the coffee they give you to drink and the plentiful meals? But with what object are they fattening you? An honest girl couldn't swallow the food, for she'd know what she was being fed for. You're in debt here, and, of course, you'll always be in debt, and you will go on being in debt to the very end, till the visitors here begin to scorn you. And that'll happen soon enough. Don't rely upon your youth—all that flies by express here, you know. You'll be kicked out. And not simply kicked out; long before that the madam will begin nagging at you, scolding you, abusing you, as though you had not sacrificed your health for her, had not thrown away your youth and your soul for her benefit, but as though you had ruined her, beggared her, robbed her. And don't expect anyone to take your part: the others, your companions, will attack you, too, to win her favor, for all are in slavery here, and here they have lost all conscience and pity long ago. They have become utterly vile, and nothing on earth is viler, more loathsome, and more insulting than their abuse. And you're laying down everything here, unconditionally, youth and health and beauty and hope, and at twenty-two you will look like a woman of five-and-thirty, and you'll be lucky if you're not diseased; pray to God to save you from that! No doubt you are thinking now that you have a fine time and no work to do! Yet there is no work harder or more dreadful in the world or ever has been. One would think that the heart alone would be worn out with tears. And you won't dare to say a word, not half a word, when they drive you away from here; you'll go away as though you were to blame. You'll change to another house, then to a third, then somewhere else, till you come down at last to the Hay Market. There you'll be beaten at every turn; that's good manners there, the visitors don't know how to be friendly without beating you. You don't believe that it's so hateful there? Go and look for yourself some time, you can see with your own eyes. Once, one New Year's Day, I saw a woman at a door. They had turned her out as a joke, to give her a taste of the frost because she had been crying so much, and they shut the door behind her. At nine o'clock in the morning she was already quite drunk, disheveled, half naked, covered with bruises, her face was powdered but she had a black eye, blood was trickling from her nose and her teeth; some cabman had just given her a drubbing. She was sitting on the stone steps, a salt fish of some sort in her hand; she was crying, wailing something about her luck and slapping the fish on the steps, and cabmen and drunken soldiers were crowding in the doorway taunting her. You don't believe that you'll ever get to be like that? I'd be sorry to believe it, too, but how do you know—maybe ten years, eight years ago, that very woman with the salt fish came here fresh as a cherub, innocent, pure, knowing no evil, blushing at every word. Perhaps she was like you, proud, ready to take offense, not like the others; perhaps she looked like a queen, and knew what happiness was in store for the man who should love her and whom she should love. Do you see how it ended? And what if at that very moment when she was pounding her salted fish on the filthy steps, drunken and disheveled—what if at that very moment she recalled the early days of her purity in her father's house, when she used to go to school and the neighbor's son watched for her on the way, declaring that he'd love her as long as he lived, that he'd devote his life to her, and when they vowed to love one another for ever and be married as soon as they were grown up! No, Liza, it would be happy for you if you were to die soon of tuberculosis in some corner, in some cellar like that woman just now. In the hospital, do you say? You'll be lucky if they take you, but what if you are still of use to the madam here? Tuberculosis is a queer disease; it's not like fever. The patient goes on hoping till the last minute and says he's all right. He deludes himself. And that just suits your madam. Never doubt it, that's how it is. You've sold your soul, and what is more, you owe money, so you daren't say a word. But when you're dying, everyone will abandon you, everyone will turn away from you, for then there will be nothing to get from you. What's more, they will reproach you for cumbering the place, for being so long over dying. However you beg you won't get a drink of water without abuse: 'Whenever are you going off, you nasty hussy, you won't let us sleep with your moaning, you make the gentlemen sick.' That's true, I've heard such things said myself. They will thrust you dying into the filthiest corner in the cellar—in the damp and the darkness; what will your thoughts be, lying there alone? When you die, strange hands will lay you out, with grumbling and impatience; no one will bless you, no one will sigh for you, all they want is to get rid of you as soon as possible; they'll buy a coffin, drag you to the grave as they did that poor woman today, and celebrate your memory at some pothouse. There'll be sleet, filth, melting snow in the grave—no need to put themselves out for you. 'Let her down, Vanuha. It's just like her luck—even here she's upside down, the hussy. Tauten the rope, you scalawag.' 'It's all right as it is.' 'All right, is it? Why, she's on her side! She was a fellow creature, after all! But, never mind, throw the earth on her.' And they won't care to waste much time quarreling over you. They'll throw on the wet blue clay as quick as they can and go off to the pothouse—and there all memory of you on earth will end; other women have children to go to their graves, fathers, husbands. But for you there'll be never a tear, nor a sigh, nor any remembrance; no one in the whole world will ever come to you, your name will vanish from off the face of the earth—as though you'd never existed, never been born at all! Nothing but filth and mud, however you knock at your coffin lid at night, when the dead arise, however you cry: 'Let me out, kind people, to live in the light of day! My life was no life at all; my life was thrown away like a dishclout; it was drunk away in the pothouse at the Hay Market; let me out, kind people, to live in the world again!' "

And I worked myself up to such a pitch that I began to have a lump in my throat myself, and . . . and all at once I stopped, sat up in dismay, and, bending over apprehensively, began to listen with a beating heart. I had reason to be worried.

I had felt for some time that I was turning her soul inside out and rending her heart, and—and the more I was convinced of it, the more eagerly I desired to gain my object as quickly and as effectually as possible. It was the exercise of my skill that carried me away; yet it was more than mere sport.

I knew I was speaking stiffly, artificially, even bookishly; in fact, I could not speak except "like a book." But that did not trouble me: I knew, I felt that I should be understood and that this very bookishness might be a help. But now, having attained my effect, I was suddenly panic-stricken. Never before had I witnessed such despair! She was lying on her face, thrusting her face into the pillow and clutching at it with both hands. Her heart was being rent. Her youthful body was shuddering all over as though in convulsions. Suppressed sobs rent her bosom and suddenly burst out in weeping and wailing, whereupon she buried her face deeper in the pillow: she did not want anyone here, not a living soul, to know of her anguish and her tears. She bit the pillow, bit her hand till it bled (I saw that afterward), or, plunging her fingers into her disheveled hair, seemed rigid with the effort of restraint, holding her breath and clenching her teeth. I started to say something, begging her to calm herself, but felt that I did not dare; and all at once, in a sort of cold shiver, almost in terror, began fumbling in the dark, trying hurriedly to get dressed and then go. It was dark: though I tried my best I could not finish dressing quickly. Suddenly I felt a box of matches and a candlestick with a whole candle in it. As soon as the room was lighted up, Liza sprang up, sat up in bed, and with a contorted face, with a half-insane smile, looked at me almost senselessly. I sat down beside her and took her hands; she came to herself, made an impulsive movement toward me, would have caught hold of me, but did not dare, and slowly bowed her head before me.

"Liza, my dear, I was wrong—forgive me, my dear," I began, but she squeezed my hand in her fingers so tightly that I felt I was saying the wrong thing and stopped.

"This is my address, Liza. Come to me."

"I'll come," she answered resolutely, her head still bowed.

"But now I am going, good-by—till we meet again."

I got up. She, too, stood up and suddenly flushed all over, gave a shudder, snatched up a shawl that was lying on a chair, and muffled herself in it to her chin. As she did this she gave another sickly smile, blushed and looked at me strangely. I felt wretched; I was in haste to get away—to disappear.

"Wait a minute," she said suddenly in the passage just at the doorway, stopping me with her hand on my overcoat. She put down the candle in hot haste and ran off; evidently she had thought of something or wanted to show me something. As she ran away she flushed, her eyes shone, and there was a smile on her lips—what was the meaning of it? Against my will I waited; she came back a minute later with an expression that seemed to ask forgiveness for something. In fact, it was not the same face, not the same look as the evening before—sullen, mistrustful, and obstinate. Her eyes now were imploring, soft, and at the same time trustful, caressing, timid. The expression with which children look at people they are very fond of, of whom they are asking a favor. Her eyes were a light hazel, they were lovely eyes, full of life, and capable of expressing love as well as sullen hatred.

Making no explanation, as though I, as a sort of higher being, must understand everything without explanations, she held out a piece of paper to me. Her whole face was positively beaming at that instant with naïve, almost childish triumph. I unfolded it. It was a letter to her from a medical student or someone of that sort—a very highflown and flowery, but extremely respectful, love letter. I don't recall the words now, but I remember well that through the highflown phrases there was apparent a genuine feeling, which could not be feigned. When I had finished reading it I met her glowing, questioning, and childishly impatient eyes fixed upon me. She fixed her eyes upon my face and waited impatiently for what I should say. In a few words, hurriedly, but with a sort of joy and pride, she explained to me that she had been to a dance somewhere in a private house, a family of "very nice people, *who knew nothing,* absolutely nothing, for she had only come here so lately, and it was only through chance she'd gotten in here . . . and she hadn't made up her mind to stay and was certainly going away as soon as she'd paid her debt. . . ." And the student had been at that party and had danced with her all evening. He had talked to her, and it turned out that he'd known her in the old days at Riga when he was a child, they had played together, but a very long time ago—and he knew her parents, but *about this* he knew nothing, nothing whatever, and had no suspicion! And the day after the dance (three days ago) he had sent her that letter through the friend with whom she had gone to the party . . . and . . . well, that was all.

She dropped her shining eyes with a sort of bashfulness as she finished.

The poor girl was keeping that student's letter as a precious treasure, and had run to fetch it, her only treasure, because she did not want me to go away without knowing that she, too, was honestly and genuinely loved; that she, too, was addressed respectfully. No doubt that letter was destined to lie in her box and lead to nothing. But none the less I am certain that she would keep it all her life as a precious treasure, as her pride and justification, and now at such a minute she had thought of that letter and brought it with naïve pride to raise herself in my eyes that I might see; that I, too, might think well of her. I said nothing, pressed her hand, and went out. I very much longed to get away. I walked all the way home, in spite of the fact that the snow was still falling in heavy melting flakes. I was exhausted, shattered, in bewilderment. But behind the bewilderment the truth was already glinting. The loathsome truth.

VIII

It was some time, however, before I consented to recognize that truth. Waking up in the morning after some hours of heavy, leaden sleep, and immediately realizing all that had happened on the previous day, I was positively amazed at my last night's *sentimentality* with Liza, at all those "outcries of horror and pity." "To think of having such an attack of womanish hysteria, pah!" I concluded. And what did I thrust my address upon her for? What if she comes? Let her come, though; it doesn't matter. But *obviously,* that was not now the chief and the most important matter: I had to make haste and at all costs save my reputation in the eyes of Zvercov and Simonov as quickly as possible; that was the chief business. And I was so taken up that morning that I actually forgot all about Liza.

First of all I had at once to repay what I had borrowed the day before from Simonov. I resolved on a desperate measure: to borrow fifteen rubles at once from Anton Antonich. As luck would have it, he was in the best of moods that morning and gave me the sum right away, without waiting to be asked twice. I was so delighted at this that, as I signed the I O U with a swaggering air, I told him casually that the night before "I'd been hitting it up with some friends at the Hôtel de Paris; we were giving a farewell party to a comrade, in fact, I might say a friend of my childhood, and you know—a desperate rake, fearfully spoilt—of course, he belongs to a good family, and has considerable means, a brilliant career; he's witty, charming, a regular Don Juan, you understand; we drank an extra half-dozen and—"

And it went off all right; all this was uttered very casually, unconstrainedly, and complacently.

On reaching home I promptly wrote to Simonov.

To this hour I am lost in admiration when I recall the truly gentlemanly, good-humored, candid tone of my letter. With tact and good breeding and, above all, entirely without superfluous words, I blamed myself for all that had happened. I defended myself, "if I really may be allowed to defend myself," by alleging that being utterly unaccustomed to wine, I had been intoxicated with the first glass, which I said I had drunk before they arrived, while waiting for them at the Hôtel de Paris between five and six o'clock. I begged Simonov's pardon in particular. I asked him to convey my explanations to all the others, especially to Zvercov, whom "I seemed to remember insulting as though in a dream." I added that I would have called upon all of them myself, but my head ached, and besides I could not face them. I was particularly pleased with a certain lightness, almost nonchalance (strictly within the bounds of politeness, however), which was apparent in my style, and better than any possible arguments gave them at once to understand that I took rather an independent view of "all that unpleasantness last night," that I was by no means so utterly crushed as you, my friends, probably imagine, but on the contrary looked upon it as a gentleman serenely respecting himself should. "On a young hero's past no censure is cast!"

"There is actually an aristocratic playfulness about it!" I thought admiringly as I read over the letter. And it's all because I am an intellectual and cultured man! Another man in my place would not have known how to extricate himself, but here I have gotten out of it and am again as jolly as ever, and all because I am "a cultured and educated man of our day." And, indeed, perhaps everything was due to the wine yesterday. H'm! No, it wasn't the wine. I hadn't drunk anything at all between five and six when I was waiting for them. I had lied to Simonov; I had lied shamelessly; and indeed I wasn't ashamed now. Hang it all, though, the great thing was that I was rid of the mess.

I put six rubles in the letter, sealed it up, and asked Apollon to take it to Simonov. When he learned that there was money in the letter, Apollon became more respectful and agreed to take it. Toward evening I went out for a walk. My head was still aching and dizzy after yesterday. But as evening came on and the twilight deepened, my impressions and, following them, my thoughts grew more and more different and confused. Something was not dead within me, in the depths of my heart and conscience it would not die, and it evinced itself in acute depression. For the most part I jostled my way through the most crowded business streets, along Meshchanski Street, along Sadovyi Street, and in Yusupov Garden. I always liked particularly sauntering along these streets in the dusk, just when there were crowds of working people of all sorts going home from their daily work, with faces looking cross from worry. What I liked was just that cheap bustle, that bald prose. On this occasion the jostling of the streets irritated me more than ever. I could not make out what was wrong with me, I could not find the clue, something seemed rising up in my soul continually, painfully, and refusing to be appeased. I returned home completely upset. It was just as though some crime were lying on my conscience.

The thought that Liza was coming worried me continually. It seemed queer to me that of all my recollections of yesterday this, seemingly, tormented me especially, quite by itself, as it were. Everything else I had quite succeeded in forgetting by evening; I dismissed it all and was still perfectly satisfied with my letter to Simonov. But on this point I was not satisfied at all. It was as though I were worried only by Liza. "What if she comes?" I thought incessantly. "Well, it doesn't matter, let her come! H'm, it's horrid that she should see how I live, for instance. Yesterday I seemed such a hero to her, while now—h'm! It's horrid, though, that I have let myself go so; my room looks like a beggar's. And I brought myself to go out to dinner in such a suit! And my leatheroid sofa with the stuffing sticking out, and my dressing gown which won't cover me, it's so tattered. And she'll see all this—and Apollon, too. That beast is certain to insult her. He'll fasten upon her in order to be rude to me. And, of course, I'll be panic-stricken as usual; I'll begin bowing and scraping before her and pulling my dressing gown about me; I'll begin smiling, telling lies. Oh, the loathsomeness of it all! And it isn't the loathsomeness that matters most! There's something more important, more loathsome, viler! Yes, viler! And to put on that dishonest lying mask again!"

When I reached that thought I fired up all at once.

"Why dishonest? How dishonest? I was speaking sincerely last night.

I remember there was real feeling in me, too. What I wanted was to excite an honorable feeling in her. . . . Her crying was a good thing; it'll have a good effect."

Yet I could not feel at ease. All that evening, even when I had come back home, even after nine o'clock, when I calculated that Liza could not possibly come, she still haunted me, and what was worse she came back to my mind always in the same attitude. One moment out of all that had happened last night stood vividly before my imagination: the moment when I struck a match and saw her pale, distorted face, with its look of torture. And what a pitiful, what an unnatural, what a distorted smile she had at that moment! But I did not know then that fifteen years later I should still see Liza in my imagination, always with the pitiful, distorted, incongruous smile which was on her face at that moment.

Next day I was ready again to look upon it all as nonsense, due to overexcited nerves, and, above all, as *exaggerated*. I was always conscious of that weak point of mine, and sometimes very much afraid of it. "I exaggerate everything; that's where I go wrong," I repeated to myself every hour. But, however, "Liza will very likely come all the same" was the refrain with which all my reflections ended. I was so uneasy that I sometimes flew into a fury: "She'll come, she's certain to come!" I cried, dashing about the room, "if not today then tomorrow; she'll find me out! The damnable romanticism of these pure hearts! Oh, the vileness—oh, the silliness—oh, the stupidity of these "wretched sentimental souls"! Why, how could one fail to understand? How could one?

But at this point I stopped short, and in great confusion, at that.

And how few, how few words, I thought, in passing, were needed; how little of the idyllic (and affectedly, bookishly, artificially idyllic too) had sufficed to turn a whole human life at once according to my will. That's virginity, to be sure! Freshness of soil!

At times a thought occurred to me, to go to her to "tell her all," and beg her not to come to me. But this thought stirred up such wrath in me that I believed I would have crushed that "damned" Liza if she had chanced to be near me at the time. I would have insulted her, have spat at her, have turned her out, have struck her!

One day passed, however, then another and another; she did not come and I began to grow calmer. I felt particularly bold and cheerful after nine o'clock. I even sometimes began dreaming and rather sweetly: I, for instance, became Liza's salvation, simply through her coming to me and my talking to her. I developed her, educated her. Finally, I noticed that she loved me, loved me passionately. I pretended not to understand (I don't know, however, why I pretended—just for effect, perhaps). At last all in confusion, transfigured, trembling and sobbing, she flung herself at my feet and said that I was her savior, and that she loved me better than anything in the world. I was amazed, but— "Liza," I said, "can you imagine that I have not noticed your love? I saw it all, I divined it, but I did not dare to approach you first, because I had an influence over you and was afraid that you would force yourself, from gratitude, to respond to my love, would try to rouse in your heart a feeling which was perhaps absent, and I did not wish that—because it would be tyranny. It would be indelicate [in short, I launched off at that point into Continental, inexplicably lofty subtleties à la George Sand], but now, now you are mine, you are my creation, you are pure, you are good, you are my noble wife.

'And into my house, calm and fearless,
    As its full mistress walk thou in.' "

Then we began living together, went abroad, and so on and so on. In fact, in the end it seemed vulgar to my own self, and I began putting out my tongue at myself.

Besides, they won't let the hussy out, I thought. They don't let them go out very readily, especially in the evening (for some reason I fancied she would come in the evening, and at seven o'clock precisely). Though she did say she was not altogether a slave there yet, and had certain rights, so—h'm! Damn it all, she will come, she's sure to come!

It was a good thing, in fact, that Apollon distracted my attention at that time by his rudeness. He drove me beyond all patience! He was the bane of my life, the curse laid upon me by Providence. We had been squabbling continually for years, and I hated him. My God, how I hated him! I believe I had never hated anyone in my life as I hated him, especially at certain moments. He was an elderly, dignified man, who worked part of his time as a tailor. But for some unknown reason he despised me beyond all measure, and looked down upon me insufferably. Though, for that matter, he looked down upon everyone. Simply to glance at that flaxen, smoothly brushed head, at the tuft of hair he combed up on his forehead and oiled with sunflower oil, at that dignified mouth, compressed into the shape of the letter ש, made one feel one was confronting a man who never had any doubts of himself. He was a pedant, to the utmost degree, the greatest pedant I had met on this earth, and with that had a vanity befitting only Alexander of Macedonia. He was in love with every button on his coat, every nail on his fingers—absolutely in love with them, and he looked it! In his behavior to me he was a perfect tyrant, he spoke very little to me, and if he chanced to glance at me he gave me a firm, majestically self-confident and invariably sarcastic look that sometimes drove me to fury. He did his work with the air of doing me the greatest favor—though he did scarcely anything for me, and did not, indeed, consider himself bound to do anything. There could be no doubt that he looked upon me as the greatest fool on earth, and that he did not "get rid" of me was simply so he could get wages from me every month. He consented to do nothing for me for seven rubles a month. Many sins should be forgiven me for what I suffered from him.

My hatred reached such a point that sometimes his very step almost threw me into convulsions. What I loathed particularly was his lisp. His tongue must have been a little too long or something of that sort, for he continually lisped, and seemed to be very proud of it, imagining that it greatly added to his dignity. He spoke in a slow, measured tone, with his hands behind his back and his eyes fixed on the ground. He maddened me particularly when he read aloud the Psalms to himself behind his partition. Many a battle I waged over that reading! But he was awfully fond of reading aloud in the evenings, in a slow, even, singsong voice, as though over the dead. Interestingly enough, that's just how he wound up his career: he hired himself out to read the Psalms over the dead, and at the same time killed rats and made shoe-blacking. But at that time I could not get rid of him; it was as though he were chemically combined with my existence. Besides, nothing would have induced him to consent to leaving me. I could not live in furnished lodgings: my lodging was my private solitude, my shell, my cave, in which I concealed myself from all mankind, and Apollon seemed to me, for some reason, an integral part of that flat, and for seven years I could not turn him away.

To be two or three days behind with his wages, for instance, was impossible. He would have made such a fuss that I wouldn't have known where to hide my head. But I was so exasperated with everyone during those days that I made up my mind for some reason and with some object to *punish* Apollon and not to pay him for a fortnight the wages that were due him. I had for a long time—for the last two years—been intending to do this, simply in order to teach him not to give himself airs before me, and to show him that if I liked I could withhold his wages. I proposed to say nothing to him about it, and was indeed purposely silent, in order to score off his pride and force him to be the first to speak of his wages. Then I would take the seven rubles out of a drawer, show him I had the money put aside on purpose, but that I wouldn't, I wouldn't, I simply wouldn't pay him his wages; I wouldn't, just because that was "my wish," because "I was master, and it was for me to decide," because he had been disrespectful, because he had been rude; but if he were to ask respectfully I might be softened and give it to him, otherwise he might wait another fortnight, another three weeks, a whole month.

But angry as I was, he nevertheless got the better of me. I could not hold out for four days. He began as he always did in such cases, for there had been such cases already, there had been attempts (and it may be observed I knew all this beforehand, I knew his nasty tactics by heart). He would begin by fixing upon me an exceedingly severe stare, keeping it up for several minutes at a time, particularly on meeting me or seeing me out of the house. If I held out and pretended not to notice these stares he would, still in silence, proceed to further tortures. All at once, *à propos* of nothing, he would glide softly into my room, when I was pacing up and down or reading, stand at the door, one hand behind his back and one foot back of the other, and fix upon me a stare more than severe, utterly contemptuous. If I suddenly asked him what he wanted he would make me no answer but continue staring at me persistently for some seconds, then, with a peculiar compression of his lips and a most significant air, deliberately turn around and deliberately go back to his room. Two hours later he would come out again, and again present himself before me in the same way. Sometimes I was so infuriated I did not even ask him what he wanted but simply raised my head sharply and imperiously and began staring back at him. We stared at one another for two minutes; at last he turned with deliberation and dignity and went back again for two hours.

If I were still not brought to reason by all this but persisted in my revolt, he would suddenly begin sighing while he looked at me, long, deep sighs as though measuring by them the depths of my moral degradation, and, of course, it ended at last by his triumphing completely: I raged and shouted, but still was forced to do what he wanted.

This time the usual staring maneuvers had scarcely begun when I lost my temper and flew at him in a fury. I was irritated beyond endurance, and not only on his account.

"Wait!" I cried in a frenzy as he was slowly and silently turning, with one hand behind his back, to go to his room. "Wait! Come back, come back, I tell you!" and I must have screamed so unnaturally that he turned around and even looked at me with some wonder. However, he persisted in saying nothing, and that infuriated me.

"How dare you come and look at me like that without being sent for? Answer me!"

After looking at me calmly for half a minute, he began turning round again.

"Wait!" I roared, running up to him. "Don't stir! There. Answer, now—what did you come to look at?"

"If you have any order to give me it's my duty to carry it out," he answered after another silent pause, with a slow, measured lisp, raising his eyebrows and calmly twisting his head from side to side, all this with exasperating composure.

"That's not what I'm asking you about, you torturer!" I shouted, turning crimson with anger. "I'll tell you myself why you came here. You see, I don't give you your wages, but you are so proud you don't want to bow down and ask for them, and so you come to punish me with your stupid stares, to worry me, and you have no sus-pi-cion how stupid it is—stupid, stupid, stupid, stupid!"

He would have turned around again without a word, but I seized him.

"Listen," I shouted to him, "here's the money, do you see, here it is [I took it out of the table drawer], here are the seven rubles, in full, but you're not going to get them. You—are—not—going—to —get—them until you come respectfully with bowed head and beg my pardon. You hear?"

"That cannot be," he answered with the most preternatural self-confidence.

"It shall be so," I said. "I give you my word of honor it shall be!"

"And there's nothing for me to beg your pardon for," he went on, as though he had not noticed my exclamations at all. "And, besides, you called me a 'torturer,' for which I can summons you to the police station at any time, for an insulting action."

"Go, summons me," I roared. "Go at once, this very minute, this very second! You are a torturer all the same! A torturer!"

But he merely looked at me, then turned, and, regardless of my loud calls to him, walked to his room with an even step and without looking around.

"If it had not been for Liza nothing of this would have happened," I decided inwardly. Then, after waiting a minute, I went myself behind his screen with a dignified and solemn air, though my heart was beating slowly and violently.

"Apollon," I said quietly and emphatically, though I was breathless, "go at once without a minute's delay and fetch the police officer."

He had meanwhile settled himself at his table, put on his spectacles, and picked up some garment he was mending. But, hearing my order, he burst into a guffaw.

"At once, go this minute! Go on or else you can't imagine what will happen."

"You are certainly out of your mind," he observed without even raising his head, lisping as deliberately as ever and threading his needle. "Whoever heard of a man sending for the police against himself? And as for being frightened—you are upsetting yourself about nothing, for nothing will come of it."

"Go!" I shrieked, shaking him by the shoulder. I felt I would strike him in a minute.

But I did not notice the door from the passage softly and slowly open at that instant and a figure come in, stop short, and begin staring at us in perplexity. I glanced, nearly swooned with shame, and rushed back to my room. There, clutching at my hair with both hands, I leaned my head against the wall and stood thus motionless.

Two minutes later I heard Apollon's deliberate footsteps.

"There's some woman asking for you," he said, looking at me with peculiar severity. Then he stood aside and let in Liza. He would not go away, but stared at us sarcastically.

"Go away, go away," I commanded in desperation. At that moment my clock began whirring and wheezing and struck seven.

IX

And into my house, calm and fearless,
As its full mistress walk thou in.

I stood before her crushed, crestfallen, revoltingly confused, and I believe I smiled as I did my utmost to wrap myself in the folds of my ragged quilted dressing gown—exactly as, in a fit of depression, I had imagined the scene not long before. After standing over us for a couple of minutes Apollon went away, but that did not put me any more at ease. What made it worse was that she, too, was overwhelmed with confusion—more so, in fact, than I might have expected. Overwhelmed at the sight of me, of course.

"Sit down," I said mechanically, moving a chair up to the table, and I sat down on the sofa. She obediently seated herself at once and gazed at me open-eyed, evidently expecting something from me at once. This naïveté of expectation drove me to fury, but I restrained myself.

She ought to have tried not to notice, as though everything had been as usual, while instead of that, she. . . . And I dimly felt that I should make her pay dearly for *all this*.

"You have found me in a strange position, Liza," I began, stammering and knowing that this was the wrong way to begin. "No, no, don't imagine anything," I cried, seeing that she had suddenly flushed. "I am not ashamed of my poverty. On the contrary, I regard my poverty with pride. I am poor but honorable. One can be poor and honorable," I mumbled. "However . . . Would you like tea?"

"No"—she was about to refuse.

"Wait a minute."

I leaped up and ran to Apollon. I had to get out of the room somehow.

"Apollon," I whispered in feverish haste, flinging down before him the seven rubles which had remained all the time in my clenched fist, "here are your wages. See, I give them to you; but for that you must come to my rescue: bring me tea and a dozen zwieback from the restaurant. If you won't go, you'll make me a miserable man! You don't know who this woman is. This is—everything! You may be imagining something—but you don't know what that woman is!"

Apollon, who had already sat down to his work and put on his spectacles again, at first glanced askance at the money without speaking or putting down his needle; then, without paying the slightest attention to me or making any answer, he went on busying himself with his needle, which he had not yet threaded. I waited before him for three minutes with my arms crossed à la Napoleon. My temples were dank with sweat. I was pale, I felt. But, thank God, he must have been moved to pity, looking at me. Having threaded his needle he deliberately got up from his seat, deliberately moved back his chair, deliberately took off his spectacles, deliberately counted the money, and, finally asking me over his shoulder: "Shall I get enough for two?", deliberately walked out of the room. As I was going back to Liza the thought occurred to me: Shouldn't I run away just as I was in my dressing gown, no matter where, and then let come what might?

I sat down again. She looked at me uneasily. For some minutes we were silent.

"I will kill him," I shouted suddenly, striking the table with my fist so that the ink spurted out of the inkstand.

"What are you saying!" she cried, starting.

"I will kill him! Kill him!" I shrieked, suddenly striking the table in absolute frenzy and at the same time fully understanding how stupid it was to be so frenzied. "You don't know, Liza, what a torturer he is to me. He is my torturer. He went just now to fetch something; he—"

And suddenly I burst into tears. It was an hysterical attack. How ashamed I felt in the midst of my sobs! But still I could not restrain them.

She was frightened.

"What's the matter? What's wrong?" she cried, fussing about me.

"Water, give me water! Over there!" I muttered faintly, though I was inwardly conscious that I could have got on very well without water and without muttering faintly. But I was what is called *putting on an act,* to save appearances, though the attack was a genuine one.

She gave me water, looking at me in bewilderment. At that moment Apollon brought in the tea. It suddenly seemed to me that this commonplace, prosaic tea was horribly undignified and paltry after all that had happened, and I blushed crimson. Liza looked at Apollon with positive alarm. He went out without a glance at either of us.

"Liza, do you despise me?" I asked, looking at her fixedly, trembling with impatience to know what she was thinking.

She was confused and did not know what to answer.

"Drink your tea," I said to her angrily. I was angry with myself, but, of course, it was she who would have to pay for it. A horrible spite against her suddenly surged up in my heart; I believe I could have killed her. To revenge myself on her I swore inwardly not to say a word to her all the time. "She is the cause of it all," I thought.

Our silence lasted for five minutes. The tea stood on the table; we did not touch it. I had got to the point of purposely refraining from breaking the silence in order to embarrass her further; it was awkward for her to begin. Several times she glanced at me with mournful perplexity. I was obstinately silent. I was, of course, myself the chief sufferer, because I was fully conscious of the disgusting meanness of my spiteful stupidity, and yet at the same time I could not restrain myself.

"I want to—get away from there altogether," she began, to break the silence in some way, but, poor girl, that was just what she ought not to have spoken about at such a stupid moment to a man as stupid as I was. My heart positively ached with pity for her tactless and unnecessary straightforwardness. But something hideous at once stifled all compassion in me; it even provoked me to greater venom. I did not care what happened. Another five minutes passed.

"Perhaps I am in your way," she began with timidity, hardly audibly, and was getting up.

But as soon as I saw this first impulse of wounded dignity I positively trembled with spite, and at once burst out:

"Why have you come to me? Tell me that, please?" I began, gasping for breath and disregarding all logical connection in my words. I longed to have it all out at once, at one sweep; I did not even trouble how to begin. "Why have you come? Answer me, answer me!" I cried, hardly knowing what I was doing. "I'll tell you, my good girl, why you have come. You've come because I talked sentimental bosh to you that time. So now you are soft as butter and longing for fine sentiments again. But you may as well know that I was laughing at you then. And I'm laughing at you now. Why are you shuddering? Yes, I was laughing at you! I had been insulted just before, at dinner, by the fellows who came that evening before me. I came to you, meaning to thrash one of them, an officer. But I didn't succeed, I didn't find him; I had to avenge the insult on someone to get even; you turned up, I vented my spleen on you and laughed at you. I had been humiliated, so I wanted to humiliate; I had been treated like a rag, so I wanted to show my power. That's what it was, and you imagined I had come there on purpose to save you. Yes? You imagined that? You imagined that?"

I knew that she would perhaps be muddled and not take it all in exactly, but I knew, too, that she would grasp the gist of it, very well indeed. And so, in fact, she did. She turned white as linen, tried to say something, and her lips worked painfully; but she sank on a chair as though she had been felled by an ax. And all the time afterward she listened to me with her lips parted and her eyes wide open, shuddering in awful terror. The cynicism, the cynicism of my words overwhelmed her.

"Save you!" I went on, jumping up from my chair and dashing up and down the room before her. "Save you from what? But perhaps I myself am worse than you. Why didn't you throw it in my teeth when I was giving you that sermon: 'But what did you yourself come here for? Was it to read me a sermon?' Power, power was what I wanted then, sport was what I wanted; I wanted to wring out your tears, your humiliation, your hysteria—that was what I wanted then! Of course, I couldn't keep it up then, because I'm a foolishly wretched creature, I was frightened, and, the devil knows why, foolishly gave you my address. Afterward, before I got home, I was cursing and swearing at you because of that address; I hated you already because of the lies I had told you. Because I only like playing with words, only dreaming. But, do you know, what I really want is that you should all go to hell. That's what I want. I want peace; yes, I'd sell the whole world for a copper, straight off, if only I'd be left in peace. Is the world to go to pot or am I to go without my tea? I say that the world may go to pot for all I care, so long as I always get my tea. Did you know that or not? Well, anyway, I know that I'm a blackguard, a scoundrel, an egoist, a sluggard. Here I've been shuddering for the last three days at the thought of your coming. And do you know what has worried me particularly for these three days? That I posed as such a hero to you, and now you would see me in a wretched, torn dressing gown, beggarly, loathsome. I told you just now that I was not ashamed of my poverty; well, you may as well know that I am ashamed of it. I am ashamed of it more than of anything, more afraid of it than of being found out if I were a thief, because I am as touchy as though I had been flayed, and the very air blowing on me hurts. Surely by now you must realize that I shall never forgive you for having found me in this wretched dressing gown, just as I was flying at Apollon like a spiteful cur. The savior, the former hero, was flying like a mangy, unkempt sheep dog at his flunky, and the flunky was jeering at him! And I shall never forgive you for the tears I could not help shedding before you just now, like some silly woman put to shame! And for what I am confessing to you now I'll never forgive *you* either! Yes—you must answer for it all because you turned up like this, because I am a blackguard, because I am the nastiest, stupidest, absurdest, and most envious of all the worms on earth, who are not a bit better than I am, but, the devil knows why, are never embarrassed, while I shall always be insulted by every louse. That is my doom! And what is it to me that you don't understand a word of this? And what do I care, what do I care about you, and whether you go to ruin there or not? Do you understand? How I'll hate you now after saying this, for having been here and listening. Why, it's not once in a lifetime a man speaks out like this, and then it is in hysterics! What more do you want? Why do you still stand confronting me, after all this? Why are you upsetting me? Why don't you go?"

But at this point a strange thing happened. I was so accustomed to thinking and imagining everything from books, and to picturing everything in the world to myself just as I had made it up in my dreams beforehand, that I could not all at once take in this strange circumstance. What happened was this: Liza, insulted and crushed by me, understood a great deal more than I imagined. She understood from all this what a woman understands first of all, if she feels genuine love, that is, that I was myself unhappy.

The frightened and wounded expression on her face was followed first by a look of sorrowful perplexity. When I began calling myself a scoundrel and a blackguard and my tears flowed (the tirade was accompanied throughout by tears), her whole face worked convulsively. She was on the point of getting up and stopping me; when I finished she took no notice of my shouting: "Why are you here, why don't you go away?" but realized only that it must have been very bitter for me to say all this. Besides, she was so crushed, poor girl; she considered herself infinitely beneath me; how could she feel anger or resentment? She suddenly leaped up from her chair with an irresistible impulse and held out her hands, yearning toward me, though still timid and not daring to move forward. At this point there was a revulsion in my heart, too. Then she suddenly rushed to me, threw her arms around me, and burst into tears. I, too, could not restrain myself and sobbed as I never had before.

"They won't let me—I can't be good!" I managed to articulate; then I went to the sofa, fell on it face downward, and sobbed on it for a quarter of an hour in genuine hysterics. She came close to me, put her arms around me, and stayed thus, motionless. But the trouble was that the hysterics could not go on forever, and (I am writing the loathsome truth) lying face down on the sofa with my face thrust into my nasty leatheroid cushion, I began by degrees to be aware of a faraway, involuntary but irresistible feeling that it would be awkward now for me to raise my head and look Liza straight in the face. Why was I ashamed? I don't know, but I was ashamed. The thought, too, came into my overwrought brain that our parts now were completely reversed, that she was now the heroine, while I was just such a crushed and humiliated creature as she had been before me that night—four days before. And all this came into my mind during the minutes I was lying on my face on the sofa.

My God! Surely I was not envious of her then.

I don't know, to this day I cannot decide, and at the time, of course, I was still less able than now to understand, what I was feeling. I cannot get on without domineering and tyrannizing over someone, but . . . there is no explaining anything by reasoning and so it is useless to reason.

I mastered myself, however, and raised my head; I had to do so sooner or later. And I am convinced to this day that it was just because I was ashamed to look at her that another feeling was suddenly kindled and flamed up in my heart—a feeling of mastery and possession. My eyes gleamed with passion and I gripped her hands tightly. How I hated her and how I was drawn to her at that minute! The one feeling intensified the other. It was almost like an act of vengeance. At first there was a look of amazement, even of terror on her face, but only for one instant. She warmly and rapturously embraced me.

X

A quarter of an hour later I was rushing up and down the room in frenzied impatience; from minute to minute I went up to the screen and peeped through the crack at Liza. She was sitting on the ground with her head leaning against the bed, and must have been crying. But she did not go away, and that irritated me. This time she understood it all. I had insulted her finally, but . . . there's no need to describe it. She realized that my outburst of passion had been simply revenge, a fresh humiliation, and that to my earlier, almost causeless hatred was added now a *personal hatred,* born of envy. Though I do not maintain positively that she understood all this distinctly; but she certainly did fully understand that I was a despicable man, and, what was worse, incapable of loving her.

I know I shall be told that this is incredible—but it is incredible to be as spiteful and stupid as I was; it may be added that it was strange I should not love her, or, at any rate, appreciate her love. Why is it strange? In the first place, by then I was incapable of love, for I repeat, with me loving meant tyrannizing and showing my moral superiority. I have never in my life been able to imagine any other sort of love, and have nowadays come to the point of sometimes thinking that love really consists in the right—freely given by the beloved—to tyrannize over her.

Even in my underground dreams I did not imagine love except as a struggle. I began it always with hatred and ended it with moral subjugation, and afterward I never knew what to do with the subjugated object. And what is there to wonder at in that, since I had succeeded in so corrupting myself, since I was so out of touch with "real life," as to have actually thought of reproaching her and putting her to shame for having come to me to hear "fine sentiments"; and did not even guess that she had come, not to hear fine sentiments but to love me, because to a woman all reformation, all salvation from any sort of ruin, and all moral renewal, is contained in love and can only show itself in that form.

I did not hate her so much, however, when I was dashing about the room and peeping through the crack in the screen. I was only insufferably oppressed by her being here. I wanted her to disappear. I wanted "peace," to be left alone in my underground world. Real life oppressed me with its novelty so much that I could hardly breathe.

But several minutes passed and she still remained, without stirring, as though she were unconscious. I had the shamelessness to tap softly on the screen as though to remind her. She started, sprang up, and flew to seek her kerchief, her hat, her coat, as though making her escape from me. Two minutes later she came from behind the screen and, with heavy eyes, looked at me. I gave a spiteful grin, which was forced, however, to *keep up appearances,* and turned away from her eyes.

"Good-by" she said, going toward the door.

I ran up to her, seized her hand, opened it, thrust something in it, and closed it again. Then I turned at once and dashed away in haste to the other corner of the room to avoid seeing her, at any rate.

I did mean a moment ago to tell a lie—to write that I did this accidentally, not knowing through foolishness, through having lost my head, what I was doing. But I don't want to lie, and so I'll say right out that I opened her hand and put the money in it from spite. It came into my head to do this while I was dashing up and down the room and she was sitting behind the screen. But this I can say for certain: though I did that cruel thing purposely, it was not an impulse from the heart, but came from my evil brain. This cruelty was so affected, so purposely made up, so completely a product of the brain, of books, that I could not even keep it up a minute—first I dashed away to avoid seeing Liza, and then in shame and despair rushed after her. I opened the door in the passage and began listening.

"Liza! Liza!" I cried on the stairs, but in a low voice, not boldly.

There was no answer, but I fancied I heard her footsteps, lower down on the stairs.

"Liza!" I cried more loudly.

No answer. But at that minute I heard the unwieldy outer glass door open heavily with a creak and slam violently, the sound echoing up the stairs.

She had gone. I went back to my room hesitatingly. I felt horribly oppressed.

I stood still at the table, beside the chair on which he had sat, and looked aimlessly before me. A minute passed, suddenly I started; straight before me on the table I saw—in short, I saw a crumpled blue five-ruble note, the one I had thrust into her hand a minute before. It was the same note; it could be no other, there was no other in the flat. So she had managed to fling it from her hand on the table at the moment when I had dashed into the corner furthest from her.

Well! I might have expected that she would do that. Might I have expected it? No, I was such an egoist, I was so lacking in respect for my fellow creatures that I could not even imagine she would do so. I could not endure it. A minute later I flew like a madman to dress, flinging on what I could at random and ran headlong after her. She could not have got two hundred paces away when I ran out into the street.

It was a still night, and the snow was coming down thick and falling almost perpendicularly, covering the pavement and the empty street as though with a pillow. There was no one in the street; not a sound was to be heard. The street lamps gave a disconsolate and ineffectual glimmer. I ran two hundred paces to the street intersection and stopped short.

Where had she gone? And why was I running after her?

Why? To fall down before her, to sob with remorse, to kiss her feet, to entreat her forgiveness! I longed for that, my whole breast was being rent to pieces, and never, never shall I recall that moment with indifference. "But—what for?" I thought. Should I not begin to hate her, perhaps, even tomorrow, just because I had kissed her feet today?

Should I give her happiness? Had I not recognized that day, for the hundredth time, what I was worth? Should I not torture her?

I stood in the snow, gazing into the troubled darkness, and pondered this.

"And will it not be better," I mused fantastically afterward at home, stifling the living pang of my heart with fantastic dreams—"will it not be better that she should keep the resentment of the insult forever? Resentment—why, it is purification; it is a most stinging and painful consciousness! Tomorrow I should have defiled her soul and have exhausted her heart, while now the feeling of insult will never die in her heart, and however loathsome the filth awaiting her, the feeling of insult will elevate and purify her through hatred. H'm! Perhaps, too, by forgiveness. . . . Will all that make things easier for her, though?"

And, indeed, I will ask an idle question here on my own account: Which is better—cheap happiness or exalted sufferings? Well, which *is* better?

So I dreamed as I sat at home that evening, almost dead with the pain in my soul. Never had I endured such suffering and remorse, yet could there have been the faintest doubt when I ran out from my lodging that I should turn back halfway?

I never met Liza again and I have heard nothing of her. I will add, too, that I remained for a long time afterward pleased with the phrase about the benefit from resentment and hatred in spite of the fact that I almost fell ill from misery.

Even now, so many years later, all this is somehow a very evil memory. I have many evil memories now, but—hadn't I better end my "Notes" here? I believe I made a mistake in beginning to write them; anyway, I have felt ashamed all the time I've been writing this story. So it's hardly literature as much as a corrective punishment. Why, to tell long stories, showing how I have spoiled my life through morally rotting in my cubbyhole, through lack of fitting environment, through divorce from real life and rankling spite in my underground world, would certainly not be interesting; a novel needs a hero, and all the traits for an antihero are *expressly* gathered together here, and (what matters most) it all produces an unpleasant impression, for we are all divorced from life, we are all cripples, every one of us, more or less.

We are so divorced from it that we feel at once a sort of loathing for real life, and so cannot bear to be reminded of it. Why, we have come almost to look upon real life as an effort, almost as hard work, and we are all privately agreed that it is better in books. And why do we fuss and fume sometimes? Why are we perverse, asking for something else, without ourselves knowing what? It would be the worse for us if our petulant prayers were answered. Come, try, give any one of us, for instance, a little more independence, untie our hands, widen the spheres of our activity, relax the control and we—yes, I assure you—we'd be begging to be under control again at once. I know that you will very likely be angry with me for that, and will begin shouting and stamping. Speak for yourself, you will say, and for your miseries in your underground holes, and don't dare to say "all of us." Excuse me, gentlemen, I'm not justifying myself with that "all of us."

As for what concerns me in particular, I have in my life only carried to an extreme what you have not dared to carry halfway, and what's more, you have taken your cowardice for good sense, and have found comfort in deceiving yourselves. So that perhaps, after all, there is more life in me than in you. Look into it more carefully! Why, we don't even know what living means now, what it is, and what it is called. Leave us alone without books and we'll be lost and in confusion at once. We'll not know what to join to, what to cling to, what to love and what to hate, what to respect and what to despise. We are oppressed at being men—men with real individual flesh and blood, we are ashamed of it, we think it a disgrace and try to contrive to be some sort of impossible generalized man. We are stillborn, and for generations past have been begotten not by living fathers, and that suits us more and more. We are developing a taste for it. Soon we shall contrive to be born from an idea somehow. But enough; I don't want to write more from *underground*.

[*The notes of this paradoxalist do not end here, however. He could not refrain from going on with them, but it seems to us that we may stop here.*]

Michael Eugraphovich
Saltycov
"M. Shchedrin"
1 8 2 6 – 1 8 8 9

THE SALTYCOVS are described both as an ancient noble family and as middle-class landowners. Michael's mother seems to have been very much of a tyrannical terror; the satirist himself has given a merciless portrait of her in one of his works. His entire outlook on life was formed by a Bible which fell into his hands as a child, making him sense the abyss between the Book's desired truth and vulgar reality and opening his eyes to the nature of hypocrisy. After two years at the aristocratic Moscow Institute he entered the Alexandrovski Lyceum. Since Pushkin's day each graduating class had followed the custom of choosing a future Pushkin from its midst; in 1844 the choice fell on Saltycov. Upon graduation he entered the civil service, with very much the same idealism as Gogol's, and later on was to experience the same disenchantment that Gogol had

felt. But whereas Gogol had broken with the civil service very quickly, Saltycov had, by 1858, worked himself up to a Lieutenant-Governorship, and did not resign (to devote himself entirely to literature) until 1868.

He wrote his first poem in 1841, but soon abandoned poetry for satire. His first story appeared in 1847. His *Mixed Affair* is quite weak as compared with his later work, but, published in the fateful year of 1848 (he was involved in the Petrashevski circle, just as Dostoievski was), it was enough to rouse such wrath in the authorities that he was banished to a provincial hellhole for eight years.

He attained fame with his *Provincial Sketches,* which created a most profound impression. Although these character studies of bureaucrats were scathingly described by Pisarev, the extreme Nihilist (in an article that has become famous) as "flowers of naïve humor," the perceptive Chernyshevski wrote of them and their author: "Their purpose is not at all to expose venal bureaucrats; they are, rather, a truthful, artistic picture of a milieu in which the conditions branded by the author are not only possible but actually unavoidable. No one has chastised social vices in words more bitter, no one has exposed our social sores to us with such mercilessness."

His writings are a satirical chronicle (unbroken for twoscore years) of Russian society. They are the most exquisite—and virulent—analysis of Czarist Russia. He has himself listed some of his targets: "the law of the club, double-dealing, lying, rapacity, perfidy, empty-headedness." Venal authority, serf-owning squirearchy, feral bourgeoisie, weak and poltroonish intellectuals—his satire was a puissant weapon against them all at a time when all struggle seemed unavailing. He depicted with amazing vividness the disintegration and decay of the Russian nobility. *The Mon-Repos Retreat* is the opening note in a funeral march of which the ax-strokes in Chekhov's *The Cherry Orchard* are the last. And in this genre *The Golovlev Family* (1872-1876) towers even over *Oblomov* (supreme as that novel is on another score) and all but dwarfs Bunin's *Dry Valley. The Golovlev Family* is his greatest book; it places him in the forefront of Russian realists. It has become an undisputed classic—ranked by some as equal to *Dead Souls.*

But it is as a virtuoso of artistic satire that he is supreme; as a master of *pure* satire he is greater even than Gogol. And until the utter reformation of mankind topples the world's great satirists into oblivion, his place among them is secure. (His universality the reader can judge for himself from the selection here given.)

His *Fairy Tales* (*Vices and Virtues* is one of these) are an unforgettable, unsurpassed work of genius. They are profound in concept, amusing in their inexhaustible good humor, and at the same time tragic in their brilliant, venomous wit, their genial malice. Their style is perfect. Saltycov himself called it Aesopic; he had to evolve a special one—colloquial, allusive, connotative, neologistic—as a mask of "naïve humor" against the censorship. And of course Saltycov's style is another "despair of translators"—which may account for his obscurity in English.

The "master of that laughter which makes man wise," who valued personal liberty and human dignity above all else, had no mean share in drawing up the indictment of old Russia—that indictment of which Dostoievski was the last word.

The Virtues and the Vices

THE VIRTUES and the Vices were at daggers drawn from the times of old. The Vices led a merry life and did their business cleverly, whereas the life of the Virtues was more on the drab side, but then they were cited as an example for emulation in all the *A B C's* and school readers. Yet just the same, on the quiet, they used to think: "There, if only we, too, could manage to turn a nice little deal or two, the way the Vices do!" And truth compels us to say they did just that under the cover of the general hubbub.

It is difficult to say what lay at the very beginning of their feud, or who had been the first to start it. It looks as if the Virtues had been the instigators. Sin, now, was spry and ever so wise in all sorts of shrewd dodges. When he started covering space with great strides, like a fleet steed, and strutting about through all the wide world in his cloths-of-gold and his silks—why, the Virtues just couldn't catch up with him. And having failed in keeping up with him and his many children, the Vices, they got good and sore.

"Very well," they shook their fists at Sin, "strut about in your silks and satins, you insolent scalawag! Us, we'll be respected even in sackcloth and tatters!"

But all the answer the Vices made to them was:

"Go ahead and be respected, and God be with ye!"

The Virtues couldn't take all those sneers and they began lacing it into the Vices on all the highways and byways. They'd come out in their sackcloth rags and tatters on to some fork of the roads and start pestering the passers-by: "Ain't it true, now, all you honest folk, that we're near and dear to you even in our rags?"

But the passers-by would answer them:

"My, but there's an awful lot of you old beggarwomen sprung up of late! On your way, now, and don't be keeping us back! God will provide for you!"

Translated by Bernard Guilbert Guerney. Copyright, 1943, by the Vanguard Press, Inc.

The Virtues also took a stab at turning to the guardians of law and order for co-operation.

"Where's your eyes? Look at what a loose rein you've given to the public. Why, first thing you know, it'll be mired up to its ears in Vices!"

But all the guardians knew was to stand there and touch their caps to the Vices. And so the Virtues were left out in the cold; all they could do was to threaten in vexation:

"Just you wait! You'll get a long stretch at hard labor in Siberia for your goin's-on!"

But the Vices, in the meanwhile, were dashing forrarder and forrarder all the time—and not only that, but bragging about it, too.

"You sure have found something to scare us with!" they taunted. "Hard labor, indeed! As for us, it's maybe yes and maybe no, but you've been in hard labor up to your ears ever since you was born! Lookit them spiteful things! Skin and bones, but just see how their eyes glitter. They snap their teeth at the pie, but don't know how to go about gettin' a holt of it!"

In short, the feud grew worse and worse with every day. Ever so many times matters came to a pitched battle, but even here Fortune betrayed the Virtues, practically every time. The Vices would get the upper hand and clap the Virtues in irons: "Stay there and don't be raising no fuss, you troublemakers!" And stay there they would, until the administrative powers would step in and set them free.

It was during one of these battles that Simple Simon, happening to pass by, stopped and said to the combatants:

"My, but you're silly—so silly! Why in the world are you committing such mayhem on one another? For in the beginning all of you alike were MERE ATTRIBUTES, and it was only later on, because of human sloppiness and chicanery, that Virtues and Vices came about. Some Attributes were squeezed hard, others were given a free swing—and so the wheels and thingumabobs in the mechanism got out of order. And confusion, dissension, and sorrow came to reign in the world. . . . But here's what you do: turn to the source primeval: perhaps you may actually get together on some point!"

That's what Simple Simon said, and after that he went on his way to the Treasury, to pay his income tax.

Whether it was that Simple Simon's words had an effect upon them, or whether the powder had run out and they couldn't go on with the fight, the fact remains that the warriors put their swords back in their scabbards and got to thinking.

However, it was the Virtues that did most of the thinking, because their bellies had shrunk from hunger; but as for the Vices, no sooner had the bugles sounded to cease fighting than they wandered off to attend to their scoundrelly affairs and began started living gloriously.

"It's all well and good for Simple Simon to shoot his mouth off about *Attributes*—" Humility was the first to speak up. "We know all about them *Attributes* as well as he does! But then, there's some Attributes as struts about in velvet, and eats off of gold services, whilst there's others what walks around in shabby ticking and have to sit all day long without a bite to eat. It ain't no skin off of Simple Simon's nose: he's stuffed his guts with chaff and feels righteous; but you can't take old birds like us in with chaff—we know a hawk from a handsaw!"

"Besides, what's all this stuff about *Attributes?*" Decorum voiced his uneasiness. "Isn't this some sort of a trap? There'd always been Virtues and there'd always been Vices; this business has been going on for hundreds of thousands of years, and hundreds of thousands of big thick books have been written about it, but, no, he's got to come spang out with it: 'Attributes!' No, you just try and tackle those hundreds of thousands of books and you'll see what a cloud of dust will rise from them!"

They deliberated and deliberated and finally decided: Decorum had spoken truly. For how many thousands of millenniums had the Virtues been held Virtues and the Vices Vices! How many thousands of books had been written about that, what mountains of paper and oceans of ink had been used up! The Virtues had always stood on the right hand, the Vices on the left, and suddenly, according to Simple Simon's fool speech, you've got to renounce everything and call yourselves some sort of *Attributes!* Why, it was almost the same thing as renouncing the rights of your status and calling yourself *man!* As for being simple, simple enough it was—but then simplicity at times is worse than thievery. Just go and touch something in all simplicity, and from the very first step you'll fall into such an incomputable number of pitfalls that, like as not, you'll leave your head behind you!

No, there was no use in thinking about *Attributes,* but as for seeking a compromise of some sort (or making a deal, as they say), that might be good business. Such a deal as might both cheer up the Virtues and be right up the Vices' alley. For, after all, even the Vices must have had a scare thrown into them from time to time.

There, just the other day, Lust had been caught *in flagrante delicto* in a bathhouse, and proceedings had been instituted, and that very same night Fornication had been thrown down several flights of stairs in nothing but his underwear. And was it so long ago that Latitudinarianism had been in full and magnificent flower, yet now it had been torn up, root and all? Consequently, it wouldn't be disadvantageous even for the Vices to make a deal.

"My dear ladies and gentlemen! Wouldn't some one of you care to make a motion? Who has some sort of an . . . er . . . little expedient in mind?"

The first to respond to this call was an ancient little codger, whom they called Experience (there are two Experiences: one Vicious, the other Virtuous; well, this fellow was Virtuous Experience). And he had a proposition:

"You will have to find," he told his fellow Virtues, "an invaluable someone who would be respected by the Virtues and, at the same time, one whom the Vices would not shy away from. And you send him for a parley into the enemy's camp."

They started looking about and, naturally, came across what they wanted. They found two dark horses: Moderation and Accuracy. Both of them hung out in the back lots of the places settled by the Virtues, theirs being the portion of all orphans, but they bootlegged moonshine and, on the sly, received the Vices at their shebang.

However, the first time the Virtues came a cropper. Their dark horses were both none too impressive and far too yielding to carry out the problem imposed upon them. Hardly had they appeared at the camp of the Vices, hardly had they wound up for their long-winded discourse: "Little by little does it; slow but sure—" when the whole horde of Vices started gobbling at them:

"We've heard all them sayings, now, many's the time. You've been stalking us with them oats for a long time now, but that ain't our fare! Git goin', you poor little things, and God go with ye! Don't run up no board-bill around here!"

And, just as if to show the Virtues that you couldn't put anything over on them, they went on an all-night bender at the Samarkand Tavern, and in the morning, as they were leaving, they caught Abstinence and Chastity, and what they did to those poor girls was so very low-down that even the Tatar waiters at the Samarkand couldn't get over it: "Nice gents, yet lookit what they're doin'!"

It was then that the Virtues grasped that this matter was serious, and that they'd have to tackle it in real earnest.

There had sprouted up among them about that time a creature of a neuter gender: nor fish nor flesh nor good red herring; nor knight nor lady, but just a little pinch of each. It had sprouted, straightened up, and burst into flower. And the name of this indeterminate intermediate was also of the neuter gender: Hypocrisy.

Everything about this creature was an enigma, beginning with its origin. The old-timers used to say that once upon a time Resignation and Lechery had come to know each other in a dark hallway, and that this was the fruit of that union. That fruit the Virtues had watered and nurtured communally, and then had placed it in the boarding school run by Mme. Commeilfaut, a Frenchwoman. This surmise as to its origin was also borne out by Hypocrisy's outward semblance, inasmuch as, although it never went about otherwise than with its eyes cast down to the floor, close observers had noted more than once that lecherous shadows ran rather often over its face, while its buttocks, on occasion, would quiver in a way that was even *very* far from decorous. Indubitably, Mme. Commeilfaut's boarding school was to a considerable degree to blame for this outward equivoque. There Hypocrisy had mastered all the major subjects: *walking a chalked line,* and *not letting butter melt in your mouth,* and *getting under somebody's skin*—everything in short, that assures a virtuous life. But at the same time it had not escaped the influence of the cancan, with which influence the walls and the very air of the boarding school were saturated. But, besides that, Mme. Commeilfaut had gummed up things still more by imparting to Hypocrisy the details concerning its parents. About the father, Lechery, she confessed that he was *mauvais ton* and impudent—he tried to pinch everybody. About the mother, Resignation, she admitted that, although Resignation was not at all stunning in looks, she nevertheless cried out so charmingly whenever she was pinched that even such Vices as were not given to amatory pinching (such as Venality, Insolence-in-Office, Despondence, and the like)—well, even they could not deny themselves this pleasure.

And it was none other than precisely this neuter being, which kept its eyes cast down on the floor, yet kept looking all around with wanton glances from under its lowered eyelids, whom the Virtues chose to enter into parleys with the Vices, and to invent a common *modus vivendi* under which both the one group and the other might lead a free and easy life.

"Yes, but do you know how to act the way we do?" Gallant Behavior had the notion of putting the creature through a preliminary examination.

"Who, me?" Hypocrisy was amazed. "Why, this is how I'd go about it—"

And before the Virtues had a chance to think, Hypocrisy already had its darling little eyes cast down and its tiny hands folded on its bosom, and the daintiest blush mantling its innocent-looking little cheeks. Just a virgin, and that's all there was to it!

"Look at the cunning creature! Well, now, and what about their ways—the way the Vices act?"

But Hypocrisy did not even bother answering this question. In an instant it had perpetrated something that no one could clearly perceive, yet realistic to such a degree that Penetration could only spit in disgust.

And thereafter they all resolved, without a single dissenting vote, to have pettifogger Shyster execute a general power-of-attorney for the prosecution of the Virtues' affairs and to put it in Hypocrisy's hands.

When you tackle something, don't try to back out; no matter how bitter the pill was to take, yet the Virtues had to sue the Vices for pardon. So Hypocrisy went off to their vile rookery and, for very shame, didn't know which way to avert its eyes. "This abomination has spread all over now!" it complained aloud, but mentally added: "My, what a fine life the Vices are leading!" And, sure enough, Hypocrisy hadn't gone even a mile from the habitation of the Virtues when it could sniff a sea at full tide on all sides of it. Peals of laughter, and dancing, and games; the very air was filled with the din of revelry. And what an outstanding town the Vices had built for themselves: spacious, well-lighted, with streets and lanes, with squares and boulevards. Here was Perjury Street, there Treason Square, and over there, actually, Disgrace Boulevard. The Father of Lies Himself ran a dive there, dispensing slander over the bar and for home consumption.

But no matter how merrily the Vices lived, no matter how experienced they were in all low-down matters, yet when they laid eyes on Hypocrisy even they had to gasp. To look at her, she was, for all the world, a sure enough virgin; but whether she really was that the Devil himself could not make out. Even the Father of Lies, who thought there was no vileness in the world which he could not surpass—well, even his eyes were popping out.

"Well," he admitted, "it was in vain I dreamed that there was no one in the world more harmful than I. Where do I come in? There it is, the real venom, now! My forte is brazening things out; that's why—not often, it's true, but just from time to time—that's why they give me the bum's rush and chuck me down all the stairs. But this treasure, once it clings to you, you'll never get shut of! It will enmesh you so, will entwine you so, that it'll never let you go till it has sucked you bone-dry!"

Nevertheless, no matter how great the enthusiasm that had been aroused by Hypocrisy, even here dissension could not be avoided. The more substantial citizens among the Vices (the aborigines), who valued above all else the traditions of antiquity (such pillars as Sophistry, Inanity, Pride, Misanthropy, and their ilk), not only refrained from going to meet Hypocrisy but warned others likewise.

"A true Vice has no need of concealment," said they, "but himself carries his banner high and awe-inspiringly. What substantially new thing can Hypocrisy reveal to us that we haven't known and practiced since the very start of time? Absolutely none. On the contrary, it will teach us dangerous subterfuges and will compel us, if not to be outright ashamed of ourselves, then, in any event, to assume an air of being ashamed. *Caveant Consules!* Up to now we have had a sufficiency of firm and faithful followers, but eventually they, too, beholding our subterfuges, may say: 'The Vices sure must have gotten into a jam, since they'll soon have to deny their own selves!' And they'll turn away from us Vices—turn away they will! There, you'll see!"

Thus spake the inveterate Vices-Catos, who recognized no new tendencies, nor enticements, nor conditions. Having been born on a dunghill, they preferred to suffocate in the dung, as long as they would not have to depart from the traditions of their grandsires.

These were followed by another category of Vices who likewise did not evince any particular enthusiasm at meeting Hypocrisy; however, not because the latter went against their grain, but because they already, even without the intermediacy of Hypocrisy, had secret relations with the Virtues. To this category belonged Perfidy, Disloyalty, Treachery, Tale Bearing, Chicanery, and the like. They burst into no cheers of triumphant greeting, broke into no plaudits, offered no *vivas,* but merely winked to Hypocrisy on the sly, as much as to say: "Welcome!"

Be all that as it may, Hypocrisy's triumph was nevertheless assured. The youthful element, in the persons of Fornication, Inebriation, Barroom-Brawling, and so on, immediately called a meeting and met the truce-bearer with such ovations that Sophistry found himself compelled to cease his grousing forever.

"You only go upsetting everybody, you nasty old men!" the youngsters shouted at the elders. "We want to live, but you give us the willies!

We'll get into some school reader [this was especially enticing], will shine in the salons! The nice old ladies will simply love us!"

In a word, grounds for agreement were found at once, so that when Hypocrisy, on returning in due time, submitted a report to the Virtues, it was unanimously admitted that every reason for the existence of the Virtues and Vices as separate and inimical groups was set aside for all time. Nevertheless, they hadn't the hardihood to abrogate the old nomenclature. How could you tell, maybe it might even come in handy again? Instead, they decided to use it with such discretion that it would be perceptible to everybody that the names covered nothing but dust and ashes.

From that time forth great hospitality sprang up between the Vices and the Virtues. If Dissoluteness felt a yen to stay a while with Abstinence, he'd offer his arm to Hypocrisy—and Abstinence, having already caught sight of them from afar, would greet them:

"Welcome! Step right in! We was talkin' about you just the other day—"

Or the other way around. If Abstinence felt a yen to try some tasty Lenten dish at Dissoluteness', she'd offer her arm to Hypocrisy—and Dissoluteness already had his door flung wide open:

"Welcome! Step right in! Just the other day we was talkin' about you—"

On fast days they'd treat each other with Lenten dainties; on days when fasting was relaxed they'd treat each other with forbidden ones. With one hand they'd make the sign of the cross; with the other they'd do outrageous things. One eye would be turned up to heaven on high, the other would be lusting ever so busily and unceasingly. For the first time the Virtues came to know frailties—but the Vices didn't lose out on the deal, either. On the contrary, they were saying to all and sundry: "Never have we known any such tempting dainties as we now enjoy in passing!"

As for Simple Simon, he can't get it through his head even to this day: How come the Virtues and the Vices had so willingly made peace through Hypocrisy, when it would have been far more natural to meet on the common ground that both the one group and the other were really nothing but *Attributes*—and let it go at that!

Count Leo Nicolaievich
Tolstoi
1 8 2 8 - 1 9 1 0

~

> He [Tolstoi] is on very indeterminate terms with God, but at times they
> remind me of the terms of "two bears in one lair."
>
> GORKI

> Dear and beloved Leo Nicolaievich: I have not written you for a long
> time, for I have been, and am now, lying on my deathbed. I cannot get
> well; that is out of the question. But I write to tell you how glad I am
> to have been a contemporary of yours, and to make my last earnest re-
> quest. My friend, resume your literary work. . . . Oh, how happy I
> should be if I could believe that my supplication would prevail with
> you. My friend, our great national writer, grant my request!
>
> TURGENEV

THOSE LANDOWNING *boyari*, the Tolstois, are as interwoven with the tapestry of Russian history as the Pushkins and Turgenevs; the Tolstoi family has produced three major writers, the greatest of them being, of course, Leo, who is credited by excellent critical opinion with no fewer than three of the "world's greatest" novels. He was born at Yasnaya Polyana—Radiant [or Se-rene] Meadow—in the Province of Tula, and was orphaned at nine. In 1843 he entered the University of Kazan, to study Oriental languages, but in 1844 began to study law; he did not finish, however, leaving the University in 1847. He stayed at Radiant Meadow until 1851, when he entered the army (as a Cadet of Artillery) in the Caucasus, where he saw action in skirmishes with the mountaineers. In 1852 he began his literary career with *Childhood,* published by Necrassov in *The Contemporary.* He took part in the Crimean War; the only gain Russia realized from that disastrous campaign was the *Sebastopol Sketches* of the young Tolstoi.

In 1856 he settled in Petersburg, writing a series of stories evincing disillusionment with existing social conditions. The appearance of Tolstoi as a writer was hailed enthusiastically, but he kept very much to himself. In 1857 he resigned his commission and visited Germany, France, Italy, and England. The next trip abroad was in 1859, to study schools, welfare institutions—and jails; 1860 is marked by the death of his brother Nicholas (literally in his arms) and the beginning of his work on *War and Peace* (written at Radiant Meadow and published 1864-69). In 1861 he had his most serious quarrel with Turgenev, which almost led to a duel. In 1862, at thirty-four, he married the eighteen-year-old Sophia Andreievna, daughter of Dr. Behrs, and went back to Radiant Meadow. Here begins the stage of educating the peasants in a model school, and editing *Radiant Meadow,* a periodical devoted to expounding Tolstoi's views, which at the time were actually regarded as radical. (It was Tolstoi himself who said: "We'll do almost anything in the world for the toiler—except get off his back.")

Anna Karenina was published 1873-76. Levin, in that novel, is the portrait of Tolstoi at this stage of his life. Roughly, the death of Tolstoi the Artist and the birth of Tolstoi the Man coincided with the publication of the final portion of *Anna Karenina.* The contradictions due to a heart overflowing with humanity but under the guidance of a mind filled with skepticism became more pronounced.

It is a woeful error but a common one to regard *all* of Tolstoi's writings as literature, merely because they bear his great name. But the Tolstoi who was Pushkin's green-oak-on-a-curved-seashore is not Tolstoi Stylites. The rabid Tolstoians object, naturally, to this theorem; the dichotomy, none the less, is complete.

Ten years were taken from Dostoievski's creative life by Siberia. Ten years were taken from Tolstoi's creative life by his exclusive interest in his religious ideas. He wrote practically nothing worthy of the name of literature from the final publication of *Anna Karenina* in 1876 until 1886, when his *Death of Ivan Ilyich* appeared. The Tolstoians jubilantly chided those who had maintained that their god had ceased to be an artist. "See," they said, "his train has come out of the tunnel at last!" Whether it actually had or not, is something the reader can best judge for himself.

Of course, the case of Tolstoi is not so appalling as Dostoievski's. Tolstoi had his masterpieces already behind him; he was not afflicted by epilepsy; he was not only in a position to write, but to write in comfort; if he chose to carry bricks he could do so in a wheelbarrow, as a seigniorial whim; he did not have to lug them with the skirts of a convict's blouse for a hod, under the knout of a prison guard. And Tolstoi was in a position to put his later works in the public domain (a dubious generosity that hardly benefited anybody but the publishers), instead of having to sell most of his early copyrights and a contract for a new novel for fifteen hundred dollars, as Dostoievski had to do. On the other hand, Tolstoi used the powerful weapon of his world-wide fame to castigate Czarism, Orthodoxy, and militarism with impunity, although not even he could escape either the political or the spiritual censorships: his later, nonliterary works had to be published outside of Russia or, like *What is My Faith?* and *My Confession*, had only an illegal (though enormous) circulation in his native land. And to Tolstoi's eternal credit it must be pointed out that he was excommunicated by the Orthodox Church (1901), instead of indulging in mystical nonsense about Slavic Orthodoxy like Dostoievski.

Nor was the effect of religion as harrowing in Tolstoi's case as in Gogol's. Gogol committed the unbelievable stupidity of *Choice Passages from Correspondence with Friends;* Tolstoi published (Geneva, 1880-81) *A Criticism of Dogmatic Theology*—one of the most important works of Tolstoi the Man.

Of course, nothing in this sketch is meant as a disparagement of Tolstoi the Man, the Moralist. It is merely pointed out that Tolstoi the Man, the Moralist, great as his written or

recorded moralities may be, is not Tolstoi the Literary Artist. And if he did not deliberately abandon art, art certainly abandoned him. In one instance we have his own word for it, as reported by his Boswell, Maude: "When I asked Tolstoi what he thought of the tale (*Walk in the Light While There is Light*), he said: 'I never hear it mentioned without feeling ashamed of myself. It is thoroughly inartistic.' "

No literary artist has ever divagated into religiosity without losing his literary artistry; and literary standards should no more be applied to the latter-day Tolstoi than to Mary Baker Eddy or Joanna Southcott.

From *War and Peace* to Sunday-school stories, theological tracts, and rehashing the Bible; from *Anna Karenina* to pleas for vegetarianism and fulminations against liquor and tobacco; from *Yardstick* to a condemnation of all art (including all he had himself written up to his getting religion, with the exception of two stories), that did not earn the approval of that supreme critic of the arts, the "unperverted country peasant." *Degeneration* and *What is Art?*; Tolstoi and Nordau, bracketed. Wine, woman, and song have never wrought a comparable debacle in all literature.

Tolstoianism (a mixture of back-to-the-soil-and-the-simple-life-ism, petit-bourgeoisie-and-muzhik Christian anarchism, and negative Christianity and vegetarianism, finally jelling into a semi-intellectual, semi-peasant sectarianism) was, it may be admitted, a necessary and not entirely ineffectual movement in Czarist Russia. Even today it has its followers—but so has Fletcherism. Again, there is absolutely no impugnment here of Tolstoi's utter sincerity and partial renunciations, nor any minimizing of his stature as a moralist. It is merely pointed out that not even a Tolstoi could reconcile personal metaphysics with impossible social conditions, or transform a pink plaster into an effective remedy. Dostoievski became the darling of the reactionaries; Tolstoi the Man has been taken over by the anarchists. And, ironically, Tolstoi's two greatest sermons—*War and Peace* and *Anna Karenina*—were delivered by Tolstoi the Artist, a Titan among creative Titans.

His death at a wayside railroad station after his Oedipus-like exodus from Radiant Meadow occasioned political demonstrations throughout Russia, while the removal of his living, protective presence led to unspeakable persecutions of Tolstoians by the Russian Church and State.

Some critic has said, wittily if unkindly, that Tolstoi was apparently given to the world solely for the purpose of comparison and contrast with Dostoievski. The best of such antithetical works is Merezhcovski's *Tolstoi as Man and Artist, with an Essay on Dostoievski,* available, though incompletely, in an anonymous English version.

Tolstoi's works, with but few exceptions, are available in numerous English translations, the best being those done, *con amore,* by Louise and Aylmer Maude.

Obviously, the ideal representation for Tolstoi would be *War and Peace,* all 600,000 words of it. Or *Anna Karenina,* which runs to only half a million words. But since neither of these ideals is hardly feasible in an anthology until Gutenberg's invention is improved by the addition of elasticity, it has been thought best to resort to an approximation of an *alpha* and *omega* selectivity for Tolstoi. *Yardstick* (1861) shows him at the height of his creative power; as sheer storytelling it can hardly be surpassed. It is Tolstoi in love with life and the forces of life; in the field of animal stories, an extremely rich one in Russian literature (perhaps because in Russia it was the horse that was man's best friend, rather than the dog), *Yardstick* is one of the supreme examples. *The Death of Ivan Ilyich* may be called the swan song of Tolstoi as creative artist, merging into Tolstoi-Ecclesiastes, and is also a supreme achievement. The other two stories are thoroughly typical of Tolstoi the preacher. Both were, significantly, published in the same year as *The Death of Ivan Ilyich* (1886). *The Imp and the Crust* is, strictly speaking, a temperance tract —but what a tract! It shows Tolstoi as a master of the fairy tale, a genre that has enticed so many of the great writing Russians. And *How Much Land Does a Man Need?* will always remain one of the great moralities. It is Tolstoi in his austerest, most objective vein.

Yardstick

THE STORY OF A HORSE

Dedicated to the Memory of M. A. Stahovich[1]

I

EVER HIGHER and higher rose the sky, ever wider spread the dawn glow, the dull silver of the dew turned paler and paler, there was less and less life to the sickle of the moon, the forest was becoming more and more resonant. Men were beginning to get up out of their sleep, and in the seigniorial stable yard one heard more and more frequently equine snorting, much to-do in the straw, and even the angry high-pitched whinnying of the huddled horses, foolishly quarrelsome over something or other.

"Ho-o-o! You've got plenty of time, even if you're starved," said the old drover, quickly opening the creaking gates. "Where you goin'?" he swung at a filly that tried to get through the gates.

Nester the drover was clad in a cossackeen girdled with a belt of inlaid leather; the lash of his whip was wound around his left shoulder, and a towel holding a loaf of bread was tucked in at his belt. He was carrying a saddle and a bridle in his arms.

The horses were not in the least frightened and took no offense at the drover's mocking tone; they made believe they were utterly indifferent and leisurely walked away from the gates, except for one old mare, a dark bay with a flowing mane, who laid back an ear and flung her croup around quickly. At which a very young filly, standing behind,

Translated especially for this work by Bernard Guilbert Guerney. Copyright, 1943, by the Vanguard Press, Inc.

[1] The subject was conceived by M. A. Stahovich, author of *At Night* and *The Horseman,* and was transmitted to Tolstoi by A. A. Stahovich.—*Editor.*

whom the matter did not concern in any way, squealed and backed up against the first horse she could find.

"Ho!" the drover cried out still more loudly and threateningly, and went to a corner of the yard.

Of all the horses in the paddock (about a hundred), the least impatience was evinced by a skewbald gelding standing by himself under an overhang in a corner and, with his eyes half closed, licking an oaken post of the shed. Nobody knows just what taste the skewbald gelding found in it, but his air was serious and thoughtful enough as he went through this performance.

"Keep up your shenanigans, you!" The drover addressed him without changing his tone, walking up to him and putting the saddle and a greasy saddlecloth in the manure near the animal.

The skewbald gelding stopped licking the post and, without stirring, contemplated Nester for a long time. He did not give him a horse-laugh, did not get into a temper, did not frown, but merely distended his whole belly and sighed, ever so heavily, and turned away. The drover put an arm about the gelding's neck and put a bridle on him.

"What are you sighing about?" asked Nester.

The gelding twitched his tail, as though to say: "Nothing in particular, Nester." Nester put the saddlecloth on him and then the saddle; meanwhile the gelding laid back his ears, probably by way of expressing his displeasure, but he was merely cursed as "Trash!"—after which the saddle girths were tightened. At this the gelding sucked himself full of wind, but a finger was thrust in his mouth and he received a blow with the knee in his belly and had to let the wind out. Despite this, when the shabrack girth was being tightened, he once more laid back his ears and even looked over his shoulder. Even though he knew that it would not help, he nevertheless deemed it necessary to express his discomfort at this and would always demonstrate against it. When he was fully saddled, he thrust out his right foreleg, which had fallen asleep, and took to champing at the bit, also through some peculiar considerations of his own, for it was high time he knew that the bit could not possibly have any savor.

Nester set his foot in the shortened stirrup and clambered up on the gelding, unwound the lash of his whip from his shoulder, freed his cossackeen from under his knees, settled down in the saddle with a peculiar coachman's-hunter's-drover's seat, and gave a tug at the reins. The gelding lifted up his head, evincing his readiness to go wherever he was bid, but did not budge from the spot. He knew that before starting out there would yet be much yelling from his back, that there would be commands to the other drover, Vasska, and to the horses. And, sure enough, Nester began shouting:

"Vasska! Hey, Vasska! Did you let the brood mares out, or didn't you? Where you headin' for, you devil! Ho-o-o! Are you asleep or what? Open them gates! Let the brood mares out first," and so on.

The gates creaked. Vasska, surly and sleepy, holding his horse by a halter, stood near the gatepost and let the horses through. The horses, following one another, stepping daintily over the straw and sniffing it, began going through the gate: fillies, dock-maned yearling stallions, suckling foals, and gravid brood mares, the latter cautiously, one by one, maneuvering their heavy bellies through the gates. They crowded through, now and then in twos and threes, laying their heads over the backs of those ahead and with their legs becoming livelier in the gateway, for which they received hearty oaths from the drovers every time. The suckling foals at times threw themselves at the feet of brood mares who were not their own dams, and neighed ringingly in response to the choppy, rumbling calls of the brood mares.

One very young mischievous filly, as soon as she'd gotten outside the gates, bent her head down and off to one side, bucked with her croup and squealed, but just the same could not get up courage enough to get ahead of closely dappled gray old Zhuldyba, who, as always, went staidly at the very head, at a quiet, ponderous gait, her belly shifting from side to side.

In a few minutes the paddock, which had been so full of life, became sadly desolate, the posts of the empty shed stuck up depressingly, and all one could see was rumpled, manure-strewn straw. No matter how familiar this picture of desolation was to the skewbald gelding, it had, in all probability, a depressing effect upon him. Slowly, as though he were bowing, he lowered and then lifted his head, sighed as deeply as the shabrack girth would allow him and, shuffling his bent, stiff legs, ambled off after the drove, bearing old Nester on his bony back.

"I know what's coming next; as soon as we get out on the road he'll start striking a flint and then light up his stubby brier with its brass rim and a cap on a small chain," the gelding was thinking. "I'm glad enough, because in the early morning, while the dew is still on the grass, I find the smell of his pipe pleasant and it reminds me of much that was likewise pleasant; the only thing vexing me, though, is that once the old man gets the pipe between his teeth he always gets in a cocky mood, imagines he's the Lord knows what, and then sits sideways—sideways, without fail, yet it's that side which hurts me. However, God be with him, it's nothing new for me to suffer for the pleasure of others; I have even begun to find some sort of horsy satisfaction in it. Let the poor fellow preen himself. For he can feel chipper only as long as nobody sees him; let him sit sideways," reasoned the gelding and, stepping cautiously on his gnarled legs, walked in the middle of the road.

I I

Having gotten the drove to the river, along which the horses were to graze, Nester dismounted and unsaddled the gelding. The drove in the meanwhile had already begun to scatter slowly over the yet ungrazed meadow, covered with dew and a mist rising both from the meadow and the river curving around it.

Nester took the bit off the skewbald gelding and then scratched his throatlatch, in response to which the gelding shut his eyes as a sign of gratitude and pleasure.

"So you like that, you old hound!" Nester remarked.

The gelding, however, did not in the least like this caress, and it was only out of considerateness that he pretended to find it agreeable; he tossed his head as a sign of assent. But suddenly, altogether unexpectedly and for no reason whatsoever, probably supposing that too great familiarity might give the skewbald gelding false notions of his importance, Nester without any preliminaries thrust the gelding's head away from him and, swinging the bridle hard, dealt the gelding's bony leg a very painful blow with the buckle and, without a word, went up on a hillock, to a tree stump near which he usually sat.

But even though this action had hurt the skewbald gelding's feelings, he did not betray this in any way and, slowly switching his scanty tail and sniffing something or other, nibbling the grass now and then only by way of diversion, ambled off to the river. Paying no attention whatsoever to the cavortings of the morn-gladdened fillies or the dock-tailed yearling stallions and suckling foals around him, and knowing that the best thing of all for one's health, especially at his age, was first of all to drink heartily on an empty stomach, and only then to graze, he chose a spot on the bank where it was least steep and there was most room and, wetting his hoofs and fetlocks, thrust his muzzle in the water and began sucking in the water through his torn lips, twitching his fast-filling sides and swinging, from pleasure, his scanty skewbald tail, with the stump all but exposed.

A chestnut filly, always ready to start something, who was forever teasing the ancient and playing all sorts of nasty tricks upon him, this time waded up to him as though she had some business of her own to attend to there, but really for the sole purpose of muddying the water before his muzzle. But the skewbald had already drunk his fill and, as though not noticing the chestnut filly's intention, calmly, one after the other, drew out his legs, which had sunk in the silt, shook his head and, going off to one side from the younger element, began to graze. Shifting his legs in all sorts of ways and without trampling down any grass unnecessarily, he grazed for almost three hours, almost without straightening up. Having filled himself up so that his belly hung down like a sack from his gaunt, steep ribs, he distributed his weight on all his four ailing legs in such a way as to minimize their aches and pains—especially his right foreleg, which was the weakest of all—and dozed off.

There is an old age which is majestic, there is a vile one, and there is a pitiful old age. There is an old age that is both majestic and vile. The old age of the skewbald gelding was precisely of the last sort.

The gelding was of great height—not less than fifteen hands. Originally his color had been pied—black and white; that is what he *had* been, but now the raven-black spots had turned a dirty chestnut. His markings consisted of three patches. One was on the head (with an irregular bald spot on the side of the nose), reaching halfway down the neck. His mane, long and with plenty of burrs in it, was irregularly white and tending to chestnut. A second patch went along the right side and halfway down to the belly; the third patch was on the croup, taking in some of the tail and reaching halfway down the thighs. What was left of his tail was whitish, streaked. The big, bony head (with deep hollows over the eyes and a black drooping lower lip that had been torn at some time in the past) hung heavy and low on a neck that was bent from gauntness and seemed to be of wood. The drooping lower lip exposed the blackish tongue, held by the teeth off to one side, and the yellow stumps of the ground-down lower teeth. The ears, one of which was nicked, drooped low at the sides and twitched lazily only at rare intervals, to shoo off the flies that clung to them. A tuft of the forelock, which was still long, hung behind one ear; the large forehead was depressed and rough: the skin hung down in bags at the broad jowls. The sinews on neck and head had become knotted, quivering and trembling at the least touch of a fly. The expression of the face was austerely patient, deeply thoughtful, and betrayed suffering.

The forelegs were bent in a bow at the knees; there were bouillons on both hoofs, while on the leg where the dirty chestnut patch reached halfway down there was a lump as big as your fist. The hind legs were fresher, but had been galled at the thighs, evidently a long time ago, and the hair no longer grew there. All four legs seemed disproportionately long owing to the gauntness of the body. The ribs, although steep enough, were very much in evidence, and the skin was so tightly drawn over them that it seemed to have dried up in the hollows between them. The withers and the back were crisscrossed with traces of old beatings, while toward the croup there was a fresh sore, swollen and suppurating; the black stump of the tail, with the vertebrae clearly defined, stuck out long and almost hairless. On the chestnut-colored croup there was an old wound, the size of a palm, grown over with white hair—it looked something like a bite. Another wound, healed into a scar, could be seen on the foreshoulder. The hocks and the tail were soiled from a chronic disorder of the stomach. The hair all over the body, even though it was short, was up on end. But, despite the repulsive old age of this horse, one involuntarily stopped in thought after one glance at it, while a judge of horseflesh would say right off that this had been a remarkably good horse in its day. Such a judge would even have said that there was but one breed in Russia which could have produced such broad bones, such enormous cannons, such hoofs, such slenderness of leg bones, such a set of the neck—and, chiefest of all, such a skull—an eye so large, black, and clear, such thoroughbred plexuses of veins about the head and neck, and such fine hide and hair.

There was, in reality, something majestic about the figure of this horse and about its horrible conjunction of the repulsive signs of decrepitude (intensified by the parti-coloring of the hair) and the mannerisms, the expression of self-confidence and serenity due to a consciousness of beauty and power.

Like a living ruin he stood solitary in the middle of the dew-covered meadow, while not far from him could be heard the youthful neighing and whinnying and stamping and snorting of the scattering drove.

III

The sun had already climbed above the forest and was vividly sparkling on the grass and the bends of the river. The dew was evaporating and gathering into drops; the last of the morning mist was dissipating like light smoke. The small clouds were curly, but there was no wind yet. The green rye, the ears forming into tubes, was bristling beyond the river, and there was a smell of fresh verdure and flowers. The cuckoo was sending forth its hoarse call from the forest, and Nester, sprawled out on his back, was reckoning up how many more years he had left to live. The larks were rising up over rye and meadow. A belated rabbit got right in among the drove and then loped out into the open and froze near a bush, listening.

Vasska had dozed off, his head down in the grass; the fillies, roaming ever wider, skirted him and scattered down the slope. The older mares, snorting, laid a light trail through the dew and were constantly looking for a spot where none would intrude upon them; they were no longer grazing, however, but merely making their dessert on tasty herbs and grass shoots. The whole drove was imperceptibly moving in a single direction.

And again old Zhuldyba, staidly stepping out in front of the others, showed them the possibility of further progress. Midge, a young raven-black mare who had foaled for the first time, was incessantly neighing, choppingly and rumblingly, and, with tail up, snorted at her lilac-black suckling colt; young Silky Girl, her hide sleek and glossy, her head so low that her black, silky forelock covered her forehead and eyes, was toying with the grass—she'd nibble it and stop and tap her dew-wet foot with its downy fetlock. One of the older suckling colts, with his stubby, curly tail lifted up like a panache, probably inventing a game for himself, had, for the twenty-sixth time by now, galloped around his dam, who kept calmly nibbling the grass, having already managed to get used to the nature of her son, and only now and then looking at him out of the corner of her great dark eye.

One of the smallest sucklings, black, big-headed, with his forelock sticking up between his ears as if he were astonished, and his little tail still twisted to the side in which it had been turned in his dam's belly, with ears cocked and his eyes stolid, stood rooted, intently watching the colt who was galloping and backing, and one could not tell whether the baby was staring in envy or condemning the other for his performance. Some colts were sucking, nuzzling the teats; some, for no known reason, despite the calls of their dams, jog-trotted awkwardly in a directly opposite direction, as though in search of something, and then, for some purpose equally unknown, stopped and neighed in ear-piercing despair; some wallowed on their sides; some were learning to graze; some were scratching themselves behind their ears with their hind legs. Two other gravid mares were walking apart and, slowly shifting their feet, were still grazing. Evidently their condition was respected by all, and none of the younger element ventured to approach and intrude on them. But if some mischievous fillies did get the notion of coming near, a mere twitch of ear and tail sufficed to show such hussies the entire indecorum of such conduct.

The dock-maned yearling stallions and the yearling fillies pretended that they were already mature and staid; they cavorted but rarely and got into gay companies. They grazed with decorum, arching their closely cropped necks like swans and, as though they, too, had tails, waved their docked stumps. Just like the full-grown horses, they laid down, rolled in the grass or scratched one another. The gayest company of all consisted of two- and three-year-olds and unmated mares. Almost all of these went about together in a separate maidenly throng. One could hear stamping, squealing, neighing, snorting among them. They came together, put their heads on one another's shoulders, sniffed one another, cavorted, and at times, lifting up their tails like trumpets, half at jog trot, half at a canter, proudly and coquettishly pranced before their sister fillies.

The first beauty and instigator among all these youngsters was the chestnut filly. Whatever she started, the others followed suit; wherever she went, thither would the whole throng of beauties go as well. The mischief-maker was in a particularly playful mood this morning. This streak of gaiety had come upon her just as it comes upon men. Even at the drenching place, having had her joke at the expense of the ancient, she had started running along through the water, made believe she had been startled by something, had gasped and then dashed off for all she was worth over the field, so that Vasska had had to gallop off after her and all the others who had followed at her heels.

After which, having grazed a little, she had begun to roll, then to tease the equine crones by walking in front of their noses; then had cut off a suckling and had started chasing him, as if she would bite him. The dam had become frightened and stopped grazing, the suckling bawled heartrendingly, but the mischief-maker did him no harm whatsoever, having merely thrown a good scare into him and staged a spectacle for her sister fillies, who regarded her pranks with a sympathetic eye. After that she got the notion of turning the head of an inoffensive little roan whom a peasant was using to plow a field beyond the rye. She proudly took her stand, leaning somewhat to one side, lifted up her head, shook herself, and neighed sweetly, tenderly, and long. And there was an expression of mischievousness and of emotion and of a certain longing in that neigh. There was in it desire, and a promise of love and a longing therefor.

There, a land rail among the thick reeds passionately calls his mate to him as he darts from place to place; there are the cuckoo and the quail singing of love, and the flowers send their fragrant pollen to one another through their messenger the wind.

"For I, too, am young and beautiful and strong," said the neighing of the mischievous filly, "yet up to now it has not been given to me to experience the delight of this emotion, and not only has it not been given to me, but never a lover—not one!—has yet beheld me."

And the neighing, fraught with so much significance, aroused a pensive and youthful echo from bottom land and field and was borne from afar to the little roan. He cocked up his ears and stopped. The peasant kicked him with his bast sandal, but the little roan was bewitched by the silvery sound of the distant neighing, and he neighed in his turn. The peasant became angered, pulled at the traces, and kicked him in the belly so hard with the bast sandal that the neigh was cut short, and the roan plodded on. But the roan now had a feeling that was both delectable and sad, and from beyond the growing rye for a long time yet there were borne to the drove the sounds of the neigh the roan had begun and of the angry voice of the peasant.

If from the mere sound of this call the little roan could have lost his senses to the extent of forgetting his duty, what would have befallen him if he could have seen the mischief-maker in all her beauty, could have seen how she, with her ears cocked, her nostrils distended, sucking in the air, and yearning to be off somewhere, her whole young and beautiful body quivering, was calling him?

But the mischief-maker did not spend much time in thinking of her impressions. When the call of the roan had died away she neighed mockingly again and, lowering her head, began pawing the ground, after which she went to awaken and tease the skewbald gelding. The skewbald gelding was an eternal martyr and butt for these happy youngsters. He suffered more from those youngsters than from men. He did no evil either to the ones or the others. Men were motivated by needing him—but why did the young horses torture him?

IV

He was old, they were young; he was gaunt, they were feeling their oats; he was woebegone, they were gay. Therefore he was an alien, an outsider, altogether a different being, and it was out of the question to pity him. Horses feel pity only for their own selves and only rarely for those in whose skin they might easily imagine themselves. But then, was the skewbald gelding to blame because he was old and emaciated and disfigured?

It would seem not, yet, according to equine standards, he was to blame, and those who were always in the right were only those who were strong, young, and happy, those who had everything ahead of them, those whose every muscle quivered and whose tail went up like a stake from utterly uncalled-for expenditures of energy. It is even possible that the skewbald gelding himself understood this and during his calm moments agreed that he was to blame, that he had already lived his life, that he had to pay for that life; but he was a horse, after all, and often could not refrain from feeling insults, sadness, and indignation as he looked at this younger element, punishing him for that very thing which they all would be subject to toward the end of life. An aristocratic feeling was also one cause of the horses' pitilessness. Every horse in the drove traced his or her pedigree either through sire or dam from the famous Sour Cream Pitcher, whereas no one knew what line the skewald was from; the skewbald was a newcomer, bought three years ago at a fair for eighty paper bills.

The chestnut filly, as though she were strolling about, walked up to the very nose of the skewbald gelding and nudged him. He already knew what was coming and, without opening his eyes, laid his ears back and bared his teeth. The filly turned her croup to him and made believe she was about to kick him. He opened his eyes and walked off in a different direction. He no longer wanted to sleep and fell to grazing. The mischief-maker, accompanied by her sister fillies, approached him anew. A two-year-old filly, very stupid and marked with a star on her forehead, who always imitated the chestnut and followed her in everything, came up with her and, as imitators always do, began overdoing the very same thing the instigator was doing.

The chestnut had a way of walking up as if she were minding her own business and passing by the gelding's very nose, with never a look at him, so that he absolutely did not know whether he should get angry or not, and this was really funny. She went through this performance this time as well, but the filly with the starred forehead, who was following the chestnut and was in a particularly gay mood, struck the gelding right in the chest. He again bared his teeth, squealed, and with a spirit that could hardly be expected from him, made a dash for her and bit her on the thigh. The little starred filly backed with her whole croup, and backed hard, striking painfully the ancient's barrel-staved, prominent ribs. The ancient actually rattled in his throat, was about to throw himself at her, but then changed his mind and, with a heavy sigh, walked off to one side. The entire youthful element of the drove must have taken as a personal affront the impertinence which the skewbald had permitted himself against the starred filly, and for all the rest of that day they absolutely would not allow him to graze and would not give him a moment's peace, so that the drover had to calm them down several times and could not understand what had gotten into them.

The gelding felt so hurt that he walked up of his own accord to Nester when the old man got ready to bring the drove back, and the old horse felt happier and calmer when he was saddled and mounted.

God knows what the ancient gelding was thinking about as he bore the ancient Nester on his back. Whether he was reflecting with bitterness on the relentless and cruel younger element, or whether he was forgiving those who had wronged him, with that contemptuous and taciturn pride peculiar to ancients, the fact remains that he did not betray his reflections all the way home.

On this evening some cronies had come to visit Nester and, as he was driving the horses past the huts of the house serfs, he noticed a horse and cart hitched near his front steps. Having coralled the drove, he was in such a hurry that he let the gelding into the yard without taking the saddle off and, after yelling to Vasska to unsaddle him, locked the gates and went off to his cronies.

Whether as a consequence of the insult inflicted on the star-marked filly, a great-granddaughter of Sour Cream Pitcher, by the "scabby trash" bought at a horsefair and knowing neither his sire nor dam, and therefore insulting the aristocratic feelings of the whole paddock, or as a consequence of the gelding's still carrying a high saddle without a mount and therefore presenting a strangely fantastic spectacle for the horses, the fact remains that something out of the ordinary went on in the paddock that night. All the horses, young and old, pursued the gelding with their teeth bared, chasing him all over the yard; there were sounds of hoofs kicking against his gaunt sides, and heavy groaning. The gelding could not bear this any more; he could no longer avoid the kicks. He stopped in the middle of the yard; his face expressed the revolting, weak malevolence of impotent old age, followed by despair; he laid back his ears—and suddenly something happened that made all the horses quiet down abruptly. Vyazopuriha, the oldest mare of all, approached, sniffed the gelding, and sighed. The gelding sighed as well. . . .

V

In the middle of the yard, flooded by the light of the moon, stood the tall, gaunt figure of the gelding still carrying a high saddle with an upright, knobbed pommel. The other horses stood around him without stirring and in profound silence, as though they had learned something new from him, something out of the ordinary. And they truly had learned something new, something unexpected.

Here is what they learned from him.

NIGHT THE FIRST

Yes, I am the son of Amiable I and Country Wife. According to the pedigree my name is Muzhik I. I am Muzhik I according to the pedigree, I am Yardstick in street talk, so nicknamed by the crowd for my long and sweeping stride, the equal of which was not to be found in all Russia. By birth there is not in the world a horse of better blood than mine. I'd never have told you this. What would be the use? You wouldn't have recognized me, just as Vyazopuriha failed to recognize me, even though she had been at the Hrenovo stud with me, and who only now has acknowledged me. You wouldn't believe me even now, if it weren't for the testimony of this Vyazopuriha. I'd never tell you this. I've no need of horsy commiseration. But you wanted this. Yes, I'm that Yardstick whom the lovers of horseflesh are searching for and cannot find, that Yardstick whom the Count himself used to know and whom he got out of his stud because I humiliated Swan, his favorite stallion.

When I was foaled I didn't know what *skewbald* meant—I thought I was just a horse. The first remark about my coat made, I remember, a deep impression upon me and my dam.

I must have been foaled late at night; toward morning, licked down by my dam, I was already standing on my legs. I remember that I was constantly wishing for something, and that everything seemed exceedingly amazing to me and, at the same time, exceedingly simple. Our stalls were in a long, warm corridor with a gate of latticework, through which you could see everything.

My dam offered me her teats, but I was still so innocent that I kept nuzzling now her forelegs, now her udder. Suddenly my dam looked around at the latticed door and, stepping over me, stood aside. The day groom was looking into our stalls through the lattice.

"Look at that, will you—Country Wife has foaled," said he, and began to lift the latch. He walked over the fresh-strewn straw and put his arms around me. "Just look, Taras," he shouted. "What a skewbald—just like a magpie."

I struggled free from him and stumbled to my knees.

"What a little devil!"

My dam felt uneasy; she did not come to my defense, however, but merely walked a little off to one side after a heavy, heavy sigh. The grooms came and began looking me over. One of them ran off to inform the head groom.

They all laughed, looking at my markings, and gave me all sorts of odd names. Not only I, but my mother, too, did not understand the meaning of their words. Up to now in my immediate line, as well as among all those of my blood, there had never been a single skewbald. We didn't think there was anything bad about that. As for my build and strength, they were praised by all even then.

"Look at how spry he is," said one of the grooms. "There's no holding him."

Some time later the head groom came and began to wonder at my color; he actually seemed disappointed.

"Who in the world did a great freak like that take after?" he commented. "The General will never let him stay at the stud. Eh, Country Wife, you sure have fixed my wagon for me," he turned to my dam; "if you'd at least foaled him with a star marking—but, no, it had to be an out-and-out skewbald!"

My dam made no answer and, as females always do in such cases, sighed again.

"And who the devil did he take after?—he looks just like a muzhik," the head groom went on. "You can't have a disgrace like that hanging around the stud. And yet he's good-looking—right good-looking!" he was saying—and so said they all as they looked at me.

A few days later the General himself came; he took one look at me— and again for some reason all were horrified by something—and swore both at me and my dam for the color of my coat.

"And yet he's good-looking—right good-looking!" said everyone who looked at me.

Until spring we foals lived in the mares' quarters, each one with his dam—only when the snow on the paddock roofs had already begun to thaw in the sun did they begin to let us out with our dams into the wide yard, strewn with fresh straw, but this was only rarely. Here for the first time I came to know all those of my blood, both near and far removed. Here I saw all the famous brood mares of the time coming out with their sucklings from the different wickets. Here were Dutchwoman, Midge (own daughter to Sour Cream Pitcher), Scarlet Fever, Good and Quiet—a mount, she was; all celebrities of that day, they all gathered there with their sucklings, ambled about in the sun, rolled in the freshly laid straw and sniffed one another, just as common horses do. I can't forget to this day the appearance of that paddock, filled with the beauties of that period. You would have seen there that same Vyazopuriha, who was then only a one-year-old, a charming, gay, and spirited filly, but—and this isn't said to offend her—despite the fact that she's considered a blooded rarity among you, she was at that time one of the poorest horses of that brood.

My piebaldness, which men disliked so, proved very much to the liking of horses; they all surrounded me, admired me, and made overtures to me. I was already beginning to forget what men said of my piebaldness and felt happy. But I soon came to know the first grief in my life, and the cause of it was my dam. When it had already begun to thaw, when the sparrows were chirruping under the sheds and one felt more keenly the spring in the air, my dam began to change in her treatment of me.

Her whole manner changed: either she would suddenly become playful, running through the yard, which was utterly unbecoming to one of her respectable age, or she would become moody and take to neighing, or she would bite and kick out at her sister mares, or start sniffing me and snorting in dissatisfaction, or, coming out into the sun, she would lay her head on the shoulder of her cousin, Merchant's Lady, and for a long while would scratch the other's back and thrust me away from her teats.

One day the head groom came, ordered a halter put on her, and she was led out of the stable; she neighed; I answered her and darted after her, but she did not even look back at me. Taras, the groom, put his arms about me just as they were shutting the door after my dam had been led out.

I made a dash, knocking the groom down in the straw, but the door was shut, and all I heard was the constantly receding neighing of my dam. And in that neighing I no longer heard her call to me—what I heard was expressive of something else. In answer to her neigh there came a mighty answering one from a distance—as I learned later, it was that of Goodfellow I, who, with a groom on either side of him, was going to an assignation with my dam.

I don't remember how Taras left our stall—I was far too sad; I felt I had lost my dam's love forever. And all because I was skewbald, I thought, remembering what men said about my coat, and such rancor overcame me that I took to knocking my head and knees against the walls of the stall, and kept doing that until I was all in a sweat and had stopped from exhaustion.

After some time my dam came back to me. I heard her coming at a hand gallop, with an unusual stride, down the aisle and to our stall. They opened the wicket for her, and I did not recognize her, she had grown so much younger and handsomer. She sniffed me all over, snorted, and began a choppy, rumbling neigh. By her whole air I saw that she did not love me.

She told me how handsome Goodfellow I was, and about her love for him. These assignations went on, and the relations between my dam and myself were becoming cooler and cooler.

Soon we were let out to graze. From that time on I learned new joys, which replaced for me the loss of my dam's love. I had play-mates, both colts and fillies. All of us learned together how to graze, to neigh just as the adults did, and, with our tails up, to prance around our dams. That was a happy period. Everything was forgiven me, everybody admired my looks and regarded with tolerance anything I might do. This did not last long.

Soon thereafter something horrible happened to me.

The gelding heaved a sigh, ever so deep a sigh, and walked away from the other horses.

Dawn had already begun. The gates creaked; Nester entered. The drover fixed the saddle on the gelding and drove all the horses out to pasture.

VI

NIGHT THE SECOND

As soon as the horses had been driven into the yard, they again crowded about the gelding.

In the month of August my dam and I were separated (the gelding went on). Nor did I feel any particular grief. I saw that my mother was already heavy with a younger brother, the famous Mustachio, and I was no longer what I had once been. I wasn't jealous, but I felt that I was becoming colder toward her. Besides, I knew that after leaving my dam I would go into the quarters where all the colts were kept, where we were stalled in twos and threes and where we young fellows were let out for an airing daily, all of us in a crowd.

There I shared the same stall with Dear Lad. Dear Lad was a mount, and subsequently the Emperor rode on him, and he was portrayed in paintings and statues. At that time he was just a plain suckling with a sleek fine coat, a small neck as arched as a swan's, and legs straight and slender, like harp strings. He was always jolly, kindhearted and amiable; he was always ready to play, to lick you, and to try pranks on horse or man. We became friends, perforce, living together as we did, and that friendship continued through all our youth. He was jolly and lightheaded. Even then he was becoming the great lover, flirting with the fillies and laughing at my innocence. And to my misfortune I began imitating him, out of vanity, and was soon all taken up with love. And this early inclination of mine was the cause of the greatest change in my destiny. It so happened that I became infatuated. . . .

Vyazopuriha was older than I by a year, she and I were especially friendly, but toward the end of fall I noticed that she was fighting shy of me—

However, I'm not going to tell you the whole unfortunate story of my love; she herself remembers my insane infatuation, which ended for me in the most important change in my life.

The drovers took to chasing her and beating me. One evening they drove me into a special stall; I neighed all through the night, as though I had a premonition of what would take place on the morrow.

In the morning there came to the corridor of my stall the General himself, the head groom, the grooms and the drovers, and there was a terrible uproar. The General was bawling out the head groom, the head groom was making excuses for himself, saying that he'd given no orders to let me have my way, but that the grooms had done so of their own accord. The General said he'd have all of 'em horsewhipped, but that you couldn't keep colts stalled all the time. Then they quieted down and left. I did not understand a thing, but I saw that they had something or other in mind for me. . . .

The day after that my neighing days were over and done with forever; I became that which I am now. The whole world changed in my eyes. Everything lost its appeal for me; I withdrew into myself and became reflective. At first everything was distasteful to me. I ceased even drinking, eating, and walking about; as for play, it goes without saying I didn't even think of it. At times I'd get the notion into my head of kicking up my heels, of cavorting a little, of neighing a little; but immediately the fearful question would occur to me: What for? What's the use? And my last strength would desert me.

Once, of an evening, I was being led home at the time when the drove was coming home from pasture. Even from afar I caught sight of a cloud of dust with vague, familiar outlines of all the brood mares in our stud. I heard cheerful, choppy neighing and the stamping of hoofs. I stopped, despite the fact that the rope of the halter by which the groom was pulling me was cutting into my neck, and began looking at the approaching drove, as one looks at happiness lost forever and gone beyond retrieve. They were nearing, and I made out, one after the other, all the familiar, beautiful, majestic, healthy, well-fed figures. Here and there some of them also turned around to look at me. I did not feel the pain from the halter the groom was tugging at. I forgot myself and involuntarily, through old memories, began to neigh and started running at a trot. But my neighing echoed sadly, mirth-provokingly, and absurdly. Those in the drove did not start laughing loudly, but I noticed that many of them, out of decency, turned away from me. They, evidently, felt not only aversion but pity and conscience-struck shame, but above all, they felt like laughing at me. They found something funny about my scrawny, unimpressive neck (I had lost weight at that time), my great head, my long, awkward legs, and the silly jog-trot gait in which I had, through my habit of old, begun to cavort around my groom. None responded to my neighing; all turned away from me. I suddenly understood everything—understood to what an extent I had forever become far removed from all of them, and I do not remember how I came home in the wake of the groom.

Even before, I had already evinced an inclination to gravity and pondering; but now there was a decisive overturn in me. My markings, which aroused such strange contempt in men, my fearful, unexpected misfortune, and also my somehow anomalous position at the stud, which I felt but as yet could not explain to myself no matter how I tried, compelled me to withdraw into myself. I pondered deeply on the injustice of men, who were condemning me because I was a skewbald; I pondered deeply about the inconstancy of maternal love—and female love in general, and the dependence of that love on physical conditions; and, chiefly, I pondered deeply over the qualities of that strange breed of animals with whom we are so closely bound and whom we call men —those qualities out of which issued that anomalousness of my position at the stud, which I felt but could not understand.

The significance of this anomalousness and of the human qualities upon which it was based was revealed to me by the following incident.

It was in winter, during the holidays. For a whole day I was given no fodder and was not drenched. As I learned later, this was because our groom was drunk. That same day the head groom came to my stall, saw that there was no fodder, began to swear in the vilest of vile words about the absent groom, and then went away.

The next day the groom, with another one, a crony of his, came into our stable to give us hay. I noticed that he was particularly pale and woebegone—especially about the look of his long back was there something significant and calling forth one's compassion.

He angrily tossed the hay in the rack. I was about to reach with my head over his shoulder, but he hit me with his fist on the nose so painfully that I leaped back. Whereupon he kicked me with his boot in the belly.

"If it hadn't been for this scabby creature nothin' would have happened," said he.

"Why, how come?" asked the other groom.

"Never fear, he don't go checking up on the Count's horses, but he visits his own hoss twice a day."

"Why, did they give him that there skewbald, now?" asked the other.

"Whether they sold it to him or made him a present of it—who the hell knows. If you was to starve all of the Count's horses to death, nothin' would happen; but how dared I not give *his* yearling any fodder? 'Lie down,' says he, and did he larrup me! There's no Christianity in him. Has more pity for a brute beast than a human bein'. He wears no cross on him, it's easy to see; he counted the lashes himself, the monster! The General himself never gave me no dose like that; he crisscrossed my whole back with welts. You can see he ain't got a Christian's soul."

That which they were saying about a whipping and Christianity I understood well; but it was utterly obscure to me then what the words "*his own* colt, *his* colt," meant, from which I saw that people presupposed some sort of connection between me and the head groom. What that connection consisted of I could not at that time grasp, no matter how I tried. It was only considerably later, when they separated me from the other horses, that I understood what was meant. At that time I simply could not understand the significance of calling *me* the property of a man. The words "*My* horse" referred to me, a living horse, and seemed to me just as strange as "My land," "My air," "My water."

However, these words had an enormous influence upon me. I kept thinking of this without cease, and only long after the most diversified dealings with men did I come to understand, at last, the significance which men ascribe to these queer words. Their significance is this: Men are guided in life not by deeds but by words. They do not love the opportunity of doing or not doing a thing so much as they love the opportunity of speaking about different objects in words agreed upon among themselves. Such words, which are considered very important among them, are really nothing but words, and their gist lies in the one word *my*, which they apply to different things, beings and objects—even to land, to men, and to horses. They agree among themselves that only one of them may say *my* about one particular thing. And he who can apply *my* to the greatest number of things in this game agreed upon among themselves is considered the happiest. *Why* that is so I don't know, but so it is. Formerly I tried for a long time to explain this to myself by some direct gain they may derive, but this explanation proved to be unjust.

Many of those men who called me, for instance, their horse, never rode me, but it was wholly different people who did ride me. It was also not they who fed me, but entirely others. The good things, again, were not done to me by those who called me their horse, but by coachmen, veterinaries, and, in general, outsiders. Subsequently, having widened the circle of my observations, I became convinced that it is not only concerning us horses that the concept of *my* has no other basis save a low and brute human instinct, which among them is called the sense or right of property. Man says "The house is mine," and never lives in it, but merely worries about the building and maintenance of the house. A merchant says: "My shop, my dry-goods shop," for instance, and doesn't own a suit of the best material to be found in that shop of his.

There are men who call land theirs, yet have never set eyes on that land and have never trodden it. There are men who call other men theirs, but yet have never set eyes on the other men, and their sole relation to those other men consists of doing them evil.

There are men who call women their women or wives, but these women live with other men who do not own them. And men do not strive in life to do that which they consider good, but toward calling as many things as possible *theirs.*

Now I am convinced that the distinction between us and men consists of just that. And therefore, to say nothing whatsoever about our other points of superiority over men, we can through this alone boldly say that in the scale of living creatures we stand higher than men: the activity of men—at least of those whom I've had to do with—is guided by words, whereas ours is guided by horse sense.

And so the head groom had received this right to say *my horse* about me, and because of that he had horsewhipped the groom. This discovery made a strong impression on me, and together with those thoughts and opinions which my pied color called forth in men, and the reflectiveness called forth in me by my dam's betrayal, compelled me to become the serious and deeply reflective gelding I am.

I was thrice misfortunate: I was a skewbald, I was a gelding, and people had gotten the notion that I belonged not to God and to myself, as is natural to every living creature, but that I belonged to the head groom.

The consequences of the notion they'd gotten about me were many.

The first one, for instance, was that I was kept apart, had better fodder, was exercised more often, and was put earlier in harness, than the others. I was first harnessed when I was going on my third year. I remember how, the first time the head groom himself, who imagined that I belonged to him, began to harness me amid a crowd of grooms, expecting me to be obstreperous or to balk. They tied ropes all over me before backing me in between the shafts; they put a broad cross of leather on my back and tied it to the shafts, so that I might not throw myself back on my croup, whereas all I was waiting for was to show my eagerness and love for work.

They wondered because I started off like a veteran horse. They began pacing me and I began to practice trotting. With every day I scored greater successes, so that three months later the General himself and many others were praising my stride. But what a strange thing: precisely because they imagined I was not my own but belonged to the head groom, my stride took on for them an entirely different significance.

The stallions, my brethren, were driven on the track; they were paced and clocked; men came out to watch them, they were driven in gilded sulkies, expensive horsecloths were thrown over them. I was driven in the unpretentious sulky of the head groom, when he had business in Chesmenka and other farms. All this was due to my being a skewbald, but chiefly because I was, in their opinion, not the Count's but the head groom's own.

Tomorrow, if we're still alive, I'll tell you what was the most important consequence to me of this right of property which the head groom imagined he had over me.

All that day the horses treated Yardstick with respect. But Nester's treatment of him was as rough as ever. The muzhik's little roan stallion began neighing as soon as he was nearing the drove, and the chestnut filly was coquetting again.

VII

NIGHT THE THIRD

The new moon was already born, and its slender, narrow sickle lit up the figure of Yardstick, standing in the middle of the yard; the horses *were crowding* around him.

The most important—and astonishing—consequence for me of my being not the Count's, not God's, but the head groom's (the skewbald went on), was that that which constitutes our chief merit—a spirited stride—became the cause of my banishment.

They were pacing Swan around the course when the head groom drove me up from Chesmenka and stopped near the course. Swan went past us. He was going well, but just the same he was showing off: there wasn't in him that efficiency which I had worked out for myself: that faculty of having another foot come up the second the first touches the ground, and of not having the least effort go to waste but to have every effort carry you forward. Swan passed by us. I started going onto the track; the head groom did not hold me back.

"What say—want to try out my skewbald dog?" he shouted, and when Swan came up to us again he let me go. The other had already gotten up speed, and so I fell back at the first lap, but in the second I began gaining on him, began drawing near his sulky, began to run side by side with him—and got ahead of him. I tried it again—with the same result. I was the more spirited. And this threw everybody into panic. The General asked that I be sold as quickly as possible and as far away as possible, so as to see nor hide nor hair of me. "Or else the Count will find out, and there'll be trouble"—that's what he said.

And I was sold to a jobber as a shaft horse. I didn't stay on the jobber's hands long. I was bought by a Hussar, who had come for a remount.

All this was so unjust, so cruel, that I was glad when I was led out of Hrenovo and parted forever from all that was near and dear to me. I felt far too sad among them. Before them lay love, honors, freedom; before me—work and humiliation, and humiliation and work, to the end of my life! For what? For that I was skewbald, and because, for that reason, I had had to become somebody's horse.

Yardstick could not tell them more of his story that evening. There was an occurrence in the paddock which created a great stir among all the horses. Merchant's Lady, a gravid mare who was overdue with her foaling, and who had been an attentive listener to Yardstick's story since its beginning, suddenly turned around and slowly walked under the shed, where she began to groan so loudly that she attracted the attention of all the horses; she lay down, then she got up again, and again lay down. The old brood mares understood what was happening to her, but the youngsters were all excited and, leaving the gelding, surrounded the ailing mare. Toward morning there was a new colt, swaying on its wobbly legs. Nester shouted for the head groom, and the mare with her foal were led off to the day stable, while the rest of the horses were driven out without them.

VIII

NIGHT THE FOURTH

In the evening, when the gates were closed and everything had quieted down, the skewbald went on as follows:

Many are the observations, both of men and of horses, that I managed to make during the time I was passing from hand to hand. I stayed the longest of all with two owners: the Prince, who was an officer in the Hussars, and a little crone who lived near the church of Nicola of the Presentation.

At the Hussar officer's I passed the best time of my life.

Even though he was the cause of my perdition, even though he never loved anything or anybody, I love him now and I loved him then for precisely that reason.

What I liked about him precisely was that he was handsome, happy, rich, and because of that loved no one.

You will understand this lofty equine feeling of ours! His coldness, my dependence upon him, lent particular ardor to my love for him. "Kill me, founder me," I used to think in those days when both his luck and mine ran high, "and I'll be all the happier for that."

He had bought me from the jobber, to whom the head groom had sold me, for eight hundred rubles. The Hussar had bought me because nobody had any pied horses.

He had a mistress. I knew this because I carried him to her every day; I carried her, too, and at times carried the two of them together.

His mistress was a Venus and he was an Adonis. And I loved both of them for that. And I lived well.

Here's how my life went: in the morning the groom would come to attend to me—not the coachman himself, mind you, but a groom. This hostler was a young boy, fresh from the country. He'd open the door, let out all the horsy fumes and vapor, get rid of the manure, take off the horsecloths, and then begin to run a brush over my body and knock out small rows of whitish fluff and the like on the floor joist, which was all splintery from caulks. I'd nibble at his sleeve, just in horseplay, and paw. Then, one by one, we were brought up to the trough of cold water, and the lad contemplated admiringly my markings, that he had worked at so hard, or my leg, as straight as an arrow, with its broad hoof, and my sleek croup and back, so smooth and broad you could bed on it. Hay was tossed up into the high racks, oats were poured into the mangers of oak. Then Theophan, the head coachman, would arrive.

The master and the coachman resembled each other. Neither one feared anything or loved anybody, except his own self, and for that reason everybody loved them. Theophan walked about in a red shirt and plush trousers and a sleeveless jacket. I loved it when, of holidays, in that jacket and with his hair slicked down with pomatum, he would walk into the stable and call out: "There, you brute creature, you're forgettin' yourself!" and would prod my thigh with the handle of the pitchfork, yet never painfully, however, but merely as a joke. I'd immediately appreciate the joke and, cocking back an ear, would click my teeth.

We had a coal-black stallion, one of a pair. Of nights they would team me up in harness with him, among others. This Regimental had no sense of humor, but was out-and-out mean, mean as the Devil. I stood in the stall next to his, with just the barrier between us, and many's the tough fight we had. But Theophan wasn't afraid of him. He used to walk straight up to him and yell at him; it looked as if the black would kill him, but, no, he'd side-step, and Theophan would clap the harness right on him.

At one time he and I were teamed up, and we dashed down Kusnetski Bridge, which isn't a bridge at all but a great street. Neither the master nor the coachman was afraid: they laughed, shouted at the people, and held us back, and turned us this way and that—so in the end the black didn't succeed in running over anybody.

It was in their service that I lost my best points and half my life. That's where they overdrenched me and ruined my legs and feet. But despite everything that was the best period of my life! At noon they'd come, harness me, grease my hoofs, slick down my forelock and mane, and back me in between the shafts.

The sleigh was of reed-work, upholstered in velvet; the harness had little silver buckles on it; the reins were of silk and, at the same time, filleted. The harness was such that when all the traces, all the little straps and things, were put on and fastened in place, you couldn't tell where the harness ended and the horse began. They'd harness us in the coach house. Theophan would enter, with his behind broader than his shoulders, with a red belt that reached up to his armpits; he'd look over the harness, take his seat, fix his robe, put his feet in the footrests, pass some joke or other, always heft his whip, with which he hardly ever even flicked me, but just for the sake of etiquette, and would say: "Let 'er go!" And, with every stride a frolic, I'd start out of the gate; and the cook, who'd come out with the slops, and the muzhik who'd brought firewood into the yard, would stand watching with goggling eyes.

Theophan would drive out, ride back and forth a little, and pull up. The flunkies would come out, other coachmen drove up. And they'd start talking. Everybody waited; sometimes we'd stand for three hours at the front entrance, going for a little ride occasionally and then pulling up again.

At last there'd be a noise in the entry; gray-headed Tihon with his little potbelly would run out in his livery coat: "Drive up!" At that time they didn't have that coarse way of saying: "Come on!" as though I didn't know that it's customary to go onward and not backward. Theophan would make a kissing sound with his lips and drive up closer; the Prince would come out, hurriedly and nonchalantly, as though there was nothing astonishing about that sleigh, or about the horse, or about Theophan, who'd straighten up his back and hold his arms in so rigid a way that it seemed impossible for him to keep it up for long. The Prince would come out in a shako and a uniform overcoat with a collar of silvery beaver, which hid his handsome face with its fresh color and black eyebrows, a face that never should have been hidden. He'd come out with his sword, spurs, and the brass-tipped heels of his galoshes jingling, walking over the carpet as though he were in a hurry and paying no attention to me or to Theophan—whom everybody, except himself, was looking at and admiring. Theophan would make that kissing noise with his lips, I'd lean into my harness, and at a round honest pace we'd drive up to wherever we were going and pull up; I'd look at the Prince out of the corner of my eye and toss my blooded head and fine forelock. If the Prince were in good spirits he'd jest with Theophan; Theophan would reply in kind, turning his handsome head around just the least bit and, without lowering his arms, make a barely perceptible move with his reins, which was nevertheless perfectly comprehensible to me, and *thud, thud, thud!*—I'd run, ever more sweepingly, quivering in every muscle and throwing the snow and mire back against the dashboard. At that time there was none of that coarse way of shouting: "Ho-o-o!" as though the coachman had a bellyache or something, but there was an esoteric phrase: "Watch out, now!"—"Watch out, now!" Theophan would shout from time to time, and the common folk would hug the wall and stop and crane their necks, looking around at the handsome gelding, the handsome driver, and the handsome master.

I was especially fond of overtaking a trotter. When we, Theophan and I, used to catch sight in the distance of a rig worthy of our exertion, we, flying like a whirlwind, would gradually float nearer and nearer. By now, spattering mire far beyond the sleigh, I'd evened up with the occupant and was snorting over his head; then I'd even up with the driver's seat, with the front shaft; then I no longer saw the horse, and only heard his hoofbeats falling farther and farther behind. But the Prince and Theophan and I, we all kept silent and made believe that we were simply out for a ride, minding our own business, that we weren't even noticing riders with gentle horses when we came across them. I was fond of overtaking a good trotter, but I also loved to meet up with one. One instant, a sound, a glance—and we had already gone apart and each one was flying solitarily on his own way. . . .

The gates creaked, and the voices of Nester and Vasska were heard.

NIGHT THE FIFTH

The weather began to change. It was overcast, there was no dew of mornings, but it was still warm and the midges simply stuck to one. As soon as the drove had been corralled, the horses gathered about the skewbald, and he ended his story as follows:

My happy life soon came to an end. I had lived thus for only two years. At the end of the second winter occurred the most joyous event in my life, and after it my greatest misfortune. This was at Shrovetide. I took the Prince to the races. Satin-Smooth and Bullock were to run off a race. I don't know what went on in the clubhouse. But I know that the Prince came out and ordered Theophan to drive on into the track. I remember I was led into the track and placed there, and then Satin-Smooth was placed alongside. Satin-Smooth was in regular racing rig, but I came on just as I was, drawing a city sleigh. At a turn I showed him my heels. I was greeted by loud laughter and roars.

When I was led off I was followed by a crowd. And five men or so were offering the Prince thousands of rubles. He merely laughed, showing his white teeth.

"No," he was saying, "this isn't a horse but a friend; I wouldn't take a mountain of gold for him. *Au revoir,* gentlemen!"

He unbuttoned the apron and got into the sleigh.

"To Ostezhenka!"

His mistress had her apartment there. And we flew off.

That was the last happy day for the Prince and me. We came to her. He called her *his*. But she'd fallen in love with some other man and had gone off with him. The Prince found this out at her apartment. It was five o'clock, and without unharnessing me he went off after her. I was given the whip, something that had never been done to me before, and was let out at a gallop. For the first time I changed my pace clumsily and became ashamed of myself; I wanted to correct it but suddenly I heard the Prince shouting in a voice that was not his own: "Let him have it!" And the whip whistled and cut me, and I galloped off, my hind legs striking against the metal of the dashboard.

We caught up with her sixteen miles farther on. I had brought him where he wanted, but I trembled all night long and could not eat a mouthful. In the morning they drenched me. I drank, and forever ceased to be the horse I had been. I was sick; they tortured and maimed me—curing me, as men call it. My hoofs sloughed off, I got bouillons, and my legs became bowed; my chest caved in, and there was listlessness and weakness all through my body. I was sold to a coper. He fed me up on carrots and something else, and made me over into something else that did not resemble me but that could take in someone who didn't know much about horses. There was no longer any strength, any speed left in me.

Besides that, the coper used to torture me every time any buyers came, by walking into my stall and starting in to lash me with a great whip and frighten me, so that he threw me into a frenzy. Then he'd rub down the welts from the whip and lead me out.

A little old crone bought me from the coper. She was forever riding to Nicola of the Presentation, and she used to whip her coachman. The coachman actually cried in my stall. And I learned that tears have a pleasant, salty taste. Then the little crone died. Her estate manager took me to the country and sold me to a dry-goods peddler; then I overate on wheat and became sicker than ever. I was sold to a muzhik. With him I had to plow and went almost without eating, and my leg was almost cut off by a plowshare. I was sick again. A gypsy got me in a swap. He tortured me horribly and at last sold me to the manager of this stud. And here I am. . . .

They were all silent. A drizzle began to fall.

I X

As the drove was coming home the next evening it was met by the owner and a guest of his. Zhuldyba, as she was nearing home, looked out of the corner of her eye at the two male figures: one was that of the young owner, in a straw hat; the other was that of a military man, tall, stout, bloated. The old mare looked out of the corner of her eye at the men and, crowding the owner, went past him; the others—the youngsters —became flustered and got in a huddle, especially when the owner and his guest deliberately walked in right among the horses, pointing something out to each other and talking.

"That dappled gray mare I bought from Voyecov," the owner was saying.

"And whose is that black filly with the white legs? Damn good-looking," the guest was saying. They looked over many of the horses, making them run and stop. They noticed the chestnut filly, too.

"This is one of the Hrenov breed left over, one of their mounts," the owner pointed out.

They could not examine all the horses as they went past. The owner shouted for Nester, and the old man, hastily prodding the sides of the skewbald with his heels, started forward at a jog trot. The skewbald hobbled, leaning heavily on one leg, but it was evident that he would under no circumstances have raised any protest even if he were ordered to run just as he was doing, as long as his strength lasted, and to the end of the world. He was ready even to gallop, and actually made a start with his right leg.

"There, I dare say there's no better horse in Russia than this mare," said the owner, pointing out one. The guest praised her. The owner began bustling, dashing, showing the horses and giving the history and breed of each horse.

The guest evidently felt bored listening to him and was trying to think of some questions, so that he might seem interested in all this.

"Yes, yes," he kept saying absent-mindedly.

"Just take a look," the owner was saying without heeding the other, "look at those legs. She came dear, but I have a three-year-old from her, already running."

"Does he run well?" asked the guest.

In this manner they went over almost all the horses, and there was nothing more to show. And they fell silent.

"Well, what do you say—shall we go?"

"Let's."

They went through the gates. The guest was glad the exhibition was at an end and that he'd go into the house, where he'd be able to have a bite, a drink, a smoke, and he became visibly more cheerful.

As they were passing by Nester, who, sitting on the skewbald, was awaiting further orders, the guest slapped the croup of the skewbald with his big, puffy hand.

"There's a painted fellow," said he. "I had just such a skewbald—remember, I was telling you about him?"

The host, perceiving that it was not his horses the guest was speaking about, ceased even to listen but, looking over his shoulder, kept watching his drove.

Suddenly, over his very ear, he heard a stifled, weak, senile neighing. It was the skewbald who had sent up this neigh, then paused, and, as though becoming ashamed, cut it short.

Neither the guest nor the host paid any attention to this neigh and went on to the house.

Yardstick had recognized in the bloated old man his beloved master, Serpuhovskoi, the erstwhile brilliant Croesus and Adonis.

X

The rain kept on drizzling. It was gloomy in the paddock, but it was quite otherwise in the manor house. A sumptuous evening tea was set on the table in the sumptuous reception room. The host, the hostess, and their newly arrived guest were seated at the table.

The hostess, who was pregnant (which was very noticeable because of her bulging abdomen, her straight, shoulders-back pose, her stoutness, and particularly her eyes, great eyes that were meekly and sol-emnly directed inwardly), was officiating at the samovar.

The host was holding in his hands a box of special cigars, aged for ten years, such as no one else had, according to his words, and was about to boast of them before his guest. The host was an Adonis of twenty-five, fresh, well-groomed, well-combed. At home he wore a new, roomy, substantial suit that had been tailored in London. He had large, expensive charms on his watch chain. His cuff links were large, like-wise massive, of gold, mounted with turquoise. His imperial was *à la Napoléon III,* and the mousetail tips of his mustache were pomatumed and stuck out in a manner that could have originated only in Paris.

The hostess had on a dress of silky muslin patterned with huge gay bouquets. There was some sort of special golden pins in her thick ruddy hair, not quite all of it her own but beautiful nevertheless. There were many bracelets on her arms and many rings on her fingers, and every one of them was expensive.

The samovar was of silver, the table service of the finest china. A flunky, magnificent in his swallowtail and white vest and tie, stood at the door like a carven image, awaiting orders. The furniture was of bentwood and brightly lacquered; the wallpaper was dark, with a large flower design. Near the table, with her silver collar tinkling, lay an unusually slender greyhound bitch, which had an unusually hard Eng-lish name that was but poorly pronounced by both hosts, who knew no English. In a corner, flooded over with flowers, stood an *incrusté* grand piano. Newness, luxuriousness, and rarity were wafted from it. Everything was good, but upon everything lay a peculiar tinge of su-perfluousness, of riches and an absence of intellectual interests.

The host was a sportive hunter, a sturdy and sanguine fellow, one of those whose breed never dies out; they ride about in sable-lined over-coats, toss expensive bouquets to actresses, drink the most expensive wines of the very latest brand, in the most expensive hotels, give prizes in their names, and keep the most expensive ——.

Their visitor, Nikita Serpuhovskoi, was a man past his forties, tall, stout, bald-headed, with a great mustache and great side whiskers. He must have been very handsome at one time. Now he had evidently come down, physically and morally and pecuniarily.

He was so deep in debts that he had to go to work to avoid being put away. He was now on his way to a provincial town to superintend a stud farm. His influential relatives had managed to procure this post for him.

He was dressed in a military jacket and blue trousers. The jacket and trousers were of a sort which none but a rich man would have had tailored for him; the same applied to his linen; his watch, too, was British. His boots had some sort of wondrous soles, as thick as your finger.

Nikita Serpuhovskoi had during his lifetime run through an estate of two million and had run up a hundred and twenty thousand of debts on top of that. When one bites off a chunk like that there always remains a sweep in life, affording one credit and the possibility of living another decade or so almost in luxury.

The decade or so was already waning and the sweep coming to an end, and life was becoming a sad thing for Nikita. He was already beginning to tipple, that is, to become tipsy from wine, which had never happened to him in former days. But, correctly speaking, his tippling really had neither beginning nor end. Most of all his decline was perceptible in the uneasiness of his glances (his eyes were becoming uncontrollably shifty) and the hesitancy of his intonations and movements. This restlessness struck one all the more because, evidently, it had come upon him recently, because it was evident that he had been long accustomed, throughout his life, not to fear anybody or anything, and that now he had recently come through heavy sufferings to this fear, which was so foreign to his nature.

The host and the hostess noticed this; they exchanged understanding looks, evidently deferring a detailed discussion on this subject only until bedtime, and bore with poor Nikita. And even were attentive to him.

The sight of the young host's happiness humiliated Nikita and, as he recalled his own irretrievable past, made him feel a sickly envy.

"Does cigar smoke bother you, Mary?" he asked, turning to the lady with that special tone acquired only through vast worldly experience, a tone polite, friendly, but not quite respectful, in which men who know the world speak to kept women in contradistinction to wives. Not that he wanted to insult her. On the contrary, now he would rather have ingratiated himself with her and her master, although he would not under any circumstances have admitted this to himself. But he had already become habituated to talking like that to such women. He knew that she herself would have wondered, would have been insulted, even, were he to treat her as a born lady. Also, it was necessary to hold in reserve a certain nuance of a polite tone for the lawful wife of one who was his equal. He was always respectful with real ladies, but not because he shared any of the so-called convictions which are promulgated in the magazines (he never read all that trash about respect for the personality of each individual, about the insignificance of marriage, and so on), but because all decent people act like that, and he was a decent person, even though a fallen one.

He took a cigar. But the host, committing a gaucherie, took a whole handful of cigars and offered them to his guest.

"No, you'll see how good they are. Take 'em."

Nikita put the cigars aside with his hand, and in his eyes there was a flicker, barely perceptible, of offense and shame.

"Thanks." He took out his cigar case. "Try mine."

The hostess was a sensitive woman. She perceived Nikita's feelings and hastened to start a conversation with him:

"I like cigars very much. I'd smoke them myself if there weren't plenty of people around me smoking them."

And she smiled her beautiful, kindly smile. He smiled in answer, but without assurance. He had two front teeth missing.

"No, you take this one," the host, who was not at all sensitive, persisted. "The others are milder. *Fritz, bringen Sie noch eine Kiste,*" he said, *"dort zwei."* [1]

The flunky, a German, brought another box.

"Which do you like best? Strong ones? These are very good. Take all of 'em," he kept thrusting them upon Nikita.

He was evidently glad that there was somebody before whom he could boast of his rare possessions and did not notice anything out of the way. Serpuhovskoi lit his cigar and hastened to go on with the conversation that had been started.

"Well, how much did you have to pay for Satin-Smooth?" he asked.

"He came high—no less than five thousand. But at least I'm safe now. What offspring he has, I must say!"

"Do they run?" asked Serpuhovskoi.

"They run well. Just the other day his son took three purses: In Tula, Moscow, and Petersburg. He ran against Voyecov's Raven-Black, too. That rat of a jockey balled him up with four different gaits, or he'd have left the other at the post."

"He's a trifle cheesy. Too much Dutch in him—that's what I'll tell you," said Serpuhovskoi.

"Well, what do you think brood mares are for? I'll show you tomor-

---

[1] "Fritz, bring another box. There are two there."

row. For Good Girl I gave three thousand, and two thousand for Tender Lady."

And again the host began to enumerate his riches. The hostess perceived that Serpuhovskoi found this oppressive and that he was only pretending to listen.

"Are you going to have more tea?" she asked the host.

"I am not," said the host, and went on talking. She got up; the host stopped her, took her around, and kissed her.

Serpuhovskoi, as he looked at them, and also for their benefit, attempted a smile that was not at all natural, but when the host got up and, with his arm around the hostess, took her as far as the portière, Nikita's face suddenly changed, he sighed heavily, and a sudden expression of despair appeared on his bloated face. One could see even rancor upon it.

The host returned and, smiling, sat down opposite Nikita. They were silent for a while.

XI

"Yes, you were saying you bought him at Voyecov's," said Serpuhovskoi, with apparent nonchalance.

"Yes. I was speaking of Satin-Smooth. I was wanting to buy some mares at Dubovitski's. But all he had left were scrubs."

"He went up the flue," said Serpuhovskoi—and suddenly stopped and looked around him. He had recalled that he owed twenty thousand to this very fellow who had gone up the flue. And if it came to saying that anyone had gone up the flue, then they must certainly be saying it about him. He broke out laughing.

Both were again silent for a long while. The host was running over in his head the things of which he might boast before his guest; Serpuhovskoi was trying to think of some way to show that he did not consider himself as having gone up the flue. But both found their thoughts functioning slowly, despite the fact that they were trying to encourage themselves with cigar smoke.

"Say, when do we have a drink?" Serpuhovskoi was thinking.

"I absolutely must have a drink, or else a fellow can die from boredom with him," the host was thinking.

"Well, now, are you going to stay here long?" asked Serpuhovskoi.

"Why, another month or so. Well, shall we have supper, or what? Supper ready, Fritz?"

They went into the dining room. There, under a lamp, stood a table set with candles and the most unusual delicacies: siphons with tiny dolls for tops, unusual wines in carafes, unusual appetizers, and unusual vodka. They had a drink, ate, drank some more, ate some more, and the conversation caught on. Serpuhovskoi became flushed and began talking without any hesitancy.

They talked about women. Who had what kind: Gypsy, ballet girl, Frenchwoman.

"Well, now, have you left Mattie?" asked the host.

This was the kept woman who had ruined Serpuhovskoi.

"It wasn't I who did the leaving but she. Ah, brother, when I think of what I've sent down the drain in my lifetime! Now I'm glad, really, when a thousand comes my way; I'm glad, really, when I get away from everybody. Can't stand it in Moscow. Ah, what's the use of talking!"

The host was bored listening to Serpuhovskoi. He wanted to talk about himself—to boast. Whereas Serpuhovskoi wanted to talk about himself—about his brilliant past. The host poured out wine for him, and waited till the other would be through, so as to tell the other about himself, how his stud was now so arranged as nobody had arranged one before. And that his Mary loved him not for his money alone, but that she loved him with her heart.

"I wanted to tell you that at my stud farm—" he was just about to launch forth. But Serpuhovskoi interrupted him.

"There was a time, I may say," he began, "when I loved and knew how to live. You're speaking about racing, for instance; well, now, tell me—what's your most spirited horse?"

The host was glad of this opportunity to speak some more of his stud farm and had just begun, but Serpuhovskoi again interrupted him.

"Yes, yes," he said. "For with you stud owners all this is only for the sake of vanity, and not for pleasure, not for the full life. But that wasn't the way with me. There, I was telling you a while ago that I once had a harness horse, a skewbald, of the same markings as the one your drover was riding. Oh, what a horse! You wouldn't know; this was in 'forty-two; I'd just come to Moscow and went to a jobber, and what do I see but a skewbald gelding. With all the good points. The price? A thousand. He was to my liking, I took him and began riding him. I never had, and you, too, haven't, and never will have, a horse like that. I never knew a horse better for riding, or for strength or beauty. You were a boy then, you couldn't know, but you must have heard, I think. All Moscow knew him."

"Yes, I've heard," the host answered grudgingly, "but I wanted to tell you about my own horses—"

"So you've heard, have you? I bought him just so, without pedigree, without any certificate; it was only later that I found out. Voyecov and I tracked it down. He was the son of Amiable I; they called him Yard-stick on account of the even way he measured off the ground. Because of his markings he was taken out of the Hrenovo stud and given to the head groom, who gelded him and sold him to a jobber. There are no such horses nowadays, my little friend! 'Ah, the time that has been! Ah, my youth!' " He sang from a gypsy song. He was beginning to get tipsy. "Eh, it was a good time. I was twenty-five, I had eighty thousand a year, I hadn't a single gray hair then, all my teeth were like pearls. No matter what I tackled I succeeded at—and it has all come to an end—"

"Well, horses weren't as spirited then," said the host, availing himself of the pause. "I'll tell you this, that my first foals started walking when they were only—"

"Your horses! Why, they were more spirited then—"

"How do you mean, more spirited?"

"More spirited. I remember it all as if it were right now. I left Moscow for the races on this skewbald. I had no racers of my own. I didn't like racers; I had blooded horses: General Cholier, Mohammed. The skewbald I used for driving. My driver was a fine fellow; I loved him. He drank himself to the devil, too. So I came to the track.

" 'Serpuhovskoi,' they tell me, 'when will you ever get yourself a stable of racers?' 'The devil take your gee-gees,' I told 'em. 'I've a skewbald I drive that'll beat all of yours.' 'Oh, no, he won't!' 'I'll bet you a thousand.' We struck hands on it, and let 'em race. He beat 'em by five seconds; won a thousand-ruble bet for me. But that's nothing! I made sixty-six miles in three hours with a team of three blooded horses. All Moscow knows that."

And Serpuhovskoi began to lie so neatly and ceaselessly that the host hadn't a chance to put in a single word and sat with a dismal face opposite the other, and kept pouring wine into the other's glass and his own, as his sole diversion.

It had already begun to dawn. But they still sat on. The host was excruciatingly bored. He got up.

"If it's time to sleep, it's time to sleep," said Serpuhovskoi, getting up and swaying, and, puffing hard, he went to the room assigned to him.

The master was in bed with his mistress.

"No, he's impossible. He got drunk and started lying without stopping for breath."

"And he's paying attention to me."

"I'm afraid he'll be asking for money."

Serpuhovskoi was lying in bed with all his clothes on and was puffing hard.

"Looks as if I'd lied a great deal," it occurred to him. "Well, what's the odds! The wine is good, but he's a great swine. Something of the shopkeeper about him. And I, too, am a great swine," he said to himself and broke into laughter. "There was a time when I kept women, now I am being kept. Yes, Winckler's frau is keeping me. I accept money from her. Well, it serves him right. However, you ought to undress. But you'll never get your boots off." "Hey, hey there!" he called out, but the man who had been assigned to wait on him had long since gone off to sleep.

He sat up, took off his jacket and vest and managed somehow to clamber out of his trousers; but as for the boots, he could not pull them off for the longest time—his flabby belly was in the way. Somehow or other he dragged off one boot; with the other he struggled, struggled, got all out of breath and all tuckered out. And thus, with one foot stuck in the boot leg, he slumped over and started snoring, filling the whole room with the reek of tobacco, wine, and filthy senility.

XII

If Yardstick recalled anything else on this night, he was distracted by Vasska. Vasska threw a horsecloth over him and galloped off. Until morning he kept him hitched near the pothouse door, next to a muzhik's horse. They licked each other. In the morning the gelding was in the drove again and kept scratching all the time.

"Somehow or other I'm itching much too much," he thought.

Five days went by. A horse doctor was called in.

"Scabs. Let him be sold to the gypsies."

"What for? Cut his throat—only he must be got rid of at once."

The morning was windless and clear. The drove went out to the pasture. Yardstick was left behind. A frightful man arrived—gaunt, filthy, in a long black overcoat splattered with something or other. He was a knacker. He took hold of Yardstick's rope halter, without as much as a look at him, and led him off. Yardstick went along calmly, without looking back, dragging his legs as always and scraping his croup against the straw.

When they had come out of the gates he pulled in the direction of the well, but the knacker jerked him back and said:

"No need of that."

The knacker and Vasska, who was walking behind them, came to a little hollow back of a brick barn and, as though there was something special about this most ordinary spot, they halted, and the knacker, passing the halter to Vasska, took off his long coat, rolled up his sleeves, and got out of his bootleg a knife and a whetstone. The gelding stretched his head toward the halter, wanting to munch it out of boredom, but it was too far to reach. He sighed and closed his eyes. His lower lip drooped, the ground-down yellow teeth were exposed, and he began dozing off to the sounds of the knife being whetted. Only his right foreleg, aching so from its suppurating sore and held off to one side, quivered now and then. Suddenly he was taken under the jowls and his head was lifted up. He opened his eyes. There were two hounds in front of him. One was sniffing in the direction of the knacker; the other just sat, looking at the gelding, as though it were expecting something, and that something was to come precisely from him. The gelding glanced at the hounds and began rubbing his cheek against the hand that was holding him.

"They want to cure me, probably," he thought. "Let 'em!"

And, true enough, he felt that something had been done to his throat. He felt pain; he shuddered, kicked out with one leg, but held himself back and waited for what would come next. What came next was that something wet began to pour out in a great stream on his neck and chest. He heaved a sigh that distended his sides. And he began to feel easier—far easier.

All the heaviness of his life was being eased!

He shut his eyes and began lowering his head to one side—no one was holding him. Then his legs began to shake, his whole body swayed. He was not so much frightened as astonished.

Everything had become so new. He was astonished, tried to dart forward, upward. But instead of that his legs, having stirred from their stance, began to weave, he started keeling over to one side and, wanting to shift his feet, slumped forward and on to his left side.

The knacker bided his time, until the spasms had ceased, drove the hounds away when they came closer, and then took the gelding by his legs, turned him over and on to his back and, having ordered Vasska to hold one of the legs, began the flaying.

"That, too, was a hoss," said Vasska.

"If he'd been better fed the hide would be a good one," said the knacker.

That evening the drove passed over the hill, and those horses who were going along the edge on the left could see something red below, around which the dogs were fussing worrisomely and over which ravens and kites were flying to and fro. One dog, its forepaws hard against the carrion, with head swinging from side to side, was tearing off with a rending sound that which it had sunk its fangs into. The chestnut filly halted, stretched out her head and neck, and for long sniffed in the air. It was all they could do to drive her off.

At dawn, in a ravine in the old forest, on a grassy dell in a hollow, the big-headed wolf cubs were howling joyously. There were five of them: four almost of the same size, but the fifth a tiny fellow with a head as big as his body. The gaunt she-wolf, whose hair was shedding, came out of the bushes, dragging her full belly with pendant teats along the ground, and squatted opposite her cubs. The cubs took their places facing her in a half circle. She went up to the smallest and, getting down on one knee and lowering her muzzle, went through a few spasmodic movements and, opening her fanged maw, strained and hawked out a large piece of horseflesh. The larger cubs crowded her, but she made a threatening move toward them and let the smallest one have the whole piece. The little fellow, as though he were wrathful, growlingly tucked the horse meat under him and began wolfing it. In the same way the she-wolf hawked up meat for another cub, and a third, and the others; she fed all the five, and then lay down facing them, and rested.

In a week there were only a great skull and two cannon bones knocking about near the brick barn; all the rest had been dragged away. When summer was coming on, a muzhik who was gathering bones for fertilizer took away these cannon bones and the skull as well, and made good use of them.

Serpuhovskoi's dead body, still walking about this world, eating and drinking, was put away in the earth considerably later. Neither his hide, nor flesh, nor bones were found to be of any use.

And even as for twenty years by now his dead body, still walking about the world, had been a great burden to everybody, so even the putting away of his body in the earth was only an extra hardship for people. He had long since become utterly unnecessary to anybody, he had long since become a burden to all, but still the dead burying the dead found it necessary to clothe this puffy body, which had immediately begun to putrefy, in a military uniform, well made of good cloth, to put good, well-made boots on it, to lay it away in a new, well-made coffin, with the freshest of little tassels at four of the corners, then place this new coffin in another, a casket of lead, and haul it off to Moscow, and there to unearth ancient human bones, and precisely there hide this putrefying body, swarming with maggots, in its new uniform and well-polished boots, and then throw earth over the whole business.

1861.

The Death of Ivan Ilyich

I

DURING A RECESS in the Melvinski trial in the large building of the Law Courts the judiciary and the public prosecutor met in Ivan Egorovich Shebek's chambers, where the conversation turned on the celebrated Krasovski case. Fedor Vassilievich warmly maintained that it was not subject to their jurisdiction. Ivan Egorovich maintained the contrary, while Peter Ivanovich, not having entered into the discussion at the start, took no part in it but looked through the *Gazette* which had just been handed in.

Translated by Louise and Aylmer Maude. Revised.

"Gentlemen," he said, "Ivan Ilyich has died!"

"You don't say so!"

"Here, read it yourself," replied Peter Ivanovich, handing Fedor Vassilievich the paper still damp from the press. Surrounded by a black border were the words: "Praskovya Fedorovna Golovina, with profound sorrow, informs relatives and friends of the demise of her beloved husband Ivan Ilyich Golovin, Member of the Court of Justice, which occurred on February 4 of this year 1882. The funeral will take place on Friday at one o'clock in the afternoon."

Ivan Ilyich had been a colleague of the gentlemen present and was liked by them all. He had been ill for some weeks with an illness said to be incurable. His post had been kept open for him, but there had been conjectures that in case of his death Alexeiev might receive his appointment, and that either Vinnicov or Shtabel would succeed Alexeiev. So on receiving the news of Ivan Ilyich's death the first thought of each of the gentlemen in those chambers was of the changes and promotions it might occasion among themselves or their acquaintances.

"I'll be sure to get Shtabel's place or Vinnicov's," thought Fedor Vassilievich. "I was promised that long ago, and the promotion means an extra eight hundred rubles a year for me besides the allowance."

"Now I must apply for my brother-in-law's transfer from Kaluga," thought Peter Ivanovich. "My wife will be very glad, and then she won't be able to say that I never do anything for her relatives."

"I thought he'd never leave his bed again," Peter Ivanovich said aloud. "It's very sad."

"But what really was the matter with him?"

"The doctors couldn't say—at least they could, but each of them said something different. When last I saw him I thought he was getting better."

"And I haven't been to see him since the holidays. I always meant to go."

"Had he any property?"

"I think his wife had a little—but something quite trifling."

"We'll have to go to see her, but they live so terribly far away."

"Far away from you, you mean. Everything's far away from your place."

"You see, he never can forgive my living on the other side of the river," said Peter Ivanovich, smiling at Shebek. Then, still talking of the distances between different parts of the city, they returned to the Court.

Besides considerations as to the possible transfers and promotions likely to result from Ivan Ilyich's death, the mere fact of the death of a near acquaintance aroused, as usual, in all who heard of it the complacent feeling that "It's he who's dead and not I."

Each one thought or felt: "Well, he's dead, but I'm alive!" But the more intimate of Ivan Ilyich's acquaintances, his so-called friends, could not help thinking also that they would now have to fulfill the very tiresome demands of propriety by attending the funeral service and paying a visit of condolence to the widow.

Fedor Vassilievich and Peter Ivanovich had been his nearest acquaintances. Peter Ivanovich had studied law with Ivan Ilyich and had considered himself under obligations to him.

Having told his wife at dinnertime of Ivan Ilyich's death, and of his conjecture that it might be possible to get her brother transferred to their circuit, Peter Ivanovich sacrificed his usual nap, put on his evening clothes, and drove to Ivan Ilyich's house.

At the entrance stood a carriage and two cabs. Leaning against the wall in the hall downstairs near the coat rack was a coffin lid covered with cloth of gold, ornamented with gold cord and tassels that had been polished up with metal powder. Two ladies in black were taking off their fur cloaks. Peter Ivanovich recognized one of them as Ivan Ilyich's sister, but the other was a stranger to him. His colleague Schwartz was just coming downstairs, but on seeing Peter Ivanovich enter he stopped and winked at him, as if to say: "Ivan Ilyich has made a mess of things—not like you and me."

Schwartz's face with his fashionable whiskers, and his slim figure in evening dress, had as usual an air of elegant solemnity which contrasted with the playfulness of his character and had a special piquancy here, or so it seemed to Peter Ivanovich. He allowed the ladies to precede him and slowly followed them upstairs. Schwartz did not come down but remained where he was, and Peter Ivanovich understood that he wanted to arrange where they should play bridge that evening. The ladies went upstairs to the widow's room, and Schwartz, with seriously compressed lips but a playful look in his eyes, indicated by a twitch of his eyebrows the room to the right where the body lay.

Peter Ivanovich, like everyone else on such occasions, entered feeling uncertain what he would have to do. All he knew was that at such times it is always safe to cross oneself. But he was not quite sure whether one should make obeisances while doing so. He therefore adopted a middle course. On entering the room he began crossing himself and made a slight movement resembling a bow. At the same time, as far as the motion of his head and arm allowed, he surveyed the room. Two young men—apparently nephews, one of whom was a high-school pupil—were leaving the room, crossing themselves as they did so. An old woman was standing motionless, and a lady with strangely arched eyebrows was saying something to her in a whisper. A vigorous, resolute clerical person in a frock coat was reading something in a loud voice with an expression that precluded any contradiction. The butler's assistant, Gerasim, stepping lightly in front of Peter Ivanovich, was strewing something on the floor. Noticing this, Peter Ivanovich was immediately aware of the faint odor of a decomposing body.

The last time he had called on Ivan Ilyich, Peter Ivanovich had seen Gerasim in the study. Ivan Ilyich had been particularly fond of him and he had been performing the duty of a sick nurse.

Peter Ivanovich continued to make the sign of the cross, slightly inclining his head in an intermediate direction between the coffin, the reader, and the icons on the table in a corner of the room. Afterward, when it seemed to him that this movement of his arm in crossing himself had gone on too long, he stopped and began to look at the corpse.

The dead man lay, as dead men always lie, in a specially cumbrous way, his rigid limbs sunk in the soft cushions of the coffin, with the head forever bowed on the pillow. His yellow waxen brow with bald patches over his sunken temples was thrust up in the way peculiar to the dead, the protruding nose seeming to press on the upper lip. He was much changed and had grown even thinner since Peter Ivanovich had last seen him, but, as is always the case with the dead, his face was handsomer and above all more dignified than when he was alive. The expression on the face said that what was necessary had been accomplished, and accomplished rightly. Besides this, there was in that expression a reproach and a warning to the living. This warning seemed to Peter Ivanovich out of place, or at least not applicable to him. He felt a certain discomfort and so he hurriedly crossed himself once more and turned and went out of the door—too hurriedly and too regardless of propriety, as he himself was aware.

Schwartz was waiting for him in the adjoining room with legs spread wide apart and both hands toying with his top hat behind his back. The mere sight of that playful, well-groomed, and elegant figure refreshed Peter Ivanovich. He felt that Schwartz was above all these happenings and would not surrender to any depressing influences. His very look said that this incident of a church service for Ivan Ilyich could not be a sufficient reason for infringing the order of the session—in other words, that it would certainly not prevent his unwrapping a new pack of cards and shuffling them that evening while a footman placed four fresh candles on the table: in fact, that there was no reason for supposing that this incident would hinder their spending the evening agreeably. Indeed, he said this in a whisper as Peter Ivanovich passed him, proposing that they should meet for a game at Fedor Vassilievich's. But apparently Peter Ivanovich was not destined to play bridge that evening. Praskovya Fedorovna (a short, fat woman who, despite all efforts to the contrary, had continued to broaden steadily from her shoulders downward and who had the same extraordinarily arched eyebrows as the lady who had been standing by the coffin), dressed all in black, her head covered with lace, came out of her own room with some other ladies, conducted them to the room where the dead body lay, and said: "The service will begin immediately. Please go in."

Schwartz, making an indeterminate bow, stood still, evidently neither accepting nor declining this invitation. Praskovya Fedorovna, recognizing Peter Ivanovich, sighed, went close up to him, took his hand, and said: "I know you were a true friend to Ivan Ilyich—" and looked at him, awaiting some suitable response. And Peter Ivanovich knew that, just as it had been the right thing to cross himself in that room, what he had to do here was to press her hand, sigh, and say: "Believe me—" So he did all this and as he did it felt that the desired result had been achieved: that both he and she were touched.

"Come with me. I want to speak to you before it begins," said the widow. "Give me your arm."

Peter Ivanovich gave her his arm, and they went to the inner rooms, passing Schwartz, who winked at Peter Ivanovich commiseratingly.

"That kills our bridge game. Don't object if we find another player. Perhaps you can cut in when you do escape," said his playful look.

Peter Ivanovich sighed still more deeply and despondently, and Praskovya Fedorovna pressed his arm gratefully. When they reached the drawing room, upholstered in pink cretonne and lighted by a dim lamp, they sat down at the table—she on a sofa and Peter Ivanovich on a low, soft ottoman, the springs of which yielded spasmodically under his weight. Praskovya Fedorovna had been on the point of warning him to take another seat, but felt that such a warning was out of keeping with her present condition and so changed her mind. As he sat down on the ottoman Peter Ivanovich recalled how Ivan Ilyich had arranged this room and had consulted him regarding this pink cretonne with green leaves. The whole room was full of furniture and knickknacks, and on her way to the sofa the lace of the widow's black shawl caught on the carved edge of the table. Peter Ivanovich rose to detach it, and the springs of the ottoman, relieved of his weight, rose also and gave him a bounce. The widow began detaching her shawl herself, and Peter Ivanovich again sat down, suppressing the rebellious springs of the ottoman under him. But the widow had not quite freed herself, and Peter Ivanovich got up again, and again the ottoman rebelled and even creaked. When this was all over she took out a clean cambric handkerchief and began to weep. The episode with the shawl and the struggle with the ottoman had cooled Peter Ivanovich's emotions, and he sat there with a sullen look on his face. This awkward situation was interrupted by Sokolov, Ivan Ilyich's butler, who came to report that the plot in the cemetery that Praskovya Fedorovna had chosen would cost two hundred rubles. She stopped weeping and, looking at Peter Ivanovich with the air of a victim, remarked in French that it was very hard for her. Peter Ivanovich made a silent gesture signifying his full conviction that it must indeed be so.

"You may smoke," she said in a magnanimous yet crushed voice, and turned to discuss with Sokolov the price of the plot for the grave.

Peter Ivanovich, while lighting his cigarette, heard her inquiring very circumstantially into the prices of different plots in the cemetery and finally decide which she would take. When that was done she gave instructions about engaging the choir. Sokolov then left the room.

"I look after everything myself," she told Peter Ivanovich, shifting the albums that lay on the table; and noticing that the table was endangered by his cigarette ash, she immediately passed him an ash tray, saying as she did so: "I consider it an affectation to say that my grief prevents my attending to practical affairs. On the contrary, if anything can —I won't say console me, but rather distract me—it is seeing to everything concerning him." She again took out her handkerchief as if preparing to cry, but suddenly, as if mastering her feeling, she shook herself and began to speak calmly. "But there's something I want to talk to you about."

Peter Ivanovich bowed, keeping under control the springs of the ottoman, which immediately began quivering under him.

"He suffered terribly the last few days."

"Did he?" asked Peter Ivanovich.

"Oh, terribly! He screamed unceasingly, not for minutes but for hours. For the last three days he screamed incessantly. It was unendurable. I cannot understand how I bore it; you could hear him three rooms off. Oh, what I have suffered!"

"Is it possible that he was conscious all that time?" asked Peter Ivanovich.

"Yes," she whispered. "To the last moment. He took leave of us a quarter of an hour before he died, and asked us to take Volodya away."

The thought of the sufferings of this man he had known so intimately, first as a laughing little boy, then as a schoolmate, and later as a grown-up colleague, suddenly struck Peter Ivanovich with horror, despite an unpleasant consciousness of his own and this woman's dissimulation. He again saw that brow, and that nose pressing down on the upper lip, and felt personal fear.

"Three days of frightful suffering and then death! Why, that might suddenly, at any time, happen to me," he thought, and for a moment felt terrified. But—he did not himself know how—the customary reflection at once occurred to him that this had happened to Ivan Ilyich and not to him, and that it should not and could not happen to him, and that to think that it could would be yielding to depression, which he ought not to do, as Schwartz's expression plainly showed. After which reflection Peter Ivanovich felt reassured, and began to ask with interest about the details of Ivan Ilyich's death, as though death were an accident natural to Ivan Ilyich but certainly not to himself.

After many details of the really dreadful physical sufferings Ivan Ilyich had endured (which details he learned only from the effect those sufferings had produced on Praskovya Fedorovna's nerves), the widow apparently found it necessary to get down to business.

"Oh, Peter Ivanovich, how hard it is! How terribly, terribly hard!" and she again began to weep.

Peter Ivanovich sighed and waited for her to finish blowing her nose. When she had done so he said: "Believe me—" and she again began talking and brought out what was evidently her chief concern with him—namely, to question him as to how she could obtain a grant of money from the Government on the occasion of her husband's death. She made it appear that she was asking Peter Ivanovich's advice about her pension, but he soon saw that she already knew about that to the minutest detail, even better than he did himself. She knew how much could be got out of the Government in consequence of her husband's death, but wanted to find out whether she could not possibly extract something more. Peter Ivanovich tried to think of some means of doing so, but after reflecting for a while and, out of propriety, condemning the Government for its niggardliness, he said he thought that nothing more could be got. Then she sighed and evidently began to devise means of getting rid of her visitor. Noticing this, he put out his cigarette, rose, pressed her hand, and went out into the anteroom.

In the dining room, where the clock stood that Ivan Ilyich had liked so much and had bought at an antique shop, Peter Ivanovich met a priest and a few acquaintances who had come to attend the service, and he recognized Ivan Ilyich's daughter, a handsome young woman. She was in black, and her slim figure appeared slimmer than ever. She had a gloomy, determined, almost angry expression, and bowed to Peter Ivanovich as though he were in some way to blame. Behind her, with the same offended look, stood a wealthy young man, an Examining Magistrate, whom Peter Ivanovich also knew and who was her fiancé, as he had heard. He bowed mournfully to them and was about to pass into the death chamber, when from under the stairs appeared the figure of Ivan Ilyich's schoolboy son, who was extremely like his father. He seemed a young Ivan Ilyich, such as Peter Ivanovich remembered him when they had studied law together. His tear-stained eyes had in them the look one sees in the eyes of boys of thirteen or fourteen who are not pure-minded. When he saw Peter Ivanovich he scowled morosely and shamefacedly. Peter Ivanovich nodded to him and entered the death chamber. The service began: candles, groans, incense, tears and sobs. Peter Ivanovich stood looking gloomily down at his feet. He did not look once at the dead man, did not yield to any depressing influence, and was one of the first to leave the room. There was no one in the anteroom, but Gerasim darted out of the dead man's room, rummaged with his strong hands among the fur coats to find Peter Ivanovich's, and helped him on with it.

"Well, friend Gerasim," said Peter Ivanovich, so as to say something. "It's a sad affair, isn't it?"

"It's God's will. We'll all come to it some day," answered Gerasim, displaying his teeth—the even, white teeth of a healthy peasant—and, like a man in the thick of urgent work, he briskly opened the front door, called the coachman, helped Peter Ivanovich into the sleigh, and sprang back to the front steps, as if in readiness for what he had to do next.

Peter Ivanovich found the fresh air particularly pleasant after the smells of incense, the dead body, and carbolic acid.

"Where to, Sir?" asked the driver.

"It's not too late even now. I'll call on Fedor Vassilievich," thought Peter Ivanovich.

He accordingly drove there and found the players just finishing the first rubber, so that it was quite convenient for him to cut in.

II

Ivan Ilyich's life had been most simple and most ordinary, and therefore most terrible.

He had been a member of the Court of Justice, and died at the age of forty-five. His father had been an official who, after serving in various ministries and departments in Petersburg, had made the sort of career which brings men to positions from which by reason of their long service they cannot be dismissed, though they are obviously unfit to hold any responsible post, and for whom, therefore, posts are specially created which, though fictitious, carry salaries of from six to ten thousand rubles that are not fictitious, and in receipt of which they live on to a great age.

Such had been the Privy Councilor and superfluous member of various superfluous institutions, Ilya Ephimovich Golovin.

He had three sons, of whom Ivan Ilyich was the second. The oldest son was following in his father's footsteps, only in another department, and was already approaching that stage in the service at which a similar sinecure would be reached. The third son was a failure. He had ruined his prospects in a number of posts and was now serving in the Department of Railroads. His father and brothers, and still more their wives, not merely disliked meeting him, but avoided remembering his existence unless compelled to do so. His sister had married Baron Greff, a Petersburg official of her father's type. Ivan Ilyich was *le phénix de la famille,* as people said. He had been neither as cold and formal as his elder brother nor as wild as the younger, but was a happy mean between them—an intelligent, polished, lively, and agreeable man. He had studied with his younger brother at the School of Law, but the latter had failed to complete the course and was expelled when he was in the fifth class. Ivan Ilyich finished the course well. Even when he was at the School of Law he was just what he remained for the rest of his life: a capable, cheerful, good-natured, and sociable man, though strict in the fulfillment of what he considered to be his duty: and he considered his duty to be what was so considered by those in authority. Neither as a boy nor as a man was he a toady, but from early youth was by nature attracted to people of high station as a midge is drawn to the light, assimilating their ways and views of life and establishing friendly relations with them. All the enthusiasms of childhood and youth passed without leaving much trace on him; he succumbed to sensuality, to vanity, and latterly to the liberalism of the highest classes, but always within limits which his instinct unfailingly indicated to him as correct.

At school he had done things which had formerly seemed to him very horrid and made him feel disgusted with himself when he did them; but when later on he saw that such actions were done by people of good position and that they did not regard them as wrong, he was able not exactly to regard them as right, but to forget about them entirely or not to be at all troubled at remembering them.

Having graduated from the School of Law and qualified for the tenth rank of the Civil Service, and having received money from his father for his equipment, Ivan Ilyich had ordered for himself clothes at Scharmer's, the fashionable tailor's, hung a medallion inscribed *respice finem* on his watch chain, taken leave of his professor and the Prince who was patron of the school, had a farewell dinner with his comrades at Donon's first-class restaurant, and with his new and fashionable portmanteau, linen, clothes, shaving and other toilet appliances, and a traveling rug, all purchased at the best shops, set off for one of the provinces where, through his father's influence, he had been attached to the Governor as an official for special service.

In the province Ivan Ilyich soon arranged as easy and agreeable a position for himself as he had had at the School of Law. He performed his official tasks, made his career, and at the same time amused himself pleasantly and decorously. Occasionally he paid official visits to country districts, where he behaved with dignity both to his superiors and his inferiors, and performed the duties entrusted to him, which related chiefly to the Sectarians,[1] with an exactness and incorruptible honesty of which he could not but feel proud.

In official matters, despite his youth and taste for frivolous gaiety, he was exceedingly reserved, punctilious, and even severe; but in society he was often amusing and witty, and always good-natured, correct in

---

[1] See note appended to Belinski's *Letter to Gogol.—Editor.*

his manner, and a *bon enfant,* as the Governor and his wife—with whom he was like one of the family—used to say of him.

In the province he had an affair with a lady who made advances to the elegant young lawyer, and there had also been a milliner; and there were carousals with aides-de-camp who visited the district, and after-supper visits to a certain outlying street of doubtful reputation; and there was, too, some obsequiousness to his chief and even to his chief's wife, but all this was done with such a tone of good breeding that no hard names could be applied to it. It all came under the heading of the French saying: *"Il faut que jeunesse se passe."* [1] It was all done with clean hands, in clean linen, with French phrases, and, above all, among people of the best society and consequently with the approval of people of rank.

Thus did Ivan Ilyich serve for five years, and then there came a change in his official life. The new and reformed judicial institutions were introduced, and new men were needed. Ivan Ilyich became such a new man. He was offered the post of Examining Magistrate, and he accepted it, though the post was in another province and obliged him to give up the connections he had formed and to make new ones. His friends met to give him a send-off; they had a group photograph taken and presented him with a silver cigarette case, and he set off to his new post.

As Examining Magistrate Ivan Ilyich was just as *comme il faut* and decorous a man, inspiring general respect and capable of separating his official duties from his private life, as he had been when acting as an official on special service. His duties now as Examining Magistrate were far more interesting and attractive than before. In his former position it had been pleasant to wear an undress uniform made by Scharmer, and to pass through the crowd of petitioners and officials who were timorously awaiting an audience with the Governor, and who envied him as with a free and easy gait he went straight into his chief's private room to have a cup of tea and a cigarette with him. But not many people had then been directly dependent on him—only police officials and the Sectarians when he went on special missions—and he liked to treat them politely, almost as comrades, as if he were letting them feel that he who had the power to crush them was treating them in this simple, friendly way. There were then but few such people.

But now, as an Examining Magistrate, Ivan Ilyich felt that everyone without exception, even the most important and self-satisfied, was in

---

[1] Youth must have its fling.

his power, and that he need only write a few words on a sheet of paper with a certain heading, and this or that important, self-satisfied person would be brought before him in the role of an accused person or a witness, and, if he did not choose to allow him to sit down, would have to stand before him and answer his questions. Ivan Ilyich never abused his power; he tried, on the contrary, to soften its expression, but the consciousness of it and of the possibility of softening its effect supplied the chief interest and attraction of his office. In his work itself, especially in his examinations, he very soon acquired a method of eliminating all considerations irrelevant to the legal aspect of the case, and reducing even the most complicated case to a form in which it would be presented on paper only in its externals, completely excluding his personal opinion of the matter, while, above all, observing every prescribed formality. The work was new, and Ivan Ilyich had been one of the first men to apply the new Code of 1864.[1]

On taking up the post of Examining Magistrate in a new town, he made new acquaintances and connections, placed himself on a new footing, and assumed a somewhat different tone. He took up an attitude of rather dignified aloofness toward the provincial authorities, but picked out the best circle of legal gentlemen and wealthy gentry living in the town and assumed a tone of slight dissatisfaction with the Government, of moderate liberalism, and of enlightened citizenship. At the same time, without at all altering the elegance of his dress, he ceased shaving his chin and allowed his beard to grow as it pleased.

Ivan Ilyich settled down very pleasantly in this new town. The society there, which inclined toward opposition to the Governor, was friendly, his salary was larger, and he began to play *vint,* a variation of bridge, which he found added not a little to the pleasure of life, for he had a capacity for cards, played good-humoredly, and calculated rapidly and astutely, so that he usually won.

After living there for two years he met his future wife, Praskovya Fedorovna Mihel, who was the most attractive, clever, and brilliant girl of the set in which he moved, and among other amusements and relaxations from his labors as Examining Magistrate, Ivan Ilyich established light and playful relations with her.

While he had been an official on special service he had been accustomed to dance, but now as an Examining Magistrate it was exceptional for him to do so. If he danced now, he did it as if to show that though

---

[1] The emancipation of the serfs in 1861 was followed by a thorough all-round reform of judicial proceedings.—A. M.

he served under the reformed order of things, and had reached the fifth official rank, yet when it came to dancing he could do it better than most people. So at the end of an evening he sometimes danced with Praskovya Fedorovna, and it was chiefly during these dances that he captivated her. She fell in love with him. He had had at first no definite intention of marrying, but when the girl fell in love with him he said to himself: "Really, why shouldn't I marry?"

Praskovya Fedorovna came of a good family, was not bad-looking, and had some little property. Ivan Ilyich might have aspired to a more brilliant match, but even this was good. He had his salary, and she, he hoped, would have an equal income. She was well connected and was a sweet, pretty, and thoroughly correct young woman. To say that he had married because he had fallen in love with her and found that she sympathized with his views of life would be as incorrect as to say that he married because his social circle approved of the match. He was swayed by both these considerations: the marriage gave him personal satisfaction, and at the same time it was considered the right thing by the most highly placed of his associates.

So Ivan Ilyich got married.

The preparations for marriage and the beginning of married life, with its conjugal caresses, the new furniture, new crockery, and new linen, were very pleasant until his wife became pregnant—so that he had begun to think that marriage would not impair the easy, agreeable, gay, and always decorous character of his life, approved of by society and regarded by himself as natural, but would even improve it. But from the first months of his wife's pregnancy, something new, unpleasant, depressing, and unseemly, and from which there was no way of escape, unexpectedly showed itself.

His wife, without any reason—*de gaieté de cœur,* as Ivan Ilyich expressed it to himself—began to disturb the pleasure and propriety of their life. She began to be jealous without any cause, expected him to devote all his attention to her, found fault with everything, and made coarse and ill-mannered scenes.

At first he hoped to escape from the unpleasantness of this state of affairs by the same easy and decorous relation to life that had served him heretofore: he tried to ignore his wife's disagreeable moods, continued to live in his usual easy and pleasant way, invited friends to his house for a game of cards, and also tried going out to his club or spending his evenings with friends. But one day his wife began upbraiding him so vigorously, using such coarse words, and continued to abuse him every time he did not fulfill her demands so resolutely and with such evident determination not to give way till he submitted—that is, till he stayed at home and was bored just as she was—that he became alarmed. He now realized that matrimony—at any rate with Praskovya Fedorovna—was not always conducive to the pleasures and amenities of life, but on the contrary often infringed both upon comfort and propriety, and that he must therefore entrench himself against such infringement. And he began to seek for means of doing so. His official duties were the one thing that impressed Praskovya Fedorovna, and by means of his official work and the duties attached to it he began struggling with his wife to secure his own independence.

With the birth of their child, the attempts to feed it and the various failures in doing so, and with the real and imaginary illnesses of mother and child, in which Ivan Ilyich's sympathy was demanded but about which he understood nothing, the need of securing for himself an existence outside his family life became still more imperative.

As his wife grew more irritable and exacting and Ivan Ilyich transferred the center of gravity of his life more and more to his official work, so did he grow to like his work better and become more ambitious than before.

Very soon, within a year of his wedding, he had realized that marriage, though it may add some comforts to life, is in fact a very intricate and difficult affair toward which, in order to perform one's duty—that is, to lead a decorous life approved of by society—one must adopt a definite attitude, just as toward one's official duties.

And he evolved such an attitude toward married life. He only required of it those conveniences—dinner at home, housewife, and bed—which it could give him, and, above all, that propriety of external forms required by public opinion. For the rest, he looked for lighthearted pleasure and propriety, and was very thankful when he found them, but if he met with antagonism and querulousness he at once retired into his separate fenced-off world of official duties, where he found satisfaction.

Ivan Ilyich was esteemed a good official, and after three years was made Assistant Public Prosecutor. His new duties, their importance, the possibility of indicting and imprisoning anyone he chose, the publicity his speeches received, and the success he had in all these things, made his work still more attractive.

More children came. His wife became more and more querulous and ill-tempered, but the attitude Ivan Ilyich had adopted toward his home life rendered him almost impervious to her grumbling.

After seven years' service in that town he was transferred to another province as Public Prosecutor. They moved, but were short of money, and his wife did not like the place they moved to. Though the salary was higher, the cost of living was greater, besides which, two of their children died, and family life became still more unpleasant for him.

Praskovya Fedorovna blamed her husband for every inconvenience they encountered in their new home. Most of the conversations between husband and wife, especially as to the children's education, led to topics which recalled former disputes, and those disputes were apt to flare up again at any moment. There remained only those rare periods of amorousness which still came to them at times but did not last long. These were islets at which they anchored for a while and then again set out upon that ocean of veiled hostility which showed itself in their aloofness from each other. This aloofness might have grieved Ivan Ilyich had he considered that it ought not to exist, but he now regarded the position as normal, and even made it the goal at which he aimed in family life. His aim was to free himself more and more from those unpleasantnesses and to give them a semblance of harmlessness and propriety. He attained this by spending less and less time with his family, and when obliged to be at home he tried to safeguard his position by the presence of outsiders.

The chief thing, however, was that he had his official duties. The whole interest of his life now centered in the official world, and that interest absorbed him. The consciousness of his power, being able to ruin anybody he wished to ruin, the importance, even the external dignity of his entry into court, or meetings with his subordinates, his success with superiors and inferiors, and, above all, his masterly handling of cases, of which he was conscious—all this gave him pleasure and filled his life, together with chats with his colleagues, dinners, and bridge. So that on the whole his life continued to flow as he considered it should do—pleasantly and properly.

Thus things continued for another seven years. His eldest daughter was already sixteen, another child had died, and only one son was left, a schoolboy and a subject of dissension. Ivan Ilyich wanted to enter him in the School of Law, but to spite him Praskovya Fedorovna entered him at the High School. The daughter had been educated at home and had turned out well: the boy did not learn badly either.

III

Thus had Ivan Ilyich lived for seventeen years after his marriage. He was already a public prosecutor of long standing, and had declined several proposed transfers while awaiting a more desirable post, when an unanticipated and unpleasant occurrence quite upset the peaceful course of his life. He was expecting to be offered the post of Presiding Judge in a university town, but Happe somehow came to the front and obtained the appointment instead. Ivan Ilyich became irritable, reproached Happe, and quarreled both with him and with his immediate superiors—who became colder to him and again passed him over when other appointments were made.

This was in 1880, the hardest year of Ivan Ilyich's life. It was then that it became evident, on the one hand, that his salary was insufficient for his family to live on, and, on the other, that he had been forgotten, and not only this, but that what was for him the greatest and most cruel injustice appeared to others a quite ordinary occurrence. Even his father did not consider it his duty to help him. Ivan Ilyich felt himself abandoned by everyone, and also felt that all regarded his position with a salary of thirty-five hundred rubles [about $1,750] as quite normal and even fortunate. He alone knew that with the consciousness of the injustices done him, with his wife's incessant nagging, and with the debts he had contracted by living beyond his means, his position was far from normal.

In order to save money that summer he obtained leave of absence and went with his wife to live in the country at her brother's place.

In the country, without his work, he experienced ennui for the first time in his life, and not only ennui but intolerable depression, and he decided that it was impossible to go on living like that, and that it was necessary to take energetic measures.

Having passed a sleepless night pacing up and down the veranda, he decided to go to Petersburg and bestir himself, in order to punish those who had failed to appreciate him and to get transferred to some other ministry.

Next day, despite many protests from his wife and her brother, he started for Petersburg with the sole object of obtaining a post with a salary of five thousand rubles a year. He was no longer bent on any particular department, or tendency, or kind of activity. All he now wanted was an appointment to another post with a salary of five thousand rubles, either in the administration, in the banks, with the Department of Railroads, in one of the Empress Maria's institutions, or even in the Customs—but it had to carry with it a salary of five thousand rubles and be in a ministry other than that in which they had failed to appreciate him.

And this quest of his was crowned with remarkable and unexpected success. At Kursk an acquaintance of his, F. I. Ilyin, got into the first-class carriage, sat down beside Ivan Ilyich, and told him of a telegram just received by the Governor of Kursk announcing that a change was about to take place in the ministry: Peter Ivanovich was to be superseded by Ivan Semenovich.

The proposed change, apart from its significance for Russia, had a special significance for Ivan Ilyich, because by bringing forward a new man, Peter Petrovich, and consequently his friend Zachar Ivanovich, things became highly favorable for Ivan Ilyich, since Zachar Ivanovich was a friend and a colleague of his.

In Moscow this news was confirmed, and on reaching Petersburg Ivan Ilyich found Zachar Ivanovich and received a definite promise of an appointment in his former Department of Justice.

A week later he telegraphed to his wife: "Zachar in Miller's place. Receiving appointment on presentation of report."

Thanks to this change of personnel, Ivan Ilyich had unexpectedly obtained an appointment in his former ministry which placed him two stages above his former colleagues, besides giving him five thousand rubles salary and three thousand five hundred rubles for expenses connected with his removal. All his ill humor toward his former enemies and the whole department vanished, and Ivan Ilyich was completely happy.

He returned to the country more cheerful and contented than he had been for a long time. Praskovya Fedorovna also cheered up, and a truce was arranged between them. Ivan Ilyich told her how he had been feted by everybody in Petersburg, how all those who had been his enemies were put to shame and now fawned on him, how envious they were of his appointment, and how much everybody in Petersburg had liked him.

Praskovya Fedorovna listened to all this and appeared to believe it. She did not contradict anything, but merely went ahead with plans for their life in the town into which they were going. Ivan Ilyich saw with delight that these plans were his plans, that he and his wife agreed, and that, after a stumble, his life was regaining its due and natural character of pleasant lightheartedness and decorum.

He had come back for a short time only, for he had to take up his new duties on the tenth of September. Moreover, he needed time to settle into the new place, to move all his belongings from the province, and to buy and order many additional things: in a word, to make such arrangements as he had resolved on, which were almost exactly what Praskovya Fedorovna, too, had decided on.

Now that everything had happened so fortunately, and that he and his wife were at one in their aims, and moreover saw so little of one another, they got on together better than they had done since the first years of marriage. Ivan Ilyich had thought of taking his family away with him at once, but the insistence of his wife's brother and her sister-in-law, who had suddenly become particularly amiable and friendly to him and his family, induced him to depart alone.

So he departed, and the cheerful state of mind induced by his success and by the harmony between his wife and himself, the one intensifying the other, did not leave him. He found a delightful house, just the thing both he and his wife had dreamed of. Spacious, lofty reception rooms in the old style, a convenient and dignified study, rooms for his wife and daughter, a study for his son—it might have been specially built for them. Ivan Ilyich himself superintended the arrangements, chose the wallpapers, supplemented the furniture (preferably with antiques, which he considered particularly *comme il faut*), and supervised the upholstering. Everything progressed and progressed and approached the ideal he had set himself: even when things were only half completed they exceeded his expectations. He saw what a refined and elegant character, free from vulgarity, it would all have when it was ready.

On falling asleep he pictured to himself how the reception room would look. Looking at the yet unfinished drawing room he could see the fireplace, the screen, the whatnot, the dainty chairs dotted here and there, the dishes and plates on the walls, and the bronzes, as they would be when everything was in place. He was pleased by the thought of how his wife and daughter, who shared his taste in these matters, would be impressed. They were certainly not expecting as much. He had been particularly successful in finding, and buying cheaply, antiques which gave a particularly aristocratic character to the whole place. But in his letters he intentionally understated everything in order to be able to surprise them. All this so absorbed him that his new duties—though he liked his official work—interested him less than he had expected. Sometimes he even had moments of absent-mindedness during the Court sessions, and would consider whether he should have straight or curved cornices for his curtains. He was so interested in all this that he often did things himself, rearranging the furniture or rehanging the curtains. Once when mounting a stepladder to show the upholsterer, who did not understand, how he wanted the hangings draped, he made a false step and slipped, but being a strong and agile man he had clung on and merely bruised his side against the window frame. The bruised place was painful, but the pain soon passed, and he felt particularly bright and well just then. He wrote: "I feel fifteen years younger." He thought he would have everything ready by September, but things dragged on till mid-October. But the result was charming not only in his eyes but in those of everyone who saw it.

In reality it was just what one usually sees in the houses of people of moderate means who want to put up a rich front and therefore succeed only in resembling others like themselves: there were damasks, dark wood, plants, rugs, and dull and polished bronzes—all the things people of a certain class have in order to resemble other people of the same class. His house was so like the others that it would never have been noticed, but to him it all seemed to be quite exceptional. He was very happy when he met his family at the station and brought them to the newly furnished house, all lit up, with a footman in a white tie opening the door into a hall decorated with plants, and when they went on into the drawing room and his study, uttering exclamations of delight. He conducted them everywhere, drank in their praises eagerly, and beamed with pleasure. At tea that evening, when Praskovya Fedorovna, among other things, asked him about his fall, he laughed and showed them how he had gone flying and had frightened the upholsterer.

"It's a good thing I'm something of an athlete. Another man might have been killed, but I merely bruised myself, right here; it hurts when you touch it, but it's passing off already—it's only a bruise."

So they began living in their new home—which, as always happens, when they got thoroughly settled, they found to be just one room short; the increased income, too, was bound to be, as is always the case, just a trifle (some five hundred rubles) too small. But it was all very fine.

Things went particularly well at first, before everything was finally arranged and while something had still to be done: this thing bought, that thing ordered, another thing moved, and something else adjusted.

Though there were some disputes between husband and wife, they were both so well satisfied and had so much to do that it all passed off without any serious quarrels. When nothing was left to arrange, things became rather dull and something seemed to be lacking, but by that time they were making acquaintances, forming habits, and life was growing fuller.

Ivan Ilyich spent his mornings at the law court and came home to dinner, and at first he was generally in a good humor, though he occasionally became irritable, precisely on account of his house. (Every spot on the tablecloth or the upholstery, and every broken window-blind string, irritated him. He had devoted so much trouble to arranging it all that every disturbance of it distressed him.) But on the whole his life ran its course as he believed life should do: easily, pleasantly, and decorously.

He got up at nine, drank his coffee, read the paper, and then put on his undress uniform and went to the law court. There the harness in which he worked had already been stretched to fit him, and he donned it without a hitch: petitioners, inquiries at the chancery, the chancery itself, and the sessions, both public and administrative. In all this the thing was to exclude everything fresh and vital, which always disturbs the regular course of official business, and to admit only official relations with people, and then only on official grounds. A man would come, for instance, wanting some information; Ivan Ilyich, as one in whose sphere the matter did not lie, would have nothing to do with him: but if the man had some business with him in his official capacity, something that could be expressed on officially stamped paper, he would do everything, positively everything, he could within the limits of such relations, and in doing so would maintain the semblance of friendly human relations, that is, would observe the amenities of life. As soon as the official relations ended, so did everything else.

Ivan Ilyich possessed in the highest degree this capacity of separating his real life from the official side of affairs and not mixing the two, and by long practice and natural aptitude had brought it to such a pitch that sometimes, in the manner of a virtuoso, he would even allow himself to let the human and official relations mingle. He let himself do this just because he felt that he could at any time he chose resume the strictly official attitude again and drop the human relations. And he did it all easily, pleasantly, correctly, and even artistically. In the intervals between the sessions, he smoked, drank tea, chatted a little about politics, a little about general topics, a little about cards, but most of all about official appointments. Tired, but with the feelings of a virtuoso—that of a first violin who has played his part in an orchestra with precision—he would return home to find that his wife and daughter had been out paying calls, or had a visitor, and that his son had been to school, had done his homework with his tutor, and was duly learning what was taught at high school. Everything was as it should be.

After dinner, if they had no visitors, Ivan Ilyich sometimes read a book that was being much discussed at the time, and in the evening settled down to work—that is, he read official papers, compared the depositions of witnesses, and noted the paragraphs of the Code applying to them. This was neither dull nor amusing. It was dull when he might have been playing bridge, but if no bridge were available it was at any rate better than doing nothing or sitting with his wife. His chief pleasure was giving little dinners to which he invited men and women of good social position, and just as his drawing room resembled all other drawing rooms, so did his enjoyable little parties resemble all other such parties.

Once they even gave a dance. He enjoyed it, and everything went off well, except that it led to a violent quarrel with his wife about the cakes and sweets. Praskovya Fedorovna had made her own plans, but Ivan Ilyich had insisted on getting everything from an expensive confectioner and ordered too many cakes, and the quarrel occurred because some of those cakes were left over and the confectioner's bill had come to forty-five rubles. It was a great and disagreeable quarrel. Praskovya Fedorovna called him "a fool and an imbecile," and he had clutched at his head and made angry allusions to divorce.

But the dance itself had been enjoyable. The best people attended, and Ivan Ilyich had danced with Princess Trufonova, a sister of the distinguished founder of the "Bear my Burden" Society.

The pleasures connected with his work were pleasures of ambition; his social pleasures were those of vanity; but his greatest pleasure was playing bridge. He acknowledged that whatever disagreeable incident happened in his life, the pleasure that beamed like a ray of light above everything else was to sit down to bridge with good players, not noisy partners, and of course to four-handed bridge (with five players it was annoying to be the dummy, though one pretended not to mind), to play a clever and serious game (when the cards allowed it) and then to sup and have a glass of wine. After a game of bridge, especially if he had won a little (to win a large sum was unpleasant), Ivan Ilyich went to bed in specially good humor.

Thus did they live. They had formed a circle of acquaintances among the best people and were visited by people of importance and by young folk. In their views as to their acquaintances, husband, wife and daughter were in entire agreement, and tacitly and unanimously kept at arm's length and shook off the various shabby friends and relations who, with much show of affection, gushed into the drawing room with Japanese plates hung on the walls. Soon these shabby friends ceased to obtrude themselves and only the best people remained in the Golovins' set.

Young men made up to Lisa, and Petrishchev, an Examining Magistrate and Dmitri Ivanovich Petrishchev's son and sole heir, began to be so attentive to her that Ivan Ilyich had already spoken to Praskovya Fedorovna about it, and considered whether they should not arrange a party for them, or get up some private theatricals.

Thus did they live, and all went well, without change, and life flowed pleasantly.

IV

They were all in good health. It could hardly be called ill health if Ivan Ilyich sometimes complained that he had a queer taste in his mouth and felt some discomfort in his left side.

But this discomfort increased and, though not exactly painful, grew into a sense of pressure in his side, accompanied by ill humor. And his irritability became worse and worse and began to mar the agreeable, easy, and correct life that had become established in the Golovin family. Quarrels between husband and wife became more and more frequent, and soon the ease and amenity disappeared and even the decorum was barely maintained. Scenes again became frequent, and very few of those islets remained on which husband and wife could meet without an explosion. Praskovya Fedorovna now had good reason to say that her husband's temper was trying. With characteristic exaggeration she said he had always had a dreadful temper, and that it had needed all her good nature to put up with it for twenty years. It was true that now the quarrels were started by him. His bursts of temper always came just before dinner, often just as he began on his soup. Sometimes he noticed that a plate or dish was chipped, or that the food was not right, or his son put his elbow on the table, or his daughter's hair was not done as he liked it, and for all this he blamed Praskovya Fedorovna.

At first she used to answer and say disagreeable things to him, but once or twice he fell into such a rage at the beginning of dinner that she realized it was due to some physical derangement brought on by taking food, and so she restrained herself and did not answer, but merely hurried to get the dinner over with. She regarded this self-restraint as highly praiseworthy. Having come to the conclusion that her husband had a dreadful temper and made her life miserable, she began to feel sorry for herself, and the more she pitied herself the more she hated her husband. She began to wish he would die; yet she did not want him to die, because then his salary would cease. And this irritated her against him still more. She considered herself dreadfully unhappy just because not even his death could save her, and though she concealed her exasperation, that hidden exasperation of hers increased his irritation also.

After one scene in which he had been particularly unfair and after which he had said in explanation that he certainly was irritable but that it was due to his not being well, she said that if he was ill it should be attended to, and insisted on his going to see a celebrated doctor.

He went. Everything took place as he had expected and as it always does. There was the usual waiting and the important air assumed by the doctor, with which he was so familiar (resembling that which he himself assumed in court), and the sounding and listening, and the questions which called for answers that were foregone conclusions and were evidently unnecessary, and the look of importance which implied that "if only you put yourself in our hands we will arrange everything —we know indubitably how it has to be done, always in the same way for everybody alike." It was all just as it was in the law court. The doctor put on just the same air toward him as he himself put on toward an accused person.

The doctor said that so-and-so indicated that this and that was going on inside the patient, but if the investigation of so-and-so did not confirm this, then he must assume this-that-and-the-other. If he assumed this-that-and-the-other, then—and so on. To Ivan Ilyich only one question was important: Was his case serious or not? But the doctor ignored that inappropriate question. From his point of view it was not the one under consideration; the real question was to decide between a floating kidney, chronic catarrh, or appendicitis. It was not a question of Ivan Ilyich's life or death, but one between a floating kidney and an inflamed appendix. And that question the doctor solved brilliantly, as it seemed to Ivan Ilyich, in favor of the appendix, with the reservation that should an examination of the urine give fresh indications the matter would be reconsidered. All this was just what Ivan Ilyich had himself brilliantly accomplished a thousand times in dealing with men on trial. The doctor summed up just as brilliantly, looking over his spectacles triumphantly and even gaily at the accused. From the doctor's summing up Ivan Ilyich concluded that things were bad, but that for the doctor, and perhaps for everybody else, it was a matter of indifference, though for him it was bad. And this conclusion struck him painfully, arousing in him a great feeling of pity for himself and of bitterness toward the doctor's indifference to a matter of such importance.

He said nothing of this, but arose, placed the doctor's fee on the table, and remarked with a sigh: "We sick people probably often put inappropriate questions. But tell me, in general, is this complaint dangerous or not?"

The doctor looked at him sternly over his spectacles with one eye, as if to say: "Prisoner, if you will not keep to the questions put to you, I shall be obliged to have you removed from the court."

"I've already told you what I consider necessary and proper. The analysis may show something more." And the doctor bowed.

Ivan Ilyich went out slowly, seated himself disconsolately in his sleigh, and drove home. All the way home he was going over what the doctor had said, trying to translate those complicated, obscure, scientific phrases into plain language and find in them an answer to the question: "Is my condition bad? Is it very bad? Or is there as yet nothing much wrong?" And it seemed to him that the meaning of what the doctor had said was that it was very bad. Everything in the streets seemed depressing. The cabmen, the houses, the passers-by, and the shops were all dismal. His ache, this dull gnawing ache that never ceased for a moment, seemed to have acquired a new and more serious significance from the doctor's dubious remarks. Ivan Ilyich now watched that ache with a new and oppressive feeling.

He reached home and began to tell his wife about it. She listened, but in the middle of his account his daughter came in with her hat on, ready to go out with her mother. She sat down reluctantly to listen to this tedious recital but could not stand it long, and her mother, too, did not hear him to the end.

"Well, I'm very glad you went," she said. "Mind, now, and take your medicine regularly. Give me the prescription and I'll send Gerasim to the druggist's." And she went to get ready for going out.

While she was in the room he had hardly taken time to breathe, but he sighed deeply when she left it.

"Well," he thought, "perhaps it isn't so bad after all."

He began taking his medicine and following the doctor's directions, which had been altered after the examination of the urine. It had turned out that there was a contradiction between the indications drawn from the examination of the urine and the symptoms that showed themselves. It turned out that what was happening differed from what the doctor had told him, and that he had either forgotten, or blundered, or hidden something from him. He could not, however, be blamed for that, and Ivan Ilyich still obeyed his orders implicitly and at first derived some comfort from doing so.

From the time of his visit to the doctor, Ivan Ilyich's chief occupation was the exact fulfillment of the doctor's instructions regarding hygiene and the taking of medicine, and the observation of his pain and his excretions. His chief interests came to be people's ailments and people's health. When sickness, deaths, or recoveries were mentioned in his presence, especially when the illness resembled his own, he listened with agitation which he tried to hide, asked questions, and applied what he heard to his own case.

The pain did not decrease, but Ivan Ilyich made efforts to force himself to think that he was better. And he could do this as long as nothing agitated him. But as soon as he had any unpleasantness with his wife, any lack of success in his official work, or held bad cards at bridge, he became at once acutely aware of his disease. He had formerly borne such mischances, hoping soon to adjust what was wrong, to master it and attain success, or make a grand slam. But now every mischance upset him and plunged him into despair. He would say to himself: "There now, just as I was beginning to get better and the medicine had begun to take effect, comes this accursed misfortune or unpleasantness!" And he was furious with the mishap, or with the people who were causing the unpleasantness and killing him, for he felt that this fury was killing him, yet could not restrain it. One would have thought it should have been clear to him that this exasperation with circumstances and people aggravated his illness, and that he ought therefore to ignore unpleasant occurrences. But he drew the very opposite conclusion: he said that he needed peace, and he watched for everything that might disturb it and became irritable at the slightest infringement of it. His condition was rendered worse by the fact that he read medical books and consulted doctors. The progress of his disease was so gradual that he could deceive himself when comparing one day with another—the difference was so slight. But when he consulted the doctors it seemed to him that he was getting worse, and even very rapidly. Yet despite this he was consulting them continually.

That month he went to see another celebrity, who told him almost the same thing as the first had done, but put his questions rather differently, and the interview with this celebrity merely increased Ivan Ilyich's doubts and fears. A friend of a friend of his, a very good doctor, diagnosed his illness again quite differently from the others, and though he predicted recovery, his questions and suppositions bewildered Ivan Ilyich still more and increased his doubts. A homeopathist diagnosed the disease in yet another way, and prescribed medicine which Ivan Ilyich took secretly for a week. But after a week, not feeling any improvement and having lost confidence both in the former doctor's treatment and in this one's, he became still more despondent.

One day a lady acquaintance mentioned a cure wrought by a miracle-working icon. Ivan Ilyich caught himself listening attentively and beginning to believe that this miraculous cure had actually occurred. This incident alarmed him. "Has my mind really weakened to such an extent?" he asked himself. "Nonsense! It's all rubbish. I mustn't give way to nervous fears but, having chosen a doctor, must keep strictly to his treatment. That's what I'll do. Now it's all settled. I won't think about it, but will follow the treatment seriously till summer, and then we'll see. From now there must be no more of this wavering!" This was easy to say but impossible to carry out. The pain in his side oppressed him and seemed to grow worse and more incessant, while the taste in his mouth grew more and more peculiar. It seemed to him that his breath had a disgusting smell, and he was conscious of a loss of appetite and strength. There was no deceiving himself: something terrible, new, and more important than anything before in his life, was taking place within him, of which he alone was aware. Those about him did not understand or would not understand it, but thought everything in the world was going on as usual. This tormented Ivan Ilyich above all. He saw that his household, especially his wife and daughter, who were in a perfect whirl of visiting, did not understand anything of all this and were annoyed that he was so depressed and so exacting, as if he were to blame for it.

Though they tried to disguise it, he saw that he was an obstacle in their path, and that his wife had adopted a definite line in regard to his illness and kept to it regardless of anything he said or did. Her attitude was this: "You know," she would say to her friends, "Ivan Ilyich can't do as other people do, and keep to the treatment prescribed for him. One day he'll take his drops and keep strictly to his diet and go to bed in good time, but the next day, unless I watch him, he'll suddenly forget his medicine, eat sturgeon—which is forbidden—and sit up playing cards till one o'clock in the morning."

"Oh, come, when was that?" Ivan Ilyich would ask in vexation. "Only once, at Peter Ivanovich's."

"And yesterday, with Shebek."

"Well, even if I hadn't stayed up, this pain would have kept me awake."

"Be that as it may, you'll never get well like that, but will always make us wretched."

Praskovya Fedorovna's attitude to Ivan Ilyich's illness, as she expressed it both to others and to him, was that it was his own fault and was another of the annoyances he caused her. Ivan Ilyich felt that this opinion escaped her involuntarily—but that did not make it any easier for him.

At the law court, too, he noticed, or thought he noticed, a strange attitude toward himself. It sometimes seemed to him that people were watching him inquisitively, as a man whose place might soon be vacant. Then again, his friends would suddenly begin to chaff him in a friendly way about his low spirits, as if the awful, horrible, and unheard-of thing that was going on within him, incessantly gnawing at him and irresistibly drawing him away, was a very agreeable subject for jests. Schwartz in particular irritated him by his jocularity, vivacity, and *savoir-faire,* which reminded him of what he himself had been ten years ago.

Friends came to make up a set and sat down to cards. They dealt, bending the new cars to soften them, and he sorted the diamonds in his hand and found he had seven. His partner said: "No trumps," and supported him with two diamonds. What more could be wished for? Everything ought to be jolly and lively. They would make a grand slam. But suddenly Ivan Ilyich would become conscious of that gnawing pain, that taste in his mouth, and it seemed ridiculous that in such circumstances he should feel pleasure at making a grand slam.

He looked at his partner, Michael Michaelovich, who rapped the table with his strong hand and instead of snatching up the tricks pushed the cards courteously and indulgently toward Ivan Ilyich, so that the latter might have the pleasure of gathering them up without the trouble of stretching out his hand for them. "Does he think I'm too weak to stretch out my arm?" thought Ivan Ilyich, and forgetting what he was doing he overtrumped his partner, missing the grand slam by three tricks. And what was most awful of all was that he saw how upset Michael Michaelovich was about it, but did not himself care. And it was dreadful to realize why he did not care.

They all saw that he was suffering, and said: "We can stop if you're tired. Take a rest." Lie down? No, he wasn't tired at all, and he finished the rubber. All were gloomy and silent. He felt that he had diffused this gloom over them and could not dispel it. They had supper and went away, and he was left alone with the consciousness that his life was poisoned and was poisoning the lives of others, and that this poison did not weaken but penetrated more and more deeply into his whole being.

With this consciousness, and with physical pain besides the terror, he must go to bed, often to lie awake the greater part of the night. Next morning he had to get up again, dress, go to the law court, speak, and write; or, if he did not go out, spend at home those twenty-four hours a day each of which was a torture. And he had to live thus all alone on the brink of an abyss, with no one who understood or pitied him.

V

Thus one month passed, and then another. Just before the New Year his brother-in-law came to town and stayed at their house. Ivan Ilyich was at the law court, and Praskovya Fedorovna had gone shopping. When Ivan Ilyich came home and entered his study he found his brother-in-law there—a healthy, florid man—unpacking his portmanteau. He raised his head on hearing Ivan Ilyich's footsteps and looked up at him for a moment without a word. That stare told Ivan Ilyich everything. His brother-in-law opened his mouth to utter an exclamation of surprise, but checked himself, and that action confirmed it all.

"I have changed, eh?"

"Yes, there is a change."

And after that, try as he would to get his brother-in-law to return to the subject of his looks, the latter would say nothing about it.

Praskovya Fedorovna came home, and her brother went out to her. Ivan Ilyich locked the door and began to examine himself in the glass, first full face, then in profile. He took up a portrait of himself taken with his wife and compared it with what he saw in the glass. The change in him was immense. Then he bared his arms to the elbow, looked at them, drew the sleeves down again, sat down on an ottoman, and grew blacker than night.

"No, no, this won't do!" he said to himself, and jumped up, went to the desk, took up some law papers and began to read them, but could not continue. He unlocked the door and went into the reception room. The door leading to the drawing room was shut. He approached it on tiptoe and eavesdropped.

"No, you're exaggerating!" Praskovya Fedorovna was saying.

"Exaggerating! Don't you see it? Why, he's a dead man! Look at his eyes—there's no light in them. But what's wrong with him?"

"No one knows. Nicolaevich [that was another doctor] said something, but I don't know what. And Leshchetitski [this was the celebrated specialist] said quite the contrary—"

Ivan Ilyich tiptoed away, went to his own room, lay down, and began musing: "It must be the kidney, a floating kidney." He recalled all the doctors had told him of how it had detached itself and swayed about. And by an effort of imagination he tried to catch that kidney and arrest it and support it. So little was needed for this, it seemed to him. "No, I'll go to see Peter Ivanovich again." [That was the friend whose friend was a doctor.] He rang, ordered the carriage, and got ready to go.

"Where are you going, Jean?" asked his wife, with a specially sad and exceptionally kind look.

This exceptionally kind look and the French form of his first name irritated him. He looked morosely at her.

"I must go to see Peter Ivanovich."

He went to see Peter Ivanovich, and together they went to see the latter's friend, the doctor. He was in, and Ivan Ilyich had a long talk with him.

Reviewing the anatomical and physiological details of what in the doctor's opinion was going on inside him, he understood it all.

There was something, a small thing, in the vermiform appendix. It might all come out right. Only stimulate the energy of one organ and check the activity of another, then absorption would take place and everything would come out right. He got home rather late for dinner, and conversed cheerfully as he ate it, but could not for a long time bring himself to go back to work in his room. At last, however, he went to his study and did what was necessary, but the consciousness that he had put something aside—an important, intimate matter which he would revert to when his work was done—never left him. When he had finished his work he remembered that this intimate matter was the thought of his vermiform appendix. But he did not give himself up to it, and went to the drawing room for tea.

There were callers there, including the Examining Magistrate who was a desirable match for his daughter, and they were conversing, playing the piano, and singing. Ivan Ilyich, as Praskovya Fedorovna remarked, spent that evening more cheerfully than usual, but he never for a moment forgot that he had postponed the important matter of the appendix. At eleven o'clock he said good night and went to his bedroom. Since his illness he had slept alone in a small room next to his study. He undressed and picked up a novel by Zola, but instead of reading it he fell into thought, and in his imagination that desired improvement in the vermiform appendix occurred. There was the absorption and evacuation and the re-establishment of normal activity.

"Yes, that's it!" he said to himself. "One need only assist nature, that's all." He remembered his medicine, rose, took it, and lay down on his back watching for the beneficent action of the medicine and its lessening of the pain. "I need only take it regularly and avoid all injurious influences. I'm already feeling better, much better." He began feeling his side: it was not painful to the touch. "There, I really don't feel it. It's much better already." He put out the light and turned on his side. "The appendix is getting better, absorption is going on." Suddenly he felt the old, familiar, dull, gnawing pain, stubborn and severe. There was the same familiar loathsome taste in his mouth. His heart sank and he felt dazed. "My God! My God!" he muttered. "Again, again! And it will never cease." And suddenly the matter presented itself in a quite different aspect. "The vermiform appendix! The kidney!" he said to himself. "It's not a question of appendix or kidney, but of life and—death. Yes, life was there and now it's going, going, and I can't stop it. Yes. Why deceive myself? Isn't it obvious to everyone but me that I'm dying, and that it's only a question of weeks, days—it may happen this moment. There was light, and now there is darkness.

I was here and now I'm going there! Where?" A chill came over him, his breathing ceased, and he felt only the throbbing of his heart.

"When I am no more, what will there be? There'll be nothing. Then where shall I be when I am no more? Can this be dying? No, I don't want to die!" He jumped up and tried to light the candle, felt for it with trembling hands, dropped candle and candlestick on the floor, and fell back on his pillow.

"What's the use? It makes no difference," he said to himself, staring with wide-open eyes into the darkness. "Death. Yes, death. And none of them knows or wishes to know it, and they have no pity for me. Now they're playing." (He heard through the door the distant sound of a song and its accompaniment.) "It's all the same to them, but they will die, too! Fools! I first, and they later, but it'll be the same for them. And now they are having a fine time—the beasts!"

Anger choked him, and he was agonizingly, unbearably miserable. "It's impossible that all men have been doomed to suffer this awful horror!" He raised himself.

"Something must be wrong. I must calm myself—must think it all over from the beginning." And he again began thinking. "Yes, the beginning of my illness: I hit my side, but I was still quite well that day and the next. It hurt a little, then rather more. I saw the doctors; this was followed by despondency and anguish, and more doctors, and I drew nearer to the abyss. My strength grew less and I kept coming nearer and nearer, and now I have wasted away and there's no light in my eyes. I think of the appendix—but this is death! I think of my appendix getting better, and all the while death is right here! Can it really be death?"

Again terror seized him, and he gasped for breath. He leaned down and began feeling for the matches, pressing with his elbow against the stand beside the bed. It was in his way and hurt him, he grew furious with it, pressed on it still harder, and upset it. Breathless and in despair, he fell on his back, expecting death to come immediately.

Meanwhile the visitors were leaving. Praskovya Fedorovna was seeing them off. She heard something fall and came in.

"What's happened?"

"Nothing. I knocked the stand over accidentally."

She went out and returned with a candle. He lay there panting heavily, like a man who has run a thousand yards, and stared upward at her with a fixed look.

"What is it, Jean?"

"No-o-thing. I upset it." ("Why say anything? She won't understand," he thought.)

And in truth she did not understand. She picked up the stand, lit his candle, and hurried away to see another visitor off. When she came back he still lay on his back, looking upward.

"What is it? Do you feel worse?"

"Yes."

She shook her head and sat down.

"Do you know, Jean, I think we must ask Leshchetitski to come and see you here."

This meant calling in the famous specialist, regardless of expense. He smiled malevolently and said "No." She remained a little longer and then went up to him and kissed his forehead.

While she was kissing him he hated her from the bottom of his soul and with difficulty refrained from pushing her away.

"Good night. God send you sound sleep."

"Yes."

VI

Ivan Ilyich saw that he was dying, and he was in continual despair.

In the depth of his heart he knew he was dying, but not only was he not accustomed to the thought, he simply did not and could not grasp it.

The syllogism he had learnt from Kiezewetter's *Logic:* "Caius is a man, men are mortal, therefore Caius is mortal," had always seemed to him correct as applied to Caius, but certainly not as applied to Ivan Ilyich. That Caius—man in the abstract—was mortal was perfectly correct, but he wasn't Caius, not an abstract man, but a creature quite, quite apart from all others. He had been little Vanya, with a mamma and a papa, with Mitya and Volodya, with toys, a coachman and a nurse, afterward with Katenka and with all the joys, griefs, and delights of childhood, boyhood, and youth. What did Caius know of the smell of that striped leather ball Vanya had been so fond of? Had Caius kissed his mother's hand like that, and did the silk of her dress rustle so for Caius? Had he rioted like that at school when the pastry was bad? Had Caius been in love like that? Could Caius preside at a session the way he did? "Caius really was mortal, and it was right for him to die; but for me, little Vanya, Ivan Ilyich, with all my thoughts and emotions, it's altogether a different matter. It cannot be that I ought to die. That would be too terrible."

That was how he felt.

"If I had to die like Caius I'd have known it was so. An inner voice would have told me so, but there was nothing of the sort in me and I and all my friends felt that our case was quite different from that of Caius. And now here it is!" he said to himself. "It can't be. It's impossible! Yet here it is. How is that? How is one to understand it?"

He could not understand it, and tried to drive this false, incorrect, morbid thought away and to replace it by other proper and healthy thoughts. But that thought, and not the thought only but the reality itself, seemed to come and confront him.

And to replace that thought he called up a succession of others, hoping to find in them some support. He tried to get back into the former current of thoughts that had once screened the thought of death from him. But strange to say, all that had formerly shut off, hidden, and destroyed his consciousness of death no longer had that effect.

He now spent most of his time in attempting to re-establish that old current. He would say to himself: "I will take up my duties again—after all, I used to live by them." And banishing all doubts he would go to the law court, enter into conversation with his colleagues, and sit at ease as was his wont, scanning the crowd with a thoughtful look and leaning both his emaciated arms on the arms of his oak chair; bending over as usual to a colleague and drawing his papers nearer, he would interchange whispers with him, and then suddenly raising his eyes and sitting erect would pronounce certain words and open the proceedings.

But suddenly in the midst of those proceedings the pain in his side, regardless of the stage the proceedings had reached, would begin its own gnawing work. He would turn his attention to it and try to drive the thought of it away, but without success. *It* would come and stand before him and look at him, and he would be petrified and the light would die out of his eyes, and he would again begin asking himself whether *It* alone was true. And his colleagues and subordinates would see with surprise and distress that he, the brilliant and subtle judge, was becoming confused and making mistakes. He would shake himself, try to pull himself together, manage somehow to bring the sitting to a close, and return home with the sorrowful consciousness that his judicial labors could not as formerly hide from him what he wanted them to hide, and could not deliver him from *It*. And what was worst of all was that *It* drew his attention to *Itself*, not in order to make him take some action, but only that he should look at *It*, look *It* straight in the face: look at *It* and, without doing anything, suffer inexpressibly.

And to save himself from this condition Ivan Ilyich looked for consolations—new screens—and new screens were found and for a while seemed to save him, but then they immediately fell to pieces or rather became transparent, as if *It* penetrated them and nothing could veil *It*.

In these latter days he would go into the drawing room he had arranged—that drawing room where he had fallen and for the sake of which (how bitterly ridiculous it seemed) he had sacrificed his life—for he knew that his illness had originated with that injury. He would enter and see that something had scratched the polished table. He would look for the cause of this and find that it was an album, whose bronze ornamentation had got bent. He would take up the expensive album which he had lovingly arranged, and feel vexed with his daughter and her friends for their untidiness—for the album was torn here and there and some of the photographs had been reinserted upside down. He would put it carefully in order and bend the ornamentation back into position. Then it would occur to him to place all those things in another corner of the room, near the plants. He would call the footman, but his daughter or wife would come to help him. They would not agree, and his wife would contradict him, and he would dispute and grow angry. But that was all right, for then he did not think about *It*. *It* was invisible then.

But then, when he was moving something himself, his wife would say: "Let the servants do it. You'll hurt yourself again." And suddenly *It* would flash through the screen and he would see *It*. Just a flash of *It*, and he hoped *It* would disappear, but he would involuntarily pay attention to his side. *"It* sits there as before, gnawing just the same!" And he could no longer forget *It*, but could distinctly see *It* looking at him from behind the flowers. "What's all this for?"

"It really is so! I lost my life over that curtain as I might have done when storming a fort. Is that possible? How terrible and how stupid. It can't be true! It can't—but it is."

He would go to his study, lie down, and again be alone with *It*: face to face with *It*. And nothing could be done with *It* except to look at *It* and shudder.

VII

How it happened is impossible to say, because it came about step by step, unnoticed, but in the third month of Ivan Ilyich's illness his wife, his daughter, his son, his acquaintances, the doctors, the servants, and above all he himself, were aware that the whole interest he had for other people was whether he would soon vacate his place, and at last release the living from the discomfort caused by his presence, and be himself released from his sufferings.

He slept less and less. He was given opium and hypodermic injections of morphine, but this did not relieve him. The dull depression he experienced in a somnolent condition at first gave him a little relief, but only as something new; afterward it became as distressing as the pain itself or even more so.

Special foods were prepared for him by the doctors' orders, but all those foods became increasingly distasteful and disgusting to him.

For his excretions also special arrangements had to be made, and this was a torment to him every time—a torment from the uncleanliness, the unseemliness, and the smell, and from knowing that another person had to take part in it.

But it was just through this most unpleasant matter that Ivan Ilyich obtained comfort. Gerasim, the butler's young assistant, always came in to carry away the bedpan. Gerasim was a clean, fresh peasant lad, grown stout on citified fare, and always cheerful and bright. At first the sight of him, in his clean Russian peasant costume, engaged in that disgusting task, embarrassed Ivan Ilyich.

Once, when he got up from the pan, too weak to draw up his trousers, he dropped into a soft armchair and looked with horror at his bare, flaccid thighs with the muscles so sharply marked on them.

Gerasim, with a firm light tread, his heavy boots emitting a pleasant smell of tar and fresh winter air, came in wearing a clean Hessian apron, the sleeves of his print shirt tucked up over his strong bare young arms, and refraining from looking at his sick master out of consideration for his feelings, restraining the joy of life that beamed from his face, he went up to the pan.

"Gerasim!" Ivan Ilyich called him in a weak voice.

Gerasim started, evidently afraid he might have committed some blunder, and with a rapid movement turned his fresh, kind, simple young face, which was just showing the first downy signs of a beard.

"Yes, Sir?"

"That must be very unpleasant for you. You must forgive me. I'm helpless."

"Oh, why, Sir?" and Gerasim's eyes beamed and he showed his glistening white teeth. "What's a little trouble? It's a case of illness with you, Sir."

And his deft strong hands did their accustomed task, and he went out of the room stepping lightly. Five minutes later he as lightly returned.

Ivan Ilyich was still sitting in the same position in the armchair.

"Gerasim," he said when the latter had replaced the freshly washed utensil, "please come here and help me." Gerasim went up to him. "Lift me up. It is hard for me to get up, and I have sent Dmitrii away."

Gerasim went up to him, grasped his master with his strong arms deftly but gently, in the same way that he walked—lifted him, supported him with one hand, and with the other drew up his trousers and would have set him down again, but Ivan Ilyich asked to be led to the sofa. Gerasim, without an effort and without apparent pressure, led him, almost lifting him, to the sofa and placed him on it.

"Thank you. How easily and well you do it all!"

Gerasim smiled again and turned to leave the room. But Ivan Ilyich felt such a comfort in his presence that he did not want to let him go.

"One thing more, please move up that chair. No, the other one— under my feet. It is easier for me when my feet are raised."

Gerasim brought the chair, set it down gently in place, and raised Ivan Ilyich's legs on to it. It seemed to Ivan Ilyich that he felt better while Gerasim was holding up his legs.

"It's better when my legs are higher," he said. "Place that cushion under them."

Gerasim did so. He again lifted the legs and placed them back, and again Ivan Ilyich felt better while Gerasim held his legs. When he set them down Ivan Ilyich fancied he felt worse.

"Gerasim," he said, "are you busy now?"

"Not at all, Sir," said Gerasim, who had learned from the towns- people how to speak to gentlefolk.

"What have you still to do?"

"What have I to do? I've done everything except chopping the logs for tomorrow."

"Then hold my legs up a bit higher, can you?"

"Of course I can. Why not?" And Gerasim raised his master's legs higher, and Ivan Ilyich thought that in that position he did not feel any pain at all.

"And how about the logs?"

"Don't trouble about that, Sir. There's plenty of time."

Ivan Ilyich told Gerasim to sit down and hold his legs, and began to talk to him. And strange to say it seemed to him that he felt better while Gerasim held his legs up.

After that Ivan Ilyich would sometimes call Gerasim and get him to hold his legs on his shoulders, and he liked talking to him. Gerasim did it all easily, willingly, simply, and with a good nature that touched Ivan Ilyich. Health, strength, and vitality in other people were offensive to him, but Gerasim's strength and vitality did not mortify but soothed him.

What tormented Ivan Ilyich most was the deception, the lie, which for some reason they all accepted, that he was not dying but was simply ill, and that he only need keep quiet and undergo treatment and then the results would be very good. He, however, knew that, do what they would, nothing would come of it, only still more agonizing suffering and death. This deception tortured him—their not wishing to admit what they all knew and what he knew, but wanting to lie to him concerning his terrible condition, and wishing and forcing him to participate in that lie. Those lies—lies enacted over him on the eve of his death and destined to degrade this awful, solemn act to the level of their visitings, their curtains, their sturgeon for dinner—were a terrible agony for Ivan Ilyich. And, strangely enough, many times when they were going through their antics over him he had been within a hair's-breadth of calling out to them: "Stop lying! You know and I know that I'm dying. Then at least stop lying about it!" But he had never had the spirit to do it.

The awful, terrible act of his dying was, he could see, reduced by those about him to the level of a casual, unpleasant, and almost indecorous incident (as if someone entered a drawing room diffusing an unpleasant odor), and this was done by that very decorum which he had served all his life long. He saw that no one felt for him, because no one even wished to grasp his position. Only Gerasim recognized it and pitied him, and so Ivan Ilyich felt at ease only with him. He felt comforted when Gerasim supported his legs (sometimes all night long) and refused to go to bed, saying: "Don't you worry, Ivan Ilyich, I'll get sleep enough later on," or when he suddenly became familiar and exclaimed: "If you weren't sick it would be another matter, but as it is, why should I grudge a little trouble?" Gerasim alone did not lie; everything showed that he alone understood the facts of the case and did not consider it necessary to disguise them, but simply felt sorry for his emaciated and enfeebled master. Once when Ivan Ilyich was sending him away he even said straight out: "We shall all of us die, so why should I grudge a little trouble?"—expressing the fact that he did not think his work burdensome, because he was doing it for a dying man and hoped someone would do the same for him when his time came.

Apart from this lying, or because of it, what most tormented Ivan Ilyich was that no one pitied him as he wished to be pitied. At certain moments after prolonged suffering he wished most of all (though he would have been ashamed to confess it) for someone to pity him as a sick child is pitied. He longed to be petted and comforted. He knew he was an important functionary, that he had a beard turning gray, and that therefore what he longed for was impossible, but still he longed for it. And in Gerasim's attitude toward him there was something akin to what he wished for, and so that attitude comforted him. Ivan Ilyich wanted to weep, wanted to be petted and cried over, and then his colleague Shebek would come, and instead of weeping and being petted Ivan Ilyich would assume a serious, severe, and profound air, and by force of habit would express his opinion on a decision of the Court of Appeals and would stubbornly insist on that view. This falsity around him and within him did more than anything else to poison his last days.

VIII

It was morning. He knew it was morning because Gerasim had gone, and Peter the footman had come and put out the candles, drawn back one of the curtains, and begun quietly to tidy up. Whether it was morning or evening, Friday or Sunday, made no difference, it was all just the same: the gnawing, unmitigated, agonizing pain, never ceasing for an instant, the consciousness of life inexorably waning but not yet extinguished, the approach of that ever dreaded and hateful Death which was the only reality, and always the same falsity. What were days, weeks, hours, in such a case?

"Will you have some tea, Sir?"

"He wants things to be regular, and wishes the gentlefolk to drink tea in the morning," thought Ivan Ilyich, but all he said was "No."

"Wouldn't you like to move to the sofa, Sir?"

"He wants to tidy up the room, and I'm in the way. I am uncleanliness and disorder," he thought, but all he said was:

"No, leave me alone."

The man went on bustling about. Ivan Ilyich stretched out his hand. Peter came up, ready to help.

"What is it, Sir?"

"My watch."

Peter took the watch, which was close at hand, and gave it to his master.

"Half-past eight. Are they up?"

"No, Sir, except Vladimir Ivanich [the son], who's gone to school. Praskovya Fedorovna ordered me to wake her if you asked for her. Shall I do so?"

"No, there's no need."—"Perhaps I'd better have some tea," he thought, and added aloud: "Yes, bring me some tea."

Peter went to the door, but Ivan Ilyich dreaded being left alone. "How can I keep him here? Oh, yes, my medicine."—"Peter, give me my medicine."—"Why not? Perhaps it may still do me some good." He took a spoonful and swallowed it. "No, it won't help. It's all tomfoolery, all deception," he decided as soon as he became aware of the familiar, sickly, hopeless taste. "No, I can't believe in it any longer. But the pain, why this pain? If it would only cease just for a moment!" And he moaned. Peter turned toward him. "It's all right. Go and fetch me some tea."

Peter went out. Left alone, Ivan Ilyich groaned not so much with pain, terrible though that was, as from mental anguish. Always and forever the same, always these endless days and nights. If only it would come quicker. If only *what* would come quicker? Death, darkness? No, no! Anything rather than death!

When Peter returned with the tea on a tray, Ivan Ilyich stared at him for a time in perplexity, not realizing who and what he was. Peter was disconcerted by that look, and his embarrassment brought Ivan Ilyich to himself.

"Oh, tea! All right, put it down. Only help me to wash and put on a clean shirt."

And Ivan Ilyich began to wash. With pauses for rest, he washed his hands and then his face, cleaned his teeth, brushed his hair, and looked in the glass. He was terrified by what he saw, especially by the limp way in which his hair clung to his pallid forehead.

While his shirt was being changed he knew that he would be still more frightened at the sight of his body, so he avoided looking at it. Finally he was ready. He drew on a dressing gown, wrapped himself in a plaid, and sat down in the armchair to take his tea. For a moment he felt refreshed, but as soon as he began to drink the tea he was again aware of the same taste, and the pain also returned. He finished it with an effort, and then lay down, stretching out his legs, and dismissed Peter.

Always the same. Now a spark of hope flashes up, then a sea of despair rages, and always the pain; always pain, always despair, and always the same. When alone he had a dreadful and distressing desire to call someone, but he knew beforehand that with others present it would be still worse. "Another dose of morphine—to lose consciousness. I'll tell him, this doctor, that he must think of something else. It's impossible, impossible, to go on like this."

An hour passes like that, and then another. But now there is a ring at the door bell. Perhaps it's the doctor? It is. He comes in, fresh, hearty, plump, and cheerful, with that look on his face which seems to say: "There, now, you're in a panic about something, but we'll arrange it all for you directly!" The doctor knows this expression is out of place here, but he has put it on once for all and can't take it off—like a man who has put on a frock coat in the morning to pay a round of calls.

The doctor rubs his hands vigorously and reassuringly.

"Brr! How cold it is! There's such a sharp frost; just let me warm myself!" he says, as if it were only a matter of waiting till he was warm, and then he would put everything right.

"Well, now, how are you?"

Ivan Ilyich feels that the doctor would like to say: "Well, how are our affairs?" but that even he feels that this would not do, and says instead: "What sort of a night have you had?"

Ivan Ilyich looks at him as much as to say: "Really, don't you ever become ashamed of lying?" But the doctor does not wish to understand this question, and Ivan Ilyich says: "Just as terrible as ever. The pain never leaves me and never subsides. If only something—"

"Yes, you sick people are always like that. There, now, I think I'm warm enough. Even Praskovya Fedorovna, who's so particular, could find no fault with my temperature. Well, now I can say good morning," and the doctor presses his patient's hand.

Then, dropping his former playfulness, he begins with a most serious face to examine the patient, feeling his pulse and taking his temperature, and then begins the tapping and auscultation.

Ivan Ilyich knows quite well and definitely that all this is nonsense and pure humbug, but when the doctor, getting down on one knee, leans over him, putting his ear first higher then lower, and performs various gymnastic movements over him with a significant expression on his face, Ivan Ilyich submits to it all as he used to submit to the speeches of the lawyers, though he knew very well that they were all lying and why they were lying.

The doctor, kneeling on the sofa, was still sounding him when Praskovya Fedorovna's silk dress swished at the door and she was heard scolding Peter for not having let her know of the doctor's arrival.

She came in, kissed her husband, and at once proceeded to prove that she had been up a long time already, and only owing to a misunderstanding failed to be there when the doctor arrived.

Ivan Ilyich looked at her, scrutinized her from head to toe, and set down against her the whiteness and plumpness and cleanness of her hands and neck, the gloss of her hair, and the sparkle of her vivacious eyes. He hated her with his whole soul. And the thrill of hatred he felt for her made him suffer from her touch.

Her attitude toward him and his disease was still the same. Just as the doctor had adopted a certain relation to his patient which he could not abandon, so had she formed one toward her husband—that he wasn't doing something he ought to do and was himself to blame, and that she reproached him lovingly for this—and she could not now change that attitude.

"You see, he doesn't listen to me and doesn't take his medicine at the proper time. And, above all, he lies in a position that is no doubt bad for him—with his legs up."

She described how he made Gerasim hold up his legs.

The doctor smiled with a disdainful affability that said: "What's to be done? These sick people do have foolish fancies of that kind, but we must forgive them."

When the examination was over the doctor looked at his watch, and then Praskovya Fedorovna announced to Ivan Ilyich that of course he could do as he pleased, but she had sent today for a celebrated specialist who would examine him and have a consultation with Michael Danilovich (their regular doctor).

"Please don't raise any objections. I'm doing this for my own sake," she said ironically, letting it be felt that she was doing it all for his sake and said this only not to leave him any right to refuse. He remained silent, knitting his brows. He felt that he was so surrounded and involved in a mesh of falsity that it was hard to unravel anything.

Everything she did for him was entirely for her own sake, and she told him she was doing for herself what she actually was doing for herself, as if that was so incredible that he must understand the opposite.

At half-past eleven the celebrated specialist arrived. Again the tapping began and the significant conversations in his presence and in another room, about the kidneys and the appendix, and the questions and answers, with such an air of importance that again, instead of the real question of life and death which now alone confronted him, the question arose of a kidney and an appendix which were not behaving as they ought to and would now be attacked by Michael Danilovich and the specialist and forced to amend their ways.

The celebrated specialist took leave of him with a serious though not hopeless look, and in reply to the timid question which Ivan Ilyich, with eyes glistening with fear and hope, put to him, as to whether there was a chance of recovery, said that he could not vouch for it, but there was a possibility. The look of hope with which Ivan Ilyich watched the doctor go out was so pathetic that Praskovya Fedorovna, seeing it, actually wept as she left the room to hand the doctor his fee.

The gleam of hope kindled by the doctor's encouragement did not last long. The same room, the same pictures, curtains, wallpaper, medicine bottles, were all there, and the same aching suffering body, and Ivan Ilyich began to moan. They gave him a subcutaneous injection, and he sank into oblivion.

It was twilight when he came to. They brought him his dinner and he swallowed, with difficulty, some beef tea, and then everything was the same again, and night was coming on.

After dinner, at seven o'clock, Praskovya Fedorovna came into the room in evening dress, her full bosom pushed up by her corset, and with traces of powder on her face. She had reminded him in the morning that they were going to the theater. Sarah Bernhardt was visiting the town, and they had a box, which he had insisted on their taking. Now he had forgotten about it, and her evening gown offended him, but he concealed his vexation when he remembered that he had himself insisted on their securing a box and going because it would be an instructive and aesthetic pleasure for the children.

Praskovya Fedorovna had come in, self-satisfied but yet with a rather guilty air. She sat down and asked how he was but, as he saw, only for the sake of asking and not in order to learn about it, knowing that there was nothing to learn—and then went on to what she really wanted to say: that she would not on any account have gone, but that the box had been taken, and Helen and their daughter were going, as well as Petrishchev (the Examining Magistrate, their daughter's fiancé), and that it was out of the question to let them go alone; but that she would have much preferred to sit with him for a while; and he must be sure to follow the doctor's orders while she was away.

"Oh, and Fedor Petrovich [the fiancé] would like to come in. May he? And Lisa?"

"All right."

Their daughter came in in full evening dress, her fresh young flesh exposed (making a show of that very flesh which in his own case caused so much suffering), strong, healthy, evidently in love, and having but little patience with illness, suffering, and death, because they interfered with her happiness.

Fedor Petrovich came in, too, in full dress, his hair curled à la Capoul, a tight stiff collar round his long sinewy neck, an enormous white shirt front and narrow black trousers tightly stretched over his strong thighs. He had one white glove tightly drawn on, and was holding his opera hat.

Following him the schoolboy crept in unnoticed, in a new uniform, poor little fellow, and wearing gloves. Terribly dark shadows showed under his eyes, the meaning of which Ivan Ilyich knew well.

His son had always seemed pathetic to him, and now it was dreadful to see the boy's frightened look of pity. It seemed to Ivan Ilyich that Vassya was the only one besides Gerasim who understood and pitied him.

They all sat down and again asked how he was. A silence ensued. Lisa asked her mother about the opera glasses, and there was an altercation between mother and daughter as to who had taken them and where they had been put. This occasioned some unpleasantness.

Fedor Petrovich inquired of Ivan Ilyich whether he had ever seen Sarah Bernhardt. Ivan Ilyich did not at first catch the question, but then replied: "No; have you seen her before?"

"Yes, in *Adrienne Lecouvreur.*"

Praskovya Fedorovna mentioned some roles in which Sarah Bernhardt was particularly good. Her daughter disagreed. Conversation sprang up as to the splendor and realism of her acting—the sort of conversation that is always repeated and is always the same.

In the midst of the conversation Fedor Petrovich glanced at Ivan Ilyich and became silent. The others also looked at him and grew silent. Ivan Ilyich was staring with glittering eyes straight before him, evidently indignant with them. This had to be rectified, but it was impossible to do it. The silence had to be broken, but for a time no one dared to break it, and they all became afraid that the conventional deception would suddenly become obvious and the truth become plain to all. Lisa was the first to pluck up courage and break that silence, but by trying to hide what everybody was feeling she betrayed it:

"Well, if we're going, it's time to start," she said, looking at her watch, a present from her father, and with a faint and significant smile at Fedor Petrovich pertaining to something known only to them. She got up with a swish of her dress.

They all rose, said good night, and went away.

When they had gone it seemed to Ivan Ilyich that he felt better; the falsity had gone with them. But the pain remained—that same pain and that same fear that made everything monotonously alike, nothing harder and nothing easier. Everything was worse.

Again minute followed minute and hour followed hour. Everything remained the same and there was no cessation. And the inevitable end of it all became more and more terrible.

"Yes, send Gerasim here," he replied to a question Peter asked.

IX

His wife returned late at night. She came in on tiptoe, but he heard her, opened his eyes, and made haste to close them again. She wished to send Gerasim away and to sit with him herself, but he opened his eyes and said: "No, go away."

"Are you in great pain?"

"It's always the same."

"Take some opium."

He agreed and took some. She went away.

Till about three in the morning he was in a state of stupefied misery. It seemed to him that he and his pain were being thrust into a narrow, deep black sack, but though they were pushed further and further in they could not be pushed to the bottom. And this, terrible enough in itself, was accompanied by suffering. He was frightened, yet wanted to fall through the sack; he struggled yet co-operated. And suddenly he broke through, fell, and regained consciousness. Gerasim was sitting at the foot of the bed dozing quietly and patiently, while he himself lay with his emaciated stockinged legs resting on Gerasim's shoulders; the same shaded candle was there and the same unceasing pain.

"Go away, Gerasim," he whispered.

"It's all right, Sir. I'll stay a while."

"No. Go away."

He removed his legs from Gerasim's shoulders, turned sideways onto his arm, and felt sorry for himself. He only waited till Gerasim had gone into the next room and then restrained himself no longer but wept like a child. He wept on account of his helplessness, his terrible loneliness, the cruelty of man, the cruelty of God, and the absence of God.

"Why hast Thou done all this? Why hast Thou brought me here? Why, why dost Thou torture me so terribly?"

He did not expect any answer and yet wept because there was no answer and could be none. The pain again grew more acute, but he did not stir and did not call. He said to himself: "Go on! Strike me! But what is it for? What have I done to Thee? What is it for?"

Then he grew quiet and not only ceased weeping but even held his breath and became all attention. It was as though he were listening not to an audible voice but to the voice of his soul, to the current of thoughts arising within him.

"What is it you want?" was the first clear conception capable of expression in words that he heard.

"What do you want? What do you want?" he repeated to himself.

"What do I want? To live and not to suffer," he answered.

And again he listened with such concentrated attention that even his pain did not distract him.

"To live? How?" asked his inner voice.

"Why, to live as I used to—well and pleasantly."

"As you lived before, well and pleasantly?" the voice repeated.

And in imagination he began to recall the best moments of his pleasant life. But, strange to say, none of those best moments of his pleasant life now seemed at all what they had then seemed—none of them except the first recollections of childhood. There, in childhood, there had been something really pleasant with which it would be possible to live if it could return. But the child who had experienced that happiness existed no longer; it was like a reminiscence of someone else.

As soon as the period began which had produced the present Ivan Ilyich, all that had then seemed joys now melted before his sight and turned into something trivial and often nasty.

And the further he departed from childhood, and the nearer he came to the present, the more worthless and doubtful were the joys. This began with the School of Law. A little that was really good was still found there—there was lightheartedness, friendship, and hope. But in the upper classes there had already been fewer of such good moments. Then during the first years of his official career, when he was in the service of the Governor, some pleasant moments again occurred: they were the memories of love for a woman. Then all became confused and there was still less of what was good; later on again there was still less that was good, and the further he went, the less there was. His marriage, a mere accident, then the disenchantment that followed it, his wife's bad breath and her sensuality and hypocrisy; then that deadly official life and those preoccupations about money, a year of it, and two, and ten, and twenty, and always the same thing. And the longer it lasted, the more deadly it became. "It's just as if I'd been going downhill while I imagined I was going up. And that's really what it was. I was going up in public opinion, but to the same extent life was ebbing away from me. And now it's all done, and there is only death.

"Then what does it mean? Why? It can't be that life is so senseless and horrible. But if it really has been so horrible and senseless, why must I die and die in agony? There's something wrong!

"Maybe I didn't live as I ought to have done," it suddenly occurred to him. "But how could that be, when I did everything properly?" he replied, and immediately dismissed from his mind this, the sole solution of all the riddles of life and death, as something quite impossible.

"Then what do you want now? To live? Live how? Live as you lived in the law court when the court attendant proclaimed: 'His Honor, His Honor, the Judge!' he repeated to himself. 'Here he is—His Honor! His Honor, the Judge!' But I'm not guilty!" he exclaimed angrily. "What is it for?" And he ceased crying but, turning his face to the wall, continued to ponder on the same question: Why, and for what purpose, was there all this horror? But however much he pondered, he found no answer. And whenever the thought occurred to him, as it often did, that it all resulted from his not having lived as he ought to have lived, he at once recalled the correctness of his whole life and dismissed so strange an idea.

X

Another fortnight passed. Ivan Ilyich no longer left his sofa now. He would not lie in bed but lay on the sofa, facing the wall nearly all the time. He suffered ever the same unceasing agonies and in his loneliness pondered always on the same insoluble question: "What is this? Can it be that this is death?" And an inner voice answered: "Yes, it is death."

"Why these sufferings?" And the voice answered: "For no reason— they just are." Beyond and besides this there was nothing.

From the very beginning of his illness, ever since he had first been to see the doctor, Ivan Ilyich's life had been divided between two contrary and alternating moods: now it was despair and the expectation of this uncomprehended and terrible death, and now hope and an intently interested observation of the functioning of his organs. Now before his eyes there was only a kidney or an intestine that temporarily evaded its duty, and now only that incomprehensible and dreadful death from which it was impossible to escape.

These two states of mind had alternated from the very beginning of his illness, but the further it progressed, the more doubtful and fantastic became his conception of the kidney, and the more real his sense of impending death.

He had but to call to mind what he had been three months before and what he was now, to see with what regularity he had been going downhill, for every possibility of hope to be shattered.

Latterly, during that loneliness in which he found himself as he lay with his face to the back of the sofa, a loneliness in the midst of a populous town and surrounded by numerous acquaintances and relations but that yet could not have been more complete anywhere—either at the bottom of the sea or under the earth—during that terrible loneliness he had lived only in memories of the past. Pictures of his past rose before him one after the other. They always began with what was nearest in time and then went back to what was most remote—to his childhood—and rested there. If he thought of the stewed prunes that had been offered him that day, his mind went back to the raw shriveled French plums of his childhood, their peculiar flavor and the flow of saliva when he sucked their stones, and along with the memory of that taste came a whole series of memories of those days: his nurse, his brother, and their toys. "No, I mustn't think of that. It's too painful," he said to himself, and brought himself back to the present—to the button on the back of the sofa and the creases in its morocco. "Morocco is expensive, but it does not wear well: there had been a quarrel about it. It was a different kind of quarrel and a different kind of morocco that time when we tore father's portfolio and were punished, and mamma brought us some tarts." And again his thoughts dwelt on his childhood, and again it was painful, and he tried to banish them and fix his mind on something else.

Then again together with that chain of memories another series passed through his mind—of how his illness had progressed and grown worse. There also, the farther back he looked, the more life there had been. There had been more of what was good in life and more of life itself. The two merged together. "Just as the pain went on getting worse and worse, so my life grew worse and worse," he thought. "There's one bright spot there at the back, at the beginning of life, and afterward all becomes blacker and blacker and proceeds more and more rapidly—in inverse ratio to the square of the distance from death," thought Ivan Ilyich. And the example of a stone falling downward with increasing velocity entered his mind. Life, a series of increasing sufferings, flies farther and farther toward its end—the most terrible suffering. "I'm flying—" He shuddered, shifted his body, and tried to resist, but was already aware that resistance was impossible, and again with eyes weary of gazing but unable to cease seeing what was before them, he stared at the back of the sofa and waited—awaited that dreadful fall and shock and destruction.

"Resistance is impossible!" he said to himself. "If I could only understand what it's all for! But that, too, is impossible. An explanation would be possible if it could be said that I haven't lived as I ought to. But it's impossible to say that," and he remembered all the legality, rectitude and propriety of his life. "That, at any rate, certainly can't be admitted," he thought, and his lips smiled ironically as if someone could see that smile and be taken in by it. "There is no explanation! Agony, death. . . . What for?"

XI

Another two weeks went by in this way, and during that fortnight an event occurred that Ivan Ilyich and his wife had desired. Petrishchev formally proposed. It happened in the evening. The next day Praskovya Fedorovna came into her husband's room considering how best to inform him of it, but that very night there had been a fresh change for the worse in his condition. She found him still lying on the sofa but in a different position. He lay on his back, groaning and staring fixedly straight in front of him.

She began to remind him of his medicines, but he turned his eyes toward her with such a look that she did not finish what she was saying, so great an animosity, to her in particular, did that look express.

"For Christ's sake, let me die in peace!" he said.

She would have gone away, but just then their daughter came in and went up to say good morning. He looked at her as he had done at his wife, and in reply to her inquiry about his health said drily that he would soon free them all of himself. They were both silent, and after sitting with him for a while went away.

"Is it our fault?" Lisa said to her mother. "Just as if we were to blame! I'm sorry for papa, but why should we be tortured?"

The doctor came at his usual time. Ivan Ilyich answered "Yes" and "No," never taking his angry eyes from him, and at last said: "You know you can do nothing for me, so leave me alone."

"We can ease your sufferings."

"You can't even do that. Let me be."

The doctor went into the drawing room and told Praskovya Fedorovna that the case was very serious, and that the only recourse left was opium to allay her husband's sufferings, which must be terrible.

It was true, as the doctor said, that Ivan Ilyich's physical sufferings were terrible, but worse than the physical sufferings were his mental sufferings, which were his chief torture.

His mental sufferings were due to the fact that that night, as he looked at Gerasim's sleepy, good-natured face with its prominent cheek bones, the question suddenly occurred to him: "What if my whole life *has* really been wrong?"

It occurred to him that what had appeared perfectly impossible before—namely, that he had not spent his life as he should have done—might after all be true. It occurred to him that his scarcely perceptible attempts to struggle against what was considered good by the most highly placed people, those scarcely noticeable impulses which he had immediately suppressed, might have been the real thing, and all the rest false. And his professional duties and the whole arrangement of his life and of his family, and all his social and official interests, might all have been false. He tried to defend all those things to himself and suddenly felt the weakness of what he was defending. There was nothing to defend.

"But if that's so," he said to himself, "and I'm leaving this life with the consciousness that I have lost all that was given me, and it's impossible to rectify it—what then?"

He lay on his back and began to pass his life in review in quite a new way. In the morning when he saw first his footman, then his wife, then his daughter, and then the doctor, their every word and movement confirmed to him the awful truth that had been revealed to him during the night. In them he saw himself—all that for which he had lived—and saw clearly that it was not real at all, but a terrible and huge deception which had hidden both life and death. This consciousness intensified his physical suffering tenfold. He groaned and tossed about, and pulled at his clothing which choked and stifled him. And he hated them on that account.

He was given a large dose of opium and became unconscious, but at noon his sufferings began again. He drove everybody away and tossed from side to side.

His wife came to him and said:

"Jean, my dear, do this for me. It can't do any harm and often helps. Healthy people often do it—"

He opened his eyes wide.

"What? Take communion? Why? It's unnecessary! However—" She began to cry.

"Yes, do, my dear. I'll send for our priest. He's such a lovely man."

"All right. Very well," he muttered.

When the priest came and heard his confession, Ivan Ilyich was softened and seemed to feel a relief from his doubts, and consequently from his sufferings, and for a moment there came a ray of hope. He again began to think of his vermiform appendix and the possibility of correcting it. He received the sacrament with tears in his eyes.

When they laid him down again afterward he felt a moment's ease, and the hope that he might live awoke in him again. He began to think of the operation that had been suggested to him. "To live! I want to live!" he said to himself.

His wife came in to congratulate him after his communion, and when, uttering the usual conventional words, she added:

"You feel better, don't you?"—he, without looking at her, said: "Yes."

Her dress, her figure, the expression of her face, the tone of her voice, all revealed the same thing. "This is wrong, it's not as it should be. All you have lived for, and still live for, is falsehood and deception, hiding life and death from you." And as soon as he admitted that thought, his hatred and his agonizing physical suffering again sprang up, and with that suffering a consciousness of the ineluctable, approaching end. And to this was added a new sensation of grinding, shooting pain and a feeling of suffocation.

The expression of his face when he had uttered that "Yes" had been dreadful. Having uttered it, he looked her straight in the eyes, turned over on his face with a rapidity extraordinary in his weak state, and shouted:

"Go away! Go away and leave me alone!"

XII

From that moment the screaming began that continued for three days, and was so terrible that one could not hear it without horror even through two closed doors. At the moment he answered his wife he realized that he was lost, that there was no return, that the end had come, the very end, and his doubts were still unsolved and remained doubts.

"Oh! Oh! Oh!" he cried in various intonations. He had begun by screaming: "I won't have it! I won't!" and continued screaming on the letter *o*.

For three whole days, during which time did not exist for him, he struggled in that black sack into which he was being thrust by an invisible, resistless force. He struggled as a man condemned to death struggles in the hands of the executioner, though knowing that he cannot save himself. And every moment he felt that despite all his efforts he was drawing nearer and nearer to what terrified him. He felt that his agony was due to his being thrust into that black opening and still more to his not being able to get right into it. He was hindered from getting into it by his conviction that his life had been a good one. That very justification of his life held him fast and prevented his moving forward, and it caused him most torment of all.

Suddenly some force struck him in the chest and side, making it still harder to breathe, and he fell through the hole, and there at the bottom was a light. What had happened to him was like the sensation one sometimes experiences in a railway carriage when one thinks one is going backward, while one is really going forward, and suddenly becomes aware of the real direction.

"Yes, it was all not the right thing," he said to himself, "but that doesn't matter. It can be so. But what *is* the right thing?" he asked himself, and suddenly grew quiet.

This occurred at the end of the third day, two hours before his death. Just then his schoolboy son had crept softly in and gone up to the bedside. The dying man was still screaming desperately and waving his arms. His hand fell on the boy's head, and the boy caught it, pressed it to his lips, and began to cry.

At that very moment Ivan Ilyich fell through and caught sight of the light, and it was revealed to him that though his life had not been what it should have been, this could still be rectified. He asked himself: "What *is* the right thing?" and grew still, listening. Then he felt that someone was kissing his hand. He opened his eyes, looked at his son, and felt sorry for him. His wife came up to him, and he glanced at her. She was gazing at him open-mouthed, with undried tears on her nose and cheeks and a despairing look on her face. He felt sorry for her, too.

"Yes, I'm making them wretched," he thought. "They're sorry, but it will be better for them when I die." He wished to say this but had not the strength to utter it. "Besides, why speak? I must act," he thought. With a look at his wife, he indicated his son and said: "Take him away—sorry for him—sorry for you, too—" He tried to add: "Forgive me," but said "Forego—" and waved his hand, knowing that He whose understanding mattered would understand.

And suddenly it grew clear to him that what had been oppressing him and would not leave him was all dropping away at once from two sides, from ten sides, and from all sides. He was sorry for them, he must act so as not to hurt them: release them and free himself from these sufferings. "How good and how simple!" he thought. "And the pain?" he asked himself. "What has become of it? Where are you, my pain?"

He turned his attention to it.

"Yes, here it is. Well, what of it? Let the pain be. And death—where is it?"

He sought his former accustomed fear of death and did not find it. "Where is it? What death?" There was no fear because he could not find death.

In place of death there was light.

"So that's what it is!" he suddenly exclaimed aloud. "What joy!"

To him all this happened in a single instant, and the meaning of that instant did not change. For those present his agony continued for another two hours. Something rattled in his throat, his emaciated body twitched, then the gasping and rattle became less and less frequent.

"It's all over!" said someone near him.

He heard these words and repeated them in his soul.

"Death is all over," he said to himself. "It's no more!"

He drew in a breath, stopped in the midst of a sigh, stretched out, and died.

March 25, 1886.

The Imp and the Crust

A POOR PEASANT set out early one morning to plow, taking with him for his breakfast a crust of bread. He got his plow ready, wrapped the bread in his coat, put it under a bush, and set to work. After a while, when his horse was tired and he was hungry, the peasant fixed the plow, let the horse loose to graze, and went to get his coat and his breakfast.

He lifted the coat, but the bread was gone! He looked and looked, turned the coat over, shook it out—but the bread was gone. The peasant couldn't make this out at all.

Translated by Louise and Aylmer Maude. Revised.

"That's strange," thought he. "I saw no one, but all the same some-one has been here and has taken the bread!"

It was an imp who had stolen the bread while the peasant was plow-ing, and at that moment he was sitting behind the bush, waiting to hear the peasant swear and call on the Devil.

The peasant was sorry to lose his breakfast, but: "It can't be helped," said he. "After all, I shan't die of hunger! No doubt whoever took the bread needed it. May it do him good!"

And he went to the well, had a drink of water, and rested a bit. Then he caught his horse, harnessed it, and began plowing again.

The imp was crestfallen at not having made the peasant sin, and he went to report what had happened to the Devil, his master.

He came to the Devil and told how he had taken the peasant's bread, and how the peasant instead of cursing had said: "May it do him good!"

The Devil was angry, and replied: "If the man got the better of you, it was your own fault—you don't understand your business! If the peasants, and their wives after them, take to that sort of thing, it'll be all up with us. The matter can't be left like that! Go back at once," said he, "and put things right. If in three years you don't get the better of that peasant, I'll have you ducked in holy water!"

The imp was frightened. He scampered back to earth, thinking how he could redeem his fault. He thought and thought, and at last hit upon a good plan.

He turned himself into a laboring man and went and took service with the poor peasant. The first year he advised the peasant to sow wheat in a marshy place. The peasant took his advice and sowed in the marsh. The year turned out a very dry one, and the crops of the other peasants were all scorched by the sun, but the poor peasant's wheat grew thick and tall and full-eared. Not only had he grain enough to last him for the whole year, but he had much left over besides.

The next year the imp advised the peasant to sow on the hill; and it turned out a wet summer. Other people's wheat was beaten down and rotted and the ears did not fill; but the peasant's crop, up on the hill, was a fine one. He had more grain left over than before, so that he did not know what to do with it all.

Then the imp showed the peasant how he could mash the grain and distil spirit from it; and the peasant made strong drink, and began to drink it himself and to give it to his friends.

So the imp went to the Devil, his master, and boasted that he had made up for his failure. The Devil said that he would come and see for himself how the case stood.

He came to the peasant's house, and saw that the peasant had invited his well-to-do neighbors and was treating them to drink. His wife was offering the drink to the guests, and as she handed it round she stumbled against the table and spilled a glassful.

The peasant was angry and scolded his wife: "What do you mean, you slut? Do you think it's ditchwater, you cripple, that you must go pouring good stuff like that over the floor?"

The imp nudged the Devil, his master, with his elbow: "See," said he, "that's the man who did not grudge his only crust!"

The peasant, still railing at his wife, began to carry the drink round himself. Just then a poor peasant returning from work came in uninvited. He greeted the company, sat down, and saw that they were drinking. Tired with his day's work, he felt that he, too, would like a drop. He sat and sat, and his mouth kept watering, but the host instead of offering him any only muttered: "I can't find drink for everyone who comes along."

This pleased the Devil; but the imp chuckled and said, "Wait a bit, there's more to come yet!"

The rich peasants drank, and their host drank, too. And they began to make false, oily speeches to one another.

The Devil listened and listened, and praised the imp.

"If," said he, "the drink makes them so foxy that they begin to cheat each other, they will soon all be in our hands."

"Wait for what's coming," said the imp. "Let them have another glass all round. Now they are like foxes, wagging their tails and trying to get round one another, but presently you will see them like savage wolves."

The peasants had another glass each, and their talk became wilder and rougher. Instead of oily speeches, they began to abuse and snarl at one another. Soon they took to fighting, and punched one another's noses. And the host joined in the fight and he, too, got well beaten.

The Devil looked on and was much pleased at all this.

"This is first-rate!" said he.

But the imp replied: "Wait a bit—the best is yet to come. Wait till they have had a third glass. Now they're raging like wolves, but let them have one more glass and they'll be like swine.'

The peasants had their third glass, and became quite like brutes. They muttered and shouted, not knowing why, and not listening to one another.

Then the party began to break up. Some went alone, some in twos, and some in threes, all staggering down the street. The host went out to speed his guests, but he fell on his nose into a puddle, smeared himself from top to toe, and lay there grunting like a hog.

This pleased the Devil still more.

"Well," said he, "you've hit on a first-rate drink, and have quite made up for your blunder about the bread. But now tell me how this drink is made. You must first have put in fox's blood; that was what made the peasants sly as foxes. Then, I suppose, you added wolf's blood; that's what made them fierce like wolves. And you must have finished off with swine's blood, to make them behave like swine."

"No," said the imp, "that wasn't the way I did it. All I did was to see that the peasant had more grain than he needed. The blood of the beasts is always in man; but as long as he has only enough grain for his needs the blood is kept within bounds. While that was the case, the peasant did not grudge his last crust. But when he had grain left over, he looked for ways of getting pleasure out of it. And I showed him a pleasure—drinking! And when he began to turn God's good gifts into spirits for his own pleasure—the fox's, wolf's, and swine's blood in him all came out. If only he goes on drinking, he'll always be a beast!"

The Devil praised the imp, forgave him for his former blunder, and advanced him to a post of high honor.

1886.

How Much Land Does a Man Need?

I

AN ELDER SISTER came to visit her younger sister in the country. The elder was married to a shopkeeper in town, the younger to a peasant in the village. As the sisters sat over their tea talking, the elder began to

Translated by Louise and Aylmer Maude. Revised.

boast of the advantages of town life, saying how comfortably they lived there, how well they dressed, what fine clothes her children wore, what good things they ate and drank, and how she went to the theater, promenades, and entertainments.

The younger sister was piqued, and in turn disparaged the life of a shopkeeper, and stood up for that of a peasant.

"I wouldn't change my way of life for yours," said she. "We may live roughly, but at least we're free from worry. You live in better style than we do, but though you often earn more than you need, you're very likely to lose all you have. You know the proverb, 'Loss and gain are brothers twain.' It often happens that people who're wealthy one day are begging their bread the next. Our way is safer. Though a peasant's life is not a rich one, it's long. We'll never grow rich, but we'll always have enough to eat."

The elder sister said sneeringly:

"Enough? Yes, if you like to share with the pigs and the calves! What do you know of elegance or manners! However much your good man may slave, you'll die as you live—on a dung heap—and your children the same."

"Well, what of that?" replied the younger sister. "Of course our work is rough and hard. But on the other hand, it's sure, and we need not bow to anyone. But you, in your towns, are surrounded by temptations; today all may be right, but tomorrow the Evil One may tempt your husband with cards, wine, or women, and all will go to ruin. Don't such things happen often enough?"

Pahom, the master of the house, was lying on the top of the stove and he listened to the women's chatter.

"It is perfectly true," thought he. "Busy as we are from childhood tilling mother earth, we peasants have no time to let any nonsense settle in our heads. Our only trouble is that we haven't land enough. If I had plenty of land, I shouldn't fear the Devil himself!"

The women finished their tea, chatted a while about dress, and then cleared away the tea things and lay down to sleep.

But the Devil had been sitting behind the stove, and had heard all that had been said. He was pleased that the peasant's wife had led her husband into boasting, and that he had said that if he had plenty of land he would not fear the Devil himself.

"All right," thought the Devil. "We'll have a tussle. I'll give you land enough; and by means of that land I'll get you into my power."

II

Close to the village there lived a lady, a small landowner who had an estate of about three hundred acres. She had always lived on good terms with the peasants until she engaged as her manager an old soldier, who took to burdening the people with fines. However careful Pahom tried to be, it happened again and again that now a horse of his got among the lady's oats, now a cow strayed into her garden, now his calves found their way into her meadows—and he always had to pay a fine.

Pahom paid up, but grumbled, and, going home in a temper, was rough with his family. All through that summer Pahom had much trouble because of this manager, and he was actually glad when winter came and the cattle had to be stabled. Though he grudged the fodder when they could no longer graze on the pasture land, at least he was free from anxiety about them.

In the winter the news got about that the lady was going to sell her land and that the keeper of the inn on the high road was bargaining for it. When the peasants heard this they were very much alarmed.

"Well," thought they, "if the innkeeper gets the land, he'll worry us with fines worse than the lady's manager. We all depend on that estate."

So the peasants went on behalf of their village Council and asked the lady not to sell the land to the innkeeper, offering her a better price for it themselves. The lady agreed to let them have it. Then the peasants tried to arrange for the village Council to buy the whole estate, so that it might be held by them all in common. They met twice to discuss it, but could not settle the matter; the Evil One sowed discord among them and they could not agree. So they decided to buy the land individually, each according to his means; and the lady agreed to this plan as she had to the other.

Presently Pahom heard that a neighbor of his was buying fifty acres, and that the lady had consented to accept one-half in cash and to wait a year for the other half. Pahom felt envious.

"Look at that," thought he, "the land is all being sold, and I'll get none of it." So he spoke to his wife.

"Other people are buying," said he, "and we must also buy twenty acres or so. Life is becoming impossible. That manager is simply crushing us with his fines."

So they put their heads together and considered how they could manage to buy it. They had one hundred rubles laid by. They sold a colt and one half of their bees, hired out one of their sons as a farm hand, and took his wages in advance; borrowed the rest from a brother-in-law, and so scraped together half the purchase money.

Having done this, Pahom chose a farm of forty acres, some of it wooded, and went to the lady to bargain for it. They came to an agreement, and he shook hands with her upon it and paid her a deposit in advance. Then they went to town and signed the deeds, he paying half the price down, and undertaking to pay the remainder within two years.

So now Pahom had land of his own. He borrowed seed, and sowed it on the land he had bought. The harvest was a good one, and within a year he had managed to pay off his debts both to the lady and to his brother-in-law. So he became a landowner, plowing and sowing his own land, making hay on his own land, cutting his own trees, and feeding his cattle on his own pasture. When he went out to plow his fields, or to look at his growing corn, or at his grass meadows, his heart would fill with joy. The grass that grew and the flowers that bloomed there seemed to him unlike any that grew elsewhere. Formerly, when he had passed by that land, it had appeared the same as any other land, but now it seemed quite different.

III

So Pahom was well contented, and everything would have been right if the neighboring peasants would only not have trespassed on his wheatfields and meadows. He appealed to them most civilly, but they still went on: now the herdsmen would let the village cows stray into his meadows, then horses from the night pasture would get among his corn. Pahom turned them out again and again, and forgave their owners, and for a long time he forbore to prosecute anyone. But at last he lost patience and complained to the District Court. He knew it was the peasants' want of land, and no evil intent on their part, that caused the trouble, but he thought:

"I can't go on overlooking it, or they'll destroy all I have. They must be taught a lesson."

So he had them up, gave them one lesson, and then another, and two or three of the peasants were fined. After a time Pahom's neighbors began to bear him a grudge for this, and would now and then let their cattle on to his land on purpose. One peasant even got into Pahom's wood at night and cut down five young lime trees for their bark. Pahom, passing through the wood one day, noticed something white. He came nearer and saw the stripped trunks lying on the ground, and close by stood the stumps where the trees had been. Pahom was furious.

"If he'd only cut one here and there it would have been bad enough," thought Pahom, "but the rascal has actually cut down a whole clump. If I could only find out who did this, I'd get even with him."

He racked his brains as to who it could be. Finally he decided: "It must be Simon—no one else could have done it." So he went to Simon's homestead to have a look around, but he found nothing, and only had an angry scene. However, he now felt more certain than ever that Simon had done it, and he lodged a complaint. Simon was summoned. The case was tried, and retried, and at the end of it all Simon was acquitted, there being no evidence against him. Pahom felt still more aggrieved, and let his anger loose upon the Elder and the Judges.

"You let thieves grease your palms," said he. "If you were honest folk yourselves you wouldn't let a thief go free."

So Pahom quarreled with the judges and with his neighbors. Threats to burn his hut began to be uttered. So though Pahom had more land, his place in the community was much worse than before.

About this time a rumor got about that many people were moving to new parts.

"There's no need for me to leave my land," thought Pahom. "But some of the others may leave our village and then there'd be more room for us. I'd take over their land myself and make my estate somewhat bigger. I could then live more at ease. As it is, I'm still too cramped to be comfortable."

One day Pahom was sitting at home, when a peasant, passing through the village, happened to drop in. He was allowed to stay the night, and supper was given him. Pahom had a talk with this peasant and asked him where he came from. The stranger answered that he came from beyond the Volga, where he had been working. One word led to another, and the man went on to say that many people were settling in those parts. He told how some people from his village had settled there. They had joined the community there and had had twenty-five acres per man granted them. The land was so good, he said, that the rye sown on it grew as high as a horse, and so thick that five cuts of a sickle made a sheaf. One peasant, he said, had brought nothing with him but his bare hands, and now he had six horses and two cows of his own.

Pahom's heart kindled with desire.

"Why should I suffer in this narrow hole, if one can live so well elsewhere?" he thought. "I'll sell my land and my homestead here, and with the money I'll start afresh over there and get everything new. In this crowded place one is always having trouble. But I must first go and find out all about it myself."

Toward summer he got ready and started out. He went down the Volga on a steamer to Samara, then walked another three hundred miles on foot, and at last reached the place. It was just as the stranger had said. The peasants had plenty of land: every man had twenty-five acres of communal land given him for his use, and anyone who had money could buy, besides, at a ruble-and-a-half an acre, as much good freehold land as he wanted.

Having found out all he wished to know, Pahom returned home as autumn came on, and began selling off his belongings. He sold his land at a profit, sold his homestead and all his cattle, and withdrew from membership in the village. He only waited till the spring, and then started with his family for the new settlement.

IV

As soon as Pahom and his family reached their new abode, he applied for admission into the Council of a large village. He stood treat to the Elders and obtained the necessary documents. Five shares of communal land were given him for his own and his sons' use: that is to say—125 acres (not all together, but in different fields) besides the use of the communal pasture. Pahom put up the buildings he needed and bought cattle. Of the communal land alone he had three times as much as at his former home, and the land was good wheat-land. He was ten times better off than he had been. He had plenty of arable land and pasturage, and could keep as many head of cattle as he liked.

At first, in the bustle of building and settling down, Pahom was pleased with it all, but when he got used to it he began to think that even here he hadn't enough land. The first year he sowed wheat on his share of the communal land and had a good crop. He wanted to go on sowing wheat, but had not enough communal land for the purpose, and what he had already used was not available, for in those parts wheat is sown only on virgin soil or on fallow land. It is sown for one or two years, and then the land lies fallow till it is again overgrown with steppe grass. There were many who wanted such land, and there was not enough for all, so that people quarreled about it. Those who were better off wanted it for growing wheat, and those who were poor wanted it to let to dealers, so that they might raise money to pay their taxes. Pahom wanted to sow more wheat, so he rented land from a dealer for a year. He sowed much wheat and had a fine crop, but the land was too far from the village—the wheat had to be carted more than ten miles. After a time Pahom noticed that some peasant-dealers were living on separate farms and were growing wealthy, and he thought:

"If I were to buy some freehold land and have a homestead on it, it would be a different thing altogether. Then it would all be fine and close together."

The question of buying freehold land recurred to him again and again.

He went on in the same way for three years, renting land and sowing wheat. The seasons turned out well and the crops were good, so that he began to lay by money. He might have gone on living contentedly, but he grew tired of having to rent other people's land every year, and having to scramble for it. Wherever there was good land to be had, the peasants would rush for it and it was taken up at once, so that unless you were sharp about it you got none. It happened in the third year that he and a dealer together rented a piece of pasture land from some peasants, and they had already plowed it up, when there was some dispute and the peasants went to law about it, and things fell out so that the labor was all lost.

"If it were my own land," thought Pahom, "I should be independent, and there wouldn't be all this unpleasantness."

So Pahom began looking out for land which he could buy, and he came across a peasant who had bought thirteen hundred acres, but having got into difficulties was willing to sell again cheap. Pahom bargained and haggled with him, and at last they settled the price at fifteen hundred rubles, part in cash and part to be paid later. They had all but clinched the matter when a passing dealer happened to stop at Pahom's one day to get feed for his horses. He drank tea with Pahom, and they had a talk. The dealer said that he was just returning from the land of the Bashkirs, far away, where he had bought thirteen thousand acres of land, all for a thousand rubles. Pahom questioned him further, and the dealer said:

"All one has to do is to make friends with the chiefs. I gave away about one hundred rubles' worth of silk robes and carpets, besides a case of tea, and I gave wine to those who would drink it; and I got the land for less than three kopecks an acre." And he showed Pahom the title deed, saying:

"The land lies near a river, and the whole steppe is virgin soil."

Pahom plied him with questions, and the dealer said:

"There's more land there than you could cover if you walked a year, and it all belongs to the Bashkirs. They're as simple as sheep, and land can be got almost for nothing."

"There, now," thought Pahom, "with my one thousand rubles, why should I get only thirteen hundred acres, and saddle myself with a debt besides? If I take it out there, I can get more than ten times as much for my money."

V

Pahom inquired how to get to the place, and as soon as the grain dealer had left him, he prepared to go there himself. He left his wife to look after the homestead, and started on his journey, taking his hired man with him. They stopped at a town on their way and bought a case of tea, some wine, and other presents, as the grain dealer had advised.

On and on they went until they had gone more than three hundred miles, and on the seventh day they came to a place where the Bashkirs had pitched their round tents. It was all just as the dealer had said. The people lived on the steppe, by a river, in felt-covered tents. They neither tilled the ground nor ate bread. Their cattle and horses grazed in herds on the steppe. The colts were tethered behind the tents, and the mares were driven to them twice a day. The mares were milked, and from the milk kumiss was made. It was the women who prepared the kumiss, and they also made cheese. As far as the men were concerned, drinking kumiss and tea, eating mutton, and playing on their pipes was all they cared about. They were all stout and merry, and all the summer long they never thought of doing any work. They were quite ignorant, and knew no Russian, but were good-natured enough.

As soon as they saw Pahom, they came out of their tents and gathered around their visitor. An interpreter was found, and Pahom told them he had come about some land. The Bashkirs seemed very glad; they took Pahom and led him into one of the best tents, where they made him sit on some down cushions placed on a carpet, while they sat around him. They gave him some tea and kumiss, and had a sheep killed, and gave him mutton to eat. Pahom took presents out of his cart and distributed them among the Bashkirs, and divided the tea amongst them. The Bashkirs were delighted. They talked a great deal among themselves, and then told the interpreter what to say.

"They wish to tell you," said the interpreter, "that they like you, and that it's our custom to do all we can to please a guest and to repay him for his gifts. You have given us presents, now tell us which of the things we possess please you best, that we may present them to you."

"What pleases me best here," answered Pahom, "is your land. Our land is crowded and the soil is worn out, but you have plenty of land, and it is good land. I never saw the likes of it."

The interpreter told the Bashkirs what Pahom had said. They talked among themselves for a while. Pahom could not understand what they were saying, but saw that they were much amused and heard them shout and laugh. Then they were silent and looked at Pahom while the interpreter said:

"They wish me to tell you that in return for your presents they will gladly give you as much land as you want. You have only to point it out with your hand and it is yours."

The Bashkirs talked again for a while and began to dispute. Pahom asked what they were disputing about, and the interpreter told him that some of them thought they ought to ask their Chief about the land and not act in his absence, while others thought there was no need to wait for his return.

VI

While the Bashkirs were disputing, a man in a large fox-fur cap appeared on the scene. They all became silent and rose to their feet. The interpreter said: "This is our Chief himself."

Pahom immediately fetched the best dressing gown and five pounds of tea, and offered these to the Chief. The Chief accepted them, and seated himself in the place of honor. The Bashkirs at once began telling him something. The Chief listened for a while, then made a sign with his head for them to be silent, and addressing himself to Pahom, said in Russian:

"Well, so be it. Choose whatever piece of land you like; we have plenty of it."

"How can I take as much as I like?" thought Pahom. "I must get a deed to make it secure, or else they may say: 'It is yours,' and afterward may take it away again."

"Thank you for your kind words," he said aloud. "You have much land, and I only want a little. But I should like to be sure which portion is mine. Could it not be measured and made over to me? Life and death are in God's hands. You good people give it to me, but your children might wish to take it back again."

"You are quite right," said the Chief. "We will make it over to you."

"I heard that a dealer had been here," continued Pahom, "and that you gave him a little land, too, and signed title deeds to that effect. I should like to have it done in the same way."

The Chief understood.

"Yes," replied he, "that can be done quite easily. We have a scribe, and we will go to town with you and have the deed properly sealed."

"And what will be the price?" asked Pahom.

"Our price is always the same: one thousand rubles a day."

Pahom did not understand.

"A day? What measure is that? How many acres would that be?"

"We do not know how to reckon it out," said the Chief. "We sell it by the day. As much as you can go around on your feet in a day is yours, and the price is one thousand rubles a day."

Pahom was surprised.

"But in a day you can get around a large tract of land," he said.

The Chief laughed.

"It will all be yours!" said he. "But there is one condition: If you don't return on the same day to the spot whence you started, your money is lost."

"But how am I to mark the way that I have gone?"

"Why, we shall go to any spot you like, and stay there. You must start from that spot and make your round, taking a spade with you. Wherever you think necessary, make a mark. At every turning, dig a hole and pile up the turf; then afterward we will go around with a plow from hole to hole. You may make as large a circuit as you please, but before the sun sets you must return to the place you started from. All the land you cover will be yours."

Pahom was delighted. It was decided to start early next morning. They talked·a while, and after drinking some more kumiss and eating some more mutton, they had tea again, and then the night came on. They gave Pahom a feather bed to sleep on, and the Bashkirs dispersed for the night, promising to assemble the next morning at daybreak and ride out before sunrise to the appointed spot.

VII

Pahom lay on the feather bed, but could not sleep. He kept thinking about the land.

"What a large tract I'll mark off!" thought he. "I can easily do thirty-five miles in a day. The days are long now, and within a circuit of thirty-five miles what a lot of land there will be! I'll sell the poorer land, or let it to peasants, but I'll pick out the best and farm it myself. I'll buy two ox teams and hire two more laborers. About a hundred and fifty acres shall be plowland, and I'll pasture cattle on the rest."

Pahom lay awake all night, and dozed off only just before dawn. Hardly were his eyes closed when he had a dream. He thought he was lying in that same tent and heard somebody chuckling outside. He wondered who it could be, and rose and went out, and he saw the Bashkir Chief sitting in front of the tent holding his sides and rolling about with laughter. Going nearer to the Chief, Pahom asked: "What are you laughing at?" But he saw that it was no longer the Chief, but the grain dealer who had recently stopped at his house and had told him about the land. Just as Pahom was going to ask: "Have you been here long?" he saw that it was not the dealer, but the peasant who had come up from the Volga, long ago, to Pahom's old home. Then he saw that it was not the peasant either, but the Devil himself with hoofs and horns, sitting there and chuckling, and before him lay a man, prostrate on the ground, barefooted, with only trousers and a shirt on. And Pahom dreamed that he looked more attentively to see what sort of man it was lying there, and he saw that the man was dead, and that it was himself. Horror-struck, he awoke.

"What things one dreams about!" thought he.

Looking around he saw through the open door that the dawn was breaking.

"It's time to wake them up," thought he. "We ought to be starting."

He got up, roused his man (who was sleeping in his cart), bade him harness, and went to call the Bashkirs.

"It's time to go to the steppe to measure the land," he said.

The Bashkirs rose and assembled, and the Chief came, too. Then they began drinking kumiss again, and offered Pahom some tea, but he would not wait.

"If we are to go, let's go. It's high time," said he.

VIII

The Bashkirs got ready and they all started: some mounted on horses and some in carts. Pahom drove in his own small cart with his servant and took a spade with him. When they reached the steppe, the red dawn was beginning to kindle. They ascended a hillock (called by the Bashkirs a *shikhan*) and, dismounting from their carts and their horses, gathered in one spot. The Chief came up to Pahom and, stretching out his arm toward the plain:

"See," said he, "all this, as far as your eye can reach, is ours. You may have any part of it you like."

Pahom's eyes glistened: it was all virgin soil, as flat as the palm of your hand, as black as the seed of a poppy, and in the hollows different kinds of grasses grew breast-high.

The Chief took off his fox-fur cap, placed it on the ground, and said:

"This will be the mark. Start from here, and return here again. All the land you go around shall be yours."

Pahom took out his money and put it on the cap. Then he took off his outer coat, remaining in his sleeveless undercoat. He unfastened his girdle and tied it tight below his stomach, put a little bag of bread into the breast of his coat, and, tying a flask of water to his girdle, he drew up the tops of his boots, took the spade from his man, and stood ready to start. He considered for some moments which way he had better go— it was tempting everywhere.

"No matter," he concluded, "I'll go toward the rising sun."

He turned his face to the east, stretched himself, and waited for the sun to appear above the rim.

"I must lose no time," he thought, "and it's easier walking while it's still cool."

The sun's rays had hardly flashed above the horizon when Pahom, carrying the spade over his shoulder, went down into the steppe.

Pahom started walking neither slowly nor quickly. After having gone a thousand yards he stopped, dug a hole, and placed pieces of turf one on another to make it more visible. Then he went on; and now that he had walked off his stiffness he quickened'his pace. After a while he dug another hole.

Pahom looked back. The hillock could be distinctly seen in the sunlight, with the people on it, and the glittering iron rims of the cartwheels. At a rough guess Pahom concluded that he had walked three miles. It was growing warmer; he took off his undercoat, slung it across his shoulder, and went on again. It had grown quite warm now; he looked at the sun—it was time to think of breakfast.

"The first shift is done, but there are four in a day, and it's too soon yet to turn. But I'll just take off my boots," said he to himself.

He sat down, took off his boots, stuck them into his girdle, and went on. It was easy walking now.

"I'll go on for another three miles," thought he, "and then turn to the left. This spot is so fine that it would be a pity to lose it. The further one goes, the better the land seems."

He went straight on for a while, and when he looked around, the hillock was scarcely visible and the people on it looked like black ants, and he could just see something glistening there in the sun.

"Ah," thought Pahom, "I have gone far enough in this direction; it's time to turn. Besides, I'm in a regular sweat, and very thirsty."

He stopped, dug a large hole, and heaped up pieces of turf. Next he untied his flask, had a drink, and then turned sharply to the left. He went on and on; the grass was high, and it was very hot.

Pahom began to grow tired: he looked at the sun and saw that it was noon.

"Well," he thought, "I must have a rest."

He sat down, and ate some bread and drank some water; but he did not lie down, thinking that if he did he might fall asleep. After sitting a little while, he went on again. At first he walked easily; the food had strengthened him; but it had become terribly hot and he felt sleepy. Still he went on, thinking: "An hour to suffer, a lifetime to live."

He went a long way in this direction also, and was about to turn to the left again, when he perceived a damp hollow: "It would be a pity to leave that out," he thought. "Flax would do well there." So he went on past the hollow and dug a hole on the other side of it before he made a sharp turn. Pahom looked toward the hillock. The heat made the air hazy: it seemed to be quivering, and through the haze the people on the hillock could scarcely be seen.

"Ah," thought Pahom, "I have made the sides too long; I must make this one shorter." And he went along the third side, stepping faster. He looked at the sun: it was nearly halfway to the horizon, and he had not yet done two miles of the third side of the square. He was still ten miles from the goal.

"No," he thought, "though it will make my land lopsided, I must hurry back in a straight line now. I might go too far, and as it is I have a great deal of land."

So Pahom hurriedly dug a hole and turned straight toward the hillock.

IX

Pahom went straight toward the hillock, but he now walked with difficulty. He was exhausted from the heat, his bare feet were cut and bruised, and his legs began to fail. He longed to rest, but it was impossible if he meant to get back before sunset. The sun waits for no man, and it was sinking lower and lower.

"Oh, Lord," he thought, "if only I have not blundered trying for too much! What if I am too late?"

He looked toward the hillock and at the sun. He was still far from his goal, and the sun was already near the rim of the sky.

Pahom walked on and on; it was very hard walking, but he went quicker and quicker. He pressed on, but was still far from the place. He began running, threw away his coat, his boots, his flask, and his cap, and kept only the spade which he used as a support.

"What am I to do?" he thought again. "I've grasped too much and ruined the whole affair. I can't get there before the sun sets."

And this fear made him still more breathless. Pahom kept on running; his soaking shirt and trousers stuck to him, and his mouth was parched. His breast was working like a blacksmith's bellows, his heart was beating like a hammer, and his legs were giving way as if they did not belong to him. Pahom was seized with terror lest he should die of the strain.

Though afraid of death, he could not stop.

"After having run all that way they will call me a fool if I stop now," thought he.

And he ran on and on, and drew near and heard the Bashkirs yelling and shouting to him, and their cries inflamed his heart still more. He gathered his last strength and ran on.

The sun was close to the rim of the sky and, cloaked in mist, looked large, and red as blood. Now, yes, now, it was about to set! The sun was quite low, but he was also quite near his goal. Pahom could already see the people on the hillock waving their arms to make him hurry. He could see the fox-fur cap on the ground and the money in it, and the Chief sitting on the ground holding his sides. And Pahom remembered his dream.

"There's plenty of land," thought he, "but will God let me live on it? I have lost my life, I have lost my life! Never will I reach that spot!"

Pahom looked at the sun, which had reached the earth: one side of it had already disappeared. With all his remaining strength he rushed on, bending his body forward so that his legs could hardly follow fast enough to keep him from falling. Just as he reached the hillock it suddenly grew dark. He looked up—the sun had already set!

He gave a cry: "All my labor has been in vain," thought he, and was about to stop, but he heard the Bashkirs still shouting, and remembered that though to him, from below, the sun seemed to have set, they on the hillock could still see it. He took a long breath and ran up the hillock. It was still light there. He reached the top and saw the cap. Before it sat the Chief, laughing and holding his sides. Again Pahom remembered his dream, and he uttered a cry: his legs gave way beneath him, he fell forward and reached the cap with his hands.

"Ah, that's a fine fellow!" exclaimed the Chief. "He has gained much land!"

Pahom's servant came running up and tried to raise him, but he saw that blood was flowing from his mouth. Pahom was dead.

The Bashkirs clicked their tongues to show their pity.

His servant picked up the spade and dug a grave long enough for Pahom to lie in, and buried him in it.

Six feet from his head to his heels was all he needed.

1886.

Nicholas Semyonovich
Lescov
1 8 3 1 – 1 8 9 5

LESCOV is a striking example of the author who becomes established as a classic through popular acclaim rather than contemporary critical opinion. He is great not merely as a Russian storyteller; it is only the bar of language that prevents wider recognition of him as one of the great storytellers of the world.

After a background of hard struggle from his teens on, in Civil Service and elsewhere, Lescov began writing as a provincial journalist in 1860; by 1862 he was able to continue journalism in Petersburg. Here one of his articles was misinterpreted by the radicals, who, ably assisted by the critics, began to boycott him. His first short story (his popularity is based largely on his stories, while his *Cathedral Folk* is the greatest favorite among his novels) appeared in 1863. *No Way Out,* a novel, published the following year, widened

the breach, again without much justice on the part of the radicals. Lescov did not throw up the sponge and go abroad, as Turgenev did under similar circumstances; his next novel, *At Daggers Drawn* (1870-71), lives up to its title. But Lescov was never really a reactionary; during his latter years he began to publish in the mildly leftist periodicals. One of his satirical stories of life among the priests (a long and remarkable series) led to the loss of a government sinecure.

Toward the end of his life he became a devout Tolstoian; his Christianity, however, is of a more subjective, warmer nature than the chill, theoretical Christianity of the master of the Radiant Meadow. Tolstoi, incidentally, was one of the sincerest admirers of Lescov's work, but nevertheless criticized his lack of self-discipline as a writer.

Lescov has been called the most Russian of the Russian writers. His greatest charm (at least for the Russian) is his language, peculiarly his own, and a point of departure in Russian literature. He reveled in raciness, picturesqueness, vigor, colloquialisms, oddities of trade and professional cant, earthy yet poetical folk expressions, and actual (for the most part delightful) plays upon words. This is not at all as horrendous as it may sound, but it does give the inept translators another chance to drag out that abominated and worn-out excuse, known in the trade as "the despair of translators," and may help to account for his being a practically unknown quantity to the English reader, even though two or three volumes of Lescov are available in English. He is vivid, grotesque (often bizarre), colorful, a master of character-drawing, a great humorist, and unique in a number

of ways; many of his stories have wonder and magic. The best way of conveying an idea of Lescov as a writer is to compare him with Goya as an artist.

All things considered, he can best be represented here by *Lady Macbeth of Mtsensk* (which he labels as a sketch). It is indisputably one of the greatest short stories in all literature; the reader cannot help but perceive its kinship to classic Greek tragedy. The translator, instead of wasting her energies in despair, has succeeded, to a great extent, in conveying the author's famous style, which he has here kept under full artistic curb. The story was used as the libretto for Shostakovich's opera (performed in this country some years ago in Cleveland and at the Metropolitan Opera House in New York), and was dramatized and performed with great success on the Soviet stage within the last few years.

Lady Macbeth of Mtsensk

Sing your first song blushingly.

FOLK SAYING

I

NOW AND THEN, in our parts, we are confronted with such characters that, no matter how many years may have passed since one's encounter with them, one can never recall some of them without a spiritual shudder. And distinctly belonging to the number of such characters is

Translated especially for this work by Ethel O. Bronstein. Copyright, 1943, by the Vanguard Press, Inc.

Katerina Lvovna Ismailova, a merchant's wife, who in her day played out a fearful drama, after which our gentry, echoing the quip of some wag, took to calling her *Lady Macbeth—of the Mtsensk District.*

Katerina Lvovna, although not a born beauty, was a woman of very pleasing appearance. She was only in her twenty-fourth year; though not very tall, she was well built, with a throat that seemed carved of marble, her shoulders well rounded, her bosom firm, her nose straight and fine, her eyes black and lively, her forehead white and high, and hair so black that it was actually blue-black. She had been married off to one of our merchants, Ismailov of Touskary, which is in the province of Kursk, not for love or from any inclination but merely because Ismailov had courted her; for she was a poor girl and did not have much chance to pick and choose suitors. The household of the Ismailovs was not one of the least in our town; they carried on a trade in the finest wheat flour, maintained a big mill in the district on lease, had a profitable orchard near town, and, in the town itself, a well-built house. All in all, they were a well-to-do trading clan. Moreover, the family was not at all extensive, consisting of the father-in-law, Boris Timotheievich Ismailov, a man nigh eighty by now and long widowed; his son, Zinovii Borisich, Katerina's husband, himself a man of well over fifty; and Katerina herself—and that was all. In the fifth year of Katerina's marriage to Zinovii she was still childless. Nor had Zinovii had any children by his first wife, with whom he had lived some twenty years before becoming widowed and then marrying Katerina. He thought and hoped that God might at least bless his second marriage with an heir to his trading name and fortune, but he proved equally unlucky in the matter with Katerina.

This childlessness distressed Zinovii very much, and not him alone but the old man, Boris, as well; it saddened even Katerina deeply. For one thing, the infinite boredom reigning in the merchant's closed-up dwelling, with its high fence and loosed watchdogs, more than once induced in the young wife an ennui bordering on stupefaction, and she would have been glad, God knows how glad, to nurse a little baby; for another, she was fed up with reproaches: Why did you have to go and get married; what for did you tether a man's destiny, you barren ewe?—just as if she really had committed some crime against her husband, her father-in-law, and even against their honest trading clan.

Despite all its plenty and comfort, Katerina's life in the house of her father-in-law was of the loneliest. She rarely went visiting, and even when she did go out with her husband among his merchant friends it was no pleasure. They were strict folk: they'd watch how she sat down, how she behaved, and how she got up; yet Katerina was by nature high-spirited and, having spent her girlhood in poverty, she was used to simplicity and freedom: she would have liked to run over to the river with water buckets and to bathe in her shift under the wharf, or to pelt some passing youth with polly-seed shells through the wicket; but here it was all different. Her father-in-law and her husband would get up with the very dawn, would drench themselves with tea by six in the morning, and then be off about their business, while she, all by her lonely self, roamed idly from room to room. All was neat, all was quiet and bare; the lampads glowed before the holy images; but nowhere in the house was there a living sound or a human voice.

Katerina would roam through the empty rooms, and then roam some more, start yawning from boredom, and mount the narrow stairs to the conjugal chamber, situated in the high, rather small mezzanine. Here, too, she would sit for a spell, idly watching the hemp being weighed or the fine wheaten flour being poured out in the warehouses; again she would feel like yawning, and be glad thereat: she'd take a nap for an hour or two, but when she awoke there was the same boredom, Russian boredom, the boredom of a merchant household—such boredom that, so they say, one is glad to try self-strangulation by way of diversion. Katerina was no great lover of reading; moreover, as to books, save for the Kiev compilation of *Lives of the Holy Fathers,* there was nary a one in the house.

It was a boresome life that Katerina lived in the prosperous house of her father-in-law for all of the five years of her life with an unaffectionate husband; but, as usual, none paid the slightest attention to this boredom of hers.

II

In the sixth year of Katerina's marriage the dam at the Ismailov mill broke. Just then, as if for spite, a great deal of work had been brought to the mill, yet the breach turned out to be enormous: the water had receded below the lower beam, and all attempts at stopgap repairs proved unsuccessful. Zinovii gathered the folk from all around the region at the mill, and stayed there himself, never stirring from the spot; the old man directed their affairs in town on his own, and Katerina pined at home the livelong day all by her lone self. At first she was even more bored without her husband, but then this began to seem even better: she felt freer by herself. Her heart had never turned to him particularly, and without him there was at least one less to order her about.

One day Katerina happened to be sitting in her attic, at her little window, yawning and yawning, not thinking of anything in particular, until at last she grew ashamed of her yawning. Outside in the courtyard it was such glorious weather: warm, bright, gay, and through the green wooden palings of the garden she could see the frisky little birds flitting from twig to twig.

"Now, just why did I get to yawning so?" Katerina wondered. "Guess I might as well get up and go out into the yard or take a stroll through the garden."

Katerina threw an old jacket of brocaded silk over her shoulders and went out.

Outside it was so bright and the air was so invigorating, while on the raised porch near the warehouses there was ever so much gay, loud laughter!

"What are you so gay about?" Katerina asked her father-in-law's clerks.

"Well, you see, Ekaterina Lvovna, our mother, we've been weighing a live sow," answered an old clerk.

"What sow?"

"Oh, that sow Axinia, which bore her son Vassilii but didn't invite us to no christening," she was informed brashly and gaily by a youth with a bold, handsome face framed in curls black as pitch, and a barely sprouting beard.

At that minute, out of a flour bin suspended from the beam of the scales, there peeped out the fat phiz of the rosy-cheeked cook Axinia.

"You fiends, you sleek devils!" scolded the cook, trying to catch hold of the iron beam and clamber out of the swinging bin.

"Before her dinner she weighs nigh unto three hundred pounds, but let her eat a bale of hay, and we'll run out of weights!" the handsome youth explained again and, having overturned the bin, dumped the cook out onto some sacks piled in a corner.

The countrywoman, scolding playfully, began putting herself to rights.

"Well, now, how much of me would there be?" joked Katerina and, grasping the ropes, got up on the platform of the scales.

"A little short of a hundred and fifteen pounds," answered the same handsome lad, by the name of Serghei, throwing a weight onto the scales. "That's a marvel!"

"What are you marveling at?"

"That you pull the beam down even that much, Katerina Lvovna. The way I figger, a man ought to carry you all day in his arms, and even then he wouldn't tire but would only find it a pleasure for himself."

"What, don't you think I'm human? You'd get tired just the same," Katerina, unused to such talk, answered him, blushing faintly and feeling a sudden access of desire to chatter away and to have her fill of merry, playful talk.

"Never, by God! I'd carry you even to Araby the blessed," was Serghei's retort to her remark.

"That's no way to figger, young fellow," said an ordinary little peasant who was measuring out the flour. "Just what does the weight in us amount to? Do you think it's our flesh that does things? The weight of our flesh, dear man, don't mean nothin'; it's our strength, our strength that does things—not our flesh!"

"Why, when I was a girl, I was ever so strong," said Katerina, again unable to restrain herself. "It wasn't every man could overpower me, either."

"Very well, let's have your tiny hand, if that's the case," the handsome lad requested.

Katerina was taken aback but nevertheless held out her hand.

"Ouch, let go my ring—that hurts!" Katerina cried out as Serghei squeezed her hand in his, and with her free hand shoved against his chest. The lad let go the mistress's hand and, from her shove, swerved two paces to the side.

"Hmm—now go ahead and talk about women!" marveled the undersized peasant.

"Oh, no, you just let us come to grips," Serghei suggested, tossing back his curls.

"Well, come on," answered Katerina, grown gay by now, and raised her dainty elbows.

Serghei took his young mistress around and hugged her firm bosom to his red shirt. Katerina had barely moved her shoulders, but Serghei had already lifted her from the floor, held her up in his arms, pressed her close, and set her gently down on an upturned measure.

Katerina had not succeeded in marshaling her vaunted prowess. Red as red could be, as she sat on the measure she adjusted the jacket which had fallen off her shoulders, and quietly left the warehouse, while Serghei cleared his throat with just the right touch of bravado and called out:

"There, you blessed idiots! Let the flour pour, don't rest on your oar; if there's aught to spare we'll get our share!"

Just as though he had paid no attention whatsoever to what had just happened!

"What a hound for women he is, that damned Serezhka!" Axinia the cook informed her, plodding after Katerina. "That thief's got everything: build, face, good looks. Take any woman you like—that scoundrel will get around her right off; he'll get around her and bring her to sin. And as for being untrue, the scoundrel's untrue as untrue can be!"

"Well, now, Axinia, what about . . . is your boy living?" the young mistress was saying as she walked ahead of her.

"He's alive, mother mine, alive and kicking—what's he got to worry about? When they're not wanted, that's just when they got a good hold on life, you see."

"And whom did you get him by?"

"Who knows? He just happened, like; when you've got a lot of friends things is bound to happen."

"Has he been with us long, this lad?"

"Who's that? Serghei, d'you mean?"

"Yes."

"About a month. He used to work for the Konchonovs before, but the master chased him out." Axinia lowered her voice and added: "They do say he made love to the mistress herself. . . . There, the thrice-anathematized soul, he's *that* bold!"

III

A warm, milky-white dusk lay over the town. Zinovii hadn't yet returned from working on the repairs of the dam. Nor was Katerina's father-in-law at home; he'd gone to the birthday party of an old friend and left word not to expect him even for supper. Katerina, having nothing to do, supped early, opened her little attic window, and, leaning against the jamb, cracked polly-seeds. The hands in the kitchen had eaten their supper and were scattering over the courtyard on their way to bed: some to the barns, some to the granaries, some to the tall, fragrant hay-ricks. Serghei was the very last to leave the kitchen. He made the rounds of the yard, unchained the watchdogs, whistled, and, walking past Katerina's window, glanced up at her and made a low bow.

"Good evening," Katerina said to him softly from her dormer window—and the yard became hushed as a wilderness.

"Mistress!" someone called two minutes later outside Katerina Lvovna's locked door.

"Who is it?" she asked, frightened.

"Please not to be afeared: it's me, Serghei," answered the clerk.

"What do you want, Serghei?"

"I've something to ask of your graciousness, Katerina Ilvovna; I want to ask your grace about a certain little matter—let me in for just a minute."

Katerina Lvovna turned the key and admitted Serghei.

"What is it?" she asked, going back to her dormer window.

"I came to you, Katerina Ilvovna, to ask if you mightn't have some little book for me to read. It's ever so boresome."

"I have no books of any kind, Serghei: I don't read," answered Katerina.

"It's so boresome!" Serghei complained.

"Why should *you* be bored?"

"Saving your presence, why shouldn't I be bored? I'm a young man; we live here just as it might be in some monastery, and all I can see ahead, till the coffin-lid is clamped down on me, is that I must perish in a solitude like this. At times I'm even driven to downright despair."

"Why don't you get married?"

"Get married? Easier said nor done. Whom can I marry here? I don't stack up to much, no wealthy man's daughter would marry me; and because of our poverty, Katerina Ilvovna, as you yourself may know, all our women are uneducated. As if they could understand rightly about love! There, just deign to see what the ideas of even the rich are. Now you, I may say, would be naught but a solace to any man of feelings, yet here they are, keeping you like a canary in a cage."

"It's true, I'm lonely," escaped from Katerina.

"How could you help but be bored, Ma'am, living the life you do? Even supposing you did have someone on the side, just like others do in your situation, it would be impossible for you even to see him."

"Well, now, you're going . . . a little too far. If I'd had a little baby, now—there, that would make me happy, I think."

"But you see, if you'll allow me to point this out, there's got to be something back of a baby—it don't just come of itself. Don't you think I understand, after living so many years among my masters and seeing the kind of life the merchants' womenfolk live? There's a song that goes: 'Without your own true love life is but longing sad,' and that longing, I must tell you, Katerina Ilvovna, touches my own heart so to the quick that I could take it and cut it out of my breast with a knife of chilled steel and throw it at your little feet. And then I'd feel easier, a hundred times easier."

"What's all this you're telling me about your heart? It's nothing to me. You'd better be on your way."

"No, please, mistress," uttered Serghei, his whole body quivering as he took a step toward Katerina. "I know, I see and even feel and understand greatly, that you haven't any easier a time of it in this world than I; the only thing is that now—" he said all this in a single breath—"now, this minute, all this lies in your own hands and in your power."

"What are you after? What is it? Why did you come here to me? I'll throw myself out the window," Katerina was saying, feeling herself in the unbearable grip of an indescribable fear and clutching at the window sill with her hand.

"My incomparable one, my very life! Why throw yourself out the window?" Serghei whispered with easy assurance and, tearing the young mistress away from the window, clasped her hard.

"Oh! Oh! Let me go!" softly moaned Katerina, weakening under Serghei's ardent kisses, even as, beyond her will, she snuggled against his mighty body.

Serghei picked his young mistress up in his arms as if she were a baby and bore her off into a dark corner.

Silence enveloped the room, broken only by the ticking of the pocket watch of Katerina's husband, hanging above the headboard of her bed; but that was no hindrance whatsoever.

"Go," Katerina was saying half an hour later, without looking at Serghei as she rearranged her disheveled hair before a small mirror.

"Why in the world should I leave here now?" Serghei answered in a happy voice.

"My father-in-law will lock the doors."

"Eh, my soul, my soul! What sort of people have you been dealing with, that they can find their way to a woman only by a door? As for me, whether I'm coming to you or going from you, there's doors for me everywhere," answered the lad, indicating the posts that supported the balcony.

IV

Zinovii had been away from home for a week, and that whole week his wife had whiled each night away, till the white dawn broke, with Serghei.

Much wine from the father-in-law's cellar was drunk during those same nights in the bedroom of Zinovii Borisich, and many sweet sweets eaten, and many a kiss sipped from the young mistress' honeyed lips, and much toying with black curls was there on the soft pillows. But no road runs smooth all the way; there's also rough going here and there.

Sleep would not come to Boris Timotheich; the old man wandered about the quiet house in his nightshirt of lurid calico; he came to one window, came to another, looked out, and there below him, slipping quiet as quiet down a post under his daughter-in-law's window, was the red shirt of that fine lad Serghei. Boris Timotheich dashed out and grabbed the Lothario by his legs. The latter swung back, as if to plant a haymaker on his master's ear, he was so vexed, but held back, after deciding there would be a row.

"Tell me," said Boris Timotheich, "where was you at, you thief?"

"Where was I, says he! Wherever it was, I'm not there now, Boris Timotheich, my dear Sir," answered Serghei.

"You spent the night in my daughter-in-law's room?"

"As to that, master, once again—I know where I spent the night; but here's what, Boris Timotheich, you take my word for it; you can't bring back what's past; don't you go bringing shame down on your decent merchant household, at least. Just you tell me what you want of me now? What satisfaction would you like?"

"I'd like, you varmint, for to give you five hundred lashes," answered Boris Timotheich.

"Mine was the guilt—your will be done," the gallant agreed. "Tell me where I'm to follow you; have yourself a good time—lap up my blood."

So old Boris led Serghei to a small stone storeroom he had, and he lashed away at him with a quirt till there was no more strength left in him. Not a groan did Serghei let out of him, but he did chew up half the shirt-sleeve he'd sunk his teeth into.

And after that old Boris left Serghei lying in that storeroom, until his back, beaten so livid that it looked like cast iron, might heal, shoved in a clay pitcher of water, snapped shut the big lock, and sent for his son.

But, even in our time, six miles over the byroads of Russia are not to be traversed rapidly, whereas Katerina could no longer bear to pass an extra hour without Serghei. She had developed suddenly in all the fullness of her awakened nature and had become so resolute that there was no restraining her. She ferreted out Serghei's whereabouts, talked things over with him through the iron door, and dashed off in search of the keys.

"Let Serghei go, Father dear," she appealed to her father-in-law.

The old man simply turned green. Never had he expected such brazen daring from his sinful but always, up to now, submissive daughter-in-law.

"What are you up to, you so-and-so?" he began shaming Katerina.

"Let him go," she said. "I swear to you on my conscience that there's been nothing wrong between us yet."

" 'No wrong!' says she!"—and he just plain ground his teeth. "And what was you two passing your time at up there of nights? Fluffing up your husband's pillows?"

But she wouldn't let him be, harping on her one note: Let him go, and let him go.

"If that's the way you'd have it," said old Boris, "then get this: when your husband gets back, we'll flog you with our own hands out in the stable, honest wife that you are; and as for him, I'll send that low-down villain to prison tomorrow."

That's what Boris Timotheich decided; the only thing was that his decision was never carried out.

V

That night old Boris ate some mushrooms with buckwheat porridge, and after that heartburn set in; he was seized with sudden pain in the pit of his stomach; he was racked by dreadful vomiting spells, and toward morning he died, and, as it happened, in the very same way that the rats died in his warehouses, for whose benefit Katerina would always prepare a special mess with her own hands, using a dangerous white powder that was entrusted into her keeping.

Katerina freed her Serghei from the old man's stone storeroom and, without the least shame, before the eyes of all the people, made him comfortable in her husband's bed to recover from her father-in-law's beatings, whilst the father-in-law himself was, without any delay, interred with all Christian rites. Remarkably enough, no doubts occurred to anyone: if Boris Timotheich died, why, then, die he did, after eating mushrooms, just as did so many others after eating them. Old Boris was buried in all haste without even waiting for his son, for the weather at that time of year was sultry, and the messenger had not found Zinovii Borisich at the mill. He had chanced to get some forest land cheap, more than sixty miles still further, had gone to look at it, and hadn't told anyone clearly just where he was going.

Having disposed of this matter, Katerina became completely unbridled. She had never been one of your timid women, but now one could not at all divine what she had in mind; she went about bold as you please, managed everything about the house, and simply wouldn't let Serghei go a step from her side. Everyone on the place began wondering at all this, but Katerina managed to get on the right side of each in her openhanded way, and all wondering ceased at once.

"There's shenanigans going on," they surmised, "betwixt the mistress and Serghei, and that's that. That's her affair, now, and she's the one that'll have to answer for it."

And in the meantime Serghei had gotten his health back, and his suppleness, and again, like the bravest of brave fellows, had begun circling like a very falcon over Katerina, and again began their ever so pleasant life. But time was rolling on not for them alone: Zinovii Borisich, the much-wronged husband, was hastening home after his prolonged absence.

VI

After dinner it was as hot as hell itself out of doors, and the nimble flies were unbearably pesky. Katerina closed the shutters of her bedroom window and, in addition, hung a woolen kerchief on the inside, and then lay down with Serghei, to rest on the high bed, such as all merchants favor. Katerina hovered between sleep and waking; but whichever it was, she felt her face bathed in sweat, and each breath she drew coming so hot, so hard. She felt it was high time for her to wake up, to go out into the garden to drink tea, yet get up she could not, for the life of her. Finally the cook came and knocked on the door:

"The coals is dying out," she said, "in the samovar under the apple tree."

With a great effort she turned over on her side, and then began caressing a tomcat. For there was a tomcat rubbing himself in between her and Serghei, a right handsome tomcat, gray, well-grown, and as fat as fat . . . with whiskers on him like on a tax-bailiff. Katerina began rumpling his bushy fur, while he kept shoving his muzzle at her, thrusting his blunt nose into her resilient breast, and purring, like he was singing a song, ever so soft and low, dealing with her love. "And how did this great big cat ever get in here, and why?" Katerina wondered. "I put some cream to stand on the window sill here; he'll lap it all up for sure, the low-down creature. I must chase him out," she decided, and wanted to seize the tomcat and throw him out, but he just kept slipping through her fingers, like a mist. "Just the same, where did that tomcat ever come from?" Katerina reasoned in her nightmare. "We've never had a tomcat of any kind in our bedroom, and yet see what a one has made his way in here!" Again she wanted to lay hands on that tomcat, and again he just wasn't there. "Oh, but whatever is this? Come, is this a tomcat at all?" it occurred to Katerina. A sudden panic seized her and drove all sleep and drowsiness from her. Katerina glanced about the chamber—there was no tomcat whatsoever, only her handsome Serghei lying there, pressing her breast to his hot face with his strong hand.

Katerina sat up in bed; she kept kissing and kissing Serghei; she fondled him and fondled him, then tidied the rumpled feather bed and went off into the garden to drink tea; the sun in the meantime had gone down altogether, and a wonderful, enchanted evening was descending on an earth that had been so impregnated with heat.

"I overslept," said Katerina to Axinia, and sat down on a rug under an apple tree in blossom to drink tea. "What do you suppose it means, Axinia dear?" she asked the cook, the while she herself wiped a saucer with a dish towel.

"What does what mean, mother o' mine?"

"It weren't just a dream—but some tomcat or other kept creeping up to me, for all the world like it was all real. What does it mean?"

"What's all this you're saying?"

"Honest, there was a tomcat creeping up on me."

Katerina told her all about how the tomcat had been creeping up to her.

"And what for did you have to go and pet him?"

"Well, now, why ask me? I don't myself know why I petted him."

"It's something to wonder at, sure enough!"

"I myself can't stop marveling at it."

"This must certainly mean that someone's going to get at you, or that something else of the sort will come about."

"Yes, but just what exactly?"

"Well, *exactly* what it is is something that no one, my dear friend, can explain to you—not exactly; the only thing is that something's bound to happen."

"I kept seeing the crescent moon in my sleep, and then that cat," Katerina went on.

"The crescent moon—that means a little one."

Katerina Lvovna turned red.

"Wouldn't you like me to send Serghei down here to you, darling?" insinuated Axinia, who was simply dying to become her confidante.

"Oh, well," answered Katerina, "that's a good idea, too; go send him here; I'll give him tea."

"That's what I say—send him here," Axinia settled the matter, and waddled off like a duck to the garden wicket.

Katerina told Serghei as well about the cat.

"Just a daydream," Serghei told her.

"How come this daydream never happened to me before now, Serezha?"

"There's lot of things never happened before! Time was when all I could do was just look at you out of the corner of my eye and pine away, but now look at how things are! I possess all of your white body."

Serghei embraced Katerina, twirled her in the air, and, playfully, threw her down on the soft rug.

"Oh, but I'm dizzy," Katerina began. "Serezha, come here! Sit down here near me," she called, then stretched herself languorously in a voluptuous pose.

Bending down, the gallant crept in under the low apple tree, overflowing with white blossoms, and sat down on the rug at Katerina's feet.

"So you pined for me, did you, Serezha?"

"If you only knew how I pined!"

"What was it like? Tell me about it."

"How can one tell about it? Is it possible to explain how one pines? I yearned for you."

"How is it then, Serezha, that I didn't feel how you were killing yourself for me? For they say you can feel that."

Serghei let this pass in silence.

"How was it, then, that you kept singing songs, if you longed for me so? Never fear, I heard you singing on that raised porch," Katerina kept on questioning as she caressed him.

"What if I did sing songs? A mosquito sings its whole lifetime, but it ain't for joy," Serghei answered drily.

A pause ensued. Katerina was filled with supreme rapture by these confessions of Serghei's. She wanted to talk, but Serghei knit his brows and was taciturn.

"Just look, Serezha, it's paradise, paradise for fair!" exclaimed Katerina, looking out through the screen of blossom-laden branches of the apple tree at the clear blue sky, in which hung a serene full moon.

The moonlight, making its way through the leaves and blossoms of the apple tree, flickered over Katerina's face and her whole figure in fantastic specks of white as she lay there flat on her back; the air was still, save that a light, warm little breeze was barely stirring the drowsy leaves and bore far and wide the delicate fragrance of grasses and trees in flower. The air was filled with a certain languor, conducive to sloth, self-indulgence, and obscure desires.

Katerina, getting no answer, became quiet again and kept gazing at the sky through the pale-pink blossoms of the apple tree. Serghei was silent, too, but it wasn't the sky that absorbed him. Encircling his knees with both hands, he was staring with concentration at his boots.

What a golden night! Calm, light, fragrance, and a beneficent, life-giving warmth! Far away, beyond the ravine, behind the garden, someone started a tuneful song; near the fence, in the thickly planted orchard of bird-cherry trees, a nightingale struck up its song, trilling loudly; in its cage atop a tall pole a sleepy quail began its delirious notes, while behind the walls of the stable a fat horse snorted drowsily, and, over the pasture behind the garden fence, a pack of dogs swept by and vanished in the vague, black shadow of the half-ruined old barns where salt was stored.

Katerina lifted herself up a little on her elbow and glanced at the tall grass in the garden—and the grass seemed to be shimmering with the moon's brilliance as the wan light scintillated against the blossoms and leaves of the trees. Those fantastic, bright moon-specks had gilded the grass all over, and they flickered over it so, they quivered so, as if they were living butterflies of fire, or as if the grass under the trees had been taken in the moon's net and were swaying from side to side.

"Oh, Serezha, what a delight all this is!" Katerina cried out as she looked about her.

Serghei threw an indifferent glance at the scene.

"Why are you so cast down, Serezha? Or have you wearied even of my love?"

"Why talk nonsense?" Serghei answered drily and, bending down, kissed Katerina lazily.

"You're untrue, Serezha," said Katerina jealously. "You're fickle."

"I won't even take those words as having anything to do with me," Serghei answered in a calm tone.

"Then why do you kiss me like that?"

Serghei didn't even bother answering this.

"It's only husbands and wives," Katerina went on, playing with his curls, "that flick the dust off each other's lips that way. Kiss me so that the young blossoms on this apple tree over us will shower down to the ground."

"There, that's it, that's it," Katerina whispered, entwining her lover and kissing him with passionate abandon.

"Listen, Serezha, to what I'm going to tell you," Katerina began after a little while. "Why does everyone, with one voice, say that you're untrue?"

"Who's so willing to bark and lie like that about me?"

"Well, that's what people say."

"Maybe I have been untrue to them that were altogether worthless."

"And why, you fool, did you have to get mixed up with worthless ones? You oughtn't to make love at all to any woman that's worthless."

"Go ahead and talk! Is love also one of those things that you go into calculatingly? It's temptation alone that's at work. You just break a commandment with one of them, simple as you please, without any intentions or anything—and there she is, hanging about your neck. And there's love for you!"

"Listen, then, Serezha! I don't know a thing about all those others before me, and I don't want to know anything about them; there's just this: since you yourself seduced me into this love of ours, and since you know yourself that I went into it as much through your cunning as through my own desire—I tell you, Serezha, that if ever you play me false, if ever you leave me for any other, no matter who she may be, I'll never—forgive me, friend of my heart!—but I'll never part from you alive."

Serghei started.

"But, Katerina Ilvovna, light of my life!" he began. "Just take a good look at our affair. You've noticed just now how thoughtful I've been, but you don't stop to think that I can't help it. For all you know, my heart may be all clotted over with blood."

"Tell me, Serezha, tell me your sorrow!"

"What's there to tell about! In the first place, in a little while, with the Lord's blessing, your husband will bob up, and you, Serghei Philipich, get out of here, take yourself off to the back yard where the lads are playing their music, and watch, from behind the shed, how the little lamp burns in Katerina Ilvovna's bedroom, how she fluffs up the downy bed and lies down to rest with her lawful Zinovii Borisich."

"That'll never be!" Katerina drawled out gaily, with a wave of her little hand.

"Why won't it! But the way I see it, there's actually no way you can get out of it. And yet I, too, Katerina Ilvovna, have a heart of my own and can perceive my own torment."

"Come now, you've talked enough of that."

This expression of Serghei's jealousy was very welcome to Katerina, and, with a burst of laughter, she went back to her kissing.

"And in the second place," continued Serghei, ever so gently disengaging his head from Katerina's arms, bared to her shoulders—"in the second place, I must tell you also that my position, which is of the humblest, may have compelled me, many's the time, to consider things this way and that. If I were, so to speak, your equal, if I were some gentleman or some merchant, I'd never part from you while there's life in me, Katerina Ilvovna. But as things are, judge for yourself, what sort of man am I next to you? When I'll see shortly how he'll take you by your little white hand and lead you to your chamber, I'll have to bear it all in my heart and maybe, because of it, become for the rest of my life a man I myself despise. Katerina Ilvovna! You see, I'm not like those others to whom nothing matters so long as they get their delight from a woman. I feel what love really is and how, like a black snake, it sucks out my heart."

"Why do you keep explaining all this to me?" Katerina interrupted him.

She began to feel sorry for Serghei.

"Katerina Ilvovna! How can I help explaining all this? How can I? When perhaps everything has been made clear and reported in writing to your husband, when, maybe not only so far off but actually on the very morrow, there won't be nor sight nor sound of Serghei around here."

"No, no, don't even talk of that, Serezha! It can never be; no matter what happens I can never be left without you." Katerina soothed him with the same caresses as before. "If it ever comes to that . . . either he is fated to leave this life or I am, but you'll stay with me."

"That can't possibly be, Katerina Ilvovna," answered Serghei mournfully, and with a sad shake of his head. "I'm sorry myself I'm alive because of this love. If I loved someone of no more worth than myself, I might be content. Is it possible for me to keep you always as my own true love? Is it any honor for you, now, to be my mistress? I'd like to be your husband before a sacred, eternal shrine: then, even though I might always think myself your inferior, I'd still be able to show everybody in public how my wife esteems me because of my respect for her—"

Katerina was befogged by these words of Serghei, this jealousy of his, this wish of his to marry her—a wish always agreeable to a woman, no matter how brief her bond with a man before marriage. Katerina was ready now for Serghei's sake to go through fire and deep water, or into a dungeon, or to be crucified. So deeply had he made her fall in love with him that there were no limits to her devotion to him. She was beside herself in her joy; her blood seethed, and she could no longer bear to listen to anything. She quickly stopped Serghei's lips with her palm and, pressing his head close to her breast, began:

"Well, I know now how I'll even make a merchant of you and start living with you all fit and proper. Just don't grieve me over nothing at all, so long as our affairs haven't yet come to a head."

And again the kisses began, and the caresses.

The old clerk, sleeping in the shed, began hearing despite his deep sleep, in the still of the night, now whispering and low laughter, as if somewhere mischievous children were conspiring to play as evil a jest as possible on feeble old age, now laughter, ringing and gay, as though lake nixies were tickling some victim. And this proceeded from Katerina, plashing in the moonlight as in water, and rolling about on the soft rug, and frolicking and playing with her husband's young clerk. The tender white blossoms of the tufted apple tree showered and showered down on them, until at last their shower ceased. And in the meantime the brief summer night was passing, the moon had hidden behind the steep roof of the tall warehouses and was looking at the earth askance, more and more dully; from the roof of the kitchen an ear-piercing feline duet arose, followed by spitting and angry snarling, after which two or three cats, losing their footing, rolled noisily down the stack of lathwood leaning against the roof.

"Let's go to bed," said Katerina slowly, as if exhausted, rising from the rug and, just as she had been lying there, in only her chemise and white petticoats, went through the merchantly yard, now all still, as if in the stillness of death, while Serghei, behind her, carried the little rug and her blouse, which she, in her playfulness, had cast off.

VII

No sooner had Katerina blown out the candle and, all undressed, laid herself down on the soft featherbed, than sleep engulfed her completely. Katerina, having had her fill of play and joyance, fell asleep so deeply that her foot slept, and her hand slept, yet again she heard through her sleep that the door had apparently opened again and, like a heavy old boot, the familiar cat fell on the bed.

"Now, just what sort of visitation is this business of the cat?" the tired Katerina reasoned. "I turned the key of that door myself, on purpose, the window is closed—yet here he is again. I'm going to throw him out this minute." Katerina was about to get up, but her drowsy hands and feet would not serve her; and in the meantime the cat walked all over her, and his purring was so very wondrous that he seemed to be uttering human speech. Katerina felt as if tiny ants were running all up and down her body.

"No," she thought, "there's no other help for it; tomorrow I'll have to sprinkle the bed with holy water, for this is a most astonishing sort of cat that's taken to haunting me."

But there was that purr-purring at her very ear; he thrust his muzzle right up against her, and said: "Come, what sort of cat am I!" said he. "Whatever makes you think that! It's ever so clever of you to figure, Katerina Lvovna, that I'm no tomcat at all, for what I really am is that well-reputed trader, Boris Timotheich. It's just that I don't feel very well right now, all my dainty guts has split inside of me from the good things my daughter-in-law treated me to. And so you see," he purred, "that's why I've shrunk so, and now show myself as a tomcat to them as can't rightly tell what I really am. Well, and how are you living and doing now in our house, Katerina Lvovna? Are you carrying out all your commandments faithfully? I've made my way from the graveyard on purpose just to have a look at how you and Serghei Philipich keep your husband's bed warm. But, after all, *purr-purr,* I don't see a thing. Don't you be afeared of me: you see, from the feast you treated me to, my dear little eyes have crawled out of my head as well. Look into my eyes, deary-dear, don't you be afeared!"

Katerina did look, and began to scream at the top of her voice. The tomcat was again lying between her and Serghei, and the head on that tomcat was the head of Boris Timotheievich, just as big as the head of the dead man had been, and, instead of each eye, a fiery circle whirled and turned, whirled and turned, every which way!

Serghei awoke, calmed Katerina down, and went back to sleep, but sleep had forsaken her—and it was just as well.

She was lying there, her eyes wide open, when suddenly she heard that someone had apparently made his way into the yard by climbing over the gates. There, the dogs had made a dash for whoever it was, but then quieted down—probably they had begun to fawn on the arrival. Then, another minute passed, and the iron latch clicked below, and the door opened. "Either I'm imagining all these sounds, or my Zinovii Borisich has come back—he must have opened the door with his extra key," thought Katerina, and hastily nudged Serghei.

"Listen, Serezha," she said, while she raised herself on her elbow and pricked up her ears.

Someone was indeed approaching the locked door of the bedroom, walking softly up the stairs, cautiously shifting his weight from foot to foot.

Katerina sprang quickly off the bed, just in her chemise, and opened the dormer window. That same moment Serghei, in his bare feet, sprang out on the balcony and wound his legs about the post down which he had slid more than once from the bedroom of his master's wife.

"No, no need of that—no need of that! You lie down here . . . don't stir from here," whispered Katerina, and threw out after him his footgear and clothing, while she dived back under the blanket and lay there, and waited.

Serghei obeyed Katerina; he didn't slide down the post but instead hid snugly under the wooden overhang of the small balcony.

Katerina, meanwhile, heard her husband approach the door, and, holding his breath, stand there listening. She could even hear the quickened beating of his jealous heart; yet it wasn't pity but malicious laughter that seized on Katerina.

"Go look for yesterday," she addressed her husband mentally, smiling and breathing as evenly as an innocent babe.

This went on for about ten minutes; but finally Zinovii Borisich grew tired of standing by the door and listening to his wife sleeping: he knocked on the door.

"Who's there?" Katerina called out, not too soon, and in an apparently sleepy voice.

"One of your own," Zinovii responded.

"Is that you, Zinovii Borisich?"

"Yes, it's me! As if you don't hear me!"

Katerina jumped up, just as she had been lying, in her chemise, let her husband into the chamber, and again sprang back into the warm bed.

"It gets chilly just before dawn, somehow," she remarked, wrapping herself up in the blanket.

Zinovii Borisich entered, looking about him, said a prayer before the icon, lit a candle, and took another look around.

"How are you doing—getting along all right?" he asked his wife.

"Nothing to complain about," answered Katerina and, sitting up, began putting on a loose calico blouse.

"You want me to fix up a samovar, I guess?" she asked.

"Don't bother; call Axinia—let her fix it up."

Katerina put her slippers on her bare feet and ran out. She did not return for half an hour. During that time she herself had gotten the charcoal to glowing under the small samovar and, ever so quietly, had dashed over to Serghei on the small balcony.

"Stay here," she whispered to him.

"What's the use of sitting here?" Serghei asked, also in a whisper.

"Oh, how brainless you are! You stay here till I tell you different."

And Katerina herself made him sit down again in his former place.

Meanwhile Serghei, outside on the balcony, could hear everything that was going on in the bedroom. He heard the door close again as Katerina came back to her husband. He could hear every blessed word.

"What were you puttering about so long?" Zinovii asked his wife.

"I was fixing up the samovar," she answered calmly.

A pause followed. Serghei could hear Zinovii putting his frock coat away on a hanger. Then he washed himself, snorting and splashing water in all directions; there, he has asked for a towel; the conversation has begun again.

"Well, just how was it you buried my father?" the husband inquired.

"Just like that," answered his wife; "he died, and they buried him."

"But it was so unexpected!"

"God alone knows," answered Katerina, and began clattering the cups.

Zinovii walked mournfully about the room.

"And how did you pass your time here?" Zinovii again questioned his wife.

"Everyone knows what our pleasures are like here, I guess; we don't go to balls, nor to theayters neither."

"And it looks as if you didn't take much pleasure in seeing your husband, for that matter," Zinovii was starting up, eyeing her askance.

"We're no newlyweds, you and me, to be rushing at each other mad with love when we meet. How do you expect me to be overcome with joy? I fuss and run my feet off all day, just to pleasure you."

Katerina ran out again to fetch the samovar and again dashed over to Serghei, tugged at him, and said:

"Stop yawning! Keep your eyes open, Serezha!"

Serghei had no clear idea of what all this was leading up to but, just the same, he became alert.

Katerina returned, and there was Zinovii, kneeling on the bed and hanging up his silver traveling-watch with its beadwork fob on the wall above the headboard.

"How come, Katerina Lvovna, that you've made up the bed for two, when you were here all by your lonesome?" he suddenly asked his wife, somehow oddly.

"Why, I was waiting for you all along," answered Katerina, looking at him calmly.

"And I thank you kindly for that same. Now here's a certain object: how come it got in your feather bed?"

Zinovii Borisovich picked up from the bed sheet a small knitted woolen belt that belonged to Serghei and, holding it up by one end, dangled it before his wife's eyes.

Katerina didn't hesitate in the least.

"I found it in the garden," she said, "and caught up my skirt with it."

"Yes!" Zinovii pronounced with peculiar emphasis. "We've also heard a thing or two about those skirts of yours."

"And just what was it you heard?"

"Oh, all about your good works!"

"There's been no such thing."

"Well, we'll go into that later, we'll go into all of it," answered Zinovii, shoving his empty cup over to his wife.

Katerina let that pass in silence.

"We'll bring all those affairs of yours out into the light, Katerina Lvovna," Zinovii added after a long pause, raising his eyebrows at his wife.

"Your Katerina isn't the sort that's easy scairt. She's not so very scairt of that," she answered.

"What's that? What's that?" cried Zinovii, raising his voice.

"Never mind . . . I don't cry my cabbages twice," answered his wife.

"No, you'd better watch out! You've gotten pretty talkative while you were here alone, somehow!"

"And just why shouldn't I be talkative?" Katerina came back at him.

"You'd do better to keep more of an eye on yourself."

"I've got nothing to keep an eye on myself about. Just because someone with a long tongue carries tales to you, I don't have to stand for all sorts of abuse! That's something new, sure enough!"

"Long tongues or no, but your amours here are pretty well known."

"What amours of mine?" Katerina shouted, genuinely incensed.

"I know which."

"Well, if you know, go ahead: speak more plainly!"

Zinovii made no answer and again shoved his empty cup over to his wife.

"There's nothing to talk about, it looks like," Katerina declared with scorn, provocatively tossing a teaspoon on her husband's saucer. "Well, go on, go on, tell me whom they told you about? Who's this lover that I prefer to you?"

"You'll find out—don't be in such a hurry."

"What, has someone been barking and lying to you about Serghei —is that it?"

"We'll find out, we'll find out, Katerina Lvovna, my fine lady. No one has taken away our rights over you, and no one can take 'em away. . . . You'll come around to telling me all about yourself—"

"Ugh! I can't stand this!" Katerina cried out, gritting her teeth, and, blenching white as linen, suddenly sprang out of the door.

"Well, here he is," she announced a few seconds later, leading Serghei into the room by his sleeve. "Question him and me, since you know so much. Maybe you'll find out even more than you'd like!"

Zinovii Borisich was actually disconcerted. He looked first at Serghei, leaning against the doorpost, then at his wife, who had calmly sat down with her arms crossed on the edge of the bed; he had no idea of what all this was leading up to.

"What are you doing, you snake?" he barely managed to say, without rising from his armchair.

"Question us about what you know so well," Katerina answered him brazenly. "You thought you'd threaten me with a beating," she continued, her eyes blinking ominously, "but that'll never be; and as for me, I may have known what to do even before these promises of yours, and that's what I'm going to do with you."

"What's this? Get out!" Zinovii shouted at Serghei.

"Well, well!" Katerina taunted him.

She quickly and deftly locked the door, shoved the key into her pocket, and again lounged on the bed in her loose blouse.

"Well, now, Serezhechka, come, come here, my own dear," she beckoned the clerk over to her.

Serghei tossed back his curls and boldly sat down next to the mistress of the house.

"Oh, Lord! My God! What is this? What are you about, you heathen?" Zinovii cried out, turning all purple and rising from his armchair.

"What? Don't you like it? Just look at him, look at my bright-eyed falcon, see how beautiful he is!"

Katerina burst out laughing and kissed Serghei passionately in front of her husband.

That very instant her cheek blazed from a resounding slap, and Zinovii flung himself toward the open dormer window.

VIII

"Aha! So that's it! Well, my dear friend, I thank you! That's all I've been waiting for!" cried out Katerina, "Well, now, evidently things will have to go my way and not yours—"

With a single motion she thrust Serghei away from her, threw herself quickly at her husband, and, before Zinovii had time to jump to the window, she clutched his throat from behind with her slim fingers and, as if he were a sheaf of freshly cut hemp, hurled him to the floor.

Crashing heavily and striking the back of his head against the floor with full force, Zinovii went out of his head entirely. He had never anticipated such a swift dénouement. This first violence his wife had used against him showed him that she was ready for anything, if she might but rid herself of him, and that his present position was dangerous in the extreme. Zinovii realized this instantly in the moment of his fall and didn't cry out, knowing that his voice would not reach anybody's ear but might only hasten the outcome. He silently moved his eyes, and rested them, with an expression of malice, reproach, and agony, on his wife, whose slim fingers were squeezing his throat hard.

Zinovii did not defend himself; his arms, with fists clenched hard, lay stretched out and were jerking spasmodically. One of them was quite free; Katerina had pressed the other to the floor with one of her knees.

"Hold him," she whispered, unperturbed, to Serghei, and then turned back to her husband.

Serghei sat down on his master, pressed down both his arms with his own knees, and was about to grasp his throat from under Katerina's hands, but at that very instant he himself cried out desperately. At the sight of the man who had wronged him so a lust for blood-vengeance aroused all of Zinovii's remaining strength; he put forth a terrific effort, wrenched his pinioned hands from under Serghei's knees and, clutching Serghei's raven curls, sank his teeth like a beast into Serghei's throat. But that didn't last long: Zinovii immediately groaned hard and let his head drop.

Katerina, pale, hardly breathing at all, stood over her husband and her lover; in her right hand was a heavy molded candlestick, which she was holding by the top with the heavier end down. Along Zinovii's temple and cheek ruby-red blood was running down like a very fine thread.

"Call the priest—" Zinovii got out in a dull moan, turning his head with loathing as far away as possible from Serghei, who was sitting on him. "I want to be shriven," he got out even less articulately, shuddering, and looking askance at the warm blood coagulating under his hair.

"You'll do well enough as you are," Katerina said in a whisper; then, to Serghei: "Come, we've bothered with him enough, get a good grip on his throat."

There was a rattle in Zinovii's throat.

Katerina bent over, squeezed with her own hands the hands of Serghei about her husband's throat, and laid her ear to Zinovii's breast. Five silent minutes later she rose:

"Enough," she said. "He's got his."

Serghei got up, too, and drew a deep breath. Zinovii was lying dead, his windpipe crushed, his temple split. Under the left side of his head there was a small splotch of blood, which, however, no longer flowed from the small wound, now clotted and choked with hair.

Serghei carried Zinovii Borisich down into a wine cellar built under that very same stone storeroom wherein the late Boris Timotheich had not so long ago locked up Serghei himself, and returned to the attic. Meanwhile Katerina, the sleeves of her blouse rolled up and her skirt hitched high, was painstakingly cleaning up with soap and washrag the blood stain left by Zinovii on the floor of his bedchamber. The water had not yet grown cold in the samovar used to make the poisoned tea with which Zinovii had been warming his blessed little propertied soul, and the stain washed out without a trace.

Katerina picked up the little brass rinsing bowl of the samovar and the soapy washcloth.

"Come, give me some light," she said to Serghei as she went to the door. "Lower—let the light fall lower," she said, closely examining every floor board over which Serghei had had to drag Zinovii all the way to the wine cellar.

Only in two places on the painted floor were there two tiny splotches, each no bigger than a cherry. Katerina rubbed them with the washcloth and they disappeared.

"There, serves you right—don't go creeping up on your wife like a thief; don't be lying in wait for her," Katerina uttered, straightening up and looking over her shoulder toward the stone storeroom.

"Now it's over and done with," said Serghei, and shuddered at the sound of his own voice.

When they returned to the bedroom the dawn was piercing the eastern sky in a thin, rosy streak and, lightly gilding the blossom-clad apple trees, peeped into Katerina's room through the green palings of the garden fence.

Out in the yard the old clerk, his sheepskin jacket thrown over his shoulders, yawning and crossing himself, was making his way from the shed to the kitchen.

Katerina carefully drew the shutter up by its tape and took in Serghei with a searching look, as if to look into and know his very soul.

"Well, and so you're a merchant now," she said, laying her white hands on Serghei's shoulders.

Serghei said not a word in answer.

His lips quivered, and his whole body was shaking in a fit of ague. But as for Katerina, it was only her lips that felt cold.

In a couple of days great calluses appeared on Serghei's hands from the crowbar and the heavy spade; but then Zinovii Borisich had been so tidily put away in his own cellar that, without the help of his widow or her lover, none could ever find him till the dread Day of Resurrection.

IX

Serghei went about with his throat swathed in a scarlet kerchief. Meanwhile, before the marks left on Serghei's throat by the teeth of Boris had healed, the absence of Katerina's husband had become a matter of anxious comment. Serghei himself began talking about him even more frequently than the others. He'd sit down of an evening with the lads on a bench, and begin:

"Really, now, fellows, how is it our master still isn't here?"

The others would wonder in their turn.

Just then word came from the mill that the master had hired horses and set out for home long since. The coachman who had driven him told how Zinovii had seemed upset and had dismissed him somehow oddly: about two miles before they reached the town, near the monastery, he had left the cart, picked up his carpetbag, and gone off. Hearing a tale like that, they were all puzzled even more.

Zinovii Borisich had vanished, and that was all there was to it.

Searches and investigations were set in motion, but they didn't reveal anything: the merchant seemed to have vanished into thin air. All that could be learned from the testimony of the coachman, who had been arrested, was that the merchant had left him at the monastery by the river and gone off. The matter was not clarified, but in the meantime Katerina, the widow-woman, was living peacefully and quite freely with Serghei. There were surmises that Zinovii Borisich was now here, now there; but just the same Zinovii did not return, and Katerina knew, better than anyone else, that there never would or could be any returning for him.

Thus a month passed, and a second, and a third, and Katerina began to feel herself heavy with child.

"Our wealth is safe, Serezhechka; I have an heir for you," she imparted to Serghei, and then proceeded to petition the Town Council: Things were thus and so, and she felt and knew she was pregnant, and in the meantime the Ismailov affairs were at a standstill; they must give her all authority in business matters and free access to all the property.

It was unthinkable that such a business enterprise should go to rack and ruin. Katerina was her husband's lawful wife; there were no great or suspicious debts; it therefore seemed her petition should be granted. And grant it they did.

And so Katerina lived and queened it, and, following her example, they'd already taken to dignifying Serega as Serghei Philipich, when bang! like a bolt from the blue came a new worriment. A letter from the townships of Liven came to the mayor of our town, stating that the funds with which Boris Timotheich had operated had not been entirely his own: the greater portion of the moneys handled by him belonged not to him but to a young nephew, a minor, Fedor Zaharov Lyamin; and the letter added that this business must be adjudicated and not put into the hands of Katerina alone. This notice arrived; the mayor discussed it with Katerina, and then, in a week, lo and behold! a little old lady with a small boy arrived from the Livens.

"I," she announced, "am a cousin of the late Boris Timotheievich, and this is my nephew, Fedor Lyamin."

Katerina received them.

Serghei, observing from the courtyard this arrival and the reception accorded the newcomers by Katerina, turned white as a priest's alb.

"What's wrong with you?" the mistress of the house asked him when, having followed the guests in, he stopped in the hall, observing them.

"Nary a thing," answered the clerk, turning from the hall into the entry. "I was just thinking, these folks from Liven are odd and not even," he said with a sigh, shutting the outer door behind him.

"Well, what do we do now?" Serghei Philipich asked Katerina Lvovna that night as they sat around the samovar. "Now, Katerina Ilvovna, our whole affair, yours and mine, turns to dust and ashes."

"Why 'dust and ashes,' Serezha?"

"Because everything's going to be divided up now. What will be left for us to manage with?"

"Why, Serezha! Are you afraid you won't get enough?"

"I'm not thinking of my share; I just doubt that we can still be happy."

"How do you mean? Why shouldn't we be happy, Serezha?"

"Because, the way I love you, I'd like to see you a real lady, and not living the way you used to before," answered Serghei Philipich. "And now everything's coming out arsy-versy; with so much less capital, we'll have to get along on even less than we did before."

"But do you think it makes any difference to me, Serezhechka?"

"That's just it, Katerina Ilvovna; maybe it's all right with you, but never with me, since I respect you so much; and then, too, it would pain me terribly to have this happen before the eyes of other people, mean and envious as they are. You can do as you please, of course; but I'm convinced that in such circumstances I could never be happy."

And Serghei went on and on, harping on the one note to Katerina, that on account of Fedya Lyamin he had become the unhappiest of men, deprived of the possibility of elevating and honoring her, Katerina Ilvovna, before her whole mercantile world. Serghei always brought the talk around to the conclusion that, if it weren't for this Fedya, there would be nor mete nor bound to their happiness when and if within the nine months after the disappearance of her husband Katerina gave birth to her baby and came into the entire estate.

X

Then Serghei abruptly stopped even mentioning the heir. No sooner had such talk been cut off from the lips of Serghei, than Fedya Lyamin took root in both the mind and heart of Katerina. She actually brooded and became undemonstrative even to Serghei. Whether she was asleep, or going about her household affairs, or praying to her God, there was always the one thing on her mind: "How can this be? Sure, now, why must I lose all my wealth because of this boy? I've suffered so much, have taken so much sin on my soul," Katerina kept thinking, "whilst he, without any trouble to himself at all, just comes here and takes everything away from me. . . . And it wouldn't be so bad if it were at least a grown man—but a child, a mere boy . . ."

Outdoors the early frosts had begun. There was no news, naturally, from anywhere at all concerning Zinovii Borisich. Katerina was getting stout, and continued to go about brooding; and in the town tongues were wagging away, clacking day and night on her account, seeking the why and the wherefore: How come the young Ismailova, who'd been a barren ewe all this while, and getting thinner and leaner with every day, had now all of a sudden begun to swell out in front? And in the meantime the young heir, Fedya Lyamin, kept playing in the courtyard, in his light squirrel jacket, breaking up the ice in the shallow holes.

"Now, then, Fedor Ignatich, now there, my fine merchant's son!" Axinia, the cook, would shout to him as she ran through the yard. "Is it a nice thing for a merchant's son like you to be messing in them there puddles?"

And so the co-heir who was embarrassing to Katerina and to the object of her love kept gamboling like an innocent kid, and slept even more innocently at the side of his overfond great-aunt, never thinking or guessing that he had crossed anyone's path or lessened-worsened anyone's happiness.

Finally, Fedya ran about so much that he caught chickenpox and, with it, a painful cold in the chest; and the boy was put to bed. At first they treated him with herbs and grasses, but then the doctor was sent for.

He began coming to the house, began prescribing remedies, and they began administering them to the little boy every hour; now his great-aunt would do it and now, at her request, Katerina.

"Be so kind," she'd say, "Katerina dear; I know, mother o' mine, that you yourself are getting too heavy to move about much; that you yourself are waiting for whatever God may send you; but be so kind."

Katerina didn't refuse the old woman. Whenever the latter went to attend vespers, or to an all-night service to pray for "the young one, Fedor, lying on his bed of pain," or to early mass to receive a bit of holy wafer in his behalf, Katerina would sit with the sick boy, and give him drink, and administer his medicine to him on time.

And that's how the little crone went to vespers and to the all-night mass on the eve of the Feast of the Presentation, having asked Katerina, dear, to look after little Fedya. By this time the boy was already on the mend.

So Katerina entered Fedya's room, and there he was, sitting up in bed in his light squirrel jacket and reading the *Lives of the Holy Fathers.*

"What is it you're reading, Fedya?" Katerina asked him as she made herself comfortable in an armchair.

"I'm reading about the lives of the Holy Fathers, Aunty."

"Do you like them?"

"Very much, Aunty."

Katerina leaned on her arm and fell to watching Fedya as he moved his lips. And suddenly it was as if the demons had rent their chains and altogether taken possession of her former thoughts: how much evil this boy was causing her, and how fine it would be if he weren't around.

"What would it matter, now," Katerina pondered. "He's sick as it is; he has to be taking medicine . . . and what don't happen during an illness? . . . All anybody could say would be that the doctor had hit on the wrong medicine."

"Is it time for your medicine, Fedya?"

"If you please, Aunty," answered the boy, and, having downed the spoonful, added: "these descriptions of the saints are ever so interesting, Aunty."

"Go on, keep on reading," Katerina let fall, and, throwing an icy glance around the room, let it rest on the windows with their frosty designs. "I've got to order them to close the shutters," she said, and went out into the parlor, from there into the drawing room, and then upstairs to her own room, where she sat down.

Within five minutes Serghei, silent, and dressed in a dandified fur-lined jacket trimmed with soft seal, came up to her.

"The windows shuttered?" Katerina asked him.

"They are," Serghei answered curtly, removed the thief from the candlewick with the snuffers, and took up his stand beside the stove.

Silence set in.

"Tonight's services won't be over soon, will they?" asked Katerina.

"Tomorrow's a great holy day; the service will be a long one," Serghei answered.

There was another pause.

"I've got to go down to Fedya; he's all alone there," Katerina announced, getting up.

"All alone?" Serghei asked her, looking at her from under his brows.

"All alone," she answered him in a whisper. "Why, what of it?"

And from eye to eye there passed between them a flash as of chain lightning; but neither said another word to the other.

Katerina went down; she made the round of the empty rooms; quiet reigned everywhere, the icon-lamps burned with an even glow, her own shadow ran ahead and spread across the walls; the shuttered windows had begun to thaw and were shedding water like tears. Fedya was sitting up in bed, reading. Seeing Katerina, he merely said:

"Aunty, please put this book away and give me that one from the icon-stand."

Katerina carried out the boy's request and handed him the book.

"Don't you think you ought to go to sleep, Fedya?"

"No, Aunty. I'm going to wait up for my great-aunt."

"Why should you wait up for her?"

"She promised to bring me a blessed wafer from the all-night mass."

Katerina suddenly blenched; her own child stirred for the first time under her heart. And a chill ran through it. She stood a while in the middle of the room and then went out, rubbing her cold hands.

"There!" she whispered, entering her bedroom quietly and finding Serghei in his former place by the stove.

"Well?" Serghei asked in a scarcely audible tone. And something caught in his throat.

"He's all alone."

Serghei knit his eyebrows and began to breathe heavily.

"Let's go," said Katerina, turning sharply toward the door.

Serghei quickly took off his boots and asked:

"What should I take with me?"

"Nothing." Katerina barely breathed her answer and quietly drew him after her by the hand.

XI

The sick boy shuddered and let his book fall on his lap when Katerina came into his room for the third time.

"What's the matter, Fedya?"

"Oh, Aunty, something scared me," he answered, smiling tremulously and shrinking in a corner of the bed.

"But whatever scared you?"

"Who was that with you, Aunty?"

"Where? No one came with me, little darling."

"No one?"

The boy stretched himself to the foot of the bed and, screwing up his eyes, looked in the direction of the door through which his aunt had entered, and was reassured.

"I guess I must have just imagined it," he said.

Katerina stood still, her elbow resting on the headboard of her nephew's bed.

Fedya looked at his aunt and remarked to her that she seemed all pale for some reason.

In answer to this remark Katerina coughed deliberately and looked expectantly at the door leading into the parlor. The only sound that came from there was that of a floor board creaking.

"I'm reading the life of my patron saint, Aunty—Fedor, soldier and martyr. How pleasing he made himself to God!"

Katerina stood there, silent.

"Would you like to sit down, Aunty, and I'll read it over to you?" her nephew wheedled.

"Wait a bit; I'll be right back; I just want to look after the icon-lamp in the drawing room," answered Katerina, and went out with short, hurried steps.

The whispering that began in the parlor was faint as could be but, amid the pervading quiet, it reached the sensitive ear of the child.

"Aunty! Why, what's going on? Whom are you whispering with there?" cried out the boy, with tears in his voice. "Come here, Aunty— I'm afraid!" he called again a second later, even more tearfully, and he thought he heard Katerina, in the parlor, say "All right," which the boy took to be meant for him.

"What are you afraid of?" Katerina asked him in a rather hoarse voice, coming in with a determined tread and placing herself so that her body hid the door into the parlor from the sick boy. "Lie down," she said to him right after this.

"But I don't want to, Aunty."

"No, you lie down, Fedya—listen to me, lie down . . . it's time," Katerina repeated.

"But what's all this for, Aunty! I don't want to lie down at all."

"No, you lie down, lie down," Katerina told him, in a voice that had changed again and was unsteady, and, seizing the boy under the armpits, laid him down at the head of the bed.

In that same instant Fedya screamed frantically: he had caught sight of Serghei, pale, barefoot, entering the room.

Katerina clapped her palm over the mouth the terrified child had opened wide in horror, and called out sharply:

"Come on, hurry up—hold him straight, so's he won't struggle!"

Serghei took hold of Fedya by his arms and legs, while Katerina, with a single motion, covered the small, childish face of the victim with a large down pillow and fell on it with her firm, resilient breast.

For four minutes or so, a silence as of the grave pervaded the room.

"He's finished," Katerina said in a whisper, but she had barely straightened up, about to restore everything to order, when the walls of the quiet house which had concealed so many crimes shook from deafening blows: the windows jarred, the floors swayed, the slender chains on which the image-lamps hung wavered and sent fantastic shadows scurrying over the walls.

Serghei shuddered and ran off as fast as his legs would carry him; Katerina flung herself after him, while the noise and hubbub followed them. It seemed as if unearthly forces were rocking the sinful house to its foundations.

Katerina feared that Serghei, spurred on by terror, might run outdoors and betray himself by his panic, but he dashed straight for the stairs leading to the attic.

Serghei had run up a few steps when, in the dark, he crashed head-on into a half open door and, with a groan, flew down, beside himself with superstitious terror.

"Zinovii Borisich! Zinovii Borisich!" he muttered as he flew head-first down the stairs, drawing Katerina, whom he had knocked off her feet, after him.

"Where?" she asked.

"There, he flew by right over us on a sheet of iron! There, there he is again!" and Serghei screamed. "That's him thundering—there, he's thundering again!"

By now it was evident that innumerable hands were pounding at all the windows facing the street, while someone was trying to break down the door.

"You fool! Get up, you fool!" cried Katerina, and no sooner were the words out than she herself streaked off to Fedya, arranged the head of the dead boy in a completely natural position on the pillows, as if he were asleep, and with a firm hand opened the door which a whole mob was trying to break down.

It was a fearful sight. Katerina looked over the heads of the crowd besieging the stoop, and saw line after line of strangers climbing over the high fence into the yard, while the whole street groaned with their excited talk.

Before Katerina had a chance to realize anything, the mob surrounding the stoop had bowled her over and swept her into the inner rooms.

XII

And here is how all this excitement had come about: an enormous number of worshipers was wont to attend, on the eve of any of the twelve high holy days, all the churches in the town where Katerina Lvovna lived, which, even though it was provincial, was nevertheless a fairly large industrial one, and as for any church where holy communion was to be received in the morning, why, there was no room therein for even a worm to turn. In such a church there is usually a choir singing, made up of young mercantile bloods, with their own special choirmaster.

Our townfolk are devout and zealous toward the church of God; and for that reason they are artistic in their own way: churchly splendor and the harmonious, "organistic" singing form for them one of their loftiest and purest delights. Wherever the choir sings, there will be gathered almost half the town, especially the mercantile youth: clerks, boys, dandies, artisans from the factories and mills, and even the masters of the factories and mills themselves, with their better halves. All would gather in the same church; everyone wanted, even though he had to stand outside on the porch, or under a window in hellish heat or crackling frost, to hear an octave sung in organ tones, or a bold tenor bringing out the most capricious of grace notes.

There was to be holy communion in the parish church of the Ismailovs, in commemoration of the Presentation of the Most Blessed Virgin; and therefore on the eve of this holy day, at the very time that the scene with Fedya, described above, was taking place, the youth of the whole town was to be found at that church. As they left in a noisy crowd, they discussed the merits of the well-known tenor and the chance blunders of the equally famous bass.

But not all were taken up with these vocalistic topics; there were those in the crowd who were interested in other matters as well.

"There, now, fellows, there's some mighty queer things going the rounds about the young Ismailov woman," began a young mechanic who had been imported from Petersburg by one of the merchants for his steam mill, as they approached the Ismailov house. "They're saying," he went on, "that there ain't a minute goes by but she's loving up Serghei—that's their clerk, now."

"Aw, everybody knows that," said a blue nankeen, sheepskin-lined jacket. "Come to think of it, she weren't even in church tonight!"

"Church? What are you talking about? That wicked young creature has so besmirched herself that she no longer fears God, nor her own conscience, nor the eyes of decent folk."

"Look: there's a light in their house," said the mechanic, pointing to a streak of light between the shutters.

"Take a look through the crack, see what they're up to!" several voices encouraged him.

The mechanic, supported by the shoulders of two of his friends, had barely put his eye to the crack of the shutter when he cried out at the top of his voice:

"Brothers! They're strangling someone there—friends, they're strangling someone!"

And the mechanic began pounding desperately on the shutters with his hands. Half a score of the others followed his example and, jumping up to the windows, also fell to hammering away with their fists.

The crowd increased with every instant, and that is how the already described siege of the Ismailov house had come about.

"I seen it myself; I seen it with me own eyes," the mechanic testified as he stood over the dead Fedya. "The child was laying thrown down on his bed, while the two of them was strangling him."

Serghei was taken to the precinct house that very evening, while Katerina was led off to her room upstairs, where two guards were set over her.

Unbearable cold pervaded the home of the Ismailovs: the stoves were not going, the door was never closed for a minute, one dense crowd of curiosity seekers was succeeded by another. All of them went to look at Fedya lying in his coffin, and at another, a larger coffin, its lid completely covered by a wide pall. A little white satin wreath lay on

Fedya's forehead, concealing the red line left by the autopsy performed on the skull. The medicolegal examination had revealed that Fedya had died of suffocation, and Serghei, led up to his corpse, at the very first words of the priest concerning dread Judgment Day and the punishment awaiting the unrepentant, burst into tears, and, opening up his soul, confessed not only to the murder of Fedya but also begged them to dig up Zinovii Borisich, whom he had interred without benefit of clergy. The body of Katerina Lvovna's husband, covered with dry sand, had not yet decomposed completely: they exhumed him and laid him in an oversized coffin. As his accomplice in both these crimes, Serghei named, to the horror of all, the young mistress of the house.

Katerina Lvovna had but the one answer to all questions: "I don't know; I have no knowledge of all this."

Serghei was made to bear witness against her at a confrontation. Having listened to his confessions, Katerina looked at him with mute amazement, yet without wrath, and said with indifference:

"Since he's so willing to tell all about it, there's no use in my denying anything: I murdered them."

"But what for?" they questioned her.

"For him," she answered, indicating Serghei, who hung his head.

The accused were jailed, and the horrible affair, which had aroused universal interest and indignation, was quickly settled. By the end of February the sentence of the Criminal Court was read out to Serghei and to Katerina Lvovna, widow of a merchant of the third guild; they had been condemned to be whipped in the market place of their town, after which both were to be transported to hard labor in Siberia. At the beginning of March, on a bitter frosty morning, the executioner counted off the designated number of lividly purple wales on Katerina's bared white back, then beat out Serghei's share on his shoulders as well, and branded his handsome face with the triple Cain-mark of the convict.

During all this time, for some reason or other, Serghei aroused far more public sympathy than Katerina. Besmeared and all in blood, he stumbled time and again as he came down from the black scaffold, whereas Katerina came down staidly, her only concern being to keep her coarse shift and rough convict coat from sticking to her back.

Even in the prison hospital, when they showed her her baby, all she said was: "Oh, who needs him?" And, turning away to the wall, with never a moan, never a complaint, she slumped, breast down, on the hard bunk.

XIII

The convoy of convicts in which Serghei and Katerina found themselves set out when spring appeared only on the calendar, while the sun, according to the proverb, "shone bright enough but didn't warm much."

Katerina's child was given into the keeping of the little crone, Boris Timotheievich's cousin, for, since he was considered the legitimate male issue of the convicted woman's slain husband, the child now remained the sole heir of the entire estate of the Ismailovs. Katerina was quite content with this arrangement and gave the child up with complete indifference. Her love for its father, like the love of many inordinately passionate women, was in no measure transferred to his child.

But, for that matter, nothing existed for her, nor light, nor darkness, nor evil, nor good, nor sorrow, nor gladness; she understood nothing and loved no one—not even herself. She waited with impatience for one thing only: for the convoy to set out on the road, for there she hoped to see her Serezhechka again; and as for the child, she forgot it completely.

Katerina's hopes did not deceive her: Serghei, loaded with heavy chains and branded, left the prison gates in the same small group as she.

Man becomes accustomed to any situation, however repulsive, and retains in it, so far as possible, the capacity to pursue his meager joys. But Katerina had no need to become accustomed to anything: she was seeing Serghei again, and with him even the road that led to a convict's life was abloom with happiness.

Katerina had taken very little of value with her in her bag made of ticking, and even less in actual money. But even long before they had reached Nizhni-Novgorod she had distributed it all among the corporals convoying the prisoners, to be able to plod alongside Serghei on the road, and to stand for an hour or so embracing him in the dark night, in some chill blind corner of a halting-station's narrow hallway.

But the only thing was that Katerina's branded lover had become very unaffectionate to her, somehow: if he said anything, he seemed to tear every word out of himself; he set but little value on these secret meetings with her, for which she had to go without her food and drink, expending from her lean purse the small coins she needed for herself, and he even said, more than once:

"You'd do better, instead of going out to dust the corners in the hallway with me, if you were to offer me the money you give the corporal."

"All I gave him was five-and-twenty kopecks, Serezhenka," Katerina pleaded.

"And isn't five-and-twenty kopecks money? You haven't found so many of those same coins lying on the road, have you? But you've given away not a few, I guess."

"But then, Serezha, we were able to see each other."

"Well, does it come easy, does it make us happy, to see each other after such torments, now? I've a mind to curse my very life, let alone a meeting like this!"

"But to me nothing matters, Serezha, so long as I can see you."

"That's all foolishness," answered Serghei.

At times Katerina would bite her lips till they bled at such replies, while at others, in the darkness of these nocturnal meetings, tears of rancor and grief would appear even in her eyes, not much given to weeping; but she endured everything, let everything pass in silence, and was eager to deceive her own self.

Thus, in these new relations to each other, they reached Nizhni-Novgorod. Here their convoy was combined with another bound for Siberia from the Moscow region.

In this large reinforcement, among a multitude of all sorts, there were, in the female contingent, two exceedingly interesting characters: one was Thiona, a soldier's wife from Yaroslavl, such a splendid, voluptuous woman, tall, with a heavy black braid, and languid hazel eyes, shaded, as with a mysterious veil, by thick eyelashes; the other, a seventeen-year-old sharp-featured little blonde, with delicately rosy skin, a tiny mouth, dimples on her fresh cheeks, and tawny-golden curls willfully escaping around her forehead from under the convict's kerchief of ticking. This girl was called Sonetka by the rest of the convicts.

The beauty Thiona was of a gentle and lethargic disposition. She was known to everyone in her gang, and none of the men was particularly overjoyed at his success in making a conquest of her, nor was any one of them aggrieved to see that she crowned with equal success every other seeker after her favors.

"Our aunt Thiona is the most kindhearted of women; she'll never hurt anyone's feelings," all the male convicts maintained jestingly and unanimously.

But Sonetka was of another sort entirely.

Of her they said:

"She's an eel: she'll twist and she'll squirm, but you'll never grasp her firm."

Sonetka had taste; she was fastidious—and even, perhaps, very fastidious; she wished to have passion served to her, not as a raw mushroom, but with a piquant, spicy sauce, with sufferings and with sacrifices, whereas Thiona was the very essence of Russian simplicity, too lazy even to say to any man: "Get away from me," and who knew but one thing: that she was a female woman. Such women are highly appreciated among brigand bands, convict gangs, and the Social-Democratic communes of Petersburg.

The advent of these two women when their convoy was combined with that of Serghei and Katerina had a tragic significance for the latter.

XIV

From the very first days of the augmented convoy's progress from Nizhni to Kazan, Serghei very obviously set about getting into the good graces of Thiona, the soldier's wife, and encountered no insuperable setback. Thiona, the languid beauty, didn't make Serghei languish, just as, in her kindhearted way, she didn't make any man languish. At the third or fourth way-station, as soon as the early dusk had fallen, Katerina had, by bribery, arranged a meeting with her Serezhechka and was now lying sleepless, waiting for the corporal on duty to come in at any moment, nudge her softly, and whisper to her: "Run along and make it snappy!" The door opened once, and some woman or other darted into the corridor; again it opened, and again another of the female convicts lost no time in jumping up from her sleeping-bench, and likewise vanished in the wake of her guide; finally someone tugged at the coarse convict coat with which Katerina had covered herself. The young woman quickly got up from the sleeping-bench that had been so smoothly polished by so many convict bodies, threw her coat over her shoulders, and nudged the guard standing in front of her to guide her.

As Katerina walked along the corridor, faintly lit in only one spot by a purblind wick in a shallow saucer of tallow, she stumbled over two or three couples, who made themselves as unnoticeable as possible from a distance. As she passed the male convicts' quarters she caught restrained laughter coming through the little window cut into the door.

"Listen to 'em whinnying!" mumbled the guide to Katerina and, taking hold of her shoulders, shoved her into a nook and withdrew.

One of Katerina's groping hands felt a coarse coat and a beard; her other hand touched the burning face of a woman.

"Who is it?" Serghei asked in a low voice.

"But what are you doing here? Who's that with you?"

In the dark, Katerina tore the kerchief off her rival's head. The latter slipped aside, dashed away, and, stumbling over someone in the corridor, sped away like the wind.

A chorus of laughter burst out from the men's ward.

"You villain!" Katerina whispered, and slapped Serghei's face with the corners of the kerchief she had torn from the head of his new love.

Serghei was about to raise his hand to her, but Katerina had already flitted as light as a shadow down the corridor and grasped the knob of her cell door. The laughter from the men's section which followed her was repeated so loudly that the guard, who was standing apathetically opposite the flickering wick in its saucer and spitting at the toe of his boot to pass the time, raised his head and barked out: "Quiet, you!"

Katerina lay down silently and stayed thus, never stirring, until morning came. She wanted to say to herself: "I don't love him any more," and felt that she loved him more passionately, more deeply, than ever. And before her eyes appeared, again and again, the same picture: that of his right palm trembling under the head of *that other,* his left hand clasping the *other's* glowing shoulders.

The poor woman began to cry and, beyond her will, longed for that same palm to be under her head at that very minute, for that other hand to be clasping her shoulders, now shaking hysterically.

"You might give me back my kerchief, at least," Thiona, the soldier's wife, wakened her in the morning.

"Oh, so it was you?"

"Give it back to me, please!"

"But why are you coming between us?"

"Why, how am I doing that? Do you think there's any such great love between us, or anything really so important, that you need get angry about it?"

Katerina thought a moment, then took from under her pillow the kerchief she had torn off that night, and, throwing it to Thiona, turned her face to the wall.

Her heart grew lighter.

"*Fui!*" she said to herself. "Am I to be actually jealous of this painted tub? The hell with her! It's disgusting for me even to compare myself with her!"

"Look here, Katerina Ilvovna, here's what I'll tell you," Serghei was saying to her the next day, as they were on their way again, "please get it through your head that, in the first place, I'm no Zinovii Borisich for you and, in the second, that you're no longer the wife of an important merchant; so, as a favor to me, don't you go putting on any airs. I got no use for a butting she-goat."

Katerina made no answer to this and for a week she walked side by side with Serghei without their exchanging a glance or a word. Since she was the offended one, she persisted in maintaining her dignity and didn't want to take the first step toward reconciliation in this, her first, quarrel with Serghei.

In the meantime, while Katerina remained angry at Serghei, he began casting sheep's eyes at the white-skinned, petite Sonetka and making playful overtures to her. He'd bow to her and say: "Our best to you!" or he'd smile at her, or, as they met, contrive to put his arm around her and hug her. Katerina saw all this, and her heart seethed all the more within her.

"Should I make up with him, I wonder?" Katerina mused as she stumbled along without seeing the ground beneath her feet.

But now more than ever her pride would not let her be the first to make overtures of peace. And in the meantime Serghei dangled ever more persistently after Sonetka, and it was already becoming evident to everyone that the unattainable Sonetka, who had been twisting like an eel right along, but whom there was no getting a hold of, was suddenly becoming easier to handle, somehow.

"See, you were complaining about me," Thiona happened to say to Katerina one day, "yet what did I do to you? Mine was a chance affair; it came, and it's gone and past; but you'd better watch out for this Sonetka."

"To hell with this pride of mine: I'll make up with him this very day," Katerina decided, by now thinking only of the cleverest way to go about this peacemaking.

But it was Serghei himself who extricated her from this difficult situation.

"Ilvovna!" he called her at the next halting place. "Come out to me tonight for just a minute; I've business with you."

Katerina let this pass in silence.

"Well, now, are you still angry at me, by any chance? Won't you come out?"

Katerina again made no answer.

But Serghei, as did everyone else who observed Katerina, noticed, as they were approaching the convoy station, that she began hanging around the chief corporal, and that she slipped him seventeen kopecks that had been given her in charity on the road.

"Soon as I can get it together, I'll give you ten more," Katerina pleaded.

The corporal hid the money in the cuff of his overcoat:

"All right," he said.

Serghei, when these negotiations were over, grunted and winked at Sonetka.

"Oh, you, Katerina Ilvovna!" he said, embracing her as they were going up the steps of the convoy station. "There's not another woman in all this world, lads, that can compare with this one!"

Katerina both blushed and panted from happiness.

It was barely night when the door opened quietly; she simply leapt through it; she was quivering, and her hands groped, seeking Serghei in the dark corridor.

"My Kate!" Serghei breathed, embracing her.

"Oh, you, my evil one!" Katerina answered through her tears, and clung to him with her lips.

The guard was walking up and down the corridor, stopping every now and then to practice spitting on his boots, and then started walking anew; the worn-out convicts snored away behind their doors, a mouse was nibbling away at a quill somewhere under the stove, the crickets were chirping away for all they were worth, vying with one another, but Katerina was still in seventh heaven.

But the raptures abated, and the inevitable prose made itself heard.

"I'm in deadly pain; from my ankle to my knee, my bones nag and nag," complained Serghei, sitting with Katerina on the floor in a corner of the corridor.

"Well, how can it be helped, Serezhechka?" she asked, snuggling under a fold of his coat.

"Unless . . . maybe I should ask them to put me in the hospital at Kazan?"

"Oh, whatever are you saying, Serezha!"

"Well, what else is there when I'm sick to death?"

"But how can you stay behind while they drive me on ahead?"

"Well, what can I do? I'm telling you that chain chafes me, it chafes me so, as if all of it were eating into the bone. It might help if I tried wearing wool stockings for a while," Serghei let fall a minute later.

"Stockings? I still have a new pair of stockings, Serezha."

"Well, what could be better!" Serghei responded.

Katerina, without saying another word, dashed into her room, rummaged around under the sleeping bench for her bag, and hurried back to Serghei with a pair of heavy blue woolen stockings, with bright clocks—stockings for the manufacture of which the town of Bolcov is so justly celebrated.

"With them on it won't be bad at all," Serghei declared as he left Katerina, taking her last pair of stockings with him.

Katerina, happy now, returned to her hard bench and fell fast asleep.

She didn't hear how, after her return, Sonetka went out into the corridor, nor how she came back from there quietly only just before morning.

All this took place two stages before Kazan.

X·V

A chill, inclement day, with gusts of wind and rain mixed with snow, dourly greeted the gang setting out from the gates of the stuffy convoy station. Katerina set out stoutheartedly enough, but no sooner had she joined her own line than she began to shake all over and turned green. Everything grew dark before her eyes; every joint began to nag, and her knees failed her. There was Sonetka standing before Katerina, sporting the blue woolen stockings with the bright clocks that Katerina knew so well.

Katerina started off along the road just as if there were no life in her; only her eyes were alive as they looked frightfully at Serghei and never left him, not even for a wink.

At the first halting place she walked calmly up to Serghei, whispered "Villain!"—and without the least warning spat right in his eyes.

Serghei was about to hurl himself at her, but the others held him back.

"Just you wait!" was all he said, and he wiped his face.

"Never mind; she's sure not afraid to stand up to you!" the other convicts taunted Serghei, and Sonetka's trilling laugh was especially merry.

This little intrigue to which Sonetka had yielded was developing entirely to her taste.

"You're not going to get away with this just like that!" Serghei threatened Katerina.

Exhausted by the bad weather and the distance covered, Katerina, her soul shattered, slept fitfully that night on the benches in the convoy station and never heard when two men entered the women's ward.

Upon their entrance Sonetka raised herself fom her sleeping-bench, silently indicated Katerina to them with her hand, lay down again, and wrapped herself up in her convict coat.

That same instant Katerina's coat was thrown up over her head, and a stout, doubled rope's end, wielded with all of a muzhik's strength, began to flail her back, covered only by her rough shift.

Katerina cried out, but her voice could not be heard through the coat that muffled her head. She tried to break away, but with no more success, for a sturdy convict was sitting on her shoulders and holding her arms fast.

"Fifty," finally counted off a voice which no one found any difficulty in identifying as the voice of Serghei, and the nocturnal visitors vanished together through the door.

Katerina freed her head and jumped up: there was no one there; but not far away someone was sniggering in malicious joy under her coat. Katerina recognized Sonetka's laugh.

This affront was beyond all bounds, nor were there any bounds to the feeling of rancor that began to seethe at that moment in the soul of Katerina. She surged forward, out of her mind, and, still out of her mind, fell on the breast of Thiona, who caught her as she fell.

On that full breast which, so short a while before, had delighted with its depraved sweetness Katerina's faithless lover, she now wept out her unbearable grief and, as a child would to its mother, she clung to her foolish and oversoft rival. They were equals at last: both equalized in value and both cast off.

They were equals! . . . Thiona, submitting to the first-come whim, and Katerina, consummating the drama of her love.

But by now, to tell the truth, nothing was any longer an affront to Katerina. Having exhausted her tears, she grew hard, as if turned to stone, and with wooden calmness was getting ready to go out to the muster-call.

The drum rolled: *thump-thumpety-thumpety-thump;* the drab convicts, in irons and without, tumbled out into the courtyard: Serghei was there, and Thiona, and Sonetka, and Katerina, and the Old-Faith Schismatic in the same irons with a Jew, and the Pole on the same chain with a Tatar.

At first they were all in one throng, but presently straightened out into some semblance of order and started off.

It was a most cheerless picture: a handful of human beings torn away from the world and bereft of the slightest shadow of any hope for a better future, drowning in the cold, black mud of the unpaved highway. Everything around them was hideous to the verge of horror; the never-ending mud, the leaden sky, and the sodden willows that had shed their every leaf, and the raven, with its feathers all ruffled, perching among their starkly outflung branches. The wind would now moan, now rage, then wail and roar.

In these hellish, soul-rending sounds that completed the horror of the picture resounded the words of the Biblical Job: "Let the day perish wherein I was born!" and the counsel of his wife: "Curse God and die!"

Whoever would not hearken to these words, whoever is not tempted but is rather frightened by the thought of death even in so dismal a situation, must needs strive to silence these wailing voices by something even more hideous. Your simple, common man understands this excellently well: at such a time he gives full freedom to all his bestial simplicity, begins to clown, to make cruel sport of himself, of all men, of all sensibility. None too tender even without that, he becomes doubly vicious.

"Well, my fine merchant's lady, is your worthy self still enjoying good health?" Serghei insolently asked Katerina, after the gang had just left the village where they had stopped overnight, losing sight of it behind a sodden knoll.

With these words, turning at once to Sonetka, he covered her with the folds of his coat and began to sing in an exaggerated falsetto:

"A small russet head flits by in the shadow of the casement;
You are not asleep, my mischief; you are not asleep, my torment;
I will hide you in my cloak, so none may see or notice."

And, as he sang these words, Serghei took Sonetka around and kissed her loudly before the whole gang of convicts. . . .

Katerina saw all this, yet without really seeing it: by now she was walking along like a being bereft of all life. The others began nudging her and pointing out to her how indecently Serghei was carrying on with Sonetka. Katerina became the butt of their gibes.

"Leave her be," Thiona would intervene whenever anyone of the gang tried to make fun of Katerina as she stumbled along. "Can't you see, you devils, that the woman is sick as can be?"

"She must have got her little feet wet," a young convict waxed witty.

"Everybody knows these ladies of the merchant class: they're brought up ever so delicately," Serghei rose to the occasion. "To be sure," he kept up the badinage, "if she had a pair of warm dainty stockings it wouldn't matter so much."

It was just as though Katerina stirred out of her sleep.

"You crawling snake!" she said, goaded beyond endurance. "Laugh at me, you low-down scoundrel—go ahead and laugh at me!"

"Oh, no, my fine merchant's lady, I don't mean to laugh at you at all, but since Sonetka there is selling such really fine stockings, why, I just thought maybe our fine merchant's lady might want to buy a pair."

This drew much laughter. Katerina stepped along like a wound-up automaton.

The weather was worsening all the time. Out of the gray clouds that covered the sky snow began to fall in wet flakes which melted as they touched the ground and made the mud still deeper, still more insufferably hard to wade through. Finally, a dark leaden streak appeared ahead; its outer edge was indistinguishable. That streak was the Volga. A strongish wind wandered over the Volga and drove the slow-rising, wide-mawed dark waves to and fro.

The gang of thoroughly drenched, thoroughly chilled convicts slowly neared the river-crossing and stopped, awaiting the ferry barge.

The barge, dripping and dark, drew up; the guards began to embark the convicts.

"They say someone on this barge has some vodka to sell," remarked one of the convicts when, bespattered with the flakes of wet snow, the barge pushed off from the shore and began to roll on the billows of the enraged river.

"Well, now, sure enough, it would be a shame to miss a chance at a little something to wet your whistle," Serghei responded and, persecuting Katerina for Sonetka's amusement, added: "What do you say, my fine merchant's lady? What about treating us to a shot of vodka, for old friendship's sake? Don't be stingy. Just remember, my dearest, our former love, how you and me, my joy, would while the time away together; how, through the long autumn nights, you and me would sit together; how we'd send your dear kith and kin off to their eternal rest, all by ourselves, with never a priest or deacon for to help us."

Katerina was shivering all over from the cold. Besides the cold, which penetrated through her sodden clothes to her very bones, something else was affecting Katerina's whole being. Her head was burning, as if actually on fire; the pupils of her eyes were dilated, animated by a wandering, sharp glitter, and fixed immovably on the rolling waves.

"Say, I could do with a little vodka; it's so cold I can't stand it," Sonetka trilled like a little silver bell.

"Come on, my merchant's lady, why not treat us!" Serghei kept nagging.

"Oh, you! Where's your conscience?" Thiona called out, shaking her head in reproach.

"That's not at all to your credit," a young convict by the name of Gordiushka came to her support.

"If you have no conscience about her, you might at least have some before the others!"

"Why, you world's mattress!" Serghei yelled at Thiona. "You and your conscience! Why, do you expect my conscience to bother me over *her*? I may never have loved her, even, but now—why, this worn slipper of Sonetka's is dearer to me than that foul face of hers—the skinned cat! What have you to say to that? Let her love slew-mouthed Gordiushka there; or—" here he cautiously looked around at a mounted milksop in his Caucasian felt cloak and military cap with a cockade, and added: "or, better still, let her get around that convoy officer—at least under his cloak she won't get soaked from the rain."

"And everyone'll call her an officer's lady!" Sonetka's voice again trilled like a little silver bell.

"That's right! . . . And it would be child's play for her to get enough for a pair of stockings," Serghei followed suit.

Katerina did not defend herself; she stared even more fixedly at the waves, and her lips moved. Through the loathsome speeches of Serghei she could hear the rumbling and groaning that arose from the yawning and plashing billows. And suddenly, out of one breaking billow the livid head of Boris Timotheievich appeared before her; out of another her husband peered, and then began to rock, clasping Fedya, whose head was drooping. Katerina wanted to recall a prayer and moved her lips, but what her lips whispered was: "How you and me would while the time away together; how, through the long autumn nights, you and me would sit together; how we'd send folks out of this great wide world with cruel deaths."

Katerina Lvovna was shivering. Her wandering gaze was becoming concentrated and wild. Once or twice her hands stretched aimlessly into space, only to drop back. Another minute—and suddenly her whole body began to rock; never taking her eyes from one of the dark waves, she bent down, seized Sonetka by the legs, and, in a single move, hurled herself and the girl over the side of the barge.

Everyone was petrified with astonishment.

Katerina Lvovna appeared on the crest of a wave and plunged down again; a second wave brought up Sonetka.

"The boat hook! Throw over the boat hook!" the cry went up on the barge.

The heavy boat hook on its long rope whirled up in the air and fell into the water. Sonetka had again gone down out of sight. Two seconds later, quickly carried away by the backwash of the barge, she again flung up her arms; but at the same time, out of another wave, Katerina Lvovna rose almost waist-high above the water, hurled herself at Sonetka as a strong pike might hurl itself at a feebly resisting dace, and neither came up again.

Vsevolod Michailovich
Garshin
1 8 5 5 – 1 8 8 8

POET, short-story writer, and initiator in Russian literature of the social-psychological novelette, the form that was later on brought to such perfection by Chekhov, V. M. Garshin laid the foundation of his literary reputation with *Four Days* (1877), a war story surpassing even *The Red Badge of Courage.* He was wounded in the Russo-Turkish War (1877-78), and was in the forefront as a fighter against absolutism.

He committed suicide, during a fit of depression, by leaping down a stairwell.

Life

A YOUNG DISCIPLE asked of that saintly sage, Jiaffar:

"Master, what is life?"

In silence the master turned back the soiled sleeve of his sackcloth burnoose and showed the disciple a revolting sore that was eating into his arm.

And, at that very time, the nightingales were trilling in full song, and all Seville was fragrant with the sweet odor of roses.

January 12, 1881.

B. G. G.

Alexis Maximovich
Peshcov
"Maxim Gorki"

1 8 6 8 — 1 9 3 6

THE WRITER who became famous under the pen name of Maxim Gorki (Maxim Bitter) is one of Russia's Great Self-Taught. He lost his father (an upholsterer) at four, and his mother at seven. His entire formal schooling lasted for five months, at the age of seven; thereafter he learned from men and books; as a reader he was probably more omnivorous than even Samuel Johnson. The schooling was broken off by his being apprenticed to a shoemaker; two months later, after fearfully scalding himself, he was apprenticed to a draftsman. Here the pattern of his adventurous youth (save that it began earlier and was much harsher) becomes similar to the youth-patterns of such writers as Istrati, Kuprin, or our own Mark Twain or Jack London—although it should be definitely understood that Gorki is *not* the Russian Jack London. (Many of

Gorki's works are, naturally, autobiographical; the reader is referred, in particular, to *Childhood* and *My Universities*.)

He became a scullion on a Volga steamer, where the chef, an ex-corporal and a great drunkard, but also very intelligent, taught him how to read and write, a great deal about books, and a little about cooking. Then came another spell at draftsmanship, engraving, icon-painting (and icon-peddling), apple-selling, working as a railroad watchman. At sixteen, in Kazan, he tried to enter school, but free education was not the fashion in Russia at the time. It was at this period that he had to earn his daily bread (literally) by working in a cellar bakery; besides learning to bake bread he mastered the ancient art of pretzel-bending. (A rereading of *Twenty-Six Men and One Girl* is suggested at this point.) Here, too, he was initiated into the revolutionary movement, and was first arrested in 1889.

Leaving Kazan, he tramped through all of the South and Southeast of Russia. In 1890, at Nizhni-Novgorod (since renamed Gorki) he became law-clerk to M. A. Lanin, who did a great deal for his education, and whom Gorki always gratefully remembered as his greatest benefactor. In 1891 he again started off on his wanderings; this is the well-known Volga-boatman period, when he hauled barges together with another unknown, Fedor Chaliapin. Gorki had been keeping a diary since the age of ten, but now he began writing in earnest. And in 1892, while he was working at a railroad repair shop in Tiflis, *Makar Chudra,* his first story, was published under the now famous pen name in a local newspaper.

In 1894 he returned to Nizhni, where he became a provincial journalist, and next year met Korolenco, who helped him break into the "thick-paper" magazines with *Chelkash.* Despite his increasing reputation he did not abandon journalism until, with the publication of his collected short stories in 1898, his success became overwhelming. He attained celebrity not only in Russia but abroad. In Petersburg (1899-1901) he became more active than ever as a revolutionary, and was the mainstay of the radical periodical *Life,* to which he contributed, among other things, *Thoma Gordeiev* and, above all, *The Song of the Stormy Petrel,* a poem prophesying the approach-

ing revolution but bringing about the immediate suppression of the review and the author's arrest and banishment to Arzamas.

In 1902 *The Lowest Depths* was produced, under Stanislavski, and attained enormous popularity not only in Russia but throughout the world. (It is here given, without any grace notes, as a living and enduring play.)

In January, 1905, Gorki was arrested and confined in that forcing-bed of Russian literature, the Fortress of SS Peter and Paul, for taking part in a protest against Bloody Sunday ($^{1/9}$ O. S./$_{1/22}$ N. S.) the opening of the Revolution of 1905), which imprisonment in its turn caused a world-wide protest. After his release he did not at all desist, but took a very active part in the armed rebellion in the December of the same year in Moscow. In 1906, after a series of triumphant receptions in Finland and Scandinavia, he was met with ovations in New York. When it was discovered, however, that his wife (a great actress) was his wife only at common law, Gorki was unable to find a single hotel to put him up for even a night. The press (which edified all America with the Stanford White murder the same year) became a yelping, baying pack; the gentle William Dean Howells and that firebrand-under-wraps, Mark Twain, who had charge of a banquet in honor of Gorki, turned tail and scurried off on all fours—in interesting contrast to the gentle Chekhov and outspoken Korolenco who, in 1902, when Gorki's election to the Academy of Science was rescinded, were not afraid to stand up on their hind legs and resign as Academicians as a protest against Nicholas II.[1]

Gorki had pulmonary tuberculosis, which compelled him to live for long periods at Capri; he went there in 1907 and did not return to Russia until 1913. (The help he rendered when Messina was devastated by earthquake and tidal wave in 1908 was enormous, yet only a small part of the concrete good he did throughout his life.) During World War I he was antimilitaristic, and in 1917 accepted the Revolution, although not without certain differences of opinion. From then to the very end of his life he performed miracles in preserving the existent Russian culture and bringing into being a new one.

In 1921 his health again compelled him to live in Capri, where, however, he remained as active as ever; he returned to Russia permanently in 1929; his forty-year jubilee as a writer was celebrated throughout the Soviets in 1932.

There have been innumerable studies comparing and contrasting Tolstoi and Dostoievski; a fascinating one could be written about Gorki and Tolstoi. Both loved their Russia; each one tried to save it in his own way: Tolstoi through passivity and spirituality, Gorki through action and practicality. Tolstoi made

the grand but inutile gesture of renouncing his enormous royalties; Gorki spent his fabulous earnings as a writer in financing the revolutionary movement. But the most impressive difference is that there was no rupture in Gorki: Gorki the man kept growing in stature as an artist to the very end. You will find no story in Gorki preaching that the muzhik is badly off only when he has too much bread, or that if the muzhik will only keep a miraculous taper burning at the horse's tail if he's made to work on a holiday, Something or Somebody will see to it that the inhuman overseer will meet with a particularly messy, nasty death.

As writer, Gorki has been given as many labels as Polonius gave to the drama. He has been called a realist, a romanticist, a romantic realist, and a realistic romanticist. His popularity can hardly be accounted for by the novelty of milieu and characters in his early writings: Uspenski, Zlatovretski, and Levitov had written of the dregs of society before, although perhaps not appealingly or objectively, and such stories by no means preponderate in Gorki's work, although, regrettably enough, it is precisely for these stories of philosophical tramps and noblehearted prostitutes that Gorki has become best known abroad. He himself disliked this early vein of his, these "truthful lies." Gorki the humorist and, above all, Gorki the poet, with his affirmation of the grandeur and

---

[1] It is a pity that Gorki's *The City of the Yellow Devil, A High-Priest of Morals, A King of the Republic*, etc., are hardly likely ever to appear in English; they are superb Americana for the Year of the Great Thaw.

beauty of life, remains unknown outside of Russia, and his marvelous descriptions of steppe, sea, and sun remain the sole property of the Russians. (It is a source of particular satisfaction to represent Gorki here with *The Clown,* in a light that will probably be novel to the reader.)

Vulgarity, according to Gorki, was sworn enemy to Chekhov. And Gorki himself directed all his wonderfully keen and penetrating powers of observation, all his capacity for truth-telling, against what he was a sworn foe of, what he had the utmost detestation for, and regarded as the source of all vulgarity—*meshchantstvo,* which is but mildly rendered by *bourgeoisie.*

Chekhov, in his *Sea Gull,* gave Russia a symbol of the receding past. Gorki, in his *Song of the Stormy Petrel,* offered a symbol of protest and revolt and, in his *Song of the Falcon,* loosed a symbol of faith in a glorious future.

The Clown

ONE DAY, as I was going through one of the passages of a circus, I happened to look in at the open door of a clown's dressing room and, becoming interested in him, stopped. In a long frock coat, wearing an opera hat and gloves, with a slender cane under his armpit, he was standing in front of a mirror and, raising his hat with a beautiful gesture of his dexterous hand, was bowing and scraping before his mirrored reflection.

Noticing in the mirror my astonished face, he quickly turned around to me and said with a smile, pointing a finger at his face in the mirror:

"I—I! Yes?"

Then he moved aside; his reflection in the mirror vanished; he slowly passed his hand through the air and spoke anew:

"I no more! Understand?"

I did not grasp this by-play, became embarrassed, and went off, followed by his soft laughter, but from that moment on the clown assumed an unusual and disquieting interest for me.

He was an Englishman, middle-aged, with dark eyes, exceedingly adroit and amusing in the arena, in the center of the dark funnel of the circus. His smooth, spare face seemed to me significant and clever, while his ringing voice sounded mocking, well-nigh unpleasant in my

Translated by Bernard Guilbert Guerney. Copyright, 1943, by the Vanguard Press, Inc.

ears when the clown, performing on the tanbark of the arena just like a huge tomcat, called out broken Russian words.

After those bows in front of the mirror I began shadowing him; during the intermissions I hung around the narrow door of his dressing room, observing him as he applied clown-white to his face or rubbed black and red grease paint off it as he sat before his mirror. No matter what he may have been doing, he always talked to himself or hummed, whistling some song that was always one and the same.

I saw him in the barroom drinking vodka in small sips, and heard him ask the bartender in broken Russian:

"What time?"

"Ten to twelve."

"Oh, that hard! But not hard is—" and he began to count: *"Od-din, duva, tiri, chertiri.* Most easy is *chertiri!"*

He tossed a silver coin on the zinc bar and went out into the street humming: *"Tiri, chertiri—tiri, chertiri!"*

He always strolled about by himself, while I tailed him like a detective, and it seemed to me that this man lived an especial, mysterious life and that he looked upon everything in a way that could never be mine. At times I tried to imagine myself in England: understood by no one, fearfully alien to everything, deafened by the mighty din of a life unfamiliar to me—would I be able to live with just as calm a smile, on terms of friendship only with myself, as this stalwart, graceful dandy lived?

I invented sundry incidents in which this Englishman played the rôle of a gallant hero, I adorned him with all the virtues known to me, and admired him. He reminded me of Dickens' people, obdurate in evil and good.

Once, in the daytime, as I was crossing a bridge over the Oka, I happened to see him sitting on the edge of one of the pontoons, fishing; I stopped and watched him until he was all through. Every time he hooked a ruff or a perch he would pull it out, bring it close to his face and whistle ever so softly into the fish's mouth, after which he would carefully take it off the hook and throw it back in the water. Whenever he baited his hook with a worm he would say something to it, and if a rowboat came out from under the bridge the clown would doff his small, brimless cap and bow amiably to the strangers—and, if he was answered, would pull a dreadfully astonished face, with his eyebrows raised high. In general he knew how to amuse himself and, evidently, loved to do so.

Another time I saw him up on a hill, in the small garden of the Church of the Assumption. He was looking down on the fair, which seemed driven in like a wedge between the Volga and the Oka; he was holding his slender cane and, running his fingers over it as if it were a flute, was softly whistling something. The muffled, confused din of a life alien to him was floating up from the Volga and the fair toward the sultry sky. Steamers, barges, rowboats crept with difficulty over the filthy water, over the iridescent petroleum blotches; whistles and metallic scraping reached his ears; somebody's broad palms were smacking the water, mightily and fast, while in the distance, beyond the bends of the river, there was a forest fire, and the dully red sun—shorn of its rays, a bald sun—hung motionless in the smoky sky.

Tapping his cane against the trunk of a tree the clown began singing, ever so softly, as if he were chanting a prayer: *"One, dawn, lawn, dear—"*

His face was pensive and serious, his eyebrows contracted; the strange sounds of his song evoked in me a certain apprehensive mood: I wanted to escort him safely home, to the fair.

Suddenly a surly, shaggy dog bobbed up from somewhere. It went past the clown, sat down two steps away from him on the dusty grass, and, after a prolonged yawn, gave him a sidelong look. The clown straightened up and, putting the cane up to his shoulder, as if it were a gun and not a cane, aimed it at the animal.

"Urrr," the dog emitted a low growl.

"Rrr-haow!" the clown answered it in excellent canine language. The dog got up and slunk away in a huff, while the clown looked back and, noticing me under a tree, winked at me amiably.

He was dressed like a dandy, as always, in a long gray coat with trousers to match; he had on a glossy opera hat and was beautifully shod. I thought to myself that only a clown, having dressed himself so aristocratically, could behave himself like an urchin out in public. And, in general, it seemed to me that this man, alien to everybody, deprived of his language, felt himself so free amid the bustle of the town and the fair only because he was a clown.

He trod the sidewalks like an important personage, without yielding his right of way to anybody, stepping aside only for women. And I saw that whenever anybody in the crowd brushed against him with elbow or shoulder he always, calmly and squeamishly, dusted off something with his gloved hand from the spot the stranger had touched.

The grave Russians and the others collided without paying much attention to the matter and, even when they ran full tilt into one another, face to face, did not excuse themselves, did not lift their caps or hats with a polite gesture. In the walk of these grave people there was something unseeing, something burden-laden; anybody could see that these people were in a hurry and that they had no time to give the right of way to one another.

But the clown strutted about insouciantly, like a glutted raven on a battlefield, and it seemed to me that he wanted to abash and annihilate everybody in his way by his politeness. This—or it may have been something else about him—provoked an unpleasant feeling within me.

Naturally, he saw that people are rude; he understood that, in passing, they insulted one another with vile oaths—he could not but see and understand this. But he passed through the torrents of humanity rushing over the sidewalks as though he did not see anything, and I thought angrily: "You're putting on an act; I don't believe you."

But I considered myself absolutely insulted when I once noticed this dandy helping a drunkard who had been knocked down by a horse to get up, placing him on his feet, and immediately thereafter, his fingers working ever so meticulously, peeling off his yellow gloves and throwing them into the mud.

The gala performance at the circus ended after midnight. It was the end of August; an autumn rain, as fine as powdered glass, was falling from the black void over the monotonous rows of the fair's structures. The turbid blotches of the street lamps dissolved in the damp air. The wheels of the hired carriages rumbled over the worn cobbles of the roadway; the horde of gallery gods was yelling as it poured out of the side exits of the circus.

The clown came out into the street in a long, shaggy overcoat, with a cap to match, and his slender cane tucked under his armpit. After a look into the darkness overhead he took his hands out of his pockets, turned up the collar of his overcoat, and, as unhurriedly as ever yet with brisk steps, started to cross the square.

I knew that he was staying at a hotel not far from the circus, but he was walking away from his quarters.

I could hear him whistling as I walked behind him.

Reflections of light drowned in the puddles amid the cobbles of the roadway; black horses overtook us, the water sloshing under the tires of carriage wheels; music poured torrentially out of tavern windows; women squealed in the darkness. The shiftless, dissolute night of the fair was beginning.

Young ladies floated along the sidewalk like ducks; they accosted the men, and their voices were hoarse from the damp.

There, one of them accosted the clown; in a bass that sounded like a deacon's she invited him to come along with her. He took a step back, snatched the cane out from under his armpit, and, holding it like a saber, silently pointed it straight at the woman's face. She cursed and leaped aside, while he, without hastening his steps, turned a corner and went down a street that was as straight as a taut guitar string. Somewhere far ahead of us some people were laughing, feet were scraping over the brick sidewalk, and a feminine voice was painfully squealing.

A score of steps—and I saw, in the dim light of a street lamp, that three of the fair watchmen were fussing on the sidewalk, amusing themselves with a woman, taking her around, mauling and hugging her, and passing her from hand to hand. The woman was squealing just like a tiny dog; she stumbled, swaying as the huge paws pushed her, and the whole width of the sidewalk was taken up with the to-do of these drab, dank people.

As the clown walked up to them he took his cane anew from under his armpit, and anew began using it like a sword, quickly and deftly pointing it at the faces of the watchmen.

They began to growl, heavily stomping on the bricks of the sidewalk but without making way for the clown; then one of them threw himself under his feet, calling out hoarsely:

"Grab him!"

The clown fell; the disheveled woman made a headlong dash past him, adjusting her skirt as she ran and cursing hoarsely:

"Sonsabitches! Basta'ds!"

"Tie him up!" a voice commanded ferociously. "Ah-ha, so you'd use a stick, would you?"

The clown ringingly cried out something in a foreign language; he was lying face down on the sidewalk and his heels were kicking the back of the man sitting astride the small of the clown's back, twisting his arms backward.

"Oho, you devil! Lift him up! Take him away!"

Leaning against a cast-iron pillar supporting the roof of an arcade I saw three figures, closely linked in the darkness, going off into the raw distance of the street—going off slowly and swayingly, as though the wind were impelling them.

The watchman who had been left behind had lit a match and, squatting on his heels, was searching for something on the sidewalk.

"Go easy!" he said, when I approached. "Don't step on my whistle; I dropped it."

"Who's the fellow they took away?" I asked.

"Oh, nobody in particular!"

"What did he do?"

"He wouldn't have been took if he hadn't been up to something—"

I had an unpleasant feeling, a sense of injury; but just the same, I remember, I thought triumphantly: "There, now!"

A week later I saw the clown again. He was rolling about the arena like a tomcat in motley; he shouted, he leaped about.

But it appeared to me that he was performing not so well as before, not so entertainingly.

And, as I watched him, I felt myself guilty in some way.

The Lowest Depths

CHARACTERS

MICHAEL IVANOV KOSTYLEV, *Keeper of the lodging house;* 54

MEDVEDEV, *policeman, Uncle of Vassilissa and Natasha;* 50

VASSKA PEPEL, 28

ANDREW MITRICH KLESHCH, *Locksmith;* 40

BUBNOV, *Capmaker;* 45

SATIN } *approximately the same*
The ACTOR } *age, under* 40

The BARON, 33

LUKE, *a Pilgrim;* 60

ALESHKA, *Shoemaker;* 20

CROOKED WEN }
TATAR } *Roustabouts*

Several Tramps: *Walk-ons*

VASSILISSA KARPOVNA, *Wife of Kostylev;* 26

NATASHA, *her Sister;* 20

ANNA, *Wife of Kleshch;* 30

NASTYA, *a Professional Woman;* 24

DOUGH PAN, *a Huckstress of dumplings; under* 40

Several Women: *Walk-ons*

ACT I

A cavernous basement. Massive ceiling; stone arches, sooty and with the plaster peeling. Back, center, door into entry. Light is away from spectators, and falls from a square window near ceiling, right. Corner, right, is taken up with PEPEL'S *room, partitioned off with deal; near door of this room is* BUBNOV'S *bunk. In the corner, left, is a huge, square Russian stove (usually built like a kiln, of bricks and white-washed); in the stone wall, left, is door into kitchen, where* DOUGH PAN, NASTYA *and the* BARON *live. Near the wall, between the stove and door, is a wide bed, screened with a curtain of dirty calico. There are bunks all along the walls. Toward the foot, left, is a block of wood with a vise and a small anvil, and another, smaller block near by. Sitting on it, with the anvil before him, is* KLESHCH, *fitting keys to old locks. At his feet are two huge rings of wire, holding hundreds of keys, a battered white-metal samovar, a hammer and files. In the middle of the lodging house stands a big table, with two benches and a tabouret; all these are unpainted and dirty.* DOUGH PAN *is presiding, with a samovar before her; also seated at the table are the* BARON, *chewing a crust of black bread, and* NASTYA, *on the tabouret, reading a tattered book, with her elbows propped up on the table.* ANNA, *lying on the curtained-off bed, is coughing.*

BUBNOV, *sitting on his bunk, is measuring an old pair of trousers, ripped apart at the seams, against a hat block squeezed between his knees, planning the best way to cut the cloth into caps. Near by is a torn hatbox, to cut visors from, scraps of oilcloth, and rags.* SATIN *has just awakened; he lies on his bunk, grousing. The* ACTOR, *out of sight on top of the oven, is fussing and coughing.*

The beginning of spring. Morning.

BARON: Continue!

DOUGH PAN: "Oh, no, darling," I says, "you get away from me with that stuff. I been all through it," I says, "and I wouldn't go to the altar now if you was to tempt me with the world and all!"

BUBNOV (*to* SATIN): What are you bellyaching about? (SATIN *growls again.*)

DOUGH PAN: "What—me, a free woman," I says, "and my own boss, and I should go on somebody else's passport and give myself up for a slave—oh, no!" Why, if he was to be an American prince I wouldn't think of marrying him!

KLESHCH: You lie!

DOUGH PAN: Wha-at!

KLESHCH: You lie! You'll get hitched to Abie.

BARON (*snatching book away from* NASTYA *and reading the title*): "Fatal Love"—(*Goes off into peals of laughter.*)

NASTYA (*holding her hand out for the book*): Give me that! Give it back to me! There, stop annoying me. (BARON *watches her, waving the book out of her reach.*)

DOUGH PAN (*to* KLESHCH): Why, you readheaded goat! Where do you get off telling me I lie? Why, where do you get off speaking so fresh to me?

BARON (*hitting* NASTYA *over the head with the book*): You're a fool, Nastka.

NASTYA (*snatching the book away*): Give me that!

KLESHCH: My, what a great lady! But as for Abie, you're going to get hitched to him. That's all you're waiting for.

DOUGH PAN: Of course! Sure! What else! But as for you, you've driven your wife so hard she's half dead—

KLESHCH: Shut your mouth, you old bitch! It's none of your business.

DOUGH PAN: Aha! You can't stand the truth.

BARON: They're off. Nastka, where do you think you are now?

NASTYA (*without raising her head*): Oh, go away!

ANNA (*putting her head out from behind the curtain*): The day has begun. For God's sake don't yell! Stop cursing one another—

KLESHCH: She's off on her whining—

ANNA: Not a day passes by without that. You might at least let me die in peace.

BUBNOV: Noise don't interfere with dying.

DOUGH PAN (*approaching* ANNA): Say, how did you ever manage to live with a scrooge like that?

ANNA: Leave off. . . . Leave me alone.

DOUGH PAN: We-ell! Eh, you long-suffering creature! Your chest, now—has it let up any?

BARON: Say, Dough Pan—time to be going to the market place.

DOUGH PAN: We're going right away. (*To* ANNA.) Care for some good hot dumplin's? I'll give you some.

ANNA: No. Thanks, just the same. What's the use my eating?

DOUGH PAN: You just go ahead and eat 'em, now. Hot stuff makes you feel better. I'll put some aside for you in a bowl. If you should feel like it any time, go ahead and eat 'em! (*To the* BARON.) Come along, my fine gentleman! (*To* KLESHCH.) Ugh, you foul devil! (*Goes off into kitchen.*)

ANNA (*coughing*): Oh, Lord.

BARON (*gently tapping the nape of* NASTYA'S *neck*): Drop that, you big ninny!

NASTYA (*mumbling*): Get away from me. I'm not bothering you. (*The* BARON, *softly whistling, follows* DOUGH PAN *into the kitchen.*)

SATIN (*raising himself a little on his bunk*): Just who was it beat me up yesterday?

BUBNOV: Why, does it make any difference to you?

SATIN: You're right, at that. But what was it they beat me up for?

BUBNOV: You was playing cards, wasn't you?

SATIN: I was that—

BUBNOV: That's just what they beat you up for.

SATIN: The low-down b-b-bums!

ACTOR (*showing his head on top of the stove*): They'll kill you for good one of these days.

SATIN: My, but is your head made out of wood!

ACTOR: How do you figure that out?

SATIN: Ever hear of anybody getting killed two days in a row?

ACTOR (*after reflecting a few moments*): I don't get it. Why not?

KLESHCH: Be that as it may, you'd better get down off of there and tidy up the place. Why should you be taking it so easy?

ACTOR: That's none of your business.

KLESHCH: Well, you just wait till Vassilissa gets here; she'll show you whose business it is.

ACTOR: The hell with Vassilissa! It's the Baron's turn to tidy up today. Hey, Baron!

BARON (*emerging from kitchen*): I haven't the time to tidy up. I'm going to the market place with Dough Pan.

ACTOR: That doesn't concern me. You can go to jail, for all I care. After all, it's your turn to sweep up. I'm not going to do anybody else's work.

BARON: Well, the hell with you. Nastenka will sweep up. Hey, you—Fatal Love! Wake up! (*Takes book away from* NASTYA.)

NASTYA (*getting up*): What do you want? Let me have that back! Always making trouble. And yet he's a gentleman!

BARON (*returning the book to her*): Nastya, sweep up for me? All right? (*Returns to kitchen.*)

NASTYA (*going into kitchen*): Sure thing! Watch me do it!

DOUGH PAN (*in the kitchen doorway, to* BARON): You just come along; they'll tidy up without you. Listen, Actor, when you're asked to do something, you just go ahead and do it. I guess it won't kill you!

ACTOR: Well . . . it's always me! I can't understand why—

BARON (*emerging from kitchen, under a yoke with a basket at each end; there is a large pot, covered with rags, in each basket*): They're kind of heavy today, somehow—

SATIN: What did you have to go and be born a Baron for?

DOUGH PAN (*to* ACTOR): Mind you, now—you sweep up! (*Exit into entry—but lets the* BARON *precede her.*)

ACTOR (*crawling down from the stove*): Breathing dust is bad for me. (*With pride.*) My organism is poisoned with alcohol. (*Sits down on a bunk and falls into a brown study.*)

SATIN (*mockingly, and relishing the big words*): Organism. . . . Organon. . . .

ANNA: Andrei Mitrich—

KLESHCH: What now?

ANNA: Dough Pan left some dumplings in the kitchen. You take 'em.

KLESHCH (*approaching her*): Why, aren't you going to eat 'em?

ANNA: I don't feel like it. What's the use of my eating? You work; you've got to have food.

KLESHCH: Are you afraid? Don't be afraid; maybe you'll still—

ANNA: Go ahead and eat 'em! I'm in a bad way. Looks as if it won't be long now—

KLESHCH (*going away*): Never mind. You may get up on your feet yet. Things like that do happen! (*Exit into kitchen.*)

ACTOR (*loudly, as though he had suddenly awakened*): Yesterday, at the clinic, the Doctor says to me: "Your organism," he says, "is thoroughly poisoned with alcohol!"

SATIN (*grinning*): Organon—

ACTOR (*bent on having his own way*): Not organon, but or-ga-ni-sm!

SATIN (*mouthing the word*): Sicambrian!

ACTOR (*with an "I-give-you-up!" gesture toward* SATIN): Eh, with you it's always double talk. I'm telling you this in all seriousness. Yes. If the organism is poisoned, it means that it's harmful for me to sweep the floor—to breathe in the dust—

SATIN (*in the same vein*): Microbiotics! (*Sniggers.*)

BUBNOV: What are you battin' about?

SATIN: Just words. And I know still another one: Trans-cen-den-tal.

BUBNOV: What may that be?

SATIN: Don't know. I've forgotten.

BUBNOV: Why do you use it, then?

SATIN: Just so. Brother, I'm fed up with all human words. Fed up with all our words! I've heard every one of 'em—thousands of times, for sure!

ACTOR: There's a scene in the tragedy of *Hamlet* that goes, "Words, words, words. . . ." A good thing, that drama. I played one of the gravediggers in it.

KLESHCH (*emerging from the kitchen*): Are you going to start playing with the broom soon?

ACTOR: None of your business. (*Beating his breast.*)

> The fair Ophelia! Nymph, in thy orisons,
> Be all my sins remember'd.

(*A muffled uproar, shouts, shrill sound of a policeman's whistle, are heard, off, somewhere in the distance.* KLESHCH *sits down to his work, scraping away with a file.*)

SATIN: I love words I can't understand—odd words. When I was a youngster I used to work in a telegraph office. I read a lot of books.

BUBNOV: So you were a telegraph operator, too?

SATIN: I was. There are very good books—and no end of curious words. I was a well-educated man—do you know that?

BUBNOV: So I've heard—a hundred times! Well, supposing you was—what a great thing! Me, now, I was a fur dresser, had my own establishment. My hands was that yellow from dye; I used to dye furs, so my hands was all yellow—my arms, too, right up to the elbows! I was beginning to think I'd never wash 'em clean to my dying day, that I'd just die with my hands and arms all yellow. But now, there they are; my hands are just plain dirty. Yes, Sir!

SATIN: Well, what else were you?

BUBNOV: Why, nothing else.

SATIN: What are you driving at?

BUBNOV: I just said it . . . by way of example. It turns out that no matter how you paint yourself on the outside, it'll all rub off. Yes, Sir—it'll all rub off.

SATIN: A-ah! All my bones are aching!

ACTOR (*clasping his knees as he sits up on the bunk*): Education is all bosh; the main thing is talent. I knew a certain actor; it was all he could do to spell out his parts, but he played heroes in such a way he made the audience bring the house down——

SATIN: Bubnov, let me have five kopecks! That's all!

BUBNOV: All I've got to my name is two kopecks.

ACTOR: What I'm saying is that talent is what a leading man needs. And talent is faith in your own self, in your own power.

SATIN: You give me five kopecks, and I'll believe that you're a talented man, a hero, a crocodile, a constable. Kleshch, give me five kopecks!

KLESHCH: Go to hell! There's a lot of your sort around here.

SATIN: What are you cursing for? Besides, you haven't got a copper, I know.

ANNA: Andrei Mitrich! I'm stifling. . . . I feel so bad——

KLESHCH: Well, what can I do?

BUBNOV: Open the door into the entry——

KLESHCH: Fine! You're sitting on your bunk, but me, I'm almost on the floor. You let me sit in your place, and then go ahead and open the door. But me, I've got a cold as it is.

BUBNOV (*unruffled*): I don't need that door open. It's your wife that's askin' for it.

KLESHCH (*glumly*): There's lots of people asking for lots of things.

SATIN: Eh, but my head is buzzing! And why must people go socking other people over the bean?

BUBNOV: They don't sock you only over the bean, but all the rest of the body as well. (*Getting up.*) I got to go out and buy me some thread. Say, we haven't seen our landlords for a long spell today, somehow. Just as though they'd croaked. (*Exit.* ANNA *coughs.* SATIN *is lying down, with his hands clasped behind his head.*)

ACTOR (*going up to* ANNA, *after dismally surveying the room*): Well, how are things? Bad?

ANNA: It's stifling in here.

ACTOR: Want me to help you out into the entry? Very well, get up. (*Helps her up, throws some sort of ragged garment over her shoulders, and, supporting her, leads her toward entry.*) There, there, keep your chin up! I'm sick myself—all poisoned with alcohol——

KOSTYLEV (*appearing in the entry doorway*): Going for a promenade? Ah, what a fine couple—an old ram and a little lamb——

ACTOR: You just stand aside. Can't you tell sick people when you come across them?

KOSTYLEV: Pass, if you please! (*Exeunt* ACTOR *and* ANNA. KOSTYLEV, *humming something on the psalm-snuffling side, looks suspiciously over his lodging house and, cocking his head to the left, seems to be listening to something going on in* PEPEL'S *room.* KLESHCH *clanks his keys and scrapes away with his file ferociously as he watches the landlord furtively.*) Scraping away, are you?

KLESHCH: What?

KOSTYLEV: Scraping away, I said? (*Pause.*) Er-er . . . now . . . what was it I wanted to ask you? (*Quickly and in a low voice.*) My wife hasn't been here?

KLESHCH: Haven't seen her.

KOSTYLEV (*cautiously drawing nearer to the door of* PEPEL'S *room*): Just see how much of my space you're taking up for the two rubles a month! A bed, and where you yourself sit. Yes, Sir! Enough for all of five rubles, by God! I'll have to tack on half a ruble a month to your rent—

KLESHCH: Why not take a noose, now, and just throw it around my neck and strangle me? You're going to croak soon, and yet you never think of anything but half-rubles—

KOSTYLEV: Why go strangling you? Who'd get any benefit out of it? The Lord be with you; live on and enjoy life, for all of me. But just the same I'll tack on another half-ruble to your rent: it'll buy some oil for an icon-lamp . . . and this my offering will burn before a holy image. . . . That offering will do for me, in atonement of my sins, and for you as well. For you yourself never think of your sins. And that's that. Eh, Andy, but you're an evil-tempered man! Your wife has wasted away because of your evil deeds. Nobody loves you, or respects you; your work is rasping on the nerves, upsetting everybody—

KLESHCH (*shouting*): What are you after? Did you come here to madden me? (SATIN *emits a loud growl.*)

KOSTYLEV (*with a shudder*): What's gotten into you, friend?

ACTOR (*entering*): I made her comfortable out in the entry, and wrapped her up.

KOSTYLEV: What a kindhearted man you are, brother! That's a good deed; it'll be credited to your account—

ACTOR: When?

KOSTYLEV: In the other world, little brother. There everything, every deed of ours, is accounted for.

ACTOR: Well, you might reward me right here and now for my goodness.

KOSTYLEV: Why, how could I do that?

ACTOR: Knock off half of what I owe you.

KOSTYLEV: Hee-hee! You're always joking, dear man, always fooling around. For how can anyone compare kindness of heart with money? Kindness is above all good things, whilst your debt to me is nothing but a debt. Therefore, you must pay it to me. Your kindness to an old man like me must be shown to me without any reward.

ACTOR: You're a swindler, old man. (*Exit into kitchen.* KLESHCH *gets up and goes into entry.*)

KOSTYLEV (*to* SATIN): Did you see that rasping fellow? He run off, hee-hee! He don't have much love for me.

SATIN: Who has—outside of the Devil?

KOSTYLEV (*with a sly smile*): What a foul-mouthed fellow! And yet I love all of you. I understand that you are all my brethren, miserable, unfit for anything, all lost. . . . (*Suddenly and briskly.*) But—what about Vasska? Is he in?

SATIN: Take a look.

KOSTYLEV (*walking up to door of* PEPEL'S *room and knocking*): Vassya! (ACTOR *appears in kitchen doorway; he is chewing something.*)

PEPEL (*off*): Who's there?

KOSTYLEV: It's me—me, Vassya.

PEPEL: What do you want?

KOSTYLEV (*moving to one side of door*): Open up.

SATIN (*without looking at* KOSTYLEV): He'll open up—and there she'll be. (*The* ACTOR *guffaws.*)

KOSTYLEV (*in a low, worried voice*): Eh? Who's there? What . . . what are you up to?

SATIN: What? Are you talking to me?

KOSTYLEV: What did you say?

SATIN: Oh, I was just talking—to myself.

KOSTYLEV: Watch your step, brother! A joke's a joke, but don't go too far! Yes! (*Pounds on door.*) Vassilii!

PEPEL (*opening door*): Well? What are you disturbing me for?

KOSTYLEV (*peeking into* PEPEL'S *room*): I. . . . You see—

PEPEL: Did you bring the money?

KOSTYLEV: I have some business with you.

PEPEL: Did you bring the money?

KOSTYLEV: What money? Hold on—

PEPEL: The money—seven rubles for the watch. What about it?

KOSTYLEV: What watch, Vassya? Why, you know——

PEPEL: You look out, now! Yesterday, in front of witnesses, I sold you a watch for ten rubles; three I got——come across with the other seven! What are you batting your eyes at me for? Snooping around, disturbing people——yet you don't know your own business!

KOSTYLEV: Shhh. . . . Don't fly off the handle, Vassya. That watch, now, is——

PEPEL: Stolen.

KOSTYLEV (*sternly*): I don't receive stolen goods. How can you say such a thing?

PEPEL (*grabbing* KOSTYLEV *by the shoulder*): What did you bother me for? What do you want?

KOSTYLEV: Why . . . I don't want a thing. I'll go. If that's the way you act——

PEPEL: Get going; bring me the money!

KOSTYLEV (*going out*): What a rough crowd! My, my! (*Exit.*)

ACTOR: What a comedy!

SATIN: That's swell! I like it.

PEPEL: What was he up to?

SATIN (*laughing*): Don't you get it? He's looking for his wife. Say, why don't you bump him off when you have a little time to spare, Vassilii?

PEPEL: I should spoil my life over a louse like that.

SATIN: No, you do it a smart way. Then marry Vassilissa; you'll be our landlord——

PEPEL: That'd be just too lovely! Not only will you sell all my property to booze with but, through my kindness of heart, will sell me out as well to get money for more booze. (*Sits down on bunk.*) The bastard, he woke me up. And I was having a swell dream, too: seems like I was fishing, and I hooked the most enormous trout you ever did see! A trout the like of which comes only in a dream. And there I was, playing him, and me afraid the line will break! And I got the landing net all set: There, I thought, I'll land him right away——

SATIN: That was no trout; it was Vassilissa.

ACTOR: He landed Vassilissa a long time ago.

PEPEL (*angrily*): Go to hell, the both of you——and take her along with you!

KLESHCH (*coming in from entry*): It's as cold as a son-of-a-bitch!

ACTOR: How is it you didn't bring Anna in? She'll freeze to death.

KLESHCH: Natashka took her along to their kitchen.

ACTOR: The old devil will chase her out.

KLESHCH (*sitting down to his work*): Oh, Natashka will bring her back.

SATIN: Vassilii, give me five kopecks!

ACTOR (*to* SATIN): Eh, you and your five kopecks! Give us twenty kopecks, Vassya!

PEPEL: I'd better give it to you quick—before you ask me for a whole ruble. Here you are! (*Hands some silver to* ACTOR.)

SATIN: Gibraltar! There are no better people on earth than thieves!

KLESHCH (*glumly*): Money comes easy to them. They don't work.

SATIN: Money comes easy to lots of people, but there aren't many that part with it easy. Work? You arrange things so that work will be a pleasure for me; I'll go to work then—maybe. . . . Yes—could be! When work is a pleasure life is good! When work is a task, life is slavery. (*To* ACTOR.) Hey, there, Sardanapalus! Come on!

ACTOR: Come on, Nebuchadnezzar! I'll get as drunk as forty thousand drunkards! (*Exit, with* SATIN.)

PEPEL (*yawning*): Well, how's your wife?

KLESHCH: Looks like it'll be over soon. (*Pause.*)

PEPEL: I'm looking at you—and it seems like all your scraping is for nothing.

KLESHCH: Well, what am I to do?

PEPEL: Not a thing.

KLESHCH: How am I going to eat, then?

PEPEL: People do manage to get along somehow—

KLESHCH: The people here? What sort of people are they? Rag, tag, and bobtail; the honey-bucket brigade. People! I'm a workingman; it goes against me just to look at 'em. I been working ever since I was a youngster. You're thinking that I'll never escape out of here? I'll crawl out; I'll leave my skin behind, but crawl out I will. There, you wait . . . till my wife dies. I've lived on here for half a year—yet it's been the same as six years!

PEPEL: Nobody here is any worse than you. You oughtn't to say such things.

KLESHCH: No worse! They live without honor, without conscience—

PEPEL (*apathetically*): And what would they be doing with honor, with conscience? You can't pull either honor or conscience over your legs instead of boots. Honor and conscience is for them that has the rule over others, and power.

BUBNOV (*entering*): Oo-ooh! I'm chilled!

PEPEL: Bubnov, have you got a conscience?

BUBNOV: Wha-at! Conscience, did you say?

PEPEL: Well, yes.

BUBNOV: What do I need a conscience for? I'm no rich man.

PEPEL: There, I'm saying that very same thing! It's the rich that stand in need of honor and conscience. Yes! But Kleshch is giving us hell: We got no conscience, says he.

BUBNOV: Why, what does he want—is he after borrowing some?

PEPEL: He's got a lot of his own.

BUBNOV (*to* KLESHCH): You're selling it, then? Well, you won't find no customers for it here. If it was some busted hatboxes I'd buy 'em off you—and then only on the cuff.

PEPEL (*instructively*): You're a fool, Andy! You ought to hear Satin on the subject of conscience. Or else the Baron.

KLESHCH: I've nothing to talk with them about.

PEPEL: They're smarter than you—even though they're drunks.

BUBNOV: And when a fellow's drunk and smart, there's two good points to him.

PEPEL: Satin says that every man wants his neighbor to have a conscience, but, you see, nobody finds it to his advantage to have any. And that's right. (*Enter* NATASHA, *followed by* LUKE, *with a staff in his hand, a knapsack over his shoulders, and a small pot and teakettle dangling at his belt.*)

LUKE: Good health to all you honest folk!

PEPEL (*stroking his mustache*): Ah, Natasha!

BUBNOV (*to* LUKE): They were honest folk—but that was spring before last.

NATASHA: Here's our new lodger.

LUKE: It don't make no difference to me! I respect crooks, too. To my way of thinkin' there ain't a flea to be found that's bad all around; all of 'em are black little things, all of 'em go hoppety-hop! And that's that. And now, deary, where am I to make myself to home?

NATASHA (*indicating door into kitchen*): Go in there, Grandpa.

LUKE: Thanks, little girl. If that's the place, that's the place. Any place where it's warm is to an old man the place where he was born.

PEPEL (*gallantly*): What an interesting little old man you've brought, Natasha—

NATASHA: More interesting than you. Andrei! Your wife is in our kitchen; you come and fetch her, later on.

KLESHCH: All right, I'll come.

NATASHA: You might sort of . . . treat her a little kinder. For it won't be long now—

KLESHCH: I know.

NATASHA: Yes, you know! But knowing isn't enough; you've got to understand. For it's a fearful thing to be dying.

PEPEL: But you take me now, I'm not afraid.

NATASHA: Oh, sure! Brave, you are!

BUBNOV (*whistling in surprise*): They sold me rotten thread!

PEPEL: Really, I'm not afraid. I could meet my death right now. Take a knife, strike me right through the heart, and I'll die without letting a peep out of me! I'd even die with joy—because the blow would be dealt by a pure hand—

NATASHA (*making her exit*): You go and try that on some other girls.

BUBNOV (*plaintively drawling*): Yep—the thread's all rotten.

NATASHA (*in the door to the entry*): Don't forget about your wife, Andrei.

KLESHCH: All right. (*Exit* NATASHA.)

PEPEL: A good wench!

BUBNOV: Not at all a bad young lady.

PEPEL: Why is she . . . like that to me? Throwing me aside? For she'll go to the dogs here anyway.

BUBNOV: She will—because of you.

PEPEL: Because of me? Why? I feel sorry for her.

BUBNOV: Like a wolf for a lamb?

PEPEL: You lie! I feel very sorry for her. It's a tough life for her here, I can see that.

KLESHCH: Wait till Vassilissa sees you carrying on a conversation with her.

BUBNOV: Vassilissa? Ye-es; she don't give up anything that's hers without a fight. She's one tough baby.

PEPEL (*lying down on the bunk*): Go to hell, both of you! Prophets!

KLESHCH: You'll see. Just wait!

LUKE (*singing in the kitchen in a low, snuffling voice, wringing the last lugubrious drop out of every syllable*):

> In the mi-i-idle of the ni-i-ight
> You can't se-e-e- the ro-o-oad for to ta-a-ake—

KLESHCH (*going off into the entry*): Listen to him howl. Another nuisance—

PEPEL: And yet why do I feel blue? Why do I get these fits of the blues? You live on and on; everything's great! And suddenly it's like you took a chill; you get the blues—

BUBNOV: So you've got the blues? Mm-mmm!

PEPEL: Yes, by God!

LUKE (*still singing*): Eh, you just can't se-e-e the ro-o-oad for to ta-a-ake—

PEPEL: Hey, there, old-timer!

LUKE (*peering out of kitchen door*): Who, me?

PEPEL: Yes, you. Don't sing.

LUKE (*emerging from kitchen*): Don't you like it?

PEPEL: I like it when people sing well.

LUKE: That means, then, I'm not singing well?

PEPEL: It follows—

LUKE: See that! And I was thinkin' I was singing well. There, it always works out like that: a man may be thinking to himself: "I'm doing wonders!" Then he wakes up: people ain't so satisfied—

PEPEL (*laughing*): There you are! That's it!

BUBNOV: You say you're blue—and you're laughing your head off.

PEPEL: Why, what's it to you? You raven—

LUKE: Who's blue, now?

PEPEL: Me, that's who. (*Enter* BARON.)

LUKE: See that! And there, in the kitchen, there's a young lady sitting, reading a book and crying! Honest! The tears is just running down her face. And I says to her: "What's it all about—eh, darlin'?" And she says: "I feel sorry." "Who you feelin' sorry for?" I says. "Why," she says, "for the people in this here book."—There, that's what a person occupies herself with, eh? Evidently that's also because of the blues—

BARON: That woman's a fool.

PEPEL: Have you had tea yet, Baron?

BARON: I have. Continue!

PEPEL: Would you like me to treat you to a half-bottle?

BARON: Naturally. Continue!

PEPEL: Get down on all fours like a dog and bark.

BARON: You fool! What are you—a millionaire? Or are you drunk?

PEPEL: No, you go ahead and bark a little—it'll amuse me. You're a gentleman; there was a time when you didn't think our kind human —and all that sort of thing—

BARON: Very well; continue!

PEPEL: What for? So now I'll make you act like a dog and bark, and you'll do it, too—for you will, won't you?

BARON: I will not! You blockhead! What pleasure could it afford you, when I myself know that I've become just a little short of being worse than you? You might force me to crawl around on all fours, only I'm on the same level as you.

BUBNOV: Right!

LUKE: And I'll say it, too—good for him!

BUBNOV: What has been, has been; while all that's left don't matter a damn. There are no lords and masters here; the color's run off of everything; there's nothing but the naked human creature remaining.

LUKE: All are equal, then? And you, dear man—were you a Baron?

BARON: And what may *this* be? Who are you, scarecrow?

LUKE (*laughing*): I've seen a Count, in my time, and a Grand Duke. But it's the first time I meet up with a Baron—and even then he's shop-worn.

PEPEL (*roaring with laughter*): And yet you had me groggy that time, Baron!

BARON: Time you were a little wiser, Vassilii.

LUKE (*with a sigh*): Eh-heh! I take a look at you, little brothers of mine, and the way you live, now, is. . . . (*With pain.*) My, my!

BUBNOV: The way we live is such, that, the moment you get up in the morning, you set up a howl—

BARON: We've lived better, too . . . yes! I used to wake up in the morning and have my coffee in bed. Coffee—with cream! Yes!

LUKE: Yet all men are human bein's! No matter how you pretend, no matter how you twist and turn, a man you were born, and a man you'll die. And the more I look, the more I see that people are becoming more intelligent, more interestin' like. And although their life is growin' worse and worse, yet they want everythin' to be better and better. A stubborn lot, mankind!

BARON: Who may you be, old-timer? Where did you bob up from?

LUKE: Me, now?

BARON: Are you a pilgrim?

LUKE: All of us here on earth are pilgrims. They say—so I've heard —that even this earth of ours is a pilgrim in the sky.

BARON (*sternly*): All that is so, yes; but have you got a passport?

LUKE (*after due reflection*): And who may you be? A dick?

PEPEL (*gleefully*): That was a honey, old-timer! Well, dear Baron, did you get yours that time?

BUBNOV: Ye-es, the gentleman got his.

BARON (*embarrassed*): There, why raise a fuss? I'm only joking, old-timer! I myself haven't got any papers—

BUBNOV: You lie!

BARON: That is, I have papers, but they're no damned good.

LUKE: All those papers of all sorts—they're all no good.

PEPEL: Let's go to a ginmill, Baron!

BARON: I'm right with you there! Well, good-by, old-timer. You old swindler!

LUKE: It takes all kinds to make this world, dear man.

PEPEL (*in doorway of entry*): Well, are we going, or what? (*Exit.* BARON *hurries after him.*)

LUKE: Was the man a Baron, for a fact?

BUBNOV: Who knows anything about him? He's a gentleman, that's true. And even now he'll keep on and on, and then all of a sudden show that he is a gentleman. Hasn't got over it yet, evidently.

LUKE: Gentlemanliness is something like smallpox, you might say: a man may get rid of it, but the marks remain.

BUBNOV: Not a bad fellow, just the same. Only once in a while he'll kick up his heels—like about your passport, for instance.

ALESHKA (*entering, with plenty under his belt, and an accordeon in his hands; he is whistling*): Howya, fellows!

BUBNOV: What are you hollerin' about?

ALESHKA: 'Scuse me . . . f'give me! Can I help it if I'm p'lite?

BUBNOV: Off on a bender again?

ALESHKA: And how! Mediakin, the police captain, he chased me out of his precinct just now, and he says, "I don't want to see nor hide nor hair of you out in the street," he says. No, Siree! I'm a man of character, I am. And my boss he just snaps and snorts at me. But what's a boss? (*With a contemptuous snort.*) Juss a misunderstandin', thass all. He's a rum-hound, my boss is. But I'm the sort of man who don't want nothin'! I don't want nothin'—and thass all there's to it! There, take me for a ruble and twenty kopecks! But me, I don't want nothin'! (NASTYA *comes out of kitchen.*) You give me a million, and I wouldn't touch it. But when it comes to having a pal that's no more than a boozehound bossing it over a good man like me—I won't have that neither! I jush plain won't stand for nothin' like that! (NASTYA, *standing in kitchen doorway, shakes her head as she watches* ALESHKA.)

LUKE (*good-naturedly*) : Eh, lad, you sure are all in a muddle!

BUBNOV: Human foolishness.

ALESHKA (*sprawling out on the floor*) : There, go ahead and gobble me up! But me, I don't wish for nothin'! I'm a desperate man, I am. Jush explain to me—am I worse'n anybody else? Why am I worse'n anybody else? There, Mediakin he says to me, "Keep off the streets, or I'll smash your puss in for you!" But I'm going jush the same; I'll go and lie down right in the middle of the gutter: go ahead and run me over! Me, I don't wish for nothin'!

NASTYA: The poor little fellow! Still so young, and yet he's already acting up like that.

ALESHKA (*catching sight of her and getting up on his knees*) : Young lady! Mademoiselle! *Parlez français . . . prix courant. . . .* Boy, am I having a time!

NASTYA (*in a loud whisper through entry door*) : Vassilissa!

VASSILISSA (*quickly opening door, to ALESHKA*) : You here again?

ALESHKA: Greetings . . . and welcome—

VASSILISSA: I told you, you puppy, never to show your face here—but you had to come here again?

ALESHKA: Vassilissa Karpovna, would you like me to play a funeral march for you?

VASSILISSA (*giving his shoulder a shove*) : Get out!

ALESHKA (*moving toward entry door*) : Hold on! You mushtn't act like that! A funeral march . . . learned it jush the other day! Bran-new music. . . . Hold on! You mushtn't act like that!

VASSILISSA: I'll show you whether I must or not! I'll sic the whole street against you, you damned heathen, you! You're too young to be yapping about me—

ALESHKA (*running out*) : Very well, I'll go away!

VASSILISSA (*to* BUBNOV) : Don't let him set foot in here! You hear me?

BUBNOV: I'm no watchman for you.

VASSILISSA: I don't give a hang who you are! You're living here out of charity—don't forget that! How much do you owe me?

BUBNOV (*calmly*) : Haven't reckoned it up.

VASSILISSA: Watch out—I'll reckon it up for you!

ALESHKA (*popping entry door open and yelling*) : Well, I ain't afraid of you, Vassilissa Karpovna! I ain't afraid, no Siree! (*Hides in kitchen*—LUKE *laughs.*)

VASSILISSA: Who may you be?

LUKE: Just passing through. A pilgrim.

VASSILISSA: Lodging here for the night, or going to live here?

LUKE: I'll see.

VASSILISSA: Your passport!

LUKE: Why not—

VASSILISSA: Let's have it!

LUKE: I'll bring it. I'll bring it up to your place.

VASSILISSA: Passing through, sure! Why don't you say you're a fly-by-night—it'd be nearer the truth, now.

LUKE (*with a sigh*): My, you ain't at all a kindly soul, mother. (VASSILISSA *goes toward door of* PEPEL'S *room.*)

ALESHKA (*peeping out of the kitchen, in a whisper*): Is she gone? Eh?

VASSILISSA (*turning on him*): You still here? (ALESHKA *whistles and hides.* NASTYA *and* LUKE *laugh.*)

BUBNOV (*to* VASSILISSA): He ain't around.

VASSILISSA: Who do you mean?

BUBNOV: Vasska.

VASSILISSA: Did I ask you about him?

BUBNOV: I see you looking all over—

VASSILISSA: I'm watching out so's everything in order—you understand? How is it this place hasn't been swept up yet? How many times have I given orders that the place should be kept clean?

BUBNOV: It's the Actor's turn to sweep up.

VASSILISSA: I'm not concerned with whose turn it is! But if the sanitation inspectors ever come here and slap on a fine, I'll fire all of you out of here on the spot.

BUBNOV (*calmly*): And where will you get your living from then?

VASSILISSA: I don't want a single speck of dust around here! (*On her way into kitchen turns on* NASTYA.) What are you sticking there for? Why is your puss all swollen? Why do you stand there like a log? Sweep up the floor! Did you see Nathalie? Was she here?

NASTYA: Don't know. Haven't seen her.

VASSILISSA: Was my sister here, Bubnov?

BUBNOV: Why, she brought that there fellow— (*Nodding toward* LUKE.)

VASSILISSA: Was—he here?

BUBNOV: Vassilii? He was. She was talking with Kleshch—Natasha was.

VASSILISSA: I wasn't asking you whom she was talking with! There's dirt everywhere. Up to your neck. Eh, you swine! I want this place cleaned up—you hear me? (*Exit quickly.*)

BUBNOV: What a savage animal that creature is!

LUKE: She won't stand for no fooling, that one.

NASTYA: Anyone would turn into a wild beast, living such a life. You tie any living person to such a husband as she's got—

BUBNOV: Oh, she isn't tied to him with any dead knot!

LUKE: Does she always . . . explode . . . like that?

BUBNOV: Always. She's come to see her lover, you see, and he ain't around.

LUKE: So she felt hurt. Oho-ho! What a lot of all sorts of people are bossing the earth . . . and they frighten one another with all sorts of frightening things, and still there ain't no order in their life . . . and no cleanliness. . . .

BUBNOV: Everybody wants everything to be right as rain but they're short on brains. However, the place ought to be swept up. Nastya, you ought to busy yourself with that!

NASTYA: Oh, sure! What am I—a chambermaid for all of you? (*After a short silence.*) There, I'm going to get drunk today! And how!

BUBNOV: That, too, is a good idea.

LUKE: How come, young lady, you want to get drunk? Just a while back you was cryin'; now you say you're going to get drunk!

NASTYA (*challengingly*): Well, when I get drunk I'll be crying again . . . and that's that!

BUBNOV: Not much to it.

LUKE: But what's your reason, tell me that? For just so, without a reason, even a pimple won't come up. (NASTYA *keeps silent, shaking her head.*) So-o. Eh-heh, my dear folk! Whatever is going to become of you? Well, guess I'll sweep a little here. Where's your broom?

BUBNOV: In the entry, behind the door. (LUKE *goes out into entry.*) Nastenka!

NASTYA: What?

BUBNOV: Why did Vassilissa go for Aleshka like that?

NASTYA: He was saying about her that Vasska is fed up with her and that he wants to throw her over—and get her sister Natasha for himself. I'm getting out of here—to some other place.

BUBNOV: What for? Where are you going?

NASTYA: I'm fed up. I'm one too many here.

BUBNOV (*calmly*): You're one too many anywheres. And besides, all people on this earth are one too many. (NASTYA *shakes her head, gets up, and goes out quietly into the entry. Enter* MEDVEDEV, *followed by* LUKE, *with a broom*.)

MEDVEDEV (*to* LUKE): I don't seem to know you—

LUKE: What about all the others—do you know them?

MEDVEDEV: It's my duty to know everybody in my precinct. But as for you—well, I don't know you.

LUKE: That, Uncle, is because the whole world hasn't found room for itself in your precinct. There's a little bit left over outside of it. (*Goes off into kitchen*.)

MEDVEDEV (*walking up to* BUBNOV): True enough, my precinct's not so great—even though it's worse than any big one. Just now, before my shift changed, I carted Aleshka over to the station house. He's laid himself out, you understand, in the middle of the gutter, plays on his accordeon, and keeps bawling: "I don't want nothing—I don't wish for nothing!" There's horses goin' past and traffic in general; he might have been run over by the wheels, and so on. A riotous lad. Well, so I up and put him away. Very fond of being disorderly, he is.

BUBNOV: Coming to play checkers tonight?

MEDVEDEV: I'll come. Mm-yes. . . . But what about—Vasska?

BUBNOV: Nothing. Everything the same way.

MEDVEDEV: He's getting along, then?

BUBNOV: Why shouldn't he be. He's allowed to get along.

MEDVEDEV (*dubiously*): He is? (LUKE *walks out into entry, carrying a pail*.) Mm. . . . There's been talk going around . . . about Vasska. You haven't heard?

BUBNOV: I hear all sorts of talk.

MEDVEDEV: About Vassilissa, it seems. You haven't noticed anything?

BUBNOV: Noticed what?

MEDVEDEV: Just so—in general. Maybe you know, but you're just lying to me? Because everybody is in on it. (*Sternly*.) You mustn't lie, brother.

BUBNOV: Why should I lie?

MEDVEDEV: Watch your step, then! Ah, the sons-of-bitches! They're saying that Vasska and Vassilissa . . . you know. But what's it to me? I'm not her father; I'm only her uncle. Why laugh at me? (*Enter* DOUGH PAN.) What's come over people now—they make fun of everything! (*Noticing* DOUGH PAN.) Aha! So you're here!

DOUGH PAN: My most charming garrison! He was pestering me on the market place again, Bubnov, wanting me to marry him.

BUBNOV: Go to it—what more do you want? He's got money, and he's still a husky lover.

MEDVEDEV: Who, me? Ho-ho!

DOUGH PAN: Oh, you gray-coat! No, don't you go touching me on my sore spot! I've been through that there, my little darlin'. For a woman to marry is the same as jumpin' into a hole in the ice in the middle of winter: you do it only once, but you'll remember it as long as you live.

MEDVEDEV: Hold on, now; there's all kinds of husbands.

DOUGH PAN: But then I'm always the same. Just as soon as my darling little husband croaked—may he rot in Hell!—why, I just sat all by myself for a whole day, out of pure joy; I sat there and I plain couldn't believe my good luck.

MEDVEDEV: If your husband used to beat you—for nothing, that is —you should have complained to the police.

DOUGH PAN: I complained to God for eight years running—and He didn't help me.

MEDVEDEV: Wife-beating is forbidden now. There's strict laws about everything now, and regulations. You mustn't beat up anybody just so; people are beaten only to maintain law and order.

LUKE (*leading in* ANNA *from entry*): There, now, we've managed to creep so far. Eh, you! How can anybody in such a weak condition go about by herself? Where's your place?

ANNA (*indicating bed*): Thanks, Grandpa.

DOUGH PAN: There she is—a married woman! Take a good look at her!

LUKE: The little woman is in an altogether weak state. She's walkin' about in the entry, catchin' at the walls, and moanin'. Why do you let her go out by herself?

DOUGH PAN: We didn't keep a sharp enough lookout, father—forgive us! And her mustard pot has evidently gone out for a good time.

LUKE: There, you're laughing. And yet how can anyone abandon a person in this place? A person—no matter what he or she's like—is still worth something—

MEDVEDEV: She ought to be under observation! Suppose she ups and dies? There'll be no end of red tape over it. She ought to be watched!

LUKE: Right you are, Capt—

MEDVEDEV: Mm-yes. . . . Although I'm not really a captain yet.

LUKE: You don't say! And yet your appearance is of the most heroic! (*Much noise and great stamping of feet out in the entry. Distant, muffled shouts.*)

MEDVEDEV: What's going on—a row?

BUBNOV: Sounds like it.

DOUGH PAN: Go and take a look.

MEDVEDEV: I'll have to go, at that. Eh, duty, duty! And why do they always part people when they're having a fight? They'd stop of themselves anyway—for fighting is tiring work. They ought to be allowed to fight each other freely, as much as each one can stomach; then there'd be less fighting, for they'd remember their beatings longer.

BUBNOV (*getting down off his bunk*): You might put that up to your superiors.

KOSTYLEV (*throwing open the entry door and yelling to* MEDVEDEV): Come on, Abram! Vassilissa is killing Natashka! Come on! (DOUGH PAN, MEDVEDEV, and BUBNOV *dash out into the entry.* LUKE, *shaking his head, follows them with his eyes.*)

ANNA: Oh, Lord! Poor Natashenka!

LUKE: Who's doing all that fightin' there?

ANNA: The landladies . . . they're sisters.

LUKE (*drawing nearer to* ANNA): Are they dividing something, or what?

ANNA: They're fighting just so. Both of them are well fed, healthy—

LUKE: What's your name, now?

ANNA: Anna. I look at you—and you look like my father . . . my dear father . . . he was just so kind . . . soft—

LUKE: I've been through the mill, plenty—that's why I'm so soft! (*Laughs, quaveringly.*)

Curtain

ACT II

Same setting. Night.

SATIN, *the* BARON, CROOKED WEN, *and the* TATAR *are on the bunks near the stove, playing cards.* KLESHCH *and the* ACTOR *are watching the game.* BUBNOV, *on his bunk, is playing checkers with* MEDVEDEV. LUKE *is sitting on a tabouret near* ANNA'S *bed.*

The lodginghouse is illuminated by two lamps: one hangs on the wall, near the cardplayers; the other is on BUBNOV'S *bunk.*

TATAR: One more time I playing—then no more I playing.

BUBNOV: Hey, Wen—sing! (*Starts off.*) "The sun rises and the sun sets—"

CROOKED WEN (*chiming in*): "But my prison sees no light—"

BUBNOV and CROOKED WEN (*together*):

> And the sentries, always watching—e-eh!
> Guard my window day and night—

ANNA: Beatings . . . insults . . . I've never known anything but that— Never!

LUKE: Eh, little one! Don't you be downhearted!

MEDVEDEV: It's not your turn! Watch out!

BUBNOV: A-ah! Right you are, right you are!

TATAR (*shaking his fist at* SATIN): What for you wanting to hide card? I having eyes. Eh, you!

CROOKED WEN: Cut it out, Hassan! They'll trim us no matter what we do. Go ahead and sing, Bubnov!

ANNA: I can't remember a time when I had a square meal. I shivered over each mouthful. I went in fear and trembling all my life. I went through tortures . . . so's I wouldn't eat more than anybody else. All my life I walked about in rags—all my miserable life. What for?

LUKE: Eh, you little child! Are you tired out? It don't matter!

ACTOR: Play the jack—the jack, you devil!

BARON: And here's our king.

KLESHCH: Those two always have the better cards.

SATIN: It's a little habit we have.

MEDVEDEV: Make that one a king.

BUBNOV: Well, I've got one, too!

ANNA: And now I'm dying.

KLESHCH: So that's what they're up to! (*To the* TATAR.) Prince, stop playing! Stop it, I'm telling you!

ACTOR: Doesn't he catch on without you?

BARON: Watch out, Andy, or I'll send you straight to hell!

TATAR: Deal 'em one time more! The pitcher, she went to the well one time too much, she broke herself—and I being the same! (KLESHCH, *shaking his head, walks over to* BUBNOV'S *bunk.*)

ANNA: I keep on thinking all the time: Lord! Can it be that there, too, in the other world, torment is to be my lot? Can it be the same there, too?

LUKE: It won't be anything like that there! You just lie still. There won't be anything there! You'll have plenty of rest there. Bear a little while longer. Everybody has to bear with things in life—every human being bears with life in his own way. (*Gets up and goes into kitchen with rapid steps.*)

BUBNOV (*starts singing*): "You can watch me all you want to—"

CROOKED WEN (*chiming in*): "In my cell I will remain—"

BUBNOV and CROOKED WEN (*harmonizing*):

> Though I'm longing for my freedom—*eh!*
> Yet I cannot break my chain—

TATAR (*yells*): Hey! You shoving card up sleeve!

BARON (*embarrassed*): Well, now . . . what do you want me to do—shove it up my nose?

ACTOR (*soothingly*): Prince, you're mistaken! Nobody, ever, does such things—

TATAR: I seeing him! Shark! I not playing!

SATIN (*collecting the cards*): You get away from us, Hassan. You knew all about us being crooks. So what did you want to play for?

BARON: You lost two rubles, but you raise three rubles' worth of fuss. And he's a Prince, too!

TATAR (*with heat*): You got to playing honestly!

SATIN: Whatever for?

TATAR: What you meaning, what for?

SATIN: Yes, just that—whatever for?

TATAR: You not knowing?

SATIN: No, I don't know. Do you? (*The* TATAR, *enraged, spits in disgust.* ALL *laugh uproariously at him.*)

CROOKED WEN (*benignantly*): You're a funny duck, Hassan! Just get this through your head, will you? If they were to start leading an honest life they'd croak from hunger inside of three days.

TATAR: What that having do with me! You got to living honestly!

CROOKED WEN: So you've started that record! Let's better go and have tea! (*To* BUBNOV.) Hey, Bubnov! (*Begins song.*) "Ee-eh—my chains, my heavy chains—"

BUBNOV (*chiming in*): "Iron sentries, you guard well—"

CROOKED WEN: C'mon, Hassanka! (*Sings, in a low voice, as he exits.*) "I can't bend you, I can't rend you—" (*The* TATAR *shakes his fist at the* BARON *and follows his friend.*)

SATIN (*laughing, to the* BARON): You, Your Highness, have again triumphantly put your royal foot in it. An educated man, yet you don't know how to palm a card—

BARON (*shrugging his shoulders*): The devil knows how that card slipped up.

ACTOR: No talent, no faith in yourself . . . and without that nobody ever accomplished anything.

MEDVEDEV: I have one king to your two. Mm-yes!

BUBNOV: Even one's good enough if you know your stuff. Go ahead and play! Make your move!

KLESHCH: You've lost the game, Abram Ivanich!

MEDVEDEV: That's none of your business—understand? And keep your yap shut.

SATIN: My winnings are fifty-three kopecks.

ACTOR: The three kopecks are mine. But, come to think of it, what do I need three kopecks for?

LUKE (*entering from kitchen*): There, you've trimmed the Tatar. Are you going out for a little vodka?

BARON: Come along with us.

SATIN: I'd like to see how you are when you get drunk.

LUKE: No better than when I'm sober.

ACTOR: Come on, old-timer. I'll declaim some couplets for you.

LUKE: What's them things?

ACTOR: Poetry—do you understand?

LUKE: Poet-ry? And what would I be doing with it—with this poetry, now?

ACTOR: It's funny stuff. And, at times, sad—

SATIN: Well, coupletist, are you coming along? (*Exit, with* BARON.)

ACTOR: You go ahead—I'll catch up with you! Here, for example, old-timer, is something from a certain poem—I've forgotten the beginning . . . I've forgotten it! (*Rubs his forehead.*)

BUBNOV: That did it! Your king is cooked! It's your turn!

MEDVEDEV: I didn't make the right move, God damn it!

ACTOR: Formerly, old-timer, when my organism wasn't all poisoned with alcohol, I used to have a good memory. But now, there it is . . . curtains! It's curtains for me. I always recited that poem with great success—amid thunderous applause! You . . . you don't know what applause is. Brother, it's the same as vodka! I used to come on, strike a pose like this— (*assumes pose*) strike a pose like this . . . and— (*Falls silent.*) Can't recall a thing—can't recall a single word! The poem I loved best of all . . . Bad, isn't it, old-timer?

LUKE: Well, what can there be good about it, when you've forgotten something you loved? One's whole soul is in what one loves.

ACTOR: I have drunk away my soul, old-timer. I'm done for, brother. But why am I done for? Because I had no faith in myself. I'm all washed up!

LUKE: Oh, now, why? You take a cure. Listen to me—they can cure you of drinking nowadays. For nothing, little brother! There's a special clinic, like, built just for hard drinkers—so's to cure 'em, for nothing. They've realized, you see, that even a drunkard is also a man, and are actually glad when he wants to take the cure. So there you be—go to it! Go there.

ACTOR (*pensively*): Where should I go? Where is this place?

LUKE: Why—it's in a certain town. What do they call it? It's got such an odd name. Say, I'll get the name of the town for you! The only thing, now, is this: you get yourself ready in the meantime. Hold yourself back! Get a grip on yourself and bear up. And later on you'll cure yourself—and start life anew. A good thing to start anew, eh, brother? Just make up your mind—and it's done, in two shakes of a lamb's tail!

ACTOR (*smiling*): To start anew! From the very beginning. . . . A good thing, that. Ye-es. Start anew. (*Laughs.*) Well—yes! (*Both with doubt and eagerness.*) I can do it! For I can do it, eh?

LUKE: And why not? Man can do everything—as long as he gets the desire to do it.

ACTOR (*as though suddenly awakening*): You're a queer duck! Good-by for now. (*Whistles.*) Little old-timer, good-by! (*Exit.*)

ANNA: Grandpa!

LUKE: What is it, Mother?

ANNA: Talk to me a little.

LUKE (*approaching* ANNA'S *bed*): All right, let's have a little conversation. (KLESHCH *looks around him, walks up in silence to his wife, looks at her, and makes certain gestures, as if he wanted to communicate something to her.*) What is it, little brother?

KLESHCH (*in a low voice*): Nothing. (*Slowly walks over to entry door, stands a few seconds before it, and then goes out.*)

LUKE (*following* KLESHCH *with his eyes*): It's hard for your man now.

ANNA: I've no mind for him now.

LUKE: Did he use to beat you?

ANNA: Sure thing. It's because of him, I guess, that I took sick.

BUBNOV: My wife used to have a lover; he was a good hand at checkers, the skunk!

MEDVEDEV: Mm-mm. . . .

ANNA: Grandpa, darling! I feel so down in the mouth—

LUKE: It's nothing! That comes on before dyin', little girl. It's nothing, darlin'. You keep on hopin'. There, now, you'll die, and you'll be at rest. You'll have no need of anything any more—and nothin' to fear! Quiet, rest—lie there to your heart's content! Death, now—it sets everything to rest. She is kindly to us. "When life doth cease, then comes peace," they say; and that's the truth, darlin'! For where is a person to rest on this earth otherwise? (*Enter* PEPEL. *He is a little tipsy, disheveled, gloomy. Takes seat on bunk near door to his room and sits there silently and motionlessly.*)

ANNA: And how are things there—is there torment there, too?

LUKE: There'll be nothing! Nothing! Have faith. Peace—and nothing more! You will be summoned before the Lord, and they'll say, "Lord, behold, thy handmaiden Anna is come to Thee now—"

MEDVEDEV (*sternly*): How come you know what they'll say there? Eh, you— (PEPEL, *at the sound of* MEDVEDEV'S *voice, raises his head and listens.*)

LUKE: Naturally I know, Captain—

MEDVEDEV (*in a conciliatory tone*): Mm—yes! Well . . . that's your affair. Although . . . I'm not really a captain yet—

BUBNOV: I'm taking two of your pieces.

MEDVEDEV: Eh, you! I hope you—

LUKE: And the Lord will look upon you gently, kindly, and He'll say, "I know this Anna! There," He'll say, "lead this Anna into Paradise! Let her find peace there. I know she's led a very hard life, that she is very tired. Peace be unto Anna!"

ANNA (*gasping*): Grandpa . . . you darling . . . if only it would be like that! If only . . . there were peace. Not to feel anything!

LUKE: You won't! There'll be nothing there! Have faith. Die with joy, without worrying. Death, I'm telling you, is to us like a mother to her little ones—

ANNA: But . . . maybe . . . maybe I'll get well—eh?

LUKE (*with a dubious smile*): What for? To undergo torment again?

ANNA: Well—a little while longer! To live just a little while! If there isn't going to be any torment . . . there . . . you can bear it here. You can!

LUKE: There'll be nothing there! Just simply—

PEPEL (*getting up*): Right! And then again, maybe it ain't!

ANNA (*frightened*): Oh, Lord—

LUKE: Ah, there, handsome!

MEDVEDEV: Who's that hollering?

PEPEL (*walking up to him*): Me! What about it?

MEDVEDEV: You're hollering for nothing, that's what! A man ought to behave himself peaceful—

PEPEL: Eh, what a thickheaded oaf! And he's an uncle, at that! Ho-ho!

LUKE (*to* PEPEL, *quietly*): Listen, stop yelling! There's a woman dying here. She's got one foot in the grave—don't go upsetting her.

PEPEL: I'll do it out of respect for you, Grandfather, if you like! You're all right, brother! You're swell at telling lies—it's a pleasure to hear you tell them fairy tales. Go ahead and lie, it don't matter. There's so little that's pleasant in this world!

BUBNOV: The woman, now—is she really dyin'?

LUKE: It don't look like she was foolin'.

BUBNOV: That means she'll stop coughing, then. Her cough was most upsettin'. I'm taking two pieces!

MEDVEDEV: Ah, may you rot in hell!

PEPEL: Abram!

MEDVEDEV: Don't you go callin' me by my first name!

PEPEL: Abrashka! Is Natasha ailing?

MEDVEDEV: What's it to you?

PEPEL: No, really, tell me—did Vassilissa beat her up bad?

MEDVEDEV: There again—what's it to you? That's a family affair. And who may you be?

PEPEL: It don't matter who I be, but—if I feel like it, you'll never set eyes on Natashka again!

MEDVEDEV (*abandoning the game*): What's that you're saying? Whom are you talking about? That my niece should—oh, you thief!

PEPEL: A thief, sure—but it ain't you that ever caught me!

MEDVEDEV: Wait! I'll catch you—and it won't be long—

PEPEL: You do and you'll bring grief on all your family. Do you think I'm going to keep my mouth shut before the prosecutor? You can't make a wolf over! They'll ask me, "Who put you up to stealing and showed you where to steal?"—"Mishka Kostylev and his wife!"—

"Who acted as receiver for the stolen goods?"—"Mishka Kostylev and his wife!"

MEDVEDEV: You're lying! They won't believe you.

PEPEL: They'll believe me—'cause it's the truth! And I'll get you tangled up in it, too—ha! I'll ruin all of you, you devils—you'll see!

MEDVEDEV (*nonplused*): You're lying! And . . . you're lying! And . . . what harm have I done you? You mad dog—

PEPEL: And what good have you ever done me?

LUKE: 'At's it!

MEDVEDEV (*to* LUKE): You—what are you croaking about? What's it all to you? This is a family affair!

BUBNOV (*to* LUKE): Leave 'em be! It's not for you and me they're tyin' them hangman's nooses.

LUKE: Why, I didn't mean no harm. All I'm sayin' is that if you ain't done good to somebody you acted badly—

MEDVEDEV (*failing to understand him*): Just remember that! All of us here . . . know one another, but as for you—who may you be? (*Exit quickly, with a snort of anger.*)

LUKE: That gent sure got angry. Oho-ho, your affairs, brothers, as far as I can see . . . are all in a muddle.

PEPEL: He ran off to complain to Vassilissa.

BUBNOV: You're horsing around, Vassilii. You got too much courage in your system, somehow. Watch out; courage is well enough when you're going for a hay ride—but here it don't belong at all. They'll skin you alive.

PEPEL: Oh, no! You can't take us Yaroslavl men right off with your bare hands. If it's goin' to be war, then we'll wage a war!

LUKE: Really, now, lad, you ought to leave this place behind you.

PEPEL: Where am I to go? Well, now, you tell me where?

LUKE: Go to—Siberia!

PEPEL: Ehe! No, I'll wait a bit, until they send me to that there Siberia at the government's expense—

LUKE: Now, you just listen to me—you go there! There you can get on the right road. They need fellows like you there!

PEPEL: My road has been laid down for me! My father sat all his life in jails and he bade me to do the same. Even when I was little—well, even then they called me a thief, and the son of a thief—

LUKE: And yet it's a fine land, is Siberia! A land of gold! Whosoever has got his health and his wits will find himself as snug as a bug in a rug there.

PEPEL: Why are you lyin' all the time for, old-timer?

LUKE: What did you say?

PEPEL: Have you become deaf? What are you lyin' for, I said.

LUKE: Just what am I lyin' about, now?

PEPEL: About everything. With you things are fine there, and things are fine here—for you're lyin'! For what reason?

LUKE: Believe me, now. Go and take a look for yourself. You'll thank me. What are you knocking around here for? And—why are you hankering so badly after the truth? My goodness! Maybe that same truth, now, will hit you like a club over the head.

PEPEL: Why, it's all one to me! If it's a club, let it be a club!

LUKE: What a queer fellow! Why kill yourself?

BUBNOV: What are the both of you battin' about? Can't understand it. What sort of truth do you need, Vasska? And what for? You know the truth about yourself. And everybody else knows it, for the matter of that.

PEPEL: Hold on; stop your croaking. Let him tell me. Listen, old-timer: is there a God? (LUKE, *smiling, keeps silent.*)

BUBNOV: People live like they were so many chips floatin' on the river, and chips is what's thrown aside when houses are built.

PEPEL (*still after* LUKE): Well? Is there? Tell me!

LUKE (*in a low voice*): If you believe, there is; if you don't, there ain't. Whatever you believe in, that thing is. (PEPEL, *without a word, stares at the old man stubbornly and in bewilderment.*)

BUBNOV: I'm going out for some tea—coming along to the gin mill? (*Trying to arouse* PEPEL.) Hey, there!

LUKE (*to* PEPEL): Why are you staring?

PEPEL: Just so. Hold on, now! That means, then—

BUBNOV: I'm going by myself then. (*Goes toward entry door, where he encounters* VASSILISSA.)

PEPEL: So then . . . you . . .

VASSILISSA (*to* BUBNOV): Is Nastasia here?

BUBNOV: No. (*Exit.*)

PEPEL: Ah—so you've come—

VASSILISSA (*walking up to* ANNA): Still living?

LUKE: Don't disturb her.

VASSILISSA: You again? What are you sticking around here for?

LUKE: I can leave, if need be—

VASSILISSA (*going toward door of* PEPEL's *room*): Vassilii, I have business to talk over with you! (*Goes into* PEPEL's *room.* LUKE *walks up to entry door, opens it, and slams it shut, loudly; then he cautiously climbs up on a bunk, and from there on top of the stove.*) Vassya, come here!

PEPEL: I won't. I don't feel like it.

VASSILISSA: Well, what is it? What are you angry about?

PEPEL: I've got the blues. I'm fed up with all this damned business.

VASSILISSA: And are you fed up with . . . me, too?

PEPEL: And you, too. (VASSILISSA *emerges, draws the shawl snugger around her shoulders, pressing her hands to her breast; she goes to* ANNA'S *bed, cautiously peeps in behind curtain, and returns to* PEPEL.) Well, go ahead and spill it.

VASSILISSA: What's the use of saying anything? There's no forcing you to be kind—and it ain't in my nature to beg for kindness. Thanks for coming out with the truth.

PEPEL: What truth?

VASSILISSA: Why, about being fed up with me—or ain't that the truth? (PEPEL *watches her in silence. She draws closer to him.*) Why are you staring? Don't you recognize me?

PEPEL (*with a sigh*): You're beautiful, Vasska. (*She puts her hand on his neck, but he shakes it off by moving his shoulder away.*) But my heart never went out to you . . . And I slept with you, and all—yet you never were to my liking—

VASSILISSA (*softly*): So-o. We-ell—

PEPEL: Well, there's nothing for us to talk about. Nothing. Go away from me.

VASSILISSA: Has another taken your eye?

PEPEL: None of your business. Even if she did, I ain't goin' to call you in as a matchmaker.

VASSILISSA (*significantly*): And that's a pity. Maybe I might even have made the match.

PEPEL (*suspiciously*): With whom?

VASSILISSA: You know—why pretend? Vassilii, I'm a straight shooter. (*In a lower tone.*) I won't conceal it—you've wronged me. It's as though you'd lashed me with a whip, for no good reason on earth. You said you loved me, and then, all of a sudden—

PEPEL: Not all of a sudden at all. I've been like that a long time. You've no soul in you, wench. A woman must have a soul in her. We're beasts; what we need—well, we got to be trained. But you—what have you trained me to?

VASSILISSA: That which is no longer there. I know human beings aren't masters of their own selves. You don't love me any more—well and good! So be it, then.

PEPEL: Well, that means it's all over. We've parted peacefully, without a row—and that's swell!

VASSILISSA: No, hold on! After all . . . when I was your woman . . . I was expectin' all the time that you'd help me clamber out of this filthy bog—that you'd set me free of my husband, my uncle, of all the life here. And maybe it weren't you I loved, Vassya; maybe what I loved in you was this hope, this plan of mine. You understand? I was expectin' that you'd drag me out—

PEPEL: You ain't no nail; I'm no pliers. I was thinkin' myself that you, bein' smart—for you *are* smart! You're slick!

VASSILISSA (*bending close to him*): Vassya, let's . . . help each other—

PEPEL: How could we?

VASSILISSA (*softly, vehemently*): My sister—you like her, I know—

PEPEL: That's why you beat her, you beast! Watch out, Vasska! Don't you touch her—

VASSILISSA: Hold on. Don't fly off the handle! It can all be done on the quiet, in a nice way. Would you like to marry her? And I'll even give you money, to boot—three hundred! If I get more together, I'll give you more.

PEPEL (*edging away from her*): Hold on—what's all this? What for?

VASSILISSA: Set me free of my husband! Take that noose from around my neck!

PEPEL: So *that's* it! Oho-ho! That's sure a nifty scheme you've thought up. That means the husband will be put away in his coffin and the lover in prison for life, whilst you yourself—

VASSILISSA: Vassya! Why prison? Don't do it yourself—use your pals! And even if you was to do it yourself, who'd find out? Think—there's Nathalie! You'll have money—you'll go off somewhere. You'll free me forever. And if my sister won't be around me, it will be a good thing for her. It's—it's hard for me to see her. I feel mean against her, because of you—and I can't hold myself in; I torture the wench, I beat her—beat her so that I cry myself, out of pity for her. Yet beat her I do! And—I'll go on beating her!

PEPEL: You beast! Boasting of what a beast you are.

VASSILISSA: I ain't boasting—just telling the truth. Think it over, Vassya. You had to sit in jail twice because of my husband—because of his greedy nature. He's hanging on to me like a bedbug—he's been sucking my blood for four years! And what sort of a husband is he for a woman like me? He's bearin' down on Natashka; she's a beggar, he says. And he's poison to everybody—

PEPEL: That's a cunning net you're spinning—

VASSILISSA: Everything is plain in my words. Only a fool wouldn't understand what I'm after—(KOSTYLEV *enters cautiously and steals forward.*)

PEPEL (*to* VASSILISSA): Well—you can go!

VASSILISSA: Think it over. (*Catching sight of her husband.*) What do you want? Did you come after me? (PEPEL *jumps up and stares at* KOSTYLEV *wildly.*)

KOSTYLEV: It's me—me! And are you here . . . by yourselves? Just having a little talk, eh? (*Suddenly stamps his feet and squeals wildly at his wife.*) Vasska . . . you low-down, beggarly . . . hide! (*Becomes frightened at his own outcry, which is met by silence and immobility.*) Lord forgive me! You have again brought me to sin, Vassilissa. I'm looking for you all over. (*Again squealing.*) Time to go to bed! You forgot to put oil into the lamps before the holy images! You beggar . . . you swine! (*Waves his quivering hands before her threateningly.* VASSILISSA *walks slowly toward the entry door, looking over her shoulder at* PEPEL.)

PEPEL (*to* KOSTYLEV): *You*—get going! Git!

KOSTYLEV (*shouts*): I'm boss here! Git yourself—you! Thief—

PEPEL (*in a stifled voice*): Mishka, git going—

KOSTYLEV: Don't you dare! I'm boss here! I'll fix you—(PEPEL *grabs him by the back of his collar and shakes him. There is much noisy turning on top of the stove, and an exceedingly high-pitched yawn.* PEPEL *releases* KOSTYLEV, *and the old man runs out into the entry, shouting.*)

PEPEL (*leaping up on the bunk next to the stove*): Who's there? Who's on top there?

LUKE (*putting out his head*): What did you say?

PEPEL: You!

LUKE (*unperturbed*): Me—me myself. Oh, Lord Jesus Christ!

PEPEL (*shutting entry door, looking for the bolt and not finding it*): Oh, hell! Get down off of there, old-timer!

LUKE: Right away! I'm getting off—

PEPEL (*roughly*): What did you crawl on top of there for?

LUKE: And where should I have gone?

PEPEL: Why—didn't you go out into the hall?

LUKE: Brother, it's cold out in the hall for an old man like me.

PEPEL: You—overheard?

LUKE: Sure I heard! How could one help overhearing it! Or am I deef? Eh, lad, luck is comin' your way! It's comin' right at you!

PEPEL (*suspiciously*): What luck? In what way?

LUKE: Well, because I'd crawled up on top there.

PEPEL: So. . . . But why did you start twisting and turning?

LUKE: Because it got too hot for me, that's why—lucky for your orphaned state. Then, again, I figured to myself, watch out the lad don't make a mistake—and strangle a poor old man like me—

PEPEL: Ye-es. . . . I might have done that same. I hate spying—

LUKE: What's so complicated about that? Nothing hard about it. There's many a mistake like that being made—

PEPEL (*smiling*): What are you drivin' at? Have you made any mistake like that, or what?

LUKE: Lad, you listen to what I'm tellin' you! This woman ought to be put out of your life! You just tell yourself: No! Don't let her near you. As for her husband, she'll get him out of this world herself, and more cleverly than you ever would—yes! Don't you listen to her—the she-devil! Look at me—what do I look like? Baldy-headed! And for why? From all these different women, now. I knew more of 'em, of these women, now, than I had hairs on my head. And this here Vassilissa, now—she's worse nor any loco-weed!

PEPEL: I don't rightly know—whether to say thanks to you, or whether you're also—

LUKE: Don't you say anything! You won't say anything better than I've told you! You listen to me: Whichever one here you like the better, take her by the arm and scram out of here—on the double-quick! Get away! Get away from here!

PEPEL (*glumly*): There's no understanding people—which ones are good, which bad. A man can't understand anything.

LUKE: What's there to understand? Man lives every which way. The way his heart is set, that's the way he goes. Today he's good; on the morrow he's bad! But if that young wench has really got holt of your soul—go off with her, and that's that. Or else go off by your own self. You're a young fellow—you'll have time to saddle yourself with a woman.

PEPEL (*taking* LUKE *by the shoulder*): No, you tell me why you're doing all these things—

LUKE: Wait—let go of me. I'm goin' to take a look at Anna; she was breathing much too hard—(*Goes to* ANNA'S *bed, draws the curtain aside, looks in, and puts his hand on* ANNA. PEPEL *follows him with his eyes, thoughtfully yet absent-mindedly.* LUKE *makes the sign of the cross over himself.*) Jesus Christ, Most Merciful! Accept in peace the soul of this Thy handmaiden Anna, now newly come before Thee—

PEPEL (*softly*): Dead? (*Does not approach bed, but cranes his neck to look at it.*)

LUKE (*softly*): Her troubles are over! But where's her man now?

PEPEL: At some ginmill, probably—

LUKE: He ought to be told.

PEPEL (*with a shudder*): I have no love for dead people—

LUKE (*going toward entry door*): Why love them? It's the living that ought to be loved—the living—

PEPEL: I'm going along with you.

LUKE: Afraid?

PEPEL: I have no love for 'em—(*They hasten out. The room is empty, still. There is a muffled noise, intermittent and hard to explain, on the other side of the entry door.*)

ACTOR (*enters, halting in entry door, forgetting to close it behind him, and shouting, as he holds on to the doorposts*): Hey there, old-timer! Where are you? I've remembered that poem. Lissen! (*Takes two staggering paces forward and, striking a pose, recites.*)

> Messieurs! If the path to sacred truth
> All of this world were unable to find,
> All hail to the madman whose bright-glowing mind
> With its golden dream mankind would soothe.

(NATASHA *appears in doorway behind the* ACTOR): Hey, old-timer!

> If the sun our poor earthly globe's path
> On the morrow should fail to enlighten,
> On the morrow the whole world would brighten
> From some thought that a madman's mind hath!

NATASHA (*laughing*): You scarecrow! Stewed to the gills!

ACTOR (*turning around to her*): A-ah, it's you? But where's the little old-timer—the darling little old-timer? There is, ap—ap—parently nobody here. Farewell, Natasha! Aye, fare thee well!

NATASHA (*coming into room*): You haven't said hello yet, but you're already saying good-by—

ACTOR (*barring her way*): I'm going away, leaving. Comes the spring, and I shall no longer be here—

NATASHA: Let me through. Where are you off to?

ACTOR: I am off to seek that city . . . to cure myself. Thou, too, Ophelia. . . . Get thee to a nunnery! There is, you understand, a clinic for . . . for or-gan-isms. For drunkards. A mosh excellent clinic! All of marble—and with a marble floor. Light, everything clean, good food—all free. And the floor, too, is of marble—yes! I will find the place, cure myself—and will be a new man. I would breed from hence occasions. I am on the path to a new birth, as King . . . King Lear says. Natasha, my stage name is Sverchcov-Zavolzhski. Never a soul knows that—never a soul! I have no name here. Do you understand how humiliating it is to lose one's name? Even dogs have names to call them by—(NATASHA *carefully walks around the* ACTOR, *stops near* ANNA'S *bed, and looks at her.*) If a man has no name, he doesn't exist—

NATASHA: Look, dear man—why, she's dead—

ACTOR (*shaking his head*): Impossible!

NATASHA (*taking a step back*): Honest to God she is! Have a look!

BUBNOV (*in entry doorway*): Have a look at what?

NATASHA: Anna, now—she's dead!

BUBNOV: That means her coughing is over. (*Goes to* ANNA'S *bed, takes a look, goes to his own bunk.*) You gotta tell Kleshch—it's his affair.

ACTOR: I'll go—I'll tell him. She's lost her name! (*Exit.*)

NATASHA (*standing in the middle of the room*): There . . . I'll be the same, too, some day—lying in a basement . . . beaten to death—

BUBNOV (*spreading nondescript rags over his bunk*): What's that? What are you muttering about?

NATASHA: Just so—talking to myself.

BUBNOV: Waitin' for Vasska? Watch out, Vasska will break your head for you—

NATASHA: Why, isn't it all the same who breaks it? It's better if he does it, after all.

BUBNOV (*lying down*): Well, it's your own lookout.

NATASHA: There, it's a good thing she died—yet it's a pity. Lord, what did this being live for?

BUBNOV: It's the same way for everybody: they're born, they live a while, they die. I, too, will die. And so will you. What's there to be sorry about? (*Enter* LUKE, *the* TATAR, CROOKED WEN, *and* KLESHCH; *he brings up the very rear, slowly, shrinking into himself.*)

NATASHA: Shh! Anna—

CROOKED WEN: We've heard. The Kingdom of Heaven be hers, if she's dead.

TATAR (*to* KLESHCH): Must be taking out! Taking out in hall! Here dead must not being—live person sleeping here.

KLESHCH (*in a low voice*): We'll take her out—

CROOKED WEN (*to* TATAR): You think there'll be a bad smell coming from her? There won't be any—not from her; she got all dried up while still living.

NATASHA: Lord, if they'd only pity her a little . . . if only somebody had a good word of some sort to say for her! Oh, you!

LUKE: Don't you take offense at it, girl—they don't mean nothin'. Where do they . . . where do we get off pityin' the dead! Eh, deary, we don't pity the livin'; we don't know how to pity our own selves— what's the use!

BUBNOV: And another thing—death ain't afraid of words. Sickness is afraid of words, but death? No!

TATAR (*backing away*): Police should calling.

CROOKED WEN: Police—there's something you gotta have. Have you let the police know, Kleshch?

KLESHCH: No. She must be buried—and all I got is forty kopecks—

CROOKED WEN: Well, in a case like that, borrow. Or we'll make a collection—this one five kopecks, that one as much as he can. But let the police know—quick as you can! Or else they'll think you bumped off the woman, or somethin'. (*Goes to bunk where the* TATAR *is lying by now, and gets ready to lie down with him.*)

NATASHA (*going toward* BUBNOV'S *bunk*): There, she'll be coming to me in my dreams now. I always dream of the dead. I'm afraid to go home by myself; it's dark out in the hall—

LUKE (*following her out*): You watch out for the living, I'm telling you.

NATASHA: See me home, Grandpa.

LUKE: Come on. Come on—I'll see you home. (*Exeunt both. Pause.*)

CROOKED WEN: Oh-ho-o! Hassan, my friend, it's going to be spring soon. The farm folk in their villages are fixin' their plows and harrows —gettin' ready for plowing. . . . But us? Hey, Hassan? He's snoozin' already, the damned Mahomet—

BUBNOV: Tatars like to have their sleep.

KLESHCH (*standing in the middle of the lodginghouse*): What am I to do now?

CROOKED WEN: Lie down and sleep—that's about all you *can* do.

KLESHCH (*quietly*): But—what about her? (*Nobody answers him. Enter* SATIN *and* ACTOR.)

ACTOR (*shouting*): Old-timer! Hither, noble and truehearted Kent!

SATIN: Here comes the great traveler! H-ho!

ACTOR: It's all settled and decided! Old-timer, where's that town? Where are you?

SATIN: Fata Morgana! The old man told you a pack of lies! There is nothing! There are no towns, there are no people—there isn't a thing!

ACTOR: You lie!

TATAR (*jumping up*): Where is owner this place? I going to owner this place! No can sleep, he no can taking money. Dead peoples, drunken peoples! (*Exit quickly.* SATIN *whistles after him.*)

BUBNOV: Go to bed, fellows, don't make any noise. Night is for sleeping.

ACTOR (*catching sight of* ANNA'S *bed*): Aye—what have we here? Aha! The dead. . . . "Our nets, dragging, have dredged up a body dead—" Poem by . . . by . . . Pushkin? Pushkin? N-no! B-ber-anger!

SATIN (*shouting*): The dead can't hear! The dead can't feel! Shout! Roar! The dead can't hear—(LUKE *appears in entry doorway.*)

Curtain

ACT III

A wasteland. Back yards, cluttered with all sorts of rubbish and over-grown with burdock. At back, a high fire-retarding wall of baked brick. It bars any view of the sky. Near it are elder bushes. At right is the timbered wall of some outbuilding—barn or stable. At left, a gray wall, with vestiges of plaster—belonging to the house in the basement of which is the lodging place of the KOSTYLEVS. *This wall is at an angle, so that its rear corner juts out almost to the center of the wasteland. Between it and the red brick wall is a narrow passage. There are two windows in the gray wall: one on a level with the ground, the other a little short of five feet above the lower, and nearer the fire-wall. Near the house wall is a sledge, with the runners turned up; there is also a log, a little over nine feet long. At the wall, right, is a pile of weather-beaten boards and beams.*

Evening; the sun is setting, casting a reddish glow over the fire-wall.

Early spring—there are traces of recently thawed snow; the black twigs of the elder bushes are devoid of buds.

NATASHA *and* NASTYA *are sitting side by side on the log.* LUKE *and the* BARON *are on the upturned sledge.* KLESHCH *is lying on the lumber at right.* BUBNOV'S *far from prepossessing face is framed by the window near the ground.*

NASTYA (*with her eyes shut and swaying her head in time with the words of her story, which she is telling in almost a singsong*): So then, he comes at night into the garden, into a summerhouse, now, as we had made up . . . and me, I'm expectin' him a long time, and I'm shiverin' all over from fear and trouble. He, too, is shiverin' all over—and white as chalk, and there's a ree-volver in his hand—

NATASHA (*chewing polly-seeds*): My! It looks like the truth, what they say about students; they're a desperate lot.

NASTYA: And he says to me in a dreadful voice, he says: "My precious love—"

BUBNOV: Haw-haw! Precious?

BARON: Hold on! If you don't like it, close your ears, but don't keep others back from lying. Continue!

NASTYA: "My love," he says, "I cannot get my fill of gazing upon you. My parents," says he, "won't give their consent to my espousing you . . . and threaten to curse me everlastingly for the love I bear you. Well, for that reason," says he, "I am obligated to take my own life." And his ree-volver, now, is so-o tremendous, and loaded with ten bullets! "Farewell," he says, "amiable friend of my heart! I have come to an unalterable decision; I absolutely cannot live without you." And I answers him, "My never-to-be-forgotten friend . . . Felix—"

BUBNOV (*in astonishment*): Wha-at! What did you say? P'leece?

BARON (*going off into peals of laughter*): Oh, Nastya! Come . . . come! Why, last time it was Gaston!

NASTYA (*jumping up*): Keep quiet, both of you! You miserable creatures! Oh, you homeless dogs! For . . . can you understand . . . love? Real love? But I knew love—and it was real! (*To the* BARON):

You, you insignificant thing! *You* an educated man—you say you used to have your coffee in bed—

LUKE: Look here, you two! Don't interfere. Have some respect for a person; it isn't what one says that matters; what matters is why a person says anything! Tell your story, girl; don't mind anything.

BUBNOV: Lay it on good and thick, you crow; go ahead with your story!

BARON: Well, go on!

NATASHA: Don't you listen to them—what do they amount to? They're doing that out of jealousy. They haven't anything to say about themselves, that's why.

NASTYA (*sitting down again*): I don't want to go on. I'm not saying another word. If they don't believe me—if they laugh at me—(*Cutting her speech off abruptly she is silent for a few seconds; then, shutting her eyes again, she resumes, loudly and with warmth, waving her hand in time with her words and just as though she were hearkening to distant music.*) And so, I answer him, "Joy of my life! You who are as a shining crescent moon to me! For me, too, it is entirely impossible to live on in this world without you—inasmuch as I love you madly, and shall go on loving you, as long as this heart beats within my breast! But," I says, "do not do away with your youthful life! How precious it must be to your parents, whose whole joy and pride you are! Forsake me! It would be best that I perish—out of yearning for you, you who are my life . . . Let it be me alone . . . I am . . . you know what . . . Let it be me, then. . . . I am going to perdition anyways—so it don't matter! I am no good at all . . . and there's nothing left for me . . . nothing!" (*Buries her face in her hands and weeps noiselessly.*)

NATASHA (*in a low voice, as she turns away*): Don't cry. You mustn't! (LUKE, *with a smile, strokes* NASTYA'S *head.*)

BUBNOV (*roaring with laughter*): Oh, ain't she a caution? Eh?

BARON (*also laughing*): Do you think it's the gospel truth, Grandpa? All this is out of that book, "Fatal Love!" All this is so much bosh! Leave her alone!

NATASHA: Why, what's it to you? You! Keep your trap shut—since God has already done you in.

NASTYA (*furiously*): You lost soul! You empty creature! Where do you keep your soul?

LUKE (*taking* NASTYA *by the hand*): Let's come away, deary! It don't matter—don't get worked up over it! I know. I believe you!

You've got the right on your side, and not them! If you believe that you've experienced real love—why, then, it means you have! You have! And as for your boy friend there, don't be angry at him. Maybe he's laughing just out of envy. Probably he never knew anything of the sort—real love, that is—or anything! Let's go!

NASTYA (*clasping her hands to her breast*): Grandpa, I swear to God all this happened! It all happened! He was a student—a Frenchman. They called him Little Gaston—he had a little black beard— (*Stroking an imaginary beard.*) Walked about in patent-leather boots. . . . May thunder strike me on this spot if that ain't so! And how he loved me! How he loved me!

LUKE: I know. Never mind! I believe you! He wore patent-leather boots, you say? My, my, my! Well, now, and did you love him in your turn? (*Both turn corner of gray wall.*)

BARON: My, but is that young lady stupid! Good-natured, yes, but stupid—unbearably so!

BUBNOV: And how is it that a person should love to lie so? She's always acting as if she was facin' a public prosecutor—really!

NATASHA: Evidently the lie is more pleasant than the truth. I my-self—

BARON: What about yourself? Go on—yes?

NATASHA: I think up things—and wait—

BARON: Wait for what?

NATASHA (*smiling in confusion*): Nothing in particular. For instance, I think that on the morrow someone . . . out of the ordinary . . . will come. Or else that something—also unusual—will happen. I am waiting for a long time. I'm always waiting. But when you really come down to it—what can one expect? (*Pause.*)

BARON (*with a slight sneer*): There's nothing to expect—I expect nothing! Everything . . . has already happened! It is past—done with! Continue!

NATASHA: Or else I imagine to myself that on the morrow I am going to . . . die suddenly. And from that thought I get a creepy feeling. It's good to imagine about death in the summertime . . . you can always be killed by lightning—

BARON: Life is hard for you. It's all because of your sister. She's got the Devil's own nature!

NATASHA: But for whom isn't life hard? It's bad for everybody— I can see that.

KLESHCH (*lying motionless and taking no part in the conversation all this time, now suddenly springing to his feet*) : For everybody? You lie! Not everybody! If it were bad for everybody—well and good! It wouldn't hurt a body so much then—yes!

BUBNOV: What's got into you? The Devil prod you with his horns? Look at you—what a howl you set up! (KLESHCH *lies down in his place again, and keeps growling.*)

BARON: Er . . . I'll have to go to Nastenka and make up. If I don't make up, she won't give me anything to get drunk on.

BUBNOV: Mmm. . . . People like to lie. As for Nastenka, the thing is easy to understand! She's gotten used to putting paint on her puss— so she wants to put paint on her soul as well—to touch the soul up, too, with a rosy blush. But as for the others—why do they go and do it? There's Luke, for example; he lies a whole heap—and that without doing any good to himself. He's an old man already—what does he want to be lyin' for?

BARON (*fleering a little, as he starts going off*) : All people have rather drab little souls. All of them wish to put on a little rouge—

LUKE (*emerging from around the corner of the gray wall*) : You're a gentleman—why do you go upsetting the wench? You oughtn't to be interferin' with her. Let her have a good time crying. For she's sheddin' them tears for her own pleasure—what harm does it do you?

BARON: It's stupid, old-timer! I'm fed up with her. Today it's Felix, tomorrow it's Gaston—but always it's the same old drivel! However, I'm on my way to make up with her. (*Exit.*)

LUKE: There, go ahead and be kind to her a little. To be a little kind to a person never does no harm.

NATASHA: You're a kindly person, Grandpa. Why are you so kind?

. LUKE: Kind, says you? Well . . . if that's so, all right! Yes! (*Soft sounds of accordeon and singing behind the red brick wall.*) Girl, somebody's got to be kind, too—somebody's got to feel sorry for people! Christ, now, felt sorry for all men, and bade us do likewise. I'll tell you something: to take pity on a person in time . . . may turn out to be a fine thing. There, for instance, I once had a job as a caretaker at a country house—for a certain engineer, near the town of Tomsk, in Siberia. Well, anyway, this house was situated in a forest —a forsaken sort of place. And it was wintertime, and me all by my lone self there, in this here country house, now. It was grand! Just fine! Only, one night I hear there's somebody breakin' in—

NATASHA: Robbers?

LUKE: Just that. They're breakin' in, you understand. Yes! I picked up my gun and went out. I see two of 'em, pryin' open a window—and so taken up with their work that they don't even see me. I shout to them, "Hey, there, you! Get away from there!" But they, you understand, go for me with an ax. I give 'em full warnin', "Back up, now! Or else I'll shoot, at once!" And I train my gun now at one, now at the other. So they fall down on their knees, "Let us go now!" But me, now, I'd already gotten my dander up—because of that there ax, you know. So I says to 'em, "I was chasin' you away, you divvels, but you wouldn't go. But now," I says, "one of you get busy and break off some of them long twigs!" So they broke off an armful. "Now," I orders them, "one of you lie down, and the other flog him!" And so, just like I ordered 'em to, they flogged each other. But when they was through, they says to me, they says, "Grandpa, give us a crust of bread, for Christ's sake! We're trampin' around, with nothin' to eat!" And there's your robbers for you, deary! (*Laughs.*) And goin' for me with an ax, at that! Yes . . . good men, both of 'em. So I says to 'em, "You'd do better, you crazy divvels, if you was to ask for bread right off." But they says to me, "We got sick and tired of that; you beg and beg and nobody gives you nothin' . . . and that hurts!" And after that they just lived on with me all winter through. One of 'em—Stepan, his name was—used to take the gun and just go off into the woods. And the other—Jacob, he was called—was ailin' all the time, coughin', with never a stop. And so the three of us, you understand, watched that there country house. Comes the spring—"Good-by, Grandpa!" they tells me. And off they went—wanderin' all over Russia.

NATASHA: Escaping, were they? Convicts?

LUKE: Just that—escaped convicts. They'd run off from the penal colony. Good men, they were! If I hadn't taken pity on 'em, they might have killed me—or done some other harm. And then there'd be a trial, and prison, and Siberia—where's the good of all that? The prison couldn't teach 'em to be good, and Siberia couldn't, either. But a man could—yes! A man can teach another to be good—a very simple matter, that! (*Pause.*)

BUBNOV: Mmm . . . But me, now—I don't know how to lie! Why lie? To my way of thinkin', come out with the truth, whatever it may happen to be. Why be bashful?

KLESHCH (*suddenly jumping up again, as if he had been scalded, and shouting*): What truth? Where is it, this truth? (*Beats his hands over his rags and tatters.*) *This* is truth. No work, no strength—*that* is the truth! Shelter . . . there is no shelter! You gotta die—there's your truth. You devil! What . . . what do I need truth for? Give me a chance to draw a free breath—one free breath! Wherein am I guilty? Why has all this *truth* been wished on me? They won't let a man live— you devil! They won't let a man live—there it is, this truth!

BUBNOV: Look at how that worked him all up!

LUKE: Lord Jesus! Look here, dear man—you, now—

KLESHCH (*quivering from excitement*): You're all talking about this here tru-uth. You, old man, are consolin' everybody. *I'll* tell you— I hate everybody! And this here truth—to hell with the God damn' thing! Did you get that? Get it—may it be damned to hell! (*Runs around corner of gray wall, looking over his shoulder.*)

LUKE: My, my, my! How the man has worked himself all up! And wherever has he run off to?

NATASHA: He's as good as out of his head right now—

BUBNOV: He done that swell! Just like he was puttin' on an act on the stage. Them things happen quite often. He ain't grown used to life yet, see—

PEPEL (*coming on slowly from around corner of gray wall*): Peace unto this honest gathering! Well, Luke, you cunning holy ancient— still spinning your yarns?

LUKE: You should have seen . . . how the man was yellin' here!

PEPEL: You mean Kleshch, don't you? What's got into him? He was running as if he'd been scalded—

LUKE: You'd run, too—if your heart was overflowin' like that.

PEPEL (*taking a seat*): Don't like him. He's much too mean, and he's proud, besides. (*Mimicking* KLESHCH.) "Me, I'm a working-man!" And all the time he's being pushed down deeper and deeper, it looks like. Go ahead and work, if you like it; but what's there to be proud about? If you're goin' to put a value on men accordin' to how hard they work, then a horse is better nor any man: it draws its load— and never says a word! Natasha, are your folks home?

NATASHA: They went to the cemetery. After that they was meanin' to go to the all-night mass—

PEPEL: There, now, I was wonderin'; you're free—a rare thing for you!

LUKE (*thoughtfully, to* BUBNOV): There, you talk of truth. Truth, now—it ain't always the thing for what ails you. You can't always cure a man's soul with the truth. Here's an instance—I knew a certain man who believed in a land where righteousness prevailed—

BUBNOV: In wh-at!

LUKE: In a land of righteousness. "There must be," he used to say, "a land where righteousness prevails. That land, now, is settled with a special sort of people—good people! They respect one another; they help one another in every little thing. And everything there is fine and glorious!" And this here man, now, was all the time gettin' ready to set out—to seek this land of righteousness. He was poor, he led a hard life, but when things got so tough that a body could just lie down and give up his ghost, he still didn't lose his spirit, but all the time he'd just smile and keep on sayin', "No matter! I can still stand it! I'll wait a little longer and then forsake all this life and go off into the land of righteousness." That's the one joy he had—this land. . . .

PEPEL: Well? And did he go there?

BUBNOV: Where? Haw-haw!

LUKE: And then they sent to the place where this man was—it all took place in Siberia—they sent a man sentenced to banishment; a learned man he was. This learned man, he had books, and he had blueprints, and all sorts of fancy trimmin's. And so this fellow, he says to the learned man, he says, "Do me a favor, will you—show me where this land of righteousness is located, and which is the road to it? Right off this learned man he opened up his books, he spread out his blueprints . . . he looked and he looked—the land of righteousness wasn't nowhere to be found! All's in its right place, all the lands is shown—but there ain't no land of righteousness!

PEPEL (*in a low voice*): Well? There ain't any? (BUBNOV *is in stitches.*)

NATASHA: Hold on, you! Well, Grandpa?

LUKE: The fellow couldn't believe it. "It's got to be there," he says. "Look for it more closely! For otherwise," says he, "your books and your charts ain't of no use, if they don't show the land of righteousness." The learned man, he got into a huff over that. "My charts," he says, "is as accurate as can be, but there's no land of righteousness anywheres at all, at all." Well, now, when it come to that, the man just blew up. How come? He'd lived and he'd lived, he'd endured and endured, and kept on havin' faith all the time that there was such a land! But accordin' to them there charts it turned out there wasn't any! It was like a hold-up! And he says to the learned man, he says: "You're a low-down critter and no learned man—" And biff! he hauls off and give him one in the ear! And again! (*After a short silence.*) And after that he went home and strung himself up. (*General silence.* LUKE, *with a smile, contemplates* PEPEL *and* NATASHA.)

PEPEL (*in a low voice*): The . . . the hell with that! The story, now, ain't so cheerful.

NATASHA: The fellow couldn't stand havin' been fooled like that—

BUBNOV (*glumly*): It's all a lot of fairy tales.

PEPEL: Ye-es. And there's the land of righteousness for you. It just didn't turn out to be there, you see—

NATASHA: You feel sorry. For the man, that is—

BUBNOV: It's all a lot of liverwurst. That, too! Haw-haw! Land of righteousness! Sure, why not? (*Vanishes from window.*)

LUKE (*nodding in* BUBNOV'S *direction*): He's laughing! Eh-he! (*Pause.*) Well, you two—good luck to you! I'll be leavin' all of you shortly.

PEPEL: Where you bound for this time?

LUKE: For them fellows in the south of Russia with a topknot over their foreheads. They've discovered a new faith down there, so I've heard. I'll have to take a look at it . . . yes! Folks are forever seeking, forever longing after, some better way! Lord, grant them patience!

PEPEL: What do you think? Will they ever find it?

LUKE: Folks, you mean? They will! Whoever seeketh, findeth; whoever desireth strongly, findeth!

NATASHA: If only they would find somethin'. Think up somethin' that would be better—

LUKE: They will think up somethin'! All they need is help, little girl . . . they need respect—

NATASHA: How could I help? I myself . . . have no one to help me—

PEPEL (*with decision*): I'm . . . I'm going to talk to you once more, Natasha. There, before him—he knows all about it. Come with me!

NATASHA: Where to? Through all the prisons?

PEPEL: I told you I'd leave off thievin'! I swear to God I'll leave off! If I said so, I'll drop it! I know how to read and write; I'll go to work. (*Nods in the direction of* LUKE.) There, now, he says that one ought to go to Siberia of one's own free will. What do you say—let's go there? You think my way of livin' don't turn my stomach? Eh, Natasha! I know—I can feel . . . I kid myself along by thinkin' that there's others that are bigger thieves than I am, yet live in honor from everybody—only this don't help me none! It ain't the right thing. I don't repent. I don't believe in conscience. But there's one thing I do sense: that you gotta . . . live a different life! You gotta live a better life! A man's gotta live so's . . . to have respect for his own self—

LUKE: Right you are, dear man! May the Lord will it so! May Christ help you in that! Right—a man must have respect for his own self.

PEPEL: I've been a thief from my earliest years. Everybody was always sayin' to me: "Vasska, you thief—Vasska, you son of a thief!" Aha—so that's it! Very well, then, I'll oblige you. There, I *am* a thief! Get this, now: maybe it was out of sheer spite I became a thief. I am a thief because nobody ever had the sense to call me by any other name. Suppose you give me one—eh, Natasha?

NATASHA (*sadly*): Somehow, I don't believe . . . in any words whatsoever. And I feel restless today. There's a queer feeling in my heart—as if I was expectin' something. It's no use, Vassilii, your starting this kind of talk today—

PEPEL: What then? This isn't the first time I'm talkin' to you like this—

NATASHA: And what would be the use for me to go off with you? For, when it comes to loving you . . . I don't love you so much. Now and then you're to my liking; but there's times when it turns my stomach to look at you. I don't love you, it seems. For when people love they can't see anything bad in the one they love—but I do.

PEPEL: You'll come to love me, never fret. I'll get you used to me—you just say yes! I've been watchin' you for more than a year; I can see you're a serious-minded girl . . . and good. Someone that can be relied upon. And I fell very much in love with you! (VASSILISSA, *all in her Sunday best, appears at the window and, as she stands there, listens.*)

NATASHA: So. You fell in love with me—but what about my sister—

PEPEL (*in embarrassment*): Well, what's there to her? There's not a few . . . women like that—

LUKE: Don't you mind that, girl! If there's no bread, folks will eat weeds. If there ain't no real bread to be got, now—

PEPEL (*glumly*): You—have pity on me, now! My life ain't any too sweet. It's a wolf's life—there's little comfort in it. I'm sinkin' like I was in a quagmire—whatever I clutch at—it's all rotten. None of it will hold. Your sister, now. . . . I thought she wasn't what she is. If she weren't so greedy for money, I'd have tackled anything for her sake! If only she'd been—all mine. But it's something else she's after. It's money she's after—and freedom. And the reason she's after it is so's she can whore around. She can't help me. But you—you're like a young fir tree; you may bend but won't break—

LUKE: And I'll say it, too. Marry him, little girl—marry him! He's not a bad lad—a good lad! The only thing you'll have to do is to remind him as often as possible that he's a good lad, so's he wouldn't forget it, see! He'll believe you. You just keep on telling him, "Vassya, now, you're a good man—don't you forget it!" You just think, darlin'; where are you to go, outside of him? Your sister's a mean beast; as for her husband, there ain't even any use sayin' anythin' about him: he's such a vile old man as is past all tellin'. And the whole life here. . . . Where are you to go? But this lad—he's staunch—

NATASHA: There isn't any place to go. I know—I thought of that. The only thing is, I don't trust anybody. Yet—there's nowheres for me to go—

PEPEL: There is one road for you. But I'll never let you set foot on it—I'd liefer kill you.

NATASHA (*smiling*): There, I'm not your wife yet, yet you're already wanting to kill me.

PEPEL (*embracing her*): Cut it out, Natasha! What does anything matter?

NATASHA (*snuggling up to him*): Well, there's one thing I'll tell you, Vassilii—there, I'm sayin' it as before God! The first time you lay a hand on me, or insult me in any other way, I won't have no pity on myself. Either I'll hang myself or—

PEPEL: May my hand wither if I ever hurt you!

LUKE: Never mind; don't have no doubts, darlin'! He needs you more'n you need him.

VASSILISSA (*through the window*): There, they've made the match! I wish you love and harmony!

NATASHA: They've come! Oh, Lord! They saw everything—oh, Vassilii!

PEPEL: What are you frightened about? Now nobody dares touch you!

VASSILISSA: Don't be afraid, Nathalia! He's not goin' to beat you. He don't know how to beat a woman—nor how to love, either. I know.

LUKE (*in a low voice*): Ah, what a woman! What a poisonous varmint—

VASSILISSA: He's much better at words—

KOSTYLEV (*emerging from around corner of gray wall*): Natashka! What you doin' here, you drone? Spreadin' gossip? Complainin' against your kith and kin? But the samovar ain't ready yet? The table ain't cleared?

NATASHA: Why, you were going to church—

KOSTYLEV: None of your business where we were going! You mind your own—and do as you're ordered!

PEPEL: Lie down, you! She's not your servant any more. Don't you go, Nathalia—don't do anythin'!

NATASHA: Don't be giving me orders—it's not time for that yet!

PEPEL (*to* KOSTYLEV): That'll do you! You've been havin' your sport over one human bein'—now it's enough! Now she's mine!

KOSTYLEV: Yours—re-eally? When did you buy her? How much did you give? (VASSILISSA *goes off into peals of laughter.*)

LUKE: Vassya! You'd better go—

PEPEL: Watch out—you're much too gay! You may be crying soon!

VASSILISSA: Oh, how dreadful! Oh, I'm so scared!

LUKE: Vassilii, go 'way! Don't you see? They're stringin' you along —tryin' to get you all worked up. Don't you understand?

PEPEL: Yes. . . . Aha! (*Nods at* KOSTYLEV, *then* VASSILISSA.) He lies—you lie! What you're wishing for will never come!

VASSILISSA: Nor will anythin' that I don't wish, Vassya!

PEPEL (*shaking his fist at her*): We'll see! (*Exit.*)

VASSILISSA (*vanishing from the window*): I'll fix a fine little wedding for you!

KOSTYLEV (*walking up to* LUKE): What are you doing, old-timer?

LUKE: Not a thing—old-timer.

KOSTYLEV: So. You're leavin', they tell me?

LUKE: Time I was—

KOSTYLEV: Where to?

LUKE: Wherever my eyes may lead me—

KOSTYLEV: Goin' vagabondin', that means. You find it hard to stay in any one place, it seems?

LUKE: You leave an ax lay too long and it'll rust, they say.

KOSTYLEV: That may be all right for an ax. But a man ought to live in one place. Men ain't supposed to live like cockroaches—each one crawlin' off wheresoever he likes. A man must settle down in some place—not go traipsin' all over the face of the earth. . . .

LUKE: But what if a man can't find a spot for hisself anywhere?

KOSTYLEV: He's a vagabond, then—a useless creature. A man must be of some use; he's got to work—

LUKE: You don't say!

KOSTYLEV: Yes. How can it be otherwise? What's a wanderer? A man who goes wanderin' is different from all others. If he be a pilgrim —the real thing, now—and may know something, or may have learned something, even then the chances are it's something nobody needs. Or even if he has come to know some truth somewhere in his wanderings—well, even then it isn't every truth that's necessary. Yes! Let him keep it all to himself—and keep mum! If he's really a pilgrim, now, he keeps mum! Or else he'll speak so that no one can understand anything. And—he don't wish for nothin', he don't butt into anythin', he don't go around confusin' people for no reason whatsoever. How people live is none of his business. He must follow a righteous life. He must live in forests, in the thickest of forests—so's no one will see him! And not hinder anyone, not judge anyone, but pray for all, for all the sins of the world—for mine, for yours—for everybody's! That's the very reason he flees from the vanity of this world—so's to pray. That's what. (*Pause.*) But you—what sort of a pilgrim are you? You ain't got no passport. A good man's gotta have a passport. All good people have passports—yes!

LUKE: There's people, and there's others. And there's also—men—

KOSTYLEV: Don't you get too—wise! Don't be puttin' any riddles to me. I'm just as smart as you be. What do you mean by people and men?

LUKE: Where's the riddle in that? I say there's soil that's not fit for sowing. And there's fertile soil: whatever you sow therein, it will bring forth. And that's the way of it, now.

KOSTYLEV: Well? What's all that for?

LUKE: There's you, for instance. Were the Lord God Himself to say to you, "Michailo! Be thou a man!"—it would still be no use, nohow; the way you are, that's the way you'll remain—

KOSTYLEV: Say! Why, do you know that my wife's uncle is in the police? And if I was to—

VASSILISSA (*entering*): Michailo Ivanovich, come and have your tea.

KOSTYLEV (*to* LUKE): You . . . tell you what: you get out! Clear out of my house!

VASSILISSA: That's right—make yourself scarce, old man! Your little tongue is much too long. Besides, who knows—maybe you're an escaped convict, or somethin'—

KOSTYLEV: This very day! I don't want nor hide nor hair of you here! Or else I'll—watch out!

LUKE: You'll call in uncle? Call in your uncle. "I've caught an escaped convict, now!" Your uncle will get a reward—all of three kopecks—

BUBNOV (*at the window*): Is there a trade goin' on here? What you askin' three kopecks for?

LUKE: They're threatenin' to sell me out, now—

VASSILISSA (*to her husband*): Come along—

BUBNOV: For three kopecks. Well, you'd better keep your eyes peeled, old-timer. They'd sell you out for even one kopeck.

KOSTYLEV (*to* BUBNOV): You! You look just like a hobgoblin peepin' out from under a stove! (*Exit, with* VASSILISSA.)

VASSILISSA (*near the angle of the gray wall*): What a lot of ignorant people—and all sorts of crooks—there are in this world!

LUKE: Enjoy your tea!

VASSILISSA (*turning around*): Hold your tongue—you loathsome-lookin' toadstool! (*Turns corner with* KOSTYLEV.)

LUKE: I'm leavin', this very night.

BUBNOV: That's the best thing. It's always best to leave in time.

LUKE: Right you are—

BUBNOV: I know. I think I saved myself a stretch at hard labor once by leavin' in time.

LUKE: No?

BUBNOV: That's the truth. Here's how it happened: my wife got mixed up with a journeyman that was workin' for me. He was a good worker, though, right clever at dyein' dog into raccoon; cat skins, too; he'd turn 'em into wallaby, or muskrat—oh, all sorts of furs. Clever fellow. Well, then, my wife got mixed up with him. And they got so stuck on each other that it looked like they'd poison me, first thing you know, or get me out of this world in some other way. I used to beat my wife—and the journeyman would beat me. And he sure fought mean! Once he tore out half my beard and broke one of my ribs for me. Well, I got mean in my own turn. One time I fetched my wife one over the bean with a metal yardstick—and, in general, there was a major war on! However, I see that nothing will come of it the way I was gettin' at it. They was getting the upper hand of me! And right there is when I got the idea of doing my wife in. I got the idea fixed in my head right well! But I came to my senses in time. I left—

LUKE: It's best that way! Let 'em keep on makin' raccoons out of dog skins there!

BUBNOV: The only thing was, the shop, now, was in my wife's name—and I was left out in the cold, the way you see me now! Although, to tell the truth, I'd have lost the shop through drink anyway. I'm fond of hard drink, you see.

LUKE: Hard drink, eh? So that's it!

BUBNOV: None worse! Once I start pouring the stuff down, I'll drink through all I got; all I'll have left is my own hide. Then, too, I'm lazy. It's simply a sin the way I dislike work! (*Enter* SATIN *and the* ACTOR, *arguing.*)

SATIN: Bosh! You won't go anywhere! It's all the Devil's own twaddle! Say, old-timer, what stuff have you been putting into the ears of this burned-out candle end?

ACTOR: You lie! Look, Grandpa, tell him he lies! I *am* going. Today I worked; I cleaned the streets—and didn't touch a drop! How is that? And here's the coin— (*Shows some silver.*) All of thirty kopecks —and me perfectly sober!

SATIN: It's unnatural, that's what it is! Let me have that silver—I'll spend it on drink. Or else lose it at cards. (*Stretches hand toward coins.*)

ACTOR: Get away from that! That's for my fare!

LUKE (*to* SATIN): And what are you tryin' to mislead him for?

SATIN (*declaiming*): "Oh tell me, thou prophet, beloved of the gods, what the future in store for me holds?" I've been cleaned out, brother—down to my undershirt. Not everything is lost yet, Grandpa —the world still holds card sharks who are smarter than I am!

LUKE: You're a jolly fellow, Constantine—so agreeable!

BUBNOV: Hey, Hamlet! Come over here. (ACTOR *goes to window and squats on his heels before it. He and* BUBNOV *converse in very low tones.*)

SATIN: Brother, I was very entertaining when I was young! It's a pleasure to recall it! Just a devil of a fellow! I danced magnificently, played on the stage, liked to make people laugh. It was glorious!

LUKE: How is it you got off your right path?

SATIN: What an inquisitive little fellow you are, old-timer! You'd like to know everything. But why?

LUKE: A body wants to grasp what human affairs are, now. For I look at you, and I can't understand it! You're so brave, Constantine, far from stupid—and then, all of a sudden—

SATIN: Prison, Grandpa! I spent four years and seven months sitting in prison. And after you've been in prison there's no way out for you!

LUKE: Oho-ho! And what was you in for?

SATIN: For a low-down scoundrel! I killed a scoundrel because of my quick temper—he irked me. And it was in jail that I learned how really to play cards.

LUKE: And did you kill him because of a woman?

SATIN: Because of my own sister. However, you'd better lay off me! I don't like being interrogated. And—all this was long ago. My sister— died. Must be nine years ago by now. Brother, my sister was one grand person.

LUKE: You sure take your life easy! But, just a while ago, that locksmith set up such a howl! My, my, my!

SATIN: Kleshch?

LUKE: The same. There ain't no work, he was yellin'; there ain't anything!

SATIN: He'll get used to it. What am I to do for amusement now?

LUKE (*softly*): Look! Here he comes. (KLESHCH *walks on slowly, with head cast down.*)

SATIN: Hey, there, widower! Why so down in the mouth? What are you trying to think up?

KLESHCH: I'm thinking, what am I to do? I have no tools; the funeral ate everything up.

SATIN: Here's my advice: don't do a damn' thing. Just stick around and cumber the earth.

KLESHCH: It's all well and good for *you* to talk. Me, I still have some shame before folks—

SATIN: Drop it! Folks aren't ashamed because your life is worse than any dog's. Think this over: you won't work, I won't work; still others, by the hundred—by the thousand—everybody!—you understand?—all quit working! Nobody wants to do anything—what will happen then?

KLESHCH: Everybody will croak from starvation—

LUKE (*to* SATIN): With such talk as that you ought to join up with the folks that call theirselves Runners. There's a sect like that; Runners, they call theirselves—

SATIN: I know. They are no fools, Grandpa!

NATASHA (*her cry comes from the upper window*): What's that for? Hold on! (*Her voice rises almost to a scream.*) What's it for?

LUKE (*in alarm*): Is that Natasha? Isn't she yellin' for help? Eh? Oh, those two—

KOSTYLEV (*his shrill voice emerging from the fuss, hubbub, and the sound of breaking china, all issuing from the window of their flat*): A-ah! You heretic witch! You streetwalker, you!

VASSILISSA (*through window*): Stand back! Wait—I'll fix her. Take that! And that!

NATASHA (*through window*): They're beating me up! They're killing me!

SATIN (*directing his voice at the upper window*): Hey, there, you!

LUKE (*bustling about*): Vassilii, now! Somebody ought to call Vassya, now. Oh, Lord! Fellows—hey, fellows—

ACTOR (*running*): Wait, I'll get him right away!

BUBNOV: They've taken to beating her quite often, I must say.

SATIN: Come along, old-timer! We'll be witnesses!

LUKE (*following* SATIN): What sort of a witness would I make! What's the use! If only they'd get Vassilii here quickly as they can—

NATASHA'S VOICE: Sister! Dear sister! (*Wails, breaking off suddenly.*)

BUBNOV: They've shut her mouth. Guess I'll go for a look. (*Vanishes from window. The fuss in the* KOSTYLEV *flat subsides, apparently receding into some other room or the entry.*)

LUKE'S VOICE (*through upper window*): Hold on! (*Through upper window comes sound of a door slamming, and this sound cuts off, as if with an ax, all the hubbub. On stage everything is quiet. Dusk is falling.*)

KLESHCH (*sitting apathetically on the overturned sledge and rubbing his hands hard, then beginning to mutter something, at first indistinctly, then*): Well, what's a man to do? Gotta live! (*Loudly.*) Gotta have shelter. . . . Well? There is no shelter! There's nothin'! A man all on his own—all on his own, all there is of him! There ain't no help— (*Walks off, slowly, all bent over. A few moments of sinister silence. Then, somewhere in the narrow passage, an indistinct hubbub, a chaos of sounds, spring up. These increase, drawing nearer. Individual voices become distinguishable.*)

VASSILISSA: I'm her sister! Leggo of me!

KOSTYLEV: What right you got to do this?

VASSILISSA: You convict, you!

SATIN: Get Vasska here! Make it snappy! Sock him good, Wen! (*A police whistle, somewhere off*)

TATAR (*running out of passage; his right hand is in a sling*): What sort of law is being this—to killing off people in daytime?

CROOKED WEN (*entering, followed by* MEDVEDEV): Eh, but didn't I let him have it, just once!

MEDVEDEV (*to the* TATAR): Where do you get off, fightin'?

TATAR: And what about you? What you duty supposing to be?

MEDVEDEV (*running after the* TATAR): Hold on! Gimme back me whistle!

KOSTYLEV (*running out of passage*): Get him, Abram! Take him away! He's done murder! (DOUGH PAN *and* NASTYA *come around the corner of the gray wall, leading between them* NATASHA, *who is all disheveled.* SATIN *emerges, backing away from* VASSILISSA, *who, flailing her arms, is doing her utmost to get at her sister.* ALESHKA, *like one possessed, is hopping around her, whistling into her ears, shouting, howling. Then a few more people troop on. Nondescripts, male and female, but all in rags.*)

SATIN (*to* VASSILISSA): Where you going? You damned wildcat!

VASSILISSA: Get away from me, you convict! I'll tear her apart if I have to die for it!

DOUGH PAN (*after leading* NATASHA *off to one side*): As for you, Vassilissa—that'll do you! You ought to be ashamed of yourself! What you ragin' like a beast for?

MEDVEDEV (*grabbing* SATIN): Aha! I got you!

SATIN: Hey, Wen! Sail into 'em! Vasska! Vasska! (ALL *start milling near the passage between the red brick wall and the gray.* NATASHA *is led off to the pile of lumber, right, and made to sit down thereon.*)

PEPEL (*leaping out from the passageway and, without a word, roughly clearing a way through the crowd for himself*): Where's Nathalia? Hey, you—

KOSTYLEV (*disappearing around the corner*): Grab Vasska, Abram! Hey, fellows, help us take Vasska! The thief—the robber!

PEPEL (*pummelling the old man with sledge-hammer blows*): Ah, you—you old whoremaster! (KOSTYLEV *falls, in such a way that only the upper part of his body projects around the corner.* PEPEL *rushes to* NATASHA.)

VASSILISSA: Beat up Vasska! Darlings! Beat up the thief!

MEDVEDEV (*shouting at* SATIN): You dassn't butt in! It's a family affair! They're all related—but where do you come in?

PEPEL (*to* NATASHA): How—what did she come at you with? A knife?

DOUGH PAN: Lookit what beasts they are! They scalded the wench's legs with boilin' water!

NASTYA: They overturned the samovar.

TATAR: May be being by accident. You gotta knowing for sure. Must not saying just so—

NATASHA (*almost fainting*): Vassilii . . . take me away—hide me—

VASSILISSA: By all the saints! Look there! (*Pointing to* KOSTYLEV.) See for yourselves! He's dead! He's kilt! (ALL *crowd near the passage, around* KOSTYLEV.)

BUBNOV (*emerging from the crowd and going toward* VASSILII, *and saying in a low voice*): Vasska! The old man, now—he's—his goose is cooked!

PEPEL (*looking at* BUBNOV *as if he did not understand*): Go ahead —call somebody. He ought to be in a hospital. It's all right—I'll pay the bills!

BUBNOV: I'm telling you somebody laid the old man out for good— (*The hubbub on stage dies down, like a bonfire when water is thrown on it. Individual, low-voiced exclamations emerge.*)

VARIOUS VOICES: Is that so?— There's a mix-up for you!— Well, I'll be!— Let's beat it outta here, brother!— Oh, hell!— You gotta keep yourself in hand, now!— Clear outta here, whilst the police hasn't come! (*The crowd melts, one by one.* BUBNOV, TATAR, NASTYA, *and* DOUGH PAN *rush toward* KOSTYLEV'S *corpse.*)

VASSILISSA (*raising herself up from the ground and shouting in a triumphant voice*): He's kilt! My husband! And there's the one that kilt him! Vasska kilt him! I seen him! Darling, I seen him! Well, what do you say now, Vassya? Police!

PEPEL (*leaving* NATASHA'S *side*): Let me go. (*Clearing a path to the corpse.*) Out of my way! (*Contemplates the old man; turns to* VASSILISSA.) Well? You happy now? (*Touches corpse with the toe of his boot.*) Croaked—the old hound! Things fell out the way you wanted them. But—maybe I ought to do you in, too? (*Throws himself upon her.* SATIN *and* CROOKED WEN *make haste to grab him.* VASSILISSA *disappears in the passageway.*)

SATIN: Come to your senses!

CROOKED WEN: Whoa-a, there! Not so fast!

VASSILISSA (*emerging again*): Well, now, Vassya, my dear friend? There's no shaking off one's fate. Police! Blow your whistle, Abram!

MEDVEDEV: They've torn my whistle off, the devils!

ALESHKA: Here it is! (*Blows whistle.* MEDVEDEV *runs after him.*)

SATIN (*bringing* PEPEL *over to* NATASHA): Don't let it get you down, Vasska. Murder in a fight—it don't amount to nothin'! You won't get much of a stretch.

VASSILISSA: Hold Vasska! He did the killin'—I seen him!

SATIN: I hit the old man about three times myself—it wouldn't have taken much to finish him! Call me as a witness, Vasska—

PEPEL: I don't have to justify myself. What I got to do is put the skids under Vassilissa. And put them under her I will! She was puttin' me up to kill her husband—she was puttin' me up to it!

NATASHA (*suddenly and loudly*): Aha! Now I got it! Is that it, Vassilii? Fine people! They was actin' in cahoots! My sister and him! They was in cahoots! It's them that framed up the whole thing. Is that it, Vassilii? That's . . . that's why you was talkin' to me just a while ago? So's she might overhear everything? Fine people? She's his . . . sweetheart—you all know that—everybody knows it! They're in cahoots! It's her that talked him into killin' her husband—her husband was in their way . . . and I, too, was in their way. And so they maimed me—

PEPEL: Nathalia, what are you sayin'? What are you sayin'!

SATIN: What the hell's goin' on here!

VASSILISSA: You lie! She's lyin'! I . . . He, Vasska, kilt him!

NATASHA: They're in cahoots! May you be damned! Both of you!

SATIN: Well, now, this is some show! Watch your step, Vassilii! They'll pull you under, the two of them.

CROOKED WEN: I just can't get it through my head! Well, well! The things that go on!

PEPEL: Nathalia! Can it be that you really mean it? That you really believe that I . . . and she—

SATIN: My God, Natasha, you ought to—realize what's what—

VASSILISSA (*from the passageway*): They kilt my husband, Your Honor! Vasska Pepel, a thief—he done the killin', Officer, Your Honor! I seen it—everybody seen it—

NATASHA (*darting about, almost out of her senses*): Good people— my sister and Vasska done the killing! Hey, there, officers! Listen to me. . . . It's her, my own sister, that put him up to it . . . talked him into it! Her own sweetheart—there he is, damn him! They done the killin'! Take 'em . . . bring 'em to trial! Take me along, too—put me in prison . . . for Christ's own sake, put me in prison!

Curtain

ACT IV

Setting same as ACT I. PEPEL'S *room, however, is no longer in evidence; the partitions have been dismantled. And the place formerly occupied by* KLESHCH *no longer shows the block and anvil.*

The TATAR *is lying in the corner formerly taken up by* PEPEL'S *room, tossing and turning, and, at rare intervals, groaning.* KLESHCH *is seated at the table, repairing an accordeon, from time to time trying the chords. Seated at the other end of the table are* SATIN, *The* BARON, *and* NASTYA. *Standing before them is a bottle of vodka, three bottles of beer, and the heel of a big loaf of black broad. The* ACTOR *is tossing and turning on top of the stove, frequently coughing.*

Night. The scene is lighted by a lamp standing in the middle of the table.

Strong wind, off.

KLESHCH: Yes-ss. So he just up and made himself scarce during all that mix-up.

BARON: Vanished from the police. Like unto smoke that riseth from before a fire—

SATIN (*in the same declamatory vein*): Even as sinners vanish from before the righteous!

NASTYA: He was a nice little old man. But you—you ain't human. You're just so much rust!

BARON (*drinking*): To your health, Milady!

SATIN: Curious old codger! Yes! There, now, Nastenka fell in love with him.

NASTYA: Well, so I did. Yes, I came to love him! That's true. He saw everything—understood everything—

SATIN (*laughing*): And, in general, he was for many people the same thing as mush is for the toothless—

BARON (*laughing in his turn*): Or a plaster for boils!

KLESHCH: He had pity for others. But you, now—there's no pity in you—

SATIN: What good would it do you if I were to pity you?

KLESHCH: You might . . . you might—well, not exactly pity me— you might keep from hurting me—

TATAR (*sitting up on his bunk and rocking his sore hand as if it were a baby*): Old man was a good man. He having the law of the soul in him. Who having the law of soul in him is good! Who losing that law is lost!

BARON: What law is that, Prince?

TATAR: A law like that. All difference kind of law. You know what law—

BARON: Go on!

TATAR: Do not hurting any man—there being the law!

SATIN: That goes under the heading of: Penal Code, Criminal and Corrective.

BARON: And also: Penal Statutes, Within the Jurisdiction of Justices of the Peace.

TATAR: Koran naming it. Your Koran must having that law. The soul must being the Koran—yes!

KLESHCH (*testing the sound of the accordeon*): Hell, it hisses! However, it's the truth the Prince is telling you. One ought to live according to the law—according to the Gospel—

SATIN: Go ahead—who's stopping you?

BARON: Give it a try.

TATAR: Mahomet giving the Koran, saying: There being the law! Do like is being wrote here! Then coming time when Koran not being enough—that time giving its own law, a new law. Every time giving its own law—

SATIN: Well, yes! The time has come and has given us the Penal Code. A stout law! It'll be a long time before you wear it out!

NASTYA (*thumping her tumbler against the table*): Really, now— why do I go on living here—among the likes of you? I'll go away. I'll go off somewhere—to the ends of the earth.

BARON: Without any shoes, Milady?

NASTYA: Mother-naked! If I have to go crawling on all fours!

BARON: That will be most picturesque, Milady—provided it's on all fours—

NASTYA: Yes, I'll even go crawling! Only not to see your homely-lookin' puss! Ah, but I'm disgusted with everythin'! All life—all people!

SATIN: If you do start out, you might take the Actor along with you. He's getting ready to set out in the same direction. He's gotten wind of the fact that just a half a mile this side of the earth there is a clinic for organons—

ACTOR (*thrusting his head out from the top of the stove*): Or-ga-ni-sms, you blockhead!

SATIN: For organons poisoned with alcohol—

ACTOR: Yes! He'll go away! He'll go away—you'll see!

BARON: Who is *he,* Sir?

ACTOR: Me!

BARON: *Merci,* servant of the goddess—what's her name? The goddess of drama, of tragedy—what did they call her?

ACTOR: A muse, you bonehead! Not a goddess, but a muse!

SATIN: Lachesis? Hera? Aphrodite? Atropos? The Devil alone can tell which is which! It's all the old-timer's doing. He's the one that got the Actor all steamed up. You understand, Baron?

BARON: The old man is stupid!

ACTOR: Ignoramuses! Savages! Mel-po-me-ne is the muse you're thinking of! You heartless creatures! You'll see—he'll go away! "Surfeit yourselves, ye benighted minds!"—that's from a poem by Beranger . . . yes! He'll find a place for himself where there is no—no—

BARON: Where there is nothing, Sir?

ACTOR: Yes! Nothing! "This pit my grave shall be, none other seek; Here I am dying, grown powerless and weak . . ." What are you living for? What for?

BARON: Hey, you—"Kean, or Genius and Dissoluteness"—that's a drama by Dumas *père!* Stop yelling!

ACTOR: You lie! I'll keep on yelling all I want to!

NASTYA (*lifting her head up from the table and waving her arms*): Keep right on! Let 'em hear you!

BARON: Where's the sense in that, Milady?

SATIN: Leave 'em alone, Baron! To hell with 'em! Let 'em shout— let 'em break their heads! Let 'em! There must be some sense to it. Don't hinder a human bein', as the old-timer used to say. Yes, it's he, the old bag of wind, who has soured our fellow-inmates on us.

KLESHCH: He beckoned them on somewhere—but he himself didn't tell them what the road was—

BARON: The old man is a charlatan—

NASTYA: You lie! Charlatan yourself!

BARON: Hush your mouth, Milady!

KLESHCH: He had no great love for the truth, the old man didn't. He rose up against the truth, no end—and that's as it should be! Sure enough—what sort of truth is this? Even without it it's hard enough to draw a breath. There's the Prince—his hand, now, got crushed whilst he was workin'. That hand, now, will have to be sawn off clean, I hear. And there's your truth for you!

SATIN (*thumping his fist on the table*): Silence! You're dumb cattle, all of you! Keep still about the old man, you blockheads! (*More calmly.*) You, Baron, are worse than all of them! You don't savvy a thing—yet you shoot off your yap! The old man is *not* a faker. What is truth? Man—there's your truth! He grasped that—but not you! You're as thick as they come. I understand the old man—yes! He did lie—but it was out of pity for you, may the devil take you! There are many people who lie out of pity for their fellow-creatures. I know—I used to read a lot! They lie—beautifully, inspiredly, stirringly! There is the lie that consoles, the lie that makes one reconciled—the lie that justifies the overload that crushes the hand of a roustabout—and pins the blame on him who is dying from hunger! I know what lying is! Whoever is weak of soul, and whoever lives by sucking the sap out of others—to them the lie is a necessity. Some it sustains; others wrap themselves up in it. But as for him who is his own master, who is independent and doesn't devour that which is not his own—what need has he of the lie? Truth is the God of the free man!

BARON: Bravo! Beautifully, splendidly said! I agree. You speak like—like a respectable person!

SATIN: Why shouldn't a cardsharp speak well occasionally, if respectable persons speak like—card-sharps? Yes. There's a great deal I've forgotten—but there's still a thing or two I *do* know! The old man? He's a clever old thing! He had the same effect upon me as—acid has on an old and dirt-encrusted coin. Let's drink to his health! Fill the glasses! (NASTYA *fills a tumbler with beer and hands it to* SATIN. *He smiles slightly.*) The old man lived from within himself; he looked upon everything with his own eyes. Once I happened to ask him, "Grandpa, why do people live?" (*Tries to speak in* LUKE'S *voice and imitates his mannerisms.*) "Why, now," he said, "people live for somethin' better, dear little lad! There, let's say, live the carpenters—and they're rag, tag, and bobtail, all on 'em! And, lo and behold you, a certain carpenter is born amongst them—such a carpenter that the world hasn't seen his like yet; he's head and shoulders over everybody, and there's no equal to him amongst all the carpenters. He places his form and his visage, as it were, upon all carpentry, and right off moves the whole trade twenty years ahead. And the same way with all them others—locksmiths, now—shoemakers and other working people. And all them that sow and reap, and even the lords and masters—all live for the better. Everyone thinks he's goin' through life for hisself, yet it turns out that he's livin' for better things! For a hundred years, or mebbe more, they live only for the coming of a better man!" (NASTYA *is staring fixedly at* SATIN'S *face.* KLESHCH *ceases working on the accordeon and is also listening. The* BARON, *with his head bent low, is noiselessly tapping his fingers on the table. The* ACTOR, *practically off the top of the stove now, is cautiously trying to clamber down to the bunk beneath.*) "All, my dear little lad, all without exception, are livin' for somethin' better! And that's the very reason why every human bein' ought to be respected. For after all, it ain't known to us just who he may be, why he was born, and what he can do. Mebbe he was born for our happiness—for our great benefit? And we ought, most of all, to respect children—the little ones! The little ones need space! Don't you hinder the children from livin'! Respect 'em, make things easy for 'em—for the children, now!" (*Pause.*)

BARON (*thoughtfully*): Mmm . . . so. For better things? That reminds me of our family. An old family—from the times of Catherine the Great. Nobles! Warriors! Emigrés from France. They served, they rose ever higher and higher. During the reign of Nicholas the First my Grandfather, Gustav Debille, held a high post, had wealth—hundreds of serfs, thoroughbreds, chefs—

NASTYA: You lie! There wasn't anythin' of the kind!

BARON (*jumping to his feet*): Wha-at! We-ell—continue!

NASTYA: There wasn't anythin' of the kind!

BARON (*screaming*): A mansion in Moscow! A mansion in Petersburg! Coaches—coaches with escutcheons! (KLESHCH *warily picks up the accordeon, rises, and walks off to one side, whence he observes the scene.*)

NASTYA: There wasn't.

BARON: Quiet, you! There were flunkies by the score, I'm telling you!

NASTYA (*gloating*): There—was—not!

BARON: I'll kill you—

NASTYA (*getting set for flight*): There weren't no coaches!

SATIN: Leave off, Nastenka! Don't get his dander up—

BARON: Wait, you trash! My grandfather—

NASTYA: There weren't no grandfather! There weren't anything! (SATIN *roars with laughter.*)

BARON (*worn out by his wrath, slumping back on the bench*): Satin, tell her—tell this bimmy—so you, too, are laughing? You, too, don't believe me? (*Screams in despair, thumping his fists on the table.*) All of this was, the devil take both of you!

NASTYA (*gloating*): Aha, so you're howling, are you? Have you understood now how a person feels when you don't believe 'em?

KLESHCH (*coming back to table*): I thought there was goin' to be a fight.

TATAR: A-ah, people silly! Very bad.

BARON: I cannot allow people to—to make sport of me like that! I have proof— (*to* NASTYA)—documents, you devil!

SATIN: Shove 'em in an ash can. And forget about your grandfather's coaches. You won't get anywhere in the coach of the time that has been.

BARON: But how dare she—

NASTYA: You *don't* say! How dast I!

SATIN: You see, she does dare! Just wherein is she worse than you? Even though it's a sure bet that in her past there were not only no coaches but no grandfather—and not even a father and a mother—

BARON (*calming down*): The devil take you! You know how to discourse calmly. But in my case, it seems, there isn't any firmness—

SATIN: Put in a supply. It's a handy gadget. (*Pause.*) Nastya, have you been to the hospital?

NASTYA: What for?

SATIN: To see Natasha.

NASTYA: You sure do remind yourself of things! She was let out, ages ago—let out, and disappeared! She's nowhere to be found.

SATIN: That means she's been let out—for good.

KLESHCH: It would be interestin' to know—who'll dig whose grave deeper? Vasska Vassilissa's, or she his?

NASTYA: Vassilissa will squirm out of it! She's foxy. But Vasska— he'll get the book thrown at him.

SATIN: All you get for manslaughter in a fight is a stretch in prison.

NASTYA: A pity! It'd be better if he got hard labor. All of you ought to be sentenced to hard labor. Swept away, like so much rubbish, into a deep pit somewheres!

SATIN (*astonished*): What are you up to? Has the Devil gotten into you?

BARON: There, I'll give her one on the ear for being so fresh!

NASTYA: Try it! Just touch me!

BARON: I'll try, all right!

SATIN: Cut it out! Don't touch her. "Don't hurt no human bein'!" I can't get that old man out of my head! (*Roars with laughter.*) "Don't hurt no human bein'!" But what if I have been hurt once—and that one hurt was enough to last me all my life? What then? Forgive? Forgive nothing! Forgive nobody—

BARON (*to* NASTYA): You've got to understand this: I'm not your kind. You are—filth!

NASTYA: Oh, you miserable creature! Why, you—you live off of me, like a worm off an apple! (*A uniform explosion of laughter from the men.*)

KLESHCH: Ah, what a fool! What a little apple!

BARON: You just can't be angry at her! What an idiot!

NASTYA: Laughing, are you? You lie! You don't feel like laughing!

ACTOR (*somberly*): Let them have it!

NASTYA: If I only could! I'd take you, and— (*Picks up a cup from the table and smashes it against the floor.*) That's what I'd do to you!

TATAR: What for breaking dishes? Eh-eh, woodenhead!

BARON (*rising*): No—I'm going to—teach her manners right away!

NASTYA (*running off*): To hell with all of you!

SATIN (*calling after her*): Hey, there! That's enough! Whom are you trying to scare? And just what's up, after all?

NASTYA: You wolves, you! May you all croak! Wolves!

ACTOR (*somberly*): Amen!

TATAR: Ugh-ugh! Russian woman—bad-tempered woman! Fresh. Too free! Tatar woman—no! Tatar woman knowing law!

KLESHCH: What she needs is a good dusting.

BARON: Low-down . . . creature!

KLESHCH (*testing the accordeon*): Done! But its owner ain't here yet. That lad is going to hell with himself.

SATIN: Have a drink now!

KLESHCH: Thanks! Time to hit the hay, too.

SATIN: Getting used to us?

KLESHCH (*takes some vodka, then goes to his bunk in the corner*): 'Tain't so bad. People are people wherever you go. At first a body can't see that. Then you take a closer look, and it turns out people are people everywhere. 'Tain't so bad! (*The* TATAR *spreads something over his bunk, gets down on his knees, and prays.*)

BARON (*indicating The* TATAR *to* SATIN): Look!

SATIN: Leave him alone! He's a good fellow, don't bother him! (*Laughs loudly.*) I'm in a kindly mood today—the devil knows why!

BARON: You're always in a kindly mood—when you get some likker in you. And intelligent!

SATIN: When I'm drunk I like everything. Ye-es. What's he doing—praying? Splendid! A man may believe—or he may not believe—that's his own affair! A man is free—he pays for everything himself; for belief, for unbelief, for love, for intellect. Man himself settles the score—and for that reason he is free! Man—there's the truth! What is man? It's not I, not you, not they—no! It's you, I, they, the old man, Napoleon, Mahomet—all in one! (*Draws a human outline in the air with his finger.*) Understand? This is something enormous! In it are all the beginnings and all the ends. Everything is within man—everything is for man! Only man exists; as for all the rest, it's the work of his hands and his mind! (*Spells out.*) M-a-n! That's magnificent! That has a proud sound! M-a-n! You must respect man! Not pity him—not degrade him with pity. You must respect him! Let's drink to Man, Baron! (*Rises.*) It's a fine thing—to feel yourself a man! I am a convict, a murderer, a cardsharp—well, yes! When I pass through a street, people look at me as at a crook; they step aside and look around—and many a time they say to me, "Scoundrel! Faker! Work!" Work? What for? So as to have a full belly? (*Laughs loudly.*) I've always despised people who expend too much thought on having full bellies. That isn't the heart of the matter, Baron! It isn't! Man is above that! Man is above a full belly!

BARON (*shaking his head*): You are discoursing. That's a good thing—it must warm the heart. I lack that sort of thing. I can't do it! (*Looks around him, then speaks softly, cautiously.*) Brother, there are times when I am—afraid. You understand? I'm scared stiff. Because—what's going to happen later?

SATIN (*pacing room*): Nonsense? Whom has man to fear?

BARON: Do you know, ever since I can remember myself . . . there's been some sort of a haze in my head. I have never understood anything. I feel—embarrassed, somehow. It seems to me that all my life all I've been doing is changing from one suit to another—but to what end? I can't understand it! I studied; I wore the uniform of an aristocratic school. But what was it I studied? Can't remember. I married; that meant putting on a morning coat, and then a lounging robe. The wife I took unto myself was a vile creature—and why did I ever do it? Can't understand. I went through all my property—every bit of it!—whereupon I wore some sort of pepper-and-salt coat and rusty-looking trousers. But how did I come to ruin myself? Didn't notice. I had a post with the Treasury Department—uniform coat, and a cap with a cockade. I embezzled government funds—and so they put the convict's floppy denim on me. After that I put on *these* sartorial gems. And all this came about as if in a dream. Eh? Funny, isn't it?

SATIN: Not very. Stupid, rather.

BARON: Yes. I, too, think it's stupid. And yet—I must have been born for something. Eh?

SATIN (*laughing*): Probably. Man is born for better things! (*Nods head.*) That way everything is fine!

BARON: This—Nastenka! She ran off—where to? Should I go and see . . . where she is? After all, she is— (*Exit. Pause.*)

ACTOR: Hey, Tatar! (*Pause.*) Prince! (TATAR *turns his head.*) Pray . . . for me.

TATAR: What is it?

ACTOR (*in a lower voice*): For me . . . pray!

TATAR (*after a short silence*): Yourself—pray.

ACTOR (*quickly climbing off stove, going up to table, pouring vodka for himself with a trembling hand, and then all but running out into the entry*): I'm off!

SATIN (*calling after* ACTOR): Hey, there, you Sicambrian! Where are you off to? (*Sends a shrill whistle after the* ACTOR. *Enter* MEDVEDEV, *in a woman's quilted jacket, and* BUBNOV; *the latter has a string of pretzels in one hand and several sun-cured fish in the other; there is a bottle of vodka under his arm and another bottle sticks out of a side pocket of his jacket. Both revelers are tipsy, but not too much so.*)

MEDVEDEV: A camel is . . . a sort of an ass! Only he ain't got no ears.

BUBNOV: Aw, can that! You yourself are a sort of an ass.

MEDVEDEV: It ain't got no ears whatsoever, a camel ain't. It hears through its nostrils—

BUBNOV (*to* SATIN): My friend! I been lookin' for you through all the ginmills and beer joints! Take a bottle—my hands is all full.

SATIN: Try putting the pretzels on the table—that'll free one hand.

BUBNOV (*testing the theory*): It works! Oh, you—Edison! Look at him! There he is—in person! Eh? There's a lad who knows all the answers!

MEDVEDEV: Crooks are all smart—I know! They can't get along without they got brains. A good man, now, he's good even if he's foolish; but a bad one, he absolutely must have brains. But about a camel, now, you're all wet. It's a saddle animal—it ain't got no horns— and it ain't got no teeth—

BUBNOV: Where's all the people? Why's there nobody around? Hey, crawl out of your holes—it's my treat! Who's that in the corner?

SATIN: Will it take you long to spend your last copper on drink? You scarecrow!

BUBNOV: Oh, it won't take me long! This time I didn't accumulate no great capital. Hey, Crooked Wen! Where's Wen?

KLESHCH (*walking up to the table*): He ain't around.

BUBNOV (*with appropriate mimicry*): Grrr! Watchdog! Gobble gobble, gobble! Like a tom-turkey! Stop barking, stop grumbling! Drink, have a good time, keep your chin up! I'm treatin' everybody! Brother, I love to treat! If I was rich, I'd—I'd start a free ginmill! By God, I would! With music, and there'd be a whole choir! Drop in, drink, eat, listen to the singin'—make your souls rejoice! You fellows without a copper to your names—c'mon over to me free ginmill! As for you, Satin—as for you—here, take half of all my capital! That's what!

SATIN: You give me all of it right now—

BUBNOV: All my capital? Right now? Here y'are! There's a ruble—and here's twenty kopecks more—some five-kopeck pieces—a few coppers—it's all yours!

SATIN: Very well, then! Your money will be safer with me. I'll gamble with it.

MEDVEDEV: I'm witness to the transaction: the money's been given to you for safekeeping. What's the amount?

BUBNOV: You? You're a camel. We don't need no witnesses—

ALESHKA (*entering barefooted*): Fellows, I got me feet all wet—

BUBNOV: Come and wet your throat, then! That's the best cure of all! You're a swell guy—you sing and make music—that's shplendid! But as for drinkin'—you ain't doin' the right thing at all, at all. Drinkin' is bad for you.

ALESHKA: All I have to do is take one look at you to see that. But it's only when you're stewed that you look like a human bein'. Kleshch! Did you fix my accordeon? (*Sings, as he does the Cossack dance.*)

> Eh, if this here mug
> Weren't so sweet and smug,
> Me lady friend would never
> Love me up and hug!

I've caught a chill, fellows! It's co-old!

MEDVEDEV: Mmm-yes! And supposin' I was to ask you who your lady friend is?

BUBNOV: Lay off of him! Brother, you're all washed up now. You ain't no p'leeceman no more—that's all over! Neither a p'leeceman nor an uncle—

ALESHKA: But just plain aunty's husband!

BUBNOV: One of your nieces is in prison; the other's dyin'—

MEDVEDEV (*with proud dignity*): You lie. She ain't dyin'—I got her listed as missin' without clues! (SATIN *goes off into roars of laughter.*)

BUBNOV: It's all the same thing, brother! A man without nieces ain't no uncle!

ALESHKA (*with a sweeping bow*): Your Excellency! Grand Drum Major to a Dowager She-goat (*Sings.*)

> Me girl friend has the money,
> I'm broke as broke can be;
> But I am spry and funny,
> She calls me honey-bunny!

It's cold, fellows! (*Enter* CROOKED WEN; *then—to the end of the act—others, men and women, trickle in; they undress and settle in the bunks as they grumble to themselves.*)

CROOKED WEN: What did you run off for, Bubnov?

BUBNOV: Come here! Sit down. Let's sing together, brother! My favorite song—eh?

TATAR: Nighttime for sleep! Singing songs for daytime!

SATIN: Oh, never mind that, Prince. You come over here!

TATAR: What are you meaning, never mind? Noise will being. When songs singing noise is being—

BUBNOV (*going to him*): How's the hand doing, Prince? Have they cut off your hand yet?

TATAR: What for? We waiting a while yet; maybe not having to cut. Hand not made of iron—not taking long to cut—

CROOKED WEN: You're in a *yaman,* like you Tatars say; in a bad way, Hassanka! Without a hand you won't be any good! Our kind is valued only for our hands and backs. If the hand ain't there—there ain't no man! Your chances ain't worth a pinch of snuff. Come on and have a drink—and that's that!

DOUGH PAN (*entering*): Ah, my dear fellow-tenants! You got no idea what it's like out—you got no idea! Cold, slush. My policeman here? Hey, there, master mind!

MEDVEDEV: Here!

DOUGH PAN: Wearin' my jacket again? And it looks like you were a little stewed, eh? What's the grand idea?

MEDVEDEV: It's a birthday party—Bubnov's! And—it's cold, slushy—

DOUGH PAN: I'll make you watch your step, you! Slush! Stop cuttin' up. Go to bed, now!

MEDVEDEV (*going off into the kitchen*): Sleep is something I could do with. I want to sleep—it's time!

SATIN: How come you're so strict with him?

DOUGH PAN: There ain't no other way, dear friend. A man like that you gotta be strict with. I took him for a lover, thinkin' he'd be of some good to me—since he's a military man, sort of, whereas you folks are all ornery, and me bein' only a woman. But what does he do but take to drink! That don't benefit me none!

SATIN: You didn't use very good judgment in choosing a helpmate—

DOUGH PAN: No, it's best that way! You wouldn't want to live with me—you ain't the sort! But even if you should get to livin' with me, it wouldn't last more'n a week—you'd lose me at cards, chitterlings and all!

SATIN (*roaring with laughter*): Right you are, landlady! I would gamble you away!

DOUGH PAN: There, you see! Aleshka!

ALESHKA: Here I be!

DOUGH PAN: You been talking about me?

ALESHKA: Me? All the time—all the time, so help me! "There's a woman, for you!" I tell 'em. "An amazing woman! Three hundred and sixty-five pounds of flesh, fat, bone—and not an ounce of brains!"

DOUGH PAN: There you lie! When it comes to brains I got too much, actually. No, but why do you say I beat my policeman a lot?

ALESHKA: I think you must have been beating him, since you were pulling his hair—

DOUGH PAN (*laughing*): You fool! You ought to see there's no use washing dirty linen before everybody! And, again, that hurts him. It's because of your talk that he's taken to drinking—

ALESHKA: So it must be true what they say—even a hen will take to drink! (SATIN *and* KLESHCH *burst into laughter.*)

DOUGH PAN: Ugh, you scalawag! What sort of a man are you. Aleshka?

ALESHKA: The very first sort! Good all around! Whichever way the winds blow, that's the way I go!

BUBNOV (*near* TATAR'S *bunk*) : Come on, Prince! We won't let you sleep anyway. We're going to sing—all night long! Hey, Crooked Wen!

CROOKED WEN: Sing, did you say? Could be!

ALESHKA: And I'll play the tunes for you.

SATIN: And we'll listen!

TATAR (*smiling*) : Well, Bubna, you old Shaitan! Let's have a glass. We will drinking, will having a good time—when death coming, we will dying!

BUBNOV: Fill a glass for him, Satin! Sit down, Crooked Wen! Eh, brothers! Is it much a man needs? There, I've put a drink or two under my belt and I'm happy. Hey, Wen, start singing—my favorite song! I'll start singing it—and crying—

CROOKED WEN (*leads off*) : "The sun rises and the sun sets—"

BUBNOV (*quickly chiming in*) : "But my prison knows no light—"

BARON (*flinging open the entry door and calling from the threshold*) : Hey! All of you! Come on! Come on out! There—out in the back lots! The Actor went and hanged himself! (*General silence. All stare at the* BARON. NASTYA *appears behind him, then, with staring eyes, goes slowly to the table.*)

SATIN (*in a quiet voice*) : Eh! He had to go and spoil our song— the fool!

Final Curtain

Anton Pavlovich
Chekhov
1 8 6 0 — 1 9 0 4

＊ ＊

> I recently reread almost all of Chekhov. And everything in him is won-
> drous. . . . Chekhov as an artist is beyond comparison with former Rus-
> sian writers—with Turgenev, Dostoievski, or with me.
>
> TOLSTOI, quoted by
>
> P. A. SERGHEIENCO (1904)

> Beautifully simple, he [Chekhov] loved everything simple, genuine,
> sincere. . . . Hating all that was vulgar and filthy, he described all
> the vilenesses of life in the noble language of a poet, with the gentle
> smile of a humorist.
>
> GORKI

ANTON CHEKHOV, the son of an ex-serf who kept a general store, was born in Taganrog (in the south of Russia), where he went through the gymnasium (and received sixty per cent in an examination on the Russian language). In the closely knit family he was a veritable Yorick; some of the domestic tomfooleries were subsequently incorporated in his early work. In his 'teens he was madly in love with the theater; he took the part of the *Mayor* in a home production of *The Inspector General.*

He entered the University of Moscow in 1879 and was graduated in medicine in 1884, but did not practice long nor regularly; later, when importunate admirers insisted on consulting him as a doctor, he utilized the gold pieces received as fees (the prescriptions were generally kept as autographs) for his innumerable charities.

The family became impoverished, and to support it and finance his studies Chekhov became an out-and-out humorist and superb parodist for the newspapers and comic weeklies; his first story appeared in 1880. He resorted to a number of pen names, since he wanted to reserve his real name for medical articles; the most famous pseudonym, and the one by which he is still affectionately called, was Antosha Chehonte, a nickname he had received from an instructor in theology during his schooldays; the one he enjoyed most was The Man Without a Spleen; a pen name which originated in a typesetter's error; a letter to one of his brothers is signed Schiller Shakespearovich Goethe. (Incidentally, one brother, Alexander, also contributed to the humorous periodicals, while another, Nicolai, drew for them.)

1886 was a year of transition for Chekhov; he was becoming a "serious" or "thick-paper" writer. His first full-length play, *Ivanov,* was produced and was greeted both with wild applause and loud hisses—it was an unqualified success only three years later, when it was given under a different management. In the same year he established his reputation with *Motley Stories.* (This is usually cited as his first book, but that honor belongs to *Stories of Melpomene,* brought out two years before at the author's expense.)

Chekhov had the usual trouble with the censorship; his first dramatic effort, *On the Highway* (a one-act dramatization of a short story of his) never saw the stage, for it was suppressed as "too dismal and filthy" —in reality, it showed a gentleman who had ruined himself through drink, and gentlemen were, at that time, sacrosanct in Russia; nor was the playlet published until after the author's death. He also had the courage to resign (together with Korolenco and others) as an Academician when, in 1902, the Academy of Science, under pressure from the government, rescinded its election of Gorki.

In 1890 Chekhov (one of the comparatively few Russian authors to escape prison and exile) journeyed to the island of Sakhalin, then Russia's Devil's Island, where he saw men chained to wheelbarrows and the strappado in use; he talked with and cross-indexed every one of the ten-thousand population of convicts and penal settlers. The resultant book, with the name of the island for title, is a pioneering study in penology, a devastating indictment of Czarist Russia's inhumanity to Russians, and contains fascinating thumbnail sketches of some of Russia's most fantastic master-criminals.

The last half of the '90's and the early 1900's came to be considered the era of the *Chekhovian mood*—a yearning, during a period of hopeless national stagnation and reaction, for something better ("Moscow! Moscow!"), the era of the *Chekhovian dove-gray cloak.* (The reader is entitled to know these catch-phrases for his own appraisement. Chekhov himself discounted them enormously; when a lady, well-dressed, handsome, and with plenty of well-fed flesh on her solid bones, assumed the *Chekhov tone* and complained to him: "Life is so drab, Anton Pavlovich! Everything is so gray: people, sky, sea; even the flowers seem gray to me. And there are no desires—the soul is weary. Just as if it were a disease of some sort—" he interrupted her with conviction: "It is a disease, Ma'am! It even has a Latin name—they call it *morbus pretendialis.*")

The awesome triumvirate of Tolstoi, Dostoievski, and Turgenev changed to the somewhat less austere one of Chekhov, Gorki, and Tolstoi.

The Sea Gull had a history similar to that of *Ivanov;* in 1896 it was hissed off the stage; in 1898, as produced by Stanislavski at the Moscow Art Theater, it was a gigantic success. 1901 is marked by the production of *The Three Sisters,* and by Chekhov's marriage to Olga Knipper, creator of *Mary* in that play, and of *Nastya* in *The Lowest Depths.* The first night of *The Cherry Orchard* (January 17, 1904), to which he was forcibly brought for the third-act curtain, coincided with the author's forty-fourth birthday and was turned not only into a birthday celebration but an anticipatory jubilee (he had been writing for almost twenty-five years).

This was the culminating point of his career as a writer. Chekhov had had pulmonary tuberculosis since 1883, at least, and had been forced to live at Yalta, in the Crimea (1898-

1904) and elsewhere where the climate was more suitable for his lungs than in his beloved Moscow, to which he was always drawn; there had also been repeated trips abroad in search of health. The last one was to Badenweiler, in the Black Forest, where he died July 2, 1904.

The last scene in the career of the author of *Oysters* was as fantastic, as exquisitely ironic as anything he ever wrote. "Vulgarity," Gorki tells us, "was his enemy; all his life had he contended with it; it was vulgarity he had mocked and depicted with a dispassionate, sharp-pointed pen.... And vulgarity avenged itself upon him with a most abominable little prank. . . . The coffin of the writer 'tenderly loved' by all Moscow was brought home in some sort of green-painted freight-car, with a sign in large letters on its sliding door: FOR OYSTERS. Part of the small throng which had gathered to receive the body of the writer went off after the coffin of General Keller, which had been brought back from Manchuria, wondering greatly why Chekhov was being buried to the strains of a military band. When the error was cleared up, there were slight smiles and giggling from the more lighthearted ones. Chekhov's coffin was followed by a hundred or so—no more; very memorable were two lawyers, both in brand-new footwear and gay cravats. Walking behind them I heard one speaking of the intelligence of the dog. . . . And some lady in a lilac dress, walking under a lacy parasol, was assuring an old man in horn-rimmed spectacles: 'Ah, he was amazingly charming, and so witty. . . .'

"The dirty-green blotch of that freight-car seems to me nothing else save the huge grin of vulgarity, triumphant over its wearied foe."

Chekhov not merely perfected the Russian short story but advanced the form throughout the world. Ninety-five per cent of his stories are sheer perfection. *A Work of Art* is given here as a specimen of Chekhov's pure humor; *Chorus Lady,* as characteristic of Chekhov in transition: if one cares to go deeper than the sugar-coating of the amusing situation, one can come upon the "bitter core of reproach."

As playwright, Chekhov is the creator of his own, individual drama—the untheatrical theater, substituting mood and atmosphere for plot and claptrap, transmuting static material into lyricity. His *Cherry Orchard* has been proclaimed the greatest play since Shakespeare, and his *Three Sisters* as the supreme play of all time and throughout the world.

Chekhov himself maintained that his plays were really light comedies. That view finds support in none other than Andreiev: "Do not believe that *The Three Sisters* is a pessimistic play, engendering only despair and fruitless melancholy. It is a radiant, fine play. . . . Take pity on the sisters . . . and, in passing, join in their summoning cry: 'To Moscow!' To Moscow! To the light! To life, freedom and happiness!"

As for the alleged melancholy per-meating his work, Chekhov wrote somewhere that, to the Russian writer, melancholy was what the humble potato is to a skilled French chef—it can be dished out in two hundred different ways. And while writing was no easier a taskmistress to him than to any other genuine writer, one memoirist, G. S. Petrov, quotes Chekhov on Chekhov (at least in his beginnings) : "I wrote as a bird sings. I'd sit down and write. Without thinking of how to write or about what. My things wrote themselves. I could write at any time I liked. To write a sketch, a story, a skit cost me no labor. I, like a young calf or a colt let out into the freedom of a green and radiant pasture, leaped, cavorted, kicked up my heels. . . . I laughed myself and made those around me laugh. I came to grips with life and, without wasting much thought on it, tossed it this way and that. I pinched it, tickled it, grabbed its sides, poked my finger in its ribs, in its breast; I slapped it on the belly. I felt gay myself—and, from the sidelines, the result must have been very funny."

The main characteristics of Chekhov's unusual talent were a psychological insight (more merciful and hopeful than Dostoievski's), keen observation, a bright, gentle, fresh humor, pity, understanding—and fine irony and exquisite skepticism rather than the glibly touted melancholy. His ideal was a healthy, cultured society—not merely for Russia but for all mankind.

Work of Art

HUGGING UNDER HIS ARM a something wrapped up in No. 223 of the *Stock Exchange News,* Sasha Smirnov (his mother's only son) put on a mawkishly solemn mien and entered the consulting room of Dr. Koshelcov.

"Ah, my dear young fellow!" the Doctor greeted him. "Well, how do we feel? What's the good word?"

Sasha took to blinking his eyes, placed his hand on his heart, and spoke in a voice pulsating with emotion:

"Sir, my mother sends you her regards and told me to thank you. I am my mother's only son—and you have saved my life . . . you have pulled me through a dangerous illness and . . . we both hardly know how to thank you."

"There, that'll do, youngster!" the Doctor cut him short, yet at the same time feeling ever so pleased. "I've done no more than anybody else would have in my place."

"I am my mother's only son. We are poor people and, of course, cannot pay you for your services and . . . we feel very much put out about it, Doctor. But just the same, my mother and I—I am my mother's only son—we earnestly beg you to accept as a token of our gratitude this—this object, which—a most valuable object, of antique bronze— a rare work of art—"

"Oh, but you really shouldn't have done this!" the Doctor made a wry face. "There, why did you have to go and do it?"

"No, really, you mustn't refuse it, please," Sasha kept on mumbling, in the meanwhile undoing the parcel. "By refusing it you will hurt not only my dear mother's feelings but my own. It's a very fine object—of antique bronze. It has come down to us from my dear late father, and we treasured it as a precious remembrance. My dear father used to buy up antique bronzes and sell them to connoisseurs. And now my dear mother and I are in the same line."

Translated by Bernard Guilbert Guerney. Copyright, 1943, by *Encore* and published here by courtesy of that magazine and Dent Smith, its editor.

Sasha unwrapped the object and placed it, in solemn triumph, on the Doctor's desk. It was a candelabrum, rather squat, of antique bronze and artistic workmanship. It depicted a group: two decidedly female figures, standing on a pedestal in the costume of Eve and in poses for the description of which I have neither the powers nor a suitable temperament. The two nudes were smiling coquettishly and, in general, had such an air about them that it seemed as if, were it not for their bounden duty of propping up the candelabrum, they would have skipped off their pedestal and staged such a debauch in the room as, reader, it is unseemly even to think of.

After but one glance at the gift the Doctor fell to scratching the back of his right ear meditatively, grunted, and hesitantly blew his nose.

"Yes, it really is an exquisite object," he murmured, "but—how am I to put it?—not quite the thing . . . not at all for general perusal, so to say. . . . This is no longer *décolletée* but the deuce knows what."

"Oh, now, just why do you say that?"

"The tempter himself, that old serpent, couldn't have thought up anything nastier. Why, if you were to keep such a case of delirium tremens on the desk it would mean defiling the whole apartment!"

"What strange views you have on art, Doctor!" Sasha took umbrage at the remark. "Why, it's an artistic object—just take a look at it! There is so much beauty and elegance about it that the soul becomes filled with reverent awe and tears well up in one's throat! When one beholds such beauty one forgets all things earthly. . . . Just take a look—what mobility, what ethereal masses, what expressiveness!"

"I understand all that very well, my dear fellow," the Doctor broke in on him, "but, after all, I'm a family man. I have little ones running around here; I have lady patients!"

"Of course, if one looks at it from the point of view of the mob," Sasha conceded, "then, of course, this highly artistic object appears in a different light. . . . But, Doctor, rise above the mob! All the more so since by your refusal you will deeply grieve not only my dear mother but me. I am my mother's only son—you have saved my life. We are relinquishing to you the thing we hold most precious and—and my only regret is that the mate to this candelabrum is missing."

"Thanks, my dear friend, I am most grateful. Regards to your dear mother . . . but really, by God, you can judge for yourself—I have little ones running around here; I have lady patients. Oh, well, let it stay! For there's no arguing with you."

"Why, there's really nothing to argue about," Sasha rejoiced. "Just put the candelabrum here—right next to this vase. There! What a pity, though, that the mate to it is missing! What a pity! Well, good-by, Doctor!"

After Sasha's departure the Doctor contemplated the candelabrum a long time, scratching the back of his right ear and pondering.

"A superb object, indisputably," he reflected, "and it would be a pity just to chuck it out. . . . But as for leaving it around the house, that's simply out. . . . Hmm! What a dilemma! Whom could I present or contribute it to?"

After a great deal of reflection he remembered a good friend of his, one Uhov, a lawyer, who had done some legal work for him and to whom he was consequently indebted.

"That will be just the thing," the Doctor decided. "Since he's a friend of mine he wouldn't feel right taking money from me, and it would be most appropriate for me to make him a present of this object. I'll cart this fiendish thing over to his place! Besides, he's single and none too serious-minded."

Without any further delay the Doctor put on his things, took the candelabrum, and set out for Uhov's.

"Greetings, my friend!" said he, finding the lawyer at home. "I'm here to . . . to thank you, brother, for your efforts. You won't take any money, so you might at least accept this trifling object. There you are, brother! A little thing—but no end magnificent!"

On catching sight of the trifling object the lawyer became indescribably delighted.

"What an item!" he guffawed. "Ah, the devil take it all! What clever devils there are, to think up a thing like that! Wonderful! Amazing! Wherever did you get anything so fascinating?"

However, after having vented his delight, the lawyer cast a wary glance toward the door:

"The only thing is, brother," he announced, "you'll have to take your present back. I won't accept it."

"Why?" the Doctor became apprehensive.

"Oh, just so. . . . My mother drops in on me; I have lady clients, and, besides, I'd feel ashamed before the house help."

"Never, never, never! You dare not refuse!" the Doctor flailed his arms. "You would be behaving like a swine if you did! It's an object of art. What mobility . . . what expressiveness! . . . . I won't even discuss the matter! You would offend me by refusing it."

"If only it were daubed over in the right places—or if one could stick on fig-leaves here and there—"

But the Doctor took to flailing his arms harder than ever, made a hasty getaway from Uhov's place, and, satisfied with having been able to get the gift off his hands, went home.

After the Doctor's departure the lawyer looked over the candelabrum thoroughly, his fingers caressing it as he turned it every which way and, just as the Doctor had done, racked his head as to what he could do with the present.

"It's a beautiful thing," he cogitated, "and it would be a pity just to throw it out, yet at the same time it wouldn't be proper to keep it around the place. The best thing would be to make a present of it to somebody. . . . Here's what: I'll make an offering of this candelabrum to Shashkin, the comedian, this very evening. The scoundrel is crazy about things like that, and, appropriately enough, it's his benefit tonight."

No sooner said than done. That evening the candelabrum, painstakingly wrapped, was ceremoniously presented to Shashkin. And all evening long the comedian's dressing room was under assault by males who came to admire the present and was filled by an incessant enraptured din and by laughter that sounded like neighing. But if any actress approached the door, asking: "May I come in?"—the comic's hoarse voice would be raised in instant warning: "No, no, honey! I'm not decent!"

But once the performance was over, the comedian took to shrugging his shoulders and gesturing hopelessly:

"There, now," he said repeatedly, "where am I to put this abomination? Why, I room with a respectable family! I have actresses calling on me! It isn't like photographs—you can't hide *that* in a desk drawer!"

"Why, you just go ahead and sell it, Sir," his dresser advised him, helping him to change into his street clothes. "There's an old woman at the edge of the town who makes a business of buying up old bronzes. Take the trolley there and ask for Smirnova. Everybody knows her."

The comedian followed the good advice.

Two days later the Doctor happened to be sitting in his consulting room and, with a finger to his brow, was meditating on the gall and its acids. Suddenly the door burst open and Sasha Smirnov flew into the room. He was beaming, radiant, and his whole being exuded happiness. And in his hands he held a something wrapped up in a newspaper.

"Doctor!" he began, gasping. "Imagine my delight! It's just your good fortune—we've succeeded in acquiring a mate to your candelabrum! Is my dear mother happy! I am my mother's only son . . . you saved my life—"

And Sasha, quivering with grateful emotion, placed the candelabrum before the Doctor.

The Doctor let his jaw drop, was about to say something, but didn't say a thing. He couldn't find his tongue.

The Chorus Lady

ONCE, WHEN SHE HAD been somewhat younger, and better in looks and voice, Nicholas Kolpacov, who adored her, happened to be sitting in the attic-room of the country house where she was staying for the summer. It was insufferably hot and stifling. Kolpacov had just dined and finished off a whole bottle of indifferent port; he was out of sorts and did not feel at all well. Both of them were bored stiff and merely marking time until the heat abated and they would be able to go out for a stroll.

Suddenly and unexpectedly someone rang the front doorbell. Kolpacov, who was in shirtsleeves and house slippers, sprang up and looked at Pasha questioningly.

"The postman, probably, or maybe one of my girl friends," said the songstress.

Kolpacov would have been embarrassed neither before any of Pasha's girl friends nor any postmen, but, just to be on the safe side, he grabbed up his clothes in an armful and went off into an adjoining room, while Pasha hurried to open the door. To her great surprise the person standing on the threshold was neither the postman nor a girl friend but some unknown woman—young, handsome, dressed like a lady, and, to all appearances, of the respectable sort.

The stranger was pale and breathing hard, as though after a climb up a long flight of stairs.

Translated by Bernard Guilbert Guerney. Copyright, 1943, by *Encore* and published here by courtesy of that magazine and Dent Smith, its editor.

"What is it you wish?" asked Pasha.

The lady did not answer at once. She took a step forward, looked over the room slowly, and took a seat with the air of one unable to keep on her feet because of fatigue or poor health; then, for a long while, her pale lips merely moved, as she tried to say something.

"Is my husband with you?" she asked at last, raising her great eyes with their reddened, tear-stained lids and fixing them on Pasha.

"What husband?" Pasha got out in a whisper, and suddenly grew so scared that she felt her hands and feet turn cold. "What husband?" she repeated, beginning to tremble.

"*My* husband—Nicholas Kolpacov."

"N-no . . . no, Ma'am. I—I don't know anything about any husbands."

A minute went by in silence. The stranger passed a handkerchief several times over her pale lips and, in order to overcome an inward tremor, held her breath, while Pasha stood before her without stirring, as though she were rooted to the spot, and stared at her caller with incomprehension and fear.

"So he isn't here, you say?" asked the lady, this time in a firm voice and with an odd sort of smile.

"I—I don't know whom you're asking for."

"You are vile—and low, and abominable," murmured the stranger, eying Pasha with hatred and aversion. "Yes, yes . . . you are vile. I am very, very glad to be able to tell you this to your face at last!"

Pasha sensed that she was making an impression of something vile, something hideous, upon this lady in black with her wrathful eyes and her white, slender fingers, and she became ashamed of her own plump red cheeks, of the freckles on her nose and the bang dangling over her forehead. This bang simply would not stay in place, no matter how she combed it. And it seemed to her that if she were a skinny little thing, without quite so much powder plastered on her face, and minus that bang, why, it might have been possible to hide the fact that she wasn't respectable, and it wouldn't be so terrible and shameful to be standing before a strange, mysterious lady.

"Where is my husband?" the lady went on. "However, whether he's here or not is immaterial to me, but I must inform you that an embezzlement has been revealed, and that they are looking for Nicholas. . . . They want to arrest him. There, that's all your doing!"

The lady stood up and, in great agitation, traversed the room. Pasha stared at her and, out of sheer fright, could not grasp a thing.

"They'll find him this very day and arrest him," declared the lady, emitting something between a snivel and a whimper, and one could sense in this sound both injury and exasperation. "I know who brought him to such a horrible pass. You are vile, abominable! You repulsive, meretricious creature!" (The lady's lips writhed and her nose wrinkled in aversion.) "I am powerless—listen to me, you low woman! . . . I am powerless, you have greater power than I—yet there is One to intercede for my children and for me! God sees all things! He is just! He will demand an accounting from you for my every tear, for all the sleepless nights I have spent! A time will come when you shall remember me!"

Another silence ensued. The lady paced the room and wrung her hands, while Pasha kept staring at her dully, unable to comprehend anything and expecting her to do something dreadful.

"I don't know a thing, Ma'am," she managed to say, and suddenly broke into tears.

"You lie!" the lady raised her voice, her eyes flashing malevolently at the girl. "I know everything! I've known about you a long time now! I know that all last month he spent every day hanging around here!"

"Very well. So what? What does it signify? I've lots of gentlemen calling on me, but I ain't holding nobody here against their will. He's free to come here of his own free will."

"An embezzlement has been revealed, I am telling you! He has embezzled money that doesn't belong to him where he works! For the sake of—of such a one as yourself—for *your* sake he has dared to commit a crime. Listen," said the lady in a resolute voice, halting before Pasha and facing her squarely, "it's impossible that you should be utterly devoid of principles; true, you live only to inflict evil, which is your purpose—yet it's inconceivable that you can have fallen so low as not to have even a trace of human feeling left in you! He has a wife, he has children. . . . If he should be convicted and sent up, why, his children and I would starve to death. Do understand this! Yet at the same time there is a way to save both him and us from poverty and disgrace. If I were to bring in nine hundred rubles today—well, they will not bother him. Nine hundred rubles—no more!"

"What nine hundred rubles?" Pasha asked in a stifled voice. "I . . . I don't know a thing about any such amount. . . . I never took none of it."

"I am not asking you for nine hundred rubles. You have no money, and besides, I don't need anything that is really yours. It's something else I'm asking of you. Men usually make valuable gifts to—the likes of you. Let me have back only those things which my husband made you a present of."

"Why, Ma'am, he never made me a present of anything!" Pasha protested shrilly, beginning to understand.

"Where is the money, in that case? He has squandered not only his own money but mine, and that of others. Where has it all gone to, then? See here—I'm begging you! I was all wrought up and told you a great many unpleasant things—well, I apologize. You must hate me, I know, but if you are at all capable of compassion, *do* put yourself in my place! Give those things back to me, I implore you!"

"Hmm. . . ." said Pasha and shrugged her shoulders. "I'd do it with pleasure, but—may God punish me if I lie!—he never gave me a thing. Cross my heart—you gotta believe me. Hold on, though—you're right." The songstress became embarrassed. "He did bring me a trinket or two, as it happens. There, I'll let you have 'em, if you like."

Pasha pulled out one of the small drawers of her dressing-table and drew out therefrom a pinchbeck bracelet and a skimpy little ring set with an imitation ruby.

"There!" she said, offering these things to her visitor.

The lady became offended. She flared up, and a spasm ran over her face.

"Come, what are you offering me?" she asked. "It isn't alms I'm asking of you but that which isn't your property—that which, taking advantage of your position, you extracted from my husband, that weak, unfortunate being! . . . Thursday, when I saw you with my husband on the boat-landing, you had on expensive brooches and bracelets. So there's no use at all in your playing an innocent little lamb before me! I am begging you for the last time: will you give me those things or not?"

"Really, I swear to God, what a strange person you are!" remarked Pasha, beginning to take offense in her turn. "I swear to you that outside of this bracelet and this little ring I never laid my eyes on anything from your Nicholas. All he ever brought me was French pastry."

"French pastry!" The unknown lady smiled wryly. "There isn't a thing at home for the children to eat—but there is French pastry here. You absolutely refuse to make restitution of those things?"

Receiving no answer, the lady sat down and, pondering over something, stared fixedly at one spot.

"What's to be done now?" she asked herself. "If I fail to raise the nine hundred, he is ruined, and my children and I with him. Should I kill this abominable creature—or get down on my knees before her, perhaps?"

The aristocratic lady pressed a handkerchief to her face and broke into sobs.

"I beg you!" the chorus girl heard her say through her sobs. "Why, you have bankrupted my husband and brought him to ruin—save him, then! You may have no compassion for him, but then there are the children . . . the children! Wherein are the children to blame?"

Pasha vividly imagined an indeterminate number of tiny tots, huddling out on the sidewalk and crying from hunger, and she began to sob in her turn.

"But what can I do, Ma'am?" she asked. "You say that I am an abominable creature and that I bankrupted your Nicholas, but I'm telling you—I swear to you, as before the only true God—that I never had any good out of him whatsoever! Motya is the only girl in our whole chorus that's got a rich fellow keeping her, but as for all the rest of us, why, we just get along on coffee and. Your Nicholas is a well-educated and refined gentleman; so, I went ahead and let him come here. Us girls gotta do it—there's no way out."

"I am begging you for those things! Those things—give them to me! I am weeping—humiliating myself. There, I'll get down on my knees, if you like! There!"

Pasha cried out in fright and waved her arms in protest. She felt that this pale, handsome lady who spoke so grand, just like on the stage, was really capable of getting down on her knees before her—precisely because of her pride, of her nobility, so as to exalt herself and humiliate the chorine.

"Very well, I'll give you my things!" Pasha began to bustle about. "Only I didn't get 'em off of your Nicholas! I got 'em from my other gentleman friends. Suit yourself, Ma'am."

Pasha pulled out the top drawer of a bureau and got out of it a brooch set with diamonds, a string of corals, and several rings and bracelets, and handed all of them over to the lady.

"Take 'em, if you wish, only I never had any good out of your husband. Take 'em, get rich off of me!" Pasha went on, hurt by the other's threat to get down on her knees. "But if you're so high and noble—his lawful wife, now—why, you ought to have a better hold on him. That's what you ought to do! I didn't lead him on to come to me; he come of his own self."

The lady, through her tears, looked the proffered things over.

"This isn't all," she objected. "This won't fetch even five hundred—"

Pasha impulsively tossed out of the bureau drawer an additional gold watch, a cigar case, and a pair of man's cuff links:

"There!" she said, spreading her hands. "I haven't another thing left—not if you was to search the place!"

Her visitor heaved a sigh, wrapped the things up in a tiny handkerchief with trembling hands, and, without as much as a word, without even a nod, walked out.

The door of the adjoining room opened and Kolpacov emerged. He was pale and, from time to time, tossed his head nervously, as though he had just taken a very bitter dose; his eyes glistened with tears.

"What things did you ever bring me?" Pasha pounced on him. "And when, may I ask?"

"Things, indeed! What do those things matter?" he managed to say, with a toss of his head. "My God! She wept before *you,* she humiliated herself!"

"I'm asking you—what things did you ever bring me?" Pasha screamed.

"My God, she—so decent, so proud and pure—she even wanted to get down on her knees before this—this trollop! And *I* brought her to this! I let this happen!"

He clutched his head.

"No, I shall never forgive myself this!" he groaned. "I shan't forgive myself! Get away from me, you—you trash!" he cried out with repugnance, backing away from Pasha and warding her off with shaking hands. "She wanted to get down on her knees—and before whom? Before *you!* Oh, my God!"

He quickly dressed himself and, squeamishly edging away from Pasha, made his way to the door and walked out.

Pasha threw herself down on the bed and broke into noisy weeping. By now she felt sorry about her things, which she had given away in the heat of the moment, and at the same time she felt hurt.

She recalled how, three years back, a certain butter-and-egg man had beaten her up for no good reason on earth.

And she broke into still noisier weeping.

The Three Sisters

CHARACTERS

OLGA ⎫
IRENE ⎬ The SISTERS PROZOROV
MARY ⎭
BARON TUZENBACH
DOCTOR CHEBUTYKIN
CAPTAIN SOLIONNYI
ANPHISSA
PHERAPONT
LIEUTENANT COLONEL VERSHININ
ANDREW PROZOROV

KULYGHIN
NATHALIE
PHEDOTIK
RODE
Maid
Soldiers
Military Officers (2)
Musicians (1 m., 1 f.)
Bobby

ACT I, Scene 1

At the PROZOROVS'. *A provincial reception room with a colonnade, beyond which can be seen a large dining room, where a table is being set for lunch.*

Noon; bright and sunny out of doors.

OLGA, *in a blue dress (the uniform of an instructress in a girls' high school), does not leave off correcting composition books, whether she is standing still or pacing the room.*

MARY, *in a black dress, a small hat on her lap, sits reading a book.*

IRENE, *in a white dress, is standing, deep in thought.*

OLGA: Father died exactly a year ago to the day; the fifth of May—your birthday, Irene. It was very cold; there was actually snow falling then. It seemed to me I would never live through it; you were lying

Translated by Bernard Guilbert Guerney. This translation was first performed October 14, 1939, by the Surry Theatre, under the sponsorship of Dwight Deere Wiman, at the Longacre Theatre, New York. Copyright, 1939, 1943, by the Translator. In its present publication this play is intended solely for the reading public, all rights being retained by the Translator, care of Vanguard Press, Inc.

in a faint, just as if you were dead. But there, a year's gone by, and we recall all that lightly; you're already wearing white—and your face is radiant. (*Clock strikes twelve.*) The clock was striking then, too, in just the same way. (*Pause.*) There was music, I remember, while they were carrying father's coffin along; there was a salvo of guns at the cemetery. He was a general and commanded a whole brigade—but, just the same, there weren't many people to see him off. However, it was raining at the time. Raining hard, and there was snow, too.

IRENE: Why recall all this? (BARON TUZENBACH, CHEBUTYKIN, *and* SOLIONNYI *appear beyond colonnade, near table in dining room.*)

OLGA: It's warm today; you can keep the windows open—but the birches haven't put out their leaves yet. Father got his brigade and left Moscow, taking us with him, all of eleven years ago, but—and I still remember this so well!—everything in Moscow right now, at the beginning of May, is already in bloom; it's warm, and everything is flooded with sunlight. Eleven years have passed, and yet I remember everything there as though we'd left it only yesterday. Good Lord! This morning when I awoke, I saw the flood of light. I saw spring— and joy began to riot in my soul; I longed, passionately, for the place where I was born.

CHEBUTYKIN (*sarcastically, to* SOLIONNYI) : A fat chance!

TUZENBACH (*also to* SOLIONNYI) : All this is nonsense, of course. (MARY, *absorbed in her book, is whistling a snatch of song under her breath.*)

OLGA: Stop whistling, Mary! How can you? (*Pause.*) I have to teach at the high school every day and then tutor until nighttime—that must be why I have these constant headaches, and my thoughts are already those of an old woman. And really, during these four years I've been teaching, I've felt as if both strength and youth were leaving me— day by day, drop by drop. And I have but one dream that grows and becomes stronger all the time—

IRENE: To go to Moscow. To sell the house, to have done with everything here—and then, off to Moscow—

OLGA: Yes! To be off to Moscow, as quickly as possible. (CHEBUTY-KIN *and* TUZENBACH *laugh.*)

IRENE: Our brother will become a professor probably—he won't go on living here at any rate. But then, there's the hitch about poor Mary—

OLGA: Mary can visit us in Moscow every year, and stay the whole summer. (MARY *is still softly whistling her song.*)

IRENE: God willing, everything will work out right. (*Looks out of the window.*) Beautiful weather today. I don't know what makes my soul feel so radiant! I remembered this morning that it was my birthday and suddenly felt joy, and recalled my childhood, when mother was still alive. And what wonderful thoughts stirred me—what thoughts!

OLGA: You're all aglow today—you seem extraordinarily beautiful. Mary is beautiful, too. Andrew would look well, too, if it weren't for his having filled out so much; it isn't at all becoming to him. But I . . . I've aged, I've lost a great deal of weight; it might be because I get angry at the girls in school. There, today I'm free, I'm staying home— and my head doesn't ache; I feel I'm younger than I was yesterday. I'm twenty-eight, but the only thing is. . . . Everything is for the best, everything comes from the hands of God—yet it seems to me if I were to marry and spend every day at home it would be much better. (*Pause.*) I would love my husband.

TUZENBACH (*to* SOLIONNYI): You talk such bosh—I'm fed up listening to you. (*Entering reception room.*) Forgot to tell you. Vershinin—that's our new battery commander—will be paying you a visit today. (*Sits down at piano.*)

OLGA: Oh, really? I'm very glad to hear it.

IRENE: Is he an old man?

TUZENBACH: No, he's not so very old. Forty—or forty-five, at the most. (*Playing softly.*) A fine fellow, to judge by appearances. Not a fool, that's one thing sure. Only he talks a lot.

IRENE: Is he interesting?

TUZENBACH: Yes, so-so—only he has a wife, a mother-in-law . . . and two little girls. A second marriage, at that. He goes around paying calls, and everywhere he goes he tells them he has a wife and two little girls. He'll say the same thing here, too. His wife is some sort of a dim-wit, with a long girlish braid; she utters nothing but highfalutin sentiments, she philosophizes, and every so often stages an attempt at suicide—evidently to spite her husband. Me, I'd have left a woman like that long ago, but he puts up with her and merely complains.

SOLIONNYI (*entering from the dining room with* CHEBUTYKIN): I can make a lift of only fifty-five pounds with one hand, whereas I can lift one hundred and eighty pounds, or even two hundred and fifteen, if I use both hands. From this I conclude that two men are not twice as strong as one, but three times as strong, or even stronger—

CHEBUTYKIN (*reading a newspaper as he walks along*): "To stop falling hair . . . a quarter of an ounce of naphthalene to half a bottle of alcohol. . . . Dissolve and use daily. . . ." (*Writing in a notebook.*) We'll make a note of it! (*To* SOLIONNYI.) Well, now, I'm telling you: you stick a small cork into a little bottle, and then pass a tiny glass tube through. Then you take just the tiniest pinch of the commonest, most ordinary alum—

IRENE: Chebutykin—darling Chebutykin!

CHEBUTYKIN: What is it, my little girl, my dearest?

IRENE: Tell me, why am I so happy today? Just as though I were under sail; a blue sky spreads wide over me, with great white birds soaring. Why is all this? Why?

CHEBUTYKIN (*kissing her hands tenderly*): My white bird. . . .

IRENE: When I awoke this morning and got up and washed, it suddenly began to seem to me that everything in the world was clear, and that I knew the right way to live. Darling, I know everything now. Man must work; he must toil in the sweat of his brow, no matter who or what he may be, and in that alone do the meaning and purpose of his life lie, and of his happiness, his raptures. How splendid it is to be a laborer who rises when it is barely light and breaks stones out in the street, or to be a shepherd, or a teacher teaching little children, or an engineer guiding a locomotive. . . . Good Lord—to be not only a man . . . it's better to be an ox, it's better to be just a horse, as long as one works, than to be a young woman who gets up at noon, drinks coffee in bed, and then spends two hours primping. . . . Oh, how horrible that is! You know the thirst one occasionally feels during a hot spell? Well, that's how compelling my newborn desire to work is. And if I won't get up early and work hard, you can just drop me as a friend—

CHEBUTYKIN (*gently*): I will, I will. . . .

OLGA: Father trained us to get up at seven. Now Irene wakes up at seven—and lies in bed and broods over something or other until nine, at least. And what a serious face she has! (*Laughs.*)

IRENE: You've gotten used to regarding me as a little girl, and it seems strange to you when my face is serious. I am twenty!

TUZENBACH: This longing for toil—oh, my God, how I understand it! I haven't done an honest stitch of work in all my life. I was born in Petersburg, that bleak and frivolously vain city, in a family which never knew what work meant or had the least notion of any cares. I remember when I used to come home from my corps a flunky would pull off my boots for me, while I carried on like a crank and my mother watched me in reverent awe. I was guarded from toil. But they hardly succeeded in safeguarding me—hardly! The time is come, a juggernaut is moving upon us, a great cleansing storm is brewing, which is coming and is already near and will soon blow away from our social structure all sloth, and apathy, and prejudice against toil, and the rottenness of tedium. I am going to work—and some twenty-five or thirty years from now not a soul but will be working. Not a soul!

CHEBUTYKIN: *I* won't be.

TUZENBACH: *You* don't count.

SOLIONNYI (*to* TUZENBACH): Twenty-five years from now you'll no longer be in this world—glory be to God. In two or three years you'll cash in from a stroke, or I'll blow up and put a bullet through your forehead, my angel. (*Takes a perfume atomizer out of his pocket and sprays his shirt front and hands.*)

CHEBUTYKIN (*laughing*): But really, now, I've never worked at anything. Soon as I left the university I didn't do another lick of work. Why, I've never even read a single book through—all I read was newspapers. (*Takes another newspaper out of his pocket.*) There— I know from the papers that there was a certain writer, by the name of So-and-so—but hanged if I know just what it was he wrote. . . . God knows what it was. (*A knocking on the ceiling of the apartment below is heard.*) That's a signal for me to come down; someone must have come to see me. I'll be back right away; just a little patience— (*Exits hurriedly, grooming his beard.*)

IRENE: He must be up to something.

TUZENBACH: Right! He went off with such a solemn expression— evidently he'll be back in a minute with a present for you.

IRENE: How very provoking.

OLGA: Yes, it's dreadful. He's always doing silly things like that.

MARY (*reciting to herself*): "A green oak grows on a curved shore. . . . A gold chain is about it wound. . . . A gold chain is about it wound. . . ." (*Gets up; hums very softly.*)

OLGA: You aren't at all in a jolly mood today, Mary. (MARY, *still humming, puts on her hat.*) Where are you off to?

MARY: Home.

IRENE: That's a peculiar way to act—

TUZENBACH: Leaving a birthday party like this.

MARY: What's the difference. . . . I'll come this evening. Good-by, dearest—(*Kisses* IRENE.) Again I wish you health—I wish you happiness. Time was, when father was alive, that thirty or forty of his officers would come to us every time we had a birthday party and there would be a great fuss; but today you can count the guests on the fingers of one hand, and everything's as quiet as in a graveyard. I'm going. I've got the blues today and I don't feel so chipper, so don't you mind me. (*Smiling through her tears.*) We'll have a talk later on, but let it be good-by for the present, darling—I want to crawl off somewhere.

IRENE (*displeased*): There, how you act—

OLGA (*crying in sympathy*): I understand you, Mary.

SOLIONNYI: When a man philosophizes, you'll get philosophy—or sophistry, at any rate; but when a woman philosophizes—or if two women have a go at it—then you get . . . but I guess I'd better keep my fingers crossed! (*Suits business to speech.*)

MARY: Just what do you mean by that, you horrid, dreadful creature?

SOLIONNYI: Oh, not a thing! (*Quoting.*) "He had hardly made a sound when the bear struck him to the ground!" (*Pause.*)

MARY (*angrily, to* OLGA): Do stop blubbering!

ANPHISSA (*entering, to* PHERAPONT, *who follows her in, carrying a birthday cake*): This way, old-timer. Come right in—your boots are clean enough. (*To* IRENE.) From the Town Council—from Protopopov. A birthday cake, now.

IRENE: Thank you—and thank him for me. (*Takes cake from* PHERAPONT.)

PHERAPONT: Eh?

IRENE (*louder*): Thank him for me!

OLGA (*to* ANPHISSA): See that he gets some cake, nurse. Go, Pherapont, they'll give you some cake in the kitchen.

PHERAPONT: Eh?

ANPHISSA: Come on, Pherapont, old-timer—come on! (*Exit, with* PHERAPONT.)

MARY: I don't much like this Protopopov—this Michael, or whatever his first name is. You oughtn't to invite him.

IRENE: I didn't.

MARY: Well, that's fine. (*Enter* CHEBUTYKIN, *followed by an* ORDERLY *carrying a silver samovar; there is a general expression of surprise and vexation.*)

OLGA (*putting her hands up to hide her smile*): A samovar! This is awful! (*Goes toward table in dining room.*)

IRENE: Chebutykin, darling, what are you up to?

TUZENBACH (*laughing*): I told you!

CHEBUTYKIN: My darlings, my beautiful girls, you're all I have, you're the dearest thing in all this world to me. I'll soon be sixty; I'm an old man—a lonely, insignificant old man. . . . There's nothing worth while about me save this love for you, and if it weren't for you I'd long since have put a stop to my cluttering up this earth. . . . (*To* IRENE.) My darling, my little girl, I've known you from the day you were born. I dandled you in my arms. . . . I loved your mother, who is now dead—

IRENE: But why such extravagant presents?

CHEBUTYKIN (*through his tears, with vexation*): Extravagant presents. . . . Oh, you! (*To the* ORDERLY, *indicating table in dining room.*) Put the samovar over there. (*Teasingly mimicking* IRENE.) Extravagant presents! (ORDERLY *carries samovar into dining room, then exits.*)

ANPHISSA (*entering and passing through reception room*): Darlings, there's a strange colonel just come in. He's already taken off his coat, children, and is heading this way. Irene, dearest, do you be kind and a polite little girl. (*As she exits.*) It's time for lunch long since—oh, Lord!

TUZENBACH: It must be Vershinin. (*As* VERSHININ *enters.*) Lieutenant Colonel Vershinin!

VERSHININ (*to* MARY *and* IRENE): I have the honor of presenting myself: I am Vershinin. I am very, very happy to be with you at last. How you girls have grown—my, my!

IRENE: Do be seated, please. We're most delighted.

VERSHININ (*jovially*): I'm most happy—most happy. Yes—but there were three of you—all sisters. I remember—three little girls. I don't remember their faces any more, but I do remember very well that Colonel Prozorov, your father, had three little girls, and that I saw them with my own eyes. How time does fly! My, my, how it does fly!

TUZENBACH: Colonel Vershinin hails from Moscow.

IRENE: From Moscow? You're from Moscow?

VERSHININ: Yes, that's where I'm from. Your late father commanded a battery there while I was an officer in the same brigade. (*To* MARY.) Your face, now—I do remember it a little, I think.

MARY: Yet I don't remember you!

IRENE: Olga! Olga! (*Calling into the dining room.*) Olga, do come here! (OLGA *enters the reception room from the dining room.* IRENE *addresses her, with an introductory gesture toward* VERSHININ.) The Colonel, it turns out, is from Moscow.

VERSHININ: You must be Olga, then—the eldest. . . . And you are Mary. . . . And you are Irene, the youngest—

OLGA: You are from Moscow?

VERSHININ: Yes. I not only studied in Moscow but began my service there; I served there for a long time; at last I got the battery here—had myself transferred here, as you see. I don't remember you, to tell the truth; all I do remember is that there were three of you—three sisters. Your father, however, has remained in my memory; there, I have but to shut my eyes, and I see him as plain as if he were standing before me. I used to call on you in Moscow—

OLGA: I thought I remembered everybody, but now—

VERSHININ: My first name is Alexander—

IRENE: So you come from Moscow . . . what a surprise!

OLGA: Why, we're going to move there.

IRENE: We ought to be there by autumn—we think. It's our native city—we were born there, all of us. On Old Basmannaya Street— (*Both* IRENE *and* OLGA *laugh for joy.*)

MARY: What an unexpected find—somebody from our home town. (*Becoming animated.*) I've recalled it all now! Don't you remember, Olga, how we used to talk of the "lovelorn Major" in our house? You were a lieutenant at the time and in love with some girl or other, and, for some reason, everybody was teasing you by calling you "Major"—

VERSHININ (*laughing*): That's it, that's it! The "lovelorn Major"— that's just how it was—

MARY: You had only a mustache then. . . . Oh, how you have aged! (*Plaintively.*) How you have aged!

VERSHININ: Yes. . . . When I was called the "lovelorn Major" I was still young, I was in love. Things are different now.

OLGA: But you haven't a single gray hair yet! You've grown older— but you aren't old yet.

VERSHININ: Just the same, I'm going on forty-three. Did you leave Moscow long ago?

IRENE: Eleven years ago. There, now, Mary—what are you crying for, you funny girl? (*Through her own tears.*) First thing you know, I'll start crying, too.

MARY: I don't mean anything by it. (*To* VERSHININ.) And what street did you live on?

VERSHININ: On Old Basmannaya.

OLGA: Why, so did we—

VERSHININ: At one time I lived on German Street—just a stroll to the Red Barracks. There's a gloomy bridge on the way; the water under the bridge is noisy. You'd get downhearted if you were all alone.

(*Pause.*) But here—how wide, how full the river is! A wonderful river!

OLGA: Yes—only it's so cold here. It's so cold here, and then there are the mosquitoes—

VERSHININ: Oh, come now! There's such a hearty, fine, Slavic climate here. A forest, a river—and there are birches, too. The dear birches, so demure—I love them more than all the other trees. It's fine living here. Only it's so odd that the nearest railroad station is all of fourteen miles from here. And nobody can tell you why that's so.

SOLIONNYI: But *I* can tell you why. (*All look at him.*) It's because if the station were near it wouldn't be far, and if it's far, then it means that it isn't near—

TUZENBACH (*breaking the awkward silence*): He's quite a wit.

OLGA (*to* VERSHININ): Now I've also remembered you. Yes, I remember you.

VERSHININ: I knew your mother.

CHEBUTYKIN: A fine soul she was—may the Kingdom of Heaven be hers.

IRENE: Mamma's buried in Moscow.

OLGA: At the New Nunnery of the Virgin—

MARY: Just imagine—I'm already beginning to forget her face. And in just the same way people will fail to remember us. They, too, will forget.

VERSHININ: Yes. They'll forget. For such is our fate; there's no help for it. That which to us seems serious, significant, of the utmost importance—the time will come, and it will be forgotten, or will seem of no importance whatsoever. (*Pause.*) And—this is interesting—we can't at all tell now just what, precisely, will be considered exalted, important, and what will be considered pathetic, ludicrous. For instance, didn't the discoveries of Copernicus or, let's say, of Columbus, seem at first unnecessary, ludicrous, while some empty-headed twaddle, written by some crackpot or other, seemed to be the eternal truth? And it can come to pass that our life today, to which we reconcile ourselves so, will in time seem strange, cumbersome, stupid, far from clean— even sinful, perhaps—

TUZENBACH: Who knows? But still, it may be that this very life of ours will be styled exalted and that it will be honored in memory. There are no tortures now, no wholesale executions, no invasions . . . yet at the same time how much suffering there is!

SOLIONNYI (*in a high-pitched voice and clowning through the mo-*

tions of throwing chicken-feed): Here, chick, chick, chick! You don't have to feed the Baron—just let him spout philosophy—

TUZENBACH: Let me alone—I beg of you. (*Moves to another seat.*) And, after all, you are very boring.

SOLIONNYI (*in the same high-pitched voice and repeating business*): Here, chick, chick, chick!

TUZENBACH (*to* VERSHININ): The sufferings we see today—and there are so many of them!—nevertheless testify to a certain uplift in morals to which society has already attained—

VERSHININ: Yes, yes, of course.

CHEBUTYKIN: You have just said, Baron, that our life will be called exalted; but, just the same, people are so mean-spirited, so small— (*Getting up.*) Just see how small *I* am. If only to console me, you must say that my life is an exalted, comprehensible thing. (*A violin, playing a hackneyed classic none too brilliantly, is heard, off.*)

MARY: That's Andrew playing—our brother.

IRENE: He's the scholar of the family. He'll be a professor—probably. Papa was a military man, but his son has chosen scholarship as a career—

MARY: At father's wish.

OLGA: We teased him to death today. He's a little in love, I think—

IRENE: With one of the local girls. She'll be paying us a visit today, in all probability.

MARY: My, how she dresses! It isn't merely bad taste, or being behind the fashion—she's just plain pathetic. Last time it was some sort of a weird, bright, yellowish skirt, with such vulgar, skimpy trimming —and topped off with a red blouse! And her cheeks are scrubbed— positively scrubbed. Andrew isn't really in love—I can't admit that, for, after all, he has taste—but he's simply teasing us, just so, clowning around. I heard yesterday that she's going to marry Protopopov, the Chairman of the Town Council. And that would be just too perfect. (*Calling at one of the side doors.*) Andrew, come in here! Just for a minute, dear! (ANDREW *enters.*)

OLGA: This is my brother, Andrew.

VERSHININ (*bowing*): Lieutenant Colonel Vershinin.

ANDREW (*returning the bow and mopping his forehead*): You have come to take command of the battery here?

OLGA: Just imagine, Andrew—the Colonel is from Moscow!

ANDREW: Really? In that case I felicitate you—my dear little sisters won't give you much rest.

VERSHININ: I've already succeeded in boring your sisters.

IRENE: Just look at this photograph frame Andrew gave me as a present today! (*Shows gimcrack frame to* VERSHININ.) He made it all by himself.

VERSHININ (*examining the frame, and hardly knowing what comment to make*): Yes . . . it's quite—

IRENE: And that little frame there, over the piano—he made that, too. (ANDREW, *with a gesture of annoyance and self-depreciation, edges away.*)

OLGA: He's not only the scholar of the family but also plays the violin and turns out all sorts of things with a jigsaw—in a word, he's handy all around. Don't go, Andrew! That's a habit of his—always going off by himself. Come over here! (MARY *and* IRENE, *laughing, take* ANDREW *by the arms and bring him back.*)

MARY: Come on, come on!

ANDREW: Do let me alone, please.

MARY: What a funny fellow! Why, we used to call the Colonel the "lovelorn Major"—and he was never the least bit angry.

VERSHININ: Not in the least!

MARY: Well, I want to call you the "lovelorn fiddler"!

IRENE: Or the "lovelorn professor."

OLGA: He's in love! Our Andrew's in love!

IRENE (*applauding*): Bravo, bravo! *Bis!* Our Andrew's in love!

CHEBUTYKIN (*approaching* ANDREW *from behind and putting both arms around his waist*): " 'Tis but for love that Nature us created!" (*Laughs loudly; he is still carrying a newspaper around with him.*)

ANDREW: There, that'll do, that'll do—(*Mops his face.*) I haven't slept a wink all night, and right now I'm not entirely myself, so to say. I read until four and then lay down—but it wasn't much use. I kept thinking of one thing and another—and suddenly it was day—breaking early, with the sunlight simply streaming into the bedroom. (*Irrelevantly, after a brief but awkward pause.*) During the summer, while I'm here, I'd like to translate a certain book from the English.

VERSHININ: Why, do you know English?

ANDREW: Yes. Father—God rest his soul!—simply overwhelmed us with education. It's both amusing and silly, yet I must confess that after his death I really began to put on weight, and now you see me grown actually fat in a single year, just as if my body had been released from under a crushing weight. Thanks to Father my sisters and I know

French, German, and English—while Irene knows Italian as well. But at what a cost all that was attained!

MARY: To know three extra languages in this town is an uncalled-for luxury. And not a luxury, even, but some sort of an uncalled-for appendage—like an extra finger on each hand, let's say. We know such a great deal that is superfluous!

VERSHININ: There, now! (*Laughing.*) So you know a great deal that is superfluous, do you? It seems to me that there isn't—and that there can't be—any town so dull and dismal that it would find an intelligent, cultured person unnecessary. Let's suppose that among the population of a hundred thousand in this town—which is backward and crude, of course—there are only three such persons as yourselves. It goes without saying that you'll never overcome the benighted mass surrounding you; during the course of your lifetime you will, little by little, have to retreat and become lost in this horde of a hundred thousand; life will stifle you, but still you shall not vanish, shall not remain utterly without influence; after you there will appear six others, perhaps, such as yourselves, then twelve, and so on, until at last such people as yourselves will become the majority. In two or three hundred years life on this earth will become unimaginably splendid, amazing. Man has need of such a life, and if it doesn't exist as yet he must nevertheless have a premonition of it, must await it, dream of it, prepare for it; he must, toward that end, both perceive and know more than his grandsire and his sire perceived and knew. (*Laughs.*) And yet you complain that a great deal of what you know is superfluous!

MARY (*taking off her hat*): I'm staying for lunch.

IRENE (*with a sigh*): Really, somebody ought to write all this down. (ANDREW *is no longer on, having gone off unperceived.*)

TUZENBACH: After many years, you say, life on this earth will be splendid, amazing. That's true enough. Yet to have some share in it now, even though remotely, one must prepare for it, one must work—

VERSHININ (*getting up*): Yes. But, I say, what a lot of flowers you have here! (*Looks about him.*) And a wonderful home. I envy you! Why, all my life I've had to knock around in miserable flats, with just a chair or two, a sofa, and stoves that are forever smoking. That's precisely what has been lacking in my life—flowers such as these. (*Rubbing his hands.*) Oh, well, what does it matter!

TUZENBACH: Yes, one must work. I'll bet you're thinking it's the Teuton in me, turned soft and sentimental. But I give you my word,

I'm a Russian and can't even speak German. My father belonged to the Orthodox Church. . . . (*Pause.*)

VERSHININ (*pacing the floor*): I often think: what if one were to begin his life all over again—and consciously, at that? What if the first life, already lived through, were merely a rough draft, so to say, while the other were a clean copy! Then every man jack of us, I'm thinking, would strive, first of all, not to repeat himself; at the least, he would create a different life-setting for himself, he would create for himself a home such as this, with flowers, with plenty of light. . . . I have a wife and two little girls; besides that, my wife is a delicate creature, and so on and so on. Well, now, if I were to live my life all over again, from scratch, I wouldn't marry—never, never!

KULYGHIN (*entering and approaching* IRENE—*he is in a uniform frock coat*): My dear sister—for I consider you such—permit me to congratulate you on your birthday and to wish you, in all sincerity, and from the very bottom of my heart, health, and all that a girl of your years may wish for. And, likewise, to offer you this book. (*Hands* IRENE *a book.*) A Brief History of our High School for the last fifty years—written by myself. A most trifling book, composed for lack of anything better to do—but you read it just the same. Greetings, gentlemen! (*To* VERSHININ.) My name is Kulyghin; I am an instructor at the high school here. Also one of the town's officials. (*To* IRENE.) In this book you will find a list of all those who have graduated from our high school during the last fifty years. *Feci, quod potui, faciant meliora potentes.* (*Kisses* MARY.)

IRENE: Why, you already gave me one of these books—at Easter.

KULYGHIN (*laughing*): You don't say! In that case, let me have it back—or, better still, give it to the Colonel. Do take it, Colonel. You'll read it some day when you're bored.

VERSHININ (*taking the proffered book from* IRENE): Thank you. (*As he gets ready to leave.*) I'm most happy to have made your acquaintance—

OLGA: You aren't leaving? You mustn't—you mustn't!

IRENE: You'll stay for lunch. Please!

OLGA: I implore you!

VERSHININ (*with a bow*): Apparently I've dropped in on your birthday party. Forgive me for not felicitating you; I didn't know. (*Goes off with* OLGA *into the dining room.*)

KULYGHIN: Today, ladies and gentlemen, is Sunday—the day of rest. Let us rest, then; let us make merry, each one in keeping with his or her years and position. Rugs ought to be removed for the summer and put away till winter. It might be advisable to use insecticide on them, or naphthalene. The Romans were a stalwart race, because they knew how to toil—and also how to rest; they believed in *mens sana in corpore sano*. Their life followed certain recognized forms. As the Director of our school puts it: "The chief thing in every life is the form it takes." That which loses its form comes to its end—and the same holds true in our everyday life as well. (*Takes* MARY *around the waist, laughing as he does so*.) Mary loves me. My wife loves me. And the curtains also ought to be put away, together with the rugs. I'm feeling gay today; I am in excellent spirits. Mary, we have a date at the Director's at four today. A walking trip is being arranged for the instructors and their families.

MARY: I'm not going.

KULYGHIN (*in a hurt tone*): Why not, Mary darling?

MARY: I'll tell you about it later—(*Angrily*.) All right, I'll go; only get away from me, please! (*Walks away from* KULYGHIN.)

KULYGHIN: And after that we'll spend the evening at the Director's. Despite the poor state of his health, this man strives, first and foremost, to be social. An excellent, radiant personality. A splendid fellow. Yesterday, after the conference, he said to me: "I am tired, Theodore— tired!" (*Looks at wall clock, then at his watch*.) "Yes," he says, "I am tired!"—just like that. (*Violin plays, off*.)

OLGA: Ladies and gentlemen, come to lunch, if you please! And don't overlook the cake!

KULYGHIN: Ah, Olga darling—my darling! Yesterday I worked from early morning until late at night and became ever so tired—yet today I feel happy. (*Goes into dining room, toward table*.) Yes, darling. . . .

CHEBUTYKIN (*putting newspaper in his pocket and grooming beard*): Cake, did you say? Splendid!

MARY (*sternly, to* CHEBUTYKIN): Only watch out—don't you drink a drop today. Do you hear? Drink is bad for you.

CHEBUTYKIN: Oh, now! That's all over and done with as far as I'm concerned. It's two years now since I've gone on a bender. (*Impatiently*.) Eh, sweetheart—what difference does it make?

MARY: Just the same, don't you dare to drink. Don't you dare! (*Angrily, but low enough for her husband not to hear*.) Damn! Another evening of unmitigated boredom at the Director's!

TUZENBACH: I wouldn't go, in your place. And that's that.

CHEBUTYKIN: Don't you go, sweet.

MARY: It's all very well for you to say "Don't go". . . . What a confounded, unbearable life! (*Goes into dining room.*)

CHEBUTYKIN (*walking over to her*): Oh, I wouldn't say that!

SOLIONNYI (*passing into dining room*): Here—chick, chick, chick! . . .

TUZENBACH (*to* SOLIONNYI): There, that's enough. That'll do.

SOLIONNYI: Here, chick, chick, chick!

KULYGHIN (*jovially*): Your health, Colonel! I am a pedagogue, and one of the family here—Mary's husband. She's a good soul—a very good soul—

VERSHININ (*indicating one of the bottles on the table*): I'll have some of that dark stuff—(*Drinks.*) Your health! (*To* OLGA.) I feel so fine here—(*Only* IRENE *and* TUZENBACH *remain in the reception room now.*)

IRENE: Mary isn't her own self today. She married Kulyghin when she was only eighteen, and he seemed the wisest of men to her. But things don't look the same now. He may be the kindest of men—but not the wisest.

OLGA (*impatiently*): Andrew! Do come out at last!

ANDREW (*off*): Right away. (*Enters and goes to table.*)

TUZENBACH (*to* IRENE): What are you thinking of?

IRENE: Oh, nothing in particular. I not only dislike but actually fear this Solionnyi. He never says anything but stupid things—

TUZENBACH: He *is* a queer duck. I feel sorry for him and vexed at the same time—but sorry, mostly. He strikes me as being shy. Whenever we're alone he can be very intelligent and kind, but in society he's a brute and a bully. Don't go now; let them get seated in the meantime. Let me be near you for a while. What are you thinking of? (*Pause.*) You aren't twenty; I'm not thirty yet. How many years still remain ahead of us—a long, long succession of days, filled with my love for you—

IRENE: Don't speak of love to me, Nicholas.

TUZENBACH (*disregarding her words*): Mine is a passionate longing for life, for struggle, for toil, and this longing in my soul is blended with love of you, Irene, and, as if by design, you are splendid and beautiful, and life, too, seems to me splendid and beautiful! What are you thinking of?

IRENE: Life is splendid and beautiful, you say. Yes—but what if it only *seems* so? Life hasn't been splendid and beautiful to us three sisters yet; it has been stifling us, as if it were a patch of weeds. . . . Why, I am actually in tears—and that's entirely uncalled for—(*Dabs her face quickly; smiles.*) One must toil—toil. That's why we're down at the mouth and have such a gloomy outlook on life—because we don't know what toil means. We were begotten of people who despised toil—

NATHALIE (*entering—she has on a pink dress, but the sash is green*): What—sitting down to lunch already? I must be late! (*Throws a fleeting glance in a mirror; primps.*) My hair isn't done so badly, I think—(*Catching sight of* IRENE.) Irene, darling! Congratulations! (*Kisses her, hard and lingeringly.*) You've so many guests here . . . really, I feel out of place. How d'you do, Baron!

OLGA (*stepping into the reception room*): Well, if it isn't Nathalie, at last! How are you, dear! (*They kiss.*)

NATHALIE: Congratulations! But you have so many people here . . . I feel horribly embarrassed—

OLGA: Come, now! We're all friends here. (Sotto voce, *shocked.*) Why, you're wearing a green sash, actually! My dear, that isn't at all nice!

NATHALIE: Why, is that a bad omen?

OLGA: No; it's simply unbecoming and . . . odd, somehow—

NATHALIE (*in a weepy voice*): Really? But then, it isn't *really* green. . . . It's an off-shade, rather— (*Follows* OLGA *into dining room.* IRENE *and* TUZENBACH *also join the others, leaving the reception room deserted. All in the dining room sit down to lunch.*)

KULYGHIN: Here's wishing you a fine young man, Irene. Time you were getting married.

CHEBUTYKIN: And here's wishing you a nice young man, too, Nathalie.

KULYGHIN: Nathalie already has a nice young man.

MARY (*rapping a fork against her plate*): Guess I may as well toss off a little drink, too. We live but once, whatever our life may be like! Let 'er rip!

KULYGHIN: You wouldn't get more than D in conduct.

VERSHININ: I say, this is a fine liqueur. What is it made of?

SOLIONNYI: Cockroaches.

IRENE (*in a tearful voice*): Ugh! Ugh! How disgusting!

OLGA: We're having roast turkey and apple pie for supper. Glory be, I'm home all day today, and all evening. . . . Come tonight, gentlemen.

VERSHININ: Permit me to come tonight, too!

IRENE: By all means.

NATHALIE: There's nothing formal about the people here.

CHEBUTYKIN: " 'Tis but for love that Nature us created!" (*Laughs.*)

ANDREW (*angrily*): Do stop it, all of you! I'm surprised you aren't fed up with all this. (*Enter* PHEDOTIK, *with camera, and* RODE, *carrying a large basket of flowers.*)

PHEDOTIK: I say, they're already having lunch.

RODE (*boomingly, and lisping*): Already at lunch? Yes, so they are!

PHEDOTIK: Hold it for just a minute! (*Snaps a picture.*) One! Hold it just a little longer— (*Snaps another picture.*) Two! Now I'm all done! (PHEDOTIK *and* RODE *pick up the basket and go into dining room, where they are met with noisy greetings.*)

RODE (*boomingly*): I congratulate you! I wish you the best of everything—oh, just everything! The weather is positively charming today—simply perfection itself. I spent the whole morning hiking with the high-school lads. I am the physical culture instructor at the high school, you know.

PHEDOTIK (*as he snaps* IRENE): You may move now—it's perfectly all right. You look so intriguing today. (*Taking a humming top out of his pocket.*) Here's a humming top for you, by the way. It has a wonderful sound.

IRENE: Why, how charming!

MARY: "A green oak grows on a curved shore. . . . A gold chain is about it wound. . . . A gold chain is about it wound—" (*In a weepy voice.*) Oh, why do I keep on saying that? Those lines have been haunting me ever since morning—

KULYGHIN: There are thirteen at table!

RODE (*boomingly*): Come, ladies and gentlemen, can it be possible that you attach any significance to superstitions? (*General laughter.*)

KULYGHIN: If there are thirteen at table, it means that some people in love are present. (*To* CHEBUTYKIN.) Can it be you, by any chance? (*General laughter.*)

CHEBUTYKIN: I am an old sinner . . . but just why Nathalie should be so confused—well, that's something I absolutely cannot understand! (*Loud laughter.* NATHALIE *dashes out of the dining room, with* ANDREW *after her.*)

ANDREW: Come, now, don't pay any attention to them! Wait! Hold on, I beg you—

NATHALIE: I'm ashamed . . . I don't know what's come over me—

but they're making a laughingstock out of me. My leaving the table just now was impolite, but I couldn't help it. . . . I couldn't— (*Buries her face in her hands.*)

ANDREW: Dearest, I beg you, I implore you, don't excite yourself. I assure you they're merely joking—out of the kindness of their hearts. My dear, my beautiful one, they're all kind, all sincere, and they love both of us. Come over here to the window where they can't see us— (*Looks about him.*)

NATHALIE: I am so unused to society!

ANDREW: Oh, youth—wonderful, gloriously beautiful youth! My dear, my beautiful one—don't upset yourself so! Believe me—I want you to believe. . . . I feel so fine; my soul is filled with love, with ecstasy. . . . Oh, nobody can see us! Nobody! Why—just why—I fell in love with you, or when I fell in love with you . . . oh, I can't understand any of it! My dear, my sweet, my pure one—be my wife! I love you—I love you . . . as no one has ever loved anyone before— (*They kiss.* PHEDOTIK *and* RODE *enter and, catching sight of* NATHALIE *and* ANDREW *kissing, stop short.*)

Curtain

ACT I, Scene 2

Same as Scene 1.
About two years later.
An accordeon is playing, off, evidently out of doors, so softly that it can hardly be heard.
No lights.

NATHALIE (*entering with a candle, in a house robe, crossing over to the door of* ANDREW'S *room and pausing there*): What are you doing, Andrew? Reading? It's all right—don't mind little me; I merely looked in— (*Goes to opposite door, opens it, peeps in, then shuts it again.*) I'm afraid of a fire—

ANDREW (*entering, with a book in his hand*): What are you doing, Nathalie?

NATHALIE: Just looking around—I'm afraid of a fire. It's Shrove-tide now; the servants are all dizzy—first thing you know something may happen. Yesterday, around midnight, I was passing through the dining room—and there was a candle burning. And, no matter how I tried, I couldn't get at who had left it burning like that! (*Setting down her candle.*) What time is it?

ANDREW (*glancing at his watch*): Quarter past eight.

NATHALIE: Olga and Irene aren't home yet. Still out. Working all the time, the poor darlings. Olga and her Pedagogical Council; Irene and her telegraph office— (*Sighs.*) This morning I said to your sister: "Irene, darling," I said, "you *must* take care of yourself." But she won't even listen. A quarter past eight, you say? I'm afraid our Bobby isn't at all well. Why does his skin feel so cold? Yesterday he ran a temperature, but today he's cold all over. . . . I'm so frightened!

ANDREW: It isn't anything, Nathalie. The boy is all right.

NATHALIE: Just the same, maybe we'd better put him on a diet. I'm afraid. And tonight I heard them saying some maskers were expected. It would be better if they didn't come, Andrew.

ANDREW: Really, I don't know. After all, they were asked to come.

NATHALIE: This morning, when our little baby boy woke up, he looked at me—and suddenly smiled! That means he must have recognized me. "Bobby," I said to him, "how are you? How are you, darling?" And did he laugh! Children know what's what—they know right well. So that's settled, then, Andrew—I'll tell them not to let the maskers in.

ANDREW (*hesitatingly*): Why, it all depends on what my sisters want to do. They're in authority here.

NATHALIE: They'll agree, too—I'll tell them. They're kindhearted— (*Leaving.*) I ordered some buttermilk for supper. The doctor says you ought to have nothing but buttermilk, otherwise you'll never reduce. (*Pausing.*) Bobby's skin feels so cold. I'm afraid he's cold in his room, most likely. He ought to be moved to another room—until the weather gets warmer, at least. Irene's room, for instance, is just the very thing for a baby; it isn't the least bit damp, and it gets the sun all day long. I must speak to her; she can share Olga's room for the time being. It won't matter, really; she's away all day; she merely sleeps here. . . . (*Pause.*) Andrew, darling, why don't you say something?

ANDREW: Oh, it's nothing; I was just thinking. Besides, there's really nothing to say—

NATHALIE: Oh . . . there's something I wanted to tell you. . . . Oh, yes—Pherapont is waiting; he came from the Town Council and asked to see you.

ANDREW (*yawning*): Call him in. (*Exit* NATHALIE. ANDREW, *bending over the candle* NATHALIE *has left behind, reads his book.* PHERAPONT *enters; he is in an old, tattered coat, with the collar turned up; his ears are tied around with a bandanna.* ANDREW *looks up.*) How are you, old friend? What was it you wanted to see me about?

PHERAPONT: The Chairman sent along this book and some papers or other. Here you are— (*Hands* ANDREW *a ledger and a large bulging envelope.*)

ANDREW: Thanks. That's fine. But how is it you didn't get here earlier? Why, it's going on nine now.

PHERAPONT: Eh?

ANDREW (*louder*): I'm saying you've come late—it's going on nine now.

PHERAPONT: Sure enough. It was still light, though, when I got here, but they wouldn't let me see you. "Master's busy," they kept on tellin' me. "Oh, well, it don't matter," thinks I. "If he's busy, he's busy; I ain't in no hurry to get anywheres." (*Under the impression that* ANDREW *is asking him something.*) Eh?

ANDREW: It's nothing. (*Riffling the pages of his book.*) Tomorrow's Friday, and we really have no meeting, but I'll go anyway. It'll give me something to do. It's so boring to stay at home— (*Pause.*) Oh, grandpa, how strangely life changes—how life takes you in! Today, out of sheer boredom, for sheer lack of anything to do, I picked up this book—nothing more than old lectures at the university!—and I had to laugh. . . . Good Lord! I am Secretary of the Town Council, that same Council over which Protopopov presides; I am Secretary now, and the utmost I can hope for is to become an actual member of that Council! I am to be a member of the Town Council—*I*, who every night dream that I am a professor at the University of Moscow, a celebrated scholar of whom all Russia is proud!

PHERAPONT: I couldn't rightly tell you. . . . My hearin's not so good now—

ANDREW: If your hearing were all it should be, perhaps I wouldn't be talking like this before you. Yet talk to someone I must—but my wife doesn't understand, and as for my sisters, I'm afraid of them for some reason—afraid that they'll make fun of me, will humiliate me. . . . I'm not a drinking man; I'm not fond of hanging around bars; but what a thrill I would get right now just from sitting a while at Tyestov's, in Moscow, or at the Moscow Grand Café, old-timer!

PHERAPONT: Speakin' of Moscow—a contractor feller was tellin' us at the Council the other day that there was some merchants or other in Moscow that threw a pancake party; well, now, one of 'em et forty of them pancakes in a row, and he just up and died, it seems like. Forty, it may have been, or maybe even fifty. I disremember which.

ANDREW: In Moscow you can sit in the enormous dining room of some restaurant; nobody knows you and you don't know anybody, yet at the same time you don't feel yourself a stranger. But here you know everybody and everybody knows you, yet you're a stranger—a stranger. . . . A stranger, and all alone—

PHERAPONT: Eh? (*Pause.*) And the same contractor feller was tellin' us—mebbe he's lyin', at that—that there's a great, big cable stretched right acrosst all of Moscow—

ANDREW: What in the world for?

PHERAPONT: I couldn't rightly say. That's what the contractor feller was tellin' us.

ANDREW: Nonsense. (*Turning the pages of his book.*) Were you ever in Moscow?

PHERAPONT (*after a pause*): No, I weren't. God hasn't dealt me any such hand as that. (*Pause.*) Can I go?

ANDREW: You may. Good-by. (*Exit* PHERAPONT.) You'll come tomorrow and pick up these papers. . . . You may go now. (*Looking up from his book at last.*) Why, he's gone! (*Doorbell rings.*) Yes, that's how things go. . . . (*Stretches himself and shuffles off listlessly into his own room. A* NURSE *is singing, off, evidently lulling a child to sleep. Enter* MARY *and* VERSHININ. *A little later, as they are talking, a* MAID *enters and lights candles and a lamp.*)

MARY: I don't know. (*Pause.*) I really don't know. Of course, habit plays an important part. After father died, for instance, for a long time we could not get used to the fact that we no longer had orderlies. But even aside from habit, it seems to me that it's simply a sense of justice which speaks within me. Perhaps it may not hold true in other places, but in our town the most decent, the finest, and best-educated people are army men.

VERSHININ: I'm thirsty. I wouldn't mind having tea.

MARY (*glancing at her watch*): It will be served soon. I was married off when I was eighteen, and I was awed by my husband because he was a teacher, whereas I was just out of high school. At that time he seemed to me awfully erudite, clever, and important. But now, unfortunately, things aren't like that.

VERSHININ: Yes. . . . I see.

MARY: I'm not referring to my husband—I've grown used to him. But, in general, there are so many boorish, unpleasant, uncultured people among the civilians. Boorishness upsets me; it offends me; I suffer when I see someone lacking tact, lacking gentleness or politeness. Whenever I chance to be among teachers—my husband's colleagues—why, I simply suffer.

VERSHININ: Yes. . . . But it seems to me that there isn't any difference, that civilians and military men are just about equally interesting—at least in this town! If you'll listen to a local intellectual, whether he is a civilian or a military man, all you'll learn is that he's at the end of his rope about his wife, that he is at the end of his rope about his household, that he is at the end of his rope about his property, that he is at the end of his rope about his horses. . . . An exalted plane of thought is inherent in the highest degree in the Russian—but tell me, why does he strike such a low mark in life? Why?

MARY: Yes—why?

VERSHININ: Why is he at the end of his rope about his children, about his wife? And why are his wife and children at the end of their rope about *him?*

MARY: You are a little out of sorts today.

VERSHININ: Perhaps. I haven't had lunch yet—haven't eaten a thing since morning. One of my daughters is ailing a little, and when my little girls are ailing I am overwhelmed with anxiety, my conscience tortures me because I have given them such a mother as theirs. Oh, if you just could have seen her today! What a paltry creature! We started squabbling at seven in the morning and at nine I slammed the door and left. (*Pause.*) I never speak of all this, and it's strange that I should complain only to you. (*Kisses her hand.*) Don't be angry at me. I have nobody—nobody!—but you— (*Pause.*)

MARY: What a noise the fire makes! Just before Father died, the chimney in our house was humming. There, just like that.

VERSHININ: Are you superstitious?

MARY: Yes.

VERSHININ: That's strange. (*Kisses her hand.*) You are a glorious, wonderful woman. Glorious, wonderful! It's dark here—yet I can see how your eyes sparkle—

MARY (*changing her seat*): It's lighter here—

VERSHININ: I am in love—in love—in love! I love your eyes, every movement you make, which I see in my dreams. . . . Glorious, wonderful woman!

MARY (*laughing softly*): When you speak to me like that I laugh, even though I feel frightened. Don't say such things again, I beg you— (*In an undertone.*) But no—go on. . . . What difference does it make to me— (*Buries her face in her hands.*) What difference does it make to me. . . . Somebody's coming this way—speak of something else— (IRENE *and* TUZENBACH *enter through dining room.*)

TUZENBACH: I have a three-story family name. They call me Baron Tuzenbach-Krone-Altschauer, but I am a Russian and of the Orthodox Church, just as you are. There is very little that is German left in me— unless it be the perseverance, the persistence with which I haunt you. I see you home every night—

IRENE: How tired I am!

TUZENBACH: And I'll be calling for you at the telegraph office and seeing you home every single day; I'll keep it up for ten years, for twenty years—until you drive me away— (*Joyfully, catching sight of* MARY *and* VERSHININ.) There you are! How are you?

IRENE: Well, I'm home at last. (*To* MARY.) Just a little while ago a lady came into the office to send a telegram to her brother in Saratov —her son died today—and she couldn't, for the life of her, remember her brother's address. So in the end I sent the message off without any street number—just to Saratov. Crying, she was. And, for no reason at all, I became rude to her. "I'm busy!" I told her. The whole thing was so stupid.—Is it tonight the maskers are coming?

MARY: Yes.

IRENE (*sinking into an armchair*): I want to rest a little. I'm all in.

TUZENBACH (*with a smile*): When you come home from work you seem such a young, unhappy little thing! (*Pause.*)

IRENE: I'm all in. No, I don't like the telegraph office—I don't like it.

MARY: You've lost weight. . . . (*Whistles under her breath.*) You've grown younger—and at the same time you're looking like a tomboy.

TUZENBACH: It's because of the way she does her hair.

IRENE: I'll have to look for another job; this one isn't at all to my taste. That which I wanted so much, that which I dreamed of, is the very thing lacking about it. Toil without poetry, without ideals— (*Knocking from the floor below.*) That's Doctor Chebutykin knocking! (*To* TUZENBACH.) Be a good fellow—answer him. I can't . . . I'm all in. (TUZENBACH *knocks on floor.*) He'll be up right away. We ought to take certain measures. Yesterday the Doctor and our

Andrew were at the club and lost at cards again. They say Andrew lost two hundred.

MARY (*apathetically*) : Well, what are we to do this time?

IRENE: He lost two weeks ago; he lost last December. If only he would lose everything as quickly as possible we might get out of this town. Good Lord, I dream of Moscow every night; I've simply gone mad on the subject. (*Laughs.*) We're going there in June, and until June there's still—February, March, April, May—almost half a year!

MARY: The main thing is, Nathalie mustn't find out about the money Andrew lost.

IRENE: I don't think that will make much difference to her. (CHEBUTYKIN, *obviously just up from an after-dinner nap, enters the dining room; he grooms his beard, then sits down at the table and takes a newspaper out of his pocket.*)

MARY: There, he's arrived. Has he paid his rent?

IRENE (*laughing*) : No. He hasn't paid a copper in eight months. Forgotten all about it, evidently.

MARY (*laughing in her turn*) : With what dignity he sits there! (*All laugh. Pause.*)

IRENE (*to* VERSHININ) : Why are you so quiet?

VERSHININ: I don't know. I feel like having tea. My kingdom for a glass of tea! I haven't eaten a thing since morning—

CHEBUTYKIN: Oh, Irene!

IRENE: What is it?

CHEBUTYKIN: Come here, please. *Venez ici.* (IRENE goes to CHEBUTYKIN *and sits down at the table.*) I can't be without you. (IRENE *lays out a game of solitaire.*)

VERSHININ: Oh, well, if we aren't getting any tea let's indulge in a little philosophizing.

TUZENBACH: Let's. What about?

VERSHININ: What about? Let's daydream a little . . . about that life, for instance, which will come after us, in two or three hundred years, say.

TUZENBACH: Well, why not? After us men will fly through the air; the cut of our coats will change; they'll discover a sixth sense, perhaps, and develop it—but life will still remain the same: a life of hardship, filled with mysteries—and happiness. And a thousand years from now man will be sighing in the selfsame way: "Ah, but life is hard!" —and at the same time, just as now, he will be afraid of death and averse to it.

VERSHININ (*after brief thought*): How shall I put it to you? It seems to me that everything upon this earth must change little by little, and that it is already changing before our eyes. After the lapse of two hundred, three hundred—or even a thousand years, let's say, since the point does not lie in the actual period of time—a new, happy life will come. We will have no part in this life, of course, yet we are living for the sake of that life now, we are working for it—yes, we are even suffering for it; we are creating it, and in that alone lies the aim—and, if you like, the happiness—of our being here on earth. (MARY *laughs softly.*)

TUZENBACH: What are you laughing at?

MARY: I don't know. I've been laughing all day today, from the very morning.

VERSHININ (*to* TUZENBACH): I finished the same school you did; I did not go to a university, however. I read a great deal, but don't know how to choose books and perhaps do not read at all the things I should; yet at the same time, the longer I live, the more I want to know. My hair is turning gray, I am almost an old man—yet I know little—oh, how little! But still it seems to me that I know that which is most important and real—that I know it thoroughly. And how I would like to prove to you that happiness is not for us, that there mustn't be any, and that there won't be. . . . We must merely work, on and on, but as for happiness—it is the lot of our distant posterity. (*Pause.*) If not for me, then at least for the descendants of my descendants. (PHEDOTIK *aud* RODE *appear in the dining room; they sit down and begin to hum softly, to the strumming of a guitar.*)

TUZENBACH: According to you one must not even dream of happiness! But what if I *am* happy?

VERSHININ: No!

TUZENBACH (*throwing up his hands and laughing*): Evidently we don't understand each other. Well, how am I to convince you? (MARY *laughs softly.* TUZENBACH *threatens her with his finger.*) Go ahead and laugh! (*To* VERSHININ.) Not only after two or three hundred but even after a million years life will remain the same as it has always been; it does not change; it remains constant, following laws of its own which are no affair of ours—or which we will never learn, at least. There are certain beautiful birds—cranes, for instance—that fly on and on, and no matter what ideas, exalted or petty, may go through their heads, they'll still keep right on flying, yet never know why they're flying or where. They are flying and will go on flying, no matter what bird-philosophers may arise among them; and they'll let 'em philosophize to their hearts' content—as long as they themselves may fly—

MARY: Still, there must be some meaning?

TUZENBACH: A meaning, did you say? There, the snow is falling. What is the meaning of that? (*Pause.*)

MARY: It seems to me that man must have faith, or must seek faith; otherwise his life is void—void. . . . To live—and yet not know why cranes fly, why children are born, why there are stars in the sky. . . . One has to know why one lives, or else all things are paltry—just so much chaff. (*Pause.*)

VERSHININ: Still, I regret my youth has passed—

MARY: Gogol has said somewhere: "Life on this earth is a bore, gentlemen!"

TUZENBACH: And I would say: "It's mighty hard to argue with you, my friends!" I wash my hands of you.

CHEBUTYKIN (*reading from his newspaper*): "A Balzac was married in Berdichev—" (IRENE *is humming softly.*) I really must write that down in my book— (*Making an entry in his notebook.*) "A Balzac was married in Berdichev—" (*Resumes reading his newspaper.*)

TUZENBACH (*to Mary*): The die is cast. Do you know that I've handed in my resignation?

MARY: Yes—so I've heard. And I fail to see anything good about it. I don't like civilians.

TUZENBACH: No matter. (*Standing up.*) I'm no Adonis—what sort of a military figure do I cut? Oh, well, it doesn't matter, anyway. . . . I am going to work. Oh—to work but one day in my life so as to come home in the evening dead tired, fall in exhaustion on my bed, and go off to sleep at once! (*Passing into dining room.*) How soundly working men must sleep!

PHEDOTIK (*to* IRENE): I just bought some colored crayons for you —at the best place in town. And this little knife—

IRENE: You've taken to treating me like a little girl—but I'm grown up now. (*Takes crayons and knife; then, with delight.*) How charming!

PHEDOTIK: And I bought one for myself, too . . . there, have a look . . . here's one blade . . . here's another . . . and a third—this thingamajig is for picking the wax out of your ears . . . and these little scissors are for clipping your nails—

RODE (*boomingly*): How old are you, Doctor?

CHEBUTYKIN: Who, me? Thirty-three! (*General laughter.*)

PHEDOTIK: Here, let me show you a different kind of solitaire— (*Lays out the cards for* IRENE. ANPHISSA *brings in a samovar; she fusses around it. A little later* NATHALIE *puts in an appearance; she, too, fusses around the table.* SOLIONNYI *arrives and, after greeting everybody, takes a seat at the table.*)

VERSHININ: I say, though—what a wind!

MARY: Yes. I'm sick of the winter. I've forgotten by now what summer is like.

IRENE: This game will come out right. Which means that we're going to Moscow—

PHEDOTIK: No, it won't work out. See—the eight turned up on the deuce of spades—(*Laughs.*) That means you won't get to Moscow.

CHEBUTYKIN (*reading from his newspaper*): "Tsitsicar. An epidemic of smallpox is reported to be raging here."

ANPHISSA (*approaching* MARY): Come, Mary, have some tea, darling. (*To* VERSHININ.) If you please, Your Honor—forgive me, Sir, I've forgotten your name—

MARY: Bring me a cup here, nurse. I'm not going in there.

IRENE: Nurse!

ANPHISSA: Coming, coming!

NATHALIE: Even babies at the breast understand things excellently. "How d'you do, Bobby?" I say to him. "How d'you do, darling?" And he looks up at me in *such* an odd way! You may think it's the mother in me speaking, but no, no, I assure you! He's an unusual child.

SOLIONNYI: If it were *my* child I'd fry him brown on a skillet and eat him. (*Takes his glass into the reception room and takes a seat in a corner.*)

NATHALIE (*burying her face in her hands*): You ill-bred brute!

MARY: You're lucky if you don't notice whether it's winter now or summer. It seems to me that if I were in Moscow I would regard the weather with indifference—

VERSHININ: The last few days I've been reading the diary of a certain French politician—a Premier—which he wrote in prison. This Premier was sentenced in the Panama scandal. With what ecstasy, what rapture he speaks of the birds he sees through the window of his cell, and which he had never noticed before, at the time he was Premier! Now, of course, since he has been set at liberty, he no longer notices the birds, just as he didn't notice them before he went to prison. And in precisely the same way you won't notice Moscow when you'll be living there. Happiness doesn't exist and never will exist for us—we merely long for it.

TUZENBACH (*picking up an empty candy box from the table*): Why, where did all the candy go to?

IRENE: Solionnyi ate it.

TUZENBACH: All of it?

ANPHISSA (*to* VERSHININ, *as she brings the tea*): A note for you, Sir.

VERSHININ: For me? (*Taking the note.*) From one of my girls— (*Reading note.*) Yes, naturally! (*To* MARY.) Excuse me; I'll leave as unobtrusively as I can. I won't have tea—(*Gets up, agitated.*) The same old story.

MARY: What is it? It isn't a secret, is it?

VERSHININ (*in a low voice*): My wife has taken poison again. I'll have to go. I'll leave without anybody noticing me. All this is horribly unpleasant. (*Kissing* MARY'S *hand.*) My glorious, beloved, splendid woman. . . . I'll go this way, as quietly as possible— (*Leaves.*)

ANPHISSA: Where's he off to now? And just when I had served the tea, too. What a man!

MARY (*flaring up*): Get away from me! You don't give me a moment's rest with your nagging—(*Goes to table, carrying her cup.*) I'm fed up with you, old lady!

ANPHISSA: Why get so offended? Darling!

ANDREW (*off*): Anphissa!

ANPHISSA (*mimicking*): "Anphissa!" It's all very well for you to be sitting there, yelling your head off—(*Exit.*)

MARY (*at the table, angrily*): I wish you'd give me a chance to sit down! (*Mixing up* IRENE'S *cards.*) Spreading your cards all over the table! We're supposed to be having tea!

IRENE: You have a vile temper, Mary dear.

MARY: Don't talk to me then! Don't touch me!

CHEBUTYKIN (*laughing*): Don't touch her! Don't touch her!

MARY (*turning on him*): You're sixty, and yet you're forever spouting the damnedest stuff, like a little boy—

NATHALIE (*sighing*): Mary, dearest, why use such expressions in conversation? With your beautiful appearance—I'm being absolutely frank with you—you would be simply fascinating in any good social setting, if it weren't for your language. *Je vous prie, pardonnez moi, Marie, mais vous avez des manières un peu grossières. . . .*

TUZENBACH (*trying to restrain his laughter*): May I have . . . may I have . . . that's cognac over there, I think—

NATHALIE: *Il paraît que mon Bobby déjà ne dort pas*—he must have waked up. He isn't at all well today. Excuse me, I'm going to him— (*Leaves.*)

IRENE: But where has Vershinin gone?

MARY: Home. Something's up with his wife again.

TUZENBACH (*approaching* SOLIONNYI, *with a decanter of cognac in his hand*): You're forever moping by yourself, mulling over something or other—and nobody can understand what it is exactly. There, let's make up. Let's have a shot of cognac. (*They drink.*) I'll have to play the piano all night tonight—probably all sorts of trashy stuff. Oh, well, let come what may!

SOLIONNYI: Why should we make up? I didn't quarrel with you.

TUZENBACH: You always make me feel that something is up between us. Yours is a strange nature, I must say.

SOLIONNYI (*declaiming*): "I may be strange, but who is not? Be thou not wroth, Aleko! . . ."

TUZENBACH: What in the world has Pushkin to do with it? (*Pause.*)

SOLIONNYI: When I'm alone with someone, things aren't so bad, I'm like everybody else; but in a gathering I'm glum, bashful, and . . . I talk all sorts of rot. Just the same, I'm more honest and more honorable than lots of others—lots! And I can prove it.

TUZENBACH: I'm often angry at you; whenever we're at some gathering you're constantly picking on me; but still, for some reason, I am fond of you. Come what may, I'm going to get drunk tonight. Let's drink!

SOLIONNYI: Let's. (*They drink.*) I never had anything against you, Baron. But my nature is the same as Lermontov's. (*Softly.*) I even look a little like Lermontov—so they tell me. (*Takes a perfume flask from his pocket and douses some perfume on his hands.*)

TUZENBACH: I'm handing in my resignation. Finis! I've been thinking and thinking it over for five years and have come to a decision at last. I'm going to work.

SOLIONNYI (*declaiming*): "Be thou not wroth, Aleko. . . . Forget thy dreams—forget!" (*While they are speaking,* ANDREW *enters quietly with a book and sits down near a candle.*)

TUZENBACH: Yes, I'm going to work.

CHEBUTYKIN (*going toward the reception room with* IRENE): And the banquet also was Caucasian—leek soup and, for the meat course, a roast called *chehertma*—

SOLIONNYI: *Cheremsha* isn't meat at all, but a vegetable something like our leek—

CHEBUTYKIN: No, my angel. *Chehertma* isn't leek, but roasted mutton—

SOLIONNYI: And I'm telling you that *cheremsha* is leek—

CHEBUTYKIN: And I'm telling you that *chehertma* is mutton!

SOLIONNYI: And I'm telling that *cheremsha* is leek—

CHEBUTYKIN: Why should I argue with you? You've never lived in the Caucasus and you've never eaten *chehertma*.

SOLIONNYI: I never have because I can't stand it. *Cheremsha* gives off the same odor as garlic.

ANDREW (*imploringly*): Enough, gentlemen! I beg you!

TUZENBACH: When are the maskers coming?

IRENE: They promised to be here about nine; that means they ought to be here any minute.

TUZENBACH (*taking* ANDREW *around the waist, half-singing*): "Oh, my shanty, oh, my shanty—oh, my shanty, new and good—"

ANDREW (*dancing as he chimes in*): "New and good, of maple wood!"

CHEBUTYKIN (*dancing*): "With a lattice like a hood!" (*General laughter.*)

TUZENBACH (*kissing* ANDREW): Let's drink, the devil take it! Let's drink to closer ties, Andrew. I'm coming along with you. On to Moscow, Andrew—to the university!

SOLIONNYI: Which one? There are two universities in Moscow.

ANDREW: There's only one university in Moscow.

SOLIONNYI: And I'm telling you there are two universities—

ANDREW: Let there be three. The more the merrier.

SOLIONNYI: There are two universities in Moscow! (*Murmurs of indignation and much hushing.*) There are two universities in Moscow —the old and the new. But if you don't like to listen, if what I say irritates you, then I can just hush up. I can even go off into another room— (*Stalks off through one of the side doors.*)

TUZENBACH: Bravo, bravo! (*Laughs.*) Begin, ladies and gentlemen—I'm sitting down to play! Funny fellow, this Solionnyi! (*Sits down at piano; plays a waltz.*)

MARY (*dancing by herself*): The Baron's drunk, the Baron's drunk, the Baron's drunk!

NATHALIE (*entering, and beckoning to* CHEBUTYKIN): Oh, Doctor! (*Speaks to him about something in a low voice, then goes out quietly.*)

CHEBUTYKIN *taps* TUZENBACH *on the shoulder and whispers something in his ear.*)

IRENE: What's up?

CHEBUTYKIN: Time we were going. Take good care of yourselves!

TUZENBACH: Good night. Time to be going.

IRENE: Wait, wait! But what about the maskers?

ANDREW (*in confusion*): There won't be any. . . . You see, my dear, Nathalie says that Bobby isn't at all well, and for that reason . . . in short, I don't know—it doesn't much matter to me—

IRENE (*shrugging her shoulders*): Bobby isn't well!

MARY: Let 'er rip! They're giving us the gate—so we'll have to go. (*To* IRENE.) It isn't Bobby with whom there's something wrong, but with herself—(*taps her forehead*)—right here! . . . The little bourgeoise! (ANDREW *sneaks off to his room, right.* CHEBUTYKIN *follows him. The others are getting ready to leave.*)

PHEDOTIK: What a pity! I was planning to spend the whole evening here, but since the little one isn't well, then, naturally. . . . I'll bring him some toys tomorrow—

RODE (*boomingly*): Today I purposely took a good nap after dinner—I thought I was going to dance all night. Why, it's only nine now!

MARY: Let's get out of here—we'll talk things over outside. We'll decide on ways and means. (*A general exchange of such phrases as* "Good-by!" *and* "Keep well!" *All leave.* ANPHISSA *and a* MAID *come on, clear away the things from the table and, after extinguishing the lights, go off. A* NURSE *is heard singing a lullaby.* ANDREW, *wearing overcoat and hat, enters stealthily, followed by* CHEBUTYKIN.)

CHEBUTYKIN: Never managed to marry, somehow, because life flashed by like a gleam of lightning—and also because I was madly in love with your mother, who had married by then—

ANDREW: One oughtn't to marry. One oughtn't—because it's a deadly bore.

CHEBUTYKIN: That may very well be—but then there's loneliness. Philosophize all you want to, but loneliness, my dear fellow, is a frightful thing. Although, when you come right down to it . . . it makes absolutely no difference, of course!

ANDREW: Let's get out of here as fast as we can.

CHEBUTYKIN: But what's the rush? We'll get there in plenty of time.

ANDREW: I'm afraid my wife may stop me.

CHEBUTYKIN: Ah!

ANDREW: I'm not going to play tonight; I'll just hang around. I don't feel very well. What am I to do for my shortness of breath, Doctor?

CHEBUTYKIN: No use even asking me! I don't remember, my dear fellow . . . I don't know—

ANDREW: Let's go through the kitchen. (*Exeunt. Doorbell rings; a little later it rings again. Voices and laughter, off. Enter* IRENE, *followed by* ANPHISSA.)

IRENE: Who can that be?

ANPHISSA (*in a whisper*): It's the maskers. (*Another ring.*)

IRENE: Tell them there's nobody home, nurse darling. They'll have to excuse us. (ANPHISSA *goes out.* IRENE *thoughtfully paces the room; she is agitated.*)

SOLIONNYI (*entering, and then stopping short*): Nobody here. . . . Why, where is everybody?

IRENE: They've gone home.

SOLIONNYI: That's odd. Are you all alone?

IRENE: Yes. (*Pause.*) Good-night.

SOLIONNYI: A little while ago I behaved without sufficient restraint—tactlessly. But you aren't like all the others; you are noble, pure; you can perceive the truth. . . . You, and you alone, can understand me. I am in love—profoundly, infinitely in love—

IRENE: Good-by. Do go.

SOLIONNYI: I cannot live without you— (*Following her about.*) Oh, my bliss! (*With tears in his voice.*) Oh, my happiness! Those magnificent, wonderful, amazing eyes, such as I have never beheld in any other woman—

IRENE (*coldly*): Stop it!

SOLIONNYI: This is the first time I speak of my love for you, and it is just as if I were not upon this earth but on some other planet. (*Rubbing his forehead.*) Oh, well, what does it matter! One can't win anybody's affection by force, of course. But I won't brook any rivals more fortunate than I—I won't! I swear to you by all that's holy that I will kill any rival of mine. . . . Oh, my wonderful one!

NATHALIE (*crossing the room with a candle, peeping in at a couple of doors, and finally passing by the door of* ANDREW'S *room*): Andrew must have retired. Let him read in peace. (*To* SOLIONNYI): You must really excuse me; I didn't know you were here, or I would have put on something more appropriate—(*Indicates her negligée.*)

SOLIONNYI: I don't mind in the least. Good-by! (*Exit.*)

NATHALIE: You must be all tired out, my poor, dear little girl. (*Kisses* IRENE.) You ought to go to bed early.

IRENE: Is Bobby asleep?

NATHALIE: Yes. But he's restless. By the way, darling, I've been meaning to have a little talk with you, but either you're always away, or I have no time. . . . It seems to me that Bobby finds it cold and damp in the room we're now using as a nursery—and your room would be such a fine one for a baby. Dearest, my own darling, do move into Olga's room and share it with her!

IRENE (*failing to grasp what* NATALIE *is saying*): Move where? (*A sleigh with jingle-bells is heard driving up to the house.*)

NATHALIE: You'll be in the same room with Olga, and I'll give your room to Bobby for the time being. He's such a little doll; today I said to him: "Bobby, you're mine! Mine!" And he looks up at me with those adorable, darling eyes of his—(*Doorbell rings.*) That must be Olga. How late she is! (MAID *enters, walks up to* NATHALIE, *and whispers something into her ear.*) Protopopov? What a queer fellow! Protopopov has just driven up; he's inviting me to take a ride in his troika— (*Laughs.*) What strange creatures men are! (*Bell rings again.*) That must be somebody else. Perhaps I really should take a a little ride—for a quarter of an hour or so—(*To* MAID.) Tell him I'll be ready in a minute. (*A third ring.*) See who that is, somebody! It's Olga, probably. (*Exit.* MAID *runs off.* IRENE *is sitting, deep in thought. Enter* KULYGHIN *and* OLGA, *with* VERSHININ *behind them.*)

KULYGHIN: There, now! And yet they said there was going to be a party here this evening!

VERSHININ: That's strange. I left just a little while ago—about half an hour, say—and they were expecting some maskers—

IRENE: They're all gone.

KULYGHIN: Has Mary left, too? Where did she go? And why is Protopopov waiting downstairs in his troika? Whom is he waiting for?

IRENE: Stop bombarding me with questions. I'm all in.

KULYGHIN: My, what a cranky girl!

OLGA: How can any conference last so long. . . . I'm at the end of my rope. My head, my head—my head is splitting—(*Sits down.*) Andrew lost two hundred at cards yesterday. The whole town is talking about it.

KULYGHIN: Yes, I got tired out at the conference, too. (*Sits down.*)

VERSHININ: My wife got the bright idea just now of throwing a scare into me—she almost poisoned herself. Everything turned out all right, and I was glad and thought I would have a little rest. . . . But I'll have to go, won't I? Well, allow me to extend my best wishes for the holidays! (*To* KULYGHIN.) Let's go somewhere, just the two of us. I can't remain at home—I absolutely can't. . . . Let's go!

KULYGHIN: I'm tired out. I won't go. (*Gets up.*) All tired out! Did my wife go home?

IRENE: Probably.

KULYGHIN (*kissing* IRENE'S *hand*): Good-by, then. I intend resting all day tomorrow—and the day after. My best wishes for the holidays. (*Going off.*) I'm dying for some tea. I was planning on spending the evening in pleasant company, and now—*O, fallacem hominum spem!* Use the accusative in conjunction with an exclamation—

VERSHININ: I'll go by myself then. (*Whistles as he leaves with* KULYGHIN.)

OLGA: My head's splitting. . . . Oh, my head! Andrew has lost at cards again . . . the whole town is talking about it. . . . I'm going to lie down. (*Going off.*) Tomorrow I am free. Oh, my God, what a pleasure that is! Tomorrow I'm free—and I'm free the day after tomorrow. . . . My head's splitting. . . . Oh, my head— (*Goes off.*)

IRENE (*left alone on stage*): They're all gone. Not a soul left. (*An accordeon is playing out in the street. Lullaby, off.*)

NATHALIE (*entering in fur coat and hat, and passing through dining room, followed by* MAID): I'll be back in half an hour. I'm just going for a little ride. (*Leaves.*)

IRENE (*now utterly alone, yearningly*): Moscow! Moscow! Moscow!

Curtain

ACT II

Two years later.

Bedroom of IRENE *and* OLGA. *Bed, right; another, left; each one has a screen.*

About three in the morning. Tocsin, off; evidently the alarm it is sounding is for a fire that began a long time ago.

It is apparent that no one in the house has even thought of going to bed.

MARY *is lying down on a divan; she is dressed in her usual black. Enter* OLGA *and* ANPHISSA.

ANPHISSA: They're down below now, settin' under the staircase. I says to them, I says: "Come upstairs, do! How can you carry on like that?"—but they just keep on crying. "We don't know where our daddy is," they says to me. "God forbid," says they, "but maybe he got burned up!" What ideas they get into their little heads! And there's some other folks out in the courtyard. . . . And they, too, haven't a rag to cover themselves with—

OLGA (*taking dresses out of a closet*): Here, take this gray dress . . . and this one . . . this blouse, too. And take this skirt as well, nurse darling. Good God, what's going on! It looks as if some streets have been absolutely gutted. Take this dress—and this—(*Tossing the dresses over* ANPHISSA'S *arm.*) The poor Vershinins! They're terribly frightened; their house all but burned down. Let them spend the night here—they mustn't be allowed to go home. Poor Phedotik has lost everything in the fire; he hasn't a stitch left—

ANPHISSA: Maybe you'd better call Pherapont, Olga dear—I mayn't be able to lug all these the whole way—

OLGA (*ringing*): You can ring and ring—they'll never answer. (*Opening door and calling down.*) Come on up, whoever is there! (*A window, red with the glow of a conflagration, can be glimpsed through the opened door. A fire engine clangs past the house.*) How horrible all this is! And how sick I am of it all—(*To* PHERAPONT, *as he enters.*) Here, take these—bring them down. There are two young ladies sitting under the staircase—give them these . . . and this, too—

PHERAPONT: Right, Miss! In the year eighteen-twelve all Moscow was in flames, too. Lordy, Lordy! Was them Frenchies surprised!

OLGA: There, run along with you!

PHERAPONT: Right, Miss! (*Exit.*)

OLGA: Give everything away, nurse darling. We don't need anything—get rid of all this. . . . I'm so tired I can hardly keep on my feet. . . . The Vershinins must not be allowed to go home! The little girls can lie down in the reception room, and we'll put their father downstairs, in the Baron's apartment. Phedotik can also be put up at the Baron's—or let him sleep in our dining room. . . . The Doctor's drunk, as if for spite, so you can't put anybody in his apartment. And Vershinin's wife can also sleep in the reception room.

ANPHISSA (*wearily*) : Olga, my darling little girl, don't drive me out! Don't drive me out!

OLGA: You say such silly things, nurse. Nobody's driving you out.

ANPHISSA (*putting her head on* OLGA'S *breast*) : My own, my precious. I work, I sweat. . . . I'll get feeble; then they'll say: "Go on—git!" But where am I to go? Where? I'm eighty . . . goin' on eighty-two—

OLGA: You just sit down for a while, nurse darling. You're all in, my poor dear—(*Making* ANPHISSA *sit down.*) Rest a while, dearest. You've turned so pale!

NATHALIE (*entering*) : They're saying in town that a committee to help the victims of the fire ought to be formed as quickly as possible. Well, why not? It's a splendid idea. On general principles the poor ought to be helped with all speed possible—it's a duty of those who are better off. Bobby and little Sophie are sleeping—sleeping just as if there was absolutely nothing happening. We have so many people all over the house—you stumble over them whichever way you turn. There's influenza in town now—I'm afraid the little ones may catch it.

OLGA (*paying no attention to her*) : You can't see the fire from this room; it's peaceful in here.

NATHALIE. Yes. . . . My hair must be a sight. (*Before a mirror.*) They say I've put on weight—but it isn't true! Not in the least! Why, Mary's asleep—she's all tired out, the poor dear. (*To* ANPHISSA, *with cold fury.*) Don't you dare sit in my presence! Get up! Get out of here! (ANPHISSA *gets out. Pause.*) I simply can't understand why on earth you keep this old creature!

OLGA (*taken aback*) : Pardon me, but I also can't understand what you're saying—

NATHALIE: She's of no earthly use here. She's a countrywoman and belongs in some village. . . . What sort of pampering is this? I like order in the house! There must be no superfluous people in a household! (*Stroking* OLGA'S *cheek.*) You're all in, poor darling! Our Chief Instructress is all in! When my little Sophie grows up and enters the high school I'll be in such awe of you—

OLGA: I won't be Chief Instructress.

NATHALIE: They'll elect you, Olga darling. It's all settled.

OLGA: I'll decline. I can't fill the post. It's beyond my strength. (*Taking a glass of water.*) You treated Nurse so rudely just now. I'm sorry, but I'm in no condition to stand such things. Everything is dark before my eyes—

NATHALIE (*in agitation*) : Forgive me, Olga—forgive me! I didn't mean to offend you— (MARY *gets up, picks up a pillow, and walks out, demonstratively.*)

OLGA: Do understand, my dear. . . . Our upbringing may have been peculiar, perhaps, but I can't endure this. Such treatment has a depressing effect on me; I get ill. . . . I simply lose heart!

NATHALIE: Forgive me, forgive me— (*Kisses* OLGA.)

OLGA: Every rude action, even the slightest, every tactless word, upsets me—

NATHALIE: I often say more than I should, that's true; but you must agree, my dear, that she might live in the country—

OLGA: She has been with us for thirty years now.

NATHALIE: But look, she can no longer work! Either I don't understand you, or you refuse to understand me. She's no longer fit for work —all she does is sleep or sit around.

OLGA: Well, let her sit around.

NATHALIE (*amazed*): What do you mean—let her sit around? Why, she's a servant, isn't she? (*With tears in her voice.*) I can't understand you, Olga. I have a nurse, I have a wet-nurse; we have a maid and a cook—what do we want an old woman for in addition? What for? (*Tocsin, off.*)

OLGA: I've aged ten years in this one night.

NATHALIE: We must come to an understanding, Olga. You're at the school, I am at home; you have your job at school, my job is to run the household. And if I say anything about the servants I know what I'm talking about; I-know-what-I-am-talk-ing-a-bout. . . . And by tomorrow this old thief, this old scarecrow, must be out of the house— (*Stamping her foot.*) The old witch! Don't you dare to exasperate me! Don't you dare! (*Suddenly checking herself.*) Really, unless you move downstairs we'll be always quarreling. This is dreadful.

KULYGHIN (*entering*): Where's Mary? Time she were home. The fire is dying down, they say. (*Stretching.*) Only one block burned down, but then there was a wind and it looked at first as if the whole town was burning. (*Takes a seat.*) I'm tired out. My dear little Olga, I often think that if I hadn't married Mary I would have married you. Little Olga. . . . You're very pretty! I'm at the end of my rope. (*Sits up and listens.*)

OLGA: What is it?

KULYGHIN: As if for spite, the Doctor's gone on a bender; he's horribly drunk. As if for spite! (*Gets up.*) There, he's coming up, I think.

Do you hear him? Yes, he's coming here— (*Laughs.*) Really, what a man he is! I'm going to keep out of sight. (*Goes in a corner, behind door of closet.*) What a villain!

OLGA: He kept away from drink for two years—and now he suddenly goes and gets drunk. (*Goes with* NATHALIE *to back of room.*)

CHEBUTYKIN (*enters; without staggering, just as if he were sober, takes a turn about the room, stops, looks about him, then goes to washstand and begins washing his hands, speaking glumly*) : May the devil take them . . . and break them . . . all of 'em. . . . They think I'm a doctor, that I can cure all their ills and pains, when I know absolutely nothing, have forgot everything I ever did know, and remember nothing—absolutely nothing! (NATHALIE *and* OLGA *tiptoe out without his perceiving it.*) Devil take it all. Last Wednesday I attended a woman out in the sticks; she died—and I am guilty of her death. Yes. . . . I did know a thing or two twenty-five years ago, but now I know nothing. Nothing. Maybe I'm not even a man, but merely pretending now that I have hands and feet—and a head; maybe I don't even exist, but it merely seems to me that I walk about, eat, sleep— (*Weeps.*) Oh, only not to exist! (*Glumly, as he stops weeping.*) What the devil. . . . A couple of days ago, at the club, they got to talking; they mentioned Shakespeare, Voltaire; I'd never read them, not a blessed word, but I put on a knowing air, as if I had read them. And there were others there who did the very same thing I did. How vulgar—low-down! And I reminded myself of the woman I had done to death on Wednesday . . . and I reminded myself of everything else as well—and everything in my soul became snarled, vile, abominable. And I went off . . . off on a bender. (*Enter* IRENE, VERSHININ, *and* TUZENBACH; *the last is wearing civilian clothes, new and of the latest cut.*)

IRENE: Let's sit here for a while. No one will come in here.

VERSHININ: If it hadn't been for the soldiers the whole town would have burned down. Good lads! (*Rubbing his hands with satisfaction.*) Finest people on earth. Eh, what splendid lads they are!

KULYGHIN (*approaching them*) : What time is it, gentlemen?

TUZENBACH: It's going on four. Day is breaking already.

IRENE: They're all sitting in the dining room; nobody's leaving. And that Solionnyi of yours is sitting there, too— (*To* CHEBUTYKIN.) You ought to go to bed, Doctor.

CHEBUTYKIN: Not at all, not at all . . . thank you! (*Grooms his beard.*)

KULYGHIN (*laughing*) : My, but the Doctor is stewed! (*Slapping*

CHEBUTYKIN *on the back.*) Good boy! *In vino veritas,* as the ancients used to say.

TUZENBACH: They're after me to arrange a concert for the benefit of the fire victims.

IRENE: Oh, whom could you get to perform—

TUZENBACH: It could be arranged, if one really wanted to do it. Mary plays the piano marvelously, in my opinion.

KULYGHIN: She does play marvelously!

IRENE: She's forgotten how to play by now. Hasn't played in three years—or four.

TUZENBACH: There's absolutely nobody in this town who understands music—not a soul. But I—I understand music, and I assure you, upon my word of honor, that Mary plays superbly—almost with genius.

KULYGHIN: Right you are, Baron. I love her very much, my Mary. She's a fine person.

TUZENBACH: To be able to play so magnificently, yet at the same time realize that no one—no one!—understands you. . . .

KULYGHIN (*with a sigh*): Yes. . . . But would it be dignified for her to take part in a public concert? (*Pause.*) After all, gentlemen, I know nothing about such things. Perhaps it may actually be all right. I must admit that our Director is a kind man—even exceptionally kind —and most intelligent, but still, he holds to certain views. . . . Of course, it is really none of his affair, but still, if you wish, I may have a talk with him, perhaps. (CHEBUTYKIN *picks up a porcelain clock and examines it.*)

VERSHININ: I mussed myself all up at the fire; I must look like nothing on earth. (*Pause.*) Yesterday I heard, just in passing, that they want to transfer our brigade to some out-of-the-way point. Some say to Poland; others, to Chita.

TUZENBACH: I also heard that. Well, what will we do then? The whole town will become desolate.

IRENE: Well, we'll leave the town, too!

CHEBUTYKIN (*as the clock slips out of his hands and crashes against the floor*): Smashed to smithereens— (*Pause. All are upset and embarrassed.*)

KULYGHIN (*picking up the pieces*): Oh, Doctor, Doctor! To break such a valuable object! You get zero—with a minus—in conduct!

IRENE: That clock belonged to our mother.

CHEBUTYKIN: Maybe. . . . If it belonged to your mother, well and good. Maybe I didn't break it, but it merely seems that I broke it. Maybe it merely seems to us that we exist, but in reality we aren't here at all. I don't know anything; no one knows anything— (*Near the doorway.*) What are you looking at? Nathalie is carrying on a bit of a romance with Protopopov, and yet you don't see anything. . . . You sit here, now, and don't see anything, and yet Nathalie is carrying on with Protopopov— (*Sings.*) "Zis for you, and zat for you—" (*Exit.*)

VERSHININ: Yes. (*Laughs.*) Really, how strange all this is! (*Pause.*) When the fire started I dashed home as fast as I could. I get near our house, and I see that it's safe, and unharmed, and not in danger, but that my two little girls are standing in the doorway in nothing but their underthings; their mother isn't with them; people are rushing to and fro, horses are dashing about, and the dogs, and the faces of my girls show alarm, horror, supplication—I can't tell you what they showed— my heart contracted when I saw their faces. "My God," I thought, "what those girls will have to go through during the course of their long lives!" I grab them, I run, yet I keep on thinking of only one thing—what they'll have to live through in this world! (*Tocsin. Pause.*) I come here—and find their mother, screaming, raging— (*Enter* MARY, *carrying a pillow, and sits down on divan.*) And while my little girls were standing in that doorway, in nothing but their underthings, and the street glowed red from the fire—why, it occurred to me that something like this must have been taking place ever so long ago, when an enemy would come swooping down unexpectedly, and pillage and put whole cities to the torch. . . . And yet in reality what a difference there is between that which is and that which was! And a little more time will pass, some two or three hundred years, say, and men will look upon this, our present life, in the same way, both with fear and a contemptuous smile—all that which exists now will seem clumsy, and cumbersome, and most uncomfortable, and strange. Oh, most assuredly, what a life it will be—what a life! (*Laughs.*) Forgive me; I've again plunged into philosophizing. Do let me keep on with it, my friends. I have a dreadful longing to philosophize—that's the sort of mood I'm in. (*Pause.*) You all seem to be asleep. . . . And so I say: what a life it will be! You can imagine it for yourselves. At present there are only three such people as you, but in the generations to come there shall be more and more, ever more and more, and the time will come when all things will change to conform with your ways, when people will live in keeping with your ways, and then you, too, will become quaint, antiquated; people will be born who will be better than you. . . . (*Laughs.*) Today I'm in some sort of a peculiar mood. I want to live—I want to, devilishly so— (*Sings.*) "Love all obey, both young and old; its yearnings are as purest gold—" (*Laughs.*)

MARY (*hums*): *Tram-tam-tam*—

VERSHININ (*humming in response*): *Tam-tam*—

MARY (*ending the musical phrase on a rising, questioning note*): *Tra-ta-ra?* . . .

PHEDOTIK (*dancing as he enters*): I'm burned out, I'm burned out, I'm burned out!

IRENE: What's the joke? Are you completely burned out?

PHEDOTIK: Clean as a whistle. Nary a thing left. The guitar burned up, and the camera burned up, and all my letters. I had a little notebook I wanted to make you a present of—well, that burned, too.

IRENE (*to* SOLIONNYI *as he enters*): No, please, you'll really have to leave. You can't come in here.

SOLIONNYI: How is it the Baron can come in, but not I?

VERSHININ: Really, I must be going. (*To* SOLIONNYI.) How is the fire?

SOLIONNYI: Dying down, they say. It seems downright strange to me—how is it the Baron can come in, but not I? (*Takes out a perfume atomizer and sprays himself.*)

VERSHININ (*hums*): *Tram-tam-tam*—

MARY (*humming in response*): *Tram-tam.* . . .

VERSHININ (*laughing, to* SOLIONNYI): Let's go down to the dining room.

SOLIONNYI: Very well, then! We'll make a note of it. "This could be so much plainer made, but of mad geese I am afraid—" (*Glaring at* TUZENBACH.) Here—chick, chick, chick! (*Goes out with* VERSHININ *and* PHEDOTIK.)

IRENE: Look—this Solionnyi has filled the whole room with smoke — (*In surprise.*) Why, the Baron is asleep! Baron! Baron!

TUZENBACH (*waking up with a start*): I am tired, I must say. It's that brickmaking plant. . . . No, I'm not delirious; I am really going into a brickmaking plant soon—to start working. I've already talked things over there. (*To* IRENE, *tenderly.*) You are so pale, so gloriously beautiful, so seductive! It seems to me that your pallor glows in the dark, like light. You are sad, you are dissatisfied with life—oh, let us go on together, let us work together!

MARY: Baron, you will have to leave the room—

TUZENBACH (*laughing*): Are you here? I can't see. (*Kissing* IRENE'S *hand.*) Good-by; I'm going. I'm looking at you now and I recall how, sometime in the long ago, on your birthday, you—so energetic, so gay—were speaking of the joys of work. . . . And what a happy life shimmered like a mirage before us then! Where is it? (*Again kissing* IRENE'S *hand.*) There are tears in your eyes. . . . Go to bed now; it's already dawn. Morning is beginning. If I were only allowed to give up my life for you!

MARY: Do go, Baron! Really, now—

TUZENBACH: I'm going! (*Goes out.*)

MARY (*lying down*): Are you asleep, Fedor?

KULYGHIN (*with a start*): Eh?

MARY: You ought to go home.

KULYGHIN: My dear Mary, my darling Mary—

IRENE: She's all in. You ought to let her rest, Fedya.

KULYGHIN: I'll go right away. My wife is a fine, splendid woman! I love you, my only one—

MARY (*exasperated*): *Amo, amas, amat; amamus, amatis, amant—*

KULYGHIN (*laughing*): No, really, she's amazing. I've been married to you for all of seven years, yet it seems to me as if we were married only yesterday. 'Pon my word! No, really, you're an amazing woman. I am content, I am content, I am content!

MARY: I'm bored stiff, I'm bored stiff, I'm bored stiff—(*Sits up.*) And here's something I can't get out of my head—it's simply disgraceful. It's just like a thorn in my side—I can't keep quiet about it. I'm speaking of Andrew. He has mortgaged this house at the bank and his wife has raked in all the money, and yet the house doesn't belong to him alone but to all four of us! He ought to realize that if he has any decency in him.

KULYGHIN: Oh, now, Mary! Why should you bother yourself about that? Andrew is in debt up to his ears—well, God be with him!

MARY: At any rate, it's disgraceful. (*Lies down again.*)

KULYGHIN: You and I aren't poor. I work; I teach at the high school, and also tutor on the side. I am an honest man. And a simple one. . . . *Omnia mea mecum porto,* as they say.

MARY: I'm not at all in need, but the injustice of it makes me angry. (*Pause.*) Do go, Fedor!

KULYGHIN (*kissing* MARY): You're tired; rest for half an hour or so, while I sit somewhere and wait for you. Take a nap— (*Going.*) I am content, I am content, I am content! (*Goes out.*)

IRENE: But really now, how shallow our Andrew has become, how insipid and old he has grown with that woman! At one time he was preparing himself for a professorship, yet yesterday he was boasting that he has at last landed as a member of the—Town Council! He is a member of the Council—and Protopopov is Chairman! The whole town is talking and laughing its head off—and he's the only one who knows nothing and sees nothing. And right now everybody has run to the fire—but he mopes in his room and doesn't pay the least attention to what's happening. All he does is play on his fiddle. (*In an attack of nerves.*) Oh, how horrible, horrible—horrible! (*Bursts into tears.*) I can't, I can't stand it any more! I can't, I can't! (OLGA *enters and starts putting her dressing table in order.* IRENE *sobs loudly.*) Throw me out, throw me out—I can't stand it any more!

OLGA (*frightened*): What are you saying? What are you saying, darling!

IRENE (*still sobbing*): Where's everything gone to? Where? Where is it? Oh, my God, my God! I've forgotten—forgotten everything. Everything is jumbled in my head. I can't remember what the Italian word for "window" is—or for "ceiling," say. . . . I'm forgetting everything, I'm forgetting things every day, yet life is slipping away and will never return—never; never will we get to Moscow! I can see that we won't go there—

OLGA: Darling, darling—

IRENE (*restraining herself*): Oh, I am unhappy. I can't work—I won't work. Enough—enough! I worked as a telegraph clerk; now I am working at the Town Council, and I detest and despise everything they give me to do. I am already going on twenty-four; I've been working for a long time now, and my brain has dried up, I have become thin, have lost my looks, have grown old, and there is nothing left for me—nothing, no satisfaction of any sort—yet time passes and it seems as if you were withdrawing from a beautiful life, going back further and further, into some sort of an abyss. I am in despair, and just why I'm still alive, why I haven't killed myself up to now, is something I can't understand—

OLGA: Don't cry, my little girl, don't cry. I, too, am suffering.

IRENE: I'm not crying—I'm not crying. Enough! There, I'm not crying any more. That's all . . . that's all!

OLGA: Darling, I'm telling you as a sister, as a friend; if you want my advice—marry the Baron! (IRENE *weeps softly.*) Why, you respect him, you value him highly. He isn't handsome, it's true, but he's so decent, so clean. After all, one doesn't marry for love but in order to do one's duty. I, at least, think so, and I'd marry without love. No matter who might want me, I'd marry him anyway, as long as he were decent. Why, I'd even marry an old man—

IRENE: I was waiting all this time . . . we'd go to live in Moscow, there I would meet the man who was really meant for me. I dreamed of him, I loved him! But it turned out to be all nonsense—all nonsense—

OLGA (*embracing* IRENE): My beautiful sister, my darling, I understand everything. When the Baron left the service and came to see us in civilian clothes he looked so plain to me that I actually broke into tears. He asked me: "Why are you crying?" What was I to tell him? But if God were so to ordain it that you were to marry him, I would be happy then. Then it would be a different matter—an altogether different matter. (NATHALIE, *carrying a candle, crosses stage silently, from door, right, and exits at door, left.*)

MARY: She pussyfoots around as if she were a firebug or something.

OLGA: Mary, you're being silly. The silliest one in our family is you. You must excuse me for saying so, please. (*Pause.*)

MARY: I want to make a confession, dear sisters. My soul is in torment. I will confess before you and then never speak of it again—not to a soul. I'll tell you this very minute—(*Softly.*) This is my secret, yet you must know all. I cannot keep silent— (*Pause.*) I am in love—in love. . . . I love that man. You saw him just now. Well, what's the use of keeping anything back? In short, I love Vershinin—

OLGA (*going behind the screen near her bed*): Drop it! I can't hear you anyway.

MARY: What am I to do, then? (*Clutches her head.*) He seemed odd to me at first, then I felt sorry for him—then I came to love him . . . came to love him for his voice, for the things he said, for his misfortunes, for his two little girls—

OLGA (*from behind her screen*): I can't hear you, I tell you! No matter what silly things you might say, I still can't hear you.

MARY: Eh, you're silly, Olga. I'm in love; such, then, is my fate. Such, then, is my lot. And he loves me also. All that is frightful. Yes? That isn't at all *nice*, is it? (*Pulls* IRENE *by the arm, drawing her near.*) Oh, my darling! How will we ever get through our life; whatever will become of us? When you read some novel or other, it all seems old stuff, and everything is so easy to understand; but it's when you fall in love yourself that you realize that nobody knows anything, and that each one must decide for one's own self. My darlings, my sisters! I have confessed to you; now I'm going to be silent. I'm going to be like Gogol's madman from now on! "Silence—silence. . . ." (*Enter AN-DREW, with* PHERAPONT *following him.*)

ANDREW (*angrily*): What is it you want? I can't understand you.

PHERAPONT (*impatiently, hovering in the doorway*): I've already told you ten times, Andrew Sergheievich—

ANDREW: First of all, I'm not "Andrew Sergheievich" to you, but "Your Honor!"

PHERAPONT: The firemen, Your Honor, beg leave to drive to the river through your garden. As it is, they have to go round about all the time. Regular nuisance, it is—

ANDREW: Very well. Tell them it's all right. (*Exit* PHERAPONT.) I'm fed up with them. Where's Olga? (OLGA *walks out from behind her screen.*) Sorry, but I had to come to you—let me have a key for the cupboard. I've mislaid mine somewhere. You have a small key that'll fit. (OLGA *hands him a key.* IRENE *withdraws behind her screen. Pause.*) What an enormous fire! It's beginning to die down now. The devil! This Pherapont got on my nerves so—but just the same that was a stupid thing to tell him: "Your Honor!" (*Pause.*) Well, why don't you say something, Olga? (*Pause.*) It's time you quit sulking like that and stopped acting so nonsensically, so . . . cantankerously! You're here, Mary, and so's Irene; well, that's just fine—let's have it out, once and for all, then. What have you all got against me? What is it?

OLGA: Drop it, Andrew. We'll have an explanation tomorrow. (*In agitation.*) What an excruciating night!

ANDREW (*with exceeding uneasiness*): Don't excite yourself. I'm asking you, in all calmness: What have you got against me? Come right out with it!

VERSHININ (*singing, off*): *Tram-tam-tam!*

MARY (*loudly, eagerly, as she gets up*): *Tra-ta-ta!* . . .Good-by, Olga, and God keep you! (*Darts behind* IRENE'S *screen and kisses her.*) Sleep well! Good-by, Andrew. Go, now; the girls are tired out. You can have your explanation tomorrow. (*Exit.*)

OLGA: Really, Andrew, let's put it off till tomorrow— (*Goes behind her screen.*) Time to sleep.

ANDREW: I'll have my say and then go. Right away. In the first place, you all have something against Nathalie—my wife!—and I've noticed that from the very day I married her. Nathalie is a splendid, sincere person, straightforward and noble. That's my opinion. I love and respect my wife—do you understand that? I respect her, and I demand that others respect her as well. I repeat, she is a sincere, noble person, and all your dissatisfaction, if you'll forgive me for saying so, is so much childish caprice— (*Pause.*) In the second place, you seem to be wrought up, somehow, over the fact that I'm not a professor, that I don't go in for scholarship. But I'm serving as an administrator, I am a member of the Town Council, and this my service I consider just as sacred and exalted as the pursuit of academic honors. I am a member of the Town Council and proud of it, if you want to know something— (*Pause.*) In the third place. . . . I also have this to tell you. . . . I did mortgage the house without having first obtained your consent. In that I am guilty, yes, and I beg you to forgive me. I was impelled to do so by debts . . . thirty-five thousand. . . . I don't play cards any more—I dropped them long ago; but the chief extenuation I have to offer in my defense is that you girls are single, that you receive Father's pension, whereas I had no . . . income, so to speak— (*Pause.*)

KULYGHIN (*looking in at the door*): Mary isn't here? (*Anxiously.*) Where can she be then? That's odd— (*Hurries away.*)

ANDREW: They aren't listening. . . . Nathalie is a splendid, sincere person— (*Paces floor in silence; then stops.*) When I took a wife I thought we'd be happy—that we'd all be happy—but oh, my God! (*Weeps.*) My darling sisters—dear sisters—don't believe me! Don't believe me! (*Rushes off.*)

KULYGHIN (*in the doorway, anxiously*): Where's Mary? Mary isn't here? This is astonishing! (*Hurries away. Tocsin. Stage clear. Knocking from below.*)

IRENE (*behind her screen*): Olga! Who's that knocking on the floor below?

OLGA (*also from behind her screen*): That's Doctor Chebutykin. He's drunk.

IRENE: What an uneasy night! (*Pause.*) Olga! (*Looks out from behind her screen.*) Did you hear what Vershinin was saying? The brigade is being shifted from here—they're transferring it to some distant point—

OLGA: Those are just rumors.

IRENE: We'll be left all alone then. . . . Olga!

OLGA: Well?

IRENE: Darling, dearest—I respect, I appreciate the Baron; he's a splendid person; I'll marry him, I agree—only let's go to Moscow! I implore you—let's go! There's nothing better on earth than Moscow! Let's go, Olga! Let's go!

Curtain

ACT III

Autumn, same year. High noon.

An old garden on the PROZOROV *grounds. A long path, with firs on each side, and a vista of a river, with a forest on its other bank. Terrace of the house, right, with a table cluttered with glasses and bottles; it is apparent that champagne was flowing freely here just a little before.*

At rare intervals PASSERS-BY *go through garden to river; five* SOLDIERS *march by rapidly.*

CHEBUTYKIN, *in a beatific mood which does not desert him throughout the act, is sitting in an armchair in the garden, marking time till he is called; he is now wearing a military cap and has a walking stick with him.* IRENE, KULYGHIN (*with a decoration around his neck but minus his mustache*), *and* TUZENBACH *are standing on the terrace, seeing* PHEDOTIK *and* RODE *off—both of these officers are in service uniforms, and are about to step down from the terrace into the garden.*

TUZENBACH (*embracing* PHEDOTIK): You're a good fellow; you and I got along so well. (*Embracing* RODE). Good-by once more . . . my dear fellow!

IRENE: *Au revoir!*

PHEDOTIK: Not *au revoir* but good-by—we'll never see each other again!

KULYGHIN: Who knows! (*Dabs at his eyes; then smiles.*) There, I've turned on the tears, too—

IRENE: We'll meet again some day.

PHEDOTIK: Ten or fifteen years from now? But we'll hardly recognize each other then—we'll merely exchange nods coldly— (*Snapping a picture.*) Hold it! . . . One more, for the last time—

RODE (*embracing* TUZENBACH): We'll never see each other again— (*Kissing* IRENE'S *hand.*) Thanks for everything! Everything!

PHEDOTIK (*in irritation*): Don't be in such a rush!

TUZENBACH: We'll see each other again, God willing. Do write us. Write, without fail.

RODE (*taking in the garden with a sweeping gaze*): Good-by, trees! (*Halloos.*) Ho-o-o, there!— (*Waits for echo.*) Good-by, echo!

KULYGHIN: First thing you know you'll get married there, in Poland. And your Polish wife will hug you and call you *"Kochane!"* (*Laughs.*)

PHEDOTIK (*glancing at his watch*): There's less than an hour left. Solionnyi is the only one in our battery going on the barge, for we're with the main troops. Three batteries are leaving today as a division; tomorrow three more will leave—and then peace and quiet will reign throughout the town—

TUZENBACH: And so will a horrible boredom.

RODE (*to* KULYGHIN): But isn't your wife here?

KULYGHIN: Mary's in the garden.

PHEDOTIK: I'd like to say good-by to her.

RODE: Good-by; I must go, or else I'll start blubbering— (*Quickly embraces* TUZENBACH *and* KULYGHIN *and kisses* IRENE'S *hand.*) We've had such a fine time here—

PHEDOTIK (*to* KULYGHIN): Here's something to remember me by— a little notebook, pencil and all! We'll go down to the river this way— (PHEDOTIK *and* RODE *take a few steps, then both look back.*)

RODE (*hallooing*): Ho-o-o-o, there!"

KULYGHIN (*shouting back*): Good-by! (*In the back of the garden* PHEDOTIK *and* RODE *encounter* MARY *and bid her good-by; she walks off with them.*)

IRENE: They're gone. . . . (*Seats herself on the bottom step of terrace.*)

CHEBUTYKIN: Yet they forgot to say good-by to me.

IRENE: But why should you complain?

CHEBUTYKIN: Well, I forgot myself somehow. However, I'll see them again soon—I'm leaving tomorrow. Yes, there's only one short day left. In a year they'll retire me; I'll come here again and finish my days near you. There's only one short year left till I'll be getting my pension. (*Puts the newspapers he had been reading in his pocket and takes out another one.*) I'll come back to you and reform my way of life—but radically! I'll become such a quiet little old man, such a good . . . good-natured, venerable little old man—

IRENE: Well, you really should change your way of living, you old darling. You ought to—somehow.

CHEBUTYKIN: Yes. I feel I ought to. (*Sings softly.*) *Tarara-boom-deray*. . . . *Tarara-boom-deray*. . . .

KULYGHIN: The Doctor's incorrigible—incorrigible!

CHEBUTYKIN: Ah, if I could but be put through a course of training at your hands! Then I'd emerge as a very paragon—

IRENE: Fedor has shaved off his mustache—and now I can't bear to look at him!

KULYGHIN: Why, what's wrong with that?

CHEBUTYKIN: I'm strongly tempted to say what your face looks like now, but I'm in no position to do so.

KULYGHIN: Come, what's the matter with being clean shaven? It's the accepted thing. Our Principal shaves his mustache—and I shaved mine off, too, as soon as I became the head of a department. Nobody likes the idea, but it doesn't affect me in the least. I am content. Mustache or no, I am still content— (*Takes a seat.* ANDREW, *at back, comes on and wheels a baby carriage with a sleeping infant, back and forth.*)

IRENE: Doctor, my darling, my own—I'm horribly worried. You were on Main Street last night—tell me, what happened there?

CHEBUTYKIN: What happened? Why, nothing. Just a trifling incident. (*Keeps on reading his newspaper.*) It doesn't amount to anything!

KULYGHIN: They're saying, now, that apparently Solionnyi and the Baron met yesterday near the theater—

TUZENBACH: Don't go any further! Really, now— (*Makes a gesture of resignation and goes into house.*)

KULYGHIN: —near the theater. Solionnyi began picking on the Baron, and the Baron couldn't take it; he came out with something offensive—

CHEBUTYKIN: I know nothing about it. It's all tommyrot.

KULYGHIN: An instructor in a certain seminary wrote "Tommyrot!" on a student's composition—but the handwriting was so illegible that the student took it for a Latin expression of approval—(*laughter*)— amazingly funny, that. Well, they're saying that Solionnyi is apparently in love with Irene, and that he has, so it seems, come to hate the Baron. That's easy to understand. Irene is a splendid girl. She even resembles Mary—the same thoughtful type. Only your character is gentler, Irene. However, Mary also has a splendid character. I love her—my Mary. (*Hallooing, off, in the depth of the garden.*)

IRENE (*with a shudder*): Everything seems to frighten me today somehow. (*Pause.*) I've got everything ready. I'm sending my things off after dinner. The Baron and I are getting married tomorrow—and the very same day we're going off to the brickmaking plant—and the day after I start right in teaching. The new life is beginning. God will help me somehow! When I was taking my examination for a teacher's license I actually wept for joy—for the surpassing love I felt— (*Pause.*) The van ought to be along for my things any minute—

KULYGHIN: That's all very well—only somehow all this seems lacking in seriousness. Mere ideas—and very little that is serious. However, my best wishes to you, with all my heart.

CHEBUTYKIN (*greatly moved*): My fine, splendid girl, my precious! All of you have gone far; there's no catching up with you. I've been left behind, like a migrating bird that has grown too old and is unable to fly any farther. Fly on, my darlings—fly on, and God be with you! (*Pause.*) Just the same, what a pity it is you shaved off your mustache.

KULYGHIN: You might let up on the subject! (*Pause.*) There, the soldiers will leave us today, and everything will go on as of old. No matter what they may say, Mary is a fine, sincere woman; I am very much in love with her and I thank my lucky stars. People are born under different stars. . . . There's a certain Kozyrev clerking in the Excise Office here. He and I studied together—he was let out from the fifth grade in high school because he couldn't master *ut consecutivum*. Now he is in terrible straits, and in bad health, and whenever I run across him I say: "Greetings, *ut consecutivum*!"—"Yes," he answers me, "just so—*ut consecutivum*"—and coughs at the same time. But I, now—why, luck has been coming my way all my life; I am content; there, I even have the Cross of St. Stanislas—Second Class—and now I myself teach this same *ut consecutivum* to others. Of course, I am a clever person, much cleverer than others, but that isn't the basis of my content— (The Maiden's Prayer, *played amateurishly on a piano, comes floating out of the house.*)

IRENE: Well, tomorrow I won't have to be listening to the *Maiden's Prayer,* at any rate. And I won't have to be tripping up over this Protopopov at every step, either! (*Pause.*) Why, Protopopov is sitting there in the reception room this very minute; he *would* have to come today, too—

ANDREW: The Chief Instructress hasn't arrived yet?

IRENE: No. Somebody went to get her. If you only knew how hard it is for me to live here alone, without Olga. She has a room at the high school and is taken up with her work all day long, but I'm alone, and bored, and haven't a thing to do, and I hate the room I'm in. I had actually decided that if I wasn't fated to live in Moscow things would have to go on just the way they were. It was my fate, evidently. Nothing to be done about it. Everything depends upon the will of God. It's true the Baron has proposed to me. Well, why not? I thought it over and came to a decision. He's a fine man—even an amazingly fine man. And it was just as though my soul sprouted wings; I was filled with joy, I felt lighthearted, and I again felt the urge to work—to work! But then something happened yesterday; there's something mysterious hanging over my head—

CHEBUTYKIN: Tommyrot!

NATHALIE (*through window*): Here's the Chief Instructress now!

KULYGHIN (*to* IRENE): The Chief Instructress has arrived. Let's go in. (*Goes into house with* IRENE.)

CHEBUTYKIN (*reading his newspaper and singing softly*): Tara-ra . . . boom-*deray*. . . . Tara-ra . . . boom-*deray!* (MARY *approaches.* ANDREW, *back, wheels baby carriage across.*)

MARY: There you are, sitting, sitting—always sitting—

CHEBUTYKIN: Why, what's wrong with that?

MARY (*taking a seat*): Oh, not a thing! (*Pause.*) Did you love my mother?

CHEBUTYKIN: Very much.

MARY: And did she love you?

CHEBUTYKIN (*after a pause*): That's something I don't remember any longer now.

MARY: My man here? That's how Martha, a cook we once had, used to speak of her policeman—"My man." Is my man here?

CHEBUTYKIN: Not yet.

MARY: When you snatch at happiness by fits and starts—little bit by little bit—and then lose it, as I have—why, little by little you become coarse, mean-tempered. (*Pointing to her breast.*) I'm all seething inside— (*Contemplating brother* ANDREW, *who is wheeling his baby carriage by.*) There's Andrew, our dear little brother. All the hopes we had for him are over and done with. It took thousands of men to raise up a great bell; no end of toil and money had been spent on it—but it suddenly fell and smashed. Suddenly, without rhyme or reason. And that's Andrew for you.

ANDREW: I wonder when things will quiet down in this house at last. What noise!

CHEBUTYKIN: We won't have long to wait now. (*Looks at his watch.*) It's an antique—with chimes— (*Winds watch; it chimes.*) The

First, Second, and Fifth batteries are leaving at one sharp. (*Pause.*) And
I'm leaving tomorrow.

ANDREW: For good?

CHEBUTYKIN: Don't know. I may come back here in a year's time.
However, the devil alone knows. It really doesn't matter— (*A harp
and a violin are playing somewhere in the distance.*)

ANDREW: The town will die out. As if a lid were clamped down
on it. (*Pause.*) Something happened in town yesterday. Near the theater. Everybody's talking about it, yet I don't know a thing.

CHEBUTYKIN: It doesn't amount to anything. A trifling stupid mix-
up. Solionnyi started picking on the Baron, and the latter blew up and
insulted him, and the upshot was that Solionnyi was obliged to challenge him to a duel. (*Looks at his watch.*) Just about time for it; at
half-past twelve, in that grove there—you can see it across the river.
Bang-bang! (*Laughs.*) Solionnyi imagines he's Lermontov—he even
writes poems. But, all joking aside, this is his third duel.

MARY: Whose third duel?

CHEBUTYKIN: Solionnyi's.

MARY: But what about the Baron?

CHEBUTYKIN: What do you want to know about the Baron?

MARY: Everything's muddled in my head. . . . Just the same, they
oughtn't to be allowed to go through with it. He may wound the Baron,
or even kill him.

CHEBUTYKIN: The Baron's a fine fellow, but one Baron more or less
—what does it matter? Let 'em bang away! What does it really matter?
(*Hallooing, beyond the garden.*) He can wait. That's Skvortzov calling
me—he's one of the seconds. He's waiting in a boat. (*Pause.*)

ANDREW: In my opinion it's downright immoral either to take part
in a duel or to attend one, even in the capacity of a doctor.

CHEBUTYKIN: It merely seems that way. We have no being; nothing
in this world has any being; we don't exist—it merely seems to us that
we exist. . . . And what does it all matter!

MARY: That's how they talk, talk, talk, all day long—(*Going.*)
We're living in a climate where the snow is likely to start falling without the least provocation, but, as if that weren't bad enough, there are
all these eternal disquisitions—(*Stopping.*) I won't go into the house—
I can't go there. When Vershinin comes, let me know—(*Going down
the garden path.*) There, the birds are migrating already—(*Looking
upward.*) Swans or wild geese. . . . My darlings—my happy creatures! (*Exit.*)

ANDREW: Our house will become dead. The officers will go away, you will go away, my sister will marry, and I'll be left all alone in the house.

CHEBUTYKIN: But what about your wife? (PHERAPONT *enters with some papers.*)

ANDREW: My wife—is my wife. She's sincere, decent—kind, if you like; but, with all that, there's something about her that debases her into a petty, unperceptive animal—a sort of coarse little animal, you know. At any rate, she isn't human. I'm telling you this as my friend—the only being to whom I can open up my heart. I love Nathalie, true enough, but at times she strikes me as amazingly vulgar, and on such occasions I go out of my head. I can't understand for what reason I love her so much or why I love her at all—or, at least, why I loved her once—

CHEBUTYKIN (*getting up*): I'm leaving tomorrow, brother; it may be that we'll never see each other again, so here's my advice to you. You know what? Grab your hat, take down your walkin' cane, and go—and keep on going, without as much as looking back once. And the farther off you go, the better. (SOLIONNYI *crosses at back, with two* OFFICERS; *catching sight of* CHEBUTYKIN, SOLIONNYI *goes toward him. The* OFFICERS *keep on going.*)

SOLIONNYI: It's time, Doctor! It's half past twelve already. (*Exchanges greetings with* ANDREW.) We have to go right now. I'm fed up with the whole lot of you! If anybody asks for me, Andrew, you tell 'em I'll be right back—(*Sighs, as* ANDREW *in a huff wheels his carriage away.*) Oh, oh, oh! "He had hardly made a sound when the bear struck him to the ground!" (*Going with* CHEBUTYKIN.) What are you grousing about, old-timer?

CHEBUTYKIN (*resenting the familiarity*): Say!

SOLIONNYI: How do you feel?

CHEBUTYKIN (*petulantly*): With my fingers!

SOLIONNYI: No need of you fretting, old-timer. I'll just indulge myself a little; I'll merely wing him, like a woodcock. (*Takes out flagon and sprays perfume on his hands.*) There, I've used up a whole bottle, but they still have an odor about them. My hands have a charnel odor about them— (*Pause.*) So-o. Do you remember the lines: "Yet for a storm the sail still yearns—as though in storms one found repose!"

CHEBUTYKIN (*burlesquing him*): Yes. "He had hardly made a sound when the bear struck him to the ground!" (*Exit with* SOLIONNYI. *Hallooing in depth of garden. Enter* ANDREW *and* PHERAPONT.)

PHERAPONT: Here's some papers has to be signed—

ANDREW (*nervously*): Get away from me! Get away! I beg you! (*Goes off with his baby carriage.*)

PHERAPONT: That's just what papers is for—they're meant to be signed—(*Trails despondently after* ANDREW. *Enter* IRENE *and* TUZEN-BACH, *the latter wearing a straw hat.*)

KULYGHIN (*crossing stage as he shouts*): Ma-ary! Oh, Ma-a-ry! (*Exit.*)

TUZENBACH: There, apparently, is the only man in town who's glad the military men are leaving.

IRENE: That's easy to understand. (*Pause.*) Our town will become desolate now.

TUZENBACH: Dearest, I won't be gone long—

IRENE: Where are you going?

TUZENBACH: I have to be in town to—to see some of my friends off.

IRENE: That's not true. Nicholas, why are you so absent-minded today? (*Pause.*) What happened yesterday near the theater?

TUZENBACH (*with an impatient movement*): I'll be back in an hour and be with you again—(*Kissing her hands.*) I can't get my fill of gazing at you—(*Studying her face.*) It's five years now that I'm in love with you and I still can't get used to the idea, and you seem more and more gloriously beautiful to me. What splendid, wonderful hair! What eyes! I'll carry you off with me tomorrow; we'll work, we'll be rich, my dreams will take on new life. You will be happy. The only thing is—the only thing!—you do not love me!

IRENE: That does not lie in my power. I shall be your wife, both faithful and submissive—but there isn't any love. What can I do? (*Weeps.*) I haven't been in love even once in all my life. Oh, I used to dream so about love; I have been dreaming of love for a long time, all my days and nights, but my soul is like a priceless piano that is locked—and the key to which is lost. (*Pause.*) You seem upset.

TUZENBACH: I didn't sleep all night. There's nothing in my life so dreadful that it can haunt me, and it's only this lost key which torments my soul and won't let me sleep. Say something to me— (*Pause.*) Say something to me!

IRENE: Say what? What can I say to you? Just what?

TUZENBACH: Anything.

IRENE: Don't! Don't! (*Pause.*)

TUZENBACH: What trifles, what silly little details, can at times take on significance in one's life, without rhyme or reason. You laugh at them, just as you always did, you consider them trifles, and yet you stick to them and feel that you haven't the strength to drop them. Oh, let's not talk of all this! I'm in a gay mood. As if I were seeing these firs, these maples, these birches for the first time in my life, and as if everything were regarding me with curiosity—and expectancy. What beautiful trees—and, really, how beautiful life must be when they're so near you! (*Hallooing, off*) I must go—it's time. There's a tree that has withered—yet it sways together with the others in the wind, just the same. And so it seems to me that if I, too, should die, I shall nevertheless play a part in life, in one way or another. Good-by, my darling— (*Kisses her hands.*) Those papers of yours you gave me—you'll find them lying on my desk, under the calendar.

IRENE: I'm going along with you.

TUZENBACH (*perturbed*): No, no! (*Walks off rapidly; stops as he reaches garden path.*) Irene!

IRENE: What is it?

TUZENBACH (*at a loss as to what to say*): I—I didn't have any coffee today. Tell them to have some ready for me. (*Hastens away.* IRENE *stands in deep thought for a while, then withdraws into depth of garden and sits down on a swing.* ANDREW *wheels in the baby carriage, with* PHERAPONT *dogging his steps.*)

PHERAPONT: Them papers ain't mine, now, but the Government's. I didn't think them up out of my own head—

ANDREW: Oh, where is it, where has my past gone to, when I was young, lighthearted, intellectual, when I dreamed and thought exquisitely, when my present and my future were made radiant by hope? Why, when we have barely begun to live, do we grow tedious, drab, uninteresting, slothful, apathetic, useless, miserable? Our town is in existence for almost two hundred years now, it contains a hundred thousand inhabitants—and there's not a one among them that doesn't resemble all the others, not a soul, either in the past or at present, that has ever been chivalrous, not a single scholar, not a single artist, not a being even in the least outstanding, who might arouse envy or a passionate desire of emulation. All they do is eat, drink, sleep, and then die. They breed others and these, too, eat, drink, sleep, and, so as not to become stultified from boredom, diversify their life with vile gossip, with drink, with cards, with pettifogging. And the wives deceive their husbands, while the husbands lie to themselves and others, making believe that they see nothing, that they hear nothing. And the general, insuperable vulgarity influences and oppresses the children, and the divine spark expires within them, and they become the same pitiful, ambulating corpses, all of them as alike as maggots, that their fathers and mothers are—(*Turning on* PHERAPONT.) What do you want?

PHERAPONT: Eh? Why, these here papers has to be signed—

ANDREW: I'm fed up with you!

PHERAPONT (*handing papers to* ANDREW): The doorman of the Treasury was telling us just now—it seems like there was a frost of two hundred degrees in Moscow this winter—

ANDREW: The present is detestable; but then, when I think of the future, how fine I feel! I become so buoyant, so unconstrained, and in the distance the light begins to break, I see freedom, I see myself and my children being freed from slothfulness, freed from stuffing ourselves with roast-goose-and-cabbage and swilling cider, freed from snoring for hours after such dinners, and from vile parasitism—

PHERAPONT: Two thousand folk was froze to death, it seems like. The people, he was tellin' us, was frightened to death. In Moscow, that was—or maybe it was Petersburg; I disremember which.

ANDREW (*overcome by an emotion of tenderness*): My dear sisters, my wonderful sisters—(*With tears in his voice.*) Mary, my sister—

NATHALIE (*through window*): Who's talking so loudly? Is it you, Andy? You'll wake up little Sophie! *Il ne faut pas faire du bruit, la Sophie est dormée déjà. Vous êtes un ours.* (*Losing her temper completely.*) If you want to talk, you'll have to hand the carriage over to somebody else. Pherapont, take the carriage from the master!

PHERAPONT: Right-o, Ma'am! (*Relieves* ANDREW *of baby carriage.*)

ANDREW (*flabbergasted*): I wasn't talking loudly—

NATHALIE (*off, near window, caressingly*): Bobby! Bobby is a naughty little boy! Bobby is a *bad* little boy!

ANDREW (*glancing through the papers, to* PHERAPONT): Very well; I'll look 'em over, sign whatever is necessary, and then you can carry them back to the office. (*Goes into house, examining the papers.* PHERAPONT *wheels baby carriage into depth of garden.*)

NATHALIE (*off, at window*): Bobby, what's your mother's name? Why, you darling—darling! And who's this? It's your Aunt Olga! Come on, say "Hello, Olga," to your aunt! (WANDERING MUSICIANS— *a man and a girl—appear and play on a violin and a harp.* VERSHININ, OLGA, *and* ANPHISSA *emerge from house and for a minute or so listen in silence.* IRENE *approaches.*)

OLGA: Our garden must be a public thoroughfare, the way everybody walks and drives through it. Nurse, give something to these musicians—

ANPHISSA (*giving some coins to the musicians*) : Go, and God's blessing go with you, my dears. (MUSICIANS *bow and go off.*) A bitter lot,
these folk has. It ain't a full belly that makes 'em play. Hello, Irene;
dearest! (*Kisses her.*) My, my, am I living high now, little girl! Am I!
I'm staying at the high school with Olga—God has willed it so for my
old age. Never have I lived so in all my born days, sinner that I am.
A great, big apartment, and at the government's expense, at that, and
there's a little room, with a little bed, all to myself. I wake up in the
middle of the night—and oh, Lord, and Mother of God, there ain't
a happier person nor myself in all the world!

VERSHININ (*to* OLGA, *after a glance at his watch*) : We're leaving
right away. Time I was going. (*Pause.*) Best wishes to you in everything—everything! Where is—

IRENE: Mary is somewhere there, out in the garden. I'll go and look
for her.

VERSHININ: That would be most kind of you. I haven't much time.

ANPHISSA: I'll go and look, too. (*Calls.*) Oh, Ma-a-ary-y-y! (*Keeps
calling as she goes off into depth of garden with* IRENE.)

VERSHININ: All things must come to an end, sometime. And so here
we are, parting. (*Glances at his watch.*) The whole town tendered us
something in the nature of a farewell luncheon; we drank champagne,
the mayor delivered a speech, I ate and listened, but my soul was here,
among you—(*Looks around the garden.*) I have grown used to you.

OLGA: Shall we see each other again—ever?

VERSHININ: Probably not. (*Pause.*) My wife and both of my little
girls will spend about two months more here; please, if anything
should happen, or if something has to be done—

OLGA: Yes, yes, of course. Set your mind at rest. (*Pause.*) Tomorrow
there will no longer be a solitary soldier left in the whole town; everything will become a memory, and, of course, a new life will begin for
us—(*Pause.*) Everything is turning out contrary to the way we'd want
it. I didn't want to become Chief Instructress—and still I became one.
Moscow isn't for us, then—

VERSHININ: Oh, well! Thank you for everything. Forgive me if there
was anything not just so. . . . I've had a great deal—oh, a very great
deal!—to say; well, forgive me that, too; remember no evil of me—

OLGA (*dabbing at her eyes*) : How is it Mary isn't coming yet?

VERSHININ: What else am I to tell you in farewell? What shall I
philosophize about for a bit? (*Laughs.*) Life is hard. To many of us
it appears to be a dead end, and hopeless, but still, it must be confessed,

it's becoming ever clearer, brighter, and apparently the time isn't far off when it will become altogether radiant. (*Glances at his watch.*) It's time! Time for me to go. In former times mankind was taken up with wars, filling its existence with military campaigns, forays, conquests; but now it has outlived all that, although an enormous void has been left behind, there being nothing as yet to fill it; humanity is passionately seeking this something and, of course, will eventually find it. Ah, if that something would but come as speedily as possible! (*Pause.*) You know, if only education could be coupled with industriousness, and industriousness with education—(*Glances at his watch.*) However, it's really time for me to go—

OLGA: Here she comes. (*Enter* MARY.)

VERSHININ: I came to say good-by—(OLGA *draws off a little to one side, so as not to intrude on their farewells.*)

MARY (*looking directly at* VERSHININ): Good-by—(*They kiss—for a long time.*)

OLGA: There, there—(MARY *is violently sobbing.*)

VERSHININ: Write me. Don't forget me! Let me go now. It's time I went. Take her, Olga! It's time I . . . went now . . . I'm late—(*Greatly moved, he kisses* OLGA'S *hands, then once more embraces* MARY *and quickly leaves.*)

OLGA: There, Mary! Stop it, darling!

KULYGHIN (*entering, and stopping in embarrassment*): Never mind, let her cry a while—let her. My beautiful Mary, my good Mary! You're my wife, and I am content, come what may. I'm not complaining, I'm not making a single reproach to you. . . . There, even Olga is witness to that. We'll begin to live our old life, and I won't say a single word to you, or make a single insinuation—

MARY (*restraining her sobs*): "A green oak grows on a curved shore. . . . A gold chain is about it wound. . . . A chain of gold? A gold chain?" I'm going out of my mind! "A green oak grows on a curved shore—"

OLGA: Calm yourself, Mary! Calm yourself! Get her some water—

MARY: I'm not crying any more—

KULYGHIN: She isn't crying any more; she's a good girl—(*A pistol shot, muffled by the distance.*)

MARY: "A green oak grows on a curved shore. . . . A gold chain. . . . Green gold shore. . . . A green oak grows. . . ." I'm all mixed up—(*Drinks a little water from tumbler* KULYGHIN *holds for her.*) What a failure my life has been! I have no need of anything more now.

I'll calm down in a minute. What does it matter? . . . What does "on a curved shore" mean? Why has that phrase stuck in my head? My thoughts are all mixed up—(*Enter* IRENE.)

OLGA: Calm yourself, Mary. There, that's a clever girl! Let's go in the house.

MARY (*furiously*): I'm not going in there! (*Sobs, but at once restrains herself.*) I no longer enter that house, and I don't intend to do so now.

IRENE: Let's just sit together for a while; we don't have to say anything. Why, I'm leaving tomorrow—(*Pause.*)

KULYGHIN: I took these false whiskers away from one of the boys in the third grade today—(*Takes out and puts on false mustache and beard.*) I must look like our instructor in German—(*Laughs.*) Don't I? Little boys are so funny!

MARY: You really do look like that German in your school.

OLGA (*laughing*): Yes! (MARY *weeps again.*)

IRENE: There, now, Mary!

KULYGHIN: I really do look very much like him.

NATHALIE (*entering, to* MAID, *who follows her on*): What? Oh, Protopopov can sit with little Sophie; as for Bobby, let Andrew Sergheievich wheel him about a bit. Children are such a nuisance—(*To* IRENE.) So you're leaving tomorrow. . . . What a pity. Do stay for another week or so. (*Lets out a little scream as she catches sight of the disguised* KULYGHIN. KULYGHIN *takes off false whiskers.*) Oh, you! You frightened me out of my wits. (*To* IRENE.) I've grown so used to you—why, do you think it will be easy for me to part with you? I'm going to have Andrew and his fiddle shifted to your room—let him scrape away! And we'll put little Sophie in his room. She's a wonderful, *wonderful* child! What a little doll that girl is! Today she looked up at me with *such* darling little eyes, and she says: "Ma-mma!"

KULYGHIN: A splendid child—quite true.

NATHALIE: That means tomorrow I'll be all by myself here. (*Sighs.*) I'll give orders, first of all, to chop down all those firs along that path, then that maple over there. Those trees look so ugly when evening comes—(*To* IRENE.) Darling, that sash isn't in the least becoming to you—it's in bad taste. You ought to wear something sort of light. And I'll give 'em orders to plant a lot of little flowers—little flowers, you know, and there will be so much fragrance—(*Sternly.*) What's that fork doing on the bench? (*On her way into the house, to the* MAID *following her.*) What's that fork doing on the bench, I'm asking you? (*From within, shouting.*) Don't you dare talk back to me!

KULYGHIN: She has a full head of steam on today! (*Military march, off.*—ALL *listen to it.*)

OLGA: They're going away. (*Enter* CHEBUTYKIN.)

MARY: All our friends are going away. Well, what of it? *Bon voyage!* (*To her husband.*) Time to go home. Where's my hat—and my cape?

KULYGHIN: I took them inside. I'll bring them out right away. (*Goes in house.*)

OLGA: Yes, we can all go home now. It's time.

CHEBUTYKIN (*entering*): Olga Serghcievna!

OLGA: What is it? (*Pause.*) What is it?

CHEBUTYKIN: Nothing. . . . I really don't know how to tell you— (*Whispers in her ear.*)

OLGA (*extremely horrified*): It isn't possible!

CHEBUTYKIN: Yes—what a thing to happen! I'm tired out; I'm at the end of my rope; I can't talk any more—(*With vexation.*) However, what difference does it make!

MARY: What happened?

OLGA (*embracing* IRENE): This is a dreadful day. . . . I don't know how to tell you, dearest—

IRENE: What is it? Tell me quickly—what is it? For God's sake!

CHEBUTYKIN: The Baron was killed in a duel just now.

IRENE (*softly weeping*): I knew it, I knew it—

CHEBUTYKIN (*seating himself on a bench in the depth of the garden*): I'm tired out! (*Taking a newspaper out of his pocket.*) Let 'em cry a bit—(*Sings softly.*) *Tarara-boom-deray . . . Tarara-boom-deray!* What does anything matter? (*The three sisters stand together in a close embrace.*)

MARY: Oh, how that music sounds! They are going away from us; one has already gone, never to return—never! We will be left all alone, to begin our life over again. We have to go on living. . . . We have to go on—

IRENE (*putting her head on* OLGA'S *breast*): A time will come, and everybody will learn why all this is, what all this suffering is for; there will be no mysteries of any kind; but in the meanwhile we will have to go on living. We must work—only work! Tomorrow I'll go away by myself; I'll teach at the school and give up my whole life to those who may possibly need it. It is autumn now; winter will be here soon;

it will cover everything with snow—but I'll go on working—I'll go on working—

OLGA (*embracing both her sisters*): The music sounds so gay, so brave, and one wants to live so much! Oh, my God! Time will pass, and we'll depart forever; they'll forget us, forget our faces, our voices, and how many there were of us, but our sufferings will be transmuted into joy for those who shall be living after us; happiness and peace will come upon earth, and men will say a kind word for those who are living now, and will bless them. Oh, my dear sisters, our life is not over yet! Let us go on living! The music sounds so gay, so joyous, and only a little while more, it seems, and we shall learn why we are living, why we are suffering. . . . If we could but know—if we could but know! (*The music plays more and more softly.* KULYGHIN, *gay, smiling, enters carrying* MARY'S *hat and cape.* ANDREW *comes on, wheeling the baby carriage, with* BOBBY *sitting up in it.*)

CHEBUTYKIN (*singing softly*): *Tarara-boom-deray!* . . . *Tararaboom-deray!* (*Reading his newspaper.*) What does it all matter! What does it all matter!

OLGA: If we could but know! If we could but know!

Final Curtain

Dmitrii Sergheievich
Merezhcovski

1 8 6 5 - 1 9 4 1

THE MAN WHO has been called the most encyclopedic mind of this generation was born on one of the small islands near Petersburg; as a child he passed the winters in a house built at the time of Peter the Great, and within sight of that Czar's palace, his log cabin, and his church. Merezhcovski was a mystic and wrote poetry (and criticism) before his teens; his first poem was published in 1882, and he always maintained that he had been poorly welcomed in Russian literature. He received his education at the end of the '70's and the beginning of the '80's—the era of the severest Classicism. He first came into contact with the Government at the University of Petersburg: a Molière club he had organized was raided by the political police, and he escaped exile only through the influence of his father. At the end of the '90's Merezhcovski founded a religious and philosophi-

cal society, encouraged by his wife, the famous poetess Zinaida Hippius; needless to add, this society was likewise suppressed. And in 1908 his *Paul I* was closed down by the authorities after the first performance, while the manuscript of *Alexander I* was confiscated.

It was Merezhcovski (among many others) who wrote that Orthodoxy and the order existing in old Russia were inseparably bound up with each other, and that Christianity could be attained there only if Autocracy and Orthodoxy were alike done away with. Nevertheless, he became an émigré after the Revolution. He died in the Nazi-occupied South of France.

When the present writer saw him (and Zinaida Hippius) at Antibes in 1931 he seemed, against the tawny earth and indigo-blue waves of the Mediterranean, a veritable Tithonus. And when he commented on Kuprin, the latter's comment on Merezhcovski came to mind: "Dmitrii Sergheievich is the greatest of scholars, but—well, he's not quite the most creative of writers."

As poet, Merezhcovski championed the moderns, but the Symbolists more so than the Decadents.

Peter the Great is, naturally, a favorite subject in Russian art, especially in literature. Merezhcovski is best known as critic and, above all, as historical novelist. The vignette selected shows him at his best in this genre. It is taken from *Peter and Alexis* (Chapter IV, Book IV: "The Inundation"), *The Antichrist* volume of the superb *Christ and Antichrist* triptych, which took twelve years in the writing. (The first part is *Julian the Apostate: The Death of the Gods*; the second, *The Romance of Leonardo da Vinci: The Gods Resurgent*.) The Peter and Alexis parallel to the David and Absalom, father-against-son-and-son-against-father situation presents Merezhcovski with an opportunity for that study in contrasts between strength and weakness, for that Dostoievskian play of love and hatred within the soul of each proponent, which Merezhcovski delights in. Elsewhere in the book he has given Alexei's background, allegedly in the Czarevich's own confession: "The reason for my disobedience to my father was that

from my infancy I lived with my mother and her women, where I learned nought but indoor amusements. . . . The people about me, seeing my inclination to indulgence in bigotry and in conversation with priests and blackfriars, visiting them frequently and drinking with them, not only did not hinder me but even did the like in my company. And they did estrange me from my father." Later in the story Alexis flees abroad, is accused of conspiring with foreign powers to usurp his father's throne, and is lured back to Russia by Peter Andreievich Tolstoi, an Anacreon-and-Ovid-translating diplomat, working through a wench-Venus whom Alexei had wronged.

Absalom dangled in an oak; it was a stranger who took three darts in his hand and thrust them through the heart of Absalom while he was yet alive. It was Alexis' own father who snatched the knout from the hangman to wield it with a giant's strength on the back of his son as he hanged on a strappado. In the scene here given we find the strong father confronting a weak son, whom Peter the father loves as his *zoon,* and whom Peter the Czar abhors as a sloven, a drone, a sluggard, as a weakling unable to be a successor in the paramount task of building a new Russia.

Peter and Alexis

PETER WAS SAYING to Alexis:

"When the war with the Swedes began—oh, what great routs we suffered because of our lack of skill; with what bitterness and patience did we have to go through our schooling, until we deservedly beheld that same enemy, before whom we once trembled, now trembling still more before us! All of which hath been attained through the poor efforts of myself and other true sons of Russia. And to this day we eat bread in the sweat of our first father, Adam. As much as in our power lay did we toil, like unto Noah, over the ark of Russia, having always but one thing in mind—that Russia might be glorious before all the world. But when, after contemplating this joy bestowed by God upon our Fatherland, I do look upon my line of succession, I am consumed by a bitter grief almost equal to my joy, seeing thee altogether unfitted for the conduct of matters of state—"

As he had been going up the staircase of the Winter Palace, and passed the grenadier standing sentry duty near the doors leading to the little office or workroom of the Czar, Alexis had experienced, as he always did before his interviews with his father, an unreasoning animal fear. Everything grew dark before his eyes, his teeth chattered, his legs gave way under him; he was afraid he would fall.

But in proportion as his father went on, in a calm, even tone, with his lengthy, evidently premeditated speech, which he seemed to have gotten down by heart, Alexis was growing calmer. Everything was congealing, petrifying within him—and again it was all one to him, as though his father were not speaking to him nor about him.

The Czarevich stood like a soldier, eyes front, his arms along the seams of his trousers; he was listening, and at the same time was not, stealthily scrutinizing the room with a distracted and apathetic curiosity. Turning-lathes, carpenter's tools, astrolabes, water levels, compasses, globes and other mathematical, artillery, and fortification appliances

Translated by Bernard Guilbert Guerney. Copyright, 1931, by the Modern Library, Inc., and used here through courtesy of the publisher. Revised.

cluttered the cramped little office, giving it the air of a ship's cabin. Along the walls, paneled in dark oak, hung the seascapes of the Dutch master Adam Silo, beloved of Peter; seascapes "useful for acquiring a knowledge of the art of seamanship." These were all objects familiar to the Czarevich since childhood, engendering in him a whole series of recollections: upon a newspaper sheet—a Dutch *News Current*—lay great, round, metal-rimmed spectacles, twined around with a blue silk thread in order not to rub the bridge of the nose; alongside was a nightcap of white ribbed dimity, with a green tassel, which Aleshka had once happened to tear off when he had been playing with it—but at that time his father had not become angered: he had merely put aside the ukase he had been writing and had immediately sewed the tassel on with his own hands.

Peter was seated at a table piled high with papers, in an old, high-backed, leather armchair, near an exceedingly heated stove. He had on a blue dressing gown, faded and much worn, which the Czarevich remembered seeing even before the Battle of Poltava, with the same patch of a brighter color upon a spot burned through by a pipe; he also wore a jersey of red wool, with white bone buttons. One of these was broken off, only half remaining; the Czarevich recognized it, and counted it—a thing he always did, for some reason or other, during the lengthy admonitions of his father; it was the sixth button, counting from below; his smallclothes were of coarse blue woolen stuff; he had on gray darned stockings of worsted and old slippers trodden down at the heels. The Czarevich scrutinized all of these trifles, so familiar, so homely—and so remote. The face of Batiushka was the only thing he could not see. Through the window, beyond which the snowy, smooth expanse of the Neva gleamed whitely, an oblique ray of the yellow wintry sun fell between them—slender, short, sharp, like a sword. It divided them and screened them from each other. In the quadrangle of sunlight which the windowpane cast on the floor, at the very feet of the Czar, slept his favorite little bitch, the red-pelted Lizetta, curled up in a ball. And the Czar spoke on in an even, monotonous voice, somewhat hoarse because of his cough—just as though he were reading a written ukase:

"God is not to blame for thy incapacity, inasmuch as He hath not deprived thee of reason, nor hath He taken away thy bodily strength; even though thou art not of a strong nature, still thou art no weakling; but, worst of all, thou wilt not even hear of matters military, through which we have come from darkness to light, and because of which we are now respected in the world, where before we were not even known. I am not teaching thee to be eager for war without any lawful cause, but to love matters military, and in every way possible to further and learn them, inasmuch as the military science is one of the two things indispensable for governing—to wit, order and defense. From a contempt of war general ruin is bound to follow, of which we have a clear example in the fall of the Greek Empire. Have they not perished because they abandoned their arms and, overcome by love of peace alone, being desirous of living in tranquillity, ever yielded to their adversary? Has not this tranquillity of theirs given them over into never-ending bondage to tyrants? But if thou hast at the back of thy mind the idea that generals can direct military affairs according to thy will, that is not true reasoning, inasmuch as everybody looks to the leader, so as to fall in with his likes: whatever the man at the head likes, the others like as well; but that which he turns away from, the others also care naught for. Besides, having no heart therefor, thou studiest naught and thus art ignorant of matters military. And, without knowing how to command others, how canst thou render their deserts to the deserving and punish the laggards without understanding all the factors of their calling? Thou wilt be forced merely to gape at them—to gape at them like a fledgling. Dost thou put forth thy weak health as an excuse for being unable to bear the toils of a military life? But even that is no reason, inasmuch as it is not hard work that I desire so much as willingness, which no illness could deprive thee of. Art thou harboring the thought that there are many who do not go to the wars themselves, yet whose affairs are well run? True, although they do not go themselves, yet they have the will to do so; take the late French king, Louis, who did not often go to the wars himself, yet had such a great zeal therefor, and evinced such fine strategies, that his warring was called a theater and school of the world. Nor was it solely for war that he showed a zeal, but even for other matters, and for various industries, through all of which he made his realm celebrated above all others! Putting all of these factors before thee, I shall revert to what I said first, in speaking of thee. Inasmuch as I am but a man, and subject to death—"

The sunbeam which separated them faded away, and Alexis glanced into the face of Peter. It had changed greatly—as if years and not merely a month had gone by since he had seen his father last. At that time Peter had been in the full bloom of his powers and manhood; now he was almost an old man. And the Czarevich realized that his father's illness had not been assumed; that probably he had actually been nearer death than the Czarevich (and all of them) had thought. About his denuded skull (his front hair had fallen out), the pouches under his eyes, the jutting lower jaw—about the whole pale-yellow puffy face, seemingly swollen and bloated, there was something ponderous, crushing, frozen, as in a death mask. Only in the exceedingly bright glitter—like the glitter of inflammation—of the enormous eyes, widened like those of a caged bird of prey, eyes so prominent that they seemed to bulge out, was there an expression of former youthfulness. Yet that very expression was now infinitely weary, weak, almost pitiable.

And Alexis also realized that even though he had thought a great deal about the death of his father, and had awaited and desired that death, he had never really grasped its significance, as though not believing that his father could actually die. Only now, for the first time, did he suddenly come to believe. And there was incomprehension in this emotion, and a new, never heretofore experienced fear, no longer for himself, but for his father: What must death be like to such a man? How would he meet death?

"Inasmuch as I am but a man, and subject to death," Peter went on, "to whom should I bequeath this which I have planted with the help of the All-Highest, and which has already grown to some extent? To him who hath made himself like unto the wicked and slothful servant in the Gospels, who hid his talent in the earth—that is to say, who cast from him all that God gave him? And I must also dwell upon that evil and stubborn nature of thine. For how greatly have I not upbraided thee for this—and not only upbraided, but even chastised? And, too, have I not e'en refused to speak with thee—actually for years at a time? Yet nought of this availed, nought is of any good; everything was in vain, everything went by the board, and thou dost not want to do anything save to take thy ease at home, make merry forever—as if thou wert not of our house, being contrary in all things! For while, on the one hand, thou hast the kingly blood of a high lineage, on the other hand thou hast vile opinions, like the lowest of low varlets, ever communing with shiftless folk from whom thou canst learn nought save evil and abominable ways. And wherewithal dost thou repay thy father for having brought thee into the world? Dost thou help me in these my griefs and trials, so unbearable, now that thou hast attained years of maturity? Nay, not so—which is known to all men! Rather, thou hatest my works, which I do for the people of my nation, without sparing my health, and, verily, thou shalt be a destroyer of these works after me! Pondering upon all of this with bitterness, and perceiving that I cannot incline thee toward good, I have thought it best to make known to thee my last testament, and to bide a while longer, hoping that thou wilt reform—yet not hypocritically, but truly. But if not, be it known to thee—"

At these words he was taken by a coughing fit—prolonged, excruciating, a residue of his illness. His face turned scarlet, his eyes were popping out, the sweat stood out on his forehead, and his veins were swollen. He was suffocating—and, from his frantic and vain efforts to clear his throat, he strangled still more, as little children do, who do not know how to cough. In this blending of the childish and the senile there was something both laughable and awful.

Lizetta awoke and fixed an intelligent and seemingly pitying gaze upon her master. The Czarevich also glanced at his father, and suddenly something poignant—most poignant—pierced his heart, just as if it had been stung:

"Even a dog has pity, whereas I—" he said to himself.

Peter finally managed to clear his throat, spat, cursed roundly in his usual indecent oath, and, wiping the sweat and tears from his face with his handkerchief, at once went on from the very place where he had stopped. And, although his voice was now still hoarser, it was as dispassionate and even as before, as though he were reading a written ukase:

"I therefore affirm—be it known to thee—"

The handkerchief chanced to fall out of his hands. He was about to bend down in order to pick it up, but Alexis forestalled him. He darted over, picked it up, and handed it over to his father. And this little service suddenly recalled to him that timid, tender, almost enamored emotion which he had at one time felt for his father.

"Batiushka!" he exclaimed, with such expressiveness of voice and face that Peter looked at him intently, only to drop his eyes immediately. "God sees, I have nothing crafty against thee on my conscience; but as for depriving me of the succession, I crave it myself, because of my weakness. For what would it profit me to take upon my shoulders that which I cannot bear? For how could I ever do it! And then, too, Batiushka . . . how could I ever wish that thou—that thou shouldst? . . . Oh, Lord!"

His voice broke; he lifted up his hands despairingly, convulsively, as though he wanted to clutch his head—and froze so, all pale and trembling, with a strange, distracted smile on his lips. He himself knew not what this was; he merely sensed, growing, welling up within him, a something that was striving, with a shattering force, to escape from his bosom. One word, one glance, one sign from his father, and the son would have fallen down at his feet, would have embraced them, would have begun to sob with such tears that the fearful wall between them would have crumbled, would have melted away like ice under the sun. He would have explained everything, finding such words that his father would have forgiven him, would have understood how Alexei had loved him all his life—him alone—and that he still loved him, more than ever, nor asked for anything save to be allowed to love his father, to die for him, if the latter would but just once take pity upon him, and say, as he used to say during the Czarevich's childhood, pressing him to his heart: "Alesha, my darling little boy!"

"Drop this childishness!" resounded the voice of Peter. It was rough, but somehow the roughness seemed assumed, for in reality it was uncertain and trying to cover up that uncertainty. "Do not make excuses—of any sort. Show us faithfulness by thy works; as for words, they are not worthy of belief. For even the Scripture sayeth: Neither can a corrupt tree bring forth good fruit—" [1]

Peter was looking to one side, avoiding Alexis' eyes; yet at the same time something was flitting, quivering over his face as though, through a death mask, one could glimpse a living face, a face all too dear, all too familiar to the Czarevich. But Peter had already managed to overcome his emotion. As he talked, his face was becoming ever more deathlike, his voice ever firmer and more merciless.

"Nowadays drones are not held very highly. He that eateth bread, yet profiteth not God, the Czar, and the Fatherland, is like to a worm, which turneth everything to corruption and worketh only abomination, being not of the least good to men. Even the Apostle proclaimeth: If any would not work, neither should he eat;[2] and the sluggard shall be accursed. Whereas thou hast shown thyself to be a ne'er-do-well—"

Alexis practically did not hear his words. But every sound wounded his soul and cut into it with unbearable pain, as a knife cuts into the living flesh. This was akin to murder. He wanted to cry out, to stop his father, yet he felt that the latter would not understand anything, would not hear him. Again a wall was rising, an abyss was yawning, between them. And his father was receding from him, ever farther and farther with every word, ever more irretrievably, even as the dead leave the living.

[1] St. Matthew, vii, 18.
[2] II Thessalonians, iii, 10.

Finally even his pain abated. Everything again turned to stone within him; again nothing mattered to him. He was merely languishing from a sleepy tedium, induced by this dead voice, which no longer even wounded but merely sawed raspingly, like a dull blade.

In order to end matters, to break away as soon as possible, he chose a moment of silence to make a long-considered answer, delivering it with the same dead expression of countenance, and the same dead voice, that Batiushka had used:

"Most Gracious Sovereign and Batiushka! I have nought to say save this: if thou art pleased to deprive me, because of my unfitness, of the succession to the crown of Russia, let thy will be done. I implore you most humbly, Sire, to do so, since I perceive myself to be unfit and incapable for this high post, inasmuch as I am of quite poor memory, without which nought can be accomplished, for all my powers, mental and bodily, have become debilitated through sundry ailments, and have made me unfit to rule such a people, which hath need of a sounder man than I. Therefore, I would have no pretensions to succeed to the rule of Russia after you; even if I had no brother, but all the more so since there is one now, for which God be thanked, and to whom God grant health. Nor shall I have any pretensions in the future, in which I call God to witness to my soul; and, as a true acknowledgment, I am ready to write this oath in my own hand. I entrust my children to you; as for myself, I want nought save subsistence until my death."

A silence fell. In the stillness of the wintry noonday one could hear only the measured, brassy ticking of the wall clock's pendulum.

"Thy renunciation is but procrastination, and not real!" Peter finally uttered. "For, since thou art unafraid now, and dost not regard highly the admonitions of thy father, how wilt thou keep my behests after me? As for thy taking an oath, 'tis not worthy of belief, because of the obdurateness of thy heart. One may also cite the words of David: All men are liars.[1] Also, even though thou shouldst want to follow my behests, certain longbeards, priests, and holy ancients, who, because of their idle life are none too well off now, will be able to sway and compel thee, inasmuch as thou art very partial to them. As for remaining, as thou fain wouldst, neither fish, flesh, nor good red herring— 'tis impossible. Therefore, thou must either mend thy ways and, without any hypocrisy, make thyself worthy to be my successor, inasmuch as my spirit cannot be at rest without one, all the more so now, since my health hath grown poor, or else take vows as a monk—"

[1] Psalm CXVI, 11.

Alexis, his eyes cast down, kept silent. His face now seemed as much of a death mask as the face of Peter. Mask against mask—and in both there was an unexpected, strange, seemingly spectral resemblance: a similarity of contrasts. It was as though the broad, round, puffy face of Peter, reflected in the long and gaunt face of Alexis, as in a concave mirror, had become monstrously narrowed, elongated.

Peter, too, kept silent, but on his right cheek, at the corner of his mouth and of his eye—over the entire right side of his face—a rapid tic or twitching began: gradually increasing, it changed into a convulsion, which made his face, neck, shoulder, arm and leg writhe. Many considered him subject to the falling sickness, or even demoniacally possessed, because of these convulsive cramps, which were forerunners of attacks of frenzied rage. Alexis could not look at his father without horror during such moments. But now he was calm, just as though girt about by an invisible, impenetrable armor. What else could Batiushka do to him? Kill him? Let him! Why, was not that which he had just done to him worse than murder?

"Why art thou silent?" Peter suddenly cried out, striking his fist on the table in one of the convulsive spasms which shook all his body. "Beware, Aleshka! Dost think I do not know thee? I know thee, brother —I can see thee through and through! Hast thou risen up against thy own blood, thou whelp? Dost wish thy father's death? Ugh, thou snake in the grass, thou accursed bigot! 'Tis from the priests and the holy ancients, never fear, that thou hast learned such politics! 'Tis not in vain that the Savior enjoined His Apostles to fear no one, yet enjoined them most particularly concerning this: Beware ye, said He, of the leaven of the Pharisees—[1] which is the hypocrisy of the monks, their dissimulation—"

A sinuous, evil sneer sparkled in the downcast eyes of the Czarevich. He barely restrained himself from asking his father as to the meaning of the substitution of dates in the *Declaration to My Son*—that of October 11 instead of October 22. From whom, now, had Batiushka learned this dissimulation, this knavery, worthy of Petka the clerk, Petka the lout, or of Fedosska, "the prince of this world," with his "most divinely wise craftiness," his "celestial politics"?

"One more admonition—the last," Peter began again in his former voice—even, almost dispassionate, restraining his convulsion through an unbelievable effort. "Consider everything thoroughly and, having

[1] St. Luke, xii, 1; also St. Matthew, xvi, 6 and 11, and St. Mark, viii, 15.

come to a resolution, give me thy answer without any delay. But if not, then let it be known unto thee that I shall absolutely deprive thee of the succession. For if gangrene were to set in in my finger, must I not lop if off, even though it be part of my body? Thus will I lop off even thee, like to a gangrenous member! And think not that I am saying this merely to affright thee: verily, before God, I will fulfill what I say. For I have not spared my life, nor do I spare it now, for my people and for my Fatherland. How, then, can I spare thee, thou worthless one? Better a worthy stranger than one of the blood who is worthless. Therefore we reiterate: one of two things must be definitely done: either mend thy ways, or else take the tonsure. But shouldst thou do neither—"

Peter drew himself up to his full gigantic height. Convulsions were again overcoming him: his head was trembling, his arms and legs jerking. The death mask of his face, with its unblinking, inflamed gaze, yet grimacing as if it were indulging in merry-andrew antics, was horrible. One heard the muffled growling of a beast in his voice.

"But shouldst thou do neither, I shall treat thee as a malefactor!"

"I desire monkhood, and beg your gracious consent," uttered the Czarevich in a quiet, firm voice.

He was lying. Peter knew he was lying. And Alexis knew that his father knew this. The malevolent joy of revenge filled the soul of the Czarevich. In his infinite submission there was infinite contumacy. Now the son was stronger than the father; the weakling was stronger than the strong man. Of what benefit to the Czar would be his son's taking the tonsure? "The cowl is not nailed on to the head—it can e'en be taken off." Today a monk—tomorrow a Czar. Batiushka's bones would turn in the grave when his son would make mock of him, would squander, ruin everything, leaving not a single stone standing upon another, sending Russia to perdition. He should be not tonsured but slain, extirpated, wiped off the face of the earth.

"Get thee gone!" Peter moaned out in impotent frenzy.

The Czarevich raised his eyes and looked at his father point-blank, from under his brows: thus a wolf cub stares at an old wolf, its young fangs bared, its back bristling. Their glances crossed, like swords in a duel, and the father's gaze fell, just as if it had broken, like a knife striking granite.

And he again launched his low roar, like a wounded beast, and with a maternal oath suddenly raised his fist above the head of his son, ready to hurl himself upon him, ready to maul him, to kill him.

Suddenly a tiny, tender, and strong hand descended upon Peter's shoulder.

The Empress Ekaterina Alexeievna had long been eavesdropping at the door of the room, and had made attempts to spy through the keyhole. Katenka was inquisitive. As always, she came to the rescue of her spouse at the moment of greatest danger. She had opened the door noiselessly and stolen up to him from behind, on tiptoe.

"Petenka! Batiushka!" she began, with a humble air, which was yet somewhat jocose and humoring, such as kindly wet-nurses use in speaking to stubborn children, or nurses use with the sick. "Do not fash thyself, Petenka; break not thy heart, my dearest, or else thou wilt tire thyself out beyond thy strength and then take to thy bed again and fall sick. As for thee, Czarevich, do go—do go, my own, and God be with thee! Thou canst see our Sovereign is not feeling well."

Peter turned around, caught sight of the calm, almost jolly face of Katenka, and at once came to his senses. The uplifted arms fell and hung down as if of wood, and the whole huge, corpulent body sank into an armchair, just as if an age-old tree had crashed down, cut at its very roots.

Alexis regarded his father point-blank, as before, from under his brows; stooping, shrunk into himself, just as if he had his back up, like one beast against another, he was slowly backing toward the exit, and only on the very threshold did he suddenly make a quick turn, opening the door and going out.

As for Katenka, she perched sideways on the arm of the chair, embraced Peter's head, and pressed it to her bosom—a full bosom, as soft as a cushion: the bosom of a real foster mother. Side by side with his sallow, ailing, almost aged face, the rosy-cheeked face of Katenka seemed altogether young—all in little downy birthmarks, resembling beauty spots, with its charming little prominences and dimples, and arched sable eyebrows, and painstakingly curled ringlets of dyed black hair upon her low brow, and large, rather bulgy eyes, with the unchanging smile one always finds on the portraits of royalty. However, on the whole she resembled not so much a Czaritza as a German tavern-maid or a Russian soldier-woman—a laundress, as the Czar himself styled her, who accompanied her "old man" on all his campaigns, "doing" for him with her own hands; and, when he had "the colic fits," it was she who made hot compresses for him, rubbed down his abdomen with the unguents prescribed by Blumentrost, and physicked him.

No one save Katenka could tame these fits of insane, regal wrath, which those about him dreaded so much.

Clasping his head with one hand, she stroked his hair with the other, to the unvarying, soothing refrain of: "Petenka, Batiushka, my darling, dearest little friend of my heart!" She was like a mother lulling a sick child—and like a lion tamer fondling one of his beasts. Under this measured, soft caress the Czar was growing calmer, as if he were falling asleep. His bodily convulsions were abating. It was only the death mask of his face, now altogether turned to stone, with the eyes shut, which still twitched occasionally, as though it were grimacing like a merry-andrew's.

Katenka had been followed into the room by a little monkey—brought as a present to Lizanka, the youngest Czarevna, by a certain Dutch skipper. This madcap jackanapes, following the Czaritza like some page, strove to catch the train of her dress, as though it wanted to lift it up with bold shamelessness. But, catching sight of Lizetta, it grew frightened and leaped on the table, and from the table onto the sphere which represented the course of celestial luminaries according to the system of Copernicus. The slender brass arcs bent under the beastie, the globe of the universe emitted a soft tinkle—whereupon the monkey leaped still higher, to the very top of the upright English clock, in its cabinet of tulipwood and glass. The last beam of the sun fell upon the clock, and the pendulum, as it swayed, flashed like lightning. It was a long time since Jocko had seen the sun. As if trying to recall something, it looked with melancholy wonder at the alien, wan, wintry sun, and puckered up its eyes and made funny little faces, as though mimicking the convulsions on the face of Peter. And dreadful was the resemblance of the merry-andrew grimaces on these two faces: that of the tiny beast and that of the great Czar.

Alexis was on his way home.

He was in that state in which people who have had a leg or an arm amputated find themselves: coming to, they try to feel the place where the member had been and perceive that it is no longer there. Thus did the Czarevich feel about that spot in his soul where his love for his father had been—and perceived that it no longer existed. "I'll lop thee off like to a gangrenous member," he recalled Batiushka's utterance. It was as though, together with his love, everything had been taken from the Czarevich. There was a void: no hope, no fear, no sorrows, no joy—everything was a void, vacuous and frightful.

Leonid Nicolaievich
Andreiev
1 8 7 1 - 1 9 1 9

THE WRITER WHO, next to Dostoiev-ski, has done most to give Russian literature its hardly merited reputation for morbidity was born in a provincial, semi-intellectual bureaucratic family; his father was a surveyor, his mother (like Necrassov's) a Pole. His student days were marked by extreme hardship, hereditary dipsomania, an unsuccessful love affair, and three attempts at suicide (in one he laid himself under a train but escaped unharmed, in another he shot himself near the heart, and was left with a cardiac disorder which was the ultimate cause of his death). In 1891 he studied at the University of Petersburg, changing to the University of Moscow in 1893; by 1897 he was practicing law, reporting crime, and writing humorous newspaper copy. Whatever his writings may be like, he is described as having been personally neither gloomy nor a solitary, but amiable and sociable.

Andreiev's first productions were stories—brief, realistic, saturated with Chekhovian and Gorkian psychology, and tinged with a somewhat sentimental humanism. His first story appeared in 1895, and he was one of the many authors encouraged by Gorki; he did not win recognition, however, until the appearance of his first volume of short stories in 1901. The next two or three years were the happiest in his life; he had married and was being hailed as the rising hope of the new Realism. In 1905 he received the accolade bestowed on almost every worth-while pre-Revolutionary Russian writer, when, by lending his apartment for a revolutionary meeting, he brought upon himself repressions by the government. (Andreiev saw actually four epochs of Russian history: the last years of the tyrannical Alexander III's reign [it was the nightmarish atmosphere of this period that induced the 1894 attempt at suicide, in which Andreiev injured his heart], the ascension of the footling, charlatan-haunted Nicholas II, the Russo-Japanese War and the Revolution of 1905 that came in its wake, and the Revolution [or Revolutions] of 1917.) Much of his best and most characteristic work was done before 1905, which year marks the beginning of his exceptional popularity; it began to wane in 1908, but persisted until 1914, despite the sneering attitude of many critics.

His first wife died in 1906, and although he remarried, his irregular mode of life, his hard drinking, his fads (like Bunin, he tried painting), his extravagance, would all seem to indicate that he was anything but a happy man. He lived on a grand scale in a house of fantastic architecture at Kuokkala (Finland); feverish spells of writing for days and nights at a stretch and completing novels and dramas in remarkably short periods were succeeded by months of idleness.

From 1914 to 1918 he edited a reactionary paper, which was especially virulent between February and November of 1917. He died in Finland (his heart succumbing from the shock caused by a bomb falling too near his house), an irreconcilable foe of the Soviets.

Necrassov, in Alexander II's day, put a rhetorical question in the title of one of his great poems: *Who Can Live Happy and Free in Russia?* Andreiev's writings, under Nicholas II, gave the obvious answer: A man can only either die or exist like a bivalve under the Czars. His *Thought* is the negative pole to Kuprin's *Happiness.* (Chekhov's *The Bet* hovers between these two stories.) Madness and horror (the opening words of *Red Laughter,* and a refrain of the story) are, according to Andreiev, the only possible reactions to man's realization of the truth; man's mind is a black night of madness (*The Black Masks*); he symbolized mankind as a mob of monsters and madmen groveling in despair before an unsurmountable *Wall.* Negation, nihilism, annihilation, death, and nonentity—these are the only reality. Everything was useless: Russian life, society, morality, culture; Science (*To the Stars*); Love of Humanity (*Anathema, The Ocean*); Religion (*Savva, Judas Iscariot*); Life—and even Death! (*Lazarus*); Revolution (*The General, Thus It Has Been, King Hunger, When the King Loses His Head, Darkness*). On the other hand, he has paid due and sincere homage to revolutionaries, at least, in *The Seven That Were Hanged* and *The Marseillaise.*

His attitude to revolution in general was regarded with particular disfavor; he was accused of resolving his inner conflicts with too passive a submission to social reality, criticized for a superficial though pungent simplification and intensification of the profound dialectics and sophistries of Dostoievski, upbraided for negating all too easily all the supposititious ways out of the social blind alleys. He was called everything from defeatist to the gravedigger of the revolutionary impulses of the *intelligentsia,* since he asserted that it was not worth while struggling or having faith in anything. His treatment at the hands of the aesthetic symbolists and others was none too kind: Merezhcovski laughed at him as "this popular and influential barbarian"; Tolstoi wrote: "Andreiev plays boogymans—yet I'm not in the least frightened"; Bunin called him a tiger—in a taxidermist's window.

Modern criticism, however, has weighed Andreiev more coolly and dispassionately, and while it does not regard him as peer to Schopenhauer or Leopardi, it nevertheless does not consider him merely a vest-pocket Dostoievski or a Russian Poe. It sums him up as an absorbingly interesting, authentic, and sincere writer, a fair number of whose works insures him not too obscure a niche in the pantheon of Russian literature.

Lazarus is an example of Andreiev at his macabre best, while *Ben Tobith* is a saber worthy of being placed by the side of the *Procurator of Judaea* rapier. About one-third of Andreiev's work is available in English, although some of his best and most powerful things have never been published in English. He is exceptionally fortunate (for the most part) in his translators, particularly in Archibald J. Wolfe, Avrahm Yarmolinsky, and John Cournos.

Lazarus

I

WHEN LAZARUS left the grave where, for three days and three nights, he had been under the enigmatical sway of Death, and returned alive to his dwelling, for a long time no one noticed in him those sinister peculiarities which, as time went on, made his very name a horror. Gladdened unspeakably by the sight of him who had been returned to life, those near to him caressed him unceasingly, and satiated their burning desire to serve him, by their solicitude for his food and drink and garments. And they dressed him gorgeously, in bright colors of hope and laughter, and when, like to a bridegroom in his bridal vestures, he sat again among them at the table, and again ate and drank,

Translated by Avrahm Yarmolinsky. From *Lazarus.* (Published by the Stratford Company.)

they wept, overwhelmed with tenderness. And they summoned the neighbors to look at him who had risen miraculously from the dead. These came and shared the serene joy of the hosts. Strangers from far-off towns and hamlets came and adored the miracle in tempestuous words. Like to a beehive was the house of Mary and Martha.

Whatever was found new in Lazarus' face and gestures was thought to be some trace of a grave illness and of shocks recently experienced. Evidently, the destruction wrought by death on the corpse had been merely arrested by some miraculous power, for its effects were still apparent, and what death had succeeded in doing with Lazarus' face and body was like an artist's unfinished sketch seen under thin glass. On Lazarus' temples, under his eyes, and in the hollows of his cheeks lay a deep and cadaverous lividness; cadaverously blue also were his long fingers, and around his fingernails, grown long in the grave, the livid hue had become purple and dark. On his lips the skin, swollen in the grave, had burst in places, and thin, reddish cracks were formed, shining as though covered with transparent mica. And he had grown stout. His body, puffed up in the grave, retained its monstrous size and showed those frightful swellings in which one sensed the presence of the rank moisture of decomposition. But the heavy corpse-like odor which permeated Lazarus' graveclothes, and, it seemed, his very body, soon entirely disappeared, the livid spots on his face and hands grew paler, and the reddish cracks closed up, although they never disappeared altogether. That is how Lazarus looked when he appeared before people, in his second life, but his face looked natural to those who had seen him in the coffin.

In addition to the changes in his appearance, Lazarus' temper seemed to have undergone a transformation, but this circumstance startled no one and attracted no attention. Before his death Lazarus had always been cheerful and carefree, fond of laughter and a merry joke. It was because of this brightness and cheerfulness, with not a touch of malice and darkness, that the Master had grown so fond of him. But now Lazarus had grown grave and taciturn, he never jested himself, nor responded with laughter to other people's jokes; and the words which he uttered, very infrequently, were the plainest, most ordinary and necessary words, as devoid of depth and significance as those sounds with which animals express pain and pleasure, thirst and hunger. They were the words that one can say all one's life, and yet they give no indication of what pains and gladdens the depths of the soul.

Thus, with the face of a corpse which for three days had been under

the heavy sway of death, dark and taciturn, already appallingly transformed, but still unrecognized by anyone in his new self, he was sitting
at the festal table, among friends and relatives, and his gorgeous
nuptial garments glittered with yellow gold and bloody scarlet. Broad
waves of jubilation, now soft, now tempestuously sonorous, surged
around him; warm glances of love were reaching out for his face, still
cold with the coldness of the grave; and a friend's warm palm caressed
his livid, heavy hand. Musicians had been summoned, and they made
merry music on tympanum and pipe, on cithara and harp. It was as
though bees were humming, grasshoppers chirring, and birds warbling
over the happy house of Mary and Martha.

I I

One of the guests incautiously lifted the veil. By a thoughtless word
he broke the serene charm and uncovered the truth in all its naked
ugliness. Ere the thought formed itself in his mind, his lips uttered
with a smile:

"Why dost thou not tell us what happened in the beyond?"

And all grew silent, startled by the question. It was as if it occurred
to them only now that for three days Lazarus had been dead, and
they looked at him, anxiously awaiting his answer. But Lazarus kept
silence.

"Thou dost not wish to tell us?" wondered the man. "Is it so terrible
there?"

And again his thought came after his words. Had it been otherwise,
he would not have asked this question, which at that very moment
oppressed his heart with its insufferable horror. Uneasiness seized all
present, and with a feeling of heavy weariness they awaited Lazarus'
words, but he was silent, sternly and coldly, and his eyes were lowered.
And, as if for the first time, they noticed the frightful lividness of his
face and his repulsive obesity. On the table, as though forgotten by
Lazarus, rested his bluish-purple wrist, and to this all eyes turned
as if it were from it that the awaited answer was to come. The musicians were still playing, but now the silence reached them, too, and
even as water extinguishes scattered embers so were their merry tunes
extinguished in the silence. The pipe grew silent; the voices of the
sonorous tympanum and the murmuring harp died away; and, as if

its strings had burst, the cithara answered with a tremulous, broken note. Silence.

"Thou dost not wish to say?" repeated the guest, unable to check his chattering tongue. But the stillness remained unbroken, and the bluish-purple hand rested motionless. And then he stirred slightly and everyone felt relieved. He lifted up his eyes, and lo! straightway embracing everything in one heavy glance, fraught with weariness and horror, he looked at them—Lazarus, who had arisen from the dead.

It was the third day since Lazarus had left the grave. Ever since then many had experienced the pernicious power of his eye, but neither those who were crushed by it forever, nor those who found the strength to resist in it the primordial sources of life (which is as mysterious as death), ever could explain the horror which lay motionless in the depth of his black pupils. Lazarus looked calmly and simply with no desire to conceal anything; he looked coldly, as one who is infinitely indifferent to those alive. Many carefree people came close to him without noticing him, and only later did they learn with astonishment and fear who that calm stout man was, who walked slowly by, almost touching them with his gorgeous and dazzling garments. The sun did not cease shining when he was looking, nor did the fountain hush its murmur, and the sky overhead remained cloudless and blue. But the man under the spell of his enigmatical look heard no more the fountain and saw not the sky overhead. Sometimes he wept bitterly, sometimes he tore his hair and in frenzy called for help; but more often it came to pass that apathetically and quietly he began to die, and so he languished many years, before everybody's very eyes, wasted away, colorless, flabby, dull, like a tree silently drying in a stony soil. And of those who gazed at him, the ones who wept madly sometimes felt again the stir of life; the others never.

"So thou dost not wish to tell us what thou hast seen yonder?" repeated the man. But now his voice was impassive and dull, and deadly gray weariness showed in Lazarus' eyes. And deadly gray weariness covered like dust all the faces, and with dull amazement the guests stared at one another and did not understand wherefore they had gathered here and were sitting at the rich table. The talk ceased. They thought it was time to go home, but could not overcome the flaccid lazy weariness which glued their muscles, and they kept on sitting there, yet apart and torn away from one another, like pale fires scattered over a dark field.

But the musicians were paid to play, and again they took their instruments, and again tunes full of studied mirth and studied sorrow began to flow and to rise. They unfolded the customary melody, but the guests hearkened in dull amazement. Already they knew not wherefore it was necessary nor why it was well that people should pluck strings, inflate their cheeks, blow into slender pipes, and produce a bizarre, many-voiced noise.

"What vile music," said someone.

The musicians took offense and left. Following them, the guests left one after another, for night was already come. And when placid darkness encircled them and they began to breathe with more ease, suddenly Lazarus' image loomed up before each one in formidable radiance: the livid face of a corpse, graveclothes gorgeous and resplendent, a cold look, in the depths of which lay motionless an unknown horror. As though petrified, they were standing far apart, and darkness enveloped them, but in the darkness blazed brighter and brighter the supernatural vision of him who for three days had been under the enigmatical sway of death. For three days had he been dead: thrice had the sun risen and set, but he had been dead; children had played, streams had murmured over pebbles, the wayfarer had stirred up the hot dust in the highroad—but he had been dead. And now he was again among them; he touched them, he looked at them— looked at them! And through the black disks of his pupils, as through darkened glass, stared the unknowable Beyond.

III

No one was taking care of Lazarus, for no friends, no relatives were left to him, and the great desert which encircled the Holy City came near the very threshold of his dwelling. And the desert entered his house and stretched on his couch, like a wife, and extinguished the fires. No one was taking care of Lazarus. One after the other his sisters —Mary and Martha—forsook him. For a long while Martha was loath to abandon him, for she knew not who would feed him and pity him; she wept and prayed. But one night, when the wind was roaming in the desert and with a soughing sound the cypresses were bending over the roof, she dressed noiselessly and left the house secretly. Lazarus probably heard the door slam; it banged against the side-post under the gusts of the desert wind, but he did not rise to go out and to look at her who was abandoning him. All the night long the cypresses soughed over his head and the door thumped plaintively, letting in the cold, greedy desert.

Like a leper he was shunned by everyone, and it was proposed to tie a bell to his neck, as is done with lepers, to warn people against sudden meetings. But someone remarked, growing frightfully pale, that it would be too horrible if by night the tinkling of Lazarus' bell were suddenly heard under the windows—and so the project was abandoned.

And since he did not take care of himself, he would probably have starved to death, had not the neighbors brought him food in fear of something that they sensed but vaguely. The food was brought to him by children; they were not afraid of Lazarus, nor did they mock him with naïve cruelty, as children are wont to do with the wretched and miserable. They were indifferent to him, and Lazarus answered them with the same coldness; he had no desire to caress their fine black curls nor to look into their innocent shining eyes. Given up to Time and to the desert, his house was crumbling down, and long since had his famishing, lowing goats wandered away to the neighboring pastures. And his bridal garments became threadbare. Ever since that happy day, when the musicians played, he had worn them unaware of the difference of the new and the worn. The bright colors grew dull and faded; vicious dogs and the sharp thorns of the desert had turned the soft fabric into rags.

By day, when the merciless sun slew all things alive, and even scorpions sought shelter under stones and writhed there in a mad desire to sting, he sat motionless under the sun's rays, his livid face and his uncouth, bushy beard lifted up, bathing in the fiery flood.

When people still talked to him, he was once asked:

"Poor Lazarus, doth it please thee to sit thus and to stare at the sun?"

And he had answered:

"Yes, it doth."

So strong, it seemed, was the cold of his three days' grave, so deep the darkness, that there was no heat on earth to warm Lazarus, nor a splendor that could brighten the darkness of his eyes. That is what came to the mind of those who spoke to Lazarus, and with a sigh they left him.

And when the scarlet, flattened globe would sink lower, Lazarus would set out for the desert and walk straight toward the sun, as though striving to reach it. He always walked straight toward the sun, and those who tried to follow him and to spy upon what he was doing at night in the desert retained in their memory the black silhouette of a tall stout man against the red background of an enormous flattened disk. Night pursued them with her horrors, and so they did not learn of Lazarus' doings in the desert, but the vision of black on red was forever branded on their brains. Just as a beast with a splinter in its eye furiously rubs its muzzle with its paws, so they, too, foolishly rubbed their eyes, but what Lazarus had given was indelible, and Death alone could efface it.

But there were people who lived far away who never saw Lazarus and knew of him only by report. With daring curiosity, which is stronger than fear and feeds upon it, with hidden mockery, they would come to Lazarus as he sat in the sun and enter into conversation with him. By this time Lazarus' appearance had changed for the better and was not so terrible. The first minute they snapped their fingers and thought of how stupid the inhabitants of the Holy City were; but when the short talk was over and they started homeward, their looks were such that the inhabitants of the Holy City recognized them at once and said:

"Look, there is one more madman on whom Lazarus has set his eye," and they shook their heads regretfully, and lifted up their arms.

There came brave, intrepid warriors, with clanging weapons; happy youths came with laughter and song; busy tradesmen, jingling their money, ran in for a moment, and haughty priests leaned their staffs against Lazarus' door, and they were all strangely changed as they came back. The same terrible shadow swooped down upon their souls and gave a new appearance to the old familiar world.

Those who still had the desire to speak, expressed their feelings thus:

All things tangible and visible grew hollow, light, and transparent—similar to lightsome shadows in the darkness of night;

for that great darkness, which encompasses the whole cosmos, was dispersed neither by the sun nor by the moon and the stars, but like an immense black shroud enveloped the earth and, like a mother, embraced it;

it penetrated all the bodies, it penetrated iron and stone—and the particles of the bodies having lost their ties, grew lonely; and it penetrated into the depth of the particles, and the particles of particles became lonely;

for that great void, which encompasses the cosmos, was not filled by things visible: neither by the sun, nor by the moon and the stars, but reigned boundless, penetrating everywhere, severing body, particle from particle;

in the void hollow trees spread hollow roots; in the void temples, palaces, and houses loomed up, threatening a phantasmal fall—loomed up and they were hollow; and in the void men moved about restlessly, but they were light and hollow as shadows;

for, Time was no more, and the beginning of all things came near their end: the building was still being built, and builders were still hammering away, and its ruins were already seen and the void in its place; a man was still being born, but already funeral candles were burning at his head, and now they were extinguished, and there was the void in place of the man and of the funeral candles;

and wrapped by void and darkness the man in despair trembled in the face of the Horror of the Infinite.

Thus spake the men who had still a desire to speak. But, surely, much more could have been told by those who wished not to speak, and died in silence.

IV

At that time there lived in Rome a renowned sculptor. In clay, marble, and bronze he wrought bodies of gods and men, and such was their beauty that people called them immortal. But he himself was discontented and asserted that there was something even more beautiful that he could not make concrete either in marble or in bronze.

"I have not yet gathered the glowing of the moon, nor have I drunk my fill of sunshine," he was wont to say, "and there is no soul in my marble, no life in my beautiful bronze."

And when on moonlit nights he slowly walked along the road, crossing the black shadows of cypresses, his white tunic flitting under the moon, those who met him would laugh in a friendly way and say:

"Art thou going to gather moonlight, Aurelius? Why, then, didst thou not fetch baskets?"

And he would answer, laughing and pointing to his eyes:

"Here are the baskets wherein I gather the sheen of the moon and the glimmer of the sun."

And so it was; the moon glimmered in his eyes and the sun sparkled therein. But he could not translate them into marble, and herein lay the serene tragedy of his life.

He was descended from an ancient patrician race, had a good wife and children, and suffered from no want.

When the obscure rumor about Lazarus reached him, he consulted his wife and friends and undertook the far journey to Judaea to see him who had miraculously risen from the dead. He was somewhat weary in those days and he hoped that the road would sharpen his blunted senses. What was said of Lazarus did not frighten him: he had pondered much over Death, did not like it, but he disliked also those who confused it with life.

"On this side lies life with its splendor of beauty, on the other— Death with its enigma," he pondered, "and man can conceive naught better while he is alive than to delight in life and in the beauty of all things living."

And he even had a vainglorious desire to convince Lazarus of the truth of his own view and restore his soul to life, as his body had been restored. This seemed so much easier because the rumors, timorous and strange, did not convey the whole truth about Lazarus and but vaguely warned against something frightful.

Lazarus had just risen from a rock in order to follow the sun which was setting in the desert, when a rich Roman attended by an armed slave approached him and addressed him in a sonorous tone of voice:

"Lazarus!"

And Lazarus beheld a superb face, lit with glory, and he beheld bright raiment, and precious stones sparkling in the sun. The red light lent to the Roman's face and head the appearance of gleaming bronze —this also Lazarus noticed. He resumed obediently his place and lowered his weary eyes.

"Yea, thou art ugly, my poor Lazarus," quietly said the Roman, playing with his golden chain. "Thou art even horrible, my poor friend, and Death was not idle that day when thou didst fall so heedlessly into its clutches. But thou art as stout as a barrel, and, as the great Caesar used to say, stout people are not ill-tempered; to tell the truth, I don't understand why men fear thee. Permit me to spend the night in thy house; the hour is late, and I have no shelter."

Never had anyone asked Lazarus' hospitality.

"I have no bed," said he.

"I am somewhat of a soldier and I can sleep sitting," the Roman answered. "We shall build a fire."

"I have no fire."

"Then we shall have our talk in the darkness, like two friends. I think thou wilt find a bottle of wine."

"I have no wine."

The Roman laughed.

"Now I see why thou art so somber and dislikest thy second life. No wine! Why, then we shall do without it: there are words that make the head go round better than any Falernian."

By a sign he dismissed the slave, and they remained all alone. And again the sculptor started speaking, but it was as if, together with the setting sun, life had left his words, and they grew pale and hollow, as if they staggered on unsteady feet, as if they stumbled and fell, drunk with the heavy lees of weariness and despair. And black chasms grew up between the words—like far-off hints of the great void and the great darkness.

"Now I am thy guest, and thou wilt not be unkind to me, Lazarus!" said he. "Hospitality is the duty even of those who for three days were dead. Three days, I was told, thou didst rest in the grave. There it must be cold—and that is whence comes thy ill habit of going without fire and wine. As for me, I like fire; it grows dark here so rapidly. . . . The lines of thy eyebrows and forehead are quite, quite interesting: they are like ruins of strange palaces, buried in ashes after an earthquake. But why dost thou wear such ugly and queer garments? I have seen bridegrooms in thy country, and they wear such clothes—so mirthprovoking, so frightful. But thou art no bridegroom, art thou?"

The sun had already disappeared, a monstrous black shadow came running from the east—it was as if gigantic bare feet had begun swishing through the sand, and the wind sent a cold wave along the spine.

"In the darkness thou seemest still bigger, Lazarus, as if thou hadst grown stouter in these few moments. Dost thou feed on darkness, Lazarus? I would fain have a little fire—at least a little fire, a little fire. I feel somewhat chilly, your nights are so barbarously cold. Were it not so dark, I should say that thou wert looking at me, Lazarus. Yes, it seems to me, thou art. Why, thou art looking at me, I feel it—but there, thou art smiling."

Night came and filled the air with heavy blackness.

"How well it will be, when the sun will rise tomorrow anew! I am a great sculptor, as thou mayst know; that is what my friends call me. I create. Yes, that is the word. But I need daylight. I give life to the cold marble, I melt sonorous bronze in fire, in the bright, hot fire. . . . Why didst thou touch me with thy hand?"

"Come," said Lazarus. "Thou art my guest."

And they went to the house. And a long night enveloped the earth.

The slave, seeing that his master did not come, went to seek him, when the sun was already high in the sky. And he beheld his master side by side with Lazarus: in profound silence were they sitting right under the dazzling and scorching rays of the sun and looking upward. The slave began to weep and cried out:

"My Master! What hath befallen thee, Master?"

The very same day Aurelius left for Rome. On the way the sculptor was pensive and taciturn, staring attentively at everything—the men, the ship, the sea, as though trying to retain something. On the high sea a storm burst over them, and all through it Aurelius stayed on deck and eagerly scanned the seas looming near and then sinking with a thud.

At home his friends were frightened at the change which had taken place in Aurelius, but he calmed them, saying meaningly:

"I have found it."

And without changing the dusty clothes he had worn on his journey, he fell to work, and the marble obediently resounded under his sonorous hammer. Long and eagerly worked he, admitting no one, until one morning he announced that the work was ready and ordered his friends to be summoned, severe critics and connoisseurs of art. And to meet them he put on bright and gorgeous garments, that glittered with the yellow of gold and the scarlet of dyed byssus.

"Behold my work," said he thoughtfully.

His friends glanced, and a shadow of profound sorrow covered their faces. It was something monstrous, deprived of all the lines and shapes familiar to the eye, but not without a hint at some new, strange image.

On a thin, crooked twig, or rather on an ugly likeness of a twig, rested askew a blind, ugly, shapeless, outspread mass of something utterly and inconceivably distorted, a mad leap of wild and bizarre fragments, all feebly and vainly striving to part from one another. And, as if by chance, beneath one of the wildly rent salients a butterfly was chiseled with divine skill, all airy loveliness, delicacy, and beauty, with transparent wings, which seemed to tremble with an impotent desire to take flight.

"Wherefore this wonderful butterfly, Aurelius?" said somebody falteringly.

"I know not," was the sculptor's answer.

But it was necessary to tell the truth, and one of his friends who loved him best said firmly:

"This is ugly, my poor friend. It must be destroyed. Give me the hammer."

And with two strokes he broke the monstrous mass into pieces, leaving only the infinitely delicate butterfly untouched.

From that time on Aurelius created nothing. With profound indifference he looked at marble and bronze, and on his former divine works, whereon everlasting beauty rested. With the purpose of arousing his former fervent passion for work and awakening his deadened soul, his friends took him to see other artists' beautiful works, but he remained as indifferent as before, and no smile warmed his tightened lips. And only after listening to lengthy talks about beauty would he retort wearily and indolently:

"But all this is a lie."

And by day, when the sun was shining, he went into his magnificent, skillfully laid-out garden and, having found a place without shadow, he exposed his bare head to the glare and heat. Red and white butterflies fluttered around; from the crooked lips of a drunken satyr water streamed down with a splash into a marble cistern, but he sat motionless and silent—like a pallid reflection of him who, in the far-off distance, at the very gates of the stony desert, sat under the fiery sun.

V

And now it came to pass that the great, deified Augustus himself summoned Lazarus. The Imperial messengers dressed him gorgeously, in solemn nuptial clothes, as if Time had legalized them, and he was to remain until his very death the bridegroom of an unknown bride. It was as though an old, rotting coffin had been gilded and furnished with new, gay tassels. And men, all in trim and bright attire, rode after him, as if in bridal procession indeed, and those at the head trumpeted loudly, bidding people to clear the way for the Emperor's messengers. But Lazarus' way was deserted: his native land cursed the hateful name of him who had miraculously risen from the dead, and people scattered at the very news of his appalling approach. The solitary voice of the brass trumpets sounded in the motionless air, and the wilderness alone responded with its languid echo.

Then Lazarus went by sea. And his was the most magnificently arrayed and the most mournful ship that ever mirrored itself in the azure waves of the Mediterranean Sea. Many were the travelers aboard, but like a tomb was the ship, all silence and stillness, and the despairing water sobbed at the steep, proudly curved prow. All alone sat Lazarus, exposing his head to the blaze of the sun, silently listening to the murmur and splash of the wavelets, and the seamen and messengers sat far from him, a vague group of weary shadows. Had the thunder burst and the wind attacked the red sails, the ship would probably have perished, for none of those aboard had either the will or the strength to struggle for life. With a supreme effort some mariners would reach the board and eagerly scan the blue, transparent deep, hoping to see a naiad's pink shoulder flash in the hollow of an azure wave, or a drunken gay centaur dash along and in frenzy splash the wave with his hoof. But the sea was like a wilderness, and the deep was mute and deserted.

With utter indifference did Lazarus set his feet on the streets of the Eternal City. As though all her wealth, all the magnificence of her palaces built by giants, all the resplendence, beauty, and music of her refined life were but the echo of the wind in the wilderness, the reflection of the desert's shifting sands. Chariots were dashing along, and through the streets moved throngs of the strong, fair, proud builders of the Eternal City and haughty participants in its life; a song sounded; fountains and women laughed their pearly laughter; drunken philosophers harangued, and the sober listened to them with a smile; hoofs pounded the stone pavements. And surrounded by cheerful noise, a stout, heavy man was moving along, a chilling blotch of silence and despair, and on his way he sowed disgust, anger, and vague, gnawing weariness. "Who dares to be sad in Rome?" the citizens wondered indignantly, and frowned. In two days the entire city already knew all about him who had miraculously risen from the dead, and apprehensively shunned him.

But some daring people there were who wanted to test their strength, and Lazarus obeyed their imprudent summons. Kept busy by state affairs, the Emperor constantly delayed the reception, and seven days did he who had risen from the dead go about visiting others.

And Lazarus came to a cheerful winebibber, and the host met him with laughter on his lips:

"Drink, Lazarus, drink!" shouted he. "Would not Augustus laugh to see thee drunk!"

And half-naked drunken women laughed, and rose petals fell on

Lazarus' livid hands. But then the winebibber looked into Lazarus' eyes, and his gaiety ended forever. Drunk did he remain for the rest of his life; never did he drink aught, yet he remained drunk. But, instead of the gay reveries which wine brings with it, frightful dreams began to haunt him, the sole food of his stricken spirit. Day and night he lived in the noisome vapors of his nightmares, and death itself was not more frightful than its raving, monstrous forerunners.

And Lazarus came to a youth and his beloved, who loved each other and were most beautiful in their passion. Proudly and strongly embracing his love, the youth said with soft compassion:

"Look upon us, Lazarus, and share our joy. Is there aught stronger than love?"

And Lazarus looked. And for the rest of their life they kept on loving each other, but their passion grew gloomy and joyless, like those funereal cypresses whose roots feed on the decay of the graves and whose black summits in a still evening hour seek in vain to reach the sky. Thrown by the unknown forces of life into each other's embraces, they mingled tears with kisses, voluptuous pleasures with pain, and they felt themselves doubly slaves, obedient slaves to life, and patient servants of the silent Nothingness. Ever united, ever severed, they blazed like sparks and like sparks lost themselves in the boundless dark.

And Lazarus came to a haughty sage, and the sage said to him:

"I know all the horrors thou canst reveal to me. Is there aught thou canst frighten me with?"

But before long the sage felt that the knowledge of horror was far from being horror itself, and that the vision of death was not Death. And he felt that wisdom and folly are equal before the face of Infinity, for Infinity knows them not. And it vanished, the dividing-line between knowledge and ignorance, between truth and falsehood, between upper and nether, and shapeless thought hung suspended in the void. Then the sage clutched his gray head and cried out frantically:

"I cannot think! I cannot think!"

Thus, under the indifferent glance of him who had miraculously risen from the dead, perished everything that serves to affirm life, its significance and joys. And it was suggested that it was dangerous to let him look upon the Emperor, that it was better to kill him, and, having buried him secretly, to tell the Emperor that he had disappeared none knew whither. Already swords were being whetted, and youths devoted to the public welfare prepared for the murder, when Augustus ordered Lazarus to be brought before him next morning, thus destroying the cruel plans.

If there was no way of getting rid of Lazarus, at least it was possible to soften the terrible impression his face produced. With this in view, skillful painters, tonsorialists, and artists were summoned, and all night long they busied themselves over the head of Lazarus. They trimmed his beard, curled it, and gave it a neat, agreeable appearance. By means of pigments they concealed the corpse-like lividness of his hands and face. Repulsive were the wrinkles of suffering that furrowed his aged face, and they were puttied, painted, and smoothed; then, over the smooth background, wrinkles of good-tempered laughter and pleasant, carefree mirth were skillfully painted with fine brushes.

Lazarus submitted indifferently to everything that was done to him. Soon he was turned into a becomingly stout, venerable old man, into a quiet and kind grandfather of numerous offspring. It seemed that the smile, with which only a while ago he had been telling funny stories, was still lingering on his lips, and that in the corner of each eye was still lurking that serene kindliness which is the companion of old age. But they dared not change his nuptial garments, and they could not change his eyes, two dark and frightful panes through which the incomprehensible Beyond itself was gazing upon men.

VI

Lazarus was not moved by the magnificence of the Imperial palace. It was as though he saw no difference between the crumbling house closely pressed by the desert, and the stone palace, solid and fair, and indifferently he passed into it. And the hard marble of the floors he trod grew similar to the shifting sand of the desert, and the multitude of richly dressed and haughty men became like void air under his glance. No one looked into his face as Lazarus passed by, fearing to fall under the appalling influence of his eyes; but when the sound of his heavy footsteps had sufficiently died down, the courtiers raised their heads and with fearful curiosity scrutinized the figure of a stout, tall, slightly bent old man, who was slowly penetrating into the very heart of the Imperial palace. Were Death itself passing, it would be faced with no greater fear: for until then the dead alone knew Death, and those alive knew Life only—and there was no bridge between them.

But this extraordinary man, although alive, knew Death, and enigmatical, appalling, was his accursed knowledge.

"Woe," people thought, "he will take the life of our great, deified Augustus," and they sent curses after Lazarus, who meanwhile kept on advancing into the interior of the palace.

Already did the Emperor know who Lazarus was, and prepared to meet him. But the Monarch was a brave man, and felt his own tremendous unconquerable power, and in his fateful duel with him who had miraculously risen from the dead he did not want to invoke human help. And so he met Lazarus face to face.

"Lift not thine eyes upon me, Lazarus," he commanded. "I have heard that thy face is like that of the Medusa and turns into stone whomsoever thou lookest at. Now, I wish to see thee and have a talk with thee, before I turn into stone," he added in a tone of regal jocoseness, not devoid of fear.

Coming close to Lazarus, he carefully examined his face and his strange festal garments. And, although Augustus had a keen eye, he was deceived by the appearance of Lazarus.

"So. Thou dost not appear terrible, my venerable old man. But the worse for us, if horror assumes such a respectable and pleasant air. Now let us have a talk."

Augustus sat, and questioning Lazarus as much with his eyes as with words, started the conversation:

"Why didst thou not greet me upon thy entering?"

"I knew not it was needful," Lazarus answered with indifference.

"Art thou a Christian?"

"Nay."

Augustus nodded his head in approval.

" 'Tis well. I like not the Christians. They shake the tree of life ere it is covered with fruit, and scatter its fragrant bloom to the winds. But who art thou?"

"I was dead," answered Lazarus with a visible effort

"So I have heard. But who art thou now?"

Lazarus was silent, but at last repeated in a tone of weary apathy:

"I was dead."

"Listen to me, stranger," said the Emperor, distinctly and severely giving utterance to the thought that had come to him at the beginning, "my realm is the realm of Life, my people are of the living, not of the dead. Thou art one too many here. I know not who thou art nor what thou sawest there; but if thou liest, I hate thy lies, and if thou tellest the truth, I hate thy truth. In my bosom I feel the throb of life; I feel strength in my arm, and my proud thoughts, like eagles, pierce the space. And yonder is the shelter of my rule; under the protection of laws created by me people live and toil and rejoice. Dost thou hear the battle cry, the challenge men throw into the face of the future?"

Augustus, as in prayer, stretched forth his arms and exclaimed solemnly:

"Be blessed, O great and divine Life!"

Lazarus was silent, and with growing sternness the Emperor went on:

"Thou art not wanted here, miserable scrap snatched from under Death's teeth, thou inspirest weariness and disgust with life; like a caterpillar in the fields, thou devourest the rich ear of joy and spewest forth the drivel of despair and sorrow. Thy truth is like a rusty sword in the hands of a mighty murderer—and as a murderer thou shalt be executed. But before that let me look into thine eyes. Perchance 'tis only cowards who fear them, whereas in the brave they awake the thirst for strife and victory; in that case thou shalt be rewarded and not executed. Now look at me, Lazarus."

At first it appeared to the deified Augustus that a friend was looking at him—so soft, so tenderly fascinating was Lazarus' gaze. It held a promise not of horror but sweet rest, and the Infinite seemed to the Emperor a tender mistress, a compassionate sister, a mother. But stronger and stronger grew its embraces, and already the mouth, greedy for kisses, interfered with the Monarch's breathing, and already to the surface of the soft tissues of the body came the iron of the bones and tightened the merciless circle, and unknown fangs, blunt and cold, touched his heart and languidly sank therein.

"It pains me," said the deified Augustus, turning pale. "Yet look at me, Lazarus, look at me."

It was as though ponderous gates, ever closed, were slowly moving apart, and through the increasing interstice the appalling horror of the Infinite were pouring out, slowly and steadily. Like two shadows they entered the shoreless void and the unfathomable darkness; they extinguished the sun, ravished the earth from under the feet and the roof from overhead. No more did the congealed heart ache.

"Look on, look on, Lazarus," Augustus commanded, tottering.

Time stood still, and the beginning of each thing grew frightfully near to its end. The throne of Augustus, but recently raised up, crumbled down, and the Void was already in the place of that throne and of Augustus. Noiselessly did Rome itself crumble into dust and a new city stood on its site, and it, too, was swallowed by the void. Like fantastic giants cities, states, and countries fell and vanished in the void darkness—and with utmost indifference did the insatiable black maw of the Infinite swallow them.

"Cease!" the Emperor commanded.

In his voice already sounded a note of indifference; his hands dropped in languor, and in the vain struggle with the onrushing darkness his eagle-like eyes now blazed up, now dimmed.

"Thou hast slain me, Lazarus," said he in a spiritless, feeble voice.

And these words of hopelessness saved him. He remembered his people, whose shield he was destined to be, and keen salutary pain pierced his deadened heart.

"They are doomed to death," he reflected wearily. "Bleak shades in the darkness of the Infinite," he reflected, and horror grew within him. "Fragile vessels with living, seething blood, with hearts that know sorrow, and great joy also," he reflected within his heart, and tenderness pervaded it.

Thus pondering and oscillating between the poles of Life and Death, he slowly came back to life, to find in its sufferings and in its joys a shield against the darkness of the Void and the horror of the Infinite.

"Nay, thou hast not slain me, Lazarus," said he firmly, "but 'tis I who will take thy life. Get thee gone!"

That evening the deified Augustus partook of his meats and wines with particular joy. Now and then his lifted hand remained hovering in the air, and a dull glimmer replaced the bright sheen of his eagle-like eyes. It was the cold wave of Horror that surged at his feet. Defeated, but not undone, ever awaiting its hour, that Horror stood at the Emperor's bedside like a black shadow that pervaded all his life; it swayed his nights but yielded the days to the sorrows and joys of Life.

The following day the public executioner seared with a hot iron the eyes of Lazarus. Thereafter he was sent back to his native land. The deified Augustus dared not kill him.

Lazarus returned to the desert, and the wilderness met him with the hissing breath of its wind and the heat of its blazing sun. Again he sat on a rock, his uncouth, bushy beard lifted up, and the two black holes that had been his eyes stared at the sky with an expression of dull terror. Afar off the Holy City stirred noisily and restlessly, but around him everything was deserted and mute. No one approached the place where dwelt he who had miraculously risen from the dead, and long since his neighbors had forsaken their houses. Driven by the executioner's red-hot iron into the depth of his skull, his accursed knowledge hid there in ambush. As though leaping out of that ambush it plunged its thousand invisible eyes into man—and none dared look upon Lazarus.

And in the evening, when the sun, reddening and expanding, would come nearer and nearer the western horizon, the blinded Lazarus would slowly follow it. He would stumble against the rocks and fall, obese and weak as he was, would rise heavily to his feet and walk on again; and against the red screen of the sunset his black body and outspread hands would form a monstrous likeness of a cross.

And it came to pass that once he went out and did not come back. Thus seemingly ended the second life of him who had for three days been under the enigmatical sway of Death and had risen miraculously from the dead.

Ben-Tobith

ON THAT DREAD DAY, when a universal wrong was wrought, and Jesus Christ was crucified between two thieves on Golgotha—on that day the teeth of Ben-Tobith, a trader of Jerusalem, had begun to ache unbearably from the earliest hours of the morning.

That toothache had begun even the day before, toward evening: at first his right jaw had begun to pain him slightly, while one tooth (the one just before the wisdom tooth) seemed to have become a little higher and, whenever the tongue touched it, felt a trifle painful. After supper, however, the ache had subsided entirely; Ben-Tobith forgot all about it and felt rather on good terms with the world—he had made a profitable deal that day, exchanging his old ass for a young and strong one, was in a very merry mood, and had not considered the ill-boding symptoms of any importance.

And he had slept very well and most soundly, but just before the dawn something had begun to trouble him, as though someone were rousing him to attend to some very important matter, and when Ben-

Translated by Bernard Guilbert Guerney. Copyright, 1943, by the Vanguard Press, Inc.

Tobith angrily awoke, his teeth were aching, aching frankly and malevolently, in all the fullness of a sharp and piercing pain. And by now he could not tell whether it was only the tooth that had bothered him yesterday or whether other teeth had also made common cause with it: all his mouth and his head were filled with a dreadful sensation of pain, as though he were compelled to chew a thousand red-hot, sharp nails.

He took a mouthful of water from a clay jug: for a few moments the raging pain vanished; the teeth throbbed and undulated, and this sensation was actually pleasant in comparison with what he had felt before. Ben-Tobith lay down anew, bethought him of his newly-acquired young ass, reflected how happy he would be if it were not for those teeth of his, and tried his best to fall asleep. But the water had been warm, and five minutes later the pain returned, raging worse than before, and Ben-Tobith sat up on his pallet and swayed to and fro like a pendulum. His whole face puckered up and was drawn toward his prominent nose, while on the nose itself, now all white from his torments, hung a bead of cold sweat.

And thus, swaying and groaning from his pain, did he greet the first rays of that sun which was fated to behold Golgotha with its three crosses and then grow dim from horror and grief.

Ben-Tobith was a good man and a kindly, with little liking for wronging anybody, yet when his wife awoke he told her many unpleasant things, even though he was barely able to open his mouth, and complained that he had been left alone like a jackal, to howl and writhe in his pain. His wife accepted the unmerited reproaches with patience, since she realized that they were not uttered from an evil heart, and brought him many excellent remedies, such as purified rat droppings, to be applied to the cheek, a pungent infusion of scorpions, and a true shard of the tablets of the law, splintered off at the time Moses had shattered them.

The rat droppings eased the pain a little, but not for long; it was the same way with the infusion and the shard, for each time, after a short-lived relief, the pain returned with new vigor. And during the brief moments of respite Ben-Tobith consoled himself by thinking of the young ass and making plans concerning it, while at such times as his teeth worsened he moaned, became wroth with his wife, and threatened to dash his brains out against a stone if the pain would not abate. And all the while he kept pacing up and down the flat roof of his house, but avoided coming too near the edge thereof for very shame, since his whole head was swathed, like a woman's, in a shawl.

The children came running to him several times and, speaking very fast, told him something or other about Jesus of Nazareth. Ben-Tobith would stop his pacing and listen to them for a few moments with his face puckering but then stamp his foot in anger and drive them from him; he was a kindhearted man and loved children, but now he was wroth because they annoyed him with all sorts of trifles.

Nor was that the only unpleasant thing: the street, as well as all the roofs near by, were crowded with people who did not have a single thing to do, apparently, but stare at Ben-Tobith with his head swathed, like a woman's, in a shawl. And he was just about to come down from the roof when his wife told him:

"Look there—they're leading the robbers. Maybe that will make thee forget thy pain."

"Leave me in peace, woman. Canst thou not see how I suffer?" Ben-Tobith answered her surlily.

But the words of his wife held out a vague hope that his toothache might let up, and he grudgingly approached the parapet of his roof. Putting his head to one side, shutting one eye and propping up his sore cheek with his hand, he made a wry, weepy face, and looked down.

An enormous mob, raising great dust and an incessant din, was going helter-skelter through the narrow street that ran uphill. In the midst of this mob walked the malefactors, bending under the weight of their crosses, while the lashes of the Roman legionaries writhed over their heads like black serpents. One of the condemned—that fellow with the long, light hair, his seamless chiton all torn and stained with blood —stumbled against a rock that had been thrown under his feet and fell. The shouts grew louder, and the motley crowd, like an iridescent sea, closed over the fallen man.

Ben-Tobith shuddered from pain—it was just as though someone had plunged a red-hot needle into his tooth and then given that needle a twist for good measure. He let out a long-drawn moan: "Oo-oo-oo!" and left the parapet, wryly apathetic and in a vile temper.

"Hearken to them screaming!" he enviously mumbled, picturing to himself the widely open mouths, with strong teeth that did not ache, and imagined what a shout he himself would set up if only he were well.

And because of that mental picture his pain became ferocious, while his head bobbed fast, and he began to low like a calf: "Moo-oo-oo!"

"They say He restored sight to the blind," said Ben-Tobith's wife, who was glued to the parapet, and she skimmed a pebble toward the spot where Jesus, who had risen to his feet under the lashes, was now slowly moving.

"Yea, verily! If he would but rid me of my toothache it would suffice," Ben-Tobith retorted sarcastically, and added with a bitterness begotten of irritation: "Look at the dust they are raising! For all the world like a drove of cattle. Somebody ought to take a stick to them and disperse them! Take me downstairs, Sarah."

The good wife turned out to be right: the spectacle had diverted Ben-Tobith somewhat, although it may have been the rat droppings that had helped at last, and he succeeded in falling asleep. And when he awoke, the pain had practically vanished, and there was only a gumboil swelling on his right jaw, so small a gumboil that one could hardly notice it. His wife said that it was altogether unnoticeable, but Ben-Tobith smiled slyly at that: he knew what a kindhearted wife he had, and how she liked to say things that would please the hearer. Samuel the tanner, a neighbor, dropped in, and Ben-Tobith took him to see his young ass and listened with pride to the tanner's warm praises of the animal and its master.

Later on, heeding the plea of the inquisitive Sarah, the three of them set out for Golgotha, to have a look at the crucified. On the way Ben-Tobith told Samuel all about his misery from the very beginning, how last night he had felt a nagging ache in his right jaw, and how he had awakened in the night from the frightful pain. To make his recital graphic he assumed an expression of suffering, shut his eyes, tossed his head and moaned, while the gray-bearded Samuel shook his head commiseratingly and declared:

"Tsk-tsk-tsk! How that must have hurt!"

Ben-Tobith was so gratified by the sympathetic reception accorded to his story that he repeated it, and then went back to the remote time when his first tooth had begun to bother him—just one, a lower, on his left jaw. And thus, in animated talk, they reached Golgotha.

The sun, condemned to shed its light upon the world on that dread day, had already set beyond the distant knolls, and a ruddy scarlet streak was glowing like a bloodstain in the west. Against this background the crosses showed dark and indistinct, while some figures glimmered vague and white as they knelt at the foot of the central cross.

The people had long since dispersed; it was turning chill, and Ben-Tobith, after a casual glance at the crucified malefactors, took Samuel by the arm and discreetly headed him for home. He was in a particularly eloquent mood, and he wanted to round out the story of his toothache.

Thus did they wend their way homeward, and Ben-Tobith, to the accompaniment of Samuel's sympathetic nods and exclamations, assumed an expression of suffering, tossed his head, and moaned artfully, the while, from out the deep ravines, from the distant, sunparched plains, the black night rose. As though it would screen from the sight of heaven the great malefaction the earth had wrought.

1903

Freedom [1]

IF I SHOULD gather from all the world all the goodly words that men have among them—tender speeches, sonorous songs—and loose them like a flock of birds into the joyous air;

If I should gather all the smiles of children, the laughter of women whom none had yet wronged, the caresses of gray-haired mothers, the hard handclasp of a friend—and fashion all these into an incorruptible wreath for some splendidly beautiful head;

If I should go all the earth over and gather all the flowers, whichsoever ones there are on this earth—in the forests, in the fields and meadows, in the gardens of rich men, in the depths of the waters, on the blue bottom of the ocean; if I should gather all the precious glittering stones, if I should unearth them in impassable ravines, in the darkness of deep mines, pluck them out of kings' crowns and the earlobes of rich women—and pile all these, both stones and flowers, in one glittering hill;

If I should gather all the fires, whichsoever ones there are burning in all creation—all lights, all rays, all flare-ups, explosions, soft radiances—and with the glow of a single great conflagration illumine the universes as they shudder:

Yea, even then I still would not name thee, would not crown, would not glorify thee fitly, Freedom!

B. G. G.

[1] From *The Day of Wrath*.

Theodore Kusmich
𝔗eternicov
"Theodore Sologub"

1 8 6 3 — 1 9 2 7

TETERNICOV (the pen name Sologub should not be confused with the name of another writer, Count Vladimir Alexandrovich Sollogub) is labeled as the greatest and most exquisite of the earlier Symbolists and the foremost of the Decadents. His parentage (mother, a domestic servant; father, varyingly described as shoemaker, tailor) is regarded as unforgivable by critics of the aristocratic persuasion. If this fellow (a schoolmaster, and most of the time a provincial schoolmaster, at that) had to write, why couldn't he have been a Hogg, or a Burns? Instead, the august Mirski ranks his verse as the most refined and most delicate of modern Russian poetry, and we are driven to seeking imperfect analogies in Wilde, Blake, the Spasmodics, and the Parnassians. At the present writing the Editor can recall no writer stranger in Russian literature—even though that literature boasts of a Briussov. In prose or verse, the tinge of demonism, or even of Satanism, is generally present. But if Sologub's writing is a weird, unwholesome flower, if his hypersensitive muse is "ascetically monstrous," blame it almost wholly on the poisoned soil, on the nightmare atmosphere of Czarism—Alexander III's, to be plainer.

Sologub made his debut in 1896 with a volume of poems, a collection of short stories, and a novel, but it was not until the publication in 1907 of his greatest novel, *The Lesser Demon,* that he achieved general recognition and a success that enabled him to abandon teaching. Not the least of his literary achievements was the translation of *Droll Stories.* Sologub is one of the many classical refutations of the artists-in-uniform hoax:

in 1923 his sixtieth anniversary was marked by a public celebration in Leningrad (then Petrograd), although his literary creed remained unchanged to his death.

A considerable quantity of Solo-gub's prose is available in English, fortunately for the most part in the able translations of Cournos. Five poems are included in the Deutsch and Yarmolinsky anthology, *Russian Poetry*.

The Amphora

In an amphora brightly patterned
A slave bears wine somberly,
His path uneven is, unlanterned,
Dark, too, the heaven's canopy.
With his eyes straining and each step slow
Through the half-murk he gropes ahead;
One misstep: thick the wine will flow
And, staining, on his bosom spread.

Thus my own urn, long filled with sorrows,
I bear. The bane of memories
(Dread bane more poignant than barbed arrows),
Lurks treacherous within its lees.
By ways most devious, with utmost care
I bear my vessel filled with ill,
Fearful some hand, touching it unware,
May on my bosom its wine spill.

B. G. G.

Vanquish All Your Gladness

VANQUISH all your gladness,
Mortify your laughter.
All that holds joy's sweetness
Dooms in the hereafter.
Mortify your gladness,
Vanquish all your laughter.
Who is it that laughs now?
Children, gods and fools.
Be ye, then, austere. Vow
To be wisdom's tools!
Let the children laugh now,
And the gods, and fools.

B. G. G.

Three Gobs of Spit

A MAN was walking along and happened to spit. Three times. All in the same place.

The man went on. The gobs of spit remained.

And one of the gobs of spit said:

"We are here—but the man is not."

And the second said:

"He is gone."

And the third:

"That is the only thing he came here for—to plant us here. We are the purpose of man's life. He is gone. But we remain."

B. G. G.

Ivan Alexeievich
Bunin

1 8 7 7 -

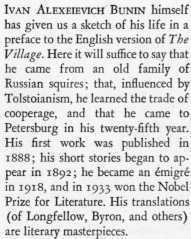

IVAN ALEXEIEVICH BUNIN himself
has given us a sketch of his life in a
preface to the English version of *The
Village*. Here it will suffice to say that
he came from an old family of
Russian squires; that, influenced by
Tolstoianism, he learned the trade of
cooperage, and that he came to
Petersburg in his twenty-fifth year.
His first work was published in
1888; his short stories began to appear in 1892; he became an émigré
in 1918, and in 1933 won the Nobel
Prize for Literature. His translations
(of Longfellow, Byron, and others)
are literary masterpieces.

Bunin is unique in Russian literature in several respects, and distinctly
of the *aristoi* in either Russian or universal letters. As a literary figure he
strikes one, almost irresistibly, as a
French Academician in stature—and
we find that in the old Russia he was
"one of the Twelve Honorary Academicians, who correspond to the
French Immortals." He strikes one
not as a Slav but as a Gaul who has
chosen impeccable Russian as his medium. The obvious objection is that
he has not the Gallic verve—to which
the obvious retort is that there have
been French writers who were very
far from sprightly.

It is odd how few of his stories are
told in the first person; still more
curious is it to observe how many of
his stories deal with Death, directly
or obliquely. Kuprin has been called
the Poet of Life; Bunin might, with
equal justice, be styled the Poet of
Death. He is more than half in love
with Death—and that not necessarily
easeful death. He can extract the
honey of wormwood poetry even out
of the brutal and brutish death of a
peasant. Yet the accusation of morbidity, only too readily aimed against
Russian writers, would hardly hold
against him. Is there anywhere a
more eager paean to life than his *The*

Cicadas? Death to Bunin is part of, as well as a sequel to, life: the obverse of a medal he yearns to decipher. Perhaps the difference between the two Poets can best be shown thus: Kuprin can write a perfectly delightful, life-imbued sketch about the famous Canine Cemetery in Paris; Bunin does a ghastly, absorbing yet chill piece about the functioning of a French crematorium.

And besides Death, his particular province is Love. But here, too, he prefers to pose peculiar situations. He may not have all the fiendish insight of Dostoievski, but very few writers today wield as delicate a psychological scalpel as the author of *The Grammar of Love.* "After all, the creepiest thing in the world is the soul of man," as he points out in *A Creepy Story.*

Nor has the present writer much patience with clichés about Bunin's "profoundly Russian" outlook on religion. He is a greater cosmopolite than even Turgenev was and, if anything, is imbued with Oriental mysticism. Best of all, his religious and artistic beliefs are summed up in his quotation from Saadi: "I strove to view the face of the earth and leave thereon the impress of my soul."

His style is chill, hard, brilliant, like rock-crystal. He wanted to be a painter, and a painter he is, even in giving his reaction to *sounds.* He is ever aloof, ever objective. Since he has steered fairly clear of literary schools and movements, Russian criticism is at a loss for a precise label; the nearest is "Neo-Realist."

The supreme example of his short-story writing is *The Gentleman from San Francisco.* It has become justly celebrated as a world masterpiece. Its popularity (an odd term in connection with Bunin!) is due primarily to its universality. A great deal of Bunin's work is available in English.

Nothing is definitely known of Bunin's present fate; he is supposed to be still in the South of France. A few of his latest stories, which have miraculously and mysteriously reached New York, where they have been published in the original, testify to nothing but an artist's indomitable will to function despite all and any conditions.

The reader who is fond of the short story is particularly commended to the volume from which the subjoined story is taken, and to *The Elaghin Affair and Other Stories* (both published by Alfred A. Knopf, Inc.).

The Gentleman from San Francisco

Alas, alas, that great city Babylon, that mighty city!
THE APOCALYPSE

THE GENTLEMAN from San Francisco—neither at Naples nor at Capri had anyone remembered his name—was going to the Old World for two whole years, with wife and daughter, solely for the sake of pleasure.

He was firmly convinced that he was fully entitled to rest, to pleasure, to prolonged and comfortable travel, and to not a little else besides. For such a conviction he had his reasons—that, in the first place, he was rich, and, in the second, that he was only now beginning to live, despite his eight-and-fifty years. Until now he had not lived but had merely existed—not at all badly, it is true, but, nevertheless, putting all his hopes on the future. He had labored with never a pause for rest—the coolies, whom he had imported by whole thousands, well knew what this meant!—and finally he saw that much had already been accomplished, that he had almost come abreast of those whom he had at one time set out to emulate, and he decided to enjoy a breathing space. It was a custom among the class of people to which he belonged to commence their enjoyment of life with a journey to Europe, to India, to Egypt. He, too, proposed to do the same. Of course, he desired, first of all, to reward himself for his years of toil; however, he rejoiced on account of his wife and daughter as well. His wife had never been distinguished for any special sensitiveness to new impressions—but then, all elderly American women are fervid travelers. As for his daughter—a girl no longer in her first youth, and somewhat sickly—travel was a downright necessity for her: to say nothing of the benefit to her health, were there no fortuitous encounters during travels? It is while traveling that one may at times sit at table with a billionaire, or scrutinize frescoes by his side.

Translated by Bernard Guilbert Guerney. Reprinted from *The Gentleman from San Francisco and Other Stories* by Ivan Bunin by permission of and special arrangement with Alfred A. Knopf, Inc. Copyright, 1935, by Alfred A. Knopf, Inc.

The itinerary worked out by the gentleman from San Francisco was an extensive one. In December and January he hoped to enjoy the sun of Southern Italy, the monuments of antiquity, the *tarantella,* the serenades of strolling singers, and that which men of his age relish with the utmost finesse: the love of little, youthful Neapolitaines, even though it be given not entirely without ulterior motives; he contemplated spending the Carnival in Nice, in Monte Carlo, whither the very pick of society gravitates at that time—that very society upon which all the benefits of civilization depend: not merely the cut of tuxedos, but, as well, the stability of thrones, and the declaration of wars, and the prosperity of hotels—Monte Carlo, where some give themselves up with passion to automobile and sail races; others to roulette; a third group to that which it is the custom to call flirting; a fourth, to trapshooting, in which the pigeons, released from their cotes, soar up most gracefully above emerald-green swards, against the background of a sea that is the color of forget-me-nots—only, in the same minute, to strike against the ground as little, crumpled clods of white. . . . The beginning of March he wanted to devote to Florence; about the time of the Passion of Our Lord to arrive at Rome, in order to hear the *Miserere* there; his plans also embraced Venice, and Paris, and bullfighting in Seville, and sea bathing in the British Isles, and Athens, and Constantinople, and Palestine, and Egypt, and even Japan —of course, be it understood, already on the return trip. . . . And everything went very well at first.

It was the end of November; almost as far as Gibraltar it was necessary to navigate now through an icy murk, now amidst a blizzard of wet snow; but the ship sailed in all safety and even without rolling; the passengers the steamer was carrying proved to be many, and all of them people of note; the ship—the famous "Atlantida"—resembled the most expensive of European hotels, with all conveniences: an all-night bar, Turkish baths, a newspaper of its own—and life upon it flowed in accordance with a most complicated system of regulations: people got up early, to the sounds of bugles, stridently resounding through the corridors at that dark hour when day was so slowly and inimically dawning over the grayish-green desert of waters, ponderously turbulent in the mist. Putting on their flannel pajamas, the passengers drank coffee, chocolate, cocoa; then they got into marble baths, did their exercises, inducing an appetite and a sense of well-being, performed their toilet for the day, and went to breakfast. Until eleven one was supposed to promenade the decks vigorously, inhaling the fresh coolness of the ocean, or to play at shuffleboard and other games for the sake of arousing the appetite anew, and, at eleven, to seek sustenance in bouillon and sandwiches; having refreshed themselves, the passengers perused their newspaper with gusto and calmly awaited lunch, a meal still more nourishing and varied than the breakfast. The next two hours were sacred to repose—the decks were then encumbered with *chaises longues,* upon which the travelers reclined, covered up with plaids, contemplating the cloud-flecked sky and the foaming hummocks flashing by over the side, or else pleasantly dozing off; at five o'clock, refreshed and put in good spirits, they were drenched with strong fragrant tea, served with cookies; at seven they were apprized by bugle signals of a dinner of nine courses. . . . And thereupon the gentleman from San Francisco, in an access of animal spirits, would hurry to his resplendent *cabine de luxe* to dress.

In the evening the tiers of the "Atlantida" gaped through the dusk as though they were fiery, countless eyes, and a great multitude of servants worked with especial feverishness in the kitchens, sculleries, and wine vaults. The ocean, heaving on the other side of the walls, was awesome; but none gave it a thought, firmly believing it under the sway of the captain—a red-haired man of monstrous bulk and ponderousness, always seeming sleepy, resembling, in his uniform frock coat with its golden chevrons, an enormous idol; it was only very rarely that he left his mysterious quarters to appear in public. A siren on the forecastle howled every minute in hellish sullenness and whined in frenzied malice, but not many of the diners heard the siren—it was drowned by the strains of a splendid stringed orchestra, playing exquisitely and ceaselessly in the two-tiered hall, decorated with marble, its floors covered with soft rugs, festively flooded with the lights of crystal lusters and gilded *girandoles,* filled to overflowing with diamond-bedecked ladies in *décolletée* and men in tuxedos, graceful waiters and deferential *maîtres d'hôtel*—among whom one, who took orders for wines exclusively, even walked about with a chain around his neck, like a Lord Mayor. A tuxedo and perfect linen made the gentleman from San Francisco appear very much younger. Spare, not tall, clumsily but strongly built, groomed until he shone, and moderately animated, he sat in the aureate-pearly refulgence of this palatial room, at a table with a bottle of amber Johannisberger, with countless goblets, small and large, of the thinnest glass, with a curly bouquet of curly hyacinths. There was something of the Mongol about his yellowish face with clipped silvery mustache; his large teeth gleamed with gold fillings; his stalwart, bald head glistened like old ivory. Rich, yet in keeping with her years, was the dress of his wife— a big woman, expansive and calm; elaborate, yet light and diaphanous, with an innocent frankness, was that of his daughter—tall, slender, with magnificent hair, exquisitely dressed, with breath aromatic from violet cachous, and with the tenderest of tiny, rosy pimples about her lips and between her shoulder blades, just the least bit powdered. . . .

The dinner lasted for two whole hours, while after dinner there was dancing in the ballroom, during which the men—the gentleman from San Francisco among their number, of course—with their feet cocked up, determined, upon the basis of the latest political and stock-exchange news, the destinies of nations, smoking Havana cigars and drinking *liqueurs* until they were crimson in the face, seated in the bar, where the waiters were Negroes in red jackets, the whites of their eyes resembling hard-boiled eggs with the shell off. The ocean, with a dull roar, was moiling in black mountains on the other side of the wall; the snow-gale whistled mightily through the sodden rigging; the whole steamer quivered as it mastered both the gale and the mountains, sundering to either side, as though with a plow, their shifting masses, that again and again boiled up and reared high, with tails of foam; the siren, stifled by the fog, was moaning with a deathly anguish; the lookouts up in their crow's-nest froze from the cold and grew dazed from straining their attention beyond their strength. Like to the grim and sultry depths of the infernal regions, like to their ultimate, their ninth circle, was the womb of the steamer, below the water line—that womb where dully gurgled the gigantic furnaces, devouring with their incandescent maws mountains of hard coal, cast into them by men stripped to the waist, purple from the flames, and with smarting, filthy sweat pouring over them; whereas here, in the bar, men threw their legs over the arms of their chairs with never a care, sipping cognac and *liqueurs,* and were wafted among clouds of spicy smoke as they indulged in well-turned conversation; in the ball-room everything was radiant with light and warmth and joy; the dancing couples were now awhirl in waltzes, now twisting in the tango— and the music insistently, in some delectably shameless melancholy, was suppliant always of the one, always of the same thing. . . . There was an ambassador among this brilliant throng—a lean, modest little old man; there was a great man of riches—clean-shaven, lanky, of indeterminate years, and with the appearance of a prelate, in his dress coat of an old-fashioned cut; there was a well-known Spanish writer;

there was a world-celebrated beauty, already just the very least trifle faded and of an unenviable morality; there was an exquisite couple in love with each other, whom all watched with curiosity and whose happiness was unconcealed: *he* danced only with *her;* sang—and with great ability—only to *her* accompaniment; and everything they did was carried out so charmingly that the captain was the only one who knew that this pair was hired by Lloyd's to play at love for a good figure and that they had been sailing for a long time, now on one ship, now on another.

At Gibraltar everybody was gladdened by the sun—it seemed to be early spring; a new passenger, whose person aroused the general interest, made his appearance on board the "Atlantida"—he was the hereditary Prince of a certain Asiatic kingdom, traveling incognito; a little man who somehow seemed to be all made of wood, even though he was alert in his movements; broad of face, with narrow eyes, in gold-rimmed spectacles; a trifle unpleasant through the fact that his skin showed through his coarse black mustache like that of a cadaver; on the whole, however, he was charming, unpretentious, and modest. On the Mediterranean Sea there was a whiff of winter again; the billows ran high, and were as multicolored as the tail of a peacock; they had snowy-white crests, lashed up—although the sun was sparkling brightly and the sky was perfectly clear—by a *tramontana,* a chill northern wind from beyond the mountains, that was joyously and madly rushing to meet the ship. . . . Then, on the second day, the sky began to pale, the horizon became covered with mist, land was nearing; Ischia, Capri appeared; through the binoculars Naples— lumps of sugar strewn at the foot of some dove-colored mass—could be seen; while over it and this dove-colored mass were visible the ridges of distant mountains, vaguely glimmering with the dead whiteness of snows. There was a great number of people on deck; many of the ladies and gentlemen had already put on short, light fur coats, with the fur outside; Chinese boys, never contradictory and never speaking above a whisper, bow-legged striplings with pitch-black queues reaching to their heels and with eyelashes as long and thick as those of young girls, were already dragging, little by little, sundry plaids, canes, and portmanteaus and grips of alligator hide toward the companionways.

The daughter of the gentleman from San Francisco was standing beside the Prince, who had been, through a fortuitous circumstance, presented to her yesterday evening, and she pretended to be looking intently into the distance, in a direction he was pointing out to her, telling, explaining something or other to her, hurriedly and quietly. On account of his height he seemed a boy by contrast with others— he was queer and not at all prepossessing of person, with his spectacles, his derby, his English greatcoat, while his scanty mustache looked just as if it were of horsehair, and the swarthy, thin skin seemed to be drawn tightly over his face and somehow had the appearance of being lacquered—but the young girl was listening to him, without understanding, in her agitation, what he was saying; her heart was thumping from an incomprehensible rapture before his presence and from pride that he was speaking with her and not some other. Everything about him that was different from others—his lean hands, his clear skin, under which flowed the ancient blood of kings, even his altogether unpretentious, yet somehow distinctively neat, European dress —everything held a secret, inexplicable charm, evoked a feeling of amorousness. Ask for the gentleman from San Francisco himself—he, in a high silk hat, in gray spats over patent-leather shoes, kept on glancing at the famous beauty who was standing beside him—a tall blonde of striking figure, her eyes painted in the latest Parisian fashion; she was holding a diminutive, hunched-up, mangy lap dog on a silver chain and was chattering to it without cease. And the daughter, in some vague embarrassment, tried not to notice her father.

Like all Americans of means, he was very generous on his travels, and, like all of them, believed in the full sincerity and good will of those who brought him food and drink with such solicitude, who served him from morn till night, forestalling his least wish; of those who guarded his cleanliness and rest, lugged his things around, summoned porters for him, delivered his trunks to hotels. Thus had it been everywhere, thus had it been on the ship, and thus was it to be in Naples as well. Naples grew, and drew nearer; the musicians, the brass of their instruments flashing, had already clustered upon the deck and suddenly deafened everybody with the triumphant strains of a march; the gigantic captain, in his full-dress uniform, appeared upon his stage and, like a condescending heathen god, waved his hand amiably to the passengers—and to the gentleman from San Francisco it seemed that it was for him alone that the march so beloved by proud America was thundering, that it was he whom the captain was felicitating upon a safe arrival. And every other passenger felt similarly about himself—or herself. And when the "Atlantida" did finally enter the harbor, had heaved to at the wharf with her many-tiered mass, black with people, and the gangplanks clattered down—what a multitude of porters and their helpers in caps with gold braid, what a multitude of different *commissionaires,* whistling gamins, and strapping ragamuffins with packets of colored postal cards in their hands, made a rush toward the gentleman from San Francisco, with offers of their services! And he smiled, with a kindly contemptuousness, at these ragamuffins as he went toward the automobile of precisely that hotel where there was a possibility of the Prince's stopping as well, and drawled through his teeth, now in English, now in Italian:

"Go away! * *Via!*"

Life at Naples at once assumed its wonted, ordered current; in the early morning, breakfast in the somber dining room with its damp draft from windows opening on some sort of stony little garden; the sky was usually overcast, holding out but little promise, and there was the usual crowd of guides at the door of the vestibule; then came the first smiles of a warm, rosy sun; there was, from the high hanging balcony, a view of Vesuvius, enveloped to its foot by radiant morning mists, and of silver-and-pearl eddies on the surface of the Bay, and of the delicate contour of Capri against the horizon; one could see tiny burros, harnessed in twos to little carts, running down below over the quay, sticky with mire, and detachments of diminutive soldiers marching off to somewhere or other to lively and exhilarating music. Next came the procession to the waiting automobile and the slow progress through populous, narrow, and damp corridors of streets, between tall, many-windowed houses; the inspection of lifelessly clean museums, evenly and pleasantly, yet bleakly, lit, seemingly illuminated by snow; or of cool churches, smelling of wax, which everywhere and always contain the same things: a majestic portal, screened by a heavy curtain of leather, and inside—silence, empty vastness, unobtrusive little flames of a seven-branched candelabrum glowing redly in the distant depths, on an altar bedecked with laces; a solitary old woman among the dark wooden pews; slippery tombstones underfoot; and somebody's *Descent from the Cross*—inevitably a celebrated one.

At one o'clock there was luncheon upon the mountain of San Martino, where, toward noon, gathered not a few people of the very first quality, and where the daughter of the gentleman from San Francisco had once almost fainted away for joy, because she thought she saw the Prince sitting in the hall, although she already knew

* English in the original. The same applies to the other phrases in this story marked with asterisks. *Translator.*

through the newspapers that he had left for a temporary stay at Rome. At five came tea at the hotel, in the showy salon, so cosy with its rugs and flaming fireplaces; and after that it was already time to get ready for dinner—and once more came the mighty, compelling reverberation of the gong through all the floors; once more the processions in indian file of ladies in *décolletée,* rustling in their silks upon the staircases and reflected in all the mirrors; once more the palatial dining room, widely and hospitably opened, and the red jackets of the musicians upon their platform, and the black cluster of waiters about the *maître d'hôtel,* who, with a skill out of the ordinary, was ladling some sort of thick, roseate soup into plates. . . . The dinners, as everywhere else, were the crowning glory of each day; the guests dressed for them as for a rout, and these dinners were so abundant in viands, and wines, and mineral waters, and sweets, and fruits, that toward eleven o'clock at night the chambermaids were distributing through all the corridors rubber bags with hot water to warm sundry stomachs.

However, the December of that year proved to be not altogether a successful one for Naples; the porters grew confused when one talked with them of the weather, and merely shrugged their shoulders guiltily, muttering that they could not recall such another year— although it was not the first year that they had been forced to mutter this and to urge in extenuation that "something terrible is happening everywhere"; there were unheard-of storms and torrents of rain on the Riviera; there was snow in Athens; Etna was also all snowed over and was aglow of nights; tourists were fleeing from Palermo in all directions, escaping from the cold. The morning sun deceived the Neapolitans every day that winter: toward noon the sky became gray and a fine rain began falling, but growing heavier and colder all the time; at such times the palms near the entrance of the hotel glistened as though they were of tin, the town seemed especially dirty and cramped, the museums exceedingly alike; the cigar stumps of the corpulent cabmen, whose rubber coats flapped in the wind like wings, seemed to have an insufferable stench, while the energetic snapping of their whips over their scrawny-necked nags was patently false; the footgear of the *signori* sweeping the rails of the tramways seemed horrible; the women, splashing through the mud, their black-haired heads bared to the rain, appeared hideously short-legged; as for the dampness and the stench of putrid fish from the sea foaming at the quay—they were a matter of course. The gentleman and the lady from San Francisco began quarreling in the morning; their daughter either walked about pale, with a headache, or, coming to life again, went into raptures over everything, and was at such times both charming and beautiful: beautiful were those tender and complex emotions which had been awakened within her by meeting that homely man through whose veins flowed uncommon blood; for, after all is said and done, perhaps it is of no real importance just what it is, precisely, that awakens a maiden's soul —whether it be money, or fame, or illustrious ancestry. . . .

Everybody affirmed that things were entirely different in Sorrento, in Capri—there it was both warmer and sunnier, and the lemon trees were in blossom, and the customs were more honest, and the wine was more natural. And so the family from San Francisco determined to set out with all its trunks to Capri, and, after seeing it all, after treading the stones where the palace of Tiberius had once stood, after visiting the faerylike caverns of the Azure Grotto and hearing the bagpipers of Abruzzi, who for a whole month preceding Christmas wander over the island and sing the praises of the Virgin Mary, they meant to settle in Sorrento.

On the day of departure—a most memorable one for the family from San Francisco!—there was no sun from the early morning. A heavy fog hid Vesuvius to the very base; this gray fog spread low over the leaden heaving of the sea that was lost to the eye at a distance of half a mile. Capri was entirely invisible—as though there had never been such a thing in the world. And the little steamer that set out for it was so tossed from side to side that the family from San Francisco was laid prostrate upon the divans in the sorry general cabin of this tub, their feet wrapped up in plaids and their eyes closed from nausea. Mrs. suffered—so she thought—more than anybody; she was overcome by seasickness several times; it seemed to her that she was dying, whereas the stewardess, who always ran up to her with a small basin— she had been, for many years, day in and day out, rolling on these waves, in freezing weather and in torrid, and yet was still tireless and kind to everybody—merely laughed. Miss was dreadfully pale and held a slice of lemon between her teeth; now she could not have been cheered even by the hope of a chance encounter with the Prince at Sorrento, where he intended to be about Christmas. Mr., who was lying on his back, in roomy overcoat and large cap, never unlocked his jaws all the way over; his face had grown darker and his mustache whiter, and his head ached dreadfully: during the last days, thanks to the bad weather, he had been drinking too heavily of evenings, and had too much admired the "living pictures" in dives of *recherché* libertinage. But the rain kept lashing against the jarring port-holes, the water from them running down on the divans; the wind, howling, bent the masts, and at times, aided by the onslaught of a wave, careened the little steamer entirely to one side, and then something in the hold would roll with a rumble.

During the stops, at Castellamare, at Sorrento, things were a trifle more bearable, but even then the rocking was fearful—the shore, with all its cliffs, gardens, *pini* or pines, its pink and white hotels and hazy mountains clad in curly greenery, swayed up and down as if on a swing; boats bumped up against the sides of the ship; sailors and steerage passengers were yelling vehemently; somewhere, as though it had been crushed, a baby was wailing and smothering; a raw wind was blowing in at the door; and, from a swaying boat with a flag of the Hotel Royal, a lisping gamin was screaming, luring travelers: "Kgoya-al! Hotel Kgoya-al! . . ." And the gentleman from San Francisco, feeling that he was an old man—which was but proper— was already thinking with sadness and melancholy of all these Royals, Splendids, Excelsiors, and of these greedy, insignificant manikins, reeking of garlic, that are called Italians.

Once, having opened his eyes and raised himself from the divan, he saw, underneath the craggy steep of the shore, a cluster of stone hovels, moldy through and through, stuck one on top of another near the very edge of the water, near boats, near all sorts of rags, tins, and brown nets—hovels so miserable that, at the recollection that this was that very Italy he had come hither to enjoy, he felt despair. . . . Finally, at twilight, the dark mass of the island began to draw near, seemingly bored through and through by little red lights near its base; the wind became softer, warmer, more fragrant; over the abating waves, as opalescent as black oil, golden pythons flowed from the lanterns on the wharf. . . . Then came the sudden rumble of the anchor, and it fell with a splash into the water; the ferocious yells of the boatmen, vying with one another, floated in from all quarters— and at once the heart grew lighter, the lights in the general cabin shone more brightly, a desire arose to eat, to drink, to smoke, to be stirring. . . . Ten minutes later the family from San Francisco had descended into a large boat; within fifteen minutes it had set foot upon the stones of the wharf, and had then got into a bright little railway car and to its buzzing started the ascent of the slope, amid the stakes of the vineyards, half-crumbled stone enclosures, and wet, gnarled orange trees, some of them under coverings of straw—trees with thick, glossy foliage and aglimmer with the orange fruits; all these objects were sliding downward, past the open windows of the little car, toward the base of the mountain. . . . Sweetly smells the earth of Italy after rain, and her every island has its own, its especial aroma!

The island of Capri was damp and dark on this evening. But now it came into life for an instant; lights sprang up here and there, as always on the steamer's arrival. At the top of the mountain, where stood the station of the funicular, there was another throng of those whose duty lay in receiving fittingly the gentleman from San Francisco. There were other arrivals also, but they merited no attention—several Russians, who had taken up their abode in Capri—absent-minded because of their bookish meditations, unkempt, bearded, spectacled, the collars of their old drap overcoats turned up; and a group of long-legged, long-necked, round-headed German youths in Tyrolean costumes, with canvas knapsacks slung over their shoulders—these latter stood in need of nobody's services, feeling themselves at home everywhere, and were not at all generous in their expenditures. The gentleman from San Francisco, on the other hand, who was calmly keeping aloof from both the one group and the other, was immediately noticed. He and his ladies were bustlingly assisted to get out, some men running ahead of him to show him the way: he was surrounded anew by urchins, and by those robust Caprian wives who carry on their heads the portmanteaus and trunks of respectable travelers. The wooden pattens of these women clattered over a *piazetta* that seemed to belong to some opera, an electric globe swaying above it in the damp wind; the rabble of urchins burst into sharp, birdlike whistles—and, as though on a stage, the gentleman from San Francisco proceeded in their midst toward some medieval arch, underneath houses that had become welded into one mass, beyond which a little echoing street—with the tuft of a palm above flat roofs on its left, and with blue stars in the black sky overhead—led slopingly to the grand entrance of the hotel, glittering ahead. . . . And again it seemed that it was in honor of the guests from San Francisco that this damp little town of stone on a craggy little island of the Mediterranean Sea had come to life, that it was they who had made so happy and affable the proprietor of the hotel, that it was they only who had been waited for by the Chinese gong that now began whanging its summons to dinner through all the floors of the hotel the instant they had set foot in the vestibule.

The proprietor, a young man of haughty elegance, who had met them with a polite and exquisite bow, for a minute dumfounded the gentleman from San Francisco: having glanced at him, the gentleman from San Francisco suddenly recalled that just the night before, among the rest of the confusion of images that had beset him in his sleep, he had seen precisely this gentleman—just like him, down to the least detail: in the same sort of exquisite cutaway coat, and with the same pomaded and painstakingly combed head. Startled, he was almost taken aback; but since, from long, long before, there was not even a mustard seed of any sort of so-called mystical emotions left in his soul, his astonishment was dimmed the same instant; passing through a corridor of the hotel, he spoke jestingly to his wife and daughter of this strange coincidence of dream and reality. And only his daughter glanced at him with alarm at that moment: her heart suddenly contracted from sadness, from a feeling of their loneliness upon this foreign, dark island—a feeling so strong that she almost burst into tears. But still she said nothing of her feelings to her father—as always.

An exalted personage—Rais XVII—who had been visiting Capri, had just taken his departure, and the guests from San Francisco were given the same apartments that he had occupied. To them was assigned the handsomest and most expert chambermaid, a Belgian, whose waist was slenderly and firmly corseted, and who wore a little starched cap that looked like a pronged crown; also, the stateliest and most dignified of flunkies, a fiery-eyed Sicilian, swarthy as coal; and the nimblest of bellboys, the short and stout Luigi—a fellow who was very fond of a joke, and who had changed many places in his time. And a minute later there was a slight tap at the door of the room of the gentleman from San Francisco—the French *maître d'hôtel* had come to find out if the newly arrived guests would dine, and, in the event of an answer in the affirmative—of which, however, there was no doubt—to inform them that the *carte du jour* consisted of crawfish, roast beef, asparagus, pheasants, and so forth. The floor was still rocking under the gentleman from San Francisco—so badly had the atrocious little Italian steamer tossed him about—but, without hurrying, with his own hands, although somewhat clumsily from being unaccustomed to such things, he shut a window that had banged upon the entrance of the *maître d'hôtel* and had let in the odors of the distant kitchen and of the wet flowers in the garden, and with a leisurely precision replied that they would dine, that their table must be placed at a distance from the door, at the farthest end of the dining room, that they would drink local wine and champagne—moderately dry and only slightly chilled. The *maître d'hôtel* concurred in every word of his, in intonations most varied, having, however, but one significance—that there was never a doubt, nor could there possibly be any, about the correctness of the wishes of the gentleman from San Francisco, and that everything would be carried out punctiliously. In conclusion he inclined his head and asked deferentially:

"Will that be all, Sir?"

And, having received a long-drawn-out "Yes" * in answer, he added that the *tarantella* would be danced in the vestibule today—the dancers would be Carmella and Giuseppe, known to all Italy, and to "the entire world of tourists."

"I have seen her on post cards," said the gentleman from San Francisco in a voice devoid of all expression. "About this Giuseppe, now—is he her husband?"

"Her cousin, sir," answered the *maître d'hôtel*.

And, after a little wait, after considering something, the gentleman from San Francisco dismissed him with a nod.

And then he began his preparations anew, as though for a wedding ceremony: he turned on all the electric lights, filling all the mirrors with reflections of light and glitter, of furniture and opened trunks; he began shaving and washing, ringing the bell every minute, while other impatient rings from his wife's and daughter's rooms floated through the entire corridor and interrupted his. And Luigi, in his red apron, was rushing headlong to answer the bell, with an ease peculiar to many stout men, the while he made grimaces of horror that made the chambermaids, running by with glazed porcelain pails in their hands, laugh till they cried. Having knocked on the door with his knuckles, he asked with an assumed timidity, with a respectfulness that verged on idiocy:

"*Ha sonato, signore?* (Did you ring, Sir?)"

And from the other side of the door came an unhurried, grating voice, insultingly polite:

"Yes, come in. . . ." *

What were the thoughts, what were the emotions of the gentleman from San Francisco on this evening, that was of such portent to him? He felt nothing exceptional—for the trouble in this world is just that everything is apparently all too simple! And even if he had sensed within his soul that something was impending, he would, nevertheless, have thought that this thing would not occur for some time to come—in any case, not immediately. Besides that, like everyone who has gone through the rocking of a ship, he wanted very much to eat, was anticipating with enjoyment the first spoonful of soup, the first mouthful of wine, and performed the usual routine of dressing even with a certain degree of exhilaration that left no time for reflections.

Having shaved and washed himself, having inserted several artificial teeth properly, he, standing before a mirror, wetted the remnants of his thick, pearly-gray hair and plastered it down around his swarthy yellow skull, with brushes set in silver; drew a suit of cream-colored silk underwear over his strong old body, beginning to be full at the waist from excesses in food, and put on silk socks and dancing slippers on his shriveled, splayed feet; sitting down, he put in order his black trousers, drawn high by black silk braces, as well as his snowy-white shirt, with the bosom bulging out; put the links through the glossy cuffs, and began the torturous pursuit of the collar button underneath the stiffly starched collar. The floor was still swaying beneath him, the tips of his fingers pained him greatly, the collar button at times nipped hard the flabby skin in the hollow under his Adam's apple, but he was persistent, and finally, his eyes glittering from the exertion, his face all livid from the collar that was choking his throat—a collar far too tight—he did contrive to accomplish his task, and sat down in exhaustion in front of the pier glass, reflected in it from head to foot, a reflection that was repeated in all the other mirrors.

"Oh, this is dreadful!" he muttered, letting his strong bald head drop, and without trying to understand, without reflecting, just what, precisely, was dreadful; then, with an accustomed and attentive glance, he inspected his stubby fingers, with gouty hardenings at the joints, and his convex nails of an almond color, repeating, with conviction: "This is dreadful. . . ."

But at this point the second gong sonorously, as in some heathen temple, reverberated through the entire house. And, getting up quickly from his seat, the gentleman from San Francisco tightened his collar with the necktie and his stomach by means of the low-cut vest, put on his tuxedo, drew out his cuffs, scrutinized himself once more in the mirror. . . . This Carmella, swarthy, with eyes which she knew well how to use most effectively, resembling a mulatto woman, clad in a dress of many colors, with the color of orange predominant, must dance exceptionally, he reflected. And, stepping briskly out of his room and walking over the carpet to the next one—his wife's—he asked, loudly, if they would be ready soon?

"In five minutes, Dad!" a girl's voice, ringing and by now gay, responded from the other side of the door.

"Very well," said the gentleman from San Francisco.

And, leisurely, he walked down red-carpeted corridors and staircases, descending in search of the reading room. The servants he met stood aside and hugged the wall to let him pass, but he kept on his way as though he had never even noticed them. An old woman who was late for dinner, already stooping, with milky hair, but *décolletée* in a light-gray gown of silk, was hurrying with all her might, but drolly, in a henlike manner, and he easily outstripped her. Near the glass doors of the dining room, where all the guests had already assembled and were beginning their dinner, he stopped before a little table piled with boxes of cigars and Egyptian cigarettes, took a large Manila cigar, and tossed three *lire* upon the little table; upon the closed veranda he glanced, in passing, through the open window; out of the darkness he felt a breath of the balmy air upon him, thought he saw the tip of an ancient palm that had flung wide across the stars its fronds, which seemed gigantic, heard the distant, even noise of the sea floating in to him. . . . In the reading room—snug, quiet, and illuminated only above the tables, some gray-haired German was standing, rustling the newspapers—unkempt, resembling Ibsen, in round silver spectacles and with the astonished eyes of a madman. Having scrutinized him coldly, the gentleman from San Francisco sat down in a deep leather chair in a corner near a green-shaded lamp, put on his pince-nez, twitching his head because his collar was choking him, and hid himself completely behind the newspaper sheet. He rapidly ran through the headlines of certain items, read a few lines about the never-ceasing Balkan war, with an accustomed gesture turned the newspaper over— when suddenly the lines flared up before him with a glassy glare, his neck became taut, his eyes bulged, the pince-nez flew off his nose. . . . He lunged forward, tried to swallow some air—and gasped wildly; his lower jaw sank, lighting up his entire mouth with the reflection of the gold fillings; his head dropped back on his shoulder and began to sway; the bosom of his shirt bulged out like a basket—and his whole body, squirming, his heels catching the carpet, slid downward to the floor, desperately struggling with Someone.

Had the German not been in the reading room, the personnel of the hotel would have managed, quickly and adroitly, to hush up this dreadful occurrence; instantly, through back passages, seizing him by the head and feet, they would have rushed off the gentleman from San

Francisco as far away as possible—and never a soul among the guests would have found out what he had been up to. But the German had dashed out of the reading room with a scream—he had aroused the entire house, the entire dining room. And many jumped up from their meal, overturning their chairs; many, paling, ran toward the reading room. "What—what has happened?" was heard in all languages—and no one gave a sensible answer, no one comprehended anything, since even up to now men are amazed most of all by death, and will not, under any circumstances, believe in it. The proprietor dashed from one guest to another, trying to detain those who were running away and to pacify them with hasty assurances that this was just a trifling occurrence, a slight fainting spell of a certain gentleman from San Francisco. . . . But no one listened to him; many had seen the waiters and bellboys tearing the necktie, the vest, and the rumpled tuxedo off this gentleman, and even, for some reason or other, the dancing slippers off his splayed feet, clad in black silk. But he was still struggling. He was still obdurately wrestling with death; he absolutely refused to yield to her, who had so unexpectedly and churlishly fallen upon him. His head was swaying, he rattled hoarsely, like one with his throat cut; his eyes had rolled up, like a drunkard's. . . . When he was hurriedly carried in and laid upon a bed in room No. 43—the smallest, the poorest, the dampest, and the coldest, situated at the end of the bottom corridor—his daughter ran in, with her hair down, in a little dressing gown that had flown open, her bosom, raised up by the corset, uncovered; then his wife, big and ponderous, already dressed for dinner— her mouth rounded in terror. . . . But by now he had ceased even to bob his head.

A quarter of an hour later everything in the hotel had assumed some semblance of order. But the evening was irreparably spoiled. Some guests, returning to the dining room, finished their dinner, but in silence, with aggrieved countenances, while the proprietor would approach now one group, now another, shrugging his shoulders in polite and yet impotent irritation, feeling himself guilty without guilt, assuring everybody that he understood very well "how unpleasant all this was," and pledging his word that he would take "all measures within his power" to remove this unpleasantness. It was necessary to call off the *tarantella*, all unnecessary electric lights were switched off, the majority of the guests withdrew into the bar, and it became so quiet that one heard distinctly the ticking of the clock in the vestibule, whose sole occupant was a parrot, dully muttering something, fussing in his cage before going to sleep, contriving to doze off at last with one claw ludicrously stretched up to the upper perch. . . . The gentleman from San Francisco was lying upon a cheap iron bed, under coarse woolen blankets, upon which the dull light of a single bulb beat down from the ceiling. An icebag hung down to his moist and cold forehead. The livid face, already dead, was gradually growing cold; the hoarse rattling, expelled from the open mouth, illuminated by the reflection of gold, was growing fainter. This was no longer the gentleman from San Francisco rattling—he no longer existed—but some other. His wife, his daughter, the doctor, and the servants were standing about, gazing at him dully. Suddenly, that which they awaited and feared was consummated—the rattling ceased abruptly. And slowly, slowly, before the eyes of all, a pallor flowed over the face of the man who had died, and his features seemed to grow finer, to become irradiated, with a beauty which had been rightfully his in the long ago. . . .

The proprietor entered. *"Già è morto,"* said the doctor to him in a whisper. The proprietor, his face dispassionate, shrugged his shoulders. The wife, down whose cheeks the tears were quietly coursing, walked up to him and timidly said that the deceased ought now to be carried to his own room.

"Oh, no, Madam," hastily, correctly, but now without any amiability and not in English, but in French, retorted the proprietor, who was not at all interested now in such trifling sums as the arrivals from San Francisco might leave in his coffers. "That is absolutely impossible, Madam," said he, and added in explanation that he valued the apartments occupied by them very much; that, were he to carry out her wishes, everybody in Capri would know it, and the tourists would shun those apartments.

The young lady, who had been gazing at him strangely, sat down on a chair and, stuffing a handkerchief into her mouth, burst into sobs. The wife dried her tears immediately, her face flaring up. She adopted a louder tone, making demands in her own language, and still incredulous of the fact that all respect for them had been completely lost. The proprietor, with a polite dignity, cut her short: if Madam was not pleased with the customs of the hotel, he would not venture to detain her; and he firmly announced that the body must be gotten away this very day, at dawn, that the police had already been notified, and one of the police officers would be here very soon and would carry out all the necessary formalities. Was it possible to secure even a common coffin in Capri, Madam asked? Regrettably, no—it was beyond possibility, and no one would be able to make one in time. It would be necessary to have recourse to something else. . . . For instance—English soda water came in large and long boxes. . . . It was possible to knock the partitions out of such a box. . . .

At night the whole hotel slept. The window in Room No. 43 was opened—it gave out upon a corner of the garden where, near a high stone wall with broken glass upon its crest, a phthisic banana tree was growing; the electric light was switched off; the key was turned in the door, and everybody went away. The dead man remained in the darkness—the blue stars looked down upon him from the sky, a cricket with a pensive insouciance began his song in the wall. . . . In the dimly lit corridor two chambermaids were seated on a window sill, at some darning. Luigi, in slippers, entered with a pile of clothing in his arms.

"Pronto? (All ready?)" he asked solicitously, in a ringing whisper, indicating with his eyes the fearsome door at the end of the corridor. And he waved his hand airily in that direction. . . . *"Partenza!"* he called out in a whisper, as though he were speeding a train, the usual phrase used in Italian depots at the departure of trains—and the chambermaids, choking with silent laughter, let their heads sink on each other's shoulder.

Thereup, hopping softly, he ran up to the very door, gave it the merest tap, and, inclining his head to one side, in a low voice asked with the utmost deference:

"Ha sonato, signore?"

And, squeezing his throat, thrusting out his lower jaw, in a grating voice, slowly and sadly, he answered his own question, as though from the other side of the door:

"Yes, come in. . . ." *

And at dawn, when it had become light beyond the window of room No. 43, and a humid wind had begun to rustle the tattered leaves of the banana tree; when the blue sky of morning had lifted and spread out over the Island of Capri, and the pure and clear-cut summit of Monte Solaro had grown aureate against the sun that was rising beyond the distant blue mountains of Italy; when the stonemasons, who were repairing the tourists' paths on the island, had set out to work— a long box that had formerly been used for soda water was brought to room No. 43. Soon it became very heavy, and was pressing hard against the knees of the junior porter, who bore it off briskly on a one-horse cab over the white paved highway that sinuously wound to and fro over the slopes of Capri, among the stone walls and the vineyards, ever downward, to the very sea. The cabby, a puny little man with reddened eyes, in an old, wretched jacket with short sleeves, and in trodden-down shoes, was undergoing the aftereffects of drink—he had diced the whole night through in a *trattoria,* and kept on lashing his sturdy little horse, tricked out in the Sicilian fashion, with all sorts of little bells livelily jingling upon the bridle with its tufts of colored wool and upon the brass points of its high pad; with a yard-long feather stuck in its cropped forelock—a feather that shook as the horse ran. The cabby kept silent; he was weighed down by his shift-lessness, his vices—by the fact that he had, that night, lost to the last mite all those coppers with which his pockets had been filled. But the morning was fresh; in air such as this, with the sea all around, under the morning sky, the aftereffects of drink quickly evaporate and a man is soon restored to a carefree mood, and the cabby was furthermore consoled by that unexpected sum, the opportunity to earn which had been granted him by some gentleman from San Francisco, whose lifeless head was bobbing from side to side in the box at his back. . . . The little steamer—a beetle lying far down below, against the tender and vivid deep-blue with which the Bay of Naples is so densely and highly flooded—was already blowing its final whistles, that reverberated loudly all over the island, whose every bend, every ridge, every stone, was as distinctly visible from every point as if there were absolutely no such thing as atmosphere. Near the wharf the junior porter was joined by the senior, who was speed-ing with the daughter and wife of the gentleman from San Francisco in his automobile—they were pale, with eyes hollow from tears and a sleepless night. And ten minutes later the little steamer was again chugging through the water, again running toward Sorrento, toward Castellamare, carrying away from Capri, for all time, the family from San Francisco. . . . And again peace and quiet resumed their reign upon the island.

Upon this island, two thousand years ago, had lived a man who had become completely enmeshed in his cruel and foul deeds, who had for some reason seized the power over millions of people in his hands, and who, having himself lost his head at the senselessness of this power and from the fear of death by assassination lurking in ambush behind every corner, had committed cruelties beyond all measure—and humankind has remembered him for all time; and those who, in their collusion, just as incomprehensively and, in substance, just as cruelly as he, reign at present in power over this world, gather from all over the earth to gaze upon the ruins of that stone villa where he had dwelt on one of the steepest ascents of the island. On this splendid morning all those who had come to Capri for just this purpose were still sleeping in the hotels, although toward their entrances were already being led little mouse-gray burros with red saddles, upon which, after awaking and sating themselves with food, Americans and Germans, men and women, young and old, would again clamber upon ponderously this day, and after whom would again run the old Caprian beggarwomen, with sticks in their gnarled hands —would run over stone paths, and always uphill, up to the very summit of Mount Tiberio.

Set at rest by the fact that the dead old man from San Francisco, who had likewise been planning to go with them but instead of that had only frightened them with a *memento mori,* had already been shipped off to Naples, the travelers slept on heavily, and the quiet of the island was still undisturbed, the shops in the city were still shut. The market place on the *piazetta* alone was carrying on traffic—in fish and greens; and the people there were all simple folk, among whom, without anything to do, as always, was standing Lorenzo the boatman, famous all over Italy—a tall old man, a carefree rake and a handsome fellow, who had served more than once as a model to many artists; he had brought, and had already sold for a song, two lobsters that he had caught that night and which were already rustling in the apron of the cook of that very hotel where the family from San Francisco had passed the night, and now he could afford to stand in calm idleness even until the evening, looking about him with a kingly bearing (a little trick of his), consciously picturesque with his tatters, clay pipe, and a red woolen *beretta* drooping over one ear.

And along the precipices of Monte Solaro, upon the ancient Phoenician road hewn out of the crags, down its stone steps, two mountaineers of Abruzzi were descending from Anacapri. One had bagpipes under his leathern mantle—a large bag made from the skin of a she-goat, with two pipes; the other had something in the nature of wooden Pan's-reeds. They went on—and all the land, joyous, splendid, sunflooded, spread out below them: the stony humps of the island, which was lying almost in its entirety at their feet; and that faerylike deep blue in which it was aswim; and the radiant morning vapors over the sea, toward the east, under the blinding sun, that was now beating down hotly, rising ever higher and higher; and, still in their morning vagueness, the mistily azure massive outlines of Italy, of her mountains near and far, whose beauty human speech is impotent to express. . . . Halfway down the pipers slackened their pace; over the path, within a grotto in the craggy side of Monte Solaro, all illumined by the sun, all bathed in its warmth and glow, in snowy-white raiment of gypsum, and in a royal crown, golden-rusty from inclement weathers, stood the Mother of God, meek and gracious, Her orbs lifted up to heaven, to the eternal and happy abodes of Her thrice-blessed Son. The pipers bared their heads, put their reeds to their lips—and there poured forth their naïve and humbly jubilant praises to the sun, to the morning, to Her, the Immaculate Intercessor for all those who suffer in this evil and beautiful world, and to Him Who had been born of Her womb in a cavern at Bethlehem, in a poor shepherd's shelter in the distant land of Judaea. . . .

Meanwhile, the body of the dead old man from San Francisco was returning to its home, to a grave on the shores of the New World. Having gone through many humiliations, through much human neglect, having wandered for a week from one port warehouse to another, it had finally gotten once more on board that same famous ship upon which but so recently, with so much deference, he had been borne to the Old World. But now he was already being concealed from the quick —he was lowered in his tarred coffin deep into the black hold. And once more the ship was sailing on and on upon its long sea voyage. In the nighttime it sailed past the Island of Capri, and, to one watching them from the island, there was something sad about the ship's lights slowly disappearing over the dark sea. But upon the ship itself, in its brilliant *salons* resplendent with lusters and marbles, there was a crowded ball that night, as usual.

There was a ball on the second night also, and on the third—again in the midst of a raging snowstorm, whirling over an ocean booming like a funeral mass, and heaving in mountains trapped out in mourning by the silver spindrift. The innumerable fiery eyes of the ship that was retreating into the night and the snow gale were barely visible for the snow to the Devil watching from the crags of Gibraltar, from the stony gateway of two worlds. The Devil was as enormous as a cliff, but the ship was still more enormous than he; many-tiered, many-funneled, created by the pride of the New Man with an ancient heart. The snow gale smote upon its rigging and wide-throated funnels, hoary from the snow, but the ship was steadfast, firm, majestic—and awesome. Upon its topmost deck were reared, in their solitude among the snowy whirlwinds, those snug, dimly lit chambers where, plunged in a light and uneasy slumber, was its ponderous guide, who resembled a heathen idol, reigning over the entire ship. He heard the pained howlings and the ferocious squealings of the storm-stifled siren, but soothed himself by the proximity of that which, in the final summing up, was incomprehensive even to himself, that which was on the other side of his wall: that large cabin, which had the appearance of being armored and was being constantly filled by the mysterious rumbling, quivering, and crisp sputtering of blue flames, flaring up and exploding around the pale-faced operator with a metal half-hoop upon his head. In the very depths, in the under-water womb of the "Atlantida," were the thirty-thousand-pound masses of boilers and of all sorts of other machinery—dully glittering with steel, hissing out steam and exuding oil and boiling water—of that kitchen, made red-hot from infernal furnaces underneath, wherein was brewing the motion of the ship. Forces, fearful in their concentration, were bubbling, were being transmitted to its very keel, into an endlessly long catacomb, into a tunnel, illuminated by electricity, wherein slowly, with an inexorability that was crushing to the human soul, was revolving within its oily couch the gigantean shaft, exactly like a living monster that had stretched itself out in this tunnel. Meanwhile, amidship the "Atlantida," its warm and luxurious cabins, its dining halls and ballrooms, poured forth radiance and joyousness, were humming with the voices of a well-dressed gathering, were sweetly odorous with fresh flowers, and the strains of the stringed orchestra were their song. And again excruciatingly writhed and at intervals came together among this throng, among this glitter of lights, silks, diamonds, and bared feminine shoulders, the supple pair of hired lovers; the sinfully modest, very pretty young woman, with eyelashes cast down, with a chaste coiffure, and the well-built young man, with black hair that seemed to be pasted on, with his face pale from powder, shod in the most elegant of patent-leather footgear, clad in a tight-fitting dress coat with long tails—an Adonis who resembled a huge leech. And none knew that, already for a long time, this pair had grown weary of languishing dissemblingly in their blissful torment to the sounds of the shamelessly sad music—nor that, far below, at the bottom of the black hold, stood a tarred coffin, in close proximity to the somber and sultry depths of the ship that was toilsomely overpowering the darkness, the ocean, the snowstorm. . . .

1915

Alexander Ivanovich

Kuprin

1 8 7 0 - 1 9 3 8

Perhaps the greatest of living Russian novelists is Kuprin—exalted, hysterical, sentimental, Rabelaisian Kuprin.

STEPHEN GRAHAM (1916)

ALEXANDER IVANOVICH KUPRIN was born in a provincial town in Central Russia. He began his schooling at six, going on to the Second Cadet Corps in Moscow and, finally, after graduation from a military school, he entered the army. Dropping out after a few years, he was, by turns, poet, columnist, roustabout, surveyor, actor, singer, choir-singer, factory worker, medical student, hunter, and fisherman on the Black Sea. In a thinly veiled self-portrait in *Yama* he also mentions stoking on the Sea of Azov, circus-riding, tobacco-growing, typesetting and carpentering.

If Chekhov is the *Wunderkind* of Russian literature, Kuprin is decidedly its *enfant terrible*. But whereas Chekhov's· mantle is dovegray, Kuprin wears a coat of many colors. He received his cachet early in his career from none other than Leo Tolstoi: "Kuprin is the only man of the rising generation who writes with truth and sincerity." He began writing in 1884, but did not gain recognition until 1896, with *Moloch* (a story of factory life) ; his first collection of stories appeared in 1903; *The Duel,* a novel exposing the bestial senselessness of army life (and clericalism) created a furore and made him famous, coming as it did in 1905, after the defeat of Russia's graft-ridden armed forces at the hands of the Japanese. His *Yama:*

The Pit (1904-14-15-29) made him world-famous and, despite all censors and censorships, sold in millions of copies in practically as many languages as *Robinson Crusoe*.

Kuprin has been styled, and most aptly, the Poet of Life. Amphitheatrov called him a highly talented disciple of Chekhov and heir to Chekhov's sincerity and fine atomistic style, and compared him as an artistic storyteller with Tolstoi before the latter's conversion to religion. (Kuprin will in no instance suffer if you compare his *Horse Thieves* with Chekhov's story of the same name; or his *Emerald* with Tolstoi's *Yardstick*; or his *Golden Rooster* with Bunin's *The Third Cock-Crow*; or even his *Lestrygonians* with the *Hunting Sketches* of Turgenev!)

Purely as a storyteller, and leaving all matters of style and literary stature out of the question, Kuprin ranks with the greatest. (Perhaps that is why he has written so keenly and appreciatively of Kipling and London.) His range of subjects is enormous; his powers of observation and his versatility are extraordinary. Some of his picaresques (such as *The Insult,* showing all the thieving skills and techniques, or *Off the Street,* a monologue) are sheer *tours de force.* In *The Liquid Sun* he is an innovator, with Briussov and Alexei Tolstoi, of the pseudoscientific thriller in Russia. He writes of newspapermen, bohemians, priests, thieves, prostitutes, army men, muzhiks, Jews, Tatars, gypsies, actors, clowns, circus people, athletes, merchants, jockeys, fishermen, hunters, sailors. And all *con*

amore. There are sentimental stories and humorous stories (and parodies) ; animal stories and flower stories, stories for children—and for neuropaths; one story is dedicated to a circus clown, another to a jockey— and a third to a race horse. His popularity was fantastic: the publication of a new Kuprin story was bill-posted like a circus; his eating (and drinking) exploits were the talk of Petersburg.

When the present writer saw him in 1931, Kuprin was editing a Russian periodical in Paris at some munificent sum in francs which amounted to $2.40 a week. He was no longer the Kuprin of the Café Vienna in Petersburg, but was still the Poet of Life. Merely to see Rastelli juggling for an hour and a half at the Cirque Medrano would be a memorable experience enough; to see him and at the same time hear Kuprin's *expertise* on the great art of juggling as demonstrated by a genius was a unique one.

He was at the time dreaming of returning to Russia disguised as a Tatar—he was very proud of his Tatar blood. (He had left Russia along with the staff of Yudenich, just as Bunin had left it with Denikin.) But he returned to the Soviets openly (about 1936) and was met with open arms and acclamation; special new editions of his works were brought out, and he wrote with amazement of the New Russia. He had realized his dream, and died in his native land.

The worst one can say of Kuprin is that he is, occasionally, oversentimental; the harshest criticism of him is Merezhcovski's personal comment (a perfect companion-piece to Kuprin's comment on Merezhcovski): "Alexander Ivanovich is superb as a creative artist, but, really, he is hardly top-notch as a scholar."

But, whatever his shortcomings, boring the reader is not one of them. It is almost impossible to be anything but fascinated with Kuprin; he is vigorous and invigorating, and his boundless wonder at the infinite spectacle of life, his love of life and the fullness thereof, make him the perfect antidote to Dostoievski. If the reader should surmise that the Editor considers him the most lovable of the great writing Russians, the reader will not have surmised wrongly.

The nine volumes of Kuprin available in English represent about a quarter of his work. Fortunately, only one of these translations (*Sasha*) is utterly incompetent; unfortunately, it contains some of Kuprin's best stories, not translated into English elsewhere.

The Bracelet of Garnets

L. van Beethoven
2 Son. (Op. 2, No. 2.)
Largo Appassionato

I

IN THE MIDDLE of August, just before the birth of the new moon, came those spells of abominable weather which are so peculiar to the northern marge of the Black Sea. Now, for days on end, a thick fog would

Translated by Bernard Guilbert Guerney. Copyright, 1943, by the Vanguard Press, Inc.

lie heavy over earth and sea, and at such times the enormous siren of the lighthouse would bellow day and night, for all the world like an infuriated bull. Or, from morning till night, a drizzle fell, fine as water-dust, transforming the clayey roads and paths into uniform black mud, in which carts and carriages would become stuck for a long time. Or else a fierce hurricane would start blowing from the Nor'-west, from the direction of the steppes; because of it the tips of the trees swayed, bending low and then straightening up, just like waves in a storm; the iron roofs of the villas rumbled of nights, and it sounded as if some-one were running over them in ironshod boots, the window frames shook, doors banged, and there was wild yowling in the hearth-chimneys. Several fishing barks had lost their way at sea, while two had not returned at all: only a fortnight later were the bodies of the fisher-men cast up on different spots along the shore.

The residents of the suburban seaside resort—for the most part Greeks and Jews, in love with life and mercurial, like all Southerners—were hastily shifting to town. Over the highway, now grown quaggy, stretched an endless succession of moving vans, loaded to overflowing with all sorts of household effects: mattresses, divans, trunks, chairs, washstands, samovars. It was a sorry, sad and, at the same time, a repulsive sight to look through the cheesecloth turbidity of the rain at these pitiful belongings, which seemed so shabby, grimy, and beggarly —to look at the chambermaids and cooks perched upon the sodden tar-paulins atop the moving vans, with such things as flatirons, tins and baskets in their hands—to look at the sweat-covered, exhausted horses, forever halting, their knees trembling, steaming and with their sides heaving hard—to look at the hoarsely cursing drivers, wrapped up in matting against the rain. It was still sadder to see the forsaken summer villas, with their suddenly acquired roominess, their emptiness and barrenness, their mangled flower beds, broken windowpanes, aban-doned dogs, and all sorts of vacation-time rubbish—cigarette and cigar butts, scraps of paper, shards, little boxes and medicine bottles.

Toward the beginning of September, however, the weather changed, suddenly and abruptly. There suddenly came the time of calm, un-clouded days, so clear, sunny and warm that not even July had their like. Upon the dried, mown fields, upon their prickly, yellowed stubble, summer gossamer began to gleam with the glitter of mica. The trees, now once more at peace, were shedding their yellow leaves, noiselessly and submissively.

Princess Vera Nicolaievna Sheyina, wife of the local Marshal of Nobility, had been unable to move from her summer residence, since the alterations in her town house had not yet been completed. And now she rejoiced exceedingly over the coming of the enchanting days, the serenity, the solitude, the pure air, the twittering of the swallows flocking on the telegraph wires preparatory to their migration, and the caressing, briny breeze, blowing faintly from the sea.

II

Besides, today—the seventeenth of September—was her birthday. Through the endearing, distant recollections of childhood she always loved this day, and always expected it to bring some happiness, some wonder. Her husband, as he was leaving for the city that morning on urgent matters, had placed upon her little night-table a case containing splendid earrings of pear-shaped pearls, and this present had put her in a still gayer mood.

She was all alone in the house. Her bachelor brother, Nicolai, who ordinarily lived with them, had also gone off to town—to appear at court, where he was an assistant District Attorney. Her husband had promised to bring home only a few people to dinner, and those only their most intimate friends. It was rather fortunate that her birthday coincided with vacation time. In town they would have had to go to the expense of a grand formal dinner—even, likely as not, that of a ball; whereas here in the country house they could manage with the very least expenditures. Prince Sheyin, notwithstanding his prominent position in society—and, perhaps, even owing to it—could barely make ends meet. His enormous family estate had been all but ruined by his ancestors, yet one had of necessity to live above one's means—to hold receptions, contribute to charities, dress well, keep horses, and so forth. Princess Vera, whose former passionate love for her husband had long since passed into a sense of firm, faithful, true friendship, put forth every exertion to help the Prince ward off complete financial ruin. Without his perceiving it, she denied herself in many things and, as far as possible, economized in household matters.

Just now she was walking in the garden and, with garden shears, was carefully cutting flowers for the dinner table. The flower beds had become thinned out and had a disorderly appearance. Varicolored and dark-scarlet clove-gillyflowers were blooming their last, as were the stock-flowers, half in blossoms and half in slender, green pods that gave off an odor of cabbage; the rose bushes still yielded—for the third time this summer—buds and roses, but already dwarfed and rare, just as though they had degenerated. But then the dahlias, peonies, and asters bloomed in full pomp, with their chilly, haughty beauty, diffusing through the vibrant air their autumnal herbaceous, pensive fragrance. The other flowers, after their luxuriant love and their inordinate maternity of summer, were gently showering countless seeds of future life upon the ground.

The familiar sounds of a three-toned automobile horn came from the road. It was Anna Nicolaievna Friesse, Vera's sister, driving up; she had promised that morning over the telephone to come and help the Princess with household tasks and in receiving the guests.

Her fine sense of hearing had not deceived Vera. She went to meet her sister. In a few minutes an elegant limousine came to an abrupt stop near the gates of the country house and the chauffeur, nimbly hopping off his seat, flung the car door open.

The sisters kissed each other joyously. From their earliest childhood they had been attached to each other in warm and considerate friendship. In appearance they were unlike each other, to the verge of oddity. The elder, Vera, with her tall, sinuous figure, her tender yet chill and proud face, her splendidly beautiful although rather large hands, and that enchanting slope of the shoulders which may be seen in antique miniatures, had taken after her mother, who had been an English beauty. The younger, Anna, had on the other hand inherited the Mongolian blood of her father, a Tatar Prince, whose grandfather had become a Christian only at the beginning of the nineteenth century, and whose proud line went back to none other than Tamerlane—or Lang-Temir, as her father proudly styled in Tatar this great blood-ogre. She was half a head shorter than her sister, somewhat broad in the shoulders, very much alive, frivolous, and much given to mockery. Her face was of a pronounced Mongol type, with rather noticeable cheekbones, small narrow eyes (which, to boot, she was forever puckering up because of her nearsightedness), and a haughty expression about the tiny, sensuous mouth—especially the full lower lip, a trifle outthrust. Nevertheless, this face captivated one with some elusive and incomprehensible charm, which lay, perhaps, in her smile, and, perhaps, in the deep muliebrity of all the features—also, perhaps, in a piquant, provokingly coquettish mimicry. Her graceful homeliness incited and attracted the attention of men far more frequently and powerfully than the aristocratic beauty of her sister.

She was married to a very rich and very stupid man who did nothing whatsoever but was connected with some benevolent institution and bore the title of Gentleman-in-Waiting. She could not stand her husband, but just the same had borne him two children, a boy and a girl, after which she had resolved to have no more—and had stuck to her resolution. But as for Vera, she avidly longed for children and even—so it seemed to her—the more the merrier; yet for some reason she had none, and morbidly and vehemently adored her sister's pretty and anemic little children, always decorous and obedient, with pale, pasty faces and curled, flaxen, doll-like hair.

Anna was made up entirely of jolly lackadaisicalness and endearing (occasionally even strange) contradictions. She willingly yielded to the riskiest flirtations in all the capitals and all the health resorts of Europe, yet was never unfaithful to her husband, whom, however, she contemptuously held up to ridicule, both to his face and behind his back; she was extravagant, inordinately fond of games of chance, of dances, of dangerous thrills and piquant sights, and visited dubious cafés when abroad; yet at the same time she was distinguished by her generous kindliness and a deep, sincere piety, which had even impelled her to adopt Catholicism in secret. Her back, bosom, and shoulders were of rare beauty; when setting out for grand affairs she exposed herself far beyond the limits permitted by decorum and fashion, yet it was said that under her low décolletée she always wore a hair shirt.

Vera, however, was severely simple, coldly and somewhat haughtily amiable to everybody, independent, and regally calm.

III

"My God, how charming everything is here! How charming!" Anna was saying, walking with quick and small steps along the path with her sister. "If possible, let's sit a while on the little bench over the precipice. It's such a long while since I've seen the sea. And what wonderful air—one has but to breathe it and the heart rejoices. Last summer in the Crimea, at Miskhora, I made an amazing discovery. Do you know what odor sea water gives off at high tide? It smells of mignonettes—if you can imagine such a thing."

"You're a dreamer," Vera smiled kindly.

"No, no, I also remember the time when everybody laughed at me because I said that moonlight has a certain rosy tinge. But just the other day Boritski, the artist—the same chap who's doing my portrait—agreed that I was right, and that artists have long known this."

"This artist—is he your new infatuation?"

"You're always inventing something of the sort!" Anna began laughing and, quickly approaching the very brink of the precipice that fell in a sheer wall deep to the sea far below, looked downward and suddenly cried out in horror and staggered back with a blanched face.

"Oh, how high!" she uttered in a voice quavering and suddenly growing faint. "When I look down from such a height I always feel a delectable and hateful sensation in my breasts. And my toes feel pinched. And yet it draws me—it draws me—"

She was about to lean once more over the precipice, but her sister stopped her.

"Anna, my dear, for God's sake! My own head turns when you lean over. Sit down, I beg you."

"Oh, very well, very well; there, I've sat down! But do look—what beauty, what joy; one simply can't tire of looking at it. If you but knew how grateful I am to God for all the miracles He has wrought for us!"

Both fell into thought for a moment. Far, far below them lay the sea. From the bench one could not see the shore, and because of that the sensation of the infinity and grandeur of the sea's expanse was still further intensified. The water was caressingly calm and of a joyous blue, showing lightly in slanting smooth streaks only where the current was, and passing into a richly blue, deep color at the horizon.

The fishing boats, which the eye could distinguish only with difficulty, so tiny did they seem, were immovably slumbering on the smooth expanse of the sea, not far from shore; while farther on, without moving forward, as though it were floating motionless in the air, was a three-masted ship, clad from the tips of its masts to its deck in graceful sails, bellying in the wind.

"I understand you," said the elder sister thoughtfully. "But in my case the feeling is unlike yours, somehow. When I first see the sea after a long time, it not only agitates me but also makes me rejoice, and overwhelms me. As though I were seeing, for the first time, a tremendous, solemn miracle. But later, when I grow used to it, it begins to crush me with its flat void. I feel depression when I look at it, and shortly try to avoid looking at it further. It becomes a bore."

Anna smiled.

"What are you smiling at?" asked the sister.

"Last summer," said Anna slyly, "a great cavalcade of us set out from Yalta to Uch-Kosh. It lies beyond the forestry reservations, above the waterfall. At first we ran into a cloud: it was very damp and we could see but poorly, but we kept on mounting even higher, up a steep, narrow path between pines. And, somehow, suddenly, the forest came to an end, and we emerged from the mist. Just imagine the picture: a narrow little platform on the crag, and, at our feet, a precipice. The hamlets below seemed no bigger than matchboxes; the forests and gardens looked like stubby grass. The whole region goes down to the sea, just like a relief map. And, farther on—the sea! For fifty, for a hundred miles ahead. It seemed to me that I was hovering in the air and that, at any second, I would start flying. What beauty—what buoyancy! I turned around and, enraptured, said to the guide: 'Splendid, isn't it, Seid-Ogli?' But he merely clicked his tongue: 'Eh, leddy, what a bore all this are to me. Ev-ery day we see him.' "

"Thanks for the comparison," Vera laughed. "No, what I meant to convey is merely that we Northerners are never fated to grasp the bewitching beauty of the sea. I love the forest. Do you remember the forest in our Egorovsk? Could it possibly ever become tedious? Those pines! And what mosses! And what of the poisonous mushrooms? They looked as if they were made of red satin and embroidered with white pearls. How quiet it was—and cool."

"I have no great preferences; I love everything," answered Anna. "But most of all I love my little sister, my level-headed Verenka. There are but the two of us in the world."

She embraced her elder sister and snuggled up to her, cheek to cheek. And suddenly she recalled something.

"My, how very silly I am! Here we are, sitting and discussing nature just as in a novel, and yet I've forgotten all about my present. Here, look! I'm only afraid you mayn't like it."

She took out of her small handbag a tiny notebook in a striking binding; against a background of blue velvet, rubbed and turned drab from time, wound a dull gold design in filigree, of rare intricacy, exquisiteness and beauty—evidently a labor of love from the hands of some skillful and patient artist. The book was attached to a small gold chain, as fine as a thread; the leaves in the middle had been replaced by tablets of elephant ivory.

"What a splendid thing! Bewitching!" said Vera, and kissed her sister. "Thank you. Wherever did you acquire such a treasure?"

"In a certain antique shop. Surely you know my weakness for rummaging among old odds and ends. That's how I stumbled upon this prayer book. Look—can you see how the ornament here forms the figure of the Cross? True, I found only the binding—everything else I had to think up: the leaves, the clasps, the pencil. But Molineux absolutely refused to understand me, no matter how I explained things to him. The clasps were supposed to be in the same style as the entire design, of old, dull gold, finely carved—but God knows what he made out of them. But then the little chain is an authentic Venetian one, very ancient."

Vera caressingly stroked the exquisite binding.

"What profound antiquity! How old can this book be?" she asked.

"I'm afraid to give any exact date. About the end of the seventeenth century, or the middle of the eighteenth."

"How strange," said Vera with a pensive smile. "Here I am holding in my hand an object which, perhaps, touched the hands of the Marquise de Pompadour, or of Antoinette the Queen herself. . . . But do you know, Anna—it's only you who could have gotten the puckish idea of making a lady's notebook out of a prayerbook. However, let's go and see what's going on in the house."

They went toward the house over a great stone terrace, screened on all sides by dense espaliers of Isabella grapes. The black, copious clusters, emitting a faint odor of garden strawberries, hung heavily among the greenery, here and there touched with gold by the sun. A green half-light was diffused through the whole terrace, making the two feminine faces suddenly appear pale.

"Are you going to order the tables to be set here?" asked Anna.

"Why, I thought of that myself. But the evenings are so cool now; the dining-room would be better. However, the men can come out here to smoke."

"Anybody interesting coming?"

"I don't know yet. All I know is that Grandfather will be here."

"Ah, darling Grandfather! How lovely!" Anna cried out and clapped her hands. "It seems as if I haven't seen him for a century."

"Vassya's sister is coming, and, I believe, Professor Speshnicov. I thought I'd simply go mad yesterday, Annenka. You know that both the Professor and Grandfather like a good dinner, but you can't buy anything either here or in town, for love or money. Luka managed to obtain some quail—probably had ordered some hunter he knows to get them—and is now planning to do something with them. We managed to get some roast beef that isn't so bad. Ah, the inevitable roast beef! The lobsters, though, are very good."

"Come, now, things aren't so *very* bad. Don't upset yourself. However, confidentially, you yourself have a weakness for dainty eating."

"But there will also be an uncommon thing or two. This morning a fisherman brought in what they call a sea-rooster. It's simply some sort of a monster! Actually frightful to look at."

Anna, who was inordinately curious, immediately demanded that the sea-rooster be brought for her to look at.

Luka, the tall, clean-shaven, yellow-faced chef, came with a large, oval white tub, which he carried with difficulty and great care by the two projecting ears, being afraid of splashing water on the parquet floor.

"Twelve and a half pounds, Your Highness," said he, with the pride peculiar to chefs. "We weighed it a little while ago."

The fish was too large for the tub and was lying on the bottom, with its tail turned up. Its scales gave off a sheen of gold, its fins were of a bright red color, while spreading at right angles from its enormous, ravenous maw were two long wings of tender blue, pleated like fans. The sea-rooster was still alive, and its gills were working hard.

The younger sister cautiously touched the head of the fish with her little finger. But the sea-rooster suddenly plashed with its tail, and Anna jerked her hand away with a squeal.

"Please not to worry, Your Highness; everything will be done first class," said the chef, evidently understanding Vera's apprehensions. "Just now a Bulgarian brought in two muskmelons. Pineapple variety. Something in the nature of cantaloupes, like, only they're 'way more aromatic. And I'd also like to ask Your Highness what sauce you'd care to order served with this here rooster: Tatar or Polonaise? Or maybe simply with buttered toast?"

"Do as you know best. You can go now," the Princess dismissed him.

IV

The guests began arriving after five. Prince Vassilii Lvovich brought with him his widowed sister, Liudmilla Lvovna, a Dyrassova by marriage—a corpulent, kindhearted, and unusually silent woman; a worldly, young, rich good-for-nothing and roué, one Vassiuchuk, whom the whole town knew under that familiar name—he was the life of every party because of his ability to sing and declaim, as well as to put on *tableaux vivants,* pageants and charity bazaars; Jennie Reiter, the famous pianiste, who had been Princess Vera's closest friend in the Smolnyi Institute, and Vera's brother, Nicolai Nicolaievich. After that, Anna's husband arrived in a car with the clean-shaven, stout, hideously huge Professor Speshnicov, and Von Zeck, the Lieutenant Governor. The latest of all to arrive was General Anossov, in a fine hired landau, accompanied by two officers: Staff Colonel Ponomarev—a prematurely aged, gaunt, jaundiced man, exhausted by overwhelming administrative tasks, and Lieutenant Bahtinski of the Hussar Guards, who was celebrated in Petersburg as the best of dancers and an incomparable cotillon leader.

General Anossov, an obese, tall, silvery ancient, was ponderously getting down from the footrest, holding with one hand to a bar on the driver's seat and with the other to the back of the carriage. In his left hand he held an ear-trumpet and in his right a rubber-tipped cane. He had a big, coarse, red face with a fleshy nose, and with that good-natured, grandiose expression, just the least bit contemptuous, in his puckered-up eyes, with radiating, puffy semicircles around them, which is peculiar to manly and simple people who have faced danger and death frequently and close at hand. Both sisters, recognizing him from afar, ran up to the carriage at precisely the right moment to hold him up under the arms on either side, half in jest and half in earnest.

"Just as if . . . I were a high ecclesiastic!" said the General, in a kindly, rather hoarse voice.

"Grandpa—dear little Grandpa!" Vera was saying in a tone of light reproach. "We expect you every day, and yet you never as much as show your face."

"Grandpa has lost all conscience in our South," Anna began laughing. "One might, at least, remember one's goddaughter. But no, you carry on like a Don Juan, you shameless fellow, and have forgotten that we even exist."

The General, baring his majestic head, kissed the hands of each sister in turn, then kissed their cheeks, and, once more, their hands.

"My dear little girls! Hold on, don't scold!" he was saying, gasping at every word, due to his asthma of many years. " 'Pon my word . . . all these miserable pill-dispensers . . . made me bathe my rheumatics all summer long . . . in some sort of filthy cranberry jelly . . . that had an awful smell . . . and they didn't succeed in washing 'em out of me after all. . . . You're the first people . . . I'm visiting. . . . Awfully glad to see you. . . . How are things? You, Verochka, are altogether an English lady . . . you've taken on . . . an absolute resemblance to your departed mother. . . . When are you going to invite me to stand godfather?"

"Oh, never, Grandpa, I'm afraid—"

"Don't give up hope . . . you've all life ahead of you. Pray to God. . . . But you, Anya, haven't changed a bit. . . . Even at sixty . . . you'll be the selfsame giddy grasshopper. I almost forgot. Allow me to present *Messieurs les officiers*—"

"I had the honor long ago!" said Colonel Ponomarev, bowing.

"I was presented to the Princess in Petersburg," the Hussar chimed in.

"Well, in that case, Anya, may I present to you Lieutenant Bahtinski. A dancer and a rowdy, but a good cavalryman. Bahtinski, take out of the carriage whatever is there, my dear fellow . . . let's go, my little ones. . . . What are you going to feed us with, Verochka? After . . . the sea-bathing regimen . . . I have the appetite of a lieutenant just out of military school."

General Anossov had been the devoted friend and a companion on the field of battle to the late Prince Mirza-Bulat-Tuganovski. All his tender friendship and love he had, after the Prince's death, transferred to the daughters of his friend. He had known them when they had been mere tots, and had even been godfather to Anna, the younger. At that time—even as at present—he had been commandant of the great but practically superseded fortress in the town of K——, and had been almost a daily visitor at the Tuganovski home. The children simply deified him for his indulgences, his presents, his box seats for the circus and theater, and because nobody could be as fascinating a playmate as Anossov. But, most enchanting of all, and the most firmly impressed upon their minds, had been his stories of military campaigns, encounters, and bivouac stands, of victories and retreats, of death, wounds, and cruel frosts—leisurely, epically calm, simplehearted stories, told between evening tea and that tedious hour when the children would be called to bed.

In the light of present-day ways this fragment of antiquity appeared as a titanic and an unusually picturesque figure. In him were combined precisely those simple but touching and profound traits which even in his time were far more often to be met with among the rank and file than among officers, those purely Russian muzhik traits which, taken as a whole, produce an exalted type, a type that at times makes our soldier not only invincible, but actually a protomartyr, almost a saint—traits consisting of a guileless, naïve faith, a radiant, simple-heartedly cheerful view of life, a cool and practical valor, resignation in the face of death, pity for the vanquished, an infinite patience, and an astounding physical and moral endurance.

Anossov, beginning with the Polish War, had participated in all campaigns except the one against the Japanese. He would have gone to this war as well without any vacillations, but he had not been called, and he had always had a rule that was great because of its modesty: Do not thrust yourself upon death until it calls you. During his entire term of service he not only had not flogged, but had not even as much as struck, a single soldier. At the time of the Polish Insurrection he had on one occasion refused to shoot the prisoners, despite the personal order of the commander of the regiment. "I not only will have a spy shot," he had declared, "but, if you order me to, will kill him person-ally. But these fellows are prisoners, and I can't do it." And so simply, so respectfully had he said this, looking straight into the eyes of the chief officer with his clear, unwavering gaze, without a hint of chal-lenge or posing, that, instead of being himself turned over to a firing squad, he was left in peace.

In the War of 1877-79 he had very rapidly risen to the rank of colonel, notwithstanding the fact that he had had but little education, or, as he himself expressed it, "had finished only the bears' academy," or the school of hard knocks. He had taken part in the crossing of the Danube, had gone through the Balkans, undergone the siege at Shipka, and had been in the last attack on Plevna; he had been wounded seriously once and four times lightly, and, besides all that, had gotten a cruel contusion of the head from a grenade splinter. Radetski and Skobelev had known him personally, and bore themselves toward him with exceptional respect. It was of none other than him that Skobelev had happened to say: "I know of one officer who is far braver than I—and that's Major Anossov."

He came back from the wars practically deaf, thanks to the grenade splinter, with an impaired foot, from which, during the Balkan march, three frostbitten toes had been amputated, and with the cruelest rheu-matism, a souvenir of his life in Shipka. After two years of peaceful life they had tried to put him on the shelf by retiring him, but Anossov had gotten his back up. At this juncture the military chief of the district came in very handily, helping him with his influence; this official had been an eyewitness of his coolheaded courage at the crossing of the Danube. It was decided in Petersburg not to bring grief to the meritorious Colonel, and he was given a life tenure as Commandant in the town of K——, a post rather honorary than strictly necessary for purposes of defending the state.

In the town everyone knew him, from the highest to the lowest, and everybody smiled good-naturedly at his frailties, his habits, and his manner of dressing. He always went unarmed, in an old-fashioned frock coat, in a cap with a large brim and an enormous, straight visor, a cane in his right hand, an ear trumpet in his left, and inevitably convoyed by two pug dogs grown lazy, fat, and asthmatic, with the tips of their tongues always lolling between their clenched teeth. If, during his usual daily morning stroll, he happened to meet any acquaintances, pedestrians several blocks away could hear the Commandant shouting, and the pug dogs accompanying him by barking in chorus.

Like many deaf people, he was a passionate devotee of the opera and, occasionally, during some languorous duet or other, his decisive bass would reverberate through the entire theater: "Ah, but he took that *do* clean, the devil take it! Easy as cracking a nut!" A ripple of restrained laughter would pass through the theater, but the General did not even suspect it: in all naïveness he thought that he had exchanged a fresh impression in a whisper with the person next to him.

In his capacity of Commandant he rather frequently, together with his wheezing pug dogs, visited the main guardhouse, where officers under arrest were quite cozily recuperating from military hardships with the help of whist, tea, and anecdotes. He closely interrogated each one: "What's your name? Who sent you here? For how long? What for?" At times, altogether unexpectedly, he would praise an officer for a brave action, even though it had been contrary to the regulations; at times he would fall to dragging the offender over the coals, shouting so that he could be heard out in the street. But, having had his fill of shouting, without any transition or pause he would inquire from where the officer's dinners were brought in, and how much he paid. There were occasions when some erring second lieutenant, sent for a long session from some hole so godforsaken that it had not even a guardhouse of its own, would confess that he, through his impecuniosity, had to get along on the soldiers' mess. Anossov would immediately see to it that the poor fellow had his dinners brought to him from the Commandant's own house, which was no more than two hundred steps away from the guardhouse.

And it was in the town of K—— that he had drawn near to the Tuganovski family, and had become attached to the children with such close ties that it had become a psychic necessity for him to see them every evening. If the young ladies happened to be out somewhere, or if his duties detained the General himself, he would be sincerely downcast, and could not find a place for himself in the great Commandant's house. Every summer he obtained leave of absence and passed a whole month at Egorovsk, a country estate of the Tuganovskis, at a distance of some thirty-odd miles from K——.

He had transferred all the hidden tenderness of his soul and the need for a heartfelt love to these youngsters—and especially to the girls. He himself had been married on a time, but so long ago that he had actually forgotten about it. Even before the last war his wife had run away from him with a strolling player, captivated by his velvet coat and lace cuffs. The General had sent her a pension up to her very death, but would not let her into his house, in spite of tearful scenes and letters filled with repentance. They had had no children.

V

Contrary to expectations, the evening was so calm and warm that the candles on the terrace and in the dining room burned with unwavering flames. Prince Vassilii Lvovich amused everybody at table. He had an unusual and individual ability in telling a story. He would take as the basis of his story some true episode, whose chief dramatic personage would be some one of those present, or one of their mutual acquaintances, but he would lay the colors on so thick, and at the same time would speak with such a serious mien and in such a matter-of-fact tone, that his audience split its sides with laughter. Today he had told of Nicolai Nicolaevich's wedding to a certain rich and handsome lady— a wedding that had not come off. All he had for a basis was the fact that the lady's husband had not wanted to give her a divorce. But as the Prince told it, truth was miraculously interwoven with invention. He made the serious, always somewhat prim Nicolai run through the streets at night in his stocking feet, with his shoes under his arm. At some corner or other the young man had been detained by a policeman, and it was only after a long and tempestuous altercation that Nicolai had succeeded in proving he was an assistant District Attorney and not a night prowler. The wedding, according to the storyteller's words, had failed to come off by a hair's breadth, for at the most crucial moment a band of desperate perjurers who had taken part in the affair had suddenly struck, demanding an addition to the pay for their work. Nicolai, out of miserliness (and he really was somewhat miserly), and also since he was opposed on principle to all labor plots and strikes, had refused point-blank to pay anything extra, referring the strikers to a specific law statute, confirmed by an opinion of a court of appeals. Thereupon the perjurers, whose ire had been aroused, in answer to the customary question as to whether any man knew of any reasons which would prevent the consummation of the marriage, answered in a chorus: "Yes, we do know. All that we have testified to at the trial under oath is a lie from beginning to end, to utter which the Attorney had forced us, through threats and coercion. As for the husband of this lady, we, as persons in the know, can say of him only that he is the most respectable man in the world, as chaste as Joseph, and of an angelic disposition."

Having struck on the vein of wedding stories, Prince Vassilii also did not spare Gustav Ivanovich Friesse, Anna's husband: he told how on the very day after the wedding he had appeared to demand, with the help of the police, that his bride be put out of her parents' home, as one not having an individual passport, and that she be installed in her lawful husband's place of residence. The only true element in this story was the fact that during the first days of her married life Anna had had to be ceaselessly near her mother, who had fallen ill (Vera had had to hurry to her place in the South), while poor Gustav gave himself up to despondence and despair.

They all laughed. Anna, too, smiled with her eyes puckered. Gustav Ivanovich laughed loudly and in rapture, and his thin face, with the shiny skin drawn tightly over it, the scanty, light hair slicked down, and the eye-sockets sunk in, resembled a skull that had bared the vilest set of teeth in its grin. To this day he adored Anna, even as on the first day of their married life; he always tried to sit next to her, to touch her unperceived, and courted her in such an enamored and smug manner that one felt sorry and embarrassed on his account.

Just before getting up from the table, Vera Nicolaievna mechanically counted the guests. There proved to be thirteen at table. She was superstitious and thought to herself: "That's bad, really! How is it it never entered my head even once to count them over? And it's Vassya's fault; he didn't tell me a thing over the phone."

Whenever there was an intimate gathering at the Sheyins' or at Friesse's, it was the usual thing to play poker after dinner, since both sisters were almost ridiculously fond of games of chance. Because of this, special rules had been actually worked out at both homes. Ivory chips of a determined value were distributed equally among all the players, and the game lasted until such time as all the chips passed into a single pair of hands—the game would then be over for the evening, no matter how the partners might insist upon its continuation. To draw chips more than once was strictly prohibited. Such severe laws had been drawn out of practical experience, to curb both the Princess Vera and Anna Nicolaievna, whose gambling fever knew no restraint. The aggregate losses rarely came to more than a hundred or two.

They sat down to poker this time as well. Vera, who was not taking part in the game, was about to go out on the terrace, where the table was being set for tea, when suddenly a chambermaid called her out of the dining room with a somewhat mysterious air.

"What is it, Dasha?" asked the Princess Vera with displeasure, passing into her tiny study, adjoining her bedchamber. "Why have you such a silly air? And whatever are you twirling in your hands?"

Dasha laid on the table a small quadrangular object, neatly wrapped in white paper, and painstakingly banded with a narrow pink ribbon.

"Honest to God, I ain't to blame, Your Highness," she began to babble, her cheeks flaring up a bright red from a sense of injury. "He came and said—"

"Who is this 'he'?"

"A redcap, Your Highness—a messenger."

"And then?"

"He came into the kitchen, and placed this here thing on a table. 'Give that,' says he, 'to your missus. But,' says he, 'it must be put into her own hands!' I asks him who it's from. And he says: 'It's all explained inside the package.' And with that remark he run off."

"Go and catch up with him."

"It's too late, Your Highness. He come in the middle of the dinner— only I couldn't make up my mind to disturb you, Your Highness. That would be half an hour ago."

"Very well, then, you may go."

She cut the ribbon with a pair of scissors and threw it into the wastebasket, together with the paper on which the address had been written.

Unwrapped, the object proved to be a small jewelry case of red plush, evidently fresh from some shop. Vera lifted the small lid, lined with pale-blue silk, and saw, pressed into black velvet, an oval bracelet of gold and, within its circle, a note, quaintly folded into a pretty, octagonal shape. She quickly unfolded the bit of paper. The handwriting appeared familiar to her, but, like a true woman, she immediately put the note to one side to look at the bracelet.

It was of gold of low caratage, very thick but hollow and, on the outside, covered all over with small, old-fashioned, badly polished garnets. However, rising in the center of the bracelet, set around some sort of odd, small green stone, were five splendidly beautiful garnets, cut *en cabochon* and each about the size of a pea. When Vera, through a chance move, turned the bracelet just right under the light of an electric lamp, enchanting deep-red living fires suddenly began to glow within them, deep under their smooth, egg-shaped surfaces.

"Just like blood!" reflected Vera, with unexpected disquietude.

Then she remembered the letter and picked it up. She read the following lines, written in a small, magnificently calligraphic hand:

"Your Highness, Most Esteemed Princess Vera Nicolaievna!

"Respectfully felicitating You on the radiant and joyous Day of Your Good Angel, I venture to transmit to You my humble offering— the offering of a faithful slave."

"Ah—it's that fellow!" thought Vera, with displeasure. Just the same, she read the letter through to the very end. . . .

"I never would permit myself to offer You anything chosen by me personally; to do so I have neither the right nor the necessary fine taste, nor—I confess—the money. However, I suppose that there is not to be found in all the world a treasure worthy of adorning You.

"This bracelet, however, belonged to my great-grandmother, while the last to wear it was my departed mother. In the center, among the big stones, You will perceive a green one. This is a quite rare sort of garnet—a green garnet. According to an old tradition preserved in our family, it has the property of bestowing the gift of second sight on the women wearing it, and of driving away their oppressive thoughts; as for men, it safeguards them from violent death.

"All the stones have been reset as faithfully as possible from their old silver setting, and you may be assured that none has worn this bracelet before you.

"You are at liberty to throw out this ludicrous plaything immediately, or to make a present of it to somebody, but I still will be happy even in that Your hands have touched it.

"I implore You not to be wroth with me. I turn red at the recollection of my impertinence of seven years back, when I dared to write foolish and wild letters to You, who were at that time a young lady, and even to expect an answer to them. Now there remains within me only veneration, an eternal worship, and the devotion of a slave. All I can do now is to wish You happiness in Your every moment, and to rejoice if You are happy. In my mind I bow down to the ground before the furniture upon which you sit, the parquet floor You tread; the trees that You brush by in Your passing, the maid to whom You speak. It is not even envy that I feel—either toward human beings or inanimate things.

"Once more I implore forgiveness for having disturbed You with a long, uncalled-for letter.

"Your humble servant, unto death, and beyond death,

G. S. Zh."

"Should I show it to Vassya or not? And, if I do show it—when? Now—or after the guests have gone? No, better do it later; now not only this unhappy creature would be ridiculous, but I with him."

Thus did the Princess Vera reflect, and could not take her eyes off the five crimson fires, quivering deep within the five garnets.

VI

It was all they could do to make Colonel Ponomarev sit down to poker. He said that he did not know this game, that, as a general thing, he did not recognize gambling even in jest, that he liked and knew comparatively well only whist. However, he could not withstand the entreaties, and at long last consented.

At first it was necessary to teach and correct him, but he got to know the rules of poker quickly enough, and not more than half an hour passed before all the chips were stacked in front of him.

"You can't do that!" said Anna, comically offended. "You might at least have let us have a little excitement."

Three of the guests—Speshnicov, the Colonel, and the Lieutenant Governor, a rather stolid, respectable, and boring German—were the sort of people whom Vera positively did not know how to entertain or what to do with. She made up a whist party for them, calling on Gustav Ivanovich to be the fourth. Anna, from afar, to show her gratitude, let her lids drop over her eyes, and her sister immediately understood her. Everybody knew that unless Gustav Ivanovich was immediately pinned to cards he would hover about his wife all evening, just as if he were tied to her skirts, baring his rotten teeth in his death's-head face and spoiling his wife's mood.

Now the evening began to run smoothly, without constraint and in animation. Vassiuchuk, to the accompaniment of Jennie Reiter, sang in a low voice Italian folk *canzonetti* and the *Oriental Songs* of Rubinstein. He had only a small voice, but of a pleasant timbre, true and under full control. Jennie Reiter, a very exacting musician, always accompanied him willingly. However, it was said that Vassiuchuk was paying court to her.

In the corner, upon a sofa, Anna was desperately coquetting with the Hussar. Vera walked up and, with a smile, eavesdropped.

"No, no, please don't laugh," Anna was saying gaily, puckering up her charming, provoking Tatar eyes at the officer. "You, of course, consider it work to fly at a breakneck pace at the head of your squadron, and to take the hurdles at steeplechases. But just take a look at our work. For example, we have just finished with a lottery for charity. Do you think that was easy? Shame on you! The crowd, the air filled with smoke, all sorts of janitors, cabbies, and I don't know what the others were called. And all annoyed us with complaints: this is wrong and that wasn't right. And the livelong day you have to stand on your feet. And there's still a concert ahead of you for the Benefit of Impecunious Female White Collar Workers, and after that a White Ball—"

"At which, I dare hope, you won't refuse me a mazurka?" put in Bahtinski and, making a slight bow, clicked his spurs under his chair.

"Thank you! But my sorest spot—the sorest spot of all—is our asylum. An asylum for vicious children—do you understand?"

"Oh, I understand perfectly. Must be dreadfully amusing—"

"Stop it—aren't you ashamed of laughing at such things? But do you understand just what is the unfortunate part of it for us? We want to shelter these unfortunate children, with their souls filled with hereditary vices and bad examples; we want to warn them, to show them kindness—"

"Hm!"

"—to raise their morals, to awaken in their souls a consciousness of duty. Do you follow me? And so, every day, the children are brought to us in their hundreds, their thousands; yet, among all of them, there isn't a single vicious one! If you ask the parents whether their child is vicious, they actually get insulted! Can you imagine such a thing? And so the asylum has been opened, dedicated, and everything is in readiness—and there's never an inmate, boy or girl! One might as well offer a prize for every vicious infant delivered—"

"Anna Nicolaievna," the Hussar interrupted her, seriously and insinuatingly. "Why offer prizes? You can have me, free. 'Pon my word, you'll never find a more vicious infant!"

"Stop! One can't talk with you seriously." She burst into laughter, throwing herself against the back of the sofa, her eyes glittering.

Prince Vassilii Lvovich, sitting at a big round table, was showing to his sister, Anossov, and his brother-in-law an album of family caricatures he had drawn himself. All four were laughing wholeheartedly, and little by little this laughter drew over to them all the guests who were not taken up with cards.

The album might have served as a supplement of illustrations to the satirical stories of Prince Vassilii. With his imperturbable calm he showed, for example: The History of the Love Adventures of the Brave General Anossov in Turkey, Bulgaria, and Other Countries— The Adventures of *le Petit Maître* Prince Nicolai Bulat-Tuganovski at Monte Carlo, and so forth.

"You will see right away, ladies and gentlemen, a brief description of the life of our most beloved sister, Liudmilla Lvovna," he was saying, casting a quick, mocking glance at his sister. " 'Part One.. Childhood. The child grew; they called her Lima.' "

The page of the album was adorned by the figure of a girl, drawn in a deliberately childish manner—the face was in profile, yet had two eyes, with broken short lines sticking out from under the skirt in lieu of feet, the arms outflung and the fingers spread out.

"No one *ever* called me Lima," Liudmilla Lvovna began laughing.

" 'Part Two. First Love. A junker in the Cavalry is offering on his knees, to the fair Lima, a poem of his own workmanship. It contains lines that are veritable pearls in their beauty:

'Thy foot, made in such splendid fashion,
Doth manifest unearthly passion!—'

"And right here you have an authentic representation of the foot.

"And in this episode the junker is trying to persuade the innocent

Lima to elope from her parental home. And, in this—the elopement itself. And this, now, is a critical situation: 'Wrathful Father Overtakes Fugitives. Junker pusillanimously throws Blame on Meek Lima:

> 'While thou wert primping, a precious hour sped by,
> And lo, the dread pursuit to us is drawing nigh. . . .
> Deal with it as you may see fit,
> While I into the bushes flit!' "

The History of the Maiden Lima was followed by a new tale: Princess Vera and the Enamored Telegraph Clerk.

"Only the illustrations for this touching poem, in pen and ink and colored crayons, are ready as yet. The text is in preparation."

"This must be something new," commented Anossov. "I haven't seen it yet."

"The latest out. The newest thing on the book marts."

Vera touched his shoulder lightly:

"That's unnecessary—better not show it."

But Vassilii Lvovich either had not heard what she said, or had not attached any importance to it.

"The beginning goes back to prehistoric times. On a certain splendid day in May a certain maiden, by the name of Vera, receives by post a letter headed by two billing doves. Here's the letter—and here are the doves.

"The letter contains an ardent confession of love, written in defiance of all rules of orthography. It begins thus: 'Beauteous Blonde—you who are . . . a tempestuous sea of flame seething within my breast. Your glance, like a venomous serpent, has sunk its fangs into my tortured soul'—and so on, and so on. At the end there is a modest signature: 'I may be classed as but a poor telegraph clerk, yet my feelings are worthy of My Lord George. I dare not reveal my full name—it is far too unseemly. I sign myself merely with my initials—P. P. Zh. I beg of you to answer me by mail, care of General Delivery.' And here, ladies and gentlemen, you may see even the portrait of the telegraph clerk himself, very successfully executed in colored crayons.

"The heart of Vera has been transpierced (here is the heart, and here's the arrow). But, like a decorous and well-brought-up miss, she shows the letter to her respected parents, as well as to the friend of her childhood and her bridegroom, that handsome young man, Vassya Sheyin. And here is the illustration. Of course, in time, the drawings will be accompanied by explanations in verse.

"Vassya Sheyin, sobbing, returns to Vera the betrothal ring he had given her in exchange for hers. 'I dare not stand in the way of your happiness,' says he, 'but, I implore you, do not take any decisive step hastily. Think, reflect, make sure of yourself and of him. My child, you know not life, and, like a moth, are flying into the bright flame. But I—alas!—I know what the cold and hypocritical world is like. Know, that telegraph clerks are fascinating but crafty. It affords them an inexplicable delight to beguile with their proud beauty and their false sentiments some inexperienced victim and then cruelly mock her.'

"Half a year passes. In the whirlwind of life's waltz Vera gradually forgets her admirer and marries the handsome young Vassya— but the telegraph clerk does not forget her. And lo, he disguises himself as a chimney sweep and, after covering himself with soot, penetrates into the boudoir of the Princess Vera. The marks of four fingers and a thumb and of two lips have been left, as you perceive, everywhere: upon the rugs, upon the pillows, upon the wallpaper, and even on the parquet floor.

"Here he is, disguised as a countrywoman, getting a place in our kitchen as a common dishwasher. However, the excessive affability of Luka, the chef, compels him to resort to flight.

"Here you see him—in a madhouse. And here he has taken the tonsure of a monk. But each day he undeviatingly dispatches passionate letters to Vera. And where his tears fall on the paper, there the ink spreads out in blots.

"Finally he dies, but before his death he bequeaths for transmission to Vera two buttons of his telegraphic uniform, and a perfume bottle— filled to the brim with his tears—"

"Ladies and gentlemen, who wants tea?" asked Vera Nicolaievna.

VII

The prolonged autumnal sunset had burned itself out. The last small streak of dark crimson, as narrow as a chink, which had glowed at the very edge of the horizon between a livid cloud and the earth, at last expired. Neither the earth, nor the trees, nor the sky was distinguishable by now. The great stars alone quivered like eyelashes overhead amid the black night, and the bluish beam of the lighthouse rose straight up in a slender pillar and seemed to shatter with a splash there, against the cupola of heaven, in a tenuous, misty circle of light. Night moths beat against the glass candle shades. The white, starry flowers of tobacco plants near the palisade sent forth their fragrance still more sharply out of the darkness and the freshness of night.

Speshnicov, the Lieutenant Governor, and Colonel Ponamarev had long since taken their departure, after promising to send the horses back from the trolley stop for the Commandant. The remaining guests were seated on the terrace. The sisters compelled General Anossov, despite his protests, to put on an overcoat, and they wrapped his feet up in a warm plaid. Before him stood a bottle of Pommard, his favorite red wine; Vera sat on one side of him, and Anna on the other. They solicitously looked after the General, filling his slender goblet with the heavy, thick wine, moving the matches toward him, slicing off pieces of cheese for him, and so on. The old Commandant was purring from bliss.

"Yes, Sir. . . . Autumn, autumn, autumn," the old man was saying, his eyes fixed on the flame of a candle, and he thoughtfully shook his head. "Autumn. There, it's time for me to be packing up as well. Ah, but what a pity it is! The beautiful days have just arrived. A fellow could live on and on at the seashore, in quiet, and ever so peacefully—"

"Well, do live with us a while, Grandpa," said Vera.

"Can't, my darling—can't. Duty. . . . My leave of absence has expired. But what's the use of talking, it would be fine! Just notice how the roses smell, now. I can smell them from here. But in the summer time, during the hot spells, there wasn't one fragrant blossom —except for white acacia. And even that had a candy-like smell."

Vera took out of a small vase two rosebuds, a pink and a carmine, and inserted them in the buttonhole of the Commandant's overcoat.

"Thanks, Verochka." Anossov bent his head toward his lapel, sniffed the flowers, and suddenly smiled with a fine, aged smile.

"We came, I remember, to Bucharest, and billeted ourselves in quarters. Well, one day I'm walking along the street, when suddenly a strong odor of roses was wafted toward me. I stopped, and saw a splendid crystal flagon of attar of roses standing between two soldiers. They had already greased their boots with it, as well as their gunlocks. 'What's that you've got there?' I asked them. 'Some sort of oil, Your Honor; we put it in the buckwheat porridge, but it's no good, it just makes your mouth all raw—yet it's got a grand smell!' I gave them all of a ruble, and they surrendered their find to me with pleasure. There wasn't more than half the oil left by now, but, judging by the high price the stuff fetches, what was left was worth twenty gold pieces. The soldiers, being pleased, added: 'And here, Your Honor, is also some kind of Turkish peas—no matter how long we cook 'em, the damned things won't get soft.' The 'damned things' were coffee-beans. I told them: 'This is good only for Turks—it isn't fit for soldiers.' Lucky they didn't get a bellyful of opium. I saw whole cakes of it in some places, trampled right into the mud."

"Grandpa, tell us frankly," Anna begged him, "tell us, did you ever experience fear during battles? Were you ever afraid?"

"Strange as it may seem, Annochka, I was afraid, and yet I wasn't. Don't you believe the fellow who tells you he was never afraid, and that the whistling of bullets is for him the sweetest of music. Such a chap is either a psychopath or a braggart. All men alike are afraid— but one man will go all to pieces from fear, while another will keep himself well in hand. And, d'you see—the fright always remains the same, whereas the ability to hold yourself in check will constantly grow—and that's how you get the heroes and the daredevils. So-o. But there was one time when I was frightened almost to death."

"Do tell us, Grandpa," both sisters begged him in chorus.

To this day they listened to Anossov's stories with the same rapture as in their early childhood. Anna, involuntarily, even spread her elbows on the table, altogether like a child, and laid her chin on the heels of her palms, placed closely together. There was a certain homely charm in his unhurried and naïve story-telling. And the very turns of the phrases in which he conveyed his military reminiscences, in his case willy-nilly, took on an odd, cumbersome, somewhat bookish character, just as though he were telling his story after some beloved, ancient stereotype.

"The story is very short," Anossov obliged. "It took place in Shipka, in winter—after I already had received my contusion in the head. There were four of us living in a sod hut. And that's just where my dreadful adventure befell me. One morning, just on getting out of bed, I got the notion that my name wasn't Jacob but Nicolai, and there wasn't any way I could change that idea. Realizing that I was about to lose my mind, I shouted for some water to be brought to me, soaked my head in it, and my reason returned."

"I can well imagine, Jacob Michailovich, how many conquests you made among the women there," said Jennie Reiter. "You, probably, were very handsome in your youth."

"Oh, our Grandpa is an Adonis even now!" cried out Anna.

"I was no Adonis," said Anossov, with a calm smile. "But then, they never turned up their noses at me, either. There was, for instance, a very touching incident in that same Bucharest. When we entered it, the inhabitants saluted us on the main square with salvos of cannon-fire, which shattered many windows; those which had had glasses of water placed on the sills, however, remained undamaged. And how did I find this out? Well, here's how. When I came to the quarters assigned to me I saw a low little cage standing on the window sill; there was a crystal bottle of large proportions atop the cage, with clear water in which goldfish were swimming, and in their midst was a canary on a perch. A canary in water! This astounded me, but, on closer inspection, I saw that the bottle had a broad bottom, with a hollow space in it, so that the canary could freely fly in through the open top of the cage and perch there. After that I had to admit to myself that I wasn't any too bright about surmising things.

"I entered the house, and there I saw the prettiest little Bulgarian girl. I presented my billeting ticket to her and, at the same time, asked her why their windows were undamaged after all that cannonading, and she explained to me that it was because of the water taking up the vibrations. And she also explained about the canary—that's how slow I must have looked. And so, in the middle of our conversation, a spark passed between us, something like an electric spark, and I felt that I'd fallen in love at first sight—ardently and irretrievably."

The old man fell silent and carefully sipped a little of the dark wine.

"But, after all, didn't you explain your feelings to her after that?" asked the pianist.

"Hm . . . of course we had an explanation. . . . But not in words. This is how it came about—"

"Grandpa, I do hope you won't make us blush?" Anna put in, laughing slyly.

"No, no—the romance was of the most respectable sort. You see, everywhere we were billeted the inhabitants made exceptions and added stipulations, but in Bucharest the inhabitants were on such a friendly footing with us that on one occasion, when I began to play the fiddle, the girls immediately put on their best things and came for a dance, and after that this became a daily occurrence.

"One evening, while the dancing was going on by the light of the moon, I went into the entry, where my little Bulgarian girl had gone as well. Upon catching sight of me she began pretending that she was sorting the dried rose-petals which, I must tell you, the denizens thereabouts gather in whole bagfuls. But I embraced her, pressed her to my heart, and kissed her a number of times.

"From then on, whenever the moon and the stars appeared in the sky, I'd hasten to my beloved and, in her presence, forget all the workaday cares for the time being. But when we had to march away from those regions, we vowed eternal love for each other—and bade farewell to each other forever."

"And is that all?" asked Liudmilla Lvovna, in disappointment.

"Why, what more would you have?" retorted the Commandant.

"No, Jacob Michailovich—you must forgive me, but that isn't love; rather just a bivouac adventure of an army officer."

"I don't know, my dear—really, 'pon my word, I don't know whether this was love, or some other feeling—"

"Yes, but. . . . Do tell me—is it possible that you really never loved with a genuine love? You know, that love which—well, which . . . in a word . . . a holy, pure, eternal love, a love not of this earth. Is it possible that you haven't experienced it?"

"Really, I wouldn't be able to answer you," hesitated the old man, getting up from his chair. "Probably I haven't loved. In the beginning there never was time: youth, sprees, cards, fighting. It seemed there would never be an end to life, to youth and health. But then I looked around—and I saw that I was already a crumbling ruin. And now, Verochka, don't be keeping me any longer. I'll make my adieux. My dear Hussar," he turned to Bahtinski, "the night is warm—let's walk to meet the carriage."

"And I'll go along with you, Grandpa," said Vera.

"And I," Anna added quickly.

Before leaving, Vera approached her husband and said to him, quietly:

"Go and take a look. There's a red jewel case in the little drawer of my desk, and inside it a letter. Read it over."

VIII

Anna walked in front with Bahtinski, while some twenty paces behind them walked the Commandant, with Vera on his arm. The night was so black that during the first few minutes, until their eyes became accustomed to it after the light, their feet had to grope for the path. Anossov, who, despite his years, had preserved an amazing keenness of sight, had to help his companion. From time to time he caressed with his big, cold hand that of Vera, which was lying in the crook of his arm.

"This Liudmilla Lvovna is rather funny," the General suddenly began speaking, as though continuing the course of his thoughts aloud. "How many times I have observed in life that, no sooner does fifty strike for a lady—and especially if she be a widow or an old wench—than she is simply drawn to hang around about somebody else's love affair. She either spies, gets malicious joy over mishaps, and gossips, or shoves her nose in, trying to arrange the happiness of others, or else dishes out goo about exalted love. But what I mean to say is that people in our day have forgotten how to love. I can't see any real love around. And even in my time I didn't see any!"

"Why, how can that be, Grandpa?" Vera contradicted gently, giving his hand a gentle squeeze. "Why all this slander? You were married yourself. Therefore you must have loved, after all?"

"That doesn't mean a thing, Verochka. Do you know how I came to get married? I saw a little girl, as dewy as dewy can be, sitting near me. When she breathed, her bosom simply heaved under her little blouse. She'd let her eyelashes drop—such long, long eyelashes—and then blush furiously all over. And the skin on her cheeks was ever so soft; her little neck was so white, and virginal, and her hands were such soft, warm little hands. Ah, the Devil take it! And there were her papa and mamma snooping around, eavesdropping behind doors, contemplating you with such sad, doglike, devoted eyes. And when you were leaving the house, there were those quick, snatched kisses in the doorway. At tea her little foot used to touch you under the table, as if by chance. Well, your goose was cooked. 'My dear Nikita Antonych, I have come to you to seek your daughter's hand. Believe me, she is a holy being. . . .' Well, papa's eyes are already moist, and he's all set to kiss you. 'My dear fellow, I have long surmised this! Well, may God send you every blessing! Only see that you guard this treasure well.' And then, inside of three months, the holy treasure is walking about in a tattered dressing gown, with her bare feet in slippers; whatever little hair she has, thin and unkempt, is in curlpapers; she's as bitchy as a cook with the orderlies, poses before young officers, lisping, squealing, rolling up her eyes. For some reason or other she calls her husband

'Jacques' in the presence of others. Like this, through the nose, drawing it out languishingly: 'J-a-a-acques!' A spendthrift, an actress, a sloven, a glutton. And her eyes are lying—always lying! Now it's over and done with, all shaken down and settled to the bottom. At heart I'm even grateful to that ham actor. Glory be to God, there were no children—"

"Did you forgive your wife and the man, Grandpa?"

"Forgive isn't the word, Verochka. At first I was like one violently insane. Had I laid my eyes on them then, I would, of course, have killed them both. But later, little by little, it all passed away, and there was nothing left save contempt. And that's a good thing. God has delivered me from any extra bloodshed. And, besides that, I escaped the usual lot of the majority of husbands. Just what would I have been but for this vile happening? A pack mule, an ignominious yes-man, a shield, a milch cow, a screen—some sort of a domestic necessity. No! Everything worked out for the best, Verochka."

"No, no, Grandpa—you really must forgive me, but, after all, the former hurt still speaks in you. And you apply your unfortunate experience to all humanity. Why, take Vassya and myself, for instance. Could our marriage possibly be called unhappy?"

Anossov kept silent for a rather long while. Then he drawled out unwillingly:

"Very well, then . . . let's say it's an exception. But then, why do people marry in the majority of cases? Let's take the woman. It's a disgrace to be left a spinster, especially when all your girl friends have already landed husbands. It's hard to feel you're an extra mouth to feed in the family. Then there's the desire to be the mistress of a household, its chief personage, a lady, and independent. In addition there's the need—a downright physical need—of maternity, and of building one's own nest. As for the men, they have other motives. In the first place, the weariness bred of a bachelor life, of disorder in one's rooms, of tavern dinners, of dirt, cigarette stubs, torn and odd underclothes, of debts, of unceremonious companions, and so on and so on. In the second place, one feels that family life is more advantageous, wholesome and economical. In the third place, one thinks: There, children will come; I, now, shall die, but a part of me will still be left on earth . . . something in the nature of an illusion of immortality. In the fourth place, there's the seductiveness of innocence, as in my case. Besides that, there are also occasional thoughts of the dowry. But where is this love, now? Love that is unavaricious, self-denying, expecting no reward? That love of which it is said that it is 'strong as death'? You understand? The sort of love for which one would perform any exploit, give up one's life—face martyrdom—that love which is not at all a task, but pure joy? Hold on, hold on, Vera—are you going to spring your Vassya on me again? Really, I do love him. He's a good lad. Who knows, perhaps the future will show his love in the light of great beauty. But I want you to understand the sort of love I'm speaking of. Love must be a tragedy. It is the greatest mystery in the world. No worldly comforts, considerations, and compromises must touch it."

"Have you ever witnessed such a love, Grandpa?" asked Vera softly.

"No," the old man answered decisively. "True, I know two instances that approach it. But one was dictated by folly, while the other . . . was just so-so . . . sort of sour. Solely through pity. If you like, I'll tell you. It won't take long."

"Please do, Grandpa."

"Very well, then. In a certain regiment of our division (only it wasn't our regiment), the colonel had a wife. Her phiz, I must tell you, Verochka, was against all nature. Bony, red-haired, she was; lanky, all skin and bones, with a huge mouth on her. The plaster simply trickled off her face, the way it does in an old city house. And yet, you understand, a sort of regimental Messalina: temperament, imperiousness, contempt for people, passion for variety. And, to top it all off—a morphine fiend.

"And so, one autumn day an ensign is sent to this regiment—fresh out of the oven, he was altogether a sparrow fledgling, all yellow around the mouth, just out of the military academy. After a month, this old mare had taken absolute possession of him. He's her page, he's her servant, he's her slave, he's her eternal partner and gallant at every dance; he totes her fan and her handkerchief; in nothing but his skimpy little uniform he hops out into the frost to call her carriage. A horrible thing, this, when a fresh and pure urchin lays his first love at the feet of an experienced, imperious harridan, old in depravity. Even if he has immediately leaped out unharmed, you can put him down as lost in the future, just the same. It stamps him for life.

"By Christmas he had already palled upon her. She came back to one of her former, tested passions. But he couldn't help himself. He trailed her, like some apparition. He was all fagged out, emaciated, grown black in the face. To put it in highfalutin style, 'death was already writ large upon his lofty brow.' He was terribly jealous of her. They say he stood for hours at a stretch under her windows.

"And so, one day in spring, they arranged some sort of a regimental May Day, or picnic. I knew both her and him personally, but I was not present at this occurrence. As is always the case on such occasions, there'd been a great deal of drinking. They were coming back at night on foot, following a railroad track. Suddenly, a freight train came toward them. It came along very slowly, puffing up a rather steep incline, the whistle blowing all the time. And so, just as the lights of the locomotive came up with the party, she suddenly whispered in the ensign's ear: 'You're forever saying that you love me. And yet, if I were to command you, you still wouldn't throw yourself under the train.' But he, without answering a word, started off at a run—and drops right under the train. They say that he had calculated the leap perfectly, precisely in the way of the front and rear wheels—so that he would have been neatly sliced in halves. But some idiot or other got the idea of holding him back and pushing him away. But he couldn't overcome the ensign by force. And so the latter, since his hands were gripping the rails, had both of them lopped off at the wrists."

"Oh, how horrible!" Vera cried out.

"He had to leave the service. His comrades scraped up a little something for him, so he could go away. To stay on in the town wouldn't have been quite right for him—he'd be a living, visible reproach, always before her and the whole regiment. And the man was done for, in the most abominable fashion. Became a beggar. Froze to death somewhere in Petersburg, on a wharf.

"As for the other case—it was altogether pitiful. And the woman was the very same sort as the first, only young and good-looking. Her conduct was very, very bad. No matter how lightly we regarded these domestic romances, still it went against our grain. But as for the husband, nothing mattered to him. He knew, he saw everything, and said nothing. His friends hinted around, but he merely gave them the brush-off. 'Drop it, drop it. It doesn't bother me—it doesn't bother me. As long as Lenochka is happy!' What a dolt!

"In the end, she formed a strong attachment with Lieutenant Vishnyacov, a subaltern in their company. And thus three of them lived together in a polyandrous marriage—just as though it were the most legal form of wedlock. And at this juncture our regiment was shifted to the front. Our ladies saw us off; she, too, saw us off, and really, one felt ashamed even to watch the scene. If only, for the sake of decency, she'd looked even once at her husband; but no, she hung on the neck of her lieutenant, like the Evil One on a withered pussy willow, and would not go away from him. In farewell, when we were already seated in the cars and the train had started, why—the shameless creature!—she actually called out to her husband: 'Remember, now—take care of Volodya! If anything happens to him, I'll leave the house and never come back—and I'll take the children along!'

"Perhaps you think that this captain was some sort of a rag? A wishy-washy fellow? That he had the soul of a grasshopper? Not a bit of it. He was a brave soldier. Under the Green Mountains he led his company six times against a Turkish redoubt, and of all the two hundred men under him he had only fourteen left. Twice wounded, he refused to go to the dressing station. That's the sort he was. The soldiers worshiped him like a god.

"But she had commanded him. His Lenochka had commanded him!

"And so he tended this coward and loafer Vishnyacov—this drone that yielded no honey; he tended him like a nurse, like a mother. At the night stands, under the rain and in the mud, he wrapped him up in his own overcoat. He went in his place to lay mines, while the other lay at his ease in a dugout or played stuss. Of nights he inspected the sentry posts in Vishnyacov's stead. And notice this, Verunya—this was at the time when the bashi-bazouks were cutting off our pickets just as simply as a farmer's wife cuts off cabbage heads in her truck garden. By God, even though it be a sin to recall it, yet we all rejoiced when we learned that Vishnyacov had given up the ghost because of typhoid, in the hospital."

"Well, what about women, Grandpa—have you ever met women who loved?"

"Oh, of course, Verochka. I'll even go farther; I am convinced that almost every woman is capable of the highest heroism in love. Stop to think: even as she kisses, embraces, yields, she is *already* a mother. To her, if she loves, love holds the entire meaning of life—holds all of creation! But she is not at all to blame for the fact that love among mankind has taken on such vulgar forms and has come down to being simply some sort of everyday convenience, a minor diversion. It's the men that are to blame; they're surfeited at twenty; they have the bodies of chicks and the souls of rabbits; they are incapable of strong desires, of heroic deeds, of tenderness in or adoration before love. People say all these existed in former days. And even if they didn't, haven't they been dreamed of and yearned for by the best minds and souls of mankind—the poets, romanticists, musicians, artists? Just the other day I was reading the story of little Mary Lescaut and the Cavalier de

Grieux. . . . Would you believe it, I was drenched in tears! Well, do tell me, my dear, as your conscience prompts you—doesn't every woman, in the very depths of her heart, dream of such a love—single, all-forgiving, ready for all things, humble and self-denying?"

"Oh, of course, of course, Grandpa!"

"But, if it isn't there, women go in for revenge. Another thirty years or so will pass. I shan't see the time, but you, Verochka, may see it. Mark my words: thirty years or so from now women will assume unheard-of power in the world. They'll dress themselves like Hindu idols. They'll trample upon us men as if we were so many despised, prostrate slaves. The harebrained whims and caprices of those women will become excruciating laws for us. And all this because we, for whole generations, did not know how to bow down before love and revere it. That will be their revenge. You know the physical law: the force of reaction is equal to the force of action."

After a brief silence, he added:

"Do tell me, Verochka—unless you find it painful—what's this business about the telegraph clerk Prince Vassilii was speaking of today? You know how he is; how much truth is there in it, and how much invention?"

"Why, does it interest you, Grandpa?"

"It's all up to you—all up to you, Vera. If for some reason you find it distasteful—"

"Why, not at all. I'll tell you with pleasure."

And she told the Commandant, in full detail, about some madman or other who had begun pursuing her with his love even two years before her marriage.

She had not seen him even once, and did not know even his name. He merely wrote to her, and signed his letters G.S. Zh. Once he let slip the fact that he worked in some governmental department or other as the pettiest of clerks; he had not mentioned a word about any telegraph office. Evidently he was constantly watching her, because in his letters he indicated exactly where she spent her evenings, in what society, and how she had been dressed. In the beginning his letters had been of a vulgar and curiously ardent nature, even though they were quite chaste. But on one occasion ("By the by, Grandpa, don't let a word of this slip to anyone in our circle—no one knows anything about this"), Vera had written him, asking him not to make things difficult for her with his amatory effusions. Since that time he had become silent on the subject of love and had taken to writing only at rare intervals: at Easter, at New Year's, and on her birthdays. Princess Vera also told about the present he had sent her today, and also repeated, almost word for word, the strange letter of her mysterious worshiper.

"Ye-es," drawled out the Commandant at last. "Perhaps this is simply an abnormal chap, a maniac, yet—who knows?—perhaps your path in life, Verochka, has been crossed by precisely such a love as every woman dreams of and of which men are less capable than women. Wait, now! Do you see any lanterns moving ahead of us? My carriage, most probably."

At the same time they heard behind them the throaty yapping of an automobile, and the road, furrowed with wheels, began to glow with a white, acetylene light. Gustav Ivanovich drove up.

"Annochka. I fetched your things along. Get in," said he. "Would Your Excellency permit me to drive you home?"

"No, thanks, my dear fellow," the Commandant answered. "I have no great love for that machine. All it does is shake you up and smell bad, but there's no pleasure in it. Well, good-by, Vera. I'm going to come often now," he said, kissing Vera's hands and forehead.

All made their adieux. Friesse brought Vera Nicolaievna to the gates of her villa, then, quickly swinging around, vanished in the darkness with his roaring and snorting car.

I X

It was with an unpleasant feeling that Princess Vera went up the steps of the terrace and into the house. Even from afar she heard the booming voice of her brother Nicolai and caught sight of his tall, gaunt figure, rapidly pacing from one end of the room to the other. Her husband was seated at a card-table and, with his big, light-haired, closely cropped head bent low, was drawing with chalk upon the green cloth.

"I've been insisting on this a long time!" Nicolai was saying in irritation, and his right hand made a gesture as if he were throwing some invisible weight to the ground. "I have been long insisting that a stop must be put to these fool letters. Even before Vera married you I maintained that you two were amusing yourselves with them like little children, finding them merely funny. And here, by the by, is Vera herself.

Vassilii Lvovich and myself, Verochka, are discussing right now this madman of yours—your P.P. Zh. I find this correspondence insolent and low."

Vera turned red at these words and sat down on the divan, in the shadow of a potted palm.

"There hasn't been any correspondence whatsoever," Sheyin stopped him coldly. "He was the only one who wrote."

"I apologize for the expression," said Vera's brother, and again cast to the ground some invisible great weight, just as though he had snatched it off his breast.

"Well, I can't understand why you call him *mine*," put in Vera, encouraged by her husband's support. "He's just as much yours as he is mine—"

"Very well, I apologize once more. In a word, all I want to say is that an end must be put to his preposterous actions. The matter, in my opinion, is passing beyond those bounds where one may laugh and draw amusing little pictures. Believe me, if there is anything which I am concerned and perturbed about, it's nothing but Vera's good name—and yours, Vassilii Lvovich."

"Well, there, Nick, you've gone just a little too far," retorted Sheyin.

"Perhaps, perhaps. But both of you risk finding yourselves in a ridiculous situation, and that without much trouble."

"I fail to see just how," said the Prince.

"Just imagine that this idiotic bracelet—" here Nicolai lifted the red case a little from the table and immediately let it drop squeamishly in its place—"this little monstrosity, right up some country priest's alley, may remain on our hands, or that we chuck it out, or make a present of it to one of the maids. Then, in the first place, P.P. Zh. can boast to his friends or comrades that the Princess Vera Nicolaievna Sheyina accepts his presents, and, in the second place, he'll be encouraged to further exploits at the very first opportunity. Tomorrow, he'll send a diamond ring, the day after, a string of pearls, and then, first thing you know, he's up for embezzlement or forgery, while Prince and Princess Sheyin are subpoenaed as witnesses. A charming situation!"

"No, no—the bracelet must be returned without fail!" Vassilii Lvovich exclaimed.

"I think so as well," concurred Vera, "and that as soon as possible. But how is it to be done? Why, we don't know either his name or his address."

"Oh, that's altogether a trifling matter!" Nicolai Nicolaievich retorted disparagingly. "We know the fellow's initials. P.P.Zh.—is that right, Vera?"

"G.S. Zh."

"There, that's splendid. Besides that, we know that he works in some government bureau. That's absolutely sufficient. No later than tomorrow I'll get hold of a city directory and track down a government clerk or some other Civil Service worker with those initials. If for any reason I fail to find him, I'll just call in a police detective and order him to track down the man. If any difficulty arises, I have in my hands this bit of paper with his handwriting. In short, by two o'clock tomorrow afternoon I'll know the exact name and address of this gay young blade, and even the hours when he can be found home. And, once I find this out, we'll not only return his treasure to him tomorrow, but also take certain measures so that he'll never remind us of his existence again."

"What are you thinking of doing?" asked Prince Vassilii.

"What am I thinking of doing? I'll go to the Governor and ask him—"

"No; anybody but the Governor. You know what our relations are. There we'd be in positive danger of finding ourselves in a ridiculous situation."

"Very well, then. I'll go to the Colonel of Gendarmes. We belong to the same club. Just let him summon this Romeo and throw a good scare into him. You know how he does that? He puts his index finger right under the culprit's nose; the Colonel never moves the hand at all, but wags just that one finger, and shouts at the same time: 'I-won't-stand-for-anything-of-that-sort-Sir!' "

"Ugh! Resorting to gendarmes!" Vera made a wry face.

"Right you are, Vera," the Prince quickly agreed with her. "It might be best not to mix in any outsiders in this business. It would give rise to rumors and gossip. We all know well what our town is like. All of us live in glass houses. It might be better if I were to go myself to this . . . youngster. Although, God knows, he may be all of sixty. I'll hand the bracelet back to him and read him a good stiff lecture."

"In that case, I'll come along with you," Nicolai Nicolaievich quickly cut him short. "You're much too soft. Leave it to me to have a talk with him. And now, my friends," he took out his pocket-watch and glanced at it, "you will excuse me if I go to my room for just a minute. I can hardly keep on my feet, yet there are still two cases I have to look over."

"For some reason I've become sorry for this unfortunate," Vera said hesitatingly.

"There's no reason to feel sorry for him!" Nicolai responded sharply, turning around in the doorway. "If a man in our circle had permitted himself such an action as sending this bracelet and letter, Prince Vassilii would have challenged him to a duel. And if he didn't, I would. And in the good old days I simply would have ordered him to be taken to the stable and given a good beating with birch rods. Wait for me in your office tomorrow, Vassilii Lvovich; I'll get in touch with you by phone."

X

The spittle-covered staircase smelt of mice, cats, kerosene, and washing. Before they reached the sixth floor, Prince Vassilii Lvovich stopped.

"Wait a little," said he to his brother-in-law. "Let me catch my breath. Ah, Nick, we oughtn't to do this!"

They went up two more flights. It was so dark on the staircase landing that Nicolai Nicolaievich had to light two matches before he could make out the number of the flat.

When he rang, the door was opened by a corpulent woman with gray eyes and white hair, whose torso was bent somewhat forward—evidently because of some physical affliction.

"Is Mr. Zheltcov at home?" asked Nicolai Nicolaievich.

The woman, in alarm, ran her eyes from one man to the other and then back again. The respectable appearance of both must have reassured her.

"He's at home—please come in," said she, opening the door. "First door to the left."

Prince Bulat-Tuganovski knocked three times, quickly and resolutely. He heard some sort of a rustle within, and knocked again.

"Come in," a faint voice responded.

The room was very low, but very wide and long, almost square in shape. Two round windows, altogether like portholes, admitted the feeblest of lights. As a matter of fact, the whole room resembled the main cabin of some tramp steamer. Along one wall stood a rather narrow bed; along the other a very big and broad divan, covered with a tattered yet splendid Tehin rug; in the middle was a table, covered with a colorful Ukrainian cloth.

They could not make out the occupant's face at first: he was standing with his back to the light and, in his embarrassment, was rubbing his hands. He was tall, spare; his long hair was soft and downy.

"Mr. Zheltcov, if I am not mistaken?" Nicolai Nicolaievich asked superciliously.

"Yes. This is a great pleasure. Allow me—"

He took two steps toward Tuganovski, with his hand outstretched but, at that same moment, as though not noticing his greeting, Nicolai Nicolaievich turned around completely to face Sheyin:

"I told you we were not mistaken."

Zheltcov's thin, nervous fingers fidgeted with the front of his short and shabby brown jacket, buttoning and unbuttoning it. Finally he managed to utter with difficulty, indicating the divan and bowing awkwardly:

"Won't you be so kind—please be seated."

Now they could see him whole—exceedingly pale, with a tender face, like a girl's, with blue eyes and a stubborn childlike chin, with a deep dimple in the middle; he was around thirty—or thirty-five, perhaps.

"Thank you," Prince Sheyin said very simply, as he scrutinized him very attentively.

"*Merci,*" Nicolai Nicolaievich answered curtly. And both remained standing. "We have come to you for just a few minutes, all in all. This is Prince Vassilii Lvovich Sheyin, the Marshal of Nobility for the district. My name is Mirza-Bulat-Tuganovski. I'm the assistant District Attorney. The matter which we will have the honor of discussing with you concerns both the Prince and myself alike—or, rather, the Prince's wife, who is also my sister."

Zheltcov, utterly confused, suddenly sank down on the divan and babbled through lips that had become lifeless: "Please sit down, gentlemen. I beg you"—but, probably recalling that he had already extended that same invitation and that it had gone unheeded, he leapt up, hurried to the window and, ruffling his hair, resumed his place there. And again his trembling hands began running up and down the front of his coat, worrying the buttons, plucking his light, reddish mustache, unnecessarily touching his face.

"I am at your service, Your Highness," he said dully, gazing at Vassilii Lvovich with entreaty in his eyes.

But Sheyin kept silent. It was Nicolai Nicolaievich who began:

"In the first place, permit us to return your property," said he and, getting the red jewel case out of his pocket, laid it meticulously on the table. "Of course, it does honor to your taste, but we would most strenuously request that there may be no repetition of such surprises in the future."

"Forgive me. I realize myself that I am very much at fault," Zheltcov uttered in a whisper, looking at the floor and turning red. "Perhaps you will permit me to offer you a glass of tea?"

"You see, Mr. Zheltcov," Nicolai Nicolaievich went on, as though he had not caught Zheltcov's last words, "I am very glad that I found you to be a decent man, a gentleman, capable of catching one's meaning at a mere hint. And I think that we'll arrive at an immediate understanding. If I am not mistaken, you have been pursuing Princess Vera Nicolaievna for about seven or eight years by now—isn't that so?"

"Yes," answered Zheltcov softly, and lowered his eyelashes reverently.

"And up to this time we have taken no measures whatsoever against you, although—you must agree—this not only could, but should, have been done. Isn't that so?"

"Yes."

"Yes. But by your last action—the sending of this very bracelet of garnets, to be precise—you have overstepped the final limits of our patience. D'you understand? The final limits. I shan't conceal from you that our first thought was to turn to the aid of the authorities, but we have not done this, and I am very glad we have not, inasmuch as— I repeat—I have immediately perceived you to be a man not without noble impulses—"

"Pardon me—how did you put that?" Zheltcov suddenly asked with interest, and broke into laughter. "You wanted to turn to the authorities? Was that precisely how you put it?"

He thrust his hands in his pockets, seated himself comfortably in a corner of the divan, got out a cigarette case and matches and lit a cigarette.

"And so, you said that you wanted to resort to the help of the authorities? You will excuse me, Prince, if I sit?" he turned to Sheyin. "Well, Sir, what's next?"

The Prince moved a chair up to the table and sat down. Without taking his eyes off this strange man, he contemplated his face with perplexity and an avid, grave curiosity.

"But you see, my dear chap, there's always time for that measure,"

Nicolai Nicolaievich went on with an easy effrontery. "To intrude into a family of strangers—"

"Pardon me if I interrupt you—"

"No, pardon *me*, but it will be *I* who'll have to interrupt you—" the attorney almost shouted.

"Just as you please. Speak on. I am listening. But I have a few words to say to Prince Vassilii Lvovich."

And, without paying any further attention to Tuganovski, he said:

"The most difficult moment of my life has now come. And, Prince, I must speak to you without any conventionalities. You will hear me to the end?"

"I am listening," said Sheyin. "Oh, Nick, do keep still a while!" said he impatiently, noting Tuganovski's wrathful gesture, and turned to Zheltcov: "Go ahead."

Zheltcov gasped for air for a few seconds, as though he were suffocating, then began, suddenly and rapidly, as though he had plunged off a precipice. His jaws alone moved; his lips seemed still and white, like those of a dead man:

"It is hard to utter such . . . a phrase . . . that I love your wife. But seven years of hopeless and—respectful—love give me the right to do so. I agree that in the beginning, when Vera Nicolaievna was still unmarried, I used to write foolish letters to her, and even expected an answer to them. I agree that my last action—namely, the sending of the bracelet—was a still greater folly. But . . . there, I am looking straight into your eyes, and I feel that you will understand me: I know that it is not within my power ever to cease loving her. Tell me, Prince— we will take it for granted that this is unpleasant to you—but tell me, what would you do to put an immediate end to this feeling of mine? Drive me out of this town to some other, as Nicolai Nicolaievich has just suggested? What difference would that make? Even there I'd go on loving Vera Nicolaievna just as I do here. Lock me up in a prison? But even in prison I would find means of letting her know of my existence. That leaves but one solution—death. If that is what you wish, I will accept death in any form you prefer."

"Instead of attending to the matter at hand, we are indulging in some sort of melodramatic elocution," said Nicolai Nicolaievich, putting on his hat. "The long and the short of it is this: You are offered a choice of two things—either you absolutely forgo annoying Vera Nicolaievna, or, if you do not agree to this, we take certain measures which our position, our friends, and so forth, enable us to take."

Zheltcov, however, did not even glance in his direction, although he had heard his words. He turned to Prince Vassilii Lvovich and asked:

"Will you permit me to leave you for ten minutes or so? I won't conceal from you that I'm going to call Princess Vera Nicolaievna on the telephone. I assure you I'll repeat to you everything that I will be able to."

"You may go," said Sheyin.

When Vassilii Lvovich and Tuganovski were left alone, the latter immediately flew at his brother-in-law.

"This is no way to go about it!" he shouted, with the gesture that made him look as if he were throwing some invisible object off his chest with his right hand. "This is absolutely no way! I warned you that I was going to do all the talking when we got down to business. Instead of that you went all to pieces and allowed him to go on and on about his feelings. I could have settled the whole business in a few words—"

"Wait," said Prince Vassilii Lvovich. "All this will be cleared up right away. The main thing is that I still see his face, and I feel that this man is incapable of deliberate deceit and lying. And, really, if you stop and think, Nick—is he to blame because of love? And can anyone control such an emotion as love—an emotion which up to this day has never found anyone who could expound it?" The Prince mused a while before going on: "I feel sorry for the man. And it isn't only that I am sorry—but, mind you, I feel that I am present at some tremendous tragedy of the soul, and I can't play the buffoon here."

"That is decadence," said Nicolai Nicolaievich.

Ten minutes later Zheltcov came back. His eyes glistened, and there was profundity in them, as though they were brimming with unshed tears. And it was obvious that he had forgotten all about worldly etiquette, about precedence in sitting down, and that he had ceased worrying about being a gentleman. And again, with an aching, nervous sensitiveness, Prince Sheyin grasped all this.

"I am ready," said Zheltcov, "and on the morrow you will hear no more of me. As far as you are concerned, it will be as if I had died. But there is one condition—it is to *you* I am speaking, Prince Vassilii Lvovich: you see, I've embezzled public funds and, willy-nilly, I'll have to run away from this city. Permit me to write one more letter—the last—to Princess Vera Nicolaievna—"

"No! If you're through, you're through. No more letters!" Nicolai Nicolaievich began to shout.

"Very well; write it," said Sheyin.

"And that is all," uttered Zheltcov, with a superior smile. "You will hear no more of me and, of course, will never again see me. Princess Vera Nicolaievna did not want to talk to me at all. When I asked her if I could remain in the city, so that I might see her, if only at rare intervals—without, of course, ever letting her see me—her answer was: 'Oh, if you only knew what a bore all this business has become to me! Please put an end to it as quickly as you can!' And so I am putting an end to this business. I've done everything I could, I believe."

That evening, on reaching his villa, Vassilii Lvovich gave his wife a very exact account of his interview with Zheltcov, without omitting anything. It was as if he felt himself obligated to do so.

Vera, although she was upset, was not surprised, nor did she become embarrassed.

That night, when her husband came to her bed, she suddenly said to him, as she turned her face to the wall: ·

"Leave me alone. I know that this man will kill himself."

XI

Princess Vera Nicolaievna hardly ever read the newspapers, because, in the first place, they smudged her hands, and, in the second, she could never make out current newspaperese.

But fate made her open a newspaper at precisely the page and at the very column with the short paragraph headed: A MYSTERIOUS DEATH:

"G. S. Zheltcov, a clerk in the Comptroller's Department, committed suicide yesterday, at or about seven in the evening. According to the findings of a special investigation, the clerk's suicide was due to an embezzlement of public funds. In any event, such an embezzlement is mentioned in the note left by the suicide. Since the testimony of witnesses has established that the act was deliberate and of his own free will, it has been decided not to send the body to the Morgue for an autopsy."

"Why did I have a premonition of this?" Vera thought to herself. "Of precisely this tragic way out? And what was this—love or madness?"

She spent the whole day in walking about the flower garden and the orchard. The disquiet which increased within her from minute to minute apparently would not let her remain in one spot. And all her thoughts were fettered to that unknown man whom she had never seen, and now was hardly likely ever to see—to this ludicrous P.P. Zh., as they called him.

" 'Who knows—perhaps your path in life has been crossed by a genuine, self-denying, true love,' " she recalled the words of Anossov.

At six the postman arrived. This time Vera Nicolaievna recognized Zheltcov's handwriting and, with a tenderness which she did not expect from herself, unfolded his letter:

"I am not to blame, Vera Nicolaievna," Zheltcov wrote, "that it pleased God to send me, as an enormous happiness, my love for You. Everything has worked out so that nothing in life interests me—neither politics, nor science, nor philosophy, nor solicitude for the future happiness of humanity; for me the whole of life consists only of You. And now I feel that, like some unwelcome wedge, I have cut into your life. If You can, forgive me this. Today I am going away, and shall never return, and there will be nothing to remind You of me.

"I am infinitely grateful to You for merely being on this earth. I have tested myself; this is no malady, no maniacal idea: this is love, a love which it has pleased God to bestow upon me for some reason.

"Let it be said that I was ludicrous in your eyes, and in the eyes of your brother, Nicolai Nicolaievich. Departing, I say in rapture: *Yea, sanctified be Thy name.*

"Eight years ago I first saw You at a circus, in a box and, right then, from the very first second, I said to myself: I love her, because in all this world there is nothing like to her, there is nothing better; there is neither beast, nor plant, nor star, nor any human being more splendidly beautiful than You, or more tender. It is as if all the beauty of the earth has become incarnate within You. . . .

"Just consider—what was I to do? Run off to another city? My heart would, just the same, have been near You, at your feet; every moment of the day filled with You, with the thought of You, with dreams of You . . . a sweet delirium. I am very much ashamed about my foolish bracelet and blush when I think of it. Well, what of it? It was a mistake. I can imagine what an impression it must have made upon your guests!

"In ten minutes I am going away; I will have time only to affix a stamp and to mail this letter, for I would not trust anybody else to do it. I urge You to burn this letter. I have just now made a fire and am committing to the flames all that is most dear to me, all that life has held for me: your handkerchief, which, I confess, I stole—You forget it on a chair, at a ball; your note—oh, how I kissed it!—in which You forbade me to write you; the catalogue of an art exhibition—You held that catalogue in your hand for a while and then forgot it on a chair when you left. . . . *Finis.* I have severed everything, but nevertheless I think, and am even convinced, that You will think of me again. If You do, then . . . I know You are very fond of music; I have seen You most frequently at Beethoven recitals—well, if You do think of me again, then play, or order to be played for You, the Sonata in D Major, No. 2, Op. 2.

"I do not know how to end this letter. From the very depths of my soul I thank You because You were the sole joy of my life—its sole consolation—its sole thought. May God grant You happiness, and let nothing transient and worldly trouble your splendidly beautiful soul. I kiss your hands.

G. S. Zh."

She came to her husband with her eyes red from tears and her lips puffy and, having shown him the letter, said:

"I do not want to conceal anything from you, but I feel that something horrible has forced itself into our life. Probably you and Nicolai have done something you shouldn't have."

Prince Sheyin read the letter through attentively, refolded it neatly, and, after a long silence, said:

"I have no doubt of this man's sincerity; and, even more than that, I dare not analyze his feelings toward you."

"He died?" asked Vera.

"Yes—he died. I will say that he loved you, and that he was not mad in the least. I never took my eyes off him, and saw his every movement, every change on his face. And for him life did not exist without you. It seemed to me that I was in the presence of an enormous agony, such agony as men die from, and I almost realized that the man before me was a dead man. Do you understand, Vera? I did not know how to act, what I was to do—"

"Tell me, Vassenka," Vera Nicolaievna interrupted him, "would you feel hurt if I went to the city and had a look at his body?"

"No, no, Vera—please do, I beg of you. I'd go myself, except that Nicolai has spoiled everything for me. I am afraid I would feel myself out of place."

XII

Vera Nicolaievna left her carriage two blocks before she came to Lutheran Street. She found Zheltcov's quarters without any great difficulty. A gray-eyed old woman, very corpulent and wearing silver-rimmed spectacles, came in answer to her ring and, just as she had done yesterday, asked:

"Whom did you wish to see?"

"Mr. Zheltcov," said the Princess.

Probably her costume—her hat, gloves, and the somewhat imperious tone—must have produced a great impression upon the landlady. She grew talkative:

"If you please, if you please—there, the first door to the left—right there! He left us so suddenly. So it was embezzlement, let's say. He should have told me of it. You know how much one can accumulate, letting rooms out to bachelors. But still, I could have managed to scrape up six or seven hundred and put it up for him. If you but knew, Pani, what a splendid man he was! For eight years I had him as a lodger, and I didn't think of him as a roomer at all but as if he were my own son."

There was a chair right in the entry, and Vera sank down on it.

"I'm a friend of your late roomer," she said, choosing each word carefully. "Tell me something about the last minutes of his life—about what he did, and said."

"Pani, two gentlemen came here and talked with him for a very long time. Then he explained that they had offered him the place of an estate manager. Then Pan Zheltcov ran out to telephone, and when he came back he was ever so cheerful. Then those two gentlemen went away, while he sat down and started writing a letter. Then he went and dropped the letter in a mailbox, and then we heard a sound as if somebody had shot off a child's pistol. We didn't pay any attention to it at all. He always had his tea at seven in the evening. Lukeria—that's our maid—she comes and knocks: he don't answer; then she knocks again, and then once more. And so we had to break down his door—but he was already dead."

"Tell me something about the bracelet," Vera Nicolaievna demanded.

"Ah, ah, ah—the bracelet! Why, I'd actually forgot. How do you happen to know about it? Before writing the letter, he came to me and said: 'Are you a Roman Catholic?'—I says: 'Yes, I'm a Roman Catholic.' Then he says: 'You have a charming custom—' them's the very words he used: a charming custom—'you have a charming custom of hanging rings, necklaces, and other gifts on the image of the Mother of God. So please grant my request—can you hang this bracelet on Her icon?' I promised him I'd do so."

"Will you show him to me?" asked Vera.

"If you please, if you please, Pani. There, that's his door—the first to the left. They wanted to carry him off to the Morgue today, but he's got a brother, so he begged and begged until they allowed him to give the body a Christian burial. If you please, if you please—right this way."

Vera summoned all her strength and opened the door. There were three wax candles burning in the room, which was filled with the odor of labdanum. The table on which Zheltcov's body was lying was placed obliquely across the room; his head was resting very low: the pillow thrust under it was so skimpy and small that it seemed to have been deliberately palmed off on the corpse—there, what does anything matter to a dead man? There was profound gravity upon his closed eyes, and his lips were smiling beatifically and uncaringly, as though before his parting with life he had come to know some deep and delectable mystery, which had been a solution to all his life as a mortal. She recalled having seen that same expression of being at peace with the world upon the death masks of two great sufferers: Pushkin and Napoleon.

"If you say so, Pani, I'll go away," suggested the old woman, and one could catch in her tone something exceedingly intimate.

"Yes, I'll call you later," said Vera, and as soon as the landlady had left, took out of a small side pocket of her blouse a large red rose, lifted up the head of the corpse a little with her left hand, while with her right she placed the flower under it. At that second she realized that that love of which every woman dreams had gone by her. She recalled the words of General Anossov concerning eternal, extraordinary love— almost prophetic words. And, putting the hair back from the dead man's forehead to either side, she squeezed his temples hard between her hands and kissed his cold, moist forehead with a long, friendly kiss.

As she was leaving, the landlady addressed her in a fawning, characteristically Polish tone:

"Pani, I can see that you are not like all the others, that you haven't come here out of mere curiosity. The late Pan Zheltcov told me long before his death: 'If I should happen to die, and a certain lady should come to look at my body, you tell her that Beethoven's best work is—' he even wrote it down for me on purpose. Here's the paper—have a look—"

"Let me see it," said Vera Nicolaievna, and suddenly burst into tears.

"You must excuse me, but this impression of death is so oppressive that I cannot restrain myself."

And she read the words written in the familiar hand:

L. van Beethoven. Son. No. 2, Op. 2. Largo Appassionato.

XIII

Vera Nicolaievna returned home only late in the evening, and was glad that she found neither her husband nor brother at home.

But she did find Jennie Reiter waiting for her and, agitated by all she had seen and heard, Vera ran to her and, kissing the large, beautiful hands of the pianiste, cried out:

"Jennie, darling, I beg of you—play something for me!" and immediately went out of the room into the flower garden and sat down on a bench.

Not even for a second did she doubt that Jennie would play that very passage from the Second Sonata which this dead man with the ludicrous family name of Zheltcov had asked her to have played.

And so it was. From the very first chord she recognized this extraordinary work, unique in its profundity. And her soul seemed somehow to be cleft in two. She thought on the instant of that great love which had gone by her, such a love as is repeated only once in a thousand years. She recalled the words of General Anossov, and asked herself why this man had compelled her to listen to precisely this work of Beethoven's, and that against her will? And words were taking form in her mind. They were synchronized in her thoughts with the music to such an extent that it seemed as if they were distiches, each one of them closing with the words: *Yea, sanctified be Thy name.*

"Hearken, I shall show Thee now, in tender sounds, a life that submissively and joyously dedicated itself to torments, sufferings, and death. No complaint, no reproach, no pang of self-pride did. I know. Before Thy face I am but the one prayer: *Yea, sanctified be Thy name.*

"Yea, I foresee suffering, blood, and death. And I think that it is hard for the body to part with the soul, but, Splendidly Beautiful One, .praise be to Thee—passionate praise and gentle love. *Yea, sanctified be Thy name.*

"I recall Thy every step, Thy smile, Thy every glance—the sound of Thy footsteps. With a delectable grief—a gentle, splendidly beautiful grief—are my last recollections surrounded. But I shall cause Thee no grief. I depart alone, in silence—so hath it pleased God and fate. *Yea, sanctified be Thy name.*

"At the pre-mortal, sad hour I pray but to Thee alone. Life might have been splendidly beautiful for me as well. Murmur not, poor heart—murmur not. In my soul I call upon death, but within my heart I am filled with praise of Thee: *Yea, sanctified be Thy name.*

"Thou knowest not, nor do the people about Thee know, how splendidly beautiful Thou art. The clock strikes. 'Tis time. And, dying, in the grievous hour of parting with life, I none the less chant: *Glory unto Thee!*

"Behold, it cometh, all-pacifying Death; yet I still say: *Glory to Thee! . . .*"

Princess Vera embraced the trunk of an acacia, nestled close to it, and wept. The tree quivered softly. A light wind sprang up and, as though commiserating with her, began to sough among the leaves. The starflowers of the tobacco plants sent forth a more pungent fragrance. . . . And, at the same time, the amazing music, as though submitting to her grief, went on:

"Calm Thyself, dearest one—calm Thyself, calm Thyself. Dost Thou remember me? Dost remember? For Thou art my sole and my last love. Calm Thyself, I am with Thee. Think of me—and I shall be with Thee, inasmuch as we have loved each other for but one instant, yet for all eternity. Dost Thou remember me? Dost remember? Dost remember? Lo, I feel Thy tears. Calm Thyself. My sleep is so sweet, sweet, sweet. . . ."

Jennie Reiter, having finished playing, came out of the room and caught sight of the Princess sitting on a bench, all in tears.

"What is the matter with you?" asked the pianiste.

Vera, her eyes glistening with tears, fell to kissing Jennie's face, lips, eyes—uneasily, in real agitation—saying:

"No, no—he has forgiven me now. Everything is well."

Arcadii Timotheich
Averchenco
1 8 8 1 – 1 9 2 5

AVERCHENCO began his career by writing "straight" stories that compare favorably with Kuprin and Chekhov, but he is primarily known as a humorist. He founded and edited that fabulous weekly, *Satyricon* (1906-17) ; his clever and fantastic skits and one-act plays formed the backbone of the repertoires of the Crooked Mirror and Chauve Souris theater-cabarets in Petersburg. He became an émigré in 1917, and died in Constantinople.

The case of Averchenco is perhaps the most curious refutation of the many canards of the professional Soviet-haters. A Soviet pamphlet-library of world-humor, of enormous circulation, devotes several numbers to Averchenco (at least seven)— including the stories from his most virulent counterrevolutionary volume, *Twelve Knives in the Back of the Revolution.*

However, despite his being a funnyman who was not afraid to be funny, and despite the universality of his humor, only five or six of his hundreds of stories have achieved publication in English—and then only in magazines.

Both the story and the playlet here given show his predominant trait: a masterly grasp of grotesquerie and extravagance of situation.

The Young Man Who Flew Past

A PSYCHO-DRAMA
IN THE LIFE OF MAN

THIS SAD and tragic history began thus:

Three persons, in three different poses, were carrying on an animated conversation on the sixth floor of a large stone house.

The woman, with plump, beautiful arms, was holding a bed sheet to her breast, forgetting that a bed sheet could not do double duty and cover her shapely bare knees at the same time. The woman was crying, and in the intervals between sobs she was saying:

"Oh, John! I swear to you I'm not guilty! He set my head in a whirl, he seduced me—and, I assure you, all against my will! I resisted—"

One of the men, still in his hat and overcoat, was gesticulating wildly and speaking reproachfully to the third person in the room:

"Scoundrel! I'm going to show you right now that you will perish like a cur and the law will be on my side! You shall pay for this meek victim! You reptile! You base seducer!"

The third in this room was a young man who, although not dressed with the greatest meticulousness at the present moment, bore himself, nevertheless, with great dignity.

"I? Why, I have not done anything—I . . ." he protested, gazing sadly into an empty corner of the room.

"You haven't? Take this, then, you scoundrel!"

The powerful man in the overcoat flung open the window giving out upon the street, gathered the young man who was none too meticulously dressed into his arms, and heaved him out.

Finding himself flying through the air, the young man bashfully buttoned his vest, and whispered to himself in consolation:

"Never mind! Our failures merely serve to harden us!"

And he kept on flying downward.

Translated by Bernard Guilbert Guerney. Copyright, 1943, by the Translator.

He had not yet had time to reach the next floor (the fifth) in his flight, when a deep sigh issued from his breast.

A recollection of the woman whom he had just left poisoned with its bitterness all the delight in the sensation of flying.

"My God!" thought the young man. "Why, I loved her! And she could not find the courage even to confess everything to her husband! God be with her! Now I can feel that she is distant, and indifferent to me."

With this last thought, he had already reached the fifth floor and, as he flew past a window he peeked in, prompted by curiosity.

A young student was sitting reading a book at a lopsided table, his head propped up in his hands.

Seeing him, the young man who was flying past recalled his life; recalled that heretofore he had passed all his days in worldly distractions, forgetful of learning and books; and he felt drawn to the light of knowledge, to the discovery of nature's mysteries with a searching mind, drawn to admiration before the genius of the great masters of words.

"Dear, beloved student!" he wanted to cry out to the man reading, "you have awakened within me all my dormant aspirations, and cured me of the empty infatuation with the vanities of life, which have led me to such a grievous disenchantment on the sixth floor. . . ."

But, not wishing to distract the student from his studies, the young man refrained from calling out, flying down to the fourth floor instead, and here his thoughts took a different turn.

His heart contracted with a strange, sweet pain, while his head grew dizzy—from delight and admiration.

A young woman was sitting at the window of the fourth floor and, with a sewing machine before her, was at work upon something.

But her beautiful white hands had forgotten about work at the present moment, and her eyes—blue as cornflowers—were afar off, pensive and dreamy.

The young man could not take his eyes off this vision, and some new feeling, great and mighty, spread and grew within his heart.

And he understood that all his former encounters with women had been no more than empty infatuations, and that only now he understood that strange, mysterious word—Love.

And he was attracted to the quiet, domestic life; to the endearments of a being beloved beyond words; to a smiling existence, joyous and peaceful.

The next story, past which he was flying at the present moment, confirmed him still more in his inclination.

In the window of the third floor he saw a mother who, singing a quiet lullaby and laughing, was bouncing a plump, smiling baby; love, and a kind, motherly pride were sparkling in her eyes.

"I, too, want to marry the girl on the fourth floor, and have just such rosy, plump children as the one on the third floor," mused the young man, "and I would devote myself entirely to my family and find my happiness in this self-sacrifice."

But the second floor was now approaching. And the picture which the young man saw in a window of this floor forced his heart to contract again.

A man with disheveled hair and wandering gaze was seated at a luxurious writing table. He was gazing at a photograph in a frame before him; at the same time, he was writing with his right hand, and holding a revolver in his left, pressing its muzzle to his temple.

"Stop, madman!" the young man wanted to call out. "Life is so beautiful!" But some instinctive feeling restrained him.

The luxurious appointments of the room, its richness and comfort, led the young man to reflect that there is something else in life which could disrupt even all this comfort and contentment, as well as a whole family; something of the utmost force—mighty, terrific. . . .

"What can it be?" he wondered with a heavy heart. And, as if on purpose, Life gave him a harsh, unceremonious answer in a window of the first floor, which he had now reached.

Nearly concealed by the draperies, a young man was sitting at the window, sans coat and vest; a half-dressed woman was sitting on his knees, lovingly entwining the head of her beloved with her round, rosy arms, and passionately hugging him to her magnificent bosom. . . .

The young man who was flying past remembered that he had seen this woman (well-dressed) out walking with her husband—but this man was decidedly not her husband. Her husband was older, with curly black hair, half-gray, while this man had beautiful fair hair.

And the young man recalled his former plans: of studying, after the student's example; of marrying the girl on the fourth floor; of a peaceful, domestic life, à la the third—and once more his heart was heavily oppressed.

He perceived all the ephemerality, all the uncertainty of the happiness of which he had dreamed; beheld, in the near future, a whole procession of young men with beautiful fair hair about his wife and himself; remembered the torments of the man on the second floor, and the measures which he had taken to free himself from these torments—and he understood.

"After all I have witnessed, living is not worth while! It is both foolish and tormenting," thought the young man, with a sickly, sardonic smile; and, contracting his eyebrows, he determinedly finished his flight to the very sidewalk.

Nor did his heart tremble when he touched the flagging of the pavement with his hands and, breaking these now useless members, he dashed out his brains against the hard, indifferent stone.

And, when the curious gathered around his motionless body, it never occurred to any of them what a complex drama the young man had lived through just a few moments before.

The Man with a Green Necktie

CHARACTERS

CHETVERORUCOV—*a minor official*   SANDOMIRSKI—*a traveling salesman*
SOPHIA—*his wife*   THE STRANGER

SCENE—*A second-class railway compartment.* SANDOMIRSKI *is sitting and reading a comic paper.* CHETVERORUCOV *and* SOPHIA *are just sitting. All three are bored and yawning.*

SOPHIA (*yawning*): Oh, Lord—what a bore!

CHETVERORUCOV: Stop yawning! (*Yawns in his turn.*) There, you see, I've caught it from you! (*Yawns again.*)

SANDOMIRSKI (*yawning*): Oh, yes, it is something of a bore. A long trip is always boring. (*Looks through window.*) I wonder what station this is?

CHETVERORUCOV (*also looking out*): We'll see in a minute. (*Rub-*

bing the window with his coatsleeve.) There, now, that's better! (*Reads*) "For Men On—" No, that's not it!

SOPHIA (*yawns*): How I hate traveling!

CHETVERORUCOV (*yawning*): Stop grumbling! It's bad enough as it is!

SANDOMIRSKI (*yawning*): Yes. I wouldn't call this gay.

THE STRANGER (*enters. He has on a rough overcoat and traveling cap, and wears a bright green necktie. Making a polite and all-embracing bow, he addresses the married couple, indicating a seat next to them*): May I? (CHETVERORUCOV, *displeased, makes room for him.*)

SOPHIA: By all means!

SANDOMIRSKI (*muttering*): Who the devil sent him? (THE STRANGER *makes himself comfortable and becomes absorbed in a newspaper. A pause, followed by the whistling of the locomotive, and the rumbling of wheels.*)

SOPHIA (*yawning*): Five hours more of this! Five hours of deathly boredom!

CHETVERORUCOV (*sententiously*): Travel by rail is monotonous, and it is precisely this monotony that tires one.

THE STRANGER (*putting his paper aside, examining his fellow travelers closely, and breaking into low, subdued laughter*): So you're all bored, are you? I know the reason for your boredom! You're bored because you're not what you pretend to be—and that *is* a dreadful bore!

SANDOMIRSKI (*in a huff*): What do you mean, Sir? I assure you, I, as a person of intelligence—

THE STRANGER (*interrupting him with a smile*): We—none of us—are what we pretend to be! You, now—who are you?

SANDOMIRSKI: Who—me? I represent the firm of Evans and Crumble, with a line of broadcloths, knitted fabrics, and corduroys.

THE STRANGER (*with a peal of laughter*): Why, I knew you'd think of the most ridiculous thing! There, now—why do you fib, both to yourself and others? You, a Cardinal, attached to the Papal Court at the Vatican, and yet you deliberately use this Crumble fellow as a mask!

SANDOMIRSKI (*frightened and astonished*): The Vatican? Me?

THE STRANGER: Vatican or no—you are still a Cardinal! Don't try to fool me! I know that you're one of the cleverest and craftiest individuals of our times. I've heard a thing or two about you!

SANDOMIRSKI: Pardon me, but I find these . . . jests . . . un-called-for!

THE STRANGER (*laying a heavy hand on his shoulder and assuming a stern air*): Giuseppe, you can't take me in! Instead of all this silly talk, I'd prefer to hear you speak of the Vatican, of the mode of life there, and of your successes among the pious ladies of the Italian nobility.

SANDOMIRSKI (*aghast*): Let me go! What *is* this?

THE STRANGER (*threateningly clapping a hand over* SANDOMIRSKI'S *mouth*): Sh-h-h! You mustn't yell—there's a lady present! (*Resumes his seat, plucks out a revolver, and covers* SANDOMIRSKI *with it*): Giuseppe, I'm the kindest of fellows at heart—but I can't bear to have a hypocrite, a sham, an impostor sitting next to me! (SOPHIA, *frightened, shrinks into a corner.* CHETVERORUCOV *attempts to stand up— but a gesture from* THE STRANGER *fixes him once more in his place.*) Friends, calm yourselves! All I demand from this fellow is that he confess his true identity.

SANDOMIRSKI (*trembling*): I'm a traveling salesman—

THE STRANGER: You lie, Giuseppe! You're a Cardinal! (*Aims his revolver.*)

CHETVERORUCOV (*to* SANDOMIRSKI, *in a whisper*): Can't you see whom you have to deal with? He's a madman! Go on—tell him you're a Cardinal!

SANDOMIRSKI (*in a desperate whisper*): But I am *not* a Cardinal!

CHETVERORUCOV (*to* THE STRANGER, *ingratiatingly*): He feels embarrassed about admitting to you that he's a Cardinal. But, in all probability, he *is* a Cardinal!

THE STRANGER (*eagerly*): There—didn't I tell you? Don't you find that there's something Cardinalish about his face?

CHETVERORUCOV (*readily falling in with* THE STRANGER'S *mood*): There—there is! But, really—is it worth your while to get so worked up over it?

THE STRANGER (*petulantly—and juggling his revolver*): Well, let me hear *him* say he is!

SANDOMIRSKI (*with a shriek of despair*): Very well, then—very well! There—I *am* a Cardinal!

THE STRANGER (*with a triumphant flourish of his gun*): You see? I told you so! *All* men and women are not what they seem! Give me your blessing, Your Reverence! (SANDOMIRSKI *hesitatingly shrugs his shoulders, then extends both his hands and flutters them over* THE STRANGER'S *head.* SOPHIA *laughs loudly.*)

SANDOMIRSKI: Why all this laughter? (*To* THE STRANGER.): Sir, let me go out for just a moment.

THE STRANGER: Oh, no, I won't! I want you to tell me about some amusing little intrigue of yours with certain of the fair lambs in your flock.

SANDOMIRSKI: What *are* you talking about? What intrigues could I possibly—(THE STRANGER *puts his gun to* SANDOMIRSKI'S *temple.*) Oh, well, of course, there was an affair or two. . . . But hardly anything worth telling about—

THE STRANGER: Tell me, anyway!

SANDOMIRSKI: Take your gun away, and I will! Well, which shall it be? There was the time when a certain beautiful lady fell in love with me—

THE STRANGER (*eagerly*): A Countess?

SANDOMIRSKI: Very well—she was a Countess. "Myron—I mean Giuseppe," she says to me, "I love you something awful!" We exchanged kisses—

THE STRANGER: Oh, no—you must go more into details! Where did you meet her, and how was this great emotion aroused within you?

SANDOMIRSKI (*wearily*): We were at a ball. She had on a dress— you know, sort of white, with huge roses all over it. Some Ambassador or other had introduced us to each other. I said to her: "Countess, what a pretty little thing you are—"

THE STRANGER (*sternly cutting him short*): Come, what sort of a yarn are you spinning? Why, how could you, one of the cloth, be at a ball?

SANDOMIRSKI: Oh, well, you could hardly call it a ball—just a modest evening at home! She says to me: "Giuseppe, I am miserable! I would like to communicate at your church—"

THE STRANGER: You mean "to confess," not "communicate"?

SANDOMIRSKI: Well, yes—"to confess." "Very well," I said, "you may come!" And so she did, and said: "Giuseppe, you must forgive me, but I love you—"

THE STRANGER: What a frightfully stupid story! Your fellow passengers have evinced no interest whatsoever in it! If all of the Pope's Cardinals are like you, I don't envy His Holiness in the least (*To* CHETVERORUCOV.) I can't understand how you can permit such an interesting woman as your wife to be bored, when you have such a splendid gift—

CHETVERORUCOV (*timidly apprehensive*): Gift? What gift?

THE STRANGER: Your voice, of course! My word, but you're a shrewd article! Do you imagine because that cap hanging up there indicates that you are an official, nobody can surmise that you are really a celebrated baritone, who has garnered ever so many laurels in all the capitals of the world?

CHETVERORUCOV (*with a sickly smile*): You are mistaken. I really am a minor official, and this is my wife, Sophia—

THE STRANGER (*shifting the muzzle of his gun to cover* CHETVERORUCOV): Cardinal, what is your opinion? Is this man an official or a celebrated baritone?

SANDOMIRSKI (*with malicious glee*): Oh, a baritone, assuredly!

THE STRANGER: There, you see? Out of the mouths of babes and Cardinals! Do sing something for us, *maestro!* I implore you!

CHETVERORUCOV (*babbling helplessly*): I don't know how . . . My voice, I assure you, is most abominable—

THE STRANGER (*laughing wildly*): The modesty of true talent!

CHETVERORUCOV: I assure you—

THE STRANGER: Sing, the devil take you! Sing!

CHETVERORUCOV (*eying his wife timidly and singing very much off-key*):

"Out of the stars and the night,
Out of the sun and the dew,
Out of the dark and the light,
I have wrought all my dreams of you—"

THE STRANGER: You sing well! Your salary must run into four figures. Or even five! D'you know, no matter what you may say, music hath charms to soothe the savage breast. Isn't that so, Cardinal?

SANDOMIRSKI: Oh, most decidedly!

THE STRANGER: There, my friends—you see? You had hardly stopped pretending, had hardly become yourselves, than your mood brightened, and your boredom seems to have vanished! For you aren't bored—are you?

SANDOMIRSKI (*sighing*): Good heavens, no! This is all so jolly—no end! (*Laughs unconvincingly.*)

THE STRANGER: I'm *so* glad! I notice, dear Madam, that your pretty little face, too, wears another expression now. The most dreadful thing in life, my friends is sham—pretense. And so I have made these gentlemen take their masks off. One proved to be a Cardinal—the other a baritone. Am I right, Cardinal?

SANDOMIRSKI: You talk Gospel truth.

THE STRANGER: Most awful of all is the falsehood one finds in everything. It envelops us in our swaddling clothes; it accompanies us at every step; we breathe it—we carry it about upon our faces, upon our bodies. Therefore, Madam, I respectfully venture to request that you take off your dress! It conceals that which is the most splendidly beautiful thing in all the world—the body. . . . (*Points his revolver at* CHETVERORUCOV *and, looking point-blank at* SOPHIA, *gently resumes.*) Be so kind—disrobe! Surely, your husband can have no objection to that?

CHETVERORUCOV (*in a quavering voice, as he eyes the revolver*): I . . . I . . . I have nothing against it! I . . . I, too, love b-b-beauty! You may, Sophia—just a little. (*Sniggers.*)

SOPHIA (*casting a look of scorn at her husband and getting up resolutely, although with hysterical laughter*): Ah! So that's it? Very well, then! I, too, love beauty—and despise cowardice. I will disrobe for you. However, do order your Cardinal to turn away.

THE STRANGER (*sternly*): Cardinal! You, as one of spiritual calling, may not contemplate the vision of visions! Put that paper over your head! (SANDOMIRSKI *does so.*)

CHETVERORUCOV (*babbling*): Sophy . . . not too much . . . please!

SOPHIA: Leave me alone! (*She takes off her dress. To* THE STRANGER.) There! I *am* interesting—am I not? If you wish to kiss me, you may ask my husband for permission—he'll undoubtedly grant it!

THE STRANGER: Baritone! May I have your permission to salute, most respectfully, one of the finest women I have ever met? (CHETVERORUCOV, *speechless, looks at* THE STRANGER *in horror.*) Madam, he evidently has nothing against it! I shall, most respectfully, kiss your hand.

SOPHIA: Why the hand? Let us simply kiss! For you *do* find me attractive?

THE STRANGER (*enraptured*): You make me infinitely happy! (*They kiss—ardently. The locomotive whistles; the train slows down—then stops.* SOPHIA *dresses hastily.* THE STRANGER *picks up his things.*) You, Cardinal—and you, baritone! The train stops here for five minutes. During these five minutes I'll be standing on the platform, with the gun cocked in my coat pocket. Should either one of you take a step out of this compartment, I'll shoot him like a dog! Is that understood?

SANDOMIRSKI (*groaning*): Oh, go, go! (THE STRANGER *exits. There is a pause—all three seem rooted to their places. The locomotive whistles once more. A uniformed arm, holding a note, is thrust into the*

compartment. SANDOMIRSKI *snatches the note and reads it aloud.*)
"Confess you weren't bored! My original yet effective method of making travel by rail seem shorter has the additional advantage of compelling each passenger to show himself (or herself) in his (or her) true colors. There were four of us: a fool, a coward, a courageous woman, and myself—a droll fellow, and the life of the party! Baritone, kiss the Cardinal for me!"

Slow Curtain

Valerii Yacovlevich
Briussov

1 8 7 3 - 1 9 2 4

"Reading Briussov is a tremendous enjoyment. . . . He, in contradistinction to many, many poets—either dismal, or like tinkling guitars,
or like singing Gypsies in low taverns (even Block!)—demands from
the reader unusual sensitiveness and exaltation. . . . He will afford
you, the reader, the opportunity of eliciting images vivid to the verge of
hallucination—images that flare up before you. . . . And what enormous variety, what a panorama, what a glittering kaleidoscope of those
images will pass before you as you turn Briussov's pages!"

A. LUNACHARSKI

GRANDSON OF a serf who, after buying his freedom, had amassed a fortune, and son of an emancipated serf
who squandered it, this poet (some
of whose most fascinating poems are
far too curious—to put it mildly—
ever to appear in English) made his
debut in print at sixteen—with a defense of the totalizator. He had begun plucking the "flowers of evil,"
according to his own phrase and confession, at twelve, and began writing
even before that, block-printing
"scientific articles," stories and poems
—he first wrote poetry at the age of
eight. Under the influence of the
Parnassians he tried to implant Symbolism in Russia, beginning with
1894, and within ten years was the
acknowledged head of the Russian
Symbolists. He received his greatest
encouragement, as a writer outside
of any particular clique, from Gorki.

A superb craftsman, Briussov regarded writing, especially poetry, as
no more than a trade, and fostered
its technics and development; extremely versatile—poet, novelist,
short story writer, dramatist, critic,
prosodist, literary historian, editor,

publisher—he yet remained an individualist as artist. He was extremely prolific: exclusive of posthumous publications, his books run to more than eighty. A remarkable linguist, he knew even Sanscrit, and, as translator, handled superbly (to mention a few) Poe, Wilde, French lyricists of the nineteenth century, Verhaeren, Maeterlinck, Verlaine, d'Annunzio, Ausonius, Homer—and the poets of Armenia. In 1914 he was a war correspondent. His most interesting project, perhaps, was the one he began shortly before his death: an edition of Pushkin, wherein Briussov undertook to complete the rough and unfinished drafts of the great poet.

As man, Briussov was with and of the Revolution from its beginning to his death.

The short story here given is from *The Republic of the Southern Cross and Other Stories* (McBride, N.Y., 1919). In justice to the anonymous translator it must be said that the revision is so extensive as to amount practically to a new translation.

The Republic of the Southern Cross

THERE HAS lately appeared a whole series of accounts of the dreadful catastrophe which has befallen the Republic of the Southern Cross. They are strikingly at variance with one another and give numerous details of a manifestly fantastic and improbable nature. Obviously, the writers of these accounts have lent too ready an ear to the narratives of the survivors from Star City, the inhabitants of which, as it is common knowledge now, were all stricken with a psychical disorder. For that reason we consider it opportune to give herewith a summary of all the reliable evidence to date concerning this disaster at the South Pole.

The Republic of the Southern Cross came into being some forty years ago—a development of the three hundred steel mills established in the South Polar regions. In a general notice, sent to each and every government throughout the world, the new state put forth its claims to all lands, whether mainland or island, within the limits of the Antarctic Circle, as also to all parts of such lands extending beyond it. It announced its readiness to purchase from the various other states involved the lands which those states might consider to be under their special protectorate. The claims of the new Republic did not meet with any opposition on the part of the fifteen great powers of the world. Disputed points concerning certain islands lying entirely outside the Polar Circle, yet closely related to the South Polar state, were settled by special treaties. On the fulfillment of the various formalities, the Republic of the Southern Cross was admitted into the family of the world states, and its diplomatic representatives were recognized by all governments.

The chief city of the Republic, called Star City, was situated at the actual Pole itself. At that imaginary point through which the earth's axis passes and all the meridians of the earth become one, stood the City Hall, and the dome with its pointed turrets looked upon the nadir of the heavens. The streets of the city extended along the meridians branching from the City Hall, and these meridians were intersected by other streets in concentric circles. The height of the buildings was uniform, as was also their external architecture. The walls were without windows, since all the buildings, as well as the streets, were artificially lighted by electricity. Because of the severity of the climate, an impenetrable and opaque roof had been constructed over the whole city, with powerful air-conditioning units that insured a constant change of air. These regions have but one day and one night in the year, each one lasting six months. And the temperature of the streets was also artificially maintained at the same level throughout all the seasons of the year.

According to the last census, the population of Star City had reached two and a half million. The whole of the remaining population of the Republic, numbering fifty million, was concentrated in the neighborhood of the ports and manufacturing centers. These other points were also noted for the settlement of millions of people in cities which, in their external characteristics, were reminiscent of Star City. Thanks to an ingenious application of electric power, the entrance to the regional harbors remained ice-free and accessible all the year round. Funicular trains, electrically operated, connected the most populated parts of the Republic, and every day tens of thousands of passengers and millions of kilograms of freight were carried by them from one town to another. The hinterland of the country remained uninhabited. Travelers looking out of the train windows could see nothing but depressing wastes below, white in winter and overgrown with wretched-looking grass during the three months of summer. All wild life had long since been exterminated, and the country itself produced no means of sustenance for its population. But the bustling life of the ports and industrial centers was all the more remarkable. In order to convey an idea of this life it will perhaps suffice to say that of late years approximately seven-tenths of the world output of metals has come from the state mines of the Republic.

The Constitution of the Republic, to all outward appearance, seemed to be the realization of ultimate democracy. But the only fully enfranchised citizens were the workers in the metal industry, who numbered about sixty per cent of the whole population. All mills and mines were the property of the state. The life of the miners and affiliated workers was made easy by all possible comforts, conveniences, and even luxuries. Placed at their disposal, aside from magnificent accommodations and a recherché cuisine, were various educational institutions and means of cultural entertainment: libraries, museums, theaters, concert auditoria, halls for all types of sport, and so forth. The number of working hours per day was extremely short. The training and education of children, the dispensing of medical and legal aid, as well as the ministry of the different religious cults, were all assumed by the state. Ample provision for all the needs—and even the whims— of the workers for the state having been arranged, no wages were paid; but the families of citizens who had served twenty years in mine or mill, or who in their years of work had died or become enfeebled, received pensions for life, on condition that they did not leave the Republic. From among the workers, by universal ballot, the Representatives to the Law-Making Chamber were elected, and this Chamber had cognizance of all questions pertaining to the political life of the country—without having the power, however, to alter its fundamental laws.

It must be said that this democratic exterior concealed the purely autocratic tyranny of the shareholders and directors of a former trust. While yielding to others the places of deputies in the Chamber, they never failed to place their own candidates as directors of the mines and mills. And in the hands of the Board of Directors the economic life of the country was concentrated. The Directorate received all the contracts and assigned them to the different mines and mills for fulfillment; it purchased the materials and machinery for the work; all business management was in its hands. It handled immense sums of money, running into the billions. The Law-Making Chamber merely certified the entries of debits and credits in the operation of the plants and mines, the accounts being submitted to it for that purpose, and the balance on these accounts greatly exceeded the entire budget of the Republic. The influence of this Board of Directors in the international relations of the Republic was immense. Its decisions could make or break whole countries. The prices fixed by it determined the wages of millions among the laboring masses throughout the world. And, moreover, the influence of the Board, though indirect, was always decisive in the internal affairs of the Republic. The Law-Making Chamber, in fact, appeared to be no more than the humble servant of the will of the Board.

For the maintenance of power in its own hands the Board was obliged to regulate implacably the entire life of the country. Though having every appearance of liberty, the life of the citizens was actually standardized down to even the most minute details. The buildings throughout all the towns of the Republic were restricted to one unvarying pattern, fixed by law. The decoration of all buildings used by the workers, though luxurious to a degree, was strictly uniform. Every man, woman, and child received exactly the same food at exactly the same time. The clothes issued at the government stores never varied, and for decades at a stretch were of the same unchanging cut. At a signal from the City Hall, at a set hour, a strict curfew was enforced. The entire press of the country was under the thumb of a rigorous censorship. No articles directed against the dictatorship of the Board were permitted to see the light. But, as a matter of fact, the entire country was so convinced of the benevolence of this dictatorship that the linotypers would have refused on their own account to set any articles criticizing the Board. The mines and plants were overrun with the Board's stool pigeons. At the slightest manifestation of discontent against the Board these stool pigeons hastened to arrange meetings and, with impassioned oratory, to dissuade the doubters. The fact that the life of the workers in the Republic was the envy of the entire world was, of course, a disarming argument. It is said that in cases of persistent agitation by certain individuals the Board did not hesitate to resort to assassination. At any rate, during the whole existence of the Republic, the universal ballot of the citizens had never brought into power a single deputy who was hostile to the Directorate.

The population of Star City was composed chiefly of workers who had fulfilled their span of service. They were, so to say, shareholders in the government. The means which they received from the state permitted them to live opulently. It is not astonishing, therefore, that Star City was considered one of the gayest capitals in the world. For various entrepreneurs and entertainers it was a veritable gold mine.

The world's celebrities brought their talents hither. Here the best operas, the best concerts, the best exhibitions were to be found; here the best-informed newspapers (within the obvious limitations) were published. The shops of Star City were amazing in the richness and choice of their stocks, the restaurants in the luxury of their menus and the superb skill of service. Resorts of vice, where every form of depravity invented in either the ancient or the modern world was to be found, abounded. However, the governmental regulation of life was maintained in Star City as well. It is true that the decorations of living quarters and the fashions in wearing apparel were not so rigidly adhered to, but the curfew remained in force, a rigorous censorship of the press was kept up, and numerous stool pigeons were employed by the Board. Order was officially maintained by a People's Police, but the secret police of the all-cognizant Board functioned side by side with it.

Such was, in its general character, the mode of life in the Republic of the Southern Cross and in its Capital. The problem of the future historian will be to determine to what extent that mode of life was responsible for the outbreak and spread of that fatal disease which brought about the ruin of Star City and with it, it may well be, that of the whole young Republic.

The first cases of the *contradiction mania* were observed in the Republic some twenty years ago. At that time it bore the character of a rare and sporadic affliction. Nevertheless, the local psychiatrists were greatly interested therein and have given a circumstantial account of its symptoms at the International Medical Congress at Lhasa, where several reports on it were read. Subsequently it was, somehow or other, forgotten, even though there was never any difficulty in finding cases of it in the psychiatric clinics of Star City. The mental disorder derived its name from the fact that its victims consistently contradicted their wishes by their actions, desiring to do one thing but saying and doing another. (The scientific label of the disease is *mania contradicens*.) It begins with fairly mild symptoms, generally those of characteristic aphasia. The stricken persons, instead of saying "Yes," say "No"; wishing to utter something caressing, they will splutter abuse, and so on. The majority of them also will begin to contradict themselves by their behavior: intending to go to the left they turn to the right; thinking to raise a hat brim in order to see better, they would pull it down over the eyes instead, and so forth. As the disease develops, contradiction overtakes the whole of the bodily and spiritual life of the patient, exhibiting infinite diversity conformable with the individual's idiosyncrasies. In general, the speech of the patient becomes unintelligible and his actions are absurd. The normality of the physiological functions of the organism is disturbed. While acknowledging the irrationality of his behavior, the victim nevertheless falls into a state of extreme excitement bordering upon actual insanity. Many commit suicide, sometimes in fits of manic depression, sometimes in moments of psychic lucidity. Others perish from an influx of blood to the brain. In almost all cases the disorder is fatal; cases of recovery are rare in the extreme.

The *mania contradicens* assumed an epidemic character at Star City during the middle months of this year. Up to that time the number of cases had never exceeded two per cent of the total number of patients in the hospitals. But this proportion suddenly soared to *twenty-five per cent* during the month of May (or the Autumn Month, as it is called in the Republic) and it continued to increase during the succeeding months with as great rapidity. By the middle of June there were already two per cent *of the whole population*—that is, some fifty thousand persons—officially certified as suffering from *contradiction*. No detailed statistical data of any later date is available to us. The hospitals overflowed. The number of doctors on the spot proved to be altogether insufficient. And, moreover, the doctors themselves, as well as the nurses in the hospitals, were also affected by the malady. In a very short while there was no one to whom to appeal for medical aid, and a correct record of patients became impossible. The evidence given by eyewitnesses agrees, however, on one point: it was impossible to find any family or group in which someone was not afflicted. The number of sound people rapidly decreased as panic caused a wholesale exodus from the Capital, yet the number of those stricken increased. It is probably true that by the month of August all who remained in Star City were down with this psychical disorder.

It is possible to follow the first developments of the epidemic through the columns of the local newspapers, the headings of which were in ever larger type as the mania grew. Since the detection of the disease in its early stages was most difficult, the chronicle of the first days of the epidemic is full of comic incidents. A conductor on one of the city's subways, instead of taking fares from the passengers, went around giving them money himself. A policeman whose duty it was to regulate traffic spent his whole day in snarling it. A visitor in a gallery, as he walked from room to room, turned all the pictures with their faces to the wall.

(This item is rather dubious: it is stated specifically that the exhibition was one of trans-post-sur-surrealistic paintings.) A newspaper page, proofread by one already touched with the disease, was printed the next morning full of the most amusing absurdities. At a concert, the violinist, attacked by the disorder, suddenly interrupted the harmonious efforts of the orchestra with the most dreadful dissonances. A very, very long series of such happenings gave plenty of scope for the witticisms of the local columnists. But several instances of a different type of phenomena caused the jokes to come to an abrupt stop. The first was that of a doctor, overcome by the disease, who prescribed poison for a girl under his care, thus bringing about her death. For three days the newspapers were filled with this occurrence. Then two nurses, who had taken forty-one children for an airing in one of the city's parks, were attacked by *contradiction* and cut the throats of all their young charges. This event staggered the whole city. But, on the evening of the same day, two victims of the malady turned a machine gun taken from one of the armories against the populace, killing and injuring some five hundred people.

After this, all the newspapers and civic bodies in the city called peremptorily for prompt measures against the epidemic. At a special session of the Board of Directors and the Law-Making Chamber sitting together it was decided to call in doctors from other cities and outside the Republic, to enlarge the existing hospitals and construct new ones, and to build barracks everywhere for the isolation of the sufferers, to print and distribute half a million copies of a pamphlet on the disease, its symptoms, and methods of cure, to organize a special street patrol of doctors and orderlies throughout the city to render first aid to those who had not been removed from private quarters. It was likewise decided to run special trains every day on all the funiculars for the removal of the patients, since the doctors were of the opinion that change of air was one of the best remedies. Similar measures were undertaken at the same time by various associations, societies, and clubs. A Society for Combating the Epidemic was actually formed, and the members thereof gave themselves up to the work with remarkable self-devotion. But, in spite of all these measures, the epidemic gained ground with each day, overcoming in its progress old men and little children, active workers and the superannuated, the chaste and the debauched. And soon society as a whole was enveloped in the elemental terror of the unheard-of calamity.

The hegira from Star City commenced. At first only a few fled, and these were the leading dignitaries—the Directors, the Deputies of the Law-Making Chamber, who made all haste to send their families to cities in the south of Australia and Patagonia. Following these, the floating elements of the population fled, those aliens who had so gladly sojourned in the "gayest city of the Southern Hemisphere"—theatrical artists, businessmen, cocottes. When the epidemic showed no signs of abating, even the shopkeepers fled. They hurriedly sold off their goods and left their empty premises to the will of Fate. With them, naturally, went the bankers, the theater and restaurant owners, the newspaper and magazine editors and publishers. At last even the permanent residents were impelled to leave. According to law, the departure of workers from the Republic was forbidden, under penalty of losing their pensions, but, just the same, the number of deserters began to increase. The employees of the city institutions fled, the militia fled, so did the pharmacists and even the doctors. The desire for flight became a veritable mania in its turn. Everyone who was in a position to do so fled.

The stations of the funiculars were jammed with immense crowds; train tickets fetched enormous sums and could be held only by fighting. One had to pay no less than a fortune for a place on one of the dirigibles, each of which could take only ten passengers. At the moment of train departures, newcomers would break into the compartments and take up places which they refused to relinquish except through the application of brute force. Mobs stopped the trains which had been arranged especially for victims of the disease, dragged the latter out of the cars and then compelled the engine drivers to go on. From the end of May, all train service, except between the Capital and the ports, ceased to operate. The trains left Star City packed like sardine boxes, the passengers standing on the steps and in the passageways, some even venturing to cling on the outside, despite the fact that, with the speed the electric funiculars of the day had attained, any person doing such a rash thing risked being suffocated. The steamship lines of Australia, South America and South Africa amassed inordinate riches transporting refugees from the Republic to other lands. The two air-transport companies of the Republic which ran the dirigibles waxed no less prosperous, accomplishing, as they did, ten trips a day and bearing away from Star City the last belated millionaires.

On the other hand, trains arrived at Star City practically empty; it was impossible to persuade people to come to work at the Capital at any wages; the only rare arrivals were eccentric globe-trotters and seekers of new thrills. It is computed that from the beginning of the exodus to the twenty-second of June, when the regular train services ceased, a million and a half persons—that is, almost two-thirds of the entire population—passed out of Star City by the six funicular systems.

By his enterprise, courage, and strength of will, one man earned eternal fame for himself—and that was the Chairman of the Board of Directors, Horace Deville. At the extraordinary session of the fifth of June, Deville had been elected, both by the Board and by the Law-Making Chamber, as Dictator over the city, and was given the title of Chief. He had sole control of the city treasury, of the militia, and of all municipal institutions. It was at this time that the decision was reached to remove the government of the Republic and all the archives from Star City to a northern port. The name of Horace Deville should be written in letters of gold among the most heroic names of history. For six weeks did he struggle with the growing anarchy in the city. He succeeded in gathering around him a group of helpers as selfless as himself. He was able to enforce discipline, both in the militia and in the municipal services generally, for a considerable time, though these bodies were terrified by the general disaster and decimated by the epidemic. Hundreds of thousands owe their escape to Horace Deville, who, thanks to his energy and powers of organization, made it possible for them to leave. He lightened the misery of the last days for thousands of others, making it possible for them to die in hospitals, carefully looked after, and not merely stoned or clubbed to death by some mad mob.

And Deville preserved for mankind a chronicle of the catastrophe, for one cannot but consider as a chronicle his short but all-important telegrams, sent several times a day from Star City to the temporary seat of the government of the Republic at a northern port. Deville's first deed on becoming Chief of the city was an attempt to restore calm among the population. He issued manifestoes proclaiming that the psychical infection was most easily contracted by people in a state of excitement, and he called upon all sound and well-balanced persons to exercise their authority to restrain those of weaker fiber and the nervous ones. Next, Deville utilized the Society for Combating the Epidemic and placed under the authority of its members all public places, theaters, meetinghouses, squares and other public thoroughfares. During these days hardly an hour passed without the discovery of new cases. Whichever way one looked, one saw faces or whole groups of faces manifestly expressive of abnormality. The greater number of victims, once they realized their condition, evinced an immediate desire for help. But under the influence of the disorder this desire expressed itself in various types of hostile action against the nearest bystanders. The stricken persons wished to hasten home or to a hospital, but instead of doing this they fled in fright to the outskirts of the city. The thought would occur to them of asking a passer-by to do something for them, yet instead of that they would seize him by the throat. In this way many persons were strangled, struck down, or injured with knife or stick. Consequently any crowd, whenever it found itself in the presence of a sufferer from *contradiction,* would take to its heels. It was at such moments that the members of the Society would appear on the scene, take the sick person into custody, and then calm and take him or her to the nearest hospital; it was also their work to reason with the crowds and explain that there really was no danger, that the general disaster had simply spread a little further, and that it was their duty to combat it to the full extent of their powers.

The sudden seizures of persons in the audiences of theaters or meeting places often led to the most tragic catastrophes. Once, at an opera performance, there was a mass seizure of hundreds of people who, instead of expressing their approval of the singers, rushed pell-mell on to the stage and scattered blows right and left.[1] At the Grand Dramatic Theater an actor whose part called for suicide by a pistol shot fired the pistol several times at the audience. The pistol was, of course, loaded with blank cartridges, but the shots had such an effect on the nerves of the spectators that it hastened the outbreak of the disorder in many in whom it had been merely latent. In the crush which ensued several score were killed. But the worst catastrophe of all took place at the Theater of Fireworks. The militia posted there as a fire brigade suddenly set fire to the stage and to the screens through which the various lighting effects were obtained. No less than two hundred of the spectators, mostly children, were burned or crushed to death. After this occurrence Horace Deville closed every theater and concert auditorium in the city.

By now, the thieves and bandits constituted a grave danger to the citizens, since in the general disorganization the undesirable elements were able to carry their depredations to great lengths. It is said that a number of them had come to Star City from other countries. Some simulated the mania in order to escape punishment, but others felt no

---

[1] The name of the opera performed is withheld in all reports of the occurrence— most probably through censorship.

necessity of making any pretense at disguising their open robberies. Gangs of thieves entered the abandoned shops, broke into private dwellings, and simply took the more valuable objects or demanded gold; they stopped people in the streets and stripped them of their valuables, such as watches, rings, bracelets, money. And the robberies were accompanied by outrages of every sort, even of the most disgusting nature. The Chief dispatched companies of militia to hunt down the criminals, but these guardians of law and order did not dare to enter into open conflict with the lawbreakers. There were dreadful moments when the malady would suddenly manifest itself in one or more among either the militia or the criminals—or both—and friend would turn his weapon against friend.

At first the Chief simply expelled from the city the criminals who fell under arrest. But the wardens in charge of the prison trains liberated them, in order to sell the places in the train they might have taken up, whereupon the Chief was obliged to condemn the criminals to death. Thus, after a lapse of almost three centuries, capital punishment was once more introduced upon earth. In June a general scarcity of indispensable food and medicines began to make itself felt. The imports by funicular transportation dwindled; all manufacturing within the city was practically at a standstill. Deville organized the city bakeries and the distribution of bread and meat to the population. The same communal tables that had been so long established at the plants and mines were now set up in the very Capital. However, it was impossible to find sufficient staffs for the kitchens and the service. Some voluntary workers toiled until they fell down from exhaustion, and even the number of these volunteers diminished. The city's crematoria were going full blast night and day, yet the number of corpses increased instead of decreasing. Finding dead bodies abandoned in the streets and in the houses became a common occurrence. The municipal services —such as telegraph, telephone, and mail communications, electric lighting, water supply, sanitation, and all the rest—were attended to by fewer and fewer people. Yet it is astonishing how much Deville succeeded in accomplishing. He looked after everything and everyone. It is easy to guess that he never knew a moment's rest. And all those who were saved testify unanimously that his activity was beyond all praise.

Toward the middle of June the shortage of manpower on the funiculars began to be felt. There were not enough engine drivers or conductors. On the seventeenth of July the first wreck took place on the

Southwestern Line, caused by the seizure of the engine driver. In a paroxysm of the attack he plunged the train over a precipice on to a glacier, and almost all the passengers were killed or maimed. News of this was brought to Star City by the next train, and it came like a thunderbolt. A hospital train was immediately dispatched; it brought back the dead and injured—and toward the evening of the same day news spread of a similar catastrophe on the First Line. Two of the funicular systems connecting Star City with the outside world were disorganized. Wreck crews were sent out from Star City and from North Port to repair the lines, but this was almost impossible, owing to the winter temperature. There was no hope of train service resuming on these two lines—at least not in the near future.

These catastrophes were simply the forerunners of new ones. The more worried the engine drivers became, the more receptive they were to the disorder and to the repetition of the same error their predecessors had made. Merely because they were afraid of wrecking a train, they wrecked it. During the five days from the eighteenth to the twenty-second of June seven passenger trains came to grief. Literally thousands of passengers were killed outright, perished from their injuries, or starved to death unrescued amid the snowy, icy wastes. Only very few had sufficient strength to return to Star City through their own exertions. The six main lines connecting Star City with the outside world were put entirely out of commission. One of these lines had been practically destroyed by an enraged mob, the excuse given being that the trains were run exclusively for the rich. The others were wrecked one by one, the disorder probably attacking not merely the drivers but all the crews. The population of Star City was at this juncture approximately six hundred thousand. For some time their sole means of communication with the outside world had been the telegraph.

On the twenty-fourth of June, the Metropolitan subway ceased to run. On the twenty-sixth, all telephone service was discontinued. On the twenty-seventh, all the pharmacies, except the largest, centrally located one, were closed. On the first of July, all the residents in the outlying parts of the city were commanded to move into the central districts, for the better maintenance of order, more efficient distribution of food, and prompter rendering of medical aid. Suburban dwellers left their own quarters and settled in those recently abandoned by the fugitives. All sense of property vanished. No one regretted leaving his own house to take up his abode in somebody else's. Nevertheless, burglars and bandits did not disappear, though perhaps one would now call them demented creatures rather than criminals. They went on stealing, and great caches of gold and other loot have been discovered in the deserted houses where they had hidden them— together with precious stones scattered about the decomposing body of the thief himself.

It is astonishing, but even in the midst of universal destruction life tended to keep to its former courses. There still were shopkeepers who kept their places open and sold for incredible sums the luxuries, flowers, books, guns, and other wares which they had preserved. Purchasers threw down their unnecessary gold ungrudgingly and the miserly merchants squirreled it, God knows why. Speak-easy dives still existed, with wine, woman, song, and cards, where unfortunates sought refuge and strove to forget the dread reality. There the sound mingled with the afflicted, but no record has remained of the scenes which must have taken place. Two or three newspapers still tried to preserve the signifi- cance of the printed word in the midst of the desolation. Copies of these newspapers are being sold now at ten and twenty times their original value and are undoubtedly destined to become bibliophilic rarities of the first degree.[1] Their columns mirror faithfully the horrors prevalent in the stricken city, described in the midst of the reigning madness and set by half-mad linotypers. There were reporters who took notes of what was happening in the city, editorial writers who debated hotly the state of affairs, and even columnists who endeavored to lighten these tragic days. But the dispatches received from outside countries, telling as they did of a real, normal life, caused the souls of Star City's newspaper readers to fall into despair.

There were desperate attempts to escape. At the beginning of July a veritable host of women and children, led by one John Dew, decided to set out on foot for Londontown, the nearest inhabited place. Deville understood the madness of this attempt but could not stop the people, and himself supplied them with warm clothing and provisions. This whole horde of about two thousand was lost in the snowy wastes and the perpetual Polar night. A certain Whiting began to preach a more heroic remedy: this was to kill off all those afflicted with the mania,

[1] Only six years after the date of the above account the Blue Faun Book Shop of New York sold a far-from-mint copy of the *Star City Dispatch* for the twenty-eighth of June for $325, while at a recent auction in London a run of the (Star City) *Inquirer,* complete from May first to July thirteenth (established by Brierley as the day of its suspension), fetched, in only a fair state, £673, the successful bidder reselling it almost immediately on the spot at a fifty per cent advance.—*Editor.*

after which, he maintained, the epidemic would cease. He found a considerable body of adherents—however, in those dark days any proposal, no matter how wild, how inhuman, would have obtained attention as long as it promised deliverance in any way. Whiting and his friends broke into every house in the city and did away with whatever victims of the mania they found. They massacred the patients in the hospitals—they even killed those who were merely suspected of being unsound. Brigands and lunatics joined themselves to these bands of idealistic assassins. The whole city became their arena. It was during these difficult days that Horace Deville organized his co-workers into a military force, inspired them with his courage, and set out to fight the Whitingites. This affair lasted several days. Hundreds of men fell on either side, till at last Whiting himself was captured. He was manifestly in the last stages of *mania contradicens* and, instead of going to the scaffold, was taken to a hospital where he shortly died a miserable death.

On the eighth of July came one of the worst calamities. The control man at the Central Power Station smashed all the generating motors. The electric light failed, and the whole city was plunged into utter darkness. As there was no other means of lighting and heating the city, the people were left in a helpless plight. Deville had, however, foreseen such an eventuality and had accumulated a considerable quantity of torches and fuel. Bonfires were lighted in all the streets. Flashlights were distributed by the tens of thousands. But these miserable lights could not illumine the gigantic perspectives of Star City, or the highways running in a straight line for scores of kilometers, or the gloomy heights of the towering buildings. With the coming of the darkness the last traces of discipline in the city disappeared. Terror and madness at last took full possession of all souls. The sound could not be distinguished from the sick. A dreadful orgy of despair began.

The moral sense of the people declined with astonishing rapidity. Culture slipped off them like a delicate bark and revealed man wild and naked, as the man-beast he was. All sense of right was lost; force alone was acknowledged. For women, the only law became that of desire and indulgence. The most virtuous matrons behaved like the most abandoned women, with no continence or fidelity, and used the vile language of the tavern. Young girls ran about the streets, demented and wanton. Drunkards staged drinking bouts in the ruined wine cellars, not in the least distressed if a corpse was sprawling among the bottles. All this was constantly aggravated by fresh outbreaks of the disease. Most lamentable was the situation of the children, abandoned by their parents to the will of Fate. They died of hunger, of injuries after assault, and were killed both deliberately and by accident. It is even affirmed that cannibalism took place.

At this ultimate stage of the tragedy Horace Deville could not, of course, extend help to the entire population. But he did arrange shelter in the City Hall for those who still retained their reason. All entrances to the building were barricaded, and sentries were constantly on guard. There was food and water for three thousand people for forty days. Deville, however, had only eighteen hundred people in the building, and though there must have been other people with sound minds in the town, they could not have known what Deville was doing, and remained in hiding in the houses. Many must have resolved to remain indoors to the very end, and, later, many bodies were found of those who had died of hunger in their solitude. It is remarkable that among those who took refuge in the City Hall there were very few new cases of the malady. Deville was able to maintain discipline in his small community. He kept to the last a diary of all that happened, and that diary, together with the telegrams he had sent, furnishes the most reliable source of evidence as to the catastrophe. The diary was discovered in a secret closet in the City Hall, where the most precious documents were kept. The last entry refers to the twentieth of July. Deville writes that a literally frenzied mob is assaulting the building, and that he is obliged to fire pistol shots at the people. "What I am hoping for," he writes, "I know not. No help can be expected before the spring. And we haven't the food to keep us alive until spring. But I will do my duty until the very end." These were the last recorded words of Deville—truly noble words!

It must be added that on the twenty-first of July the mob took the City Hall by storm, and that its defenders were all either killed or scattered. The body of Deville has not yet been found, and there is no reliable evidence available as to just what took place in the city after the twenty-first. It must be conjectured, from the state in which the city was found, that anarchy had reached its very limits. The gloomy streets, flickeringly lit up by the glare of bonfires of furniture and books, can be imagined. (Fire was obtained by striking iron on flint.) Hordes of madmen and drunkards danced wildly about these bonfires. Men and women drank together, passing the common cup from lip to lip. The worst scenes of sensuality were so common a spectacle that they hardly aroused interest. Some sort of dark, atavistic instinct animated the souls of these townsmen and, half-naked, unwashed, unkempt, they danced the dances of their remote ancestors, the contemporaries of the cave bears, and sang the same wild songs as did the troglodyte hordes when they fell with stone axes upon some mammoth making his last stand. With songs, with incoherent outcries, with idiotic laughter, mingled the cries of those who had lost the power to express in words their own delirious dreams; mingled with these were the moans, as well, of those in the throes of death. Sometimes dancing gave way to fighting—for a cask of wine, for a woman, or simply for no reason at all, in a fit of madness brought on by the emotions of *contradiction*. There was nowhere to flee; the same dreadful scenes were everywhere; everywhere were the same orgies, the same fights, the same brutal gaiety or brutal rage—or else, absolute darkness, which seemed even more dreadful, even more unbearable to the staggered imagination.

Star City became an immense black coffer in which were some thousands of beings bearing a certain resemblance to man, abandoned in air polluted by hundreds of thousands of corpses, where among the living there was not a soul that had any intuition of its own situation. This was a city of those bereft of their senses, a gigantic madhouse, the greatest and most revolting bedlam which the world has ever known. And the madmen destroyed one another, stabbed or strangled one another, died of madness, died of horror, died of hunger, and of all the pestilences which reigned in the polluted air.

It goes without saying that the government of the Republic did not remain indifferent to the great calamity which had befallen the Capital. But it soon became very clear that no help whatever could be rendered. No doctors, nurses, administrators, or workers of any kind would agree to go to Star City. After the breakdown of funicular service and even of air transport it was, of course, impossible to get there, the climatic conditions being too great an obstacle. Moreover, the attention of the government was soon taken up by cases of *mania contradicens* appearing in other cities of the Republic. In some of these the malady threatened to take on the same epidemic character, and social panic set in that was akin to the conditions in Star City itself. A mass exodus from the more populated parts of the Republic commenced. Work in all mines and plants came to a standstill and the entire industrial life of the country faded away. Thanks, however, to strong measures promptly taken, the progress of the mania was arrested in these towns, and nowhere did it reach the proportions it attained at the Capital.

The anxiety with which the whole world followed the misfortunes of the young Republic is well known. At first no one even dreamed that the disaster could grow to the extent it did, and the dominant feeling had been that of curiosity. The chief newspapers throughout the world (and in that number our own *Northern European Evening News*) sent their own special correspondents to Star City to write up the epidemic. Many of these brave knights of the typewriter became victims of their own professional obligations. When the news became more alarming, various foreign governments and philanthropic societies offered their services to the Republic. Some sent troops, others doctors, still others money; but the catastrophe developed with such rapidity that all these good-will offerings proved of little avail. After the breakdown of the funicular systems the only information out of Star City was conveyed in the telegrams sent by the Chief. These telegrams were transmitted to the ends of the earth and printed in billions of copies. Even after the wrecking of the entire electrical system the telegraph service lasted a few days longer, thanks to the accumulators in the powerhouse. There is no accurate information as to why the telegraph service ceased altogether; perhaps the apparatus was destroyed. The last telegram of Horace Deville was that of the twenty-seventh of June. From that date on, for almost six weeks, humanity remained without news of the Republic's Capital.

During July, several attempts were made to reach Star City by air. Several new dirigibles and airplanes were received by the Republic. But for a long time all efforts to reach the Capital failed. At last, however, Thomas Billy, the famous ace of World War VI, succeeded in flying to the unfortunate city. He picked up from the roof of the city a man and a woman in an extreme state of hunger and mental collapse. Looking through the air vents, Billy saw that the streets were plunged in absolute darkness, but he heard savage cries and concluded that there were still living beings, more or less human, within the city. However, he did not dare to gyroscope into the city itself.

Toward the end of August one funicular line was put in order as far as the station of Lissis, a hundred and five kilometers from Star City. A detachment of men, well armed and bearing food and first-aid medical kits, entered the town through the northwestern gates. They, however, could not penetrate further than the first few blocks of buildings because of the dreadful atmosphere. They had to work step by step, in gas masks, clearing the streets of bodies and disinfecting the air as they went. Whatever few people they encountered were completely irresponsible. They resembled wild animals and had to be hunted down and held by force. About the middle of September, funicular service to Star City was once more established, and trains ran on regular schedules.

At the time of writing, the greater part of the city has already been cleared. Electric light and heating are once more in working order. The only section of the city which has not yet been dealt with is the American quarter, but it is thought that there is not a single living being there. About ten thousand people have been saved, but the majority of these is apparently beyond cure. Those who have recovered to any degree evince a strong disinclination to speak of the experience they have lived through. Furthermore, their stories are full of incongruities and most frequently find no confirmation in documentary evidence. Various newspapers of the last days of July have been found. The latest to date, that of the twenty-second of July, gives the news of the death of Horace Deville and invites the survivors to seek shelter in City Hall. There are extant, indeed, some sheets dated in August, but the matter printed thereon makes it clear that the author (who was probably setting his own delirium in type) was quite irresponsible. The discovery of Horace Deville's diary, already noted, contains a regular chronicle of events from the twenty-eighth of June to the twentieth of July. The frenzy that prevailed throughout the city during the last days is luridly evidenced by the discoveries made in the streets and buildings. Mutilated bodies everywhere: bodies of those who had starved to death, of those who had suffocated, of those who had been unspeakably murdered by the insane—and even of those who had been half-eaten. Bodies were found in the most unexpected places: in the tunnels of the Metropolitan subway, in sewers, in various sheds, even inside boilers. The interiors of most of the buildings had been wrecked, and the loot which the robbers had found it impossible to dispose of had been hidden in secret rooms and buried in basements.

It will certainly be several months before Star City becomes habitable once more. This city, which could accommodate three million people, now has a population of only thirty thousand workers, all engaged in clearing, repairing, and disinfecting the streets and buildings. A considerable number of the former inhabitants who had fled are, however, coming back in considerable numbers to seek the bodies of their kin and to glean whatever remains of lost fortunes. Several tourists, attracted by the amazing spectacle of the desolated city, have also arrived. A few entrepreneurs have opened hotels and are doing fairly well. A small night club is about to open, the talent for which has already been engaged.

In keeping with its long-standing policy of *FIRST* NEWS *FIRST*, the *Northern European Evening News* has engaged the services of Mr. Mark Lewis Evans, the noted author and explorer, as Special Correspondent, and hopes to print in the very near future his circumstantial reports of all the fresh discoveries which may be made in the stricken Capital of the Republic of the Southern Cross.

Litany

THE GLOWING of thy eyes I beatify!
In my delirium it did upon me shine.

The smiling of thy lips I beatify!
It did intoxicate, like unto wine.

The venom of thy kiss I beatify!
To all my thoughts, my dreams, 'twas poison keen.

The scythe of thy caress I beatify!
All of my soul's past thou didst with it glean.

The fire of thy love I beatify!
Joyous I plunged into its blazing bed.

The twilight of thy soul I beatify!
For over me its dark wing thou didst spread.

For all, for all, I thee do beatify:
For grief; for pain; for horror of long days;

For that, in thy steps, I drew to Eden nigh—
For that, though barred, I through its portals gaze!

B. G. G.

Her Knees

HER KNEES I kiss. The bending shadows cease
Being entities, and, kissing, us enfold.
All earthly things a diffident silence hold:
We are the meaning of sighs lost on a breeze,
We are the canorous verses of a rondeau old.

Brother of hallowed times! Singer forgot, untold!
To song thou didst entrust thy sorrow and unease—
And lo! This day to me thy verse extolled
            Her knees.

Crownèd in thorns my days, yet their mold
Fashioned one hour of lilac-wreathed ease. . . .
As fair Sulamith found her spouse's threshold,
As Alexander found the door to Helen's sweet surcease—
So my lips found, sweeter an hundredfold,
            Her knees. . . .
                        B. G. G.

Birds of Fury

BIRDS of fury soaring upon fiery, flaming pinions,
Flew o'er the white portals of Heaven's pure dominions;
Fiery reflections leapt on marble and porphyry—
Then the feathered pilgrims sped again and flew oversea.

But upon the marble pure of the threshold virginal
Something glowing kept, crept on, scarlet and unnatural;
And beneath the portaled vaults, of adamants, eternal,
The angels all quaffed deep of sins secret and infernal.
                        B. G. G.

Anna Ahmatova

1 8 8 9 –

AHMATOVA is the pen name of Anna Andreievna Gorenco, an early member of the Acmeists or Adamists, who, while acknowledging Symbolism as a "worthy sire" (they were also kindred to the Ego-Futurists), sought to reform it by substituting for its mysticism a firm, clear view of life. Many of the subsequent members of the group went over to neoclassicism. The poet N. Gumilev, Ahmatova's husband, was one of the first in the group, and her first volume of poems, *Evening,* was issued in 1912, the year of the formation of the group. Her poetry is marked by subjectivity, lyricism, and a simplicity that is really anything but simple. Ahmatova was decidedly not one of those poets who abandoned their Russia when the Revolution toppled their ivory towers.

The Gray-Eyed King

Glory to my pain that nought can allay!
The gray-eyed king met his death yesterday.

The stifling fall evening glowed dully red;
My husband came home, and stolidly said:

"You know, he had on his gray hunting cloak;
They came on his body near the old oak.

The queen is so young! I pity her plight;
Her hair turned to silver just overnight."

He found on the shelf his pipe, charred and rough,
Lit it, and then to his night shift went off.

Now I shall wake my small girl from her sleep
And into her gray eyes gaze long and deep,

Hearing the tall poplars whisper to me:
"No more on this earth your king will you see. . . ."

B. G. G.

Alexander Alexandrovich
Block

1 8 8 0 — 1 9 2 1

ALEXANDER ALEXANDROVICH BLOCK, predominantly a lyricist, was one of the foremost representatives of Russian Symbolism. Although he was composing verse at five, he did not begin writing seriously until eighteen; in his high-school and early university days he wanted to be an actor. He was first inspired by Zhucovski; subsequently, he was greatly influenced by Soloviev and Briussov. His first book of poems appeared in 1904; through fear of clerical censorship it was necessary to clear it through a provincial censorship office. His poetical play, *Show Booth,* was produced by Meyerhold in 1906.

During the revolution of 1905, Block carried the red banner at the head of a procession. 1917 saw him at the front; he met the October Revolution with rapture and was with and of that Revolution until he died (of a heart ailment) in the days when his country was still being blockaded.

Out of words current in the streets, out of catch-phrases and *chastushki* (nonsensical quatrains, street songs with a punch-line something like the limerick's), using assonances and deliberately outrageous rhymes, this exquisite poet fashioned (in a single night, the legend claims) a comparatively short poem that succeeds in doing what Carlyle tried to accomplish in several ponderous tomes: epitomizing a Revolution. And epitomizing all revolutions: bloody, bestial, and glorious; ghastly in their humors, unbridled, and stern.

The Twelve is not merely Block's greatest poem, or a great Russian poem; it has become, since its writing in January, 1918, one of the great poems in the world.

The Twelve

I

BLACK the night.
White the snow.
Blow, wind! blow!—
You can't keep on your feet—hold tight!
Blow, wind, blow—
Over all of God's world go!

Watch the wind swirl
The white, fluffy snow.
Snow on top, thin ice below.
Watch out—don't trip;
Better walk slow.
Ah, the poor fellow—he sure did slip!

From tower to tower
Stretches a thick twine.
On this twine hangs a sign:
To the Ratifying Assembly—All Power!
A little crone, in despair, is groaning, keening—
She simply cannot grasp the placard's full meaning:
Where is the need of such a huge sign?
There's enough cloth in that canvas square
Many a good lad's boots for to line—
For our lads have no clothes and their feet are bare. . . .

Like an old hen the crone
Surmounts a snowdrift both deep and wet:
"Oh, Mother of God, defend your own!
Oh, them Bolsheviks will be the death of me yet!"

Translated by Bernard Guilbert Guerney. Copyright, 1943, by the Vanguard Press,
Inc.

The wind is most ornery!
The frost is as fierce.
The bourzhui on the corner, he
Turns his coat collar right up to his ears.

And who is this? Hair long, unsheared,
And he mumbles into his beard:
"The treacherous swine!
Russia is through!"
Some writing gent, paid a penny a line—
Now not a sou.

And there, through snowdrifts slinking,
Goes a cassocked roly-poly:
Why so sad, so shrinking,
Comrade Holy?

Remember your old tricks?
How proudly you would stalk,
Your belly, outthrust, bore a crucifix
And shone on all the folk.

Two ladies meet and walk side by side;
The one in caracul voices her woes:
"We just cried *and* cried—"
She slips—*wham!* There she goes,
Stretched out from her head to her toes!
Upsy-daisy!
Lift her, now—go easy!

The wind is bracing,
And evil, and fine,
Under skirts racing,
Bearing off, torn into shreds,
The huge canvas sign:
To the Ratifying Assembly—All Power!
And every word it spreads:

". . . We, too, had a parley . . .
. . . In that house, 'cross the way . . .

. . . And in conclusion
. . . Made a resolution:
Ten rubles for time, twenty-five for all night . . .
. . . No girl will take less; it wouldn't be right . . .
. . . C'mon, dearic, let's hit the hay. . . ."

It's getting late.
The street is forsaken—
Save for a tramp
By the cold overtaken;
And the whistling wind will not abate.

"Hey, you poor scamp!
Come here, I say—
Let's kiss, old unshaven! . . ."

"Give me bread!"
"What comes after that, hey?
Git! On your way!"

Black, black the sky overhead.

Rancor, rancor to make one weep,
To make one's blood seethe in dismay,
Rancor sanctified, rancor black and deep . . .

Comrade, on this day
Vigil keep!

II

The wind roams free, the snowflakes flutter;
Twelve men are marching in the gutter.

Their rifle-straps are black, yet glow;
They shall have lights where'er they go!

Their caps are crumpled; they smoke, they gripe;
By rights their backs should have the convict's stripe!

> Liberty, Liberty!
> Eh, eh, no crosses on 'em hang!
> *Bang—bang—bang!*

Comrades, it's cold, cold as can be!

"Well, Vanka and Katka are hitting the booze—
She's got plenty of Kerenski bills in her shoes!"

"Vanka is rich now; he's rich—and how!"
"Vanka was one of us; he's a soldier lad now!"
"C'mon, Vanka, bourzhui, son-of-a-bitch!
Try my girl's kisses—ain't she a witch?"

> Liberty, liberty!
> Eh, eh, no crosses on 'em hang!

"So Katka is busy in Vanka's flat?
What's she so busy with—tell me, what?"
> *Bang—bang—bang!*

They shall have lights where'er they go!
Their rifle-straps on shoulders glow.

In revolution march abreast!
Your foe knows neither sleep nor rest!

Grip rifle, friend; don't show the white feather:
Let Holy Russia have it; fire all together—

> At Russia stolid, unrefined,
> With huts unfit for humankind,
> With her big, broad, fat behind!

> Eh, eh, no crosses on 'em hang!

III

So our lads laid down their tools,
The Red Army for to serve,
The Red Army for to serve—
And to die like fightin' fools!

Eh, the troubles we have borne!
Ain't we got fun?
A uniform all torn
And an Austrian gun!

To bring all bourzhuis to ruination
We'll fan a world-wide conflagration—
World conflagration, fed by blood.
Bless us, O Lord!

IV

Snowflakes swirl, runners skirl:
Vanka's out with his girl!
On the shafts small lanterns
Glow.
Eh, eh, let 'er go!

His army coat is a disgrace—
And what a silly-looking face!
He twirls, twirls his black mustache—
One more twirl, one more twirl,
Joking with his Kitty girl.

Vanka—my, he's broad of shoulder!
Vanka—my, no man talks bolder!
Watch him hugging that fool girl,
Setting her head in a whirl!

She is lolling back in style
Giving him the pearly smile.
Oh, you Kitty, my sweet Kitty—
Your plump face is no end pretty!

V

"On your neck, my darling Kitty,
A knife-scar has not yet healed;
Under your breasts, darling Kitty,
That fresh scratch can't be concealed!

"Eh, eh, dance and smile!
Your legs sure the eye beguile!

"What lace undies you wore—
Wear 'em, wear 'em, be in style!
For officers you played the whore—
Whore on, whore, on, for a while!

"Eh, eh, whore a while—
Till you turn my heart to bile!

"There was that officer—recall?
He did not escape the knife . . .
You got no memory at all?
I'll refresh it, you low-life!

"I'll give it a trial—
Just lie down with me a while!

"Spats of suede you once was sporting;
You liked chocolates—and how!
With cadets you went cavorting—
With plain sojers cavort now!

"Eh, eh, sin a while—
Then the soul won't feel so vile!"

V I

. . . Again the turnout onward dashes;
The driver yells, and flies, and lashes . . .
"Hold on, hold on! Help me, Andrei!
And you, Pete, run behind the sleigh!"

Bang—bangety—bang—bang—bang—bang—bang!
The stirred up snow-motes in the cold air hang.

Driver—and Vanka—race the sleigh . . .
"Fire one more shot! Now! That's the way!"

Bangety-bang! "Now you will know
How with another's gal to go!"

. . . .

"He's run away! Just wait, you trash—
Tomorrow I will cook your hash!"

But where is Kitty? Dead, dead, dead:
The bullet went right through her head.

"You glad now, Kitty?"—"Not a peep!
Lie in the snow, you carrion cheap!"

In revolution march abreast!
Your foe knows neither sleep nor rest!

V I I

And again the twelve go marching,
Each with rifle slung in place;
The poor murderer alone
Tries to hide his guilty face.

He strides faster, ever faster—
He has not recovered yet;
Winds his muffler tighter, tighter—
If he only could forget . . .

"Come on, friend, what's got you down?
You ain't your own self as yet!"
"Come on now, Petie, you old clown—
Is it Kitty you regret?"

"Oh, my friends, she was my steady;
Why, I loved that wench no end . . .
Many nights, black nights and heady,
With that wench I used to spend!

"For the deviltry alone
Gleaming in her eyes of fire,
For a mole that scarlet shone
When her body I'd admire—
Like a fool I've killed my own
Dearest one—my heart's desire!"

"Why, you bitch! So that's your worry!
What are you—a woman? Hey?
Want to spill your heart-throb story?
Well, not at *this* time of day!
We can't now play nursie with you—
Not in this earth-shaking year!
Greater burdens strain our sinew—
Think that over, comrade dear!"

Thereupon his restless pace
To his comrades' pace Pete slows—
And again lifts up his face,
Off his shoulders worry throws.

Eh, eh, no harm is done
Just to have a little fun!

Lock up every house door tight—
There'll be robberies tonight!

Open every cellar wide—
Tonight all the beggars ride!

VIII

Oh, the troubles we have borne!

What weariness weary,
    Deathly, dreary!

How the time will pass, somehow
    I will watch, I will watch. . . .

And for pastime head and brow
    I will scratch, I will scratch. . . .

Some polly seeds to chew, now,
    I will snatch, I will snatch. . . .

I will slit the throat, I vow,
    Of some wretch, of some wretch. . . .

You'd better fly, you bourzhui crow!
    I'll let your blood flow,
    To avenge one I know—
    Her brows like the sloe . . .
Lo-ord—re-hest—the—so-houl—of—thi-his Tha-hy
                                    handmaiden!

What
    weariness!

IX

The towers brood in the still night,
No more is heard the city's din;
Not a policeman is in sight—
"Lads, paint the town, though there's no gin!"

A bourzhui at a crossing, shrinking,
Tries hard to warm his nose and hands;
With tucked-in tail, famished, slinking,
A mangy hound beside him stands.

Starved like the dog, the bourzhui pale
Stands silent, like a question mark;
Like mongrel hound with tucked-in tail
The old world heels him in the dark.

X

"That is sure a growing blizzard—
What a blizzard, what a blizzard!
To see four steps off a wizard
Would be needed! Nasty as a buzzard's gizzard!"

The snow like a cyclone swirls,
The snow in upright pillars whirls.

"Holy Savior, how it's snowing!"
"Hey, Pete, watch out where you're going!
Did any golden altar screen
Save you from committing sin?
From the neck up you are dead—
Get some sense into your head!
Ain't your hands with dried blood gritty,
Just because you loved poor Kitty?"

In revolution march abreast!
Your foe is near—he knows no rest!

Ahead, ahead, ahead—
          All ye who earn your bread!

XI

Unblessed, the twelve march steady,
Into the distance going;
For all things set and ready,
For nothing pity knowing.

Their rifles they all train
Upon their unseen foe,
At every blind lane
Where wind and blizzard blow,
And where their boots remain
Stuck in soft, drifted snow. . . .

    A flag—red—
    Makes eyes ache.

    Measured tread
    Makes earth quake.

    Hark! The dread
    Foe may wake . . .

And the blizzard blinds their sight
    Day and night
    Without let . . .

Ahead, ahead—
          All ye who earn your bread!

XII

. . . They march on with sovereign tread . . .
"Who's that, now? Come on out!"
'Tis the wind, far off ahead,
Trying the red flag to rout . . .

A deep snowdrift lies ahead:
"Who's in there? Hey, come on out!"
Just a hungry hound, half-dead,
Skulks behind them as they shout . . .

"Mangy mutt, don't hang around—
Or you'll feel my bayonet!
The old world is a scabby hound—
Git! A beating's all you'll get!"

It still skulks, nor will give ground,
Tail tucked in and wolf-fangs bare—
Hungry hound, mongrel hound!
"Hey, there, answer! Who goes there?"

"That red flag—who waves it so?"
"It's so dark—can't see at all!"
"Who's that running? See him go,
Hiding behind every wall?"

"It's no use; come on out, friend—
I will get you, live or dead!"
"You'll fare poorly in the end,
For we'll fill you full of lead!"

Bang—bang—bang! And echo only
Mid the houses loudly rang,
While the blizzard, laughing snowily,
Pealed and shrieked and howled and sang.

Bang—bang—bang!
Bang—bang—bang! . . .

. . . Thus they their sovereign march pursue:
Behind them skulks the hound half-dead;
Ahead (with flag of sanguine hue)—
    Invisible within the storm,
    Immune from any bullet's harm,
Walking with laden step and gentle
In snowy, pearl-strewn mantle,
    With small, white roses garlanded—
Jesus the Christ walks at their head.

Vladimir Vladimirovich
Mayacovski

1 8 9 3 – 1 9 3 0

BORN IN GEORGIA (his native city of Bagdadi is now called Mayacovski), this poet had an early taste of Czarist oppression and was a revolutionary throughout his life. He took an active part in the Revolution of 1905 (at the age of twelve); from the age of thirteen he had to make his own living. In 1908 he left the *gymnasia*; the same year he was arrested for working with an underground printing plant, and the eleven months in prison gave him an opportunity to read and start writing poetry. His age (fifteen) saved him from a worse sentence. Next year, he was arrested twice, but served only six months. From 1910 to 1914 he studied painting; in 1912 he issued, with others, the famous Futurist Manifesto, *A Slap in the Face of Public Taste,* a much-needed pronouncement which, while it did not entirely clear the poetical air, did decidedly startle and shock the Symbolists, *et al.,* who were getting quite stuffy. (Mayacovski's group consisted of Cubo-Futurists, not to be confused with Ego-Futurists or others.)

He was violently opposed to World War I; the Revolution (one of his poems prophesied it would come in 1916) he met with open arms, taking part in the fighting, and in a comparatively short time drawing three thousand different posters and writing six thousand rhymed squibs. In 1925 he visited the United States and Mexico; there were other trips abroad, in 1927 and 1929. A jubilee exhibition of his twenty years' work was held in 1930. His suicide (brought on either by a prolonged attack of grippe or an unsuccessful love affair—or both) was a great shock, especially in view of his condemnation of the suicide of Yessenin. As a poet, Mayacovski was a great innovator, versatile, prolific, and effective; his poems and plays are for the most part satirical. His popularity was (and still is) enormous.

Both of the subjoined poems

demonstrate how effectively this poet used his chief weapon of satire—even though he wielded it like a bludgeon, rather than a rapier. The term Cadet, in the shorter poem, is a sobriquet for a Constitutional Democrat, the pre-Revolutionary equivalent of a parlor-Red (or Pink), a teacup revolutionary.

Block's *The Twelve* was the poem of the Revolution, but Mayacovski was *the* Poet of the Revolution.

Black and White

If you view
    Havana
        with sight-seeing gringos,
The land is a
    paradise,
        nothing is wanting:
Under the
    palms
        stand one-legged flamingos;
Collario blooms all
        Vedado
           is flaunting.

But in
    Havana
        all's sharply divided:
The whites have the
        dollars—
        and do all the bossing,
But the blacks—not a
        cent.
        So Willie provided
Himself with a
    broom,
        and stands sweeping a crossing.

All his life Willie's
                 sweeping, and beyond all
                                    doubt
By itself the
          dust would fill an ocean-deep
                                    bin:
That's the reason that Willie's
                            hair all
                                  fell out,
And that is the reason Willie's
                          belly
                              fell in.

Willie's
       joys
          form but a dull, meager spectrum:
Six hours of
          sleep
             is his notion of fun,
And, with
        luck,
            some thief, or the man who inspects rum,
May toss the poor Negro a
                        cent
                            on the run.

Would it help
            things at all if man walked on his
                                          head?
There surely must be some way all this
                                    dust
                                        to subdue!
Yet man's head has thousands of
                            hairs
                                 to help spread
Dust, but of
          legs
             man has never more than just two.

Gay
   Prado
      runs past with its scents and refrains;
Now rising, now falling, come the
             strains
                   of hot jazz;
The man who is not
          overburdened with
                 brains
Might think
     Havana
        is where lost Paradise was.

But few
     sinuosities
          bless Willie's brain—
Not
  much
     can be reaped there, for not much has been sown;
One thing, and one only, does his
             mind
                retain,
But that one is
     deep-graven,
          like a monument's stone:

"White man eats
     Pineapples
          ripened and juicy—
Black man eats
     pineapples
          rotted with wet;
White man gets
     light work,
          for he can be choosy—
Black man does
     hard work,
          for that's all he can get."

Few were the
           problems
                     that haunted poor Willie,
But one was
          most knotty—
                    the knottiest of all,
And when
        it
             would get him, it drove him nigh silly—
So silly, the
          broom
                from his black hands would fall.

And it came to pass that the
                       greatest
                            of kings—
The King of Sugar—
                   while Willie wrestled with
                                        doubt,
Had to come calling, dressed in
                          snowy-white
                                   things,
At the Cigar King's
               main office,
                        near where Willie hung out.

The
   Negro
        accosted the blubbery dandy:
"I beg your pardon,
               Sir,
                    My dear Mister Bigger—
But why must sugar, that's   .
                      white as white
                                can be,
Be grown, hauled and milled by a
                          black, black
                                   nigger?

Black
    seegars
        don't look right in a face that is white—
They seem far more
        fitten
            in a face that's all black;
And if
    sugar
        is what gives you such delight,
Why don't you at growin' it
            yourself
                take a crack?"

Now, a
    question
        like that you don't just let go;
The Sugar King's face from
            white
                turned all yellow;
He whirled on his
        heel
            with a haymaker blow,
Then, discarding his gloves, he left the
                black
                    fellow.

All around Willie wondrous
            botany
                grows,
Green
    over his head interlace the
                bananas;
With his hand he wipes off the
                blood
                    from his nose
(On what Willie makes you just *can't*
                buy
                    bandannas).

Willie felt his
        jaw,
                snorted his broken nose,
And then picked up his
                broom. How could he
                        ever learn
That
    Negroes
           who try such a question to pose,
Should address it to
                Moscow,
                    to the Comintern?

Little Parlor–Red Riding Hood

Once on a time there lived a Cadet,
And this Cadet always sported a little Red hat.

Save this little Red hat that he'd fallen heir to,
Divvel a bit else of him was Red in hue.

No sooner he'd hear that Rev'lution somewheres had come
Than he'd trot out that hat and perch it right on his dome.

Long lived the Cadets without care or much bother—
The son, and the father, and likewise grandfather.

But one day a fierce wind over all the land spread
And of that Cadet's Red hat it left nary a shred,

Making him neutral-hued. And the wolves of Rev'lution
Seeing him thus, just *pounced* on that there Rooshian.

And that was the end of that little Cadet:
Down to his cuff links the poor feller was et.

Children, remember, when you play "politicians,"
That wolves revolutin' are but poor dietitians.

                                B. G. G.

Michael Michaelovich
Zoshchenco

1 8 9 5 -

THE LEADING Soviet humorist was born in the Ukraine, the son of an artist. He studied law at the University of Petersburg but did not finish, volunteering for the front in 1914, where he served as an officer and was gassed and wounded. After the Revolution he wandered all over Russia, and was, in turn, carpenter, fur trapper, shoemaker's apprentice, telephone operator, policeman, detective, gambler, clerk, actor. In 1918 he volunteered again—for the Red Army.

In 1921, he helped form the famous Serapion Brotherhood literary circle, and published his first story in 1922.

His humorous stories (their brevity and casual anecdotage is deceptive; they are, for the most part, really stories) usually deal with the post-Revolutionary Ivan Q. Public, his tribulations and contretemps.

And Zoshchenco, like Lescov before him and, to a slighter extent, Shchedrin-Saltycov, has worked out a language of his own which contributes to the humor of the situation. That language is motley, picturesque, broken—and pulsating. Like all great humorists too faithful to their time, Zoshchenco may have to pay the penalty of comparative neglect in the future, but at present he remains the most popular Soviet humorist. That popularity attests, above all, to the Russian's ability not merely to laugh but to laugh at himself.

However, Zoshchenco has already paid one penalty of the humorist; he had begun (like most Russian humorists) with "straight" stories in the great tradition (the tragicomedy of some of these is akin to Gogol's), has made a number of curious literary experiments and excursions, and has done (and is doing) serious work—but all this is obscured by his hundreds of humorous stories, skits, parodies.

The two stories here given should be of general appeal, in any language; *Tooth-Jerking* may, in particular, interest those who have had not unsimilar experience with health-insurance and hospitalization schemes outside of Russia.

A volume of Zoshchenco is available in English, which will give the reader at least a skeletal idea of his stories, if not of his style.

Tooth-Jerking

THIS YEAR Egorych's teeth got in a bad way. They started falling out.

Of course, the years go on of themselves. The organism, so to say, falls into ruin. Bone structure, probably owing to the impermanence of prewar materials, becomes weatherbeaten.

To cut it short, then, this year the teeth of Ivan Egorych Kolbassiev, who lived in our house, began to crumble and fall out.

One of his teeth, now, it's true enough, he had had knocked out for him during a conversation. But the others began falling without waiting for the coming of any events, as it were. The man might be chewing something, let's say, or talking about the wages he could make and, in general, there mightn't be anybody at all in his immediate vicinity, yet the teeth would be trickling out of his mouth. Downright amazing. Six teeth he lost, in a short time.

The only thing was, Egorych wasn't afraid of that at all. He didn't give a hang about being left toothless. He was one of those fellows who are insured all around. They'd always be obliged to replace his teeth.

That's the sort of ideas he went through life with. And he used to say:

"I never," he'd say, "feel tight about teeth. You can knock 'em right out. If it came to anything else, now, or if you wanted to sock me in the nose, I'd never allow it; but as far as teeth are concerned I feel free and easy. Us fellows who are insured are always quite easy on that score."

And so, you understand, when Ivan Egorych lost six of his teeth he

Translated by Bernard Guilbert Guerney. Copyright, 1943, by the Vanguard Press, Inc.

decided on a thorough repair job. He took all the policies and documents along and went to the clinic— I think that's what they called it.

In the clinic they told him: "By all means. We can set 'em in. The only thing is, we've got a rule: there must be eight teeth missing. If it's more than that—well, our loss is your gain. But the clinic don't take on none of them small repair jobs."

Egorych, he tells 'em: "I got six missing."

"No," they tell him, "can't do a thing for you in that case, Comrade. You just bide your time."

That's when Egorych got mad, actually.

"Why," he says, "what am I supposed to do? Knock the rest of me teeth out with a bat or something?"

"Knocking 'em out," they tell him, "is unnecessary. Why interfere with nature? Wait a while; maybe you'll be fortunate enough to have them fall out by themselves."

Egorych went home thoroughly flabbergasted.

"That dental business was the one thing I had nothing to worry about, and now to have such unexpected things coming up, you know!" he reflected.

So Egorych began biding the time when his superfluous, unauthorized teeth would fall out.

In a short while, one of them did that very thing. And Egorych himself began monkeying with another and putting it to rights—with a rasp—and at last pried it loose from the place where it had been roosting so long.

Egorych made a beeline for that clinic.

"Now," he tells them, just as if he were shopping at a drugstore, "there's exactly eight teeth missing."

"By all means," they tell him, "we can oblige you now. How are your teeth—are the eight missing all in a row? Or how? For we have a proviso to that effect: the teeth must be missing in an unbroken series. If they aren't missing all in a row, but the gaps are scattered all over, we can't undertake anything—because a citizen like that, dentally considered, is still able to chew; occlusion, and all that."

Egorych, he says: "No, they ain't all in a row."

"In that case," they tell him, "we're in no position to do anything for you."

Egorych didn't say a thing to that; all he did was to gnash his remaining teeth and walk out of that clinic.

"Eh, now," he thought to himself, "what untoward things will turn up! My soul was so nice and peaceful, but now it's anything but that."

Right now Egorych leads a quiet life, is on a liquid diet, and cleans what's left of his teeth—with a special little brush—three times a day.

In that respect, one of the clinic's rules turned out to be a good thing.

The Agitator

GREGORY KOSSONOSSOV, janitor in an aviation school, was going off on a furlough to his native village.

"Well, now, Comrade Kossonossov," his friends urged him just before he left, "when you get back to your village don't forget to do a little agitating for the cause of aviation. You just tell the peasants how flying is developing—like as not they may chip in for a plane."

"You just leave that to me," Kossonossov assured them. "I'll agitate, all right. I won't say but that it might be different if it were anything else, but when it comes to aviation I'll tell 'em what's what, don't you fret."

It was a fine day in autumn when he arrived at the village, and he lost little time in going to the village Soviet.

"I've just come from the city, and I'd like to do a little agitating," he informed the chairman. "Could you stage a meeting?"

"Why not?" the chairman agreed. "You just trot along; I'll get 'em together tomorrow."

On the following day the chairman got the farmer folk together in the firehouse. Kossonossov came in, bowed to the assembly, and, being unused to speechmaking, began in a quavering voice:

"It's like this, see. . . . Aviation, Comrades, is. . . . Well, now, you may not be well up on politics, so suppose I start off with a few words on that. Right here is Germany, let's say, and here you have England. And here is Russia, and over there—well, now, generally speaking—"

Translated by Morris Spiegel. Copyright, 1943, by the Vanguard Press, Inc.

"What are you driving at, friend?" came from the audience.

"What am I driving at?" Kossonossov became provoked. "Why, aviation, that's what! Aviation is forging ahead all the time, that's what! Now, then: here is Russia, see? And over here is China—"

The peasants listened glumly.

"Stop stalling!" someone in the back of the hall called out.

"I'm not stalling," Kossonossov answered. "I'm talking about aviation. It's growing by leaps and bounds, Comrades. No use saying it ain't. What's right is right. There's no use arguing—"

"You aren't making yourself clear enough," the chairman called out. "Suppose you get a little closer to the masses, Comrade."

Kossonossov stepped forward a trifle and, rolling a cigarette from a scrap of newspaper, made a fresh start:

"Here's how things stand, Comrades. First they build the planes, then they fly 'em. You know—through the air. Of course, now and then, one of 'em won't stay up in the air and will go *kerplunk* to the ground. Like Comrade Yernilikin the pilot, for instance. He went up, all right, but then he plunked down so hard you could have used a matchbox for a coffin for what was left of him—"

"Well, nacherly," one of the peasants piped up. "Man ain't no bird."

"Why, that's just what I'm trying to tell you." Kossonossov rejoiced at this support. "If a bird flops, it don't give a hang; a flip of the wings, and it's off again. But a man is hard up against it. Another flier, Comrade Popcov, also took to the air; everything was going swell when *bingo!* his motor stalled on him. Boy, did *he* flop!"

"Yes?" the peasants became inquisitive.

"I'll say he did! And then there was the time when another fellow plunged down right amongst the trees, and he hung there like a little baby, bawling—no end of fun, that was. Oh, there's all sorts of things happening right along. Take the time that muley cow got mixed up with the propeller. . . . Clip-clip, chop-chop—frankfurters! You couldn't unscramble her horns from her teats. Dogs have a habit of getting in the way every so often, too—"

"What about hosses?" some of the peasants wanted to know. "Do hosses ever get tangled up with them contraptions, friend?"

"Sure thing!" Kossonossov agreed heartily. "Hosses too—nothing out of the way about that."

"Why, the damned so-and-so's!" someone raged. "What will they think up next? Slaughter hosses, will they?"

"That's the very thing I been telling you right along, Comrades—

aviation is making great strides. You ought to get together, now, and chip in for one—"

"Chip in for what, friend?" asked the peasants.

"For an airplane, of course," Kossonossov patiently explained.

Grimly smiling, the peasants filed out of the hall.

Proverbs

Proverbs are salt; Russian proverbs are salt-and-pepper. One proverbialist who held the highest opinion of them was none other than Catherine the Great (although it must be owned she was rather on the Polonius side); Dahl (see the introductory note on Turgenev) did pioneering and very important work with his first-hand collection of thirty-eight thousand. The present handful, from many and various sources, was selected, translated (for the greatest part), and arranged by the Editor.

Woman and Marriage

A woman has more tricks than a house has bricks.

A woman laughs when she can, but cries whenever she wishes.

One woman is a market; two are a fair.

Where the Devil can't do anything, he sends a woman in his stead.

Between a woman's *no* and *yes* there's no room for a needle to pass.

Women are long of hair but short of sense.

If granny weren't granny, she'd be a grandfather.

Jealousy and Love are sisters.

Pray once when going to the wars; pray twice when going to sea; but pray thrice when going to get married.

The first wife is sent by God, the second by man, the third by the Devil.

There's only one wicked woman in all this world—and she's the one a man marries.

Twice is a wife dear to her husband: when he carries her in over the threshold, and when he carries her out feet first.

When a man gets married, his love is buried.

If you're looking for trouble, marry a young widow.

Never marry a priest's daughter.

Cabbage soup thick, a wife good and meek—what else need any man seek?

A wife is no balalaika; you can't put her on the shelf after playing.

A crab is no fish among fish; a bat is no bird among birds; a hen-pecked man is no man among men.

Luck

Fortune and Misfortune are next-door neighbors.

Go fast, and you'll catch up with misfortune; walk slow, and it will catch up with you.

A pocketful of luck is better than a sackful of wisdom.

If you're lucky, even your roosters will lay eggs.

When luckless Makar goes in the forest all the pine cones fall on him.

There'll be a holiday up our alley, too, some day.

Money

Only a hammer of gold can open a door of iron.

When money speaks, Truth keeps its mouth shut.

Samson was a man of might, yet even he could not pay money before he had it.

The bear dances, but the Gypsy bear-leader takes the money.

Dear medicine is sure to benefit—if not the sick man, then the apothecary.

Keep a thing seven years and it's bound to come in handy.

He gives nuts to a squirrel when it has lost its teeth.

He'd flay a flea.

You can't flay the same bull twice.

In the next world, usurers will have to count red-hot coins with their bare hands.

Don't trust a landlord till he's six feet under.

The seller needs but one eye; the buyer a hundred.

Even in hell the muzhik will have to wait on the landlord, feeding the fire under the landlord's caldron.

Folly, Sloth, and Hard Drink

The Good Lord Himself keeps an eye on fools.

Fools you never reap nor sow—just of themselves they always grow.

It's a fool mouse that knows but one hole.

An empty sack won't stand up.

An obliging fool is worse than any foe.

A fool would ask for a drink if he were drowning.

When the head is thick it's the feet that suffer.

There's no wise answer to a fool's question.

Teaching a fool is like giving medicine to a dead man.

A man's a fool to make his doctor his heir.

You can't buy wisdom abroad if there's none at home.

He went to clip the sheep and came home without his coat.

He goes fishing for stars shining on water—with a sieve.

When a muzhik brews beer, the Devil stands by with a pail.

A good sleep will cure a drunkard, but a fool never.

If all fools wore white caps we'd look like a flock of sheep.

"Come on, lazybones, there's hardboiled eggs for dinner!"—"Are the shells off 'em?"

The drunkard and the laggard have seven Sundays a week.

A soldier can't find a place either in Heaven or Hell: he's too rowdy for Heaven, and he'd drink all the devils in Hell under the table.

The drunkard may be in church, but folks will think he's at the pot-house just the same.

Drink at table, not behind a door.

To a drunkard the ocean is only knee-deep.

Characterizations

What's good for the Russian is death for the German.

The Russian is clever, but always too late.

The German may be a good fellow, but it's better to hang him.

A Gypsy tells the truth but once in his life—and even then he's sorry.

Spit in his eyes, and he'll say it's dew from Heaven.

He's as stupid as a cork.

You and me's related—we dried our rags in the same sun.

Animal Saws

Where there are no fish, even a crawfish can pass itself for a fish.

Not every fish can be a sturgeon.

If you're a rooster, crow; if you're a hen, lay eggs.

The ravens don't peck one another's eyes out.

Only an eagle can look straight at the sun.

A cow may be black, but it gives white milk.

You can pull and pull, but you can't milk a bull.

Act like a sheep if you want to bring a wolf.

A fox counts chickens even in its sleep.

When a wolf asks a goat to dine, the goat ought to decline.

Make friends with the wolf—but keep your ax handy.

Lie down with dogs and you'll get up with fleas.

A horse has four legs, yet it stumbles just the same.

The wolf hunts, but he's also hunted.

He shot at a crow and hit a cow.

———————

Worldly Wisdom

A father's blessing won't sink in water nor will fire burn it.

He who adds but a straw to the widow's thatch pleases God.

It took but one spark to set Moscow on fire.

Napoleon wasn't scorched, but he left Moscow just the same.

An empty belly has deaf ears.

A full belly turns a deaf ear to learning.

Stone is hard, but the bread of strangers is harder.

If you scald yourself with milk, you'll blow to cool water.

A spoonful of tar is enough to spoil a cask of honey.

The bashful beggar goes hungry.

If you worry about crows, you'll never sow millet.

If you're afraid of wolves, don't go in the forest.

The bell calls to church, but you'll never see it inside one.

Better a misstep than a slip of the tongue.

A good reputation stands still; a bad one runs.

You can sew up a shirt but not your neighbor's mouth.

Calumny is like coal—it either burns you or besmirches you.

Let dogs bark—the wind bears their barking away.

———————

A good friend is better than a hundred relatives.

A thousand friends are all too few; one enemy is one too many.

A new friend is an uncracked nut.

———————

Measure your cloth ten times—you can cut it but once.

You can't put fire out with straw.

No matter how you cut and sew, the seams are bound to show.

He who's never been to sea doesn't know what trouble can be.

The elbow is near, but try to bite it.

Make haste only in catching fleas.

If a man knew where he'd fall, he'd have a pillow handy.

If you tickle yourself you can laugh when you like.

When you die, even a grave is comfortable.

A man can bear any burden, provided it's on somebody else's shoulders.

When you die, the man who blows your horn is buried with you.

A man's thoughts may be roving far and wide, but death is ever at his side.

It's a nuisance to go alone, even to drown oneself.

A man can get used to everything but hanging.

The squires fight—and the peasants are wounded.

The official picks up his pen—the peasant starts praying, and birds fall from the sky.

Officials have good jobs waiting for them in the next world; they're made full-time devils the minute they die.

Age and youth know not the same truth.

There is no cure for death.

No man can die two deaths, and no man can escape one.

A man can get used even to Hell.

Even crooked sticks burn right.

The greatest Czar must be put to bed with a shovel at last.

Religion

If God is with you, you can cross the ocean; if He isn't, don't cross your threshold.

Pray to God, but keep rowing toward shore.

Pray to God, but don't get sassy to the Devil either.

Put a good word in now and then even for the Devil—you never know whom you may please.

Born, baptized, married, or in the earth laid—always the priest has to be paid.

Don't ask any change from a priest or for any remnants from a tailor.

If there weren't any thunder, the muzhik would never think of crossing himself.

Man does what he can; God what He wills.

As long as there's a bog there'll be devils aplenty.

A fool shoots; God guides the bullet.

Crime and Punishment

A judge and a belly ask without words.

Be righteous before God; be wealthy before a judge.

If you have a hundred rubles, the law is on your side.

Any stick will do to beat a thief, but only a ruble can help you with an official.

Don't fear the Law but the judge.

Laws are straight, but judges are crooked.

The Law is like an axle—you can turn it whichever way you please, if you give it plenty of grease.

A rich man is always in the right when a poor man sues.

It's only the poor thieves that get hanged.

You lose your time stealing from a thief.

It's a poor thief that steals from his neighbor.

They blame the wolf, but it's the Gypsy that got the horse.

No man is a thief till he's caught.

Better to beg than steal, but better to work than beg.

Even the thief prays to God, but it's the Devil that gets hold of his prayers.

The Russian Word

Even as an incomputable host of churches, of monasteries, with cupolas, bulbous domes, and crosses is scattered all over holy and devout Russia, so does an incomputable multitude of tribes, generations, peoples swarm, flaunt their motley and scurry across the face of the earth. And every folk that bears within itself the pledge of mighty forces, that is endowed with the creative aptitudes of the soul, with a vivid individuality of its own and with other gifts of God—each such folk has become singularly distinguished by some word all its own, through which, expressing any subject whatsoever, it reflects in that expression a part of its own character. With a profound knowledge of the heart and a wise grasp of life will the word of the Englishman echo; like an airy dandy will the impermanent word of the Frenchman flash and then burst into smithereens; finically, intricately will the German contrive his intellectually gaunt word, which is not within the easy reach of all men. But there is never a word which can be so sweeping, so boisterous, which would burst out so, from out the very heart, which would seethe so, and quiver and throb so much like a living thing, as an aptly uttered Russian word!

G O G O L , *Dead Souls*

Book One, Chapter V